THE ABA STANDING COMMITTEE ON LAW AND NATIONAL SECURITY

THE U.S. INTELLIGENCE COMMUNITY LAW SOURCEBOOK

A Compendium of National Security Related Laws and Policy Documents

2013 EDITION

ANDREW BORENE, ADAM PEARLMAN,
AND HARVEY RISHIKOF, EDITORS

AMERICAN BAR ASSOCIATION
Defending Liberty
Pursuing Justice

Cover design by ABA Publishing

17 16 15 14 13 5 4 3 2 1

Cataloging-in-Publication Data is on file with the Library of Congress

ISBN: 978-1-62722-263-1

Discounts are available for books ordered in bulk. Special consideration is given to state bars, CLE programs, and other bar-related organizations. Inquire at Book Publishing, ABA Publishing, American Bar Association, 321 North Clark Street, Chicago, Illinois 60654.

www.ShopABA.org

U.S. Intelligence Community Law Sourcebook 2013 Edition

Editors: Andrew Borene, Adam Pearlman and Harvey Rishikof

TABLE OF CONTENTS

This section provides a selection of relevant new commentary on law related to the US Intelligence Community in 2013, in the form of relevant U.S. Government officials' publicly available speeches or remarks. It is designed to provide context of public issues that professionals in the field faced during the current publication period.

1. This book includes the President's comments as prepared. A full transcript of the remarks, as delivered, is available online at: http://www.whitehouse.gov/the-press-office/2013/05/23/remarks-president-national-defense-university.

This section provides a selected overview of laws, executive orders, and policy related to the U.S. Intelligence Community in 2013. It is designed to provide a general picture of the law of the community.

2. For the entire Act, *see* the 2012 edition of *The U.S. Intelligence Community Law Sourcebook.*

---

3. For enhanced coverage of Executive Orders related to detention and Guantanamo Bay, *see* the 2011 edition of *The U.S. Intelligence Community Law Sourcebook* Detention and Interrogation Policy Annex.

4, Executive Order 13636 related to critical infrastructure cybersecurity appears in the Cybersecurity Annex, *infra*.

5. A joint ODNI/DoD press release "Under Secretary of Defense for Intelligence to be Dual-Hatted as Director of Defense Intelligence" (ODNI News Release No. 16-07, DoD News Release No. 637-07) is included in this publication. This Memorandum of Agreement has been annotated as "For Official Use Only," a copy of the actual document can be obtained by authorized government users at: https://usdi.dtic.mil/usdi_docs/keyref/usdi_keyref.cfm.

Detention Annex[6]

---

6. A broader compilation of U.S. Detention Policy & Law can be found in the 2012 edition of *The U.S. Intelligence Community Law Sourcebook*. It has been reduced to greater specificity this year.

7. The published rules of these committees are included for reference on Congressional role in the oversight and specific legislative process related to the U.S. intelligence community.

DEDICATION

This publication is dedicated to all of our national security professionals, both to civilians and those in uniform.

We work and rest more safely because you stand watch. Thank you for your service to our great Republic.

ABOUT THE AMERICAN BAR ASSOCIATION'S STANDING COMMITTEE ON LAW AND NATIONAL SECURITY

The American Bar Association Standing Committee on Law and National Security conducts studies, sponsors programs and conferences and coordinates working groups on law and national security-related issues, including the legal responses to terrorism, the restructuring of the intelligence community and its role in law enforcement, and operational international law in the conduct of the military. These activities assist policymakers, educate lawyers, the media and the public, and enable the Committee to make recommendations to the American Bar Association. The Committee's website is **www.abanet.org/natsecurity**.

The Standing Committee on Law and National Security is comprised of eleven members appointed by the American Bar Association President for staggered three-year terms. Currently the committee is chaired by James McPherson. It is assisted by an Advisory Committee, Counselors to the Committee, and liaisons from ABA entities. Since 1962 the Standing Committee has sustained an unwavering commitment to educating the Bar and the public on the importance of the Rule of Law in preserving the freedoms of our democracy and shaping our national security system.

Founded by five farsighted individuals, including Chicago lawyer Morris I. Leibman and then-ABA President and later Supreme Court Justice Lewis J. Powell, the Standing Committee focuses on legal aspects of national security with particular attention in recent years to the issues raised by the legal responses to terrorist events and intelligence challenges.

From its inception, the Standing Committee has pursued its objectives through a diverse program of scholarship, conferences, workshops, and publications. One measure of the Committee's effectiveness is the rapid growth in recent years of the field it pioneered. For example, the number of accredited law schools offering courses or seminars on national security law has increased from 1 in 1974, to 7 in 1984, to 83 in 1994—more than a ten-fold increase in the past decade. By 1990, there were three separate law school casebooks on "national security law." Today, almost every accredited law school has one or more offerings in this field.

Over the years, the Standing Committee has included among its members individuals who have served as Senators and Representatives, Director of Central Intelligence, Secretary of the Army, Deputy Secretary of Labor, ambassadors, legal advisers to the Department of State and National Security Council, general counsels to the Department of Defense, Central Intelligence Agency, National Security Agency, several military services, and key congressional committees; and a diverse range of prominent scholars from the nation's preeminent law schools.

ACKNOWLEDGMENTS

As the editors, we must give credit to many others for their time, assistance, and advice.

As always, any value this sourcebook provides is undoubtedly a result of the input of this group of colleagues, friends, organizations, and willing experts who help us to varying degrees with feedback, criticism, and support.

The editors are especially grateful for the research assistance of Pierre Hines, a law student at Georgetown University Law Center, U.S. Army veteran, and member of the Truman National Security Project's Defense Council. His research was thorough and timely, doubtless as a result of his passion for the project.

We'd also like to thank the following staff members of the American Bar Association: Holly McMahon, the Staff Director of the Standing Committee on Law and National Security, along with Richard Paszkiet in publishing. Also, the members, advisors, and counselors associated with the ABA's Standing Committee on Law and National Security provided advice on shaping this and future editions.

Former CIA attorney George Jameson has been especially helpful in lending his deep personal knowledge of the evolution of the intelligence community, Congressional oversight, and the needs of practitioners.

Credit must go to the organizational supporters of this work, especially the American Bar Association, its Standing Committee on Law and National Security.

Also, a resounding thank you must go to Ben Wittes of Brookings Institution along with law professors Bobby Chesney and Ken Anderson, and the other editors and contributors to Lawfare, who have begun building and maintaining a vitally important electronic resource. They are building an incredible collection of resources not only for those who enjoy this print book, but across the fields of national security law and policy.

As always, if any readers or reviewers have ideas for improvement in future editions, please do not hesitate to contact us through the ABA or the committee's website at: **www.abanet.org/natsecurity**.

ABOUT THE EDITORS OF THE 2013 U.S. INTELLIGENCE COMMUNITY LAW SOURCEBOOK

Editor-in-Chief, U.S. Intelligence Community Law Sourcebook
Andrew Borene

Andrew Borene is an attorney with experience in business, law, and government. He serves as an executive with ReconRobotics, Inc. and advises other high-tech businesses in the national security space. He is also an Adjunct Professor of Political Science at Macalester College, where he teaches National Security Policy. He is President of the Twin Cities Chapter of the Association for Unmanned Vehicle Systems, is an executive board member with the FBI's InfraGard Alliance in Minnesota, and is a corporate constituent of U.S. State Department's Overseas Advisory Council. He maintains a security clearance as a consultant with Adventium Labs, and serves on the Defense Council of the Truman National Security Project.

Formerly an Associate Deputy General Counsel at the U.S. Department of Defense, Andrew has also been adjunct faculty at the University of Minnesota, and has supported the U.S. intelligence community as a program management executive with LexisNexis.

Before 9/11, Andrew began his professional career as a Public Finance Associate at Wells Fargo & Co., later serving on active duty as a U.S. Marine intelligence officer with the 1st Marine Division, including combat service in Iraq and subsequently as the executive officer for its Headquarters & Service Company at Camp Pendleton. He was a U.S. Department of State funded fellow to study post-conflict peace-building in Northern Ireland. He was also a judicial extern in the chambers of Judge John Tunheim in U.S. District Court.

Andrew has written commentary for *The New York Times, The Hill, The Washington Times, Foreign Policy* and other publications. He has appeared on CNN, ABC News, Fox News, CBS, NPR, and BBC. He is editor-in-chief of the American Bar Association's *U.S. Intelligence Community Law Sourcebook* and contributes as an author and editor to other ABA published books on International Humanitarian Law, International Human Rights Law, and National Security Law.

Andrew holds a J.D. from the University of Minnesota Law School, a B.A. in Economics from Macalester College, and completed Harvard University's executive program in Financial Institutions for Private Enterprise Development. He is licensed to practice law in Minnesota and the District of Columbia, and admitted to the U.S. Court of International Trade and the U.S. Court of Appeals for the Federal Circuit. He is Director of Special Projects for the ABA's Standing Committee on Law & National Security.

Co-Editor, U.S. Intelligence Community Law Sourcebook
Adam Pearlman

Adam Pearlman is an Associate Deputy General Counsel for the United States Department of Defense. He has previously served in various capacities at the Department of Justice, and in law school was an intern in the White House Counsel's Office. Mr. Pearlman was part of the interagency team advising the Iraqi High Tribunal during its proceedings against Saddam Hussein and top lieutenants of his former regime. He has developed expertise in counterterrorism, criminal, and intelligence law matters, and has published articles on subjects including cybersecurity and terrorist financing.

Mr. Pearlman is a member of the Executive Committee of the Federalist Society's International and National Security Law Practice Group, and is a Vice Chairman of the ABA Section of International Law's National Security Committee, and Aerospace and Defense Industries Committee. He previously served as a chapter editor of *The International Lawyer's Year in Review*, and a Symposium Editor for the *Harvard Journal of Law and Public Policy*. Mr. Pearlman is a graduate of the University of California at Los Angeles, The George Washington University Law School, and the National Intelligence University, where he earned a Master of Science degree in strategic intelligence. His thesis, "The Iguana and the Albatross: Guantanamo's Strategy and Impact," considers intelligence, legal, and foreign policy metrics in analyzing the successes and shortcomings of holding suspected terrorists in law of war detention at Guantanamo Bay.

Editor-at-Large, U.S. Intelligence Community Law Sourcebook
Harvey Rishikof

Harvey Rishikof is immediate past chair of the American Bar Association Standing Committee on Law and National Security and currently serves as chair of its Advisory Committee. Mr. Rishikof has been a Professor of Law and National Security Studies at the National War College (NWC) in Washington, D.C. He is the former chair of the Department of National Security Strategy at the NWC and specializes in the areas of national security, civil and military courts, terrorism, international law, civil liberties, and the U.S. Constitution.

Mr. Rishikof s career includes experiences in the private sector, academia, and public service and is a lifetime member of the Council on Foreign Relations and the American Law Institute. He is the former dean of Roger Williams School of Law, and as Legal Counsel to the Deputy Director of the FBI, Rishikof focused on policies concerning national security and terrorism, and served as liaison to the Office of the Attorney General at the Department of Justice.

As Administrative Assistant to the Chief Justice of the United States Supreme Court, Mr. Rishikof, a former federal court of appeals law clerk in the Third Circuit for the Honorable Leonard I. Garth, served as chief of staff and was involved in general policy issues concerning the federal court system. In this capacity, he acted as liaison to the Executive Branch, Congress, the Federal Judicial Center, and the Administrative Office of the United States Court.

Mr. Rishikof holds a J.D. from New York University School of Law, an M.A. from Brandeis University, and a BA from McGill University. His most recent co-edited book, *The National Security Enterprise, Navigating the Labyrinth* (Georgetown Press) came out in 2011.

INTRODUCTION

This 2013 volume of the *U.S. Intelligence Community Law Sourcebook* marks the Fourth Edition of our publication. This year, we continue to develop and strengthen the volume in accord with the feedback we receive from leading national security law practitioners. We have also expanded the editorial team this year, strengthening Andrew Borene's efforts with the formally recognized additions of Adam Pearlman and Harvey Rishikof.

We continue to build upon the legacy of the publication as a helpful tool for practitioners and students who want to see important laws, policy documents, and proposed legislation evolving from year to year. Previous years' Tables of Contents will be a useful reference for those who wish to track that evolution.

The core focus of this publication will continue to be the Constitution and the laws, executive orders and policies governing the activities of the U.S. Intelligence Community in the national security enterprise that are most relevant in each year of publication. Under our Constitution these operations will always be conducted in accord with, and subject to, the rule of law.

We hope you continue to find this publication of value in knowing the lay of the law from year to year. Please contact us through American Bar Association publishing if you have suggestions for future improvements, additions and edits.

I. Context and Commentary

Remarks of President Barack Obama at the National Defense University Fort McNair, Washington, D.C. May 23, 2013

(as prepared for delivery)

The White House
Office of the Press Secretary
For Immediate Release
May 23, 2013

Remarks of President Barack Obama

It's an honor to return to the National Defense University. Here, at Fort McNair, Americans have served in uniform since 1791– standing guard in the early days of the Republic, and contemplating the future of warfare here in the 21st century.

For over two centuries, the United States has been bound together by founding documents that defined who we are as Americans, and served as our compass through every type of change. Matters of war and peace are no different. Americans are deeply ambivalent about war, but having fought for our independence, we know that a price must be paid for freedom. From the Civil War, to our struggle against fascism, and through the long, twilight struggle of the Cold War, battlefields have changed, and technology has evolved. But our commitment to Constitutional principles has weathered every war, and every war has come to an end.

With the collapse of the Berlin Wall, a new dawn of democracy took hold abroad, and a decade of peace and prosperity arrived at home. For a moment, it seemed the 21st century would be a tranquil time. Then, on September 11th 2001, we were shaken out of complacency. Thousands were taken from us, as clouds of fire, metal and ash descended upon a sun-filled morning. This was a different kind of war. No armies came to our shores, and our military was not the principal target. Instead, a group of terrorists came to kill as many civilians as they could.

And so our nation went to war. We have now been at war for well over a decade. I won't review the full history. What's clear is that we quickly drove al Qaeda out of Afghanistan, but then shifted our focus and began a new war in Iraq. This carried grave consequences for our fight against al Qaeda, our standing in the world, and—to this day—our interests in a vital region.

Meanwhile, we strengthened our defenses—hardening targets, tightening transportation security, and giving law enforcement new tools to prevent terror. Most of these changes were sound. Some caused inconvenience. But some, like expanded surveillance, raised difficult questions about the balance we strike between our interests in security and our values of privacy. And in some cases, I believe we compromised our basic values—by using torture to interrogate our enemies, and detaining individuals in a way that ran counter to the rule of law.

After I took office, we stepped up the war against al Qaeda, but also sought to change its course. We relentlessly targeted al Qaeda's leadership. We ended the war in Iraq, and brought nearly 150,000 troops home. We pursued a new strategy in Afghanistan, and increased our training of Afghan forces. We unequivocally banned torture, affirmed our commitment to civilian courts, worked to align our policies with the rule of law, and expanded our consultations with Congress.

Today, Osama bin Laden is dead, and so are most of his top lieutenants. There have been no large-scale attacks on the United States, and our homeland is more secure. Fewer of our troops are in harm's way, and over the next 19 months they will continue to come home. Our alliances are strong, and so is our standing in the world. In sum, we are safer because of our efforts.

Now make no mistake: our nation is still threatened by terrorists. From Benghazi to Boston, we have been tragically reminded of that truth. We must recognize, however, that the threat has shifted and evolved from the one that came to our shores on 9/11. With a decade of experience to draw from, now is the time to ask ourselves hard questions—about the nature of today's threats, and how we should confront them.

These questions matter to every American. For over the last decade, our nation has spent well over a trillion dollars on war, exploding our deficits and constraining our ability to nation build here at home. Our service-members and their families have sacrificed far more on our behalf. Nearly 7,000 Americans have made the ultimate sacrifice. Many more have left a part of themselves on the battlefield, or brought the shadows of battle back home. From our use of drones to the detention of terrorist suspects, the decisions we are making will define the type of nation—and world—that we leave to our children.

So America is at a crossroads. We must define the nature and scope of this struggle, or else it will define us, mindful of James Madison's warning that "No nation could preserve its freedom in the midst of continual warfare." Neither I, nor any President, can promise the total defeat of terror. We will never erase the evil that lies in the hearts of some human beings, nor stamp out every danger to our open society. What we can do—what we must do—is dismantle networks that pose a direct danger, and make it less likely for new groups to gain a foothold, all while maintaining the freedoms and ideals that we defend. To define that strategy, we must make decisions based not on fear, but hard-earned wisdom. And that begins with understanding the threat we face.

Today, the core of al Qaeda in Afghanistan and Pakistan is on a path to defeat. Their remaining operatives spend more time thinking about their own safety than plotting against us. They did not direct the attacks in Benghazi or Boston. They have not carried out a successful attack on our homeland since 9/11. Instead, what we've seen is the emergence of various al Qaeda affiliates. From Yemen to Iraq, from Somalia to North Africa, the threat today is more diffuse, with Al Qaeda's affiliate in the Arabian Peninsula—AQAP –the most active in plotting against our homeland. While none of AQAP's efforts approach the scale of 9/11 they have continued to plot acts of terror, like the attempt to blow up an airplane on Christmas Day in 2009.

Unrest in the Arab World has also allowed extremists to gain a foothold in countries like Libya and Syria. Here, too, there are differences from 9/11. In some cases, we confront state-sponsored networks like Hizbollah that engage in acts of terror to achieve political goals. Others are simply collections of local militias or extremists interested in seizing territory. While we are vigilant for signs that these groups may pose a transnational threat, most are focused on operating in the countries and regions where they are based. That means we will face more localized threats like those we saw in Benghazi, or at the BP oil facility in Algeria, in which local operatives—in loose affiliation with regional networks—launch periodic attacks against Western diplomats, companies, and other soft targets, or resort to kidnapping and other criminal enterprises to fund their operations.

Finally, we face a real threat from radicalized individuals here in the United States. Whether it's a shooter at a Sikh Temple in Wisconsin; a plane flying into a building in Texas; or the extremists who killed 168 people at the Federal Building in Oklahoma City—America has confronted many forms of violent extremism in our time. Deranged or alienated individuals—often U.S. citizens or legal residents—can do enormous damage, particularly when inspired by larger notions of violent jihad. That pull towards extremism appears to have led to the shooting at Fort Hood, and the bombing of the Boston Marathon.

Lethal yet less capable al Qaeda affiliates. Threats to diplomatic facilities and businesses abroad. Homegrown extremists. This is the future of terrorism. We must take these threats seriously, and do all that we can to confront them. But as we shape our response, we have to recognize that the scale of this threat closely resembles the types of attacks we faced before 9/11. In the 1980s, we lost Americans to terrorism at our Embassy in Beirut; at our Marine Barracks in Lebanon; on a cruise ship at sea; at a disco in Berlin; and on Pan Am Flight 103 over Lockerbie. In the 1990s, we lost Americans to terrorism at the World Trade Center; at our military facilities in Saudi Arabia; and at our Embassy in Kenya. These attacks were all deadly, and we learned that left unchecked, these threats can grow. But if dealt with smartly and proportionally, these threats need not rise to the level that we saw on the eve of 9/11.

Moreover, we must recognize that these threats don't arise in a vacuum. Most, though not all, of the terrorism we face is fueled by a common ideology—a belief by some extremists that Islam is in conflict with the United States and the West, and that violence against Western targets, including civilians, is justified in pursuit of a larger cause. Of course, this ideology is based on a lie, for the United States is not at war with Islam; and this ideology is rejected by the vast majority of Muslims, who are the most frequent victims of terrorist acts.

Nevertheless, this ideology persists, and in an age in which ideas and images can travel the globe in an instant, our response to terrorism cannot depend on military or law enforcement alone. We need all elements of national power to win a battle of wills and ideas. So let me discuss the components of such a comprehensive counter-terrorism strategy.

First, we must finish the work of defeating al Qaeda and its associated forces.

In Afghanistan, we will complete our transition to Afghan responsibility for security. Our troops will come home. Our combat mission will come to an end. And we will work with the Afghan government to train security forces, and sustain a counter-terrorism force which ensures that al Qaeda can never again establish a safe-haven to launch attacks against us or our allies.

Beyond Afghanistan, we must define our effort not as a boundless 'global war on terror'—but rather as a series of persistent, targeted efforts to dismantle specific networks of violent extremists that threaten America. In many cases, this will involve partnerships with other countries. Thousands of Pakistani soldiers have lost their lives fighting extremists. In Yemen, we are supporting security forces that have reclaimed territory from AQAP. In Somalia, we helped a coalition of African nations push al Shabaab out of its strongholds. In Mali, we are providing military aid to a French-led intervention to push back al Qaeda in the Maghreb, and help the people of Mali reclaim their future.

Much of our best counter-terrorism cooperation results in the gathering and sharing of intelligence; the arrest and prosecution of terrorists. That's how a Somali terrorist apprehended off the coast of Yemen is now in prison in New York. That's how we worked with European allies to disrupt plots from Denmark to Germany to the United Kingdom. That's how intelligence collected with Saudi Arabia helped us stop a cargo plane from being blown up over the Atlantic.

But despite our strong preference for the detention and prosecution of terrorists, sometimes this approach is foreclosed. Al Qaeda and its affiliates try to gain a foothold in some of the most distant and unforgiving places on Earth. They take refuge in remote tribal regions. They hide in caves and walled compounds. They train in empty deserts and rugged mountains.

In some of these places—such as parts of Somalia and Yemen—the state has only the most tenuous reach into the territory. In other cases, the state lacks the capacity or will to take action. It is also not possible for America to simply deploy a team of Special Forces to capture every terrorist. And even when such an approach may be possible, there are places where it would pose profound risks to our troops and local civilians– where a terrorist compound cannot be breached without triggering a firefight with surrounding tribal communities that pose no threat to us, or when putting U.S. boots on the ground may trigger a major international crisis.

To put it another way, our operation in Pakistan against Osama bin Laden cannot be the norm. The risks in that case were immense; the likelihood of capture, although our preference, was remote given the certainty of resistance; the fact that we did not find ourselves confronted with civilian casualties, or embroiled in an extended firefight, was a testament to the meticulous planning and professionalism of our Special Forces—but also depended on some luck. And even then, the cost to our relationship with Pakistan—and the backlash among the Pakistani public over encroachment on their territory—was so severe that we are just now beginning to rebuild this important partnership.

It is in this context that the United States has taken lethal, targeted action against al Qaeda and its associated forces, including with remotely piloted aircraft commonly referred to as drones. As was true in previous armed conflicts, this new technology raises profound questions—about who is targeted, and why; about civilian casualties, and the risk of creating new enemies; about the legality of such strikes under U.S. and international law; about accountability and morality.

Let me address these questions. To begin with, our actions are effective. Don't take my word for it. In the intelligence gathered at bin Laden's compound, we found that he wrote, "we could lose the reserves to the enemy's air strikes. We cannot fight air strikes with explosives." Other communications from al Qaeda operatives confirm this as well. Dozens of highly skilled al Qaeda commanders, trainers, bomb makers, and operatives have been taken off the battlefield. Plots have been disrupted that would have targeted international aviation, U.S. transit systems, European cities and our troops in Afghanistan. Simply put, these strikes have saved lives.

Moreover, America's actions are legal. We were attacked on 9/11. Within a week, Congress overwhelmingly authorized the use of force. Under domestic law, and international law, the United States is at war with al Qaeda, the Taliban, and their associated forces. We are at war with an organization that right now would kill as many Americans as they could if we did not stop them first. So this is a just war—a war waged proportionally, in last resort, and in self-defense.

And yet as our fight enters a new phase, America's legitimate claim of self-defense cannot be the end of the discussion. To say a military tactic is legal, or even effective, is not to say it is wise or moral in every instance. For the same human progress that gives us the technology to strike half a world away also demands the discipline to constrain that power—or risk abusing it. That's why, over the last four years, my Administration has worked vigorously to establish a framework that governs our use of force against terrorists—insisting upon clear guidelines, oversight and accountability that is now codified in Presidential Policy Guidance that I signed yesterday.

In the Afghan war theater, we must support our troops until the transition is complete at the end of 2014. That means we will continue to take strikes against high value al Qaeda targets, but also against forces that are massing to support attacks on coalition forces. However, by the end of 2014, we will no longer have the same need for force protection, and the progress we have made against core al Qaeda will reduce the need for unmanned strikes.

Beyond the Afghan theater, we only target al Qaeda and its associated forces. Even then, the use of drones is heavily constrained. America does not take strikes when we have the ability to capture individual terrorists - our preference is always to detain, interrogate, and prosecute them. America cannot take strikes wherever we choose—our actions are bound by consultations with partners, and respect for state sovereignty. America does not take strikes to punish individuals—we act against terrorists who pose a continuing and imminent threat to the American people, and when there are no other governments capable of effectively addressing the threat. And before any strike is taken, there must be near-certainty that no civilians will be killed or injured—the highest standard we can set.

This last point is critical, because much of the criticism about drone strikes—at home and abroad—understandably centers on reports of civilian casualties. There is a wide gap between U.S. assessments of such casualties, and non-governmental reports. Nevertheless, it is a hard fact that U.S. strikes have resulted in civilian casualties, a risk that exists in all wars. For the families of those civilians, no words or legal construct can justify their loss. For me, and those in my chain of command, these deaths will haunt us as long as we live, just as we are haunted by the civilian casualties that have occurred through conventional fighting in Afghanistan and Iraq.

But as Commander-in-Chief, I must weigh these heartbreaking tragedies against the alternatives. To do nothing in the face of terrorist networks would invite far more civilian casualties—not just in our cities at home and facilities abroad, but also in the very places –like Sana'a and Kabul and Mogadishu—where terrorists seek a foothold. Let us remember that the terrorists we are after target civilians, and the death toll from their acts of terrorism against Muslims dwarfs any estimate of civilian casualties from drone strikes.

Where foreign governments cannot or will not effectively stop terrorism in their territory, the primary alternative to targeted, lethal action is the use of conventional military options. As I've said, even small Special Operations carry enormous risks. Conventional airpower or missiles are far less precise than drones, and likely to cause more civilian casualties and local outrage. And invasions of these territories lead us to be viewed as occupying armies; unleash a torrent of unintended consequences; are difficult to contain; and ultimately empower those who thrive on violent conflict. So it is false to assert that putting boots on the ground is less likely to result in civilian deaths, or to create enemies in the Muslim world. The result would be more U.S. deaths, more Blackhawks down, more confrontations with local populations, and an inevitable mission creep in support of such raids that could easily escalate into new wars.

So yes, the conflict with al Qaeda, like all armed conflict, invites tragedy. But by narrowly targeting our action against those who want to kill us, and not the people they hide among, we are choosing the course of action least likely to result in the loss of innocent life. Indeed, our efforts must also be measured against the history of putting American troops in distant lands among hostile populations. In Vietnam, hundreds of thousands of civilians died in a war where the boundaries of battle were blurred. In Iraq and Afghanistan, despite the courage and discipline of our troops, thousands of civilians have been killed. So neither conventional military action, nor waiting for attacks to occur, offers moral safe-harbor. Neither does a sole reliance on law enforcement in territories that have no functioning police or security services—and indeed, have no functioning law.

This is not to say that the risks are not real. Any U.S. military action in foreign lands risks creating more enemies, and impacts public opinion overseas. Our laws constrain the power of the President, even during wartime, and I have taken an oath to defend the Constitution of the United States. The very precision of drones strikes, and the necessary secrecy involved in such actions can end up shielding our government from the public scrutiny that a troop deployment invites. It can also lead a President and his team to view drone strikes as a cure-all for terrorism.

For this reason, I've insisted on strong oversight of all lethal action. After I took office, my Administration began briefing all strikes outside of Iraq and Afghanistan to the appropriate committees of Congress. Let me repeat that—not only did Congress authorize the use of force, it is briefed on every strike that America takes. That includes the one instance when we targeted an American citizen: Anwar Awlaki, the chief of external operations for AQAP.

This week, I authorized the declassification of this action, and the deaths of three other Americans in drone strikes, to facilitate transparency and debate on this issue, and to dismiss some of the more outlandish claims. For the record, I do not believe it would be constitutional for the government to target and kill any U.S. citizen—with a drone, or a shotgun—without due process. Nor should any President deploy armed drones over U.S. soil.

But when a U.S. citizen goes abroad to wage war against America—and is actively plotting to kill U.S. citizens; and when neither the United States, nor our partners are in a position to capture him before he carries out a plot—his citizenship should no more serve as a shield than a sniper shooting down on an innocent crowd should be protected from a swat team

That's who Anwar Awlaki was—he was continuously trying to kill people. He helped oversee the 2010 plot to detonate explosive devices on two U.S. bound cargo planes. He was involved in planning to blow up an airliner in 2009. When Farouk Abdulmutallab—the Christmas Day bomber—went to Yemen in 2009, Awlaki hosted him, approved his suicide operation, and helped him tape a martyrdom video to be shown after the attack. His last instructions were to blow up the airplane when it was over American soil. I would have detained and prosecuted Awlaki if we captured him before he carried out a plot. But we couldn't. And as President, I would have been derelict in my duty had I not authorized the strike that took out Awlaki.

Of course, the targeting of any Americans raises constitutional issues that are not present in other strikes—which is why my Administration submitted information about Awlaki to the Department of Justice months before Awlaki was killed, and briefed the Congress before this strike as well. But the high threshold that we have set for taking lethal action applies to all potential terrorist targets, regardless of whether or not they are American citizens. This threshold respects the inherent dignity of every human life. Alongside the decision to put our men and women in uniform in harm's way, the decision to use force against individuals or groups—even against a sworn enemy of the United States—is the hardest thing I do as President. But these decisions must be made, given my responsibility to protect the American people.

Going forward, I have asked my Administration to review proposals to extend oversight of lethal actions outside of warzones that go beyond our reporting to Congress. Each option has virtues in theory, but poses difficulties in practice. For example, the establishment of a special court to evaluate and authorize lethal action has the benefit of bringing a third branch of government into the process, but raises serious constitutional issues about presidential and judicial authority. Another idea that's been suggested—the establishment of an independent oversight board in the executive branch—avoids those problems, but may introduce a layer of bureaucracy into national-security decision-making, without inspiring additional public confidence in the process. Despite these challenges, I look forward to actively engaging Congress to explore these—and other—options for increased oversight.

I believe, however, that the use of force must be seen as part of a larger discussion about a comprehensive counter-terrorism strategy. Because for all the focus on the use of force, force alone cannot make us safe. We cannot use force everywhere that a radical ideology takes root; and in the absence of a strategy that reduces the well-spring of extremism, a perpetual war—through drones or Special Forces or troop deployments—will prove self-defeating, and alter our country in troubling ways.

So the next element of our strategy involves addressing the underlying grievances and conflicts that feed extremism, from North Africa to South Asia. As we've learned this past decade, this is a vast and complex undertaking. We must be humble in our expectation that we can quickly resolve deep rooted problems like poverty and sectarian hatred. Moreover, no two countries are alike, and some will undergo chaotic change before things get better. But our security and values demand that we make the effort.

This means patiently supporting transitions to democracy in places like Egypt, Tunisia and Libya—because the peaceful realization of individual aspirations will serve as a rebuke to violent extremists. We must strengthen the opposition in Syria, while isolating extremist elements—because the end of a tyrant must not give way to the tyranny of terrorism. We are working to promote peace between Israelis and Palestinians—because it is right, and because such a peace could help reshape attitudes in the region. And we must help countries modernize economies, upgrade education, and encourage entrepreneurship—because American leadership has always been elevated by our ability to connect with peoples' hopes, and not simply their fears.

Success on these fronts requires sustained engagement, but it will also require resources. I know that foreign aid is one of the least popular expenditures—even though it amounts to less than one percent of the federal budget. But foreign assistance cannot be viewed as charity. It is fundamental to our national security, and any sensible long-term strategy to battle extremism. Moreover, foreign assistance is a tiny fraction of what we spend fighting wars that our assistance might ultimately prevent. For what we spent in a month in Iraq at the height of the war, we could be training security forces in Libya, maintaining peace agreements between Israel and its neighbors, feeding the hungry in Yemen, building schools in Pakistan, and creating reservoirs of goodwill that marginalize extremists.

America cannot carry out this work if we do not have diplomats serving in dangerous places. Over the past decade, we have strengthened security at our Embassies, and I am implementing every recommendation of the Accountability Review Board which found unacceptable failures in Benghazi. I have called on Congress to fully fund these efforts to bolster security, harden facilities, improve intelligence, and facilitate a quicker response time from our military if a crisis emerges.

But even after we take these steps, some irreducible risks to our diplomats will remain. This is the price of being the world's most powerful nation, particularly as a wave of change washes over the Arab World. And in balancing the trade-offs between security and active diplomacy, I firmly believe that any retreat from challenging regions will only increase the dangers we face in the long run.

Targeted action against terrorists. Effective partnerships. Diplomatic engagement and assistance. Through such a comprehensive strategy we can significantly reduce the chances of large scale attacks on the homeland and mitigate threats to

Americans overseas. As we guard against dangers from abroad, however, we cannot neglect the daunting challenge of terrorism from within our borders.

As I said earlier, this threat is not new. But technology and the Internet increase its frequency and lethality. Today, a person can consume hateful propaganda, commit themselves to a violent agenda, and learn how to kill without leaving their home. To address this threat, two years ago my Administration did a comprehensive review, and engaged with law enforcement. The best way to prevent violent extremism is to work with the Muslim American community—which has consistently rejected terrorism—to identify signs of radicalization, and partner with law enforcement when an individual is drifting towards violence. And these partnerships can only work when we recognize that Muslims are a fundamental part of the American family. Indeed, the success of American Muslims, and our determination to guard against any encroachments on their civil liberties, is the ultimate rebuke to those who say we are at war with Islam.

Indeed, thwarting homegrown plots presents particular challenges in part because of our proud commitment to civil liberties for all who call America home. That's why, in the years to come, we will have to keep working hard to strike the appropriate balance between our need for security and preserving those freedoms that make us who we are. That means reviewing the authorities of law enforcement, so we can intercept new types of communication, and build in privacy protections to prevent abuse. That means that—even after Boston—we do not deport someone or throw someone in prison in the absence of evidence. That means putting careful constraints on the tools the government uses to protect sensitive information, such as the State Secrets doctrine. And that means finally having a strong Privacy and Civil Liberties Board to review those issues where our counter-terrorism efforts and our values may come into tension.

The Justice Department's investigation of national security leaks offers a recent example of the challenges involved in striking the right balance between our security and our open society. As Commander-in Chief, I believe we must keep information secret that protects our operations and our people in the field. To do so, we must enforce consequences for those who break the law and breach their commitment to protect classified information. But a free press is also essential for our democracy. I am troubled by the possibility that leak investigations may chill the investigative journalism that holds government accountable.

Journalists should not be at legal risk for doing their jobs. Our focus must be on those who break the law. That is why I have called on Congress to pass a media shield law to guard against government over-reach. I have raised these issues with the Attorney General, who shares my concern. So he has agreed to review existing Department of Justice guidelines governing investigations that involve reporters, and will convene a group of media organizations to hear their concerns as part of that review. And I have directed the Attorney General to report back to me by July 12th.

All these issues remind us that the choices we make about war can impact—in sometimes unintended ways—the openness and freedom on which our way of life depends. And that is why I intend to engage Congress about the existing Authorization to Use Military Force, or AUMF, to determine how we can continue to fight terrorists without keeping America on a perpetual war-time footing.

The AUMF is now nearly twelve years old. The Afghan War is coming to an end. Core al Qaeda is a shell of its former self. Groups like AQAP must be dealt with, but in the years to come, not every collection of thugs that labels themselves al Qaeda will pose a credible threat to the United States. Unless we discipline our thinking and our actions, we may be drawn into more wars we don't need to fight, or continue to grant Presidents unbound powers more suited for traditional armed conflicts between nation states. So I look forward to engaging Congress and the American people in efforts to refine, and ultimately repeal, the AUMF's mandate. And I will not sign laws designed to expand this mandate further. Our systematic effort to dismantle terrorist organizations must continue. But this war, like all wars, must end. That's what history advises. That's what our democracy demands.

And that brings me to my final topic: the detention of terrorist suspects.

To repeat, as a matter of policy, the preference of the United States is to capture terrorist suspects. When we do detain a suspect, we interrogate them. And if the suspect can be prosecuted, we decide whether to try him in a civilian court or a Military Commission. During the past decade, the vast majority of those detained by our military were captured on the battlefield. In Iraq, we turned over thousands of prisoners as we ended the war. In Afghanistan, we have transitioned detention facilities to the Afghans, as part of the process of restoring Afghan sovereignty. So we bring law of war detention to an end, and we are committed to prosecuting terrorists whenever we can.

The glaring exception to this time-tested approach is the detention center at Guantanamo Bay. The original premise for opening GTMO—that detainees would not be able to challenge their detention—was found unconstitutional five years ago. In the meantime, GTMO has become a symbol around the world for an America that flouts the rule of law. Our allies won't cooperate with us if they think a terrorist will end up at GTMO. During a time of budget cuts, we spend $150 million each year to imprison 166 people –almost $1 million per prisoner. And the Department of Defense estimates that we must spend another $200 million to keep GTMO open at a time when we are cutting investments in education and research here at home.

As President, I have tried to close GTMO. I transferred 67 detainees to other countries before Congress imposed restrictions to effectively prevent us from either transferring detainees to other countries, or imprisoning them in the United States. These restrictions make no sense. After all, under President Bush, some 530 detainees were transferred from GTMO with Congress's support. When I ran for President the first time, John McCain supported closing GTMO. No person has ever escaped from one of our super-max or military prisons in the United States. Our courts have convicted hundreds of people for terrorism-related offenses, including some who are more dangerous than most GTMO detainees. Given my Administration's relentless pursuit of al Qaeda's leadership, there is no justification beyond politics for Congress to prevent us from closing a facility that should never have been opened.

Today, I once again call on Congress to lift the restrictions on detainee transfers from GTMO. I have asked the Department of Defense to designate a site in the United States where we can hold military commissions. I am appointing a new, senior envoy at the State Department and Defense Department whose sole responsibility will be to achieve the transfer of detainees to third countries. I am lifting the moratorium on detainee transfers to Yemen, so we can review them on a case by case basis. To the greatest extent possible, we will transfer detainees who have been cleared to go to other countries. Where appropriate, we will bring terrorists to justice in our courts and military justice system. And we will insist that judicial review be available for every detainee.

Even after we take these steps, one issue will remain: how to deal with those GTMO detainees who we know have participated in dangerous plots or attacks, but who cannot be prosecuted—for example because the evidence against them has been compromised or is inadmissible in a court of law. But once we commit to a process of closing GTMO, I am confident that this legacy problem can be resolved, consistent with our commitment to the rule of law.

I know the politics are hard. But history will cast a harsh judgment on this aspect of our fight against terrorism, and those of us who fail to end it. Imagine a future—ten years from now, or twenty years from now—when the United States of America is still holding people who have been charged with no crime on a piece of land that is not a part of our country. Look at the current situation, where we are force-feeding detainees who are holding a hunger strike. Is that who we are? Is that something that our Founders foresaw? Is that the America we want to leave to our children?

Our sense of justice is stronger than that. We have prosecuted scores of terrorists in our courts. That includes Umar Farouk Abdulmutallab, who tried to blow up an airplane over Detroit; and Faisal Shahzad, who put a car bomb in Times Square. It is in a court of law that we will try Dzhokhar Tsarnaev, who is accused of bombing the Boston Marathon. Richard Reid, the shoe bomber, is as we speak serving a life sentence in a maximum security prison here, in the United States. In sentencing Reid, Judge William Young told him, "the way we treat you…is the measure of our own liberties." He went on to point to the American flag that flew in the courtroom—"That flag," he said, "will fly there long after this is all forgotten. That flag still stands for freedom."

America, we have faced down dangers far greater than al Qaeda. By staying true to the values of our founding, and by using our constitutional compass, we have overcome slavery and Civil War; fascism and communism. In just these last few years as President, I have watched the American people bounce back from painful recession, mass shootings, and natural disasters like the recent tornados that devastated Oklahoma. These events were heartbreaking; they shook our communities to the core. But because of the resilience of the American people, these events could not come close to breaking us.

I think of Lauren Manning, the 9/11 survivor who had severe burns over 80 percent of her body, who said, "That's my reality. I put a Band-Aid on it, literally, and I move on."

I think of the New Yorkers who filled Times Square the day after an attempted car bomb as if nothing had happened.

I think of the proud Pakistani parents who, after their daughter was invited to the White House, wrote to us, "we have raised an American Muslim daughter to dream big and never give up because it does pay off."

I think of the wounded warriors rebuilding their lives, and helping other vets to find jobs.

I think of the runner planning to do the 2014 Boston Marathon, who said, "Next year, you are going to have more people than ever. Determination is not something to be messed with."

That's who the American people are. Determined, and not to be messed with.

Now, we need a strategy—and a politics –that reflects this resilient spirit. Our victory against terrorism won't be measured in a surrender ceremony on a battleship, or a statue being pulled to the ground. Victory will be measured in parents taking their kids to school; immigrants coming to our shores; fans taking in a ballgame; a veteran starting a business; a bustling city street. The quiet determination; that strength of character and bond of fellowship; that refutation of fear—that is both our sword and our shield. And long after the current messengers of hate have faded from the world's memory, alongside the brutal despots, deranged madmen, and ruthless demagogues who litter history—the flag of the United States will still wave from small-town cemeteries, to national monuments, to distant outposts abroad. And that flag will still stand for freedom.

Thank you. God Bless you. And may God bless the United States of America.

II. Statutes, Orders, and Policy Documents

THE CONSTITUTION OF THE UNITED STATES OF AMERICA

Preamble

We the People of the United States, in Order to form a more perfect Union, establish Justice, insure domestic Tranquility, provide for the common defence, promote the general Welfare, and secure the Blessings of Liberty to ourselves and our Posterity, do ordain and establish this Constitution for the United States of America.

Article 1.

Section 1

All legislative Powers herein granted shall be vested in a Congress of the United States, which shall consist of a Senate and House of Representatives.

Section 2

The House of Representatives shall be composed of Members chosen every second Year by the People of the several States, and the Electors in each State shall have the Qualifications requisite for Electors of the most numerous Branch of the State Legislature.

No Person shall be a Representative who shall not have attained to the Age of twenty five Years, and been seven Years a Citizen of the United States, and who shall not, when elected, be an Inhabitant of that State in which he shall be chosen.

Representatives and direct Taxes shall be apportioned among the several States which may be included within this Union, according to their respective Numbers, which shall be determined by adding to the whole Number of free Persons, including those bound to Service for a Term of Years, and excluding Indians not taxed, three fifths of all other Persons.

The actual Enumeration shall be made within three Years after the first Meeting of the Congress of the United States, and within every subsequent Term of ten Years, in such Manner as they shall by Law direct. The Number of Representatives shall not exceed one for every thirty Thousand, but each State shall have at Least one Representative; and until such enumeration shall be made, the State of New Hampshire shall be entitled to choose three, Massachusetts eight, Rhode Island and Providence Plantations one, Connecticut five, New York six, New Jersey four, Pennsylvania eight, Delaware one, Maryland six, Virginia ten, North Carolina five, South Carolina five and Georgia three.

When vacancies happen in the Representation from any State, the Executive Authority thereof shall issue Writs of Election to fill such Vacancies.

The House of Representatives shall choose their Speaker and other Officers; and shall have the sole Power of Impeachment.

Section 3

The Senate of the United States shall be composed of two Senators from each State, chosen by the Legislature thereof, for six Years; and each Senator shall have one Vote.

Immediately after they shall be assembled in Consequence of the first Election, they shall be divided as equally as may be into three Classes. The Seats of the Senators of the first Class shall be vacated at the Expiration of the second Year, of the second Class at the Expiration of the fourth Year, and of the third Class at the Expiration of the sixth Year, so that one third may be chosen every second Year; and if Vacancies happen by Resignation, or otherwise, during the Recess of the Legislature of any State, the Executive thereof may make temporary Appointments until the next Meeting of the Legislature, which shall then fill such Vacancies.

No person shall be a Senator who shall not have attained to the Age of thirty Years, and been nine Years a Citizen of the United States, and who shall not, when elected, be an Inhabitant of that State for which he shall be chosen.

The Vice President of the United States shall be President of the Senate, but shall have no Vote, unless they be equally divided.

The Senate shall choose their other Officers, and also a President pro tempore, in the absence of the Vice President, or when he shall exercise the Office of President of the United States.

The Senate shall have the sole Power to try all Impeachments. When sitting for that Purpose, they shall be on Oath or Affirmation. When the President of the United States is tried, the Chief Justice shall preside: And no Person shall be convicted without the Concurrence of two thirds of the Members present.

Judgment in Cases of Impeachment shall not extend further than to removal from Office, and disqualification to hold and enjoy any Office of honor, Trust or Profit under the United States: but the Party convicted shall nevertheless be liable and subject to Indictment, Trial, Judgment and Punishment, according to Law.

Section 4

The Times, Places and Manner of holding Elections for Senators and Representatives, shall be prescribed in each State by the Legislature thereof; but the Congress may at any time by Law make or alter such Regulations, except as to the Place of Choosing Senators.

The Congress shall assemble at least once in every Year, and such Meeting shall be on the first Monday in December, unless they shall by Law appoint a different Day.

Section 5

Each House shall be the Judge of the Elections, Returns and Qualifications of its own Members, and a Majority of each shall constitute a Quorum to do Business; but a smaller number may adjourn from day to day, and may be authorized to compel the Attendance of absent Members, in such Manner, and under such Penalties as each House may provide.

Each House may determine the Rules of its Proceedings, punish its Members for disorderly Behavior, and, with the Concurrence of two-thirds, expel a Member.

Each House shall keep a Journal of its Proceedings, and from time to time publish the same, excepting such Parts as may in their Judgment require Secrecy; and the Yeas and Nays of the Members of either House on any question shall, at the Desire of one fifth of those Present, be entered on the Journal.

Neither House, during the Session of Congress, shall, without the Consent of the other, adjourn for more than three days, nor to any other Place than that in which the two Houses shall be sitting.

Section 6

The Senators and Representatives shall receive a Compensation for their Services, to be ascertained by Law, and paid out of the Treasury of the United States. They shall in all Cases, except Treason, Felony and Breach of the Peace, be privileged from Arrest during their Attendance at the Session of their respective Houses, and in going to and returning from the same; and for any Speech or Debate in either House, they shall not be questioned in any other Place.

No Senator or Representative shall, during the Time for which he was elected, be appointed to any civil Office under the Authority of the United States which shall have been created, or the Emoluments whereof shall have been increased during such time; and no Person holding any Office under the United States, shall be a Member of either House during his Continuance in Office.

Section 7

All bills for raising Revenue shall originate in the House of Representatives; but the Senate may propose or concur with Amendments as on other Bills.

Every Bill which shall have passed the House of Representatives and the Senate, shall, before it become a Law, be presented to the President of the United States; If he approve he shall sign it, but if not he shall return it, with his Objections to that House in which it shall have originated, who shall enter the Objections at large on their Journal, and proceed to reconsider it. If after such Reconsideration two thirds of that House shall agree to pass the Bill, it shall be sent, together with the Objections, to the other House, by which it shall likewise be reconsidered, and if approved by two thirds of that House, it shall become a Law. But in all such Cases the Votes of both Houses shall be determined by Yeas and Nays, and the Names of the Persons voting for and against the Bill shall be entered on the Journal of each House respectively. If any Bill shall not be returned by the President within ten Days (Sundays excepted) after it shall have been presented to him, the Same shall be a Law, in like Manner as if he had signed it, unless the Congress by their Adjournment prevent its Return, in which Case it shall not be a Law.

Every Order, Resolution, or Vote to which the Concurrence of the Senate and House of Representatives may be necessary (except on a question of Adjournment) shall be presented to the President of the United States; and before the Same shall take Effect, shall be approved by him, or being disapproved by him, shall be repassed by two thirds of the Senate and House of Representatives, according to the Rules and Limitations prescribed in the Case of a Bill.

Section 8

The Congress shall have Power To lay and collect Taxes, Duties, Imposts and Excises, to pay the Debts and provide for the common Defence and general Welfare of the United States; but all Duties, Imposts and Excises shall be uniform throughout the United States;

To borrow money on the credit of the United States;

To regulate Commerce with foreign Nations, and among the several States, and with the Indian Tribes;

To establish an uniform Rule of Naturalization, and uniform Laws on the subject of Bankruptcies throughout the United States;

To coin Money, regulate the Value thereof, and of foreign Coin, and fix the Standard of Weights and Measures;

To provide for the Punishment of counterfeiting the Securities and current Coin of the United States;

To establish Post Offices and Post Roads;

To promote the Progress of Science and useful Arts, by securing for limited Times to Authors and Inventors the exclusive Right to their respective Writings and Discoveries;

To constitute Tribunals inferior to the supreme Court;

To define and punish Piracies and Felonies committed on the high Seas, and Offenses against the Law of Nations;

To declare War, grant Letters of Marque and Reprisal, and make Rules concerning Captures on Land and Water;

To raise and support Armies, but no Appropriation of Money to that Use shall be for a longer Term than two Years;

To provide and maintain a Navy;

To make Rules for the Government and Regulation of the land and naval Forces;

To provide for calling forth the Militia to execute the Laws of the Union, suppress Insurrections and repel Invasions;

To provide for organizing, arming, and disciplining the Militia, and for governing such Part of them as may be employed in the Service of the United States, reserving to the States respectively, the Appointment of the Officers, and the Authority of training the Militia according to the discipline prescribed by Congress;

To exercise exclusive Legislation in all Cases whatsoever, over such District (not exceeding ten Miles square) as may, by Cession of particular States, and the acceptance of Congress, become the Seat of the Government of the United States, and to exercise like Authority over all Places purchased by the Consent of the Legislature of the State in which the Same shall be, for the Erection of Forts, Magazines, Arsenals, dock-Yards, and other needful Buildings; And

To make all Laws which shall be necessary and proper for carrying into Execution the foregoing Powers, and all other Powers vested by this Constitution in the Government of the United States, or in any Department or Officer thereof.

Section 9

The Migration or Importation of such Persons as any of the States now existing shall think proper to admit, shall not be prohibited by the Congress prior to the Year one thousand eight hundred and eight, but a tax or duty may be imposed on such Importation, not exceeding ten dollars for each Person.

The privilege of the Writ of Habeas Corpus shall not be suspended, unless when in Cases of Rebellion or Invasion the public Safety may require it.

No Bill of Attainder or ex post facto Law shall be passed.

No capitation, or other direct, Tax shall be laid, unless in Proportion to the Census or Enumeration herein before directed to be taken.

No Tax or Duty shall be laid on Articles exported from any State.

No Preference shall be given by any Regulation of Commerce or Revenue to the Ports of one State over those of another: nor shall Vessels bound to, or from, one State, be obliged to enter, clear, or pay Duties in another.

No Money shall be drawn from the Treasury, but in Consequence of Appropriations made by Law; and a regular Statement and Account of the Receipts and Expenditures of all public Money shall be published from time to time.

No Title of Nobility shall be granted by the United States: And no Person holding any Office of Profit or Trust under them, shall, without the Consent of the Congress, accept of any present, Emolument, Office, or Title, of any kind whatever, from any King, Prince or foreign State.

Section 10

No State shall enter into any Treaty, Alliance, or Confederation; grant Letters of Marque and Reprisal; coin Money; emit Bills of Credit; make any Thing but gold and silver Coin a Tender in Payment of Debts; pass any Bill of Attainder, ex post facto Law, or Law impairing the Obligation of Contracts, or grant any Title of Nobility.

No State shall, without the Consent of the Congress, lay any Imposts or Duties on Imports or Exports, except what may be absolutely necessary for executing its inspection Laws: and the net Produce of all Duties and Imposts, laid by any State on Imports or Exports, shall be for the Use of the Treasury of the United States; and all such Laws shall be subject to the Revision and Control of the Congress.

No State shall, without the Consent of Congress, lay any duty of Tonnage, keep Troops, or Ships of War in time of Peace, enter into any Agreement or Compact with another State, or with a foreign Power, or engage in War, unless actually invaded, or in such imminent Danger as will not admit of delay.

Article 2.

Section 1

The executive Power shall be vested in a President of the United States of America. He shall hold his Office during the Term of four Years, and, together with the Vice-President chosen for the same Term, be elected, as follows:

Each State shall appoint, in such Manner as the Legislature thereof may direct, a Number of Electors, equal to the whole Number of Senators and Representatives to which the State may be entitled in the Congress: but no Senator or Representative, or Person holding an Office of Trust or Profit under the United States, shall be appointed an Elector.

The Electors shall meet in their respective States, and vote by Ballot for two persons, of whom one at least shall not lie an Inhabitant of the same State with themselves. And they shall make a List of all the Persons voted for, and of the Number of Votes for each; which List they shall sign and certify, and transmit sealed to the Seat of the Government of the United States, directed to the President of the Senate. The President of the Senate shall, in the Presence of the Senate and House of Representatives, open all the Certificates, and the Votes shall then be counted. The Person having the greatest Number of Votes shall be the President, if such Number be a Majority of the whole Number of Electors appointed; and if there be more than one who have such Majority, and have an equal Number of Votes, then the House of Representatives shall immediately choose by Ballot one of them for President; and if no Person have a Majority, then from the five highest on the List the said House shall in like Manner choose the President. But in choosing the President, the Votes shall be taken by States, the Representation from each State having one Vote; a quorum for this Purpose shall consist of a Member or Members from two-thirds of the States, and a Majority of all the States shall be necessary to a Choice. In every Case, after the Choice of the President, the Person having the greatest Number of Votes of the Electors shall be the Vice President. But if there should remain two or more who have equal Votes, the Senate shall choose from them by Ballot the Vice-President.

The Congress may determine the Time of choosing the Electors, and the Day on which they shall give their Votes; which Day shall be the same throughout the United States.

No person except a natural born Citizen, or a Citizen of the United States, at the time of the Adoption of this Constitution, shall be eligible to the Office of President; neither shall any Person be eligible to that Office who shall not have attained to the Age of thirty-five Years, and been fourteen Years a Resident within the United States.

In Case of the Removal of the President from Office, or of his Death, Resignation, or Inability to discharge the Powers and Duties of the said Office, the same shall devolve on the Vice President, and the Congress may by Law provide for the Case of Removal, Death, Resignation or Inability, both of the President and Vice President, declaring what Officer shall then act as President, and such Officer shall act accordingly, until the Disability be removed, or a President shall be elected.

The President shall, at stated Times, receive for his Services, a Compensation, which shall neither be increased nor diminished during the Period for which he shall have been elected, and he shall not receive within that Period any other Emolument from the United States, or any of them.

Before he enter on the Execution of his Office, he shall take the following Oath or Affirmation:

> "I do solemnly swear (or affirm) that I will faithfully execute the Office of President of the United States, and will to the best of my Ability, preserve, protect and defend the Constitution of the United States."

Section 2

The President shall be Commander in Chief of the Army and Navy of the United States, and of the Militia of the several States, when called into the actual Service of the United States; he may require the Opinion, in writing, of the principal Officer in each of the executive Departments, upon any subject relating to the Duties of their respective Offices, and he shall have Power to Grant Reprieves and Pardons for Offenses against the United States, except in Cases of Impeachment.

He shall have Power, by and with the Advice and Consent of the Senate, to make Treaties, provided two thirds of the Senators present concur; and he shall nominate, and by and with the Advice and Consent of the Senate, shall appoint Ambassadors, other public Ministers and Consuls, Judges of the supreme Court, and all other Officers of the United States, whose Appointments are not herein otherwise provided for, and which shall be established by Law: but the Congress may by Law vest the Appointment of such inferior Officers, as they think proper, in the President alone, in the Courts of Law, or in the Heads of Departments.

The President shall have Power to fill up all Vacancies that may happen during the Recess of the Senate, by granting Commissions which shall expire at the End of their next Session.

Section 3
He shall from time to time give to the Congress Information of the State of the Union, and recommend to their Consideration such Measures as he shall judge necessary and expedient; he may, on extraordinary Occasions, convene both Houses, or either of them, and in Case of Disagreement between them, with Respect to the Time of Adjournment, he may adjourn them to such Time as he shall think proper; he shall receive Ambassadors and other public Ministers; he shall take Care that the Laws be faithfully executed, and shall Commission all the Officers of the United States.

Section 4
The President, Vice President and all civil Officers of the United States, shall be removed from Office on Impeachment for, and Conviction of, Treason, Bribery, or other high Crimes and Misdemeanors.

Article 3.

Section 1
The judicial Power of the United States, shall be vested in one supreme Court, and in such inferior Courts as the Congress may from time to time ordain and establish. The Judges, both of the supreme and inferior Courts, shall hold their Offices during good Behavior, and shall, at stated Times, receive for their Services a Compensation which shall not be diminished during their Continuance in Office.

Section 2
The judicial Power shall extend to all Cases, in Law and Equity, arising under this Constitution, the Laws of the United States, and Treaties made, or which shall be made, under their Authority; to all Cases affecting Ambassadors, other public Ministers and Consuls; to all Cases of admiralty and maritime Jurisdiction; to Controversies to which the United States shall be a Party; to Controversies between two or more States; between a State and Citizens of another State; between Citizens of different States; between Citizens of the same State claiming Lands under Grants of different States, and between a State, or the Citizens thereof, and foreign States, Citizens or Subjects.

In all Cases affecting Ambassadors, other public Ministers and Consuls, and those in which a State shall be Party, the supreme Court shall have original Jurisdiction. In all the other Cases before mentioned, the supreme Court shall have appellate Jurisdiction, both as to Law and Fact, with such Exceptions, and under such Regulations as the Congress shall make.

The Trial of all Crimes, except in Cases of Impeachment, shall be by Jury; and such Trial shall be held in the State where the said Crimes shall have been committed; but when not committed within any State, the Trial shall be at such Place or Places as the Congress may by Law have directed.

Section 3
Treason against the United States, shall consist only in levying War against them, or in adhering to their Enemies, giving them Aid and Comfort. No Person shall be convicted of Treason unless on the Testimony of two Witnesses to the same overt Act, or on Confession in open Court.

The Congress shall have power to declare the Punishment of Treason, but no Attainder of Treason shall work Corruption of Blood, or Forfeiture except during the Life of the Person attainted.

Article 4.

Section 1
Full Faith and Credit shall be given in each State to the public Acts, Records, and judicial Proceedings of every other State. And the Congress may by general Laws prescribe the Manner in which such Acts, Records and Proceedings shall be proved, and the Effect thereof.

Section 2
The Citizens of each State shall be entitled to all Privileges and Immunities of Citizens in the several States.

A Person charged in any State with Treason, Felony, or other Crime, who shall flee from Justice, and be found in another State, shall on demand of the executive Authority of the State from which he fled, be delivered up, to be removed to the State having Jurisdiction of the Crime.

No Person held to Service or Labour in one State, under the Laws thereof, escaping into another, shall, in Consequence of any Law or Regulation therein, be discharged from such Service or Labour, But shall be delivered up on Claim of the Party to whom such Service or Labour may be due.

Section 3
New States may be admitted by the Congress into this Union; but no new States shall be formed or erected within the Jurisdiction of any other State; nor any State be formed by the Junction of two or more States, or parts of States, without the Consent of the Legislatures of the States concerned as well as of the Congress.

The Congress shall have Power to dispose of and make all needful Rules and Regulations respecting the Territory or other Property belonging to the United States; and nothing in this Constitution shall be so construed as to Prejudice any Claims of the United States, or of any particular State.

Section 4
The United States shall guarantee to every State in this Union a Republican Form of Government, and shall protect each of them against Invasion; and on Application of the Legislature, or of the Executive (when the Legislature cannot be convened) against domestic Violence.

Article 5.

The Congress, whenever two thirds of both Houses shall deem it necessary, shall propose Amendments to this Constitution, or, on the Application of the Legislatures of two thirds of the several States, shall call a Convention for proposing Amendments, which, in either Case, shall be valid to all Intents and Purposes, as part of this Constitution, when ratified by the Legislatures of three fourths of the several States, or by Conventions in three fourths thereof, as the one or the other Mode of Ratification may be proposed by the Congress; Provided that no Amendment which may be made prior to the Year One thousand eight hundred and eight shall in any Manner affect the first and fourth Clauses in the Ninth Section of the first Article; and that no State, without its Consent, shall be deprived of its equal Suffrage in the Senate.

Article 6.

All Debts contracted and Engagements entered into, before the Adoption of this Constitution, shall be as valid against the United States under this Constitution, as under the Confederation.

This Constitution, and the Laws of the United States which shall be made in Pursuance thereof; and all Treaties made, or which shall be made, under the Authority of the United States, shall be the supreme Law of the Land; and the Judges in every State shall be bound thereby, any Thing in the Constitution or Laws of any State to the Contrary notwithstanding.

The Senators and Representatives before mentioned, and the Members of the several State Legislatures, and all executive and judicial Officers, both of the United States and of the several States, shall be bound by Oath or Affirmation, to support this Constitution; but no religious Test shall ever be required as a Qualification to any Office or public Trust under the United States.

Article 7.

The Ratification of the Conventions of nine States, shall be sufficient for the Establishment of this Constitution between the States so ratifying the Same.

Done in Convention by the Unanimous Consent of the States present the Seventeenth Day of September in the Year of our Lord one thousand seven hundred and Eighty seven and of the Independence of the United States of America the Twelfth. In Witness whereof We have hereunto subscribed our Names.

George Washington—President and deputy from Virginia

New Hampshire—John Langdon, Nicholas Gilman

Massachusetts—Nathaniel Gorham, Rufus King

Connecticut—William Samuel Johnson, Roger Sherman

New York—Alexander Hamilton

New Jersey—William Livingston, David Brearley, William Paterson, Jonathan Dayton

Pennsylvania—Benjamin Franklin, Thomas Mifflin, Robert Morris, George Clymer, Thomas Fitzsimons, Jared Ingersoll, James Wilson, Gouvernour Morris

Delaware—George Read, Gunning Bedford Jr., John Dickinson, Richard Bassett, Jacob Broom

Maryland—James McHenry, Daniel of St Thomas Jenifer, Daniel Carroll

Virginia—John Blair, James Madison Jr.

North Carolina—William Blount, Richard Dobbs Spaight, Hugh Williamson

South Carolina—John Rutledge, Charles Cotesworth Pinckney, Charles Pinckney, Pierce Butler

Georgia—William Few, Abraham Baldwin

Attest: William Jackson, Secretary

Amendment 1

Congress shall make no law respecting an establishment of religion, or prohibiting the free exercise thereof; or abridging the freedom of speech, or of the press; or the right of the people peaceably to assemble, and to petition the Government for a redress of grievances.

Amendment 2

A well regulated Militia, being necessary to the security of a free State, the right of the people to keep and bear Arms, shall not be infringed.

Amendment 3

No Soldier shall, in time of peace be quartered in any house, without the consent of the Owner, nor in time of war, but in a manner to be prescribed by law.

Amendment 4

The right of the people to be secure in their persons, houses, papers, and effects, against unreasonable searches and seizures, shall not be violated, and no Warrants shall issue, but upon probable cause, supported by Oath or affirmation, and particularly describing the place to be searched, and the persons or things to be seized.

Amendment 5

No person shall be held to answer for a capital, or otherwise infamous crime, unless on a presentment or indictment of a Grand Jury, except in cases arising in the land or naval forces, or in the Militia, when in actual service in time of War or public danger; nor shall any person be subject for the same offense to be twice put in jeopardy of life or limb; nor shall be compelled in any criminal case to be a witness against himself, nor be deprived of life, liberty, or property, without due process of law; nor shall private property be taken for public use, without just compensation.

Amendment 6

In all criminal prosecutions, the accused shall enjoy the right to a speedy and public trial, by an impartial jury of the State and district wherein the crime shall have been committed, which district shall have been previously ascertained by law, and to be informed of the nature and cause of the accusation; to be confronted with the witnesses against him; to have compulsory process for obtaining witnesses in his favor, and to have the Assistance of Counsel for his defence.

Amendment 7

In Suits at common law, where the value in controversy shall exceed twenty dollars, the right of trial by jury shall be preserved, and no fact tried by a jury, shall be otherwise re-examined in any Court of the United States, than according to the rules of the common law.

Amendment 8

Excessive bail shall not be required, nor excessive fines imposed, nor cruel and unusual punishments inflicted.

Amendment 9

The enumeration in the Constitution, of certain rights, shall not be construed to deny or disparage others retained by the people.

Amendment 10

The powers not delegated to the United States by the Constitution, nor prohibited by it to the States, are reserved to the States respectively, or to the people.

Amendment 11

The Judicial power of the United States shall not be construed to extend to any suit in law or equity, commenced or prosecuted against one of the United States by Citizens of another State, or by Citizens or Subjects of any Foreign State.

Amendment 12

The Electors shall meet in their respective states, and vote by ballot for President and Vice-President, one of whom, at least, shall not be an inhabitant of the same state with themselves; they shall name in their ballots the person voted for as President, and in distinct ballots the person voted for as Vice-President, and they shall make distinct lists of all persons voted for as President, and of all persons voted for as Vice-President and of the number of votes for each, which lists they shall sign and certify, and transmit sealed to the seat of the government of the United States, directed to the President of the Senate;

The President of the Senate shall, in the presence of the Senate and House of Representatives, open all the certificates and the votes shall then be counted;

The person having the greatest Number of votes for President, shall be the President, if such number be a majority of the whole number of Electors appointed; and if no person have such majority, then from the persons having the highest numbers not exceeding three on the list of those voted for as President, the House of Representatives shall choose immediately, by ballot, the President. But in choosing the President, the votes shall be taken by states, the representation from each state having one vote; a quorum for this purpose shall consist of a member or members from two-thirds of the states, and a majority of all the states shall be necessary to a choice. And if the House of Representatives shall not choose a President whenever the right of choice shall devolve upon them, before the fourth day of March next following, then the Vice-President shall act as President, as in the case of the death or other constitutional disability of the President.

The person having the greatest number of votes as Vice-President, shall be the Vice-President, if such number be a majority of the whole number of Electors appointed, and if no person have a majority, then from the two highest numbers on the list, the Senate shall choose the Vice-President; a quorum for the purpose shall consist of two-thirds of the whole number of Senators, and a majority of the whole number shall be necessary to a choice. But no person constitutionally ineligible to the office of President shall be eligible to that of Vice-President of the United States.

Amendment 13

1. Neither slavery nor involuntary servitude, except as a punishment for crime whereof the party shall have been duly convicted, shall exist within the United States, or any place subject to their jurisdiction.
2. Congress shall have power to enforce this article by appropriate legislation.

Amendment 14

1. All persons born or naturalized in the United States, and subject to the jurisdiction thereof, are citizens of the United States and of the State wherein they reside. No State shall make or enforce any law which shall abridge the privileges or immunities of citizens of the United States; nor shall any State deprive any person of life, liberty, or property, without due process of law; nor deny to any person within its jurisdiction the equal protection of the laws.
2. Representatives shall be apportioned among the several States according to their respective numbers, counting the whole number of persons in each State, excluding Indians not taxed. But when the right to vote at any election for the choice of electors for President and Vice-President of the United States, Representatives in Congress, the Executive and Judicial officers of a State, or the members of the Legislature thereof, is denied to any of the male inhabitants of such State, being twenty-one years of age, and citizens of the United States, or in any way abridged, except for participation in rebellion, or other crime, the basis of representation therein shall be reduced in the proportion which the number of such male citizens shall bear to the whole number of male citizens twenty-one years of age in such State.
3. No person shall be a Senator or Representative in Congress, or elector of President and Vice-President, or hold any office, civil or military, under the United States, or under any

State, who, having previously taken an oath, as a member of Congress, or as an officer of the United States, or as a member of any State legislature, or as an executive or judicial officer of any State, to support the Constitution of the United States, shall have engaged in insurrection or rebellion against the same, or given aid or comfort to the enemies thereof. But Congress may by a vote of two-thirds of each House, remove such disability.

4. The validity of the public debt of the United States, authorized by law, including debts incurred for payment of pensions and bounties for services in suppressing insurrection or rebellion, shall not be questioned. But neither the United States nor any State shall assume or pay any debt or obligation incurred in aid of insurrection or rebellion against the United States, or any claim for the loss or emancipation of any slave; but all such debts, obligations and claims shall be held illegal and void.
5. The Congress shall have power to enforce, by appropriate legislation, the provisions of this article.

Amendment 15

1. The right of citizens of the United States to vote shall not be denied or abridged by the United States or by any State on account of race, color, or previous condition of servitude.
2. The Congress shall have power to enforce this article by appropriate legislation.

Amendment 16

The Congress shall have power to lay and collect taxes on incomes, from whatever source derived, without apportionment among the several States, and without regard to any census or enumeration.

Amendment 17

The Senate of the United States shall be composed of two Senators from each State, elected by the people thereof, for six years; and each Senator shall have one vote. The electors in each State shall have the qualifications requisite for electors of the most numerous branch of the State legislatures.

When vacancies happen in the representation of any State in the Senate, the executive authority of such State shall issue writs of election to fill such vacancies: Provided, That the legislature of any State may empower the executive thereof to make temporary appointments until the people fill the vacancies by election as the legislature may direct.

This amendment shall not be so construed as to affect the election or term of any Senator chosen before it becomes valid as part of the Constitution.

Amendment 18

1. After one year from the ratification of this article the manufacture, sale, or transportation of intoxicating liquors within, the importation thereof into, or the exportation thereof from the United States and all territory subject to the jurisdiction thereof for beverage purposes is hereby prohibited.
2. The Congress and the several States shall have concurrent power to enforce this article by appropriate legislation.
3. This article shall be inoperative unless it shall have been ratified as an amendment to the Constitution by the legislatures of the several States, as provided in the Constitution, within seven years from the date of the submission hereof to the States by the Congress.

Amendment 19

The right of citizens of the United States to vote shall not be denied or abridged by the United States or by any State on account of sex.

Congress shall have power to enforce this article by appropriate legislation.

Amendment 20

1. The terms of the President and Vice President shall end at noon on the 20th day of January, and the terms of Senators and Representatives at noon on the 3d day of January, of the years in which such terms would have ended if this article had not been ratified; and the terms of their successors shall then begin.
2. The Congress shall assemble at least once in every year, and such meeting shall begin at noon on the 3d day of January, unless they shall by law appoint a different day.
3. If, at the time fixed for the beginning of the term of the President, the President elect shall have died, the Vice President elect shall become President. If a President shall not have been chosen before the time fixed for the beginning of his term, or if the President elect shall have failed to qualify, then the Vice President elect shall act as President until a President shall have qualified; and the Congress may by law provide for the case wherein neither a President elect nor a Vice President elect shall have qualified, declaring who shall then act as President, or the manner in which one who is to act shall be selected, and such person shall act accordingly until a President or Vice President shall have qualified.
4. The Congress may by law provide for the case of the death of any of the persons from whom the House of Representatives may choose a President whenever the right of choice shall have devolved upon them, and for the case of the death of any of the persons from whom the Senate may choose a Vice President whenever the right of choice shall have devolved upon them.
5. Sections 1 and 2 shall take effect on the 15th day of October following the ratification of this article.
6. This article shall be inoperative unless it shall have been ratified as an amendment to the Constitution by the legislatures of three-fourths of the several States within seven years from the date of its submission.

Amendment 21

1. The eighteenth article of amendment to the Constitution of the United States is hereby repealed.
2. The transportation or importation into any State, Territory, or possession of the United States for delivery or use therein of intoxicating liquors, in violation of the laws thereof, is hereby prohibited.
3. The article shall be inoperative unless it shall have been ratified as an amendment to the Constitution by conventions in the several States, as provided in the Constitution, within seven years from the date of the submission hereof to the States by the Congress.

Amendment 22

1. No person shall be elected to the office of the President more than twice, and no person who has held the office of President, or acted as President, for more than two years of a term to which some other person was elected President shall be elected to the office of the President more than once. But this Article shall not apply to any person holding the office of President, when this Article was proposed by the Congress, and shall not prevent any person who may be holding the office of President, or acting as President, during the term

within which this Article becomes operative from holding the office of President or acting as President during the remainder of such term.

2. This article shall be inoperative unless it shall have been ratified as an amendment to the Constitution by the legislatures of three-fourths of the several States within seven years from the date of its submission to the States by the Congress.

Amendment 23

1. The District constituting the seat of Government of the United States shall appoint in such manner as the Congress may direct: A number of electors of President and Vice President equal to the whole number of Senators and Representatives in Congress to which the District would be entitled if it were a State, but in no event more than the least populous State; they shall be in addition to those appointed by the States, but they shall be considered, for the purposes of the election of President and Vice President, to be electors appointed by a State; and they shall meet in the District and perform such duties as provided by the twelfth article of amendment.
2. The Congress shall have power to enforce this article by appropriate legislation.

Amendment 24

1. The right of citizens of the United States to vote in any primary or other election for President or Vice President, for electors for President or Vice President, or for Senator or Representative in Congress, shall not be denied or abridged by the United States or any State by reason of failure to pay any poll tax or other tax.
2. The Congress shall have power to enforce this article by appropriate legislation.

Amendment 25

1. In case of the removal of the President from office or of his death or resignation, the Vice President shall become President.
2. Whenever there is a vacancy in the office of the Vice President, the President shall nominate a Vice President who shall take office upon confirmation by a majority vote of both Houses of Congress.
3. Whenever the President transmits to the President pro tempore of the Senate and the Speaker of the House of Representatives his written declaration that he is unable to discharge the powers and duties of his office, and until he transmits to them a written declaration to the contrary, such powers and duties shall be discharged by the Vice President as Acting President.
4. Whenever the Vice President and a majority of either the principal officers of the executive departments or of such other body as Congress may by law provide, transmit to the President pro tempore of the Senate and the Speaker of the House of Representatives their written declaration that the President is unable to discharge the powers and duties of his office, the Vice President shall immediately assume the powers and duties of the office as Acting President.

Thereafter, when the President transmits to the President pro tempore of the Senate and the Speaker of the House of Representatives his written declaration that no inability exists, he shall resume the powers and duties of his office unless the Vice President and a majority of either the principal officers of the executive department or of such other body as Congress may by law provide, transmit within four days to the President pro tempore of the Senate and the Speaker of the House of Representatives their written declaration that the President is unable to discharge the powers and duties of his office. Thereupon Congress shall decide the issue, assembling within forty eight hours for that purpose if not in session. If the Congress, within twenty one days after receipt of the latter written declaration, or, if Congress is not in session, within twenty one days after Congress is required to assemble, determines by two thirds vote of both Houses that the President is unable to discharge the powers and duties of his office, the Vice President shall continue to discharge the same as Acting President; otherwise, the President shall resume the powers and duties of his office.

Amendment 26

1. The right of citizens of the United States, who are eighteen years of age or older, to vote shall not be denied or abridged by the United States or by any State on account of age.
2. The Congress shall have power to enforce this article by appropriate legislation.

Amendment 27

No law, varying the compensation for the services of the Senators and Representatives, shall take effect, until an election of Representatives shall have intervened.

Authorization for Use of Military Force

Pub. L. No. 107-40, 115 Stat. 224 (2001)

JOINT RESOLUTION

To authorize the use of United States Armed Forces against those responsible for the recent attacks launched against the United States.

Whereas, on September 11, 2001, acts of treacherous violence were committed against the United States and its citizens; and

Whereas, such acts render it both necessary and appropriate that the United States exercise its rights to self-defense and to protect United States citizens both at home and abroad; and

Whereas, in light of the threat to the national security and foreign policy of the United States posed by these grave acts of violence; and

Whereas, such acts continue to pose an unusual and extraordinary threat to the national security and foreign policy of the United States; and

Whereas, the President has authority under the Constitution to take action to deter and prevent acts of international terrorism against the United States: Now, therefore, be it

Resolved by the Senate and House of Representatives of the United States of America in Congress assembled,

SECTION 1. SHORT TITLE.

This joint resolution may be cited as the 'Authorization for Use of Military Force'.

SECTION 2. AUTHORIZATION FOR USE OF UNITED STATES ARMED FORCES.

(a) IN GENERAL—That the President is authorized to use all necessary and appropriate force against those nations, organizations, or persons he determines planned, authorized, committed, or aided the terrorist attacks that occurred on September 11, 2001, or harbored such organizations or persons, in order to prevent any future acts of international terrorism against the United States by such nations, organizations or persons.

(b) War Powers Resolution Requirements—

(1) SPECIFIC STATUTORY AUTHORIZATION- Consistent with section 8(a)(1) of the War Powers Resolution, the Congress declares that this section is intended to constitute specific statutory authorization within the meaning of section 5(b) of the War Powers Resolution.

(2) APPLICABILITY OF OTHER REQUIREMENTS—Nothing in this resolution supersedes any requirement of the War Powers Resolution.

Approved September 18, 2001.

National Defense Authorization Act of 2012, Section 1021

SEC. 1021. AFFIRMATION OF AUTHORITY OF THE ARMED FORCES OF THE UNITED STATES TO DETAIN COVERED PERSONS PURSUANT TO THE AUTHORIZATION FOR USE OF MILITARY FORCE.

(a) In General—Congress affirms that the authority of the President to use all necessary and appropriate force pursuant to the Authorization for Use of Military Force (Public Law 107-40; 50 U.S.C. 1541 note) includes the authority for the Armed Forces of the United States to detain covered persons (as defined in subsection (b)) pending disposition under the law of war.

(b) Covered Persons—A covered person under this section is any person as follows:

(1) A person who planned, authorized, committed, or aided the terrorist attacks that occurred on September 11, 2001, or harbored those responsible for those attacks.

(2) A person who was a part of or substantially supported al-Qaeda, the Taliban, or associated forces that are engaged in hostilities against the United States or its coalition partners, including any person who has committed a belligerent act or has directly supported such hostilities in aid of such enemy forces.

(c) Disposition Under Law of War—The disposition of a person under the law of war as described in subsection (a) may include the following:

(1) Detention under the law of war without trial until the end of the hostilities authorized by the Authorization for Use of Military Force.

(2) Trial under chapter 47A of title 10, United States Code (as amended by the Military Commissions Act of 2009 (title XVIII of Public Law 111-84)).

(3) Transfer for trial by an alternative court or competent tribunal having lawful jurisdiction.

(4) Transfer to the custody or control of the person's country of origin, any other foreign country, or any other foreign entity.

(d) Construction—Nothing in this section is intended to limit or expand the authority of the President or the scope of the Authorization for Use of Military Force.

(e) Authorities—Nothing in this section shall be construed to affect existing law or authorities relating to the detention of United States citizens, lawful resident aliens of the United States, or any other persons who are captured or arrested in the United States.

(f) Requirement for Briefings of Congress—The Secretary of Defense shall regularly brief Congress regarding the application of the authority described in this section, including the organizations, entities, and individuals considered to be 'covered persons' for purposes of subsection (b)(2).

FEDERAL STATUTES

National Security Act of 1947

(Chapter 343; 61 Stat. 496; approved July 26, 1947)
[As Amended Through Pub. L. 110-53, Enacted August 3, 2007]

AN ACT To promote the national security by providing for a Secretary of Defense; for a National Military Establishment; for a Department of the Army, a Department of the Navy, and a Department of the Air Force; and for the coordination of the activities of the National Military Establishment with other departments and agencies of the Government concerned with the national security.

Be it enacted by the Senate and House of Representatives of the United States of America in Congress assembled,

SHORT TITLE

That this Act may be cited as the "National Security Act of 1947".

TABLE OF CONTENTS

1. Item editorially inserted.

2. This section was redesignated as section 108 by section 705(a)(2) of P.L. 102–496, but this entry in the table of contents was not repealed.

3. The item for section 109 was repealed by section 347(i)(1)(A) of Public Law 111–259.

4. Section repealed without amending table of contents

5. Item editorially inserted.

DECLARATION OF POLICY

SEC. 2. [50 U.S.C. §401] In enacting this legislation, it is the intent of Congress to provide a comprehensive program for the future security of the United States; to provide for the establishment of integrated policies and procedures for the departments, agencies, and functions of the Government relating to the national security; to provide a Department of Defense, including the three military Departments of the Army, the Navy (including naval aviation and the United States Marine Corps), and the Air Force under the direction, authority, and control of the Secretary of Defense; to provide that each military department shall be separately organized under its own

Secretary and shall function under the direction, authority, and control of the Secretary of Defense; to provide for their unified direction under civilian control of the Secretary of Defense but not to merge these departments or services; to provide for the establishment of unified or specified combatant commands, and a clear and direct line of command to such commands; to eliminate unnecessary duplication in the Department of Defense, and particularly in the field of research and engineering by vesting its overall direction and control in the Secretary of Defense; to provide more effective, efficient, and economical administration in the Department of Defense; to provide for the unified strategic direction of the combatant forces, for their operation under unified command, and for their integration into an efficient team of land, naval, and air forces but not to establish a single Chief of Staff over the armed forces nor an overall armed forces general staff.

DEFINITIONS

SEC. 3. [50 U.S.C. §401a] As used in this Act:

(1) The term "intelligence" includes foreign intelligence and counterintelligence.

(2) The term "foreign intelligence" means information relating to the capabilities, intentions, or activities of foreign governments or elements thereof, foreign organizations, or foreign persons, or international terrorist activities.

(3) The term "counterintelligence" means information gathered and activities conducted to protect against espionage, other intelligence activities, sabotage, or assassinations conducted by or on behalf of foreign governments or elements thereof, foreign organizations, or foreign persons, or international terrorist activities.

(4) The term "intelligence community" includes the following:

(A) The Office of the Director of National Intelligence.

(B) The Central Intelligence Agency.

(C) The National Security Agency.

(D) The Defense Intelligence Agency.

(E) The National Geospatial-Intelligence Agency.

(F) The National Reconnaissance Office.

(G) Other offices within the Department of Defense for the collection of specialized national intelligence through reconnaissance programs.

(H) The intelligence elements of the Army, the Navy, the Air Force, the Marine Corps, the Federal Bureau of Investigation, and the Department of Energy.

(I) The Bureau of Intelligence and Research of the Department of State.

(J) The Office of Intelligence and Analysis of the Department of the Treasury.

(K) The elements of the Department of Homeland Security concerned with the analysis of intelligence information, including the Office of Intelligence of the Coast Guard.

(L) Such other elements of any other department or agency as may be designated by the President, or designated jointly by the Director of National Intelligence and the head of the department or agency concerned, as an element of the intelligence community.

(5) The terms "national intelligence" and "intelligence related to national security"

refer to all intelligence, regardless of the source from which derived and including information gathered within or outside the United States, that—

(A) pertains, as determined consistent with any guidance issued by the President, to more than one United States Government agency; and

(B) that involves—

(i) threats to the United States, its people, property, or interests;

(ii) the development, proliferation, or use of weapons of mass destruction; or

(iii) any other matter bearing on United States national or homeland security.

(6) The term "National Intelligence Program" refers to all programs, projects, and activities of the intelligence community, as well as any other programs of the intelligence community designated jointly by the Director of National Intelligence and the head of a United States department or agency or by the President. Such term does not include programs, projects, or activities of the military departments to acquire intelligence solely for the planning and conduct of tactical military operations by United States Armed Forces.

(7) The term "congressional intelligence committees" means—

(A) the Select Committee on Intelligence of the Senate; and

(B) the Permanent Select Committee on Intelligence of the House of Representatives.

TITLE I—COORDINATION FOR NATIONAL SECURITY

NATIONAL SECURITY COUNCIL

SEC. 101. [50 U.S.C. §402]

(a) There is here established a council to be known as the National Security Council (thereinafter in this section referred to as the "Council"). The President of the United States shall preside over meetings of the Council: *Provided,* That in his absence he may designate a member of the Council to preside in his place. The function of the Council shall be to advise the President with respect to the integration of domestic, foreign, and military policies relating to the national security so as to enable the military services and the other departments and agencies of the Government to cooperate more effectively in matters involving the national security.

The Council shall be composed of[1]—

(1) the President;

(2) the Vice President;

(3) the Secretary of State;

(4) the Secretary of Defense;

(5) the Director for Mutual Security;

(6) the Chairman of the National Security Resources Board; and

---

1. The positions of Director for Mutual Security, Chairman of the National Security ResourcesBoard, Chairman of the Munitions Board, and Chairman of the Research and DevelopmentBoard have been abolished by various Reorganiztion Plans. The statutory members of the National Security Council are the President, Vice President, Secretary of State, and Secretary ofDefense.

(7) the Secretaries and Under Secretaries of other executive departments and of the military departments, the Chairman of the Munitions Board, and the Chairman of the Research and Development Board, when appointed by the President by and with the advice and consent of the Senate, to serve at his pleasure.

(b) In addition to performing such other functions as the President may direct, for the purpose of more effectively coordinating the policies and functions of the departments and agencies of the Government relating to the national security, it shall, subject to the direction of the President, be the duty of the Council—

(1) to assess and appraise the objectives, commitments, and risks of the United States in relation to our actual and potential military power, in the interest of national security, for the purpose of making recommendations to the President in connection therewith; and

(2) to consider policies on matters of common interest to the departments and agencies of the Government concerned with the national security, and to make recommendations to the President in connection therewith.

(c) The Council shall have a staff to be headed by a civilian executive secretary who shall be appointed by the President and who shall receive a compensation of $10,000 a year.[1] The executive secretary, subject to the direction of the Council, is hereby authorized, subject to the civil-service laws and the Classification Act of 1923, as amended,[2] to appoint and fix the compensation of such personnel as may be necessary to perform such duties as may be prescribed by the Council in connection with the performance of its functions.

(d) The Council shall, from time to time, make such recommendations, and such other reports to the President as it deems appropriate or as the President may require.

(e) The Chairman (or in his absence the Vice Chairman) of the Joint Chiefs of Staff may, in his role as principal military adviser to the National Security Council and subject to the direction of the President, attend and participate in meetings of the National Security Council.

(f) The Director of National Drug Control Policy may, in the role of the Director as principal adviser to the National Security Council on national drug control policy, and subject to the direction of the President, attend and participate in meetings of the National Security Council.

(g) The President shall establish within the National Security Council a board to be known as the "Board for Low Intensity Conflict". The principal function of the board shall be to coordinate the policies of the United States for low intensity conflict.

(h)(1) There is established within the National Security Council a committee to be

---

1. The specification of the salary of the head of the National Security Council staff is obsoleteand has been superseded.

2. The Classification Act of 1923 was repealed by the Classification Act of 1949. The Classifica-tion Act of 1949 was repealed by the law enacting title 5, United States Code (Public Law 89–544, Sept. 6, 1966, 80 Stat. 378), and its provisions were codified as chapter 51 and chapter53 of title 5. Section 7(b) of that Act (80 Stat. 631) provided: "A reference to a law replacedby sections 1–6 of this Act, including a reference in a regulation, order, or other law, is deemedto refer to the corresponding provision enacted by this Act."

known as the Committee on Foreign Intelligence (in this subsection referred to as the "Committee").

(2) The Committee shall be composed of the following:

(A) The Director of National Intelligence.

(B) The Secretary of State.

(C) The Secretary of Defense.

(D) The Assistant to the President for National Security Affairs, who shall serve as the chairperson of the Committee.

(E) Such other members as the President may designate.

(3) The function of the Committee shall be to assist the Council in its activities by—

(A) identifying the intelligence required to address the national security interests of the United States as specified by the President;

(B) establishing priorities (including funding priorities) among the programs, projects, and activities that address such interests and requirements; and

(C) establishing policies relating to the conduct of intelligence activities of the United States, including appropriate roles and missions for the elements of the intelligence community and appropriate targets of intelligence collection activities.

(4) In carrying out its function, the Committee shall—

(A) conduct an annual review of the national security interests of the United States;

(B) identify on an annual basis, and at such other times as the Council may require, the intelligence required to meet such interests and establish an order of priority for the collection and analysis of such intelligence; and

(C) conduct an annual review of the elements of the intelligence community in order to determine the success of such elements in collecting, analyzing, and disseminating the intelligence identified under subparagraph (B).

(5) The Committee shall submit each year to the Council and to the Director of National Intelligence a comprehensive report on its activities during the preceding year, including its activities under paragraphs (3) and (4).

(i)(1) There is established within the National Security Council a committee to be known as the Committee on Transnational Threats (in this subsection referred to as the "Committee").

(2) The Committee shall include the following members:

(A) The Director of National Intelligence.

(B) The Secretary of State.

(C) The Secretary of Defense.

(D) The Attorney General.

(E) The Assistant to the President for National Security Affairs, who shall serve as the chairperson of the Committee.

(F) Such other members as the President may designate.

(3) The function of the Committee shall be to coordinate and direct the activities of the United States Government relating to combating transnational threats.

(4) In carrying out its function, the Committee shall—

(A) identify transnational threats;
(B) develop strategies to enable the United States Government to respond to transnational threats identified under subparagraph (A);
(C) monitor implementation of such strategies;
(D) make recommendations as to appropriate responses to specific transnational threats;
(E) assist in the resolution of operational and policy differences among Federal departments and agencies in their responses to transnational threats;
(F) develop policies and procedures to ensure the effective sharing of information about transnational threats among Federal departments and agencies, including law enforcement agencies and the elements of the intelligence community; and
(G) develop guidelines to enhance and improve the coordination of activities of Federal law enforcement agencies and elements of the intelligence community outside the United States with respect to transnational threats.

(5) For purposes of this subsection, the term "transnational threat" means the following:

(A) Any transnational activity (including international terrorism, narcotics trafficking, the proliferation of weapons of mass destruction and the delivery systems for such weapons, and organized crime) that threatens the national security of the United States.
(B) Any individual or group that engages in an activity referred to in subparagraph (A).

(j) The Director of National Intelligence (or, in the Director's absence, the Principal Deputy Director of National Intelligence) may, in the performance of the Director's duties under this Act and subject to the direction of the President, attend and participate in meetings of the National Security Council.

(k) It is the sense of the Congress that there should be within the staff of the National Security Council a Special Adviser to the President on International Religious Freedom, whose position should be comparable to that of a director within the Executive Office of the President. The Special Adviser should serve as a resource for executive branch officials, compiling and maintaining information on the facts and circumstances of violations of religious freedom (as defined in section 3 of the International Religious Freedom Act of 1998), and making policy recommendations. The Special Adviser should serve as liaison with the Ambassador at Large for International Religious Freedom, the United States Commission on International Religious Freedom, Congress and, as advisable, religious nongovernmental organizations.

(l) PARTICIPATION OF COORDINATOR FOR THE PREVENTION OF WEAPONS OF MASS DESTRUCTION PROLIFERATION AND TERRORISM.—The United States Coordinator for the Prevention of Weapons of Mass Destruction Proliferation and Terrorism (or, in the Coordinator's absence, the Deputy United States Coordinator) may, in the performance of the Coordinator's duty as principal advisor to the President on all matters relating to the prevention of weapons of mass destruction proliferation and terrorism, and, subject to the direction of the President, attend and participate in meetings of the National Security Council and the Homeland Security Council.

JOINT INTELLIGENCE COMMUNITY COUNCIL

SEC. 101A. [50 U.S.C. §402-1]

(a) JOINT INTELLIGENCE COMMUNITY COUNCIL.—There is a Joint Intelligence Community Council.

(b) MEMBERSHIP.—The Joint Intelligence Community Council shall consist of the following:

(1) The Director of National Intelligence, who shall chair the Council.

(2) The Secretary of State.

(3) The Secretary of the Treasury.

(4) The Secretary of Defense.

(5) The Attorney General.

(6) The Secretary of Energy.

(7) The Secretary of Homeland Security.

(8) Such other officers of the United States Government as the President may designate from time to time.

(c) FUNCTIONS.—The Joint Intelligence Community Council shall assist the Director of National Intelligence in developing and implementing a joint, unified national intelligence effort to protect national security by—

(1) advising the Director on establishing requirements, developing budgets, financial management, and monitoring and evaluating the performance of the intelligence community, and on such other matters as the Director may request; and

(2) ensuring the timely execution of programs, policies, and directives established or developed by the Director.

(d) MEETINGS.—The Director of National Intelligence shall convene regular meetings of the Joint Intelligence Community Council.

(e) ADVICE AND OPINIONS OF MEMBERS OTHER THAN CHAIRMAN.—

(1) A member of the Joint Intelligence Community Council (other than the Chairman) may submit to the Chairman advice or an opinion in disagreement with, or advice or an opinion in addition to, the advice presented by the Director of National Intelligence to the President or the National Security Council, in the role of the Chairman as Chairman of the Joint Intelligence Community Council. If a member submits such advice or opinion, the Chairman shall present the advice or opinion of such member at the same time the Chairman presents the advice of the Chairman to the President or the National Security Council, as the case may be.

(2) The Chairman shall establish procedures to ensure that the presentation of the advice of the Chairman to the President or the National Security Council is not unduly delayed by reason of the submission of the individual advice or opinion of another member of the Council.

(f) RECOMMENDATIONS TO CONGRESS.—Any member of the Joint Intelligence

Community Council may make such recommendations to Congress relating to the intelligence community as such member considers appropriate.

DIRECTOR OF NATIONAL INTELLIGENCE

SEC. 102. [50 U.S.C. §403]

(a) DIRECTOR OF NATIONAL INTELLIGENCE.—

(1) There is a Director of National Intelligence who shall be appointed by the President, by and with the advice and consent of the Senate. Any individual nominated for appointment as Director of National Intelligence shall have extensive national security expertise.

(2) The Director of National Intelligence shall not be located within the Executive Office of the President.

(b) PRINCIPAL RESPONSIBILITY.—Subject to the authority, direction, and control of the President, the Director of National Intelligence shall—

(1) serve as head of the intelligence community;

(2) act as the principal adviser to the President, to the National Security Council, and the Homeland Security Council for intelligence matters related to the national security; and

(3) consistent with section 1018 of the National Security Intelligence Reform Act of 2004, oversee and direct the implementation of the National Intelligence Program.

(c) PROHIBITION ON DUAL SERVICE.—The individual serving in the position of Director of National Intelligence shall not, while so serving, also serve as the Director of the Central Intelligence Agency or as the head of any other element of the intelligence community.

RESPONSIBILITIES AND AUTHORITIES OF THE DIRECTOR OF NATIONAL INTELLIGENCE

SEC. 102A. [50 U.S.C. §403-1]

(a) PROVISION OF INTELLIGENCE.—

(1) The Director of National Intelligence shall be responsible for ensuring that national intelligence is provided—

(A) to the President;

(B) to the heads of departments and agencies of the executive branch;

(C) to the Chairman of the Joint Chiefs of Staff and senior military commanders;

(D) to the Senate and House of Representatives and the committees thereof; and

(E) to such other persons as the Director of National Intelligence determines to be appropriate.

(2) Such national intelligence should be timely, objective, independent of political considerations, and based upon all sources available to the intelligence community and other appropriate entities.

(b) ACCESS TO INTELLIGENCE.—Unless otherwise directed by the President, the Director of National Intelligence shall have access to all national intelligence and intelligence related to the national security which is collected by any Federal department, agency, or other entity, except as otherwise provided by law or, as appropriate, under guidelines agreed upon by the Attorney General and the Director of National Intelligence.

(c) BUDGET AUTHORITIES.—

(1) With respect to budget requests and appropriations for the National Intelligence Program, the Director of National Intelligence shall—

(A) based on intelligence priorities set by the President, provide to the heads of departments containing agencies or organizations within the intelligence community, and to the heads of such agencies and organizations, guidance for developing the National Intelligence Program budget pertaining to such agencies and organizations;

(B) based on budget proposals provided to the Director of National Intelligence by the heads of agencies and organizations within the intelligence community and the heads of their respective departments and, as appropriate, after obtaining the advice of the Joint Intelligence Community Council, develop and determine an annual consolidated National Intelligence Program budget; and

(C) present such consolidated National Intelligence Program budget, together with any comments from the heads of departments containing agencies or organizations within the intelligence community, to the President for approval.

(2) In addition to the information provided under paragraph (1)(B), the heads of agencies and organizations within the intelligence community shall provide the Director of National Intelligence such other information as the Director shall request for the purpose of determining the annual consolidated National Intelligence Program budget under that paragraph.

(3)(A) The Director of National Intelligence shall participate in the development by the Secretary of Defense of the annual budgets for the Joint Military Intelligence Program and for Tactical Intelligence and Related Activities.

(B) The Director of National Intelligence shall provide guidance for the development of the annual budget for each element of the intelligence community that is not within the National Intelligence Program.

(4) The Director of National Intelligence shall ensure the effective execution of the annual budget for intelligence and intelligence-related activities.

(5)(A) The Director of National Intelligence shall be responsible for managing appropriations for the National Intelligence Program by directing the allotment or allocation of such appropriations through the heads of the departments containing agencies or organizations within the intelligence community and the Director of the Central Intelligence Agency, with prior notice (including the provision of appropriate supporting information) to the head of the department containing an agency or organization receiving any such allocation or allotment or the Director of the Central Intelligence Agency.

(B) Notwithstanding any other provision of law, pursuant to relevant appropriations Acts for the National Intelligence Program, the Director of the Office of Management and Budget shall exercise the authority of the Director of the Office of Management and Budget to apportion funds, at the exclusive direction of the Director of National Intelligence, for allocation to the elements of the intelligence community through the relevant host executive departments and the Central Intelligence Agency. Department comptrollers or appropriate budget execution officers shall allot, allocate, reprogram, or transfer funds appropriated for the National Intelligence Program in an expeditious manner.

(C) The Director of National Intelligence shall monitor the implementation and execution of the National Intelligence Program by the heads of the elements of the intelligence community that manage programs and activities that are part of the National Intelligence Program, which may include audits and evaluations.

(6) Apportionment and allotment of funds under this subsection shall be subject to chapter 13 and section 1517 of title 31, United States Code, and the Congressional Budget and Impoundment Control Act of 1974 (2 U.S.C. §621 et seq.).

(7)(A) The Director of National Intelligence shall provide a semi-annual report, beginning April 1, 2005, and ending April 1, 2007, to the President and the Congress regarding implementation of this section.

(B) The Director of National Intelligence shall report to the President and the Congress not later than 15 days after learning of any instance in which a departmental comptroller acts in a manner inconsistent with the law (including permanent statutes, authorization Acts, and appropriations Acts), or the direction of the Director of National Intelligence, in carrying out the National Intelligence Program.

(d) ROLE OF DIRECTOR OF NATIONAL INTELLIGENCE IN TRANSFER AND REPROGRAMMING OF FUNDS.—

(1)(A) No funds made available under the National Intelligence Program may be transferred or reprogrammed without the prior approval of the Director of National Intelligence, except in accordance with procedures prescribed by the Director of National Intelligence.

(B) The Secretary of Defense shall consult with the Director of National Intelligence before transferring or reprogramming funds made available under the Joint Military Intelligence Program.

(2) Subject to the succeeding provisions of this subsection, the Director of National Intelligence may transfer or reprogram funds appropriated for a program within the National Intelligence Program to another such program.

(3) The Director of National Intelligence may only transfer or reprogram funds referred to in subparagraph (A)—

(A) with the approval of the Director of the Office of Management and Budget; and

(B) after consultation with the heads of departments containing agencies or organizations within the intelligence community to the extent such agencies or organizations are affected, and, in the case of the Central Intelligence Agency, after consultation with the Director of the Central Intelligence Agency.

(4) The amounts available for transfer or reprogramming in the National Intelligence Program in any given fiscal year, and the terms and conditions governing such transfers and reprogrammings, are subject to the provisions of annual appropriations Acts and this subsection.

(5)(A) A transfer or reprogramming of funds or personnel may be made under this subsection only if—

(i) the funds are being transferred to an activity that is a higher priority intelligence activity;

(ii) the transfer or reprogramming supports an emergent need, improves program effectiveness, or increases efficiency;

(iii) the transfer or reprogramming does not involve a transfer or reprogramming of funds to a Reserve for Contingencies of the Director of National Intelligence or the Reserve for Contingencies of the Central Intelligence Agency;

(iv) the transfer or reprogramming results in a cumulative transfer or reprogramming of funds out of any department or agency, as appropriate, funded in the National Intelligence Program in a single fiscal year—

(I) that is less than $150,000,000, and

(II) that is less than 5 percent of amounts available to a department or agency under the National Intelligence Program; and

(v) the transfer or reprogramming does not terminate an acquisition program.

(B) A transfer or reprogramming may be made without regard to a limitation set forth in clause (iv) or (v) of subparagraph (A) if the transfer has the concurrence of the head of the department involved or the Director of the Central Intelligence Agency (in the case of the Central Intelligence Agency). The authority to provide such concurrence may only be delegated by the head of the department or agency involved to the deputy of such officer.

(6) Funds transferred or reprogrammed under this subsection shall remain available for the same period as the appropriations account to which transferred or reprogrammed.

(7) Any transfer or reprogramming of funds under this subsection shall be carried out in accordance with existing procedures applicable to reprogramming notifications for the appropriate congressional committees. Any proposed transfer or reprogramming for which notice is given to the appropriate congressional committees shall be accompanied by a report explaining the nature of the proposed transfer or reprogramming and how it satisfies the requirements of this subsection. In addition, the congressional intelligence committees shall be promptly notified of any transfer or reprogramming of funds made pursuant to this subsection in any case in which the transfer or reprogramming would not have otherwise required reprogramming notification under procedures in effect as of the date of the enactment of this subsection.

(e) TRANSFER OF PERSONNEL.—

(1)(A) In addition to any other authorities available under law for such purposes, in the first twelve months after establishment of a new national intelligence center, the Director of National Intelligence, with the approval of the Director of the Office of Management and Budget and in consultation with the congressional committees of jurisdiction referred to in subparagraph (B), may transfer not more than 100 personnel authorized for elements of the intelligence community to such center.

(B) The Director of National Intelligence shall promptly provide notice of any transfer of personnel made pursuant to this paragraph to—

(i) the congressional intelligence committees;

(ii) the Committees on Appropriations of the Senate and the House of Representatives;

(iii) in the case of the transfer of personnel to or from the Department of Defense, the Committees on Armed Services of the Senate and the House of Representatives; and

(iv) in the case of the transfer of personnel to or from the Department of Justice, to the Committees on the Judiciary of the Senate and the House of Representatives.

(C) The Director shall include in any notice under subparagraph (B) an explanation of the nature of the transfer and how it satisfies the requirements of this subsection.

(2)(A) The Director of National Intelligence, with the approval of the Director of the Office of Management and Budget and in accordance with procedures to be developed by the Director of National Intelligence and the heads of the departments and agencies concerned, may transfer personnel authorized for an element of the intelligence community to another such element for a period of not more than 2 years.

(B) A transfer of personnel may be made under this paragraph only if—

(i) the personnel are being transferred to an activity that is a higher priority intelligence activity; and

(ii) the transfer supports an emergent need, improves program effectiveness, or increases efficiency.

(C) The Director of National Intelligence shall promptly provide notice of any transfer of personnel made pursuant to this paragraph to—

(i) the congressional intelligence committees;

(ii) in the case of the transfer of personnel to or from the Department of Defense, the Committees on Armed Services of the Senate and the House of Representatives; and

(iii) in the case of the transfer of personnel to or from the Department of Justice, to the Committees on the Judiciary of the Senate and the House of Representatives.

(D) The Director shall include in any notice under subparagraph (C) an explanation of the nature of the transfer and how it satisfies the requirements of this paragraph.

(3) It is the sense of Congress that—

(A) the nature of the national security threats facing the United States will continue to challenge the intelligence community to respond rapidly and flexibly to bring analytic resources to bear against emerging and unforeseen requirements;

(B) both the Office of the Director of National Intelligence and any analytic centers determined to be necessary should be fully and properly supported with appropriate levels of personnel resources and that the President's yearly budget requests adequately support those needs; and

(C) the President should utilize all legal and administrative discretion to ensure that the Director of National Intelligence and all other elements of the intelligence community have the necessary resources and procedures to respond promptly and effectively to emerging and unforeseen national security challenges.

(f) TASKING AND OTHER AUTHORITIES.—

(1)(A) The Director of National Intelligence shall—

(i) establish objectives, priorities, and guidance for the intelligence community to ensure timely and effective collection, processing, analysis, and dissemination (including access by users to collected data consistent with applicable law and, as appropriate, the guidelines referred to in subsection (b) and analytic products generated by or within the intelligence community) of national intelligence;

(ii) determine requirements and priorities for, and manage and direct the tasking of, collection, analysis, production, and dissemination of national intelligence by elements of the intelligence community, including—

(I) approving requirements (including those requirements responding to needs provided by consumers) for collection and analysis; and

(II) resolving conflicts in collection requirements and in the tasking of national collection assets of the elements of the intelligence community; and

(iii) provide advisory tasking to intelligence elements of those agencies and departments not within the National Intelligence Program.

(B) The authority of the Director of National Intelligence under subparagraph (A) shall not apply—

(i) insofar as the President so directs;

(ii) with respect to clause (ii) of subparagraph (A), insofar as the Secretary of Defense exercises tasking authority under plans or arrangements agreed upon by the Secretary of Defense and the Director of National Intelligence; or

(iii) to the direct dissemination of information to State government and local government officials and private sector entities pursuant to sections 201 and 892 of the Homeland Security Act of 2002 (6 U.S.C. §121, 482).

(2) The Director of National Intelligence shall oversee the National Counterterrorism Center and may establish such other national intelligence centers as the Director determines necessary. (3)(A) The Director of National Intelligence shall prescribe, in consultation with the heads of other agencies or elements of the intelligence community, and the heads of their respective departments, personnel policies and programs applicable to the intelligence community that—

(i) encourage and facilitate assignments and details of personnel to national intelligence centers, and between elements of the intelligence community;

(ii) set standards for education, training, and career development of personnel of the intelligence community;

(iii) encourage and facilitate the recruitment and retention by the intelligence community of highly qualified individuals for the effective conduct of intelligence activities;

(iv) ensure that the personnel of the intelligence community are sufficiently diverse for purposes of the collection and analysis of intelligence through the recruitment and training of women, minorities, and individuals with diverse ethnic, cultural, and linguistic backgrounds;

(v) make service in more than one element of the intelligence community a condition of promotion to such positions within the intelligence community as the Director shall specify; and

(vi) ensure the effective management of intelligence community personnel who are responsible for intelligence community-wide matters.

(B) Policies prescribed under subparagraph (A) shall not be inconsistent with the personnel policies otherwise applicable to members of the uniformed services.

(4) The Director of National Intelligence shall ensure compliance with the Constitution and laws of the United States by the Central Intelligence Agency and shall ensure such compliance by other elements of the intelligence community through the host executive departments that manage the programs and activities that are part of the National Intelligence Program.

(5) The Director of National Intelligence shall ensure the elimination of waste and unnecessary duplication within the intelligence community.

(6) The Director of National Intelligence shall establish requirements and priorities for foreign intelligence information to be collected under the Foreign Intelligence Surveillance Act of 1978 (50 U.S.C. §1801 et seq.), and provide assistance to the Attorney General to ensure that information derived from electronic surveillance or physical searches under that Act is disseminated so it may be used efficiently and effectively for national intelligence purposes, except that the Director shall have no authority to direct or undertake electronic surveillance or physical search operations pursuant to that Act unless authorized by statute or Executive order.

(7) The Director of National Intelligence shall perform such other functions as the President may direct.

(8) Nothing in this title shall be construed as affecting the role of the Department of Justice or the Attorney General under the Foreign Intelligence Surveillance Act of 1978.

(g) INTELLIGENCE INFORMATION SHARING.—

(1) The Director of National Intelligence shall have principal authority to ensure maximum availability of and access to intelligence information within the intelligence community consistent with national security requirements. The Director of National Intelligence shall—

(A) establish uniform security standards and procedures;

(B) establish common information technology standards, protocols, and interfaces;

(C) ensure development of information technology systems that include multi-level security and intelligence integration capabilities;

(D) establish policies and procedures to resolve conflicts between the need to share intelligence information and the need to protect intelligence sources and methods;

(E) develop an enterprise architecture for the intelligence community and ensure that elements of the intelligence community comply with such architecture; and

(F) have procurement approval authority over all enterprise architecture-related information technology items funded in the National Intelligence Program.

(2) The President shall ensure that the Director of National Intelligence has all necessary support and authorities to fully and effectively implement paragraph (1).

(3) Except as otherwise directed by the President or with the specific written agreement of the head of the department or agency in question, a Federal agency or official shall not be considered to have met any obligation to provide any information, report, assessment, or other material (including unevaluated intelligence information) to that department or agency solely by virtue of having provided that information, report, assessment, or other material to the Director of National Intelligence or the National Counterterrorism Center.

(4) Not later than February 1 of each year, the Director of National Intelligence shall submit to the President and to the Congress an annual report that identifies any statute, regulation, policy, or practice that the Director believes impedes the ability of the Director to fully and effectively implement paragraph (1).

(h) ANALYSIS.—To ensure the most accurate analysis of intelligence is derived from all sources to support national security needs, the Director of National Intelligence shall—

(1) implement policies and procedures—

(A) to encourage sound analytic methods and tradecraft throughout the elements of the intelligence community;

(B) to ensure that analysis is based upon all sources available; and

(C) to ensure that the elements of the intelligence community regularly conduct competitive analysis of analytic products, whether such products are produced by or disseminated to such elements;

(2) ensure that resource allocation for intelligence analysis is appropriately proportional to resource allocation for intelligence collection systems and operations in order to maximize analysis of all collected data;

(3) ensure that differences in analytic judgment are fully considered and brought to the attention of policymakers; and

(4) ensure that sufficient relationships are established between intelligence collectors and analysts to facilitate greater understanding of the needs of analysts.

(i) PROTECTION OF INTELLIGENCE SOURCES AND METHODS.—

(1) The Director of National Intelligence shall protect intelligence sources and methods from unauthorized disclosure.

(2) Consistent with paragraph (1), in order to maximize the dissemination of intelligence, the Director of National Intelligence shall establish and implement guidelines for the intelligence community for the following purposes:

(A) Classification of information under applicable law, Executive orders, or other Presidential directives.

(B) Access to and dissemination of intelligence, both in final form and in the form when initially gathered.

(C) Preparation of intelligence products in such a way that source information is removed to allow for dissemination at the lowest level of classification possible or in unclassified form to the extent practicable.

(3) The Director may only delegate a duty or authority given the Director under this subsection to the Principal Deputy Director of National Intelligence.

(j) UNIFORM PROCEDURES FOR SENSITIVE COMPARTMENTED INFORMATION.— The Director of National Intelligence, subject to the direction of the President, shall—

(1) establish uniform standards and procedures for the grant of access to sensitive compartmented information to any officer or employee of any agency or department of the United States and to employees of contractors of those agencies or departments;

(2) ensure the consistent implementation of those standards and procedures throughout such agencies and departments;

(3) ensure that security clearances granted by individual elements of the intelligence community are recognized by all elements of the intelligence community, and under contracts entered into by those agencies; and

(4) ensure that the process for investigation and adjudication of an application for access to sensitive compartmented information is performed in the most expeditious manner possible consistent with applicable standards for national security.

(k) COORDINATION WITH FOREIGN GOVERNMENTS.—Under the direction of the President and in a manner consistent with section 207 of the Foreign Service Act of 1980 (22 U.S.C. §3927), the Director of National Intelligence shall oversee the coordination of the relationships between elements of the intelligence community and the intelligence or security services of foreign governments or international organizations on all matters involving intelligence related to the national security or involving intelligence acquired through clandestine means.

(l) ENHANCED PERSONNEL MANAGEMENT.—

(1)(A) The Director of National Intelligence shall, under regulations prescribed by the Director, provide incentives for personnel of elements of the intelligence community to serve—

(i) on the staff of the Director of National Intelligence;

(ii) on the staff of the national intelligence centers;

(iii) on the staff of the National Counterterrorism Center; and

(iv) in other positions in support of the intelligence community management functions of the Director.

(B) Incentives under subparagraph (A) may include financial incentives, bonuses, and such other awards and incentives as the Director considers appropriate.

(2)(A) Notwithstanding any other provision of law, the personnel of an element of the intelligence community who are assigned or detailed under paragraph (1)(A) to service under the Director of National Intelligence shall be promoted at rates equivalent to or better than personnel of such element who are not so assigned or detailed.

(B) The Director may prescribe regulations to carry out this section.

(3)(A) The Director of National Intelligence shall prescribe mechanisms to facilitate the rotation of personnel of the intelligence community through various elements of the intelligence community in the course of their careers in order to facilitate the widest possible understanding by such personnel of the variety of intelligence requirements, methods, users, and capabilities.

(B) The mechanisms prescribed under subparagraph (A) may include the following:

(i) The establishment of special occupational categories involving service, over the course of a career, in more than one element of the intelligence community.

(ii) The provision of rewards for service in positions undertaking analysis and planning of operations involving two or more elements of the intelligence community.

(iii) The establishment of requirements for education, training, service, and evaluation for service involving more than one element of the intelligence community.

(C) It is the sense of Congress that the mechanisms prescribed under this subsection should, to the extent practical, seek to duplicate for civilian personnel within the intelligence community the joint officer management policies established by chapter 38 of title 10, United States Code, and the other amendments made by title IV of the Goldwater-Nichols Department of Defense Reorganization Act of 1986 (Public Law 99-433).

(4)(A) Except as provided in subparagraph (B) and subparagraph (D), this subsection shall not apply with respect to personnel of the elements of the intelligence community who are members of the uniformed services.

(B) Mechanisms that establish requirements for education and training pursuant to paragraph (3)(B)(iii) may apply with respect to members of the uniformed services who are assigned to an element of the intelligence community funded through the National Intelligence Program, but such mechanisms shall not be inconsistent with personnel policies and education and training requirements otherwise applicable to members of the uniformed services.

(C) The personnel policies and programs developed and implemented under this subsection with respect to law enforcement officers (as that term is defined in section 5541(3) of title 5, United States Code) shall not affect the ability of law enforcement entities to conduct operations or, through the applicable chain of command, to control the activities of such law enforcement officers.

(D) Assignment to the Office of the Director of National Intelligence of commissioned officers of the Armed Forces shall be considered a joint-duty assignment for purposes of the joint officer management policies prescribed by chapter 38 of title 10, United States Code, and other provisions of that title.

(m) ADDITIONAL AUTHORITY WITH RESPECT TO PERSONNEL.—

(1) In addition to the authorities under subsection (f)(3), the Director of National Intelligence may exercise with respect to the personnel of the Office of the Director of National Intelligence any authority of the Director of the Central Intelligence Agency with respect to the personnel of the Central Intelligence Agency under the Central Intelligence Agency Act of 1949 (50 U.S.C. §403a et seq.), and other applicable provisions of law, as of the date of the enactment of this subsection to the same extent, and subject to the same conditions and limitations, that the Director of the Central Intelligence Agency may exercise such authority with respect to personnel of the Central Intelligence Agency.

(2) Employees and applicants for employment of the Office of the Director of National Intelligence shall have the same rights and protections under the Office of the Director of National Intelligence as employees of the Central Intelligence Agency have under the Central Intelligence Agency Act of 1949, and other applicable provisions of law, as of the date of the enactment of this subsection.

(n) ACQUISITION AUTHORITIES.—

(1) In carrying out the responsibilities and authorities under this section, the Director of National Intelligence may exercise the acquisition and appropriations authorities referred to in the Central Intelligence Agency Act of 1949 (50 U.S.C. §403a et seq.) other than the authorities referred to in section 8(b) of that Act (50 U.S.C. §403j(b)).

(2) For the purpose of the exercise of any authority referred to in paragraph (1), a reference to the head of an agency shall be deemed to be a reference to the Director of National Intelligence or the Principal Deputy Director of National Intelligence.

(3)(A) Any determination or decision to be made under an authority referred to in paragraph (1) by the head of an agency may be made with respect to individual purchases and contracts or with respect to classes of purchases or contracts, and shall be final.

(B) Except as provided in subparagraph (C), the Director of National Intelligence or the Principal Deputy Director of National Intelligence may, in such official's discretion, delegate to any officer or other official of the Office of the Director of National Intelligence any authority to make a determination or decision as the head of the agency under an authority referred to in paragraph (1).

(C) The limitations and conditions set forth in section 3(d) of the Central Intelligence Agency Act of 1949 (50 U.S.C. §403c(d)) shall apply to the exercise by the Director of National Intelligence of an authority referred to in paragraph (1).

(D) Each determination or decision required by an authority referred to in the second sentence of section 3(d) of the Central Intelligence Agency Act of 1949 shall be based upon written findings made by the official making such determination or decision, which findings shall be final and shall be available within the Office of the Director of National Intelligence for a period of at least six years following the date of such determination or decision.

(o) CONSIDERATION OF VIEWS OF ELEMENTS OF INTELLIGENCE COMMUNITY.— In carrying out the duties and responsibilities under this section, the Director of National Intelligence shall take into account the views of a head of a department containing an element of the intelligence community and of the Director of the Central Intelligence Agency.

(p) RESPONSIBILITY OF DIRECTOR OF NATIONAL INTELLIGENCE REGARDING NATIONAL INTELLIGENCE PROGRAM BUDGET CONCERNING THE DEPARTMENT OF DEFENSE.—Subject to the direction of the President, the Director of National Intelligence shall, after consultation with the Secretary of Defense, ensure that the National Intelligence Program budgets for the elements of the intelligence community that are within the Department of Defense are adequate to satisfy the national intelligence needs of the Department of Defense, including the needs of the Chairman of the Joint Chiefs of Staff and the commanders of the unified and specified commands, and wherever such elements are performing Government-wide functions, the needs of other Federal departments and agencies.

(q) ACQUISITIONS OF MAJOR SYSTEMS.—

(1) For each intelligence program within the National Intelligence Program for the acquisition of a major system, the Director of National Intelligence shall—

(A) require the development and implementation of a program management plan that includes cost, schedule, and performance goals and program milestone criteria, except that with respect to Department of Defense programs the Director shall consult with the Secretary of Defense;

(B) serve as exclusive milestone decision authority, except that with respect to Department of Defense programs the Director shall serve as milestone decision authority jointly with the Secretary of Defense or the designee of the Secretary; and

(C) periodically—

(i) review and assess the progress made toward the achievement of the goals and milestones established in such plan; and

(ii) submit to Congress a report on the results of such review and assessment.

(2) If the Director of National Intelligence and the Secretary of Defense are unable to reach an agreement on a milestone decision under paragraph (1)(B), the President shall resolve the conflict.

(3) Nothing in this subsection may be construed to limit the authority of the Director of National Intelligence to delegate to any other official any authority to perform the responsibilities of the Director under this subsection.

(4) In this subsection:

(A) The term "intelligence program", with respect to the acquisition of a major system, means a program that—

(i) is carried out to acquire such major system for an element of the intelligence community; and

(ii) is funded in whole out of amounts available for the National Intelligence Program.

(B) The term "major system" has the meaning given such term in section 4(9) of the Federal Property and Administrative Services Act of 1949 (41 U.S.C. §403(9)).

(r) PERFORMANCE OF COMMON SERVICES.—The Director of National Intelligence shall, in consultation with the heads of departments and agencies of the United States Government containing elements within the intelligence community and with the Director of the Central Intelligence Agency, coordinate the performance by the elements of the intelligence community within the National Intelligence Program of such services as are of common concern to the intelligence community, which services the Director of National Intelligence determines can be more efficiently accomplished in a consolidated manner.

OFFICE OF THE DIRECTOR OF NATIONAL INTELLIGENCE

SEC. 103. [50 U.S.C. §403-3]

(a) OFFICE OF DIRECTOR OF NATIONAL INTELLIGENCE.—There is an Office of the Director of National Intelligence.

(b) FUNCTION.—The function of the Office of the Director of National Intelligence is to assist the Director of National Intelligence in carrying out the duties and responsibilities of the Director under this Act, the National Security Act of 1947 (50 U.S.C. §401 et seq.), and other applicable provisions of law, and to carry out such other duties as may be prescribed by the President or by law.

(c) COMPOSITION.—The Office of the Director of National Intelligence is composed of the following:

(1) The Director of National Intelligence.

(2) The Principal Deputy Director of National Intelligence.

(3) Any Deputy Director of National Intelligence appointed under section 103A.

(4) The National Intelligence Council.

(5) The General Counsel.

(6) The Civil Liberties Protection Officer.
(7) The Director of Science and Technology.
(8) The National Counterintelligence Executive (including the Office of the National Counterintelligence Executive).
(9) Such other offices and officials as may be established by law or the Director may establish or designate in the Office, including national intelligence centers.

(d) STAFF.—
(1) To assist the Director of National Intelligence in fulfilling the duties and responsibilities of the Director, the Director shall employ and utilize in the Office of the Director of National Intelligence a professional staff having an expertise in matters relating to such duties and responsibilities, and may establish permanent positions and appropriate rates of pay with respect to that staff.
(2) The staff of the Office of the Director of National Intelligence under paragraph (1) shall include the staff of the Office of the Deputy Director of Central Intelligence for Community Management that is transferred to the Office of the Director of National Intelligence under section 1091 of the National Security Intelligence Reform Act of 2004.

(e) LIMITATION ON CO-LOCATION WITH OTHER ELEMENTS OF INTELLIGENCE COMMUNITY.—Commencing as of October 1, 2008, the Office of the Director of National Intelligence may not be co-located with any other element of the intelligence community.

DEPUTY DIRECTORS OF NATIONAL INTELLIGENCE

SEC. 103A. [50 U.S.C. §403-3a]

(a) PRINCIPAL DEPUTY DIRECTOR OF NATIONAL INTELLIGENCE.—
(1) There is a Principal Deputy Director of National Intelligence who shall be appointed by the President, by and with the advice and consent of the Senate.
(2) In the event of a vacancy in the position of Principal Deputy Director of National Intelligence, the Director of National Intelligence shall recommend to the President an individual for appointment as Principal Deputy Director of National Intelligence.
(3) Any individual nominated for appointment as Principal Deputy Director of National Intelligence shall have extensive national security experience and management expertise.
(4) The individual serving as Principal Deputy Director of National Intelligence shall not, while so serving, serve in any capacity in any other element of the intelligence community.
(5) The Principal Deputy Director of National Intelligence shall assist the Director of National Intelligence in carrying out the duties and responsibilities of the Director.
(6) The Principal Deputy Director of National Intelligence shall act for, and exercise the powers of, the Director of National Intelligence during the absence or disability of the Director of National Intelligence or during a vacancy in the position of Director of National Intelligence.

(b) DEPUTY DIRECTORS OF NATIONAL INTELLIGENCE.—

(1) There may be not more than four Deputy Directors of National Intelligence who shall be appointed by the Director of National Intelligence.

(2) Each Deputy Director of National Intelligence appointed under this subsection shall have such duties, responsibilities, and authorities as the Director of National Intelligence may assign or are specified by law.

(c) MILITARY STATUS OF DIRECTOR OF NATIONAL INTELLIGENCE AND PRINCIPAL DEPUTY DIRECTOR OF NATIONAL INTELLIGENCE.—

(1) Not more than one of the individuals serving in the positions specified in paragraph (2) may be a commissioned officer of the Armed Forces in active status.

(2) The positions referred to in this paragraph are the following:

(A) The Director of National Intelligence.

(B) The Principal Deputy Director of National Intelligence.

(3) It is the sense of Congress that, under ordinary circumstances, it is desirable that one of the individuals serving in the positions specified in paragraph (2)—

(A) be a commissioned officer of the Armed Forces, in active status; or

(B) have, by training or experience, an appreciation of military intelligence activities and requirements.

(4) A commissioned officer of the Armed Forces, while serving in a position specified in paragraph (2)—

(A) shall not be subject to supervision or control by the Secretary of Defense or by any officer or employee of the Department of Defense;

(B) shall not exercise, by reason of the officer's status as a commissioned officer, any supervision or control with respect to any of the military or civilian personnel of the Department of Defense except as otherwise authorized by law; and

(C) shall not be counted against the numbers and percentages of commissioned officers of the rank and grade of such officer authorized for the military department of that officer.

(5) Except as provided in subparagraph (A) or (B) of paragraph (4), the appointment of an officer of the Armed Forces to a position specified in paragraph (2) shall not affect the status, position, rank, or grade of such officer in the Armed Forces, or any emolument, perquisite, right, privilege, or benefit incident to or arising out of such status, position, rank, or grade.

(6) A commissioned officer of the Armed Forces on active duty who is appointed to a position specified in paragraph (2), while serving in such position and while remaining on active duty, shall continue to receive military pay and allowances and shall not receive the pay prescribed for such position. Funds from which such pay and allowances are paid shall be reimbursed from funds available to the Director of National Intelligence.

NATIONAL INTELLIGENCE COUNCIL

SEC. 103B. [50 U.S.C. §403-3b]

(a) NATIONAL INTELLIGENCE COUNCIL.—There is a National Intelligence Council.

(b) COMPOSITION.—

(1) The National Intelligence Council shall be composed of senior analysts within the intelligence community and substantive experts from the public and private sector, who shall be appointed by, report to, and serve at the pleasure of, the Director of National Intelligence.

(2) The Director shall prescribe appropriate security requirements for personnel appointed from the private sector as a condition of service on the Council, or as contractors of the Council or employees of such contractors, to ensure the protection of intelligence sources and methods while avoiding, wherever possible, unduly intrusive requirements which the Director considers to be unnecessary for this purpose.

(c) DUTIES AND RESPONSIBILITIES.—

(1) The National Intelligence Council shall—

(A) produce national intelligence estimates for the United States Government, including alternative views held by elements of the intelligence community and other information as specified in paragraph (2);

(B) evaluate community-wide collection and production of intelligence by the intelligence community and the requirements and resources of such collection and production; and

(C) otherwise assist the Director of National Intelligence in carrying out the responsibilities of the Director under section 102A.

(2) The Director of National Intelligence shall ensure that the Council satisfies the needs of policymakers and other consumers of intelligence.

(d) SERVICES AS SENIOR INTELLIGENCE ADVISERS.—Within their respective areas of expertise and under the direction of the Director of National Intelligence, the members of the National Intelligence Council shall constitute the senior intelligence advisers of the intelligence community for purposes of representing the views of the intelligence community within the United States Government.

(e) AUTHORITY TO CONTRACT.—Subject to the direction and control of the Director of National Intelligence, the National Intelligence Council may carry out its responsibilities under this section by contract, including contracts for substantive experts necessary to assist the Council with particular assessments under this section.

(f) STAFF.—The Director of National Intelligence shall make available to the National Intelligence Council such staff as may be necessary to permit the Council to carry out its responsibilities under this section.

(g) AVAILABILITY OF COUNCIL AND STAFF.—

(1) The Director of National Intelligence shall take appropriate measures to ensure that the National Intelligence Council and its staff satisfy the needs of policymaking officials and other consumers of intelligence.

(2) The Council shall be readily accessible to policymaking officials and other appropriate individuals not otherwise associated with the intelligence community.

(h) SUPPORT.—The heads of the elements of the intelligence community shall, as appropriate, furnish such support to the National Intelligence Council, including the preparation of intelligence analyses, as may be required by the Director of National Intelligence.

(i) NATIONAL INTELLIGENCE COUNCIL PRODUCT.—For purposes of this section, the term "National Intelligence Council product" includes a National Intelligence Estimate and any other intelligence community assessment that sets forth the judgment of the intelligence community as a whole on a matter covered by such product.

GENERAL COUNSEL

SEC. 103C. [50 U.S.C. §403-3c]

(a) GENERAL COUNSEL.—There is a General Counsel of the Office of the Director of National Intelligence who shall be appointed by the President, by and with the advice and consent of the Senate.

(b) PROHIBITION ON DUAL SERVICE AS GENERAL COUNSEL OF ANOTHER AGENCY.—The individual serving in the position of General Counsel may not, while so serving, also serve as the General Counsel of any other department, agency, or element of the United States Government.

(c) SCOPE OF POSITION.—The General Counsel is the chief legal officer of the Office of the Director of National Intelligence.

(d) FUNCTIONS.—The General Counsel shall perform such functions as the Director of National Intelligence may prescribe.

CIVIL LIBERTIES PROTECTION OFFICER

SEC. 103D. [50 U.S.C. §403-3d]

(a) CIVIL LIBERTIES PROTECTION OFFICER.—

(1) Within the Office of the Director of National Intelligence, there is a Civil Liberties Protection Officer who shall be appointed by the Director of National Intelligence.

(2) The Civil Liberties Protection Officer shall report directly to the Director of National Intelligence.

(b) DUTIES.—The Civil Liberties Protection Officer shall—

(1) ensure that the protection of civil liberties and privacy is appropriately incorporated in the policies and procedures developed for and implemented by the Office of the Director of National Intelligence and the elements of the intelligence community within the National Intelligence Program;

(2) oversee compliance by the Office and the Director of National Intelligence with requirements under the Constitution and all laws, regulations, Executive orders, and implementing guidelines relating to civil liberties and privacy;

(3) review and assess complaints and other information indicating possible abuses of civil liberties and privacy in the administration of the programs and operations of the Office and the Director of National Intelligence and, as appropriate, investigate any such complaint or information;

(4) ensure that the use of technologies sustain, and do not erode, privacy protections relating to the use, collection, and disclosure of personal information;

(5) ensure that personal information contained in a system of records subject to

section 552a of title 5, United States Code (popularly referred to as the Privacy Act'), is handled in full compliance with fair information practices as set out in that section;

(6) conduct privacy impact assessments when appropriate or as required by law; and

(7) perform such other duties as may be prescribed by the Director of National Intelligence or specified by law.

(c) USE OF AGENCY INSPECTORS GENERAL.—When appropriate, the Civil Liberties Protection Officer may refer complaints to the Office of Inspector General having responsibility for the affected element of the department or agency of the intelligence community to conduct an investigation under paragraph (3) of subsection (b).

DIRECTOR OF SCIENCE AND TECHNOLOGY

SEC. 103E. [50 U.S.C. §403-3e]

(a) DIRECTOR OF SCIENCE AND TECHNOLOGY.—There is a Director of Science and Technology within the Office of the Director of National Intelligence who shall be appointed by the Director of National Intelligence.

(b) REQUIREMENT RELATING TO APPOINTMENT.—An individual appointed as Director of Science and Technology shall have a professional background and experience appropriate for the duties of the Director of Science and Technology.

(c) DUTIES.—The Director of Science and Technology shall—

(1) act as the chief representative of the Director of National Intelligence for science and technology;

(2) chair the Director of National Intelligence Science and Technology Committee under subsection (d);

(3) assist the Director in formulating a long-term strategy for scientific advances in the field of intelligence;

(4) assist the Director on the science and technology elements of the budget of the Office of the Director of National Intelligence; and

(5) perform other such duties as may be prescribed by the Director of National Intelligence or specified by law.

(d) DIRECTOR OF NATIONAL INTELLIGENCE SCIENCE AND TECHNOLOGY COMMITTEE.—

(1) There is within the Office of the Director of Science and Technology a Director of National Intelligence Science and Technology Committee.

(2) The Committee shall be composed of the principal science officers of the National Intelligence Program.

(3) The Committee shall—

(A) coordinate advances in research and development related to intelligence; and

(B) perform such other functions as the Director of Science and Technology shall prescribe.

NATIONAL COUNTERINTELLIGENCE EXECUTIVE

SEC. 103F. [50 U.S.C. §403-3f]

(a) NATIONAL COUNTERINTELLIGENCE EXECUTIVE.—The National Counterintelligence Executive under section 902 of the Counterintelligence Enhancement Act of 2002 (title IX of Public Law 107-306; 50 U.S.C. §402b et seq.) is a component of the Office of the Director of National Intelligence.

(b) DUTIES.—The National Counterintelligence Executive shall perform the duties provided in the Counterintelligence Enhancement Act of 2002 and such other duties as may be prescribed by the Director of National Intelligence or specified by law.

CHIEF INFORMATION OFFICER

SEC. 103G. [50 U.S.C. §403-3g]

(a) CHIEF INFORMATION OFFICER.—To assist the Director of National Intelligence in carrying out the responsibilities of the Director under this Act and other applicable provisions of law, there shall be within the Office of the Director of National Intelligence a Chief Information Officer who shall be appointed by the President, by and with the advice and consent of the Senate.

(b) CHIEF INFORMATION OFFICER OF INTELLIGENCE COMMUNITY.—The Chief Information Officer shall serve as the chief information officer of the intelligence community.

(c) DUTIES AND RESPONSIBILITIES.—Subject to the direction of the Director of National Intelligence, the Chief Information Officer shall—

- (1) manage activities relating to the information technology infrastructure and enterprise architecture requirements of the intelligence community;
- (2) have procurement approval authority over all information technology items related to the enterprise architectures of all intelligence community components;
- (3) direct and manage all information technology-related procurement for the intelligence community; and
- (4) ensure that all expenditures for information technology and research and development activities are consistent with the intelligence community enterprise architecture and the strategy of the Director for such architecture.

(d) PROHIBITION ON SIMULTANEOUS SERVICE AS OTHER CHIEF INFORMATION OFFICER.—An individual serving in the position of Chief Information Officer may not, while so serving, serve as the chief information officer of any other department or agency, or component thereof, of the United States Government.

INSPECTOR GENERAL OF THE INTELLIGENCE COMMUNITY

SEC. 103H. [50 U.S.C. 403–3h]

(a)OFFICE OF INSPECTOR GENERAL OF THE INTELLIGENCE COMMUNITY.—There is within the Office of the Director of National Intelligence an Office of the Inspector General of the Intelligence Community.

(b) PURPOSE.—The purpose of the Office of the Inspector General of the Intelligence Community is—

(1) to create an objective and effective office, appropriately accountable to Congress, to initiate and conduct independent investigations, inspections, audits, and reviews on programs and activities within the responsibility and authority of the Director of National Intelligence;

(2) to provide leadership and coordination and recommend policies for activities designed—

(A) to promote economy, efficiency, and effectiveness in the administration and implementation of such programs and activities; and

(B) to prevent and detect fraud and abuse in such programs and activities;

(3) to provide a means for keeping the Director of National Intelligence fully and currently informed about—

(A) problems and deficiencies relating to the administration of programs and activities within the responsibility and authority of the Director of National Intelligence; and

B) the necessity for, and the progress of, corrective actions; and

(4) in the manner prescribed by this section, to ensure that the congressional intelligence committees are kept similarly informed of—

(A) significant problems and deficiencies relating to programs and activities within the responsibility and authority of the Director of National Intelligence; and

(B) the necessity for, and the progress of, corrective actions.

(c) INSPECTOR GENERAL OF THE INTELLIGENCE COMMUNITY.—

(1) There is an Inspector General of the Intelligence Community, who shall be the head of the Office of the Inspector General of the Intelligence Community, who shall be appointed by the President, by and with the advice and consent of the Senate.

(2) The nomination of an individual for appointment as Inspector General shall be made—

(A) without regard to political affiliation;

(B) on the basis of integrity, compliance with security standards of the intelligence community, and prior experience in the field of intelligence or national security; and

(C) on the basis of demonstrated ability in accounting, financial analysis, law, management analysis, public administration, or investigations.

(3) The Inspector General shall report directly to and be under the general supervision of the Director of National Intelligence.

(4) The Inspector General may be removed from office only by the President. The President shall communicate in writing to the congressional intelligence committees the reasons for the removal not later than 30 days prior to the effective date of such removal. Nothing in this paragraph shall be construed to prohibit a personnel action otherwise authorized by law, other than transfer or removal.

(d) ASSISTANT INSPECTORS GENERAL.—Subject to the policies of the Director of National Intelligence, the Inspector General of the Intelligence Community shall—

(1) appoint an Assistant Inspector General for Audit who shall have the responsibility for supervising the performance of auditing activities relating to programs and activities within the responsibility and authority of the Director;

(2) appoint an Assistant Inspector General for Investigations who shall have the responsibility for supervising the performance of investigative activities relating to such programs and activities; and

(3) appoint other Assistant Inspectors General that, in the judgment of the Inspector General, are necessary to carry out the duties of the Inspector General.

(e) DUTIES AND RESPONSIBILITIES.—It shall be the duty and responsibility of the Inspector General of the Intelligence Community—

(1) to provide policy direction for, and to plan, conduct, supervise, and coordinate independently, the investigations, inspections, audits, and reviews relating to programs and activities within the responsibility and authority of the Director of National Intelligence;

(2) to keep the Director of National Intelligence fully and currently informed concerning violations of law and regulations, fraud, and other serious problems, abuses, and deficiencies relating to the programs and activities within the responsibility and authority of the Director, to recommend corrective action concerning such problems, and to report on the progress made in implementing such corrective action;

(3) to take due regard for the protection of intelligence sources and methods in the preparation of all reports issued by the Inspector General, and, to the extent consistent with the purpose and objective of such reports, take such measures as may be appropriate to minimize the disclosure of intelligence sources and methods described in such reports; and

(4) in the execution of the duties and responsibilities under this section, to comply with generally accepted government auditing.

(f) LIMITATIONS ON ACTIVITIES.—

(1) The Director of National Intelligence may prohibit the Inspector General of the Intelligence Community from initiating, carrying out, or completing any investigation, inspection, audit, or review if the Director determines that such prohibition is necessary to protect vital national security interests of the United States.

(2) Not later than seven days after the date on which the Director exercises the authority under paragraph (1), the Director shall submit to the congressional intelligence committees an appropriately classified statement of the reasons for the exercise of such authority.

(3) The Director shall advise the Inspector General at the time a statement under paragraph (2) is submitted, and, to the extent consistent with the protection of intelligence sources and methods, provide the Inspector General with a copy of such statement.

(4) The Inspector General may submit to the congressional intelligence committees any comments on the statement of which the Inspector General has notice under paragraph (3) that the Inspector General considers appropriate.

(g) AUTHORITIES.—

(1) The Inspector General of the Intelligence Community shall have direct and prompt access to the Director of National Intelligence when necessary for any purpose pertaining to the performance of the duties of the Inspector General.

(2)(A) The Inspector General shall, subject to the limitations in subsection (f), make such investigations and reports relating to the administration of the programs and activities within the authorities and responsibilities of the Director as are, in the judgment of the Inspector General, necessary or desirable.

(B) The Inspector General shall have access to any employee, or any employee of a contractor, of any element of the intelligence community needed for the performance of the duties of the Inspector General.

(C) The Inspector General shall have direct access to all records, reports, audits, reviews, documents, papers, recommendations, or other materials that relate to the programs and activities with respect to which the Inspector General has responsibilities under this section.

(D) The level of classification or compartmentation of information shall not, in and of itself, provide a sufficient rationale for denying the Inspector General access to any materials under subparagraph (C).

(E) The Director, or on the recommendation of the Director, another appropriate official of the intelligence community, shall take appropriate administrative actions against an employee, or an employee of a contractor, of an element of the intelligence community that fails to cooperate with the Inspector General. Such administrative action may include loss of employment or the termination of an existing contractual relationship.

(3) The Inspector General is authorized to receive and investigate, pursuant to subsection (h), complaints or information from any person concerning the existence of an activity within the authorities and responsibilities of the Director of National Intelligence constituting a violation of laws, rules, or regulations, or mismanagement, gross waste of funds, abuse of authority, or a substantial and specific danger to the public health and safety. Once such complaint or information has been received from an employee of the intelligence community—

(A) the Inspector General shall not disclose the identity of the employee without the consent of the employee, unless the Inspector General determines that such disclosure is unavoidable during the course of the investigation or the disclosure is made to an official of the Department of Justice responsible for determining whether a prosecution should be undertaken; and

(B) no action constituting a reprisal, or threat of reprisal, for making such complaint or disclosing such information to the Inspector General may be taken by any employee in a position to take such actions, unless the complaint was made or the information was disclosed with the knowledge that it was false or with willful disregard for its truth or falsity.

(4) The Inspector General shall have the authority to administer to or take from any person an oath, affirmation, or affidavit, whenever necessary in the

performance of the duties of the Inspector General, which oath, affirmation, or affidavit when administered or taken by or before an employee of the Office of the Inspector General of the Intelligence Community designated by the Inspector General shall have the same force and effect as if administered or taken by, or before, an officer having a seal.

(5)(A) Except as provided in subparagraph (B), the Inspector General is authorized to require by subpoena the production of all information, documents, reports, answers, records, accounts, papers, and other data in any medium (including electronically stored information, as well as any tangible thing) and documentary evidence necessary in the performance of the duties and responsibilities of the Inspector General.

(B) In the case of departments, agencies, and other elements of the United States Government, the Inspector General shall obtain information, documents, reports, answers, records, accounts, papers, and other data and evidence for the purpose specified in subparagraph (A) using procedures other than by subpoenas.

(C) The Inspector General may not issue a subpoena for, or on behalf of, any component of the Office of the Director of National Intelligence or any element of the intelligence community, including the Office of the Director of National Intelligence.

(D) In the case of contumacy or refusal to obey a subpoena issued under this paragraph, the subpoena shall be enforceable by order of any appropriate district court of the United States.

(6) The Inspector General may obtain services as authorized by section 3109 of title 5, United States Code, at rates for individuals not to exceed the daily equivalent of the maximum annual rate of basic pay payable for grade GS–15 of the General Schedule under section 5332 of title 5, United States Code.

(7) The Inspector General may, to the extent and in such amounts as may be provided in appropriations, enter into contracts and other arrangements for audits, studies, analyses, and other services with public agencies and with private persons, and to make such payments as may be necessary to carry out the provisions of this section.

(h) COORDINATION AMONG INSPECTORS GENERAL.—

(1)(A) In the event of a matter within the jurisdiction of the Inspector General of the Intelligence Community that may be subject to an investigation, inspection, audit, or review by both the Inspector General of the Intelligence Community and an inspector general with oversight responsibility for an element of the intelligence community, the Inspector General of the Intelligence Community and such other inspector general shall expeditiously resolve the question of which inspector general shall conduct such investigation, inspection, audit, or review to avoid unnecessary duplication of the activities of the inspectors general.

(B) In attempting to resolve a question under subparagraph (A), the inspectors general concerned may request the assistance of the Intelligence Community Inspectors General Forum established under paragraph (2).

In the event of a dispute between an inspector general within a department or agency of the United States Government and the Inspector General of the Intelligence Community that has not been resolved with the assistance of such Forum, the inspectors general shall submit the question to the Director of National Intelligence and the head of the affected department or agency for resolution.

(2)(A) There is established the Intelligence Community Inspectors General Forum, which shall consist of all statutory or administrative inspectors general with oversight responsibility for an element of the intelligence community.

(B) The Inspector General of the Intelligence Community shall serve as the Chair of the Forum established under subparagraph (A). The Forum shall have no administrative authority over any inspector general, but shall serve as a mechanism for informing its members of the work of individual members of the Forum that may be of common interest and discussing questions about jurisdiction or access to employees, employees of contract personnel, records, audits, reviews, documents, recommendations, or other materials that may involve or be of assistance to more than one of its members.

(3) The inspector general conducting an investigation, inspection, audit, or review covered by paragraph (1) shall submit the results of such investigation, inspection, audit, or review to any other inspector general, including the Inspector General of the Intelligence Community, with jurisdiction to conduct such investigation, inspection, audit, or review who did not conduct such investigation, inspection, audit, or review.

(i) COUNSEL TO THE INSPECTOR GENERAL.—

(1) The Inspector General of the Intelligence Community shall—

(A) appoint a Counsel to the Inspector General who shall report to the Inspector General; or

(B) obtain the services of a counsel appointed by and directly reporting to another inspector general or the Council of the Inspectors General on Integrity and Efficiency on a reimbursable basis.

(2) The counsel appointed or obtained under paragraph (1) shall perform such functions as the Inspector General may prescribe.

(j) STAFF AND OTHER SUPPORT.—

(1) The Director of National Intelligence shall provide the Inspector General of the Intelligence Community with appropriate and adequate office space at central and field office locations, together with such equipment, office supplies, maintenance services, and communications facilities and services as may be necessary for the operation of such offices.

(2)(A) Subject to applicable law and the policies of the Director of National Intelligence, the Inspector General shall select, appoint, and employ such officers and employees as may be necessary to carry out the functions, powers, and duties of the Inspector General. The Inspector General shall ensure that any officer or employee so selected, appointed, or employed has security clearances appropriate for the assigned duties of such officer or employee.

(B) In making selections under subparagraph (A), the Inspector General shall ensure that such officers and employees have the requisite training and experience to enable the Inspector General to carry out the duties of the Inspector General effectively.

(C) In meeting the requirements of this paragraph, the Inspector General shall create within the Office of the Inspector General of the Intelligence Community a career cadre of sufficient size to provide appropriate continuity and objectivity needed for the effective performance of the duties of the Inspector General.

(3) Consistent with budgetary and personnel resources allocated by the Director of National Intelligence, the Inspector General has final approval of—

(A) the selection of internal and external candidates for employment with the Office of the Inspector General; and

(B) all other personnel decisions concerning personnel permanently assigned to the Office of the Inspector General, including selection and appointment to the Senior Intelligence Service, but excluding all securitybased determinations that are not within the authority of a head of a component of the Office of the Director of National Intelligence.

(4)(A) Subject to the concurrence of the Director of National Intelligence, the Inspector General may request such information or assistance as may be necessary for carrying out the duties and responsibilities of the Inspector General from any department, agency, or other element of the United States Government.

(B) Upon request of the Inspector General for information or assistance under subparagraph (A), the head of the department, agency, or element concerned shall, insofar as is practicable and not in contravention of any existing statutory restriction or regulation of the department, agency, or element, furnish to the Inspector General, such information or assistance.

(C) The Inspector General of the Intelligence Community may, upon reasonable notice to the head of any element of the intelligence community and in coordination with that element's inspector general pursuant to subsection (h), conduct, as authorized by this section, an investigation, inspection, audit, or review of such element and may enter into any place occupied by such element for purposes of the performance of the duties of the Inspector General.

(k) REPORTS.—

(1)(A) The Inspector General of the Intelligence Community shall, not later than January 31 and July 31 of each year, prepare and submit to the Director of National Intelligence a classified, and, as appropriate, unclassified semiannual report summarizing the activities of the Office of the Inspector General of the Intelligence Community during the immediately preceding 6 month period ending December 31 (of the preceding year) and June 30, respectively. The Inspector General of the Intelligence Community shall provide any portion of the report involving a component of a department of the United States Government to the head of that department simultaneously with submission of the report to the Director of National Intelligence.

(B) Each report under this paragraph shall include, at a minimum, the following:

(i) A list of the title or subject of each investigation, inspection, audit, or review conducted during the period covered by such report.

(ii) A description of significant problems, abuses, and deficiencies relating to the administration of programs and activities of the intelligence community within the responsibility and authority of the Director of National Intelligence, and in the relationships between elements of the intelligence community, identified by the Inspector General during the period covered by such report.

(iii) A description of the recommendations for corrective action made by the Inspector General during the period covered by such report with respect to significant problems, abuses, or deficiencies identified in clause

(ii).

(iv) A statement of whether or not corrective action has been completed on each significant recommendation described in previous semiannual reports, and, in a case where corrective action has been completed, a description of such corrective action.

(v) A certification of whether or not the Inspector General has had full and direct access to all information relevant to the performance of the functions of the Inspector General.

(vi) A description of the exercise of the subpoena authority under subsection

(g)(5) by the Inspector General during the period covered by such report.

(vii) Such recommendations as the Inspector General considers appropriate for legislation to promote economy, efficiency, and effectiveness in the administration and implementation of programs and activities within the responsibility and authority of the Director of National Intelligence, and to detect and eliminate fraud and abuse in such programs and activities.

(C) Not later than 30 days after the date of receipt of a report under subparagraph (A), the Director shall transmit the report to the congressional intelligence committees together with any comments the Director considers appropriate. The Director shall transmit to the committees of the Senate and of the House of Representatives with jurisdiction over a department of the United States Government any portion of the report involving a component of such department simultaneously with submission of the report to the congressional intelligence committees.

(2)(A) The Inspector General shall report immediately to the Director whenever the Inspector General becomes aware of particularly serious or flagrant problems, abuses, or deficiencies relating to programs and activities within the responsibility and authority of the Director of National Intelligence.

(B) The Director shall transmit to the congressional intelligence committees each report under subparagraph (A) within 7 calendar days of receipt of such report, together with such comments as the Director considers appropriate. The Director shall transmit to the committees of the Senate and of the House of Representatives with jurisdiction over a department of the United States Government any portion of each report under subparagraph (A) that involves a problem, abuse, or deficiency related to a component of such department simultaneously with transmission of the report to the congressional intelligence committees.

(3)(A) In the event that—

(i) the Inspector General is unable to resolve any differences with the Director affecting the execution of the duties or responsibilities of the Inspector General;

(ii) an investigation, inspection, audit, or review carried out by the Inspector General focuses on any current or former intelligence community official who—

(I) holds or held a position in an element of the intelligence community that is subject to appointment by the President, whether or not by and with the advice and consent of the Senate, including such a position held on an acting basis;

(II) holds or held a position in an element of the intelligence community, including a position held on an acting basis, that is appointed by the Director of National Intelligence; or

(III) holds or held a position as head of an element of the intelligence community or a position covered by subsection (b) or (c) of section 106;

(iii) a matter requires a report by the Inspector General to the Department of Justice on possible criminal conduct by a current or former official described in clause (ii);

(iv) the Inspector General receives notice from the Department of Justice declining or approving prosecution of possible criminal conduct of any current or former official described in clause (ii); or

(v) the Inspector General, after exhausting all possible alternatives, is unable to obtain significant documentary information in the course of an investigation, inspection, audit, or review, the Inspector General shall immediately notify, and submit a report to, the congressional intelligence committees on such matter.

(B) The Inspector General shall submit to the committees of the Senate and of the House of Representatives with jurisdiction over a department of the United States Government any portion of each report under subparagraph (A) that involves an investigation, inspection, audit, or review carried out by the Inspector General focused on any current or former official of a component of such department simultaneously with submission of the report to the congressional intelligence committees.

(4) The Director shall submit to the congressional intelligence committees any report or findings and recommendations of an investigation, inspection, audit, or review conducted by the office which has been requested by the Chairman or Vice Chairman or ranking minority member of either committee.

(5)(A) An employee of an element of the intelligence community, an employee assigned or detailed to an element of the intelligence community, or an employee of a contractor to the intelligence community who intends to report to Congress a complaint or information with respect to an urgent concern may report such complaint or information to the Inspector General.

(B) Not later than the end of the 14calendarday period beginning on the date of receipt from an employee of a complaint or information under subparagraph (A), the Inspector General shall determine whether the complaint or information appears credible. Upon making such a determination, the Inspector General shall transmit to the Director a notice of that determination, together with the complaint or information.

(C) Upon receipt of a transmittal from the Inspector General under subparagraph (B), the Director shall, within 7 calendar days of such receipt, forward such transmittal to the congressional intelligence committees, together with any comments the Director considers appropriate.

(D)(i) If the Inspector General does not find credible under subparagraph (B) a complaint or information submitted under subparagraph (A), or does not transmit the complaint or information to the Director in accurate form under subparagraph (B), the employee (subject to clause (ii)) may submit the complaint or information to Congress by contacting either or both of the congressional intelligence committees directly.

(ii) An employee may contact the congressional intelligence committees directly as described in clause (i) only if the employee—

(I) before making such a contact, furnishes to the Director, through the Inspector General, a statement of the employee's complaint or information and notice of the employee's intent to contact the congressional intelligence committees directly; and

(II) obtains and follows from the Director, through the Inspector General, direction on how to contact the congressional intelligence committees in accordance with appropriate security practices.

(iii) A member or employee of one of the congressional intelligence committees who receives a complaint or information under this subparagraph does so in that member or employee's official capacity as a member or employee of such committee.

(E) The Inspector General shall notify an employee who reports a complaint or information to the Inspector General under this paragraph of each action taken under this paragraph with respect to the complaint or information. Such notice shall be provided not later than 3 days after any such action is taken.

(F) An action taken by the Director or the Inspector General under this paragraph shall not be subject to judicial review.

(G) In this paragraph, the term "urgent concern" means any of the following:

(i) A serious or flagrant problem, abuse, violation of law or Executive order, or deficiency relating to the funding, administration, or operation of an intelligence activity within the responsibility and authority of the Director of National Intelligence involving classified information, but does not include differences of opinions concerning public policy matters.

(ii) A false statement to Congress, or a willful withholding from Congress, on an issue of material fact relating to the funding, administration, or operation of an intelligence activity.

(iii) An action, including a personnel action described in section 2302(a)(2)(A) of title 5, United States Code, constituting reprisal or threat of reprisal prohibited under subsection (g)(3)(B) of this section in response to an employee's reporting an urgent concern in accordance with this paragraph.

(H) Nothing in this section shall be construed to limit the protections afforded to an employee under section 17(d) of the Central Intelligence Agency Act of 1949 (50 U.S.C. 403q(d)) or section 8H of the Inspector General Act of 1978 (5 U.S.C. App.).

(6) In accordance with section 535 of title 28, United States Code, the Inspector General shall expeditiously report to the Attorney General any information, allegation, or complaint received by the Inspector General relating to violations of Federal criminal law that involves a program or operation of an element of the intelligence community, or in the relationships between the elements of the intelligence community, consistent with such guidelines as may be issued by the Attorney General pursuant to subsection (b)(2) of such section. A copy of each such report shall be furnished to the Director.

(l) CONSTRUCTION OF DUTIE SREGARDING ELEMENTS OFINTELLIGENCE COMMUNITY.—Except as resolved pursuant to subsection (h), the performance by the Inspector General of the Intelligence Community of any duty, responsibility, or function regarding an element of the intelligence community shall not be construed to modify or affect the duties and responsibilities of any other inspector general having duties and responsibilities relating to such element.

(m) SEPARATE BUDGET ACCOUNT.—The Director of National Intelligence shall, in accordance with procedures issued by the Director in consultation with the congressional intelligence committees, include in the National Intelligence Program budget a separate account for the Office of the Inspector General of the Intelligence Community.

(n) BUDGET.—(1) For each fiscal year, the Inspector General of the Intelligence Community shall transmit a budget estimate and request to the Director of National Intelligence that specifies for such fiscal year—

(A) the aggregate amount requested for the operations of the Inspector General;

(B) the amount requested for all training requirements of the Inspector General, including a certification from the Inspector General that the amount requested is sufficient to fund all training requirements for the Office of the Inspector General; and

(C) the amount requested to support the Council of the Inspectors General on Integrity and Efficiency, including a justification for such amount.

(2) In transmitting a proposed budget to the President for a fiscal year, the Director of National Intelligence shall include for such fiscal year—

(A) the aggregate amount requested for the Inspector General of the Intelligence Community;

(B) the amount requested for Inspector General training;

(C) the amount requested to support the Council of the Inspectors General on Integrity and Efficiency; and

(D) the comments of the Inspector General, if any, with respect to such proposed budget.

(3) The Director of National Intelligence shall submit to the congressional intelligence committees, the Committee on Appropriations of the Senate, and the Committee on Appropriations of the House of Representatives for each fiscal year—

(A) a separate statement of the budget estimate transmitted pursuant to paragraph (1);

(B) the amount requested by the Director for the Inspector General pursuant to paragraph (2)(A);

(C) the amount requested by the Director for the training of personnel of the Office of the Inspector General pursuant to paragraph (2)(B);

(D) the amount requested by the Director for support for the Council of the Inspectors General on Integrity and Efficiency pursuant to paragraph (2)(C); and

(E) the comments of the Inspector General under paragraph (2)(D), if any, on the amounts requested pursuant to paragraph (2), including whether such amounts would substantially inhibit the Inspector General from performing the duties of the Office of the Inspector General.

CHIEF FINANCIAL OFFICER OF THE INTELLIGENCE COMMUNITY
SEC. 103I. {50 U.S.C. 403–3i]

(a) CHIEF FINANCIAL OFFICER OF THE INTELLIGENCE COMMUNITY.—To assist the Director of National Intelligence in carrying out the responsibilities of the Director under this Act and other applicable provisions of law, there is within the Office of the Director of National Intelligence a Chief Financial Officer of the Intelligence Community who shall be appointed by the Director.

(b) DUTIES AND RESPONSIBILITIES.—Subject to the direction of the Director of National Intelligence, the Chief Financial Officer of the Intelligence Community shall—

(1) serve as the principal advisor to the Director of National Intelligence and the Principal Deputy Director of National Intelligence on the management and allocation of intelligence community budgetary resources;

(2) participate in overseeing a comprehensive and integrated strategic process for resource management within the intelligence community;

(3) ensure that the strategic plan of the Director of National Intelligence—

(A) is based on budgetary constraints as specified in the Future Year Intelligence Plans and Longterm Budget Projections required under section 506G; and

(B) contains specific goals and objectives to support a performancebased budget;

(4) prior to the obligation or expenditure of funds for the acquisition of any major system pursuant to a Milestone A or Milestone B decision, receive verification from appropriate authorities that the national requirements for meeting the strategic plan of the Director have been established, and that such requirements are prioritized based on budgetary constraints as specified in the Future Year Intelligence Plans and the Long term Budget Projections for such major system required under section 506G;

(5) ensure that the collection architectures of the Director are based on budgetary constraints as specified in the Future Year Intelligence Plans and the Longterm Budget Projections required under section 506G;

(6) coordinate or approve representations made to Congress by the intelligence community regarding National Intelligence Program budgetary resources;

(7) participate in key mission requirements, acquisitions, or architectural boards formed within or by the Office of the Director of National Intelligence; and

(8) perform such other duties as may be prescribed by the Director of National Intelligence.

(c) OTHER LAW.—The Chief Financial Officer of the Intelligence Community shall serve as the Chief Financial Officer of the intelligence community and, to the extent applicable, shall have the duties, responsibilities, and authorities specified in chapter 9 of title 31, United States Code.

(d) PROHIBITION ON SIMULTANEOUS SERVICE AS OTHER CHIEF FINANCIAL OFFICER.—An individual serving in the position of Chief Financial Officer of the Intelligence Community may not, while so serving, serve as the chief financial officer of any other department or agency, or component thereof, of the United States Government.

(e) DEFINITIONS.—In this section:

(1) The term "major system" has the meaning given that term in section 506A(e).

(2) The term "Milestone A" has the meaning given that term in section 506G(f).

(3) The term "Milestone B" has the meaning given that term in section 506C(e).

CENTRAL INTELLIGENCE AGENCY

SEC. 104. [50 U.S.C. §403-4]

(a) CENTRAL INTELLIGENCE AGENCY.—There is a Central Intelligence Agency.

(b) FUNCTION.—The function of the Central Intelligence Agency is to assist the Director of the Central Intelligence Agency in carrying out the responsibilities specified in section 104A(c).

DIRECTOR OF THE CENTRAL INTELLIGENCE AGENCY

SEC. 104A. [50 U.S.C. §403-4a]

(a) DIRECTOR OF CENTRAL INTELLIGENCE AGENCY.—There is a Director of the Central Intelligence Agency who shall be appointed by the President, by and with the advice and consent of the Senate.

(b) SUPERVISION.—The Director of the Central Intelligence Agency shall report to the Director of National Intelligence regarding the activities of the Central Intelligence Agency.

(c) DUTIES.—The Director of the Central Intelligence Agency shall—

(1) serve as the head of the Central Intelligence Agency; and

(2) carry out the responsibilities specified in subsection (d).

(d) RESPONSIBILITIES.—The Director of the Central Intelligence Agency shall—

(1) collect intelligence through human sources and by other appropriate means, except that the Director of the Central Intelligence Agency shall have no police, subpoena, or law enforcement powers or internal security functions;

(2) correlate and evaluate intelligence related to the national security and provide appropriate dissemination of such intelligence;

(3) provide overall direction for and coordination of the collection of national intelligence outside the United States through human sources by elements of the intelligence community authorized to undertake such collection and, in coordination with other departments, agencies, or elements of the United States Government which are authorized to undertake such collection, ensure that the most effective use is made of resources and that appropriate account is taken of the risks to the United States and those involved in such collection; and

(4) perform such other functions and duties related to intelligence affecting the national security as the President or the Director of National Intelligence may direct.

(e) TERMINATION OF EMPLOYMENT OF CIA EMPLOYEES.—

(1) Notwithstanding the provisions of any other law, the Director of the Central Intelligence Agency may, in the discretion of the Director, terminate the employment of any officer or employee of the Central Intelligence Agency whenever the Director deems the termination of employment of such officer or employee necessary or advisable in the interests of the United States.

(2) Any termination of employment of an officer or employee under paragraph (1) shall not affect the right of the officer or employee to seek or accept employment in any other department, agency, or element of the United States Government if declared eligible for such employment by the Office of Personnel Management.

(f) COORDINATION WITH FOREIGN GOVERNMENTS.—Under the direction of the Director of National Intelligence and in a manner consistent with section 207 of the Foreign Service Act of 1980 (22 U.S.C. §3927), the Director of the Central Intelligence Agency shall coordinate the relationships between elements of the intelligence community and the intelligence or security services of foreign governments or international organizations on all matters involving intelligence related to the national security or involving intelligence acquired through clandestine means.
(g) FOREIGN LANGUAGE PROFICIENCY FOR CERTAIN SENIOR LEVEL POSITIONS IN CENTRAL INTELLIGENCE AGENCY.—

(1) Except as provided pursuant to paragraph (2), an individual may not be appointed to a position in the Senior Intelligence Service in the Directorate of Intelligence or the Directorate of Operations of the Central Intelligence Agency unless the Director of the Central Intelligence Agency determines that the individual—

(A) has been certified as having a professional speaking and reading proficiency in a foreign language, such proficiency being at least level 3 on the Interagency Language Roundtable Language Skills Level or commensurate proficiency level using such other indicator of proficiency as the Director of the Central Intelligence Agency considers appropriate; and

(B) is able to effectively communicate the priorities of the United States and exercise influence in that foreign language.

(2) The Director of the Central Intelligence Agency may, in the discretion of the Director, waive the application of paragraph (1) to any position or category of positions otherwise covered by that paragraph if the Director determines that foreign language proficiency is not necessary for the successful performance of the duties and responsibilities of such position or category of positions.

DEPUTY DIRECTOR OF THE CENTRAL INTELLIGENCE AGENCY

SEC. 104B. {50 U.S.C. 403–4c}

(a) DEPUTY DIRECTOR OF THE CENTRAL INTELLIGENCE AGENCY.—There is a Deputy Director of the Central Intelligence Agency who shall be appointed by the President.

(b) DUTIES.—The Deputy Director of the Central Intelligence Agency shall—

(1) assist the Director of the Central Intelligence Agency in carrying out the duties and responsibilities of the Director of the Central Intelligence Agency; and

(2) during the absence or disability of the Director of the Central Intelligence Agency, or during a vacancy in the position of Director of the Central Intelligence Agency, act for and exercise the powers of the Director of the Central Intelligence Agency.

RESPONSIBILITIES OF THE SECRETARY OF DEFENSE PERTAINING TO THE NATIONAL INTELLIGENCE PROGRAM

SEC. 105. [50 U.S.C. §403–5]

(a) IN GENERAL.—Consistent with the sections 102 and 102A, the Secretary of Defense, in consultation with the Director of National Intelligence, shall—

(1) ensure that the budgets of the elements of the intelligence community within the Department of Defense are adequate to satisfy the overall intelligence needs of the Department of Defense, including the needs of the Chairman of the Joint Chiefs of Staff and the commanders of the unified and specified commands and, wherever such elements are performing government wide functions, the needs of other departments and agencies;

(2) ensure appropriate implementation of the policies and resource decisions of the Director by elements of the Department of Defense within the National Intelligence Program;

(3) ensure that the tactical intelligence activities of the Department of Defense complement and are compatible with intelligence activities under the National Intelligence Program;

(4) ensure that the elements of the intelligence community within the Department of Defense are responsive and timely with respect to satisfying the needs of operational military forces;

(5) eliminate waste and unnecessary duplication among the intelligence activities of the Department of Defense; and

(6) ensure that intelligence activities of the Department of Defense are conducted jointly where appropriate.

(b) RESPONSIBILITY FOR THE PERFORMANCE OF SPECIFIC FUNCTIONS.—Consistent with sections 102 and 102A of this Act, the Secretary of Defense shall ensure—

(1) through the National Security Agency (except as otherwise directed by the President or the National Security Council), the continued operation of an effective unified organization for the conduct of signals intelligence activities and shall ensure that the product is disseminated in a timely manner to authorized recipients;

(2) through the National Geospatial-Intelligence Agency (except as otherwise directed by the President or the National Security Council), with appropriate representation from the intelligence community, the continued operation of an effective unified organization within the Department of Defense—

(A) for carrying out tasking of imagery collection;

(B) for the coordination of imagery processing and exploitation activities;

(C) for ensuring the dissemination of imagery in a timely manner to authorized recipients; and

(D) notwithstanding any other provision of law, for—

(i) prescribing technical architecture and standards related to imagery intelligence and geospatial information and ensuring compliance with such architecture and standards; and

(ii) developing and fielding systems of common concern related to imagery intelligence and geospatial information;

(3) through the National Reconnaissance Office (except as otherwise directed by the President or the National Security Council), the continued operation of an effective unified organization for the research and development, acquisition, and operation of overhead reconnaissance systems necessary to satisfy the requirements of all elements of the intelligence community;

(4) through the Defense Intelligence Agency (except as otherwise directed by the President or the National Security Council), the continued operation of an effective unified system within the Department of Defense for the production of timely, objective military and military-related intelligence, based upon all sources available to the intelligence community, and shall ensure the appropriate dissemination of such intelligence to authorized recipients;

(5) through the Defense Intelligence Agency (except as otherwise directed by the President or the National Security Council), effective management of Department of Defense human intelligence activities, including defense attaches; and

(6) that the military departments maintain sufficient capabilities to collect and produce intelligence to meet—

(A) the requirements of the Director of National Intelligence;

(B) the requirements of the Secretary of Defense or the Chairman of the Joint Chiefs of Staff;

(C) the requirements of the unified and specified combatant commands and of joint operations; and

(D) the specialized requirements of the military departments for intelligence necessary to support tactical commanders, military planners, the research and development process, the acquisition of military equipment, and training and doctrine.

(c) USE OF ELEMENTS OF DEPARTMENT OF DEFENSE.—The Secretary of Defense, in carrying out the functions described in this section, may use such elements of the Department of Defense as may be appropriate for the execution of those functions, in addition to, or in lieu of, the elements identified in this section.

ASSISTANCE TO UNITED STATES LAW ENFORCEMENT AGENCIES
SEC. 105A. [50 U.S.C. §403–5a]

(a) AUTHORITY TO PROVIDE ASSISTANCE.—Subject to subsection (b), elements of the intelligence community may, upon the request of a United States law enforcement agency, collect information outside the United States about individuals who are not United States persons. Such elements may collect such information notwithstanding that the law enforcement agency intends to use the information collected for purposes of a law enforcement investigation or counterintelligence investigation.

(b) LIMITATION ON ASSISTANCE BY ELEMENTS OF DEPARTMENT OF DEFENSE.—

(1) With respect to elements within the Department of Defense, the authority in subsection (a) applies only to the following:

(A) The National Security Agency.

(B) The National Reconnaissance Office.

(C) The National Geospatial-Intelligence Agency.

(D) The Defense Intelligence Agency.

(2) Assistance provided under this section by elements of the Department of Defense may not include the direct participation of a member of the Army,

Navy, Air Force, or Marine Corps in an arrest or similar activity.

(3) Assistance may not be provided under this section by an element of the Department of Defense if the provision of such assistance will adversely affect the military preparedness of the United States.

(4) The Secretary of Defense shall prescribe regulations governing the exercise of authority under this section by elements of the Department of Defense, including regulations relating to the protection of sources and methods in the exercise of such authority.

(c) DEFINITIONS.—For purposes of subsection (a):

(1) The term "United States law enforcement agency" means any department or agency of the Federal Government that the Attorney General designates as law enforcement agency for purposes of this section.

(2) The term "United States person" means the following:

(A) A United States citizen.

(B) An alien known by the intelligence agency concerned to be a permanent resident alien.

(C) An unincorporated association substantially composed of United States citizens or permanent resident aliens.

(D) A corporation incorporated in the United States, except for a corporation directed and controlled by a foreign government or governments.

DISCLOSURE OF FOREIGN INTELLIGENCE ACQUIRED IN CRIMINAL INVESTIGATIONS; NOTICE OF CRIMINAL INVESTIGATIONS OF FOREIGN INTELLIGENCE SOURCES

SEC. 105B. [50 U.S.C. §403–5b]

(a) DISCLOSURE OF FOREIGN INTELLIGENCE.—

(1) Except as otherwise provided by law and subject to paragraph (2), the Attorney General, or the head of any other department or agency of the Federal Government with law enforcement responsibilities, shall expeditiously disclose to the Director of National Intelligence, pursuant to guidelines developed by the Attorney General in consultation with the Director, foreign intelligence acquired by an element of the Department of Justice or an element of such department or agency, as the case may be, in the course of a criminal investigation.

(2) The Attorney General by regulation and in consultation with the Director may provide for exceptions to the applicability of paragraph (1) for one or more classes of foreign intelligence, or foreign intelligence with respect to one or more targets or matters, if the Attorney General determines that disclosure of such foreign intelligence under that paragraph would jeopardize an ongoing law enforcement investigation or impair other significant law enforcement interests.

(b) PROCEDURES FOR NOTICE OF CRIMINAL INVESTIGATIONS.—Not later than 180 days after the date of enactment of this section, the Attorney General, in consultation with the Director of National Intelligence, shall develop guidelines to ensure that after receipt of a report from an element of the intelligence community of activity of a foreign intelligence source or potential foreign intelligence source that may warrant investigation as criminal activity, the Attorney General provides notice to the Director, within a reasonable period of time, of his intention to commence, or decline to commence, a criminal investigation of such activity.

(c) PROCEDURES.—The Attorney General shall develop procedures for the administration of this section, including the disclosure of foreign intelligence by elements of the Department of Justice, and elements of other departments and agencies of the Federal Government, under subsection (a) and the provision of notice with respect to criminal investigations under subsection (b).

APPOINTMENT OF OFFICIALS RESPONSIBLE FOR INTELLIGENCE RELATED ACTIVITIES

SEC. 106.[1] [50 U.S.C. §403–6]

(a) RECOMMENDATION OF DNI IN CERTAIN APPOINTMENTS.—

(1) In the event of a vacancy in a position referred to in paragraph (2), the Director of National Intelligence shall recommend to the President an individual for nomination to fill the vacancy.

(2) Paragraph (1) applies to the following positions:

(A) The Principal Deputy Director of National Intelligence.

(B) The Director of the Central Intelligence Agency.

(b) CONCURRENCE OF DNI IN APPOINTMENTS TO POSITIONS IN THE INTELLIGENCE COMMUNITY.—

(1) In the event of a vacancy in a position referred to in paragraph (2), the head of the department or agency having jurisdiction over the position shall obtain the concurrence of the Director of National Intelligence before appointing an individual to fill the vacancy or recommending to the President an individual to be nominated to fill the vacancy. If the Director does not concur in the recommendation, the head of the department or agency concerned may not fill the vacancy or make the recommendation to the President (as the case may be). In the case in which the Director does not concur in such a recommendation, the Director and the head of the department or agency concerned may advise the President directly of the intention to withhold concurrence or to make a recommendation, as the case may be.

(2) Paragraph (1) applies to the following positions:

(A) The Director of the National Security Agency.

(B) The Director of the National Reconnaissance Office.

(C) The Director of the National Geospatial-Intelligence Agency.

(D) The Assistant Secretary of State for Intelligence and Research.

(E) The Director of the Office of Intelligence of the Department of Energy.

(F) The Director of the Office of Counterintelligence of the Department of Energy.

---

1. Section 1014 of the Intelligence Reform and Terrorism Prevention Act of 2004 (Public Law108–458; 118 Stat. 3663) amended section 106 by striking all after the heading and insertinga new subsection (a). The section designation, while it no longer exists in the law, is shownabove in order to reflect the probable intent of Congress.

(G) The Assistant Secretary for Intelligence and Analysis of the Department of the Treasury.

(H) The Executive Assistant Director for Intelligence of the Federal Bureau of Investigation or any successor to that position.

(I)[1] The Under Secretary of Homeland Security for Intelligence and Analysis.

(c) CONSULTATION WITH DNI IN CERTAIN POSITIONS.—

(1) In the event of a vacancy in a position referred to in paragraph (2), the head of the department or agency having jurisdiction over the position shall consult with the Director of National Intelligence before appointing an individual to fill the vacancy or recommending to the President an individual to be nominated to fill the vacancy.

(2) Paragraph (1) applies to the following positions:

(A) The Director of the Defense Intelligence Agency.

(B) The Assistant Commandant of the Coast Guard for Intelligence.

(C) Assistant Attorney General designated as the Assistant Attorney General for National Security under section 507A of title 28, United States Code.

NATIONAL SECURITY RESOURCES BOARD[2]

SEC. 107. [50 U.S.C. §404]

(a) The Director of the Office of Defense Mobilization,[3] subject to the direction of the President, is authorized, subject to the civil-service laws and the Classification Act of 1949,[4] to appoint and fix the compensation of such personnel as may be necessary to assist the Director in carrying out his functions.

(b) It shall be the function of the Director of the Office of Defense Mobilization to advise the President concerning the coordination of military, industrial, and civilian mobilization, including—

(1) policies concerning industrial and civilian mobilization in order to assure the most effective mobilization and maximum utilization of the Nation's manpower in the event of war.

(2) programs for the effective use in time of war of the Nation's natural and industrial resources for military and civilian needs, for the maintenance and stabilization of the civilian economy in time of war, and for the adjustment of such economy to war needs and conditions;

---

1. Margin so in law.

2. Section 107 deals with emergency preparedness. Section 50 of the Act of September 3, 1954(68 Stat. 1244), eliminated former subsection (a), relating to the establishment of the National Security Resources Board, and redesignated former subsections (b)–(d) as subsections (a)–(c).The section heading was not amended accordingly.

3. The functions of the Director of the Office of Defense Mobilization under this section which previously were transferred to the President, were delegated to the Director of the Federal Emergency Management Agency by section 4–102 of Executive Order No. 12148 (July 20, 1979,44 F.R. 43239, 50 U.S.C. App. 2251 note).

4. The Classification Act of 1949 was repealed by the law enacting title 5, United States Code (Public Law 89–544, Sept. 6, 1966, 80 Stat. 378), and its provisions were codified as chapter51 and chapter 53 of that title.

(3) policies for unifying, in time of war, the activities of Federal agencies and departments engaged in or concerned with production, procurement, distribution, or transportation of military or civilian supplies, materials, and products;

(4) the relationship between potential supplies of, and potential requirements for, manpower, resources, and productive facilities in time of war;

(5) policies for establishing adequate reserves of strategic and critical material, and for the conservation of these reserves;

(6) the strategic relocation of industries, services, government, and economic activities, the continuous operation of which is essential to the Nation's security.

(c) In performing his functions, the Director of the Office of Defense Mobilization shall utilize to the maximum extent the facilities and resources of the departments and agencies of the Government.

ANNUAL NATIONAL SECURITY STRATEGY REPORT

SEC. 108. [50 U.S.C. §404a]

(a)(1) The President shall transmit to Congress each year a comprehensive report on the national security strategy of the United States (hereinafter in this section referred to as a national security strategy report").

(2) The national security strategy report for any year shall be transmitted on the date on which the President submits to Congress the budget for the next fiscal year under section 1105 of title 31, United States Code.

(3) Not later than 150 days after the date on which a new President takes office, the President shall transmit to Congress a national security strategy report under this section. That report shall be in addition to the report for that year transmitted at the time specified in paragraph (2).

(b) Each national security strategy report shall set forth the national security strategy of the United States and shall include a comprehensive description and discussion of the following:

(1) The worldwide interests, goals, and objectives of the United States that are vital to the national security of the United States.

(2) The foreign policy, worldwide commitments, and national defense capabilities of the United States necessary to deter aggression and to implement the national security strategy of the United States.

(3) The proposed short-term and long-term uses of the political, economic, military, and other elements of the national power of the United States to protect or promote the interests and achieve the goals and objectives referred to in paragraph (1).

(4) The adequacy of the capabilities of the United States to carry out the national security strategy of the United States, including an evaluation of the balance among the capabilities of all elements of the national power of the United States to support the implementation of the national security strategy.

(5) Such other information as may be necessary to help inform Congress on matters relating to the national security strategy of the United States.

(c) Each national security strategy report shall be transmitted in both a classified and an unclassified form.

ANNUAL REPORT ON INTELLIGENCE

[Section 109 was repealed by section 347(a) of Public Law 111– 259.]

NATIONAL MISSION OF THE NATIONAL GEOSPATIAL-INTELLIGENCE AGENCY

SEC. 110. [50 U.S.C. §404e]

(a) IN GENERAL.—In addition to the Department of Defense missions set forth in section 442 of title 10, United States Code, the National Geospatial-Intelligence Agency shall support the imagery requirements of the Department of State and other departments and agencies of the United States outside the Department of Defense.

(b) REQUIREMENTS AND PRIORITIES.—The Director of National Intelligence shall establish requirements and priorities governing the collection of national intelligence by the National Geospatial-Intelligence Agency under subsection (a).

(c) CORRECTION OF DEFICIENCIES.—The Director of National Intelligence shall develop and implement such programs and policies as the Director and the Secretary of Defense jointly determine necessary to review and correct deficiencies identified in the capabilities of the National Geospatial-Intelligence Agency to accomplish assigned national missions, including support to the all-source analysis and production process. The Director shall consult with the Secretary of Defense on the development and implementation of such programs and policies. The Secretary shall obtain the advice of the Chairman of the Joint Chiefs of Staff regarding the matters on which the Director and the Secretary are to consult under the preceding sentence.

RESTRICTION ON INTELLIGENCE SHARING WITH THE UNITED NATIONS

SEC. 112. [50 U.S.C. §404g]

(a) PROVISION OF INTELLIGENCE INFORMATION TO THE UNITED NATIONS.—

(1) No United States intelligence information may be provided to the United Nations or any organization affiliated with the United Nations, or to any officials or employees thereof, unless the President certifies to the appropriate committees of Congress that the Director of National Intelligence, in consultation with the Secretary of State and the Secretary of Defense, has established and implemented procedures, and has worked with the United Nations to ensure implementation of procedures, for protecting from unauthorized disclosure United States intelligence sources and methods connected to such information.

(2) Paragraph (1) may be waived upon written certification by the President to the appropriate committees of Congress that providing such information to the United Nations or an organization affiliated with the United Nations, or to

any officials or employees thereof, is in the national security interests of the United States.

(b) ANNUAL AND SPECIAL REPORTS.—

(1) The President shall report annually to the appropriate committees of Congress on the types and volume of intelligence provided to the United Nations and the purposes for which it was provided during the period covered by the report. The President shall also report to the appropriate committees of Congress within 15 days after it has become known to the United States Government that there has been an unauthorized disclosure of intelligence provided by the United States to the United Nations.

(2) The requirement for periodic reports under the first sentence of paragraph (1) shall not apply to the provision of intelligence that is provided only to, and for the use of, appropriately cleared United States Government personnel serving with the United Nations.

(3) In the case of the annual reports required to be submitted under the first sentence of paragraph (1) to the congressional intelligence committees, the submittal dates for such reports shall be as provided in section 507.

(c) DELEGATION OF DUTIES.—The President may not delegate or assign the duties of the President under this section.

(d) RELATIONSHIP TO EXISTING LAW.—Nothing in this section shall be construed to—

(1) impair or otherwise affect the authority of the Director of National Intelligence to protect intelligence sources and methods from unauthorized disclosure pursuant to section 103(c)(7) of this Act;[1] or

(2) supersede or otherwise affect the provisions of title V of this Act.

(e) DEFINITION.—As used in this section, the term "appropriate committees of Congress" means the Committee on Foreign Relations and the Select Committee on Intelligence of the Senate and the Committee on Foreign Relations and the Permanent Select Committee on Intelligence of the House of Representatives.

DETAIL OF INTELLIGENCE COMMUNITY PERSONNEL; INTELLIGENCE COMMUNITY ASSIGNMENT PROGRAM

SEC. 113. [50 U.S.C. §404h]

(a) DETAIL.—

(1) Notwithstanding any other provision of law, the head of a department with an element in the intelligence community or the head of an intelligence community agency or element may detail any employee within that department, agency, or element to serve in any position in the Intelligence Community Assignment Program on a reimbursable or a nonreimbursable basis.

(2) Nonreimbursable details may be for such periods as are agreed to between the heads of the parent and host agencies, up to a maximum of three years,

1. The amendment made by section 1072(a)(4) of Public Law 108–458 (118 Stat. 3692) to strike "section 103(c)(6) of this Act" and insert "section 102A(i) of this Act" could not be executed be-cause the matter purported to be struck does not appear.

except that such details may be extended for a period not to exceed one year when the heads of the parent and host agencies determine that such extension is in the public interest.

(b) BENEFITS, ALLOWANCES, TRAVEL, INCENTIVES.—

(1) An employee detailed under subsection (a) may be authorized any benefit, allowance, travel, or incentive otherwise provided to enhance staffing by the organization from which the employee is detailed.

(2) The head of an agency of an employee detailed under subsection (a) may pay a lodging allowance for the employee subject to the following conditions:

(A) The allowance shall be the lesser of the cost of the lodging or a maximum amount payable for the lodging as established jointly by the Director of National Intelligence and—

(i) with respect to detailed employees of the Department of Defense, the Secretary of Defense; and

(ii) with respect to detailed employees of other agencies and departments, the head of such agency or department.

(B) The detailed employee maintains a primary residence for the employee's immediate family in the local commuting area of the parent agency duty station from which the employee regularly commuted to such duty station before the detail.

(C) The lodging is within a reasonable proximity of the host agency duty station.

(D) The distance between the detailed employee's parent agency duty station and the host agency duty station is greater than 20 miles.

(E) The distance between the detailed employee's primary residence and the host agency duty station is 10 miles greater than the distance between such primary residence and the employee's parent duty station.

(F) The rate of pay applicable to the detailed employee does not exceed the rate of basic pay for grade GS–15 of the General Schedule.

DETAIL OF OTHER PERSONNEL

SEC. 113A. [50 U.S.C. 404h–1]

Except as provided in section 904(g)(2) of the Counterintelligence Enhancement Act of 2002 (50 U.S.C. 402c(g)(2)) and section 113 of this Act, and notwithstanding any other provision of law, an officer or employee of the United States or member of the Armed Forces may be detailed to the staff of an element of the intelligence community funded through the National Intelligence Program from another element of the intelligence community or from another element of the United States Government on a reimbursable or nonreimbursable basis, as jointly agreed to by the head of the receiving element and the head of the detailing element, for a period not to exceed 2 years.

ADDITIONAL ANNUAL REPORTS FROM THE DIRECTOR OF NATIONAL INTELLIGENCE

SEC. 114. [50 U.S.C. §404i]

(a) ANNUAL REPORT ON THE SAFETY AND SECURITY OF RUSSIAN NUCLEAR FACILITIES AND NUCLEAR MILITARY FORCES.—

(1) The Director of National Intelligence shall submit to the congressional leadership on an annual basis, and to the congressional intelligence committees on the date each year provided in section 507, an intelligence report assessing the safety and security of the nuclear facilities and nuclear military forces in Russia.

(2) Each such report shall include a discussion of the following:

(A) The ability of the Government of Russia to maintain its nuclear military forces.

(B) The security arrangements at civilian and military nuclear facilities in Russia.

(C) The reliability of controls and safety systems at civilian nuclear facilities in Russia.

(D) The reliability of command and control systems and procedures of the nuclear military forces in Russia.

(3) Each such report shall be submitted in unclassified form, but may contain a classified annex.

(b) ANNUAL REPORT ON HIRING AND RETENTION OF MINORITY EMPLOYEES.—

(1) The Director of National Intelligence shall, on an annual basis, submit to Congress a report on the employment of covered persons within each element of the intelligence community for the preceding fiscal year.

(2) Each such report shall include disaggregated data by category of covered person from each element of the intelligence community on the following:

(A) Of all individuals employed in the element during the fiscal year involved, the aggregate percentage of such individuals who are covered persons.

(B) Of all individuals employed in the element during the fiscal year involved at the levels referred to in clauses (i) and (ii), the percentage of covered persons employed at such levels:

(i) Positions at levels 1 through 15 of the General Schedule.

(ii) Positions at levels above GS–15.

(C) Of all individuals hired by the element involved during the fiscal year involved, the percentage of such individuals who are covered persons.

(3) Each such report shall be submitted in unclassified form, but may contain a classified annex.

(4) Nothing in this subsection shall be construed as providing for the substitution of any similar report required under another provision of law.

(5) In this subsection, the term "covered persons" means—

(A) racial and ethnic minorities;

(B) women; and

(C) individuals with disabilities.

(c) ANNUAL REPORT ON THREAT OF ATTACK ON THE UNITED STATES USING WEAPONS OF MASS DESTRUCTION.—

(1) Not later each year than the date provided in section 507, the Director of National Intelligence shall submit to the congressional committees specified in paragraph (3) a report assessing the following:

(A) The current threat of attack on the United States using ballistic missiles or cruise missiles.

(B) The current threat of attack on the United States using a chemical, biological, or nuclear weapon delivered by a system other than a ballistic missile or cruise missile.

(2) Each report under paragraph (1) shall be a national intelligence estimate, or have the formality of a national intelligence estimate.

(3) The congressional committees referred to in paragraph (1) are the following:

(A) The congressional intelligence committees.

(B) The Committees on Foreign Relations and Armed Services of the Senate.

(C) The Committees on International Relations and Armed Services of the House of Representatives.

(d) CONGRESSIONAL LEADERSHIP DEFINED.—In this section, the term "congressional leadership" means the Speaker and the minority leader of the House of Representatives and the majority leader and the minority leader of the Senate.

LIMITATION ON ESTABLISHMENT OR OPERATION OF DIPLOMATIC INTELLIGENCE SUPPORT CENTERS

SEC. 115. [50 U.S.C. 404j]

(a) IN GENERAL.—

(1) A diplomatic intelligence support center may not be established, operated, or maintained without the prior approval of the Director of National Intelligence.

(2) The Director may only approve the establishment, operation, or maintenance of a diplomatic intelligence support center if the Director determines that the establishment, operation, or maintenance of such center is required to provide necessary intelligence support in furtherance of the national security interests of the United States.

(b) PROHIBITION OF USE OF APPROPRIATIONS.—Amounts appropriated pursuant to authorizations by law for intelligence and intelligence-related activities may not be obligated or expended for the establishment, operation, or maintenance of a diplomatic intelligence support center that is not approved by the Director of National Intelligence.

(c) DEFINITIONS.—In this section:

(1) The term "diplomatic intelligence support center"means an entity to which employees of the various elements of the intelligence community (as defined in section 3(4)) are detailed for the purpose of providing analytical intelligence support that—

(A) consists of intelligence analyses on military or political matters and expertise to conduct limited assessments and dynamic taskings for a chief of mission; and

(B) is not intelligence support traditionally provided to a chief of mission by the Director of National Intelligence.

(2) The term "chief of mission" has the meaning given that term by section 102(3) of the Foreign Service Act of 1980 (22 U.S.C. 3902(3)), and includes ambassadors at large and ministers of diplomatic missions of the United States, or persons appointed to lead United States offices abroad designated by the Secretary of State as diplomatic in nature.

(d) TERMINATION.—This section shall cease to be effective onOctober 1, 2000.

TRAVEL ON ANY COMMON CARRIER FOR CERTAIN INTELLIGENCE COLLECTION PERSONNEL

SEC. 116. [50 U.S.C. §404k]

(a) IN GENERAL.—Notwithstanding any other provision of law, the Director of National Intelligence may authorize travel on any common carrier when such travel, in the discretion of the Director—

(1) is consistent with intelligence community mission requirements, or

(2) is required for cover purposes, operational needs, or other exceptional circumstances necessary for the successful performance of an intelligence community mission.

(b) AUTHORIZED DELEGATION OF DUTY.—The Director of National Intelligence may only delegate the authority granted by this section to the Principal Deputy Director of National Intelligence, or with respect to employees of the Central Intelligence Agency, to the Director of the Central Intelligence Agency.[1]

POW/MIA ANALYTIC CAPABILITY

SEC. 117. [50 U.S.C. §404l]

(a) REQUIREMENT.—

(1) The Director of National Intelligence shall, in consultation with the Secretary of Defense, establish and maintain in the intelligence community an analytic capability with responsibility for intelligence in support of the activities of the United States relating to individuals who, after December 31, 1990, are unaccounted for United States personnel.

(2) The analytic capability maintained under paragraph (1) shall be known as the "POW/MIA analytic capability of the intelligence community".

(b) UNACCOUNTED FOR UNITED STATES PERSONNEL.—In this section, the term "unaccounted for United States personnel" means the following:

(1) Any missing person (as that term is defined in section 1513(1) of title 10, United States Code).

---

1. The amendment made by section 1072(a)(5) to strike "to the Deputy Director of Central Intelligence, or with respect to employees of the Central Intelligence Agency[,] the Director may delegate such authority to the Deputy Director for Operations" and insert "to the Principal Deputy Director of National Intelligence, or with respect to employees of the Central IntelligenceAgency, to the Director of the Central Intelligence Agency" was executed to reflect the probableintent of Congress. The comma after "Central Intelligence Agency" in the striken matter doesnot appear.

(2) Any United States national who was killed while engaged in activities on behalf of the United States and whose remains have not been repatriated to the United States.

SEMIANNUAL REPORT ON FINANCIAL INTELLIGENCE ON TERRORIST ASSETS

SEC. 118. [50 U.S.C. §404m]

(a) SEMIANNUAL REPORT.—On a semiannual basis, the Secretary of the Treasury (acting through the head of the Office of Intelligence Support) shall submit a report to the appropriate congressional committees that fully informs the committees concerning operations against terrorist financial networks. Each such report shall include with respect to the preceding six-month period—

(1) the total number of asset seizures, designations, and other actions against individuals or entities found to have engaged in financial support of terrorism;

(2) the total number of applications for asset seizure and designations of individuals or entities suspected of having engaged in financial support of terrorist activities that were granted, modified, or denied;

(3) the total number of physical searches of offices, residences, or financial records of individuals or entities suspected of having engaged in financial support for terrorist activity; and

(4) whether the financial intelligence information seized in these cases has been shared on a full and timely basis with the all departments, agencies, and other entities of the United States Government involved in intelligence activities participating in the Foreign Terrorist Asset Tracking Center.

(b) IMMEDIATE NOTIFICATION FOR EMERGENCY DESIGNATION.—In the case of a designation of an individual or entity, or the assets of an individual or entity, as having been found to have engaged in terrorist activities, the Secretary of the Treasury shall report such designation within 24 hours of such a designation to the appropriate congressional committees.

(c) SUBMITTAL DATE OF REPORTS TO CONGRESSIONAL INTELLIGENCE COMMITTEES.—In the case of the reports required to be submitted under subsection (a) to the congressional intelligence committees, the submittal dates for such reports shall be as provided in section 507.

(d) APPROPRIATE CONGRESSIONAL COMMITTEES DEFINED.—In this section, the term "appropriate congressional committees" means the following:

(1) The Permanent Select Committee on Intelligence, the Committee on Appropriations, and the Committee on Financial Services of the House of Representatives.

(2) The Select Committee on Intelligence, the Committee on Appropriations, and the Committee on Banking, Housing, and Urban Affairs of the Senate.

NATIONAL COUNTERTERRORISM CENTER

SEC. 119. [50 U.S.C. §404o]

(a) ESTABLISHMENT OF CENTER.—There is within the Office of the Director of National Intelligence a National Counterterrorism Center.

(b) DIRECTOR OF NATIONAL COUNTERTERRORISM CENTER.—

(1) There is a Director of the National Counterterrorism Center, who shall be the head of the National Counterterrorism Center, and who shall be appointed by the President, by and with the advice and consent of the Senate.

(2) The Director of the National Counterterrorism Center may not simultaneously serve in any other capacity in the executive branch.

(c) REPORTING.—

(1) The Director of the National Counterterrorism Center shall report to the Director of National Intelligence with respect to matters described in paragraph (2) and the President with respect to matters described in paragraph (3).

(2) The matters described in this paragraph are as follows:

(A) The budget and programs of the National Counterterrorism Center.

(B) The activities of the Directorate of Intelligence of the National Counterterrorism Center under subsection (h).

(C) The conduct of intelligence operations implemented by other elements of the intelligence community; and

(3) The matters described in this paragraph are the planning and progress of joint counterterrorism operations (other than intelligence operations).

(d) PRIMARY MISSIONS.—The primary missions of the National Counterterrorism Center shall be as follows:

(1) To serve as the primary organization in the United States Government for analyzing and integrating all intelligence possessed or acquired by the United States Government pertaining to terrorism and counterterrorism, excepting intelligence pertaining exclusively to domestic terrorists and domestic counterterrorism.

(2) To conduct strategic operational planning for counterterrorism activities, integrating all instruments of national power, including diplomatic, financial, military, intelligence, homeland security, and law enforcement activities within and among agencies.

(3) To assign roles and responsibilities as part of its strategic operational planning duties to lead Departments or agencies, as appropriate, for counterterrorism activities that are consistent with applicable law and that support counterterrorism strategic operational plans, but shall not direct the execution of any resulting operations.

(4) To ensure that agencies, as appropriate, have access to and receive all-source intelligence support needed to execute their counterterrorism plans or perform independent, alternative analysis.

(5) To ensure that such agencies have access to and receive intelligence needed to accomplish their assigned activities.

(6) To serve as the central and shared knowledge bank on known and suspected terrorists and international terror groups, as well as their goals, strategies, capabilities, and networks of contacts and support.

(e) DOMESTIC COUNTERTERRORISM INTELLIGENCE.—

(1) The Center may, consistent with applicable law, the direction of the President, and the guidelines referred to in section 102A(b), receive intelligence

pertaining exclusively to domestic counterterrorism from any Federal, State, or local government or other source necessary to fulfill its responsibilities and retain and disseminate such intelligence.

(2) Any agency authorized to conduct counterterrorism activities may request information from the Center to assist it in its responsibilities, consistent with applicable law and the guidelines referred to in section 102A(b).

(f) DUTIES AND RESPONSIBILITIES OF DIRECTOR.—

(1) The Director of the National Counterterrorism Center shall—

(A) serve as the principal adviser to the Director of National Intelligence on intelligence operations relating to counterterrorism;

(B) provide strategic operational plans for the civilian and military counterterrorism efforts of the United States Government and for the effective integration of counterterrorism intelligence and operations across agency boundaries, both inside and outside the United States;

(C) advise the Director of National Intelligence on the extent to which the counterterrorism program recommendations and budget proposals of the departments, agencies, and elements of the United States Government conform to the priorities established by the President;

(D) disseminate terrorism information, including current terrorism threat analysis, to the President, the Vice President, the Secretaries of State, Defense, and Homeland Security, the Attorney General, the Director of the Central Intelligence Agency, and other officials of the executive branch as appropriate, and to the appropriate committees of Congress;

(E) support the Department of Justice and the Department of Homeland Security, and other appropriate agencies, in fulfillment of their responsibilities to disseminate terrorism information, consistent with applicable law, guidelines referred to in section 102A(b), Executive orders and other Presidential guidance, to State and local government officials, and other entities, and coordinate dissemination of terrorism information to foreign governments as approved by the Director of National Intelligence;

(F) develop a strategy for combining terrorist travel intelligence operations and law enforcement planning and operations into a cohesive effort to intercept terrorists, find terrorist travel facilitators, and constrain terrorist mobility;

(G) have primary responsibility within the United States Government for conducting net assessments of terrorist threats;

(H) consistent with priorities approved by the President, assist the Director of National Intelligence in establishing requirements for the intelligence community for the collection of terrorism information; and

(I) perform such other duties as the Director of National Intelligence may prescribe or are prescribed by law.

(2) Nothing in paragraph (1)(G) shall limit the authority of the departments and agencies of the United States to conduct net assessments.

(g) LIMITATION.—The Director of the National Counterterrorism Center may not direct the execution of counterterrorism operations.

(h) RESOLUTION OF DISPUTES.—The Director of National Intelligence shall resolve disagreements between the National Counterterrorism Center and the head of a department, agency, or element of the United States Government on designations, assignments, plans, or responsibilities under this section. The head of such a department, agency, or element may appeal the resolution of the disagreement by the Director of National Intelligence to the President.

(i) DIRECTORATE OF INTELLIGENCE.—The Director of the National Counterterrorism Center shall establish and maintain within the National Counterterrorism Center a Directorate of Intelligence which shall have primary responsibility within the United States Government for analysis of terrorism and terrorist organizations (except for purely domestic terrorism and domestic terrorist organizations) from all sources of intelligence, whether collected inside or outside the United States.

(j) DIRECTORATE OF STRATEGIC OPERATIONAL PLANNING.—

(1) The Director of the National Counterterrorism Center shall establish and maintain within the National Counterterrorism Center a Directorate of Strategic Operational Planning which shall provide strategic operational plans for counterterrorism operations conducted by the United States Government.

(2) Strategic operational planning shall include the mission, objectives to be achieved, tasks to be performed, interagency coordination of operational activities, and the assignment of roles and responsibilities.

(3) The Director of the National Counterterrorism Center shall monitor the implementation of strategic operational plans, and shall obtain information from each element of the intelligence community, and from each other department, agency, or element of the United States Government relevant for monitoring the progress of such entity in implementing such plans.

NATIONAL COUNTER PROLIFERATION CENTER

SEC. 119A. [50 U.S.C. §404o-1]

(a) ESTABLISHMENT.—Not later than 18 months after the date of the enactment of the National Security Intelligence Reform Act of 2004, the President shall establish a National Counter Proliferation Center, taking into account all appropriate government tools to prevent and halt the proliferation of weapons of mass destruction, their delivery systems, and related materials and technologies.

(b) MISSIONS AND OBJECTIVES.—In establishing the National Counter Proliferation Center, the President shall address the following missions and objectives to prevent and halt the proliferation of weapons of mass destruction, their delivery systems, and related materials and technologies:

(1) Establishing a primary organization within the United States Government for analyzing and integrating all intelligence possessed or acquired by the United States pertaining to proliferation.

(2) Ensuring that appropriate agencies have full access to and receive all-source intelligence support needed to execute their counter proliferation plans or activities, and perform independent, alternative analyses.

(3) Establishing a central repository on known and suspected proliferation ac-

tivities, including the goals, strategies, capabilities, networks, and any individuals, groups, or entities engaged in proliferation.

(4) Disseminating proliferation information, including proliferation threats and analyses, to the President, to the appropriate departments and agencies, and to the appropriate committees of Congress.

(5) Conducting net assessments and warnings about the proliferation of weapons of mass destruction, their delivery systems, and related materials and technologies.

(6) Coordinating counter proliferation plans and activities of the various departments and agencies of the United States Government to prevent and halt the proliferation of weapons of mass destruction, their delivery systems, and related materials and technologies.

(7) Conducting strategic operational counter proliferation planning for the United States Government to prevent and halt the proliferation of weapons of mass destruction, their delivery systems, and related materials and technologies.

(c) NATIONAL SECURITY WAIVER.—The President may waive the requirements of this section, and any parts thereof, if the President determines that such requirements do not materially improve the ability of the United States Government to prevent and halt the proliferation of weapons of mass destruction, their delivery systems, and related materials and technologies. Such waiver shall be made in writing to Congress and shall include a description of how the missions and objectives in subsection (b) are being met.

(d) REPORT TO CONGRESS.—

(1) Not later than nine months after the implementation of this Act, the President shall submit to Congress, in classified form if necessary, the findings and recommendations of the President's Commission on Weapons of Mass Destruction established by Executive Order in February 2004, together with the views of the President regarding the establishment of a National Counter Proliferation Center.

(2) If the President decides not to exercise the waiver authority granted by subsection (c), the President shall submit to Congress from time to time updates and plans regarding the establishment of a National Counter Proliferation Center.

(e) SENSE OF CONGRESS.—It is the sense of Congress that a central feature of counter proliferation activities, consistent with the President's Proliferation Security Initiative, should include the physical interdiction, by air, sea, or land, of weapons of mass destruction, their delivery systems, and related materials and technologies, and enhanced law enforcement activities to identify and disrupt proliferation networks, activities, organizations, and persons.

NATIONAL INTELLIGENCE CENTERS

SEC. 119B. [50 U.S.C. §404o-2]

(a) AUTHORITY TO ESTABLISH.—The Director of National Intelligence may establish one or more national intelligence centers to address intelligence priorities, including, but not limited to, regional issues.

(b) RESOURCES OF DIRECTORS OF CENTERS.—

(1) The Director of National Intelligence shall ensure that the head of each national intelligence center under subsection (a) has appropriate authority, direction, and control of such center, and of the personnel assigned to such center, to carry out the assigned mission of such center.

(2) The Director of National Intelligence shall ensure that each national intelligence center has appropriate personnel to accomplish effectively the mission of such center.

(c) INFORMATION SHARING.—The Director of National Intelligence shall, to the extent appropriate and practicable, ensure that each national intelligence center under subsection (a) and the other elements of the intelligence community share information in order to facilitate the mission of such center.

(d) MISSION OF CENTERS.—Pursuant to the direction of the Director of National Intelligence, each national intelligence center under subsection (a) may, in the area of intelligence responsibility assigned to such center—

(1) have primary responsibility for providing all-source analysis of intelligence based upon intelligence gathered both domestically and abroad;

(2) have primary responsibility for identifying and proposing to the Director of National Intelligence intelligence collection and analysis and production requirements; and

(3) perform such other duties as the Director of National Intelligence shall specify.

(e) REVIEW AND MODIFICATION OF CENTERS.—The Director of National Intelligence shall determine on a regular basis whether—

(1) the area of intelligence responsibility assigned to each national intelligence center under subsection (a) continues to meet appropriate intelligence priorities; and

(2) the staffing and management of such center remains appropriate for the accomplishment of the mission of such center.

(f) TERMINATION.—The Director of National Intelligence may terminate any national intelligence center under subsection (a).

(g) SEPARATE BUDGET ACCOUNT.—The Director of National Intelligence shall, as appropriate, include in the National Intelligence Program budget a separate line item for each national intelligence center under subsection (a).

TITLE II—THE DEPARTMENT OF DEFENSE

DEPARTMENT OF DEFENSE

SEC. 201. [50 U.S.C. §408] [Subsections (a) and (b) were repealed by section 307 of Public Law 87–651 (Act of September 7, 1962, 76 Stat. 526). Subsection (c) consisted of an amendment to another Act.]

(d) [50 U.S.C. 408] Except to the extent inconsistent with the provisions of this Act, the provisions of title IV of the Revised Statutes[1]as now of hereafter amended shall

---

1. Title IV of the Revised Statutes consisted of sections 158–198 of the Revised Statutes. Sec-tions 176 and 193 are codified as sections 492–1 and 492–2 of title 31, United States Code. Theremainder of those sections have been repealed or replaced by provisions of title 5, United StatesCode, as enacted. See the "Tables" volume of the United States Code for the distribution of specific sections.

be applicable to the Department of Defense. [Sections 202–204 were repealed by section 307 of Public Law87–651 (Act of September 7, 1962, 76 Stat. 526).]

DEPARTMENT OF THE ARMY

SEC. 205. [Subsections (a), (d), and (e) were repealed by thelaw enacting titles 10 and 32, United States Code (Act of August10, 1956, 70A Stat. 676)].

(b) All laws, orders, regulations, and other actions relating to the Department of War or to any officer or activity whose title ischanged under this section shall, insofar as they are not inconsistent with the provisions of this Act, be deemed to relate to the Department of the Army within the Department of Defense or to such officer or activity designated by his or its new title.

(c) [50 U.S.C. 409(a)] the term "Department of the Army" as used in this Act shall be construed to mean the Department of theArmy at the seat of government and all field headquarters, forces, reserve components, installations, activities, and functions under the control or supervision of the Department of the Army.

DEPARTMENT OF THE NAVY

SEC. 206. (a) [50 U.S.C. 409(b)] The term "Department of theNavy" as used in this Act shall be construed to mean the Department of the Navy at the seat of government; the headquarters, United States Marine Corps; the entire operating forces of theUnited States Navy, including naval aviation, and of the United States Marine Corps, including the reserve components of such forces; all field activities, headquarters, forces, bases, installations, activities and functions under the control or supervision of the Department of the Navy; and the United States Coast Guard when operating as a part of the Navy pursuant to law.

[Subsections (b) and (c) were repealed by the law enacting titles 10 and 32, United States Code (Act of August 10, 1956, 70A Stat. 676)].

DEPARTMENT OF THE AIR FORCE

SEC. 207. [Subsections (a), (b), (d), (e), and (f) were repealed bythe law enacting titles 10 and 32, United States Code (Act of Au-gust 10, 1956, 70A stat. 676)].

(c) [50 U.S.C. 409(c)] The term "Department of the Air Force"as used in this Act shall be construed to mean the Department ofthe Air Force at the seat of government and all field headquarters, forces, reserve components, installations, activities, and functions under the control or supervision of the Department of the Air Force.

TITLE III—MISCELLANEOUS

NATIONAL SECURITY AGENCY VOLUNTARY SEPARATION

SEC. 301. 50 U.S.C. §409a

(a) SHORT TITLE.—This section may be cited as the "National Security Agency Voluntary Separation Act".

(b) DEFINITIONS.—For purposes of this section—

(1) the term "Director" means the Director of the National Security Agency; and

(2) the term "employee" means an employee of the National Security Agency, serving under an appointment without time limitation, who has been currently employed by the National Security Agency for a continuous period of at least

12 months prior to the effective date of the program established under subsection (c), except that such term does not include—

(A) a reemployed annuitant under subchapter III of chapter 83 or chapter 84 of title 5, United States Code, or another retirement system for employees of the Government; or

(B) an employee having a disability on the basis of which such employee is or would be eligible for disability retirement under any of the retirement systems referred to in subparagraph (A).

(c) ESTABLISHMENT OF PROGRAM.—Notwithstanding any other provision of law, the Director, in his sole discretion, may establish a program under which employees may, after October 1, 2000, be eligible for early retirement, offered separation pay to separate from service voluntarily, or both.

(d) EARLY RETIREMENT.—An employee who—

(1) is at least 50 years of age and has completed 20 years of service; or

(2) has at least 25 years of service, may, pursuant to regulations promulgated under this section, apply and be retired from the National Security Agency and receive benefits in accordance with chapter 83 or 84 of title 5, United States Code, if the employee has not less than 10 years of service with the National Security Agency.

(e) AMOUNT OF SEPARATION PAY AND TREATMENT FOR OTHER PURPOSES.—

(1) AMOUNT.—Separation pay shall be paid in a lump sum and shall be equal to the lesser of—

(A) an amount equal to the amount the employee would be entitled to receive under section 5595(c) of title 5, United States Code, if the employee were entitled to payment under such section; or

(B) $25,000.

(2) TREATMENT.—Separation pay shall not—

(A) be a basis for payment, and shall not be included in the computation, of any other type of Government benefit; and

(B) be taken into account for the purpose of determining the amount of any severance pay to which an individual may be entitled under section 5595 of title 5, United States Code, based on any other separation.

(f) REEMPLOYMENT RESTRICTIONS.—An employee who receives separation pay under such program may not be reemployed by the National Security Agency for the 12-month period beginning on the effective date of the employee's separation. An employee who receives separation pay under this section on the basis of a separation occurring on or after the date of the enactment of the Federal Workforce Restructuring Act of 1994 (Public Law 103–236; 108 Stat. 111) and accepts employment with the Government of the United States within 5 years after the date of the separation on which payment of the separation pay is based shall be required to repay the entire amount of the separation pay to the National Security Agency. If the employment is with an Executive agency (as defined by section 105 of title 5, United States Code), the Director of the Office of Personnel Management may, at the request of the head of the agency, waive the repayment if the individual involved possesses unique abilities and is the only qualified applicant available for the position. If the employment is with an entity in the legislative branch, the head of the entity or the appointing official may waive the repayment if the individual involved possesses unique abilities and is the only qualified applicant available for the position. If the employment is with the judicial branch, the Director of the Administrative Office of the United States Courts may waive the repayment if the individual involved possesses unique abilities and is the only qualified applicant available for the position.

(g) BAR ON CERTAIN EMPLOYMENT.—

(1) BAR.—An employee may not be separated from service under this section unless the employee agrees that the employee will not—

(A) act as agent or attorney for, or otherwise represent, any other person (except the United States) in any formal or informal appearance before, or, with the intent to influence, make any oral or written communication on behalf of any other person (except the United States) to the National Security Agency; or

(B) participate in any manner in the award, modification, or extension of any contract for property or services with the National Security Agency, during the 12-month period beginning on the effective date of the employee's separation from service.

(2) PENALTY.—An employee who violates an agreement under this subsection shall be liable to the United States in the amount of the separation pay paid to the employee pursuant to this section multiplied by the proportion of the 12-month period during which the employee was in violation of the agreement.

(h) LIMITATIONS.—Under this program, early retirement and separation pay may be offered only—

(1) with the prior approval of the Director;

(2) for the period specified by the Director; and

(3) to employees within such occupational groups or geographic locations, or subject to such other similar limitations or conditions, as the Director may require.

(i) REGULATIONS.—Before an employee may be eligible for early retirement, separation pay, or both, under this section, the Director shall prescribe such regulations as may be necessary to carry out this section.

(j) NOTIFICATION OF EXERCISE OF AUTHORITY.—The Director may[1] not make an offer of early retirement, separation pay, or both, pursuant to this section until 15 days after submitting to the congressional intelligence committees a report describing the occupational groups or geographic locations, or other similar limitations or conditions, required by the Director under subsection (h), and includes the proposed regulations issued pursuant to subsection (i).

---

1. Section 941(b)(1) of the Intelligence Authorization Act for Fiscal Year 2003 (P.L. 107–306;116 Stat. 2431) amended this subsection by striking "'REPORTING REQUIRE-MENTS.—' and all that follows through 'The Director may' and inserting 'NOTIFICATION OF EXERCISE OF AUTHORITY.—The Director may'". There was no hyphen in law within the word "Requirements". The amendment has been executed to reflect the probable intent of Congress.

(k) REMITTANCE OF FUNDS.—In addition to any other payment that is required to be made under subchapter III of chapter 83 or chapter 84 of title 5, United States Code, the National Security Agency shall remit to the Office of Personnel Management for deposit in the Treasury of the United States to the credit of the Civil Service Retirement and Disability Fund, an amount equal to 15 percent of the final basic pay of each employee to whom a voluntary separation payment has been or is to be paid under this section. The remittance required by this subsection shall be in lieu of any remittance required by section 4(a) of the Federal Workforce Restructuring Act of 1994 (5 U.S.C. §8331 note).

AUTHORITY OF FEDERAL BUREAU OF INVESTIGATION TO AWARD PERSONAL SERVICES CONTRACTS

SEC. 302. [50 U.S.C. §409b]

(a) IN GENERAL.—The Director of the Federal Bureau of Investigation may enter into personal services contracts if the personal services to be provided under such contracts directly support the intelligence or counterintelligence missions of the Federal Bureau of Investigation.

(b) INAPPLICABILITY OF CERTAIN REQUIREMENTS.—Contracts under subsection (a) shall not be subject to the annuity offset requirements of sections 8344 and 8468 of title 5, United States Code, the requirements of section 3109 of title 5, United States Code, or any law or regulation requiring competitive contracting.

(c) CONTRACT TO BE APPROPRIATE MEANS OF SECURING SERVICES.—The Chief Contracting Officer of the Federal Bureau of Investigation shall ensure that each personal services contract entered into by the Director under this section is the appropriate means of securing the services to be provided under such contract.

ADVISORY COMMITTEES AND PERSONNEL

SEC. 303. [50 U.S.C. §405]

(a) The Director of the Federal Emergency Management Agency, the Director of National Intelligence, and the National Security Council, acting through its Executive Secretary, are authorized to appoint such advisory committees and to employ, consistent with other provisions of this Act, such part-time advisory personnel as they may deem necessary in carrying out their respective functions and the functions of agencies under their control. Persons holding other offices or positions under the United States for which they receive compensation, while serving as members of such committees, shall receive no additional compensation for such service. Retired members of the uniformed services employed by the Director of National Intelligence who hold no other office or position under the United States for which they receive compensation, other members of such committees and other part-time advisory personnel so employed may serve without compensation or may receive compensation at a daily rate not to exceed the daily equivalent of the rate of pay in effect for grade GS–18 of the General Schedule established by section 5332 of title 5, United States Code, as determined by the appointing authority.

(b) Service of an individual as a member of any such advisory committee, or in any other part-time capacity for a department or agency hereunder, shall not be considered as service bringing such individual within the provisions of section 203, 205, or 207, of title 18, United States Code, unless the act of such individual, which by such section is made unlawful when performed by an individual referred to in such section, is with respect to any particular matter which directly involves a department or agency which such person is advising or in which such department or agency is directly interested.

AUTHORIZATION FOR APPROPRIATIONS

SEC. 307. [50 U.S.C. §411]

There are hereby authorized to be appropriated such sums as may be necessary and appropriate to carry out the provisions and purposes of this Act (other than the provisions and purposes of sections 102, 103, 104, 105 and titles V, VI, and VII).

DEFINITIONS

SEC. 308. [50 U.S.C. §410]

(a)[1] As used in this Act, the term "function" includes functions, powers, and duties.
(b) As used in this Act, the term, "Department of Defense" shall be deemed to include the military departments of the Army, the Navy, and the Air Force, and all agencies created under title II of this Act.

SEVERABILITY

SEC. 309. [50 U.S.C. §401 note]

If any provision of this Act or the application thereof to any person or circumstances is held invalid, the validity of the remainder of the Act and of the application of such provision to other persons and circumstances shall not be affected thereby.

EFFECTIVE DATE

SEC. 310. [50 U.S.C. §401 note]

(a) The first sentence of section 202 (a) and sections 1, 2, 307, 308, 309, and 310 shall take effect immediately upon the enactment of this Act.
(b) Except as provided in subsection (a), the provisions of this Act shall take effect on whichever of the following days is the earlier: The day after the day upon which the Secretary of Defense first appointed takes office, or the sixtieth day after the date of the enactment of this Act.

REPEALING AND SAVING PROVISIONS

SEC. 411. [50 U.S.C. §412]

All laws, orders, and regulations inconsistent with the provisions of this title are repealed insofar as they are inconsistent with the powers, duties, and responsibilities enacted hereby: *Provided,* That the powers, duties, and responsibilities of the Secretary of Defense under this title shall be administered in conformance with the

---

1. Section 307 of Public Law 87–651 (Act of September 7, 1962, 76 Stat. 526) repealed section308(a) less its applicability to sections 2, 101–103, and 303.

policy and requirements for administration of budgetary and fiscal matters in the Government generally, including accounting and financial reporting, and that nothing in this title shall be construed as eliminating or modifying the powers, duties, and responsibilities of any other department, agency, or officer of the Government in connection with such matters, but no such department, agency, or officer shall exercise any such powers, duties, or responsibilities in a manner that will render ineffective the provisions of this title.

TITLE V—ACCOUNTABILITY FOR INTELLIGENCE ACTIVITIES[1]

GENERAL CONGRESSIONAL OVERSIGHT PROVISIONS

SEC. 501. [50 U.S.C. §413]

(a)(1) The President shall ensure that the congressional intelligence committees are kept fully and currently informed of the intelligence activities of the United States, including any significant anticipated intelligence activity as required by this title.

(2) Nothing in this title shall be construed as requiring the approval of the congressional intelligence committees as a condition precedent to the initiation of any significant anticipated intelligence activity.

(b) The President shall ensure that any illegal intelligence activity is reported promptly to the congressional intelligence committees, as well as any corrective action that has been taken or is planned in connection with such illegal activity.

(c) The President and the congressional intelligence committees shall each establish such procedures as may be necessary to carry out the provisions of this title.

(d) The House of Representatives and the Senate shall each establish, by rule or resolution of such House, procedures to protect from unauthorized disclosure all classified information, and all information relating to intelligence sources and methods, that is furnished to the congressional intelligence committees or to Members of Congress under this title. Such procedures shall be established in consultation with the Director of National Intelligence. In accordance with such procedures, each of the congressional intelligence committees shall promptly call to the attention of its respective House, or to any appropriate committee or committees of its respective House, any matter relating to intelligence activities requiring the attention of such House or such committee or committees.

(e) Nothing in this Act shall be construed as authority to withhold information from the congressional intelligence committees on the grounds that providing the information to the congressional intelligence committees would constitute the unauthorized disclosure of classified information or information relating to intelligence sources and methods.

(f) As used in this section, the term "intelligence activities" includes covert actions as defined in section 503(e), and includes financial intelligence activities.

---

1. This title is also set out post at page 711 along with other materials relating to congressionaloversight of intelligence activities.

REPORTING ON INTELLIGENCE ACTIVITIES OTHER THAN COVERT ACTIONS

SEC. 502. [50 U.S.C. §413a]

(a) IN GENERAL.—To the extent consistent with due regard for the protection from unauthorized disclosure of classified information relating to sensitive intelligence sources and methods or other exceptionally sensitive matters, the Director of National Intelligence and the heads of all departments, agencies, and other entities of the United States Government involved in intelligence activities shall—

(1) keep the congressional intelligence committees fully and currently informed of all intelligence activities, other than a covert action (as defined in section 503(e)), which are the responsibility of, are engaged in by, or are carried out for or on behalf of, any department, agency, or entity of the United States Government, including any significant anticipated intelligence activity and any significant intelligence failure; and

(2) furnish the congressional intelligence committees any information or material concerning intelligence activities, other than covert actions, which is within their custody or control, and which is requested by either of the congressional intelligence committees in order to carry out its authorized responsibilities.

(b) FORM AND CONTENTS OF CERTAIN REPORTS.—Any report relating to a significant anticipated intelligence activity or a significant intelligence failure that is submitted to the congressional intelligence committees for purposes of subsection (a)(1) shall be in writing, and shall contain the following:

(1) A concise statement of any facts pertinent to such report.

(2) An explanation of the significance of the intelligence activity or intelligence failure covered by such report.

(c) STANDARDS AND PROCEDURES FOR CERTAIN REPORTS.—The Director of National Intelligence, in consultation with the heads of the departments, agencies, and entities referred to in subsection (a), shall establish standards and procedures applicable to reports covered by subsection (b).

PRESIDENTIAL APPROVAL AND REPORTING OF COVERT ACTIONS

SEC. 503. [50 U.S.C. §413b]

(a) The President may not authorize the conduct of a covert action by departments, agencies, or entities of the United States Government unless the President determines such an action is necessary to support identifiable foreign policy objectives of the United States and is important to the national security of the United States, which determination shall be set forth in a finding that shall meet each of the following conditions:

(1) Each finding shall be in writing, unless immediate action by the United States is required and time does not permit the preparation of a written finding, in which case a written record of the President's decision shall be contemporaneously made and shall be reduced to a written finding as soon as possible but in no event more than 48 hours after the decision is made.

(2) Except as permitted by paragraph (1), a finding may not authorize or sanction a covert action, or any aspect of any such action, which already has occurred.

(3) Each finding shall specify each department, agency, or entity of the United States Government authorized to fund or otherwise participate in any significant way in such action. Any employee, contractor, or contract agent of a department, agency, or entity of the United States Government other than the Central Intelligence Agency directed to participate in any way in a covert action shall be subject either to the policies and regulations of the Central Intelligence Agency, or to written policies or regulations adopted by such department, agency, or entity, to govern such participation.

(4) Each finding shall specify whether it is contemplated that any third party which is not an element of, or a contractor or contract agent of, the United States Government, or is not otherwise subject to United States Government policies and regulations, will be used to fund or otherwise participate in any significant way in the covert action concerned, or be used to undertake the covert action concerned on behalf of the United States.

(5) A finding may not authorize any action that would violate the Constitution or any statute of the United States.

(b) To the extent consistent with due regard for the protection from unauthorized disclosure of classified information relating to sensitive intelligence sources and methods or other exceptionally sensitive matters, the Director of National Intelligence and the heads of all departments, agencies, and entities of the United States Government involved in a covert action—

(1) shall keep the congressional intelligence committees fully and currently informed of all covert actions which are the responsibility of, are engaged in by, or are carried out for or on behalf of, any department, agency, or entity of the United States Government, including significant failures; and

(2) shall furnish to the congressional intelligence committees any information or material concerning covert actions which is in the possession, custody, or control of any department, agency, or entity of the United States Government and which is requested by either of the congressional intelligence committees in order to carry out its authorized responsibilities.

(c)(1) The President shall ensure that any finding approved pursuant to subsection (a) shall be reported to the congressional intelligence committees as soon as possible after such approval and before the initiation of the covert action authorized by the finding, except as otherwise provided in paragraph (2) and paragraph (3).

(2) If the President determines that it is essential to limit access to the finding to meet extraordinary circumstances affecting vital interests of the United States, the finding may be reported to the chairmen and ranking minority members of the congressional intelligence committees, the Speaker and minority leader of the House of Representatives, the majority and minority leaders of the Senate, and such other member or members of the congressional leadership as may be included by the President.

(3) Whenever a finding is not reported pursuant to paragraph (1) or (2) of this section, the President shall fully inform the congressional intelligence committees in a timely fashion and shall provide a statement of the reasons for not giving prior notice.

(4) In a case under paragraph (1), (2), or (3), a copy of the finding, signed by the President, shall be provided to the chairman of each congressional intelligence committee. When access to a finding is limited to the Members of Congress specified in paragraph (2), a statement of the reasons for limiting such access shall also be provided.

(d) The President shall ensure that the congressional intelligence committees, or, if applicable, the Members of Congress specified in subsection (c)(2), are notified of any significant change in a previously approved covert action, or any significant undertaking pursuant to a previously approved finding, in the same manner as findings are reported pursuant to subsection (c).

(e) As used in this title, the term "covert action" means an activity or activities of the United States Government to influence political, economic, or military conditions abroad, where it is intended that the role of the United States Government will not be apparent or acknowledged publicly, but does not include—

(1) activities the primary purpose of which is to acquire intelligence, traditional counterintelligence activities, traditional activities to improve or maintain the operational security of United States Government programs, or administrative activities;

(2) traditional diplomatic or military activities or routine support to such activities;

(3) traditional law enforcement activities conducted by United States Government law enforcement agencies or routine support to such activities; or

(4) activities to provide routine support to the overt activities (other than activities described in paragraph (1), (2), or (3)) of other United States Government agencies abroad.

(f) No covert action may be conducted which is intended to influence United States political processes, public opinion, policies, or media.

FUNDING OF INTELLIGENCE ACTIVITIES

SEC. 504. [50 U.S.C. §414]

(a) Appropriated funds available to an intelligence agency may be obligated or expended for an intelligence or intelligence-related activity only if—

(1) those funds were specifically authorized by the Congress for use for such activities; or

(2) in the case of funds from the Reserve for Contingencies of the Central Intelligence Agency and consistent with the provisions of section 503 of this Act concerning any significant anticipated intelligence activity, the Director of the Central Intelligence Agency has notified the appropriate congressional committees of the intent to make such funds available for such activity; or

(3) in the case of funds specifically authorized by the Congress for a different activity—

(A) the activity to be funded is a higher priority intelligence or intelligence-related activity;

(B) the need for funds for such activity is based on unforeseen requirements; and

(C) the Director of National Intelligence, the Secretary of Defense, or the Attorney General, as appropriate, has notified the appropriate congressional committees of the intent to make such funds available for such activity;

(4) nothing in this subsection prohibits obligation or expenditure of funds available to an intelligence agency in accordance with sections 1535 and 1536 of title 31, United States Code.

(b) Funds available to an intelligence agency may not be made available for any intelligence or intelligence-related activity for which funds were denied by the Congress.

(c) No funds appropriated for, or otherwise available to, any department, agency, or entity of the United States Government may be expended, or may be directed to be expended, for any covert action, as defined in section 503(e), unless and until a Presidential finding required by subsection (a) of section 503 has been signed or otherwise issued in accordance with that subsection.

(d)(1) Except as otherwise specifically provided by law, funds available to an intelligence agency that are not appropriated funds may be obligated or expended for an intelligence or intelligence-related activity only if those funds are used for activities reported to the appropriate congressional committees pursuant to procedures which identify—

(A) the types of activities for which nonappropriated funds may be expended; and

(B) the circumstances under which an activity must be reported as a significant anticipated intelligence activity before such funds can be expended.

(2) Procedures for purposes of paragraph (1) shall be jointly agreed upon by the congressional intelligence committees and, as appropriate, the Director of National Intelligence or the Secretary of Defense.

(e) As used in this section—

(1) the term "intelligence agency" means any department, agency, or other entity of the United States involved in intelligence or intelligence-related activities;

(2) the term "appropriate congressional committees" means the Permanent Select Committee on Intelligence and the Committee on Appropriations of the House of Representatives and the Select Committee on Intelligence and the Committee on Appropriations of the Senate; and

(3) the term "specifically authorized by the Congress" means that—

(A) the activity and the amount of funds proposed to be used for that activity were identified in a formal budget request to the Congress, but funds shall be deemed to be specifically authorized for that activity only to the extent that the Congress both authorized the funds to be appropriated for that activity and appropriated the funds for that activity; or

(B) although the funds were not formally requested, the Congress both specifically authorized the appropriation of the funds for the activity and appropriated the funds for the activity.

NOTICE TO CONGRESS OF CERTAIN TRANSFERS OF DEFENSE ARTICLES AND DEFENSE SERVICES

SEC. 505. [50 U.S.C. §415]

(a)(1) The transfer of a defense article or defense service, or the anticipated transfer in any fiscal year of any aggregation of defense articles or defense services, exceeding $1,000,000 in value by an intelligence agency to a recipient outside that agency shall be considered a significant anticipated intelligence activity for the purpose of this title.

(2) Paragraph (1) does not apply if—

(A) the transfer is being made to a department, agency, or other entity of the United States (so long as there will not be a subsequent retransfer of the defense articles or defense services outside the United States Government in conjunction with an intelligence or intelligence-related activity); or

(B) the transfer—

(i) is being made pursuant to authorities contained in part II of the Foreign Assistance Act of 1961, the Arms Export Control Act, title 10 of the United States Code (including a law enacted pursuant to section 7307(a) of that title), or the Federal Property and Administrative Services Act of 1949, and

(ii) is not being made in conjunction with an intelligence or intelligence-related activity.

(3) An intelligence agency may not transfer any defense articles or defense services outside the agency in conjunction with any intelligence or intelligence-related activity for which funds were denied by the Congress.

(b) As used in this section—

(1) the term "intelligence agency" means any department, agency, or other entity of the United States involved in intelligence or intelligence-related activities;

(2) the terms "defense articles" and "defense services" mean the items on the United States Munitions List pursuant to section 38 of the Arms Export Control Act (22 CFR part 121);

(3) the term "transfer" means—

(A) in the case of defense articles, the transfer of possession of those articles; and

(B) in the case of defense services, the provision of those services; and

(4) the term "value" means—

(A) in the case of defense articles, the greater of—

(i) the original acquisition cost to the United States Government, plus the cost of improvements or other modifications made by or on behalf of the Government; or

(ii) the replacement cost; and

(B) in the case of defense services, the full cost to the Government of providing the services.

SPECIFICITY OF NATIONAL INTELLIGENCE PROGRAM BUDGET AMOUNTS FOR COUNTERTERRORISM, COUNTERPROLIFERATION, COUNTERNARCOTICS, AND COUNTERINTELLIGENCE

SEC. 506. [50 U.S.C. §415a]

(a) IN GENERAL.—The budget justification materials submitted to Congress in support of the budget of the President for a fiscal year that is submitted to Congress under section 1105(a) of title 31, United States Code, shall set forth separately the aggregate amount requested for that fiscal year for the National Intelligence Program for each of the following:

(1) Counterterrorism.

(2) Counterproliferation.

(3) Counternarcotics.

(4) Counterintelligence.

(b) ELECTION OF CLASSIFIED OR UNCLASSIFIED FORM.— Amounts set forth under subsection (a) may be set forth in unclassified form or classified form, at the election of the Director of National Intelligence.

BUDGET TREATMENT OF COSTS OF ACQUISITION OF MAJOR SYSTEMS BY THE INTELLIGENCE COMMUNITY

SEC. 506A. [50 U.S.C. §415a-1]

(a) INDEPENDENT COST ESTIMATES.—

(1) The Director of National Intelligence shall, in consultation with the head of each element of the intelligence community concerned, prepare an independent cost estimate of the full life-cycle cost of development, procurement, and operation of each major system to be acquired by the intelligence community.

(2) Each independent cost estimate for a major system shall, to the maximum extent practicable, specify the amount required to be appropriated and obligated to develop, procure, and operate the major system in each fiscal year of the proposed period of development, procurement, and operation of the major system.

(3)(A) In the case of a program of the intelligence community that qualifies as a major system, an independent cost estimate shall be prepared before the submission to Congress of the budget of the President for the first fiscal year in which appropriated funds are anticipated to be obligated for the development or procurement of such major system.

(B) In the case of a program of the intelligence community for which an independent cost estimate was not previously required to be prepared under this section, including a program for which development or procurement commenced before the date of the enactment of the Intelligence Authorization Act for Fiscal Year 2004, if the aggregate future costs of development or procurement (or any combination of such activities) of the program will exceed $500,000,000 (in current fiscal year dollars), the program shall qualify as a major system for purposes of this section, and an independent cost estimate for such major system shall be prepared before the submission to Congress of the budget of the President for the first fiscal year thereafter in which appropriated funds are anticipated to be obligated for such major system.

(4) The independent cost estimate for a major system shall be updated upon—

(A) the completion of any preliminary design review associated with the major system;

(B) any significant modification to the anticipated design of the major system; or

(C) any change in circumstances that renders the current independent cost estimate for the major system inaccurate.

(5) Any update of an independent cost estimate for a major system under paragraph (4) shall meet all requirements for independent cost estimates under this section, and shall be treated as the most current independent cost estimate for the major system until further updated under that paragraph.

(b) PREPARATION OF INDEPENDENT COST ESTIMATES.—

(1) The Director shall establish within the Office of the Director of National Intelligence an office which shall be responsible for preparing independent cost estimates, and any updates thereof, under subsection (a), unless a designation is made under paragraph (2).

(2) In the case of the acquisition of a major system for an element of the intelligence community within the Department of Defense, the Director and the Secretary of Defense shall provide that the independent cost estimate, and any updates thereof, under subsection (a) be prepared by an entity jointly designated by the Director and the Secretary in accordance with section 2434(b)(1)(A) of title 10, United States Code.

(c) UTILIZATION IN BUDGETS OF PRESIDENT.—

(1) If the budget of the President requests appropriations for any fiscal year for the development or procurement of a major system by the intelligence community, the President shall, subject to paragraph (2), request in such budget an amount of appropriations for the development or procurement, as the case may be, of the major system that is equivalent to the amount of appropriations identified in the most current independent cost estimate for the major system for obligation for each fiscal year for which appropriations are requested for the major system in such budget.

(2) If the amount of appropriations requested in the budget of the President for the development or procurement of a major system is less than the amount of appropriations identified in the most current independent cost estimate for the major system for obligation for each fiscal year for which appropriations are requested for the major system in such budget, the President shall include in the budget justification materials submitted to Congress in support of such budget—

(A) an explanation for the difference between the amount of appropriations requested and the amount of appropriations identified in the most current independent cost estimate;

(B) a description of the importance of the major system to the national security;

(C) an assessment of the consequences for the funding of all programs of the National Foreign Intelligence Program in future fiscal years if the most current independent cost estimate for the major system is accurate and additional appropriations are required in future fiscal years to ensure the continued development or procurement of the major system, including the consequences of such funding shortfalls on the major system and all other programs of the National Foreign Intelligence Program; and

(D) such other information on the funding of the major system as the President considers appropriate.

(d) INCLUSION OF ESTIMATES IN BUDGET JUSTIFICATION MATERIALS.—The budget justification materials submitted to Congress in support of the budget of the President shall include the most current independent cost estimate under this section for each major system for which appropriations are requested in such budget for any fiscal year.

(e) DEFINITIONS.—In this section:

(1) The term "budget of the President" means the budget of the President for a fiscal year as submitted to Congress under section 1105(a) of title 31, United States Code.

(2) The term "independent cost estimate" means a pragmatic and neutral analysis, assessment, and quantification of all costs and risks associated with the acquisition of a major system, which shall be based on programmatic and technical specifications provided by the office within the element of the intelligence community with primary responsibility for the development, procurement, or operation of the major system.

(3) The term "major system" means any significant program of an element of the intelligence community with projected total development and procurement costs exceeding $500,000,000 (in current fiscal year dollars), which costs shall include all end-to-end program costs, including costs associated with the development and procurement of the program and any other costs associated with the development and procurement of systems required to support or utilize the program.

ANNUAL PERSONNEL LEVEL ASSESSMENTS FOR THE INTELLIGENCE COMMUNITY

SEC. 506B. [50 U.S.C. 415a–4]

(a) REQUIREMENTTOPROVIDE.—The Director of National Intelligence shall, in consultation with the head of each element of the intelligence community, prepare an annual personnel level assessment for such element that assesses the personnel levels for such element for the fiscal year following the fiscal year in which the assessment is submitted.

(b) SCHEDULE.—Each assessment required by subsection (a) shall be submitted to the congressional intelligence committees each year at the time that the President submits to Congress the budget for a fiscal year pursuant to section 1105 of title 31, United States Code.

(c) CONTENTS.—Each assessment required by subsection (a) submitted during a fiscal year shall contain the following information for the element of the intelligence community concerned:

(1) The budget submission for personnel costs for the upcoming fiscal year.

(2) The dollar and percentage increase or decrease of such costs as compared to the personnel costs of the current fiscal year.

(3) The dollar and percentage increase or decrease of such costs as compared to the personnel costs during the prior 5 fiscal years.

(4) The number of fulltime equivalent positions that is the basis for which personnel funds are requested for the upcoming fiscal year.

(5) The numerical and percentage increase or decrease of the number referred to in paragraph

(4) as compared to the number of fulltime equivalent positions of the current fiscal year.

(6) The numerical and percentage increase or decrease of the number referred to in paragraph

(4) as compared to the number of fulltime equivalent positions during the prior 5 fiscal years.

(7) The best estimate of the number and costs of core contract personnel to be funded by the element for the upcoming fiscal year.

(8) The numerical and percentage increase or decrease of such costs of core contract personnel as compared to the best estimate of the costs of core contract personnel of the current fiscal year.

(9) The numerical and percentage increase or decrease of such number and such costs of core contract personnel as compared to the number and cost of core contract personnel during the prior 5 fiscal years.

(10) A justification for the requested personnel and core contract personnel levels.

(11) The best estimate of the number of intelligence collectors and analysts employed or contracted by each element of the intelligence community.

(12) A statement by the Director of National Intelligence that, based on current and projected funding, the element concerned will have sufficient—

(A) internal infrastructure to support the requested personnel and core contract personnel levels;

(B) training resources to support the requested personnel levels; and

(C) funding to support the administrative and operational activities of the requested personnel levels.

VULNERABILITY ASSESSMENTS OF MAJOR SYSTEMS

SEC. 506C. [50 U.S.C. 415a–]

(a) INITIALVULNERABILITYASSESSMENTS.—

(1)(A) Except as provided in subparagraph (B), the Director of National Intelligence shall conduct and submit to the congressional intelligence committees an initial vulnerability assessment for each major system and its significant items of supply—

(i) except as provided in clause

(ii), prior to the completion of Milestone B or an equivalent acquisition decision for the major system; or

(ii) prior to the date that is 1 year after the date of the enactment of the Intelligence Authorization Act for Fiscal Year 2010 in the case of a major system for which Milestone B or an equivalent acquisition decision—

(I) was completed prior to such date of enactment; or

(II) is completed on a date during the 180day period following such date of enactment.

(B) The Director may submit to the congressional intelligence committees an initial vulnerability assessment required by clause (ii) of subparagraph (A) not later than 180 days after the date such assessment is required to be submitted under such clause if the Director notifies the congressional intelligence committees of the extension of the submission date under this subparagraph and provides a justification for such extension.

(C) The initial vulnerability assessment of a major system and its significant items of supply shall include use of an analysis based approach to—

(i) identify vulnerabilities;

(ii) define exploitation potential;

(iii) examine the system's potential effectiveness;

(iv) determine overall vulnerability; and

(v) make recommendations for risk reduction.

(2) If an initial vulnerability assessment for a major system is not submitted to the congressional intelligence committees as required by paragraph (1), funds appropriated for the acquisition of the major system may not be obligated for a major contract related to the major system. Such prohibition on the obligation of funds for the acquisition of the major system shall cease to apply on the date on which the congressional intelligence committees receive the initial vulnerability assessment.

(b) SUBSEQUENT VULNERABILITY ASSESSMENTS.—

(1) The Director of National Intelligence shall, periodically throughout the procurement of a major system or if the Director determines that a change in circumstances warrants the issuance of a subsequent vulnerability assessment, conduct a subsequent vulnerability assessment of each major system and its significant items of supply within the National Intelligence Program.

(2) Upon the request of a congressional intelligence committee, the Director of National Intelligence may, if appropriate, recertify the previous vulnerability assessment or may conduct a subsequent vulnerability assessment of a particular major system and its significant items of supply within the National Intelligence Program.

(3) Any subsequent vulnerability assessment of a major system and its significant items of supply shall include use of an analysis based approach and, if applicable, a testingbased approach, to monitor the exploitation potential of such system and reexamine the factors described in clauses (i) through (v) of subsection (a)(1)(C).

(c) MAJOR SYSTEM MANAGEMENT.—The Director of National Intelligence shall give due consideration to the vulnerability assessments prepared for a given major system when developing and determining the National Intelligence Program budget.

(d) CONGRESSIONAL OVERSIGHT.—

(1) The Director of National Intelligence shall provide to the congressional intelligence committees a copy of each vulnerability assessment conducted under subsection (a) or (b) not later than 10 days after the date of the completion of such assessment.

(2) The Director of National Intelligence shall provide the congressional intelligence committees with a proposed schedule for subsequent periodic vulnerability assessments of a major system under subsection (b)(1) when providing such committees with the initial vulnerability assessment under subsection (a) of such system as required by paragraph (1).

(e) DEFINITIONS.—In this section:

(1) The term "item of supply" has the meaning given that term in section 4(10) of the Office of Federal Procurement Policy Act (41 U.S.C. 403(10)).

(2) The term "major contract" means each of the 6 largest prime, associate, or Governmentfurnished equipment contracts under a major system that is in excess of $40,000,000 and that is not a firm, fixed price contract.

(3) The term "major system" has the meaning given that term in section 506A(e).

(4) The term "Milestone B" means a decision to enter into major system development and demonstration pursuant to guidance prescribed by the Director of National Intelligence.

(5) The term "vulnerability assessment" means the process of identifying and quantifying vulnerabilities in a major system and its significant items of supply.

INTELLIGENCE COMMUNITY BUSINESS SYSTEM TRANSFORMATION

SEC. 506D. [50 U.S.C. 415a–6]

(a) LIMITATIONONOBLIGATION OFFUNDS.—

(1) Subject to paragraph (3), no funds appropriated to any element of the intelligence community may be obligated for an intelligence community business system transformation that will have a total cost in excess of $3,000,000 unless—

(A) the Director of the Office of Business Transformation of the Office of the Director of National Intelligence makes a certification described in paragraph (2) with respect to such intelligence community business system transformation; and

(B) such certification is approved by the board established under subsection (f).

(2) The certification described in this paragraph for an intelligence community business system transformation is a certification made by the Director of the Office of Business Transformation of the Office of the Director of National Intelligence that the intelligence community business system transformation—

(A) complies with the enterprise architecture under subsection (b) and such other policies and standards that the Director of National Intelligence considers appropriate; or

(B) is necessary—

(i) to achieve a critical national security capability or address a critical requirement; or

(ii) to prevent a significant adverse effect on a project that is needed to achieve an essential capability, taking into consideration any alternative solutions for preventing such adverse effect.

(3) With respect to a fiscal year after fiscal year 2010, the amount referred to in paragraph (1) in the matter preceding subparagraph (A) shall be equal to the sum of—

(A) the amount in effect under such paragraph (1) for the preceding fiscal year (determined after application of this paragraph), plus (B) such amount multiplied by the annual percentage increase in the consumer price index (all items; U.S. city average) as of September of the previous fiscal year.

(b) ENTERPRISE ARCHITECTURE FOR INTELLIGENCE COMMUNITY BUSINESS SYSTEMS.—

(1) The Director of National Intelligence shall, acting through the board established under subsection (f), develop and implement an enterprise architecture to cover all intelligence community business systems, and the functions and activities supported by such business systems. The enterprise architecture shall be sufficiently defined to effectively guide, constrain, and permit implementation of interoperable intelligence community business system solutions, consistent with applicable policies and procedures established by the Director of the Office of Management and Budget.

(2) The enterprise architecture under paragraph (1) shall include the following:

(A) An information infrastructure that will enable the intelligence community to—

(i) comply with all Federal accounting, financial management, and reporting requirements;

(ii) routinely produce timely, accurate, and reliable financial information for management purposes;

(iii) integrate budget, accounting, and program information and systems; and

(iv) provide for the measurement of performance, including the ability to produce timely, relevant, and reliable cost information.

(B) Policies, procedures, data standards, and system interface requirements that apply uniformly throughout the intelligence community.

(c) RESPONSIBILITIES FOR INTELLIGENCE COMMUNITY BUSINESS SYSTEM TRANSFORMATION.—The Director of National Intelligence shall be responsible for the entire life cycle of an intelligence community business system transformation, including review, approval, and oversight of the planning, design, acquisition, deployment, operation, and maintenance of the business system transformation.

(d) INTELLIGENCE COMMUNITY BUSINESS SYSTEM INVESTMENT REVIEW.—

(1) The Director of the Office of Business Transformation of the Office of the Director of National Intelligence shall establish and implement, not later than 60 days after the enactment of the Intelligence Authorization Act for Fiscal Year 2010, an investment review process for the intelligence community business systems for which the Director of the Office of Business Transformation is responsible.

(2) The investment review process under paragraph (1) shall—

(A) meet the requirements of section 11312 of title 40, United States Code; and

(B) specifically set forth the responsibilities of the Director of the Office of Business Transformation under such review process.

(3) The investment review process under paragraph (1) shall include the following elements:

(A) Review and approval by an investment review board (consisting of appropriate representatives of the intelligence community) of each intelligence community business system as an investment before the obligation of funds for such system.

(B) Periodic review, but not less often than annually, of every intelligence community business system investment.

(C) Thresholds for levels of review to ensure appropriate review of intelligence community business system investments depending on the scope, complexity, and cost of the system involved.

(D) Procedures for making certifications in accordance with the requirements of subsection (a)(2).

(e) BUDGET INFORMATION.—For each fiscal year after fiscal year 2011, the Director of National Intelligence shall include in the materials the Director submits to Congress in support of the budget for such fiscal year that is submitted to Congress under section 1105 of title 31, United States Code, the following information:

(1) An identification of each intelligence community business system for which funding is proposed in such budget.

(2) An identification of all funds, by appropriation, proposed in such budget for each such system, including—

(A) funds for current services to operate and maintain such system;

(B) funds for business systems modernization identified for each specific appropriation; and

(C) funds for associated business process improvement or reengineering efforts.

(3) The certification, if any, made under subsection (a)(2) with respect to each such system.

(f) INTELLIGENCE COMMUNITY BUSINESS SYSTEM TRANSFORMATION GOVERNANCE BOARD.—

(1) The Director of National Intelligence shall establish a board within the

intelligence community business system transformation governance structure (in this subsection referred to as the "Board").

(2) The Board shall—

(A) recommend to the Director policies and procedures necessary to effectively integrate all business activities and any transformation, reform, reorganization, or process improvement initiatives undertaken within the intelligence community;

(B) review and approve any major update of—

(i) the enterprise architecture developed under subsection (b); and

(ii) any plans for an intelligence community business systems modernization;

(C) manage crossdomain integration consistent with such enterprise architecture;

(D) coordinate initiatives for intelligence community business system transformation to maximize benefits and minimize costs for the intelligence community, and periodically report to the Director on the status of efforts to carry out an intelligence community business system transformation;

(E) ensure that funds are obligated for intelligence community business system transformation in a manner consistent with subsection (a); and

(F) carry out such other duties as the Director shall specify.

(g) RELATION TO ANNUAL REGISTRATION REQUIREMENTS.— Nothing in this section shall be construed to alter the requirements of section 8083 of the Department of Defense Appropriations Act, 2005 (Public Law 108–287; 118 Stat. 989), with regard to information technology systems (as defined in subsection (d) of such section).

(h) RELATIONSHIP TO DEFENSE BUSINESS ENTERPRISE ARCHITECTURE.—Nothing in this section shall be construed to exempt funds authorized to be appropriated to the Department of Defense from the requirements of section 2222 of title 10, United States Code, to the extent that such requirements are otherwise applicable.

(i) RELATION TO CLINGER COHEN ACT.—

(1) Executive agency responsibilities in chapter 113 of title 40, United States Code, for any intelligence community business system transformation shall be exercised jointly by—

(A) the Director of National Intelligence and the Chief Information Officer of the Intelligence Community; and

(B) the head of the executive agency that contains the element of the intelligence community involved and the chief information officer of that executive agency.

(2) The Director of National Intelligence and the head of the executive agency referred to in paragraph (1)(B) shall enter into a Memorandum of Understanding to carry out the requirements of this section in a manner that best meets the needs of the intelligence community and the executive agency.

(j) REPORTS.—Not later than March 31 of each of the years 2011 through 2015, the Director of National Intelligence shall submit to the congressional intelligence committees a report on the compliance of the intelligence community with the requirements of this section. Each such report shall—

(1) describe actions taken and proposed for meeting the requirements of subsection (a), including—

(A) specific milestones and actual performance against specified performance measures, and any revision of such milestones and performance measures; and

(B) specific actions on the intelligence community business system transformations submitted for certification under such subsection;

(2) identify the number of intelligence community business system transformations that received a certification described in subsection (a)(2); and

(3) describe specific improvements in business operations and cost savings resulting from successful intelligence community business systems transformation efforts.

(k) DEFINITIONS.—In this section:

(1) The term "enterprise architecture" has the meaning given that term in section 3601(4) of title 44, United States Code.

(2) The terms "information system" and "information technology" have the meanings given those terms in section 11101 of title 40, United States Code.

(3) The term "intelligence community business system" means an information system, including a national security system, that is operated by, for, or on behalf of an element of the intelligence community, including a financial system, mixed system, financial data feeder system, and the business infrastructure capabilities shared by the systems of the business enterprise architecture, including people, process, and technology, that build upon the core infrastructure used to support business activities, such as acquisition, financial management, logistics, strategic planning and budgeting, installations and environment, and human resource management.

(4) The term "intelligence community business system transformation" means—

(A) the acquisition or development of a new intelligence community business system; or

(B) any significant modification or enhancement of an existing intelligence community business system (other than necessary to maintain current services).

(5) The term "national security system" has the meaning given that term in section 3542 of title 44, United States Code.

(6) The term "Office of Business Transformation of the Office of the Director of National Intelligence" includes any successor office that assumes the functions of the Office of Business Transformation of the Office of the Director of National Intelligence as carried out by the Office of Business Transformation on the date of the enactment of the Intelligence Authorization Act for Fiscal Year 2010.

REPORTS ON THE ACQUISITION OF MAJOR SYSTEMS

SEC. 506E. [50 U.S.C. 415a–7]

(a) DEFINITIONS.—In this section:

(1) The term "cost estimate"—

(A) means an assessment and quantification of all costs and risks associated with the acquisition of a major system based upon reasonably available information at the time the Director establishes the 2010 adjusted total acquisition cost for such system pursuant to subsection (h) or restructures such system pursuant to section 506F(c); and

(B) does not mean an "independent cost estimate".

(2) The term "critical cost growth threshold" means a percentage increase in the total acquisition cost for a major system of at least 25 percent over the total acquisition cost for the major system as shown in the current Baseline Estimate for the major system.

(3)(A) The term "current Baseline Estimate" means the projected total acquisition cost of a major system that is—

(i) approved by the Director, or a designee of the Director, at Milestone B or an equivalent acquisition decision for the development, procurement, and construction of such system;

(ii) approved by the Director at the time such system is restructured pursuant to section 506F(c); or

(iii) the 2010 adjusted total acquisition cost determined pursuant to subsection (h).

(B) A current Baseline Estimate may be in the form of an independent cost estimate.

(4) Except as otherwise specifically provided, the term "Director" means the Director of National Intelligence.

(5) The term "independent cost estimate" has the meaning given that term in section 506A(e).

(6) The term "major contract" means each of the 6 largest prime, associate, or Governmentfurnished equipment contracts under a major system that is in excess of $40,000,000 and that is not a firm, fixed price contract.

(7) The term "major system" has the meaning given that term in section 506A(e).

(8) The term "Milestone B" means a decision to enter into major system development and demonstration pursuant to guidance prescribed by the Director.

(9) The term "program manager" means—

(A) the head of the element of the intelligence community that is responsible for the budget, cost, schedule, and performance of a major system; or

(B) in the case of a major system within the Office of the Director of National Intelligence, the deputy who is responsible for the budget, cost, schedule, and performance of the major system.

(10) The term "significant cost growth threshold" means the percentage increase in the total acquisition cost for a major system of at least 15 percent

over the total acquisition cost for such system as shown in the current Baseline Estimate for such system.

(11) The term "total acquisition cost" means the amount equal to the total cost for development and procurement of, and systemspecific construction for, a major system.

(b) MAJOR SYSTEM COST REPORTS.—

(1) The program manager for a major system shall, on a quarterly basis, submit to the Director a major system cost report as described in paragraph (2).

(2) A major system cost report shall include the following information (as of the last day of the quarter for which the report is made):

(A) The total acquisition cost for the major system.

(B) Any cost variance or schedule variance in a major contract for the major system since the contract was entered into.

(C) Any changes from a major system schedule milestones or performances that are known, expected, or anticipated by the program manager.

(D) Any significant changes in the total acquisition cost for development and procurement of any software component of the major system, schedule milestones for such software component of the major system, or expected performance of such software component of the major system that are known, expected, or anticipated by the program manager.

(3) Each major system cost report required by paragraph (1) shall be submitted not more than 30 days after the end of the reporting quarter.

(c) REPORTS FOR BREACH OF SIGNIFICANT OR CRITICAL COST GROWTH THRESHOLDS.—If the program manager of a major system for which a report has previously been submitted under subsection (b) determines at any time during a quarter that there is reasonable cause to believe that the total acquisition cost for the major system has increased by a percentage equal to or greater than the significant cost growth threshold or critical cost growth threshold and if a report indicating an increase of such percentage or more has not previously been submitted to the Director, then the program manager shall immediately submit to the Director a major system cost report containing the information, determined as of the date of the report, required under subsection (b).

(d) NOTIFICATION TO CONGRESS OF COST GROWTH.—

(1) Whenever a major system cost report is submitted to the Director, the Director shall determine whether the current acquisition cost for the major system has increased by a percentage equal to or greater than the significant cost growth threshold or the critical cost growth threshold.

(2) If the Director determines that the current total acquisition cost has increased by a percentage equal to or greater than the significant cost growth threshold or critical cost growth threshold, the Director shall submit to Congress a Major System Congressional Report pursuant to subsection (e).

(e) REQUIREMENT FOR MAJOR SYSTEM CONGRESSIONAL REPORT.—

(1) Whenever the Director determines under subsection (d) that the total acquisition cost of a major system has increased by a percentage equal to or greater than the significant cost growth threshold for the major system, a Ma-

jor System Congressional Report shall be submitted to Congress not later than 45 days after the date on which the Director receives the major system cost report for such major system.

(2) If the total acquisition cost of a major system (as determined by the Director under subsection (d)) increases by a percentage equal to or greater than the critical cost growth threshold for the program or subprogram, the Director shall take actions consistent with the requirements of section 506F.

(f) MAJOR SYSTEM CONGRESSIONAL REPOR TELEMENTS.—

(1) Except as provided in paragraph (2), each Major System Congressional Report shall include the following:

(A) The name of the major system.

(B) The date of the preparation of the report.

(C) The program phase of the major system as of the date of the preparation of the report.

(D) The estimate of the total acquisition cost for the major system expressed in constant baseyear dollars and in current dollars.

(E) The current Baseline Estimate for the major system in constant baseyear dollars and in current dollars.

(F) A statement of the reasons for any increase in total acquisition cost for the major system.

(G) The completion status of the major system—

(i) expressed as the percentage that the number of years for which funds have been appropriated for the major system is of the number of years for which it is planned that funds will be appropriated for the major system; and

(ii) expressed as the percentage that the amount of funds that have been appropriated for the major system is of the total amount of funds which it is planned will be appropriated for the major system.

(H) The fiscal year in which the major system was first authorized and in which funds for such system were first appropriated by Congress.

(I) The current change and the total change, in dollars and expressed as a percentage, in the total acquisition cost for the major system, stated both in constant baseyear dollars and in current dollars.

(J) The quantity of end items to be acquired under the major system and the current change and total change, if any, in that quantity.

(K) The identities of the officers responsible for management and cost control of the major system.

(L) The action taken and proposed to be taken to control future cost growth of the major system.

(M) Any changes made in the performance or schedule milestones of the major system and the extent to which such changes have contributed to the increase in total acquisition cost for the major system.

(N) The following contract performance assessment information with respect to each major contract under the major system:

(i) The name of the contractor.
(ii) The phase that the contract is in at the time of the preparation of the report.
(iii) The percentage of work under the contract that has been completed.
(iv) Any current change and the total change, in dollars and expressed as a percentage, in the contract cost.
(v) The percentage by which the contract is currently ahead of or behind schedule.
(vi) A narrative providing a summary explanation of the most significant occurrences, including cost and schedule variances under major contracts of the major system, contributing to the changes identified and a discussion of the effect these occurrences will have on the future costs and schedule of the major system.

(O) In any case in which one or more problems with a software component of the major system significantly contributed to the increase in costs of the major system, the action taken and proposed to be taken to solve such problems.

(2) A Major System Congressional Report prepared for a major system for which the increase in the total acquisition cost is due to termination or cancellation of the entire major system shall include only—

(A) the information described in subparagraphs (A) through (F) of paragraph (1); and
(B) the total percentage change in total acquisition cost for such system.

(g) PROHIBITION ON OBLIGATION OF FUNDS.—If a determination of an increase by a percentage equal to or greater than the significant cost growth threshold is made by the Director under subsection
(d) and a Major System Congressional Report containing the information described in subsection(f) is not submitted to Congress under subsection (e)(1), or if a determination of an increase by a percentage equal to or greater than the critical cost growth threshold is made by the Director under subsection (d) and the Major System Congressional Report containing the information described in subsection (f) and section 506F(b)(3) and the certification required by section 506F(b)(2) are not submitted to Congress under subsection (e)(2), funds appropriated for construction, research, development, test, evaluation, and procurement may not be obligated for a major contract under the major system. The prohibition on the obligation of funds for a major system shall cease to apply at the end of the 45day period that begins on the date—

(1) on which Congress receives the Major System Congressional Report under subsection (e)(1) with respect to that major system, in the case of a determination of an increase by a percentage equal to or greater than the significant cost growth threshold (as determined in subsection (d)); or
(2) on which Congress receives both the Major System Congressional Report under subsection (e)(2) and the certification of the Director under section 506F(b)(2) with respect to that major system, in the case of an increase by a

percentage equal to or greater than the critical cost growth threshold (as determined under subsection (d)).

(h) TREATMENT OF COST INCREASES PRIOR TO ENACTMENT OF INTELLIGENCE AUTHORIZATION ACT FOR FISCAL YEAR 2010.—

(1) Not later than 180 days after the date of the enactment of the Intelligence Authorization Act for Fiscal Year 2010, the Director—

(A) shall, for each major system, determine if the total acquisition cost of such major system increased by a percentage equal to or greater than the significant cost growth threshold or the critical cost growth threshold prior to such date of enactment;

(B) shall establish for each major system for which the total acquisition cost has increased by a percentage equal to or greater than the significant cost growth threshold or the critical cost growth threshold prior to such date of enactment a revised current Baseline Estimate based upon an updated cost estimate;

(C) may, for a major system not described in subparagraph (B), establish a revised current Baseline Estimate based upon an updated cost estimate; and

(D) shall submit to Congress a report describing—

(i) each determination made under subparagraph (A);

(ii) each revised current Baseline Estimate established for a major system under subparagraph (B); and

(iii) each revised current Baseline Estimate established for a major system under subparagraph (C), including the percentage increase of the total acquisition cost of such major system that occurred prior to the date of the enactment of such Act.

(2) The revised current Baseline Estimate established for a major system under subparagraph (B) or (C) of paragraph (1) shall be the 2010 adjusted total acquisition cost for the major system and may include the estimated cost of conducting any vulnerability assessments for such major system required under section 506C.

(i) REQUIREMENTS TO USE BASE YEAR DOLLARS.—Any determination of a percentage increase under this section shall be stated in terms of constant base year dollars.

(j) FORM OF REPORT.—Any report required to be submitted under this section may be submitted in a classified form.

CRITICAL COST GROWTH IN MAJOR SYSTEMS

SEC. 506F. [50 U.S.C. 415a–8]

(a) REASSESSMENT OF MAJOR SYSTEM.—If the Director of National Intelligence determines under section 506E(d) that the total acquisition cost of a major system has increased by a percentage equal to or greater than the critical cost growth threshold for the major system, the Director shall—

(1) determine the root cause or causes of the critical cost growth, in accordance with applicable statutory requirements, policies, procedures, and guidance; and

(2) carry out an assessment of—

(A) the projected cost of completing the major system if current requirements are not modified;

(B) the projected cost of completing the major system based on reasonable modification of such requirements;

(C) the rough order of magnitude of the costs of any reasonable alternative system or capability; and

(D) the need to reduce funding for other systems due to the growth in cost of the major system.

(b) PRESUMPTION OF TERMINATION.—

(1) After conducting the reassessment required by subsection (a) with respect to a major system, the Director shall terminate the major system unless the Director submits to Congress a Major System Congressional Report containing a certification in accordance with paragraph (2) and the information described in paragraph (3). The Director shall submit such Major System Congressional Report and certification not later than 90 days after the date the Director receives the relevant major system cost report under subsection (b) or (c) of section 506E.

(2) A certification described by this paragraph with respect to a major system is a written certification that—

(A) the continuation of the major system is essential to the national security;

(B) there are no alternatives to the major system that will provide acceptable capability to meet the intelligence requirement at less cost;

(C) the new estimates of the total acquisition cost have been determined by the Director to be reasonable;

(D) the major system is a higher priority than other systems whose funding must be reduced to accommodate the growth in cost of the major system; and

(E) the management structure for the major system is adequate to manage and control the total acquisition cost.

(3) A Major System Congressional Report accompanying a written certification under paragraph (2) shall include, in addition to the requirements of section 506E(e), the root cause analysis and assessment carried out pursuant to subsection (a), the basis for each determination made in accordance with subparagraphs (A) through (E) of paragraph (2), and a description of all funding changes made as a result of the growth in the cost of the major system, including reductions made in funding for other systems to accommodate such cost growth, together with supporting documentation.

(c) ACTIONS IF MAJOR SYSTEM NOT TERMINATED.—If the Director elects not to terminate a major system pursuant to subsection (b), the Director shall—

(1) restructure the major system in a manner that addresses the root cause or causes of the critical cost growth, as identified pursuant to subsection (a), and ensures that the system has an appropriate management structure as set forth in the certification submitted pursuant to subsection (b)(2)(E);

(2) rescind the most recent Milestone approval for the major system;

(3) require a new Milestone approval for the major system before taking any action to enter a new contract, exercise an option under an existing contract, or otherwise extend the scope of an existing contract under the system, except to the extent determined necessary by the Milestone Decision Authority, on a nondelegable basis, to ensure that the system may be restructured as intended by the Director without unnecessarily wasting resources;

(4) establish a revised current Baseline Estimate for the major system based upon an updated cost estimate; and

(5) conduct regular reviews of the major system.

(d) ACTIONS IF MAJOR SYSTEM TERMINATED.—If a major system is terminated pursuant to subsection (b), the Director shall submit to Congress a written report setting forth—

(1) an explanation of the reasons for terminating the major system;

(2) the alternatives considered to address any problems in the major system; and

(3) the course the Director plans to pursue to meet any intelligence requirements otherwise intended to be met by the major system.

(e) FORM OF REPORT.—Any report or certification required to be submitted under this section may be submitted in a classified form.

(f) WAIVER.—(1) The Director may waive the requirements of subsections (d)(2), (e), and (g) of section 506E and subsections (a)(2), (b), (c), and (d) of this section with respect to a major system if the Director determines that at least 90 percent of the amount of the current Baseline Estimate for the major system has been expended.

(2)(A) If the Director grants a waiver under paragraph (1) with respect to a major system, the Director shall submit to the congressional intelligence committees written notice of the waiver that includes—

(i) the information described in section 506E(f); and

(ii) if the current total acquisition cost of the major system has increased by a percentage equal to or greater than the critical cost growth threshold—

(I) a determination of the root cause or causes of the critical cost growth, as described in subsection (a)(1); and

(II) a certification that includes the elements described in subparagraphs (A), (B), and (E) of subsection (b)(2).

(B) The Director shall submit the written notice required by subparagraph (A) not later than 90 days after the date that the Director receives a major system cost report under subsection (b) or (c) of section 506E that indicates that the total acquisition cost for the major system has increased by a percentage equal to or greater than the significant cost growth threshold or critical cost growth threshold.

(g) DEFINITIONS.—In this section, the terms "cost estimate", "critical cost growth threshold", "current Baseline Estimate", "major system", and "total acquisition cost" have the meaning given those terms in section 506E(a).

FUTURE BUDGET PROJECTIONS

SEC. 506G. [50 U.S.C. 415a–9]

(a) FUTURE YEAR INTELLIGENCE PLANS.—

(1) The Director of National Intelligence, with the concurrence of the Director of the Office of Management and Budget, shall provide to the congressional intelligence committees a Future Year Intelligence Plan, as described in paragraph (2), for—

(A) each expenditure center in the National Intelligence Program; and

(B) each major system in the National Intelligence Program.

(2)(A) A Future Year Intelligence Plan submitted under this subsection shall include the yearbyyear proposed funding for each center or system referred to in subparagraph (A) or (B) of paragraph (1), for the budget year for which the Plan is submitted and not less than the 4 subsequent fiscal years.

(B) A Future Year Intelligence Plan submitted under subparagraph (B) of paragraph (1) for a major system shall include—

(i) the estimated total lifecycle cost of such major system; and

(ii) major milestones that have significant resource implications for such major system.

(b) LONG TERM BUDGET PROJECTIONS.—

(1) The Director of National Intelligence, with the concurrence of the Director of the Office of Management and Budget, shall provide to the congressional intelligence committees a Longterm Budget Projection for each element of the intelligence community funded under the National Intelligence Program acquiring a major system that includes the budget for such element for the 5year period that begins on the day after the end of the last fiscal year for which yearbyyear pro posed funding is included in a Future Year Intelligence Plan for such major system in accordance with subsection (a)(2)(A).

(2) A Longterm Budget Projection submitted under paragraph (1) shall include—

(A) projections for the appropriate element of the intelligence community for—

(i) pay and benefits of officers and employees of such element;

(ii) other operating and support costs and minor acquisitions of such element;

(iii) research and technology required by such element;

(iv) current and planned major system acquisitions for such element;

(v) any future major system acquisitions for such element; and

(vi) any additional funding projections that the Director of National Intelligence considers appropriate;

(B) a budget projection based on effective cost and schedule execution of current or planned major system acquisitions and application of Office of Management and Budget inflation estimates to future major system acquisitions;

(C) any additional assumptions and projections that the Director of National Intelligence considers appropriate; and

(D) a description of whether, and to what extent, the total projection for each year exceeds the level that would result from applying the most recent Office of Management and Budget inflation estimate to the budget of that element of the intelligence community.

(c) SUBMISSION TO CONGRESS.—The Director of National Intelligence, with the concurrence of the Director of the Office of Management and Budget, shall submit to the congressional intelligence committees each Future Year Intelligence Plan or Longterm Budget Projection required under subsection (a) or (b) for a fiscal year at the time that the President submits to Congress the budget for such fiscal year pursuant section 1105 of title 31, United States Code.

(d) MAJOR SYSTEM AFFORDABILITY REPORT.—

(1) The Director of National Intelligence, with the concurrence of the Director of the Office of Management and Budget, shall prepare a report on the acquisition of a major system funded under the National Intelligence Program before the time that the President submits to Congress the budget for the first fiscal year in which appropriated funds are anticipated to be obligated for the development or procurement of such major system.

(2) The report on such major system shall include an assessment of whether, and to what extent, such acquisition, if developed, procured, and operated, is projected to cause an increase in the most recent Future Year Intelligence Plan and Longterm Budget Projection submitted under section 506G for an element of the intelligence community.

(3) The Director of National Intelligence shall update the report whenever an independent cost estimate must be updated pursuant to section 506A(a)(4).

(4) The Director of National Intelligence shall submit each report required by this subsection at the time that the President submits to Congress the budget for a fiscal year pursuant to section 1105 of title 31, United States Code.

(e) DEFINITIONS.—In this section:

(1) BUDGET YEAR.—The term "budget year" means the next fiscal year for which the President is required to submit to Congress a budget pursuant to section 1105 of title 31, United States Code.

(2) INDEPENDENT COST ESTIMATE; MAJOR SYSTEM.—The terms "independent cost estimate" and "major system" have the meaning given those terms in section 506A(e).

REPORTS ON SECURITY CLEARANCES

SEC. 506H. [50 U.S.C. 415a–10]

(a) QUADRENNIAL AUDIT OF POSITION REQUIREMENTS.—

(1) The President shall every four years conduct an audit of the manner in which the executive branch determines whether a security clearance is required for a particular position in the United States Government.

(2) Not later than 30 days after the completion of an audit conducted under paragraph (1), the President shall submit to Congress the results of such audit.

(b) REPORT ON SECURITY CLEARANCE DETERMINATIONS.—

(1) Not later than February 1 of each year, the President shall submit to Con-

gress a report on the security clearance process. Such report shall include, for each security clearance level—

(A) the number of employees of the United States Government who—

(i) held a security clearance at such level as of October 1 of the preceding year; and

(ii) were approved for a security clearance at such level during the preceding fiscal year;

(B) the number of contractors to the United States Government who—

(i) held a security clearance at such level as of October 1 of the preceding year; and

(ii) were approved for a security clearance at such level during the preceding fiscal year; and

(C) for each element of the intelligence community—

(i) the total amount of time it took to process the security clearance determination for such level that—

(I) was among the 80 percent of security clearance determinations made during the preceding fiscal year that took the shortest amount of time to complete; and

(II) took the longest amount of time to complete;

(ii) the total amount of time it took to process the security clearance determination for such level that—

(I) was among the 90 percent of security clearance determinations made during the preceding fiscal year that took the shortest amount of time to complete; and

(II) took the longest amount of time to complete;

(iii) the number of pending security clearance investigations for such level as of October 1 of the preceding year that have remained pending for—

(I) 4 months or less;

(II) between 4 months and 8 months;

(III) between 8 months and one year; and

(IV) more than one year;

(iv) the percentage of reviews during the preceding fiscal year that resulted in a denial or revocation of a security clearance;

(v) the percentage of investigations during the preceding fiscal year that resulted in incomplete information;

(vi) the percentage of investigations during the preceding fiscal year that did not result in enough information to make a decision on potentially adverse information; and

(vii) for security clearance determinations completed or pending during the preceding fiscal year that have taken longer than one year to complete—

(I) the number of security clearance determinations for positions as employees of the United States Government that required more than one year to complete;

(II) the number of security clearance determinations for contractors that required more than one year to complete;

(III) the agencies that investigated and adjudicated such determinations; and

(IV) the cause of significant delays in such determinations.

(2) For purposes of paragraph (1), the President may consider—

(A) security clearances at the level of confidential and secret as one security clearance level; and

(B) security clearances at the level of top secret or higher as one security clearance level.

(c) FORM.—The results required under subsection (a)(2) and the reports required under subsection (b)(1) shall be submitted in unclassified form, but may include a classified annex.

DATE OF SUBMITTAL OF VARIOUS ANNUAL AND SEMIANNUAL REPORTS TO THE CONGRESSIONAL INTELLIGENCE COMMITTEES

SEC. 507. [50 U.S.C. §415b]

(a) ANNUAL REPORTS.—

(1) The date for the submittal to the congressional intelligence committees of the following annual reports shall be the date each year provided in subsection (c)(1)(A):

(A) The annual report on intelligence required by section 109.

(B) The annual report on intelligence provided to the United Nations required by section 112(b)(1).

(C) The annual report on the protection of the identities of covert agents required by section 603.

(D) The annual report of the Inspectors Generals of the intelligence community on proposed resources and activities of their offices required by section 8H(g) of the Inspector General Act of 1978.

(E) The annual report on the acquisition of technology relating to weapons of mass destruction and advanced conventional munitions required by section 721 of the Intelligence Authorization Act for Fiscal Year 1997 (Public Law 104-293; 50 U.S.C. §2366).

(F) The annual report on commercial activities as security for intelligence collection required by section 437(c) of title 10, United States Code.

(G) The annual update on foreign industrial espionage required by section 809(b) of the Counterintelligence and Security Enhancements Act of 1994 (title VIII of Public Law 103–359; 50 U.S.C. App. §2170b(b)).

(H) The annual report on certifications for immunity in interdiction of aircraft engaged in illicit drug trafficking required by section 1012(c)(2) of the National Defense Authorization Act for Fiscal Year 1995 (22 U.S.C. §2291–4(c)(2)).

(I) The annual report on activities under the David L. Boren National Security Education Act of 1991 (title VIII of Public Law 102–183; 50 U.S.C. §1901 et seq.) required by section 806(a) of that Act (50 U.S.C. §1906(a)).

(J) The annual report on hiring and retention of minority employees in the intelligence community required by section 114(c).

(2) The date for the submittal to the congressional intelligence committees of the following annual reports shall be the date each year provided in subsection (c)(1)(B):

(A) The annual report on the safety and security of Russian nuclear facilities and nuclear military forces required by section 114(a).

(B) The annual report on the threat of attack on the United States from weapons of mass destruction required by section 114(c).

(C) The annual report on improvements of the financial statements of the intelligence community for auditing purposes required by section 114A.

(D) The annual report on counterdrug intelligence matters required by section 826 of the Intelligence Authorization Act for Fiscal Year 2003.

(b) SEMIANNUAL REPORTS.—The dates for the submittal to the congressional intelligence committees of the following semiannual reports shall be the dates each year provided in subsection (c)(2):

(1) The semiannual reports on the Office of the Inspector General of the Central Intelligence Agency required by section 17(d)(1) of the Central Intelligence Agency Act of 1949 (50 U.S.C. §403q(d)(1)).

(2) The semiannual reports on decisions not to prosecute certain violations of law under the Classified Information Procedures Act (18 U.S.C. App.) as required by section 13 of that Act.

(3) The semiannual reports on the activities of the Diplomatic Telecommunications Service Program Office (DTS–PO) required by section 322(a)(6)(D)(ii) of the Intelligence Authorization Act for Fiscal Year 2001 (22 U.S.C. §7302(a)(6)(D)(ii)).

(4) The semiannual reports on the disclosure of information and consumer reports to the Federal Bureau of Investigation for counterintelligence purposes required by section 624(h)(2) of the Fair Credit Reporting Act (15 U.S.C. §1681u(h)(2)).

(5) The semiannual provision of information on requests for financial information for foreign counterintelligence purposes required by section 1114(a)(5)(C) of the Right to Financial Privacy Act of 1978 (12 U.S.C. §3414(a)(5)(C)).

(6) The semiannual report on financial intelligence on terrorist assets required by section 118.

(c) SUBMITTAL DATES FOR REPORTS.—

(1)(A) Except as provided in subsection (d), each annual report listed in subsection (a)(1) shall be submitted not later than February 1.

(B) Except as provided in subsection (d), each annual report listed in subsection (a)(2) shall be submitted not later than December 1.

(2) Except as provided in subsection (d), each semiannual report listed in subsection (b) shall be submitted not later than February 1 and August 1.

(d) POSTPONEMENT OF SUBMITTAL.—

(1) Subject to paragraph (3), the date for the submittal of—

(A) an annual report listed in subsection (a)(1) may be postponed until March 1;

(B) an annual report listed in subsection (a)(2) may be postponed until January 1; and

(C) a semiannual report listed in subsection (b) may be postponed until March 1 or September 1, as the case may be, if the official required to submit such report submits to the congressional intelligence committees a written notification of such postponement.

(2)(A) Notwithstanding any other provision of law and subject to paragraph (3), the date for the submittal to the congressional intelligence committees of any report described in subparagraph (B) may be postponed by not more than 30 days from the date otherwise specified in the provision of law for the submittal of such report if the official required to submit such report submits to the congressional intelligence committees a written notification of such postponement.

(B) A report described in this subparagraph is any report on intelligence or intelligence-related activities of the United States Government that is submitted under a provision of law requiring the submittal of only a single report.

(3)(A) The date for the submittal of a report whose submittal is postponed under paragraph (1) or (2) may be postponed beyond the time provided for the submittal of such report under such paragraph if the official required to submit such report submits to the congressional intelligence committees a written certification that preparation and submittal of such report at such time will impede the work of officers or employees of the intelligence community in a manner that will be detrimental to the national security of the United States.

(B) A certification with respect to a report under subparagraph (A) shall include a proposed submittal date for such report, and such report shall be submitted not later than that date.

CERTIFICATION OF COMPLIANCE WITH OVERSIGHT REQUIREMENTS

SEC. 508. [50 U.S.C. 415d]

The head of each element of the intelligence community shall annually submit to the congressional intelligence committees—

(1) a certification that, to the best of the knowledge of the head of such element—

(A) the head of such element is in full compliance with the requirements of this title; and

(B) any information required to be submitted by the head of such element under this Act before the date of the submission of such certification has been properly submitted; or

(2) if the head of such element is unable to submit a certification under paragraph (1), a statement—

(A) of the reasons the head of such element is unable to submit such a certification;

(B) (B) describing any information required to be submitted by the head

of such element under this Act before the date of the submission of such statement that has not been properly submitted; and
(C) (C) that the head of such element will submit such information as soon as possible after the submission of such statement.

TITLE VI—PROTECTION OF CERTAIN NATIONAL SECURITY INFORMATION

PROTECTION OF IDENTITIES OF CERTAIN UNITED STATES UNDERCOVER INTELLIGENCE OFFICERS, AGENTS, INFORMANTS, AND SOURCES

SEC. 601. [50 U.S.C. §421]

(a) Whoever, having or having had authorized access to classified information that identifies a covert agent, intentionally discloses any information identifying such covert agent to any individual not authorized to receive classified information, knowing that the information disclosed so identifies such covert agent and that the United States is taking affirmative measures to conceal such covert agent's intelligence relationship to the United States, shall be fined under title 18, United States Code, or imprisoned not more than ten years, or both.
(b) Whoever, as a result of having authorized access to classified information, learns the identity of a covert agent and intentionally discloses any information identifying such covert agent to any individual not authorized to receive classified information, knowing that the information disclosed so identifies such covert agent and that the United States is taking affirmative measures to conceal such covert agent's intelligence relationship to the United States, shall be fined under title 18, United States Code, or imprisoned not more than five years, or both.
(c) Whoever, in the course of a pattern of activities intended to identify and expose covert agents and with reason to believe that such activities would impair or impede the foreign intelligence activities of the United States, discloses any information that identifies an individual as a covert agent to any individual not authorized to receive classified information, knowing that the information disclosed so identifies such individual and that the United States is taking affirmative measures to conceal such individual's classified intelligence relationship to the United States, shall be fined under title 18, United States Code, or imprisoned not more than three years, or both.
(d) A term of imprisonment imposed under this section shall be consecutive to any other sentence of imprisonment.

DEFENSES AND EXCEPTIONS

SEC. 602. [50 U.S.C. §422]

(a) It is a defense to a prosecution under section 601 that before the commission of the offense with which the defendant is charged, the United States had publicly acknowledged or revealed the intelligence relationship to the United States of the individual the disclosure of whose intelligence relationship to the United States is the basis for the prosecution.

(b)(1) Subject to paragraph (2), no person other than a person committing an offense under section 601 shall be subject to prosecution under such section by virtue of section 2 or 4 of title 18, United States Code, or shall be subject to prosecution for conspiracy to commit an offense under such section.

(2) Paragraph (1) shall not apply (A) in the case of a person who acted in the course of a pattern of activities intended to identify and expose covert agents and with reason to believe that such activities would impair or impede the foreign intelligence activities of the United States, or (B) in the case of a person who has authorized access to classified information.

(c) It shall not be an offense under section 601 to transmit information described in such section directly to either congressional intelligence committee.

(d) It shall not be an offense under section 601 for an individual to disclose information that solely identifies himself as a covert agent.

REPORT

SEC. 603. [50 U.S.C. §423]

(a) The President, after receiving information from the Director of National Intelligence, shall submit to the congressional intelligence committees an annual report on measures to protect the identities of covert agents, and on any other matter relevant to the protection of the identities of covert agents. The date for the submittal of the report shall be the date provided in section 507.

(b) The report described in subsection (a) shall be exempt from any requirement for publication or disclosure.

EXTRATERRITORIAL JURISDICTION

SEC. 604. [50 U.S.C. §424]

There is jurisdiction over an offense under section 601 committed outside the United States if the individual committing the offense is a citizen of the United States or an alien lawfully admitted to the United States for permanent residence (as defined in section 101(a)(20) of the Immigration and Nationality Act).

PROVIDING INFORMATION TO CONGRESS

SEC. 605. [50 U.S.C. §425]

Nothing in this title may be construed as authority to withhold information from the Congress or from a committee of either House of Congress.

DEFINITIONS

SEC. 606. [50 U.S.C. §426]

For the purposes of this title:

(1) The term "classified information" means information or material designated and clearly marked or clearly represented, pursuant to the provisions of a statute or Executive order (or a regulation or order issued pursuant to a statute or Executive order), as requiring a specific degree of protection against unauthorized disclosure for reasons of national security.

(2) The term "authorized", when used with respect to access to classified infor-

mation, means having authority, right, or permission pursuant to the provisions of a statute, Executive order, directive of the head of any department or agency engaged in foreign intelligence or counterintelligence activities, order of any United States court, or provisions of any Rule of the House of Representatives or resolution of the Senate which assigns responsibility within the respective House of Congress for the oversight of intelligence activities.

(3) The term "disclose" means to communicate, provide, impart, transmit, transfer, convey, publish, or otherwise make available.

(4) The term "covert agent" means—

(A) a present or retired officer or employee of an intelligence agency or a present or retired member of the Armed Forces assigned to duty with an intelligence agency—

(i) whose identity as such an officer, employee, or member is classified information, and

(ii) who is serving outside the United States or has within the last five years served outside the United States; or

(B) a United States citizen whose intelligence relationship to the United States is classified information, and—

(i) who resides and acts outside the United States as an agent of, or informant or source of operational assistance to, an intelligence agency, or

(ii) who is at the time of the disclosure acting as an agent of, or informant to, the foreign counterintelligence or foreign counterterrorism components of the Federal Bureau of Investigation; or

(C) an individual, other than a United States citizen, whose past or present intelligence relationship to the United States is classified information and who is a present or former agent of, or a present or former informant or source of operational assistance to, an intelligence agency.

(5) The term "intelligence agency" means the Central Intelligence Agency, a foreign intelligence component of the Department of Defense, or the foreign counterintelligence or foreign counterterrorism components of the Federal Bureau of Investigation.

(6) The term "informant" means any individual who furnishes information to an intelligence agency in the course of a confidential relationship protecting the identity of such individual from public disclosure.

(7) The terms "officer" and "employee" have the meanings given such terms by section 2104 and 2105, respectively, of title 5, United States Code.

(8) The term "Armed Forces" means the Army, Navy, Air Force, Marine Corps, and Coast Guard.

(9) The term "United States", when used in a geographic sense, means all areas under the territorial sovereignty of the United States and the Trust Territory of the Pacific Islands.

(10) The term "pattern of activities" requires a series of acts with a common purpose or objective.

TITLE VII—PROTECTION OF OPERATIONAL FILES

OPERATIONAL FILES OF THE CENTRAL INTELLIGENCE AGENCY
SEC. 701. [50 U.S.C. §431]

(a) The Director of the Central Intelligence Agency, with the coordination of the Director of National Intelligence, may exempt operational files of the Central Intelligence Agency from the provisions of section 552 of title 5, United States Code (Freedom of Information Act), which require publication or disclosure, or search or review in connection therewith.

(b) In this section, the term "operational files" means—

(1) files of the Directorate of Operations which document the conduct of foreign intelligence or counterintelligence operations or intelligence or security liaison arrangements or information exchanges with foreign governments or their intelligence or security services;

(2) files of the Directorate for Science and Technology which document the means by which foreign intelligence or counterintelligence is collected through scientific and technical systems; and

(3) files of the Office of Personnel Security which document investigations conducted to determine the suitability of potential foreign intelligence or counterintelligence sources; except that files which are the sole repository of disseminated intelligence are not operational files.

(c) Notwithstanding subsection (a) of this section, exempted operational files shall continue to be subject to search and review for information concerning—

(1) United States citizens or aliens lawfully admitted for permanent residence who have requested information on themselves pursuant to the provisions of section 552 of title 5, United States Code (Freedom of Information Act), or section 552a of title 5, United States Code (Privacy Act of 1974);

(2) any special activity the existence of which is not exempt from disclosure under the provisions of section 552 of title 5, United States Code (Freedom of Information Act); or

(3) the specific subject matter of an investigation by the congressional intelligence committees, the Intelligence Oversight Board, the Department of Justice, the Office of General Counsel of the Central Intelligence Agency, the Office of Inspector General of the Central Intelligence Agency, or the Office of the Director of National Intelligence for any impropriety, or violation of law, Executive order, or Presidential directive, in the conduct of an intelligence activity.

(d)(1) Files that are not exempted under subsection (a) of this section which contain information derived or disseminated from exempted operational files shall be subject to search and review.

(2) The inclusion of information from exempted operational files in files that are not exempted under subsection (a) of this section shall not affect the exemption under subsection (a) of this section of the originating operational files from search, review, publication, or disclosure.

(3) Records from exempted operational files which have been disseminated to and referenced in files that are not exempted under subsection (a) of this sec-

tion and which have been returned to exempted operational files for sole retention shall be subject to search and review.

(e) The provisions of subsection (a) of this section shall not be superseded except by a provision of law which is enacted after the date of enactment of subsection (a), and which specifically cites and repeals or modifies its provisions.

(f) Whenever any person who has requested agency records under section 552 of title 5, United States Code (Freedom of Information Act), alleges that the Central Intelligence Agency has improperly withheld records because of failure to comply with any provision of this section, judicial review shall be available under the terms set forth in section 552(a)(4)(B) of title 5, United States Code, except that—

(1) in any case in which information specifically authorized under criteria established by an Executive order to be kept secret in the interest of national defense or foreign relations which is filed with, or produced for, the court by the Central Intelligence Agency, such information shall be examined ex parte, in camera by the court;

(2) the court shall, to the fullest extent practicable, determine issues of fact based on sworn written submissions of the parties;

(3) when a complainant alleges that requested records are improperly withheld because of improper placement solely in exempted operational files, the complainant shall support such allegation with a sworn written submission, based upon personal knowledge or otherwise admissible evidence;

(4)(A) when a complainant alleges that requested records were improperly withheld because of improper exemption of operational files, the Central Intelligence Agency shall meet its burden under section 552(a)(4)(B) of title 5, United States Code, by demonstrating to the court by sworn written submission that exempted operational files likely to contain responsive records currently perform the functions set forth in subsection (b) of this section; and

(B) the court may not order the Central Intelligence Agency to review the content of any exempted operational file or files in order to make the demonstration required under subparagraph (A) of this paragraph, unless the complainant disputes the Central Intelligence Agency's showing with a sworn written submission based on personal knowledge or otherwise admissible evidence;

(5) in proceedings under paragraphs (3) and (4) of this subsection, the parties shall not obtain discovery pursuant to rules 26 through 36 of the Federal Rules of Civil Procedure, except that requests for admission may be made pursuant to rules 26 and 36;

(6) if the court finds under this subsection that the Central Intelligence Agency has improperly withheld requested records because of failure to comply with any provision of this section, the court shall order the Central Intelligence Agency to search and review the appropriate exempted operational file or files for the requested records and make such records, or portions thereof, available in accordance with the provisions of section 552 of title 5, United States Code (Freedom of Information Act), and such order shall be the exclusive remedy for failure to comply with this section; and

(7) if at any time following the filing of a complaint pursuant to this subsection the Central Intelligence Agency agrees to search the appropriate exempted operational file or files for the requested records, the court shall dismiss the claim based upon such complaint.

(g) DECENNIAL REVIEW OF EXEMPTED OPERATIONAL FILES—

(1) Not less than once every ten years, the Director of the Central Intelligence Agency and the Director of National Intelligence shall review the exemptions in force under subsection (a) to determine whether such exemptions may be removed from any category of exempted files or any portion thereof.

(2) The review required by paragraph (1) shall include consideration of the historical value or other public interest in the subject matter of the particular category of files or portions thereof and the potential for declassifying a significant part of the information contained therein.

(3) A complainant who alleges that the Central Intelligence Agency has improperly withheld records because of failure to comply with this subsection may seek judicial review in the district court of the United States of the district in which any of the parties reside, or in the District of Columbia. In such a proceeding, the court's review shall be limited to determining the following:

(A) Whether the Central Intelligence Agency has conducted the review required by paragraph (1) before October 15, 1994, or before the expiration of the 10-year period beginning on the date of the most recent review.

(B) Whether the Central Intelligence Agency, in fact, considered the criteria set forth in paragraph (2) in conducting the required review.

OPERATIONAL FILES OF THE NATIONAL GEOSPATIAL-INTELLIGENCE AGENCY

SEC. 702. [50 U.S.C. §432]

(a) EXEMPTION OF CERTAIN OPERATIONAL FILES FROM SEARCH, REVIEW, PUBLICATION, OR DISCLOSURE.—

(1) The Director of the National Geospatial-Intelligence Agency, with the coordination of the Director of National Intelligence, may exempt operational files of the National Geospatial-Intelligence Agency from the provisions of section 552 of title 5, United States Code, which require publication, disclosure, search, or review in connection therewith.

(2)(A) Subject to subparagraph (B), for the purposes of this section, the term "operational files" means files of the National Geospatial-Intelligence Agency (hereafter in this section referred to as "NGA") concerning the activities of NGA that before the establishment of NGA were performed by the National Photographic Interpretation Center of the Central Intelligence Agency (NPIC), that document the means by which foreign intelligence or counterintelligence is collected through scientific and technical systems.

(B) Files which are the sole repository of disseminated intelligence are not operational files.

(3) Notwithstanding paragraph (1), exempted operational files shall continue to be subject to search and review for information concerning—

(A) United States citizens or aliens lawfully admitted for permanent residence who have requested information on themselves pursuant to the provisions of section 552 or 552a of title 5, United States Code;

(B) any special activity the existence of which is not exempt from disclosure under the provisions of section 552 of title 5, United States Code; or

(C) the specific subject matter of an investigation by any of the following for any impropriety, or violation of law, Executive order, or Presidential directive, in the conduct of an intelligence activity:

(i) The congressional intelligence committees.

(ii) The Intelligence Oversight Board.

(iii) The Department of Justice.

(iv) The Office of General Counsel of NGA.

(v) The Office of the Director of NGA.

(vi) The Office of the Inspector General of the National-Geospatial Intelligence Agency.

(4)(A) Files that are not exempted under paragraph (1) which contain information derived or disseminated from exempted operational files shall be subject to search and review.

(B) The inclusion of information from exempted operational files in files that are not exempted under paragraph (1) shall not affect the exemption under paragraph (1) of the originating operational files from search, review, publication, or disclosure.

(C) Records from exempted operational files which have been disseminated to and referenced in files that are not exempted under paragraph (1) and which have been returned to exempted operational files for sole retention shall be subject to search and review.

(5) The provisions of paragraph (1) may not be superseded except by a provision of law which is enacted after the date of the enactment of this section, and which specifically cites and repeals or modifies its provisions.

(6)(A) Except as provided in subparagraph (B), whenever any person who has requested agency records under section 552 of title 5, United States Code, alleges that NGA has withheld records improperly because of failure to comply with any provision of this section, judicial review shall be available under the terms set forth in section 552(a)(4)(B) of title 5, United States Code.

(B) Judicial review shall not be available in the manner provided for under subparagraph (A) as follows:

(i) In any case in which information specifically authorized under criteria established by an Executive order to be kept secret in the interests of national defense or foreign relations is filed with, or produced for, the court by NGA, such information shall be examined ex parte, in camera by the court.

(ii) The court shall, to the fullest extent practicable, determine the issues of fact based on sworn written submissions of the parties.

(iii) When a complainant alleges that requested records are improperly withheld because of improper placement solely in exempted operational files, the complainant shall support such allegation with a sworn written submission based upon personal knowledge or otherwise admissible evidence.

(iv)(I) When a complainant alleges that requested records were improperly withheld because of improper exemption of operational files, NGA shall meet its burden under section 552(a)(4)(B) of title 5, United States Code, by demonstrating to the court by sworn written submission that exempted operational files likely to contain responsive records currently perform the functions set forth in paragraph (2).

(II) The court may not order NGA to review the content of any exempted operational file or files in order to make the demonstration required under subclause (I), unless the complainant disputes NGA's showing with a sworn written submission based on personal knowledge or otherwise admissible evidence.

(v) In proceedings under clauses (iii) and (iv), the parties may not obtain discovery pursuant to rules 26 through 36 of the Federal Rules of Civil Procedure, except that requests for admissions may be made pursuant to rules 26 and 36.

(vi) If the court finds under this paragraph that NGA has improperly withheld requested records because of failure to comply with any provision of this subsection, the court shall order NGA to search and review the appropriate exempted operational file or files for the requested records and make such records, or portions thereof, available in accordance with the provisions of section 552 of title 5, United States Code, and such order shall be the exclusive remedy for failure to comply with this subsection.

(vii) If at any time following the filing of a complaint pursuant to this paragraph NGA agrees to search the appropriate exempted operational file or files for the requested records, the court shall dismiss the claim based upon such complaint.

(viii) Any information filed with, or produced for the court pursuant to clauses (i) and (iv) shall be coordinated with the Director of National Intelligence prior to submission to the court.

(b) DECENNIAL REVIEW OF EXEMPTED OPERATIONAL FILES.—

(1) Not less than once every 10 years, the Director of the National Geospatial-Intelligence Agency and the Director of National Intelligence shall review the exemptions in force under subsection (a)(1) to determine whether such exemptions may be removed from the category of exempted files or any portion thereof. The Director of National Intelligence must approve any determination to remove such exemptions.

(2) The review required by paragraph (1)[1] shall include consideration of the

1. In section 701(g)(2), the amendment to strike "of subsection (a) of this section" and insert "paragraph (1)" made by section 922(b)(2)(E) of the National Defense Authorization Act for Fiscal Year 2004 (Public Law 108–136; 117 Stat. 1537) was executed by striking "subsection (a)of this section" and inserting "paragraph (1)" in order to reflect the probable intent of Congress.

historical value or other public interest in the subject matter of the particular category of files or portions thereof and the potential for declassifying a significant part of the information contained therein.

(3) A complainant that alleges that NGA has improperly withheld records because of failure to comply with this subsection may seek judicial review in the district court of the United States of the district in which any of the parties reside, or in the District of Columbia. In such a proceeding, the court's review shall be limited to determining the following:

(A) Whether NGA has conducted the review required by paragraph (1) before the expiration of the 10-year period beginning on the date of the enactment of this section or before the expiration of the 10-year period beginning on the date of the most recent review.

(B) Whether NGA, in fact, considered the criteria set forth in paragraph (2) in conducting the required review.

OPERATIONAL FILES OF THE NATIONAL RECONNAISSANCE OFFICE

SEC. 703. [50 U.S.C. §432a]

(a) EXEMPTION OF CERTAIN OPERATIONAL FILES FROM SEARCH, REVIEW, PUBLICATION, OR DISCLOSURE.—

(1) The Director of the National Reconnaissance Office, with the coordination of the Director of National Intelligence, may exempt operational files of the National Reconnaissance Office from the provisions of section 552 of title 5, United States Code, which require publication, disclosure, search, or review in connection therewith.

(2)(A) Subject to subparagraph (B), for the purposes of this section, the term "operational files" means files of the National Reconnaissance Office (hereafter in this section referred to as "NRO") that document the means by which foreign intelligence or counterintelligence is collected through scientific and technical systems.

(B) Files which are the sole repository of disseminated intelligence are not operational files.

(3) Notwithstanding paragraph (1), exempted operational files shall continue to be subject to search and review for information concerning—

(A) United States citizens or aliens lawfully admitted for permanent residence who have requested information on themselves pursuant to the provisions of section 552 or 552a of title 5, United States Code;

(B) any special activity the existence of which is not exempt from disclosure under the provisions of section 552 of title 5, United States Code; or

(C) the specific subject matter of an investigation by any of the following for any impropriety, or violation of law, Executive order, or Presidential directive, in the conduct of an intelligence activity:

(i) The Permanent Select Committee on Intelligence of the House of Representatives.

(ii) The Select Committee on Intelligence of the Senate.

(iii) The Intelligence Oversight Board.
(iv) The Department of Justice.
(v) The Office of General Counsel of NRO.
(vi) The Office of the Director of NRO.
(vii) The Office of the Inspector General of the NRO.

(4)(A) Files that are not exempted under paragraph (1) which contain information derived or disseminated from exempted operational files shall be subject to search and review.

(B) The inclusion of information from exempted operational files in files that are not exempted under paragraph (1) shall not affect the exemption under paragraph (1) of the originating operational files from search, review, publication, or disclosure.

(C) The declassification of some of the information contained in exempted operational files shall not affect the status of the operational file as being exempt from search, review, publication, or disclosure.

(D) Records from exempted operational files which have been disseminated to and referenced in files that are not exempted under paragraph (1) and which have been returned to exempted operational files for sole retention shall be subject to search and review.

(5) The provisions of paragraph (1) may not be superseded except by a provision of law which is enacted after the date of the enactment of this section, and which specifically cites and repeals or modifies its provisions.

(6)(A) Except as provided in subparagraph (B), whenever any person who has requested agency records under section 552 of title 5, United States Code, alleges that NRO has withheld records improperly because of failure to comply with any provision of this section, judicial review shall be available under the terms set forth in section 552(a)(4)(B) of title 5, United States Code.

(B) Judicial review shall not be available in the manner provided for under subparagraph (A) as follows:

(i) In any case in which information specifically authorized under criteria established by an Executive order to be kept secret in the interests of national defense or foreign relations is filed with, or produced for, the court by NRO, such information shall be examined ex parte, in camera by the court.

(ii) The court shall, to the fullest extent practicable, determine the issues of fact based on sworn written submissions of the parties.

(iii) When a complainant alleges that requested records are improperly withheld because of improper placement solely in exempted operational files, the complainant shall support such allegation with a sworn written submission based upon personal knowledge or otherwise admissible evidence.

(iv)(I) When a complainant alleges that requested records were improperly withheld because of improper exemption of operational files, NRO shall meet its burden under section 552(a)(4)(B) of title 5, United States Code, by demonstrating to the court by sworn written submission that exempted operational files likely to contain responsive records currently perform the functions set forth in paragraph (2).

(II) The court may not order NRO to review the content of any exempted operational file or files in order to make the demonstration required under subclause (I), unless the complainant disputes NRO's showing with a sworn written submission based on personal knowledge or otherwise admissible evidence.

(v) In proceedings under clauses (iii) and (iv), the parties may not obtain discovery pursuant to rules 26 through 36 of the Federal Rules of Civil Procedure, except that requests for admissions may be made pursuant to rules 26 and 36.

(vi) If the court finds under this paragraph that NRO has improperly withheld requested records because of failure to comply with any provision of this subsection, the court shall order NRO to search and review the appropriate exempted operational file or files for the requested records and make such records, or portions thereof, available in accordance with the provisions of section 552 of title 5, United States Code, and such order shall be the exclusive remedy for failure to comply with this subsection.

(vii) If at any time following the filing of a complaint pursuant to this paragraph NRO agrees to search the appropriate exempted operational file or files for the requested records, the court shall dismiss the claim based upon such complaint.

(viii) Any information filed with, or produced for the court pursuant to clauses (i) and (iv) shall be coordinated with the Director of National Intelligence prior to submission to the court.

(b) DECENNIAL REVIEW OF EXEMPTED OPERATIONAL FILES.—

(1) Not less than once every 10 years, the Director of the National Reconnaissance Office and the Director of National Intelligence shall review the exemptions in force under subsection (a)(1) to determine whether such exemptions may be removed from the category of exempted files or any portion thereof. The Director of National Intelligence must approve any determination to remove such exemptions.

(2) The review required by paragraph (1) shall include consideration of the historical value or other public interest in the subject matter of the particular category of files or portions thereof and the potential for declassifying a significant part of the information contained therein.

(3) A complainant that alleges that NRO has improperly withheld records because of failure to comply with this subsection may seek judicial review in the district court of the United States of the district in which any of the parties reside, or in the District of Columbia. In such a proceeding, the court's review shall be limited to determining the following:

(A) Whether NRO has conducted the review required by paragraph (1) before the expiration of the 10-year period beginning on the date of the enactment of this section or before the expiration of the 10-year period beginning on the date of the most recent review.

(B) Whether NRO, in fact, considered the criteria set forth in paragraph (2) in conducting the required review.

OPERATIONAL FILES OF THE NATIONAL SECURITY AGENCY
SEC. 704. [50 U.S.C. §432b]

(a) EXEMPTION OF CERTAIN OPERATIONAL FILES FROM SEARCH, REVIEW, PUBLICATION, OR DISCLOSURE.—The Director of the National Security Agency, in coordination with the Director of National Intelligence, may exempt operational files of the National Security Agency from the provisions of section 552 of title 5, United States Code, which require publication, disclosure, search, or review in connection therewith.

(b) OPERATIONAL FILES DEFINED.—

(1) In this section, the term "operational files" means—

(A) files of the Signals Intelligence Directorate of the National Security Agency (and any successor organization of that directorate) that document the means by which foreign intelligence or counterintelligence is collected through technical systems; and

(B) files of the Research Associate Directorate of the National Security Agency (and any successor organization of that directorate) that document the means by which foreign intelligence or counterintelligence is collected through scientific and technical systems.

(2) Files that are the sole repository of disseminated intelligence, and files that have been accessioned into the National Security Agency Archives (or any successor organization) are not operational files.

(c) SEARCH AND REVIEW FOR INFORMATION.—Notwithstanding subsection (a), exempted operational files shall continue to be subject to search and review for information concerning any of the following:

(1) United States citizens or aliens lawfully admitted for permanent residence who have requested information on themselves pursuant to the provisions of section 552 or 552a of title 5, United States Code.

(2) Any special activity the existence of which is not exempt from disclosure under the provisions of section 552 of title 5, United States Code.

(3) The specific subject matter of an investigation by any of the following for any impropriety, or violation of law, Executive order, or Presidential directive, in the conduct of an intelligence activity:

(A) The Committee on Armed Services and the Permanent Select Committee on Intelligence of the House of Representatives.

(B) The Committee on Armed Services and the Select Committee on Intelligence of the Senate.

(C) The Intelligence Oversight Board.

(D) The Department of Justice.

(E) The Office of General Counsel of the National Security Agency.

(F) The Office of the Inspector General of the Department of Defense.

(G) The Office of the Director of the National Security Agency.

(H) The Office of the Inspector General of the National Security Agency.

(d) INFORMATION DERIVED OR DISSEMINATED FROM EXEMPTED OPERATIONAL FILES.—

(1) Files that are not exempted under subsection (a) that contain information derived or disseminated from exempted operational files shall be subject to search and review.

(2) The inclusion of information from exempted operational files in files that are not exempted under subsection (a) shall not affect the exemption under subsection (a) of the originating operational files from search, review, publication, or disclosure.

(3) The declassification of some of the information contained in exempted operational files shall not affect the status of the operational file as being exempt from search, review, publication, or disclosure.

(4) Records from exempted operational files that have been disseminated to and referenced in files that are not exempted under subsection (a) and that have been returned to exempted operational files for sole retention shall be subject to search and review.

(e) SUPERCEDURE OF OTHER LAWS.—The provisions of subsection (a) may not be superseded except by a provision of law that is enacted after the date of the enactment of this section and that specifically cites and repeals or modifies such provisions.

(f) ALLEGATION; IMPROPER WITHHOLDING OF RECORDS; JUDICIAL REVIEW.—

(1) Except as provided in paragraph (2), whenever any person who has requested agency records under section 552 of title 5, United States Code, alleges that the National Security Agency has withheld records improperly because of failure to comply with any provision of this section, judicial review shall be available under the terms set forth in section 552(a)(4)(B) of title 5, United States Code.

(2) Judicial review shall not be available in the manner provided for under paragraph (1) as follows:

(A) In any case in which information specifically authorized under criteria established by an Executive order to be kept secret in the interests of national defense or foreign relations is filed with, or produced for, the court by the National Security Agency, such information shall be examined ex parte, in camera by the court.

(B) The court shall determine, to the fullest extent practicable, the issues of fact based on sworn written submissions of the parties.

(C) When a complainant alleges that requested records are improperly withheld because of improper placement solely in exempted operational files, the complainant shall support such allegation with a sworn written submission based upon personal knowledge or otherwise admissible evidence. (D)(i) When a complainant alleges that requested records were improperly withheld because of improper exemption of operational files, the National Security Agency shall meet its burden under section 552(a)(4)(B) of title 5, United States Code, by demonstrating to the court by sworn written submission that exempted operational files likely to contain responsive records currently perform the functions set forth in subsection (b).

(ii) The court may not order the National Security Agency to review the content of any exempted operational file or files in order to make the demonstration required under clause (i), unless the complainant disputes the National Security Agency's showing with a sworn written submission based on personal knowledge or otherwise admissible evidence.

(E) In proceedings under subparagraphs (C) and (D), the parties may not obtain discovery pursuant to rules 26 through 36 of the Federal Rules of Civil Procedure, except that requests for admissions may be made pursuant to rules 26 and 36.

(F) If the court finds under this subsection that the National Security Agency has improperly withheld requested records because of failure to comply with any provision of this subsection, the court shall order the Agency to search and review the appropriate exempted operational file or files for the requested records and make such records, or portions thereof, available in accordance with the provisions of section 552 of title 5, United States Code, and such order shall be the exclusive remedy for failure to comply with this section (other than subsection (g)).

(G) If at any time following the filing of a complaint pursuant to this paragraph the National Security Agency agrees to search the appropriate exempted operational file or files for the requested records, the court shall dismiss the claim based upon such complaint.

(H) Any information filed with, or produced for the court pursuant to subparagraphs (A) and (D) shall be coordinated with the Director of National Intelligence before submission to the court.

(g) DECENNIAL REVIEW OF EXEMPTED OPERATIONAL FILES.—

(1) Not less than once every 10 years, the Director of the National Security Agency and the Director of National Intelligence shall review the exemptions in force under subsection (a) to determine whether such exemptions may be removed from a category of exempted files or any portion thereof. The Director of National Intelligence must approve any determination to remove such exemptions.

(2) The review required by paragraph (1) shall include consideration of the historical value or other public interest in the subject matter of a particular category of files or portions thereof and the potential for declassifying a significant part of the information contained therein.

(3) A complainant that alleges that the National Security Agency has improperly withheld records because of failure to comply with this subsection may seek judicial review in the district court of the United States of the district in which any of the parties reside, or in the District of Columbia. In such a proceeding, the court's review shall be limited to determining the following:

(A) Whether the National Security Agency has conducted the review required by paragraph (1) before the expiration of the 10-year period beginning on the date of the enactment of this section or before the expiration of the 10-year period beginning on the date of the most recent review.

(B) Whether the National Security Agency, in fact, considered the criteria set forth in paragraph (2) in conducting the required review.

OPERATIONAL FILES OF THE DEFENSE INTELLIGENCE AGENCY
SEC. 705. [50 U.S.C. §432c]

(a) EXEMPTION OF OPERATIONAL FILES. —The Director of the Defense Intelligence Agency, in coordination with the Director of National Intelligence, may exempt operational files of the Defense Intelligence Agency from the provisions of section 552 of title 5, United States Code, which require publication, disclosure, search, or review in connection therewith.

(b) OPERATIONAL FILES DEFINED. —

(1) In this section, the term "operational files" means—

(A) files of the Directorate of Human Intelligence of the Defense Intelligence Agency (and any successor organization of that directorate) that document the conduct of foreign intelligence or counterintelligence operations or intelligence or security liaison arrangements or information exchanges with foreign governments or their intelligence or security services; and

(B) files of the Directorate of Technology of the Defense Intelligence Agency (and any successor organization of that directorate) that document the means by which foreign intelligence or counterintelligence is collected through technical systems.

(2) Files that are the sole repository of disseminated intelligence are not operational files.

(c) SEARCH AND REVIEW FOR INFORMATION. —Notwithstanding subsection (a), exempted operational files shall continue to be subject to search and review for information concerning:

(1) United States citizens or aliens lawfully admitted for permanent residence who have requested information on themselves pursuant to the provisions of section 552 or 552a of title 5, United States Code.

(2) Any special activity the existence of which is not exempt from disclosure under the provisions of section 552 of title 5, United States Code.

(3) The specific subject matter of an investigation by any of the following for any impropriety, or violation of law, Executive order, or Presidential directive, in the conduct of an intelligence activity:

(A) The Committee on Armed Services and the Permanent Select Committee on Intelligence of the House of Representatives.

(B) The Committee on Armed Services and the Select Committee on Intelligence of the Senate.

(C) The Intelligence Oversight Board.

(D) The Department of Justice.

(E) The Office of General Counsel of the Department of Defense or of the Defense Intelligence Agency.

(F) The Office of Inspector General of the Department of Defense or of the Defense Intelligence Agency.

(G) The Office of the Director of the Defense Intelligence Agency.

(d) INFORMATION DERIVED OR DISSEMINATED FROM EXEMPTED OPERATIONAL FILES.—

(1) Files that are not exempted under subsection (a) that contain information derived or disseminated from exempted operational files shall be subject to search and review.

(2) The inclusion of information from exempted operational files in files that are not exempted under subsection (a) shall not affect the exemption under subsection (a) of the originating operational files from search, review, publication, or disclosure.

(3) The declassification of some of the information contained in an exempted operational file shall not affect the status of the operational file as being exempt from search, review, publication, or disclosure.

(4) Records from exempted operational files that have been disseminated to and referenced in files that are not exempted under subsection (a) and that have been returned to exempted operational files for sole retention shall be subject to search and review.

(e) ALLEGATION; IMPROPER WITHHOLDING OF RECORDS; JUDICIAL REVIEW. —

(1) Except as provided in paragraph (2), whenever any person who has requested agency records under section 552 of title 5, United States Code, alleges that the Defense Intelligence Agency has withheld records improperly because of failure to comply with any provision of this section, judicial review shall be available under the terms set forth in section 552(a)(4)(B) of title 5, United States Code.

(2) Judicial review shall not be available in the manner provided under paragraph (1) as follows:

(A) In any case in which information specifically authorized under criteria established by an Executive order to be kept secret in the interest of national defense or foreign relations which is filed with, or produced for, the court by the Defense Intelligence Agency, such information shall be examined ex parte, in camera by the court.

(B) The court shall determine, to the fullest extent practicable, issues of fact based on sworn written submissions of the parties.

(C) When a complainant alleges that requested records were improperly withheld because of improper placement solely in exempted operational files, the complainant shall support such allegation with a sworn written submission based upon personal knowledge or otherwise admissible evidence.

(D)(i) When a complainant alleges that requested records were improperly withheld because of improper exemption of operational files, the Defense Intelligence Agency shall meet its burden under section 552(a)(4)(B) of title 5, United States Code, by demonstrating to the court by sworn written submission that exempted operational files likely to contain responsible records currently perform the functions set forth in subsection (b).

(ii) The court may not order the Defense Intelligence Agency to review the content of any exempted operational file or files in order to make the demonstration required under clause (i), unless the complainant disputes the Defense Intelligence Agency's showing with a sworn written submission based on personal knowledge or otherwise admissible evidence.

(E) In proceedings under subparagraphs (C) and (D), the parties shall not obtain discovery pursuant to rules 26 through 36 of the Federal Rules of Civil Procedure, except that requests for admission may be made pursuant to rules 26 and 36.

(F) If the court finds under this subsection that the Defense Intelligence Agency has improperly withheld requested records because of failure to comply with any provision of this subsection, the court shall order the Defense Intelligence Agency to search and review the appropriate exempted operational file or files for the requested records and make such records, or portions thereof, available in accordance with the provisions of section 552 of title 5, United States Code, and such order shall be the exclusive remedy for failure to comply with this section (other than subsection (f)).

(G) If at any time following the filing of a complaint pursuant to this paragraph the Defense Intelligence Agency agrees to search the appropriate exempted operational file or files for the requested records, the court shall dismiss the claim based upon such complaint.

(H) Any information filed with, or produced for the court pursuant to subparagraphs (A) and (D) shall be coordinated with the Director of National Intelligence before submission to the court.

(f) DECENNIAL REVIEW OF EXEMPTED OPERATIONAL FILES. —

(1) Not less than once every 10 years, the Director of the Defense Intelligence Agency and the Director of National Intelligence shall review the exemptions in force under subsection (a) to determine whether such exemptions may be removed from a category of exempted files or any portion thereof. The Director of National Intelligence must approve any determinations to remove such exemptions.

(2) The review required by paragraph (1) shall include consideration of the historical value or other public interest in the subject matter of the particular category of files or portions thereof and the potential for declassifying a significant part of the information contained therein.

(3) A complainant that alleges that the Defense Intelligence Agency has improperly withheld records because of failure to comply with this subsection may seek judicial review in the district court of the United States of the district in which any of the parties reside, or in the District of Columbia. In such a proceeding, the court's review shall be limited to determining the following:

(A) Whether the Defense Intelligence Agency has conducted the review required by paragraph (1) before the expiration of the 10year period beginning on the date of the enactment of this section or before the expiration of the 10-year period beginning on the date of the most recent review.

(B) Whether the Defense Intelligence Agency, in fact, considered the criteria set forth in paragraph (2) in conducting the required review.

(g) TERMINATION.—This section shall cease to be effective on December 31, 2007.

PROTECTION OF CERTAIN FILES OF THE OFFICE OF THE DIRECTOR OF NATIONAL INTELLIGENCE

SEC. 706. [50 U.S.C. 432d]

(a) INAPPLICABILITY OF FOIA TO EXEMPTED OPERATIONAL FILES PROVIDED TO ODNI.—

(1) Subject to paragraph (2), the provisions of section 552 of title 5, United States Code, that require search, review, publication, or disclosure of a record shall not apply to a record provided to the Office of the Director of National Intelligence by an element of the intelligence community from the exempted operational files of such element.

(2) Paragraph (1) shall not apply with respect to a record of the Office that—

(A) contains information derived or disseminated from an exempted operational file, unless such record is created by the Office for the sole purpose of organizing such exempted operational file for use by the Office;

(B) is disseminated by the Office to a person other than an officer, employee, or contractor of the Office; or

(C) is no longer designated as an exempted operational file in accordance with this title.

(b) EFFECT OF PROVIDING FILES TO ODNI.—Notwithstanding any other provision of this title, an exempted operational file that is provided to the Office by an element of the intelligence community shall not be subject to the provisions of section 552 of title 5, United States Code, that require search, review, publication, or disclosure of a record solely because such element provides such exempted operational file to the Office.

(c) SEARCH AND REVIEW FOR CERTAIN PURPOSES.—Notwithstanding subsection (a) or (b), an exempted operational file shall continue to be subject to search and review for information concerning any of the following:

(1) United States citizens or aliens lawfully admitted for permanent residence who have requested information on themselves pursuant to the provisions of section 552 or 552a of title 5, United States Code.

(2) Any special activity the existence of which is not exempt from disclosure under the provisions of section 552 of title 5, United States Code.

(3) The specific subject matter of an investigation for any impropriety or violation of law, Executive order, or Presidential directive, in the conduct of an intelligence activity by any of the following:

(A) The Select Committee on Intelligence of the Senate.

(B) The Permanent Select Committee on Intelligence of the House of Representatives.

(C) The Intelligence Oversight Board.

(D) The Department of Justice.

(E) The Office of the Director of National Intelligence.
(F) The Office of the Inspector General of the Intelligence Community.

(d) DECENNIAL REVIEW OF EXEMPTED OPERATIONAL FILES.—

(1) Not less than once every 10 years, the Director of National Intelligence shall review the exemptions in force under subsection (a) to determine whether such exemptions may be removed from any category of exempted files or any portion thereof.

(2) The review required by paragraph (1) shall include consideration of the historical value or other public interest in the subject matter of the particular category of files or portions thereof and the potential for declassifying a significant part of the information contained therein.

(3) A complainant that alleges that the Director of National Intelligence has improperly withheld records because of failure to comply with this subsection may seek judicial review in the district court of the United States of the district in which any of the parties reside, or in the District of Columbia. In such a proceeding, the court's review shall be limited to determining the following:

(A) Whether the Director has conducted the review required by paragraph (1) before the expiration of the 10year period beginning on the date of the enactment of the Intelligence Authorization Act for Fiscal Year 2010 or before the expiration of the 10year period beginning on the date of the most recent review.

(B) Whether the Director of National Intelligence, in fact, considered the criteria set forth in paragraph (2) in conducting the required review.

(e) SUPERSEDURE OF OTHER LAWS.—The provisions of this section may not be superseded except by a provision of law that is enacted after the date of the enactment of this section and that specifically cites and repeals or modifies such provisions.

(f) ALLEGATION; IMPROPER WITHHOLDING OF RECORDS; JUDICIAL REVIEW.—

(1) Except as provided in paragraph (2), whenever any person who has requested agency records under section 552 of title 5, United States Code, alleges that the Office has withheld records improperly because of failure to comply with any provision of this section, judicial review shall be available under the terms set forth in section 552(a)(4)(B) of title 5, United States Code.

(2) Judicial review shall not be available in the manner provided for under paragraph (1) as follows:

(A) In any case in which information specifically authorized under criteria established by an Executive order to be kept secret in the interests of national defense or foreign relations is filed with, or produced for, the court by the Office, such information shall be examined ex parte, in camera by the court.

(B) The court shall determine, to the fullest extent practicable, the issues of fact based on sworn written submissions of the parties.

(C)(i) When a complainant alleges that requested records were improperly withheld because of improper exemption of operational files, the Office may meet the burden of the Office under section 552(a)(4)(B) of title 5, United States Code, by demonstrating to the court by sworn written submission that exempted files likely to contain responsive records are records provided to the Office by an element of the intelligence community from the exempted operational files of such element.

(ii) The court may not order the Office to review the content of any exempted file in order to make the demonstration required under clause (i), unless the complainant disputes the Office's showing with a sworn written submission based on personal knowledge or otherwise admissible evidence.

(D) In proceedings under subparagraph (C), a party may not obtain discovery pursuant to rules 26 through 36 of the Federal Rules of Civil Procedure, except that requests for admissions may be made pursuant to rules 26 and 36 of the Federal Rules of Civil Procedure.

(E) If the court finds under this subsection that the Office has improperly withheld requested records because of failure to comply with any provision of this section, the court shall order the Office to search and review each appropriate exempted file for the requested records and make such records, or portions thereof, available in accordance with the provisions of section 552 of title 5, United States Code (commonly referred to as the Freedom of Information Act), and such order shall be the exclusive remedy for failure to comply with this section.

(F) If at any time following the filing of a complaint pursuant to this paragraph the Office agrees to search each appropriate exempted file for the requested records, the court shall dismiss the claim based upon such complaint.

(g) DEFINITIONS.—In this section:

(1) The term "exempted operational file" means a file of an element of the intelligence community that, in accordance with this title, is exempted from the provisions of section 552 of title 5, United States Code, that require search, review, publication, or disclosure of such file.

(2) Except as otherwise specifically provided, the term "Office" means the Office of the Director of National Intelligence.

TITLE VIII—ACCESS TO CLASSIFIED INFORMATION PROCEDURES

PROCEDURES

SEC. 801. [50 U.S.C 435]

(a) Not later than 180 days after the date of enactment of this title, the President shall, by Executive order or regulation, establish procedures to govern access to classified information which shall be binding upon all departments, agencies, and offices of the executive branch of Government. Such procedures shall, at a minimum—

(1) provide that, except as may be permitted by the President, no employee in the executive branch of Government may be given access to classified infor-

mation by any department, agency, or office of the executive branch of Government unless, based upon an appropriate background investigation, such access is determined to be clearly consistent with the national security interests of the United States;

(2) establish uniform minimum requirements governing the scope and frequency of background investigations and reinvestigations for all employees in the executive branch of Government who require access to classified information as part of their official responsibilities;

(3) provide that all employees in the executive branch of Government who require access to classified information shall be required as a condition of such access to provide to the employing department or agency written consent which permits access by an authorized investigative agency to relevant financial records, other financial information, consumer reports, travel records, and computers used in the performance of Government duties, as determined by the President, in accordance with section 802 of this title, during the period of access to classified information and for a period of three years thereafter;

(4) provide that all employees in the executive branch of Government who require access to particularly sensitive classified information, as determined by the President, shall be required, as a condition of maintaining access to such information, to submit to the employing department or agency, during the period of such access, relevant information concerning their financial condition and foreign travel, as determined by the President, as may be necessary to ensure appropriate security; and

(5) establish uniform minimum standards to ensure that employees in the executive branch of Government whose access to classified information is being denied or terminated under this title are appropriately advised of the reasons for such denial or termination and are provided an adequate opportunity to respond to all adverse information which forms the basis for such denial or termination before final action by the department or agency concerned.

(b)(1) Subsection (a) shall not be deemed to limit or affect the responsibility and power of an agency head pursuant to other law or Executive order to deny or terminate access to classified information if the national security so requires. Such responsibility and power may be exercised only when the agency head determines that the procedures prescribed by subsection (a) cannot be invoked in a manner that is consistent with the national security.

(2) Upon the exercise of such responsibility, the agency head shall submit a report to the congressional intelligence committees.

REQUESTS BY AUTHORIZED INVESTIGATIVE AGENCIES

SEC. 802. [50 U.S.C. §436]

(a)(1) Any authorized investigative agency may request from any financial agency, financial institution, or holding company, or from any consumer reporting agency, such financial records, other financial information, and consumer reports as may be necessary in order to conduct any authorized law enforcement investigation, counterintelligence inquiry, or security determination. Any authorized investigative agency may also request records maintained by any commercial entity within the United States pertaining to travel by an employee in the executive branch of Government outside the United States.

(2) Requests may be made under this section where—

(A) the records sought pertain to a person who is or was an employee in the executive branch of Government required by the President in an Executive order or regulation, as a condition of access to classified information, to provide consent, during a background investigation and for such time as access to the information is maintained, and for a period of not more than three years thereafter, permitting access to financial records, other financial information, consumer reports, and travel records; and

(B)(i) there are reasonable grounds to believe, based on credible information, that the person is, or may be, disclosing classified information in an unauthorized manner to a foreign power or agent of a foreign power;

(ii) information the employing agency deems credible indicates the person has incurred excessive indebtedness or has acquired a level of affluence which cannot be explained by other information known to the agency; or

(iii) circumstances indicate the person had the capability and opportunity to disclose classified information which is known to have been lost or compromised to a foreign power or an agent of a foreign power.

(3) Each such request—

(A) shall be accompanied by a written certification signed by the department or agency head or deputy department or agency head concerned, or by a senior official designated for this purpose by the department or agency head concerned (whose rank shall be no lower than Assistant Secretary or Assistant Director), and shall certify that—

(i) the person concerned is or was an employee within the meaning of paragraph (2)(A);

(ii) the request is being made pursuant to an authorized inquiry or investigation and is authorized under this section; and

(iii) the records or information to be reviewed are records or information which the employee has previously agreed to make available to the authorized investigative agency for review;

(B) shall contain a copy of the agreement referred to in subparagraph (A)(iii);

(C) shall identify specifically or by category the records or information to be reviewed; and

(D) shall inform the recipient of the request of the prohibition described in subsection (b).

(b) Prohibition of Certain Disclosure—

(1) If an authorized investigative agency described in subsection (a) certifies that otherwise there may result a danger to the national security of the United States, interference with a criminal, counterterrorism, or counterintelligence investigation, interference with diplomatic relations, or danger to the life or physical safety of any person, no governmental or private entity, or officer, em-

ployee, or agent of such entity, may disclose to any person (other than those to whom such disclosure is necessary to comply with the request or an attorney to obtain legal advice or legal assistance with respect to the request) that such entity has received or satisfied a request made by an authorized investigative agency under this section.

(2) The request shall notify the person or entity to whom the request is directed of the nondisclosure requirement under paragraph (1).

(3) Any recipient disclosing to those persons necessary to comply with the request or to an attorney to obtain legal advice or legal assistance with respect to the request shall inform such persons of any applicable nondisclosure requirement. Any person who receives a disclosure under this subsection shall be subject to the same prohibitions on disclosure under paragraph (1).

(4) At the request of the authorized investigative agency, any person making or intending to make a disclosure under this section shall identify to the requesting official of the authorized investigative agency the person to whom such disclosure will be made or to whom such disclosure was made prior to the request, except that nothing in this section shall require a person to inform the requesting official of the identity of an attorney to whom disclosure was made or will be made to obtain legal advice or legal assistance with respect to the request under subsection (a).

(c)(1) Notwithstanding any other provision of law (other than section 6103 of the Internal Revenue Code of 1986), an entity receiving a request for records or information under subsection (a) shall, if the request satisfies the requirements of this section, make available such records or information within 30 days for inspection or copying, as may be appropriate, by the agency requesting such records or information.

(2) Any entity (including any officer, employee, or agent thereof) that discloses records or information for inspection or copying pursuant to this section in good faith reliance upon the certifications made by an agency pursuant to this section shall not be liable for any such disclosure to any person under this title, the constitution of any State, or any law or regulation of any State or any political subdivision of any State.

(d) Any agency requesting records or information under this section may, subject to the availability of appropriations, reimburse a private entity for any cost reasonably incurred by such entity in responding to such request, including the cost of identifying, reproducing, or transporting records or other data.

(e) An agency receiving records or information pursuant to a request under this section may disseminate the records or information obtained pursuant to such request outside the agency only—

(1) to the agency employing the employee who is the subject of the records or information;

(2) to the Department of Justice for law enforcement or counterintelligence purposes; or

(3) with respect to dissemination to an agency of the United States, if such information is clearly relevant to the authorized responsibilities of such agency.

(f) Nothing in this section may be construed to affect the authority of an investigative agency to obtain information pursuant to the Right to Financial Privacy Act (12 U.S.C. §3401 et seq.) or the Fair Credit Reporting Act (15 U.S.C. §1681 et seq.).

EXCEPTIONS

SEC. 803. [50 U.S.C. §437]

Except as otherwise specifically provided, the provisions of this title shall not apply to the President and Vice President, Members of the Congress, Justices of the Supreme Court, and Federal judges appointed by the President.

DEFINITIONS

SEC. 804. [50 U.S.C. §438]

For purposes of this title—

(1) the term "authorized investigative agency" means an agency authorized by law or regulation to conduct a counterintelligence investigation or investigations of persons who are proposed for access to classified information to ascertain whether such persons satisfy the criteria for obtaining and retaining access to such information;

(2) the term "classified information" means any information that has been determined pursuant to Executive Order No. 12356 of April 2, 1982, or successor orders, or the Atomic Energy Act of 1954, to require protection against unauthorized disclosure and that is so designated;

(3) the term "consumer reporting agency" has the meaning given such term in section 603 of the Consumer Credit Protection Act (15 U.S.C. §1681a);

(4) the term "employee" includes any person who receives a salary or compensation of any kind from the United States Government, is a contractor of the United States Government or an employee thereof, is an unpaid consultant of the United States Government, or otherwise acts for or on behalf of the United States Government, except as otherwise determined by the President;

(5) the terms "financial agency" and "financial institution" have the meanings given to such terms in section 5312(a) of title 31, United States Code, and the term "holding company" has the meaning given to such term in section 1101(6) of the Right to Financial Privacy Act of 1978 (12 U.S.C. §3401);

(6) the terms "foreign power" and "agent of a foreign power" have the same meanings as set forth in sections 101 (a) and (b), respectively, of the Foreign Intelligence Surveillance Act of 1978 (50 U.S.C. §1801);

(7) the term "State" means each of the several States of the United States, the District of Columbia, the Commonwealth of Puerto Rico, the Commonwealth of the Northern Mariana Islands, the United States Virgin Islands, Guam, American Samoa, the Republic of the Marshall Islands, the Federated States of Micronesia, and the Republic of Palau, and any other possession of the United States; and

(8) the term "computer" means any electronic, magnetic, optical, electrochemical, or other high speed data processing device performing logical, arithmetic, or storage functions, and includes any data storage facility or communications

facility directly related to or operating in conjunction with such device and any data or other information stored or contained in such device.

TITLE IX—APPLICATION OF SANCTIONS LAWS TO INTELLIGENCE ACTIVITIES

STAY OF SANCTIONS

SEC. 901. [50 U.S.C. §441]

Notwithstanding any provision of law identified in section 904, the President may stay the imposition of an economic, cultural, diplomatic, or other sanction or related action by the United States Government concerning a foreign country, organization, or person when the President determines and reports to Congress in accordance with section 903 that to proceed without delay would seriously risk the compromise of an ongoing criminal investigation directly related to the activities giving rise to the sanction or an intelligence source or method directly related to the activities giving rise to the sanction. Any such stay shall be effective for a period of time specified by the President, which period may not exceed 120 days, unless such period is extended in accordance with section 902.

EXTENSION OF STAY

SEC. 902. [50 U.S.C. §441a]

Whenever the President determines and reports to Congress in accordance with section 903 that a stay of sanctions or related actions pursuant to section 901 has not afforded sufficient time to obviate the risk to an ongoing criminal investigation or to an intelligence source or method that gave rise to the stay, he may extend such stay for a period of time specified by the President, which period may not exceed 120 days. The authority of this section may be used to extend the period of a stay pursuant to section 901 for successive periods of not more than 120 days each.

REPORTS

SEC. 903. [50 U.S.C. §441b]

Reports to Congress pursuant to sections 901 and 902 shall be submitted promptly upon determinations under this title. Such reports shall be submitted to the Committee on International Relations of the House of Representatives and the Committee on Foreign Relations of the Senate. With respect to determinations relating to intelligence sources and methods, reports shall also be submitted to the congressional intelligence committees. With respect to determinations relating to ongoing criminal investigations, reports shall also be submitted to the Committees on the Judiciary of the House of Representatives and the Senate.

LAWS SUBJECT TO STAY

SEC. 904. [50 U.S.C. §441c]

The President may use the authority of sections 901 and 902 to stay the imposition of an economic, cultural, diplomatic, or other sanction or related action by the United States Government related to the proliferation of weapons of mass destruction, their delivery systems, or advanced conventional weapons otherwise required to be imposed by the Chemical and Biological Weapons Control and Warfare Elimination

Act of 1991 (title III of Public Law 102–182); the Nuclear Proliferation Prevention Act of 1994 (title VIII of Public Law 103– 236); title XVII of the National Defense Authorization Act for Fiscal Year 1991 (Public Law 101–510) (relating to the non-proliferation of missile technology); the Iran-Iraq Arms Nonproliferation Act of 1992 (title XVI of Public Law 102– 484); section 573 of the Foreign Operations, Export Financing Related Programs Appropriations Act, 1994 (Public Law 103–87); section 563 of the Foreign Operations, Export Financing Related Programs Appropriations Act, 1995 (Public Law 103–306); and comparable provisions.

TITLE X—EDUCATION IN SUPPORT OF NATIONAL INTELLIGENCE

SUBTITLE A—SCIENCE AND TECHNOLOGY

SCHOLARSHIPS AND WORK-STUDY FOR PURSUIT OF GRADUATE DEGREES IN SCIENCE AND TECHNOLOGY

SEC. 1001. [50 U.S.C. §441g]
(a) PROGRAM AUTHORIZED.—The Director of National Intelligence may carry out a program to provide scholarships and work-study for individuals who are pursuing graduate degrees in fields of study in science and technology that are identified by the Director as appropriate to meet the future needs of the intelligence community for qualified scientists and engineers.
(b) ADMINISTRATION.—If the Director of National Intelligence carries out the program under subsection (a), the Director shall administer the program through the Office of the Director of National Intelligence.
(c) IDENTIFICATION OF FIELDS OF STUDY.—If the Director of National Intelligence carries out the program under subsection (a), the Director shall identify fields of study under subsection (a) in consultation with the other heads of the elements of the intelligence community.
(d) ELIGIBILITY FOR PARTICIPATION.—An individual eligible to participate in the program is any individual who—

(1) either—

(A) is an employee of the intelligence community; or

(B) meets criteria for eligibility for employment in the intelligence community that are established by the Director of National Intelligence;

(2) is accepted in a graduate degree program in a field of study in science or technology identified under subsection (a); and

(3) is eligible for a security clearance at the level of Secret or above.

(e) REGULATIONS.—If the Director of National Intelligence carries out the program under subsection (a), the Director shall prescribe regulations for purposes of the administration of this section.

FRAMEWORK FOR CROSS-DISCIPLINARY EDUCATION AND TRAINING

SEC. 1002. [50 U.S.C. §441g-1] The Director of National Intelligence shall establish an integrated framework that brings together the educational components of the intelligence community in order to promote a more effective and productive intelligence community through cross-disciplinary education and joint training.

SUBTITLE B – FOREIGN LANGUAGES PROGRAM

PROGRAM ON ADVANCEMENT OF FOREIGN LANGUAGES CRITICAL TO THE INTELLIGENCE COMMUNITY

SEC. 1011. [50 U.S.C. §441j]

(a) IN GENERAL.—The Secretary of Defense and the Director of National Intelligence may jointly carry out a program to advance skills in foreign languages that are critical to the capability of the intelligence community to carry out the national security activities of the United States (hereinafter in this subtitle referred to as the Foreign Languages Program').

(b) IDENTIFICATION OF REQUISITE ACTIONS.—In order to carry out the Foreign Languages Program, the Secretary of Defense and the Director of National Intelligence shall jointly identify actions required to improve the education of personnel in the intelligence community in foreign languages that are critical to the capability of the intelligence community to carry out the national security activities of the United States and to meet the long-term intelligence needs of the United States.

EDUCATION PARTNERSHIPS

SEC. 1012. [50 U.S.C. §441j-1]

(a) IN GENERAL.—In carrying out the Foreign Languages Program, the head of a covered element of the intelligence community may enter into one or more education partnership agreements with educational institutions in the United States in order to encourage and enhance the study in such educational institutions of foreign languages that are critical to the capability of the intelligence community to carry out the national security activities of the United States.

(b) ASSISTANCE PROVIDED UNDER EDUCATIONAL PARTNERSHIP AGREEMENTS.—Under an educational partnership agreement entered into with an educational institution pursuant to this section, the head of a covered element of the intelligence community may provide the following assistance to the educational institution:

(1) The loan of equipment and instructional materials of the element of the intelligence community to the educational institution for any purpose and duration that the head of the element considers appropriate.

(2) Notwithstanding any other provision of law relating to the transfer of surplus property, the transfer to the educational institution of any computer equipment, or other equipment, that is—

(A) commonly used by educational institutions;

(B) surplus to the needs of the element of the intelligence community; and

(C) determined by the head of the element to be appropriate for support of such agreement.

(3) The provision of dedicated personnel to the educational institution—

(A) to teach courses in foreign languages that are critical to the capability of the intelligence community to carry out the national security activities of the United States; or

(B) to assist in the development for the educational institution of courses and materials on such languages.

(4) The involvement of faculty and students of the educational institution in research projects of the element of the intelligence community.

(5) Cooperation with the educational institution in developing a program under which students receive academic credit at the educational institution for work on research projects of the element of the intelligence community.

(6) The provision of academic and career advice and assistance to students of the educational institution.

(7) The provision of cash awards and other items that the head of the element of the intelligence community considers appropriate.

VOLUNTARY SERVICES

SEC. 1013. [50 U.S.C. §441j-2]

(a) AUTHORITY TO ACCEPT SERVICES.—Notwithstanding section 1342 of title 31, United States Code, and subject to subsection (b), the Foreign Languages Program under section 1011 shall include authority for the head of a covered element of the intelligence community to accept from any dedicated personnel voluntary services in support of the activities authorized by this subtitle.

(b) REQUIREMENTS AND LIMITATIONS.—

(1) In accepting voluntary services from an individual under subsection (a), the head of a covered element of the intelligence community shall—

(A) supervise the individual to the same extent as the head of the element would supervise a compensated employee of that element providing similar services; and

(B) ensure that the individual is licensed, privileged, has appropriate educational or experiential credentials, or is otherwise qualified under applicable law or regulations to provide such services.

(2) In accepting voluntary services from an individual under subsection (a), the head of a covered element of the intelligence community may not—

(A) place the individual in a policymaking position, or other position performing inherently governmental functions; or

(B) compensate the individual for the provision of such services.

(c) AUTHORITY TO RECRUIT AND TRAIN INDIVIDUALS PROVIDING SERVICES.— The head of a covered element of the intelligence community may recruit and train individuals to provide voluntary services under subsection (a).

(d) STATUS OF INDIVIDUALS PROVIDING SERVICES.—

(1) Subject to paragraph (2), while providing voluntary services under subsection (a) or receiving training under subsection (c), an individual shall be considered to be an employee of the Federal Government only for purposes of the following provisions of law:

(A) Section 552a of title 5, United States Code (relating to maintenance of records on individuals).

(B) Chapter 11 of title 18, United States Code (relating to conflicts of interest).

(2)(A) With respect to voluntary services under paragraph (1) provided by an individual that are within the scope of the services accepted under that paragraph, the individual shall be deemed to be a volunteer of a governmental entity or nonprofit institution for purposes of the Volunteer Protection Act of 1997 (42 U.S.C. §14501 et seq.).

(B) In the case of any claim against such an individual with respect to the provision of such services, section 4(d) of such Act (42 U.S.C. §14503(d)) shall not apply.

(3) Acceptance of voluntary services under this section shall have no bearing on the issuance or renewal of a security clearance.

(e) REIMBURSEMENT OF INCIDENTAL EXPENSES.—

(1) The head of a covered element of the intelligence community may reimburse an individual for incidental expenses incurred by the individual in providing voluntary services under subsection (a). The head of a covered element of the intelligence community shall determine which expenses are eligible for reimbursement under this subsection.

(2) Reimbursement under paragraph (1) may be made from appropriated or nonappropriated funds.

(f) AUTHORITY TO INSTALL EQUIPMENT.—

(1) The head of a covered element of the intelligence community may install telephone lines and any necessary telecommunication equipment in the private residences of individuals who provide voluntary services under subsection (a).

(2) The head of a covered element of the intelligence community may pay the charges incurred for the use of equipment installed under paragraph (1) for authorized purposes.

(3) Notwithstanding section 1348 of title 31, United States Code, the head of a covered element of the intelligence community may use appropriated funds or nonappropriated funds of the element in carrying out this subsection.

REGULATIONS

SEC. 1014. [50 U.S.C. §441j-3]

(a) IN GENERAL.—The Secretary of Defense and the Director of National Intelligence shall jointly prescribe regulations to carry out the Foreign Languages Program.

(b) ELEMENTS OF THE INTELLIGENCE COMMUNITY.—The head of each covered element of the intelligence community shall prescribe regulations to carry out sections 1012 and 1013 with respect to that element including the following:

(1) Procedures to be utilized for the acceptance of voluntary services under section 1013.

(2) Procedures and requirements relating to the installation of equipment under section 1013(f).

DEFINITIONS

SEC. 1015. [50 U.S.C. §441j-4] In this subtitle:

(1) The term "covered element of the intelligence community" means an agency, office, bureau, or element referred to in subparagraphs (B) through (L) of section 3(4).

(2) The term "educational institution" means—

(A) a local educational agency (as that term is defined in section 9101(26) of the Elementary and Secondary Education Act of 1965 (20 U.S.C. §7801(26)));

(B) an institution of higher education (as defined in section 102 of the Higher Education Act of 1965 (20 U.S.C. §1002) other than institutions referred to in subsection (a)(1)(C) of such section); or

(C) any other nonprofit institution that provides instruction of foreign languages in languages that are critical to the capability of the intelligence community to carry out national security activities of the United States.

(3) The term "dedicated personnel" means employees of the intelligence community and private citizens (including former civilian employees of the Federal Government who have been voluntarily separated, and members of the United States Armed Forces who have been honorably discharged, honorably separated, or generally discharged under honorable circumstances and rehired on a voluntary basis specifically to perform the activities authorized under this subtitle).

SUBTITLE C—ADDITIONAL EDUCATION PROGRAMS

ASSIGNMENT OF INTELLIGENCE COMMUNITY PERSONNEL AS LANGUAGE STUDENTS

SEC. 1021. [50 U.S.C. §441m]

(a) IN GENERAL.—The Director of National Intelligence, acting through the heads of the elements of the intelligence community, may assign employees of such elements in analyst positions requiring foreign language expertise as students at accredited professional, technical, or other institutions of higher education for training at the graduate or undergraduate level in foreign languages required for the conduct of duties and responsibilities of such positions.

(b) AUTHORITY FOR REIMBURSEMENT OF COSTS OF TUITION AND TRAINING.—

(1) The Director of National Intelligence may reimburse an employee assigned under subsection (a) for the total cost of the training described in that subsection, including costs of educational and supplementary reading materials.

(2) The authority under paragraph (1) shall apply to employees who are assigned on a full-time or part-time basis.

(3) Reimbursement under paragraph (1) may be made from appropriated or nonappropriated funds.

(c) RELATIONSHIP TO COMPENSATION AS AN ANALYST.—Reimbursement under this section to an employee who is an analyst is in addition to any benefits, allowances, travel expenses, or other compensation the employee is entitled to by reason of serving in such an analyst position.

PROGRAM ON RECRUITMENT AND TRAINING

SEC. 1022. [50 U.S.C. 441n]

(a) PROGRAM.—

(1) The Director of National Intelligence shall carry out a program to ensure that selected students or former students are provided funds to continue academic training, or are reimbursed for academic training previously obtained, in areas of specialization that the Director, in consultation with the other heads of the elements of the intelligence community, identifies as areas in which the current capabilities of the intelligence community are deficient or in which fu ture capabilities of the intelligence community are likely to be deficient.

(2) A student or former student selected for participation in the program shall commit to employment with an element of the intelligence community, following completion of appropriate academic training, under such terms and conditions as the Director considers appropriate.

(3) The program shall be known as the Pat Roberts Intelligence Scholars Program.

(b) ELEMENTS.—In carrying out the program under subsection (a), the Director shall—

(1) establish such requirements relating to the academic training of participants as the Director considers appropriate to ensure that participants are prepared for employment as intelligence professionals; and

(2) periodically review the areas of specialization of the elements of the intelligence community to determine the areas in which such elements are, or are likely to be, deficient in capabilities.

(c) USEOFFUNDS.—Funds made available for the program under subsection (a) shall be used—

(1) to provide a monthly stipend for each month that a student is pursuing a course of study;

(2) to pay the full tuition of a student or former student for the completion of such course of study;

(3) to pay for books and materials that the student or former student requires or required to complete such course of study;

(4) to pay the expenses of the student or former student for travel requested by an element of the intelligence community in relation to such program; or

(5) for such other purposes the Director considers reasonably appropriate to carry out such program.

EDUCATIONAL SCHOLARSHIP PROGRAM

SEC. 1023. [50 U.S.C. 441o]

The head of a department or agency containing an element of the intelligence community may establish an undergraduate or graduate training program with respect to civilian employees and prospective civilian employees of such element similar in purpose, conditions, content, and administration to the program that the Secretary of Defense is authorized to establish under section 16 of the National Security Agency Act of 1959 (50 U.S.C. 402 note).

INTELLIGENCE OFFICER TRAINING PROGRAM

SEC. 1024. [50 U.S.C. 441p]

(a) PROGRAMS.—

(1) The Director of National Intelligence may carry out grant programs in accordance with subsection (b) to enhance the recruitment and retention of an ethnically and culturally diverse intelligence community workforce with capabilities critical to the national security interests of the United States.

(2) In carrying out paragraph (1), the Director shall identify the skills necessary to meet current or emergent needs of the intel ligence community and the educational disciplines that will provide individuals with such skills.

(b) INSTITUTIONAL GRANT PROGRAM.—

(1) The Director may provide grants to institutions of higher education to support the establishment or continued development of programs of study in educational disciplines identified under subsection (a)(2).

(2) A grant provided under paragraph (1) may, with respect to the educational disciplines identified under subsection (a)(2), be used for the following purposes:

(A) Curriculum or program development.

(B) Faculty development.

(C) Laboratory equipment or improvements.

(D) Faculty research.

(c) APPLICATION.—An institution of higher education seeking a grant under this section shall submit an application describing the proposed use of the grant at such time and in such manner as the Director may require.

(d) REPORTS.—An institution of higher education that receives a grant under this section shall submit to the Director regular reports regarding the use of such grant, including—

(1) a description of the benefits to students who participate in the course of study funded by such grant;

(2) a description of the results and accomplishments related to such course of study; and

(3) any other information that the Director may require.

(e) REGULATIONS.—The Director shall prescribe such regulations as may be necessary to carry out this section.

(f) DEFINITIONS.—In this section:

(1) The term "Director" means the Director of National Intelligence.

(2) The term "institution of higher education" has the meaning given the term in section 101 of the Higher Education Act of 1965 (20 U.S.C. 1001).

TITLE XI—ADDITIONAL MISCELLANEOUS PROVISIONS

APPLICABILITY TO UNITED STATES INTELLIGENCE ACTIVITIES OF FEDERAL LAWS IMPLEMENTING INTERNATIONAL TREATIES AND AGREEMENTS

SEC. 1101. [50 U.S.C. 442]

(a) IN GENERAL.—No Federal law enacted on or after the date of the enactment of the Intelligence Authorization Act for Fiscal Year 2001 that implements a treaty or other international agreement shall be construed as making unlawful an otherwise lawful and authorized intelligence activity of the United States Government or its employees, or any other person to the extent such other person is carrying out such activity on behalf of, and at the direction of, the United States, unless such Federal law specifically addresses such intelligence activity.

(b) AUTHORIZED INTELLIGENCE ACTIVITIES.—An intelligence activity shall be treated as authorized for purposes of subsection (a) if the intelligence activity is authorized by an appropriate official of the United States Government, acting within the scope of the official duties of that official and in compliance with Federal law and any applicable Presidential directive.

COUNTERINTELLIGENCE INITIATIVES

SEC. 1102.

(a) INSPECTION PROCESS.—In order to protect intelligence sources and methods from unauthorized disclosure, the Director of National Intelligence shall establish and implement an inspection process for all agencies and departments of the United States that handle classified information relating to the national security of the United States intended to assure that those agencies and departments maintain effective operational security practices and programs directed against counterintelligence activities.

(b) ANNUAL REVIEW OF DISSEMINATION LISTS.—The Director of National Intelligence shall establish and implement a process for all elements of the intelligence community to review, on an annual basis, individuals included on distribution lists for access to classified information. Such process shall ensure that only individuals who have a particularized "need to know" (as determined by the Director) are continued on such distribution lists.

(c) COMPLETION OF FINANCIAL DISCLOSURE STATEMENTS REQUIRED FOR ACCESS TO CERTAIN CLASSIFIED INFORMATION.—The Director of National Intelligence shall establish and implement a process by which each head of an element of the intelligence community directs that all employees of that element, in order to be granted access to classified information referred to in subsection (a) of section 1.3 of Executive Order No. 12968 (August 2, 1995; 60 Fed. Reg. 40245; 50 U.S.C. 435 note), submit financial disclosure forms as required under subsection (b) of such section.

(d) ARRANGEMENTS TO HANDLE SENSITIVE INFORMATION.—The Director of National Intelligence shall establish, for all elements of the intelligence community, programs and procedures by which sensitive classified information relating to human intelligence is safeguarded against unauthorized disclosure by employees of those elements.

MISUSE OF THE OFFICE OF THE DIRECTOR OF NATIONAL INTELLIGENCE NAME, INITIALS, OR SEAL

SEC. 1103. [50 U.S.C. 442b]

(a) PROHIBITED ACTS.—No person may, except with the written permission of the Director of National Intelligence, or a designee of the Director, knowingly use the words ''Office of the Director of National Intelligence'', the initials ''ODNI'', the seal of the Office of the Director of National Intelligence, or any colorable imitation of such words, initials, or seal in connection with any merchandise, impersonation, solicitation, or commercial activity in a manner reasonably calculated to convey the impression that such use is approved, endorsed, or authorized by the Director of National Intelligence.

(b) INJUNCTION.—Whenever it appears to the Attorney General that any person is engaged or is about to engage in an act or practice which constitutes or will constitute conduct prohibited by subsection

(a), the Attorney General may initiate a civil proceeding in a district court of the United States to enjoin such act or practice. Such court shall proceed as soon as practicable to the hearing and determination of such action and may, at any time before final determination, enter such restraining orders or prohibitions, or take such other action as is warranted, to prevent injury to the United States or to any person or class of persons for whose protection the action is brought.

TITLE XI—ADDITIONAL MISCELLANEOUS PROVISIONS

APPLICABILITY TO UNITED STATES INTELLIGENCE ACTIVITIES OF FEDERAL LAWS IMPLEMENTING INTERNATIONAL TREATIES AND AGREEMENTS

SEC. 1101. [50 U.S.C. §442]

(a) IN GENERAL.—No Federal law enacted on or after the date of the enactment of the Intelligence Authorization Act for Fiscal Year 2001 that implements a treaty or other international agreement shall be construed as making unlawful an otherwise lawful and authorized intelligence activity of the United States Government or its employees, or any other person to the extent such other person is carrying out such activity on behalf of, and at the direction of, the United States, unless such Federal law specifically addresses such intelligence activity.

(b) AUTHORIZED INTELLIGENCE ACTIVITIES.—An intelligence activity shall be treated as authorized for purposes of subsection (a) if the intelligence activity is authorized by an appropriate official of the United States Government, acting within the scope of the official duties of that official and in compliance with Federal law and any applicable Presidential directive.

COUNTERINTELLIGENCE INITIATIVES

SEC. 1102. [50 U.S.C. §442a]

(a) INSPECTION PROCESS.—

(1) In order to protect intelligence sources and methods from unauthorized disclosure, the Director of National Intelligence shall establish and implement

an inspection process for all agencies and departments of the United States that handle classified information relating to the national security of the United States intended to assure that those agencies and departments maintain effective operational security practices and programs directed against counterintelligence activities.

(2) The Director shall carry out the process through the Office of the National Counterintelligence Executive.

(b) ANNUAL REVIEW OF DISSEMINATION LISTS.—

(1) The Director of National Intelligence shall establish and implement a process for all elements of the intelligence community to review, on an annual basis, individuals included on distribution lists for access to classified information. Such process shall ensure that only individuals who have a particularized need to know' (as determined by the Director) are continued on such distribution lists.

(2) Not later than October 15 of each year, the Director shall certify to the congressional intelligence committees that the review required under paragraph (1) has been conducted in all elements of the intelligence community during the preceding fiscal year.

(c) COMPLETION OF FINANCIAL DISCLOSURE STATEMENTS REQUIRED FOR ACCESS TO CERTAIN CLASSIFIED INFORMATION.—

(1) The Director of National Intelligence shall establish and implement a process by which each head of an element of the intelligence community directs that all employees of that element, in order to be granted access to classified information referred to in subsection (a) of section 1.3 of Executive Order No. 12968 (August 2, 1995; 60 Fed. Reg. 40245; 50

U.S.C. §435 note), submit financial disclosure forms as required under subsection (b) of such section.

(2) The Director shall carry out paragraph (1) through the Office of the National Counterintelligence Executive.

(d) ARRANGEMENTS TO HANDLE SENSITIVE INFORMATION.—The Director of National Intelligence shall establish, for all elements of the intelligence community, programs and procedures by which sensitive classified information relating to human intelligence is safeguarded against unauthorized disclosure by employees of those elements.

Intelligence Reform and Terrorism Prevention Act of 2004

(Pub. L. 108-458 of December 17, 2004; 118 Stat. 3638)

AN ACT To reform the intelligence community and the intelligence and intelligence-related activities of the United States Government, and for other purposes.

Be it enacted by the Senate and House of Representatives of the United States of America in Congress assembled,

SHORT TITLE; TABLE OF CONTENTS

SECTION 1.

(a) SHORT TITLE.—This Act may be cited as the "Intelligence Reform and Terrorism Prevention Act of 2004.

(b) TABLE OF CONTENTS.—The table of contents for this Act is as follows:

TITLE I—REFORM OF THE INTELLIGENCE COMMUNITY

SUBTITLE A—ESTABLISHMENT OF DIRECTOR OF NATIONAL INTELLIGENCE

SUBTITLE B—NATIONAL COUNTERTERRORISM CENTER, NATIONAL COUNTER PROLIFERATION CENTER, AND NATIONAL INTELLIGENCE CENTERS

SUBTITLE C—JOINT INTELLIGENCE COMMUNITY COUNCIL

SEC. 1031. Joint Intelligence Community Council.

SUBTITLE D—IMPROVEMENT OF EDUCATION FOR THE INTELLIGENCE COMMUNITY

SEC. 1041. Additional education and training requirements.
SEC. 1042. Cross-disciplinary education and training.
SEC. 1043. Intelligence Community Scholarship Program.

SUBTITLE E—ADDITIONAL IMPROVEMENTS OF INTELLIGENCE ACTIVITIES

SEC. 1051. Service and national laboratories and the intelligence community.
SEC. 1052. Open-source intelligence. SEC. 1053. National Intelligence Reserve Corps.

SUBTITLE F—PRIVACY AND CIVIL LIBERTIES

SEC. 1061. Privacy and Civil Liberties Oversight Board. SEC. 1062. Privacy and civil liberties officers.

SUBTITLE G—CONFORMING AND OTHER AMENDMENTS

SEC. 1071. Conforming amendments relating to roles of Director of National Intelligence and Director of the Central Intelligence Agency.
SEC. 1072. Other conforming amendments.
SEC. 1073. Elements of intelligence community under National Security Act of 1947.
SEC. 1074. Redesignation of National Foreign Intelligence Program as National Intelligence Program. SEC. 1075. Repeal of superseded authority.
SEC. 1076. Clerical amendments to National Security Act of 1947.
SEC. 1077. Conforming amendments relating to prohibiting dual service of the Director of the Central Intelligence Agency.
SEC. 1078. Authority to establish inspector general for the Office of the Director of National Intelligence.
SEC. 1079. Ethics matters.
SEC. 1080. Construction of authority of Director of National Intelligence to acquire and manage property and services.
SEC. 1081. General references.

SUBTITLE H—TRANSFER, TERMINATION, TRANSITION, AND OTHER PROVISIONS

SEC. 1091. Transfer of Community Management Staff.
SEC. 1092. Transfer of Terrorist Threat Integration Center.
SEC. 1093. Termination of positions of Assistant Directors of Central Intelligence.
SEC. 1094. Implementation plan.
SEC. 1095. Director of National Intelligence report on implementation of intelligence community reform.

TITLE I—REFORM OF THE INTELLIGENCE COMMUNITY

SHORT TITLE

SEC. 1001. This title may be cited as the "National Security Intelligence Reform Act of 2004".

SUBTITLE A—ESTABLISHMENT OF DIRECTOR OF NATIONAL INTELLIGENCE REORGANIZATION AND IMPROVEMENT OF MANAGEMENT OF INTELLIGENCE COMMUNITY

SEC. 1011.

(a) IN GENERAL.—Title I of the National Security Act of 1947 (50 U.S.C. §402 et seq.) is amended by striking sections 102 through 104 and inserting the following new sections: [amendments omitted here—see the National Security Act of 1947 in this book]

(b) SENSE OF CONGRESS.—It is the sense of Congress that—

(1) the human intelligence officers of the intelligence community have performed admirably and honorably in the face of great personal dangers;

(2) during an extended period of unprecedented investment and improve-

ments in technical collection means, the human intelligence capabilities of the United States have not received the necessary and commensurate priorities;

(3) human intelligence is becoming an increasingly important capability to provide information on the asymmetric threats to the national security of the United States;

(4) the continued development and improvement of a robust and empowered and flexible human intelligence work force is critical to identifying, understanding, and countering the plans and intentions of the adversaries of the United States; and

(5) an increased emphasis on, and resources applied to, enhancing the depth and breadth of human intelligence capabilities of the United States intelligence community must be among the top priorities of the Director of National Intelligence.

(c) TRANSFORMATION OF CENTRAL INTELLIGENCE AGENCY.—The Director of the Central Intelligence Agency shall, in accordance with standards developed by the Director in consultation with the Director of National Intelligence—

(1) enhance the analytic, human intelligence, and other capabilities of the Central Intelligence Agency;

(2) develop and maintain an effective language program within the Agency;

(3) emphasize the hiring of personnel of diverse backgrounds for purposes of improving the capabilities of the Agency;

(4) establish and maintain effective relationships between human intelligence and signals intelligence within the Agency at the operational level; and

(5) achieve a more effective balance within the Agency with respect to unilateral operations and liaison operations.

(d) REPORT.—

(1) Not later than 180 days after the date of the enactment of this Act, the Director of the Central Intelligence Agency shall submit to the Director of National Intelligence and the congressional intelligence committees a report setting forth the following:

(A) A strategy for improving the conduct of analysis (including strategic analysis) by the Central Intelligence Agency, and the progress of the Agency in implementing that strategy.

(B) A strategy for improving the human intelligence and other capabilities of the Agency, and the progress of the Agency in implementing that strategy.

(2)(A) The information in the report under paragraph (1) on the strategy referred to in paragraph (1)(B) shall—

(i) identify the number and types of personnel required to implement that strategy;

(ii) include a plan for the recruitment, training, equipping, and deployment of such personnel; and

(iii) set forth an estimate of the costs of such activities.

(B) If as of the date of the report under paragraph (1), a proper balance does not exist between unilateral operations and liaison operations, such report shall set forth the steps to be taken to achieve such balance.

REVISED DEFINITION OF NATIONAL INTELLIGENCE

SEC. 1012. Paragraph (5) of section 3 of the National Security Act of 1947 (50 U.S.C. §401a) is amended to read as follows:

"(5) The terms "national intelligence" and "intelligence related to national security" refer to all intelligence, regardless of the source from which derived and including information gathered within or outside the United States, that—

"(A) pertains, as determined consistent with any guidance issued by the President, to more than one United States Government agency; and "(B) that involves—

"(i) threats to the United States, its people, property, or interests;

"(ii) the development, proliferation, or use of weapons of mass destruction; or

"(iii) any other matter bearing on United States national or homeland security.".

JOINT PROCEDURES FOR OPERATIONAL COORDINATION BETWEEN DEPARTMENT OF DEFENSE AND CENTRAL INTELLIGENCE AGENCY

SEC. 1013.

(a) Development of Procedures—The Director of National Intelligence, in consultation with the Secretary of Defense and the Director of the Central Intelligence Agency, shall develop joint procedures to be used by the Department of Defense and the Central Intelligence Agency to improve the coordination and deconfliction of operations that involve elements of both the Armed Forces and the Central Intelligence Agency consistent with national security and the protection of human intelligence sources and methods. Those procedures shall, at a minimum, provide the following:

(1) Methods by which the Director of the Central Intelligence Agency and the Secretary of Defense can improve communication and coordination in the planning, execution, and sustainment of operations, including, as a minimum—

(A) information exchange between senior officials of the Central Intelligence Agency and senior officers and officials of the Department of Defense when planning for such an operation commences by either organization; and

(B) exchange of information between the Secretary and the Director of the Central Intelligence Agency to ensure that senior operational officials in both the Department of Defense and the Central Intelligence Agency have knowledge of the existence of the ongoing operations of the other.

(2) When appropriate, in cases where the Department of Defense and the Central Intelligence Agency are conducting separate missions in the same geographical area, a mutual agreement on the tactical and strategic objectives for the region and a clear delineation of operational responsibilities to prevent conflict and duplication of effort.

(b) Implementation Report- Not later than 180 days after the date of the enactment of the Act, the Director of National Intelligence shall submit to the congressional defense committees (as defined in section 101 of title 10, United States Code) and the congressional intelligence committees (as defined in section 3(7) of the National Security Act of 1947 (50 U.S.C. §401a(7))) a report describing the procedures established pursuant to subsection (a) and the status of the implementation of those procedures.

ROLE OF DIRECTOR OF NATIONAL INTELLIGENCE IN APPOINTMENT OF CERTAIN OFFICIALS RESPONSIBLE FOR INTELLIGENCE-RELATED ACTIVITIES

SEC. 1014. Section 106 of the National Security Act of 1947 (50 U.S.C. §403-6) is amended by striking all after the heading and inserting the following: [amendments omitted here—see the National Security Act of 1947 in this book]

EXECUTIVE SCHEDULE MATTERS

SEC. 1015.

(a) EXECUTIVE SCHEDULE LEVEL I.—Section 5312 of title 5, United States Code, is amended by adding at the end the following new item:
"Director of National Intelligence.".

(b) EXECUTIVE SCHEDULE LEVEL II.—Section 5313 of title 5, United States Code, is amended by adding at the end the following new items:
"Principal Deputy Director of National Intelligence. "Director of the National Counterterrorism Center. "Director of the National Counter Proliferation Center.".

(c) EXECUTIVE SCHEDULE LEVEL IV.—Section 5315 of title 5, United States Code, is amended—

(1) by striking the item relating to the Assistant Directors of Central Intelligence; and

(2) by adding at the end the following new item: "General Counsel of the Office of the National Intelligence Director.".

INFORMATION SHARING

SEC. 1016.

(a) DEFINITIONS.—In this section:

(1) HOMELAND SECURITY INFORMATION.—The term "homeland security information" has the meaning given that term in section 892(f) of the Homeland Security Act of 2002 (6 U.S.C. §482(f)).

(2) INFORMATION SHARING COUNCIL.—The term "Information Sharing Council" means the Information Systems Council established by Executive Order 13356, or any successor body designated by the President, and referred to under subsection (g).

(3) INFORMATION SHARING ENVIRONMENT.—The terms "information sharing environment" and "ISE" mean an approach that facilitates the sharing of terrorism and homeland security information, which may include any method determined necessary and appropriate for carrying out this section.

(4) PROGRAM MANAGER.—The term "program manager" means the program manager designated under subsection (f).

(5) TERRORISM INFORMATION.—The term "terrorism information"—

(A) means all information, whether collected, produced, or distributed by intelligence, law enforcement, military, homeland security, or other activities relating to—

(i) the existence, organization, capabilities, plans, intentions, vulnerabilities, means of finance or material support, or activities of foreign or international terrorist groups or individuals, or of domestic groups or individuals involved in transnational terrorism;

(ii) threats posed by such groups or individuals to the United States, United States persons, or United States interests, or to those of other nations;

(iii) communications of or by such groups or individuals; or

(iv) groups or individuals reasonably believed to be assisting or associated with such groups or individuals; and

(B) includes weapons of mass destruction information.

(6) WEAPONS OF MASS DESTRUCTION INFORMATION.—The term "weapons of mass destruction information" means information that could reasonably be expected to assist in the development, proliferation, or use of a weapon of mass destruction (including a chemical, biological, radiological, or nuclear weapon) that could be used by a terrorist organization against the United States, including information about the location of any stockpile of nuclear materials that could be exploited for use in such a weapon that could be used by a terrorist or a terrorist organization against the United States.

(b) INFORMATION SHARING ENVIRONMENT.—

(1) ESTABLISHMENT.—The President shall—

(A) create an information sharing environment for the sharing of terrorism information in a manner consistent with national security and with applicable legal standards relating to privacy and civil liberties;

(B) designate the organizational and management structures that will be used to operate and manage the ISE; and

(C) determine and enforce the policies, directives, and rules that will govern the content and usage of the ISE.

(2) ATTRIBUTES.—The President shall, through the structures described in

subparagraphs (B) and (C) of paragraph (1), ensure that the ISE provides and facilitates the means for sharing terrorism information among all appropriate Federal, State, local, and tribal entities, and the private sector through the use of policy guidelines and technologies. The President shall, to the greatest extent practicable, ensure that the ISE provides the functional equivalent of, or otherwise supports, a decentralized, distributed, and coordinated environment that—

(A) connects existing systems, where appropriate, provides no single points of failure, and allows users to share information among agencies, between levels of government, and, as appropriate, with the private sector;

(B) ensures direct and continuous online electronic access to information;

(C) facilitates the availability of information in a form and manner that facilitates its use in analysis, investigations and operations;

(D) builds upon existing systems capabilities currently in use across the Government;

(E) employs an information access management approach that controls access to data rather than just systems and networks, without sacrificing security;

(F) facilitates the sharing of information at and across all levels of security;

(G) provides directory services, or the functional equivalent, for locating people and information;

(H) incorporates protections for individuals' privacy and civil liberties;

(I) incorporates strong mechanisms to enhance accountability and facilitate oversight, including audits, authentication, and access controls;

(J) integrates the information within the scope of the information sharing environment, including any such information in legacy technologies;

(K) integrates technologies, including all legacy technologies, through Internet-based services, consistent with appropriate security protocols and safeguards, to enable connectivity among required users at the Federal, State, and local levels;

(L) allows the full range of analytic and operational activities without the need to centralize information within the scope of the information sharing environment;

(M) permits analysts to collaborate both independently and in a group (commonly known as "collective and non-collective collaboration"), and across multiple levels of national security information and controlled classified information;

(N) provides a resolution process that enables changes by authorized officials regarding rules and policies for the use, and retention of information within the scope of the information sharing environment; and

(O) incorporates continuous, real-time, and immutable audit capabilities, to the maximum extent possible.

(c) PRELIMINARY REPORT.—Not later than 180 days after the date of the enactment of this Act, the program manager shall, in consultation with the Information Sharing Council—

(1) submit to the President and Congress a description of the technological, legal, and policy issues presented by the creation of the ISE, and the way in which these issues will be addressed;

(2) establish an initial capability to provide electronic directory services, or the functional equivalent, to assist in locating in the Federal Government intelligence and terrorism information and people with relevant knowledge about intelligence and terrorism information; and

(3) conduct a review of relevant current Federal agency capabilities, databases, and systems for sharing information.

(d) GUIDELINES AND REQUIREMENTS.—As soon as possible, but in no event later than 270 days after the date of the enactment of this Act, the President shall—

(1) leverage all ongoing efforts consistent with establishing the ISE and issue guidelines for acquiring, accessing, sharing, and using information, including guidelines to ensure that information is provided in its most shareable form, such as by using tearlines to separate out data from the sources and methods by which the data are obtained;

(2) in consultation with the Privacy and Civil Liberties Oversight Board established under section 1061, issue guidelines that—

(A) protect privacy and civil liberties in the development and use of the ISE; and

(B) shall be made public, unless nondisclosure is clearly necessary to protect national security; and

(3) require the heads of Federal departments and agencies to promote a culture of information sharing by—

(A) reducing disincentives to information sharing, including over-classification of information and unnecessary requirements for originator approval, consistent with applicable laws and regulations; and

(B) providing affirmative incentives for information sharing.

(e) IMPLEMENTATION PLAN REPORT.—Not later than one year after the date of the enactment of this Act, the President shall, with the assistance of the program manager, submit to Congress a report containing an implementation plan for the ISE. The report shall include the following:

(1) A description of the functions, capabilities, resources, and conceptual design of the ISE, including standards.

(2) A description of the impact on enterprise architectures of participating agencies.

(3) A budget estimate that identifies the incremental costs associated with designing, testing, integrating, deploying, and operating the ISE.

(4) A project plan for designing, testing, integrating, deploying, and operating the ISE.

(5) The policies and directives referred to in subsection (b)(1)(C), as well as the metrics and enforcement mechanisms that will be utilized.

(6) Objective, systemwide performance measures to enable the assessment of progress toward achieving the full implementation of the ISE.

(7) A description of the training requirements needed to ensure that the ISE will be adequately implemented and properly utilized.

(8) A description of the means by which privacy and civil liberties will be protected in the design and operation of the ISE.

(9) The recommendations of the program manager, in consultation with the Information Sharing Council, regarding whether, and under what conditions, the ISE should be expanded to include other intelligence information.

(10) A delineation of the roles of the Federal departments and agencies that will participate in the ISE, including an identification of the agencies that will deliver the infrastructure needed to operate and manage the ISE (as distinct from individual department or agency components that are part of the ISE), with such delineation of roles to be consistent with—

(A) the authority of the Director of National Intelligence under this title, and the amendments made by this title, to set standards for information sharing throughout the intelligence community; and

(B) the authority of the Secretary of Homeland Security and the Attorney General, and the role of the Department of Homeland Security and the Attorney General, in coordinating with State, local, and tribal officials and the private sector.

(11) The recommendations of the program manager, in consultation with the Information Sharing Council, for a future management structure for the ISE, including whether the position of program manager should continue to remain in existence.

(f) PROGRAM MANAGER.—

(1) DESIGNATION.—Not later than 120 days after the date of the enactment of this Act, with notification to Congress, the President shall designate an individual as the program manager responsible for information sharing across the Federal Government. The individual designated as the program manager shall serve as program manager until removed from service or replaced by the President (at the President's sole discretion). The program manager, in consultation with the head of any affected department or agency, shall have and exercise governmentwide authority over the sharing of information within the scope of the information sharing environment, including homeland security information, terrorism information, and weapons of mass destruction information, by all Federal departments, agencies, and components, irrespective of the Federal department, agency, or component in which the program manager may be administratively located, except as provided by law.

(2) DUTIES AND RESPONSIBILITIES.—

(A) IN GENERAL.—The program manager shall, in consultation with the Information Sharing Council—

(i) plan for and oversee the implementation of, and manage, the ISE;

(ii) assist in the development of policies, as appropriate, to foster the development and proper operation of the ISE;

(iii) consistent with the direction and policies issued by the President, the Director of National Intelligence, and the Director of the Office of Management and Budget, issue governmentwide procedures, guidelines, instructions, and functional standards, as appropriate, for the management, development, and proper operation of the ISE;

(iv) identify and resolve information sharing disputes between Federal departments, agencies, and components; and

(v) assist, monitor, and assess the implementation of the ISE by Federal departments and agencies to ensure adequate progress, technological consistency and policy compliance; and regularly report the findings to Congress.

(B) CONTENT OF POLICIES, PROCEDURES, GUIDELINES, RULES, AND STANDARDS.—The policies, procedures, guidelines, rules, and standards under subparagraph (A)(ii) shall—

(i) take into account the varying missions and security requirements of agencies participating in the ISE;

(ii) address development, implementation, and oversight of technical standards and requirements;

(iii) take into account ongoing and planned efforts that support development, implementation and management of the ISE;

(iv) address and facilitate information sharing between and among departments and agencies of the intelligence community, the Department of Defense, the homeland security community and the law enforcement community;

(v) address and facilitate information sharing between Federal departments and agencies and State, tribal, and local governments;

(vi) address and facilitate, as appropriate, information sharing between Federal departments and agencies and the private sector;

(vii) address and facilitate, as appropriate, information sharing between Federal departments and agencies with foreign partners and allies; and

(viii) ensure the protection of privacy and civil liberties.

(g) INFORMATION SHARING COUNCIL.—

(1) ESTABLISHMENT.—There is established an Information Sharing Council that shall assist the President and the program manager in their duties under this section. The Information Sharing Council shall serve until removed from service and replaced by the President (at the sole discretion of the President) with a successor body.

(2) SPECIFIC DUTIES.—In assisting the President and the program manager in their duties under this section, the Information Sharing Council shall—

(A) advise the President and the program manager in developing policies, procedures, guidelines, roles, and standards necessary to establish, implement, and maintain the ISE;

(B) work to ensure coordination among the Federal departments and agencies participating in the ISE in the establishment, implementation, and maintenance of the ISE;

(C) identify and, as appropriate, recommend the consolidation and elimination of current programs, systems, and processes used by Federal departments and agencies to share information, and recommend, as appropriate, the redirection of existing resources to support the ISE;

(D) identify gaps, if any, between existing technologies, programs and systems used by Federal departments and agencies to share information and the parameters of the proposed information sharing environment;

(E) recommend solutions to address any gaps identified under subparagraph (D);

(F) recommend means by which the ISE can be extended to allow interchange of information between Federal departments and agencies and appropriate authorities of State and local governments;

(G) assist the program manager in identifying and resolving information sharing disputes between Federal departments, agencies, and components;

(H) identify appropriate personnel for assignment to the program manager to support staffing needs identified by the program manager; and

(I) recommend whether or not, and by which means, the ISE should be expanded so as to allow future expansion encompassing other relevant categories of information.

(3) CONSULTATION.—In performing its duties, the Information Sharing Council shall consider input from persons and entities outside the Federal Government having significant experience and expertise in policy, technical matters, and operational matters relating to the ISE.

(4) INAPPLICABILITY OF FEDERAL ADVISORY COMMITTEE ACT.—The Information Sharing Council (including any subsidiary group of the Information Sharing Council) shall not be subject to the requirements of the Federal Advisory Committee Act (5 U.S.C. App.).

(5) DETAILEES.—Upon a request by the Director of National Intelligence, the departments and agencies represented on the Information Sharing Council shall detail to the program manager, on a reimbursable basis, appropriate personnel identified under paragraph (2)(H).

(h) PERFORMANCE MANAGEMENT REPORTS.—

(1) IN GENERAL.—Not later than two years after the date of the enactment of this Act, and not later than June 30 of each year thereafter, the President shall submit to Congress a report on the state of the ISE and of information sharing across the Federal Government.

(2) CONTENT.—Each report under this subsection shall include—

(A) a progress report on the extent to which the ISE has been implemented, including how the ISE has fared on the performance measures and whether the performance goals set in the preceding year have been met;

(B) objective system-wide performance goals for the following year;

(C) an accounting of how much was spent on the ISE in the preceding year;

(D) actions taken to ensure that procurement of and investments in systems and technology are consistent with the implementation plan for the ISE;

(E) the extent to which all terrorism watch lists are available for combined searching in real time through the ISE and whether there are consistent standards for placing individuals on, and removing individuals from, the watch lists, including the availability of processes for correcting errors;

(F) the extent to which State, tribal, and local officials are participating in the ISE;

(G) the extent to which private sector data, including information from owners and operators of critical infrastructure, is incorporated in the ISE, and the extent to which individuals and entities outside the government are receiving information through the ISE;

(H) the measures taken by the Federal government to ensure the accuracy of information in the ISE, in particular the accuracy of information about individuals;

(I) an assessment of the privacy and civil liberties protections of the ISE, including actions taken in the preceding year to implement or enforce privacy and civil liberties protections; and

(J) an assessment of the security protections used in the ISE.

(i) AGENCY RESPONSIBILITIES.—The head of each department or agency that possesses or uses intelligence or terrorism information, operates a system in the ISE, or otherwise participates (or expects to participate) in the ISE shall—

(1) ensure full department or agency compliance with information sharing policies, procedures, guidelines, rules, and standards established under subsections (b) and (f);

(2) ensure the provision of adequate resources for systems and activities supporting operation of and participation in the ISE;

(3) ensure full department or agency cooperation in the development of the ISE to implement government-wide information sharing; and

(4) submit, at the request of the President or the program manager, any reports on the implementation of the requirements of the ISE within such department or agency.

(j) REPORT ON THE INFORMATION SHARING ENVIRONMENT.—

(1) IN GENERAL.—Not later than 180 days after the date of enactment of the Implementing Recommendations of the 9/11 Commission Act of 2007, the President shall report to the Committee on Homeland Security and Governmental Affairs of the Senate, the Select Committee on Intelligence of the Senate, the Committee on Homeland Security of the House of Representatives, and the Permanent Select Committee on Intelligence of the House of Representatives on the feasibility of—

(A) eliminating the use of any marking or process (including "Originator Control") intended to, or having the effect of, restricting the sharing of information within the scope of the information sharing environment, including homeland security information, terrorism information, and weapons of mass destruction information, between and among participants in the information sharing environment, unless the President has—

(i) specifically exempted categories of information from such elimination; and

(ii) reported that exemption to the committees of Congress described in the matter preceding this subparagraph; and

(B) continuing to use Federal agency standards in effect on such date of enactment for the collection, sharing, and access to information within the scope of the information sharing environment, including homeland security information, terrorism information, and weapons of mass destruction information, relating to citizens and lawful permanent residents;

(C) replacing the standards described in subparagraph (B) with a standard that would allow mission-based or threat-based permission to access or share information within the scope of the information sharing environment, including homeland security information, terrorism information, and weapons of mass destruction information, for a particular purpose that the Federal Government, through an appropriate process established in consultation with the Privacy and Civil Liberties Oversight Board established under section 1061, has determined to be lawfully permissible for a particular agency, component, or employee (commonly known as an "authorized use" standard); and

(D) the use of anonymized data by Federal departments, agencies, or components collecting, possessing, disseminating, or handling information within the scope of the information sharing environment, including homeland security information, terrorism information, and weapons of mass destruction information, in any cases in which—

(i) the use of such information is reasonably expected to produce results materially equivalent to the use of information that is transferred or stored in a nonanonymized form; and

(ii) such use is consistent with any mission of that department, agency, or component (including any mission under a Federal statute or directive of the President) that involves the storage, retention, sharing, or exchange of personally identifiable information.

(2) DEFINITION.—In this subsection, the term 'anonymized data' means data in which the individual to whom the data pertains is not identifiable with reasonable efforts, including information that has been encrypted or hidden through the use of other technology.

(k) ADDITIONAL POSITIONS.—The program manager is authorized to hire not more than 40 full-time employees to assist the program manager in—

(1) activities associated with the implementation of the information sharing environment, including—

(A) implementing the requirements under subsection (b)(2); and

(B) any additional implementation initiatives to enhance and expedite the creation of the information sharing environment; and

(2) identifying and resolving information sharing disputes between Federal departments, agencies, and components under subsection (f)(2)(A)(iv).

(l) AUTHORIZATION OF APPROPRIATIONS.—There is authorized to be appropriated to carry out this section $30,000,000 for each of fiscal years 2008 and 2009.

ALTERNATIVE ANALYSIS OF INTELLIGENCE BY THE INTELLIGENCE COMMUNITY

SEC. 1017.

(a) IN GENERAL.—Not later than 180 days after the effective date of this Act, the Director of National Intelligence shall establish a process and assign an individual or entity the responsibility for ensuring that, as appropriate, elements of the intelligence community conduct alternative analysis (commonly referred to as "red-team analysis") of the information and conclusions in intelligence products.

(b) REPORT—Not later than 270 days after the effective date of this Act, the Director of National Intelligence shall provide a report to the Select Committee on Intelligence of the Senate and the Permanent Select Committee of the House of Representatives on the implementation of subsection (a).

PRESIDENTIAL GUIDELINES ON IMPLEMENTATION AND PRESERVATION OF AUTHORITIES

SEC. 1018. The President shall issue guidelines to ensure the effective implementation and execution within the executive branch of the authorities granted to the Director of National Intelligence by this title and the amendments made by this title, in a manner that respects and does not abrogate the statutory responsibilities of the heads of the departments of the United States Government concerning such departments, including, but not limited to:

(1) the authority of the Director of the Office of Management and Budget; and

(2) the authority of the principal officers of the executive departments as heads of their respective departments, including, but not limited to, under—

(A) section 199 of the Revised Statutes (22 U.S.C. §2651);

(B) title II of the Department of Energy Organization Act (42 U.S.C. §7131 et seq.);

(C) the State Department Basic Authorities Act of 1956;

(D) section 102(a) of the Homeland Security Act of 2002 (6 U.S.C. §112(a)); and

(E) sections 301 of title 5, 113(b) and 162(b) of title 10, 503 of title 28, and 301(b) of title 31, United States Code.

ASSIGNMENT OF RESPONSIBILITIES RELATING TO ANALYTIC INTEGRITY

SEC. 1019.

(a) ASSIGNMENT OF RESPONSIBILITIES.—For purposes of carrying out section 102A(h) of the National Security Act of 1947 (as added by section 1011(a)), the Director of National Intelligence shall, not later than 180 days after the date of the enactment of this Act, assign an individual or entity to be responsible for ensuring that finished intelligence products produced by any element or elements of the intelligence community are timely, objective, independent of political considerations, based upon all sources of available intelligence, and employ the standards of proper analytic tradecraft.

(b) RESPONSIBILITIES.—

(1) The individual or entity assigned responsibility under subsection (a)—

(A) may be responsible for general oversight and management of analysis and production, but may not be directly responsible for, or involved in, the specific production of any finished intelligence product;

(B) shall perform, on a regular basis, detailed reviews of finished intelligence product or other analytic products by an element or elements of the intelligence community covering a particular topic or subject matter;

(C) shall be responsible for identifying on an annual basis functional or topical areas of analysis for specific review under subparagraph (B); and

(D) upon completion of any review under subparagraph (B), may draft lessons learned, identify best practices, or make recommendations for improvement to the analytic tradecraft employed in the production of the reviewed product or products.

(2) Each review under paragraph (1)(B) should—

(A) include whether the product or products concerned were based on all sources of available intelligence, properly describe the quality and reliability of underlying sources, properly caveat and express uncertainties or confidence in analytic judgments, properly distinguish between underlying intelligence and the assumptions and judgments of analysts, and incorporate, where appropriate, alternative analyses; and

(B) ensure that the analytic methodologies, tradecraft, and practices used by the element or elements concerned in the production of the product or products concerned meet the standards set forth in subsection (a).

(3) Information drafted under paragraph (1)(D) should, as appropriate, be included in analysis teaching modules and case studies for use throughout the intelligence community.

(c) ANNUAL REPORTS.—Not later than December 1 each year, the Director of National Intelligence shall submit to the congressional intelligence committees, the heads of the relevant elements of the intelligence community, and the heads of analytic training departments a report containing a description, and the associated findings, of each review under subsection (b)(1)(B) during such year.

(d) CONGRESSIONAL INTELLIGENCE COMMITTEES DEFINED.—In this section, the term "congressional intelligence committees" means—

(1) the Select Committee on Intelligence of the Senate; and

(2) the Permanent Select Committee on Intelligence of the House of Representatives.

SAFEGUARD OF OBJECTIVITY IN INTELLIGENCE ANALYSIS

SEC. 1020.

(a) IN GENERAL.—Not later than 180 days after the effective date of this Act, the Director of National Intelligence shall identify an individual within the Office of the Director of National Intelligence who shall be available to analysts within the Office of the Director of National Intelligence to counsel, conduct arbitration, offer recommendations, and, as appropriate, initiate inquiries into real or perceived problems of analytic tradecraft or politicization, biased reporting, or lack of objectivity in intelligence analysis.

(b) REPORT. —Not later than 270 days after the effective date of this Act, the Director of National Intelligence shall provide a report to the Select Committee on Intelligence of the Senate and the Permanent Select Committee on Intelligence of the House of Representatives on the implementation of subsection (a).

SUBTITLE B—NATIONAL COUNTERTERRORISM CENTER, NATIONAL COUNTER PROLIFERATION CENTER, AND NATIONAL INTELLIGENCE CENTERS

NATIONAL COUNTERTERRORISM CENTER

SEC. 1021. Title I of the National Security Act of 1947 (50 U.S.C. §402 et seq.) is amended by adding at the end the following new section:

[amendments omitted here—see the National Security Act of 1947 in this book]

NATIONAL COUNTER PROLIFERATION CENTER

SEC. 1022. Title I of the National Security Act of 1947, as amended by section 1021 of this Act, is further amended by adding at the end the following new section:

[amendments omitted here—see the National Security Act of 1947 in this book]

NATIONAL INTELLIGENCE CENTERS

SEC. 1023. Title I of the National Security Act of 1947, as amended by section 1022 of this Act, is further amended by adding at the end the following new section:

[amendments omitted here—see the National Security Act of 1947 in this book]

SUBTITLE C—JOINT INTELLIGENCE COMMUNITY COUNCIL

JOINT INTELLIGENCE COMMUNITY COUNCIL

SEC. 1031. Title I of the National Security Act of 1947 (50 U.S.C. §402 et seq.) is amended by inserting after section 101 the following new section:

[amendments omitted here—see the National Security Act of 1947 in this book]

SUBTITLE D—IMPROVEMENT OF EDUCATION FOR THE INTELLIGENCE COMMUNITY

ADDITIONAL EDUCATION AND TRAINING REQUIREMENTS

SEC. 1041.

(a) FINDINGS.—Congress makes the following findings:

(1) Foreign language education is essential for the development of a highly-skilled workforce for the intelligence community.

(2) Since September 11, 2001, the need for language proficiency levels to meet required national security functions has been raised, and the ability to comprehend and articulate technical and scientific information in foreign languages has become critical.

(b) LINGUISTIC REQUIREMENTS.—

(1) The Director of National Intelligence shall—

(A) identify the linguistic requirements for the Office of the Director of National Intelligence;

(B) identify specific requirements for the range of linguistic skills necessary for the intelligence community, including proficiency in scientific and technical vocabularies of critical foreign languages; and

(C) develop a comprehensive plan for the Office to meet such requirements through the education, recruitment, and training of linguists.

(2) In carrying out activities under paragraph (1), the Director shall take into account education grant programs of the Department of Defense and the Department of Education that are in existence as of the date of the enactment of this Act.

(3) Not later than one year after the date of the enactment of this Act, and annually thereafter, the Director shall submit to Congress a report on the requirements identified under paragraph (1), including the success of the Office of the Director of National Intelligence in meeting such requirements. Each report shall notify Congress of any additional resources determined by the Director to be required to meet such requirements.

(4) Each report under paragraph (3) shall be in unclassified form, but may include a classified annex.

(c) PROFESSIONAL INTELLIGENCE TRAINING.—The Director of National Intelligence shall require the head of each element and component within the Office of the Director of National Intelligence who has responsibility for professional intelligence training to periodically review and revise the curriculum for the professional intelligence training of the senior and intermediate level personnel of such element or component in order to—

(1) strengthen the focus of such curriculum on the integration of intelligence collection and analysis throughout the Office; and

(2) prepare such personnel for duty with other departments, agencies, and elements of the intelligence community.

CROSS-DISCIPLINARY EDUCATION AND TRAINING.

SEC. 1042. Title X of the National Security Act of 1947 (50 U.S.C. §441g) is amended by adding at the end the following new section:
[amendments omitted here—see the National Security Act of 1947 in this book]
165 INTELLIGENCE REFORM AND TERRORISM PREVENTION ACT OF 2004

INTELLIGENCE COMMUNITY SCHOLARSHIP PROGRAM

SEC. 1043. Title X of the National Security Act of 1947, as amended by section 1042 of this Act, is further amended by adding at the end the following new section:

[amendments omitted here—see the National Security Act of 1947 in this book]

SUBTITLE E—ADDITIONAL IMPROVEMENTS OF INTELLIGENCE ACTIVITIES

SERVICE AND NATIONAL LABORATORIES AND THE INTELLIGENCE COMMUNITY

SEC. 1051. The Director of National Intelligence, in cooperation with the Secretary of Defense and the Secretary of Energy, should seek to ensure that each service laboratory of the Department of Defense and each national laboratory of the Department of Energy may, acting through the relevant Secretary and in a manner consistent with the missions and commitments of the laboratory—

(1) assist the Director of National Intelligence in all aspects of technical intelligence, including research, applied sciences, analysis, technology evaluation and assessment, and any other aspect that the relevant Secretary considers appropriate; and

(2) make available to the intelligence community, on a community-wide basis—

(A) the analysis and production services of the service and national laboratories, in a manner that maximizes the capacity and services of such laboratories; and

(B) the facilities and human resources of the service and national laboratories, in a manner that improves the technological capabilities of the intelligence community.

OPEN SOURCE INTELLIGENCE

SEC. 1052.

(a) SENSE OF CONGRESS—It is the sense of Congress that—

(1) the Director of National Intelligence should establish an intelligence center for the purpose of coordinating the collection, analysis, production, and dissemination of open-source intelligence to elements of the intelligence community;

(2) open-source intelligence is a valuable source that must be integrated into the intelligence cycle to ensure that United States policymakers are fully and completely informed; and

(3) the intelligence center should ensure that each element of the intelligence community uses open-source intelligence consistent with the mission of such element.

(b) REQUIREMENT FOR EFFICIENT USE BY INTELLIGENCE COMMUNITY OF OPENSOURCE INTELLIGENCE.—The Director of National Intelligence shall ensure that the intelligence community makes efficient and effective use of open-source information and analysis.

(c) REPORT—Not later than June 30, 2005, the Director of National Intelligence shall submit to the congressional intelligence committees a report containing the decision of the Director as to whether an open-source intelligence center will be established. If the Director decides not to establish an open-source intelligence center, such report shall also contain a description of how the intelligence community will use open-source intelligence and effectively integrate open-source intelligence into the national intelligence cycle.

(d) CONGRESSIONAL INTELLIGENCE COMMITTEES DEFINED.—In this section, the term "congressional intelligence committees' means—

(1) the Select Committee on Intelligence of the Senate; and

(2) the Permanent Select Committee on Intelligence of the House of Representatives.

NATIONAL INTELLIGENCE RESERVE CORPS

SEC. 1053.

(a) ESTABLISHMENT.—The Director of National Intelligence may provide for the establishment and training of a National Intelligence Reserve Corps (in this section referred to as "National Intelligence Reserve Corps") for the temporary reemployment on a voluntary basis of former employees of elements of the intelligence community during periods of emergency, as determined by the Director.

(b) ELIGIBLE INDIVIDUALS.—An individual may participate in the National Intelligence Reserve Corps only if the individual previously served as a full time employee of an element of the intelligence community.

(c) TERMS OF PARTICIPATION.—The Director of National Intelligence shall prescribe the terms and conditions under which eligible individuals may participate in the National Intelligence Reserve Corps.

(d) EXPENSES.—The Director of National Intelligence may provide members of the National Intelligence Reserve Corps transportation and per diem in lieu of subsistence for purposes of participating in any training that relates to service as a member of the Reserve Corps.

(e) TREATMENT OF ANNUITANTS.—

(1) If an annuitant receiving an annuity from the Civil Service Retirement and Disability Fund becomes temporarily reemployed pursuant to this section, such annuity shall not be discontinued thereby.

(2) An annuitant so reemployed shall not be considered an employee for the purposes of chapter 83 or 84 of title 5, United States Code.

(f) TREATMENT UNDER OFFICE OF DIRECTOR OF NATIONAL INTELLIGENCE PERSONNEL CEILING.—A member of the National Intelligence Reserve Corps who is reemployed on a temporary basis pursuant to this section shall not count against any personnel ceiling applicable to the Office of the Director of National Intelligence.

SUBTITLE F—PRIVACY AND CIVIL LIBERTIES

PRIVACY AND CIVIL LIBERTIES OVERSIGHT BOARD

SEC. 1061.

(a) IN GENERAL.—There is established as an independent agency within the executive branch a Privacy and Civil Liberties Oversight Board (referred to in this section as the 'Board').

(b) FINDINGS.—Consistent with the report of the National Commission on Terrorist Attacks Upon the United States, Congress makes the following findings:

(1) In conducting the war on terrorism, the Government may need additional powers and may need to enhance the use of its existing powers.

(2) This shift of power and authority to the Government calls for an enhanced system of checks and balances to protect the precious liberties that are vital to our way of life and to ensure that the Government uses its powers for the purposes for which the powers were given.

(3) The National Commission on Terrorist Attacks Upon the United States correctly concluded that 'The choice between security and liberty is a false choice, as nothing is more likely to endanger America's liberties than the success of a terrorist attack at home. Our history has shown us that insecurity threatens liberty. Yet, if our liberties are curtailed, we lose the values that we are struggling to defend.'.

(c) PURPOSE.—The Board shall—

(1) analyze and review actions the executive branch takes to protect the Nation from terrorism, ensuring that the need for such actions is balanced with the need to protect privacy and civil liberties; and

(2) ensure that liberty concerns are appropriately considered in the development and implementation of laws, regulations, and policies related to efforts to protect the Nation against terrorism.

(d) FUNCTIONS.—

(1) ADVICE AND COUNSEL ON POLICY DEVELOPMENT AND IMPLEMENTATION.—The Board shall—

(A) review proposed legislation, regulations, and policies related to efforts to protect the Nation from terrorism, including the development and adoption of information sharing guidelines under subsections (d) and (f) of section 1016;

(B) review the implementation of new and existing legislation, regulations, and policies related to efforts to protect the Nation from terrorism, including the implementation of information sharing guidelines under subsections (d) and (f) of section 1016;

(C) advise the President and the departments, agencies, and elements of the executive branch to ensure that privacy and civil liberties are appropriately considered in the development and implementation of such legislation, regulations, policies, and guidelines; and

(D) in providing advice on proposals to retain or enhance a particular governmental power, consider whether the department, agency, or element of the executive branch has established—

(i) that the need for the power is balanced with the need to protect privacy and civil liberties;

(ii) that there is adequate supervision of the use by the executive branch of the power to ensure protection of privacy and civil liberties; and

(iii) that there are adequate guidelines and oversight to properly confine its use.

(2) OVERSIGHT.—The Board shall continually review—

(A) the regulations, policies, and procedures, and the implementation of the regulations, policies, and procedures, of the departments, agencies, and elements of the executive branch relating to efforts to protect the Nation from terrorism to ensure that privacy and civil liberties are protected;

(B) the information sharing practices of the departments, agencies, and elements of the executive branch relating to efforts to protect the Nation from terrorism to determine whether they appropriately protect privacy and civil liberties and adhere to the information sharing guidelines issued or developed under subsections (d) and (f) of section 1016 and to other governing laws, regulations, and policies regarding privacy and civil liberties; and

(C) other actions by the executive branch relating to efforts to protect the Nation from terrorism to determine whether such actions—

(i) appropriately protect privacy and civil liberties; and

(ii) are consistent with governing laws, regulations, and policies regarding privacy and civil liberties.

(3) RELATIONSHIP WITH PRIVACY AND CIVIL LIBERTIES OFFICERS.—The Board shall—

(A) receive and review reports and other information from privacy officers and civil liberties officers under section 1062;

(B) when appropriate, make recommendations to such privacy officers and civil liberties officers regarding their activities; and

(C) when appropriate, coordinate the activities of such privacy officers and civil liberties officers on relevant interagency matters.

(4) TESTIMONY.—The members of the Board shall appear and testify before Congress upon request.

(e) REPORTS.—

(1) IN GENERAL.—The Board shall—

(A) receive and review reports from privacy officers and civil liberties officers under section 1062; and

(B) periodically submit, not less than semiannually, reports—

(i)(I) to the appropriate committees of Congress, including the Committee on the Judiciary of the Senate, the Committee on the Judiciary of the House of Representatives, the Committee on Homeland Security and Governmental Affairs of the Senate, the Committee on Homeland Security of the House of Representatives, the Committee on Oversight and Government Reform of the House of Representatives, the Select Committee on Intelligence of the Senate, and the Permanent Select Committee on Intelligence of the House of Representatives; and

(II) to the President; and

(ii) which shall be in unclassified form to the greatest extent possible, with a classified annex where necessary.

(2) CONTENTS.—Not less than 2 reports submitted each year under paragraph (1)(B) shall include—

(A) a description of the major activities of the Board during the preceding period;

(B) information on the findings, conclusions, and recommendations of the Board resulting from its advice and oversight functions under subsection (d);

(C) the minority views on any findings, conclusions, and recommendations of the Board resulting from its advice and oversight functions under subsection (d);

(D) each proposal reviewed by the Board under subsection (d)(1) that—

(i) the Board advised against implementation; and

(ii) notwithstanding such advice, actions were taken to implement; and

(E) for the preceding period, any requests submitted under subsection (g)(1)(D) for the issuance of subpoenas that were modified or denied by the Attorney General.

(f) INFORMING THE PUBLIC.—The Board shall—

(1) make its reports, including its reports to Congress, available to the public to the greatest extent that is consistent with the protection of classified information and applicable law; and

(2) hold public hearings and otherwise inform the public of its activities, as appropriate and in a manner consistent with the protection of classified information and applicable law.

(g) ACCESS TO INFORMATION.—

(1) AUTHORIZATION.—If determined by the Board to be necessary to carry out its responsibilities under this section, the Board is authorized to—

(A) have access from any department, agency, or element of the executive branch, or any Federal officer or employee of any such department, agency, or element, to all relevant records, reports, audits, reviews, documents, papers, recommendations, or other relevant material, including classified information consistent with applicable law;

(B) interview, take statements from, or take public testimony from personnel of any department, agency, or element of the executive branch, or any Federal officer or employee of any such department, agency, or element;

(C) request information or assistance from any State, tribal, or local government; and

(D) at the direction of a majority of the members of the Board, submit a written request to the Attorney General of the United States that the Attorney General require, by subpoena, persons (other than departments, agencies, and elements of the executive branch) to produce any relevant information, documents, reports, answers, records, accounts, papers, and other documentary or testimonial evidence.

(2) REVIEW OF SUBPOENA REQUEST.—

(A) IN GENERAL.—Not later than 30 days after the date of receipt of a request by the Board under paragraph (1)(D), the Attorney General shall—

(i) issue the subpoena as requested; or

(ii) provide the Board, in writing, with an explanation of the grounds on which the subpoena request has been modified or denied.

(B) NOTIFICATION.—If a subpoena request is modified or denied under subparagraph (A)(ii), the Attorney General shall, not later than 30 days after the date of that modification or denial, notify the Committee on the Judiciary of the Senate and the Committee on the Judiciary of the House of Representatives.

(3) ENFORCEMENT OF SUBPOENA.—In the case of contumacy or failure to obey a subpoena issued pursuant to paragraph (1)(D), the United States district court for the judicial district in which the subpoenaed person resides, is served, or may be found may issue an order requiring such person to produce the evidence required by such subpoena.

(4) AGENCY COOPERATION.—Whenever information or assistance requested under subparagraph (A) or (B) of paragraph (1) is, in the judgment of the Board, unreasonably refused or not provided, the Board shall report the circumstances to the head of the department, agency, or element concerned without delay. The head of the department, agency, or element concerned shall ensure that the Board is given access to the information, assistance, material, or personnel the Board determines to be necessary to carry out its functions.

(h) MEMBERSHIP.—

(1) MEMBERS.—The Board shall be composed of a fulltime chairman and 4 additional members, who shall be appointed by the President, by and with the advice and consent of the Senate.

(2) QUALIFICATIONS.—Members of the Board shall be selected solely on

the basis of their professional qualifications, achievements, public stature, expertise in civil liberties and privacy, and relevant experience, and without regard to political affiliation, but in no event shall more than 3 members of the Board be members of the same political party. The President shall, before appointing an individual who is not a member of the same political party as the President, consult with the leadership of that party, if any, in the Senate and House of Representatives.

(3) INCOMPATIBLE OFFICE.—An individual appointed to the Board may not, while serving on the Board, be an elected official, officer, or employee of the Federal Government, other than in the capacity as a member of the Board.

(4) TERM.—Each member of the Board shall serve a term of 6 years, except that—

(A) a member appointed to a term of office after the commencement of such term may serve under such appointment only for the remainder of such term; and

(B) upon the expiration of the term of office of a member, the member shall continue to serve until the member's successor has been appointed and qualified, except that no member may serve under this subparagraph—

(i) for more than 60 days when Congress is in session unless a nomination to fill the vacancy shall have been submitted to the Senate; or

(ii) after the adjournment sine die of the session of the Senate in which such nomination is submitted.

(5) QUORUM AND MEETINGS.—The Board shall meet upon the call of the chairman or a majority of its members. Three members of the Board shall constitute a quorum.

(i) COMPENSATION AND TRAVEL EXPENSES.—

(1) COMPENSATION.—

(A) CHAIRMAN.—The chairman of the Board shall be compensated at the rate of pay payable for a position at level III of the Executive Schedule under section 5314 of title 5, United States Code.

(B) MEMBERS.—Each member of the Board shall be compensated at a rate of pay payable for a position at level IV of the Executive Schedule under section 5315 of title 5, United States Code, for each day during which that member is engaged in the actual performance of the duties of the Board.

(2) TRAVEL EXPENSES.—Members of the Board shall be allowed travel expenses, including per diem in lieu of subsistence, at rates authorized for persons employed intermittently by the Government under section 5703(b) of title 5, United States Code, while away from their homes or regular places of business in the performance of services for the Board.

(j) STAFF.—

(1) APPOINTMENT AND COMPENSATION.—The chairman of the Board, in accordance with rules agreed upon by the Board, shall appoint and fix the

compensation of a full-time executive director and such other personnel as may be necessary to enable the Board to carry out its functions, without regard to the provisions of title 5, United States Code, governing appointments in the competitive service, and without regard to the provisions of chapter 51 and subchapter III of chapter 53 of such title relating to classification and General Schedule pay rates, except that no rate of pay fixed under this subsection may exceed the equivalent of that payable for a position at level V of the Executive Schedule under section 5316 of title 5, United States Code.

(2) DETAILEES.—Any Federal employee may be detailed to the Board without reimbursement from the Board, and such detailee shall retain the rights, status, and privileges of the detailee's regular employment without interruption.

(3) CONSULTANT SERVICES.—The Board may procure the temporary or intermittent services of experts and consultants in accordance with section 3109 of title 5, United States Code, at rates that do not exceed the daily rate paid a person occupying a position at level IV of the Executive Schedule under section 5315 of such title.

(k) SECURITY CLEARANCES.—

(1) IN GENERAL.—The appropriate departments, agencies, and elements of the executive branch shall cooperate with the Board to expeditiously provide the Board members and staff with appropriate security clearances to the extent possible under existing procedures and requirements.

(2) RULES AND PROCEDURES.—After consultation with the Secretary of Defense, the Attorney General, and the Director of National Intelligence, the Board shall adopt rules and procedures of the Board for physical, communications, computer, document, personnel, and other security relating to carrying out the functions of the Board.

(l) TREATMENT AS AGENCY, NOT AS ADVISORY COMMITTEE.— The Board—

(1) is an agency (as defined in section 551(1) of title 5, United States Code); and

(2) is not an advisory committee (as defined in section 3(2) of the Federal Advisory Committee Act (5 U.S.C. App.)).

(m) AUTHORIZATION OF APPROPRIATIONS.—There are authorized to be appropriated to carry out this section amounts as follows:

(1) For fiscal year 2008, $5,000,000.

(2) For fiscal year 2009, $6,650,000.

(3) For fiscal year 2010, $8,300,000.

(4) For fiscal year 2011, $10,000,000.

(5) For fiscal year 2012 and each subsequent fiscal year, such sums as may be necessary.

SENSE OF CONGRESS ON DESIGNATION OF PRIVACY AND CIVIL LIBERTIES OFFICERS

SEC. 1062.

(a) DESIGNATION AND FUNCTIONS.—The Attorney General, the Secretary of Defense, the Secretary of State, the Secretary of the Treasury, the Secretary of Health and Human Services, the Secretary of Homeland Security, the Director of National Intelligence, the Director of the Central Intelligence Agency, and the head of any other department, agency, or element of the executive branch designated by the Privacy and Civil Liberties Oversight Board under section 1061 to be appropriate for coverage under this section shall designate not less than 1 senior officer to serve as the principal advisor to—

(1) assist the head of such department, agency, or element and other officials of such department, agency, or element in appropriately considering privacy and civil liberties concerns when such officials are proposing, developing, or implementing laws, regulations, policies, procedures, or guidelines related to efforts to protect the Nation against terrorism;

(2) periodically investigate and review department, agency, or element actions, policies, procedures, guidelines, and related laws and their implementation to ensure that such department, agency, or element is adequately considering privacy and civil liberties in its actions;

(3) ensure that such department, agency, or element has adequate procedures to receive, investigate, respond to, and redress complaints from individuals who allege such department, agency, or element has violated their privacy or civil liberties; and

(4) in providing advice on proposals to retain or enhance a particular governmental power the officer shall consider whether such department, agency, or element has established—

(A) that the need for the power is balanced with the need to protect privacy and civil liberties;

(B) that there is adequate supervision of the use by such department, agency, or element of the power to ensure protection of privacy and civil liberties; and

(C) that there are adequate guidelines and oversight to properly confine its use.

(b) EXCEPTION TO DESIGNATION AUTHORITY.—

(1) PRIVACY OFFICERS.—In any department, agency, or element referred to in subsection (a) or designated by the Privacy and Civil Liberties Oversight Board, which has a statutorily created privacy officer, such officer shall perform the functions specified in subsection

(a) with respect to privacy.

(2) CIVIL LIBERTIES OFFICERS.—In any department, agency, or element referred to in subsection (a) or designated by the Board, which has a statutorily created civil liberties officer, such officer shall perform the functions specified in subsection (a) with respect to civil liberties.

(c) SUPERVISION AND COORDINATION.—Each privacy officer or civil liberties officer described in subsection (a) or (b) shall—

(1) report directly to the head of the department, agency, or element concerned; and

(2) coordinate their activities with the Inspector General of such department, agency, or element to avoid duplication of effort.

(d) AGENCY COOPERATION.—The head of each department, agency, or element shall ensure that each privacy officer and civil liberties officer—

(1) has the information, material, and resources necessary to fulfill the functions of such officer;

(2) is advised of proposed policy changes;

(3) is consulted by decision makers; and

(4) is given access to material and personnel the officer determines to be necessary to carry out the functions of such officer.

(e) REPRISAL FOR MAKING COMPLAINT.—No action constituting a reprisal, or threat of reprisal, for making a complaint or for disclosing information to a privacy officer or civil liberties officer described in subsection (a) or (b), or to the Privacy and Civil Liberties Oversight Board, that indicates a possible violation of privacy protections or civil liberties in the administration of the programs and operations of the Federal Government relating to efforts to protect the Nation from terrorism shall be taken by any Federal employee in a position to take such action, unless the complaint was made or the information was disclosed with the knowledge that it was false or with willful disregard for its truth or falsity.

(f) PERIODIC REPORTS.—

(1) IN GENERAL.—The privacy officers and civil liberties officers of each department, agency, or element referred to or described in subsection (a) or (b) shall periodically, but not less than quarterly, submit a report on the activities of such officers—

(A)(i) to the appropriate committees of Congress, including the Committee on the Judiciary of the Senate, the Committee on the Judiciary of the House of Representatives, the Committee on Homeland Security and Governmental Affairs of the Senate, the Committee on Oversight and Government Reform of the House of Representatives, the Select Committee on Intelligence of the Senate, and the Permanent Select Committee on Intelligence of the House of Representatives;

(ii) to the head of such department, agency, or element; and

(iii) to the Privacy and Civil Liberties Oversight Board; and

(B) which shall be in unclassified form to the greatest extent possible, with a classified annex where necessary.

(2) CONTENTS.—Each report submitted under paragraph (1) shall include information on the discharge of each of the functions of the officer concerned, including—

(A) information on the number and types of reviews undertaken;

(B) the type of advice provided and the response given to such advice;

(C) the number and nature of the complaints received by the department, agency, or element concerned for alleged violations; and

(D) a summary of the disposition of such complaints, the reviews and inquiries conducted, and the impact of the activities of such officer.

(g) INFORMING THE PUBLIC.—Each privacy officer and civil liberties officer shall—

(1) make the reports of such officer, including reports to Congress, available to the public to the greatest extent that is consistent with the protection of classified information and applicable law; and

(2) otherwise inform the public of the activities of such officer, as appropriate and in a manner consistent with the protection of classified information and applicable law.

(h) SAVINGS CLAUSE.—Nothing in this section shall be construed to limit or otherwise supplant any other authorities or responsibilities provided by law to privacy officers or civil liberties officers.

SUBTITLE G—CONFORMING AND OTHER AMENDMENTS

CONFORMING AMENDMENTS RELATING TO ROLES OF DIRECTOR OF NATIONAL INTELLIGENCE AND DIRECTOR OF THE CENTRAL INTELLIGENCE AGENCY

SEC. 1071.

(a) NATIONAL SECURITY ACT OF 1947.—

(1) The National Security Act of 1947 (50 U.S.C. §401 et seq.) is amended by striking "Director of Central Intelligence" each place it appears in the following provisions and inserting "Director of National Intelligence":

(A) Section 101(h)(2)(A) (50 U.S.C. §402(h)(2)(A)).

(B) Section 101(h)(5) (50 U.S.C. §402(h)(5)).

(C) Section 101(i)(2)(A) (50 U.S.C. §402(i)(2)(A)).

(D) Section 101(j) (50 U.S.C. §402(j)).

(E) Section 105(a) (50 U.S.C. §403-5(a)).

(F) Section 105(b)(6)(A) (50 U.S.C. §403-5(b)(6)(A)).

(G) Section 105B(a)(1) (50 U.S.C. §403-5b(a)(1)).

(H) Section 105B(b) (50 U.S.C. §403-5b(b)), the first place it appears.

(I) Section 110(b) (50 U.S.C. §404e(b)).

(J) Section 110(c) (50 U.S.C. §404e(c)).

(K) Section 112(a)(1) (50 U.S.C. §404g(a)(1)).

(L) Section 112(d)(1) (50 U.S.C. §404g(d)(1)).

(M) Section 113(b)(2)(A) (50 U.S.C. §404h(b)(2)(A)).

(N) Section 114(a)(1) (50 U.S.C. §404i(a)(1)).

(O) Section 114(b)(1) (50 U.S.C. §404i(b)(1)).

(P) Section 115(a)(1) (50 U.S.C. §404j(a)(1)).

(Q) Section 115(b) (50 U.S.C. §404j(b)).

(R) Section 115(c)(1)(B) (50 U.S.C. §404j(c)(1)(B)).

(S) Section 116(a) (50 U.S.C. §404k(a)).

(T) Section 117(a)(1) (50 U.S.C. §404l(a)(1)).

(U) Section 303(a) (50 U.S.C. §405(a)), both places it appears.

(V) Section 501(d) (50 U.S.C. §413(d)).

(W) Section 502(a) (50 U.S.C. §413a(a)).

(X) Section 502(c) (50 U.S.C. §413a(c)).

(Y) Section 503(b) (50 U.S.C. §413b(b)).
(Z) Section 504(a)(3)(C) (50 U.S.C. §414(a)(3)(C)).
(AA) Section 504(d)(2) (50 U.S.C. §414(d)(2)).
(BB) Section 506A(a)(1) (50 U.S.C. §415a-1(a)(1)).
(CC) Section 603(a) (50 U.S.C. §423(a)).
(DD) Section 702(a)(1) (50 U.S.C. §432(a)(1)).
(EE) Section 702(a)(6)(B)(viii) (50 U.S.C. §432(a)(6)(B)(viii)).
(FF) Section 702(b)(1) (50 U.S.C. §432(b)(1)), both places it appears.
(GG) Section 703(a)(1) (50 U.S.C. §432a(a)(1)).
(HH) Section 703(a)(6)(B)(viii) (50 U.S.C. §432a(a)(6)(B)(viii)).
(II) Section 703(b)(1) (50 U.S.C. §432a(b)(1)), both places it appears.
(JJ) Section 704(a)(1) (50 U.S.C. §432b(a)(1)).
(KK) Section 704(f)(2)(H) (50 U.S.C. §432b(f)(2)(H)).
(LL) Section 704(g)(1)) (50 U.S.C. §432b(g)(1)), both places it appears.
(MM) Section 1001(a) (50 U.S.C. §441g(a)).
(NN) Section 1102(a)(1) (50 U.S.C. §442a(a)(1)). (OO) Section 1102(b)(1) (50 U.S.C. §442a(b)(1)). (PP) Section 1102(c)(1) (50 U.S.C. §442a(c)(1)). (QQ) Section 1102(d) (50 U.S.C. §442a(d)).

(2) That Act is further amended by striking "of Central Intelligence" each place it appears in the following provisions:
(A) Section 105(a)(2) (50 U.S.C. §403-5(a)(2)).
(B) Section 105B(a)(2) (50 U.S.C. §403-5b(a)(2)).
(C) Section 105B(b) (50 U.S.C. §403-5b(b)), the second place it appears.

(3) That Act is further amended by striking "Director" each place it appears in the following provisions and inserting "Director of National Intelligence":
(A) Section 114(c) (50 U.S.C. §404i(c)).
(B) Section 116(b) (50 U.S.C. §404k(b)).
(C) Section 1001(b) (50 U.S.C. §441g(b)).
(D) Section 1001(c) (50 U.S.C. §441g(c)), the first place it appears.
(E) Section 1001(d)(1)(B) (50 U.S.C. §441g(d)(1)(B)).
(F) Section 1001(e) (50 U.S.C. §441g(e)), the first place it appears.

(4) Section 114A of that Act (50 U.S.C. §404i-1) is amended by striking "Director of Central Intelligence" and inserting "Director of National Intelligence, the Director of the Central Intelligence Agency"

(5) Section 504(a)(2) of that Act (50 U.S.C. §414(a)(2)) is amended by striking "Director of Central Intelligence" and inserting "Director of the Central Intelligence Agency".

(6) Section 701 of that Act (50 U.S.C. §431) is amended—
(A) in subsection (a), by striking "Operational files of the Central Intelligence Agency may be exempted by the Director of Central Intelligence"

and inserting "The Director of the Central Intelligence Agency, with the coordination of the Director of National Intelligence, may exempt operational files of the Central Intelligence Agency"; and

(B) in subsection (g)(1), by striking "Director of Central Intelligence" and inserting "Director of the Central Intelligence Agency and the Director of National Intelligence".

(7) The heading for section 114 of that Act (50 U.S.C. §404i) is amended to read as follows:

"ADDITIONAL ANNUAL REPORTS FROM THE DIRECTOR OF NATIONAL INTELLIGENCE".

(b) CENTRAL INTELLIGENCE AGENCY ACT OF 1949.—

(1) The Central Intelligence Agency Act of 1949 (50 U.S.C. §403a et seq.) is amended by striking "Director of Central Intelligence" each place it appears in the following provisions and inserting "Director of National Intelligence":

(A) Section 6 (50 U.S.C. §403g).

(B) Section 17(f) (50 U.S.C. §403q(f)), both places it appears.

(2) That Act is further amended by striking "of Central Intelligence" in each of the following provisions:

(A) Section 2 (50 U.S.C. §403b).

(B) Section 16(c)(1)(B) (50 U.S.C. §403p(c)(1)(B)).

(C) Section 17(d)(1) (50 U.S.C. §403q(d)(1)).

(D) Section 20(c) (50 U.S.C. §403t(c)).

(3) That Act is further amended by striking "Director of Central Intelligence" each place it appears in the following provisions and inserting "Director of the Central Intelligence Agency":

(A) Section 14(b) (50 U.S.C. §403n(b)).

(B) Section 16(b)(2) (50 U.S.C. §403p(b)(2)).

(C) Section 16(b)(3) (50 U.S.C. §403p(b)(3)), both places it appears.

(D) Section 21(g)(1) (50 U.S.C. §403u(g)(1)).

(E) Section 21(g)(2) (50 U.S.C. §403u(g)(2)).

(c) CENTRAL INTELLIGENCE AGENCY RETIREMENT ACT.—Section 101 of the Central Intelligence Agency Retirement Act (50 U.S.C. §2001) is amended by striking paragraph (2) and inserting the following new paragraph (2):

"(2) DIRECTOR.—The term "Director" means the Director of the Central Intelligence Agency.".

(d) CIA VOLUNTARY SEPARATION PAY ACT.—Subsection (a)(1) of section 2 of the Central Intelligence Agency Voluntary Separation Pay Act (50 U.S.C. §2001 note) is amended to read as follows:

"(1) the term "Director" means the Director of the Central Intelligence Agency;".

(e) FOREIGN INTELLIGENCE SURVEILLANCE ACT OF 1978.—(1) The Foreign Intelligence Surveillance Act of 1978 (50 U.S.C. §1801 et seq.) is amended by striking "Director of Central Intelligence" each place it appears and inserting "Director of National Intelligence".

(f) CLASSIFIED INFORMATION PROCEDURES ACT.—Section 9(a) of the Classified Information Procedures Act (5 U.S.C. App.) is amended by striking "Director of Central Intelligence" and inserting "Director of National Intelligence".

(g) INTELLIGENCE AUTHORIZATION ACTS.—

(1) PUBLIC LAW 103-359- Section 811(c)(6)(C) of the Counterintelligence and Security Enhancements Act of 1994 (title VIII of Public Law 103-359) is amended by striking "Director of Central Intelligence" and inserting "Director of National Intelligence".

(2) PUBLIC LAW 107-306-

(A) The Intelligence Authorization Act for Fiscal Year 2003 (Public Law 107-306) is amended by striking "Director of Central Intelligence, acting as the head of the intelligence community," each place it appears in the following provisions and inserting "Director of National Intelligence":

(i) Section 313(a) (50 U.S.C. §404n(a)).

(ii) Section 343(a)(1) (50 U.S.C. §404n-2(a)(1))

(B) That Act is further amended by striking "Director of Central Intelligence" each place it appears in the following provisions and inserting "Director of National Intelligence":

(i) Section 904(e)(4) (50 U.S.C. §402c(e)(4)).

(ii) Section 904(e)(5) (50 U.S.C. §402c(e)(5)).

(iii) Section 904(h) (50 U.S.C. §402c(h)), each place it appears.

(iv) Section 904(m) (50 U.S.C. §402c(m)).

(C) Section 341 of that Act (50 U.S.C. §404n-1) is amended by striking "Director of Central Intelligence, acting as the head of the intelligence community, shall establish in the Central Intelligence Agency" and inserting "Director of National Intelligence shall establish within the Central Intelligence Agency".

(D) Section 352(b) of that Act (50 U.S.C. §404-3 note) is amended by striking "Director" and inserting "Director of National Intelligence".

(3) PUBLIC LAW 108-177-

(A) The Intelligence Authorization Act for Fiscal Year 2004 (Public Law 108-177) is amended by striking "Director of Central Intelligence" each place it appears in the following provisions and inserting "Director of National Intelligence":

(i) Section 317(a) (50 U.S.C. §403-3 note).

(ii) Section 317(h)(1).

(iii) Section 318(a) (50 U.S.C. §441g note).

(iv) Section 319(b) (50 U.S.C. §403 note).

(v) Section 341(b) (28 U.S.C. §519 note).

(vi) Section 357(a) (50 U.S.C. §403 note).

(vii) Section 504(a) (117 Stat. 2634), both places it appears.

(B) Section 319(f)(2) of that Act (50 U.S.C. §403 notc) is amended by striking "Director" the first place it appears and inserting "Director of National Intelligence".

(C) Section 404 of that Act (18 U.S.C. §4124 note) is amended by striking "Director of Central Intelligence" and inserting "Director of the Central Intelligence Agency".

OTHER CONFORMING AMENDMENTS

SEC. 1072.

(a) NATIONAL SECURITY ACT OF 1947.—

(1) Section 101(j) of the National Security Act of 1947 (50 U.S.C. §402(j)) is amended by striking "Deputy Director of Central Intelligence" and inserting "Principal Deputy Director of National Intelligence".

(2) Section 105(a) of that Act (50 U.S.C. §403-5(a)) is amended by striking "The Secretary" in the matter preceding paragraph (1) and inserting "Consistent with sections 102 and 102A, the Secretary".

(3) Section 105(b) of that Act (50 U.S.C. §403-5(b)) is amended by striking "103 and 104" in the matter preceding paragraph (1) and inserting "102 and 102A".

(4) Section 112(d)(1) of that Act (50 U.S.C. §404g(d)(1)) is amended by striking "section 103(c)(6) of this Act" and inserting "section 102A(i) of this Act".

(5) Section 116(b) of that Act (50 U.S.C. §404k(b)) is amended by striking "to the Deputy Director of Central Intelligence, or with respect to employees of the Central Intelligence Agency, the Director may delegate such authority to the Deputy Director for Operations" and inserting "to the Principal Deputy Director of National Intelligence, or with respect to employees of the Central Intelligence Agency, to the Director of the Central Intelligence Agency".

(6) Section 506A(b)(1) of that Act (50 U.S.C. §415a-1(b)(1)) is amended by striking "Office of the Deputy Director of Central Intelligence" and inserting "Office of the Director of National Intelligence".

(7) Section 701(c)(3) of that Act (50 U.S.C. §431(c)(3)) is amended by striking "Office of the Director of Central Intelligence" and inserting "Office of the Director of National Intelligence".

(8) Section 1001(b) of that Act (50 U.S.C. §441g(b)) is amended by striking "Assistant Director of Central Intelligence for Administration" and inserting "Office of the Director of National Intelligence".

(b) CENTRAL INTELLIGENCE AGENCY ACT OF 1949.—Section 6 of the Central Intelligence Agency Act of 1949 (50 U.S.C. §403g) is amended by striking "section 103(c)(7) of the National Security Act of 1947 (50 U.S.C. §4033(c)(7))" and inserting "section 102A(i) of the National Security Act of 1947".

(c) CENTRAL INTELLIGENCE AGENCY RETIREMENT ACT.—Section 201(c) of the Central Intelligence Agency Retirement Act (50 U.S.C. §2011(c)) is amended by striking "paragraph (6) of section 103(c) of the National Security Act of 1947 (50 U.S.C. §403-3(c)) that the Director of Central Intelligence" and inserting "section 102A(i) of the National Security Act of 1947 (50 U.S.C. §403-3(c)(1)) that the Director of National Intelligence".

(d) INTELLIGENCE AUTHORIZATION ACTS.—

(1) PUBLIC LAW 107-306-

(A) Section 343(c) of the Intelligence Authorization Act for Fiscal Year 2003 (Public Law 107-306; 50 U.S.C. §404n-2(c)) is amended by striking "section 103(c)(6) of the National Security Act of 1947 (50 U.S.C. §403-3((c)(6))" and inserting "section 102A(i) of the National Security Act of 1947 (50 U.S.C. §403-3(c)(1))".

(B)(i) Section 902 of that Act (also known as the Counterintelligence Enhancements Act of 2002) (50 U.S.C. §402b) is amended by striking "President" each place it appears and inserting "Director of National Intelligence".

(ii) Section 902(a)(2) of that Act is amended by striking "Director of Central Intelligence" and inserting "Director of the Central Intelligence Agency".

(C) Section 904 of that Act (50 U.S.C. §402c) is amended—

(i) in subsection (c), by striking "Office of the Director of Central Intelligence" and inserting "Office of the Director of National Intelligence"; and

(ii) in subsection (l), by striking "Office of the Director of Central Intelligence" and inserting "Office of the Director of National Intelligence".

(2) PUBLIC LAW 108-177-

(A) Section 317 of the Intelligence Authorization Act for Fiscal Year 2004 (Public Law 108-177; 50 U.S.C. §403-3 note) is amended—

(i) in subsection (g), by striking "Assistant Director of Central Intelligence for Analysis and Production" and inserting "Deputy Director of National Intelligence"; and

(ii) in subsection (h)(2)(C), by striking "Assistant Director" and inserting "Deputy Director of National Intelligence".

(B) Section 318(e) of that Act (50 U.S.C. §441g note) is amended by striking "Assistant Director of Central Intelligence for Analysis and Production" and inserting "Deputy Director of National Intelligence".

ELEMENTS OF INTELLIGENCE COMMUNITY UNDER NATIONAL SECURITY ACT OF 1947

SEC. 1073. Paragraph (4) of section 3 of the National Security Act of 1947 (50 U.S.C. §401a) is amended to read as follows:

"(4) The term "intelligence community" includes the following: "(A) The Office of the Director of National Intelligence. "(B) The Central Intelligence Agency. "(C) The National Security Agency. "(D) The Defense Intelligence Agency. "(E) The National Geospatial-Intelligence Agency. "(F) The National Reconnaissance Office. "(G) Other offices within the Department of Defense for the collection of specialized national intelligence through reconnaissance programs. "(H) The intelligence elements of the Army, the Navy, the Air Force, the Marine Corps, the Federal Bureau of Investigation, and the Department of Energy. "(I)

The Bureau of Intelligence and Research of the Department of State. "(J) The Office of Intelligence and Analysis of the Department of the Treasury. "(K) The elements of the Department of Homeland Security concerned with the analysis of intelligence information, including the Office of Intelligence of the Coast Guard. "(L) Such other elements of any other department or agency as may be designated by the President, or designated jointly by the Director of National Intelligence and the head of the department or agency concerned, as an element of the intelligence community.".

REDESIGNATION OF NATIONAL FOREIGN INTELLIGENCE PROGRAM AS NATIONAL INTELLIGENCE PROGRAM

SEC. 1074.

(a) REDESIGNATION.—Paragraph (6) of section 3 of the National Security Act of 1947 (50 U.S.C. §401a) is amended by striking "Foreign".

(b) CONFORMING AMENDMENTS.—

(1)(A) Section 506 of the National Security Act of 1947 (50 U.S.C. §415a) is amended—

(i) in subsection (a), by striking "National Foreign Intelligence Program" and inserting "National Intelligence Program"; and

(ii) in the section heading, by striking "FOREIGN".

(B) Section 105 of that Act (50 U.S.C. §403-5) is amended—

(i) in paragraphs (2) and (3) of subsection (a), by striking "National Foreign Intelligence Program" and inserting "National Intelligence Program"; and

(ii) in the section heading, by striking "FOREIGN".

(2) Section 17(f) of the Central Intelligence Agency Act of 1949 (50 U.S.C. §403q(f)) is amended by striking "National Foreign Intelligence Program" and inserting "National Intelligence Program".

REPEAL OF SUPERSEDED AUTHORITY

SEC. 1075. Section 111 of the National Security Act of 1947 (50 U.S.C. §404f) is repealed.

CLERICAL AMENDMENTS TO NATIONAL SECURITY ACT OF 1947

SEC. 1076. The table of contents in the first section of the National Security Act of 1947 is amended—

(1) by striking the items relating to sections 102 through 105 and inserting the following new items: "SEC. 101A. Joint Intelligence Community Council. "SEC. 102. Director of National Intelligence. "SEC. 102A. Responsibilities and authorities of the Director of National Intelligence. "SEC. 103. Office of the Director of National Intelligence. "SEC. 103A. Deputy Directors of National Intelligence. "SEC. 103B. National Intelligence Council. "SEC. 103C. General Counsel. "SEC. 103D. Civil Liberties Protection Officer. "SEC. 103E. Director of Science and Technology. "SEC. 103F. National Counterintelligence Executive. "SEC. 104. Central Intelligence

Agency. "SEC. 104A. Director of the Central Intelligence Agency. "SEC. 105. Responsibilities of the Secretary of Defense pertaining to the National Intelligence Program.";

(2) by striking the item relating to section 111;

(3) by striking the item relating to section 114 and inserting the following new item: "SEC. 114. Additional annual reports from the Director of National Intelligence.";

(4) by inserting after the item relating to section 118 the following new items: "SEC. 119. National Counterterrorism Center. "SEC. 119A. National Counter Proliferation Center. "SEC. 119B. National intelligence centers.

(5) by striking the item relating to section 506 and inserting the following new item: "SEC. 506. Specificity of National Intelligence Program budget amounts for counterterrorism, counterproliferation, counternarcotics, and counterintelligence."; and

(6) by inserting after the item relating to section 1001 the following new items: "SEC. 1002. Framework for cross-disciplinary education and training. "SEC. 1003. Intelligence Community Scholarship Program.".

CONFORMING AMENDMENTS RELATING TO PROHIBITING DUAL SERVICE OF THE DIRECTOR OF THE CENTRAL INTELLIGENCE AGENCY

SEC. 1077. Section 1 of the Central Intelligence Agency Act of 1949 (50 U.S.C. §403a) is amended—

(1) by redesignating paragraphs (a), (b), and (c) as paragraphs (1), (2), and (3), respectively; and

(2) by striking paragraph (2), as so redesignated, and inserting the following new paragraph (2): "(2) "Director" means the Director of the Central Intelligence Agency; and".

AUTHORITY TO ESTABLISH INSPECTOR GENERAL FOR THE OFFICE OF THE DIRECTOR OF NATIONAL INTELLIGENCE

SEC. 1078. The Inspector General Act of 1978 (5 U.S.C. App.) is amended by inserting after section 8J the following new section: "AUTHORITY TO ESTABLISH INSPECTOR GENERAL OF THE OFFICE OF THE DIRECTOR OF NATIONAL INTELLIGENCE"

SEC. 8K. If the Director of National Intelligence determines that an Office of Inspector General would be beneficial to improving the operations and effectiveness of the Office of the Director of National Intelligence, the Director of National Intelligence is authorized to establish, with any of the duties, responsibilities, and authorities set forth in this Act, an Office of Inspector General.".

ETHICS MATTERS

SEC. 1079.

(a) POLITICAL SERVICE OR PERSONNEL.—Section 7323(b)(2)(B)(i) of title 5, United States Code, is amended—

(1) in subclause (XII), by striking "or" at the end; and

(2) by inserting after subclause (XIII) the following new subclause: "(XIV) the Office of the Director of National Intelligence; or".

(b) DELETION OF INFORMATION ABOUT FOREIGN GIFTS.—Section 7342(f)(4) of title 5, United States Code, is amended—

(1) by inserting "(A)" after "(4)";

(2) in subparagraph (A), as so designated, by striking "the Director of Central Intelligence" and inserting "the Director of the Central Intelligence Agency"; and

(3) by adding at the end the following new subparagraph: "(B) In transmitting such listings for the Office of the Director of National Intelligence, the Director of National Intelligence may delete the information described in subparagraphs (A) and (C) of paragraphs (2) and (3) if the Director certifies in writing to the Secretary of State that the publication of such information could adversely affect United States intelligence sources.".

(c) EXEMPTION FROM FINANCIAL DISCLOSURES.—Section 105(a)(1) of the Ethics in Government Act (5 U.S.C. App.) is amended by inserting "the Office of the Director of National Intelligence," before "the Central Intelligence Agency".

CONSTRUCTION OF AUTHORITY OF DIRECTOR OF NATIONAL INTELLIGENCE TO ACQUIRE AND MANAGE PROPERTY AND SERVICES

SEC. 1080. Section 113(e) of title 40, United States Code, is amended—

(1) in paragraph (18), by striking "or" at the end;

(2) in paragraph (19), by striking the period at the end and inserting "; or"; and

(3) by adding at the end the following new paragraph: "(20) the Office of the Director of National Intelligence.".

GENERAL REFERENCES.

SEC. 1081.

(a) DIRECTOR OF CENTRAL INTELLIGENCE AS HEAD OF INTELLIGENCE COMMUNITY.—Any reference to the Director of Central Intelligence or the Director of the Central Intelligence Agency in the Director's capacity as the head of the intelligence community in any law, regulation, document, paper, or other record of the United States shall be deemed to be a reference to the Director of National Intelligence.

(b) DIRECTOR OF CENTRAL INTELLIGENCE AS HEAD OF CIA.—Any reference to the Director of Central Intelligence or the Director of the Central Intelligence Agency in the Director's capacity as the head of the Central Intelligence Agency in any law, regulation, document, paper, or other record of the United States shall be deemed to be a reference to the Director of the Central Intelligence Agency.

(c) COMMUNITY MANAGEMENT STAFF.—Any reference to the Community Management Staff in any law, regulation, document, paper, or other record of the United States shall be deemed to be a reference to the staff of the Office of the Director of National Intelligence.

SUBTITLE H—TRANSFER, TERMINATION, TRANSITION, AND OTHER PROVISIONS

TRANSFER OF COMMUNITY MANAGEMENT STAFF

SEC. 1091.

(a) TRANSFER.—There shall be transferred to the Office of the Director of National Intelligence such staff of the Community Management Staff as of the date of the enactment of this Act as the Director of National Intelligence determines to be appropriate, including all functions and activities discharged by the Community Management Staff as of that date.

(b) ADMINISTRATION.—The Director of National Intelligence shall administer the Community Management Staff after the date of the enactment of this Act as a component of the Office of the Director of National Intelligence under section 103 of the National Security Act of 1947, as amended by section 1011(a) of this Act.

TRANSFER OF TERRORIST THREAT INTEGRATION CENTER

SEC. 1092.

(a) TRANSFER.—There shall be transferred to the National Counterterrorism Center the Terrorist Threat Integration Center (TTIC) or its successor entity, including all functions and activities discharged by the Terrorist Threat Integration Center or its successor entity as of the date of the enactment of this Act.

(b) ADMINISTRATION.—The Director of the National Counterterrorism Center shall administer the Terrorist Threat Integration Center after the date of the enactment of this Act as a component of the Directorate of Intelligence of the National Counterterrorism Center under section 119(i) of the National Security Act of 1947, as added by section 1021(a) of this Act.

TERMINATION OF POSITIONS OF ASSISTANT DIRECTORS OF CENTRAL INTELLIGENCE

SEC. 1093.

(a) TERMINATION.—The positions referred to in subsection (b) are hereby abolished.

(b) COVERED POSITIONS.—The positions referred to in this subsection are as follows:

(1) The Assistant Director of Central Intelligence for Collection.

(2) The Assistant Director of Central Intelligence for Analysis and Production.

(3) The Assistant Director of Central Intelligence for Administration.

IMPLEMENTATION PLAN

SEC. 1094. The President shall transmit to Congress a plan for the implementation of this title and the amendments made by this title. The plan shall address, at a minimum, the following:

(1) The transfer of personnel, assets, and obligations to the Director of National Intelligence pursuant to this title.

(2) Any consolidation, reorganization, or streamlining of activities transferred to the Director of National Intelligence pursuant to this title.

(3) The establishment of offices within the Office of the Director of National Intelligence to implement the duties and responsibilities of the Director of National Intelligence as described in this title.

(4) Specification of any proposed disposition of property, facilities, contracts, records, and other assets and obligations to be transferred to the Director of National Intelligence.

(5) Recommendations for additional legislative or administrative action as the President considers appropriate.

DIRECTOR OF NATIONAL INTELLIGENCE REPORT ON IMPLEMENTATION OF INTELLIGENCE COMMUNITY REFORM

SEC. 1095.

(a) REPORT.—Not later than one year after the effective date of this Act, the Director of National Intelligence shall submit to the congressional intelligence committees a report on the progress made in the implementation of this title, including the amendments made by this title. The report shall include a comprehensive description of the progress made, and may include such recommendations for additional legislative or administrative action as the Director considers appropriate.

(b) CONGRESSIONAL INTELLIGENCE COMMITTEES DEFINED.—In this section, the term "congressional intelligence committees" means—

(1) the Select Committee on Intelligence of the Senate; and

(2) the Permanent Select Committee on Intelligence of the House of Representatives.

TRANSITIONAL AUTHORITIES

SEC. 1096.

(a) IN GENERAL.—Upon the request of the Director of National Intelligence, the head of any executive agency may, on a reimbursable basis, provide services or detail personnel to the Director of National Intelligence.

(b) TRANSFER OF PERSONNEL.—In addition to any other authorities available under law for such purposes, in the fiscal year after the effective date of this Act, the Director of National Intelligence—

(1) is authorized within the Office of the Director of National Intelligence 500 new personnel billets; and

(2) with the approval of the Director of the Office of Management and Budget, may detail not more than 150 personnel funded within the National Intelligence Program to the Office of the Director of National Intelligence for a period of not more than 2 years.

EFFECTIVE DATES

SEC. 1097.

(a) IN GENERAL.—Except as otherwise expressly provided in this Act, this title and the amendments made by this title shall take effect not later than six months after the date of the enactment of this Act.

(b) SPECIFIC EFFECTIVE DATES.—

(1)(A) Not later than 60 days after the date of the appointment of the first Director of National Intelligence, the Director of National Intelligence shall first appoint individuals to positions within the Office of the Director of National Intelligence.

(B) Subparagraph (A) shall not apply with respect to the Principal Deputy Director of National Intelligence.

(2) Not later than 180 days after the effective date of this Act, the President shall transmit to Congress the implementation plan required by section 1094.

(3) Not later than one year after the date of the enactment of this Act, the Director of National Intelligence shall prescribe regulations, policies, procedures, standards, and guidelines required under section 102A of the National Security Act of 1947, as amended by section 1011(a) of this Act.

SUBTITLE I—OTHER MATTERS

STUDY OF PROMOTION AND PROFESSIONAL MILITARY EDUCATION SCHOOL SELECTION RATES FOR MILITARY INTELLIGENCE OFFICERS

SEC. 1101.

(a) STUDY.—The Secretary of Defense shall conduct a study of the promotion selection rates, and the selection rates for attendance at professional military education schools, of intelligence officers of the Armed Forces, particularly in comparison to the rates for other officers of the same Armed Force who are in the same grade and competitive category.

(b) REPORT.—The Secretary shall submit to the Committees on Armed Services of the Senate and House of Representatives a report providing the Secretary's findings resulting from the study under subsection (a) and the Secretary's recommendations (if any) for such changes in law as the Secretary considers needed to ensure that intelligence officers, as a group, are selected for promotion, and for attendance at professional military education schools, at rates not less than the rates for all line (or the equivalent) officers of the same Armed Force (both in the zone and below the zone) in the same grade. The report shall be submitted not later than April 1, 2005.

EXTENSION AND IMPROVEMENT OF AUTHORITIES OF PUBLIC INTEREST DECLASSIFICATION BOARD

SEC. 1102.

(a) DIRECTION.—Section 703(a) of the Public Interest Declassification Act of 2000 (title VII of Public Law 106-567; 114 Stat. 2856; 50 U.S.C. §435 note) is amended—

(1) by inserting "(1)" after "ESTABLISHMENT-"; and

(2) by adding at the end the following new paragraph: "(2) The Board shall report directly to the President or, upon designation by the President, the Vice President, the Attorney General, or other designee of the President. The other designee of the President under this paragraph may not be an agency head or official authorized to classify information under Executive Order 12958, or any successor order.".

(b) PURPOSES.—Section 703(b) of that Act (114 Stat. 2856) is amended by adding at the end the following new paragraph: "(5) To review and make recommendations to the President in a timely manner with respect to any congressional request, made by the committee of jurisdiction, to declassify certain records or to reconsider a declination to declassify specific records.".

(c) RECOMMENDATIONS ON SPECIAL SEARCHES.—Section 704(c)(2)(A) of that Act (114 Stat. 2860) is amended by inserting before the period the following: ", and also including specific requests for the declassification of certain records or for the reconsideration of declinations to declassify specific records'.

(d) DECLASSIFICATION REVIEWS.—Section 704 of that Act (114 Stat. 2859) is further amended by adding at the end the following new subsection: "(e) DECLASSIFICATION REVIEWS.—If requested by the President, the Board shall review in a timely manner certain records or declinations to declassify specific records, the declassification of which has been the subject of specific congressional request described in section 703(b)(5).".

(e) NOTIFICATION OF REVIEW.—Section 706 of that Act (114 Stat. 2861) is amended by adding at the end the following new subsection: "(f) NOTIFICATION OF REVIEW.—In response to a specific congressional request for declassification review described in section 703(b)(5), the Board shall advise the originators of the request in a timely manner whether the Board intends to conduct such review.".

(f) EXTENSION.—Section 710(b) of that Act (114 Stat. 2864) is amended by striking "4 years" and inserting "8 years".

SEVERABILITY

SEC. 1103. If any provision of this Act, or an amendment made by this Act, or the application of such provision to any person or circumstance is held invalid, the remainder of this Act, or the application of such provision to persons or circumstances other those to which such provision is held invalid shall not be affected thereby.

TITLE III—SECURITY CLEARANCES SECURITY CLEARANCES; LIMITATIONS

SEC. 3002.

(a) DEFINITIONS.—In this section:

(1) CONTROLLED SUBSTANCE.—The term 'controlled substance' has the meaning given that term in section 102 of the Controlled Substances Act (21 U.S.C. 802).

(2) COVERED PERSON.—The term 'covered person' means—

(A) an officer or employee of a Federal agency;

(B) a member of the Army, Navy, Air Force, or Marine Corps who is on active duty or is in an active status; and

(C) an officer or employee of a contractor of a Federal agency.

(3) RESTRICTED DATA.—The term 'Restricted Data' has the meaning given that term in section 11 of the Atomic Energy Act of 1954 (42 U.S.C. 2014).

(4) SPECIAL ACCESS PROGRAM.—The term 'special access program' has the meaning given that term in section 4.1 of Executive Order No. 12958 (60 Fed. Reg. 19825).

(b) PROHIBITION.—After January 1, 2008, the head of a Federal agency may not grant or renew a security clearance for a covered person who is an unlawful user of a controlled substance or an addict (as defined in section 102(1) of the Controlled Substances Act (21 U.S.C. 802)).

(c) DISQUALIFICATION.—

(1) IN GENERAL.—After January 1, 2008, absent an express written waiver granted in accordance with paragraph (2), the head of a Federal agency may not grant or renew a security clearance described in paragraph (3) for a covered person who—

(A) has been convicted in any court of the United States of a crime, was sentenced to imprisonment for a term exceeding 1 year, and was incarcerated as a result of that sentence for not less than 1 year;

(B) has been discharged or dismissed from the Armed Forces under dishonorable conditions; or

(C) is mentally incompetent, as determined by an adjudicating authority, based on an evaluation by a duly qualified mental health professional employed by, or acceptable to and approved by, the United States Government and in accordance with the adjudicative guidelines required by subsection (d).

(2) WAIVER AUTHORITY.—In a meritorious case, an exception to the disqualification in this subsection may be authorized if there are mitigating factors. Any such waiver may be authorized only in accordance with—

(A) standards and procedures prescribed by, or under the authority of, an Executive order or other guidance issued by the President; or

(B) the adjudicative guidelines required by subsection (d).

(3) COVERED SECURITY CLEARANCES.—This subsection applies to security clearances that provide for access to—

(A) special access programs;

(B) Restricted Data; or

(C) any other information commonly referred to as 'sensitive compartmented information'.

(4) ANNUAL REPORT.—

(A) REQUIREMENT FOR REPORT.—Not later than February 1 of each year, the head of a Federal agency shall submit a report to the appropriate committees of Congress if such agency employs or employed a person for whom a waiver was granted in accordance with paragraph (2) during the preceding year. Such annual report shall not reveal the identity of such person, but shall include for each waiver issued the disqualifying factor under paragraph (1) and the reasons for the waiver of the disqualifying factor.

(B) DEFINITIONS.—In this paragraph:

(i) APPROPRIATE COMMITTEES OF CONGRESS.—The term 'appropriate committees of Congress' means, with respect to a report submitted under subparagraph (A) by the head of a Federal agency—

(I) the congressional defense committees;

(II) the congressional intelligence committees;

(III) the Committee on Homeland Security and Governmental Affairs of the Senate;

(IV) the Committee on Oversight and Government Reform of the House of Representatives; and

(V) each Committee of the Senate or the House of Representatives with oversight authority over such Federal agency.

(ii) CONGRESSIONAL DEFENSE COMMITTEES.—The term 'congressional defense committees' has the meaning given that term in section 101(a)(16) of title 10, United States Code.

(iii) CONGRESSIONAL INTELLIGENCE COMMITTEES.— The term 'congressional intelligence committees' has the meaning given that term in section 3 of the National Security Act of 1947 (50 U.S.C. 401a).

(d) ADJUDICATIVE GUIDELINES.—

(1) REQUIREMENT TO ESTABLISH.—The President shall establish adjudicative guidelines for determining eligibility for access to classified information.

(2) REQUIREMENTS RELATED TO MENTAL HEALTH.—The guidelines required by paragraph (1) shall—

(A) include procedures and standards under which a covered person is determined to be mentally incompetent and provide a means to appeal such a determination; and

(B) require that no negative inference concerning the standards in the guidelines may be raised solely on the basis of seeking mental health counseling.

Foreign Intelligence Surveillance Act of 1978

(Pub. L. 95–511 of October 25, 1978; 92 Stat. 1783, 50 U.S.C. ch.36 (1978), as amended (as reproduced by the ODNI Intelligence Community Legal Reference Book, 2009))

> AN ACT To authorize electronic surveillance to obtain foreign intelligence information.
>
> *Be it enacted by the Senate and House of Representatives of the United States of America in Congress assembled,*

SHORT TITLE

That this Act may be cited as the "Foreign Intelligence Surveillance Act of 1978".

TABLE OF CONTENTS

TITLE I—ELECTRONIC SURVEILLANCE WITHIN THE UNITED STATES FOR FOREIGN INTELLIGENCE PURPOSES

DEFINITIONS

SECTION 101. [50 U.S.C. §1801] As used in this title:

(a) "Foreign power" means—

(1) a foreign government or any component, thereof, whether or not recognized by the United States;

(2) a faction of a foreign nation or nations, not substantially composed of United States persons;

(3) an entity that is openly acknowledged by a foreign government or governments to be directed and controlled by such foreign government or governments;

(4) a group engaged in international terrorism or activities in preparation therefor;

(5) a foreign-based political organization, not substantially composed of United States persons;

(6) an entity that is directed and controlled by a foreign government or governments; or

(7) an entity not substantially composed of United States persons that is engaged in the international proliferation of weapons of mass destruction.

(b) "Agent of a foreign power" means—

(1) any person other than a United States person, who—

(A) acts in the United States as an officer or employee of a foreign power, or as a member of a foreign power as defined in subsection (a)(4);

(B) acts for or on behalf of a foreign power which engages in clandestine intelligence activities in the United States contrary to the interests of the United States, when the circumstances of such person's presence in the United States indicate that such person may engage in such activities in the United States, or when such person knowingly aids or abets any person in the conduct of such activities or knowingly conspires with any person to engage in such activities;

(C) engages in international terrorism or activities in preparation therefore [sic];

(D) engages in the international proliferation of weapons of mass destruction, or activities in preparation therefor; or

(E) engages in the international proliferation of weapons of mass destruction, or activities in preparation therefor for or on behalf of a foreign power; or

(2) any person who—

(A) knowingly engages in clandestine intelligence gathering activities for or on behalf of a foreign power, which activities involve or may involve a violation of the criminal statutes of the United States;

(B) pursuant to the direction of an intelligence service or network of a foreign power, knowingly engages in any other clandestine intelligence activities for or on behalf of such foreign power, which activities involve or are about to involve a violation of the criminal statutes of the United States;

(C) knowingly engages in sabotage or international terrorism, or activities that are in preparation therefor, for or on behalf of a foreign power;

(D) knowingly enters the United States under a false or fraudulent identity for or on behalf of a foreign power or, while in the United States, knowingly assumes a false or fraudulent identity for or on behalf of a foreign power; or

(E) knowingly aids or abets any person in the conduct of activities described in subparagraph (A), (B), or (C) or knowingly conspires with any person to engage in activities described in subparagraph (A), (B), or (C).

(c) "International terrorism" means activities that—

(1) involve violent acts or acts dangerous to human life that are a violation of the criminal laws of the United States or of any State, or that would be a criminal violation if committed within the jurisdiction of the United States or any State;

(2) appear to be intended—

(A) to intimidate or coerce a civilian population;

(B) to influence the policy of a government by intimidation or coercion; or

(C) to affect the conduct of a government by assassination or kidnapping; and

(3) occur totally outside the United States, or transcend national boundaries in terms of the means by which they are accomplished, the persons they appear intended to coerce or intimidate, or the locale in which their perpetrators operate or seek asylum.

(d) "Sabotage" means activities that involve a violation of chapter 105 of title 18, United States Code, or that would involve such a violation if committed against the United States.

(e) "Foreign intelligence information" means—

(1) information that relates to, and if concerning a United States person is necessary to, the ability of the United States to protect against—

(A) actual or potential attack or other grave hostile acts of a foreign power or an agent of a foreign power;

(B) sabotage, international terrorism, or the international proliferation of weapons of mass destruction by a foreign power or an agent of a foreign power; or

(C) clandestine intelligence activities by an intelligence service or network of a foreign power or by an agent of a foreign power; or

(2) information with respect to a foreign power or foreign territory that relates to, and if concerning a United States person is necessary to—

(A) the national defense or the security of the United States; or

(B) the conduct of the foreign affairs of the United States.

(f) "Electronic surveillance" means—

(1) the acquisition by an electronic, mechanical, or other surveillance device of the contents of any wire or radio communications sent by or intended to be received by a particular, known United States person who is in the United States, if the contents are acquired by intentionally targeting that United States person, under circumstances in which a person has a reasonable expectation of privacy and a warrant would be required for law enforcement purposes;

(2) the acquisition by an electronic, mechanical, or other surveillance device of the contents of any wire communication to or from a person in the United States, without the consent of any party thereto, if such acquisition occurs in the United States, but does not include the acquisition of those communications of computer trespassers that would be permissible under section 2511(2)(i) of title 18, United States Code;

(3) the intentional acquisition by an electronic, mechanical, or other surveillance device of the contents of any radio communication, under circumstances in which a person has a reasonable expectation of privacy and a warrant would be required for law enforcement purposes, and if both the sender and all intended recipients are located within the United States; or

(4) the installation or use of an electronic, mechanical, or other surveillance device in the United States for monitoring to acquire information, other than from a wire or radio communication, under circumstances in which a person has a reasonable expectation of privacy and a warrant would be required for law enforcement purposes.

(g) "Attorney General" means the Attorney General of the United States (or Acting Attorney General), the Deputy Attorney General, or, upon, the designation of the Attorney General, the Assistant Attorney General designated as the Assistant Attorney General for National Security under section 507A of title 28, United States Code.

(h) "Minimization procedures", with respect to electronic surveillance, means—

(1) specific procedures, which shall be adopted by the Attorney General, that are reasonably designed in light of the purpose and technique of the particular surveillance, to minimize the acquisition and retention, and prohibit the dissemination, of nonpublicly available information concerning unconsenting United States persons consistent with the need of the United States to obtain, produce, and disseminate foreign intelligence information;

(2) procedures that require that nonpublicly available information, which is not foreign intelligence information, as defined in subsection (c)(1), shall not be disseminated in a manner that identifies any United States person, without such person's consent, unless such person's identity is necessary to understand foreign intelligence information or assess its importance;

(3) notwithstanding paragraphs (1) and (2), procedures that allow for the retention and dissemination of information that is evidence of a crime which has been, is being, or is about to be committed and that is to be retained or disseminated for law enforcement purposes; and

(4) notwithstanding paragraphs (1), (2), and (3), with respect to any electronic surveillance approved pursuant to section 102(a), procedures that re-

quire that no contents of any communication to which a United States person is a party shall be disclosed, disseminated, or used for any purpose or retained for longer than 72 hours unless a court order under section 105 is obtained or unless the Attorney General determines that the information indicates a threat of death or serious bodily harm to any person.

(i) "United States person" means a citizen of the United States, an alien lawfully admitted for permanent residence (as defined in section 101(a)(20) of the Immigration and Nationality Act), an unincorporated association a substantial number of members of which are citizens of the United States or aliens lawfully admitted for permanent residence, or a corporation which is incorporated in the United States, but does not include a corporation or an association which is a foreign power, as defined in subsection (a) (1), (2), or (3).

(j) "United States", when used in a geographic sense, means all areas under the territorial sovereignty of the United States and the Trust Territory of the Pacific Islands.

(k) "Aggrieved person" means a person who is the target of an electronic surveillance or any other person whose communications or activities were subject to electronic surveillance.

(l) "Wire communication" means any communications while it is being carried by a wire, cable, or other like connection furnished or operated by any person engaged as a common carrier in providing or operating such facilities for the transmission of interstate or foreign communications.

(m) "Person" means any individual, including any officer or employee of the Federal Government, or any group, entity, association, corporation, or foreign power.

(n) "Contents", when used with respect to a communication, includes any information concerning the identity of the parties to such communications or the existence, substance, purport, or meaning of that communication.

(o) "State" means any State of the United States, the District of Columbia, the Commonwealth of Puerto Rico, the Trust Territory of the Pacific Islands, an any territory or possession of the United States.

(p) 'Weapon of mass destruction' means—

(1) any explosive, incendiary, or poison gas device that is designed, intended, or has the capability to cause a mass casualty incident;

(2) any weapon that is designed, intended, or has the capability to cause death or serious bodily injury to a significant number of persons through the release, dissemination, or impact of toxic or poisonous chemicals or their precursors;

(3) any weapon involving a biological agent, toxin, or vector (as such terms are defined in section 178 of title 18, United States Code) that is designed, intended, or has the capability to cause death, illness, or serious bodily injury to a significant number of persons; or

(4) any weapon that is designed, intended, or has the capability to release radiation or radioactivity causing death, illness, or serious bodily injury to a significant number of persons.'.

AUTHORIZATION FOR ELECTRONIC SURVEILLANCE FOR FOREIGN INTELLIGENCE PURPOSES

SEC. 102. [50 U.S.C. §1802]

(a)(1) Notwithstanding any other law, the President, through the Attorney General, may authorize electronic surveillance without a court order under this title to acquire foreign intelligence information for periods of up to one year if the Attorney General certifies in writing under oath that—

(A) the electronic surveillance is solely directed at—

(i) the acquisition of the contents of communications transmitted by means of communications used exclusively between or among foreign powers, as defined in section 101(a) (1), (2), or (3); or

(ii) the acquisition of technical intelligence, other than the spoken communications of individuals, from property or premises under the open and exclusive control of a foreign power, as defined in section 101(a) (1), (2), or (3);

(B) there is no substantial likelihood that the surveillance will acquire the contents of any communications to which a United States person is a party; and

(C) the proposed minimization procedures with respect to such surveillance meet the definition of minimization procedures under section 101(h); and if the Attorney General reports such minimization procedures and any changes thereto to the House Permanent Select Committee on Intelligence and the Senate Select Committee on Intelligence at least thirty days prior to their effective date, unless the Attorney General determines immediate action is required and notifies the committees immediately of such minimization procedures and the reason for their becoming effective immediately.

(2) An electronic surveillance authorized by this subsection may be conducted only in accordance with the Attorney General's certification and the minimization procedures adopted by him. The Attorney General shall assess compliance with such procedures and shall report such assessments to the House Permanent Select Committee on Intelligence and the Senate Select Committee on Intelligence under the provisions of section 108(a).

(3) The Attorney General shall immediately transmit under seal to the court established under section 103(a) a copy of his certification. Such certification shall be maintained under security measures established by the Chief Justice with the concurrence of the Attorney General, in consultation with the Director of National Intelligence, and shall remain sealed unless—

(A) an application for a court order with respect to the surveillance is made under sections 101(h)(4) and 104; or

(B) the certification is necessary to determine the legality of the surveillance under section 106(f).

(4) With respect to electronic surveillance authorized by this subsection, the Attorney General may direct a specified communication common carrier to—

(A) furnish all information, facilities, or technical assistance necessary to accomplish the electronic surveillance in such a manner as will protect its secrecy and produce a minimum of interference with the services that such carrier is providing its customers; and

(B) maintain under security procedures approved by the Attorney General and the Director of National Intelligence any records concerning the surveillance or the aid furnished which such carrier wishes to retain. The Government shall compensate, at the prevailing rate, such carrier for furnishing such aid.

(b) Applications for a court order under this title are authorized if the President has, by written authorization, empowered the Attormey General [sic] to approve applications to the court having jurisdiction under section 103, and a judge to whom an application is made may, notwithstanding any other law, grant an order, in conformity with section 105, approving electronic surveillance of a foreign power or an agent of a foreign power for the purpose of obtaining foreign intelligence information, except that the court shall not have jurisdiction to grant any order approving electronic surveillance directed solely as described in paragraph (1)(A) of subsection (a) unless such surveillance may involve the acquisition of communications of any United States person.

DESIGNATION OF JUDGES

SEC. 103. [50 U.S.C. §1803]

(a)(1) The Chief Justice of the United States shall publicly designate 11 district court judges from at least seven of the United States judicial circuits of whom no fewer than 3 shall reside within 20 miles of the District of Columbia who shall constitute a court which shall have jurisdiction to hear applications for and grant orders approving electronic surveillance anywhere within the United States under the procedures set forth in this Act, except that no judge designated under this subsection (except when sitting en banc under paragraph (2)) shall hear the same application for electronic surveillance under this Act which has been denied previously by another judge designated under this subsection. If any judge so designated denies an application for an order authorizing electronic surveillance under this Act, such judge shall provide immediately for the record a written statement of each reason for his decision and, on motion of the United States, the record shall be transmitted, under seal, to the court of review established in subsection (b).

(2)(A) The court established under this subsection may, on its own initiative, or upon the request of the Government in any proceeding or a party under section 501(f) or paragraph (4) or (5) of section 702(h), hold a hearing or rehearing, en banc, when ordered by a majority of the judges that constitute such court upon a determination that—

(i) en banc consideration is necessary to secure or maintain uniformity of the court's decisions; or

(ii) the proceeding involves a question of exceptional importance.

(B) Any authority granted by this Act to a judge of the court established under this subsection may be exercised by the court en banc. When exercising such authority, the court en banc shall comply with any requirements of this Act on the exercise of such authority.

(C) For purposes of this paragraph, the court en banc shall consist of all judges who constitute the court established under this subsection.

(b) The Chief Justice shall publicly designate three judges, one of whom shall be publicly designate as the presiding judge, from the United States district courts or courts of appeals who together shall comprise a court of review which shall have jurisdiction to review the denial of any application made under this Act. If such court determines that the application was properly denied, the court shall immediately provide for the record a written statement of each reason for its decision and, on petition of the United States for a writ of certiorari, the record shall be transmitted under seal to the Supreme Court, which shall have jurisdiction to review such decision.

(c) Proceedings under this Act shall be conducted as expeditiously as possible. The record of proceedings under this Act, including applications made and orders granted, shall be maintained under security measures established by the Chief Justice in consultation with the Attorney General and the Director of National Intelligence.

(d) Each judge designated under this section shall so serve for a maximum of seven years and shall not be eligible for redesignation, except that the judges first designated under subsection (a) shall be designated for terms of from one to seven years so that one term expires each year, and that judges first designated under subsection (b) shall be designated for terms of three, five, and seven years.

(e)(1) Three judges designated under subsection (a) who reside within 20 miles of the District of Columbia, or, if all of such judges are unavailable, other judges of the court established under subsection (a) as may be designated by the presiding judge of such court, shall comprise a petition review pool which shall have jurisdiction to review petitions filed pursuant to section 1861(f)(1) or 1881a(h)(4).

(2) Not later than 60 days after the date of the enactment of the USA PATRIOT Improvement and Reauthorization Act of 2005, the court established under subsection (a) shall adopt and, consistent with the protection of national security, publish procedures for the review of petitions filed pursuant to section 1861(f)(1) or 1881a(h)(4) by the panel established under paragraph (1). Such procedures shall provide that review of a petition shall be conducted in camera and shall also provide for the designation of an acting presiding judge.

(f)(1) A judge of the court established under subsection (a), the court established under subsection (b) or a judge of that court, or the Supreme Court of the United States or a justice of that court, may, in accordance with the rules of their respective courts, enter a stay of an order or an order modifying an order of the court established under subsection (a) or the court established under subsection (b) entered under any title of this Act, while the court established under subsection (a) conducts a rehearing, while an appeal is pending to the court established under subsection (b), or while a petition of certiorari is pending in the Supreme Court of the United States, or during the pendency of any review by that court.

(2) The authority described in paragraph (1) shall apply to an order entered under any provision of this Act.

(g)(1) The courts established pursuant to subsections (a) and (b) may establish such rules and procedures, and take such actions, as are reasonably necessary to administer their responsibilities under this Act.

(2) The rules and procedures established under paragraph (1), and any modifications of such rules and procedures, shall be recorded, and shall be transmitted to the following:

(A) All of the judges on the court established pursuant to subsection (a).

(B) All of the judges on the court of review established pursuant to subsection (b).

(C) The Chief Justice of the United States.

(D) The Committee on the Judiciary of the Senate.

(E) The Select Committee on Intelligence of the Senate.

(F) The Committee on the Judiciary of the House of Representatives.

(G) The Permanent Select Committee on Intelligence of the House of Representatives.

(3) The transmissions required by paragraph (2) shall be submitted in unclassified form, but may include a classified annex.

(i) Nothing in this Act shall be construed to reduce or contravene the inherent authority of the court established under subsection (a) to determine or enforce compliance with an order or a rule of such court or with a procedure approved by such court.

APPLICATION FOR AN ORDER

SEC. 104. [50 U.S.C. §1804]

(a) Each application for an order approving electronic surveillance under this title shall be made by a Federal officer in writing upon oath or affirmation to a judge having jurisdiction under section 103. Each application shall require the approval of the Attorney General based upon his finding that it satisfies the criteria and requirements of such application as set forth in this title. It shall include—

(1) the identity of the Federal officer making the application;

(2) the identity, if known, or a description of the specific target of the electronic surveillance;

(3) a statement of the facts and circumstances relied upon by the applicant to justify his belief that—

(A) the target of the electronic surveillance is a foreign power or an agent of a foreign power; and

(B) each of the facilities or places at which the electronic surveillance is directed is being used, or is about to be used, by a foreign power or an agent of a foreign power;

(4) a statement of the proposed minimization procedures;

(5) a description of the nature of the information sought and the type of communications or activities to be subjected to the surveillance;

(6) a certification or certifications by the Assistant to the President for National Security Affairs, an executive branch official or officials designated by the President from among those executive officers employed in the area of

national security or defense and appointed by the President with the advice and consent of the Senate, or the Deputy Director of the Federal Bureau of Investigation, if designated by the President as a certifying official —

(A) that the certifying official deems the information sought to be foreign intelligence information;

(B) that a significant purpose of the surveillance is to obtain foreign intelligence information;

(C) that such information cannot reasonably be obtained by normal investigative techniques;

(D) that designates the type of foreign intelligence information being sought according to the categories described in section 101(e); and

(E) including a statement of the basis for the certification that—

(i) the information sought is the type of foreign intelligence information designated; and

(ii) such information cannot reasonably be obtained by normal investigative techniques;

(7) a summary statement of the means by which the surveillance will be effected and a statement whether physical entry is required to effect the surveillance;

(8) a statement of the facts concerning all previous applications that have been made to any judge under this title involving any of the persons, facilities, or places specified in the application, and the action taken on each previous application; and

(9) a statement of the period of time for which the electronic surveillance is required to be maintained, and if the nature of the intelligence gathering is such that the approval of the use of electronic surveillance under this title should not automatically terminate when the described type of information has first been obtained, a description of facts supporting the belief that additional information of the same type will be obtained thereafter.

(b) The Attorney General may require any other affidavit or certification from any other officer in connection with the application.

(c) The judge may require the applicant to furnish such other information as may be necessary to make the determinations required by section 105.

(d) (1)(A) Upon written request of the Director of the Federal Bureau of Investigation, the Secretary of Defense, the Secretary of State, or the Director of National Intelligence, or the Director of the Central Intelligence Agency, the Attorney General shall personally review under subsection (a) an application under that subsection for a target described in section 101(b)(2).

(B) Except when disabled or otherwise unavailable to make a request referred to in subparagraph (A), an official referred to in that subparagraph may not delegate the authority to make a request referred to in that subparagraph.

(C) Each official referred to in subparagraph (A) with authority to make a request under that subparagraph shall take appropriate actions in advance to ensure that delegation of such authority is clearly established in the event such official is disabled or otherwise unavailable to make such request.

(2)(A) If as a result of a request under paragraph (1) the Attorney General determines not to approve an application under the second sentence of subsection (a) for purposes of making the application under this section, the Attorney General shall provide written notice of the determination to the official making the request for the review of the application under that paragraph. Except when disabled or otherwise unavailable to make a determination under the preceding sentence, the Attorney General may not delegate the responsibility to make a determination under that sentence. The Attorney General shall take appropriate actions in advance to ensure that delegation of such responsibility is clearly established in the event the Attorney General is disabled or otherwise unavailable to make such determination.

(B) Notice with respect to an application under subparagraph (A) shall set forth the modifications, if any, of the application that are necessary in order for the Attorney General to approve the application under the second sentence of subsection (a) for purposes of making the application under this section.

(C) Upon review of any modifications of an application set forth under subparagraph (B), the official notified of the modifications under this paragraph shall modify the application if such official determines that such modification is warranted. Such official shall supervise the making of any modification under this subparagraph. Except when disabled or otherwise unavailable to supervise the making of any modification under the preceding sentence, such official may not delegate the responsibility to supervise the making of any modification under that preceding sentence. Each such official shall take appropriate actions in advance to ensure that delegation of such responsibility is clearly established in the event such official is disabled or otherwise unavailable to supervise the making of such modification.

ISSUANCE OF AN ORDER

SEC. 105. [50 U.S.C. §1805]

(a) Upon an application made pursuant to section 104, the judge shall enter an ex parte order as requested or as modified approving the electronic surveillance if he finds that—

(1) the application has been made by a Federal officer and approved by the Attorney General;

(2) on the basis of the facts submitted by the applicant there is probable cause to believe that—

(A) the target of the electronic surveillance is a foreign power or an agent of a foreign power: Provided, That no United States person may be considered a foreign power or an agent of a foreign power solely upon the basis of activities protected by the first amendment to the Constitution of the United States; and

(B) each of the facilities or places at which the electronic surveillance is directed is being used, or is about to be used, by a foreign power or an agent of a foreign power;

(3) the proposed minimization procedures meet the definition of minimization procedures under section 101(h); and

(4) the application which has been filed contains all statements and certifications required by section 104 and, if the target is a United States person, the certification or certifications are not clearly erroneous on the basis of the statement made under section 104(a)(7)(E) and any other information furnished under section 104(d).

(b) In determining whether or not probable cause exists for purposes of an order under subsection (a)(2), a judge may consider past activities of the target, as well as facts and circumstances relating to current or future activities of the target.

(c) (1) SPECIFICATIONS.—An order approving an electronic surveillance under this section shall specify—

(A) the identity, if known, or a description of the specific target of the electronic surveillance identified or described in the application pursuant to section 104(a)(3) of this Act;

(B) the nature and location of each of the facilities or places at which the electronic surveillance will be directed, if known;

(C) the type of information sought to be acquired and the type of communications or activities to be subjected to the surveillance;

(D) the means by which the electronic surveillance will be effected and whether physical entry will be used to effect the surveillance; and

(E) the period of time during which the electronic surveillance is approved.

(2) DIRECTIONS.—An order approving an electronic surveillance under this section shall direct—

(A) that the minimization procedures be followed;

(B) that, upon the request of the applicant, a specified communication or other common carrier, landlord, custodian, or other specified person, or in circumstances where the Court finds, based upon specific facts provided in the application, that the actions of the target of the application may have the effect of thwarting the identification of a specified person, such other persons, furnish the applicant forthwith all information, facilities, or technical assistance necessary to accomplish the electronic surveillance in such a manner as will protect its secrecy and produce a minimum of interference with the services that such carrier, landlord, custodian, or other person is providing that target of electronic surveillance;

(C) that such carrier, landlord, custodian, or other person maintain under security procedures approved by the Attorney General and the Director of National Intelligence any records concerning the surveillance or the aid furnished that such person wishes to retain; and

(D) that the applicant compensate, at the prevailing rate, such carrier, landlord, custodian, or other person for furnishing such aid.

(3) SPECIAL DIRECTIONS FOR CERTAIN ORDERS.—An order approving an electronic surveillance under this section in circumstances where the na-

ture and location of each of the facilities or places at which the surveillance will be directed is unknown shall direct the applicant to provide notice to the court within ten days after the date on which surveillance begins to be directed at any new facility or place, unless the court finds good cause to justify a longer period of up to 60 days, of—

(A) the nature and location of each new facility or place at which the electronic surveillance is directed;

(B) the facts and circumstances relied upon by the applicant to justify the applicant's belief that each new facility or place at which the electronic surveillance is directed is or was being used, or is about to be used, by the target of the surveillance;

(C) a statement of any proposed minimization procedures that differ from those contained in the original application or order, that may be necessitated by a change in the facility or place at which the electronic surveillance is directed; and

(D) the total number of electronic surveillances that have been or are being conducted under the authority of the order.

(d)(1) An order issued under this section may approve an electronic surveillance for the period necessary to achieve its purpose, or for ninety days, whichever is less, except that

(A) 1 an order under this section shall approve an electronic surveillance targeted against a foreign power, as defined in section 101(a), (1), (2), or (3), for the period specified in the application or for one year, whichever is less, and

(B) an order under this Act for a surveillance targeted against an agent of a foreign power, who is not a United States person may be for the period specified in the application or for 120 days, whichever is less.

(2) Extensions of an order issued under this title may be granted on the same basis as an original order upon an application for an extension and new findings made in the same manner as required for an original order, except that

(A) an extension of an order under this Act for a surveillance targeted against a foreign power, a defined in paragraph (5), (6), or (7) of section 101(a), or against a foreign power as defined in section 101(a)(4) that is not a United States person, may be for a period not to exceed one year if the judge finds probable cause to believe that no communication of any individual United States person will be acquired during the period, and

(B) an extension of an order under this Act for a surveillance targeted against an agent of a foreign power who is not a United States person may be for a period not to exceed 1 year.

(3) At or before the end of the period of time for which electronic surveillance is approved by an order or an extension, the judge may assess compliance with the minimization procedures by reviewing the circumstances under which information concerning United States persons was acquired, retained, or disseminated.

(e)(1) Notwithstanding any other provision of this title, the Attorney General may authorize the emergency employment of electronic surveillance if the Attorney General—

(A) reasonably determines that an emergency situation exists with respect to the employment of electronic surveillance to obtain foreign intelligence information before an order authorizing such surveillance can with due diligence be obtained;

(B) reasonably determines that the factual basis for the issuance of an order under this title to approve such electronic surveillance exists;

(C) informs, either personally or through a designee, a judge having jurisdiction under section 103 at the time of such authorization that the decision has been made to employ emergency electronic surveillance; and

(D) makes an application in accordance with this title to a judge having jurisdiction under section 103 as soon as practicable, but not later than 7 days after the Attorney General authorizes such surveillance.

(2) If the Attorney General authorizes the emergency employment of electronic surveillance under paragraph (1), the Attorney General shall require that the minimization procedures required by this title for the issuance of a judicial order be followed.

(3) In the absence of a judicial order approving such electronic surveillance, the surveillance shall terminate when the information sought is obtained, when the application for the order is denied, or after the expiration of 7 days from the time of authorization by the Attorney General, whichever is earliest.

(4) A denial of the application made under this subsection may be reviewed as provided in section 103.

(5) In the event that such application for approval is denied, or in any other case where the electronic surveillance is terminated and no order is issued approving the surveillance, no information obtained or evidence derived from such surveillance shall be received in evidence or otherwise disclosed in any trial, hearing, or other proceeding in or before any court, grand jury, department, office, agency, regulatory body, legislative committee, or other authority of the United States, a State, or political subdivision thereof, and no information concerning any United States person acquired from such surveillance shall subsequently be used or disclosed in any other manner by Federal officers or employees without the consent of such person, except with the approval of the Attorney General if the information indicates a threat of death or serious bodily harm to any person.

(6) The Attorney General shall assess compliance with the requirements of paragraph (5).

(f) Notwithstanding any other provision of this Act, officers, employees, or agents of the United States are authorized in the normal course of their official duties to conduct electronic surveillance not targeted against the communications of any particular person or persons, under procedures approved by the Attorney General, solely to—

(1) test the capability of electronic equipment, if—

(A) it is not reasonable to obtain the consent of the persons incidentally

subjected to the surveillance;
(B) the test is limited in extent and duration to that necessary to determine to capability of the equipment;
(C) the contents of any communication acquired are retained and used only for the purpose of determining the capability of the equipment, are disclosed only to test personnel, and are destroyed before or immediately upon completion of the test; and
(D) Provided, That the test may exceed ninety days only with the prior approval of the Attorney General;

(2) determine the existence and capability of electronic surveillance equipment being used by persons not authorized to conduct electronic surveillance, if—

(A) it is not reasonable to obtain the consent of persons incidentally subjected to the surveillance;
(B) such electronic surveillance is limited in extent and duration to that necessary to determine the existence and capability of such equipment; and
(C) any information acquired by such surveillance is used only to enforce chapter 119 of title 18, United States Code, or section 705 of the Communications Act of 1934, or to protect information from unauthorized surveillance; or

(3) train intelligence personnel in the use of electronic surveillance equipment, if—

(A) it is not reasonable to—
(i) obtain the consent of the persons incidentally subjected to the surveillance;
(ii) train persons in the course of surveillances otherwise authorized by this title; or
(iii) train persons in the use of such equipment without engaging in electronic surveillance;
(B) such electronic surveillance is limited in extent and duration to that necessary to train the personnel in the use of the equipment; and
(C) no contents of any communication acquired are retained or disseminated for any purpose, but are destroyed as soon as reasonably possible.

(g) Certifications made by the Attorney General pursuant to section 102(a) and applications made and orders granted under this title shall be retained for a period of at least ten years from the date of the certification or application.

(h) No cause of action shall lie in any court against any provider of a wire or electronic communication service, landlord, custodian, or other person (including any officer, employee, agent, or other specified person thereof) that furnishes any information, facilities, or technical assistance in accordance with a court order or request for emergency assistance under this Act for electronic surveillance or physical search.

(i) In any case in which the Government makes an application to a judge under this title to conduct electronic surveillance involving communications and the judge grants such application, upon the request of the applicant, the judge shall also authorize the installation and use of pen registers and trap and trace devices, and direct the disclosure of the information set forth in section 402(d)(2).

USE OF INFORMATION

SEC. 106. [50 U.S.C. §1806]

(a) Information acquired from an electronic surveillance conducted pursuant to this title concerning any United States person may be used and disclosed by Federal officers and employees without the consent of the United States person only in accordance with the minimization procedures required by this title. No otherwise privileged communication obtained in accordance with, or in violation of, the provisions of this Act shall lose its privileged character. No information acquired from an electronic surveillance pursuant to this title may be used or disclosed by Federal officers or employees except for lawful purposes.

(b) No information acquired pursuant to this title shall be disclosed for law enforcement purposes unless such disclosure is accompanied by a statement that such information, or any information derived therefrom, may only be used in a criminal proceeding with the advance authorization of the Attorney General.

(c) Whenever the Government intends to enter into evidence or otherwise use or disclose in any trial, hearing, or other proceeding in or before any court, department, officer, agency, regulatory body, or other authority of the United States, against an aggrieved person, any information obtained or derived from an electronic surveillance of that aggrieved person pursuant to the authority of this Act, the Government shall, prior to the trial, hearing, or other proceeding or at a reasonable time prior to an effort to so disclose or so use that information or submit it in evidence, notify the aggrieved person and the court or other authority in which the information is to be disclosed or used that the Government intends to so disclose or so use such information.

(d) Whenever any State or political subdivision thereof intends to enter into evidence or otherwise use or disclose in any trial, hearing, or other proceeding in or before any court, department, officer, agency, regulatory body, or other authority of a State or a political subdivision thereof, against an aggrieved person any information obtained or derived from an electronic surveillance of that aggrieved person pursuant to the authority of this Act, the State or political subdivision thereof shall notify the aggrieved person, the court or other authority in which the information is to be disclosed or used, and the Attorney General that the State or political subdivision thereof intends to so disclose or so use such information.

(e) Any person against whom evidence obtained or derived from an electronic surveillance to which he is an aggrieved person is to be, or has been, introduced or otherwise used or disclosed in any trial, hearing, or other proceeding in or before any court, department, officer, agency, regulatory body, or other authority of the United States, a State, or a political subdivision thereof, may move to suppress the evidence obtained or derived from such electronic surveillance on the grounds that—

(1) the information was unlawfully acquired; or

(2) the surveillance was not made in conformity with an order of authorization or approval. Such a motion shall be made before the trial, hearing, or other proceeding unless there was no opportunity to make such a motion or the person was not aware of the grounds of the motion.

(f) [IN CAMERA AND EX PARTE REVIEW BY DISTRICT COURT.—] Whenever a court or other authority is notified pursuant to subsection (c) or (d), or whenever a motion is made pursuant to subsection (e), or whenever any motion or request is made by an aggrieved person pursuant to any other statute or rule of the United States or any State before any court or other authority of the United States or any State to discover or obtain applications or orders or other materials relating to electronic surveillance or to discover, obtain, or suppress evidence or information obtained or derived from electronic surveillance under this Act, the United States district court or, where the motion is made before another authority, the United States district court in the same district as the authority, shall, notwithstanding any other law, if the Attorney General files an affidavit under oath that disclosure or an adversary hearing would harm the national security of the United States, review in camera and ex parte the application, order, and such other materials relating to the surveillance as may be necessary to determine whether the surveillance of the aggrieved person was lawfully authorized and conducted. In making this determination, the court may disclose to the aggrieved person, under appropriate security procedures and protective orders, portions of the application, order, or other materials relating to the surveillance only where such disclosure is necessary to make an accurate determination of the legality of the surveillance.

(g) If the United States district court pursuant to subsection (f) determine that the surveillance was not lawfully authorized or conducted, it shall, in accordance with the requirements of law, suppress the evidence which was unlawfully obtained or derived from electronic surveillance of the aggrieved person or otherwise grant the motion of the aggrieved person. If the court determines that the surveillance was lawfully authorized and conducted, it shall deny the motion of the aggrieved person except to the extent that due process requires discovery or disclosure.

(h) Orders granting motions or requests under subsection (g), decisions under this section that electronic surveillance was not lawfully authorized or conducted, and orders of the United States district court requiring review or granting disclosure of applications, orders, or other materials relating to a surveillance shall be final orders and binding upon all courts of the United States and the several States except a United States court of appeals and the Supreme Court.

(i) In circumstances involving the unintentional acquisition by an electronic, mechanical, or other surveillance device of the contents of any communication, under circumstances in which a person has a reasonable expectation of privacy and a warrant would be required for law enforcement purposes, and if both the sender and all intended recipients are located within the United States, such contents shall be destroyed upon recognition, unless the Attorney General determines that the contents indicates a threat of death or serious bodily harm to any person.

(j) If an emergency employment of electronic surveillance is authorized under section 105(e) and a subsequent order approving the surveillance is not obtained, the judge shall cause to be served on any United States person named in the application and on such other United States persons subject to electronic surveillance as the judge may determine in his discretion it is in the interest of justice to serve, notice of—

(1) the fact of the application;

(2) the period of the surveillance; and

(3) the fact that during the period information was or was not obtained. On an ex parte showing of good cause to the judge the serving of the notice required by this subsection may be postponed or suspended for a period not to exceed ninety days. Thereafter, on a further ex parte showing of good cause, the court shall forego ordering the serving of the notice required under this subsection.

(k)(1) Federal officers who conduct electronic surveillance to acquire foreign intelligence information under this title may consult with Federal law enforcement officers or law enforcement personnel of a State or political subdivision of a State (including the chief executive officer of that State or political subdivision who has the authority to appoint or direct the chief law enforcement officer of that State or political subdivision) to coordinate efforts to investigate or protect against—

(A) actual or potential attack or other grave hostile acts of a foreign power or an agent of a foreign power;

(B) sabotage, international terrorism, or the international proliferation of weapons of mass destruction by a foreign power or an agent of a foreign power; or

(C) clandestine intelligence activities by an intelligence service or network of a foreign power or by an agent of a foreign power.

(2) Coordination authorized under paragraph (1) shall not preclude the certification required by section 104(a)(7)(B) or the entry of an order under section 105.

REPORT OF ELECTRONIC SURVEILLANCE

SEC. 107. [50 U.S.C. §1807] In April of each year, the Attorney General shall transmit to the Administrative Office of the United States Court and to Congress a report setting forth with respect to the preceding calendar year—

(a) the total number of applications made for orders and extensions of orders approving electronic surveillance under this title; and

(b) the total number of such orders and extensions either granted, modified, or denied.

CONGRESSIONAL OVERSIGHT

SEC. 108. [50 U.S.C. §1808]

(a)(1) On a semiannual basis the Attorney General shall fully inform the House Permanent Select Committee on Intelligence and the Senate Select Committees on Intelligence and the Committee on the Judiciary of the Senate concerning all electronic surveillance under this title. Nothing in this title shall be deemed to limit the authority and responsibility of the appropriate committees of each House of Congress to obtain such information as they may need to carry out their respective functions and duties.

(2) Each report under the first sentence of paragraph (1) shall include a description of—

(A) the total number of applications made for orders and extensions of orders approving electronic surveillance under this title where the nature and location of each facility or place at which the electronic surveillance will be directed is unknown;

(B) each criminal case in which information acquired under this Act has been authorized for use at trial during the period covered by such report; and

(C) the total number of emergency employments of electronic surveillance under section 105(e) and the total number of subsequent orders approving or denying such electronic surveillance.

(b) On or before one year after the effective date of this Act and on the same day each year for four years thereafter, the Permanent Select Committee on Intelligence and the Senate Select Committee on Intelligence shall report respectively to the House of Representatives and the Senate, concerning the implementation of this Act. Said reports shall include but not be limited to an analysis and recommendations concerning whether this Act should be (1) amended, (2) repealed, or (3) permitted to continue in effect without amendment.

PENALTIES

SEC. 109. [50 U.S.C. §1809]

(a) OFFENSE.—A person is guilty of an offense if he intentionally—

(1) engages in electronic surveillance under color of law except as authorized by this Act, chapter 119, 121, or 206 of title 18, United States Code, or any express statutory authorization that is an additional exclusive means for conducting electronic surveillance under section 112; or

(2) disclose or uses information obtained under color of law by electronic surveillance, knowing or having reason to known that the information was obtained through electronic surveillance not authorized by this Act, chapter 119, 121, or 206 of title 18, United States Code, or any express statutory authorization that is an additional exclusive means for conducting electronic surveillance under section 112.

(b) DEFENSE.—It is a defense to a prosecution under subsection (a) that the defendant was a law enforcement or investigative officer engaged in the course of his official duties and the electronic surveillance was authorized by and conducted pursuant to a search warrant or court order of a court of competent jurisdiction.

(c) PENALTY.—An offense in this section is punishable by a fine of not more than $10,000 or imprisonment for not more than five years, or both.

(d) JURISDICTION.—There is Federal jurisdiction over an offense under this section if the person committing the offense was an officer or employee of the United States at the time the offense was committed.

CIVIL LIABILITY

SEC. 110. [50 U.S.C. §1810] CIVIL ACTION.—An aggrieved person, other than a foreign power or an agent of a foreign power, as defined in section 101 (a) or (b)(1)(A), respectively, who has been subjected to an electronic surveillance or about whom information obtained by electronic surveillance of such person has been disclosed or used in violation of section 109 shall have a cause of action against any person who committed such violation and shall be entitled to recover—

(a) actual damages, but not less than liquidated damages of $1,000 or $100 per day for each day of violation, whichever is greater;

(b) punitive damages; and

(c) reasonable attorney's fees and other investigation and litigation costs reasonably incurred.

AUTHORIZATION DURING TIME OF WAR

SEC. 111. [50 U.S.C. §1811] Notwithstanding any other law, the President, through the Attorney General, may authorize electronic surveillance without a court order under this title to acquire foreign intelligence information for a period not to exceed fifteen calendar days following a declaration of war by the Congress.

STATEMENT OF EXCLUSIVE MEANS BY WHICH ELECTRONIC SURVEILLANCE AND INTERCEPTION OF CERTAIN COMMUNICATIONS MAY BE CONDUCTED

SEC. 112. [50 U.S.C. § 1812]

(a) Except as provided in subsection (b), the procedures of chapters 119, 121, and 206 of title 18, United States Code, and this Act shall be the exclusive means by which electronic surveillance and the interception of domestic wire, oral, or electronic communications may be conducted.

(b) Only an express statutory authorization for electronic surveillance or the interception of domestic wire, oral, or electronic communications, other than as an amendment to this Act or chapters 119, 121, or 206 of title 18, United States Code, shall constitute an additional exclusive means for the purpose of subsection (a).

TITLE II—CONFORMING AMENDMENTS

AMENDMENTS TO CHAPTER 119 OF TITLE 18, UNITED STATES CODE

SEC. 201. Chapter 119 of title 18, United States Code, is amended as follows:

(a) Section 2511(2)(a)(ii) is amended to read as follows:

> "(ii) Notwithstanding any other law, communication common carriers, their officers, employees, and agents, landlords, custodians, or other persons, are authorized to provide information, facilities, or technical assistance to persons authorized by law to intercept wire or oral communications or to conduct electronic surveillance, as defined in

section 101 of the Foreign Intelligence Surveillance Act of 1978, if the common carrier, its officers, employees, or agent, landlord, custodian, or other specified person, has been provided with—

"(A) a court order directing such assistance signed by the authorizing judge, or "(B) a certification in writing by a person specified in section 2518(7) of title or the Attorney General of the United States that no warrant or court order is required by law, that all statutory requirements have been met, and that the specified assistance is required, setting forth the period of time during which the provision of the information, facilities, or technical assistance is authorized and specifying the information, facilities, or technical assistance required. No communications common carrier, officer, employee, or agent thereof, or landlord, custodian, or other specified person shall disclose the existence of any interception or surveillance or the device used to accomplish the interception or surveillance with respect to which the person has been furnished an order or certification under this subparagraph, except as may otherwise be required by legal process and then only after prior notification of the Attorney General or to the principal prosecuting attorney of a State or any political subdivision of a State, as may be appropriate. Any violation of this subparagraph by a communication common carrier or an officer, employee, or agent thereof, shall render the carrier liable for the civil damages provided for in section 2520. No cause of action shall lie in any court against any communication common carrier, its officers, employees, or agents, landlord, custodian, or other specified person for providing information, facilities, or assistance in accordance with the terms of an order or certification under this subparagraph.".

(b) Section 2511(2) is amended by adding at the end thereof the following new provisions:

"(e) Notwithstanding any other provision of this Act or section 605 or 606 of the Communications Act of 1934, it shall not be unlawful for an officer, employee, or agent of the United States in the normal course of his official duty to conduct electronic surveillance, as defined in section 101 of the Foreign Intelligence Surveillance Act of 1978, as authorized by that Act.

"(f) Nothing contained in this chapter, or section 605 of the Communications Act of 1934, shall be deemed to affect the acquisition by the United States Government of foreign intelligence information from international or foreign communications by a means other than electronic surveillance as defined in section 101 of the Foreign Intelligence Surveillance Act of 1978, and procedures in this chapter and the Foreign Intelligence Surveillance Act of 1978 shall be the exclusive means by which electronic surveillance, as defined in section 101 of such Act, and the interception of domestic wire and oral communications may be conducted.".

(c) Section 2511(3) is repealed.

(d) Section 2518(1) is amended by inserting "under this chapter" after "communication".

(e) Section 2518(4) is amended by inserting "under this chapter" after both appearances of "wire or oral communication".

(f) Section 2518(9) is amended by striking out "intercepted" and inserting "intercepted pursuant to this chapter" after "communication".
(g) Section 2518(10) is amended by striking out "intercepted" and inserting "intercepted pursuant to this chapter" after the first appearance of "communication".
(h) Section 2519(3) is amended by inserting "pursuant to this chapter" after "wire or oral communications" and after "granted or denied".

TITLE III—PHYSICAL SEARCHES WITHIN THE UNITED STATES FOR FOREIGN INTELLIGENCE PURPOSES

DEFINITIONS

SEC. 301. [50 U.S.C. §1821] As used in this title:

(1) The terms "foreign power", "agent of a foreign power", "international terrorism", "sabotage", "foreign intelligence information", "Attorney General", "United States person", "United States", "person", weapon of mass destruction, and "State" shall have the same meanings as in section 101 of this Act, except as specifically provided by this title.

(2) "Aggrieved person" means a person whose premises, property, information, or material is the target of physical search or any other person whose premises, property, information, or material was subject to physical search.

(3) "Foreign Intelligence Surveillance Court" means the court established by section 103(a) of this Act.

(4) "Minimization procedures" with respect to physical search, means—

(A) specific procedures, which shall be adopted by the Attorney General, that are reasonably designed in light of the purposes and technique of the particular physical search, to minimize the acquisition and retention, and prohibit the dissemination, of nonpublicly available information concerning unconsenting United States persons consistent with the need of the United States to obtain, produce, and disseminate foreign intelligence information;

(B) procedures that require that nonpublicly available information, which is not foreign intelligence information, as defined in section 101(e)(1) of this Act, shall not be disseminated in a manner that identifies any United States person, without such person's consent, unless such person's identity is necessary to understand such foreign intelligence information or assess its importance;

(C) notwithstanding subparagraphs (A) and (B), procedures that allow for the retention and dissemination of information that is evidence of a crime which has been, is being, or is about to be committed and that is to be retained or disseminated for law enforcement purposes; and

(D) notwithstanding subparagraphs (A), (B), and (C), with respect to any physical search approved pursuant to section 302(a), procedures that require that no information, material, or property of a United States person shall be disclosed, disseminated, or used for any purpose or retained for longer than 72 hours unless a court order under section 304 is obtained or unless the Attorney General determines that the information indicates a threat of death or serious bodily harm to any person.

(5) "Physical search" means any physical intrusion within the United States into premises or property (including examination of the interior of property by technical means) that is intended to result in a seizure, reproduction, inspection, or alteration of information, material, or property, under circumstances in which a person has a reasonable expectation of privacy and a warrant would be required for law enforcement purposes, but does not include (A) "electronic surveillance", as defined in section 101(f) of this Act, or (B) the acquisition by the United States Government of foreign intelligence information from international or foreign communications, or foreign intelligence activities conducted in accordance with otherwise applicable Federal law involving a foreign electronic communications system, utilizing a means other than electronic surveillance as defined in section 101(f) of this Act.

AUTHORIZATION OF PHYSICAL SEARCHES FOR FOREIGN INTELLIGENCE PURPOSES

SEC. 302. [50 U.S.C. §1822]

(a)(1) Notwithstanding any other provision of law, the President, acting through the Attorney General, may authorize physical searches without a court order under this title to acquire foreign intelligence information for periods of up to one year if—

(A) the Attorney General certifies in writing under oath that—

(i) the physical search is solely directed at premises, information, material, or property used exclusively by, or under the open and exclusive control of, a foreign
power or powers (as defined in section 101(a) (1), (2), or (3));

(ii) there is no substantial likelihood that the physical search will involve the premises, information, material, or property of a United States person; and

(iii) the proposed minimization procedures with respect to such physical search meet the definition of minimization procedures under paragraphs (1) through (4) of section 301(4); and

(B) the Attorney General reports such minimization procedures and any changes thereto to the Permanent Select Committee on Intelligence of the House of Representatives and the Select Committee on Intelligence of the Senate at least 30 days before their effective date, unless the Attorney General determines that immediate action is required and notifies the committees immediately of such minimization procedures and the reason for their becoming effective immediately.

(2) A physical search authorized by this subsection may be conducted only in accordance with the certification and minimization procedures adopted by the Attorney General. The Attorney General shall assess compliance with such procedures and shall report such assessments to the Permanent Select Committee on Intelligence of the House of Representatives and the Select Commit-

tee on Intelligence of the Senate under the provisions of section 306.

(3) The Attorney General shall immediately transmit under seal to the Foreign Intelligence Surveillance Court a copy of the certification. Such certification shall be maintained under security measures established by the Chief Justice of the United States with the concurrence of the Attorney General, in consultation with the Director of National Intelligence, and shall remain sealed unless—

(A) an application for a court order with respect to the physical search is made under section 301(4) and section 303; or

(B) the certification is necessary to determine the legality of the physical search under section 305(g). (4)(A) With respect to physical searches authorized by this subsection, the Attorney General may direct a specified landlord, custodian, or other specified person to—

(i) furnish all information, facilities, or assistance necessary to accomplish the physical search in such a manner as will protect its secrecy and produce a minimum of interference with the services that such landlord, custodian, or other person is providing the target of the physical search; and

(ii) maintain under security procedures approved by the Attorney General and the Director of National Intelligence any records concerning the search or the aid furnished that such person wishes to retain.

(B) The Government shall compensate, at the prevailing rate, such landlord, custodian, or other person for furnishing such aid.

(b) Applications for a court order under this title are authorized if the President has, by written authorization, empowered the Attorney General to approve applications to the Foreign Intelligence Surveillance Court. Notwithstanding any other provision of law, a judge of the court to whom application is made may grant an order in accordance with section 304 approving a physical search in the United States of the premises, property, information, or material of a foreign power or an agent of a foreign power for the purpose of collecting foreign intelligence information.

(c) The Foreign Intelligence Surveillance Court shall have jurisdiction to hear applications for and grant orders approving a physical search for the purpose of obtaining foreign intelligence information anywhere within the United States under the procedures set forth in this title, except that no judge (except when sitting en banc) shall hear the same application which has been denied previously by another judge designated under section 103(a) of this Act. If any judge so designated denies an application for an order authorizing a physical search under this title, such judge shall provide immediately for the record a written statement of each reason for such decision and, on motion of the United States, the record shall be transmitted, under seal, to the court of review established under section 103(b).

(d) The court of review established under section 103(b) shall have jurisdiction to review the denial of any application made under this title. If such court determines that the application was properly denied, the court shall immediately provide for the record a written statement of each reason for its decision and, on petition of the United States for a writ of certiorari, the record shall be transmitted under seal to the Supreme Court, which shall have jurisdiction to review such decision.

(e) Judicial proceedings under this title shall be concluded as expeditiously as possible. The record of proceedings under this title, including applications made and orders granted, shall be maintained under security measures established by the Chief Justice of the United States in consultation with the Attorney General and the Director of National Intelligence.

APPLICATION FOR AN ORDER

SEC. 303. [50 U.S.C. §1823]

(a) Each application for an order approving a physical search under this title shall be made by a Federal officer in writing upon oath or affirmation to a judge of the Foreign Intelligence Surveillance Court. Each application shall require the approval of the Attorney General based upon the Attorney General's finding that it satisfies the criteria and requirements for such application as set forth in this title. Each application shall include—

(1) the identity of the Federal officer making the application;

(2) the identity, if known, or a description of the target of the search, and a description of the premises or property to be searched and of the information, material, or property to be seized, reproduced, or altered;

(3) a statement of the facts and circumstances relied upon by the applicant to justify the applicant's belief that—

(A) the target of the physical search is a foreign power or an agent of a foreign power;

(B) the premises or property to be searched contains foreign intelligence information; and

(C) the premises or property to be searched is or is about to be owned, used, possessed by, or is in transit to or from a foreign power or an agent of a foreign power;

(4) a statement of the proposed minimization procedures;

(5) a statement of the nature of the foreign intelligence sought and the manner in which the physical search is to be conducted;

(6) a certification or certifications by the Assistant to the President for National Security Affairs, an executive branch official or officials designated by the President from among those executive branch officers employed in the area of national security or defense and appointed by the President, by and with the advice and consent of the Senate, or the Deputy Director of the Federal Bureau of Investigation, if designated by the President as a certifying official—

(A) that the certifying official deems the information sought to be foreign intelligence information;

(B) that a significant purpose of the search is to obtain foreign intelligence information;

(C) that such information cannot reasonably be obtained by normal investigative techniques;

(D) that designates the type of foreign intelligence information being sought according to the categories described in section 101(e); and

(E) includes a statement explaining the basis for the certifications required by subparagraphs (C) and (D);

(7) where the physical search involves a search of the residence of a United States person, the Attorney General shall state what investigative techniques have previously been utilized to obtain the foreign intelligence information concerned and the degree to which these techniques resulted in acquiring such information; and

(8) a statement of the facts concerning all previous applications that have been made to any judge under this title involving any of the persons, premises, or property specified in the application, and the action taken on each previous application.

(b) The Attorney General may require any other affidavit or certification from any other officer in connection with the application.

(c) The judge may require the applicant to furnish such other information as may be necessary to make the determinations required by section 304.

(d)(1)(A) Upon written request of the Director of the Federal Bureau of Investigation, the Secretary of Defense, the Secretary of State, or the Director of National Intelligence, the Attorney General shall personally review under subsection (a) an application under that subsection for a target described in section 101(b)(2).

(B) Except when disabled or otherwise unavailable to make a request referred to in subparagraph (A), an official referred to in that subparagraph may not delegate the authority to make a request referred to in that subparagraph.

(C) Each official referred to in subparagraph (A) with authority to make a request under that subparagraph shall take appropriate actions in advance to ensure that delegation of such authority is clearly established in the event such official is disabled or otherwise unavailable to make such request.

(2)(A) If as a result of a request under paragraph (1) the Attorney General determines not to approve an application under the second sentence of subsection (a) for purposes of making the application under this section, the Attorney General shall provide written notice of the determination to the official making the request for the review of the application under that paragraph. Except when disabled or otherwise unavailable to make a determination under the preceding sentence, the Attorney General may not delegate the responsibility to make a determination under that sentence. The Attorney General shall take appropriate actions in advance to ensure that delegation of such responsibility is clearly established in the event the Attorney General is disabled or otherwise unavailable to make such determination.

(B) Notice with respect to an application under subparagraph (A) shall set forth the modifications, if any, of the application that are necessary in order for the Attorney General to approve the application under the second sentence of subsection (a) for purposes of making the application under this section.

(C) Upon review of any modifications of an application set forth under subparagraph (B), the official notified of the modifications under this paragraph shall modify the application if such official determines that such modification is warranted. Such official shall supervise the making of any modification under this subparagraph. Except when disabled or otherwise unavailable to supervise the making of any modification under the preceding sentence, such official may not delegate the responsibility to supervise the making of any modification under that preceding sentence. Each such official shall take appropriate actions in advance to ensure that delegation of such responsibility is clearly established in the event such official is disabled or otherwise unavailable to supervise the making of such modification.

ISSUANCE OF AN ORDER

SEC. 304. [50 U.S.C. §§1824]

(a) Upon an application made pursuant to section 303, the judge shall enter an ex parte order as requested or as modified approving the physical search if the judge finds that—

(1) the application has been made by a Federal officer and approved by the Attorney General;

(2) on the basis of the facts submitted by the applicant there is probable cause to believe that—

(A) the target of the physical search is a foreign power or an agent of a foreign power, except that no United States person may be considered an agent of a foreign power solely upon the basis of activities protected by the first amendment to the Constitution of the United States; and

(B) the premises or property to be searched is or is about to be owned, used, possessed by, or is in transit to or from an agent of a foreign power or a foreign power;

(3) the proposed minimization procedures meet the definition of minimization contained in this title; and

(4) the application which has been filed contains all statements and certifications required by section 303, and, if the target is a United States person, the certification or certifications are not clearly erroneous on the basis of the statement made under section 303(a)(6)(E) and any other information furnished under section 303(c).

(b) In determining whether or not probable cause exists for purposes of an order under subsection (a)(3), a judge may consider past activities of the target, as well as facts and circumstances relating to current or future activities of the target.

(c) An order approving a physical search under this section shall—

(1) specify—

(A) the identity, if known, or a description of the target of the physical search;

(B) the nature and location of each of the premises or property to be searched;
(C) the type of information, material, or property to be seized, altered, or reproduced;
(D) a statement of the manner in which the physical search is to be conducted and, whenever more than one physical search is authorized under the order, the authorized scope of each search and what minimization procedures shall apply to the information acquired by each search; and
(E) the period of time during which physical searches are approved; and

(2) direct—
(A) that the minimization procedures be followed;
(B) that, upon the request of the applicant, a specified landlord, custodian, or other specified person furnish the applicant forthwith all information, facilities, or assistance necessary to accomplish the physical search in such a manner as will protect its secrecy and produce a minimum of interference with the services that such landlord, custodian, or other person is providing the target of the physical search;
(C) that such landlord, custodian, or other person maintain under security procedures approved by the Attorney General and the Director of National Intelligence any records concerning the search or the aid furnished that such person wishes to retain;
(D) that the applicant compensate, at the prevailing rate, such landlord, custodian, or other person for furnishing such aid; and
(E) that the Federal officer conducting the physical search promptly report to the court the circumstances and results of the physical search.

(d)(1) An order issued under this section may approve a physical search for the period necessary to achieve its purpose, or for 90 days, whichever is less, except that
(A) an order under this section shall approve a physical search targeted against a foreign power, as defined in paragraph (1), (2), or (3) of section 101(a), for the period specified in the application or for one year, whichever is less, and
(B) an order under this section for a physical search targeted against an agent of a foreign power who is not a United States person may be for the period specified in the application or for 120 days, whichever is less.

(2) Extensions of an order issued under this title may be granted on the same basis as the original order upon an application for an extension and new findings made in the same manner as required for the original order, except that an extension of an order under this Act for a physical search targeted against a foreign power, as defined in paragraph (5), (6), or (7) of section 101(a), or against a foreign power, as defined in section 101(a)(4), that is not a United States person, or against an agent of a foreign power who is not a United States person, may be for a period not to exceed one year if the judge finds probable cause to believe that no property of any individual United States person will be acquired during the period.

(3) At or before the end of the period of time for which a physical search is approved by an order or an extension, or at any time after a physical search is carried out, the judge may assess compliance with the minimization procedures by reviewing the circumstances under which information concerning United States persons was acquired, retained, or disseminated.

(e)(1) Notwithstanding any other provision of this title, the Attorney General may authorize the emergency employment of a physical search if the Attorney General—

(A) reasonably determines that an emergency situation exists with respect to the employment of a physical search to obtain foreign intelligence information before an order authorizing such physical search can with due diligence be obtained;

(B) reasonably determines that the factual basis for issuance of an order under this title to approve such physical search exists;

(C) informs, either personally or through a designee, a judge of the Foreign Intelligence Surveillance Court at the time of such authorization that the decision has been made to employ an emergency physical search; and

(D) makes an application in accordance with this title to a judge of the Foreign Intelligence Surveillance Court as soon as practicable, but not more than 7 days after the Attorney General authorizes such physical search.

(2) If the Attorney General authorizes the emergency employment of a physical search under paragraph (1), the Attorney General shall require that the minimization procedures required by this title for the issuance of a judicial order be followed.

(3) In the absence of a judicial order approving such physical search, the physical search shall terminate when the information sought is obtained, when the application for the order is denied, or after the expiration of 7 days from the time of authorization by the Attorney General, whichever is earliest.

(4) A denial of the application made under this subsection may be reviewed as provided in section 103.

(5) In the event that such application for approval is denied, or in any other case where the physical search is terminated and no order is issued approving the physical search, no information obtained or evidence derived from such physical search shall be received in evidence or otherwise disclosed in any trial, hearing, or other proceeding in or before any court, grand jury, department, office, agency, regulatory body, legislative committee, or other authority of the United States, a State, or political subdivision thereof, and no information concerning any United States person acquired from such physical search shall subsequently be used or disclosed in any other manner by Federal officers or employees without the consent of such person, except with the approval of the Attorney General if the information indicates a threat of death or serious bodily harm to any person.

(6) The Attorney General shall assess compliance with the requirements of paragraph (5).

(f) Applications made and orders granted under this title shall be retained for a period of at least 10 years from the date of the application.

USE OF INFORMATION

SEC. 305. [50 U.S.C. §1825]

(a) Information acquired from a physical search conducted pursuant to this title concerning any United States person may be used and disclosed by Federal officers and employees without the consent of the United States person only in accordance with the minimization procedures required by this title. No information acquired from a physical search pursuant to this title may be used or disclosed by Federal officers or employees except for lawful purposes.

(b) Where a physical search authorized and conducted pursuant to section 304 involves the residence of a United States person, and, at any time after the search the Attorney General determines there is no national security interest in continuing to maintain the secrecy of the search, the Attorney General shall provide notice to the United States person whose residence was searched of the fact of the search conducted pursuant to this Act and shall identify any property of such person seized, altered, or reproduced during such search.

(c) No information acquired pursuant to this title shall be disclosed for law enforcement purposes unless such disclosure is accompanied by a statement that such information, or any information derived therefrom, may only be used in a criminal proceeding with the advance authorization of the Attorney General.

(d) Whenever the United States intends to enter into evidence or otherwise use or disclose in any trial, hearing, or other proceeding in or before any court, department, officer, agency, regulatory body, or other authority of the United States, against an aggrieved person, any information obtained or derived from a physical search pursuant to the authority of this Act, the United States shall, prior to the trial, hearing, or the other proceeding or at a reasonable time prior to an effort to so disclose or so use that information or submit it in evidence, notify the aggrieved person and the court or other authority in which the information is to be disclosed or used that the United States intends to so disclose or so use such information.

(e) Whenever any State or political subdivision thereof intends to enter into evidence or otherwise use or disclose in any trial, hearing, or other proceeding in or before any court, department, officer, agency, regulatory body, or other authority of a State or a political subdivision thereof against an aggrieved person any information obtained or derived from a physical search pursuant to the authority of this Act, the State or political subdivision thereof shall notify the aggrieved person, the court or other authority in which the information is to be disclosed or used, and the Attorney General that the State or political subdivision thereof intends to so disclose or so use such information.

(f)(1) Any person against whom evidence obtained or derived from a physical search to which he is an aggrieved person is to be, or has been, introduced or otherwise used or disclosed in any trial, hearing, or other proceeding in or before any court, department, officer, agency, regulatory body, or other authority of the United States, a State, or a political subdivision thereof, may move to suppress the evidence obtained or derived from such search on the grounds that—

(A) the information was unlawfully acquired; or

(B) the physical search was not made in conformity with an order of authorization or approval.

(2) Such a motion shall be made before the trial, hearing, or other proceeding unless there was no opportunity to make such a motion or the person was not aware of the grounds of the motion.

(g) Whenever a court or other authority is notified pursuant to subsection (d) or (e), or whenever a motion is made pursuant to subsection (f), or whenever any motion or request is made by an aggrieved person pursuant to any other statute or rule of the United States or any State before any court or other authority of the United States or any State to discover or obtain applications or orders or other materials relating to a physical search authorized by this title or to discover, obtain, or suppress evidence or information obtained or derived from a physical search authorized by this title, the United States district court or, where the motion is made before another authority, the United States district court in the same district as the authority shall, notwithstanding any other provision of law, if the Attorney General files an affidavit under oath that disclosure or any adversary hearing would harm the national security of the United States, review in camera and ex parte the application, order, and such other materials relating to the physical search as may be necessary to determine whether the physical search of the aggrieved person was lawfully authorized and conducted. In making this determination, the court may disclose to the aggrieved person, under appropriate security procedures and protective orders, portions of the application, order, or other materials relating to the physical search, or may require the Attorney General to provide to the aggrieved person a summary of such materials, only where such disclosure is necessary to make an accurate determination of the legality of the physical search.

(h) If the United States district court pursuant to subsection (g) determines that the physical search was not lawfully authorized or conducted, it shall, in accordance with the requirements of law, suppress the evidence which was unlawfully obtained or derived from the physical search of the aggrieved person or otherwise grant the motion of the aggrieved person. If the court determines that the physical search was lawfully authorized or conducted, it shall deny the motion of the aggrieved person except to the extent that due process requires discovery or disclosure.

(i) Orders granting motions or requests under subsection (h), decisions under this section that a physical search was not lawfully authorized or conducted, and orders of the United States district court requiring review or granting disclosure of applications, orders, or other materials relating to the physical search shall be final orders and binding upon all courts of the United States and the several States except a United States Court of Appeals or the Supreme Court.

(j)(1) If an emergency execution of a physical search is authorized under section 304(d) and a subsequent order approving the search is not obtained, the judge shall cause to be served on any United States person named in the application and on such other United States persons subject to the search as the judge may determine in his discretion it is in the interests of justice to serve, notice of—

(A) the fact of the application;

(B) the period of the search; and

(C) the fact that during the period information was or was not obtained.

(2) On an ex parte showing of good cause to the judge, the serving of the notice required by this subsection may be postponed or suspended for a period not to exceed 90 days. Thereafter, on a further ex parte showing of good cause, the court shall forego ordering the serving of the notice required under this subsection.

(k)(1) Federal officers who conduct physical searches to acquire foreign intelligence information under this title may consult with Federal law enforcement officers or law enforcement personnel of a State or political subdivision of a State (including the chief executive officer of that State or political subdivision who has the authority to appoint or direct the chief law enforcement officer of that State or political subdivision) to coordinate efforts to investigate or protect against—

(A) actual or potential attack or other grave hostile acts of a foreign power or an agent of a foreign power;

(B) sabotage, international terrorism, or the international proliferation of weapons of mass destruction by a foreign power or an agent of a foreign power; or

(C) clandestine intelligence activities by an intelligence service or network of a foreign power or by an agent of a foreign power.

(2) Coordination authorized under paragraph (1) shall not preclude the certification required by section 303(a)(6) or the entry of an order under section 304.

CONGRESSIONAL OVERSIGHT

SEC. 306. [50 U.S.C. §1826] On a semiannual basis the Attorney General shall fully inform the Permanent Select Committee on Intelligence of the House of Representatives and the Select Committee on Intelligence of the Senate and the Committee on the Judiciary of the Senate concerning all physical searches conducted pursuant to this title. On a semiannual basis the Attorney General shall also provide to those committees and the Committee on the Judiciary of the House of Representatives a report setting forth with respect to the preceding six-month period—

(1) the total number of applications made for orders approving physical searches under this title;

(2) the total number of such orders either granted, modified, or denied;

(3) the number of physical searches which involved searches of the residences, offices, or personal property of United States persons, and the number of occasions, if any, where the Attorney General provided notice pursuant to section 305(b); and

(4) the total number of emergency physical searches authorized by the Attorney General under section 304(e) and the total number of subsequent orders approving or denying such physical searches.

PENALTIES

SEC. 307. [50 U.S.C. §1827]

(a) A person is guilty of an offense if he intentionally—

(1) under color of law for the purpose of obtaining foreign intelligence information, executes a physical search within the United States except as authorized by statute; or

(2) discloses or uses information obtained under color of law by physical search within the United States, knowing or having reason to know that the information was obtained through physical search not authorized by statute, for the purpose of obtaining intelligence information.

(b) It is a defense to a prosecution under subsection (a) that the defendant was a law enforcement or investigative officer engaged in the course of his official duties and the physical search was authorized by and conducted pursuant to a search warrant or court order of a court of competent jurisdiction.

(c) An offense described in this section is punishable by a fine of not more than $10,000 or imprisonment for not more than five years, or both.

(d) There is Federal jurisdiction over an offense under this section if the person committing the offense was an officer or employee of the United States at the time the offense was committed.

CIVIL LIABILITY

SEC. 308. [50 U.S.C. §1828] An aggrieved person, other than a foreign power or an agent of a foreign power, as defined in section 101 (a) or (b)(1)(A), respectively, of this Act, whose premises, property, information, or material has been subjected to a physical search within the United States or about whom information obtained by such a physical search has been disclosed or used in violation of section 307 shall have a cause of action against any person who committed such violation and shall be entitled to recover—

(1) actual damages, but not less than liquidated damages of $1,000 or $100 per day for each day of violation, whichever is greater;

(2) punitive damages; and

(3) reasonable attorney's fees and other investigative and litigation costs reasonably incurred.

AUTHORIZATION DURING TIME OF WAR

SEC. 309. [50 U.S.C. §1829]

Notwithstanding any other provision of law, the President, through the Attorney General, may authorize physical searches without a court order under this title to acquire foreign intelligence information for a period not to exceed 15 calendar days following a declaration of war by the Congress.

TITLE IV—PEN REGISTERS AND TRAP AND TRACE DEVICES FOR FOREIGN INTELLIGENCE PURPOSES

DEFINITIONS

SEC. 401. [50 U.S.C. §1841] As used in this title:

(1) The terms "foreign power", "agent of a foreign power", "international terrorism", "foreign intelligence information", "Attorney General", "United

States person", "United States", "person", and "State" shall have the same meanings as in section 101 of this Act.

(2) The terms "pen register" and "trap and trace device" have the meanings given such terms in section 3127 of title 18, United States Code.

(3) The term "aggrieved person" means any person—

(A) whose telephone line was subject to the installation or use of a pen register or trap and trace device authorized by this title; or

(B) whose communication instrument or device was subject to the use of a pen register or trap and trace device authorized by this title to capture incoming electronic or other communications impulses.

PEN REGISTERS AND TRAP AND TRACE DEVICES FOR FOREIGN INTELLIGENCE AND INTERNATIONAL TERRORISM INVESTIGATIONS

SEC. 402. [50 U.S.C. §1842]

(a)(1) Notwithstanding any other provision of law, the Attorney General or a designated attorney for the Government may make an application for an order or an extension of an order authorizing or approving the installation and use of a pen register or trap and trace device for any investigation to obtain foreign intelligence information not concerning a United States person or to protect against international terrorism or clandestine intelligence activities, provided that such investigation of a United States person is not conducted solely upon the basis of activities protected by the first amendment to the Constitution which is being conducted by the Federal Bureau of Investigation under such guidelines as the Attorney General approves pursuant to Executive Order No. 12333, or a successor order.

(2) The authority under paragraph (1) is in addition to the authority under title I of this Act to conduct the electronic surveillance referred to in that paragraph.

(b) Each application under this section shall be in writing under oath or affirmation to—

(1) a judge of the court established by section 103(a) of this Act; or

(2) a United States Magistrate Judge under chapter 43 of title 28, United States Code, who is publicly designated by the Chief Justice of the United States to have the power to hear applications for and grant orders approving the installation and use of a pen register or trap and trace device on behalf of a judge of that court.

(c) Each application under this section shall require the approval of the Attorney General, or a designated attorney for the Government, and shall include—

(1) the identity of the Federal officer seeking to use the pen register or trap and trace device covered by the application; and

(2) a certification by the applicant that the information likely to be obtained is foreign intelligence information not concerning a United States person or is relevant to an ongoing investigation to protect against international terrorism or clandestine intelligence activities, provided that such investigation of a United States person is not conducted solely upon the basis of activities protected by the first amendment to the Constitution.

(d)(1) Upon an application made pursuant to this section, the judge shall enter an ex parte order as requested, or as modified, approving the installation and use of a pen register or trap and trace device if the judge finds that the application satisfies the requirements of this section.

(2) An order issued under this section—

(A) shall specify—

(i) the identity, if known, of the person who is the subject of the investigation;

(ii) the identity, if known, of the person to whom is leased or in whose name is listed the telephone line or other facility to which the pen register or trap and trace device is to be attached or applied;

(iii) the attributes of the communications to which the order applies, such as the number or other identifier, and, if known, the location of the telephone line or other facility to which the pen register or trap and trace device is to be attached or applied and, in the case of a trap and trace device, the geographic limits of the trap and trace order;

(B) shall direct that—

(i) upon request of the applicant, the provider of a wire or electronic communication service, landlord, custodian, or other person shall furnish any information, facilities, or technical assistance necessary to accomplish the installation and operation of the pen register or trap and trace device in such a manner as will protect its secrecy and produce a minimum amount of interference with the services that such provider, landlord, custodian, or other person is providing the person concerned;

(ii) such provider, landlord, custodian, or other person—

(I) shall not disclose the existence of the investigation or of the pen register or trap and trace device to any person unless or until ordered by the court; and

(II) shall maintain, under security procedures approved by the Attorney General and the Director of National Intelligence pursuant to section 105(b)(2)(C) of this Act, any records concerning the pen register or trap and trace device or the aid furnished; and

(iii) the applicant shall compensate such provider, landlord, custodian, or other person for reasonable expenses incurred by such provider, landlord, custodian, or other person in providing such information, facilities, or technical assistance; and

(C) shall direct that, upon the request of the applicant, the provider of a wire or electronic communication service shall disclose to the Federal officer using the pen register or trap and trace device covered by the order—

(i) in the case of the customer or subscriber using the service covered by the order (for the period specified by the order)—

(I) the name of the customer or subscriber;

(II) the address of the customer or subscriber;

(III) the telephone or instrument number, or other subscriber number or identifier, of the customer or subscriber, including any temporarily assigned network address or associated routing or transmission information;

(IV) the length of the provision of service by such provider to the customer or subscriber and the types of services utilized by the customer or subscriber;

(V) in the case of a provider of local or long distance telephone service, any local or long distance telephone records of the customer or subscriber;

(VI) if applicable, any records reflecting period of usage (or sessions) by the customer or subscriber; and

(VII) any mechanisms and sources of payment for such service, including the number of any credit card or bank account utilized for payment for such service; and

(ii) if available, with respect to any customer or subscriber of incoming or outgoing communications to or from the service covered by the order—

(I) the name of such customer or subscriber;

(II) the address of such customer or subscriber;

(III) the telephone or instrument number, or other subscriber number or identifier, of such customer or subscriber, including any temporarily assigned network address or associated routing or transmission information; and

(IV) the length of the provision of service by such provider to such customer or subscriber and the types of services utilized by such customer or subscriber.

(e)(1) Except as provided in paragraph (2), an order issued under this section shall authorize the installation and use of a pen register or trap and trace device for a period not to exceed 90 days. Extensions of such an order may be granted, but only upon an application for an order under this section and upon the judicial finding required by subsection (d). The period of extension shall be for a period not to exceed 90 days.

(2) In the case of an application under subsection (c) where the applicant has certified that the information likely to be obtained is foreign intelligence information not concerning a United States person, an order, or an extension of an order, under the section may be for a period not to exceed one year.

(f) No cause of action shall lie in any court against any provider of a wire or electronic communication service, landlord, custodian, or other person (including any officer, employee, agent, or other specified person thereof) that furnishes any information, facilities, or technical assistance under subsection (d) in accordance with the terms of an order issued under this section.

(g) Unless otherwise ordered by the judge, the results of a pen register or trap and trace device shall be furnished at reasonable intervals during regular business hours for the duration of the order to the authorized Government official or officials.

AUTHORIZATION DURING EMERGENCIES

SEC. 403. [50 U.S.C. §1843]

(a) Notwithstanding any other provision of this Act, when the Attorney General makes a determination described in subsection (b), the Attorney General may authorize the installation and use of a pen register or trap and trace device on an emergency basis to gather foreign intelligence information not concerning a United States person or information to protect against international terrorism or clandestine intelligence activities, provided that such investigation of a United States person is not conducted solely upon the basis of activities protected by the first amendment to the Constitution if—

(1) a judge referred to in section 402(b) of this Act is informed by the Attorney General or his designee at the time of such authorization that the decision has been made to install and use the pen register or trap and trace device, as the case may be, on an emergency basis; and

(2) an application in accordance with section 402 of this Act is made to such judge as soon as practicable, but not more than 7 days, after the Attorney General authorizes the installation and use of the pen register or trap and trace device, as the case may be, under this section.

(b) A determination under this subsection is a reasonable determination by the Attorney General that—

(1) an emergency requires the installation and use of a pen register or trap and trace device to obtain foreign intelligence information not concerning a United States person or information to protect against international terrorism or clandestine intelligence activities, provided that such investigation of a United States person is not conducted solely upon the basis of activities protected by the first amendment to the Constitution before an order authorizing the installation and use of the pen register or trap and trace device, as the case may be, can with due diligence be obtained under section 402 of this Act; and

(2) the factual basis for issuance of an order under such section 402 to approve the installation and use of the pen register or trap and trace device, as the case may be, exists.

(c)(1) In the absence of an order applied for under subsection (a)(2) approving the installation and use of a pen register or trap and trace device authorized under this section, the installation and use of the pen register or trap and trace device, as the case may be, shall terminate at the earlier of—

(A) when the information sought is obtained;

(B) when the application for the order is denied under section 402 of this Act; or

(C) 7 days after the time of the authorization by the Attorney General.

(2) In the event that an application for an order applied for under subsection (a)(2) is denied, or in any other case where the installation and use of a pen register or trap and trace device under this section is terminated and no order under section 402 of this Act is issued approving the installation and use of the pen register or trap and trace device, as the case may be, no information obtained or evidence derived from the use of the pen register or trap and trace

device, as the case may be, shall be received in evidence or otherwise disclosed in any trial, hearing, or other proceeding in or before any court, grand jury, department, office, agency, regulatory body, legislative committee, or other authority of the United States, a State, or political subdivision thereof, and no information concerning any United States person acquired from the use of the pen register or trap and trace device, as the case may be, shall subsequently be used or disclosed in any other manner by Federal officers or employees without the consent of such person, except with the approval of the Attorney General if the information indicates a threat of death or serious bodily harm to any person.

AUTHORIZATION DURING TIME OF WAR

SEC. 404. [50 U.S.C. §1844] Notwithstanding any other provision of law, the President, through the Attorney General, may authorize the use of a pen register or trap and trace device without a court order under this title to acquire foreign intelligence information for a period not to exceed 15 calendar days following a declaration of war by Congress.

USE OF INFORMATION

SEC. 405. [50 U.S.C. §1845]

(a)(1) Information acquired from the use of a pen register or trap and trace device installed pursuant to this title concerning any United States person may be used and disclosed by Federal officers and employees without the consent of the United States person only in accordance with the provisions of this section.

(2) No information acquired from a pen register or trap and trace device installed and used pursuant to this title may be used or disclosed by Federal officers or employees except for lawful purposes.

(b) No information acquired pursuant to this title shall be disclosed for law enforcement purposes unless such disclosure is accompanied by a statement that such information, or any information derived therefrom, may only be used in a criminal proceeding with the advance authorization of the Attorney General.

(c) Whenever the United States intends to enter into evidence or otherwise use or disclose in any trial, hearing, or other proceeding in or before any court, department, officer, agency, regulatory body, or other authority of the United States against an aggrieved person any information obtained or derived from the use of a pen register or trap and trace device pursuant to this title, the United States shall, before the trial, hearing, or the other proceeding or at a reasonable time before an effort to so disclose or so use that information or submit it in evidence, notify the aggrieved person and the court or other authority in which the information is to be disclosed or used that the United States intends to so disclose or so use such information.

(d) Whenever any State or political subdivision thereof intends to enter into evidence or otherwise use or disclose in any trial, hearing, or other proceeding in or before any court, department, officer, agency, regulatory body, or other authority of the State or political subdivision thereof against an aggrieved person any information obtained or derived from the use of a pen register or trap and trace device pursuant to this title, the State or political subdivision thereof shall notify the aggrieved person, the court or other authority in which the information is to be disclosed or used, and the Attorney General that the State or political subdivision thereof intends to so disclose or so use such information.

(e)(1) Any aggrieved person against whom evidence obtained or derived from the use of a pen register or trap and trace device is to be, or has been, introduced or otherwise used or disclosed in any trial, hearing, or other proceeding in or before any court, department, officer, agency, regulatory body, or other authority of the United States, or a State or political subdivision thereof, may move to suppress the evidence obtained or derived from the use of the pen register or trap and trace device, as the case may be, on the grounds that—

(A) the information was unlawfully acquired; or

(B) the use of the pen register or trap and trace device, as the case may be, was not made in conformity with an order of authorization or approval under this title.

(2) A motion under paragraph (1) shall be made before the trial, hearing, or other proceeding unless there was no opportunity to make such a motion or the aggrieved person concerned was not aware of the grounds of the motion.

(f)(1) Whenever a court or other authority is notified pursuant to subsection (c) or (d), whenever a motion is made pursuant to subsection (e), or whenever any motion or request is made by an aggrieved person pursuant to any other statute or rule of the United States or any State before any court or other authority of the United States or any State to discover or obtain applications or orders or other materials relating to the use of a pen register or trap and trace device authorized by this title or to discover, obtain, or suppress evidence or information obtained or derived from the use of a pen register or trap and trace device authorized by this title, the United States district court or, where the motion is made before another authority, the United States district court in the same district as the authority shall, notwithstanding any other provision of law and if the Attorney General files an affidavit under oath that disclosure or any adversary hearing would harm the national security of the United States, review in camera and ex parte the application, order, and such other materials relating to the use of the pen register or trap and trace device, as the case may be, as may be necessary to determine whether the use of the pen register or trap and trace device, as the case may be, was lawfully authorized and conducted.

(2) In making a determination under paragraph (1), the court may disclose to the aggrieved person, under appropriate security procedures and protective orders, portions of the application, order, or other materials relating to the use of the pen register or trap and trace device, as the case may be, or may require the Attorney General to provide to the aggrieved person a summary of such materials, only where such disclosure is necessary to make an accurate determination of the legality of the use of the pen register or trap and trace device, as the case may be.

(g)(1) If the United States district court determines pursuant to subsection (f) that the use of a pen register or trap and trace device was not lawfully authorized or conducted, the court may, in accordance with the requirements of law, suppress the evidence which was unlawfully obtained or derived from the use of the pen register or trap and trace device, as the case may be, or otherwise grant the motion of the aggrieved person.

(2) If the court determines that the use of the pen register or trap and trace device, as the case may be, was lawfully authorized or conducted, it may deny the motion of the aggrieved person except to the extent that due process requires discovery or disclosure.

(h) Orders granting motions or requests under subsection (g), decisions under this section that the use of a pen register or trap and trace device was not lawfully authorized or conducted, and orders of the United States district court requiring review or granting disclosure of applications, orders, or other materials relating to the installation and use of a pen register or trap and trace device shall be final orders and binding upon all courts of the United States and the several States except a United States Court of Appeals or the Supreme Court.

CONGRESSIONAL OVERSIGHT

SEC. 406. [50 U.S.C. §1846]

(a) On a semiannual basis, the Attorney General shall fully inform the Permanent Select Committee on Intelligence of the House of Representatives and the Select Committee on Intelligence of the Senate and the Committee on the Judiciary of the House of Representatives and the Committee on the Judiciary of the Senate concerning all uses of pen registers and trap and trace devices pursuant to this title.

(b) On a semiannual basis, the Attorney General shall also provide to the committees referred to in subsection (a) and to the Committees on the Judiciary of the House of Representatives and the Senate a report setting forth with respect to the preceding 6-month period—

(1) the total number of applications made for orders approving the use of pen registers or trap and trace devices under this title;

(2) the total number of such orders either granted, modified, or denied; and

(3) the total number of pen registers and trap and trace devices whose installation and use was authorized by the Attorney General on an emergency basis under section 403, and the total number of subsequent orders approving or denying the installation and use of such pen registers and trap and trace devices.

TITLE V—ACCESS TO CERTAIN BUSINESS RECORDS FOR FOREIGN INTELLIGENCE PURPOSES

ACCESS TO CERTAIN BUSINESS RECORDS FOR FOREIGN INTELLIGENCE AND INTERNATIONAL TERRORISM INVESTIGATIONS

SEC. 501. [50 U.S.C. §1861]

(a)(1) Subject to paragraph (3), the Director of the Federal Bureau of Investigation or a designee of the Director (whose rank shall be no lower than Assistant Special Agent in Charge) may make an application for an order requiring the production of any tangible things (including books, records, papers, documents, and other items) for an investigation to obtain foreign intelligence information not concerning a United States person or to protect against international terrorism or clandestine intelligence activities, provided that such investigation of a United States person is not conducted solely upon the basis of activities protected by the first amendment to the Constitution.

(2) An investigation conducted under this section shall

(A) be conducted under guidelines approved by the Attorney General under Executive Order 12333 (or a successor order); and

(B) not be conducted of a United States person solely upon the basis of activities protected by the first amendment to the Constitution of the United States.

(3) In the case of an application for an order requiring the production of library circulation records, library patron lists, book sales records, book customer lists, firearms sales records, tax return records, educational records, or medical records containing information that would identify a person, the Director of the Federal Bureau of Investigation may delegate the authority to make such application to either the Deputy Director of the Federal Bureau of Investigation or the Executive Assistant Director for National Security (or any successor position). The Deputy Director or the Executive Assistant Director may not further delegate such authority.

(b) Each application under this section

(1) shall be made to—

(A) a judge of the court established by section 103(a) of this Act; or

(B) a United States Magistrate Judge under chapter 43 of Title 28, who is publicly designated by the Chief Justice of the United States to have the power to hear applications and grant orders for the production of tangible things under this section on behalf of a judge of that court; and

(2) shall include—

(A) a statement of facts showing that there are reasonable grounds to believe that the tangible things sought are relevant to an authorized investigation (other than a threat assessment) conducted in accordance with subsection (a)(2) of this section to obtain foreign intelligence information not concerning a United States person or to protect against international terrorism or clandestine intelligence activities, such things being presumptively relevant to an authorized investigation if the applicant shows in the statement of the facts that they pertain to—

(i) a foreign power or an agent of a foreign power;

(ii) the activities of a suspected agent of a foreign power who is the subject of such authorized investigation; or

(iii) an individual in contact with, or known to, a suspected agent of a foreign power who is the subject of such authorized investigation; and

(B) an enumeration of the minimization procedures adopted by the Attorney General under subsection (g) of this section that are applicable to the retention and dissemination by the Federal Bureau of Investigation of any tangible things to be made available to the Federal Bureau of Investigation based on the order requested in such application.

(c)(1) Upon an application made pursuant to this section, if the judge finds that the application meets the requirements of subsections (a) and (b) of this section, the judge shall enter an ex parte order as requested, or as modified, approving the release of tangible things. Such order shall direct that minimization procedures adopted pursuant to subsection (g) of this section be followed.

(2) An order under this subsection—

(A) shall describe the tangible things that are ordered to be produced with sufficient particularity to permit them to be fairly identified;

(B) shall include the date on which the tangible things must be provided, which shall allow a reasonable period of time within which the tangible things can be assembled and made available;

(C) shall provide clear and conspicuous notice of the principles and procedures described in subsection (d) of this section;

(D) may only require the production of a tangible thing if such thing can be obtained with a subpoena duces tecum issued by a court of the United States in aid of a grand jury investigation or with any other order issued by a court of the United States directing the production of records or tangible things; and

(E) shall not disclose that such order is issued for purposes of an investigation described in subsection (a) of this section.

(d)(1) No person shall disclose to any other person that the Federal bureau of investigation has sought or obtained tangible things pursuant to an order under this section, other than to

(A) those persons to whom disclosure is necessary to comply with such order;

(B) an attorney to obtain legal advice or assistance with respect to the production of things in response to the order; or

(C) other persons as permitted by the Director of the Federal Bureau of Investigation or the designee of the Director.

(2)(A) A person to whom disclosure is made pursuant to paragraph (1) shall be subject to the nondisclosure requirements applicable to a person to whom an order is directed under this section in the same manner as such person.

(B) Any person who discloses to a person described in subparagraph (A), (B), or (C) of paragraph (1) that the Federal Bureau of Investigation has sought or obtained tangible things pursuant to an order under this section shall notify such person of the nondisclosure requirements of this subsection.

(C) At the request of the Director of the Federal Bureau of Investigation or the designee of the Director, any person making or intending to make a disclosure under subparagraph (A) or (C) of paragraph (1) shall identify to the Director or such designee the person to whom such disclosure will be made or to whom such disclosure was made prior to the request.

(e) A person who, in good faith, produces tangible things under an order pursuant to this section shall not be liable to any other person for such production. Such production shall not be deemed to constitute a waiver of any privilege in any other proceeding or context.

(f) [JUDICIAL REVIEW OF FISA ORDERS .—]

(1) In this subsection—

(A) the term "production order" means an order to produce any tangible thing under this section; and

(B) the term "nondisclosure order" means an order imposed under subsection (d) of this section.

(2)(A)(i) A person receiving a production order may challenge the legality of that order by filing a petition with the pool established by section 103(e)(1) of this Act. Not less than 1 year after the date of the issuance of the production order, the recipient of a production order may challenge the nondisclosure order imposed in connection with such production order by filing a petition to modify or set aside such nondisclosure order, consistent with the requirements of subparagraph (C), with the pool established by 103(e)(1) of this Act.

(ii) The presiding judge shall immediately assign a petition under clause (i) to 1 of the judges serving in the pool established by 103(e)(1) of this Act. Not later than 72 hours after the assignment of such petition, the assigned judge shall conduct an initial review of the petition. If the assigned judge determines that the petition is frivolous, the assigned judge shall immediately deny the petition and affirm the production order or nondisclosure order. If the assigned judge determines the petition is not frivolous, the assigned judge shall promptly consider the petition in accordance with the procedures established under 103(e)(2) of this Act.

(iii) The assigned judge shall promptly provide a written statement for the record of the reasons for any determination under this subsection. Upon the request of the Government, any order setting aside a nondisclosure order shall be stayed pending review pursuant to paragraph (3).

(B) A judge considering a petition to modify or set aside a production order may grant such petition only if the judge finds that such order does not meet the requirements of this section or is otherwise unlawful. If the judge does not modify or set aside the production order, the judge shall immediately affirm such order, and order the recipient to comply therewith.

(C)(i) A judge considering a petition to modify or set aside a nondisclosure order may grant such petition only if the judge finds that there is no reason to believe that disclosure may endanger the national security of the United States, interfere with a criminal, counterterrorism, or counterintelligence investigation, interfere with diplomatic relations, or endanger the life or physical safety of any person.

(ii) If, upon filing of such a petition, the Attorney General, Deputy Attorney General, an Assistant Attorney General, or the Director of the Federal Bureau of Investigation certifies that disclosure may endanger the national security of the United States or interfere with diplomatic relations, such certification shall be treated as conclusive, unless the judge finds that the certification was made in bad faith.

(iii) If the judge denies a petition to modify or set aside a nondisclosure order, the recipient of such order shall be precluded for a period of 1 year from filing another such petition with respect to such nondisclosure order.

(D) Any production or nondisclosure order not explicitly modified or set aside consistent with this subsection shall remain in full effect.

(3) A petition for review of a decision under paragraph (2) to affirm, modify, or set aside an order by the Government or any person receiving such order shall be made to the court of review established under 103(b) of this Act, which shall have jurisdiction to consider such petitions. The court of review shall provide for the record a written statement of the reasons for its decision and, on petition by the Government or any person receiving such order for writ of certiorari, the record shall be transmitted under seal to the Supreme Court of the United States, which shall have jurisdiction to review such decision.

(4) Judicial proceedings under this subsection shall be concluded as expeditiously as possible. The record of proceedings, including petitions filed, orders granted, and statements of reasons for decision, shall be maintained under security measures established by the Chief Justice of the United States, in consultation with the Attorney General and the Director of National Intelligence.

(5) All petitions under this subsection shall be filed under seal. In any proceedings under this subsection, the court shall, upon request of the Government, review ex parte and in camera any Government submission, or portions thereof, which may include classified information.

(g) MINIMIZATION PROCEDURES.—

(1) IN GENERAL.—Not later than 180 days after March 9, 2006, the Attorney General shall adopt specific minimization procedures governing the retention and dissemination by the Federal Bureau of Investigation of any tangible things, or information therein, received by the Federal Bureau of Investigation in response to an order under this subchapter.

(2) DEFINED.—In this section, the term "minimization procedures" means—

(A) specific procedures that are reasonably designed in light of the purpose and technique of an order for the production of tangible things, to minimize the retention, and prohibit the dissemination, of nonpublicly available information concerning unconsenting United States persons consistent with the need of the United States to obtain, produce, and disseminate foreign intelligence information;

(B) procedures that require that nonpublicly available information, which is not foreign intelligence information, as defined in 103(e)(1) of this Act, shall not be disseminated in a manner that identifies any United States person, without such person's consent, unless such person's identity is necessary to understand foreign intelligence information or assess its importance; and

(C) notwithstanding subparagraphs (A) and (B), procedures that allow for the retention and dissemination of information that is evidence of a crime which has been, is being, or is about to be committed and that is to be retained or disseminated for law enforcement purposes.

(h) USE OF INFORMATION.—Information acquired from tangible things received by the Federal Bureau of Investigation in response to an order under this subchapter concerning any United States person may be used and disclosed by Federal officers and employees without the consent of the United States person only in accordance with the minimization procedures adopted pursuant to subsection (g) of this section. No otherwise privileged information acquired from tangible things received by the Federal Bureau of Investigation in accordance with the provisions of this subchapter shall lose its privileged character. No information acquired from tangible things received by the Federal Bureau of Investigation in response to an order under this subchapter may be used or disclosed by Federal officers or employees except for lawful purposes.

CONGRESSIONAL OVERSIGHT

SEC. 502. [50 U.S.C. §1862]

(a) On an annual basis, the Attorney General shall fully inform the Permanent Select Committee on Intelligence of the House of Representatives and the Select Committee on Intelligence and the Committee on the Judiciary of the Senate concerning all requests for the production of tangible things under section 501 of this Act.

(b) In April of each year, the Attorney General shall submit to the House and Senate Committees on the Judiciary and the House Permanent Select Committee on Intelligence and the Senate Select Committee on Intelligence a report setting forth with respect to the preceding calendar year—

(1) the total number of applications made for orders approving requests for the production of tangible things under section 501 of this Act;

(2) the total number of such orders either granted, modified, or denied; and

(3) the number of such orders either granted, modified, or denied for the production of each of the following:

(A) Library circulation records, library patron lists, book sales records, or book customer lists.

(B) Firearms sales records.

(C) Tax return records.

(D) Educational records.

(E) Medical records containing information that would identify a person.

(c)(1) In April of each year, the Attorney General shall submit to Congress a report setting forth with respect to the preceding year—

(A) the total number of applications made for orders approving requests for the production of tangible things under section 501 of this Act; and

(B) the total number of such orders either granted, modified, or denied.

(2) Each report under this subsection shall be submitted in unclassified form.

TITLE VI—REPORTING REQUIREMENT

SEMIANNUAL REPORT OF THE ATTORNEY GENERAL

SEC. 601. [50 U.S.C. §1871]

(a) REPORT.—On a semiannual basis, the Attorney General shall submit to the Permanent Select Committee on Intelligence of the House of Representatives, the Select Committee on Intelligence of the Senate, and the Committees on the Judiciary of the House of Representatives and the Senate, in a manner consistent with the protection of the national security, a report setting forth with respect to the preceding 6-month period—

(1) the aggregate number of persons targeted for orders issued under this Act, including a breakdown of those targeted for—

(A) electronic surveillance under section 105;

(B) physical searches under section 304;

(C) pen registers under section 402;

(D) access to records under section 501;

(E) acquisitions under section 703; and

(F) acquisitions under section 704;

(2) the number of individuals covered by an order issued pursuant to section 101(b)(1)(C);

(3) the number of times that the Attorney General has authorized that information obtained under this Act may be used in a criminal proceeding or any information derived therefrom may be used in a criminal proceeding;

(4) a summary of significant legal interpretations of this Act involving matters before the Foreign Intelligence Surveillance Court or the Foreign Intelligence Surveillance Court of Review, including interpretations presented in applications or pleadings filed with the Foreign Intelligence Surveillance Court or the Foreign Intelligence Surveillance Court of Review by the Department of Justice; and

(5) copies of all decisions, orders, or opinions of the Foreign Intelligence Surveillance Court or Foreign Intelligence Surveillance Court of Review that include significant construction or interpretation of the provisions of this Act.

(b) FREQUENCY.—The first report under this section shall be submitted not later than 6 months after the date of enactment of this section. Subsequent reports under this section shall be submitted semi-annually thereafter.

(c) SUBMISSIONS TO CONGRESS.— The Attorney General shall submit to the committees of Congress referred to in subsection (a)—

(1) a copy of any decision, order, or opinion issued by the Foreign Intelligence Surveillance Court or the Foreign Intelligence Surveillance Court of Review that includes significant construction or interpretation of any provision of this Act, and any pleadings, applications, or memoranda of law associated with such decision, order, or opinion, not later than 45 days after such decision, order, or opinion is issued; and

(2) a copy of each such decision, order, or opinion, and any pleadings, applications, or memoranda of law associated with such decision, order, or opin-

ion, that was issued during the 5-year period ending on the date of the enactment of the FISA Amendments Act of 2008 and not previously submitted in a report under subsection (a).

(d) PROTECTION OF NATIONAL SECURITY.— The Attorney General, in consultation with the Director of National Intelligence, may authorize redactions of materials described in subsection (c) that are provided to the committees of Congress referred to in subsection (a), if such redactions are necessary to protect the national security of the United States and are limited to sensitive sources and methods information or the identities of targets.

(e) DEFINITIONS.— In this section:

(1) FOREIGN INTELLIGENCE SURVEILLANCE COURT.— The term 'Foreign Intelligence Surveillance Court' means the court established under section 103(a).

(2) FOREIGN INTELLIGENCE SURVEILLANCE COURT OF REVIEW.— The term 'Foreign Intelligence Surveillance Court of Review' means the court established under section 103(b).

TITLE VII—ADDITIONAL PROCEDURES REGARDING CERTAIN PERSONS OUTSIDE THE UNITED STATES

DEFINITIONS

SEC. 701. [50 U.S.C. §1881]

(a) IN GENERAL.— The terms 'agent of a foreign power', 'Attorney General', 'contents', 'electronic surveillance', 'foreign intelligence information', 'foreign power', 'person', 'United States', and 'United States person' have the meanings given such terms in section 101, except as specifically provided in this title.

(b) ADDITIONAL DEFINITIONS.—

(1) CONGRESSIONAL INTELLIGENCE COMMITTEES.— The term 'congressional intelligence committees' means—

(A) the Select Committee on Intelligence of the Senate; and

(B) the Permanent Select Committee on Intelligence of the House of Representatives.

(2) FOREIGN INTELLIGENCE SURVEILLANCE COURT.— The terms 'Foreign Intelligence Surveillance Court' and 'Court' mean the court established under section 103(a).

(3) FOREIGN INTELLIGENCE SURVEILLANCE COURT OF REVIEW; COURT OF REVIEW.— The terms 'Foreign Intelligence Surveillance Court of Review' and 'Court of Review' mean the court established under section 103(b).

(4) ELECTRONIC COMMUNICATION SERVICE PROVIDER.— The term 'electronic communication service provider' means—

(A) a telecommunications carrier, as that term is defined in section 3 of the Communications Act of 1934 (47 U.S.C. 153);

(B) a provider of electronic communication service, as that term is defined in section 2510 of title 18, United States Code;

(C) a provider of a remote computing service, as that term is defined in section 2711 of title 18, United States Code;

(D) any other communication service provider who has access to wire or electronic communications either as such communications are transmitted or as such communications are stored; or

(E) an officer, employee, or agent of an entity described in subparagraph (A), (B), (C), or (D).

(5) INTELLIGENCE COMMUNITY.— The term 'intelligence community' has the meaning given the term in section 3(4) of the National Security Act of 1947 (50 U.S.C. 401a(4)).

PROCEDURES FOR TARGETING CERTAIN PERSONS OUTSIDE THE UNITED STATES OTHER THAN UNITED STATES PERSONS

SEC. 702. [50 U.S.C. §1881a]

(a) AUTHORIZATION.— Notwithstanding any other provision of law, upon the issuance of an order in accordance with subsection (i)(3) or a determination under subsection (c)(2), the Attorney General and the Director of National Intelligence may authorize jointly, for a period of up to 1 year from the effective date of the authorization, the targeting of persons reasonably believed to be located outside the United States to acquire foreign intelligence information.

(b) LIMITATIONS.— An acquisition authorized under subsection (a)—

(1) may not intentionally target any person known at the time of acquisition to be located in the United States;

(2) may not intentionally target a person reasonably believed to be located outside the United States if the purpose of such acquisition is to target a particular, known person reasonably believed to be in the United States;

(3) may not intentionally target a United States person reasonably believed to be located outside the United States;

(4) may not intentionally acquire any communication as to which the sender and all intended recipients are known at the time of the acquisition to be located in the United States; and

(5) shall be conducted in a manner consistent with the fourth amendment to the Constitution of the United States.

(c) CONDUCT OF ACQUISITION.—

(1) IN GENERAL.—An acquisition authorized under subsection (a) shall be conducted only in accordance with—

(A) the targeting and minimization procedures adopted in accordance with subsections (d) and (e); and

(B) upon submission of a certification in accordance with subsection (g), such certification.

(2) DETERMINATION.— A determination under this paragraph and for purposes of subsection (a) is a determination by the Attorney General and the Director of National Intelligence that exigent circumstances exist because, without immediate implementation of an authorization under subsection (a), intelligence important to the national security of the United States may be lost

or not timely acquired and time does not permit the issuance of an order pursuant to subsection (i)(3) prior to the implementation of such authorization.

(3) TIMING OF DETERMINATION.— The Attorney General and the Director of National Intelligence may make the determination under paragraph (2)—

(A) before the submission of a certification in accordance with subsection (g); or

(B) by amending a certification pursuant to subsection (i)(1)(C) at any time during which judicial review under subsection (i) of such certification is pending.

(4) CONSTRUCTION.— Nothing in title I shall be construed to require an application for a court order under such title for an acquisition that is targeted in accordance with this section at a person reasonably believed to be located outside the United States.

(d) TARGETING PROCEDURES.—

(1) REQUIREMENT TO ADOPT.— The Attorney General, in consultation with the Director of National Intelligence, shall adopt targeting procedures that are reasonably designed to—

(A) ensure that any acquisition authorized under subsection (a) is limited to targeting persons reasonably believed to be located outside the United States; and

(B) prevent the intentional acquisition of any communication as to which the sender and all intended recipients are known at the time of the acquisition to be located in the United States.

(2) JUDICIAL REVIEW.— The procedures adopted in accordance with paragraph (1) shall be subject to judicial review pursuant to subsection (i).

(e) MINIMIZATION PROCEDURES.—

(1) REQUIREMENT TO ADOPT.— The Attorney General, in consultation with the Director of National Intelligence, shall adopt minimization procedures that meet the definition of minimization procedures under section 101(h) or 301(4), as appropriate, for acquisitions authorized under subsection (a).

(2) JUDICIAL REVIEW.— The minimization procedures adopted in accordance with paragraph (1) shall be subject to judicial review pursuant to subsection (i).

(f) GUIDELINES FOR COMPLIANCE WITH LIMITATIONS.—

(1) REQUIREMENT TO ADOPT.— The Attorney General, in consultation with the Director of National Intelligence, shall adopt guidelines to ensure—

(A) compliance with the limitations in subsection (b); and

(B) that an application for a court order is filed as required by this Act.

(2) SUBMISSION OF GUIDELINES.— The Attorney General shall provide the guidelines adopted in accordance with paragraph (1) to—

(A) the congressional intelligence committees;

(B) the Committees on the Judiciary of the Senate and the House of Representatives; and

(C) the Foreign Intelligence Surveillance Court.

(g) CERTIFICATION.—

(1) IN GENERAL.—

(A) REQUIREMENT.— Subject to subparagraph (B), prior to the implementation of an authorization under subsection (a), the Attorney General and the Director of National Intelligence shall provide to the Foreign Intelligence Surveillance Court a written certification and any supporting affidavit, under oath and under seal, in accordance with this subsection.

(B) EXCEPTION.— If the Attorney General and the Director of National Intelligence make a determination under subsection (c)(2) and time does not permit the submission of a certification under this subsection prior to the implementation of an authorization under subsection (a), the Attorney General and the Director of National Intelligence shall submit to the Court a certification for such authorization as soon as practicable but in no event later than 7 days after such determination is made.

(2) REQUIREMENTS.— A certification made under this subsection shall—

(A) attest that—

(i) there are procedures in place that have been approved, have been submitted for approval, or will be submitted with the certification for approval by the Foreign Intelligence Surveillance Court that are reasonably designed to—

(I) ensure that an acquisition authorized under subsection (a) is limited to targeting persons reasonably believed to be located outside the United States; and

(II) prevent the intentional acquisition of any communication as to which the sender and all intended recipients are known at the time of the acquisition to be located in the United States;

(ii) the minimization procedures to be used with respect to such acquisition—

(I) meet the definition of minimization procedures under section 101(h) or 301(4), as appropriate; and

(II) have been approved, have been submitted for approval, or will be submitted with the certification for approval by the Foreign Intelligence Surveillance Court;

(iii) guidelines have been adopted in accordance with subsection (f) to ensure compliance with the limitations in subsection (b) and to ensure that an application for a court order is filed as required by this Act;

(iv) the procedures and guidelines referred to in clauses (i), (ii), and (iii) are consistent with the requirements of the fourth amendment to the Constitution of the United States;

(v) a significant purpose of the acquisition is to obtain foreign intelligence information;

(vi) the acquisition involves obtaining foreign intelligence information from or with the assistance of an electronic communication service provider; and

(vii) the acquisition complies with the limitations in subsection (b);

(B) include the procedures adopted in accordance with subsections (d) and (e);

(C) be supported, as appropriate, by the affidavit of any appropriate official in the area of national security who is—

(i) appointed by the President, by and with the advice and consent of the Senate; or

(ii) the head of an element of the intelligence community;

(D) include—

(i) an effective date for the authorization that is at least 30 days after the submission of the written certification to the court; or

(ii) if the acquisition has begun or the effective date is less than 30 days after the submission of the written certification to the court, the date the acquisition began or the effective date for the acquisition; and

(E) if the Attorney General and the Director of National Intelligence make a determination under subsection (c)(2), include a statement that such determination has been made.

(3) CHANGE IN EFFECTIVE DATE.— The Attorney General and the Director of National Intelligence may advance or delay the effective date referred to in paragraph (2)(D) by submitting an amended certification in accordance with subsection (i)(1)(C) to the Foreign Intelligence Surveillance Court for review pursuant to subsection (i).

(4) LIMITATION.— A certification made under this subsection is not required to identify the specific facilities, places, premises, or property at which an acquisition authorized under subsection (a) will be directed or conducted.

(5) MAINTENANCE OF CERTIFICATION.— The Attorney General or a designee of the Attorney General shall maintain a copy of a certification made under this subsection.

(6) REVIEW.— A certification submitted in accordance with this subsection shall be subject to judicial review pursuant to subsection (i).

(h) DIRECTIVES AND JUDICIAL REVIEW OF DIRECTIVES-

(1) AUTHORITY.— With respect to an acquisition authorized under subsection (a), the Attorney General and the Director of National Intelligence may direct, in writing, an electronic communication service provider to—

(A) immediately provide the Government with all information, facilities, or assistance necessary to accomplish the acquisition in a manner that will protect the secrecy of the acquisition and produce a minimum of interference with the services that such electronic communication service provider is providing to the target of the acquisition; and

(B) maintain under security procedures approved by the Attorney General and the Director of National Intelligence any records concerning the acquisition or the aid furnished that such electronic communication service provider wishes to maintain.

(2) COMPENSATION.— The Government shall compensate, at the prevailing rate, an electronic communication service provider for providing informa-

tion, facilities, or assistance in accordance with a directive issued pursuant to paragraph (1).

(3) RELEASE FROM LIABILITY.— No cause of action shall lie in any court against any electronic communication service provider for providing any information, facilities, or assistance in accordance with a directive issued pursuant to paragraph (1).

(4) CHALLENGING OF DIRECTIVES.—

(A) AUTHORITY TO CHALLENGE.— An electronic communication service provider receiving a directive issued pursuant to paragraph (1) may file a petition to modify or set aside such directive with the Foreign Intelligence Surveillance Court, which shall have jurisdiction to review such petition.

(B) ASSIGNMENT.— The presiding judge of the Court shall assign a petition filed under subparagraph (A) to 1 of the judges serving in the pool established under section 103(e)(1) not later than 24 hours after the filing of such petition.

(C) STANDARDS FOR REVIEW.— A judge considering a petition filed under subparagraph (A) may grant such petition only if the judge finds that the directive does not meet the requirements of this section, or is otherwise unlawful.

(D) PROCEDURES FOR INITIAL REVIEW.— A judge shall conduct an initial review of a petition filed under subparagraph (A) not later than 5 days after being assigned such petition. If the judge determines that such petition does not consist of claims, defenses, or other legal contentions that are warranted by existing law or by a nonfrivolous argument for extending, modifying, or reversing existing law or for establishing new law, the judge shall immediately deny such petition and affirm the directive or any part of the directive that is the subject of such petition and order the recipient to comply with the directive or any part of it. Upon making a determination under this subparagraph or promptly thereafter, the judge shall provide a written statement for the record of the reasons for such determination.

(E) PROCEDURES FOR PLENARY REVIEW.— If a judge determines that a petition filed under subparagraph (A) requires plenary review, the judge shall affirm, modify, or set aside the directive that is the subject of such petition not later than 30 days after being assigned such petition. If the judge does not set aside the directive, the judge shall immediately affirm or affirm with modifications the directive, and order the recipient to comply with the directive in its entirety or as modified. The judge shall provide a written statement for the record of the reasons for a determination under this subparagraph.

(F) CONTINUED EFFECT.— Any directive not explicitly modified or set aside under this paragraph shall remain in full effect.

(G) CONTEMPT OF COURT.— Failure to obey an order issued under this paragraph may be punished by the Court as contempt of court.

(5) ENFORCEMENT OF DIRECTIVES.—

(A) ORDER TO COMPEL.— If an electronic communication service provider fails to comply with a directive issued pursuant to paragraph (1), the Attorney General may file a petition for an order to compel the electronic communication service provider to comply with the directive with the Foreign Intelligence Surveillance Court, which shall have jurisdiction to review such petition.

(B) ASSIGNMENT.— The presiding judge of the Court shall assign a petition filed under subparagraph (A) to 1 of the judges serving in the pool established under section 103(e)(1) not later than 24 hours after the filing of such petition.

(C) PROCEDURES FOR REVIEW.— A judge considering a petition filed under subparagraph (A) shall, not later than 30 days after being assigned such petition, issue an order requiring the electronic communication service provider to comply with the directive or any part of it, as issued or as modified, if the judge finds that the directive meets the requirements of this section and is otherwise lawful. The judge shall provide a written statement for the record of the reasons for a determination under this paragraph.

(D) CONTEMPT OF COURT.— Failure to obey an order issued under this paragraph may be punished by the Court as contempt of court.

(E) PROCESS.— Any process under this paragraph may be served in any judicial district in which the electronic communication service provider may be found.

(6) APPEAL.—

(A) APPEAL TO THE COURT OF REVIEW.— The Government or an electronic communication service provider receiving a directive issued pursuant to paragraph (1) may file a petition with the Foreign Intelligence Surveillance Court of Review for review of a decision issued pursuant to paragraph (4) or (5). The Court of Review shall have jurisdiction to consider such petition and shall provide a written statement for the record of the reasons for a decision under this subparagraph.

(B) CERTIORARI TO THE SUPREME COURT.— The Government or an electronic communication service provider receiving a directive issued pursuant to paragraph (1) may file a petition for a writ of certiorari for review of a decision of the Court of Review issued under subparagraph (A). The record for such review shall be transmitted under seal to the Supreme Court of the United States, which shall have jurisdiction to review such decision.

(i) JUDICIAL REVIEW OF CERTIFICATIONS AND PROCEDURES.—

(1) IN GENERAL.—

(A) REVIEW BY THE FOREIGN INTELLIGENCE SURVEILLANCE COURT.— The Foreign Intelligence Surveillance Court shall have jurisdiction to review a certification submitted in accordance with subsection (g) and the targeting and minimization procedures adopted in accordance with subsections (d) and (e), and amendments to such certification or such procedures.

(B) TIME PERIOD FOR REVIEW.— The Court shall review a certification submitted in accordance with subsection (g) and the targeting and minimization procedures adopted in accordance with subsections (d) and (e) and shall complete such review and issue an order under paragraph (3) not later than 30 days after the date on which such certification and such procedures are submitted.

(C) AMENDMENTS.— The Attorney General and the Director of National Intelligence may amend a certification submitted in accordance with subsection (g) or the targeting and minimization procedures adopted in accordance with subsections (d) and (e) as necessary at any time, including if the Court is conducting or has completed review of such certification or such procedures, and shall submit the amended certification or amended procedures to the Court not later than 7 days after amending such certification or such procedures. The Court shall review any amendment under this subparagraph under the procedures set forth in this subsection. The Attorney General and the Director of National Intelligence may authorize the use of an amended certification or amended procedures pending the Court's review of such amended certification or amended procedures.

(2) REVIEW.— The Court shall review the following:

(A) CERTIFICATION.— A certification submitted in accordance with subsection (g) to determine whether the certification contains all the required elements.

(B) TARGETING PROCEDURES.— The targeting procedures adopted in accordance with subsection (d) to assess whether the procedures are reasonably designed to-

(i) ensure that an acquisition authorized under subsection (a) is limited to targeting persons reasonably believed to be located outside the United States; and

(ii) prevent the intentional acquisition of any communication as to which the sender and all intended recipients are known at the time of the acquisition to be located in the United States.

(C) MINIMIZATION PROCEDURES.— The minimization procedures adopted in accordance with subsection (e) to assess whether such procedures meet the definition of minimization procedures under section 101(h) or section 301(4), as appropriate.

(3) ORDERS.—

(A) APPROVAL.— If the Court finds that a certification submitted in accordance with subsection (g) contains all the required elements and that the targeting and minimization procedures adopted in accordance with subsections (d) and (e) are consistent with the requirements of those subsections and with the fourth amendment to the Constitution of the United States, the Court shall enter an order approving the certification and the use, or continued use in the case of an acquisition authorized pursuant to a determination under subsection (c)(2), of the procedures for the acquisition.

(B) CORRECTION OF DEFICIENCIES.— If the Court finds that a certification submitted in accordance with subsection (g) does not contain all the required elements, or that the procedures adopted in accordance with subsections (d) and (e) are not consistent with the requirements of those subsections or the fourth amendment to the Constitution of the United States, the Court shall issue an order directing the Government to, at the Government's election and to the extent required by the Court's order—

(i) correct any deficiency identified by the Court's order not later than 30 days after the date on which the Court issues the order; or

(ii) cease, or not begin, the implementation of the authorization for which such certification was submitted.

(C) REQUIREMENT FOR WRITTEN STATEMENT.— In support of an order under this subsection, the Court shall provide, simultaneously with the order, for the record a written statement of the reasons for the order.

(4) APPEAL.—

(A) APPEAL TO THE COURT OF REVIEW.— The Government may file a petition with the Foreign Intelligence Surveillance Court of Review for review of an order under this subsection. The Court of Review shall have jurisdiction to consider such petition. For any decision under this subparagraph affirming, reversing, or modifying an order of the Foreign Intelligence Surveillance Court, the Court of Review shall provide for the record a written statement of the reasons for the decision.

(B) CONTINUATION OF ACQUISITION PENDING REHEARING OR APPEAL.—Any acquisition affected by an order under paragraph (3)(B) may continue—

(i) during the pendency of any rehearing of the order by the Court en banc; and

(ii) if the Government files a petition for review of an order under this section, until the Court of Review enters an order under subparagraph (C).

(C) IMPLEMENTATION PENDING APPEAL.— Not later than 60 days after the filing of a petition for review of an order under paragraph (3)(B) directing the correction of a deficiency, the Court of Review shall determine, and enter a corresponding order regarding, whether all or any part of the correction order, as issued or modified, shall be implemented during the pendency of the review.

(D) CERTIORARI TO THE SUPREME COURT.— The Government may file a petition for a writ of certiorari for review of a decision of the Court of Review issued under subparagraph (A). The record for such review shall be transmitted under seal to the Supreme Court of the United States, which shall have jurisdiction to review such decision.

(5) SCHEDULE.—

(A) REAUTHORIZATION OF AUTHORIZATIONS IN EFFECT.— If the Attorney General and the Director of National Intelligence seek to reauthorize or replace an authorization issued under subsection (a), the Attorney

General and the Director of National Intelligence shall, to the extent practicable, submit to the Court the certification prepared in accordance with subsection (g) and the procedures adopted in accordance with subsections (d) and (e) at least 30 days prior to the expiration of such authorization.

(B) REAUTHORIZATION OF ORDERS, AUTHORIZATIONS, AND DIRECTIVES.— If the Attorney General and the Director of National Intelligence seek to reauthorize or replace an authorization issued under subsection (a) by filing a certification pursuant to subparagraph (A), that authorization, and any directives issued thereunder and any order related thereto, shall remain in effect, notwithstanding the expiration provided for in subsection (a), until the Court issues an order with respect to such certification under paragraph (3) at which time the provisions of that paragraph and paragraph (4) shall apply with respect to such certification.

(j) JUDICIAL PROCEEDINGS.—

(1) EXPEDITED JUDICIAL PROCEEDINGS.— Judicial proceedings under this section shall be conducted as expeditiously as possible.

(2) TIME LIMITS.— A time limit for a judicial decision in this section shall apply unless the Court, the Court of Review, or any judge of either the Court or the Court of Review, by order for reasons stated, extends that time as necessary for good cause in a manner consistent with national security.

(k) MAINTENANCE AND SECURITY OF RECORDS AND PROCEEDINGS.—

(1) STANDARDS.— The Foreign Intelligence Surveillance Court shall maintain a record of a proceeding under this section, including petitions, appeals, orders, and statements of reasons for a decision, under security measures adopted by the Chief Justice of the United States, in consultation with the Attorney General and the Director of National Intelligence.

(2) FILING AND REVIEW.— All petitions under this section shall be filed under seal. In any proceedings under this section, the Court shall, upon request of the Government, review ex parte and in camera any Government submission, or portions of a submission, which may include classified information.

(3) RETENTION OF RECORDS.— The Attorney General and the Director of National Intelligence shall retain a directive or an order issued under this section for a period of not less than 10 years from the date on which such directive or such order is issued.

(l) ASSESSMENTS AND REVIEWS.—

(1) SEMIANNUAL ASSESSMENT.— Not less frequently than once every 6 months, the Attorney General and Director of National Intelligence shall assess compliance with the targeting and minimization procedures adopted in accordance with subsections (d) and (e) and the guidelines adopted in accordance with subsection (f) and shall submit each assessment to—

(A) the Foreign Intelligence Surveillance Court; and

(B) consistent with the Rules of the House of Representatives, the Standing Rules of the Senate, and Senate Resolution 400 of the 94th Congress or any successor Senate resolution—

(i) the congressional intelligence committees; and

(ii) the Committees on the Judiciary of the House of Representatives and the Senate.

(2) AGENCY ASSESSMENT.— The Inspector General of the Department of Justice and the Inspector General of each element of the intelligence community authorized to acquire foreign intelligence information under subsection (a), with respect to the department or element of such Inspector General—

(A) are authorized to review compliance with the targeting and minimization procedures adopted in accordance with subsections

(d) and (e) and the guidelines adopted in accordance with subsection (f);

(B) with respect to acquisitions authorized under subsection (a), shall review the number of disseminated intelligence reports containing a reference to a United States-person identity and the number of United States-person identities subsequently disseminated by the element concerned in response to requests for identities that were not referred to by name or title in the original reporting;

(C) with respect to acquisitions authorized under subsection (a), shall review the number of targets that were later determined to be located in the United States and, to the extent possible, whether communications of such targets were reviewed; and

(D) shall provide each such review to—

(i) the Attorney General;

(ii) the Director of National Intelligence; and

(iii) consistent with the Rules of the House of Representatives, the Standing Rules of the Senate, and Senate Resolution 400 of the 94th Congress or any successor Senate resolution—

(I) the congressional intelligence committees; and

(II) the Committees on the Judiciary of the House of Representatives and the Senate.

(3) ANNUAL REVIEW.—

(A) REQUIREMENT TO CONDUCT.— The head of each element of the intelligence community conducting an acquisition authorized under subsection (a) shall conduct an annual review to determine whether there is reason to believe that foreign intelligence information has been or will be obtained from the acquisition. The annual review shall provide, with respect to acquisitions authorized under subsection (a)—

(i) an accounting of the number of disseminated intelligence reports containing a reference to a United States-person identity;

(ii) an accounting of the number of United States-person identities subsequently disseminated by that element in response to requests for identities that were not referred to by name or title in the original reporting;

(iii) the number of targets that were later determined to be located in the United States and, to the extent possible, whether communications of such targets were reviewed; and

(iv) a description of any procedures developed by the head of such element of the intelligence community and approved by the Director of National Intelligence to assess, in a manner consistent with national security, operational requirements and the privacy interests of United States persons, the extent to which the acquisitions authorized under subsection (a) acquire the communications of United States persons, and the results of any such assessment.

(B) USE OF REVIEW.— The head of each element of the intelligence community that conducts an annual review under subparagraph (A) shall use each such review to evaluate the adequacy of the minimization procedures utilized by such element and, as appropriate, the application of the minimization procedures to a particular acquisition authorized under subsection (a).

(C) PROVISION OF REVIEW.— The head of each element of the intelligence community that conducts an annual review under subparagraph (A) shall provide such review to—

(i) the Foreign Intelligence Surveillance Court;

(ii) the Attorney General;

(iii) the Director of National Intelligence; and

(iv) consistent with the Rules of the House of Representatives, the Standing Rules of the Senate, and Senate Resolution 400 of the 94th Congress or any successor Senate resolution—

(I) the congressional intelligence committees; and

(II) the Committees on the Judiciary of the House of Representatives and the Senate.

CERTAIN ACQUISITIONS INSIDE THE UNITED STATES TARGETING UNITED STATES PERSONS OUTSIDE THE UNITED STATES

SEC. 703. [50 U.S.C. §1881b]

(a) JURISDICTION OF THE FOREIGN INTELLIGENCE SURVEILLANCE COURT.—

(1) IN GENERAL.— The Foreign Intelligence Surveillance Court shall have jurisdiction to review an application and to enter an order approving the targeting of a United States person reasonably believed to be located outside the United States to acquire foreign intelligence information, if the acquisition constitutes electronic surveillance or the acquisition of stored electronic communications or stored electronic data that requires an order under this Act, and such acquisition is conducted within the United States.

(2) LIMITATION.— If a United States person targeted under this subsection is reasonably believed to be located in the United States during the effective period of an order issued pursuant to subsection (c), an acquisition targeting such United States person under this section shall cease unless the targeted United States person is again reasonably believed to be located outside the United States while an order issued pursuant to subsection (c) is in effect. Nothing in this section shall be construed to limit the authority of the Govern-

ment to seek an order or authorization under, or otherwise engage in any activity that is authorized under, any other title of this Act.

(b) APPLICATION.—

(1) IN GENERAL.— Each application for an order under this section shall be made by a Federal officer in writing upon oath or affirmation to a judge having jurisdiction under subsection (a)(1). Each application shall require the approval of the Attorney General based upon the Attorney General's finding that it satisfies the criteria and requirements of such application, as set forth in this section, and shall include—

(A) the identity of the Federal officer making the application;

(B) the identity, if known, or a description of the United States person who is the target of the acquisition;

(C) a statement of the facts and circumstances relied upon to justify the applicant's belief that the United States person who is the target of the acquisition is—

(i) a person reasonably believed to be located outside the United States; and

(ii) a foreign power, an agent of a foreign power, or an officer or employee of a foreign power;

(D) a statement of proposed minimization procedures that meet the definition of minimization procedures under section 101(h) or 301(4), as appropriate;

(E) a description of the nature of the information sought and the type of communications or activities to be subjected to acquisition;

(F) a certification made by the Attorney General or an official specified in section 104(a)(6) that—

(i) the certifying official deems the information sought to be foreign intelligence information;

(ii) a significant purpose of the acquisition is to obtain foreign intelligence information;

(iii) such information cannot reasonably be obtained by normal investigative techniques;

(iv) designates the type of foreign intelligence information being sought according to the categories described in section 101(e); and

(v) includes a statement of the basis for the certification that—

(I) the information sought is the type of foreign intelligence information designated; and

(II) such information cannot reasonably be obtained by normal investigative techniques;

(G) a summary statement of the means by which the acquisition will be conducted and whether physical entry is required to effect the acquisition;

(H) the identity of any electronic communication service provider necessary to effect the acquisition, provided that the application is not required to identify the specific facilities, places, premises, or property at which the acquisition authorized under this section will be directed or conducted;

(I) a statement of the facts concerning any previous applications that have been made to any judge of the Foreign Intelligence Surveillance Court involving the United States person specified in the application and the action taken on each previous application; and

(J) a statement of the period of time for which the acquisition is required to be maintained, provided that such period of time shall not exceed 90 days per application.

(2) OTHER REQUIREMENTS OF THE ATTORNEY GENERAL.— The Attorney General may require any other affidavit or certification from any other officer in connection with the application.

(3) OTHER REQUIREMENTS OF THE JUDGE.— The judge may require the applicant to furnish such other information as may be necessary to make the findings required by subsection (c)(1).

(c) ORDER.—

(1) FINDINGS.— Upon an application made pursuant to subsection (b), the Foreign Intelligence Surveillance Court shall enter an ex parte order as requested or as modified by the Court approving the acquisition if the Court finds that—

(A) the application has been made by a Federal officer and approved by the Attorney General;

(B) on the basis of the facts submitted by the applicant, for the United States person who is the target of the acquisition, there is probable cause to believe that the target is—

(i) a person reasonably believed to be located outside the United States; and

(ii) a foreign power, an agent of a foreign power, or an officer or employee of a foreign power;

(C) the proposed minimization procedures meet the definition of minimization procedures under section 101(h) or 301(4), as appropriate; and

(D) the application that has been filed contains all statements and certifications required by subsection (b) and the certification or certifications are not clearly erroneous on the basis of the statement made under subsection (b)(1)(F)(v) and any other information furnished under subsection (b)(3).

(2) PROBABLE CAUSE.— In determining whether or not probable cause exists for purposes of paragraph (1)(B), a judge having jurisdiction under subsection (a)(1) may consider past activities of the target and facts and circumstances relating to current or future activities of the target. No United States person may be considered a foreign power, agent of a foreign power, or officer or employee of a foreign power solely upon the basis of activities protected by the first amendment to the Constitution of the United States.

(3) REVIEW.—

(A) LIMITATION ON REVIEW.— Review by a judge having jurisdiction under subsection (a)(1) shall be limited to that required to make the findings described in paragraph (1).

(B) REVIEW OF PROBABLE CAUSE.— If the judge determines that the facts submitted under subsection (b) are insufficient to establish probable cause under paragraph (1)(B), the judge shall enter an order so stating and provide a written statement for the record of the reasons for the determination. The Government may appeal an order under this subparagraph pursuant to subsection (f).

(C) REVIEW OF MINIMIZATION PROCEDURES.— If the judge determines that the proposed minimization procedures referred to in paragraph (1)(C) do not meet the definition of minimization procedures under section 101(h) or 301(4), as appropriate, the judge shall enter an order so stating and provide a written statement for the record of the reasons for the determination. The Government may appeal an order under this subparagraph pursuant to subsection (f).

(D) REVIEW OF CERTIFICATION.— If the judge determines that an application pursuant to subsection (b) does not contain all of the required elements, or that the certification or certifications are clearly erroneous on the basis of the statement made under subsection (b)(1)(F)(v) and any other information furnished under subsection (b)(3), the judge shall enter an order so stating and provide a written statement for the record of the reasons for the determination. The Government may appeal an order under this subparagraph pursuant to subsection (f).

(4) SPECIFICATIONS.— An order approving an acquisition under this subsection shall specify—

(A) the identity, if known, or a description of the United States person who is the target of the acquisition identified or described in the application pursuant to subsection (b)(1)(B);

(B) if provided in the application pursuant to subsection (b)(1)(H), the nature and location of each of the facilities or places at which the acquisition will be directed;

(C) the nature of the information sought to be acquired and the type of communications or activities to be subjected to acquisition;

(D) a summary of the means by which the acquisition will be conducted and whether physical entry is required to effect the acquisition; and

(E) the period of time during which the acquisition is approved.

(5) DIRECTIVES.— An order approving an acquisition under this subsection shall direct—

(A) that the minimization procedures referred to in paragraph (1)(C), as approved or modified by the Court, be followed;

(B) if applicable, an electronic communication service provider to provide to the Government forthwith all information, facilities, or assistance necessary to accomplish the acquisition authorized under such order in a manner that will protect the secrecy of the acquisition and produce a minimum of interference with the services that such electronic communication service provider is providing to the target of the acquisition;

(C) if applicable, an electronic communication service provider to maintain under security procedures approved by the Attorney General any records concerning the acquisition or the aid furnished that such electronic communication service provider wishes to maintain; and

(D) if applicable, that the Government compensate, at the prevailing rate, such electronic communication service provider for providing such information, facilities, or assistance.

(6) DURATION.— An order approved under this subsection shall be effective for a period not to exceed 90 days and such order may be renewed for additional 90-day periods upon submission of renewal applications meeting the requirements of subsection (b).

(7) COMPLIANCE.— At or prior to the end of the period of time for which an acquisition is approved by an order or extension under this section, the judge may assess compliance with the minimization procedures referred to in paragraph (1)(C) by reviewing the circumstances under which information concerning United States persons was acquired, retained, or disseminated.

(d) EMERGENCY AUTHORIZATION.—

(1) AUTHORITY FOR EMERGENCY AUTHORIZATION.— Notwithstanding any other provision of this Act, if the Attorney General reasonably determines that—

(A) an emergency situation exists with respect to the acquisition of foreign intelligence information for which an order may be obtained under subsection (c) before an order authorizing such acquisition can with due diligence be obtained, and

(B) the factual basis for issuance of an order under this subsection to approve such acquisition exists, the Attorney General may authorize such acquisition if a judge having jurisdiction under subsection (a)(1) is informed by the Attorney General, or a designee of the Attorney General, at the time of such authorization that the decision has been made to conduct such acquisition and if an application in accordance with this section is made to a judge of the Foreign Intelligence Surveillance Court as soon as practicable, but not more than 7 days after the Attorney General authorizes such acquisition.

(2) MINIMIZATION PROCEDURES.— If the Attorney General authorizes an acquisition under paragraph (1), the Attorney General shall require that the minimization procedures referred to in subsection (c)(1)(C) for the issuance of a judicial order be followed.

(3) TERMINATION OF EMERGENCY AUTHORIZATION.— In the absence of a judicial order approving an acquisition under paragraph (1), such acquisition shall terminate when the information sought is obtained, when the application for the order is denied, or after the expiration of 7 days from the time of authorization by the Attorney General, whichever is earliest.

(4) USE OF INFORMATION.— If an application for approval submitted pursuant to paragraph (1) is denied, or in any other case where the acquisition is terminated and no order is issued approving the acquisition, no information obtained or evidence derived from such acquisition, except under circumstances in which the target of the acquisition is determined not to be a United

States person, shall be received in evidence or otherwise disclosed in any trial, hearing, or other proceeding in or before any court, grand jury, department, office, agency, regulatory body, legislative committee, or other authority of the United States, a State, or political subdivision thereof, and no information concerning any United States person acquired from such acquisition shall subsequently be used or disclosed in any other manner by Federal officers or employees without the consent of such person, except with the approval of the Attorney General if the information indicates a threat of death or serious bodily harm to any person.

(e) RELEASE FROM LIABILITY.— No cause of action shall lie in any court against any electronic communication service provider for providing any information, facilities, or assistance in accordance with an order or request for emergency assistance issued pursuant to subsection (c) or (d), respectively.

(f) APPEAL.—

(1) APPEAL TO THE FOREIGN INTELLIGENCE SURVEILLANCE COURT OF REVIEW.— The Government may file a petition with the Foreign Intelligence Surveillance Court of Review for review of an order issued pursuant to subsection (c). The Court of Review shall have jurisdiction to consider such petition and shall provide a written statement for the record of the reasons for a decision under this paragraph.

(2) CERIORARI TO THE SUPREME COURT.— The Government may file a petition for a writ of certiorari for review of a decision of the Court of Review issued under paragraph (1). The record for such review shall be transmitted under seal to the Supreme Court of the United States, which shall have jurisdiction to review such decision.

(g) CONSTRUCTION.— Except as provided in this section, nothing in this Act shall be construed to require an application for a court order for an acquisition that is targeted in accordance with this section at a United States person reasonably believed to be located outside the United States.

OTHER ACQUISITIONS TARGETING UNITED STATES PERSONS OUTSIDE THE UNITED STATES

SEC. 704. [50 U.S.C. §1881c]

(a) JURISDICTION AND SCOPE.—

(1) JURISDICTION.— The Foreign Intelligence Surveillance Court shall have jurisdiction to enter an order pursuant to subsection (c).

(2) SCOPE.— No element of the intelligence community may intentionally target, for the purpose of acquiring foreign intelligence information, a United States person reasonably believed to be located outside the United States under circumstances in which the targeted United States person has a reasonable expectation of privacy and a warrant would be required if the acquisition were conducted inside the United States for law enforcement purposes, unless a judge of the Foreign Intelligence Surveillance Court has entered an order with respect to such targeted United States person or the Attorney General has authorized an emergency acquisition pursuant to subsection (c) or (d), respectively, or any other provision of this Act.

(3) LIMITATIONS.—

(A) MOVING OR MISIDENTIFIED TARGETS.— If a United States person targeted under this subsection is reasonably believed to be located in the United States during the effective period of an order issued pursuant to subsection (c), an acquisition targeting such United States person under this section shall cease unless the targeted United States person is again reasonably believed to be located outside the United States during the effective period of such order.

(B) APPLICABILITY.— If an acquisition for foreign intelligence purposes is to be conducted inside the United States and could be authorized under section 703, the acquisition may only be conducted if authorized under section 703 or in accordance with another provision of this Act other than this section.

(C) CONSTRUCTION.— Nothing in this paragraph shall be construed to limit the authority of the Government to seek an order or authorization under, or otherwise engage in any activity that is authorized under, any other title of this Act.

(b) APPLICATION.— Each application for an order under this section shall be made by a Federal officer in writing upon oath or affirmation to a judge having jurisdiction under subsection (a)(1). Each application shall require the approval of the Attorney General based upon the Attorney General's finding that it satisfies the criteria and requirements of such application as set forth in this section and shall include—

(1) the identity of the Federal officer making the application;

(2) the identity, if known, or a description of the specific United States person who is the target of the acquisition;

(3) a statement of the facts and circumstances relied upon to justify the applicant's belief that the United States person who is the target of the acquisition is—

(A) a person reasonably believed to be located outside the United States; and

(B) a foreign power, an agent of a foreign power, or an officer or employee of a foreign power;

(4) a statement of proposed minimization procedures that meet the definition of minimization procedures under section 101(h) or 301(4), as appropriate;

(5) a certification made by the Attorney General, an official specified in section 104(a)(6), or the head of an element of the intelligence community that—

(A) the certifying official deems the information sought to be foreign intelligence information; and

(B) a significant purpose of the acquisition is to obtain foreign intelligence information;

(6) a statement of the facts concerning any previous applications that have been made to any judge of the Foreign Intelligence Surveillance Court involving the United States person specified in the application and the action taken on each previous application; and

(7) a statement of the period of time for which the acquisition is required to be maintained, provided that such period of time shall not exceed 90 days per application.

(c) ORDER.—

(1) FINDINGS.— Upon an application made pursuant to subsection (b), the Foreign Intelligence Surveillance Court shall enter an ex parte order as requested or as modified by the Court if the Court finds that—

(A) the application has been made by a Federal officer and approved by the Attorney General;

(B) on the basis of the facts submitted by the applicant, for the United States person who is the target of the acquisition, there is probable cause to believe that the target is—

(i) a person reasonably believed to be located outside the United States; and

(ii) a foreign power, an agent of a foreign power, or an officer or employee of a foreign power;

(C) the proposed minimization procedures, with respect to their dissemination provisions, meet the definition of minimization procedures under section 101(h) or 301(4), as appropriate; and

(D) the application that has been filed contains all statements and certifications required by subsection (b) and the certification provided under subsection (b)(5) is not clearly erroneous on the basis of the information furnished under subsection (b).

(2) PROBABLE CAUSE.— In determining whether or not probable cause exists for purposes of paragraph (1)(B), a judge having jurisdiction under subsection (a)(1) may consider past activities of the target and facts and circumstances relating to current or future activities of the target. No United States person may be considered a foreign power, agent of a foreign power, or officer or employee of a foreign power solely upon the basis of activities protected by the first amendment to the Constitution of the United States.

(3) REVIEW.—

(A) LIMITATIONS ON REVIEW.— Review by a judge having jurisdiction under subsection (a)(1) shall be limited to that required to make the findings described in paragraph (1). The judge shall not have jurisdiction to review the means by which an acquisition under this section may be conducted.

(B) REVIEW OF PROBABLE CAUSE.— If the judge determines that the facts submitted under subsection (b) are insufficient to establish probable cause to issue an order under this subsection, the judge shall enter an order so stating and provide a written statement for the record of the reasons for such determination. The Government may appeal an order under this subparagraph pursuant to subsection (e).

(C) REVIEW OF MINIMIZATION PROCEDURES.— If the judge determines that the minimization procedures applicable to dissemination of information obtained through an acquisition under this subsection do not meet the definition of minimization procedures under section 101(h) or

301(4), as appropriate, the judge shall enter an order so stating and provide a written statement for the record of the reasons for such determination. The Government may appeal an order under this subparagraph pursuant to subsection (e).

(D) SCOPE OF REVIEW OF CERTIFICATION.— If the judge determines that an application under subsection (b) does not contain all the required elements, or that the certification provided under subsection (b)(5) is clearly erroneous on the basis of the information furnished under subsection (b), the judge shall enter an order so stating and provide a written statement for the record of the reasons for such determination. The Government may appeal an order under this subparagraph pursuant to subsection (e).

(4) DURATION.— An order under this paragraph shall be effective for a period not to exceed 90 days and such order may be renewed for additional 90-day periods upon submission of renewal applications meeting the requirements of subsection (b).

(5) COMPLIANCE.— At or prior to the end of the period of time for which an order or extension is granted under this section, the judge may assess compliance with the minimization procedures referred to in paragraph (1)(C) by reviewing the circumstances under which information concerning United States persons was disseminated, provided that the judge may not inquire into the circumstances relating to the conduct of the acquisition.

(d) EMERGENCY AUTHORIZATION.—

(1) AUTHORITY FOR EMERGENCY AUTHORIZATION.— Notwithstanding any other provision of this section, if the Attorney General reasonably determines that—

(A) an emergency situation exists with respect to the acquisition of foreign intelligence information for which an order may be obtained under subsection (c) before an order under that subsection can, with due diligence, be obtained, and

(B) the factual basis for the issuance of an order under this section exists, the Attorney General may authorize the emergency acquisition if a judge having jurisdiction under subsection (a)(1) is informed by the Attorney General or a designee of the Attorney General at the time of such authorization that the decision has been made to conduct such acquisition and if an application in accordance with this section is made to a judge of the Foreign Intelligence Surveillance Court as soon as practicable, but not more than 7 days after the Attorney General authorizes such acquisition.

(2) MINIMIZATION PROCEDURES.— If the Attorney General authorizes an emergency acquisition under paragraph (1), the Attorney General shall require that the minimization procedures referred to in subsection (c)(1)(C) be followed.

(3) TERMINATION OF EMERGENCY AUTHORIZATION.— In the absence of an order under subsection (c), an emergency acquisition under paragraph (1) shall terminate when the information sought is obtained, if the application for the order is denied, or after the expiration of 7 days from the time of authorization by the Attorney General, whichever is earliest.

(4) USE OF INFORMATION.— If an application submitted to the Court pursuant to paragraph (1) is denied, or in any other case where the acquisition is terminated and no order with respect to the target of the acquisition is issued under subsection (c), no information obtained or evidence derived from such acquisition, except under circumstances in which the target of the acquisition is determined not to be a United States person, shall be received in evidence or otherwise disclosed in any trial, hearing, or other proceeding in or before any court, grand jury, department, office, agency, regulatory body, legislative committee, or other authority of the United States, a State, or political subdivision thereof, and no information concerning any United States person acquired from such acquisition shall subsequently be used or disclosed in any other manner by Federal officers or employees without the consent of such person, except with the approval of the Attorney General if the information indicates a threat of death or serious bodily harm to any person.

(e) APPEAL.—

(1) APPEAL TO THE COURT OF REVIEW.— The Government may file a petition with the Foreign Intelligence Surveillance Court of Review for review of an order issued pursuant to subsection (c). The Court of Review shall have jurisdiction to consider such petition and shall provide a written statement for the record of the reasons for a decision under this paragraph.

(2) CERTIORARI TO THE SUPREME COURT.— The Government may file a petition for a writ of certiorari for review of a decision of the Court of Review issued under paragraph (1). The record for such review shall be transmitted under seal to the Supreme Court of the United States, which shall have jurisdiction to review such decision.

JOINT APPLICATIONS AND CONCURRENT AUTHORIZATIONS

SEC. 705. [50 U.S.C. §1881d]

(a) JOINT APPLICATIONS AND ORDERS.— If an acquisition targeting a United States person under section 703 or 704 is proposed to be conducted both inside and outside the United States, a judge having jurisdiction under section 703(a)(1) or 704(a)(1) may issue simultaneously, upon the request of the Government in a joint application complying with the requirements of sections 703(b) and 704(b), orders under sections 703(c) and 704(c), as appropriate.

(b) CONCURRENT AUTHORIZATION.— If an order authorizing electronic surveillance or physical search has been obtained under section 105 or 304, the Attorney General may authorize, for the effective period of that order, without an order under section 703 or 704, the targeting of that United States person for the purpose of acquiring foreign intelligence information while such person is reasonably believed to be located outside the United States.

USE OF INFORMATION ACQUIRED UNDER TITLE VII

SEC. 706. [50 U.S.C. §1881e]

(a) INFORMATION ACQUIRED UNDER SECTION 702.— Information acquired from an acquisition conducted under section 702 shall be deemed to be information acquired from an electronic surveillance pursuant to title I for purposes of section 106, except for the purposes of subsection (j) of such section.

(b) INFORMATION ACQUIRED UNDER SECTION 703.— Information acquired from an acquisition conducted under section 703 shall be deemed to be information acquired from an electronic surveillance pursuant to title I for purposes of section 106.

CONGRESSIONAL OVERSIGHT

SEC. 707. [50 U.S.C. §1881f]

(a) SEMIANNUAL REPORT.— Not less frequently than once every 6 months, the Attorney General shall fully inform, in a manner consistent with national security, the congressional intelligence committees and the Committees on the Judiciary of the Senate and the House of Representatives, consistent with the Rules of the House of Representatives, the Standing Rules of the Senate, and Senate Resolution 400 of the 94th Congress or any successor Senate resolution, concerning the implementation of this title.

(b) CONTENT.— Each report under subsection (a) shall include—

(1) with respect to section 702—

(A) any certifications submitted in accordance with section 702(g) during the reporting period;

(B) with respect to each determination under section 702(c)(2), the reasons for exercising the authority under such section;

(C) any directives issued under section 702(h) during the reporting period;

(D) a description of the judicial review during the reporting period of such certifications and targeting and minimization procedures adopted in accordance with subsections (d) and (e) of section 702 and utilized with respect to an acquisition under such section, including a copy of an order or pleading in connection with such review that contains a significant legal interpretation of the provisions of section 702;

(E) any actions taken to challenge or enforce a directive under paragraph (4) or (5) of section 702(h);

(F) any compliance reviews conducted by the Attorney General or the Director of National Intelligence of acquisitions authorized under section 702(a);

(G) a description of any incidents of noncompliance-

(i) with a directive issued by the Attorney General and the Director of National Intelligence under section 702(h), including incidents of noncompliance by a specified person to whom the Attorney General and Director of National Intelligence issued a directive under section 702(h); and

(ii) by an element of the intelligence community with procedures and guidelines adopted in accordance with subsections (d), (e), and (f) of section 702; and

(H) any procedures implementing section 702;

(2) with respect to section 703—
(A) the total number of applications made for orders under section 703(b);
(B) the total number of such orders—
(i) granted;
(ii) modified; and
(iii) denied; and
(C) the total number of emergency acquisitions authorized by the Attorney General under section 703(d) and the total number of subsequent orders approving or denying such acquisitions; and
(3) with respect to section 704—
(A) the total number of applications made for orders under section 704(b);
(B) the total number of such orders—
(i) granted;
(ii) modified; and
(iii) denied; and
(C) the total number of emergency acquisitions authorized by the Attorney General under section 704(d) and the total number of subsequent orders approving or denying such applications.

SAVINGS PROVISION

SEC. 708. [50 U.S.C. §1881g] Nothing in this title shall be construed to limit the authority of the Government to seek an order or authorization under, or otherwise engage in any activity that is authorized under, any other title of this Act.

TITLE VIII—PROTECTION OF PERSONS ASSISTING THE GOVERNMENT

DEFINITIONS

SEC. 801. [50 U.S.C. §1885] In this title:
(1) ASSISTANCE.— The term 'assistance' means the provision of, or the provision of access to, information (including communication contents, communications records, or other information relating to a customer or communication), facilities, or another form of assistance.
(2) CIVIL ACTION.— The term 'civil action' includes a covered civil action.
(3) CONGRESSIONAL INTELLIGENCE COMMITTEES.— The term 'congressional intelligence committees' means—
(A) the Select Committee on Intelligence of the Senate; and
(B) the Permanent Select Committee on Intelligence of the House of Representatives.
(4) CONTENTS.— The term 'contents' has the meaning given that term in section 101(n).
(5) COVERED CIVIL ACTION.— The term 'covered civil action' means a civil action filed in a Federal or State court that—
(A) alleges that an electronic communication service provider furnished assistance to an element of the intelligence community; and

(B) seeks monetary or other relief from the electronic communication service provider related to the provision of such assistance.

(6) ELECTRONIC COMMUNICATION SERVICE PROVIDER.— The term 'electronic communication service provider' means—

(A) a telecommunications carrier, as that term is defined in section 3 of the Communications Act of 1934 (47 U.S.C. 153);

(B) a provider of electronic communication service, as that term is defined in section 2510 of title 18, United States Code;

(C) a provider of a remote computing service, as that term is defined in section 2711 of title 18, United States Code;

(D) any other communication service provider who has access to wire or electronic communications either as such communications are transmitted or as such communications are stored;

(E) a parent, subsidiary, affiliate, successor, or assignee of an entity described in subparagraph (A), (B), (C), or (D); or

(F) an officer, employee, or agent of an entity described in subparagraph (A), (B), (C), (D), or (E).

(7) INTELLIGENCE COMMUNITY.— The term 'intelligence community' has the meaning given the term in section 3(4) of the National Security Act of 1947 (50 U.S.C. 401a(4)).

(8) PERSON.— The term 'person' means-

(A) an electronic communication service provider; or

(B) a landlord, custodian, or other person who may be authorized or required to furnish assistance pursuant to—

(i) an order of the court established under section 103(a) directing such assistance;

(ii) a certification in writing under section 2511(2)(a)(ii)(B) or 2709(b) of title 18, United States Code; or

(iii) a directive under section 102(a)(4), 105B(e), as added by section 2 of the Protect America Act of 2007 (Public Law 110-55), or 702(h).

(9) STATE.—The term 'State' means any State, political subdivision of a State, the Commonwealth of Puerto Rico, the District of Columbia, and any territory or possession of the United States, and includes any officer, public utility commission, or other body authorized to regulate an electronic communication service provider.

PROCEDURES FOR IMPLEMENTING STATUTORY DEFENSES

SEC. 802. [50 U.S.C. §1885a]

(a) REQUIREMENT FOR CERTIFICATION.— Notwithstanding any other provision of law, a civil action may not lie or be maintained in a Federal or State court against any person for providing assistance to an element of the intelligence community, and shall be promptly dismissed, if the Attorney General certifies to the district court of the United States in which such action is pending that—

(1) any assistance by that person was provided pursuant to an order of the court established under section 103(a) directing such assistance;

(2) any assistance by that person was provided pursuant to a certification in writing under section 2511(2)(a)(ii)(B) or 2709(b) of title 18, United States Code;

(3) any assistance by that person was provided pursuant to a directive under section 102(a)(4), 105B(e), as added by section 2 of the Protect America Act of 2007 (Public Law 110-55), or 702(h) directing such assistance;

(4) in the case of a covered civil action, the assistance alleged to have been provided by the electronic communication service provider was—

(A) in connection with an intelligence activity involving communications that was—

(i) authorized by the President during the period beginning on September 11, 2001, and ending on January 17, 2007; and

(ii) designed to detect or prevent a terrorist attack, or activities in preparation for a terrorist attack, against the United States; and

(B) the subject of a written request or directive, or a series of written requests or directives, from the Attorney General or the head of an element of the intelligence community (or the deputy of such person) to the electronic communication service provider indicating that the activity was—

(i) authorized by the President; and

(ii) determined to be lawful; or

(5) the person did not provide the alleged assistance.

(b) JUDICIAL REVIEW.—

(1) REVIEW OF CERTIFICATIONS.— A certification under subsection (a) shall be given effect unless the court finds that such certification is not supported by substantial evidence provided to the court pursuant to this section.

(2) SUPPLEMENTAL MATERIALS.— In its review of a certification under subsection (a), the court may examine the court order, certification, written request, or directive described in subsection (a) and any relevant court order, certification, written request, or directive submitted pursuant to subsection (d).

(c) LIMITATIONS ON DISCLOSURE.— If the Attorney General files a declaration under section 1746 of title 28, United States Code, that disclosure of a certification made pursuant to subsection (a) or the supplemental materials provided pursuant to subsection (b) or (d) would harm the national security of the United States, the court shall—

(1) review such certification and the supplemental materials in camera and ex parte; and

(2) limit any public disclosure concerning such certification and the supplemental materials, including any public order following such in camera and ex parte review, to a statement as to whether the case is dismissed and a description of the legal standards that govern the order, without disclosing the paragraph of subsection (a) that is the basis for the certification.

(d) ROLE OF THE PARTIES.— Any plaintiff or defendant in a civil action may submit any relevant court order, certification, written request, or directive to the district court referred to in subsection (a) for review and shall be permitted to participate in the briefing or argument of any legal issue in a judicial proceeding conducted pursuant to this section, but only to the extent that such participation does not require the disclosure of classified information to such party. To the extent that classified information is relevant to the proceeding or would be revealed in the determination of an issue, the court shall review such information in camera and ex parte, and shall issue any part of the court's written order that would reveal classified information in camera and ex parte and maintain such part under seal.

(e) NONDELEGATION.— The authority and duties of the Attorney General under this section shall be performed by the Attorney General (or Acting Attorney General) or the Deputy Attorney General.

(f) APPEAL.— The courts of appeals shall have jurisdiction of appeals from interlocutory orders of the district courts of the United States granting or denying a motion to dismiss or for summary judgment under this section.

(g) REMOVAL.— A civil action against a person for providing assistance to an element of the intelligence community that is brought in a State court shall be deemed to arise under the Constitution and laws of the United States and shall be removable under section 1441 of title 28, United States Code.

(h) RELATIONSHIP TO OTHER LAWS.— Nothing in this section shall be construed to limit any otherwise available immunity, privilege, or defense under any other provision of law.

(i) APPLICABILITY.— This section shall apply to a civil action pending on or filed after the date of the enactment of the FISA Amendments Act of 2008.

PREEMPTION

SEC. 803. [50 U.S.C. §1885b]

(a) IN GENERAL.— No State shall have authority to—

(1) conduct an investigation into an electronic communication service provider's alleged assistance to an element of the intelligence community;

(2) require through regulation or any other means the disclosure of information about an electronic communication service provider's alleged assistance to an element of the intelligence community;

(3) impose any administrative sanction on an electronic communication service provider for assistance to an element of the intelligence community; or

(4) commence or maintain a civil action or other proceeding to enforce a requirement that an electronic communication service provider disclose information concerning alleged assistance to an element of the intelligence community.

(b) SUITS BY THE UNITED STATES.— The United States may bring suit to enforce the provisions of this section.

(c) JURISDICTION.— The district courts of the United States shall have jurisdiction over any civil action brought by the United States to enforce the provisions of this section.

(d) APPLICATION.— This section shall apply to any investigation, action, or proceeding that is pending on or commenced after the date of the enactment of the FISA Amendments Act of 2008.

REPORTING

SEC. 804. [50 U.S.C. §1885c]

(a) SEMIANNUAL REPORT.— Not less frequently than once every 6 months, the Attorney General shall, in a manner consistent with national security, the Rules of the House of Representatives, the Standing Rules of the Senate, and Senate Resolution 400 of the 94th Congress or any successor Senate resolution, fully inform the congressional intelligence committees, the Committee on the Judiciary of the Senate, and the Committee on the Judiciary of the House of Representatives concerning the implementation of this title.

(b) CONTENT.— Each report made under subsection (a) shall include—

(1) any certifications made under section 802;

(2) a description of the judicial review of the certifications made under section 802; and

(3) any actions taken to enforce the provisions of section 803.

SELECTED ADDITIONAL PROVISIONS OF THE FISA AMENDMENTS ACT OF 2008

REVIEW OF PREVIOUS ACTIONS

Sec. 301.

(a) DEFINITIONS.— In this section:

(1) APPROPRIATE COMMITTEES OF CONGRESS.— The term "appropriate committees of Congress" means—

(A) the Select Committee on Intelligence and the Committee on the Judiciary of the Senate; and

(B) the Permanent Select Committee on Intelligence and the Committee on the Judiciary of the House of Representatives.

(2) FOREIGN INTELLIGENCE SURVEILLANCE COURT.— The term "Foreign Intelligence Surveillance Court" means the court established under section 103(a) of the Foreign Intelligence Surveillance Act of 1978 (50 U.S.C. 1803(a)).

(3) PRESIDENT'S SURVEILLANCE PROGRAM AND PROGRAM.— The terms "President's Surveillance Program" and "Program" mean the intelligence activity involving communications that was authorized by the President during the period beginning on September 11, 2001, and ending on January 17, 2007, including the program referred to by the President in a radio address on December 17, 2005 (commonly known as the Terrorist Surveillance Program).

(b) REVIEWS.—

(1) REQUIREMENT TO CONDUCT.— The Inspectors General of the Department of Justice, the Office of the Director of National Intelligence, the National Security Agency, the Department of Defense, and any other element of the intelligence community that participated in the President's Surveillance Program, shall complete a comprehensive review of, with respect to the oversight authority and responsibility of each such Inspector General—

(A) all of the facts necessary to describe the establishment, implementation, product, and use of the product of the Program;

(B) access to legal reviews of the Program and access to information about the Program;
(C) communications with, and participation of, individuals and entities in the private sector related to the Program;
(D) interaction with the Foreign Intelligence Surveillance Court and transition to court orders related to the Program; and
(E) any other matters identified by any such Inspector General that would enable that Inspector General to complete a review of the Program, with respect to such Department or element.

(2) COOPERATION AND COORDINATION.—
(A) COOPERATION.— Each Inspector General required to conduct a review under paragraph (1) shall—
(i) work in conjunction, to the extent practicable, with any other Inspector General required to conduct such a review; and
(ii) utilize, to the extent practicable, and not unnecessarily duplicate or delay, such reviews or audits that have been completed or are being undertaken by any such Inspector General or by any other office of the Executive Branch related to the Program.
(B) INTEGRATION OF OTHER REVIEWS.—The Counsel of the Office of Professional Responsibility of the Department of Justice shall provide the report of any investigation conducted by such Office on matters relating to the Program, including any investigation of the process through which legal reviews of the Program were conducted and the substance of such reviews, to the Inspector General of the Department of Justice, who shall integrate the factual findings and conclusions of such investigation into its review.
(C) COORDINATION.—The Inspectors General shall designate one of the Inspectors General required to conduct a review under paragraph (1) that is appointed by the President, by and with the advice and consent of the Senate, to coordinate the conduct of the reviews and the preparation of the reports.

(c) REPORTS.—
(1) PRELIMINARY REPORTS.— Not later than 60 days after the date of the enactment of this Act, the Inspectors General of the Department of Justice, the Office of the Director of National Intelligence, the National Security Agency, the Department of Defense, and any other Inspector General required to conduct a review under subsection (b)(1), shall submit to the appropriate committees of Congress an interim report that describes the planned scope of such review.
(2) FINAL REPORT.— Not later than 1 year after the date of the enactment of this Act, the Inspectors General of the Department of Justice, the Office of the Director of National Intelligence, the National Security Agency, the Department of Defense, and any other Inspector General required to conduct a review under subsection (b)(1), shall submit to the appropriate committees of Congress, in a manner consistent with national security, a comprehensive re-

port on such reviews that includes any recommendations of any such Inspectors General within the oversight authority and responsibility of any such Inspector General with respect to the reviews.

(3) FORM.— A report under this subsection shall be submitted in unclassified form, but may include a classified annex. The unclassified report shall not disclose the name or identity of any individual or entity of the private sector that participated in the Program or with whom there was communication about the Program, to the extent that information is classified.

(d) RESOURCES.—

(1) EXPEDITED SECURITY CLEARANCE.— The Director of National Intelligence shall ensure that the process for the investigation and adjudication of an application by an Inspector General or any appropriate staff of an Inspector General for a security clearance necessary for the conduct of the review under subsection (b)(1) is carried out as expeditiously as possible.

(2) ADDITIONAL PERSONNEL FOR THE INSPECTORS GENERAL.— An Inspector General required to conduct a review under subsection (b)(1) and submit a report under subsection (c) is authorized to hire such additional personnel as may be necessary to carry out such review and prepare such report in a prompt and timely manner. Personnel authorized to be hired under this paragraph—

(A) shall perform such duties relating to such a review as the relevant Inspector General shall direct; and

(B) are in addition to any other personnel authorized by law.

(3) TRANSFER OF PERSONNEL.— The Attorney General, the Secretary of Defense, the Director of National Intelligence, the Director of the National Security Agency, or the head of any other element of the intelligence community may transfer personnel to the relevant Office of the Inspector General required to conduct a review under subsection (b)(1) and submit a report under subsection (c) and, in addition to any other personnel authorized by law, are authorized to fill any vacancy caused by such a transfer. Personnel transferred under this paragraph shall perform such duties relating to such review as the relevant Inspector General shall direct.

SEVERABILITY

SEC. 401 [50 U.S.C. 1801 note] If any provision of this Act, any amendment made by this Act, or the application thereof to any person or circumstances is held invalid, the validity of the remainder of the Act, of any such amendments, and of the application of such provisions to other persons and circumstances shall not be affected thereby.

REPEALS

SEC. 403.

(a) REPEAL OF PROTECT AMERICA ACT OF 2007 PROVISIONS.—

(1) AMENDMENTS TO FISA.—

(A) IN GENERAL.—Except as provided in section 404, sections 105A,

105B, and 105C of the Foreign Intelligence Surveillance Act of 1978 (50 U.S.C. 1805a, 1805b, and 1805c) are repealed.

(B) TECHNICAL AND CONFORMING AMENDMENTS.—

(i) TABLE OF CONTENTS.—The table of contents in the first section of the Foreign Intelligence Surveillance Act of 1978 (50 U.S.C. 1801 et seq.) is amended by striking the items relating to sections 105A, 105B, and 105C.

(ii) CONFORMING AMENDMENTS.—Except as provided in section 404, section 103(e) of the Foreign Intelligence Surveillance Act of 1978 (50 U.S.C. 1803(e)) is amended—

(I) in paragraph (1), by striking "105B(h) or 501(f)(1)" and inserting "501(f)(1) or 702(h)(4)"; and

(II) in paragraph (2), by striking "105B(h) or 501(f)(1)" and inserting "501(f)(1) or 702(h)(4)".

(2) REPORTING REQUIREMENTS.—Except as provided in section 404, section 4 of the Protect America Act of 2007 (Public Law 110-55; 121 Stat. 555) is repealed.

(3) [50 USC 1803 note.] TRANSITION PROCEDURES.— Except as provided in section 404, subsection (b) of section 6 of the Protect America Act of 2007 (Public Law 110-55; 121 Stat. 556) is repealed.

(b) FISA AMENDMENTS ACT OF 2008.-

(1) [50 USC 1881 note.] IN GENERAL.—Except as provided in section 404, effective December 31, 2012, title VII of the Foreign Intelligence Surveillance Act of 1978, [50 USC 1881-1881g.] as amended by section 101(a), is repealed.

(2) [18 USC 2511 note.] TECHNICAL AND CONFORMING AMENDMENTS.-Effective December 31, 2012—

(A) the table of contents in the first section of such Act (50 U.S.C. 1801 et seq.) is amended by striking the items related to title VII;

437 FOREIGN INTELLIGENCE SURVEILLANCE ACT OF 1978

(B) except as provided in section 404, section 601(a)(1) of such Act (50 U.S.C. 1871(a)(1)) is amended to read as such section read on the day before the date of the enactment of this Act; and

(C) except as provided in section 404, section 2511(2)(a)(ii)(A) of title 18, United States Code, is amended by striking "or a court order pursuant to section 704 of the Foreign Intelligence Surveillance Act of 1978".

TRANSITION PROCEDURES

SEC. 404.

(a) TRANSITION PROCEDURES FOR PROTECT AMERICA ACT OF 2007 PROVISIONS.—

(1) CONTINUED EFFECT OF ORDERS, AUTHORIZATIONS, DIRECTIVES.—Except as provided in paragraph (7), notwithstanding any other provision of law, any order, authorization, or directive issued or made pursuant to section 105B of the Foreign Intelligence Surveillance Act of 1978, as added

by section 2 of the Protect America Act of 2007 (Public Law 11055; 121 Stat. 552), shall continue in effect until the expiration of such order, authorization, or directive.

(2) APPLICABILITY OF PROTECT AMERICA ACT OF 2007 TO CONTINUED ORDERS, AUTHORIZATIONS, DIRECTIVES.— Notwithstanding any other provision of this Act, any amendment made by this Act, or the Foreign Intelligence Surveillance Act of 1978 (50 U.S.C. 1801 et seq.)—

(A) subject to paragraph (3), section 105A of such Act, as added by section 2 of the Protect America Act of 2007 (Public Law 110-55; 121 Stat. 552), shall continue to apply to any acquisition conducted pursuant to an order, authorization, or directive referred to in paragraph (1); and

(B) sections 105B and 105C of the Foreign Intelligence Surveillance Act of 1978, as added by sections 2 and 3, respectively, of the Protect America Act of 2007, shall continue to apply with respect to an order, authorization, or directive referred to in paragraph (1) until the later of—

(i) the expiration of such order, authorization, or directive; or

(ii) the date on which final judgment is entered for any petition or other litigation relating to such order, authorization, or directive.

(3) USE OF INFORMATION.—Information acquired from an acquisition conducted pursuant to an order, authorization, or directive referred to in paragraph (1) shall be deemed to be information acquired from an electronic surveillance pursuant to title I of the Foreign Intelligence Surveillance Act of 1978 (50 U.S.C. 1801 et seq.) for purposes of section 106 of such Act (50 U.S.C. 1806), except for purposes of subsection (j) of such section.

(4) PROTECTION FROM LIABILITY.— Subsection (l) of section 105B of the Foreign Intelligence Surveillance Act of 1978, as added by section 2 of the Protect America Act of 2007, shall continue to apply with respect to any directives issued pursuant to such section 105B.

(5) JURISDICTION OF FOREIGN INTELLIGENCE SURVEILLANCE COURT.—Notwithstanding any other provision of this Act or of the Foreign Intelligence Surveillance Act of 1978 (50 U.S.C. 1801 et seq.), section 103(e) of the Foreign Intelligence Surveillance Act (50 U.S.C. 1803(e)), as amended by section 5(a) of the Protect America Act of 2007 (Public Law 110-55; 121 Stat. 556), shall continue to apply with respect to a directive issued pursuant to section 105B of the Foreign Intelligence Surveillance Act of 1978, as added by section 2 of the Protect America Act of 2007, until the later of—

(A) the expiration of all orders, authorizations, or directives referred to in paragraph (1); or

(B) the date on which final judgment is entered for any petition or other litigation relating to such order, authorization, or directive.

(6) REPORTING REQUIREMENTS.—

(A) CONTINUED APPLICABILITY.— Notwithstanding any other provision of this Act, any amendment made by this Act, the Protect America Act of 2007 (Public Law 110-55), or the Foreign Intelligence Surveillance Act of 1978 (50 U.S.C. 1801 et seq.), section 4 of the Protect America Act of

2007 shall continue to apply until the date that the certification described in subparagraph (B) is submitted.

(B) CERTIFICATION.— The certification described in this subparagraph is a certification—

(i) made by the Attorney General;

(ii) submitted as part of a semi-annual report required by section 4 of the Protect America Act of 2007;

(iii) that states that there will be no further acquisitions carried out under section 105B of the Foreign Intelligence Surveillance Act of 1978, as added by section 2 of the Protect America Act of 2007, after the date of such certification; and

(iv) that states that the information required to be included under such section 4 relating to any acquisition conducted under such section 105B has been included in a semi-annual report required by such section 4.

(7) REPLACEMENT OF ORDERS, AUTHORIZATIONS, AND DIRECTIVES.—

(A) IN GENERAL.— If the Attorney General and the Director of National Intelligence seek to replace an authorization issued pursuant to section 105B of the Foreign Intelligence Surveillance Act of 1978, as added by section 2 of the Protect America Act of 2007 (Public Law 110-55), with an authorization under section 702 of the Foreign Intelligence Surveillance Act of 1978 (as added by section 101(a) of this Act), the Attorney General and the Director of National Intelligence shall, to the extent practicable, submit to the Foreign Intelligence Surveillance Court (as such term is defined in section 701(b)(2) of such Act (as so added)) a certification prepared in accordance with subsection

(g) of such section 702 and the procedures adopted in accordance with subsections (d) and (e) of such section 702 at least 30 days before the expiration of such authorization.

(B) CONTINUATION OF EXISTING ORDERS.— If the Attorney General and the Director of National Intelligence seek to replace an authorization made pursuant to section 105B of the Foreign Intelligence Surveillance Act of 1978, as added by section 2 of the Protect America Act of 2007 (Public Law 110-55; 121 Stat. 522), by filing a certification in accordance with subparagraph (A), that authorization, and any directives issued thereunder and any order related thereto, shall remain in effect, notwithstanding the expiration provided for in subsection (a) of such section 105B, until the Foreign Intelligence Surveillance Court (as such term is defined in section 701(b)(2) of the Foreign Intelligence Surveillance Act of 1978 (as so added)) issues an order with respect to that certification under section 702(i)(3) of such Act (as so added) at which time the provisions of that section and of section 702(i)(4) of such Act (as so added) shall apply.

(8) EFFECTIVE DATE.— Paragraphs (1) through (7) shall take effect as if enacted on August 5, 2007.

(b) TRANSITION PROCEDURES FOR FISA AMENDMENTS ACT OF 2008 PROVISIONS.—

(1) ORDERS IN EFFECT ON DECEMBER 31, 2012.— Notwithstanding any other provision of this Act, any amendment made by this Act, or the Foreign Intelligence Surveillance Act of 1978 (50 U.S.C. 1801 et seq.), any order, authorization, or directive issued or made under title VII of the Foreign Intelligence Surveillance Act of 1978, as amended by section 101(a), shall continue in effect until the date of the expiration of such order, authorization, or directive.

(2) APPLICABILITY OF TITLE VII OF FISA TO CONTINUED ORDERS, AUTHORIZATIONS, DIRECTIVES.— Notwithstanding any other provision of this Act, any amendment made by this Act, or the Foreign Intelligence Surveillance Act of 1978 (50 U.S.C. 1801 et seq.), with respect to any order, authorization, or directive referred to in paragraph (1), title VII of such Act, as amended by section 101(a), shall continue to apply until the later of—

(A) the expiration of such order, authorization, or directive; or

(B) the date on which final judgment is entered for any petition or other litigation relating to such order, authorization, or directive.

(3) CHALLENGE OF DIRECTIVES; PROTECTION FROM LIABILITY; USE OF INFORMATION.— Notwithstanding any other provision of this Act or of the Foreign Intelligence Surveillance Act of 1978 (50 U.S.C. 1801 et seq.)—

(A) section 103(e) of such Act, as amended by section 403(a)(1)(B)(ii), shall continue to apply with respect to any directive issued pursuant to section 702(h) of such Act, as added by section 101(a);

(B) section 702(h)(3) of such Act (as so added) shall continue to apply with respect to any directive issued pursuant to section 702(h) of such Act (as so added);

(C) section 703(e) of such Act (as so added) shall continue to apply with respect to an order or request for emergency assistance under that section;

(D) section 706 of such Act (as so added) shall continue to apply to an acquisition conducted under section 702 or 703 of such Act (as so added); and

(E) section 2511(2)(a)(ii)(A) of title 18, United States Code, as amended by section 101(c)(1), shall continue to apply to an order issued pursuant to section 704 of the Foreign Intelligence Surveillance Act of 1978, as added by section 101(a).

(4) REPORTING REQUIREMENTS.—

(A) CONTINUED APPLICABILITY.— Notwithstanding any other provision of this Act or of the Foreign Intelligence Surveillance Act of 1978 (50 U.S.C. 1801 et seq.), section 601(a) of such Act (50 U.S.C. 1871(a)), as amended by section 101(c)(2), and sections 702(l) and 707 of such Act, as added by section 101(a), shall continue to apply until the date that the certification described in subparagraph (B) is submitted.

(B) CERTIFICATION.— The certification described in this subparagraph is a certification—

(i) made by the Attorney General;

(ii) submitted to the Select Committee on Intelligence of the Senate, the Permanent Select Committee on Intelligence of the House of Representatives, and the Committees on the Judiciary of the Senate and the House of Representatives;

(iii) that states that there will be no further acquisitions carried out under title VII of the Foreign Intelligence Surveillance Act of 1978, as amended by section 101(a), after the date of such certification; and

(iv) that states that the information required to be included in a review, assessment, or report under section 601 of such Act, as amended by section 101(c), or section 702(l) or 707 of such Act, as added by section 101(a), relating to any acquisition conducted under title VII of such Act, as amended by section 101(a), has been included in a review, assessment, or report under such section 601, 702(l), or 707.

(5) TRANSITION PROCEDURES CONCERNING THE TARGETING OF UNITED STATES PERSONS OVERSEAS.— Any authorization in effect on the date of enactment of this Act under section 2.5 of Executive Order 12333 to intentionally target a United States person reasonably believed to be located outside the United States shall continue in effect, and shall constitute a sufficient basis for conducting such an acquisition targeting a United States person located outside the United States until the earlier of—

(A) the date that authorization expires; or

(B) the date that is 90 days after the date of the enactment of this Act.

Protect America Act of 2007

(Pub. L. 110-55 of August 5, 2007; 121 Stat. 552)

To amend the Foreign Intelligence Surveillance Act of 1978 to provide additional procedures for authorizing certain acquisitions of foreign intelligence information and for other purposes.

Be it enacted by the Senate and House of Representatives of the United States of America in Congress assembled,

SHORT TITLE

SECTION 1. This Act may be cited as the "Protect America Act of 2007".

ADDITIONAL PROCEDURE FOR AUTHORIZING CERTAIN ACQUISITIONS OF FOREIGN INTELLIGENCE INFORMATION

SEC. 2. The Foreign Intelligence Surveillance Act of 1978 (50 U.S.C. §1801 et seq.) is amended by inserting after section 105 the following:

CLARIFICATION OF ELECTRONIC SURVEILLANCE OF PERSONS OUTSIDE THE UNITED STATES

SEC. 105A. Nothing in the definition of electronic surveillance under section 101(f) shall be construed to encompass surveillance directed at a person reasonably believed to be located outside of the United States.

ADDITIONAL PROCEDURE FOR AUTHORIZING CERTAIN ACQUISITIONS CONCERNING PERSONS LOCATED OUTSIDE THE UNITED STATES

SEC. 105B.

(a) Notwithstanding any other law, the Director of National Intelligence and the Attorney General, may for periods of up to one year authorize the acquisition of foreign intelligence information concerning persons reasonably believed to be outside the United States if the Director of National Intelligence and the Attorney General determine, based on the information provided to them, that—

(1) there are reasonable procedures in place for determining that the acquisition of foreign intelligence information under this section concerns persons reasonably believed to be located outside the United States, and such procedures will be subject to review of the Court pursuant to section 105C of this Act;

(2) the acquisition does not constitute electronic surveillance;

(3) the acquisition involves obtaining the foreign intelligence information from or with the assistance of a communications service provider, custodian, or other person (including any officer, employee, agent, or other specified person of such service provider, custodian, or other person) who has access to

communications, either as they are transmitted or while they are stored, or equipment that is being or may be used to transmit or store such communications;

(4) a significant purpose of the acquisition is to obtain foreign intelligence information; and

(5) the minimization procedures to be used with respect to such acquisition activity meet the definition of minimization procedures under section 101(h).

This determination shall be in the form of a written certification, under oath, supported as appropriate by affidavit of appropriate officials in the national security field occupying positions appointed by the President, by and with the consent of the Senate, or the Head of any Agency of the Intelligence Community, unless immediate action by the Government is required and time does not permit the preparation of a certification. In such a case, the determination of the Director of National Intelligence and the Attorney General shall be reduced to a certification as soon as possible but in no event more than 72 hours after the determination is made.

(b) A certification under subsection (a) is not required to identify the specific facilities, places, premises, or property at which the acquisition of foreign intelligence information will be directed.

(c) The Attorney General shall transmit as soon as practicable under seal to the court established under section 103(a) a copy of a certification made under subsection (a). Such certification shall be maintained under security measures established by the Chief Justice of the United States and the Attorney General, in consultation with the Director of National Intelligence, and shall remain sealed unless the certification is necessary to determine the legality of the acquisition under section 105B.

(d) An acquisition under this section may be conducted only in accordance with the certification of the Director of National Intelligence and the Attorney General, or their oral instructions if time does not permit the preparation of a certification, and the minimization procedures adopted by the Attorney General. The Director of National Intelligence and the Attorney General shall assess compliance with such procedures and shall report such assessments to the Permanent Select Committee on Intelligence of the House of Representatives and the Select Committee on Intelligence of the Senate under section 108(a).

(e) With respect to an authorization of an acquisition under section 105B, the Director of National Intelligence and Attorney General may direct a person to—

(1) immediately provide the Government with all information, facilities, and assistance necessary to accomplish the acquisition in such a manner as will protect the secrecy of the acquisition and produce a minimum of interference with the services that such person is providing to the target; and

(2) maintain under security procedures approved by the Attorney General and the Director of National Intelligence any records concerning the acquisition or the aid furnished that such person wishes to maintain.

(f) The Government shall compensate, at the prevailing rate, a person for providing information, facilities, or assistance pursuant to subsection (e).
(g) In the case of a failure to comply with a directive issued pursuant to subsection (e), the Attorney General may invoke the aid of the court established under section 103(a) to compel compliance with the directive. The court shall issue an order requiring the person to comply with the directive if it finds that the directive was issued in accordance with subsection (e) and is otherwise lawful. Failure to obey an order of the court may be punished by the court as contempt of court. Any process under this section may be served in any judicial district in which the person may be found.
(h)(1)(A) A person receiving a directive issued pursuant to subsection (e) may challenge the legality of that directive by filing a petition with the pool established under section 103(e)(1).

(B) The presiding judge designated pursuant to section 103(b) shall assign a petition filed under subparagraph (A) to one of the judges serving in the pool established by section 103(e)(1). Not later than 48 hours after the assignment of such petition, the assigned judge shall conduct an initial review of the directive. If the assigned judge determines that the petition is frivolous, the assigned judge shall immediately deny the petition and affirm the directive or any part of the directive that is the subject of the petition. If the assigned judge determines the petition is not frivolous, the assigned judge shall, within 72 hours, consider the petition in accordance with the procedures established under section 103(e)(2) and provide a written statement for the record of the reasons for any determination under this subsection.

(2) A judge considering a petition to modify or set aside a directive may grant such petition only if the judge finds that such directive does not meet the requirements of this section or is otherwise unlawful. If the judge does not modify or set aside the directive, the judge shall immediately affirm such directive, and order the recipient to comply with such directive.

(3) Any directive not explicitly modified or set aside under this subsection shall remain in full effect.

(i) The Government or a person receiving a directive reviewed pursuant to subsection (h) may file a petition with the Court of Review established under section 103(b) for review of the decision issued pursuant to subsection (h) not later than 7 days after the issuance of such decision. Such court of review shall have jurisdiction to consider such petitions and shall provide for the record a written statement of the reasons for its decision. On petition for a writ of certiorari by the Government or any person receiving such directive, the record shall be transmitted under seal to the Supreme Court, which shall have jurisdiction to review such decision.
(j) Judicial proceedings under this section shall be concluded as expeditiously as possible. The record of proceedings, including petitions filed, orders granted, and statements of reasons for decision, shall be maintained under security mea-

sures established by the Chief Justice of the United States, in consultation with the Attorney General and the Director of National Intelligence.
(k) All petitions under this section shall be filed under seal. In any proceedings under this section, the court shall, upon request of the Government, review ex parte and in camera any Government submission, or portions of a submission, which may include classified information.
(l) Notwithstanding any other law, no cause of action shall lie in any court against any person for providing any information, facilities, or assistance in accordance with a directive under this section.
(m) A directive made or an order granted under this section shall be retained for a period of not less than 10 years from the date on which such directive or such order is made.".

SUBMISSION TO COURT REVIEW AND ASSESSMENT OF PROCEDURES

SEC. 3. The Foreign Intelligence Surveillance Act of 1978 (50 U.S.C. §1801 et seq.) is amended by inserting after section 105B the following:

"SUBMISSION TO COURT REVIEW OF PROCEDURES

"SEC. 105C. (a) No later than 120 days after the effective date of this Act, the Attorney General shall submit to the Court established under section 103(a), the procedures by which the Government determines that acquisitions conducted pursuant to section 105B do not constitute electronic surveillance. The procedures submitted pursuant to this section shall be updated and submitted to the Court on an annual basis. "(b) No later than 180 days after the effective date of this Act, the court established under section 103(a) shall assess the Government's determination under section 105B(a)(1) that those procedures are reasonably designed to ensure that acquisitions conducted pursuant to section 105B do not constitute electronic surveillance. The court's review shall be limited to whether the Government's determination is clearly erroneous. "(c) If the court concludes that the determination is not clearly erroneous, it shall enter an order approving the continued use of such procedures. If the court concludes that the determination is clearly erroneous, it shall issue an order directing the Government to submit new procedures within 30 days or cease any acquisitions under section 105B that are implicated by the court's order. "(d) The Government may appeal any order issued under subsection (c) to the court established under section 103(b). If such court determines that the order was properly entered, the court shall immediately provide for the record a written statement of each reason for its decision, and, on petition of the United States for a writ of certiorari, the record shall be transmitted under seal to the Supreme Court of the United States, which shall have jurisdiction to review such decision. Any acquisitions affected by the order issued under subsection (c) of this section may continue during the pendency of any appeal, the period during which a petition for writ of certiorari may be pending, and any review by the Supreme Court of the United States."

REPORTING TO CONGRESS

SEC. 4. On a semi-annual basis the Attorney General shall inform the Select Committee on Intelligence of the Senate, the Permanent Select Committee on Intelligence of the House of Representatives, the Committee on the Judiciary of the Senate, and the Committee on the Judiciary of the House of Representatives, concerning acquisitions under this section during the previous 6-month period. Each report made under this section shall include—

(1) a description of any incidents of non-compliance with a directive issued by the Attorney General and the Director of National Intelligence under section 105B, to include—

(A) incidents of non-compliance by an element of the Intelligence Community with guidelines or procedures established for determining that the acquisition of foreign intelligence authorized by the Attorney General and Director of National Intelligence concerns persons reasonably to be outside the United States; and

(B) incidents of noncompliance by a specified person to whom the Attorney General and Director of National Intelligence issue a directive under this section; and

(2) the number of certifications and directives issued during the reporting period.

TECHNICAL AMENDMENT AND CONFORMING AMENDMENTS

SEC. 5.

(a) IN GENERAL.—Section 103(e) of the Foreign Intelligence Surveillance Act of 1978 (50 U.S.C. §1803(e)) is amended—

(1) in paragraph (1), by striking "501(f)(1)" and inserting "105B(h) or 501(f)(1)"; and

(2) in paragraph (2), by striking "501(f)(1)" and inserting "105B(h) or 501(f)(1)".

(b) TABLE OF CONTENTS.—The table of contents in the first section of the Foreign Intelligence Surveillance Act of 1978 (50 U.S.C. §1801 et seq.) is amended by inserting after the item relating to section 105 the following:

"105A. Clarification of electronic surveillance of persons outside the United States.

"105B. Additional procedure for authorizing certain acquisition concerning persons located outside the United States.

"105C. Submission to court review of procedures.".

EFFECTIVE DATE; TRANSITION PROCEDURES

SEC. 6.

(a) EFFECTIVE DATE.—Except as otherwise provided, the amendments made by this Act shall take effect immediately after the date of the enactment of this Act.

(b) TRANSITION PROCEDURES.—Notwithstanding any other provision of this Act, any order in effect on the date of enactment of this Act issued pursuant to the Foreign Intelligence Surveillance Act of 1978 (50 U.S.C. §1801 et seq.) shall remain in effect until the date of expiration of such order, and, at the request of the applicant, the court established under section 103(a) of such Act (50 U.S.C. §1803(a)) shall reauthorize such order as long as the facts and circumstances continue to justify issuance of such order under the provisions of the Foreign Intelligence Surveillance Act of 1978, as in effect on the day before the applicable effective date of this Act. The Government also may file new applications, and the court established under section 103(a) of the Foreign Intelligence Surveillance Act of 1978 (50 U.S.C. §1803(a)) shall enter orders granting such applications pursuant to such Act, as long as the application meets the requirements set forth under the provisions of such Act as in effect on the day before the effective date of this Act. At the request of the applicant, the court established under section 103(a) of the Foreign Intelligence Surveillance Act of 1978 (50 U.S.C. §1803(a)), shall extinguish any extant authorization to conduct electronic surveillance or physical search entered pursuant to such Act. Any surveillance conducted pursuant to an order entered under this subsection shall be subject to the provisions of the Foreign Intelligence Surveillance Act of 1978 (50 U.S.C. §1801 et seq.), as in effect on the day before the effective date of this Act.
(c) SUNSET.—Except as provided in subsection (d), sections 2, 3, 4, and 5 of this Act, and the amendments made by this Act, shall cease to have effect 180 days after the date of the enactment of this Act.
(d) AUTHORIZATIONS IN EFFECT.—Authorizations for the acquisition of foreign intelligence information pursuant to the amendments made by this Act, and directives issued pursuant to such authorizations, shall remain in effect until their expiration. Such acquisitions shall be governed by the applicable provisions of such amendments and shall not be deemed to constitute electronic surveillance as that term is defined in section 101(f) of the Foreign Intelligence Surveillance Act of 1978 (50 U.S.C. §1801(f)).

Uniting and Strengthening America by Providing Appropriate Tools Required to Intercept and Obstruct Terrorism (USA PATRIOT) Act of 2001

(Pub. L. 107-56 of October 26, 2001; 115 Stat. 272)

An Act To deter and punish terrorist acts in the United States and around the world, to enhance law enforcement investigatory tools, and for other purposes.

Be it enacted by the Senate and House of Representatives of the United States of America in Congress assembled,

SHORT TITLE AND TABLE OF CONTENTS

SECTION 1.

(a) SHORT TITLE.—This Act may be cited as the "Uniting and Strengthening America by Providing Appropriate Tools Required to Intercept and Obstruct Terrorism (USA Patriot Act) Act of 2001".

(b) TABLE OF CONTENTS.

The table of contents for this Act is as follows:

SUBTITLE B—BANK SECRECY ACT AMENDMENTS AND RELATED IMPROVEMENTS

SEC. 808. Definition of Federal crime of terrorism.
SEC. 809. No statute of limitation for certain terrorism offenses.
SEC. 810. Alternate maximum penalties for terrorism offenses.
SEC. 811. Penalties for terrorist conspiracies.
SEC. 812. Post-release supervision of terrorists.
SEC. 813. Inclusion of acts of terrorism as racketeering activity.
SEC. 814. Deterrence and prevention of cyberterrorism.
SEC. 815. Additional defense to civil actions relating to preserving records in response to Government requests.
SEC. 816. Development and support of cybersecurity forensic capabilities.
SEC. 817. Expansion of the biological weapons statute.

TITLE IX—IMPROVED INTELLIGENCE

SEC. 901. Responsibilities of Director of Central Intelligence regarding foreign intelligence collected under Foreign Intelligence Surveillance Act of 1978.
SEC. 902. Inclusion of international terrorist activities within scope of foreign intelligence under National Security Act of 1947.
SEC. 903. Sense of Congress on the establishment and maintenance of intelligence relationships to acquire information on terrorists and terrorist organizations.
SEC. 904. Temporary authority to defer submittal to Congress of reports on intelligence and intelligence-related matters.
SEC. 905. Disclosure to Director of Central Intelligence of foreign intelligence-related information with respect to criminal investigations.
SEC. 906. Foreign terrorist asset tracking center.
SEC. 907. National Virtual Translation Center.
SEC. 908. Training of government officials regarding identification and use of foreign intelligence.

TITLE X—MISCELLANEOUS

SEC. 1001. Review of the department of justice.
SEC. 1002. Sense of congress.
SEC. 1003. Definition of "electronic surveillance".
SEC. 1004. Venue in money laundering cases.
SEC. 1005. First responders assistance act.
SEC. 1006. Inadmissibility of aliens engaged in money laundering.
SEC. 1007. Authorization of funds for DEA police training in south and central Asia.
SEC. 1008. Feasibility study on use of biometric identifier scanning system with access to the FBI integrated automated fingerprint identification system at overseas consular posts and points of entry to the United States.
SEC. 1009. Study of access.

TITLE II – ENHANCED SURVEILLANCE PROCEDURES

AUTHORITY TO INTERCEPT WIRE, ORAL, AND ELECTRONIC COMMUNICATIONS RELATING TO TERRORISM

SEC. 201. Section 2516(1) of title 18, United States Code, is amended—

(1) by redesignating paragraph (p), as so redesignated by section 434(2) of the Antiterrorism and Effective Death Penalty Act of 1996 (Public Law 104-132; 110 Stat. 1274), as paragraph (r); and

(2) by inserting after paragraph (p), as so redesignated by section 201(3) of the Illegal Immigration Reform and Immigrant Responsibility Act of 1996 (division C of Public Law 104-208; 110 Stat. 3009-565), the following new paragraph:

"(q) any criminal violation of section 229 (relating to chemical weapons); or sections 2332, 2332a, 2332b, 2332d, 2339A, or 2339B of this title (relating to terrorism); or".

AUTHORITY TO INTERCEPT WIRE, ORAL, AND ELECTRONIC COMMUNICATIONS RELATING TO COMPUTER FRAUD AND ABUSE OFFENSES

SEC. 202. Section 2516(1)(c) of title 18, United States Code, is amended by striking "and section 1341 (relating to mail fraud)," and inserting "section 1341 (relating to mail fraud), a felony violation of section 1030 (relating to computer fraud and abuse),".

AUTHORITY TO SHARE CRIMINAL INVESTIGATIVE INFORMATION

SEC. 203.

(a) AUTHORITY TO SHARE GRAND JURY INFORMATION.—

(1) IN GENERAL.—Rule 6(e)(3)(C) of the Federal Rules of Criminal Procedure is amended to read as follows:

"(C)(i) Disclosure otherwise prohibited by this rule of matters occurring before the grand jury may also be made—

"(I) when so directed by a court preliminarily to or in connection with a judicial proceeding;

"(II) when permitted by a court at the request of the defendant, upon a showing that grounds may exist for a motion to dismiss the indictment because of matters occurring before the grand jury;

"(III) when the disclosure is made by an attorney for the government to another Federal grand jury;

"(IV) when permitted by a court at the request of an attorney for the government, upon a showing that such matters may disclose a violation of State criminal law, to an appropriate official of a State or subdivision of a State for the purpose of enforcing such law; or

"(V) when the matters involve foreign intelligence or counterintelligence (as defined in section 3 of the National Security Act of 1947 (50 U.S.C. §401a)), or foreign intelligence information (as defined in clause (iv) of this subparagraph), to any Federal law enforcement, intelligence, protective, immigration, national defense, or national security official in order to assist the official receiving that information in the performance of his official duties.

"(ii) If the court orders disclosure of matters occurring before the grand jury, the disclosure shall be made in such manner, at such time, and under such conditions as the court may direct.

"(iii) Any Federal official to whom information is disclosed pursuant to clause (i)(V) of this subparagraph may use that information only as necessary in the conduct of that person's official duties subject to any limitations on the unauthorized disclosure of such information. Within a reasonable time after such disclosure, an attorney for the government shall file under seal a notice with the court stating the fact that such information was disclosed and the departments, agencies, or entities to which the disclosure was made.

"(iv) In clause (i)(V) of this subparagraph, the term 'foreign intelligence information' means—

"(I) information, whether or not concerning a United States person, that relates to the ability of the United States to protect against—

"(aa) actual or potential attack or other grave hostile acts of a foreign power or an agent of a foreign power; "(bb) sabotage or international terrorism by a foreign power or an agent of a foreign power; or "(cc) clandestine intelligence activities by an intelligence service or network of a foreign power or by an agent of foreign power; or

"(II) information, whether or not concerning a United States person, with respect to a foreign power or foreign territory that relates to—

"(aa) the national defense or the security of the United States; or

"(bb) the conduct of the foreign affairs of the United States.".

(2) CONFORMING AMENDMENT.—Rule 6(e)(3)(D) of the Federal Rules of

Criminal Procedure is amended by striking "(e)(3)(C)(i)" and inserting "(e)(3)(C)(i)(I)".

(b) AUTHORITY TO SHARE ELECTRONIC, WIRE, AND ORAL INTERCEPTION INFORMATION.—

(1) LAW ENFORCEMENT.—Section 2517 of title 18, United States Code, is amended by inserting at the end the following:

"(6) Any investigative or law enforcement officer, or attorney for the Government, who by any means authorized by this chapter, has obtained knowledge of the contents of any wire, oral, or electronic communication, or evidence derived therefrom, may disclose such contents to any other Federal law enforcement, intelligence, protective, immigration, national defense, or national security official to the extent that such contents include foreign intelligence or counterintelligence (as defined in section 3 of the National Security Act of 1947 (50 U.S.C. §401a)), or foreign intelligence information (as defined in subsection (19) of section 2510 of this title), to assist the official who is to receive that information in the performance of his official duties. Any Federal official who receives information pursuant to this provision may use that information only as necessary in the conduct of that person's official duties subject to any limitations on the unauthorized disclosure of such information.".

(2) DEFINITION.—Section 2510 of title 18, United States Code, is amended by—

(A) in paragraph (17), by striking "and" after the semicolon;

(B) in paragraph (18), by striking the period and inserting "; and"; and

(C) by inserting at the end the following:

"(19) 'foreign intelligence information' means—

"(A) information, whether or not concerning a United States person, that relates to the ability of the United States to protect against—

"(i) actual or potential attack or other grave hostile acts of a foreign power or an agent of a foreign power;

"(ii) sabotage or international terrorism by a foreign power or an agent of a foreign power; or

"(iii) clandestine intelligence activities by an intelligence service or network of a foreign power or by an agent of a foreign power; or

"(B) information, whether or not concerning a United States person, with respect to a foreign power or foreign territory that relates to—

"(i) the national defense or the security of the United States; or "(ii) the conduct of the foreign affairs of the United States.".

(c) PROCEDURES.—The Attorney General shall establish procedures for the disclosure of information pursuant to section 2517(6) and Rule 6(e)(3)(C)(i)(V) of the Federal Rules of Criminal Procedure that identifies a United States person, as defined in section 101 of the Foreign Intelligence Surveillance Act of 1978 (50 U.S.C. §1801)).

(d) FOREIGN INTELLIGENCE INFORMATION.—

(1) IN GENERAL.—Notwithstanding any other provision of law, it shall be lawful for foreign intelligence or counterintelligence (as defined in section 3 of the National Security Act of 1947 (50 U.S.C. §401a)) or foreign intelligence information obtained as part of a criminal investigation to be disclosed to any Federal law enforcement, intelligence, protective, immigration, national defense, or national security official in order to assist the official receiving that information in the performance of his official duties. Any Federal official who receives information pursuant to this provision may use that information only as necessary in the conduct of that person's official duties subject to any limitations on the unauthorized disclosure of such information.

(2) DEFINITION.—In this subsection, the term "foreign intelligence information" means—

(A) information, whether or not concerning a United States person, that relates to the ability of the United States to protect against—

(i) actual or potential attack or other grave hostile acts of a foreign power or an agent of a foreign power;

(ii) sabotage or international terrorism by a foreign power or an agent of a foreign power; or

(iii) clandestine intelligence activities by an intelligence service or network of a foreign power or by an agent of a foreign power; or

B) information, whether or not concerning a United States person, with respect to a foreign power or foreign territory that relates to—

(i) the national defense or the security of the United States; or

(ii) the conduct of the foreign affairs of the United States.

CLARIFICATION OF INTELLIGENCE EXCEPTIONS FROM LIMITATIONS ON INTERCEPTION AND DISCLOSURE OF WIRE, ORAL, AND ELECTRONIC COMMUNICATIONS

SEC. 204. Section 2511(2)(f) of title 18, United States Code, is amended—

(1) by striking "this chapter or chapter 121" and inserting "this chapter or chapter 121 or 206 of this title"; and

(2) by striking "wire and oral" and inserting "wire, oral, and electronic".

EMPLOYMENT OF TRANSLATORS BY THE FEDERAL BUREAU OF INVESTIGATION

SEC. 205.

(a) AUTHORITY.—The Director of the Federal Bureau of Investigation is authorized to expedite the employment of personnel as translators to support counterterrorism investigations and operations without regard to applicable Federal personnel requirements and limitations.

(b) SECURITY REQUIREMENT.—The Director of the Federal Bureau of Investigation shall establish such security requirements as are necessary for the personnel employed as translators under subsection (a).

(c) REPORT.—The Attorney General shall report to the Committees on the Judiciary of the House of Representatives and the Senate on—

(1) the number of translators employed by the FBI and other components of the Department of Justice;

(2) any legal or practical impediments to using translators employed by other Federal, State, or local agencies, on a full, part-time, or shared basis; and

(3) the needs of the FBI for specific translation services in certain languages, and recommendations for meeting those needs.

ROVING SURVEILLANCE AUTHORITY UNDER THE FOREIGN INTELLIGENCE SURVEILLANCE ACT OF 1978

SEC. 206. Section 105(c)(2)(B) of the Foreign Intelligence Surveillance Act of 1978 (50 U.S.C. §1805(c)(2)(B)) is amended by inserting ", or in circumstances where the Court finds that the actions of the target of the application may have the effect of thwarting the identification of a specified person, such other persons," after "specified person".

DURATION OF FISA SURVEILLANCE OF NON-UNITED STATES PERSONS WHO ARE AGENTS OF A FOREIGN POWER

SEC. 207.

(a) DURATION.—

(1) SURVEILLANCE.—Section 105(e)(1) of the Foreign Intelligence Surveillance Act of 1978 (50 U.S.C. §1805(e)(1)) is amended by—

(A) inserting "(A)" after "except that"; and

(B) inserting before the period the following: ", and (B) an order under this Act for a surveillance targeted against an agent of a foreign power, as defined in section 101(b)(1)(A) may be for the period specified in the application or for 120 days, whichever is less".

(2) PHYSICAL SEARCH.—Section 304(d)(1) of the Foreign Intelligence Surveillance Act of 1978 (50 U.S.C. §1824(d)(1)) is amended by—

(A) striking "forty-five" and inserting "90";

(B) inserting "(A)" after "except that"; and

(C) inserting before the period the following: ", and (B) an order under this section for a physical search targeted against an agent of a foreign power as defined in section 101(b)(1)(A) may be for the period specified in the application or for 120 days, whichever is less".

(b) EXTENSION.—

(1) IN GENERAL.—Section 105(d)(2) of the Foreign Intelligence Surveillance Act of 1978 (50 U.S.C. §1805(d)(2)) is amended by—

(A) inserting "(A)" after "except that"; and

(B) inserting before the period the following: ", and (B) an extension of an order under this Act for a surveillance targeted

against an agent of a foreign power as defined in section 101(b)(1)(A) may be for a period not to exceed 1 year".

(2) DEFINED TERM.—Section 304(d)(2) of the Foreign Intelligence Surveil-

lance Act of 1978 (50 U.S.C. §1824(d)(2) is amended by inserting after "not a United States person," the following: "or against an agent of a foreign power as defined in section 101(b)(1)(A),".

DESIGNATION OF JUDGES

SEC. 208. Section 103(a) of the Foreign Intelligence Surveillance Act of 1978 (50 U.S.C. §1803(a)) is amended by—

(1) striking "seven district court judges" and inserting "11 district court judges"; and

(2) inserting "of whom no fewer than 3 shall reside within 20 miles of the District of Columbia" after "circuits".

SEIZURE OF VOICE-MAIL MESSAGES PURSUANT TO WARRANTS

SEC. 209. Title 18, United States Code, is amended—

(1) in section 2510—

(A) in paragraph (1), by striking beginning with "and such" and all that follows through "communication"; and

(B) in paragraph (14), by inserting "wire or" after "transmission of"; and

(2) in subsections (a) and (b) of section 2703—

(A) by striking "CONTENTS OF ELECTRONIC" and inserting "CONTENTS OF WIRE OR ELECTRONIC" each place it appears;

(B) by striking "contents of an electronic" and inserting "contents of a wire or electronic" each place it appears; and

(C) by striking "any electronic" and inserting "any wire or electronic" each place it appears.

SCOPE OF SUBPOENAS FOR RECORDS OF ELECTRONIC COMMUNICATIONS

SEC. 210. Section 2703(c)(2) of title 18, United States Code, as redesignated by section 212, is amended—

(1) by striking "entity the name, address, local and long distance telephone toll billing records, telephone number or other subscriber number or identity, and length of service of a subscriber" and inserting the following: "entity the— "(A) name; "(B) address; "(C) local and long distance telephone connection records, or records of session times and durations; "(D) length of service (including start date) and types of service utilized; "(E) telephone or instrument number or other subscriber number or identity, including any temporarily assigned network address; and "(F) means and source of payment for such service (including any credit card or bank account number), of a subscriber"; and

(2) by striking "and the types of services the subscriber or customer utilized,".

CLARIFICATION OF SCOPE

SEC. 211. Section 631 of the Communications Act of 1934 (47 U.S.C. §551) is amended—

(1) in subsection (c)(2)—

(A) in subparagraph (B), by striking "or";

(B) in subparagraph (C), by striking the period at the end and inserting "; or"; and

(C) by inserting at the end the following:

"(D) to a government entity as authorized under chapters 119, 121, or 206 of title 18, United States Code, except that such disclosure shall not include records revealing cable subscriber selection of video programming from a cable operator."; and

(2) in subsection (h), by striking "A governmental entity" and inserting "Except as provided in subsection (c)(2)(D), a governmental entity".

EMERGENCY DISCLOSURE OF ELECTRONIC COMMUNICATIONS TO PROTECT LIFE AND LIMB

SEC. 212.

(a) DISCLOSURE OF CONTENTS.—

(1) IN GENERAL.—Section 2702 of title 18, United States Code, is amended—

(A) by striking the section heading and inserting the following:

"§2702. Voluntary disclosure of customer communications or records";

(B) in subsection (a)—

(i) in paragraph (2)(A), by striking "and" at the end;

(ii) in paragraph (2)(B), by striking the period and inserting "; and"; and

(iii) by inserting after paragraph (2) the following:

"(3) a provider of remote computing service or electronic communication service to the public shall not knowingly divulge a record or other information pertaining to a subscriber to or customer of such service (not including the contents of communications covered by paragraph (1) or (2)) to any governmental entity.";

(C) in subsection (b), by striking "EXCEPTIONS.—A person or entity" and inserting "EXCEPTIONS FOR DISCLOSURE OF COMMUNICATIONS.— A provider described in subsection (a)";

(D) in subsection (b)(6)—

(i) in subparagraph (A)(ii), by striking "or";

(ii) in subparagraph (B), by striking the period and inserting "; or"; and

(iii) by adding after subparagraph (B) the following:

"(C) if the provider reasonably believes that an emergency involving immediate danger of death or serious physical injury to any person requires disclosure of the information without delay."; and

(E) by inserting after subsection (b) the following:

"(c) EXCEPTIONS FOR DISCLOSURE OF CUSTOMER RECORDS.—A provider described in subsection (a) may divulge a record or other information pertaining to a subscriber to or customer of such service (not including the contents of communications covered by subsection (a)(1) or (a)(2))—

"(1) as otherwise authorized in section 2703;

"(2) with the lawful consent of the customer or subscriber;

"(3) as may be necessarily incident to the rendition of the service or to the protection of the rights or property of the provider of that service;

"(4) to a governmental entity, if the provider reasonably believes that an emergency involving immediate danger of death or serious physical injury to any person justifies disclosure of the information; or

"(5) to any person other than a governmental entity.".

(2) TECHNICAL AND CONFORMING AMENDMENT.—The table of sections for chapter 121 of title 18, United States Code, is amended by striking the item relating to section 2702 and inserting the following:

"2702. Voluntary disclosure of customer communications or records.".

(b) REQUIREMENTS FOR GOVERNMENT ACCESS.—

(1) IN GENERAL.—Section 2703 of title 18, United States Code, is amended—

(A) by striking the section heading and inserting the following:

"2703. Required disclosure of customer communications or records";

(B) in subsection (c) by redesignating paragraph (2) as paragraph (3);

(C) in subsection (c)(1)—

(i) by striking "(A) Except as provided in subparagraph (B), a provider of electronic communication service or remote computing service may" and inserting "A governmental entity may require a provider of electronic communication service or remote computing service to";

(ii) by striking "covered by subsection (a) or (b) of this section) to any person other than a governmental entity.

"(B) A provider of electronic communication service or remote computing service shall disclose a record or other information pertaining to a subscriber to or customer of such service (not including the contents of communications covered by subsection (a) or (b) of this section) to a governmental entity' and inserting ')";

(iii) by redesignating subparagraph (C) as paragraph (2);

(iv) by redesignating clauses (i), (ii), (iii), and (iv) as subparagraphs (A), (B), (C), and (D), respectively;

(v) in subparagraph (D) (as redesignated) by striking the period and inserting "; or"; and

(vi) by inserting after subparagraph (D) (as redesignated) the following:

"(E) seeks information under paragraph (2)."; and

(D) in paragraph (2) (as redesignated) by striking "subparagraph (B)" and insert "paragraph (1)".

(2) TECHNICAL AND CONFORMING AMENDMENT.—The table of sections for chapter 121 of title 18, United States Code, is amended by striking the item relating to section 2703 and inserting the following:

"2703. Required disclosure of customer communications or records.".

AUTHORITY FOR DELAYING NOTICE OF THE EXECUTION OF A WARRANT

SEC. 213. Section 3103a of title 18, United States Code, is amended—

(1) by inserting "(a) IN GENERAL.—" before "In addition"; and

(2) by adding at the end the following:

"(b) DELAY.—With respect to the issuance of any warrant or court order under this section, or any other rule of law, to search for and seize any property or material that constitutes evidence of a criminal offense in violation of the laws of the United States, any notice required, or that may be required, to be given may be delayed if—

"(1) the court finds reasonable cause to believe that providing immediate notification of the execution of the warrant may have an adverse result (as defined in section 2705);

"(2) the warrant prohibits the seizure of any tangible property, any wire or electronic communication (as defined in section 2510), or, except as expressly provided in chapter 121, any stored wire or electronic information, except where the court finds reasonable necessity for the seizure; and

"(3) the warrant provides for the giving of such notice within a reasonable period of its execution, which period may thereafter be extended by the court for good cause shown.".

PEN REGISTER AND TRAP AND TRACE AUTHORITY UNDER FISA

SEC. 214.

(a) APPLICATIONS AND ORDERS.—Section 402 of the Foreign Intelligence Surveillance Act of 1978 (50 U.S.C. §1842) is amended—

(1) in subsection (a)(1), by striking "for any investigation to gather foreign intelligence information or information concerning international terrorism" and inserting "for any investigation to obtain foreign intelligence information not concerning a United States person or to protect against international terrorism or clandestine intelligence activities, provided that such investigation of a United States person is not conducted solely upon the basis of activities protected by the first amendment to the Constitution";

(2) by amending subsection (c)(2) to read as follows:

"(2) a certification by the applicant that the information likely to be obtained is foreign intelligence information not concerning a United States person or is relevant to an ongoing investigation to protect against international terrorism or clandestine intelligence activities, provided that such investigation of a United States person is not conducted solely upon the basis of activities protected by the first amendment to the Constitution.";

(3) by striking subsection (c)(3); and

(4) by amending subsection (d)(2)(A) to read as follows:

"(A) shall specify—

"(i) the identity, if known, of the person who is the subject of the investigation;

"(ii) the identity, if known, of the person to whom is leased or in whose name is listed the telephone line or other facility to which the pen register or trap and trace device is to be attached or applied;

"(iii) the attributes of the communications to which the order applies, such as the number or other identifier, and, if known, the location of the telephone line or other facility to which the pen register or trap and trace device is to be attached or applied and, in the case of a trap and trace device, the geographic limits of the trap and trace order.".

(b) AUTHORIZATION DURING EMERGENCIES.—Section 403 of the Foreign Intelligence Surveillance Act of 1978 (50 U.S.C. §1843) is amended—

(1) in subsection (a), by striking "foreign intelligence information or information concerning international terrorism" and inserting "foreign intelligence information not concerning a United States person or information to protect against international terrorism or clandestine intelligence activities, provided that such investigation of a United States person is not conducted solely upon the basis of activities protected by the first amendment to the Constitution"; and

(2) in subsection (b)(1), by striking "foreign intelligence information or information concerning international terrorism" and inserting "foreign intelligence information not concerning a United States person or information to protect against international terrorism or clandestine intelligence activities, provided that such investigation of a United States person is not conducted solely upon the basis of activities protected by the first amendment to the Constitution".

ACCESS TO RECORDS AND OTHER ITEMS UNDER THE FOREIGN INTELLIGENCE SURVEILLANCE ACT

SEC. 215. Title V of the Foreign Intelligence Surveillance Act of 1978 (50 U.S.C. §1861 et seq.) is amended by striking sections 501 through 503 and inserting the following:

"ACCESS TO CERTAIN BUSINESS RECORDS FOR FOREIGN INTELLIGENCE AND INTERNATIONAL TERRORISM INVESTIGATIONS

"SEC. 501.

"(a)(1) The Director of the Federal Bureau of Investigation or a designee of the Director (whose rank shall be no lower than Assistant Special Agent in Charge) may make an application for an order requiring the production of any tangible things (including books, records, papers, documents, and other items) for an investigation to protect against international terrorism or clandestine intelligence activities, provided that such investigation of a United States person is not conducted solely upon the basis of activities protected by the first amendment to the Constitution.

"(2) An investigation conducted under this section shall— "(A) be conducted under guidelines approved by the Attorney General under Executive Order 12333 (or a successor order); and "(B) not be conducted of a United States person solely upon the basis of activities protected by the first amendment to the Constitution of the United States.

"(b) Each application under this section—

"(1) shall be made to—

"(A) a judge of the court established by section 103(a); or

"(B) a United States Magistrate Judge under chapter 43 of title 28, United States Code, who is publicly designated by the Chief Justice of the United States to have the power to hear applications and grant orders for the production of tangible things under this section on behalf of a judge of that court; and

"(2) shall specify that the records concerned are sought for an authorized investigation conducted in accordance with subsection (a)(2) to obtain foreign intelligence information not concerning a United States person or to protect against international terrorism or clandestine intelligence activities.

"(c)(1) Upon an application made pursuant to this section, the judge shall enter an ex parte order as requested, or as modified, approving the release of records if the judge finds that the application meets the requirements of this section.

"(2) An order under this subsection shall not disclose that it is issued for purposes of an investigation described in subsection (a).

"(d) No person shall disclose to any other person (other than those persons necessary to produce the tangible things under this section) that the Federal Bureau of Investigation has sought or obtained tangible things under this section.

"(e) A person who, in good faith, produces tangible things under an order pursuant to this section shall not be liable to any other person for such production. Such production shall not be deemed to constitute a waiver of any privilege in any other proceeding or context.

"CONGRESSIONAL OVERSIGHT

"SEC. 502.

"(a) On a semiannual basis, the Attorney General shall fully inform the Permanent Select Committee on Intelligence of the House of Representatives and the Select Committee on Intelligence of the Senate concerning all requests for the production of tangible things under section 402. "(b) On a semiannual basis, the Attorney General shall provide to the Committees on the Judiciary of the House of Representatives and the Senate a report setting forth with respect to the preceding 6-month period—

"(1) the total number of applications made for orders approving requests for the production of tangible things under section 402; and "(2) the total number of such orders either granted, modified, or denied.".

MODIFICATION OF AUTHORITIES RELATING TO USE OF PEN REGISTERS AND TRAP AND TRACE DEVICES

SEC. 216.

(a) GENERAL LIMITATIONS.—Section 3121(c) of title 18, United States Code, is amended—

(1) by inserting "or trap and trace device" after "pen register";

(2) by inserting ", routing, addressing," after "dialing"; and

(3) by striking "call processing" and inserting "the processing and transmitting of wire or electronic communications so as not to include the contents of any wire or electronic communications".

(b) ISSUANCE OF ORDERS.—

(1) IN GENERAL.—Section 3123(a) of title 18, United States Code, is amended to read as follows:

"(a) IN GENERAL.—

"(1) ATTORNEY FOR THE GOVERNMENT.—Upon an application made under section 3122(a)(1), the court shall enter an ex parte order authorizing the installation and use of a pen register or trap and trace device anywhere within the United States, if the court finds that the attorney for the Government has certified to the court that the information likely to be obtained by such installation and use is relevant to an ongoing criminal investigation. The order, upon service of that order, shall apply to any person or entity providing wire or electronic communication service in the United States whose assistance may facilitate the execution of the order. Whenever such an order is served on any person or entity not specifically named in the order, upon request of such person or entity, the attorney for the Government or law enforcement or investigative officer that is serving the order shall provide written or electronic certification that the order applies to the person or entity being served.

"(2) STATE INVESTIGATIVE OR LAW ENFORCEMENT OFFICERS.—Upon an application made under section 3122(a)(2), the court shall enter an ex parte order authorizing the installation and use of a pen register or trap and trace device within the jurisdiction of the court, if the court finds that the State law enforcement or investigative officer has certified to the court that the information likely to be obtained by such installation and use is relevant to an ongoing criminal investigation.

"(3)(A) Where the law enforcement agency implementing an ex parte order under this subsection seeks to do so by installing and using its own pen register or trap and trace device on a packet-switched data network of a provider of electronic communication service to the pu'blic, the agency shall ensure that a record will be maintained which will identify—

"(i) any officer or officers who installed the device and any officer or officers who accessed the device to obtain information from the network;

"(ii) the date and time the device was installed, the date and time the device was uninstalled, and the date, time, and duration of each time the device is accessed to obtain information;

"(iii) the configuration of the device at the time of its installation and any subsequent modification thereof; and

"(iv) any information which has been collected by the device. To the extent that the pen register or trap and trace device can be set automatically to record this information electronically, the record shall be maintained electronically throughout the installation and use of such device.

"(B) The record maintained under subparagraph (A) shall be provided ex parte and under seal to the court which entered the ex parte order authorizing the installation and use of the device within 30 days after termination of the order (including any extensions thereof).".

(2) CONTENTS OF ORDER.—Section 3123(b)(1) of title 18, United States Code, is amended—

(A) in subparagraph (A)—

(i) by inserting "or other facility" after "telephone line"; and

(ii) by inserting before the semicolon at the end "or applied"; and

(B) by striking subparagraph (C) and inserting the following:

"(C) the attributes of the communications to which the order applies, including the number or other identifier and, if known, the location of the telephone line or other facility to which the pen register or trap and trace device is to be attached or applied, and, in the case of an order authorizing installation and use of a trap and trace device under subsection (a)(2), the geographic limits of the order; and".

(3) NONDISCLOSURE REQUIREMENTS.—Section 3123(d)(2) of title 18, United States Code, is amended—

(A) by inserting "or other facility" after "the line"; and

(B) by striking ", or who has been ordered by the court" and inserting "or applied, or who is obligated by the order".

(c) DEFINITIONS.—

(1) COURT OF COMPETENT JURISDICTION.—Section 3127(2) of title 18, United States Code, is amended by striking subparagraph (A) and inserting the following:

"(A) any district court of the United States (including a magistrate judge of such a court) or any United States court of appeals having jurisdiction over the offense being investigated; or".

(2) PEN REGISTER.—Section 3127(3) of title 18, United States Code, is amended—

(A) by striking "electronic or other impulses" and all that follows through "is attached" and inserting "dialing, routing, addressing, or signaling information transmitted by an instrument or facility from which a wire or electronic communication is transmitted, provided, however, that such information shall not include the contents of any communication"; and

(B) by inserting "or process" after "device" each place it appears.

(3) TRAP AND TRACE DEVICE.—Section 3127(4) of title 18, United States Code, is amended—

(A) by striking "of an instrument" and all that follows through the semicolon and inserting "or other dialing, routing, addressing, and signaling information reasonably likely to identify the source of a wire or electronic communication, provided, however, that such information shall not include the contents of any communication;"; and

(B) by inserting "or process" after "a device".

(4) CONFORMING AMENDMENT.—Section 3127(1) of title 18, United States Code, is amended—

(A) by striking "and"; and

(B) by inserting ", and 'contents' " after "electronic communication service".

(5) TECHNICAL AMENDMENT.—Section 3124(d) of title 18, United States Code, is amended by striking "the terms of".

(6) CONFORMING AMENDMENT.—Section 3124(b) of title 18, United States Code, is amended by inserting "or other facility" after "the appropriate line".

INTERCEPTION OF COMPUTER TRESPASSER COMMUNICATIONS

SEC. 217. Chapter 119 of title 18, United States Code, is amended—

(1) in section 2510—

(A) in paragraph (18), by striking "and" at the end;

(B) in paragraph (19), by striking the period and inserting a semicolon; and

(C) by inserting after paragraph (19) the following:

"(20) 'protected computer' has the meaning set forth in section 1030;

"(21) 'computer trespasser'— "(A) means a person who accesses a protected computer without authorization and thus has no reasonable expectation of privacy in any communication transmitted to, through, or from the protected computer; and "(B) does not include a person known by the owner or operator of the protected computer to have an existing contractual relationship with the owner or operator of the protected computer for access to all or part of the protected computer."; and

(2) in section 2511(2), by inserting at the end the following:

"(i) It shall not be unlawful under this chapter for a person acting under color of law to intercept the wire or electronic communications of a computer trespasser transmitted to, through, or from the protected computer, if—

"(I) the owner or operator of the protected computer authorizes the interception of the computer trespasser's communications on the protected computer;

"(II) the person acting under color of law is lawfully engaged in an investigation;

"(III) the person acting under color of law has reasonable grounds to believe that the contents of the computer trespasser's communications will be relevant to the investigation; and

"(IV) such interception does not acquire communications other than those transmitted to or from the computer trespasser.".

FOREIGN INTELLIGENCE INFORMATION

SEC. 218.

Sections 104(a)(7)(B) and section 303(a)(7)(B) (50 U.S.C. §1804(a)(7)(B) and 1823(a)(7)(B)) of the Foreign Intelligence Surveillance Act of 1978 are each amended by striking "the purpose" and inserting "a significant purpose".

SINGLE-JURISDICTION SEARCH WARRANTS FOR TERRORISM

SEC. 219. Rule 41(a) of the Federal Rules of Criminal Procedure is amended by inserting after "executed" the following: "and (3) in an investigation of domestic terrorism or international terrorism (as defined in section 2331 of title 18, United States Code), by a Federal magistrate judge in any district in which activities related to the terrorism may have occurred, for a search of property or for a person within or outside the district".

NATIONWIDE SERVICE OF SEARCH WARRANTS FOR ELECTRONIC EVIDENCE

SEC. 220.

(a) IN GENERAL.—Chapter 121 of title 18, United States Code, is amended—

(1) in section 2703, by striking "under the Federal Rules of Criminal Procedure" every place it appears and inserting "using the procedures described in the Federal Rules of Criminal Procedure by a court with jurisdiction over the offense under investigation"; and

(2) in section 2711—

(A) in paragraph (1), by striking "and";

(B) in paragraph (2), by striking the period and inserting "; and"; and

(C) by inserting at the end the following: "(3) the term 'court of competent jurisdiction' has the meaning assigned by section 3127, and includes any Federal court within that definition, without geographic limitation.".

(b) CONFORMING AMENDMENT.—Section 2703(d) of title 18, United States Code, is amended by striking "described in section 3127(2)(A)".

TRADE SANCTIONS

SEC. 221.

(a) IN GENERAL.—The Trade Sanctions Reform and Export Enhancement Act of 2000 (Public Law 106-387; 114 Stat. 1549A-67) is amended—

(1) by amending section 904(2)(C) to read as follows: "(C) used to facilitate the design, development, or production of chemical or biological weapons, missiles, or weapons of mass destruction.";

(2) in section 906(a)(1)—

(A) by inserting ", the Taliban or the territory of Afghanistan controlled by the Taliban," after "Cuba"; and

(B) by inserting ", or in the territory of Afghanistan controlled by the Taliban," after "within such country"; and

(3) in section 906(a)(2), by inserting ", or to any other entity in Syria or North Korea" after "Korea".

(b) APPLICATION OF THE TRADE SANCTIONS REFORM AND EXPORT ENHANCEMENT ACT.—Nothing in the Trade Sanctions Reform and Export Enhancement Act of 2000 shall limit the application or scope of any law establishing criminal or civil penalties, including any Executive order or regulation promulgated pursuant to such laws (or similar or successor laws), for the unlawful export of any agricultural commodity, medicine, or medical device to—

(1) a foreign organization, group, or person designated pursuant to Executive Order No. 12947 of January 23, 1995, as amended;

(2) a Foreign Terrorist Organization pursuant to the Antiterrorism and Effective Death Penalty Act of 1996 (Public Law 104-132);

(3) a foreign organization, group, or person designated pursuant to Executive Order No. 13224 (September 23, 2001);

(4) any narcotics trafficking entity designated pursuant to Executive Order No. 12978 (October 21, 1995) or the Foreign Narcotics Kingpin Designation Act (Public Law 106-120); or

(5) any foreign organization, group, or persons subject to any restriction for its involvement in weapons of mass destruction or missile proliferation.

ASSISTANCE TO LAW ENFORCEMENT AGENCIES

SEC. 222. Nothing in this Act shall impose any additional technical obligation or requirement on a provider of a wire or electronic communication service or other person to furnish facilities or technical assistance. A provider of a wire or electronic communication service, landlord, custodian, or other person who furnishes facilities or technical assistance pursuant to section 216 shall be reasonably compensated for such reasonable expenditures incurred in providing such facilities or assistance.

CIVIL LIABILITY FOR CERTAIN UNAUTHORIZED DISCLOSURES

SEC. 223.

(a) Section 2520 of title 18, United States Code, is amended—

(1) in subsection (a), after "entity", by inserting ", other than the United States,";

(2) by adding at the end the following: "(f) ADMINISTRATIVE DISCIPLINE.—If a court or appropriate department or agency determines that the United States or any of its departments or agencies has violated any provision of this chapter, and the court or appropriate department or agency finds that the circumstances surrounding the violation raise serious questions about whether or not an officer or employee of the United States acted willfully or intentionally with respect to the violation, the department or agency shall, upon receipt of a true and correct copy of the decision and findings of the court or appro-

priate department or agency promptly initiate a proceeding to determine whether disciplinary action against the officer or employee is warranted. If the head of the department or agency involved determines that disciplinary action is not warranted, he or she shall notify the Inspector General with jurisdiction over the department or agency concerned and shall provide the Inspector General with the reasons for such determination."; and

(3) by adding a new subsection (g), as follows:

"(g) IMPROPER DISCLOSURE IS VIOLATION.—Any willful disclosure or use by an investigative or law enforcement officer or governmental entity of information beyond the extent permitted by section 2517 is a violation of this chapter for purposes of section 2520(a).".

(b) Section 2707 of title 18, United States Code, is amended—

(1) in subsection (a), after "entity", by inserting ", other than the United States,";

(2) by striking subsection (d) and inserting the following:

"(d) ADMINISTRATIVE DISCIPLINE.—If a court or appropriate department or agency determines that the United States or any of its departments or agencies has violated any provision of this chapter, and the court or appropriate department or agency finds that the circumstances surrounding the violation raise serious questions about whether or not an officer or employee of the United States acted willfully or intentionally with respect to the violation, the department or agency shall, upon receipt of a true and correct copy of the decision and findings of the court or appropriate department or agency promptly initiate a proceeding to determine whether disciplinary action against the officer or employee is warranted. If the head of the department or agency involved determines that disciplinary action is not warranted, he or she shall notify the Inspector General with jurisdiction over the department or agency concerned and shall provide the Inspector General with the reasons for such determination."; and

(3) by adding a new subsection (g), as follows:

"(g) IMPROPER DISCLOSURE.—Any willful disclosure of a 'record', as that term is defined in section 552a(a) of title 5, United States Code, obtained by an investigative or law enforcement officer, or a governmental entity, pursuant to section 2703 of this title, or from a device installed pursuant to section 3123 or 3125 of this title, that is not a disclosure made in the proper performance of the official functions of the officer or governmental entity making the disclosure, is a violation of this chapter. This provision shall not apply to information previously lawfully disclosed (prior to the commencement of any civil or administrative proceeding under this chapter) to the public by a Federal, State, or local governmental entity or by the plaintiff in a civil action under this chapter.".

(c)(1) Chapter 121 of title 18, United States Code, is amended by adding at the end the following:

"§ 2712. Civil actions against the United States

"(a) IN GENERAL.—Any person who is aggrieved by any willful violation of this chapter or of chapter 119 of this title or of sections 106(a), 305(a), or 405(a) of the Foreign Intelligence Surveillance Act of 1978 (50 U. S.C. 1801 et seq.) may commence an action in United States District Court against the United States to recover money damages. In any such action, if a person who is aggrieved successfully establishes such a violation of this chapter or of chapter 119 of this title or of the above specific provisions of title 50, the Court may assess as damages—

"(1) actual damages, but not less than $10,000, whichever amount is greater; and

"(2) litigation costs, reasonably incurred.

"(b) PROCEDURES.—(1) Any action against the United States under this section may be commenced only after a claim is presented to the appropriate department or agency under the procedures of the Federal Tort Claims Act, as set forth in title 28, United States Code.

"(2) Any action against the United States under this section shall be forever barred unless it is presented in writing to the appropriate Federal agency within 2 years after such claim accrues or unless action is begun within 6 months after the date of mailing, by certified or registered mail, of notice of final denial of the claim by the agency to which it was presented. The claim shall accrue on the date upon which the claimant first has a reasonable opportunity to discover the violation.

"(3) Any action under this section shall be tried to the court without a jury.

"(4) Notwithstanding any other provision of law, the procedures set forth in section 106(f), 305(g), or 405(f) of the Foreign Intelligence Surveillance Act of 1978 (50 U.S.C. §1801 et seq.) shall be the exclusive means by which materials governed by those sections may be reviewed.

"(5) An amount equal to any award against the United States under this section shall be reimbursed by the department or agency concerned to the fund described in section 1304 of title 31, United States Code, out of any appropriation, fund, or other account (excluding any part of such appropriation, fund, or account that is available for the enforcement of any Federal law) that is available for the operating expenses of the department or agency concerned.

"(c) ADMINISTRATIVE DISCIPLINE.—If a court or appropriate department or agency determines that the United States or any of its departments or agencies has violated any provision of this chapter, and the court or appropriate department or agency finds that the circumstances surrounding the violation raise serious questions about whether or not an officer or employee of the United States acted willfully or intentionally with respect to the violation, the department or agency shall, upon receipt of a true and correct copy of the decision and findings of the court or appropriate department or agency promptly initiate a proceeding to determine whether disciplinary action against the officer or employee is warranted. If the head of the department or agency involved determines that disciplinary action is not warranted, he or she shall notify the Inspector General with jurisdiction over the department or agency concerned and shall provide the Inspector General with the reasons for such determination.

"(d) EXCLUSIVE REMEDY.—Any action against the United States under this subsection shall be the exclusive remedy against the United States for any claims within the purview of this section.

"(e) STAY OF PROCEEDINGS.—

(1) Upon the motion of the United States, the court shall stay any action commenced under this section if the court determines that civil discovery will adversely affect the ability of the Government to conduct a related investigation or the prosecution of a related criminal case. Such a stay shall toll the limitations periods of paragraph (2) of subsection (b).

"(2) In this subsection, the terms 'related criminal case' and 'related investigation' mean an actual prosecution or investigation in progress at the time at which the request for the stay or any subsequent motion to lift the stay is made. In determining whether an investigation or a criminal case is related to an action commenced under this section, the court shall consider the degree of similarity between the parties, witnesses, facts, and circumstances involved in the 2 proceedings, without requiring that any one or more factors be identical.

"(3) In requesting a stay under paragraph (1), the Government may, in appropriate cases, submit evidence ex parte in order to avoid disclosing any matter that may adversely affect a related investigation or a related criminal case. If the Government makes such an ex parte submission, the plaintiff shall be given an opportunity to make a submission to the court, not ex parte, and the court may, in its discretion, request further information from either party.".

(2) The table of sections at the beginning of chapter 121 is amended to read as follows:

"2712. Civil action against the United States.".

SUNSET

SEC. 224.

(a) IN GENERAL.—Except as provided in subsection (b), this title and the amendments made by this title (other than sections 203(a), 203(c), 205, 208, 210, 211, 213, 216, 219, 221, and 222, and the amendments made by those sections) shall cease to have effect on December 31, 2005.

(b) EXCEPTION.—With respect to any particular foreign intelligence investigation that began before the date on which the provisions referred to in subsection (a) cease to have effect, or with respect to any particular offense or potential offense that began or occurred before the date on which such provisions cease to have effect, such provisions shall continue in effect.

IMMUNITY FOR COMPLIANCE WITH FISA WIRETAP

SEC. 225. Section 105 of the Foreign Intelligence Surveillance Act of 1978 (50 U.S. C. 1805) is amended by inserting after subsection (g) the following: "(h) No cause of action shall lie in any court against any provider of a wire or electronic communication service, landlord, custodian, or other person (including any officer, employee, agent, or other specified person thereof) that furnishes any information, facilities, or technical assistance in accordance with a court order or request for emergency assistance under this Act.".

TITLE VIII—STRENGTHENING THE CRIMINAL LAWS AGAINST TERRORISM

DEFINITION OF DOMESTIC TERRORISM

SEC. 802.

(a) DOMESTIC TERRORISM DEFINED.—Section 2331 of title 18, United States Code, is amended—

(1) in paragraph (1)(B)(iii), by striking "by assassination or kidnapping" and inserting "by mass destruction, assassination, or kidnapping";

(2) in paragraph (3), by striking "and";

(3) in paragraph (4), by striking the period at the end and inserting "; and"; and

(4) by adding at the end the following:

"(5) the term 'domestic terrorism' means activities that— "(A) involve acts dangerous to human life that are a violation of the criminal laws of the United States or of any State; "(B) appear to be intended—

"(i) to intimidate or coerce a civilian population;

"(ii) to influence the policy of a government by intimidation or coercion; or

"(iii) to affect the conduct of a government by mass destruction, assassination, or kidnapping; and

"(C) occur primarily within the territorial jurisdiction of the United States.".

(b) CONFORMING AMENDMENT.—Section 3077(1) of title 18, United States Code, is amended to read as follows: "(1) 'act of terrorism' means an act of domestic or international terrorism as defined in section 2331;".

PROHIBITION AGAINST HARBORING TERRORISTS

SEC. 803.

(a) IN GENERAL.—Chapter 113B of title 18, United States Code, is amended by adding after section 2338 the following new section:

"§ 2339. Harboring or concealing terrorists

"(a) Whoever harbors or conceals any person who he knows, or has reasonable grounds to believe, has committed, or is about to commit, an offense under section 32 (relating to destruction of aircraft or aircraft facilities), section 175 (relating to biological weapons), section 229 (relating to chemical weapons), section 831 (relating to nuclear materials), paragraph (2) or (3) of section 844(f) (relating to arson and bombing of government property risking or causing injury or death), section 1366(a) (relating to the destruction of an energy facility), section 2280 (relating to violence against maritime navigation), section 2332a (relating to weapons of mass destruction), or section 2332b (relating to acts of terrorism transcending national boundaries) of this title, section 236(a) (relating to sabotage of nuclear facilities or fuel) of the Atomic Energy Act of 1954 (42 U.S.C. §2284(a)), or section 46502 (relating to aircraft piracy) of title 49, shall be fined under this title or imprisoned not more than ten years, or both.". "(b) A violation of this section may be prosecuted in any Federal judicial district in which the underlying offense was committed, or in any other Federal judicial district as provided by law.".

(b) TECHNICAL AMENDMENT.—The chapter analysis for chapter 113B of title 18, United States Code, is amended by inserting after the item for section 2338 the following:

"2339. Harboring or concealing terrorists.".

JURISDICTION OVER CRIMES COMMITTED AT U.S. FACILITIES ABROAD

SEC. 804. Section 7 of title 18, United States Code, is amended by adding at the end the following:

"(9) With respect to offenses committed by or against a national of the United States as that term is used in section 101 of the Immigration and Nationality Act—

"(A) the premises of United States diplomatic, consular, military or other United States Government missions or entities in foreign States, including the buildings, parts of buildings, and land appurtenant or ancillary thereto or used for purposes of those missions or entities, irrespective of ownership; and "(B) residences in foreign States and the land appurtenant or ancillary thereto, irrespective of ownership, used for purposes of those missions or entities or used by United States personnel assigned to those missions or entities.

Nothing in this paragraph shall be deemed to supersede any treaty or international agreement with which this paragraph conflicts. This paragraph does not apply with respect to an offense committed by a person described in section 3261(a) of this title.".

MATERIAL SUPPORT FOR TERRORISM

SEC. 805.

(a) IN GENERAL.—Section 2339A of title 18, United States Code, is amended—

(1) in subsection (a)—

(A) by striking ", within the United States,";

(B) by inserting "229," after "175,";

(C) by inserting "1993," after "1992,";

(D) by inserting ", section 236 of the Atomic Energy Act of 1954 (42 U.S.C. §2284)," after "of this title";

(E) by inserting "or 60123(b)" after "46502"; and

(F) by inserting at the end the following: "A violation of this section may be prosecuted in any Federal judicial district in which the underlying offense was committed, or in any other Federal judicial district as provided by law."; and

(2) in subsection (b)—

(A) by striking "or other financial securities" and inserting "or monetary instruments or financial securities"; and

(B) by inserting "expert advice or assistance," after "training,".

(b) TECHNICAL AMENDMENT.—Section 1956(c)(7)(D) of title 18, United States Code, is amended by inserting "or 2339B" after "2339A".

ASSETS OF TERRORIST ORGANIZATIONS

SEC. 806. Section 981(a)(1) of title 18, United States Code, is amended by inserting at the end the following:

"(G) All assets, foreign or domestic— "(i) of any individual, entity, or organization engaged in planning or perpetrating any act of domestic or international terrorism (as defined in section 2331) against the United States, citizens or residents of the United States, or their property, and all assets, foreign or domestic, affording any person a source of influence over any such entity or organization; "(ii) acquired or maintained by any person with the intent and for the purpose of supporting, planning, conducting, or concealing an act of domestic or international terrorism (as defined in section 2331) against the United States, citizens or residents of the United States, or their property; or

"(iii) derived from, involved in, or used or intended to be used to commit any act of domestic or international terrorism (as defined in section 2331) against the United States, citizens or residents of the United States, or their property.".

TECHNICAL CLARIFICATION RELATING TO PROVISION OF MATERIAL SUPPORT TO TERRORISM

SEC. 807. No provision of the Trade Sanctions Reform and Export Enhancement Act of 2000 (title IX of Public Law 106-387) shall be construed to limit or otherwise affect section 2339A or 2339B of title 18, United States Code.

DEFINITION OF FEDERAL CRIME OF TERRORISM

SEC. 808. Section 2332b of title 18, United States Code, is amended—

(1) in subsection (f), by inserting "and any violation of section 351(e), 844(e), 844(f)(1), 956(b), 1361, 1366(b), 1366(c), 1751(e), 2152, or 2156 of this title," before "and the Secretary"; and

(2) in subsection (g)(5)(B), by striking clauses (i) through (iii) and inserting the following:

"(i) section 32 (relating to destruction of aircraft or aircraft facilities), 37 (relating to violence at international airports), 81 (relating to arson within special maritime and territorial jurisdiction), 175 or 175b (relating to biological weapons), 229 (relating to chemical weapons), subsection (a), (b), (c), or (d) of section 351 (relating to congressional, cabinet, and Supreme Court assassination and kidnapping), 831 (relating to nuclear materials), 842(m) or (n) (relating to plastic explosives), 844(f)(2) or (3) (relating to arson and bombing of Government property risking or causing death), 844(i) (relating to arson and bombing of property used in interstate commerce), 930(c) (relating to killing or attempted killing during an attack on a Federal facility with a dangerous weapon), 956(a)(1) (relating to conspiracy to murder, kidnap, or maim persons abroad), 1030(a)(1) (relating to protection of computers), 1030(a)(5)(A)(i) resulting in damage as defined in 1030(a)(5)(B)(ii) through (v) (relating to protection of computers), 1114 (relating to killing or attempted killing of officers and employees of the United States), 1116 (relating to murder or manslaughter of foreign officials, official guests, or internationally protected persons), 1203 (relating to hostage taking), 1362 (relating to destruction of communication lines, stations, or systems), 1363 (relating to injury to buildings or property within special maritime and territorial jurisdiction of the United States), 1366(a) (relating to destruction of an energy facility), 1751(a), (b), (c), or (d) (relating to Presidential and Presidential staff assassination and kidnapping), 1992 (relating to wrecking trains), 1993 (relating to terrorist attacks and other acts of violence against mass transportation systems), 2155 (relating to destruction of national defense materials, premises, or utilities), 2280 (relating to violence against maritime navigation), 2281 (relating to violence against maritime fixed platforms), 2332 (relating to certain homicides and other violence against United States nationals occurring outside of the United States), 2332a (relating to use of weapons of mass destruction), 2332b (relating to acts of terrorism transcending national boundaries), 2339 (relating to harboring terrorists), 2339A (relating to providing material support to terrorists), 2339B (relating to providing material support to terrorist organizations), or 2340A (relating to torture) of this title; "(ii) section 236 (relating to sabotage of nuclear facilities or fuel) of the Atomic Energy Act of 1954 (42 U.S.C. §2284); or "(iii) section 46502 (relating to aircraft piracy), the second sentence of section 46504 (relating to assault on a flight crew with a dangerous weapon), section 46505(b)(3) or (c) (relating to explosive or incendiary devices, or endangerment of human life by means of weapons, on aircraft), section 46506 if homicide or attempted homicide is involved (relating to application of certain criminal laws to acts on aircraft), or section 60123(b) (relating to destruction of interstate gas or hazardous liquid pipeline facility) of title 49.".

TITLE X—MISCELLANEOUS

DEFINITION OF "ELECTRONIC SURVEILLANCE"

SEC. 1003.

Section 101(f)(2) of the Foreign Intelligence Surveillance Act (50 U.S.C. §1801(f)(2)) is amended by adding at the end before the semicolon the following: ", but does not include the acquisition of those communications of computer trespassers that would be permissible under section 2511(2)(i) of title 18, United States Code".

USA PATRIOT Improvement and Reauthorization Act of 2005

(Pub. L. 109-177 of March 9, 2006, 120 Stat. 192)

AN ACT To extend and modify authorities needed to combat terrorism, and for other purposes.

Be it enacted by the Senate and House of Representatives of the United States of America in Congress assembled,

SHORT TITLE; TABLE OF CONTENTS

SECTION 1.

(a) SHORT TITLE.—This Act may be cited as the "USA PATRIOT Improvement and Reauthorization Act of 2005".

(b) TABLE OF CONTENTS.—The table of contents for this Act is as follows:

TITLE II—TERRORIST DEATH PENALTY ENHANCEMENT

SUBTITLE A—TERRORIST PENALTIES ENHANCEMENT ACT

SUBTITLE B—FEDERAL DEATH PENALTY PROCEDURES

TITLE III—REDUCING CRIME AND TERRORISM AT AMERICA'S SEAPORTS

TITLE IV—COMBATING TERRORISM FINANCING

TITLE V—MISCELLANEOUS PROVISIONS

TITLE VI—SECRET SERVICE

TITLE VII—COMBAT METHAMPHETAMINE EPIDEMIC ACT OF 2005

SUBTITLE A—DOMESTIC REGULATION OF PRECURSOR CHEMICALS

SUBTITLE B—INTERNATIONAL REGULATION OF PRECURSOR CHEMICALS

SUBTITLE C—ENHANCED CRIMINAL PENALTIES FOR METHAMPHETAMINE PRODUCTION AND TRAFFICKING

SUBTITLE D—ENHANCED ENVIRONMENTAL REGULATION OF METHAMPHETAMINE BYPRODUCTS

SUBTITLE E—ADDITIONAL PROGRAMS AND ACTIVITIES

TITLE I—USA PATRIOT IMPROVEMENT AND REAUTHORIZATION ACT

REFERENCE TO, AND MODIFICATION OF SHORT TITLE FOR, USA PATRIOT ACT

SEC. 101.

(a) REFERENCES TO USA PATRIOT ACT.—A reference in this Act to the USA PATRIOT Act shall be deemed a reference to the Uniting and Strengthening America by Providing Appropriate Tools Required to Intercept and Obstruct Terrorism Act (USA PATRIOT Act) of 2001.

(b) MODIFICATION OF SHORT TITLE OF USA PATRIOT ACT.—Section 1(a) of the USA PATRIOT Act is amended to read as follows:

"(a) SHORT TITLE.—This Act may be cited as the 'Uniting and Strengthening America by Providing Appropriate Tools Required to Intercept and Obstruct Terrorism Act of 2001' or the 'USA PATRIOT Act'.".

USA PATRIOT ACT SUNSET PROVISIONS

SEC. 102.

(a) IN GENERAL.—Section 224 of the USA PATRIOT Act is repealed.

(b) SECTIONS 206 AND 215 SUNSET.—

(1) IN GENERAL.—Effective December 31, 2009, the Foreign Intelligence Surveillance Act of 1978 is amended so that sections 501, 502, and 105(c)(2) read as they read on October 25, 2001.

(2) EXCEPTION.—With respect to any particular foreign intelligence investigation that began before the date on which the provisions referred to in paragraph (1) cease to have effect, or with respect to any particular offense or potential offense that began or occurred before the date on which such provisions cease to have effect, such provisions shall continue in effect.

EXTENSION OF SUNSET RELATING TO INDIVIDUAL TERRORISTS AS AGENTS OF FOREIGN POWERS

SEC. 103.

Section 6001(b) of the Intelligence Reform and Terrorism Prevention Act of 2004 (Public Law 108-458; 118 Stat. 3742) is amended to read as follows:

"(b) SUNSET.—

"(1) IN GENERAL.—Except as provided in paragraph (2), the amendment made by subsection (a) shall cease to have effect on December 31, 2009.

"(2) EXCEPTION.—With respect to any particular foreign intelligence investigation that began before the date on which the provisions referred to in paragraph (1) cease to have effect, or with respect to any particular offense or potential offense that began or occurred before the date on which the provisions cease to have effect, such provisions shall continue in effect.".

SECTION 233B AND THE MATERIAL SUPPORT SECTIONS OF TITLE 18, UNITED STATES CODE

SEC. 104. Section 6603 of the Intelligence Reform and Terrorism Prevention Act of 2004 (Public Law 108-458; 118 Stat. 3762) is amended by striking subsection (g).

DURATION OF FISA SURVEILLANCE OF NON-UNITED STATES PERSONS UNDER SECTION 207 OF THE USA PATRIOT ACT

SEC. 105.

(a) ELECTRONIC SURVEILLANCE.—Section 105(e) of the Foreign Intelligence Surveillance Act of 1978 (50 U.S.C. §1805(e)) is amended—

(1) in paragraph (1)(B), by striking ", as defined in section 101(b)(1)(A)" and inserting "who is not a United States person"; and

(2) in subsection (2)(B), by striking "as defined in section 101(b)(1)(A)" and inserting "who is not a United States person".

(b) PHYSICAL SEARCH.—Section 304(d) of such Act (50 U.S.C. §1824(d)) is amended—

(1) in paragraph (1)(B), by striking "as defined in section 101(b)(1)(A)" and inserting "who is not a United States person"; and

(2) in paragraph (2), by striking "as defined in section 101(b)(1)(A)" and inserting "who is not a United States person".

(c) PEN REGISTERS, TRAP AND TRACE DEVICES.—Section 402(e) of such Act (50 U.S.C. §1842(e)) is amended—

(1) by striking "(e) An" and inserting "(e)(1) Except as provided in paragraph (2), an"; and

(2) by adding at the end the following new paragraph:

"(2) In the case of an application under subsection (c) where the applicant has certified that the information likely to be obtained is foreign intelligence information not concerning a United States person, an order, or an extension of an order, under this section may be for a period not to exceed one year.".

ACCESS TO CERTAIN BUSINESS RECORDS UNDER SECTION 215 OF THE USA PATRIOT ACT

SEC. 106.

(a) DIRECTOR APPROVAL FOR CERTAIN APPLICATIONS.—Subsection (a) of section 501 of the Foreign Intelligence Surveillance Act of 1978 (50 U.S.C. §1861(a)) is amended—

(1) in paragraph (1), by striking "The Director" and inserting "Subject to paragraph (3), the Director"; and

(2) by adding at the end the following:

"(3) In the case of an application for an order requiring the production of library circulation records, library patron lists, book sales records, book customer lists, firearms sales records, tax return records, educational records, or medical records containing information that would identify a person, the Director of the Federal Bureau of Investigation may delegate the authority to make such application to either the Deputy Director of the Federal Bureau of Investigation or the Executive Assistant Director for National Security (or any successor position). The Deputy Director or the Executive Assistant Director may not further delegate such authority.".

(b) FACTUAL BASIS FOR REQUESTED ORDER.—Subsection (b)(2) of such section is amended to read as follows:

"(2) shall include—

"(A) a statement of facts showing that there are reasonable grounds to believe that the tangible things sought are relevant to an authorized investigation (other than a threat assessment) conducted in accordance with subsection (a)(2) to obtain foreign intelligence information not concerning a United States person or to protect against international terrorism or clandestine intelligence activities, such things being presumptively relevant to an authorized investigation if the applicant shows in the statement of the facts that they pertain to—

"(i) a foreign power or an agent of a foreign power;

"(ii) the activities of a suspected agent of a foreign power who is the subject of such authorized investigation; or

"(iii) an individual in contact with, or known to, a suspected agent of a foreign power who is the subject of such authorized investigation; and

"(B) an enumeration of the minimization procedures adopted by the Attorney General under subsection (g) that are applicable to the retention and dissemination by the Federal Bureau of Investigation of any tangible things to be made available to the Federal Bureau of Investigation based on the order requested in such application.".

(c) CLARIFICATION OF JUDICIAL DISCRETION.—Subsection (c)(1) of such section is amended to read as follows:

"(c)(1) Upon an application made pursuant to this section, if the judge finds that the application meets the requirements of subsections (a) and (b), the judge shall enter an ex parte order as requested, or as modified, approving the release of tangible things. Such order shall direct that minimization procedures adopted pursuant to subsection (g) be followed.".

(d) ADDITIONAL PROTECTIONS.—Subsection (c)(2) of such section is amended to read as follows:

"(2) An order under this subsection—

"(A) shall describe the tangible things that are ordered to be produced with sufficient particularity to permit them to be fairly identified;

"(B) shall include the date on which the tangible things must be provided, which shall allow a reasonable period of time within which the tangible things can be assembled and made available;

"(C) shall provide clear and conspicuous notice of the principles and procedures described in subsection (d);

"(D) may only require the production of a tangible thing if such thing can be obtained with a subpoena duces tecum issued by a court of the United States in aid of a grand jury investigation or with any other order issued by a court of the United States directing the production of records or tangible things; and

"(E) shall not disclose that such order is issued for purposes of an investigation described in subsection (a).".

(e) PROHIBITIONS ON DISCLOSURE.—Subsection (d) of such section is amended to read as follows:

"(d)(1) No person shall disclose to any other person that the Federal Bureau of Investigation has sought or obtained tangible things pursuant to an order under this section, other than to—

"(A) those persons to whom disclosure is necessary to comply with such order;

"(B) an attorney to obtain legal advice or assistance with respect to the production of things in response to the order; or

"(C) other persons as permitted by the Director of the Federal Bureau of Investigation or the designee of the Director.

"(2)(A) A person to whom disclosure is made pursuant to paragraph (1) shall be subject to the nondisclosure requirements applicable to a person to whom an order is directed under this section in the same manner as such person.

"(B) Any person who discloses to a person described in subparagraph (A), (B), or (C) of paragraph (1) that the Federal Bureau of Investigation has sought or obtained tangible things pursuant to an order under this section shall notify such person of the nondisclosure requirements of this subsection.

"(C) At the request of the Director of the Federal Bureau of Investigation or the designee of the Director, any person making or intending to make a disclosure under this section shall identify to the Director or such designee the person to whom such disclosure will be made or to whom such disclosure was made prior to the request, but in no circumstance shall a person be required to inform the Director or such designee that the person intends to consult an attorney to obtain legal advice or legal assistance.".

(f) JUDICIAL REVIEW.—

(1) PETITION REVIEW POOL.—Section 103 of the Foreign Intelligence Surveillance Act of 1978 (50 U.S.C. §1803) is amended by adding at the end the following new subsection:

"(e)(1) Three judges designated under subsection (a) who reside within 20 miles of the District of Columbia, or, if all of such judges are unavailable, other judges of the court established under subsection (a) as may be designated by the presiding judge of such court, shall comprise a petition review pool which shall have jurisdiction to review petitions filed pursuant to section 501(f)(1).

"(2) Not later than 60 days after the date of the enactment of the USA PATRIOT Improvement and Reauthorization Act of 2005, the court established under subsection (a) shall adopt and, consistent with the protection of national security, publish procedures for the review of petitions filed pursuant to section 501(f)(1) by the panel established under paragraph (1). Such procedures shall provide that review of a petition shall be conducted in camera and shall also provide for the designation of an acting presiding judge.".

(2) PROCEEDINGS.—Section 501 of the Foreign Intelligence Surveillance Act of 1978 (50 U.S.C. §1861) is further amended by adding at the end the following new subsection:

"(f)(1) A person receiving an order to produce any tangible thing under this section may challenge the legality of that order by filing a petition with the pool established by section 103(e)(1). The presiding judge shall immediately assign the petition to one of the judges serving in such pool. Not later than 72 hours after the assignment of such petition, the assigned judge shall conduct an initial review of the petition. If the assigned judge determines that the petition is frivolous, the assigned judge shall immediately deny the petition and affirm the order. If the assigned judge determines the petition is not frivolous, the assigned judge shall promptly consider the petition in accordance with the procedures established pursuant to section 103(e)(2). The judge considering the petition may modify or set aside the order only if the judge finds that the order does not meet the requirements of this section or is otherwise unlawful. If the judge does not modify or set aside the order, the judge shall immediately affirm the order and order the recipient to comply therewith. The assigned judge shall promptly provide a written statement for the record of the reasons for any determination under this paragraph.

"(2) A petition for review of a decision to affirm, modify, or set aside an order by the United States or any person receiving such order shall be to the court of review established under section 103(b), which shall have jurisdiction to consider such petitions. The court of review shall provide for the record a written statement of the reasons for its decision and, on petition of the United States or any person receiving such order for writ of certiorari, the record shall be transmitted under seal to the Supreme Court, which shall have jurisdiction to review such decision.

"(3) Judicial proceedings under this subsection shall be concluded as expeditiously as possible. The record of proceedings, including petitions filed, orders granted, and statements of reasons for decision, shall be maintained under security measures established by the Chief Justice of the United States in consultation with the Attorney General and the Director of National Intelligence.

"(4) All petitions under this subsection shall be filed under seal. In any proceedings under this subsection, the court shall, upon request of the government, review ex parte and in camera any government submission, or portions thereof, which may include classified information.".

(g) MINIMIZATION PROCEDURES AND USE OF INFORMATION.—Section

501 of the Foreign Intelligence Surveillance Act of 1978 (50 U.S.C. §1861) is further amended by adding at the end the following new subsections:

"(g) MINIMIZATION PROCEDURES.—

"(1) IN GENERAL.—Not later than 180 days after the date of the enactment of the USA PATRIOT Improvement and Reauthorization Act of 2005, the Attorney General shall adopt specific minimization procedures governing the retention and dissemination by the Federal Bureau of Investigation of any tangible things, or information therein, received by the Federal Bureau of Investigation in response to an order under this title.

"(2) DEFINED.—In this section, the term 'minimization procedures' means—

"(A) specific procedures that are reasonably designed in light of the purpose and technique of an order for the production of tangible things, to minimize the retention, and prohibit the dissemination, of nonpublicly available information concerning unconsenting United States persons consistent with the need of the United States to obtain, produce, and disseminate foreign intelligence information;

"(B) procedures that require that nonpublicly available information, which is not foreign intelligence information, as defined in section 101(e)(1), shall not be disseminated in a manner that identifies any United States person, without such person's consent, unless such person's identity is necessary to understand foreign intelligence information or assess its importance; and "(C) notwithstanding subparagraphs (A) and (B), procedures that allow for the retention and dissemination of information that is evidence of a crime which has been, is being, or is about to be committed and that is to be retained or disseminated for law enforcement purposes.

"(h) USE OF INFORMATION.—Information acquired from tangible things received by the Federal Bureau of Investigation in response to an order under this title concerning any United States person may be used and disclosed by Federal officers and employees without the consent of the United States person only in accordance with the minimization procedures adopted pursuant to subsection (g). No otherwise privileged information acquired from tangible things received by the Federal Bureau of Investigation in accordance with the provisions of this title shall lose its privileged character. No information acquired from tangible things received by the Federal Bureau of Investigation in response to an order under this title may be used or disclosed by Federal officers or employees except for lawful purposes.".

(h) ENHANCED OVERSIGHT.—Section 502 of the Foreign Intelligence Surveillance Act of 1978 (50 U.S.C. §1862) is amended—

(1) in subsection (a)—

(A) by striking "semiannual basis" and inserting "annual basis"; and

(B) by inserting "and the Committee on the Judiciary" after "and the Select Committee on Intelligence";

(2) in subsection (b)—

(A) by striking "On a semiannual basis" and all that follows through "the preceding 6-month period" and inserting "In April of each year, the Attorney General shall submit to the House and Senate Committees on the Judiciary and the House Permanent Select Committee on Intelligence and the Senate Select Committee on Intelligence a report setting forth with respect to the preceding calendar year";

(B) in paragraph (1), by striking "and" at the end;

(C) in paragraph (2), by striking the period at the end and inserting "; and"; and

(D) by adding at the end the following new paragraph:

"(3) the number of such orders either granted, modified, or denied for the production of each of the following: "(A) Library circulation records, library patron lists, book sales records, or book customer lists. "(B) Firearms sales records. "(C) Tax return records. "(D) Educational records. "(E) Medical records containing information that would identify a person."; and

(3) by adding at the end the following new subsection:

"(c)(1) In April of each year, the Attorney General shall submit to Congress a report setting forth with respect to the preceding year— "(A) the total number of applications made for orders approving requests for the production of tangible things under section 501; and "(B) the total number of such orders either granted, modified, or denied.

"(2) Each report under this subsection shall be submitted in unclassified form.".

AUDIT ON ACCESS TO CERTAIN BUSINESS RECORDS FOR FOREIGN INTELLIGENCE PURPOSES

SEC. 106A.

(a) AUDIT.—The Inspector General of the Department of Justice shall perform a comprehensive audit of the effectiveness and use, including any improper or illegal use, of the investigative authority provided to the Federal Bureau of Investigation under title V of the Foreign Intelligence Surveillance Act of 1978 (50 U.S.C. §1861 et seq.).

(b) REQUIREMENTS.—The audit required under subsection (a) shall include—

(1) an examination of each instance in which the Attorney General, any other officer, employee, or agent of the Department of Justice, the Director of the Federal Bureau of Investigation, or a designee of the Director, submitted an application to the Foreign Intelligence Surveillance Court (as such term is defined in section 301(3) of the Foreign Intelligence Surveillance Act of 1978 (50 U.S.C. §1821(3))) for an order under section 501 of such Act during the calendar years of 2002 through 2006, including—

(A) whether the Federal Bureau of Investigation requested that the Department of Justice submit an application and the request was not submitted to the court (including an examination of the basis for not submitting the application);

(B) whether the court granted, modified, or denied the application (including an examination of the basis for any modification or denial);

(2) the justification for the failure of the Attorney General to issue implementing procedures governing requests for the production of tangible things under such section in a timely fashion, including whether such delay harmed national security;

(3) whether bureaucratic or procedural impediments to the use of such requests for production prevent the Federal Bureau of Investigation from taking full advantage of the authorities provided under section 501 of such Act;

(4) any noteworthy facts or circumstances relating to orders under such section, including any improper or illegal use of the authority provided under such section; and

(5) an examination of the effectiveness of such section as an investigative tool, including—

(A) the categories of records obtained and the importance of the information acquired to the intelligence activities of the Federal Bureau of Investigation or any other Department or agency of the Federal Government;

(B) the manner in which such information is collected, retained, analyzed, and disseminated by the Federal Bureau of Investigation, including any direct access to such information (such as access to "raw data") provided to any other Department, agency, or instrumentality of Federal, State, local, or tribal governments or any private sector entity;

(C) with respect to calendar year 2006, an examination of the minimization procedures adopted by the Attorney General under section 501(g) of such Act and whether such minimization procedures protect the constitutional rights of United States persons;

(D) whether, and how often, the Federal Bureau of Investigation utilized information acquired pursuant to an order under section 501 of such Act to produce an analytical intelligence product for distribution within the Federal Bureau of Investigation, to the intelligence community (as such term is defined in section 3(4) of the National Security Act of 1947 (50 U.S.C. §401a(4))), or to other Federal, State, local, or tribal government Departments, agencies, or instrumentalities; and

(E) whether, and how often, the Federal Bureau of Investigation provided such information to law enforcement authorities for use in criminal proceedings.

(c) SUBMISSION DATES.—

(1) PRIOR YEARS.—Not later than one year after the date of the enactment of this Act, or upon completion of the audit under this section for calendar years 2002, 2003, and 2004, whichever is earlier, the Inspector General of the Department of Justice shall submit to the Committee on the Judiciary and the Permanent Select Committee on Intelligence of the House of Representatives and the Committee on the Judiciary and the Select Committee on Intelligence of the Senate a report containing the results of the audit conducted under this section for calendar years 2002, 2003, and 2004.

(2) CALENDAR YEARS 2005 AND 2006.—Not later than December 31, 2007, or upon completion of the audit under this section for calendar years 2005 and 2006, whichever is earlier, the Inspector General of the Department of Justice shall submit to the Committee on the Judiciary and the Permanent Select Committee on Intelligence of the House of Representatives and the Committee on the Judiciary and the Select Committee on Intelligence of the Senate a report containing the results of the audit conducted under this section for calendar years 2005 and 2006.

(d) PRIOR NOTICE TO ATTORNEY GENERAL AND DIRECTOR OF NATIONAL INTELLIGENCE; COMMENTS.—

(1) NOTICE.—Not less than 30 days before the submission of a report under subsection (c)(1) or (c)(2), the Inspector General of the Department of Justice shall provide such report to the Attorney General and the Director of National Intelligence.

(2) COMMENTS.—The Attorney General or the Director of National Intelligence may provide comments to be included in the reports submitted under subsections (c)(1) and (c)(2) as the Attorney General or the Director of National Intelligence may consider necessary.

(e) UNCLASSIFIED FORM.—The reports submitted under subsections (c)(1) and (c)(2) and any comments included under subsection (d)(2) shall be in unclassified form, but may include a classified annex.

ENHANCED OVERSIGHT OF GOOD-FAITH EMERGENCY DISCLOSURES UNDER SECTION 212 OF THE USA PATRIOT ACT

SEC. 107.

(a) ENHANCED OVERSIGHT.—Section 2702 of title 18, United States Code, is amended by adding at the end the following:

"(d) REPORTING OF EMERGENCY DISCLOSURES.—On an annual basis, the Attorney General shall submit to the Committee on the Judiciary of the House of Representatives and the Committee on the Judiciary of the Senate a report containing—

"(1) the number of accounts from which the Department of Justice has received voluntary disclosures under subsection (b)(8); and

"(2) a summary of the basis for disclosure in those instances where—

"(A) voluntary disclosures under subsection (b)(8) were made to the Department of Justice; and "(B) the investigation pertaining to those disclosures was closed without the filing of criminal charges.".

(b) TECHNICAL AMENDMENTS TO CONFORM COMMUNICATIONS AND CUSTOMER RECORDS EXCEPTIONS.—

(1) VOLUNTARY DISCLOSURES.—Section 2702 of title 18, United States Code, is amended—

(A) in subsection (b)(8), by striking "Federal, State, or local"; and

(B) by striking paragraph (4) of subsection (c) and inserting the following: "(4) to a governmental entity, if the provider, in good faith, believes that an emergency involving danger of death or serious physical injury to any person requires disclosure without delay of information relating to the emergency;".

(2) DEFINITIONS.—Section 2711 of title 18, United States Code, is amended—

(A) in paragraph (2), by striking "and" at the end;

(B) in paragraph (3), by striking the period at the end and inserting "; and"; and

(C) by adding at the end the following: "(4) the term 'governmental entity' means a department or agency of the United States or any State or political subdivision thereof.".

(c) ADDITIONAL EXCEPTION.—Section 2702(a) of title 18, United States Code, is amended by inserting "or (c)" after "Except as provided in subsection (b)".

MULTIPOINT ELECTRONIC SURVEILLANCE UNDER SECTION 206 OF THE USA PATRIOT ACT

SEC. 108.

(a) INCLUSION OF SPECIFIC FACTS IN APPLICATION.—

(1) APPLICATION.—Section 104(a)(3) of the Foreign Intelligence Surveillance Act of 1978 (50 U.S.C. §1804(a)(3)) is amended by inserting "specific" after "description of the".

(2) ORDER.—Subsection (c) of section 105 of the Foreign Intelligence Surveillance Act of 1978 (50 U.S.C. §1805(c)) is amended—

(A) in paragraph (1)(A) by striking "target of the electronic surveillance" and inserting "specific target of the electronic surveillance identified or described in the application pursuant to section 104(a)(3)"; and

(B) in paragraph (2)(B), by striking "where the Court finds" and inserting "where the Court finds, based upon specific facts provided in the application,".

(b) ADDITIONAL DIRECTIONS.—Such subsection is further amended—

(1) by striking "An order approving" and all that follows through "specify" and inserting "(1) SPECIFICATIONS—An order approving an electronic surveillance under this section shall specify";

(2) in paragraph (1)(F), by striking "; and" and inserting a period;

(3) in paragraph (2), by striking "direct" and inserting "DIRECTIONS— An order approving an electronic surveillance under this section shall direct"; and

(4) by adding at the end the following new paragraph:

"(3) SPECIAL DIRECTIONS FOR CERTAIN ORDERS.—An order approving an electronic surveillance under this section in circumstances where the nature and location of each of the facilities or places at which the surveillance will be directed is unknown shall direct the applicant to provide notice to the court within ten days after the date on which surveillance begins to be directed at any new facility or place, unless the court finds good cause to justify a longer period of up to 60 days, of—

"(A) the nature and location of each new facility or place at which the electronic surveillance is directed;

"(B) the facts and circumstances relied upon by the applicant to justify the applicant's belief that each new facility or place at which the electronic surveillance is directed is or was being used, or is about to be used, by the target of the surveillance;

"(C) a statement of any proposed minimization procedures that differ from those contained in the original application or order, that may be necessitated by a change in the facility or place at which the electronic surveillance is directed; and

"(D) the total number of electronic surveillances that have been or are being conducted under the authority of the order.".

(c) ENHANCED OVERSIGHT.—

(1) REPORT TO CONGRESS.—Section 108(a)(1) of the Foreign Intelligence Surveillance Act of 1978 (50 U.S.C. §1808(a)(1)) is amended by inserting ", and the Committee on the Judiciary of the Senate," after "Senate Select Committee on Intelligence".

(2) MODIFICATION OF SEMIANNUAL REPORT REQUIREMENT ON ACTIVITIES UNDER FOREIGN INTELLIGENCE SURVEILLANCE ACT OF 1978.—Paragraph (2) of section 108(a) of the Foreign Intelligence Surveillance Act of 1978 (50 U.S.C. §1808(a)) is amended to read as follows:

"(2) Each report under the first sentence of paragraph (1) shall include a description of—

"(A) the total number of applications made for orders and extensions of orders approving electronic surveillance under this title where the nature and location of each facility or place at which the electronic surveillance will be directed is unknown;

"(B) each criminal case in which information acquired under this Act has been authorized for use at trial during the period covered by such report; and

"(C) the total number of emergency employments of electronic surveillance under section 105(f) and the total number of subsequent orders approving or denying such electronic surveillance.".

ENHANCED CONGRESSIONAL OVERSIGHT

SEC. 109.

(a) EMERGENCY PHYSICAL SEARCHES.—Section 306 of the Foreign Intelligence Surveillance Act of 1978 (50 U.S.C. §1826) is amended—

(1) in the first sentence, by inserting ", and the Committee on the Judiciary of the Senate," after "the Senate";

(2) in the second sentence, by striking "and the Committees on the Judiciary of the House of Representatives and the Senate" and inserting "and the Committee on the Judiciary of the House of Representatives";

(3) in paragraph (2), by striking "and" at the end;

(4) in paragraph (3), by striking the period at the end and inserting "; and"; and

(5) by adding at the end the following:

"(4) the total number of emergency physical searches authorized by the Attorney General under section 304(e) and the total number of subsequent orders approving or denying such physical searches.".

(b) EMERGENCY PEN REGISTERS AND TRAP AND TRACE DEVICES.—Section 406(b) of the Foreign Intelligence Surveillance Act of 1978 (50 U.S.C. §1846(b)) is amended—

(1) in paragraph (1), by striking "and" at the end;

(2) in paragraph (2), by striking the period at the end and inserting "; and"; and

(3) by adding at the end the following:

"(3) the total number of pen registers and trap and trace devices whose installation and use was authorized by the Attorney General on an emergency basis under section 403, and the total number of subsequent orders approving or denying the installation and use of such pen registers and trap and trace devices.".

(c) ADDITIONAL REPORT.—At the beginning and midpoint of each fiscal year, the Secretary of Homeland Security shall submit to the Committees on the Judiciary of the House of Representatives and the Senate, a written report providing a description of internal affairs operations at U.S. Citizenship and Immigration Services, including the general state of such operations and a detailed description of investigations that are being conducted (or that were conducted during the previous six months) and the resources devoted to such investigations. The first such report shall be submitted not later than April 1, 2006.

(d) RULES AND PROCEDURES FOR FISA COURTS.—Section 103 of the Foreign Intelligence Surveillance Act of 1978 (50 U.S.C. §1803) is amended by adding at the end the following:

"(f)(1) The courts established pursuant to subsections (a) and (b) may establish such rules and procedures, and take such actions, as are reasonably necessary to administer their responsibilities under this Act.

"(2) The rules and procedures established under paragraph (1), and any modifications of such rules and procedures, shall be recorded, and shall be transmitted to the following:

"(A) All of the judges on the court established pursuant to subsection (a).

"(B) All of the judges on the court of review established pursuant to subsection (b).

"(C) The Chief Justice of the United States.

"(D) The Committee on the Judiciary of the Senate.

"(E) The Select Committee on Intelligence of the Senate.

"(F) The Committee on the Judiciary of the House of Representatives.

"(G) The Permanent Select Committee on Intelligence of the House of Representatives.

"(3) The transmissions required by paragraph (2) shall be submitted in unclassified form, but may include a classified annex.".

JUDICIAL REVIEW OF NATIONAL SECURITY LETTERS

SEC. 115. Chapter 223 of title 18, United States Code, is amended—

(1) by inserting at the end of the table of sections the following new item:

"3511. JUDICIAL REVIEW OF REQUESTS FOR INFORMATION."; and

(2) by inserting after section 3510 the following:

"§3511. Judicial review of requests for information
"(a) The recipient of a request for records, a report, or other information under section 2709(b) of this title, section 626(a) or (b) or 627(a) of the Fair Credit Reporting Act, section 1114(a)(5)(A) of the Right to Financial Privacy Act, or section 802(a) of the National Security Act of 1947 may, in the United States district court for the district in which that person or entity does business or resides, petition for an order modifying or setting aside the request. The court may modify or set aside the request if compliance would be unreasonable, oppressive, or otherwise unlawful. "(b)(1) The recipient of a request for records, a report, or other information under section 2709(b) of this title, section 626(a) or (b) or 627(a) of the Fair Credit Reporting Act, section 1114(a)(5)(A) of the Right to Financial Privacy Act, or section 802(a) of the National Security Act of 1947, may petition any court described in subsection (a) for an order modifying or setting aside a nondisclosure requirement imposed in connection with such a request.

"(2) If the petition is filed within one year of the request for records, a report, or other information under section 2709(b) of this title, section 626(a) or (b) or 627(a) of the Fair Credit Reporting Act, section 1114(a)(5)(A) of the Right to Financial Privacy Act, or section 802(a) of the National Security Act of 1947, the court may modify or set aside such a nondisclosure requirement if it finds that there is no reason to believe that disclosure may endanger the national security of the United States, interfere with a criminal, counterterrorism, or counterintelligence investigation, interfere with diplomatic relations, or endanger the life or physical safety of any person. If, at the time of the petition, the Attorney General, Deputy Attorney General, an Assistant Attorney General, or the Director of the Federal Bureau of Investigation, or in the case of a request by a department, agency, or instrumentality of the Federal Government other than the Department of Justice, the head or deputy head of such department, agency, or instrumentality, certifies that disclosure may endanger the national security of the United States or interfere with diplomatic relations, such certification shall be treated as conclusive unless the court finds that the certification was made in bad faith.

"(3) If the petition is filed one year or more after the request for records, a report, or other information under section 2709(b) of this title, section 626(a) or (b) or 627(a) of the Fair Credit Reporting Act, section 1114(a)(5)(A) of the Right to Financial Privacy Act, or section 802(a) of the National Security Act of 1947, the Attorney General, Deputy Attorney General, an Assistant Attorney General, or the Director of the Federal Bureau of Investigation, or his designee in a position not lower than Deputy Assistant Director at Bureau headquarters or a Special Agent in Charge in a Bureau field office designated by the Director, or in the case of a request by a department, agency, or instrumentality of the Federal Government other than the Federal Bureau of Investigation, the head or deputy head of such department, agency, or instrumentality, within ninety days of the filing of the petition, shall either terminate the nondisclosure requirement or re-certify that disclosure may result in a danger to the national security of the United States, interference with a criminal, counterterrorism, or counterintelligence investigation, interference with diplomatic relations, or danger to the life or physical safety of any person. In the event of re-certification, the court may modify or set aside such a nondisclosure requirement if it finds that there is no reason to believe that disclosure may endanger the national security of the United States, interfere with a criminal, counterterrorism, or counterintelligence investigation, interfere with diplomatic relations, or endanger the life or physical safety of any person. If the recertification that disclosure may endanger the national security of the United States or interfere with diplomatic relations is made by the Attorney General, Deputy Attorney General, an Assistant Attorney General, or the Director of the Federal Bureau of Investigation, such certification shall be treated as conclusive unless the court finds that the recertification was made in bad faith. If the court denies a petition for an order modifying or setting aside a nondisclosure requirement under this paragraph, the recipient shall be precluded for a period of one year from filing another petition to modify or set aside such nondisclosure requirement.

"(c) In the case of a failure to comply with a request for records, a report, or other information made to any person or entity under section 2709(b) of this title, section 626(a) or (b) or 627(a) of the Fair Credit Reporting Act, section 1114(a)(5)(A) of the Right to Financial Privacy Act, or section 802(a) of the National Security Act of 1947, the Attorney General may invoke the aid of any district court of the United States within the jurisdiction in which the investigation is carried on or the person or entity resides, carries on business, or may be found, to compel compliance with the request. The court may issue an order requiring the person or entity to comply with the request. Any failure to obey the order of the court may be punished by the court as contempt thereof. Any process under this section may be served in any judicial district in which the person or entity may be found.

"(d) In all proceedings under this section, subject to any right to an open hearing in a contempt proceeding, the court must close any hearing to the extent necessary to prevent an unauthorized disclosure of a request for records, a report, or other information made to any person or entity under section 2709(b) of this title, section 626(a) or (b) or 627(a) of the Fair Credit Reporting Act, section 1114(a)(5)(A) of the Right to Financial Privacy Act, or section 802(a) of the National Security Act of 1947. Petitions, filings, records, orders, and subpoenas must also be kept under seal to the extent and as long as necessary to prevent the unauthorized disclosure of a request for records, a report, or other information made to any person or entity under section 2709(b) of this title, section 626(a) or (b) or 627(a) of the Fair Credit Reporting Act, section 1114(a)(5)(A) of the Right

to Financial Privacy Act, or section 802(a) of the National Security Act of 1947.
"(e) In all proceedings under this section, the court shall, upon request of the government, review ex parte and in camera any government submission or portions thereof, which may include classified information.".

CONFIDENTIALITY OF NATIONAL SECURITY LETTERS

SEC. 116.

(a) Section 2709(c) of title 18, United States Code, is amended to read:

"(c) PROHIBITION OF CERTAIN DISCLOSURE.—

"(1) If the Director of the Federal Bureau of Investigation, or his designee in a position not lower than Deputy Assistant Director at Bureau headquarters or a Special Agent in Charge in a Bureau field office designated by the Director, certifies that otherwise there may result a danger to the national security of the United States, interference with a criminal, counterterrorism, or counterintelligence investigation, interference with diplomatic relations, or danger to the life or physical safety of any person, no wire or electronic communications service provider, or officer, employee, or agent thereof, shall disclose to any person (other than those to whom such disclosure is necessary to comply with the request or an attorney to obtain legal advice or legal assistance with respect to the request) that the Federal Bureau of Investigation has sought or obtained access to information or records under this section.

"(2) The request shall notify the person or entity to whom the request is directed of the nondisclosure requirement under paragraph (1).

"(3) Any recipient disclosing to those persons necessary to comply with the request or to an attorney to obtain legal advice or legal assistance with respect to the request shall inform such person of any applicable nondisclosure requirement. Any person who receives a disclosure under this subsection shall be subject to the same prohibitions on disclosure under paragraph (1).

"(4) At the request of the Director of the Federal Bureau of Investigation or the designee of the Director, any person making or intending to make a disclosure under this section shall identify to the Director or such designee the person to whom such disclosure will be made or to whom such disclosure was made prior to the request, but in no circumstance shall a person be required to inform the Director or such designee that the person intends to consult an attorney to obtain legal advice or legal assistance.".

(b) Section 626(d) of the Fair Credit Reporting Act (15 U.S.C. §1681u(d)) is amended to read:

"(d) CONFIDENTIALITY.—

"(1) If the Director of the Federal Bureau of Investigation, or his designee in a position not lower than Deputy Assistant Director at Bureau headquarters or a Special Agent in Charge in a Bureau field office designated by the Director, certifies that otherwise there may result a danger to the national security of the United States, interference with a criminal, counterterrorism, or counterintelligence investigation, interference with diplomatic relations, or danger to the life or physical safety of any person, no consumer reporting agency or officer, employee, or agent of a consumer reporting agency shall disclose to any person (other than those to whom such disclosure is necessary to comply with the request or an attorney to obtain legal advice or legal assistance with respect to the request) that the Federal Bureau of Investigation has sought or obtained the identity of financial institutions or a consumer report respecting any consumer under subsection (a), (b), or (c), and no consumer reporting agency or officer, employee, or agent of a consumer reporting agency shall include in any consumer report any information that would indicate that the Federal Bureau of Investigation has sought or obtained such information on a consumer report.

"(2) The request shall notify the person or entity to whom the request is directed of the nondisclosure requirement under paragraph (1). "(3) Any recipient disclosing to those persons necessary to comply with the request or to an attorney to obtain legal advice or legal assistance with respect to the request shall inform such persons of any applicable nondisclosure requirement. Any person who receives a disclosure under this subsection shall be subject to the same prohibitions on disclosure under paragraph (1). "(4) At the request of the Director of the Federal Bureau of Investigation or the designee of the Director, any person making or intending to make a disclosure under this section shall identify to the Director or such designee the person to whom such disclosure will be made or to whom such disclosure was made prior to the request, but in no circumstance shall a person be required to inform the Director or such designee that the person intends to consult an attorney to obtain legal advice or legal assistance.".

(c) Section 627(c) of the Fair Credit Reporting Act (15 U.S.C. §1681v(c)) is amended to read:

"(c) CONFIDENTIALITY.—

"(1) If the head of a government agency authorized to conduct investigations of intelligence or counterintelligence activities or analysis related to international terrorism, or his designee, certifies that otherwise there may result a danger to the national security of the United States, interference with a criminal, counterterrorism, or counterintelligence investigation, interference with diplomatic relations, or danger to the life or physical safety of any person, no consumer reporting agency or officer, employee, or agent of such consumer reporting agency, shall disclose to any person (other than those to whom such disclosure is necessary to comply with the request or an attorney to obtain legal advice or legal assistance with respect to the request), or specify in any consumer report, that a government agency has sought or obtained access to information under subsection (a).

"(2) The request shall notify the person or entity to whom the request is directed of the nondisclosure requirement under paragraph (1).

"(3) Any recipient disclosing to those persons necessary to comply with the request or to any attorney to obtain legal advice or legal assistance with respect to the request shall inform such persons of any applicable nondisclosure requirement. Any person who receives a disclosure under this subsection shall be subject to the same prohibitions on disclosure under paragraph (1).

"(4) At the request of the authorized Government agency, any person making or intending to make a disclosure under this section shall identify to the requesting official of the authorized Government agency the person to whom such disclosure will be made or to whom such disclosure was made prior to the request, but in no circumstance shall a person be required to inform such requesting official that the person intends to consult an attorney to obtain legal advice or legal assistance.".

(d) Section 1114(a)(3) of the Right to Financial Privacy Act (12 U.S.C. §3414(a)(3)) is amended to read as follows:

"(3)(A) If the Government authority described in paragraph (1) or the Secret Service, as the case may be, certifies that otherwise there may result a danger to the national security of the United States, interference with a criminal, counterterrorism, or counterintelligence investigation, interference with diplomatic relations, or danger to the life or physical safety of any person, no financial institution, or officer, employee, or agent of such institution, shall disclose to any person (other than those to whom such disclosure is necessary to comply with the request or an attorney to obtain legal advice or legal assistance with respect to the request) that the Government authority or the Secret Service has sought or obtained access to a customer's financial records.

"(B) The request shall notify the person or entity to whom the request is directed of the nondisclosure requirement under subparagraph (A).

"(C) Any recipient disclosing to those persons necessary to comply with the request or to an attorney to obtain legal advice or legal assistance with respect to the request shall inform such persons of any applicable nondisclosure requirement. Any person who receives a disclosure under this subsection shall be subject to the same prohibitions on disclosure under subparagraph (A).

"(D) At the request of the authorized Government agency or the Secret Service, any person making or intending to make a disclosure under this section shall identify to the requesting official of the authorized Government agency or the Secret Service the person to whom such disclosure will be made or to whom such disclosure was made prior to the request, but in no circumstance shall a person be required to inform such requesting official that the person intends to consult an attorney to obtain legal advice or legal assistance.".

(e) Section 1114(a)(5)(D) of the Right to Financial Privacy Act (12 U.S.C. §3414(a)(5)(D)) is amended to read:

"(D) PROHIBITION OF CERTAIN DISCLOSURE.—

"(i) If the Director of the Federal Bureau of Investigation, or his designee in a position not lower than Deputy Assistant Director at Bureau headquarters or a Special Agent in Charge in a Bureau field office designated by the Director, certifies that otherwise there may result a danger to the national security of the United States, interference with a criminal, counterterrorism, or counterintelligence investigation, interference with diplomatic relations, or danger to the life or physical safety of any person, no financial institution, or officer, employee, or agent of such institution, shall disclose to any person (other than those to whom such disclosure is necessary to comply with the request or an attorney to obtain legal advice or legal assistance with respect to the request) that the Federal Bureau of Investigation has sought or obtained access to a customer's or entity's financial records under subparagraph (A).

"(ii) The request shall notify the person or entity to whom the request is directed of the nondisclosure requirement under clause (i).

"(iii) Any recipient disclosing to those persons necessary to comply with the request or to an attorney to obtain legal advice or legal assistance with respect to the request shall inform such persons of any applicable nondisclosure requirement. Any person who receives a disclosure under this subsection shall be subject to the same prohibitions on disclosure under clause (i).

"(iv) At the request of the Director of the Federal Bureau of Investigation or the designee of the Director, any person making or intending to make a disclosure under this section shall identify to the Director or such designee the person to whom such disclosure will be made or to whom such disclosure was made prior to the request, but in no circumstance shall a person be required to inform the Director or such designee that the person intends to consult an attorney to obtain legal advice or legal assistance.".

(f) Section 802(b) of the National Security Act of 1947 (50 U.S.C. §436(b)) is amended to read as follows:

"(b) PROHIBITIONS OF CERTAIN DISCLOSURE.—

"(1) If an authorized investigative agency described in subsection (a) certifies that otherwise there may result a danger to the national security of the United States, interference with a criminal, counterterrorism, or counterintelligence investigation, interference with diplomatic relations, or danger to the life or physical safety of any person, no governmental or private entity, or officer, employee, or agent of such entity, may disclose to any person (other than those to whom such disclosure is necessary to comply with the request or an attorney to obtain legal advice or legal assistance with respect to the request) that such entity has received or satisfied a request made by an authorized investigative agency under this section.

"(2) The request shall notify the person or entity to whom the request is directed of the nondisclosure requirement under paragraph (1).

"(3) Any recipient disclosing to those persons necessary to comply with the request or to an attorney to obtain legal advice or legal assistance with respect to the request shall inform such persons of any applicable nondisclosure requirement. Any person who receives a disclosure under this subsection shall be subject to the same prohibitions on disclosure under paragraph (1).

"(4) At the request of the authorized investigative agency, any person making or intending to make a disclosure under this section shall identify to the requesting official of the authorized investigative agency the person to whom such disclosure will be made or to whom such disclosure was made prior to the request, but in no circumstance shall a person be required to inform such official that the person intends to consult an attorney to obtain legal advice or legal assistance.".

VIOLATIONS OF NONDISCLOSURE PROVISIONS OF NATIONAL SECURITY LETTERS

SEC. 117. Section 1510 of title 18, United States Code, is amended by adding at the end the following:

"(e) Whoever, having been notified of the applicable disclosure prohibitions or confidentiality requirements of section 2709(c)(1) of this title, section 626(d)(1) or 627(c)(1) of the Fair Credit Reporting Act (15 U.S.C. §1681u(d)(1) or 1681v(c)(1)), section 1114(a)(3)(A) or 1114(a)(5)(D)(i) of the Right to Financial Privacy Act (12 U.S.C. §3414(a)(3)(A) or 3414(a)(5)(D)(i)), or section 802(b)(1) of the National Security Act of 1947 (50 U.S.C. §436(b)(1)), knowingly and with the intent to obstruct an investigation or judicial proceeding violates such prohibitions or requirements applicable by law to such person shall be imprisoned for not more than five years, fined under this title, or both.".

REPORTS ON NATIONAL SECURITY LETTERS

SEC. 118.

(a) EXISTING REPORTS.—Any report made to a committee of Congress regarding national security letters under section 2709(c)(1) of title 18, United States Code, section 626(d) or 627(c) of the Fair Credit Reporting Act (15 U.S.C. §1681u(d) or 1681v(c)), section 1114(a)(3) or 1114(a)(5)(D) of the Right to Financial Privacy Act (12 U.S.C. §3414(a)(3) or 3414(a)(5)(D)), or section 802(b) of the National Security Act of 1947 (50 U.S.C. §436(b)) shall also be made to the Committees on the Judiciary of the House of Representatives and the Senate.

(b) ENHANCED OVERSIGHT OF FAIR CREDIT REPORTING ACT COUNTERTERRORISM NATIONAL SECURITY LETTER.—Section 627 of the Fair Credit Reporting Act (15 U.S.C. §1681(v)) is amended by inserting at the end the following new subsection:

"(f) REPORTS TO CONGRESS.—

"(1) On a semi-annual basis, the Attorney General shall fully inform the Committee on the Judiciary, the Committee on Financial Services, and the Permanent Select Committee on Intelligence of the House of Representatives and the Committee on the Judiciary, the Committee on Banking, Housing, and Urban Affairs, and the Select Committee on Intelligence of the Senate concerning all requests made pursuant to subsection (a).

"(2) In the case of the semiannual reports required to be submitted under paragraph (1) to the Permanent Select Committee on Intelligence of the House of Representatives and the Select Committee on Intelligence of the Senate, the submittal dates for such reports shall be as provided in section 507 of the National Security Act of 1947 (50 U.S.C. §415b).".

(c) REPORT ON REQUESTS FOR NATIONAL SECURITY LETTERS.—

(1) IN GENERAL.—In April of each year, the Attorney General shall submit to Congress an aggregate report setting forth with respect to the preceding year the total number of requests made by the Department of Justice for information concerning different United States persons under—

(A) section 2709 of title 18, United States Code (to access certain communication service provider records), excluding the number of requests for subscriber information;

(B) section 1114 of the Right to Financial Privacy Act (12 U.S.C. §3414) (to obtain financial institution customer records);

(C) section 802 of the National Security Act of 1947 (50 U.S.C. §436) (to obtain financial information, records, and consumer reports);

(D) section 626 of the Fair Credit Reporting Act (15 U.S.C. §1681u) (to obtain certain financial information and consumer reports); and

(E) section 627 of the Fair Credit Reporting Act (15 U.S.C. §1681v) (to obtain credit agency consumer records for counterterrorism investigations).

(2) UNCLASSIFIED FORM.—The report under this section shall be submitted in unclassified form.

(d) NATIONAL SECURITY LETTER DEFINED.—In this section, the term "national security letter" means a request for information under one of the following provisions of law:

(1) Section 2709(a) of title 18, United States Code (to access certain communication service provider records).

(2) Section 1114(a)(5)(A) of the Right to Financial Privacy Act (12 U.S.C. §3414(a)(5)(A)) (to obtain financial institution customer records).

(3) Section 802 of the National Security Act of 1947 (50 U.S.C. §436) (to obtain financial information, records, and consumer reports).

(4) Section 626 of the Fair Credit Reporting Act (15 U.S.C. §1681u) (to obtain certain financial information and consumer reports).

(5) Section 627 of the Fair Credit Reporting Act (15 U.S.C. §1681v) (to obtain credit agency consumer records for counterterrorism investigations).

AUDIT OF USE OF NATIONAL SECURITY LETTERS

SEC. 119.

(a) AUDIT.—The Inspector General of the Department of Justice shall perform an audit of the effectiveness and use, including any improper or illegal use, of national security letters issued by the Department of Justice.

(b) REQUIREMENTS.—The audit required under subsection (a) shall include—

(1) an examination of the use of national security letters by the Department of Justice during calendar years 2003 through 2006;

(2) a description of any noteworthy facts or circumstances relating to such use, including any improper or illegal use of such authority; and

(3) an examination of the effectiveness of national security letters as an investigative tool, including—

(A) the importance of the information acquired by the Department of Justice to the intelligence activities of the Department of Justice or to any other department or agency of the Federal Government;

(B) the manner in which such information is collected, retained, analyzed, and disseminated by the Department of Justice, including any direct access to such information (such as access to "raw data") provided to any other department, agency, or instrumentality of Federal, State, local, or tribal governments or any private sector entity;

(C) whether, and how often, the Department of Justice utilized such information to produce an analytical intelligence product for distribution within the Department of Justice, to the intelligence community (as such term is defined in section 3(4) of the National Security Act of 1947 (50 U.S.C. §401a(4))), or to other Federal, State, local, or tribal government departments, agencies, or instrumentalities;

(D) whether, and how often, the Department of Justice provided such information to law enforcement authorities for use in criminal proceedings;

(E) with respect to national security letters issued following the date of the enactment of this Act, an examination of the number of occasions in which the Department of Justice, or an officer or employee of the Department of Justice, issued a national security letter without the certification necessary to require the recipient of such letter to comply with the nondisclosure and confidentiality requirements potentially applicable under law; and

(F) the types of electronic communications and transactional information obtained through requests for information under section 2709 of title 18, United States Code, including the types of dialing, routing, addressing, or signaling information obtained, and the procedures the Department of Justice uses if content information is obtained through the use of such authority.

(c) SUBMISSION DATES.—

(1) PRIOR YEARS.—Not later than one year after the date of the enactment of this Act, or upon completion of the audit under this section for calendar years 2003 and 2004, whichever is earlier, the Inspector General of the De-

partment of Justice shall submit to the Committee on the Judiciary and the Permanent Select Committee on Intelligence of the House of Representatives and the Committee on the Judiciary and the Select Committee on Intelligence of the Senate a report containing the results of the audit conducted under this subsection for calendar years 2003 and 2004.

(2) CALENDAR YEARS 2005 AND 2006.—Not later than December 31, 2007, or upon completion of the audit under this subsection for calendar years 2005 and 2006, whichever is earlier, the Inspector General of the Department of Justice shall submit to the Committee on the Judiciary and the Permanent Select Committee on Intelligence of the House of Representatives and the Committee on the Judiciary and the Select Committee on Intelligence of the Senate a report containing the results of the audit conducted under this subsection for calendar years 2005 and 2006.

(d) PRIOR NOTICE TO ATTORNEY GENERAL AND DIRECTOR OF NATIONAL INTELLIGENCE; COMMENTS.—

(1) NOTICE.—Not less than 30 days before the submission of a report under subsection (c)(1) or (c)(2), the Inspector General of the Department of Justice shall provide such report to the Attorney General and the Director of National Intelligence.

(2) COMMENTS.—The Attorney General or the Director of National Intelligence may provide comments to be included in the reports submitted under subsection (c)(1) or (c)(2) as the Attorney General or the Director of National Intelligence may consider necessary.

(e) UNCLASSIFIED FORM.—The reports submitted under subsection (c)(1) or (c)(2) and any comments included under subsection (d)(2) shall be in unclassified form, but may include a classified annex.

(f) MINIMIZATION PROCEDURES FEASIBILITY.—Not later than February 1, 2007, or upon completion of review of the report submitted under subsection (c)(1), whichever is earlier, the Attorney General and the Director of National Intelligence shall jointly submit to the Committee on the Judiciary and the Permanent Select Committee on Intelligence of the House of Representatives and the Committee on the Judiciary and the Select Committee on Intelligence of the Senate a report on the feasibility of applying minimization procedures in the context of national security letters to ensure the protection of the constitutional rights of United States persons.

(g) NATIONAL SECURITY LETTER DEFINED.—In this section, the term "national security letter" means a request for information under one of the following provisions of law:

(1) Section 2709(a) of title 18, United States Code (to access certain communication service provider records).

(2) Section 1114(a)(5)(A) of the Right to Financial Privacy Act (12 U.S.C. §3414(a)(5)(A)) (to obtain financial institution customer records).

(3) Section 802 of the National Security Act of 1947 (50 U.S.C. §436) (to obtain financial information, records, and consumer reports).

(4) Section 626 of the Fair Credit Reporting Act (15 U.S.C. §1681u) (to obtain certain financial information and consumer reports).
(5) Section 627 of the Fair Credit Reporting Act (15 U.S.C. §1681v) (to obtain credit agency consumer records for counterterrorism investigations).

USA PATRIOT ACT SECTION 214; AUTHORITY FOR DISCLOSURE OF ADDITIONAL INFORMATION IN CONNECTION WITH ORDERS FOR PEN REGISTER AND TRAP AND TRACE AUTHORITY UNDER FISA

SEC. 128.

(a) RECORDS.—Section 402(d)(2) of the Foreign Intelligence Surveillance Act of 1978 (50 U.S.C. §1842(d)(2)) is amended—

(1) in subparagraph (A)—

(A) in clause (ii), by adding "and" at the end; and

(B) in clause (iii), by striking the period at the end and inserting a semicolon;

(2) in subparagraph (B)(iii), by striking the period at the end and inserting "; and"; and

(3) by adding at the end the following:

"(C) shall direct that, upon the request of the applicant, the provider of a wire or electronic communication service shall disclose to the Federal officer using the pen register or trap and trace device covered by the order—

"(i) in the case of the customer or subscriber using the service covered by the order (for the period specified by the order)—

"(I) the name of the customer or subscriber;

"(II) the address of the customer or subscriber;

"(III) the telephone or instrument number, or other subscriber number or identifier, of the customer or subscriber, including any temporarily assigned network address or associated routing or transmission information;

"(IV) the length of the provision of service by such provider to the customer or subscriber and the types of services utilized by the customer or subscriber;

"(V) in the case of a provider of local or long distance telephone service, any local or long distance telephone records of the customer or subscriber;

"(VI) if applicable, any records reflecting period of usage (or sessions) by the customer or subscriber; and "(VII) any mechanisms and sources of payment for such service, including the number of any credit card or bank account utilized for payment for such service; and

"(ii) if available, with respect to any customer or subscriber of incoming or outgoing communications to or from the service covered by the order—

"(I) the name of such customer or subscriber;
"(II) the address of such customer or subscriber;
"(III) the telephone or instrument number, or other subscriber number or identifier, of such customer or subscriber, including any temporarily assigned network address or associated routing or transmission information; and
"(IV) the length of the provision of service by such provider to such customer or subscriber and the types of services utilized by such customer or subscriber.".

USA PATRIOT Act
Additional Reauthorizing Amendments Act of 2006

(Pub. L. No. 109-178, 120 Stat. 278)

> An Act To clarify that individuals who receive FISA orders can challenge nondisclosure requirements, that individuals who receive national security letters are not required to disclose the name of their attorney, that libraries are not wire or electronic communication service providers unless they provide specific services, and for other purposes.
>
> Be it enacted by the Senate and House of Representatives of the United States of America in Congress assembled,

SEC. 1. SHORT TITLE.
This Act may be cited as the "USA PATRIOT Act Additional Reauthorizing Amendments Act of 2006."

SEC. 2. DEFINITION.
As used in this Act, the term "applicable Act" means the Act entitled "An Act to extend and modify authorities needed to combat terrorism, and for other purposes." (109th Congress, 2d Session).

SEC. 3. JUDICIAL REVIEW OF FISA ORDERS.
Subsection (f) of section 501 of the Foreign Intelligence Surveillance Act of 1978 (50 U.S.C. 1861), as amended by the applicable Act, is amended to read as follows:

"(f)(1) In this subsection—

"(A) the term "production order" means an order to produce any tangible thing under this section; and

"(B) the term "nondisclosure order" means an order imposed under subsection (d).

"(2)(A)(i) A person receiving a production order may challenge the legality of that order by filing a petition with the pool established by section 103(e)(1). Not less than 1 year after the date of the issuance of the production order, the recipient of a production order may challenge the nondisclosure order imposed in connection with such production order by filing a petition to modify or set aside such nondisclosure order, consistent with the requirements of subparagraph (C), with the pool established by section 103(e)(1).

"(ii) The presiding judge shall immediately assign a petition under clause (i) to 1 of the judges serving in the pool established by section 103(e)(1). Not later than 72 hours after the assignment of such petition, the assigned judge shall conduct an initial review of the petition. If the assigned judge determines that the petition is frivolous, the assigned judge shall immediately deny the petition and affirm the production order or nondisclosure order. If the assigned judge determines the petition is not frivolous, the assigned judge shall promptly consider the petition in accordance with the procedures established under section 103(e)(2).

"(iii) The assigned judge shall promptly provide a written statement for the record of the reasons for any determination under this subsection. Upon the request of the Government, any order setting aside a nondisclosure order shall be stayed pending review pursuant to paragraph (3).

"(B) A judge considering a petition to modify or set aside a production order may grant such petition only if the judge finds that such order does not meet the requirements of this section or is otherwise unlawful. If the judge does not modify or set aside the production order, the judge shall immediately affirm such order, and order the recipient to comply therewith.

"(C)(i) A judge considering a petition to modify or set aside a nondisclosure order may grant such petition only if the judge finds that there is no reason to believe that disclosure may endanger the national security of the United States, interfere with a criminal, counterterrorism, or counterintelligence investigation, interfere with diplomatic relations, or endanger the life or physical safety of any person.

"(ii) If, upon filing of such a petition, the Attorney General, Deputy Attorney General, an Assistant Attorney General, or the Director of the Federal Bureau of Investigation certifies that disclosure may endanger the national security of the United States or interfere with diplomatic relations, such certification shall be treated as conclusive, unless the judge finds that the certification was made in bad faith.

"(iii) If the judge denies a petition to modify or set aside a nondisclosure order, the recipient of such order shall be precluded for a period of 1 year from filing another such petition with respect to such nondisclosure order.

"(D) Any production or nondisclosure order not explicitly modified or set aside consistent with this subsection shall remain in full effect.

"(3) A petition for review of a decision under paragraph (2) to affirm, modify, or set aside an order by the Government or any person receiving such order shall be made to the court of review established under section 103(b), which shall have jurisdiction to consider such petitions. The court of review shall provide for the record a written statement of the reasons for its decision and, on petition by the Government or any person receiving such order for writ of certiorari, the record shall be transmitted under seal to the Supreme Court of the United States, which shall have jurisdiction to review such decision.

"(4) Judicial proceedings under this subsection shall be concluded as expeditiously as possible. The record of proceedings, including petitions filed, orders granted, and statements of reasons for decision, shall be maintained under security measures established by the Chief Justice of the United States, in consultation with the Attorney General and the Director of National Intelligence.

"(5) All petitions under this subsection shall be filed under seal. In any proceedings under this subsection, the court shall, upon request of the Government, review ex parte and in camera any Government submission, or portions thereof, which may include classified information."

SEC. 4. DISCLOSURES.

(a) FISA—Subparagraph (C) of section 501(d)(2) of the Foreign Intelligence Surveillance Act of 1978 (50 U.S.C. 1861(d)(2)), as amended by the applicable Act, is amended to read as follows:

"(C) At the request of the Director of the Federal Bureau of Investigation or the designee of the Director, any person making or intending to make a disclosure under subparagraph (A) or (C) of paragraph (1) shall identify to the Director or such designee the person to whom such disclosure will be made or to whom such disclosure was made prior to the request."

(b) Title 18—Paragraph (4) of section 2709(c) of title 18, United States Code, as amended by the applicable Act, is amended to read as follows:

"(4) At the request of the Director of the Federal Bureau of Investigation or the designee of the Director, any person making or intending to make a disclosure under this section shall identify to the Director or such designee the person to whom such disclosure will be made or to whom such disclosure was made prior to the request, except that nothing in this section shall require a person to inform the Director or such designee of the identity of an attorney to whom disclosure was made or will be made to obtain legal advice or legal assistance with respect to the request under subsection (a)."

(c) Fair Credit Reporting Act—

(1) IN GENERAL—Paragraph (4) of section 626(d) of the Fair Credit Reporting Act (15 U.S.C. 1681u(d)), as amended by the applicable Act, is amended to read as follows:

"(4) At the request of the Director of the Federal Bureau of Investigation or the designee of the Director, any person making or intending to make a disclosure under this section shall identify to the Director or such designee the person to whom such disclosure will be made or to whom such disclosure was made prior to the request, except that nothing in this section shall require a person to inform the Director or such designee of the identity of an attorney to whom disclosure was made or will be made to obtain legal advice or legal assistance with respect to the request for the identity of financial institutions or a consumer report respecting any consumer under this section."

(2) OTHER AGENCIES—Paragraph (4) of section 627(c) of the Fair Credit Reporting Act (15 U.S.C. 1681v(c)), as amended by the applicable Act, is amended to read as follows:

"(4) At the request of the authorized government agency, any person making or intending to make a disclosure under this section shall identify to the requesting official of the authorized government agency the person to whom such disclosure will be made or to whom such disclosure was made prior to the request, except that nothing in this section shall require a person to inform the requesting official of the identity of an attorney to whom disclosure was made or will be made to obtain legal advice or legal assistance with respect to the request for information under subsection (a)."

(d) Right to Financial Privacy Act—

(1) IN GENERAL—Subparagraph (D) of section 1114(a)(3) of the Right to Financial Privacy Act (12 U.S.C. 3414(a)(3)), as amended by the applicable Act, is amended to read as follows:

"(D) At the request of the authorized Government authority or the Secret Service, any person making or intending to make a disclosure under this section shall identify to the requesting official of the authorized Government authority or the Secret Service the person to whom such disclosure will be made or to whom such disclosure was made prior to the request, except that nothing in this section shall require a person to inform the requesting official of the authorized Government authority or the Secret Service of the identity of an attorney to whom disclosure was made or will be made to obtain legal advice or legal assistance with respect to the request for financial records under this subsection."

(2) FEDERAL BUREAU OF INVESTIGATION—Clause (iv) of section 1114(a)(5)(D) of the Right to Financial Privacy Act (12 U.S.C. 3414(a)(5)(D)), as amended by the applicable Act, is amended to read as follows:

"(iv) At the request of the Director of the Federal Bureau of Investigation or the designee of the Director, any person making or intending to make a disclosure under this section shall identify to the Director or such designee the person to whom such disclosure will be made or to whom such disclosure was made prior to the request, except that nothing in this section shall require a person to inform the Director or such designee of the identity of an attorney to whom disclosure was made or will be made to obtain legal advice or legal assistance with respect to the request for financial records under subparagraph (A)."

(e) National Security Act of 1947—Paragraph (4) of section 802(b) of the National Security Act of 1947 (50 U.S.C. 436(b)), as amended by the applicable Act, is amended to read as follows:

"(4) At the request of the authorized investigative agency, any person making or intending to make a disclosure under this section shall identify to the requesting official of the authorized investigative agency the person to whom such disclosure will be made or to whom such disclosure was made prior to the request, except that nothing in this section shall require a person to inform the requesting official of the identity of an attorney to whom disclosure was made or will be made to obtain legal advice or legal assistance with respect to the request under subsection (a)."

SEC. 5. PRIVACY PROTECTIONS FOR LIBRARY PATRONS.

Section 2709 of title 18, United States Code, as amended by the applicable Act, is amended by adding at the end the following:

"(f) Libraries—A library (as that term is defined in section 213(1) of the Library Services and Technology Act (20 U.S.C. 9122(1)), the services of which include access to the Internet, books, journals, magazines, newspapers, or other similar forms of communication in print or digitally by patrons for their use, review, examination, or circulation, is not a wire or electronic communication service provider for purposes of this section, unless the library is providing the services defined in section 2510(15) (`electronic communication service') of this title."

This Act shall become effective immediately upon enactment.

Classified Information Procedures Act

(Pub. L. 96–456 of October 15, 1980; 94 Stat. 2025)

AN ACT To provide certain pretrial, trial, and appellate procedures for crimi]nal cases involving classified information.

Be it enacted by the Senate and House of Representatives of the United States of America in Congress assembled,

DEFINITIONS

SEC. 1. [18 U.S.C. App. §1]

(a) ''Classified information'', as used in this Act, means any information or material that has been determined by the United States Government pursuant to an Executive order, statute, or regulation, to require protection against unauthorized disclosure for reasons of national security and any restricted data, as defined in paragraph r. of section 11 of the Atomic Energy Act of 1954 (42 U.S.C. 2014(y)).

(b) ''National security'', as used in this Act, means the national defense and foreign relations of the United States.

PRETRIAL CONFERENCE

SEC. 2. [18 U.S.C. App. §2]

At any time after the filing of the indictment or information, any party may move for a pretrial conference to consider matters relating to classified information that may arise in connection with the prosecution. Following such motion, or on its own motion, the court shall promptly hold a pretrial conference to establish the timing of requests for discovery, the provision of notice required by section 5 of this Act, and the initiation of the procedure established by section 6 of this Act. In addition, at the pretrial conference the court may consider any matters which relate to classified information or which may promote a fair and expeditious trial. No admission made by the defendant or by any attorney for the defendant at such a conference may be used against the defendant unless the admission is in writing and is signed by the defendant and by the attorney for the defendant.

PROTECTIVE ORDERS

SEC. 3. [18 U.S.C. App. §3]

Upon motion of the United States, the court shall issue an order to protect against the disclosure of any classified information disclosed by the United States to any defendant in any criminal case in a district court of the United States.

DISCOVERY OF CLASSIFIED INFORMATION BY DEFENDANTS

SEC. 4. [18 U.S.C. App. §4]

The court, upon a sufficient showing, may authorize the United States to delete specified items of classified information from documents to be made available to the defendant through discovery under the Federal Rules of Criminal Procedure, to substitute a summary of the information for such classified documents, or to substitute a statement admitting relevant facts that the classified information would tend to prove. The court may permit the United States to make a request for such authorization in the form of a written statement to be inspected by the court alone. If the court enters an order granting relief following such an ex parte showing, the entire text of the statement of the United States shall be sealed and preserved in the records of the court to be made available to the appellate court in the event of an appeal.

NOTICE OF DEFENDANT'S INTENTION TO DISCLOSE CLASSIFIED INFORMATION

SEC. 5. [18 U.S.C. App. §5]

(a) Notice by Defendant.—If a defendant reasonably expects to disclose or to cause the disclosure of classified information in any manner in connection with any trial or pretrial proceeding involving the criminal prosecution of such defendant, the defendant shall, within the time specified by the court or, where no time is specified, within thirty days prior to trial, notify the attorney for the United States and the court in writing. Such notice shall include a brief description of the classified information. Whenever a defendant learns of additional classified information he reasonably expects to disclose at any such proceeding, he shall notify the attorney for the United States and the court in writing as soon as possible thereafter and shall include a brief description of the classified information. No defendant shall disclose any information known or believed to be classified in connection with a trial or pretrial proceeding until notice has been given under this subsection and until the United States has been afforded a reasonable opportunity to seek a determination pursuant to the procedure set forth in section 6 of this Act, and until the time for the United States to appeal such determination under section 7 has expired or any appeal under section 7 by the United States is decided.

(b) Failure to Comply.—If the defendant fails to comply with the requirements of subsection (a) the court may preclude disclosure of any classified information not made the subject of notification and may prohibit the examination by the defendant of any witness with respect to any such information.

PROCEDURE FOR CASES INVOLVING CLASSIFIED INFORMATION

SEC. 6. [18 U.S.C. App. §6]

(a) Motion for Hearing.—Within the time specified by the court for the filing of a motion under this section, the United States may request the court to conduct a hearing to make all determinations concerning the use, relevance, or admissibility of classified information that would otherwise be made during the trial or pretrial proceeding. Upon such a request, the court shall conduct such a hearing. Any hearing held pursuant to this subsection (or any portion of such hearing specified in the request of the Attorney General) shall be held in camera if the Attorney General certifies to the court in such petition that a public proceeding may result in the disclosure of classified information. As to each item of classified information, the court shall set forth in writing the basis for its determination. Where the United States' motion under this subsection is filed prior to the trial or pretrial proceeding, the court shall rule prior to the commencement of the relevant proceeding.

(b) Notice.—

(1) Before any hearing is conducted pursuant to a request by the United States under subsection (a), the United States shall provide the defendant with notice of the classified information that is at issue. Such notice shall identify the specific classified information at issue whenever that information previously has been made available to the defendant by the United States. When the United States has not previously made the information available to the defendant in connection with the case, the information may be described by generic category, in such forms as the court may approve, rather than by identification of the specific information of concern to the United States.

(2) Whenever the United States requests a hearing under subsection (a), the court, upon request of the defendant, may order the United States to provide the defendant, prior to trial, such details as to the portion of the indictment or information at issue in the hearing as are needed to give the defendant fair notice to prepare for the hearing.

(c) Alternative Procedure for Disclosure of Classified Information.—

(1) Upon any determination by the court authorizing the disclosure of specific classified information under the procedures established by this section, the United States may move that, in lieu of the disclosure of such specific classified information, the court order—

(A) the substitution for such classified information of a statement admitting relevant facts that the specific classified information would tend to prove; or

(B) the substitution for such classified information of a summary of the specific classified information. The court shall grant such a motion of the United States if it finds that the statement or summary will provide the defendant with substantially the same ability to make his defense as would disclosure of the specific classified information. The court shall hold a hearing on any motion under this section. Any such hearing shall be held in camera at the request of the Attorney General.

(2) The United States may, in connection with a motion under paragraph (1), submit to the court an affidavit of the Attorney General certifying that disclosure of classified information would cause identifiable damage to the national security of the United States and explaining the basis for the classification of such information. If so requested by the United States, the court shall examine such affidavit in camera and ex parte.

(d) Sealing of Records of In Camera Hearings.—If at the close of an in camera hearing under this Act (or any portion of a hearing under this Act that is held in camera) the court determines that the classified information at issue may not be disclosed or elicited at the trial or pretrial proceeding, the record of such in camera hearing shall be sealed and preserved by the court for use in the event of an appeal. The defendant may seek reconsideration of the court's determination prior to or during trial.

(e) Prohibition on Disclosure of Classified Information by Defendant, Relief for Defendant When United States Opposes Disclosure.—

(1) Whenever the court denies a motion by the United States that it issue an order under subsection (c) and the United States files with the court an affidavit of the Attorney General objecting to disclosure of the classified information at issue, the court shall order that the defendant not disclose or cause the disclosure of such information.

(2) Whenever a defendant is prevented by an order under paragraph (1) from disclosing or causing the disclosure of classified information, the court shall dismiss the indictment or information; except that, when the court determines that the interests of justice would not be served by dismissal of the indictment or information, the court shall order such other action, in lieu of dismissing the indictment or information, as the court determines is appropriate. Such action may include, but need not be limited to—

(A) dismissing specified counts of the indictment or information;

(B) finding against the United States on any issue as to which the excluded classified information relates; or

(C) striking or precluding all or part of the testimony of a witness.

An order under this paragraph shall not take effect until the court has afforded the United States an opportunity to appeal such order under section 7, and thereafter to withdraw its objection to the disclosure of the classified information at issue.

(f) Reciprocity.—Whenever the court determines pursuant to subsection (a) that classified information may be disclosed in connection with a trial or pretrial proceeding, the court shall, unless the interests of fairness do not so require, order the United States to provide the defendant with the information it expects to use to rebut the classified information. The court may place the United States under a continuing duty to disclose such rebuttal information. If the United States fails to comply with its obligation under this subsection, the court may exclude any evidence not made the subject of a required disclosure and may prohibit the examination by the United States of any witness with respect to such information.

INTERLOCUTORY APPEAL

SEC. 7. [18 U.S.C. App. §7]

(a) An interlocutory appeal by the United States taken before or after the defendant has been placed in jeopardy shall lie to a court of appeals from a decision or order of a district court in a criminal case authorizing the disclosure of classified information, imposing sanctions for nondisclosure of classified information, or refusing a protective order sought by the United States to prevent the disclosure of classified information.

(b) An appeal taken pursuant to this section either before or during trial shall be expedited by the court of appeals. Prior to trial, an appeal shall be taken within ten days after the decision or order appealed from and the trial shall not commence until the appeal is resolved. If an appeal is taken during trial, the trial court shall adjourn the trial until the appeal is resolved and the court of appeals (1) shall hear argument on such appeal within four days of the adjournment of the trial, (2) may dispense with written briefs other than the supporting materials previously submitted to the trial court, (3) shall render its decision within four days of argument on appeal, and (4) may dispense with the issuance of a written opinion in rendering its decision. Such appeal and decision shall not affect the right of the defendant, in a subsequent appeal from a judgment of conviction, to claim as error reversal by the trial court on remand of a ruling appealed from during trial.

INTRODUCTION OF CLASSIFIED INFORMATION

SEC. 8. [18 U.S.C. App. §8]

(a) Classification Status.—Writings, recordings, and photographs containing classified information may be admitted into evidence without change in their classification status.

(b) Precautions by Court.—The court, in order to prevent unnecessary disclosure of classified information involved in any criminal proceeding, may order admission into evidence of only part of a writing, recording, or photograph, or may order admission into evidence of the whole writing, recording, or photograph with excision of some or all of the classified information contained therein, unless the whole ought in fairness be considered.

(c) Taking of Testimony.—During the examination of a witness in any criminal proceeding, the United States may object to any question or line of inquiry that may require the witness to disclose classified information not previously found to be admissible. Following such an objection, the court shall take such suitable action to determine whether the response is admissible as will safeguard against the compromise of any classified information. Such action may include requiring the United States to provide the court with a proffer of the witness' response to the question or line of inquiry and requiring the defendant to provide the court with a proffer of the nature of the information he seeks to elicit.

SECURITY PROCEDURES

SEC. 9. [18 U.S.C. App. §9]

(a) Within one hundred and twenty days of the date of the enactment of this Act, the Chief Justice of the United States, in consultation with the Attorney General, the Director of Central Intelligence, and the Secretary of Defense, shall prescribe rules establishing procedures for the protection against unauthorized disclosure of any classified information in the custody of the United States district courts, courts of appeal, or Supreme Court. Such rules, and any changes in such rules, shall be submitted to the appropriate committees of Congress and shall become effective forty-five days after such submission.

(b) Until such time as rules under subsection (a) first become effective, the Federal courts shall in each case involving classified information adapt procedures to protect against the unauthorized disclosure of such information.

IDENTIFICATION OF INFORMATION RELATED TO THE NATIONAL DEFENSE

SEC. 10 [18 U.S.C. App. §10]

In any prosecution in which the United States must establish that material relates to the national defense or constitutes classified information, the United States shall notify the defendant, within the time before trial specified by the court, of the portions of the material that it reasonably expects to rely upon to establish the national defense or classified information element of the offense.

AMENDMENTS TO THE ACT

SEC. 11 [18 U.S.C. App. §11]

Sections 1 through 10 of this Act may be amended as provided in section 2076, title 28, United States Code.

ATTORNEY GENERAL GUIDELINES

SEC. 12 [18 U.S.C. App. §12]

(a) Within one hundred and eighty days of enactment of this Act, the Attorney General shall issue guidelines specifying the factors to be used by the Department of Justice in rendering a decision whether to prosecute a violation of Federal law in which, in the judgment of the Attorney General, there is a possibility that classified information will be revealed. Such guidelines shall be transmitted to the appropriate committees of Congress.

(b) When the Department of Justice decides not to prosecute a violation of Federal law pursuant to subsection (a), an appropriate official of the Department of Justice shall prepare written findings detailing the reasons for the decision not to prosecute. The findings shall include—

(1) the intelligence information which the Department of Justice officials believe might be disclosed,

(2) the purpose for which the information might be disclosed,

(3) the probability that the information would be disclosed, and

(4) the possible consequences such disclosure would have on the national security.

REPORTS TO CONGRESS

(a) Consistent with applicable authorities and duties, including those conferred by the Constitution upon the executive and legislative branches, the Attorney General shall report orally or in writing semiannually to the Permanent Select Committee on Intelligence of the United States House of Representatives, the Select Committee on Intelligence of the United States Senate, and the chairmen and ranking minority members of the Committees on the Judiciary of the Senate and House of Representatives on all cases where a decision not to prosecute a violation of Federal law pursuant to section 12(a) has been made.

(b) The Attorney General shall deliver to the appropriate committees of Congress a report concerning the operation and effectiveness of this Act and including suggested amendments to this Act. For the first three years this Act is in effect, there shall be a report each year. After three years, such reports shall be delivered as necessary.

FUNCTIONS OF ATTORNEY GENERAL MAY BE EXERCISED BY DEPUTY ATTORNEY GENERAL, THE ASSOCIATE ATTORNEY GENERAL, OR A DESIGNATED ASSISTANT ATTORNEY GENERAL

SEC. 14 [18 U.S.C. App. §14]

The functions and duties of the Attorney General under this Act may be exercised by the Deputy Attorney General, the Associate Attorney General, or by an Assistant Attorney General designated by the Attorney General for such purpose and may not be delegated to any other official.

EFFECTIVE DATE

SEC. 15 [18 U.S.C. App. §15]

The provisions of this Act shall become effective upon the date of the enactment of this Act, but shall not apply to any prosecution in which an indictment or information was filed before such date.

SHORT TITLE

SEC. 16 [18 U.S.C. App. §16]

That this Act may be cited as the ''Classified Information Procedures Act".

POSSE COMITATUS ACT

18 U.S.C. § 1385. Use of Army and Air Force as posse comitatus

Whoever, except in cases and under circumstances expressly authorized by the Constitution or Act of Congress, willfully uses any part of the Army or the Air Force as a posse comitatus or otherwise to execute the laws shall be fined under this title or imprisoned not more than two years, or both.

Freedom of Information Act

(Pub. L. No. 89-554, 80 Stat. 383, as amended (as reproduced by the ODNI Intelligence Community Legal Reference Book, 2009))

SECTION 552. PUBLIC INFORMATION; AGENCY RULES, OPINIONS, ORDERS, RECORDS, AND PROCEEDINGS.

(a) Each agency shall make available to the public information as follows:

(1) Each agency shall separately state and currently publish in the Federal Register for the guidance of the public—

(A) descriptions of its central and field organization and the established places at which, the employees (and in the case of a uniformed service, the members) from whom, and the methods whereby, the public may obtain information, make submittals or requests, or obtain decisions;

(B) statements of the general course and method by which its functions are channeled and determined, including the nature and requirements of all formal and informal procedures available;

(C) rules of procedure, descriptions of forms available or the places at which forms may be obtained, and instructions as to the scope and contents of all papers, reports, or examinations;

(D) substantive rules of general applicability adopted as authorized by law, and statements of general policy or interpretations of general applicability formulated and adopted by the agency; and

(E) each amendment, revision, or repeal of the foregoing. Except to the extent that a person has actual and timely notice of the terms thereof, a person may not in any manner be required to resort to, or be adversely affected by, a matter required to be published in the Federal Register and not so published. For the purpose of this paragraph, matter reasonably available to the class of persons affected thereby is deemed published in the Federal Register when incorporated by reference therein with the approval of the Director of the Federal Register.

(2) Each agency, in accordance with published rules, shall make available for public inspection and copying—

(A) final opinions, including concurring and dissenting opinions, as well as orders, made in the adjudication of cases;

(B) those statements of policy and interpretations which have been adopted by the agency and are not published in the Federal Register;

(C) administrative staff manuals and instructions to staff that affect a member of the public;

(D) copies of all records, regardless of form or format, which have been released to any person under paragraph (3) and which, because of the nature of their subject matter, the agency determines have become or are likely to become the subject of subsequent requests for substantially the same records; and

(E) a general index of the records referred to under subparagraph (D); unless the materials are promptly published and copies offered for sale. For records created on or after November 1, 1996, within one year after such date, each agency shall make such records available, including by computer telecommunications or, if computer telecommunications means have not been established by the agency, by other electronic means. To the extent required to prevent a clearly unwarranted invasion of personal privacy, an agency may delete identifying details when it makes available or publishes an opinion, statement of policy, interpretation, staff manual, instruction, or copies of records referred to in subparagraph (D). However, in each case the justification for the deletion shall be explained fully in writing, and the extent of such deletion shall be indicated on the portion of the record which is made available or published, unless including that indication would harm an interest protected by the exemption in subsection (b) under which the deletion is made. If technically feasible, the extent of the deletion shall be indicated at the place in the record where the deletion was made. Each agency shall also maintain and make available for public inspection and copying current indexes providing identifying information for the public as to any matter issued, adopted, or promulgated after July 4, 1967, and required by this paragraph to be made available or published. Each agency shall promptly publish, quarterly or more frequently, and distribute (by sale or otherwise) copies of each index or supplements thereto unless it determines by order published in the Federal Register that the publication would be unnecessary and impracticable, in which case the agency shall nonetheless provide copies of such index on request at a cost not to exceed the direct cost of duplication. Each agency shall make the index referred to in subparagraph (E) available by computer telecommunications by December 31, 1999. A final order, opinion, statement of policy, interpretation, or staff manual or instruction that affects a member of the public may be relied on, used, or cited as precedent by an agency against a party other than an agency only if—

(i) it has been indexed and either made available or published as provided by this paragraph; or

(ii) the party has actual and timely notice of the terms thereof.

(3) (A) Except with respect to the records made available under paragraphs (1) and (2) of this subsection, and except as provided in subparagraph (E), each agency, upon any request for records which

(i) reasonably describes such records and

(ii) is made in accordance with published rules stating the time, place, fees (if any), and procedures to be followed, shall make the records promptly available to any person.

(B) In making any record available to a person under this paragraph, an agency shall provide the record in any form or format requested by the person if the record is readily reproducible by the agency in that form or format. Each agency shall make reasonable efforts to maintain its records

in forms or formats that are reproducible for purposes of this section.
(C) In responding under this paragraph to a request for records, an agency shall make reasonable efforts to search for the records in electronic form or format, except when such efforts would significantly interfere with the operation of the agency's automated information system.
(D) For purposes of this paragraph, the term "search" means to review, manually or by automated means, agency records for the purpose of locating those records which are responsive to a request.
(E) An agency, or part of an agency, that is an element of the intelligence community (as that term is defined in section 3(4) of the National Security Act of 1947 (50 U.S.C. §401a (4))) shall not make any record available under this paragraph to—

(i) any government entity, other than a State, territory, commonwealth, or district of the United States, or any subdivision thereof; or
(ii) a representative of a government entity described in clause (i).

(4) (A) (i) In order to carry out the provisions of this section, each agency shall promulgate regulations, pursuant to notice and receipt of public comment, specifying the schedule of fees applicable to the processing of requests under this section and establishing procedures and guidelines for determining when such fees should be waived or reduced. Such schedule shall conform to the guidelines which shall be promulgated, pursuant to notice and receipt of public comment, by the Director of the Office of Management and Budget and which shall provide for a uniform schedule of fees for all agencies.

(ii) Such agency regulations shall provide that—

(I) fees shall be limited to reasonable standard charges for document search, duplication, and review, when records are requested for commercial use;
(II) fees shall be limited to reasonable standard charges for document duplication when records are not sought for commercial use and the request is made by an educational or noncommercial scientific institution, whose purpose is scholarly or scientific research; or a representative of the news media; and
(III) for any request not described in (I) or (II), fees shall be limited to reasonable standard charges for document search and duplication.

In this clause, the term 'a representative of the news media' means any person or entity that gathers information of potential interest to a segment of the public, uses its editorial skills to turn the raw materials into a distinct work, and distributes that work to an audience. In this clause, the term 'news' means information that is about current events or that would be of current interest to the public. Examples of news-media entities are television or radio stations broadcasting to the public at large and publishers of periodicals (but only if such entities qualify as disseminators of 'news') who make their products available for purchase by or subscription by or free distribution to the general public. These examples are not all-inclusive. Moreover, as methods of news delivery evolve (for example, the adoption of the electronic dissemination of newspapers through telecommunications services), such alternative media shall be considered to be news-media entities. A freelance journalist shall be regarded as working for a newsmedia entity if the journalist can demonstrate a solid basis for expecting publication through that entity, whether or not the journalist is actually employed by the entity. A publication contract would present a solid basis for such an expectation; the Government may also consider the past publication record of the requester in making such a determination.

(iii) Documents shall be furnished without any charge or at a charge reduced below the fees established under clause (ii) if disclosure of the information is in the public interest because it is likely to contribute significantly to public understanding of the operations or activities of the government and is not primarily in the commercial interest of the requester.

(iv) Fee schedules shall provide for the recovery of only the direct costs of search, duplication, or review. Review costs shall include only the direct costs incurred during the initial examination of a document for the purposes of determining whether the documents must be disclosed under this section and for the purposes of withholding any portions exempt from disclosure under this section. Review costs may not include any costs incurred in resolving issues of law or policy that may be raised in the course of processing a request under this section. No fee may be charged by any agency under this section—

(I) if the costs of routine collection and processing of the fee are likely to equal or exceed the amount of the fee; or

(II) for any request described in clause (ii) (II) or

(III) of this subparagraph for the first two hours of search time or for the first one hundred pages of duplication.

(v) No agency may require advance payment of any fee unless the requester has previously failed to pay fees in a timely fashion, or the agency has determined that the fee will exceed $250.

(vi) Nothing in this subparagraph shall supersede fees chargeable under a statute specifically providing for setting the level of fees for particular types of records.

(vii) In any action by a requester regarding the waiver of fees under this section, the court shall determine the matter de novo: Provided, That the court's review of the matter shall be limited to the record before the agency.

(viii) An agency shall not assess search fees (or in the case of a requester described under clause (ii)(II), duplication fees) under this subparagraph if the agency fails to comply with any time limit under paragraph (6), if no unusual or exceptional circumstances (as those terms are defined for purposes of paragraphs (6)(B) and (C), respectively) apply to the processing of the request.

(B) On complaint, the district court of the United States in the district in which the complainant resides, or has his principal place of business, or in which the agency records are situated, or in the District of Columbia, has jurisdiction to enjoin the agency from withholding agency records and to order the production of any agency records improperly withheld from the complainant. In such a case the court shall determine the matter de novo, and may examine the contents of such agency records in camera to determine whether such records or any part thereof shall be withheld under any of the exemptions set forth in subsection (b) of this section, and the burden is on the agency to sustain its action. In addition to any other matters to which a court accords substantial weight, a court shall accord substantial weight to an affidavit of an agency concerning the agency's determination as to technical feasibility under paragraph (2)(C) and subsection (b) and reproducibility under paragraph (3)(B).

(C) Notwithstanding any other provision of law, the defendant shall serve an answer or otherwise plead to any complaint made under this subsection within thirty days after service upon the defendant of the pleading in which such complaint is made, unless the court otherwise directs for good cause shown.

(D) Repealed. Pub. L. 98–620, title IV, §402(2), Nov. 8, 1984, 98 Stat. 3357.

(E) (i) The court may assess against the United States reasonable attorney fees and other litigation costs reasonably incurred in any case under this section in which the complainant has substantially prevailed.

(ii) For purposes of this subparagraph, a complainant has substantially prevailed if the complainant has obtained relief through either—

(I) a judicial order, or an enforceable written agreement or consent decree; or

(II) a voluntary or unilateral change in position by the agency, if the complainant's claim is not insubstantial.

(F) (i) Whenever the court orders the production of any agency records improperly withheld from the complainant and assesses against the United States reasonable attorney fees and other litigation costs, and the court additionally issues a written finding that the circumstances surrounding the withholding raise questions whether agency personnel acted arbitrarily or capriciously with respect to the withholding, the Special Counsel shall promptly initiate a proceeding to determine whether disciplinary action is warranted against the officer or employee who was primarily responsible for the withholding. The Special Counsel, after investigation and consideration of the evidence submitted, shall submit his findings and recommendations to the administrative authority of the agency concerned and shall send copies of the findings and recommendations to the officer or employee or his representative. The administrative authority shall take the corrective action that the Special Counsel recommends.

(ii) The Attorney General shall—

(I) notify the Special Counsel of each civil action described under the first sentence of clause (i); and

(II) annually submit a report to Congress on the number of such civil actions in the preceding year.

(iii) The Special Counsel shall annually submit a report to Congress on the actions taken by the Special Counsel under clause (i).

(G) In the event of noncompliance with the order of the court, the district court may punish for contempt the responsible employee, and in the case of a uniformed service, the responsible member.

(5) Each agency having more than one member shall maintain and make available for public inspection a record of the final votes of each member in every agency proceeding.

(6) (A) Each agency, upon any request for records made under paragraph (1), (2), or (3) of this subsection, shall—

(i) determine within 20 days (excepting Saturdays, Sundays, and legal public holidays) after the receipt of any such request whether to comply with such request and shall immediately notify the person making such request of such determination and the reasons therefor, and of the right of such person to appeal to the head of the agency any adverse determination; and

(ii) make a determination with respect to any appeal within twenty days (excepting Saturdays, Sundays, and legal public holidays) after the receipt of such appeal. If on appeal the denial of the request for records is in whole or in part upheld, the agency shall notify the person making such request of the provisions for judicial review of that determination under paragraph (4) of this subsection. The 20-day period under clause (i) shall commence on the date on which the request is first received by the appropriate component of the agency, but in any event not later than ten days after the request is first received by any component of the agency that is designated in the agency's regulations under this section to receive requests under this section. The 20-day period shall not be tolled by the agency except—

(I) that the agency may make one request to the requester for information and toll the 20-day period while it is awaiting such information that it has reasonably requested from the requester under this section; or

(II) if necessary to clarify with the requester issues regarding fee assessment. In either case, the agency's receipt of the requester's response to the agency's request for information or clarification ends the tolling period.

(B) (i) In unusual circumstances as specified in this subparagraph, the time limits prescribed in either clause (i) or clause (ii) of subparagraph (A) may be extended by written notice to the person making such request setting forth the unusual circumstances for such extension and the date on which a determination is expected to be dispatched. No such notice shall specify a date that would result in an extension for more than ten working days, except as provided in clause (ii) of this subparagraph.

(ii) With respect to a request for which a written notice under clause (i) extends the time limits prescribed under clause (i) of subparagraph (A), the agency shall notify the person making the request if the request cannot be processed within the time limit specified in that clause and shall provide the person an opportunity to limit the scope of the request so that it may be processed within that time limit or an opportunity to arrange with the agency an alternative time frame for processing the request or a modified request. To aid the requester, each agency shall make available its FOIA Public Liaison, who shall assist in the resolution of any disputes between the requester and the agency. Refusal by the person to reasonably modify the request or arrange such an alternative time frame shall be considered as a factor in determining whether exceptional circumstances exist for purposes of subparagraph (C).

(iii) As used in this subparagraph, "unusual circumstances" means, but only to the extent reasonably necessary to the proper processing of the particular requests—

(I) the need to search for and collect the requested records from field facilities or other establishments that are separate from the office processing the request;

(II) the need to search for, collect, and appropriately examine a voluminous amount of separate and distinct records which are demanded in a single request; or

(III) the need for consultation, which shall be conducted with all practicable speed, with another agency having a substantial interest in the determination of the request or among two or more components of the agency having substantial subject-matter interest therein.

(iv) Each agency may promulgate regulations, pursuant to notice and receipt of public comment, providing for the aggregation of certain requests by the same requestor, or by a group of requestors acting in concert, if the agency reasonably believes that such requests actually constitute a single request, which would otherwise satisfy the unusual circumstances specified in this subparagraph, and the requests involve clearly related matters. Multiple requests involving unrelated matters shall not be aggregated.

(C) (i) Any person making a request to any agency for records under paragraph (1), (2), or (3) of this subsection shall be deemed to have exhausted his administrative remedies with respect to such request if the agency fails to comply with the applicable time limit provisions of this paragraph. If the Government can show exceptional circumstances exist and that the agency is exercising due diligence in responding to the request, the court may retain jurisdiction and allow the agency additional time to complete its review of the records. Upon any determination by an agency to comply with a request for records, the records shall be made promptly available to such person making such request. Any notification of denial of any request for records under this subsection shall set forth the names and titles or positions of each person responsible for the denial of such request.

(ii) For purposes of this subparagraph, the term "exceptional circumstances" does not include a delay that results from a predictable agency workload of requests under this section, unless the agency demonstrates reasonable progress in reducing its backlog of pending requests.

(iii) Refusal by a person to reasonably modify the scope of a request or arrange an alternative time frame for processing a request (or a modified request) under clause (ii) after being given an opportunity to do so by the agency to whom the person made the request shall be considered as a factor in determining whether exceptional circumstances exist for purposes of this subparagraph.

(D) (i) Each agency may promulgate regulations, pursuant to notice and receipt of public comment, providing for multitrack processing of requests for records based on the amount of work or time (or both) involved in processing requests.

(ii) Regulations under this subparagraph may provide a person making a request that does not qualify for the fastest multitrack processing an opportunity to limit the scope of the request in order to qualify for faster processing.

(iii) This subparagraph shall not be considered to affect the requirement under subparagraph (C) to exercise due diligence.

(E) (i) Each agency shall promulgate regulations, pursuant to notice and receipt of public comment, providing for expedited processing of requests for records—

(I) in cases in which the person requesting the records demonstrates a compelling need; and

(II) in other cases determined by the agency.

(ii) Notwithstanding clause (i), regulations under this subparagraph must ensure—

(I) that a determination of whether to provide expedited processing shall be made, and notice of the determination shall be provided to the person making the request, within 10 days after the date of the request; and

(II) expeditious consideration of administrative appeals of such determinations of whether to provide expedited processing.

(iii) An agency shall process as soon as practicable any request for records to which the agency has granted expedited processing under this subparagraph. Agency action to deny or affirm denial of a request for expedited processing pursuant to this subparagraph, and failure by an agency to respond in a timely manner to such a request shall be subject to judicial review under paragraph (4), except that the judicial review shall be based on the record before the agency at the time of the determination.

(iv) A district court of the United States shall not have jurisdiction to review an agency denial of expedited processing of a request for records after the agency has provided a complete response to the request.

(v) For purposes of this subparagraph, the term "compelling need" means—

(I) that a failure to obtain requested records on an expedited basis under this paragraph could reasonably be expected to pose an imminent threat to the life or physical safety of an individual; or

(II) with respect to a request made by a person primarily engaged in disseminating information, urgency to inform the public concerning actual or alleged Federal Government activity.

(vi) A demonstration of a compelling need by a person making a request for expedited processing shall be made by a statement certified by such person to be true and correct to the best of such person's knowledge and belief.

(F) In denying a request for records, in whole or in part, an agency shall make a reasonable effort to estimate the volume of any requested matter the provision of which is denied, and shall provide any such estimate to the person making the request, unless providing such estimate would harm an interest protected by the exemption in subsection (b) pursuant to which the denial is made.

(7) Each agency shall—

(A) establish a system to assign an individualized tracking number for each request received that will take longer than ten days to process and provide to each person making a request the tracking number assigned to the request; and

(B) establish a telephone line or Internet service that provides information about the status of a request to the person making the request using the assigned tracking number, including—

(i) the date on which the agency originally received the request; and

(ii) an estimated date on which the agency will complete action on the request.

(b) This section does not apply to matters that are—

(1) (A) specifically authorized under criteria established by an Executive order to be kept secret in the interest of national defense or foreign policy and

(B) are in fact properly classified pursuant to such Executive order;

(2) related solely to the internal personnel rules and practices of an agency;

(3) specifically exempted from disclosure by statute (other than section 552b of this title), provided that such statute

(A) requires that the matters be withheld from the public in such a manner as to leave no discretion on the issue, or

(B) establishes particular criteria for withholding or refers to particular types of matters to be withheld;

(4) trade secrets and commercial or financial information obtained from a person and privileged or confidential;

(5) inter-agency or intra-agency memorandums or letters which would not be available by law to a party other than an agency in litigation with the agency;

(6) personnel and medical files and similar files the disclosure of which would constitute a clearly unwarranted invasion of personal privacy;

(7) records or information compiled for law enforcement purposes, but only to the extent that the production of such law enforcement records or information

(A) could reasonably be expected to interfere with enforcement proceedings,

(B) would deprive a person of a right to a fair trial or an impartial adjudication,

(C) could reasonably be expected to constitute an unwarranted invasion of personal privacy,

(D) could reasonably be expected to disclose the identity of a confidential source, including a State, local, or foreign agency or authority or any private institution which furnished information on a confidential basis, and, in the case of a record or information compiled by criminal law enforcement authority in the course of a criminal investigation or by an agency conducting a lawful national security intelligence investigation, information furnished by a confidential source,

(E) would disclose techniques and procedures for law enforcement investigations or prosecutions, or would disclose guidelines for law enforcement investigations or prosecutions if such disclosure could reasonably be expected to risk circumvention of the law, or

(F) could reasonably be expected to endanger the life or physical safety of any individual;

(8) contained in or related to examination, operating, or condition reports prepared by, on behalf of, or for the use of an agency responsible for the regulation or supervision of financial institutions; or

(9) geological and geophysical information and data, including maps, concerning wells. Any reasonably segregable portion of a record shall be provided to any person requesting such record after deletion of the portions which are exempt under this subsection. The amount of information deleted, and the exemption under which the deletion is made, shall be indicated on the released portion of the record, unless including that indication would harm an interest protected by the exemption in this subsection under which the deletion is made. If technically feasible, the amount of the information deleted, and the exemption under which the deletion is made, shall be indicated at the place in the record where such deletion is made.

(c) (1) Whenever a request is made which involves access to records described in subsection (b)(7)(A) and—

(A) the investigation or proceeding involves a possible violation of criminal law; and

(B) there is reason to believe that

(i) the subject of the investigation or proceeding is not aware of its pendency, and

(ii) disclosure of the existence of the records could reasonably be expected to interfere with enforcement proceedings, the agency may, during only such time as that circumstance continues, treat the records as not subject to the requirements of this section.

(2) Whenever informant records maintained by a criminal law enforcement agency under an informant's name or personal identifier are requested by a third party according to the informant's name or personal identifier, the agency may treat the records as not subject to the requirements of this section unless the informant's status as an informant has been officially confirmed.

(3) Whenever a request is made which involves access to records maintained by the Federal Bureau of Investigation pertaining to foreign intelligence or counterintelligence, or international terrorism, and the existence of the records is classified information as provided in subsection (b)(1), the Bureau may, as long as the existence of the records remains classified information, treat the records as not subject to the requirements of this section.

(d) This section does not authorize withholding of information or limit the availability of records to the public, except as specifically stated in this section. This section is not authority to withhold information from Congress.

(e) (1) On or before February 1 of each year, each agency shall submit to the Attorney General of the United States a report which shall cover the preceding fiscal year and which shall include—

(A) the number of determinations made by the agency not to comply with requests for records made to such agency under subsection (a) and the reasons for each such determination;

(B) (i) the number of appeals made by persons under subsection (a)(6), the result of such appeals, and the reason for the action upon each appeal that results in a denial of information; and

(ii) a complete list of all statutes that the agency relies upon to authorize the agency to withhold information under subsection (b)(3), the number of occasions on which each statute was relied upon, a description of whether a court has upheld the decision of the agency to withhold information under each such statute, and a concise description of the scope of any information withheld;

(C) the number of requests for records pending before the agency as of September 30 of the preceding year, and the median and average number of days that such requests had been pending before the agency as of that date;

(D) the number of requests for records received by the agency and the number of requests which the agency processed;
(E) the median number of days taken by the agency to process different types of requests, based on the date on which the requests were received by the agency;
(F) the average number of days for the agency to respond to a request beginning on the date on which the request was received by the agency, the median number of days for the agency to respond to such requests, and the range in number of days for the agency to respond to such requests;
(G) based on the number of business days that have elapsed since each request was originally received by the agency—

(i) the number of requests for records to which the agency has responded with a determination within a period up to and including 20 days, and in 20- day increments up to and including 200 days;
(ii) the number of requests for records to which the agency has responded with a determination within a period greater than 200 days and less than 301 days;
(iii) the number of requests for records to which the agency has responded with a determination within a period greater than 300 days and less than 401 days; and
(iv) the number of requests for records to which the agency has responded with a determination within a period greater than 400 days;

(H) the average number of days for the agency to provide the granted information beginning on the date on which the request was originally filed, the median number of days for the agency to provide the granted information, and the range in number of days for the agency to provide the granted information;
(I) the median and average number of days for the agency to respond to administrative appeals based on the date on which the appeals originally were received by the agency, the highest number of business days taken by the agency to respond to an administrative appeal, and the lowest number of business days taken by the agency to respond to an administrative appeal;
(J) data on the 10 active requests with the earliest filing dates pending at each agency, including the amount of time that has elapsed since each request was originally received by the agency;
(K) data on the 10 active administrative appeals with the earliest filing dates pending before the agency as of September 30 of the preceding year, including the number of business days that have elapsed since the requests were originally received by the agency;
(L) the number of expedited review requests that are granted and denied, the average and median number of days for adjudicating expedited review requests, and the number adjudicated within the required 10 days;
(M) the number of fee waiver requests that are granted and denied, and

the average and median number of days for adjudicating fee waiver determinations;

(N) the total amount of fees collected by the agency for processing requests; and

(O) the number of full-time staff of the agency devoted to processing requests for records under this section, and the total amount expended by the agency for processing such requests.

(2) Information in each report submitted under paragraph (1) shall be expressed in terms of each principal component of the agency and for the agency overall.

(3) Each agency shall make each such report available to the public including by computer telecommunications, or if computer telecommunications means have not been established by the agency, by other electronic means. In addition, each agency shall make the raw statistical data used in its reports available electronically to the public upon request.

(4) The Attorney General of the United States shall make each report which has been made available by electronic means available at a single electronic access point. The Attorney General of the United States shall notify the Chairman and ranking minority member of the Committee on Government Reform and Oversight of the House of Representatives and the Chairman and ranking minority member of the Committees on Governmental Affairs and the Judiciary of the Senate, no later than April 1 of the year in which each such report is issued, that such reports are available by electronic means.

(5) The Attorney General of the United States, in consultation with the Director of the Office of Management and Budget, shall develop reporting and performance guidelines in connection with reports required by this subsection by October 1, 1997, and may establish additional requirements for such reports as the Attorney General determines may be useful.

(6) The Attorney General of the United States shall submit an annual report on or before April 1 of each calendar year which shall include for the prior calendar year a listing of the number of cases arising under this section, the exemption involved in each case, the disposition of such case, and the cost, fees, and penalties assessed under subparagraphs (E), (F), and (G) of subsection (a)(4). Such report shall also include a description of the efforts undertaken by the Department of Justice to encourage agency compliance with this section.

(f) For purposes of this section, the term—

(1) "agency" as defined in section 551 (1) of this title includes any executive department, military department, Government corporation, Government controlled corporation, or other establishment in the executive branch of the Government (including the Executive Office of the President), or any independent regulatory agency; and

(2) 'record' and any other term used in this section in reference to information includes—

(A) any information that would be an agency record subject to the requirements of this section when maintained by an agency in any format, including an electronic format; and

(B) any information described under subparagraph (A) that is maintained for an agency by an entity under Government contract, for the purposes of records management.

(g) The head of each agency shall prepare and make publicly available upon request, reference material or a guide for requesting records or information from the agency, subject to the exemptions in subsection (b), including—

(1) an index of all major information systems of the agency;

(2) a description of major information and record locator systems maintained by the agency; and

(3) a handbook for obtaining various types and categories of public information from the agency pursuant to chapter 35 of title 44, and under this section.

(h)(1) There is established the Office of Government Information Services within the National Archives and Records Administration.

(2) The Office of Government Information Services shall—

(A) review policies and procedures of administrative agencies under this section;

(B) review compliance with this section by administrative agencies; and

(C) recommend policy changes to Congress and the President to improve the administration of this section.

(3) The Office of Government Information Services shall offer mediation services to resolve disputes between persons making requests under this section and administrative agencies as a nonexclusive alternative to litigation and, at the discretion of the Office, may issue advisory opinions if mediation has not resolved the dispute.

(i) The Government Accountability Office shall conduct audits of administrative agencies on the implementation of this section and issue reports detailing the results of such audits.

(j) Each agency shall designate a Chief FOIA Officer who shall be a senior official of such agency (at the Assistant Secretary or equivalent level).

(k) The Chief FOIA Officer of each agency shall, subject to the authority of the head of the agency—

(1) have agency-wide responsibility for efficient and appropriate compliance with this section;

(2) monitor implementation of this section throughout the agency and keep the head of the agency, the chief legal officer of the agency, and the Attorney General appropriately informed of the agency's performance in implementing this section;

(3) recommend to the head of the agency such adjustments to agency practices, policies, personnel, and funding as may be necessary to improve its implementation of this section;

(4) review and report to the Attorney General, through the head of the agency, at such times and in such formats as the Attorney General may direct, on the

agency's performance in implementing this section;

(5) facilitate public understanding of the purposes of the statutory exemptions of this section by including concise descriptions of the exemptions in both the agency's handbook issued under subsection (g), and the agency's annual report on this section, and by providing an overview, where appropriate, of certain general categories of agency records to which those exemptions apply; and

(6) designate one or more FOIA Public Liaisons.

(l) FOIA Public Liaisons shall report to the agency Chief FOIA Officer and shall serve as supervisory officials to whom a requester under this section can raise concerns about the service the requester has received from the FOIA Requester Center, following an initial response from the FOIA Requester Center Staff. FOIA Public Liaisons shall be responsible for assisting in reducing delays, increasing transparency and understanding of the status of requests, and assisting in the resolution of disputes.

Department of Defense Title 10 Authorities

CHAPTER 4 OF TITLE 10, UNITED STATES CODE UNDER SECRETARY OF DEFENSE FOR INTELLIGENCE (10 U.S.C. § 137)

SEC. 137.

(a) There is an Under Secretary of Defense for Intelligence, appointed from civilian life by the President, by and with the advice and consent of the Senate.

(b) Subject to the authority, direction, and control of the Secretary of Defense, the Under Secretary of Defense for Intelligence shall perform such duties and exercise such powers as the Secretary of Defense may prescribe in the area of intelligence.

(c) The Under Secretary of Defense for Intelligence takes precedence in the Department of Defense after the Under Secretary of Defense for Personnel and Readiness.

CHAPTER 21 OF TITLE 10, UNITED STATES CODE

SEC. 421. FUNDS FOR FOREIGN CRYPTOLOGIC SUPPORT

(a) The Secretary of Defense may use appropriated funds available to the Department of Defense for intelligence and communications purposes to pay for the expenses of arrangements with foreign countries for cryptologic support.

(b) The Secretary of Defense may use funds other than appropriated funds to pay for the expenses of arrangements with foreign countries for cryptologic support without regard for the provisions of law relating to the expenditure of United States Government funds, except that—

(1) no such funds may be expended, in whole or in part, by or for the benefit of the Department of Defense for a purpose for which Congress had previously denied funds; and

(2) proceeds from the sale of cryptologic items may be used only to purchase replacement items similar to the items that are sold; and

(3) the authority provided by this subsection may not be used to acquire items or services for the principal benefit of the United States.

(c) Any funds expended under the authority of subsection (a) shall be reported to the Select Committee on Intelligence of the Senate and the Permanent Select Committee on Intelligence of the House of Representatives pursuant to the provisions of title V of the National Security Act of 1947 (50 U.S.C. §413 et seq.). Funds expended under the authority of subsection (b) shall be reported pursuant to procedures jointly agreed upon by such committees and the Secretary of Defense.

SEC. 422. USE OF FUNDS FOR CERTAIN INCIDENTAL PURPOSES

(a) COUNTERINTELLIGENCE OFFICIAL RECEPTION AND REPRESENTATION EXPENSES.—The Secretary of Defense may use funds available to the Department of Defense for counterintelligence programs to pay the expenses of hosting foreign officials in the United States under the auspices of the Department of Defense for consultation on counterintelligence matters.

(b) PROMOTIONAL ITEMS FOR RECRUITMENT PURPOSES.—The Secretary of Defense may use funds available for an intelligence element of the Department of Defense to purchase promotional items of nominal value for use in the recruitment of individuals for employment by that element.

SEC. 423. AUTHORITY TO USE PROCEEDS FROM COUNTERINTELLIGENCE OPERATIONS OF THE MILITARY DEPARTMENTS

(a) The Secretary of Defense may authorize, without regard to the provisions of section 3302 of title 31, use of proceeds from counterintelligence operations conducted by components of the military departments to offset necessary and reasonable expenses, not otherwise prohibited by law, incurred in such operations, and to make exceptional performance awards to personnel involved in such operations, if use of appropriated funds to meet such expenses or to make such awards would not be practicable.

(b) As soon as the net proceeds from such counterintelligence operations are no longer necessary for the conduct of those operations, such proceeds shall be deposited into the Treasury as miscellaneous receipts.

(c) The Secretary of Defense shall establish policies and procedures to govern acquisition, use, management, and disposition of proceeds from counterintelligence operations conducted by components of the military departments, including effective internal systems of accounting and administrative controls.

SEC. 424. DISCLOSURE OF ORGANIZATIONAL AND PERSONNEL INFORMATION: EXEMPTION FOR SPECIFIED INTELLIGENCE AGENCIES

(a) EXEMPTION FROM DISCLOSURE.—Except as required by the President or as provided in subsection (c), no provision of law shall be construed to require the disclosure of—

(1) the organization or any function of an organization of the Department of Defense named in subsection (b); or

(2) the number of persons employed by or assigned or detailed to any such organization or the name, official title, occupational series, grade, or salary of any such person.

(b) COVERED ORGANIZATIONS.—This section applies to the following organizations of the Department of Defense:

(1) The Defense Intelligence Agency.

(2) The National Reconnaissance Office.

(3) The National Geospatial-Intelligence Agency.

(c) PROVISION OF INFORMATION TO CONGRESS.—Subsection (a) does not apply with respect to the provision of information to Congress.

SEC. 425. PROHIBITION OF UNAUTHORIZED USE OF NAME, INITIALS, OR SEAL: SPECIFIED INTELLIGENCE AGENCIES

(a) PROHIBITION.—Except with the written permission of both the Secretary of Defense and the Director of Central Intelligence, no person may knowingly use, in connection with any merchandise, retail product, impersonation, solicitation, or commercial activity in a manner reasonably calculated to convey the impression that such use is approved, endorsed, or authorized by the Secretary and the Director, any of the following (or any colorable imitation thereof):

(1) The words "Defense Intelligence Agency", the initials "DIA", or the seal of the Defense Intelligence Agency.

(2) The words "National Reconnaissance Office", the initials "NRO", or the seal of the National Reconnaissance Office.

(3) The words "National Imagery and Mapping Agency", the initials "NIMA", or the seal of the National Imagery and Mapping Agency.

(4) The words "Defense Mapping Agency", the initials "DMA", or the seal of the Defense Mapping Agency.

(5) The words "National Geospatial-Intelligence Agency", the initials "NGA," or the seal of the National Geospatial-Intelligence Agency.

(b) AUTHORITY TO ENJOIN VIOLATIONS.—Whenever it appears to the Attorney General that any person is engaged or is about to engage in an act or practice which constitutes or will constitute conduct prohibited by subsection (a), the Attorney General may initiate a civil proceeding in a district court of the United States to enjoin such act or practice. Such court shall proceed as soon as practicable to the hearing and determination of such action and may, at any time before final determination, enter such restraining orders or prohibitions, or take such other actions as is warranted, to prevent injury to the United States or to any person or class of persons for whose protection the action is brought.

SEC. 426. INTEGRATION OF DEPARTMENT OF DEFENSE INTELLIGENCE, SURVEILLANCE, AND RECONNAISSANCE CAPABILITIES

(a) ISR INTEGRATION COUNCIL.—

(1) The Under Secretary of Defense for Intelligence shall establish an Intelligence, Surveillance, and Reconnaissance Integration Council—

(A) to assist the Under Secretary with respect to matters relating to the integration of intelligence, surveillance, and reconnaissance capabilities, and coordination of related developmental activities, of the military departments, intelligence agencies of the Department of Defense, and relevant combatant commands; and

(B) otherwise to provide a means to facilitate the integration of such capabilities and the coordiation [1] of such developmental activities.

(2) The Council shall be composed of—

(A) the senior intelligence officers of the armed forces and the United States Special Operations Command;

(B) the Director of Operations of the Joint Staff; and

(C) the directors of the intelligence agencies of the Department of Defense.

(3) The Under Secretary of Defense for Intelligence shall invite the participation of the Director of Central Intelligence (or that Director's representative) in the proceedings of the Council.

(b) ISR INTEGRATION ROADMAP.—

(1) The Under Secretary of Defense for Intelligence shall develop a comprehensive plan, to be known as the "Defense Intelligence, Surveillance, and Reconnaissance Integration Roadmap", to guide the development and integration of the Department of Defense intelligence, surveillance, and reconnaissance capabilities for the 15-year period of fiscal years 2004 through 2018.

(2) The Under Secretary shall develop the Defense Intelligence, Surveillance, and Reconnaissance Integration Roadmap in consultation with the Intelligence, Surveillance, and Reconnaissance Integration Council and the Director of National Intelligence.

SEC. 427. INTELLIGENCE OVERSIGHT ACTIVITIES OF DEPARTMENT OF DEFENSE: ANNUAL REPORTS

(a) ANNUAL REPORTS REQUIRED.—

(1) Not later than March 1 of each year, the Secretary of Defense shall submit—

(A) to the congressional committees specified in subparagraph (A) of paragraph (2) a report on the intelligence oversight activities of the Department of Defense during the previous calendar year insofar as such oversight activities relate to tactical intelligence and intelligence-related activities of the Department; and

(B) to the congressional committees specified in subparagraph (B) of paragraph (2) a report on the intelligence oversight activities of the Department of Defense during the previous calendar year insofar as such oversight activities relate to intelligence and intelligence-related activities of the Department other than those specified in subparagraph (A).

(2)(A) The committees specified in this subparagraph are the following:

(i) The Committee on Armed Services and the Committee on Appropriations of the Senate.

(ii) The Permanent Select Committee on Intelligence, the Committee on Armed Services, and the Committee on Appropriations of the House of Representatives.

(B) The committees specified in this subparagraph are the following:

(i) The Select Committee on Intelligence, the Committee on Armed Services, and the Committee on Appropriations of the Senate.

(ii) The Permanent Select Committee on Intelligence and the Committee on Appropriations of the House of Representatives.

(b) ELEMENTS.—Each report under subsection (a) shall include, for the calendar year covered by such report and with respect to oversight activities subject to coverage in that report, the following:

(1) A description of any violation of law or of any Executive order or Presidential directive (including Executive Order No. 12333) that comes to the attention of any General Counsel or Inspector General within the Department of Defense, or the Under Secretary of Defense for Intelligence, and a description of the actions taken by such official with respect to such activity.

(2) A description of the results of intelligence oversight inspections undertaken by each of the following:

(A) The Office of the Secretary of Defense.

(B) Each military department.

(C) Each combat support agency.

(D) Each field operating agency.

(3) A description of any changes made in any program for the intelligence oversight activities of the Department of Defense, including any training program.

(4) A description of any changes made in any published directive or policy memoranda on the intelligence or intelligence-related activities of—

(A) any military department;

(B) any combat support agency; or

(C) any field operating agency.

(c) DEFINITIONS.—In this section:

(1) The term "intelligence oversight activities of the Department of Defense" refers to any activity undertaken by an agency, element, or component of the Department of Defense to ensure compliance with regard to requirements or instructions on the intelligence and intelligence-related activities of the Department under law or any Executive order or Presidential directive (including Executive Order No. 12333).

(2) The term "combat support agency" has the meaning given that term in section 193(f) of this title.

(3) The term "field operating agency" means a specialized subdivision of the Department of Defense that carries out activities under the operational control of the Department.

SEC. 431. AUTHORITY TO ENGAGE IN COMMERCIAL ACTIVITIES AS SECURITY FOR INTELLIGENCE COLLECTION ACTIVITIES

(a) AUTHORITY.—The Secretary of Defense, subject to the provisions of this subchapter, may authorize the conduct of those commercial activities necessary to provide security for authorized intelligence collection activities abroad undertaken by the Department of Defense. No commercial activity may be initiated pursuant to this subchapter after December 31, 2006.

(b) INTERAGENCY COORDINATION AND SUPPORT.—Any such activity shall—

(1) be coordinated with, and (where appropriate) be supported by, the Director of Central Intelligence; and

(2) to the extent the activity takes place within the United States, be coordinated with, and (where appropriate) be supported by, the Director of the Federal Bureau of Investigation.

(c) DEFINITIONS.—In this subchapter:

(1) The term "commercial activities" means activities that are conducted in a manner consistent with prevailing commercial practices and includes—

(A) the acquisition, use, sale, storage and disposal of goods and services;

(B) entering into employment contracts and leases and other agreements for real and personal property;
(C) depositing funds into and withdrawing funds from domestic and foreign commercial business or financial institutions;
(D) acquiring licenses, registrations, permits, and insurance; and
(E) establishing corporations, partnerships, and other legal entities.

(2) The term "intelligence collection activities" means the collection of foreign intelligence and counterintelligence information.

SEC. 432. USE, DISPOSITION, AND AUDITING OF FUNDS

(a) USE OF FUNDS.—Funds generated by a commercial activity authorized pursuant to this subchapter may be used to offset necessary and reasonable expenses arising from that activity. Use of such funds for that purpose shall be kept to the minimum necessary to conduct the activity concerned in a secure manner. Any funds generated by the activity in excess of those required for that purpose shall be deposited, as often as may be practicable, into the Treasury as miscellaneous receipts.

(b) AUDITS.—

(1) The Secretary of Defense shall assign an organization within the Department of Defense to have auditing responsibility with respect to activities authorized under this subchapter.

(2) That organization shall audit the use and disposition of funds generated by any commercial activity authorized under this subchapter not less often than annually. The results of all such audits shall be promptly reported to the intelligence committees (as defined in section 437 (d) of this title).

SEC. 433. RELATIONSHIP WITH OTHER FEDERAL LAWS

(a) IN GENERAL.—Except as provided by subsection (b), a commercial activity conducted pursuant to this subchapter shall be carried out in accordance with applicable Federal law.

(b) AUTHORIZATION OF WAIVERS WHEN NECESSARY TO MAINTAIN SECURITY.—

(1) If the Secretary of Defense determines, in connection with a commercial activity authorized pursuant to section 431 of this title, that compliance with certain Federal laws or regulations pertaining to the management and administration of Federal agencies would create an unacceptable risk of compromise of an authorized intelligence activity, the Secretary may, to the extent necessary to prevent such compromise, waive compliance with such laws or regulations.

(2) Any determination and waiver by the Secretary under paragraph (1) shall be made in writing and shall include a specification of the laws and regulations for which compliance by the commercial activity concerned is not required consistent with this section.

(3) The authority of the Secretary under paragraph (1) may be delegated only to the Deputy Secretary of Defense, an Under Secretary of Defense, an Assistant Secretary of Defense, or a Secretary of a military department.

(c) FEDERAL LAWS AND REGULATIONS.—For purposes of this section, Federal laws and regulations pertaining to the management and administration of Federal agencies are only those Federal laws and regulations pertaining to the following:

(1) The receipt and use of appropriated and nonappropriated funds.

(2) The acquisition or management of property or services.

(3) Information disclosure, retention, and management.

(4) The employment of personnel.

(5) Payments for travel and housing.

(6) The establishment of legal entities or government instrumentalities.

(7) Foreign trade or financial transaction restrictions that would reveal the commercial activity as an activity of the United States Government.

SEC. 434. RESERVATION OF DEFENSES AND IMMUNITIES. The submission to judicial proceedings in a State or other legal jurisdiction, in connection with a commercial activity undertaken pursuant to this subchapter, shall not constitute a waiver of the defenses and immunities of the United States.

SEC. 435. LIMITATIONS

(a) LAWFUL ACTIVITIES.—Nothing in this subchapter authorizes the conduct of any intelligence activity that is not otherwise authorized by law or Executive order.

(b) DOMESTIC ACTIVITIES.—Personnel conducting commercial activity authorized by this subchapter may only engage in those activities in the United States to the extent necessary to support intelligence activities abroad.

(c) PROVIDING GOODS AND SERVICES TO THE DEPARTMENT OF DEFENSE.— Commercial activity may not be undertaken within the United States for the purpose of providing goods and services to the Department of Defense, other than as may be necessary to provide security for the activities subject to this subchapter.

(d) NOTICE TO UNITED STATES PERSONS.—

(1) In carrying out a commercial activity authorized under this subchapter, the Secretary of Defense may not permit an entity engaged in such activity to employ a United States person in an operational, managerial, or supervisory position, and may not assign or detail a United States person to perform operational, managerial, or supervisory duties for such an entity, unless that person is informed in advance of the intelligence security purpose of that activity.

(2) In this subsection, the term "United States person" means an individual who is a citizen of the United States or an alien lawfully admitted to the United States for permanent residence.

SEC. 436. REGULATIONS

The Secretary of Defense shall prescribe regulations to implement the authority provided in this subchapter. Such regulations shall be consistent with this subchapter and shall at a minimum—

(1) specify all elements of the Department of Defense who are authorized to engage in commercial activities pursuant to this subchapter;
(2) require the personal approval of the Secretary or Deputy Secretary of Defense for all sensitive activities to be authorized pursuant to this subchapter;
(3) specify all officials who are authorized to grant waivers of laws or regulations pursuant to section 433 (b) of this title, or to approve the establishment or conduct of commercial activities pursuant to this subchapter;
(4) designate a single office within the Defense Intelligence Agency to be responsible for the management and supervision of all activities authorized under this subchapter;
(5) require that each commercial activity proposed to be authorized under this subchapter be subject to appropriate legal review before the activity is authorized; and
(6) provide for appropriate internal audit controls and oversight for such activities.

SEC. 437. CONGRESSIONAL OVERSIGHT

(a) PROPOSED REGULATIONS.—Copies of regulations proposed to be prescribed under section 436 of this title (including any proposed revision to such regulations) shall be submitted to the intelligence committees not less than 30 days before they take effect.
(b) CURRENT INFORMATION.—Consistent with title V of the National Security Act of 1947 (50 U.S.C. §413 et seq.), the Secretary of Defense shall ensure that the intelligence committees are kept fully and currently informed of actions taken pursuant to this subchapter, including any significant anticipated activity to be authorized pursuant to this subchapter.
(c) ANNUAL REPORT.—Not later each year than the date provided in section 507 of the National Security Act of 1947 (50 U.S.C. §415b), the Secretary shall submit to the congressional intelligence committees (as defined in section 3 of that Act (50 U.S.C. §401a)) a report on all commercial activities authorized under this subchapter that were undertaken during the previous fiscal year. Such report shall include (with respect to the fiscal year covered by the report) the following:
(1) A description of any exercise of the authority provided by section 433 (b) of this title.
(2) A description of any expenditure of funds made pursuant to this subchapter (whether from appropriated or non-appropriated funds).
(3) A description of any actions taken with respect to audits conducted pursuant to section 432 of this title to implement recommendations or correct deficiencies identified in such audits.
(4) A description of each corporation, partnership, or other legal entity that was established.

Homeland Security Act of 2002, §§ 101-237

(Titles I and II) (Pub. L. No. 107-296, 116 Stat. 2135), as amended

TITLE I—DEPARTMENT OF HOMELAND SECURITY

Sec. 101. [6 U.S.C. 111] EXECUTIVE DEPARTMENT; MISSION.

(a) ESTABLISHMENT.—There is established a Department of Homeland Security, as an executive department of the United States within the meaning of title 5, United States Code.

(b) MISSION.—

(1) IN GENERAL.—The primary mission of the Department is to—

(A) prevent terrorist attacks within the United States;

(B) reduce the vulnerability of the United States to terrorism;

(C) minimize the damage, and assist in the recovery, from terrorist attacks that do occur within the United States;

(D) carry out all functions of entities transferred to the Department, including by acting as a focal point regarding natural and manmade crises and emergency planning;

(E) ensure that the functions of the agencies and subdivisions within the Department that are not related directly to securing the homeland are not diminished or neglected except by a specific explicit Act of Congress;

(F) ensure that the overall economic security of the United States is not diminished by efforts, activities, and programs aimed at securing the homeland;

(G) ensure that the civil rights and civil liberties of persons are not diminished by efforts, activities, and programs aimed at securing the homeland; and

(H) monitor connections between illegal drug trafficking and terrorism, coordinate efforts to sever such connections, and otherwise contribute to efforts to interdict illegal drug trafficking.

(2) RESPONSIBILITY FOR INVESTIGATING AND PROSECUTING TERRORISM.—Except as specifically provided by law with respect to entities transferred to the Department under this Act, primary responsibility for investigating and prosecuting acts of terrorism shall be vested not in the Department, but rather in Federal, State, and local law enforcement agencies with jurisdiction over the acts in question.

Sec. 102. [6 U.S.C. 112] SECRETARY; FUNCTIONS.

(a) SECRETARY.—

(1) IN GENERAL.—There is a Secretary of Homeland Security, appointed by the President, by and with the advice and consent of the Senate.

(2) HEAD OF DEPARTMENT.—The Secretary is the head of the Department and shall have direction, authority, and control over it.

(3) FUNCTIONS VESTED IN SECRETARY.—All functions of all officers, employees, and organizational units of the Department are vested in the Secretary.

(b) FUNCTIONS.—The Secretary—

(1) except as otherwise provided by this Act, may delegate any of the Secretary's functions to any officer, employee, or organizational unit of the Department;

(2) shall have the authority to make contracts, grants, and cooperative agreements, and to enter into agreements with other executive agencies, as may be necessary and proper to carry out the Secretary's responsibilities under this Act or otherwise provided by law; and

(3) shall take reasonable steps to ensure that information systems and databases of the Department are compatible with each other and with appropriate databases of other Departments.

(c) COORDINATION WITH NON-FEDERAL ENTITIES.—With respect to homeland security, the Secretary shall coordinate through the Office of State and Local Coordination (established under section 801) (including the provision of training and equipment) with State and local government personnel, agencies, and authorities, with the private sector, and with other entities, including by—

(1) coordinating with State and local government personnel, agencies, and authorities, and with the private sector, to ensure adequate planning, equipment, training, and exercise activities;

(2) coordinating and, as appropriate, consolidating, the Federal Government's communications and systems of communications relating to homeland security with State and local government personnel, agencies, and authorities, the private sector, other entities, and the public; and

(3) distributing or, as appropriate, coordinating the distribution of, warnings and information to State and local government personnel, agencies, and authorities and to the public.

(d) MEETINGS OF NATIONAL SECURITY COUNCIL.—The Secretary may, subject to the direction of the President, attend and participate in meetings of the National Security Council.

(e) ISSUANCE OF REGULATIONS.—The issuance of regulations by the Secretary shall be governed by the provisions of chapter 5 of title 5, United States Code, except as specifically provided in this Act, in laws granting regulatory authorities that are transferred by this Act, and in laws enacted after the date of enactment of this Act.

(f) SPECIAL ASSISTANT TO THE SECRETARY.—The Secretary shall appoint a Special Assistant to the Secretary who shall be responsible for—

(1) creating and fostering strategic communications with the private sector to enhance the primary mission of the Department to protect the American homeland;

(2) advising the Secretary on the impact of the Department's policies, regulations, processes, and actions on the private sector;

(3) interfacing with other relevant Federal agencies with homeland security missions to assess the impact of these agencies' actions on the private sector;

(4) creating and managing private sector advisory councils composed of representatives of industries and associations designated by the Secretary to—

(A) advise the Secretary on private sector products, applications, and solutions as they relate to homeland security challenges; and

(B) advise the Secretary on homeland security policies, regulations, processes, and actions that affect the participating industries and associations;

(5) working with Federal laboratories, federally funded research and development centers, other federally funded organizations, academia, and the private sector to develop innovative approaches to address homeland security chal-

lenges to produce and deploy the best available technologies for homeland security missions;

(6) promoting existing public-private partnerships and developing new public-private partnerships to provide for collaboration and mutual support to address homeland security challenges;

(7) assisting in the development and promotion of private sector best practices to secure critical infrastructure;

(8) coordinating industry efforts, with respect to functions of the Department of Homeland Security, to identify private sector resources and capabilities that could be effective in supplementing Federal, State, and local government agency efforts to prevent or respond to a terrorist attack;

(9) coordinating with the Directorate of Border and Transportation Security and the Assistant Secretary for Trade Development of the Department of Commerce on issues related to the travel and tourism industries; and

(10) consulting with the Office of State and Local Government Coordination and Preparedness on all matters of concern to the private sector, including the tourism industry.

(g) STANDARDS POLICY.—All standards activities of the Department shall be conducted in accordance with section 12(d) of the National Technology Transfer Advancement Act of 1995 (15 U.S.C. 272 note) and Office of Management and Budget Circular A–119.

Sec. 103. [6 U.S.C. 113] OTHER OFFICERS.

(a) DEPUTY SECRETARY; UNDER SECRETARIES.—There are the following officers, appointed by the President, by and with the advice and consent of the Senate:

(1) A Deputy Secretary of Homeland Security, who shall be the Secretary's first assistant for purposes of subchapter III of chapter 33 of title 5, United States Code.

(2) An Under Secretary for Science and Technology.

(3) An Under Secretary for Border and Transportation Security.

(4) An Administrator of the Federal Emergency Management Agency.

(5) A Director of the Bureau of Citizenship and Immigration Services.

(6) An Under Secretary for Management.

(7) A Director of the Office of Counternarcotics Enforcement.

(8) Not more than 12 Assistant Secretaries.

(9) A General Counsel, who shall be the chief legal officer of the Department.

(b) INSPECTOR GENERAL.—There shall be in the Department an Office of Inspector General and an Inspector General at the head of such office, as provided in the Inspector General Act of 1978 (5 U.S.C. App.).

(c) COMMANDANT OF THE COAST GUARD.—To assist the Secretary in the performance of the Secretary's functions, there is a Commandant of the Coast Guard, who shall be appointed as provided in section 44 of title 14, United States Code, and who shall report directly to the Secretary. In addition to such duties as may be provided in this Act and as assigned to the Commandant by the Secretary, the duties of the Commandant shall include those required by section 2 of title 14, United States Code.

(d) OTHER OFFICERS.—To assist the Secretary in the performance of the Secretary's functions, there are the following officers, appointed by the President:

(1) A Director of the Secret Service.

(2) A Chief Information Officer.

(3) A Chief Human Capital Officer.

(4) An Officer for Civil Rights and Civil Liberties.

(5) A Director for Domestic Nuclear Detection.

(f) PERFORMANCE OF SPECIFIC FUNCTIONS.—Subject to the provisions of this Act, every officer of the Department shall perform the functions specified by law for the official's office or prescribed by the Secretary.

(e) CHIEF FINANCIAL OFFICER.—There shall be in the Department a Chief Financial Officer, as provided in chapter 9 of title 31, United States Code.

TITLE II—INFORMATION ANALYSIS AND INFRASTRUCTURE PROTECTION

Subtitle A—Directorate for Information Analysis and Infrastructure Protection; Access to Information

Sec. 201. [6 U.S.C. 121] DIRECTORATE FOR INFORMATION ANALYSIS AND INFRASTRUCTURE PROTECTION.

(a) UNDER SECRETARY OF HOMELAND SECURITY FOR INFORMATION ANALYSIS AND INFRASTRUCTURE PROTECTION.—

(1) IN GENERAL.—There shall be in the Department a Directorate for Information Analysis and Infrastructure Protection headed by an Under Secretary for Information Analysis and Infrastructure Protection, who shall be appointed by the President, by and with the advice and consent of the Senate.

(2) RESPONSIBILITIES.—The Under Secretary shall assist the Secretary in discharging the responsibilities assigned by the Secretary.

(b) ASSISTANT SECRETARY FOR INFORMATION ANALYSIS; ASSISTANT SECRETARY FOR INFRASTRUCTURE PROTECTION.—

(1) ASSISTANT SECRETARY FOR INFORMATION ANALYSIS.— There shall be in the Department an Assistant Secretary for Information Analysis, who shall be appointed by the President.

(2) ASSISTANT SECRETARY FOR INFRASTRUCTURE PROTECTION.— There shall be in the Department an Assistant Secretary for Infrastructure Protection, who shall be appointed by the President.

(3) RESPONSIBILITIES.—The Assistant Secretary for Information Analysis and the Assistant Secretary for Infrastructure Protection shall assist the Under Secretary for Information Analysis and Infrastructure Protection in discharging the responsibilities of the Under Secretary under this section.

(c) DISCHARGE OF INFORMATION ANALYSIS AND INFRASTRUCTURE PROTECTION.—The Secretary shall ensure that the responsibilities of the Department regarding information analysis and infrastructure protection are carried out through the Under Secretary for Information Analysis and Infrastructure Protection.

(d) RESPONSIBILITIES OF UNDER SECRETARY.—Subject to the direction and control of the Secretary, the responsibilities of the Under Secretary for Information Analysis and Infrastructure Protection shall be as follows:

(1) To access, receive, and analyze law enforcement information, intelligence information, and other information from agencies of the Federal Government, State and local government agencies (including law enforcement agencies), and private sector entities, and to integrate such information in order to—

(A) identify and assess the nature and scope of terrorist threats to the homeland;

(B) detect and identify threats of terrorism against the United States; and

(C) understand such threats in light of actual and potential vulnerabilities of the homeland.

(2) To carry out comprehensive assessments of the vulnerabilities of the key resources and critical infrastructure of the United States, including the performance of risk assessments to determine the risks posed by particular types of terrorist attacks within the United States (including an assessment of the probability of success of such attacks and the feasibility and potential efficacy of various countermeasures to such attacks).

(3) To integrate relevant information, analyses, and vulnerability assessments (whether such information, analyses, or assessments are provided or produced by the Department or others) in order to identify priorities for protective and support measures by the Department, other agencies of the Federal Government, State and local government agencies and authorities, the private sector, and other entities.

(4) To ensure, pursuant to section 202, the timely and efficient access by the Department to all information necessary to discharge the responsibilities under this section, including obtaining such information from other agencies of the Federal Government.

(5) To develop a comprehensive national plan for securing the key resources and critical infrastructure of the United States, including power production, generation, and distribution systems, information technology and telecommunications systems (including satellites), electronic financial and property record storage and transmission systems, emergency preparedness communications systems, and the physical and technological assets that support such systems.

(6) To recommend measures necessary to protect the key resources and critical infrastructure of the United States in coordination with other agencies of the Federal Government and in cooperation with State and local government agencies and authorities, the private sector, and other entities.

(7) To administer the Homeland Security Advisory System, including—

(A) exercising primary responsibility for public advisories related to threats to homeland security; and

(B) in coordination with other agencies of the Federal Government, providing specific warning information, and advice about appropriate protective measures and countermeasures, to State and local government agencies and authorities, the private sector, other entities, and the public.

(8) To review, analyze, and make recommendations for improvements in the policies and procedures governing the sharing of law enforcement information, intelligence information, intelligence-related information, and other information relating to homeland security within the Federal Government and between the Federal Government and State and local government agencies and authorities.

(9) To disseminate, as appropriate, information analyzed by the Department within the Department, to other agencies of the Federal Government with responsibilities relating to homeland security, and to agencies of State and local governments and private sector entities with such responsibilities in order to assist in the deterrence, prevention, preemption of, or response to, terrorist attacks against the United States.

(10) To consult with the Director of Central Intelligence and other appropriate intelligence, law enforcement, or other elements of the Federal Government to establish collection priorities and strategies for information, including law enforcement- related information, relating to threats of terrorism against the United States through such means as the representation of the Department in discussions regarding requirements and priorities in the collection of such information.

(11) To consult with State and local governments and private sector entities to ensure appropriate exchanges of information, including law enforcement-related information, relating to threats of terrorism against the United States.

(12) To ensure that—

(A) any material received pursuant to this Act is protected from unauthorized disclosure and handled and used only for the performance of official duties; and

(B) any intelligence information under this Act is shared, retained, and disseminated consistent with the authority of the Director of Central Intelligence to protect intelligence sources and methods under the National Security Act of 1947 (50 U.S.C. 401 et seq.) and related procedures and, as appropriate, similar authorities of the Attorney General concerning sensitive law enforcement information.

(13) To request additional information from other agencies of the Federal Government, State and local government agencies, and the private sector relating to threats of terrorism in the United States, or relating to other areas of responsibility assigned by the Secretary, including the entry into cooperative agreements through the Secretary to obtain such information.

(14) To establish and utilize, in conjunction with the chief information officer of the Department, a secure communications and information technology infrastructure, including data-mining and other advanced analytical tools, in order to access, receive, and analyze data and information in furtherance of

the responsibilities under this section, and to disseminate information acquired and analyzed by the Department, as appropriate.

(15) To ensure, in conjunction with the chief information officer of the Department, that any information databases and analytical tools developed or utilized by the Department—

(A) are compatible with one another and with relevant information databases of other agencies of the Federal Government; and

(B) treat information in such databases in a manner that complies with applicable Federal law on privacy.

(16) To coordinate training and other support to the elements and personnel of the Department, other agencies of the Federal Government, and State and local governments that provide information to the Department, or are consumers of information provided by the Department, in order to facilitate the identification and sharing of information revealed in their ordinary duties and the optimal utilization of information received from the Department.

(17) To coordinate with elements of the intelligence community and with Federal, State, and local law enforcement agencies, and the private sector, as appropriate.

(18) To provide intelligence and information analysis and support to other elements of the Department.

(19) To perform such other duties relating to such responsibilities as the Secretary may provide.

(e) STAFF.—

(1) IN GENERAL.—The Secretary shall provide the Directorate with a staff of analysts having appropriate expertise and experience to assist the Directorate in discharging responsibilities under this section.

(2) PRIVATE SECTOR ANALYSTS.—Analysts under this subsection may include analysts from the private sector.

(3) SECURITY CLEARANCES.—Analysts under this subsection shall possess security clearances appropriate for their work under this section.

(f) DETAIL OF PERSONNEL.—

(1) IN GENERAL.—In order to assist the Directorate in discharging responsibilities under this section, personnel of the agencies referred to in paragraph (2) may be detailed to the Department for the performance of analytic functions and related duties.

(2) COVERED AGENCIES.—The agencies referred to in this paragraph are as follows:

(A) The Department of State.

(B) The Central Intelligence Agency.

(C) The Federal Bureau of Investigation.

(D) The National Security Agency.

(E) The National Imagery and Mapping Agency.

(F) The Defense Intelligence Agency.

(G) Any other agency of the Federal Government that the President considers appropriate.

(3) COOPERATIVE AGREEMENTS.—The Secretary and the head of the agency concerned may enter into cooperative agreements for the purpose of detailing personnel under this subsection.

(4) BASIS.—The detail of personnel under this subsection may be on a reimbursable or non-reimbursable basis.

(g) FUNCTIONS TRANSFERRED.—In accordance with title XV, there shall be transferred to the Secretary, for assignment to the Under Secretary for Information Analysis and Infrastructure Protection under this section, the functions, personnel, assets, and liabilities of the following:

(1) The National Infrastructure Protection Center of the Federal Bureau of Investigation (other than the Computer Investigations and Operations Section), including the functions of the Attorney General relating thereto.

(2) The National Communications System of the Department of Defense, including the functions of the Secretary of Defense relating thereto.

(3) The Critical Infrastructure Assurance Office of the Department of Commerce, including the functions of the Secretary of Commerce relating thereto.

(4) The National Infrastructure Simulation and Analysis Center of the Department of Energy and the energy security and assurance program and activities of the Department, including the functions of the Secretary of Energy relating thereto.

(5) The Federal Computer Incident Response Center of the General Services Administration, including the functions of the Administrator of General Services relating thereto. * * * * * * *

Sec. 202. [6 U.S.C. 122] ACCESS TO INFORMATION.

(a) IN GENERAL.—

(1) THREAT AND VULNERABILITY INFORMATION.—Except as otherwise directed by the President, the Secretary shall have such access as the Secretary considers necessary to all information, including reports, assessments, analyses, and unevaluated intelligence relating to threats of terrorism against the United States and to other areas of responsibility assigned by the Secretary, and to all information concerning infrastructure or other vulnerabilities of the United States to terrorism, whether or not such information has been analyzed, that may be collected, possessed, or prepared by any agency of the Federal Government.

(2) OTHER INFORMATION.—The Secretary shall also have access to other information relating to matters under the responsibility of the Secretary that may be collected, possessed, or prepared by an agency of the Federal Government as the President may further provide.

(b) MANNER OF ACCESS.—Except as otherwise directed by the President, with respect to information to which the Secretary has access pursuant to this section—

(1) the Secretary may obtain such material upon request, and may enter into cooperative arrangements with other executive agencies to provide such material or provide Department officials with access to it on a regular or routine basis, including requests or arrangements involving broad categories of material, access to electronic databases, or both; and

(2) regardless of whether the Secretary has made any request or entered into any cooperative arrangement pursuant to paragraph (1), all agencies of the Federal Government shall promptly provide to the Secretary—

(A) all reports (including information reports containing intelligence which has not been fully evaluated), assessments, and analytical information relating to threats of terrorism against the United States and to other areas of responsibility assigned by the Secretary;

(B) all information concerning the vulnerability of the infrastructure of the United States, or other vulnerabilities of the United States, to terrorism, whether or not such information has been analyzed;

(C) all other information relating to significant and credible threats of terrorism against the United States, whether or not such information has been analyzed; and

(D) such other information or material as the President may direct.

(c) TREATMENT UNDER CERTAIN LAWS.—The Secretary shall be deemed to be a Federal law enforcement, intelligence, protective, national defense, immigration, or national security official, and shall be provided with all information from law enforcement agencies that is required to be given to the Director of Central Intelligence, under any provision of the following:

(1) The USA PATRIOT Act of 2001 (Public Law 107–56).

(2) Section 2517(6) of title 18, United States Code.

(3) Rule 6(e)(3)(C) of the Federal Rules of Criminal Procedure.

(d) ACCESS TO INTELLIGENCE AND OTHER INFORMATION.—

(1) ACCESS BY ELEMENTS OF FEDERAL GOVERNMENT.—Nothing in this title shall preclude any element of the intelligence community (as that term is defined in section 3(4) of the National Security Act of 1947 (50 U.S.C. 401a(4)), or any other element of the Federal Government with responsibility for analyzing terrorist threat information, from receiving any intelligence or other information relating to terrorism.

(2) SHARING OF INFORMATION.—The Secretary, in consultation with the Director of Central Intelligence, shall work to ensure that intelligence or other information relating to terrorism to which the Department has access is appropriately shared with the elements of the Federal Government referred to in paragraph (1), as well as with State and local governments, as appropriate.

Subtitle B—Critical Infrastructure Information

Sec. 211. [6 U.S.C. 101 note] SHORT TITLE.

This subtitle may be cited as the "Critical Infrastructure Information Act of 2002."

Sec. 212. [6 U.S.C. 131] DEFINITIONS.

In this subtitle:

(1) AGENCY.—The term "agency" has the meaning given it in section 551 of title 5, United States Code.

(2) COVERED FEDERAL AGENCY.—The term "covered Federal agency" means the Department of Homeland Security.

(3) CRITICAL INFRASTRUCTURE INFORMATION.—The term "critical infrastructure information" means information not customarily in the public domain and related to the security of critical infrastructure or protected systems—

(A) actual, potential, or threatened interference with, attack on, compromise of, or incapacitation of critical infrastructure or protected systems by either physical or computer-based attack or other similar conduct (including the misuse of or unauthorized access to all types of communications and data transmission systems) that violates Federal, State, or local law, harms interstate commerce of the United States, or threatens public health or safety;

(B) the ability of any critical infrastructure or protected system to resist such interference, compromise, or incapacitation, including any planned or past assessment, projection, or estimate of the vulnerability of critical infrastructure or a protected system, including security testing, risk evaluation thereto, risk management planning, or risk audit; or

(C) any planned or past operational problem or solution regarding critical infrastructure or protected systems, including repair, recovery, reconstruction, insurance, or continuity, to the extent it is related to such interference, compromise, or incapacitation.

(4) CRITICAL INFRASTRUCTURE PROTECTION PROGRAM.—The term "critical infrastructure protection program" means any component or bureau of a covered Federal agency that has been designated by the President or any agency head to receive critical infrastructure information.

(5) INFORMATION SHARING AND ANALYSIS ORGANIZATION.— The term "Information Sharing and Analysis Organization" means any formal or informal entity or collaboration created or employed by public or private sector organizations, for purposes of—

(A) gathering and analyzing critical infrastructure information in order to better understand security problems and interdependencies related to critical infrastructure and protected systems, so as to ensure the availability, integrity, and reliability thereof;

(B) communicating or disclosing critical infrastructure information to help prevent, detect, mitigate, or recover from the effects of a interference, compromise, or a incapacitation problem related to critical infrastructure or protected systems; and

(C) voluntarily disseminating critical infrastructure information to its members, State, local, and Federal Governments, or any other entities that may be of assistance in carrying out the purposes specified in subparagraphs (A) and (B).

(6) PROTECTED SYSTEM.—The term "protected system"—

(A) means any service, physical or computer-based system, process, or procedure that directly or indirectly affects the viability of a facility of critical infrastructure; and

(B) includes any physical or computer-based system, including a computer, computer system, computer or communications network, or any component hardware or element thereof, software program, processing instructions, or information or data in transmission or storage therein, irrespective of the medium of transmission or storage.

(7) VOLUNTARY.—

(A) IN GENERAL.—The term "voluntary", in the case of any submittal of critical infrastructure information to a covered Federal agency, means the submittal thereof in the absence of such agency's exercise of legal authority to compel access to or submission of such information and may be accomplished by a single entity or an Information Sharing and Analysis Organization on behalf of itself or its members.

(B) EXCLUSIONS.—The term "voluntary"—

(i) in the case of any action brought under the securities laws as is defined in section 3(a)(47) of the Securities Exchange Act of 1934 (15 U.S.C. 78c(a)(47))—

(I) does not include information or statements contained in any documents or materials filed with the Securities and Exchange Commission, or with Federal banking regulators, pursuant to section 12(i) of the Securities Exchange Act of 1934 (15 U.S.C. 781(I)); and

(II) with respect to the submittal of critical infrastructure information, does not include any disclosure or writing that when made accompanied the solicitation of an offer or a sale of securities; and

(ii) does not include information or statements submitted or relied upon as a basis for making licensing or permitting determinations, or during regulatory proceedings.

Sec. 213. [6 U.S.C. 132] DESIGNATION OF CRITICAL INFRASTRUCTURE PROTECTION PROGRAM.

A critical infrastructure protection program may be designated as such by one of the following:

(1) The President.

(2) The Secretary of Homeland Security.

Sec. 214. [6 U.S.C. 123] PROTECTION OF VOLUNTARILY SHARED CRITICAL INFRASTRUCTURE INFORMATION.

(a) PROTECTION.—

(1) IN GENERAL.—Notwithstanding any other provision of law, critical infrastructure information (including the identity of the submitting person or entity) that is voluntarily submitted to a covered Federal agency for use by that agency regarding the security of critical infrastructure and protected systems, analysis, warning, interdependency study, recovery, reconstitution, or other informational purpose, when accompanied by an express statement specified in paragraph (2)—

(A) shall be exempt from disclosure under section 552 of title 5, United States Code (commonly referred to as the Freedom of Information Act);

(B) shall not be subject to any agency rules or judicial doctrine regarding ex parte communications with a decision making official;

(C) shall not, without the written consent of the person or entity submitting such information, be used directly by such agency, any other Federal, State, or local authority, or any third party, in any civil action arising under Federal or State law if such information is submitted in good faith;

(D) shall not, without the written consent of the person or entity submitting such information, be used or disclosed by any officer or employee of the United States for purposes other than the purposes of this subtitle, except—

(i) in furtherance of an investigation or the prosecution of a criminal act; or

(ii) when disclosure of the information would be—

(I) to either House of Congress, or to the extent of matter within its jurisdiction, any committee or subcommittee thereof, any joint committee thereof or subcommittee of any such joint committee; or

(II) to the Comptroller General, or any authorized representative of the Comptroller General, in the course of the performance of the duties of the General Accounting Office.

(E) shall not, if provided to a State or local government or government agency—

(i) be made available pursuant to any State or local law requiring disclosure of information or records;

(ii) otherwise be disclosed or distributed to any party by said State or local government or government agency without the written consent of the person or entity submitting such information; or

(iii) be used other than for the purpose of protecting critical infrastructure or protected systems, or in furtherance of an investigation or the prosecution of a criminal act; and

(F) does not constitute a waiver of any applicable privilege or protection provided under law, such as trade secret protection.

(2) EXPRESS STATEMENT.—For purposes of paragraph (1), the term "express statement", with respect to information or records, means—

(A) in the case of written information or records, a written marking on the information or records substantially similar to the following: "This information is voluntarily submitted to the Federal Government in expectation of protection from disclosure as provided by the provisions of the Critical Infrastructure Information Act of 2002."; or

(B) in the case of oral information, a similar written statement submitted within a reasonable period following the oral communication.

(b) LIMITATION.—No communication of critical infrastructure information to a covered Federal agency made pursuant to this subtitle shall be considered to be an action subject to the requirements of the Federal Advisory Committee Act (5 U.S.C. App. 2).

(c) INDEPENDENTLY OBTAINED INFORMATION.—Nothing in this section shall be construed to limit or otherwise affect the ability of a State, local, or Federal Government entity, agency, or authority, or any third party, under applicable law, to obtain critical infrastructure information in a manner not covered by subsection (a), including any information lawfully and properly disclosed generally or broadly to the public and to use such information in any manner permitted by law.

(d) TREATMENT OF VOLUNTARY SUBMITTAL OF INFORMATION.— The voluntary submittal to the Government of information or records that are protected from disclosure by this subtitle shall not be construed to constitute compliance with any requirement to submit such information to a Federal agency under any other provision of law.

(e) PROCEDURES.—

(1) IN GENERAL.—The Secretary of the Department of Homeland Security shall, in consultation with appropriate representatives of the National Security Council and the Office of Science and Technology Policy, establish uniform procedures for the receipt, care, and storage by Federal agencies of critical infrastructure information that is voluntarily submitted to the Government. The procedures shall be established not later than 90 days after the date of the enactment of this subtitle.

(2) ELEMENTS.—The procedures established under paragraph

(1) shall include mechanisms regarding—

(A) the acknowledgement of receipt by Federal agencies of critical infrastructure information that is voluntarily submitted to the Government;

(B) the maintenance of the identification of such information as voluntarily submitted to the Government for purposes of and subject to the provisions of this subtitle;

(C) the care and storage of such information; and

(D) the protection and maintenance of the confidentiality of such information so as to permit the sharing of such information within the Federal Government and with State and local governments, and the issuance of notices and warnings related to the protection of critical infrastructure and protected systems, in such manner as to protect from public disclosure the identity of the submitting person or entity, or information that is proprietary, business sensitive, relates specifically to the submitting person or entity, and is otherwise not appropriately in the public domain.

(f) PENALTIES.—Whoever, being an officer or employee of the United States or of any department or agency thereof, knowingly publishes, divulges, discloses, or makes known in any manner or to any extent not authorized by law, any critical infrastructure information protected from disclosure by this subtitle coming to him in the course of this employment or official duties or by reason of any examination or investigation made by, or return, report, or record made to or filed with, such department or agency or officer or employee thereof, shall be fined under title 18 of the United States Code, imprisoned not more than 1 year, or both, and shall be removed from office or employment.

(g) AUTHORITY TO ISSUE WARNINGS.—The Federal Government may provide advisories, alerts, and warnings to relevant companies, targeted sectors, other governmental entities, or the general public regarding potential threats to critical infrastructure as appropriate. In issuing a warning, the Federal Government shall take appropriate actions to protect from disclosure—

(1) the source of any voluntarily submitted critical infrastructure information that forms the basis for the warning; or

(2) information that is proprietary, business sensitive, relates specifically to the submitting person or entity, or is otherwise not appropriately in the public domain.

(h) AUTHORITY TO DELEGATE.—The President may delegate authority to a critical infrastructure protection program, designated under section 213, to enter into a voluntary agreement to promote critical infrastructure security, including with any Information Sharing and Analysis Organization, or a plan of action as otherwise defined in section 708 of the Defense Production Act of 1950 (50 U.S.C. App. 2158).

Sec. 215. [6 U.S.C. 134] NO PRIVATE RIGHT OF ACTION.

Nothing in this subtitle may be construed to create a private right of action for enforcement of any provision of this Act.

Subtitle C—Information Security

Sec. 221. [6 U.S.C. 141] PROCEDURES FOR SHARING INFORMATION.

The Secretary shall establish procedures on the use of information shared under this title that—

(1) limit the redissemination of such information to ensure that it is not used for an unauthorized purpose;

(2) ensure the security and confidentiality of such information;

(3) protect the constitutional and statutory rights of any individuals who are subjects of such information; and

(4) provide data integrity through the timely removal and destruction of obsolete or erroneous names and information.

Sec. 222. [6 U.S.C. 142] PRIVACY OFFICER.

The Secretary shall appoint a senior official in the Department, who shall report directly to the Secretary, to assume primary responsibility for privacy policy, including—

(1) assuring that the use of technologies sustain, and do not erode, privacy protections relating to the use, collection, and disclosure of personal information;

(2) assuring that personal information contained in Privacy Act systems of records is handled in full compliance with fair information practices as set out in the Privacy Act of 1974;

(3) evaluating legislative and regulatory proposals involving collection, use, and disclosure of personal information by the Federal Government;

(4) conducting a privacy impact assessment of proposed rules of the Department or that of the Department on the privacy of personal information, including the type of personal information collected and the number of people affected;

(5) coordinating with the Officer for Civil Rights and Civil Liberties to ensure that—

(A) programs, policies, and procedures involving civil rights, civil liberties, and privacy considerations are addressed in an integrated and comprehensive manner; and

(B) Congress receives appropriate reports on such programs, policies, and procedures; and

(6) preparing a report to Congress on an annual basis on activities of the Department that affect privacy, including complaints of privacy violations, implementation of the Privacy Act of 1974, internal controls, and other matters.

Sec. 223. [6 U.S.C. 143] ENHANCEMENT OF NON-FEDERAL CYBERSECURITY.

In carrying out the responsibilities under section 201, the Under Secretary for Information Analysis and Infrastructure Protection shall—

(1) as appropriate, provide to State and local government entities, and upon request to private entities that own or operate critical information systems—

(A) analysis and warnings related to threats to, and vulnerabilities of, critical information systems; and

(B) in coordination with the Under Secretary for Emergency Preparedness and Response, crisis management support in response to threats to, or attacks on, critical information systems; and

(2) as appropriate, provide technical assistance, upon request, to the private sector and other government entities, in coordination with the Under Secretary for Emergency Preparedness and Response, with respect to emergency recovery plans to respond to major failures of critical information systems.

Sec. 224. [6 U.S.C. 144] NET GUARD.

The Under Secretary for Information Analysis and Infrastructure Protection may establish a national technology guard, to be known as "NET Guard", comprised of local teams of volunteers with expertise in relevant areas of science and technology, to assist local communities to respond and recover from attacks on information systems and communications networks.

Sec. 225. [6 U.S.C. 145] CYBER SECURITY ENHANCEMENT ACT OF 2002.

(a) SHORT TITLE.—This section may be cited as the "Cyber Security Enhancement Act of 2002."

(b) AMENDMENT OF SENTENCING GUIDELINES RELATING TO CERTAIN COMPUTER CRIMES.—

(1) DIRECTIVE TO THE UNITED STATES SENTENCING COMMISSION.—Pursuant to its authority under section 994(p) of title 28, United States Code, and in accordance with this subsection, the United States Sentencing Commission shall review and, if appropriate, amend its guidelines and its policy statements applicable to persons convicted of an offense under section 1030 of title 18, United States Code.

(2) REQUIREMENTS.—In carrying out this subsection, the Sentencing Commission shall—

(A) ensure that the sentencing guidelines and policy statements reflect the serious nature of the offenses described in paragraph (1), the growing incidence of such offenses, and the need for an effective deterrent and appropriate punishment to prevent such offenses;

(B) consider the following factors and the extent to which the guidelines may or may not account for them—

(i) the potential and actual loss resulting from the offense;

(ii) the level of sophistication and planning involved in the offense;

(iii) whether the offense was committed for purposes of commercial advantage or private financial benefit;

(iv) whether the defendant acted with malicious intent to cause harm in committing the offense;

(v) the extent to which the offense violated the privacy rights of individuals harmed;

(vi) whether the offense involved a computer used by the government in furtherance of national defense, national security, or the administration of justice;

(vii) whether the violation was intended to or had the effect of significantly interfering with or disrupting a critical infrastructure; and

(viii) whether the violation was intended to or had the effect of creating a threat to public health or safety, or injury to any person;

(C) assure reasonable consistency with other relevant directives and with other sentencing guidelines;

(D) account for any additional aggravating or mitigating circumstances that might justify exceptions to the generally applicable sentencing ranges;

(E) make any necessary conforming changes to the sentencing guidelines; and

(F) assure that the guidelines adequately meet the purposes of sentencing as set forth in section 3553(a)(2) of title 18, United States Code.

(c) STUDY AND REPORT ON COMPUTER CRIMES.—Not later than May 1, 2003, the United States Sentencing Commission shall submit a brief report to Congress that explains any actions taken by the Sentencing Commission in response to this section and includes any recommendations the Commission may have regarding statutory penalties for offenses under section 1030 of title 18, United States Code.

(d) EMERGENCY DISCLOSURE EXCEPTION.—

(1) * * * * * * * * * *

(2) REPORTING OF DISCLOSURES.—A government entity that receives a disclosure under section 2702(b) of title 18, United States Code, shall file, not later than 90 days after such disclosure, a report to the Attorney General stating the paragraph of that section under which the disclosure was made, the date of the disclosure, the entity to which the disclosure was made, the number of customers or subscribers to whom the information disclosed pertained, and the number of communications, if any, that were disclosed. The Attorney General shall publish all such reports into a single report to be submitted to Congress 1 year after the date of enactment of this Act.

Subtitle D—Office of Science and Technology

Sec. 231. [6 U.S.C. 161] ESTABLISHMENT OF OFFICE; DIRECTOR.

(a) ESTABLISHMENT.—

(1) IN GENERAL.—There is hereby established within the Department of Justice an Office of Science and Technology

(hereinafter in this title referred to as the "Office").

(2) AUTHORITY.—The Office shall be under the general authority of the Assistant Attorney General, Office of Justice Programs, and shall be established within the National Institute of Justice.

(b) DIRECTOR.—The Office shall be headed by a Director, who shall be an individual appointed based on approval by the Office of Personnel Management of the executive qualifications of the individual.

Sec. 232. [6 U.S.C. 162] MISSION OF OFFICE; DUTIES.

(a) MISSION.—The mission of the Office shall be—

(1) to serve as the national focal point for work on law enforcement technology; and

(2) to carry out programs that, through the provision of equipment, training, and technical assistance, improve the safety and effectiveness of law enforcement technology and improve access to such technology by Federal, State, and local law enforcement agencies.

(b) DUTIES.—In carrying out its mission, the Office shall have the following duties:

(1) To provide recommendations and advice to the Attorney General.

(2) To establish and maintain advisory groups (which shall be exempt from the provisions of the Federal Advisory Committee Act (5 U.S.C. App.)) to assess the law enforcement technology needs of Federal, State, and local law enforcement agencies.

(3) To establish and maintain performance standards in accordance with the National Technology Transfer and Advancement Act of 1995 (Public Law 104–113) for, and test and evaluate law enforcement technologies that may be used by, Federal, State, and local law enforcement agencies.

(4) To establish and maintain a program to certify, validate, and mark or otherwise recognize law enforcement technology products that conform to standards established and maintained by the Office in accordance with the National Technology Transfer and Advancement Act of 1995 (Public Law 104–113). The program may, at the discretion of the Office, allow for supplier's declaration of conformity with such standards.

(5) To work with other entities within the Department of Justice, other Federal agencies, and the executive office of the President to establish a coordinated Federal approach on issues related to law enforcement technology.

(6) To carry out research, development, testing, evaluation, and cost-benefit analyses in fields that would improve the safety, effectiveness, and efficiency of law enforcement technologies used by Federal, State, and local law enforcement agencies, including, but not limited to—

(A) weapons capable of preventing use by unauthorized persons, including personalized guns;

(B) protective apparel;

(C) bullet-resistant and explosion-resistant glass;

(D) monitoring systems and alarm systems capable of providing precise location information;

(E) wire and wireless interoperable communication technologies;

(F) tools and techniques that facilitate investigative and forensic work, including computer forensics;

(G) equipment for particular use in counterterrorism, including devices and technologies to disable terrorist devices;

(H) guides to assist State and local law enforcement agencies;

(I) DNA identification technologies; and

(J) tools and techniques that facilitate investigations of computer crime.

(7) To administer a program of research, development, testing, and demonstration to improve the interoperability of voice and data public safety communications.

(8) To serve on the Technical Support Working Group of the Department of Defense, and on other relevant interagency panels, as requested.

(9) To develop, and disseminate to State and local law enforcement agencies, technical assistance and training materials for law enforcement personnel, including prosecutors.

(10) To operate the regional National Law Enforcement and Corrections Technology Centers and, to the extent necessary, establish additional centers through a competitive process.

(11) To administer a program of acquisition, research, development, and dissemination of advanced investigative analysis and forensic tools to assist State and local law enforcement agencies in combating cybercrime.

(12) To support research fellowships in support of its mission.

(13) To serve as a clearinghouse for information on law enforcement technologies.

(14) To represent the United States and State and local law enforcement agencies, as requested, in international activities concerning law enforcement technology.

(15) To enter into contracts and cooperative agreements and provide grants, which may require in-kind or cash matches from the recipient, as necessary to carry out its mission.

(16) To carry out other duties assigned by the Attorney General to accomplish the mission of the Office.

(c) COMPETITION REQUIRED.—Except as otherwise expressly provided by law, all research and development carried out by or through the Office shall be carried out on a competitive basis.

(d) INFORMATION FROM FEDERAL AGENCIES.—Federal agencies shall, upon request from the Office and in accordance with Federal law, provide the Office with any data, reports, or other information requested, unless compliance with such request is otherwise prohibited by law.

(e) PUBLICATIONS.—Decisions concerning publications issued by the Office shall rest solely with the Director of the Office.

(f) TRANSFER OF FUNDS.—The Office may transfer funds to other Federal agencies or provide funding to non-Federal entities through grants, cooperative agreements, or contracts to carry out its duties under this section: Provided, That any such transfer or provision of funding shall be carried out in accordance with section 605 of Public Law 107–77.

(g) ANNUAL REPORT.—The Director of the Office shall include with the budget justification materials submitted to Congress in support of the Department of Justice budget for each fiscal year (as submitted with the budget of the President under section 1105(a) of title 31, United States Code) a report on the activities of the Office. Each such report shall include the following:

(1) For the period of 5 fiscal years beginning with the fiscal year for which the budget is submitted—

(A) the Director's assessment of the needs of Federal, State, and local law enforcement agencies for assistance with respect to law enforcement technology and other matters consistent with the mission of the Office; and

(B) a strategic plan for meeting such needs of such law enforcement agencies.

(2) For the fiscal year preceding the fiscal year for which such budget is submitted, a description of the activities carried out by the Office and an evaluation of the extent to which those activities successfully meet the needs assessed under paragraph (1)(A) in previous reports.

Sec. 233. [6 U.S.C. 163] DEFINITION OF LAW ENFORCEMENT TECHNOLOGY.

For the purposes of this title, the term "law enforcement technology" includes investigative and forensic technologies, corrections technologies, and technologies that support the judicial process.

Sec. 234. [6 U.S.C. 164] ABOLISHMENT OF OFFICE OF SCIENCE AND TECHNOLOGY OF NATIONAL INSTITUTE OF JUSTICE; TRANSFER OF FUNCTIONS.

(a) AUTHORITY TO TRANSFER FUNCTIONS.—The Attorney General may transfer to the Office any other program or activity of the Department of Justice that the Attorney General, in consultation with the Committee on the Judiciary of the Senate and the Committee on the Judiciary of the House of Representatives, determines to be consistent with the mission of the Office.

(b) TRANSFER OF PERSONNEL AND ASSETS.—With respect to any function, power, or duty, or any program or activity, that is established in the Office, those employees and assets of the element of the Department of Justice from which the transfer is made that the Attorney General determines are needed to perform that function, power, or duty, or for that program or activity, as the case may be, shall be transferred to the Office: Provided, That any such transfer shall be carried out in accordance with section 605 of Public Law 107–77.

(c) REPORT ON IMPLEMENTATION.—Not later than 1 year after the date of the enactment of this Act, the Attorney General shall submit to the Committee on the Judiciary of the Senate and the Committee on the Judiciary of the House of Representatives a report on the implementation of this title. The report shall—

(1) provide an accounting of the amounts and sources of funding available to the Office to carry out its mission under existing authorizations and appropriations, and set forth the future funding needs of the Office; and

(2) include such other information and recommendations as the Attorney General considers appropriate.

Sec. 235. [6 U.S.C. 165] NATIONAL LAW ENFORCEMENT AND CORRECTIONS TECHNOLOGY CENTERS.

(a) IN GENERAL.—The Director of the Office shall operate and support National Law Enforcement and Corrections Technology Centers (hereinafter in this section referred to as "Centers") and, to the extent necessary, establish new centers through a meritbased, competitive process.

(b) PURPOSE OF CENTERS.—The purpose of the Centers shall be to—

(1) support research and development of law enforcement technology;

(2) support the transfer and implementation of technology;

(3) assist in the development and dissemination of guidelines and technological standards; and

(4) provide technology assistance, information, and support for law enforcement, corrections, and criminal justice purposes.

(c) ANNUAL MEETING.—Each year, the Director shall convene a meeting of the Centers in order to foster collaboration and communication between Center participants.

(d) REPORT.—Not later than 12 months after the date of the enactment of this Act, the Director shall transmit to the Congress a report assessing the effectiveness of the existing system of Centers and identify the number of Centers necessary to meet the technology needs of Federal, State, and local law enforcement in the United States.

SEC. 236. COORDINATION WITH OTHER ENTITIES WITHIN DEPARTMENT OF JUSTICE.

Section 102 of the Omnibus Crime Control and Safe Streets Act of 1968 (42 U.S.C. 3712) is amended in subsection (a)(5) by inserting "coordinate and" before "provide".

SEC. 237. AMENDMENTS RELATING TO NATIONAL INSTITUTE OF JUSTICE.

Section 202(c) of the Omnibus Crime Control and Safe Streets Act of 1968 (42 U.S.C. 3722(c)) is amended—

(1) in paragraph (3) by inserting ", including cost effectiveness where practical," before "of projects"; and

(2) by striking "and" after the semicolon at the end of paragraph (8), striking the period at the end of paragraph

(9) and inserting "; and", and by adding at the end the following:

"(10) research and development of tools and technologies relating to prevention, detection, investigation, and prosecution of crime; and

"(11) support research, development, testing, training, and evaluation of tools and technology for Federal, State, and local law enforcement agencies."

Protection of Officers and Employees of the United States

(18 U.S.C. § 1114)

Whoever kills or attempts to kill any officer or employee of the United States or of any agency in any branch of the United States Government (including any member of the uniformed services) while such officer or employee is engaged in or on account of the performance of official duties, or any person assisting such an officer or employee in the performance of such duties or on account of that assistance, shall be punished—

(1) in the case of murder, as provided under section 1111;
(2) in the case of manslaughter, as provided under section 1112; or
(3) in the case of attempted murder or manslaughter, as provided in section 1113

Counterintelligence Enhancement Act of 2002

(Pub. L. 107-306, 116 Stat. 2432)

TITLE IX—COUNTERINTELLIGENCE ACTIVITIES

SEC. 901. SHORT TITLE; PURPOSE.

(a) SHORT TITLE.—This title may be cited as the "Counterintelligence Enhancement Act of 2002".

(b) PURPOSE.—The purpose of this title is to facilitate the note. enhancement of the counterintelligence activities of the United States Government by—

(1) enabling the counterintelligence community of the United States Government to fulfill better its mission of identifying, assessing, prioritizing, and countering the intelligence threats to the United States;

(2) ensuring that the counterintelligence community of the United States Government acts in an efficient and effective manner; and

(3) providing for the integration of all the counterintelligence activities of the United States Government.

SEC. 902. NATIONAL COUNTERINTELLIGENCE EXECUTIVE.

(a) ESTABLISHMENT.—

(1) There shall be a National Counterintelligence Executive, who shall be appointed by the President.

(2) It is the sense of Congress that the President should seek the views of the Attorney General, Secretary of Defense, and Director of Central Intelligence in selecting an individual for appointment as the Executive.

(b) MISSION.—The mission of the National Counterintelligence Executive shall be to serve as the head of national counterintelligence for the United States Government.

(c) DUTIES.—Subject to the direction and control of the President, the duties of the National Counterintelligence Executive are as follows:

(1) To carry out the mission referred to in subsection (b).

(2) To act as chairperson of the National Counterintel ligence Policy Board under section 811 of the Counterintelligence and Security Enhancements Act of 1994 (title VIII of Public Law 103–359; 50 U.S.C. 402a), as amended by section 903 of this Act.

(3) To act as head of the Office of the National Counterintelligence Executive under section 904.

(4) To participate as an observer on such boards, commit-tees, and entities of the executive branch as the President considers appropriate for the discharge of the mission and functions of the Executive and the Office of the National Counterintelligence Executive under section 904.

SEC. 903. NATIONAL COUNTERINTELLIGENCE POLICY BOARD.

(a) CHAIRPERSON.—Section 811 of the Counterintelligence and Security Enhancements Act of 1994 (title VII of Public Law 103– 359; 50 U.S.C. 402a), as amended by section 811(b)(5)(B) of this Act, is further amended—

(1) by striking subsection (b);

(2) by redesignating subsection (c) as subsection (e); and

(3) by inserting after subsection (a) the following new sub-section (b):"(b) CHAIRPERSON.—The National Counterintelligence Executive under section 902 of the Counterintelligence Enhancement Act of 2002 shall serve as the chairperson of the Board."

(b) MEMBERSHIP.—That section is further amended by inserting after subsection (b), as amended by subsection (a)(3) of this section, the following new subsection (c):

"(c) MEMBERSHIP.—The membership of the National Counterintelligence Policy Board shall consist of the following:

"(1) The National Counterintelligence Executive.

"(2) Senior personnel of departments and elements of the United States Government, appointed by the head of the department or element concerned, as follows:

"(A) The Department of Justice, including the Federal Bureau of Investigation.

"(B) The Department of Defense, including the Joint Chiefs of Staff.

"(C) The Department of State.

"(D) The Department of Energy.

"(E) The Central Intelligence Agency.

"(F) Any other department, agency, or element of the United States Government specified by the President.".

(c) FUNCTIONS AND DISCHARGE OF FUNCTIONS.—That section is further amended by inserting after subsection (c), as amended by subsection (b) of this section, the following new subsection:

"(d) FUNCTIONS AND DISCHARGE OF FUNCTIONS.—

(1) The Board shall—

"(A) serve as the principal mechanism for—

"(i) developing policies and procedures for the approval of the President to govern the conduct of counterintelligence activities; and

"(ii) upon the direction of the President, resolving conflicts that arise between elements of the Government conducting such activities; and

"(B) act as an interagency working group to—

"(i) ensure the discussion and review of matters relating to the implementation of the Counterintelligence Enhancement Act of 2002; and

"(ii) provide advice to the National Counterintelligence Executive on priorities in the implementation of the National Counterintelligence Strategy produced by the Office of the National Counterintelligence Executive under section 904(e)(2) of that Act.

"(2) The Board may, for purposes of carrying out its functions under this section, establish such interagency boards and working groups as the Board considers appropriate.".

SEC. 904. OFFICE OF THE NATIONAL COUNTERINTELLIGENCE EXECUTIVE.

(a) ESTABLISHMENT.—There shall be an Office of the National Counterintelligence Executive.

(b) HEAD OF OFFICE.—The National Counterintelligence Executive shall be the head of the Office of the National Counterintelligence Executive.

(c) LOCATION OF OFFICE.—The Office of the National Counterintelligence Executive shall be located in the Office of the Director of Central Intelligence.

(d) GENERAL COUNSEL.—

(1) There shall be in the Office of the National Counterintelligence Executive a general counsel who shall serve as principal legal advisor to the National Counterintelligence Executive.

(2) The general counsel shall—

(A) provide legal advice and counsel to the Executive on matters relating to functions of the Office;

(B) ensure that the Office complies with all applicable laws, regulations, Executive orders, and guidelines; and

(C) carry out such other duties as the Executive may specify.

(e) FUNCTIONS.—Subject to the direction and control of the National Counterintelligence Executive, the functions of the Office of the National Counterintelligence Executive shall be as follows:

(1) NATIONAL THREAT IDENTIFICATION AND PRIORITIZATION ASSESSMENT.—Subject to subsection (f), in consultation with appropriate department and agencies of the United States Government, and private sector entities, to produce on an annual basis a strategic planning assessment of the counterintelligence requirements of the United States to be known as the National Threat Identification and Prioritization Assessment.

(2) NATIONAL COUNTERINTELLIGENCE STRATEGY.—Subject to subsection (f), in consultation with appropriate department and agencies of the United States Government, and private sector entities, and based on the most current National Threat Identification and Prioritization Assessment under paragraph (1), to produce on an annual basis a strategy for the counterintelligence programs and activities of the United States Government to be known as the National Counterintelligence Strategy.

(3) IMPLEMENTATION OF NATIONAL COUNTERINTELLIGENCE STRATEGY.—To evaluate on an ongoing basis the implementation of the National Counterintelligence Strategy and to submit to the President periodic reports on such evaluation, including a discussion of any shortfalls in the implementation of the Strategy and recommendations for remedies for such shortfalls.

(4) NATIONAL COUNTERINTELLIGENCE STRATEGIC ANALYSES.—As directed by the Director of Central Intelligence and in consultation with appropriate elements of the departments and agencies of the United States Government, to oversee and coordinate the production of strategic analyses of counterintelligence matters, including the production of counterintelli-

gence damage assessments and assessments of lessons learned from counterintelligence activities.

(5) NATIONAL COUNTERINTELLIGENCE PROGRAM BUDGET.—In consultation with the Director of Central Intelligence—

(A) to coordinate the development of budgets and resource allocation plans for the counterintelligence programs and activities of the Department of Defense, the Federal Bureau of Investigation, the Central Intelligence Agency, and other appropriate elements of the United States Government;

(B) to ensure that the budgets and resource allocation plans developed under subparagraph (A) address the objectives and priorities for counterintelligence under the National Counterintelligence Strategy; and

(C) to submit to the National Security Council periodic reports on the activities undertaken by the Office under subparagraphs (A) and (B).

(6) NATIONAL COUNTERINTELLIGENCE COLLECTION AND TARGETING COORDINATION.—To develop priorities for counterintelligence investigations and operations, and for collection of counterintelligence, for purposes of the National Counterintelligence Strategy, except that the Office may not—

(A) carry out any counterintelligence investigations or operations; or

(B) establish its own contacts, or carry out its own activities, with foreign intelligence services.

(7) NATIONAL COUNTERINTELLIGENCE OUTREACH, WATCH,AND WARNING.—

(A) COUNTERINTELLIGENCE VULNERABILITY SURVEYS.—To carry out and coordinate surveys of the vulnerability of the United States Government, and the private sector, to intelligence threats in order to identify the areas, programs, and activities that require protection from such threats.

(B) OUTREACH.—To carry out and coordinate outreach programs and activities on counterintelligence to other elements of the United States Government, and the private sector, and to coordinate the dissemination to the public of warnings on intelligence threats to the United States.

(C) RESEARCH AND DEVELOPMENT.—To ensure that research and development programs and activities of the United States Government, and the private sector, direct attention to the needs of the counterintelligence community for technologies, products, and services.

(D) TRAINING AND PROFESSIONAL DEVELOPMENT.—To develop policies and standards for training and professional development of individuals engaged in counterintelligence activities and to manage the conduct of joint training exercises for such personnel.

(f) ADDITIONAL REQUIREMENTS REGARDING NATIONAL THREAT IDENTIFICATION AND PRIORITIZATION ASSESSMENT AND NATIONAL COUNTERINTELLIGENCE STRATEGY.—

(1) A National Threat Identification and Prioritization Assessment under subsection (e)(1), and any modification of such assessment, shall not go into effect until approved by the President.

(2) A National Counterintelligence Strategy under subsection(e)(2), and any modification of such strategy, shall not go into effect until approved by the President.

(3) The National Counterintelligence Executive shall submit to the congressional intelligence committees each National Threat Identification and Prioritization Assessment, or modification thereof, and each National Counterintelligence Strategy, or modification thereof, approved under this section.

(4) In this subsection, the term "congressional intelligence committees" means—

(A) the Select Committee on Intelligence of the Senate; and

(B) the Permanent Select Committee on Intelligence of the House of Representatives.

(g) PERSONNEL.—

(1) Personnel of the Office of the National Counterintelligence Executive may consist of personnel employed by the Office or personnel on detail from any other department, agency, or element of the Federal Government. Any such detail may be on a reimbursable or nonreimbursable basis, at the election of the head of the agency detailing such personnel.

(2) Notwithstanding section 104(d) or any other provision of law limiting the period of the detail of personnel on a nonreimbursable basis, the detail of an officer or employee of United States or a member of the Armed Forces under paragraph (1) on a nonreimbursable basis may be for any period in excess of one year that the National Counterintelligence Executive and the head of the department, agency, or element concerned consider appropriate.

(3) The employment of personnel by the Office, including the appointment, compensation and benefits, management, and separation of such personnel, shall be governed by the provisions of law on such matters with respect to the personnel of the Central Intelligence Agency, except that, for purposes of the applicability of such provisions of law to personnel of the Office, the National Counterintelligence Executive shall be treated as the head of the Office.

(4) Positions in the Office shall be excepted service positions for purposes of title 5, United States Code.

(h) SUPPORT.—

(1) The Attorney General, Secretary of Defense, and Director of Central Intelligence may each provide the Office of the National Counterintelligence Executive such support as may be necessary to permit the Office to carry out its functions under this section.

(2) Subject to any terms and conditions specified by the Director of Central Intelligence, the Director may provide administrative and contract support to the Office as if the Office were an element of the Central Intelligence Agency.

(3) Support provided under this subsection may be provided on a reimbursable or nonreimbursable basis, at the election of the official providing such support.

(i) AVAILABILITY OF FUNDS FOR REIMBURSEMENT.—The National Counterintelligence Executive may, from amounts available for the Office, transfer to a department or agency detailing personnel under subsection (g), or providing support under subsection (h), on a reimbursable basis amounts appropriate to reimburse such department or agency for the detail of such personnel or the provision of such support, as the case may be.

(j) CONTRACTS.—

(1) Subject to paragraph (2), the National Counterintelligence Executive may enter into any contract, lease, cooperative agreement, or other transaction that the Executive considers appropriate to carry out the functions of the Office of the National Counterintelligence Executive under this section.

(2) The authority under paragraph (1) to enter into contracts, leases, cooperative agreements, and other transactions shall be subject to any terms, conditions, and limitations applicable to the Central Intelligence Agency under law with respect to similar contracts, leases, cooperative agreements, and other transactions.

(k) TREATMENT OF ACTIVITIES UNDER CERTAIN ADMINISTRATIVE LAWS.—The files of the Office shall be treated as operational files of the Central Intelligence Agency for purposes of section 701 of the National Security Act of 1947 (50 U.S.C. 431) to the extent such files meet criteria under subsection (b) of that section for treatment of files as operational files of an element of the Agency.

(l) OVERSIGHT BY CONGRESS.—The location of the Office of the National Counterintelligence Executive within the Office of the Director of Central Intelligence shall not be construed as affecting access by Congress, or any committee of Congress, to—

(1) any information, document, record, or paper in thepossession of the Office; or

(2) any personnel of the Office.

(m) CONSTRUCTION.—Nothing in this section shall be construed as affecting the authority of the Director of Central Intelligence, the Secretary of Defense, the Secretary of State, the Attorney General, or the Director of the Federal Bureau of Investigation as provided or specified under the National Security Act of 1947 or under other provisions of law.

TITLE X—NATIONAL COMMISSION FOR REVIEW OF RESEARCH AND DEVELOPMENT PROGRAMS OF THE UNITED STATES INTELLIGENCE COMMUNITY

SEC. 1001. FINDINGS.

Congress makes the following findings:

(1) Research and development efforts under the purview of the intelligence community are vitally important to the national security of the United States.

(2) The intelligence community must operate in a dynamic, highly-challenging environment, characterized by rapid technological growth, against a growing number of hostile, technically-sophisticated threats. Research and development programs under the purview of the intelligence community are critical to ensuring that intelligence agencies, and their personnel, are provided with important technological capabilities to detect, characterize, assess, and ultimately counter the full range of threats to the national security of the United States.

(3) There is a need to review the full range of current research and development programs under the purview of the intelligence community, evaluate such programs against the scientific and technological fields judged to be of most importance, and articulate program and resource priorities for future research and development activities to ensure a unified and coherent research and development program across the entire intelligence community.

SEC. 1002. NATIONAL COMMISSION FOR THE REVIEW OF THE RESEARCH AND DEVELOPMENT PROGRAMS OF THE UNITED STATES INTELLIGENCE COMMUNITY.

(a) ESTABLISHMENT.—There is established a commission to be known as the "National Commission for the Review of the Research and Development Programs of the United States Intelligence Community" (in this title referred to as the "Commission").

(b) COMPOSITION.—The Commission shall be composed of 12 members, as follows:

(1) The Deputy Director of Central Intelligence for Community Management.

(2) A senior intelligence official of the Office of the Secretary of Defense, as designated by the Secretary of Defense.

(3) Three members appointed by the majority leader of the Senate, in consultation with the Chairman of the Select Committee on Intelligence of the Senate, one from Members of the Senate and two from private life.

(4) Two members appointed by the minority leader of the Senate, in consultation with the Vice Chairman of the Select Committee on Intelligence of the Senate, one from Members of the Senate and one from private life.

(5) Three members appointed by the Speaker of the House of Representatives, in consultation with the Chairman of the Permanent Select Committee

on Intelligence of the House of Representatives, one from Members of the House of Representatives and two from private life.

(6) Two members appointed by the minority leader of the House of Representatives, in consultation with the ranking member of the Permanent Select Committee on Intelligence of the House of Representatives, one from Members of the House of Representatives and one from private life.

(c) MEMBERSHIP.—

(1) The individuals appointed from private life as members of the Commission shall be individuals who are nationally recognized for expertise, knowledge, or experience in—

(A) research and development programs;

(B) technology discovery and insertion;

(C) use of intelligence information by national policy makers and military leaders; or

(D) the implementation, funding, or oversight of the national security policies of the United States.

(2) An official who appoints members of the Commission may not appoint an individual as a member of the Commission if, in the judgment of the official, such individual possesses any personal or financial interest in the discharge of any of the duties of the Commission.

(3) All members of the Commission appointed from private life shall possess an appropriate security clearance in accordance with applicable laws and regulations concerning the handling of classified information.

(d) CO-CHAIRS.—

(1) The Commission shall have two co-chairs, selected from among the members of the Commission.

(2) One co-chair of the Commission shall be a member of the Democratic Party, and one co-chair shall be a member of the Republican Party.

(3) The individuals who serve as the co-chairs of the Commission shall be jointly agreed upon by the President, the majority leader of the Senate, the minority leader of the Senate, the Speaker of the House of Representatives, and the minority leader of the House of Representatives.

(e) APPOINTMENT; INITIAL MEETING.—

(1) Members of the Commission shall be appointed not later than 45 days after the date of the enactment of this Act.

(2) The Commission shall hold its initial meeting on the date that is 60 days after the date of the enactment of this Act.

(f) MEETINGS; QUORUM; VACANCIES.—

(1) After its initial meeting, the Commission shall meet upon the call of the co-chairs of the Commission.

(2) Six members of the Commission shall constitute a quorum for purposes of conducting business, except that two members of the Commission shall constitute a quorum for purposes of receiving testimony.

(3) Any vacancy in the Commission shall not affect its powers, but shall be filled in the same manner in which the original appointment was made.

(4) If vacancies in the Commission occur on any day after45 days after the date of the enactment of this Act, a quorum shall consist of a majority of the members of the Commission as of such day.

(g) ACTIONS OF COMMISSION.—

(1) The Commission shall act by resolution agreed to by a majority of the members of the Commission voting and present.

(2) The Commission may establish panels composed of less than the full membership of the Commission for purposes of carrying out the duties of the Commission under this title. The actions of any such panel shall be subject to the review and control of the Commission. Any findings and determinations made by such a panel shall not be considered the findings and determinations of the Commission unless approved by the Commission.

(3) Any member, agent, or staff of the Commission may, if authorized by the co-chairs of the Commission, take any action which the Commission is authorized to take pursuant to this title.

(h) DUTIES.—The duties of the Commission shall be—

(1) to conduct, until not later than the date on whichthe Commission submits the report under section 1007(a), thereview described in subsection (i); and

(2) to submit to the congressional intelligence committees, the Director of Central Intelligence, and the Secretary of Defense a final report on the results of the review.

(i) REVIEW.—The Commission shall review the status of research and development programs and activities within the intelligence community, including—

(1) an assessment of the advisability of modifying the scope of research and development for purposes of such programs and activities;

(2) a review of the particular individual research and development activities under such programs;

(3) an evaluation of the current allocation of resourcesf or research and development, including whether the allocation of such resources for that purpose should be modified;

(4) an identification of the scientific and technological fields judged to be of most importance to the intelligence community;

(5) an evaluation of the relationship between the research and development programs and activities of the intelligence community and the research and development programs and activities of other departments and agencies of the Federal Government; and

(6) an evaluation of the relationship between the research and development programs and activities of the intelligence community and the research and development programs and activities of the private sector.

SEC. 1003. POWERS OF COMMISSION.

(a) IN GENERAL.—

(1) The Commission or, on the authorization of the Commission, any subcommittee or member thereof, may, for the purpose of carrying out the provisions of this title—

(A) hold such hearings and sit and act at such times and places, take such testimony, receive such evidence, and administer such oaths; and

(B) require, by subpoena or otherwise, the attendance and testimony of such witnesses and the production of such books, records, correspondence, memoranda, papers, and documents, as the Commission or such designated subcommittee or designated member considers necessary.

(2) Subpoenas may be issued under subparagraph (1)(B) under the signature of the co-chairs of the Commission, and may be served by any person designated by such co-chairs.

(3) The provisions of sections 102 through 104 of the Revised Statutes of the United States (2 U.S.C. 192–194) shall apply in the case of any failure of a witness to comply with any subpoena or to testify when summoned under authority of this section.

(b) CONTRACTING.—The Commission may, to such extent and in such amounts as are provided in advance in appropriation Acts, enter into contracts to enable the Commission to discharge its duties under this title.

(c) INFORMATION FROM FEDERAL AGENCIES.—The Commission may secure directly from any executive department, agency, bureau, board, commission, office, independent establishment, or instrumentality of the Government information, suggestions, estimates, and statistics for the purposes of this title. Each such department, agency, bureau, board, commission, office, establishment, or instrumentality shall, to the extent authorized by law, furnish such information, suggestions, estimates, and statistics directly to the Commission, upon request of the co-chairs of the Commission. The Commission shall handle and protect all classified information provided to it under this section in accordance with applicable statutes and regulations.

(d) ASSISTANCE FROM FEDERAL AGENCIES.—

(1) The Director of Central Intelligence shall provide to the Commission, on a nonreimbursable basis, such administrative services, funds, staff, facilities, and other support services as are necessary for the performance of the Commission's duties under this title.

(2) The Secretary of Defense may provide the Commission, on a nonreimbursable basis, with such administrative services, staff, and other support services as the Commission may request.

(3) In addition to the assistance set forth in paragraphs (1)and (2), other departments and agencies of the United States may provide the Commission such services, funds, facilities, staff, and other support as such departments and agencies consider advisable and as may be authorized by law.

(4) The Commission shall receive the full and timely cooperation of any official, department, or agency of the United States Government whose assistance is necessary for the fulfillment of the duties of the Commission under this title, including the provision of full and current briefings and analyses.

(e) PROHIBITION ON WITHHOLDING INFORMATION.—No department or agency of the Government may withhold information from the Commission on the grounds that providing the information to the Commission would constitute the unauthorized disclosure of classified information or information relating to intelligence sources or methods.

(f) POSTAL SERVICES.—The Commission may use the United States mails in the same manner and under the same conditions as the departments and agencies of the United States.

(g) GIFTS.—The Commission may accept, use, and dispose of gifts or donations of services or property in carrying out its duties under this title.

SEC. 1004. STAFF OF COMMISSION.

(a) IN GENERAL.—

(1) The co-chairs of the Commission, in accordance with rules agreed upon by the Commission, shall appoint and fix the compensation of a staff director and such other personnel as may be necessary to enable the Commission to carry out its duties, without regard to the provisions of title 5, United States Code, governing appointments in the competitive service, and without regard to the provisions of chapter 51 and subchapter III of chapter 53 of such title relating to classification and General Schedule pay rates, except that no rate of pay fixed under this subsection may exceed the equivalent of that payable to a person occupying a position at level V of the Executive Schedule under section 5316 of such title.

(2) Any Federal Government employee may be detailed to the Commission without reimbursement from the Commission, and such detailee shall retain the rights, status, and privileges of his or her regular employment without interruption.

(3) All staff of the Commission shall possess a security clearance in accordance with applicable laws and regulations concerning the handling of classified information.

(b) CONSULTANT SERVICES.—

(1) The Commission may procure the services of experts and consultants in accordance with section 3109 of title 5, United States Code, but at rates not to exceed the daily rate paid a person occupying a position at level IV of the Executive Schedule under section 5315 of such title.

(2) All experts and consultants employed by the Commission shall possess a security clearance in accordance with applicable laws and regulations concerning the handling of classified information.

SEC. 1005. COMPENSATION AND TRAVEL EXPENSES.

(a) COMPENSATION.—

(1) Except as provided in paragraph (2), each member of the Commission may be compensated at not to exceed the daily equivalent of the annual rate of basic pay in effect for a position at level IV of the Executive Schedule under section 5315 of title 5, United States Code, for each day during which that member is engaged in the actual performance of the duties of the Commission under this title.

(2) Members of the Commission who are officers or employees of the United States or Members of Congress shall receive no additional pay by reason of their service on the Commission.

(b) TRAVEL EXPENSES.—While away from their homes or regular places of business in the performance of services for the Commission, members of the Commission may be allowed travel expenses, including per diem in lieu of subsistence, in the same manner as persons employed intermittently in the Government service are allowed expenses under section 5703 of title 5, United States Code.

SEC. 1006. TREATMENT OF INFORMATION RELATING TO NATIONAL SECURITY.

(a) IN GENERAL.—

(1) The Director of Central Intelligence shall assume responsibility for the handling and disposition of any information related to the national security of the United States that is received, considered, or used by the Commission under this title.

(2) Any information related to the national security of the United States that is provided to the Commission by a congressional intelligence committee may not be further provided or released without the approval of the chairman of such committee.

(b) ACCESS AFTER TERMINATION OF COMMISSION.—Not with-standing any other provision of law, after the termination of the Commission under section 1007, only the Members and designated staff of the congressional intelligence committees, the Director of Central Intelligence (and the designees of the Director), and such other officials of the executive branch as the President may designate shall have access to information related to the national security of the United States that is received, considered, or used by the Commission.

SEC. 1007. FINAL REPORT; TERMINATION.

(a) FINAL REPORT.—Not later than September 1, 2003, the Commission shall submit to the congressional intelligence committees, the Director of Central Intelligence, and the Secretary of Defense a final report as required by section 1002(h)(2).

(b) TERMINATION.—

(1) The Commission, and all the authorities of this title, shall terminate at the end of the 120-day period beginning on the date on which the final report under subsection (a) is transmitted to the congressional intelligence committees.

(2) The Commission may use the 120-day period referred to in paragraph (1) for the purposes of concluding its activities, including providing testimony to Congress concerning the final report referred to in that paragraph and disseminating the report.

Sec. 1008. ASSESSMENTS OF FINAL REPORT.

Not later than 60 days after receipt of the final report under section 1007(a), the Director of Central Intelligence and the Secretary of Defense shall each submit to the congressional intelligence committees an assessment by the Director or the Secretary, as the case may be, of the final report. Each assessment shall include such comments on the findings and recommendations contained in the final report as the Director or Secretary, as the case may be, considers appropriate.

SEC. 1009. INAPPLICABILITY OF CERTAIN ADMINISTRATIVE PROVISIONS.

(a) FEDERAL ADVISORY COMMITTEE ACT.—The provisions of the Federal Advisory Committee Act (5 U.S.C. App.) shall not apply to the activities of the Commission under this title.

(b) FREEDOM OF INFORMATION ACT.—The provisions of section 552 of title 5, United States Code (commonly referred to as the Freedom of Information Act), shall not apply to the activities, records, and proceedings of the Commission under this title.

SEC. 1010. FUNDING.

(a) TRANSFER FROM THE COMMUNITY MANAGEMENT ACCOUNT.—Of the amounts authorized to be appropriated by this Act for the Intelligence Technology Innovation Center of the Community Management Account, the Deputy Director of Central Intelligence for Community Management shall transfer to the Director of Central Intelligence $2,000,000 for purposes of the activities of the Commission under this title.

(b) AVAILABILITY IN GENERAL.—The Director of Central Intelligence shall make available to the Commission, from the amount transferred to the Director under subsection (a), such amounts as the Commission may require for purposes of the activities of the Commission under this title.

(c) DURATION OF AVAILABILITY.—Amounts made available to the Commission under subsection (b) shall remain available until expended.

SEC. 1011. DEFINITIONS.

In this title:

(1) CONGRESSIONAL INTELLIGENCE COMMITTEES.—The term "congressional intelligence committees" means—

(A) the Select Committee on Intelligence of the Senate; and

(B) the Permanent Select Committee on Intelligence of the House of Representatives.

(2) INTELLIGENCE COMMUNITY.—The term "intelligence community" has the meaning given that term in section 3(4) of the National Security Act of 1947 (50 U.S.C. 401a(4)).

Intelligence Authorization Act for Fiscal Year 2013

Pub. L. 112–277, Title III,
§ 304, Jan. 14, 2013, 126 Stat. 2471 (50 § 403–1 note)

AN ACT

To authorize appropriations for fiscal year 2013 for intelligence and intelligence-related activities of the United States Government and the Office of the Director of National Intelligence, the Central Intelligence Agency Retirement and Disability System, and for other purposes.

Be it enacted by the Senate and House of Representatives of the United States of America in Congress assembled,

SECTION 1. SHORT TITLE; TABLE OF CONTENTS.

(a) Short Title—This Act may be cited as the 'Intelligence Authorization Act for Fiscal Year 2013'.

(b) Table of Contents—The table of contents for this Act is as follows:

SEC. 2. DEFINITIONS.
In this Act:
(1) CONGRESSIONAL INTELLIGENCE COMMITTEES—The term 'congressional intelligence committees' means—
(A) the Select Committee on Intelligence of the Senate; and
(B) the Permanent Select Committee on Intelligence of the House of Representatives.
(2) INTELLIGENCE COMMUNITY—The term 'intelligence community' has the meaning given that term in section 3(4) of the National Security Act of 1947 (50 U.S.C. 401a(4)).

TITLE I—BUDGET AND PERSONNEL AUTHORIZATIONS

SEC. 101. AUTHORIZATION OF APPROPRIATIONS.

Funds are hereby authorized to be appropriated for fiscal year 2013 for the conduct of the intelligence and intelligence-related activities of the following elements of the United States Government:

(1) The Office of the Director of National Intelligence.
(2) The Central Intelligence Agency.
(3) The Department of Defense.
(4) The Defense Intelligence Agency.
(5) The National Security Agency.
(6) The Department of the Army, the Department of the Navy, and the Department of the Air Force.
(7) The Coast Guard.
(8) The Department of State.
(9) The Department of the Treasury.
(10) The Department of Energy.
(11) The Department of Justice.
(12) The Federal Bureau of Investigation.
(13) The Drug Enforcement Administration.
(14) The National Reconnaissance Office.
(15) The National Geospatial-Intelligence Agency.
(16) The Department of Homeland Security.

SEC. 102. CLASSIFIED SCHEDULE OF AUTHORIZATIONS.

(a) Specifications of Amounts and Personnel Levels—The amounts authorized to be appropriated under section 101 and, subject to section 103, the authorized personnel ceilings as of September 30, 2013, for the conduct of the intelligence activities of the elements listed in paragraphs (1) through (16) of section 101, are those specified in the classified Schedule of Authorizations prepared to accompany the bill S. 3454 of the One Hundred Twelfth Congress.

(b) Availability of Classified Schedule of Authorizations—

(1) AVAILABILITY TO COMMITTEES OF CONGRESS—The classified Schedule of Authorizations referred to in subsection (a) shall be made available to the Committee on Appropriations of the Senate, the Committee on Appropriations of the House of Representatives, and to the President.

(2) DISTRIBUTION BY THE PRESIDENT—Subject to paragraph (3), the President shall provide for suitable distribution of the classified Schedule of Authorizations, or of appropriate portions of the Schedule, within the executive branch.

(3) LIMITS ON DISCLOSURE—The President shall not publicly disclose the classified Schedule of Authorizations or any portion of such Schedule except—

(A) as provided in section 601(a) of the Implementing Recommendations of the 9/11 Commission Act of 2007 (50 U.S.C. 415c);

(B) to the extent necessary to implement the budget; or

(C) as otherwise required by law.

SEC. 103. PERSONNEL CEILING ADJUSTMENTS.

(a) Authority for Increases—The Director of National Intelligence may authorize the employment of civilian personnel in excess of the number of positions for fiscal year 2013 authorized by the classified Schedule of Authorizations referred to in section 102(a) if the Director of National Intelligence determines that such action is necessary to the performance of important intelligence functions, except that the number of personnel employed in excess of the number authorized under such section may not, for any element of the intelligence community, exceed 3 percent of the number of civilian personnel authorized under such section for such element.

(b) Treatment of Certain Personnel—The Director of National Intelligence shall establish guidelines that govern, for each element of the intelligence community, the treatment under the personnel levels authorized under section 102(a), including any exemption from such personnel levels, of employment or assignment in—

(1) a student program, trainee program, or similar program;

(2) a reserve corps or as a reemployed annuitant; or

(3) details, joint duty, or long term, full-time training.

(c) Notice to Congressional Intelligence Committees—The Director of National Intelligence shall notify the congressional intelligence committees in writing at least 15 days prior to the initial exercise of an authority described in subsection (a).

SEC. 104. INTELLIGENCE COMMUNITY MANAGEMENT ACCOUNT.

(a) Authorization of Appropriations—There is authorized to be appropriated for the Intelligence Community Management Account of the Director of National Intelligence for fiscal year 2013 the sum of $540,721,000. Within such amount, funds identified in the classified Schedule of Authorizations referred to in section 102(a) for advanced research and development shall remain available until September 30, 2014.

(b) Authorized Personnel Levels—The elements within the Intelligence Community Management Account of the Director of National Intelligence are authorized 835 positions as of September 30, 2013. Personnel serving in such elements may be permanent employees of the Office of the Director of National Intelligence or personnel detailed from other elements of the United States Government.

(c) Classified Authorizations-

(1) AUTHORIZATION OF APPROPRIATIONS—In addition to amounts authorized to be appropriated for the Intelligence Community Management Account by subsection (a), there are authorized to be appropriated for the Community Management Account for fiscal year 2013 such additional amounts as are specified in the classified Schedule of Authorizations referred to in section 102(a). Such additional amounts for advanced research and development shall remain available until September 30, 2014.

(2) AUTHORIZATION OF PERSONNEL—In addition to the personnel authorized by subsection (b) for elements of the Intelligence Community Management Account as of September 30, 2013, there are authorized such additional personnel for the Community Management Account as of that date as are specified in the classified Schedule of Authorizations referred to in section 102(a).

TITLE II—CENTRAL INTELLIGENCE AGENCY RETIREMENT AND DISABILITY SYSTEM

SEC. 201. AUTHORIZATION OF APPROPRIATIONS.

There is authorized to be appropriated for the Central Intelligence Agency Retirement and Disability Fund for fiscal year 2013 the sum of $514,000,000.

TITLE III—GENERAL INTELLIGENCE COMMUNITY MATTERS

SEC. 301. RESTRICTION ON CONDUCT OF INTELLIGENCE ACTIVITIES.

The authorization of appropriations by this Act shall not be deemed to constitute authority for the conduct of any intelligence activity which is not otherwise authorized by the Constitution or the laws of the United States.

SEC. 302. INCREASE IN EMPLOYEE COMPENSATION AND BENEFITS AUTHORIZED BY LAW.

Appropriations authorized by this Act for salary, pay, retirement, and other benefits for Federal employees may be increased by such additional or supplemental amounts as may be necessary for increases in such compensation or benefits authorized by law.

SEC. 303. NON-REIMBURSABLE DETAILS.

Section 113A of the National Security Act of 1947 (50 U.S.C. 404h-1) is amended—

(1) by striking 'two years.' and inserting 'three years.'; and

(2) by adding at the end 'A non-reimbursable detail made under this section shall not be considered an augmentation of the appropriations of the receiving element of the intelligence community.'.

SEC. 304. AUTOMATED INSIDER THREAT DETECTION PROGRAM.

Section 402 of the Intelligence Authorization Act for Fiscal Year 2011 (Public Law 112-18; 50 U.S.C. 403-1 note) is amended—

(1) in subsection (a), by striking 'October 1, 2012,' and inserting 'October 1, 2013,'; and

(2) in subsection (b), by striking 'October 1, 2013,' and inserting 'October 1, 2014,'.

SEC. 305. SOFTWARE LICENSING.

(a) In General—Not later than 120 days after the date of the enactment of this Act, each chief information officer for an element of the intelligence community, in consultation with the Chief Information Officer of the Intelligence Community, shall—

(1) conduct an inventory of software licenses held by such element, including utilized and unutilized licenses; and

(2) report the results of such inventory to the Chief Information Officer of the Intelligence Community.

(b) Reporting to Congress—The Chief Information Officer of the Intelligence Community shall—

(1) not later than 180 days after the date of the enactment of this Act, provide to the congressional intelligence committees a copy of each report received by the Chief Information Officer under subsection (a)(2), along with any comments the Chief Information Officer wishes to provide; and

(2) transmit any portion of a report submitted under paragraph (1) involving a component of a department of the United States Government to the committees of the Senate and of the House of Representatives with jurisdiction over such department simultaneously with submission of such report to the congressional intelligence committees.

SEC. 306. STRATEGY FOR SECURITY CLEARANCE RECIPROCITY.

(a) Strategy—The President shall develop a strategy and a schedule for carrying out the requirements of section 3001(d) of the Intelligence Reform and Terrorism Prevention Act of 2004 (50 U.S.C. 435b(d)). Such strategy and schedule shall include—

(1) a process for accomplishing the reciprocity required under such section for a security clearance issued by a department or agency of the Federal Government, including reciprocity for security clearances that are issued to both persons who are and who are not employees of the Federal Government; and

(2) a description of the specific circumstances under which a department or agency of the Federal Government may not recognize a security clearance issued by another department or agency of the Federal Government.

(b) Congressional Notification—Not later than 180 days after the date of the enactment of this Act, the President shall inform Congress of the strategy and schedule developed under subsection (a).

SEC. 307. IMPROPER PAYMENTS ELIMINATION AND RECOVERY ACT OF 2010 COMPLIANCE.

(a) Plan for Compliance-

(1) IN GENERAL—The Director of National Intelligence, the Director of the Central Intelligence Agency, the Director of the Defense Intelligence Agency, the Director of the National Geospatial-Intelligence Agency, and the Director of the National Security Agency shall each develop a corrective action plan, with major milestones, that delineates how the Office of the Director of National Intelligence and each such Agency will achieve compliance, not later than September 30, 2013, with the Improper Payments Elimination and Recovery Act of 2010 (Public Law 111-204; 124 Stat. 2224), and the amendments made by that Act.

(2) SUBMISSION TO CONGRESS—Not later than 45 days after the date of the enactment of this Act—

(A) each Director referred to in paragraph (1) shall submit to the congressional intelligence committees the corrective action plan required by such paragraph; and

(B) the Director of the Defense Intelligence Agency, the Director of the National Geospatial-Intelligence Agency, and the Director of the National Security Agency shall each submit to the Committee on Armed Services of the Senate and the Committee on Armed Services of the House of Representatives the corrective action plan required by paragraph (1) with respect to the applicable Agency.

(b) Review by Inspectors General-

(1) IN GENERAL—Not later than 45 days after the completion of a corrective action plan required by subsection (a)(1), the Inspector General of each Agency required to develop such a plan, and in the case of the Director of National Intelligence, the Inspector General of the Intelligence Community, shall provide to the congressional intelligence committees an assessment of such plan that includes—

(A) the assessment of the Inspector General of whether such Agency or Office is or is not likely to reach compliance with the requirements of the Improper Payments Elimination and Recovery Act of 2010 (Public Law 111-204; 124 Stat. 2224), and the amendments made by that Act, by September 30, 2013; and

(B) the basis of the Inspector General for such assessment.

(2) ADDITIONAL SUBMISSION OF REVIEWS OF CERTAIN INSPECTORS GENERAL—Not later than 45 days after the completion of a corrective action

plan required by subsection (a)(1), the Inspector General of the Defense Intelligence Agency, the Inspector General of the National Geospatial-Intelligence Agency, and the Inspector General of the National Security Agency shall each submit to the Committee on Armed Services of the Senate and the Committee on Armed Services of the House of Representatives the assessment of the applicable plan provided to the congressional intelligence committees under paragraph (1).

SEC. 308. SUBCONTRACTOR NOTIFICATION PROCESS.

Not later than October 1, 2013, the Director of National Intelligence shall submit to the congressional intelligence committees a report assessing the method by which contractors at any tier under a contract entered into with an element of the intelligence community are granted security clearances and notified of classified contracting opportunities within the Federal Government and recommendations for the improvement of such method. Such report shall include—

(1) an assessment of the current method by which contractors at any tier under a contract entered into with an element of the intelligence community are notified of classified contracting opportunities;

(2) an assessment of any problems that may reduce the overall effectiveness of the ability of the intelligence community to identify appropriate contractors at any tier under such a contract;

(3) an assessment of the role the existing security clearance process has in enhancing or hindering the ability of the intelligence community to notify such contractors of contracting opportunities;

(4) an assessment of the role the current security clearance process has in enhancing or hindering the ability of contractors at any tier under a contract entered into with an element of the intelligence community to execute classified contracts;

(5) a description of the method used by the Director of National Intelligence for assessing the effectiveness of the notification process of the intelligence community to produce a talented pool of subcontractors;

(6) a description of appropriate goals, schedules, milestones, or metrics used to measure the effectiveness of such notification process; and

(7) recommendations for improving such notification process.

SEC. 309. MODIFICATION OF REPORTING SCHEDULE.

(a) Inspector General of the Intelligence Community—Section 103H(k)(1)(A) of the National Security Act of 1947 (50 U.S.C. 403-3h(k)(1)(A)) is amended—

(1) by striking 'January 31 and July 31' and inserting 'October 31 and April 30'; and

(2) by striking 'December 31 (of the preceding year) and June 30,' and inserting 'September 30 and March 31,'.

(b) Inspector General for the Central Intelligence Agency-

(1) IN GENERAL—Section 17(d)(1) of the Central Intelligence Agency Act of 1949 (50 U.S.C. 403q(d)(1)) is amended—

(A) by striking 'January 31 and July 31' and inserting 'October 31 and April 30';

(B) by striking 'December 31 (of the preceding year) and June 30,' and inserting 'September 30 and March 31,'; and

(C) by striking 'Not later than the dates each year provided for the transmittal of such reports in section 507 of the National Security Act of 1947,' and inserting 'Not later than 30 days after the date of the receipt of such reports,'.

(2) CONFORMING AMENDMENTS—Section 507(b) of the National Security Act of 1947 (50 U.S.C. 415b(b)) is amended—

(A) by striking paragraph (1); and

(B) by redesignating paragraphs (2), (3), and (4), as paragraphs (1), (2), and (3), respectively.

SEC. 310. REPEAL OF CERTAIN REPORTING REQUIREMENTS.

(a) Repeal of Reporting Requirements—

(1) ACQUISITION OF TECHNOLOGY RELATING TO WEAPONS OF MASS DESTRUCTION AND ADVANCED CONVENTIONAL MUNITIONS—Section 721 of the Intelligence Authorization Act for Fiscal Year 1997 (50 U.S.C. 2366) is repealed.

(2) SAFETY AND SECURITY OF RUSSIAN NUCLEAR FACILITIES AND NUCLEAR MILITARY FORCES—Section 114 of the National Security Act of 1947 (50 U.S.C. 404i) is amended—

(A) by striking subsection

(B) by striking subsection (d).

(2) REPEAL OF REPORTING REQUIREMENT REGARDINGs (a) and (d); and

(B) by redesignating subsections (b) and (c) as subsections (a) and (b), respectively.

(3) INTELLIGENCE COMMUNITY BUSINESS SYSTEMS BUDGET INFORMATION—Section 506D of the National Security Act of 1947 (50 U.S.C. 415a-6) is amended by striking subsection (e).

(3) REPEAL OF REPORTING REQUIREMENTS REGARDING SECURITY CLEARANCES—

(A) IN GENERAL—Section 506H of the National Security Act of 1947 (50 U.S.C. 415a-10) is repealed.

(B) TABLE OF CONTENTS AMENDMENT—The National Security Act of 1947 (50 U.S.C. 401 et seq.) is amended in the table of contents in the first section by striking the item relating to section 506H.

(4) MEASURES TO PROTECT THE IDENTITIES OF COVERT AGENTS—Title VI of the National Security Act of 1947 (50 U.S.C. 421 et seq.) is amended—

(A) by striking section 603; and

(B) by redesignating sections 604, 605, and 606 as sections 603, 604, and 605, respectively.

(b) Technical and Conforming Amendments-

(1) REPORT SUBMISSION DATES—Section 507 of the National Security Act of 1947 (50 U.S.C. 415b) is amended—

(A) in subsection (a)—

(i) in paragraph (1)—

(I) by striking subparagraphs (A), (C), and (D);

(II) by redesignating subparagraphs (B), (E), (F), (G), (H), and (I) as subparagraphs (A), (B), (C), (D), (E), and (F), respectively; and

(III) in subparagraph (D), as so redesignated, by striking 'section 114(c).' and inserting 'section 114(a).'; and

(ii) by amending paragraph (2) to read as follows:

'(2) The date for the submittal to the congressional intelligence committees of the annual report on the threat of attack on the United States from weapons of mass destruction required by section 114(b) shall be the date each year provided in subsection (c)(1)(B).';

(B) in subsection (c)(1)(B), by striking 'each' and inserting 'the'; and

(C) in subsection (d)(1)(B), by striking 'an' and inserting 'the'.

(2) TABLE OF CONTENTS OF THE NATIONAL SECURITY ACT OF 1947—The table of contents in the first section of the National Security Act of 1947 is amended by striking the items relating to sections 603, 604, 605, and 606 and inserting the following new items:

'Sec. 603. Extraterritorial jurisdiction.

'Sec. 604. Providing information to Congress.

'Sec. 605. Definitions.'.

TITLE IV—MATTERS RELATING TO THE CENTRAL INTELLIGENCE AGENCY

SEC. 401. WORKING CAPITAL FUND AMENDMENTS.

Section 21 of the Central Intelligence Agency Act of 1949 (50 U.S.C. 403u) is amended as follows:

(1) In subsection (b)—

(A) in paragraph (1)—

(i) in subparagraph (B), by striking 'and' at the end;

(ii) in subparagraph (C), by striking 'program.' and inserting 'program; and'; and

(iii) by adding at the end the following:

'(D) authorize such providers to make known their services to the entities specified in section (a) through Government communication channels.'; and

(B) by adding at the end the following:

'(3) The authority in paragraph (1)(D) does not include the authority to distribute gifts or promotional items.'; and

(2) in subsection (c)—

(A) in paragraph (2)(E), by striking 'from the sale or exchange of equipment or property of a central service provider' and inserting 'from the sale or exchange of equipment, recyclable materials, or property of a central service provider.'; and

(B) in paragraph (3)(B), by striking 'subsection (f)(2)' and inserting 'subsections (b)(1)(D) and (f)(2)'.

TITLE V—OTHER MATTERS

SEC. 501. HOMELAND SECURITY INTELLIGENCE PROGRAM.

There is established within the Department of Homeland Security a Homeland Security Intelligence Program. The Homeland Security Intelligence Program constitutes the intelligence activities of the Office of Intelligence and Analysis of the Department that serve predominantly departmental missions.

SEC. 502. EXTENSION OF NATIONAL COMMISSION FOR THE REVIEW OF THE RESEARCH AND DEVELOPMENT PROGRAMS OF THE UNITED STATES INTELLIGENCE COMMUNITY.

Section 1007(a) of the Intelligence Authorization Act for Fiscal Year 2003 (Public Law 107-306; 50 U.S.C. 401 note) is amended by striking 'Not later than one year after the date on which all members of the Commission are appointed pursuant to section 701(a)(3) of the Intelligence Authorization Act for Fiscal Year 2010,' and inserting 'Not later than March 31, 2013,'.

SEC. 503. PROTECTING THE INFORMATION TECHNOLOGY SUPPLY CHAIN OF THE UNITED STATES.

(a) Report—Not later than 90 days after the date of the enactment of this Act, the Director of National Intelligence shall submit to the congressional intelligence committees a report that—

(1) identifies foreign suppliers of information technology (including equipment, software, and services) that are linked directly or indirectly to a foreign government, including—

(A) by ties to the military forces of a foreign government;

(B) by ties to the intelligence services of a foreign government; or

(C) by being the beneficiaries of significant low interest or no interest loans, loan forgiveness, or other support by a foreign government; and

(2) assesses the vulnerability to malicious activity, including cyber crime or espionage, of the telecommunications networks of the United States due to the presence of technology produced by suppliers identified under paragraph (1).

(b) Form—The report required under subsection (a) shall be submitted in unclassified form, but may include a classified annex.

(c) Telecommunications Networks of the United States Defined—In this section, the term 'telecommunications networks of the United States' includes—

(1) telephone systems;

(2) Internet systems;

(3) fiber optic lines, including cable landings;
(4) computer networks; and
(5) smart grid technology under development by the Department of Energy.

SEC. 504. NOTIFICATION REGARDING THE AUTHORIZED PUBLIC DISCLOSURE OF NATIONAL INTELLIGENCE.

(a) Notification—In the event of an authorized disclosure of national intelligence or intelligence related to national security to the persons or entities described in subsection (b), the government official responsible for authorizing the disclosure shall submit to the congressional intelligence committees on a timely basis a notification of the disclosure if—

(1) at the time of the disclosure—

(A) such intelligence is classified; or

(B) is declassified for the purpose of the disclosure; and

(2) the disclosure will be made by an officer, employee, or contractor of the Executive branch.

(b) Persons or Entities Described—The persons or entities described in this subsection are as follows:

(1) Media personnel.

(2) Any person or entity, if the disclosure described in subsection (a) is made with the intent or knowledge that such information will be made publicly available.

(c) Content—Each notification required under subsection (a) shall—

(1) provide the specific title and authority of the individual authorizing the disclosure;

(2) if applicable, provide the specific title and authority of the individual who authorized the declassification of the intelligence disclosed; and

(3) describe the intelligence disclosed, including the classification of the intelligence prior to its disclosure or declassification and the rationale for making the disclosure.

(d) Exception—The notification requirement in this section does not apply to a disclosure made—

(1) pursuant to any statutory requirement, including to section 552 of title 5, United States Code (commonly referred to as the 'Freedom of Information Act');

(2) in connection with a civil, criminal, or administrative proceeding;

(3) as a result of a declassification review process under Executive Order 13526 (50 U.S.C. 435 note) or any successor order; or

(4) to any officer, employee, or contractor of the Federal government or member of an advisory committee to an element of the intelligence community who possesses an active security clearance and a need to know the specific national intelligence or intelligence related to national security, as defined in section 3(5) of the National Security Act of 1947 (50 U.S.C. 401a(5)).

(a) Record Requirement—The head of each element of the intelligence community shall ensure that such element creates and maintains a record of all authorized disclosures of classified information to media personnel, including any person or entity under contract or other binding agreement with the media to provide analysis or commentary, or to any person or entity if the disclosure is made with the intent or knowledge that such information will be made publicly available.

(b) Review by Congressional Intelligence Committees—A record under subsection (a) shall be available for review by the congressional intelligence committees in a manner jointly agreed to by the committee and the head of such element.

SEC. 503. PROCEDURES FOR CONDUCTING ADMINISTRATIVE INVESTIGATIONS OF UNAUTHORIZED DISCLOSURES.

(a) Requirement—Not later than 90 days after the date of the enactment of this Act, the Director of National Intelligence shall—

(1) establish procedures as described in subsection (b); and

(2) provide a copy of the procedures to the congressional intelligence committees.

(b) Procedures—The procedures described in this subsection are procedures that shall be implemented by each element of the intelligence community for the conduct of administrative investigations of unauthorized disclosures of classified information and shall include—

(1) designation of an office with responsibility for proactively identifying unauthorized disclosures of classified information;

(2) submission and prioritization of crimes reports to the Attorney General for purposes of criminal investigation concerning unauthorized disclosures of classified information;

(3) conduct of independent administrative investigations of unauthorized disclosures of classified information, if a criminal investigation is not pursued or is discontinued;

(4) guidelines approved by the Attorney General that authorize the Director of the F Federal Bureau of Investigation to provide relevant documents and other information in the Director's possession to appropriate elements of the intelligence community for purposes of conducting administrative investigations of the unauthorized disclosure of classified information;

(5) procedures for the heads of elements of the intelligence community to apply disciplinary measures, if appropriate, following an administrative investigation, up to and including termination of employment;

(6) in cases where an administrative investigation identifies information that may enable or inform a criminal investigation, procedures for providing such information to the Attorney General;

(7) procedures for keeping the National Counterintelligence Executive and the congressional intelligence committees informed of the status of all administrative investigations and crimes reports; and

(8) other procedures as determined by the Director.

SEC. 504. ASSESSMENT OF PROCEDURES FOR DETECTING AND PREVENTING UNAUTHORIZED DISCLOSURES.

(a) Director of National Intelligence Assessment—Not later than 120 days after the date of the enactment of this Act, the Director of National Intelligence(e) Sunset—The notification requirements of this section shall cease to be effective for any disclosure described in subsection (a) that occurs on or after the date that is one year after the date of the enactment of this Act.

SEC. 505. TECHNICAL AMENDMENTS RELATED TO THE OFFICE OF THE DIRECTOR OF NATIONAL INTELLIGENCE.

(a) Personnel Practices—Section 2302(a)(2)(C) of title 5, United States Code, is amended by striking clause (ii) and inserting the following:

> '(ii)(I) the Federal Bureau of Investigation, the Central Intelligence Agency, the Defense Intelligence Agency, the National Geospatial-Intelligence Agency, the National Security Agency, the Office of the Director of National Intelligence, and the National Reconnaissance Office; and
>
> > '(II) as determined by the President, any executive agency or unit thereof the principal function of which is the conduct of foreign intelligence or counterintelligence activities, provided that the determination be made prior to a personnel action; or'.

(b) Senior Executive Service—Section 3132(a)(1)(B) of title 5, United States Code, is amended by inserting 'the Office of the Director of National Intelligence,' after 'the Central Intelligence Agency,'.

SEC. 506. TECHNICAL AMENDMENT FOR DEFINITION OF INTELLIGENCE AGENCY.

Section 606(5) of the National Security Act of 1947 (50 U.S.C. 426) is amended to read as follows:

> '(5) The term 'intelligence agency' means the elements of the intelligence community, as that term is defined in section 3(4).'.

SEC. 507. BUDGETARY EFFECTS.

The budgetary effects of this Act, for the purpose of complying with the Statutory Pay-As-You-Go-Act of 2010, shall be determined by reference to the latest statement titled 'Budgetary Effects of PAYGO Legislation' for this Act, submitted for printing in the Congressional Record by the Chairman of the Senate Budget Committee, provided that such statement has been submitted prior to the vote on passage.

Executive Orders

Executive Order 12333—United States Intelligence Activities

As amended by Executive Orders 13284 (2003), 13355 (2004), and 13470 (2008)
46 Fed. Reg. 59,941 (Dec. 4, 1981)

Timely, accurate, and insightful information about the activities, capabilities, plans, and intentions of foreign powers, organizations, and persons, and their agents, is essential to the national security of the United States. All reasonable and lawful means must be used to ensure that the United States will receive the best intelligence possible. For that purpose, by virtue of the authority vested in me by the Constitution and the laws of the United States of America, including the National Security Act of 1947, as amended, (Act) and as President of the United States of America, in order to provide for the effective conduct of United States intelligence activities and the protection of constitutional rights, it is hereby ordered as follows:

PART 1 GOALS, DIRECTIONS, DUTIES, AND RESPONSIBILITIES WITH RESPECT TO UNITED STATES INTELLIGENCE EFFORTS

SECTION 1.1 GOALS. The United States intelligence effort shall provide the President, the National Security Council, and the Homeland Security Council with the necessary information on which to base decisions concerning the development and conduct of foreign, defense, and economic policies, and the protection of United States national interests from foreign security threats. All departments and agencies shall cooperate fully to fulfill this goal.

(a) All means, consistent with applicable Federal law and this order, and with full consideration of the rights of United States persons, shall be used to obtain reliable intelligence information to protect the United States and its interests.

(b) The United States Government has a solemn obligation, and shall continue in the conduct of intelligence activities under this order, to protect fully the legal rights of all United States persons, including freedoms, civil liberties, and privacy rights guaranteed by Federal law.

(c) Intelligence collection under this order should be guided by the need for information to respond to intelligence priorities set by the President.

(d) Special emphasis should be given to detecting and countering:

(1) Espionage and other threats and activities directed by foreign powers or their intelligence services against the United States and its interests;

(2) Threats to the United States and its interests from terrorism; and

(3) Threats to the United States and its interests from the development, possession, proliferation, or use of weapons of mass destruction.

(e) Special emphasis shall be given to the production of timely, accurate, and insightful reports, responsive to decisionmakers in the executive branch, that draw on all appropriate sources of information, including open source information, meet rigorous analytic standards, consider diverse analytic viewpoints, and accurately represent appropriate alternative views.
(f) State, local, and tribal governments are critical partners in securing and defending the United States from terrorism and other threats to the United States and its interests. Our national intelligence effort should take into account the responsibilities and requirements of State, local, and tribal governments and, as appropriate, private sector entities, when undertaking the collection and dissemination of information and intelligence to protect the United States.
(g) All departments and agencies have a responsibility to prepare and to provide intelligence in a manner that allows the full and free exchange of information, consistent with applicable law and presidential guidance.

SECTION 1.2 THE NATIONAL SECURITY COUNCIL.
(a) *Purpose*. The National Security Council (NSC) shall act as the highest ranking executive branch entity that provides support to the President for review of, guidance for, and direction to the conduct of all foreign intelligence, counterintelligence, and covert action, and attendant policies and programs.
(b) *Covert Action and Other Sensitive Intelligence Operations*. The NSC shall consider and submit to the President a policy recommendation, including all dissents, on each proposed covert action and conduct a periodic review of ongoing covert action activities, including an evaluation of the effectiveness and consistency with current national policy of such activities and consistency with applicable legal requirements. The NSC shall perform such other functions related to covert action as the President may direct, but shall not undertake the conduct of covert actions. The NSC shall also review proposals for other sensitive intelligence operations.

SECTION 1.3 DIRECTOR OF NATIONAL INTELLIGENCE. Subject to the authority, direction, and control of the President, the Director of National Intelligence (Director) shall serve as the head of the Intelligence Community, act as the principal adviser to the President, to the NSC, and to the Homeland Security Council for intelligence matters related to national security, and shall oversee and direct the implementation of the National Intelligence Program and execution of the National Intelligence Program budget. The Director will lead a unified, coordinated, and effective intelligence effort. In addition, the Director shall, in carrying out the duties and responsibilities under this section, take into account the views of the heads of departments containing an element of the Intelligence Community and of the Director of the Central Intelligence Agency.
(a) Except as otherwise directed by the President or prohibited by law, the Director shall have access to all information and intelligence described in section 1.5(a) of this order. For the purpose of access to and sharing of information and intelligence, the Director:

(1) Is hereby assigned the function under section 3(5) of the Act, to determine that intelligence, regardless of the source from which derived and including information gathered within or outside the United States, pertains to more than one United States Government agency; and

(2) Shall develop guidelines for how information or intelligence is provided to or accessed by the Intelligence Community in accordance with section 1.5(a) of this order, and for how the information or intelligence may be used and shared by the Intelligence Community. All guidelines developed in accordance with this section shall be approved by the Attorney General and, where applicable, shall be consistent with guidelines issued pursuant to section 1016 of the Intelligence Reform and Terrorism Protection Act of 2004 (Public Law 108-458) (IRTPA).

(b) In addition to fulfilling the obligations and responsibilities prescribed by the Act, the Director:

(1) Shall establish objectives, priorities, and guidance for the Intelligence Community to ensure timely and effective collection, processing, analysis, and dissemination of intelligence, of whatever nature and from whatever source derived;

(2) May designate, in consultation with affected heads of departments or Intelligence Community elements, one or more Intelligence Community elements to develop and to maintain services of common concern on behalf of the Intelligence Community if the Director determines such services can be more efficiently or effectively accomplished in a consolidated manner;

(3) Shall oversee and provide advice to the President and the NSC with respect to all ongoing and proposed covert action programs;

(4) In regard to the establishment and conduct of intelligence arrangements and agreements with foreign governments and international organizations:

(A) May enter into intelligence and counterintelligence arrangements and agreements with foreign governments and international organizations;

(B) Shall formulate policies concerning intelligence and counterintelligence arrangements and agreements with foreign governments and international organizations; and

(C) Shall align and synchronize intelligence and counterintelligence foreign relationships among the elements of the Intelligence Community to further United States national security, policy, and intelligence objectives;

(5) Shall participate in the development of procedures approved by the Attorney General governing criminal drug intelligence activities abroad to ensure that these activities are consistent with foreign intelligence programs;

(6) Shall establish common security and access standards for managing and handling intelligence systems, information, and products, with special emphasis on facilitating:

(A) The fullest and most prompt access to and dissemination of information and intelligence practicable, assigning the highest priority to detecting, preventing, preempting, and disrupting terrorist threats and activities against the United States, its interests, and allies; and

(B) The establishment of standards for an interoperable information sharing enterprise that facilitates the sharing of intelligence information among elements of the Intelligence Community;

(7) Shall ensure that appropriate departments and agencies have access to intelligence and receive the support needed to perform independent analysis;

(8) Shall protect, and ensure that programs are developed to protect, intelligence sources, methods, and activities from unauthorized disclosure;

(9) Shall, after consultation with the heads of affected departments and agencies, establish guidelines for Intelligence Community elements for:

(A) Classification and declassification of all intelligence and intelligence-related information classified under the authority of the Director or the authority of the head of a department or Intelligence Community element; and

(B) Access to and dissemination of all intelligence and intelligence-related information, both in its final form and in the form when initially gathered, to include intelligence originally classified by the head of a department or Intelligence Community element, except that access to and dissemination of information concerning United States persons shall be governed by procedures developed in accordance with Part 2 of this order;

(10) May, only with respect to Intelligence Community elements, and after consultation with the head of the originating Intelligence Community element or the head of the originating department, declassify, or direct the declassification of, information or intelligence relating to intelligence sources, methods, and activities. The Director may only delegate this authority to the Principal Deputy Director of National Intelligence;

(11) May establish, operate, and direct one or more national intelligence centers to address intelligence priorities;

(12) May establish Functional Managers and Mission Managers, and designate officers or employees of the United States to serve in these positions.

(A) Functional Managers shall report to the Director concerning the execution of their duties as Functional Managers, and may be charged with developing and implementing strategic guidance, policies, and procedures for activities related to a specific intelligence discipline or set of intelligence activities; set training and tradecraft standards; and ensure coordination within and across intelligence disciplines and Intelligence Community elements and with related nonintelligence activities. Functional Managers may also advise the Director on: the management of resources; policies and procedures; collection capabilities and gaps; processing and dissemination of intelligence; technical architectures; and other issues or activities determined by the Director.

(i) The Director of the National Security Agency is designated the Functional Manager for signals intelligence;

(ii) The Director of the Central Intelligence Agency is designated the Functional Manager for human intelligence; and

(iii) The Director of the National Geospatial-Intelligence Agency is designated the Functional Manager for geospatial intelligence.

(B) Mission Managers shall serve as principal substantive advisors on all or specified aspects of intelligence related to designated countries, regions, topics, or functional issues;

(13) Shall establish uniform criteria for the determination of relative priorities for the transmission of critical foreign intelligence, and advise the Secretary of Defense concerning the communications requirements of the Intelligence Community for the transmission of such communications;

(14) Shall have ultimate responsibility for production and dissemination of intelligence produced by the
Intelligence Community and authority to levy analytic tasks on intelligence production organizations within the Intelligence Community, in consultation with the heads of the Intelligence Community elements concerned;

(15) May establish advisory groups for the purpose of obtaining advice from within the Intelligence
Community to carry out the Director's responsibilities, to include Intelligence Community executive management committees composed of senior Intelligence Community leaders. Advisory groups shall consist of representatives from elements of the Intelligence Community, as designated by the Director, or other executive branch departments, agencies, and offices, as appropriate;

(16) Shall ensure the timely exploitation and dissemination of data gathered by national intelligence collection means, and ensure that the resulting intelligence is disseminated immediately to appropriate government elements, including military commands;

(17) Shall determine requirements and priorities for, and manage and direct the tasking, collection, analysis, production, and dissemination of, national intelligence by elements of the Intelligence Community, including approving requirements for collection and analysis and resolving conflicts in collection requirements and in the tasking of national collection assets of Intelligence Community elements (except when otherwise directed by the President or when the Secretary of Defense exercises collection tasking authority under plans and arrangements approved by the Secretary of Defense and the Director);

(18) May provide advisory tasking concerning collection and analysis of information or intelligence relevant to national intelligence or national security to departments, agencies, and establishments of the United States Government that are not elements of the Intelligence Community; and shall establish procedures, in consultation with affected heads of departments or agencies and subject to approval by the Attorney General, to implement this authority and to monitor or evaluate the responsiveness of United States Government departments, agencies, and other establishments;

(19) Shall fulfill the responsibilities in section 1.3(b)(17) and (18) of this order, consistent with applicable law and with full consideration of the rights of United States persons, whether information is to be collected inside or outside the United States;

(20) Shall ensure, through appropriate policies and procedures, the deconfliction, coordination, and integration of all intelligence activities conducted by an Intelligence Community element or funded by the National Intelligence Program. In accordance with these policies and procedures:

(A) The Director of the Federal Bureau of Investigation shall coordinate the clandestine collection of foreign intelligence collected through human sources or through human-enabled means and counterintelligence activities inside the United States;

(B) The Director of the Central Intelligence Agency shall coordinate the clandestine collection of foreign intelligence collected through human sources or through human-enabled means and counterintelligence activities outside the United States;

(C) All policies and procedures for the coordination of counterintelligence activities and the clandestine collection of foreign intelligence inside the United States shall be subject to the approval of the Attorney General; and

(D) All policies and procedures developed under this section shall be coordinated with the heads of affected departments and Intelligence Community elements;

(21) Shall, with the concurrence of the heads of affected departments and agencies, establish joint procedures to deconflict, coordinate, and synchronize intelligence activities conducted by an Intelligence
Community element or funded by the National Intelligence Program, with intelligence activities, activities that involve foreign intelligence and security services, or activities that involve the use of clandestine methods, conducted by other United States Government departments, agencies, and establishments;

(22) Shall, in coordination with the heads of departments containing elements of the Intelligence
Community, develop procedures to govern major system acquisitions funded in whole or in majority part by the National Intelligence Program;

(23) Shall seek advice from the Secretary of State to ensure that the foreign policy implications of proposed intelligence activities are considered, and shall ensure, through appropriate policies and procedures, that intelligence activities are conducted in a manner consistent with the responsibilities pursuant to law and presidential direction of Chiefs of United States Missions; and

(24) Shall facilitate the use of Intelligence Community products by the Congress in a secure manner.

(c) The Director's exercise of authorities in the Act and this order shall not abrogate the statutory or other responsibilities of the heads of departments of the United States Government or the Director of the Central Intelligence Agency. Directives issued and actions taken by the Director in the exercise of the Director's authorities and responsibilities to integrate, coordinate, and make the Intelligence Community more effective in providing intelligence related to national security shall be implemented by the elements of the Intelligence Community, provided that any department head whose department contains an element of the Intelligence

Community and who believes that a directive or action of the Director violates the requirements of section 1018 of the IRTPA or this subsection shall bring the issue to the attention of the Director, the NSC, or the President for resolution in a manner that respects and does not abrogate the statutory responsibilities of the heads of the departments.

(d) Appointments to certain positions.

(1) The relevant department or bureau head shall provide recommendations and obtain the concurrence of the Director for the selection of: the Director of the National Security Agency, the Director of the National Reconnaissance Office, the Director of the National Geospatial-Intelligence Agency, the Under Secretary of Homeland Security for Intelligence and Analysis, the Assistant Secretary of State for Intelligence and Research, the Director of the Office of Intelligence and Counterintelligence of the Department of Energy, the Assistant Secretary for Intelligence and Analysis of the Department of the Treasury, and the Executive Assistant Director for the National Security Branch of the Federal Bureau of Investigation. If the Director does not concur in the recommendation, the department head may not fill the vacancy or make the recommendation to the President, as the case may be. If the department head and the Director do not reach an agreement on the selection or recommendation, the Director and the department head concerned may advise the President directly of the Director's intention to withhold concurrence.

(2) The relevant department head shall consult with the Director before appointing an individual to fill a vacancy or recommending to the President an individual be nominated to fill a vacancy in any of the following positions: the Under Secretary of Defense for Intelligence; the Director of the Defense Intelligence Agency; uniformed heads of the intelligence elements of the Army, the Navy, the Air Force, and the Marine Corps above the rank of Major General or Rear Admiral; the Assistant Commandant of the Coast Guard for Intelligence; and the Assistant Attorney General for National Security.

(e) Removal from certain positions.

(1) Except for the Director of the Central Intelligence Agency, whose removal the Director may recommend to the President, the Director and the relevant department head shall consult on the removal, or recommendation to the President for removal, as the case may be, of: the Director of the National Security Agency, the Director of the National Geospatial-Intelligence Agency, the Director of the Defense Intelligence Agency, the Under Secretary of Homeland Security for Intelligence and Analysis, the Assistant Secretary of State for Intelligence and Research, and the Assistant Secretary for Intelligence and Analysis of the Department of the Treasury. If the Director and the department head do not agree on removal, or recommendation for removal, either may make a recommendation to the President for the removal of the individual.

(2) The Director and the relevant department or bureau head shall consult on the removal of: the Executive Assistant Director for the National Security Branch of the Federal Bureau of Investigation, the Director of the Office of

Intelligence and Counterintelligence of the Department of Energy, the Director of the National Reconnaissance Office, the Assistant Commandant of the Coast Guard for Intelligence, and the Under Secretary of Defense for Intelligence. With respect to an individual appointed by a department head, the department head may remove the individual upon the request of the Director; if the department head chooses not to remove the individual, either the Director or the department head may advise the President of the department head's intention to retain the individual. In the case of the Under Secretary of Defense for Intelligence, the Secretary of Defense may recommend to the President either the removal or the retention of the individual. For uniformed heads of the intelligence elements of the Army, the Navy, the Air Force, and the Marine Corps, the Director may make a recommendation for removal to the Secretary of Defense.

(3) Nothing in this subsection shall be construed to limit or otherwise affect the authority of the President to nominate, appoint, assign, or terminate the appointment or assignment of any individual, with or without a consultation, recommendation, or concurrence.

SECTION 1.4 THE INTELLIGENCE COMMUNITY. Consistent with applicable Federal law and with the other provisions of this order, and under the leadership of the Director, as specified in such law and this order, the Intelligence Community shall:

(a) Collect and provide information needed by the President and, in the performance of executive functions, the Vice President, the NSC, the Homeland Security Council, the Chairman of the Joint Chiefs of Staff, senior military commanders, and other executive branch officials and, as appropriate, the Congress of the United States;

(b) In accordance with priorities set by the President, collect information concerning, and conduct activities to protect against, international terrorism, proliferation of weapons of mass destruction, intelligence activities directed against the United States, international criminal drug activities, and other hostile activities directed against the United States by foreign powers, organizations, persons, and their agents;

(c) Analyze, produce, and disseminate intelligence;

(d) Conduct administrative, technical, and other support activities within the United States and abroad necessary for the performance of authorized activities, to include providing services of common concern for the Intelligence Community as designated by the Director in accordance with this order;

(e) Conduct research, development, and procurement of technical systems and devices relating to authorized functions and missions or the provision of services of common concern for the Intelligence Community;

(f) Protect the security of intelligence related activities, information, installations, property, and employees by appropriate means, including such investigations of applicants, employees, contractors, and other persons with similar associations with the Intelligence Community elements as are necessary;

(g) Take into account State, local, and tribal governments' and, as appropriate, private sector entities' information needs relating to national and homeland security;

(h) Deconflict, coordinate, and integrate all intelligence activities and other information gathering in accordance with section 1.3(b)(20) of this order; and

(i) Perform such other functions and duties related to intelligence activities as the President may direct.

SECTION 1.5 DUTIES AND RESPONSIBILITIES OF THE HEADS OF EXECUTIVE BRANCH DEPARTMENTS AND AGENCIES. The heads of all departments and agencies shall:

(a) Provide the Director access to all information and intelligence relevant to the national security or that otherwise is required for the performance of the Director's duties, to include administrative and other appropriate management information, except such information excluded by law, by the President, or by the Attorney General acting under this order at the direction of the President;

(b) Provide all programmatic and budgetary information necessary to support the Director in developing the National Intelligence Program;

(c) Coordinate development and implementation of intelligence systems and architectures and, as appropriate, operational systems and architectures of their departments, agencies, and other elements with the Director to respond to national intelligence requirements and all applicable information sharing and security guidelines, information privacy, and other legal requirements;

(d) Provide, to the maximum extent permitted by law, subject to the availability of appropriations and not inconsistent with the mission of the department or agency, such further support to the Director as the Director may request, after consultation with the head of the department or agency, for the performance of the Director's functions;

(e) Respond to advisory tasking from the Director under section 1.3(b)(18) of this order to the greatest extent possible, in accordance with applicable policies established by the head of the responding department or agency;

(f) Ensure that all elements within the department or agency comply with the provisions of Part 2 of this order, regardless of Intelligence Community affiliation, when performing foreign intelligence and counterintelligence functions;

(g) Deconflict, coordinate, and integrate all intelligence activities in accordance with section 1.3(b)(20), and intelligence and other activities in accordance with section 1.3(b)(21) of this order;

(h) Inform the Attorney General, either directly or through the Federal Bureau of Investigation, and the Director of clandestine collection of foreign intelligence and counterintelligence activities inside the United States not coordinated with the Federal Bureau of Investigation;

(i) Pursuant to arrangements developed by the head of the department or agency and the Director of the Central Intelligence Agency and approved by the Director, inform the Director and the Director of the Central Intelligence Agency, either directly or through his designee serving outside the United States, as appropriate, of clandestine collection of foreign intelligence collected through human sources or through human-enabled means outside the United States that has not been coordinated with the Central Intelligence Agency; and

(j) Inform the Secretary of Defense, either directly or through his designee, as appropriate, of clandestine collection of foreign intelligence outside the United States in a region of combat or contingency military operations designated by the Secretary of Defense, for purposes of this paragraph, after consultation with the Director of National Intelligence.

SECTION 1.6 HEADS OF ELEMENTS OF THE INTELLIGENCE COMMUNITY. The heads of elements of the Intelligence Community shall:

(a) Provide the Director access to all information and intelligence relevant to the national security or that otherwise is required for the performance of the Director's duties, to include administrative and other appropriate management information, except such information excluded by law, by the President, or by the Attorney General acting under this order at the direction of the President;

(b) Report to the Attorney General possible violations of Federal criminal laws by employees and of specified Federal criminal laws by any other person as provided in procedures agreed upon by the Attorney General and the head of the department, agency, or establishment concerned, in a manner consistent with the protection of intelligence sources and methods, as specified in those procedures;

(c) Report to the Intelligence Oversight Board, consistent with Executive Order 13462 of February 29, 2008, and provide copies of all such reports to the Director, concerning any intelligence activities of their elements that they have reason to believe may be unlawful or contrary to executive order or presidential directive;

(d) Protect intelligence and intelligence sources, methods, and activities from unauthorized disclosure in accordance with guidance from the Director;

(e) Facilitate, as appropriate, the sharing of information or intelligence, as directed by law or the President, to State, local, tribal, and private sector entities;

(f) Disseminate information or intelligence to foreign governments and international organizations under intelligence or counterintelligence arrangements or agreements established in accordance with section 1.3(b)(4) of this order;

(g) Participate in the development of procedures approved by the Attorney General governing production and dissemination of information or intelligence resulting from criminal drug intelligence activities abroad if they have intelligence responsibilities for foreign or domestic criminal drug production and trafficking; and

(h) Ensure that the inspectors general, general counsels, and agency officials responsible for privacy or civil liberties protection for their respective organizations have access to any information or intelligence necessary to perform their official duties.

SECTION 1.7 INTELLIGENCE COMMUNITY ELEMENTS. Each element of the Intelligence Community shall have the duties and responsibilities specified below, in addition to those specified by law or elsewhere in this order. Intelligence Community elements within executive departments shall serve the information and intelligence needs of their respective heads of departments and also shall operate as part of an integrated Intelligence Community, as provided in law or this order.

(a) THE CENTRAL INTELLIGENCE AGENCY. The Director of the Central Intelligence Agency shall:

(1) Collect (including through clandestine means), analyze, produce, and disseminate foreign intelligence and counterintelligence;

(2) Conduct counterintelligence activities without assuming or performing any internal security functions within the United States;

(3) Conduct administrative and technical support activities within and outside the United States as necessary for cover and proprietary arrangements;

(4) Conduct covert action activities approved by the President. No agency except the Central Intelligence Agency (or the Armed Forces of the United States in time of war declared by the Congress or during any period covered by a report from the President to the Congress consistent with the War Powers Resolution, Public Law 93-148) may conduct any covert action activity unless the President determines that another agency is more likely to achieve a particular objective;

(5) Conduct foreign intelligence liaison relationships with intelligence or security services of foreign governments or international organizations consistent with section 1.3(b)(4) of this order;

(6) Under the direction and guidance of the Director, and in accordance with section 1.3(b)(4) of this order, coordinate the implementation of intelligence and counterintelligence relationships between elements of the Intelligence Community and the intelligence or security services of foreign governments or international organizations; and

(7) Perform such other functions and duties related to intelligence as the Director may direct.

(b) THE DEFENSE INTELLIGENCE AGENCY. The Director of the Defense Intelligence Agency shall:

(1) Collect (including through clandestine means), analyze, produce, and disseminate foreign intelligence and counterintelligence to support national and departmental missions;

(2) Collect, analyze, produce, or, through tasking and coordination, provide defense and defense-related intelligence for the Secretary of Defense, the Chairman of the Joint Chiefs of Staff, combatant commanders, other Defense components, and non-Defense agencies;(3) Conduct counterintelligence activities;

(4) Conduct administrative and technical support activities within and outside the United States as necessary for cover and proprietary arrangements;

(5) Conduct foreign defense intelligence liaison relationships and defense intelligence exchange programs with foreign defense establishments, intelligence or security services of foreign governments, and international organizations in accordance with sections 1.3(b)(4), 1.7(a)(6), and 1.10(i) of this order;

(6) Manage and coordinate all matters related to the Defense Attaché system; and

(7) Provide foreign intelligence and counterintelligence staff support as directed by the Secretary of Defense.

(c) THE NATIONAL SECURITY AGENCY. The Director of the National Security Agency shall:

(1) Collect (including through clandestine means), process, analyze, produce, and disseminate signals intelligence information and data for foreign intelligence and counterintelligence purposes to support national and departmental missions;

(2) Establish and operate an effective unified organization for signals intelligence activities, except for the delegation of operational control over certain operations that are conducted through other elements of the Intelligence Community. No other department or agency may engage in signals intelligence activities except pursuant to a delegation by the Secretary of Defense, after coordination with the Director;

(3) Control signals intelligence collection and processing activities, including assignment of resources to an appropriate agent for such periods and tasks as required for the direct support of military commanders;

(4) Conduct administrative and technical support activities within and outside the United States as necessary for cover arrangements;

(5) Provide signals intelligence support for national and departmental requirements and for the conduct of military operations;

(6) Act as the National Manager for National Security Systems as established in law and policy, and in this capacity be responsible to the Secretary of Defense and to the Director;

(7) Prescribe, consistent with section 102A(g) of the Act, within its field of authorized operations, security regulations covering operating practices, including the transmission, handling, and distribution of signals intelligence and communications security material within and among the elements under control of the Director of the National Security Agency, and exercise the necessary supervisory control to ensure compliance with the regulations; and

(8) Conduct foreign cryptologic liaison relationships in accordance with sections 1.3(b)(4), 1.7(a)(6), and 1.10(i) of this order.

(d) THE NATIONAL RECONNAISSANCE OFFICE. The Director of the National Reconnaissance Office shall:

(1) Be responsible for research and development, acquisition, launch, deployment, and operation of overhead systems and related data processing facilities to collect intelligence and information to support national and departmental missions and other United States Government needs; and

(2) Conduct foreign liaison relationships relating to the above missions, in accordance with sections 1.3(b)(4), 1.7(a)(6), and 1.10(i) of this order.

(e) THE NATIONAL GEOSPATIAL-INTELLIGENCE AGENCY. The Director of the National Geospatial-Intelligence Agency shall:

(1) Collect, process, analyze, produce, and disseminate geospatial intelligence

information and data for foreign intelligence and counterintelligence purposes to support national and departmental missions;

(2) Provide geospatial intelligence support for national and departmental requirements and for the conduct of military operations;

(3) Conduct administrative and technical support activities within and outside the United States as necessary for cover arrangements; and

(4) Conduct foreign geospatial intelligence liaison relationships, in accordance with sections 1.3(b)(4),
1.7(a)(6), and 1.10(i) of this order.

(f) THE INTELLIGENCE AND COUNTERINTELLIGENCE ELEMENTS OF THE ARMY, NAVY, AIR FORCE, AND MARINE CORPS. The Commanders and heads of the intelligence and counterintelligence elements of the Army,
Navy, Air Force, and Marine Corps shall:

(1) Collect (including through clandestine means), produce, analyze, and disseminate defense and defense-related intelligence and counterintelligence to support departmental requirements, and, as appropriate, national requirements;

(2) Conduct counterintelligence activities;

(3) Monitor the development, procurement, and management of tactical intelligence systems and equipment and conduct related research, development, and test and evaluation activities; and

(4) Conduct military intelligence liaison relationships and military intelligence exchange programs with selected cooperative foreign defense establishments and international organizations in accordance with sections 1.3(b)(4), 1.7(a)(6), and 1.10(i) of this order.

(g) INTELLIGENCE ELEMENTS OF THE FEDERAL BUREAU OF INVESTIGATION. Under the supervision of the Attorney General and pursuant to such regulations as the Attorney General may establish, the intelligence elements of the Federal Bureau of Investigation shall:

(1) Collect (including through clandestine means), analyze, produce, and disseminate foreign intelligence and counterintelligence to support national and departmental missions, in accordance with procedural guidelines approved by the Attorney General, after consultation with the Director;

(2) Conduct counterintelligence activities; and

(3) Conduct foreign intelligence and counterintelligence liaison relationships with intelligence, security, and law enforcement services of foreign governments or international organizations in accordance with sections 1.3(b)(4) and 1.7(a)(6) of this order.

(h) THE INTELLIGENCE AND COUNTERINTELLIGENCE ELEMENTS OF THE COAST GUARD. The Commandant of the Coast Guard shall:

(1) Collect (including through clandestine means), analyze, produce, and disseminate foreign intelligence and counterintelligence including defense and defense-related information and intelligence to support national and departmental missions;

(2) Conduct counterintelligence activities;

(3) Monitor the development, procurement, and management of tactical intel-

ligence systems and equipment and conduct related research, development, and test and evaluation activities; and

(4) Conduct foreign intelligence liaison relationships and intelligence exchange programs with foreign intelligence services, security services or international organizations in accordance with sections 1.3(b)(4), 1.7(a)(6), and, when operating as part of the Department of Defense, 1.10(i) of this order.

(i) THE BUREAU OF INTELLIGENCE AND RESEARCH, DEPARTMENT OF STATE; THE OFFICE OF INTELLIGENCE AND ANALYSIS, DEPARTMENT OF THE TREASURY; THE OFFICE OF NATIONAL SECURITY INTELLIGENCE, DRUG ENFORCEMENT ADMINISTRATION; THE OFFICE OF INTELLIGENCE AND ANALYSIS, DEPARTMENT OF HOMELAND SECURITY; AND THE OFFICE OF INTELLIGENCE AND COUNTERINTELLIGENCE, DEPARTMENT OF ENERGY. The heads of the Bureau of Intelligence and Research, Department of State; the Office of Intelligence and Analysis, Department of the Treasury; the Office of National Security Intelligence, Drug Enforcement Administration; the Office of Intelligence and Analysis, Department of Homeland Security; and the Office of Intelligence and Counterintelligence, Department of Energy shall:

(1) Collect (overtly or through publicly available sources), analyze, produce, and disseminate information, intelligence, and counterintelligence to support national and departmental missions; and

(2) Conduct and participate in analytic or information exchanges with foreign partners and international organizations in accordance with sections 1.3(b)(4) and 1.7(a)(6) of this order.

(j) THE OFFICE OF THE DIRECTOR OF NATIONAL INTELLIGENCE. The Director shall collect (overtly or through publicly available sources), analyze, produce, and disseminate information, intelligence, and counterintelligence to support the missions of the Office of the Director of National Intelligence, including the National Counterterrorism Center, and to support other national missions.

SECTION 1.8 THE DEPARTMENT OF STATE. In addition to the authorities exercised by the Bureau of Intelligence and Research under sections 1.4 and 1.7(i) of this order, the Secretary of State shall:

(a) Collect (overtly or through publicly available sources) information relevant to United States foreign policy and national security concerns;

(b) Disseminate, to the maximum extent possible, reports received from United States diplomatic and consular posts;

(c) Transmit reporting requirements and advisory taskings of the Intelligence Community to the Chiefs of
United States Missions abroad; and

(d) Support Chiefs of United States Missions in discharging their responsibilities pursuant to law and presidential direction.

SECTION 1.9 THE DEPARTMENT OF THE TREASURY. In addition to the authorities exercised by the Office of Intelligence and Analysis of the Department of the Treasury under sections 1.4 and 1.7(i) of this order the Secretary of the

Treasury shall collect (overtly or through publicly available sources) foreign financial information and, in consultation with the Department of State, foreign economic information.

1.10 *The Department of Defense.* The Secretary of Defense shall:

(a) Collect (including through clandestine means), analyze, produce, and disseminate information and intelligence and be responsive to collection tasking and advisory tasking by the Director;

(b) Collect (including through clandestine means), analyze, produce, and disseminate defense and defense-related intelligence and counterintelligence, as required for execution of the Secretary's responsibilities;

(c) Conduct programs and missions necessary to fulfill national, departmental, and tactical intelligence requirements;

(d) Conduct counterintelligence activities in support of Department of Defense components and coordinate counterintelligence activities in accordance with section 1.3(b)(20) and (21) of this order;

(e) Act, in coordination with the Director, as the executive agent of the United States Government for signals intelligence activities;

(f) Provide for the timely transmission of critical intelligence, as defined by the Director, within the United States Government;

(g) Carry out or contract for research, development, and procurement of technical systems and devices relating to authorized intelligence functions;

(h) Protect the security of Department of Defense installations, activities, information, property, and employees by appropriate means, including such investigations of applicants, employees, contractors, and other persons with similar associations with the Department of Defense as are necessary;

(i) Establish and maintain defense intelligence relationships and defense intelligence exchange programs with selected cooperative foreign defense establishments, intelligence or security services of foreign governments, and international organizations, and ensure that such relationships and programs are in accordance with sections 1.3(b)(4), 1.3(b)(21) and 1.7(a)(6) of this order;

(j) Conduct such administrative and technical support activities within and outside the United States as are necessary to provide for cover and proprietary arrangements, to perform the functions described in sections (a) though (i) above, and to support the Intelligence Community elements of the Department of Defense; and

(k) Use the Intelligence Community elements within the Department of Defense identified in section 1.7(b) through (f) and, when the Coast Guard is operating as part of the Department of Defense, (h) above to carry out the Secretary of Defense's responsibilities assigned in this section or other departments, agencies, or offices within the Department of Defense, as appropriate, to conduct the intelligence missions and responsibilities assigned to the Secretary of Defense.

SECTION 1.11 THE DEPARTMENT OF HOMELAND SECURITY. In addition to the authorities exercised by the Office of Intelligence and Analysis of the Department of Homeland Security under sections 1.4 and 1.7(i) of this order, the

Secretary of Homeland Security shall conduct, through the United States Secret Service, activities to determine the existence and capability of surveillance equipment being used against the President or the Vice President of the United States, the Executive Office of the President, and, as authorized by the Secretary of Homeland Security or the President, other Secret Service protectees and United States officials. No information shall be acquired intentionally through such activities except to protect against use of such surveillance equipment, and those activities shall be conducted pursuant to procedures agreed upon by the Secretary of Homeland Security and the Attorney General.

SECTION 1.12 THE DEPARTMENT OF ENERGY. In addition to the authorities exercised by the Office of Intelligence and Counterintelligence of the Department of Energy under sections 1.4 and 1.7(i) of this order, the Secretary of Energy shall:

(a) Provide expert scientific, technical, analytic, and research capabilities to other agencies within the Intelligence Community, as appropriate;

(b) Participate in formulating intelligence collection and analysis requirements where the special expert capability of the Department can contribute; and

(c) Participate with the Department of State in overtly collecting information with respect to foreign energy matters.

SECTION 1.13 THE FEDERAL BUREAU OF INVESTIGATION. In addition to the authorities exercised by the intelligence elements of the Federal Bureau of Investigation of the Department of Justice under sections 1.4 and 1.7(g) of this order and under the supervision of the Attorney General and pursuant to such regulations as the Attorney General may establish, the Director of the Federal Bureau of Investigation shall provide technical assistance, within or outside the United States, to foreign intelligence and law enforcement services, consistent with section 1.3(b)(20) and (21) of this order, as may be necessary to support national or departmental missions.

PART 2 CONDUCT OF INTELLIGENCE ACTIVITIES

SECTION 2.1 NEED. Timely, accurate, and insightful information about the activities, capabilities, plans, and intentions of foreign powers, organizations, and persons, and their agents, is essential to informed decisionmaking in the areas of national security, national defense, and foreign relations. Collection of such information is a priority objective and will be pursued in a vigorous, innovative, and responsible manner that is consistent with the Constitution and applicable law and respectful of the principles upon which the United States was founded.

SECTION 2.2 PURPOSE. This Order is intended to enhance human and technical collection techniques, especially those undertaken abroad, and the acquisition of significant foreign intelligence, as well as the detection and countering of international terrorist activities, the spread of weapons of mass destruction, and espionage conducted by foreign powers. Set forth below are certain general principles that, in addition to and consistent with applicable laws, are intended to achieve the proper balance between the acquisition of essential information and protection of individual interests. Nothing in this Order shall be construed to apply to or interfere with any authorized civil or criminal law enforcement responsibility of any department or agency.

SECTION 2.3 COLLECTION OF INFORMATION. Elements of the Intelligence Community are authorized to collect, retain, or disseminate information concerning United States persons only in accordance with procedures established by the head of the Intelligence Community element concerned or by the head of a department containing such element and approved by the Attorney General, consistent with the authorities provided by Part 1 of this Order, after consultation with the Director. Those procedures shall permit collection, retention, and dissemination of the following types of information:

(a) Information that is publicly available or collected with the consent of the person concerned;

(b) Information constituting foreign intelligence or counterintelligence, including such information concerning corporations or other commercial organizations. Collection within the United States of foreign intelligence not otherwise obtainable shall be undertaken by the Federal Bureau of Investigation (FBI) or, when significant foreign intelligence is sought, by other authorized elements of the Intelligence Community, provided that no foreign intelligence collection by such elements may be undertaken for the purpose of acquiring information concerning the domestic activities of United States persons;

(c) Information obtained in the course of a lawful foreign intelligence, counterintelligence, international drug or international terrorism investigation;

(d) Information needed to protect the safety of any persons or organizations, including those who are targets, victims, or hostages of international terrorist organizations;

(e) Information needed to protect foreign intelligence or counterintelligence sources, methods, and activities from unauthorized disclosure. Collection within the United States shall be undertaken by the FBI except that other elements of the Intelligence Community may also collect such information concerning present or former employees, present or former intelligence element contractors or their present or former employees, or applicants for such employment or contracting;

(f) Information concerning persons who are reasonably believed to be potential sources or contacts for the purpose of determining their suitability or credibility;

(g) Information arising out of a lawful personnel, physical, or communications security investigation;

(h) Information acquired by overhead reconnaissance not directed at specific United States persons;

(i) Incidentally obtained information that may indicate involvement in activities that may violate Federal, state, local, or foreign laws; and

(j) Information necessary for administrative purposes.

In addition, elements of the Intelligence Community may disseminate information to each appropriate element within the Intelligence Community for purposes of allowing the recipient element to determine whether the information is relevant to its responsibilities and can be retained by it, except that information derived from signals intelligence may only be disseminated or made available to Intelligence Community elements in accordance with procedures established by the Director in coordination with the Secretary of Defense and approved by the Attorney General.

SECTION 2.4 COLLECTION TECHNIQUES. Elements of the Intelligence Community shall use the least intrusive collection techniques feasible within the United States or directed against United States persons abroad. Elements of the Intelligence Community are not authorized to use such techniques as electronic surveillance, unconsented physical searches, mail surveillance, physical surveillance, or monitoring devices unless they are in accordance with procedures established by the head of the Intelligence Community element concerned or the head of a department containing such element and approved by the Attorney General, after consultation with the Director. Such procedures shall protect constitutional and other legal rights and limit use of such information to lawful governmental purposes. These procedures shall not authorize:

(a) The Central Intelligence Agency (CIA) to engage in electronic surveillance within the United States except for the purpose of training, testing, or conducting countermeasures to hostile electronic surveillance;

(b) Unconsented physical searches in the United States by elements of the Intelligence Community other than the FBI, except for:

> (1) Searches by counterintelligence elements of the military services directed against military personnel within the United States or abroad for intelligence purposes, when authorized by a military commander empowered to approve physical searches for law enforcement purposes, based upon a finding of probable cause to believe that such persons are acting as agents of foreign powers; and
>
> (2) Searches by CIA of personal property of non-United States persons lawfully in its possession;

(c) Physical surveillance of a United States person in the United States by elements of the Intelligence
Community other than the FBI, except for:

> (1) Physical surveillance of present or former employees, present or former intelligence element contractors or their present or former employees, or applicants for any such employment or contracting; and
>
> (2) Physical surveillance of a military person employed by a non-intelligence element of a military service; and

(d) Physical surveillance of a United States person abroad to collect foreign intelligence, except to obtain significant information that cannot reasonably be acquired by other means.

SECTION 2.5 ATTORNEY GENERAL APPROVAL. The Attorney General hereby is delegated the power to approve the use for intelligence purposes, within the United States or against a United States person abroad, of any technique for which a warrant would be required if undertaken for law enforcement purposes, provided that such techniques shall not be undertaken unless the Attorney General has determined in each case that there is probable cause to believe that the technique is directed against a foreign power or an agent of a foreign power. The authority delegated pursuant to this paragraph, including the authority to approve the use of electronic surveillance as defined in the Foreign Intelligence Surveillance Act of 1978, as amended, shall be exercised in accordance with that Act.

SECTION 2.6 ASSISTANCE TO LAW ENFORCEMENT AND OTHER CIVIL AUTHORITIES. Elements of the Intelligence Community are authorized to:

(a) Cooperate with appropriate law enforcement agencies for the purpose of protecting the employees, information, property, and facilities of any element of the Intelligence Community;

(b) Unless otherwise precluded by law or this Order, participate in law enforcement activities to investigate or prevent clandestine intelligence activities by foreign powers, or international terrorist or narcotics activities;

(c) Provide specialized equipment, technical knowledge, or assistance of expert personnel for use by any department or agency, or when lives are endangered, to support local law enforcement agencies. Provision of assistance by expert personnel shall be approved in each case by the general counsel of the providing element or department; and

(d) Render any other assistance and cooperation to law enforcement or other civil authorities not precluded by applicable law.

SECTION 2.7 CONTRACTING. Elements of the Intelligence Community are authorized to enter into contracts or arrangements for the provision of goods or services with private companies or institutions in the United States and need not reveal the sponsorship of such contracts or arrangements for authorized intelligence purposes. Contracts or arrangements with academic institutions may be undertaken only with the consent of appropriate officials of the institution.

SECTION 2.8 CONSISTENCY WITH OTHER LAWS. Nothing in this Order shall be construed to authorize any activity in violation of the Constitution or statutes of the United States.

SECTION 2.9 UNDISCLOSED PARTICIPATION IN ORGANIZATIONS WITHIN THE UNITED STATES. No one acting on behalf of elements of the Intelligence Community may join or otherwise participate in any organization in the United States on behalf of any element of the Intelligence Community without disclosing such person's intelligence affiliation to appropriate officials of the organization, except in accordance with procedures established by the head of the Intelligence Community element concerned or the head of a department containing such element and approved by the Attorney General, after consultation with the Director. Such participation shall be authorized only if it is essential to achieving lawful purposes as determined by the Intelligence Community element head or designee. No such participation may be undertaken for the purpose of

influencing the activity of the organization or its members except in cases where:
(a) The participation is undertaken on behalf of the FBI in the course of a lawful investigation; or
(b) The organization concerned is composed primarily of individuals who are not United States persons and is reasonably believed to be acting on behalf of a foreign power.

SECTION 2.10 HUMAN EXPERIMENTATION. No element of the Intelligence Community shall sponsor, contract for, or conduct research on human subjects except in accordance with guidelines issued by the Department of Health and Human Services. The subject's informed consent shall be documented as required by those guidelines.

SECTION 2.11 PROHIBITION ON ASSASSINATION. No person employed by or acting on behalf of the United States Government shall engage in or conspire to engage in assassination.

SECTION 2.12 INDIRECT PARTICIPATION. No element of the Intelligence Community shall participate in or request any person to undertake activities forbidden by this Order.

SECTION 2.13 LIMITATION ON COVERT ACTION. No covert action may be conducted which is intended to influence United States political processes, public opinion, policies, or media.

PART 3 GENERAL PROVISIONS

SECTION 3.1 CONGRESSIONAL OVERSIGHT. The duties and responsibilities of the Director and the heads of other departments, agencies, elements, and entities engaged in intelligence activities to cooperate with the Congress in the conduct of its responsibilities for oversight of intelligence activities shall be implemented in accordance with applicable law, including title V of the Act. The requirements of applicable law, including title V of the Act, shall apply to all covert action activities as defined in this Order.

SECTION 3.2 IMPLEMENTATION. The President, supported by the NSC, and the Director shall issue such appropriate directives, procedures, and guidance as are necessary to implement this order. Heads of elements within the Intelligence Community shall issue appropriate procedures and supplementary directives consistent with this order. No procedures to implement Part 2 of this order shall be issued without the Attorney General's approval, after consultation with the Director. The Attorney General shall provide a statement of reasons for not approving any procedures established by the head of an element in the Intelligence Community (or the head of the department containing such element) other than the FBI. In instances where the element head or department head and the Attorney General are unable to reach agreements on other than constitutional or other legal grounds, the Attorney General, the head of department concerned, or the Director shall refer the matter to the NSC.

SECTION 3.3 PROCEDURES. The activities herein authorized that require procedures shall be conducted in accordance with existing procedures or requirements established under Executive Order 12333. New procedures, as required by Executive Order 12333, as further amended, shall be established as expeditiously as possible. All new procedures promulgated pursuant to Executive Order 12333, as amended, shall be made available to the Select Committee on Intelligence of the Senate and the Permanent Select Committee on Intelligence of the House of Representatives.

SECTION 3.4 REFERENCES AND TRANSITION. References to "Senior Officials of the Intelligence Community" or "SOICs" in executive orders or other Presidential guidance, shall be deemed references to the heads of elements in the Intelligence Community, unless the President otherwise directs; references in Intelligence Community or Intelligence Community element policies or guidance, shall be deemed to be references to the heads of elements of the Intelligence Community, unless the President or the Director otherwise directs.

SECTION 3.5 DEFINITIONS. For the purposes of this Order, the following terms shall have these meanings:

(a) *Counterintelligence* means information gathered and activities conducted to identify, deceive, exploit, disrupt, or protect against espionage, other intelligence activities, sabotage, or assassinations conducted for or on behalf of foreign powers, organizations, or persons, or their agents, or international terrorist organizations or activities.

(b) *Covert action* means an activity or activities of the United States Government to influence political, economic, or military conditions abroad, where it is intended that the role of the United States Government will not be apparent or acknowledged publicly, but does not include:

(1) Activities the primary purpose of which is to acquire intelligence, traditional counterintelligence activities, traditional activities to improve or maintain the operational security of United States Government programs, or administrative activities;

(2) Traditional diplomatic or military activities or routine support to such activities;

(3) Traditional law enforcement activities conducted by United States Government law enforcement agencies or routine support to such activities; or

(4) Activities to provide routine support to the overt activities (other than activities described in paragraph (1), (2), or (3)) of other United States Government agencies abroad.

(c) *Electronic surveillance* means acquisition of a nonpublic communication by electronic means without the consent of a person who is a party to an electronic communication or, in the case of a nonelectronic communication, without the consent of a person who is visibly present at the place of communication, but not including the use of radio direction-finding equipment solely to determine the location of a transmitter.

(d) *Employee* means a person employed by, assigned or detailed to, or acting for an element within the Intelligence Community.
(e) *Foreign intelligence* means information relating to the capabilities, intentions, or activities of foreign governments or elements thereof, foreign organizations, foreign persons, or international terrorists.
(f) *Intelligence* includes foreign intelligence and counterintelligence.
(g) *Intelligence activities* means all activities that elements of the Intelligence Community are authorized to conduct pursuant to this order.
(h) *Intelligence Community* and elements of the Intelligence Community refers to:

(1) The Office of the Director of National Intelligence;
(2) The Central Intelligence Agency;
(3) The National Security Agency;
(4) The Defense Intelligence Agency;
(5) The National Geospatial-Intelligence Agency;
(6) The National Reconnaissance Office;
(7) The other offices within the Department of Defense for the collection of specialized national foreign intelligence through reconnaissance programs;
(8) The intelligence and counterintelligence elements of the Army, the Navy, the Air Force, and the
Marine Corps;
(9) The intelligence elements of the Federal Bureau of Investigation;
(10) The Office of National Security Intelligence of the Drug Enforcement Administration;
(11) The Office of Intelligence and Counterintelligence of the Department of Energy;
(12) The Bureau of Intelligence and Research of the Department of State;
(13) The Office of Intelligence and Analysis of the Department of the Treasury;
(14) The Office of Intelligence and Analysis of the Department of Homeland Security;
(15) The intelligence and counterintelligence elements of the Coast Guard; and
(16) Such other elements of any department or agency as may be designated by the President, or designated jointly by the Director and the head of the department or agency concerned, as an element of the Intelligence Community.

(i) *National Intelligence and Intelligence Related to National Security* means all intelligence, regardless of the source from which derived and including information gathered within or outside the United States, that pertains, as determined consistent with any guidance issued by the President, or that is determined for the purpose of access to information by the Director in accordance with section 1.3(a)(1) of this order, to pertain to more than one United States Government agency; and that involves threats to the United States, its people, property, or interests; the development, proliferation, or use of weapons of mass destruction; or any other matter bearing on United States national or homeland security.

(j) *The National Intelligence Program* means all programs, projects, and activities of the Intelligence
Community, as well as any other programs of the Intelligence Community designated jointly by the Director and the head of a United States department or agency or by the President. Such term does not include programs, projects, or activities of the military departments to acquire intelligence solely for the planning and conduct of tactical military operations by United States Armed Forces.

(k) *United States person* means a United States citizen, an alien known by the intelligence element concerned to be a permanent resident alien, an unincorporated association substantially composed of
United States citizens or permanent resident aliens, or a corporation incorporated in the United States, except for a corporation directed and controlled by a foreign government or governments.

SECTION 3.6 REVOCATION. Executive Orders 13354 and 13355 of August 27, 2004, are revoked; and paragraphs 1.3(b)(9) Executive Order 12958, as amended, are inconsistent with this Order.

SECTION 3.7 GENERAL PROVISIONS.

(a) Consistent with section 1.3(c) of this order, nothing in this order shall be construed to impair or otherwise affect:

(1) Authority granted by law to a department or agency, or the head thereof; or

(2) Functions of the Director of the Office of Management and Budget relating to budget, administrative, or legislative proposals.

(b) This order shall be implemented consistent with applicable law and subject to the availability of appropriations.

(c) This order is intended only to improve the internal management of the executive branch and is not intended to, and does not, create any right or benefit, substantive or procedural, enforceable at law or in equity, by any party against the United States, its departments, agencies or entities, its officers, employees, or agents, or any other person.

Executive Order 13467— Reforming Processes Related to Suitability for Government Employment, Fitness for Contractor Employees, and Eligibility for Access to Classified National Security Information

73 Fed. Reg. 38,103 (July 2, 2008)

By the authority vested in me as President by the Constitution and the laws of the United States of America, and in order to ensure an efficient, practical, reciprocal, and aligned system for investigating and determining suitability for Government employment, contractor employee fitness, and eligibility for access to classified information, while taking appropriate account of title III of Public Law 108–458, it is hereby ordered as follows:

PART 1—POLICY, APPLICABILITY, AND DEFINITIONS

Sec. 1.1. *Policy.* Executive branch policies and procedures relating to suitability, contractor employee fitness, eligibility to hold a sensitive position, access to federally controlled facilities and information systems, and eligibility for access to classified information shall be aligned using consistent standards to the extent possible, provide for reciprocal recognition, and shall ensure cost-effective, timely, and efficient protection of the national interest, while providing fair treatment to those upon whom the Federal Government relies to conduct our Nation's business and protect national security.

Sec. 1.2. *Applicability.*
(a) This order applies to all covered individuals as defined in section 1.3(g), except that:

(i) the provisions regarding eligibility for physical access to federally controlled facilities and logical access to federally controlled information systems do not apply to individuals exempted in accordance with guidance pursuant to the Federal Information Security Management Act (title III of Public Law 107–347) and Homeland Security Presidential Directive 12; and
(ii) the qualification standards for enlistment, appointment, and induction into the Armed Forces pursuant to title 10, United States Code, are unaffected by this order.

(b) This order also applies to investigations and determinations of eligibility for access to classified information for employees of agencies working in or for the legislative or judicial branches when those investigations or determinations are conducted by the executive branch.

Sec. 1.3. *Definitions.* For the purpose of this order:
(a) "Adjudication" means the evaluation of pertinent data in a background inves-

tigation, as well as any other available information that is relevant and reliable, to determine whether a covered individual is:

(i) suitable for Government employment;

(ii) eligible for logical and physical access;

(iii) eligible for access to classified information;

(iv) eligible to hold a sensitive position; or

(v) fit to perform work for or on behalf of the Government as a contractor employee.

(b) "Agency" means any "Executive agency" as defined in section 105 of title 5, United States Code, including the "military departments," as defined in section 102 of title 5, United States Code, and any other entity within the executive branch that comes into possession of classified information or has designated positions as sensitive, except such an entity headed by an officer who is not a covered individual.

(c) "Classified information" means information that has been determined pursuant to Executive Order 12958 of April 17, 1995, as amended, or a successor or predecessor order, or the Atomic Energy Act of 1954 (42 U.S.C. 2011 *et seq.*) to require protection against unauthorized disclosure.

(d) "Continuous evaluation" means reviewing the background of an individual who has been determined to be eligible for access to classified information (including additional or new checks of commercial databases, Government databases, and other information lawfully available to security officials) at any time during the period of eligibility to determine whether that individual continues to meet the requirements for eligibility for access to classified information.

(e) "Contractor" means an expert or consultant (not appointed under section 3109 of title 5, United States Code) to an agency; an industrial or commercial contractor, licensee, certificate holder, or grantee of any agency, including all subcontractors; a personal services contractor; or any other category of person who performs work for or on behalf of an agency (but not a Federal employee).

(f) "Contractor employee fitness" means fitness based on character and conduct for work for or on behalf of the Government as a contractor employee.

(g) "Covered individual" means a person who performs work for or on behalf of the executive branch, or who seeks to perform work for or on behalf of the executive branch, but does not include:

(i) the President or (except to the extent otherwise directed by the President) employees of the President under section 105 or 107 of title 3, United States Code; or

(ii) the Vice President or (except to the extent otherwise directed by the Vice President) employees of the Vice President under section 106 of title 3 or annual legislative branch appropriations acts.

(h) "End-to-end automation" means an executive branch-wide federated system that uses automation to manage and monitor cases and maintain relevant documentation of the application (but not an employment application), investigation, adjudication, and continuous evaluation processes.

(i) "Federally controlled facilities" and "federally controlled information sys-

tems" have the meanings prescribed in guidance pursuant to the Federal Information Security Management Act (title III of Public Law 107–347) and Homeland Security Presidential Directive 12.
(j) "Logical and physical access" means access other than occasional or intermittent access to federally controlled facilities or information systems.
(k) "Sensitive position" means any position so designated under Executive Order 10450 of April 27, 1953, as amended.
(l) "Suitability" has the meaning and coverage provided in 5 CFR Part 731.

PART 2—ALIGNMENT, RECIPROCITY, AND GOVERNANCE

Sec. 2.1. *Aligned System.* (a) Investigations and adjudications of covered individuals who require a determination of suitability, eligibility for logical and physical access, eligibility to hold a sensitive position, eligibility for access to classified information, and, as appropriate, contractor employee fitness, shall be aligned using consistent standards to the extent possible. Each successively higher level of investigation and adjudication shall build upon, but not duplicate, the ones below it.
(b) The aligned system shall employ updated and consistent standards and methods, enable innovations with enterprise information technology capabilities and end-to-end automation to the extent practicable, and ensure that relevant information maintained by agencies can be accessed and shared rapidly across the executive branch, while protecting national security, protecting privacy-related information, ensuring resulting decisions are in the national interest, and providing the Federal Government with an effective workforce.
(c) Except as otherwise authorized by law, background investigations and adjudications shall be mutually and reciprocally accepted by all agencies. An agency may not establish additional investigative or adjudicative requirements (other than requirements for the conduct of a polygraph examination consistent with law, directive, or regulation) that exceed the requirements for suitability, contractor employee fitness, eligibility for logical or physical access, eligibility to hold a sensitive position, or eligibility for access to classified information without the approval of the Suitability Executive Agent or Security Executive Agent, as appropriate, and provided that approval to establish additional requirements shall be limited to circumstances where additional requirements are necessary to address significant needs unique to the agency involved or to protect national security.

Sec. 2.2. *Establishment and Functions of Performance Accountability Council.*
(a) There is hereby established a Suitability and Security Clearance Performance Accountability Council (Council).
(b) The Deputy Director for Management, Office of Management and Budget, shall serve as Chair of the Council and shall have authority, direction, and control over the Council's functions. Membership on the Council shall include the Suitability Executive Agent and the Security Executive Agent. The Chair shall select a Vice Chair to act in the Chair's absence. The Chair shall have

authority to designate officials from additional agencies who shall serve as members of the Council. Council membership shall be limited to Federal Government employees and shall include suitability and security professionals.
(c) The Council shall be accountable to the President to achieve, consistent with this order, the goals of reform, and is responsible for driving implementation of the reform effort, ensuring accountability by agencies, ensuring
the Suitability Executive Agent and the Security Executive Agent align their respective processes, and sustaining reform momentum.
(d) The Council shall:

(i) ensure alignment of suitability, security, and, as appropriate, contractor employee fitness investigative and adjudicative processes;
(ii) hold agencies accountable for the implementation of suitability, security, and, as appropriate, contractor employee fitness processes and procedures;
(iii) establish requirements for enterprise information technology;
(iv) establish annual goals and progress metrics and prepare annual reports on results;
(v) ensure and oversee the development of tools and techniques for enhancing background investigations and the making of eligibility determinations;
(vi) arbitrate disparities in procedures between the Suitability Executive Agent and the Security Executive Agent;
(vii) ensure sharing of best practices; and
(viii) advise the Suitability Executive Agent and the Security Executive Agent on policies affecting the alignment of investigations and adjudications.

(e) The Chair may, to ensure the effective implementation of the policy set forth in section 1.1 of this order and to the extent consistent with law, assign, in whole or in part, to the head of any agency (solely or jointly) any function within the Council's responsibility relating to alignment and improvement of investigations and determinations of suitability, contractor employee fitness, eligibility for logical and physical access, eligibility for access to classified information, or eligibility to hold a sensitive position.

Sec. 2.3. *Establishment, Designation, and Functions of Executive Agents.*
(a) There is hereby established a Suitability Executive Agent and a Security Executive Agent.
(b) The Director of the Office of Personnel Management shall serve as the Suitability Executive Agent. As the Suitability Executive Agent, the Director of the Office of Personnel Management will continue to be responsible for developing and implementing uniform and consistent policies and procedures to ensure the effective, efficient, and timely completion of investigations and adjudications relating to determinations of suitability and eligibility for logical and physical access.
(c) The Director of National Intelligence shall serve as the Security Executive Agent. The Security Executive Agent:

(i) shall direct the oversight of investigations and determinations of eligibility for access to classified information or eligibility to hold a sensitive position made by any agency;

(ii) shall be responsible for developing uniform and consistent policies and procedures to ensure the effective, efficient, and timely completion of investigations and adjudications relating to determinations of eligibility for access to classified information or eligibility to hold a sensitive position;

(iii) may issue guidelines and instructions to the heads of agencies to ensure appropriate uniformity, centralization, efficiency, effectiveness, and timeliness in processes relating to determinations by agencies of eligibility for access to classified information or eligibility to hold a sensitive position;

(iv) shall serve as the final authority to designate an agency or agencies to conduct investigations of persons who are proposed for access to classified information to ascertain whether such persons satisfy the criteria for obtaining and retaining access to classified information or eligibility to hold a sensitive position;

(v) shall serve as the final authority to designate an agency or agencies to determine eligibility for access to classified information in accordance with Executive Order 12968 of August 2, 1995;

(vi) shall ensure reciprocal recognition of eligibility for access to classified information among the agencies, including acting as the final authority to arbitrate and resolve disputes among the agencies involving the reciprocity of investigations and determinations of eligibility for access to classified information or eligibility to hold a sensitive position; and

(vii) may assign, in whole or in part, to the head of any agency (solely or jointly) any of the functions detailed in (i) through (vi), above, with the agency's exercise of such assigned functions to be subject to the Security Executive Agent's oversight and with such terms and conditions (including approval by the Security Executive Agent) as the Security Executive Agent determines appropriate.

(d) Nothing in this order shall be construed in a manner that would limit the authorities of the Director of the Office of Personnel Management or the Director of National Intelligence under law.

Sec. 2.4. *Additional Functions.*

(a) The duties assigned to the Security Policy Board by Executive Order 12968 of August 2, 1995, to consider, coordinate, and recommend policy directives for executive branch security policies, procedures, and practices are reassigned to the Security Executive Agent.

(b) Heads of agencies shall:

(i) carry out any function assigned to the agency head by the Chair, and shall assist the Chair, the Council, the Suitability Executive Agent, and the Security Executive Agent in carrying out any function under sections 2.2 and 2.3 of this order;

(ii) implement any policy or procedure developed pursuant to this order;

(iii) to the extent permitted by law, make available to the Performance Accountability Council, the Suitability Executive Agent, or the Security Executive Agent such information as may be requested to implement this order;

(iv) ensure that all actions taken under this order take account of the counterintelligence interests of the United States, as appropriate; and
(v) ensure that actions taken under this order are consistent with the President's constitutional authority to:
(A) conduct the foreign affairs of the United States;
(B) withhold information the disclosure of which could impair the foreign relations, the national security, the deliberative processes of the Executive, or the performance of the Executive's constitutional duties;
(C) recommend for congressional consideration such measures as the President may judge necessary or expedient; and
(D) supervise the unitary executive branch.

PART 3—MISCELLANEOUS

Sec. 3. *General Provisions.*
(a) Executive Order 13381 of June 27, 2005, as amended, is revoked. Nothing in this order shall:
(i) supersede, impede, or otherwise affect:
(A) Executive Order 10450 of April 27, 1953, as amended;
(B) Executive Order 10577 of November 23, 1954, as amended;
(C) Executive Order 12333 of December 4, 1981, as amended;
(D) Executive Order 12829 of January 6, 1993, as amended; or
(E) Executive Order 12958 of April 17, 1995, as amended; nor
(ii) diminish or otherwise affect the denial and revocation procedures provided to individuals covered by Executive Order 10865 of February 20, 1960, as amended.
(b) Executive Order 12968 of August 2, 1995 is amended:
(i) by inserting: "**Sec. 3.5.** *Continuous Evaluation.* An individual who has been determined to be eligible for or who currently has access to classified information shall be subject to continuous evaluation under standards (including, but not limited to, the frequency of such evaluation) as determined by the Director of National Intelligence."; and
(ii) by striking "the Security Policy Board shall make recommendations to the President through the Assistant to the President for National Security Affairs" in section 6.3(a) and inserting in lieu thereof "the Director of National Intelligence shall serve as the final authority";
(iii) by striking "Security Policy Board" and inserting in lieu thereof "Security Executive Agent" in each instance;
(iv) by striking "the Board" in section 1.1(j) and inserting in lieu thereof "the Security Executive Agent"; and
(v) by inserting "or appropriate automated procedures" in section 3.1(b) after "by appropriately trained adjudicative personnel".
(c) Nothing in this order shall supersede, impede, or otherwise affect the remainder of Executive Order 12968 of August 2, 1995, as amended.
(d) Executive Order 12171 of November 19, 1979, as amended, is further amended

by striking "The Center for Federal Investigative Services" in section 1–216 and inserting in lieu thereof "The Federal Investigative Services Division."

(e) Nothing in this order shall be construed to impair or otherwise affect the:

(i) authority granted by law to a department or agency, or the head thereof; or

(ii) functions of the Director of the Office of Management and Budget relating to budget, administrative, or legislative proposals.

(f) This order shall be implemented consistent with applicable law and subject to the availability of appropriations.

(g) Existing delegations of authority made pursuant to Executive Order 13381 of June 27, 2005, as amended, to any agency relating to granting eligibility for access to classified information and conducting investigations shall remain in effect, subject to the exercise of authorities pursuant to this order to revise or revoke such delegation.

(h) If any provision of this order or the application of such provision is held to be invalid, the remainder of this order shall not be affected.

(i) This order is intended only to improve the internal management of the executive branch and is not intended to, and does not, create any right or benefit, substantive or procedural, enforceable at law or in equity, by any party against the United States, its agencies, instrumentalities, or entities, its officers or employees, or any other person.

GEORGE W.BUSH

Executive Order 13475—
Further Amendments to Executive Orders 12139 and 12949 in Light of the Foreign Intelligence Surveillance Act of 1978 Amendments Act of 2008

73 Fed. Reg. 60.095 (October 7, 2008)

By the authority vested in me as President by the Constitution and the laws of the United States of America, including sections 104 and 303 of the Foreign Intelligence Surveillance Act of 1978 (50 U.S.C. 1801 et seq.), as amended by the Foreign Intelligence Surveillance Act of 1978 Amendments Act of 2008 (Public Law 110-261), it is hereby ordered as follows:

SECTION 1. Section 1-103 of Executive Order 12139 of May 23, 1979, as amended, is further amended by:
(a) striking "(7)" each place it appears and inserting in lieu thereof "(6)";
(b) adding after subsection (h) "(i) Deputy Director of the Federal Bureau of Investigation."; and
(c) by adding after the sentence that begins "None of the above officials . . .", a new sentence to read "The requirement of the preceding sentence that the named official must be appointed by the President with the advice and consent of the Senate does not apply to the Deputy Director of the Federal Bureau of Investigation."

SECTION 2. Section 3 of Executive Order 12949 of February 9, 1995, as amended, is further amended by:
(a) striking "(7)" each place it appears and inserting in lieu thereof "(6)";
(b) striking "and" at the end of subsection (g);
(c) striking the period at the end of subsection (h) and inserting in lieu thereof "; and";
(d) adding after subsection (h) "(i) Deputy Director of the Federal Bureau of Investigation."; and
(e) by adding after the sentence that begins "None of the above officials . . .", a new sentence to read "The requirement of the preceding sentence that the named official must be appointed by the President with the advice and consent of the Senate does not apply to the Deputy Director of the Federal Bureau of Investigation."

SECTION 3. This order is not intended to, and does not, create any right or benefit, substantive or procedural, enforceable at law or in equity, by any party against the United States, its agencies, instrumentalities, or entities, its officers, employees, or agents, or any other person.

GEORGE W. BUSH

Executive Order 12139—Exercise of Certain Authority Respecting Electronic Surveillance

Fed. Reg. 30,311 (May 23, 1979)

By the authority vested in me as President by Sections 102 and 104 of the Foreign Intelligence Surveillance Act of 1978 (50 U.S.C. 1802 and 1804), in order to provide as set forth in that Act (this chapter) for the authorization of electronic surveillance for foreign intelligence purposes, it is hereby ordered as follows:

SECTION 1-101. Pursuant to Section 102(a)(1) of the Foreign Intelligence Surveillance Act of 1978 (50 U.S.C. 1802(a)), the Attorney General is authorized to approve electronic surveillance to acquire foreign intelligence information without a court order, but only if the Attorney General makes the certifications required by that Section.

SECTION 1-102. Pursuant to Section 102(b) of the Foreign Intelligence Act of 1978 (50 U.S.C. 1802(b)), the Attorney General is authorized to approve applications to the court having jurisdiction under Section 103 of that Act (50 U.S.C. 1803) to obtain orders for electronic surveillance for the purpose of obtaining foreign intelligence information.

SECTION 1-103. Pursuant to Section 104(a)(7) of the Foreign Intelligence Surveillance Act of 1978 (50 U.S.C. 1804(a)(7)), the following officials, each of whom is employed in the area of national security or defense, is designated to make the certifications required by Section 104(a)(7) of the Act in support of applications to conduct electronic surveillance:

(a) Secretary of State.
(b) Secretary of Defense.
(c) Director of Central Intelligence.
(d) Director of the Federal Bureau of Investigation.
(e) Deputy Secretary of State.
(f) Deputy Secretary of Defense.
(g) Deputy Director of Central Intelligence.

None of the above officials, nor anyone officially acting in that capacity, may exercise the authority to make the above certifications, unless that official has been appointed by the President with the advice and consent of the Senate.

SECTION 1-104. Section 2-202 of Executive Order No. 12036 (set out under section 401 of this title) is amended by inserting the following at the end of that section: ''Any electronic surveillance, as defined in the Foreign Intelligence Surveillance Act of 1978, shall be conducted in accordance with that Act as well as this Order.''.

SECTION 1-105. Section 2-203 of Executive Order No. 12036 (set out under section 401 of this title) is amended by inserting the following at the end of that section: "Any monitoring which constitutes electronic surveillance as defined in the Foreign Intelligence Surveillance Act of 1978 shall be conducted in accordance with that Act as well as this Order.".

JIMMY CARTER

Executive Order 12949—Foreign Intelligence Physical Searches

60 Fed. Reg. 8,169 (Feb. 13, 1995))

By the authority vested in me as President by the Constitution and the laws of the United States, including sections 302 and 303 of the Foreign Intelligence Surveillance Act of 1978 ("Act") (50 U.S.C. 1801, *et seq.*), as amended by Public Law 103–359, and in order to provide for the authorization of physical searches for foreign intelligence purposes as set forth in the Act, it is hereby ordered as follows:

Section 1. Pursuant to section 302(a)(1) of the Act, the Attorney General is authorized to approve physical searches, without a court order, to acquire foreign intelligence information for periods of up to one year, if the Attorney General makes the certifications required by that section.

Sec. 2. Pursuant to section 302(b) of the Act, the Attorney General is authorized to approve applications to the Foreign Intelligence Surveillance Court under section 303 of the Act to obtain orders for physical searches for the purpose of collecting foreign intelligence information.

Sec. 3. Pursuant to section 303(a)(7) of the Act, the following officials, each of whom is employed in the area of national security or defense, is designated to make the certifications required by section 303(a)(7) of the Act in support of applications to conduct physical searches:

(a) Secretary of State;
(b) Secretary of Defense;
(c) Director of Central Intelligence;
(d) Director of the Federal Bureau of Investigation;
(e) Deputy Secretary of State;
(f) Deputy Secretary of Defense; and
(g) Deputy Director of Central Intelligence.

None of the above officials, nor anyone officially acting in that capacity, may exercise the authority to make the above certifications, unless that official has been appointed by the President, by and with the advice and consent of the Senate.

WILLIAM J. CLINTON

Executive Order 13383—Amending Executive Orders 12139 and 12949 in Light of Establishment of the Office of Director of National Intelligence

70 Fed. Reg. 41,933, July 15, 2005

By the authority vested in me as President by the Constitution and the laws of the United States of America, it is hereby ordered as follows:

SECTION. 1. Section 1-103 of Executive Order 12139 of May 23, 1979, is amended by:
(a) striking "(c) Director of Central Intelligence" and inserting in lieu thereof "(c) Director of National Intelligence";
(b) striking "(g) Deputy Director of Central Intelligence" and inserting in lieu thereof "(g) Director of the Central Intelligence Agency"; and
(c) adding at the end thereof "(h) Principal Deputy Director of National Intelligence.".

SECTION 2. Section 3 of Executive Order 12949 of February 9, 1995, is amended by:
(a) striking "(c) Director of Central Intelligence" and inserting in lieu thereof "Director of National Intelligence";
(b) striking "and" at the end of subsection (f);
(c) striking "(g) Deputy Director of Central Intelligence." and inserting in lieu thereof "(g) Director of the Central Intelligence Agency; and"; and
(d) adding at the end thereof "(h) Principal Deputy Director of National Intelligence.".

SECTION 3. This order is not intended to, and does not, create any right or benefit, substantive or procedural, enforceable by any party at law or in equity against the United States, its departments, agencies, entities, officers, employees, or agents, or any other person.

GEORGE W. BUSH

Executive Order 13516—Amending Executive Order 13462

74 Fed. Reg. 56,521 (Nov. 2, 2009)

By the authority vested in me as President by the Constitution and the laws of the United States of America, it is hereby ordered as follows:

Sec. 1. Executive Order 13462 of February 29, 2008, is amended as follows:
(a) by striking subsection (b) of section 2 and inserting in lieu thereof the following:

"(b) "intelligence activities" has the meaning specified in section 3.5 of Executive Order 12333 of December 4, 1981, as amended; and"

(b) by striking subsection (b) of section 3 and inserting in lieu thereof the following:

"(b) The PIAB shall consist of not more than 16 members appointed by the President from among individuals who are not full-time employees of the Federal Government."

(c) by striking subsection (c) of section 3 and inserting in lieu thereof the following:

"(c) The President shall designate a Chair or Co-Chairs from among the members of the PIAB, who shall convene and preside at meetings of the PIAB, determine its agenda, and direct its work."

(d) by inserting after subsection (b) of section 6 the following new subsection:

"(c) forward to the Attorney General information concerning intelligence activities that involve possible violations of Federal criminal laws or otherwise implicate the authority of the Attorney General;", and renumbering the subsequent subsections of section 6 accordingly.

(e) by striking subsection (a) of section 8 and inserting in lieu thereof: "To the extent permitted by law, the DNI and the heads of departments concerned shall provide such information and assistance as the PIAB and the IOB determine is needed to perform their functions under this order."

(f) by substituting "section 1.6(c) of Executive Order 12333, as amended" for "section 1.7(d) of Executive Order 12333" each time it appears in the order.

(g) by striking subsection (b) of section 11 and inserting in lieu thereof:

"(b) Any person who is a member of the PIAB or the IOB, or who is granted access to classified national security information in relation to the activities of the PIAB or the IOB, as a condition of access to such information, shall sign and comply with appropriate agreements to protect such information from unauthorized disclosure. This order shall be implemented in a manner consistent with Executive Order 12958 of April 17, 1995, as amended, and Executive Order 12968 of August 2, 1995, as amended."

Sec. 2. *General Provisions.*
(a) Nothing in this order shall be construed to impair or otherwise affect:
(i) authority granted by law to a department or agency, or the head thereof; or
(ii) functions of the Director of the Office of Management and Budget relating to budget, administrative, or legislative proposals.
(b) This order shall be implemented consistent with applicable law and subject to the availability of appropriations.
(c) This order is not intended to, and does not, create any right or benefit, substantive or procedural, enforceable at law or in equity, by any party against the United States, its departments, agencies, or entities, its officers, employees, or agents, or any other person.

BARACK OBAMA

Executive Order 13462—President's Intelligence Advisory Board and Intelligence Oversight Board

73 Fed. Reg. 11,805 (February 29, 2008)

By the authority vested in me as President by the Constitution and the laws of the United States of America, it is hereby ordered as follows:

SECTION 1. POLICY. It is the policy of the United States to ensure that the President and other officers of the United States with responsibility for the security of the Nation and the advancement of its interests have access to accurate, insightful, objective, and timely information concerning the capabilities, intentions, and activities of foreign powers.

SECTION 2. DEFINITIONS. As used in this order:
(a) "department concerned" means an executive department listed in section 101 of title 5, United States Code, that contains an organization listed in or designated pursuant to section 3(4) of the National Security Act of 1947, as amended (50 U.S.C. 401a(4));
(b) "intelligence activities" has the meaning specified in section 3.4 of Executive Order 12333 of December 4, 1981, as amended; and
(c) "intelligence community" means the organizations listed in or designated pursuant to section 3(4) of the National Security Act of 1947, as amended.

SECTION 3. ESTABLISHMENT OF THE PRESIDENT'S INTELLIGENCE ADVISORY BOARD.
(a) There is hereby established, within the Executive Office of the President and exclusively to advise and assist the President as set forth in this order, the President's Intelligence Advisory Board (PIAB).
(b) The PIAB shall consist of not more than 16 members appointed by the President from among individuals who are not employed by the Federal Government.
(c) The President shall designate a Chair from among the members of the PIAB, who shall convene and preside at meetings of the PIAB, determine its agenda, and direct its work.
(d) Members of the PIAB and the Intelligence Oversight Board (IOB) established in section 5 of this order:

(i) shall serve without any compensation for their work on the PIAB or the IOB; and

(ii) while engaged in the work of the PIAB or the IOB, may be allowed travel expenses, including per diem in lieu of subsistence, as authorized by law for persons serving intermittently in the Government (5 U.S.C. 5701-5707).

(e) The PIAB shall utilize such full-time professional and administrative staff as authorized by the Chair and approved by the President or the President's designee. Such staff shall be supervised by an Executive Director of the PIAB, appointed by the President, whom the President may designate to serve also as the Executive Director of the IOB.

SECTION 4. FUNCTIONS OF THE PIAB. Consistent with the policy set forth in section 1 of this order, the PIAB shall have the authority to, as the PIAB determines appropriate, or shall, when directed by the President:

(a) assess the quality, quantity, and adequacy of intelligence collection, of analysis and estimates, and of counterintelligence and other intelligence activities, assess the adequacy of management, personnel and organization in the intelligence community, and review the performance of all agencies of the Federal Government that are engaged in the collection, evaluation, or production of intelligence or the execution of intelligence policy and report the results of such assessments or reviews:

(i) to the President, as necessary but not less than twice each year; and

(ii) to the Director of National Intelligence (DNI) and the heads of departments concerned when the PIAB determines appropriate; and

(b) consider and make appropriate recommendations to the President, the DNI, or the head of the department concerned with respect to matters identified to the PIAB by the DNI or the head of a department concerned.

SECTION 5. ESTABLISHMENT OF INTELLIGENCE OVERSIGHT BOARD.

(a) There is hereby established a committee of the PIAB to be known as the Intelligence Oversight Board.

(b) The IOB shall consist of not more than five members of the PIAB who are designated by the President from among members of the PIAB to serve on the IOB. The IOB shall utilize such full-time professional and administrative staff as authorized by the Chair and approved by the President or the President's designee. Such staff shall be supervised by an Executive Director of the IOB, appointed by the President, whom the President may designate to serve also as the Executive Director of the PIAB.

(c) The President shall designate a Chair from among the members of the IOB, who shall convene and preside at meetings of the IOB, determine its agenda, and direct its work.

SECTION 6. FUNCTIONS OF THE IOB. Consistent with the policy set forth in section 1 of this order, the IOB shall:

(a) issue criteria on the thresholds for reporting matters to the IOB, to the extent consistent with section 1.7(d) of Executive Order 12333 or the corresponding provision of any successor order;

(b) inform the President of intelligence activities that the IOB believes:

(i)(A) may be unlawful or contrary to Executive Order or presidential directive; and

(B) are not being adequately addressed by the Attorney General, the DNI, or the head of the department concerned; or

(ii) should be immediately reported to the President.

(c) review and assess the effectiveness, efficiency, and sufficiency of the processes by which the DNI and the heads of departments concerned perform their respective functions under this order and report thereon as necessary, together

with any recommendations, to the President and, as appropriate, the DNI and the head of the department concerned;
(d) receive and review information submitted by the DNI under subsection 7(c) of this order and make recommendations thereon, including for any needed corrective action, with respect to such information, and the intelligence activities to which the information relates, as necessary, but not less than twice each year, to the President, the DNI, and the head of the department concerned; and
(e) conduct, or request that the DNI or the head of the department concerned, as appropriate, carry out and report to the IOB the results of, investigations of intelligence activities that the IOB determines are necessary to enable the IOB to carry out its functions under this order.

SECTION 7. FUNCTIONS OF THE DIRECTOR OF NATIONAL INTELLIGENCE. Consistent with the policy set forth in section 1 of this order, the DNI shall:
(a) with respect to guidelines applicable to organizations within the intelligence community that concern reporting of intelligence activities described in subsection 6(b)(i)(A) of this order:
(i) review and ensure that such guidelines are consistent with section 1.7(d) of Executive Order 12333, or a corresponding provision of any successor order, and this order; and
(ii) issue for incorporation in such guidelines instructions relating to the format and schedule of such reporting as necessary to implement this order;
(b) with respect to intelligence activities described in subsection 6(b)(i)(A) of this order:
(i) receive reports submitted to the IOB pursuant to section 1.7(d) of Executive Order 12333, or a corresponding provision of any successor order;
(ii) forward to the Attorney General information in such reports relating to such intelligence activities to the extent that such activities involve possible violations of Federal criminal laws or implicate the authority of the Attorney General unless the DNI or the head of the department concerned has previously provided such information to the Attorney General; and
(iii) monitor the intelligence community to ensure that the head of the department concerned has directed needed corrective actions and that such actions have been taken and report to the IOB and the head of the department concerned, and as appropriate the President, when such actions have not been timely taken; and
(c) submit to the IOB as necessary and no less than twice each year:
(i) an analysis of the reports received under subsection (b)(i) of this section, including an assessment of the gravity, frequency, trends, and patterns of occurrences of intelligence activities described in subsection 6(b)(i)(A) of this order;
(ii) a summary of direction under subsection (b)(iii) of this section and any related recommendations; and
(iii) an assessment of the effectiveness of corrective action taken by the DNI

or the head of the department concerned with respect to intelligence activities described in subsection 6(b)(i)(A) of this order.

SECTION 8. FUNCTIONS OF HEADS OF DEPARTMENTS CONCERNED AND ADDITIONAL FUNCTIONS OF THE DIRECTOR OF NATIONAL INTELLIGENCE.

(a) To the extent permitted by law, the DNI and the heads of departments concerned shall provide such information and assistance as the PIAB and the IOB may need to perform functions under this order.

(b) The heads of departments concerned shall:

(i) ensure that the DNI receives:

(A) copies of reports submitted to the IOB pursuant to section 1.7(d) of Executive Order 12333, or a corresponding provision of any successor order; and

(B) such information and assistance as the DNI may need to perform functions under this order; and

(ii) designate the offices within their respective organizations that shall submit reports to the IOB required by Executive Order and inform the DNI and the IOB of such designations; and

(iii) ensure that departments concerned comply with instructions issued by the DNI under subsection 7(a)(ii) of this order.

(c) The head of a department concerned who does not implement a recommendation to that head of department from the PIAB under subsection 4(b) of this order or from the IOB under subsections 6(c) or 6(d) of this order shall promptly report through the DNI to the Board that made the recommendation, or to the President, the reasons for not implementing the recommendation.

(d) The DNI shall ensure that the Director of the Central Intelligence Agency performs the functions with respect to the Central Intelligence Agency under this order that a head of a department concerned performs with respect to organizations within the intelligence community that are part of that department.

SECTION 9. REFERENCES AND TRANSITION.

(a) References in Executive Orders other than this order, or in any other presidential guidance, to the "President's Foreign Intelligence Advisory Board" shall be deemed to be references to the President's Intelligence Advisory Board established by this order.

(b) Individuals who are members of the President's Foreign Intelligence Advisory Board under Executive Order 12863 of September 13, 1993, as amended, immediately prior to the signing of this order shall be members of the President's Intelligence Advisory Board immediately upon the signing of this order, to serve as such consistent with this order until the date that is 15 months following the date of this order.

(c) Individuals who are members of the Intelligence Oversight Board under Executive Order 12863 immediately prior to the signing of this order shall be members of the Intelligence Oversight Board under this order, to serve as such consistent with this order until the date that is 15 months following the date of this order.

(d) The individual serving as Executive Director of the President's Foreign Intelligence Advisory Board immediately prior to the signing of this order shall serve as the Executive Director of the PIAB until such person resigns, dies, or is removed, or upon appointment of a successor under this order and shall serve as the Executive Director of the IOB until an Executive Director of the IOB is appointed or designated under this order.

SECTION 10. REVOCATION. Executive Order 12863 is revoked.

SECTION 11. GENERAL PROVISIONS.

(a) Nothing in this order shall be construed to impair or otherwise affect:

(i) authority granted by law to a department or agency, or the head thereof; or

(ii) functions of the Director of the Office of Management and Budget relating to budget, administrative, or legislative proposals.

(b) Any person who is a member of the PIAB or IOB, or who is granted access to classified national security information in relation to the activities of the PIAB or the IOB, as a condition of access to such information, shall sign and comply with the agreements to protect such information from unauthorized disclosure. This order shall be implemented in a manner consistent with Executive Order 12958 of April 17, 1995, as amended, and Executive Order 12968 of August 2, 1995, as amended.

(c) This order shall be implemented consistent with applicable law and subject to the availability of appropriations.

(d) This order is intended only to improve the internal management of the executive branch and is not intended to, and does not, create any right or benefit, substantive or procedural, enforceable at law or in equity, by any party against the United States, its departments, agencies or entities, its officers, employees, or agents, or any other person.

GEORGE W. BUSH

Executive Order 13526—
Classified National Security Information

Memorandum of December 29, 2009 Implementation of the Executive Order "Classified National Security Information"; Order of December 29, 2009 – Original Classification Authority, 75 Fed. Reg. 707 (Dec. 29, 2009)

By the authority vested in me as President by the Constitution and the laws of the United States of America, it is hereby ordered as follows:

PART 1 — ORIGINAL CLASSIFICATION

SECTION 1.1. CLASSIFICATION STANDARDS.

(a) Information may be originally classified under the terms of this order only if all of the following conditions are met:

(1) an original classification authority is classifying the information;

(2) the information is owned by, produced by or for, or is under the control of the United States Government;

(3) the information falls within one or more of the categories of information listed in section 1.4 of this order; and

(4) the original classification authority determines that the unauthorized disclosure of the information reasonably could be expected to result in damage to the national security, which includes defense against transnational terrorism, and the original classification authority is able to identify or describe the damage.

(b) If there is significant doubt about the need to classify information, it shall not be classified. This provision does not:

(1) amplify or modify the substantive criteria or procedures for classification; or

(2) create any substantive or procedural rights subject to judicial review.

(c) Classified information shall not be declassified automatically as a result of any unauthorized disclosure of identical or similar information.

(d) The unauthorized disclosure of foreign government information is presumed to cause damage to the national security.

SEC. 1.2. CLASSIFICATION LEVELS.

(a) Information may be classified at one of the following three levels:

(1) "Top Secret" shall be applied to information, the unauthorized disclosure of which reasonably could be expected to cause exceptionally grave damage to the national security that the original classification authority is able to identify or describe.

(2) "Secret" shall be applied to information, the unauthorized disclosure of which reasonably could be expected to cause serious damage to the national security that the original classification authority is able to identify or describe.

(3) "Confidential" shall be applied to information, the unauthorized disclosure of which reasonably could be expected to cause damage to the national security that the original classification authority is able to identify or describe.

(b) Except as otherwise provided by statute, no other terms shall be used to identify United States classified information.
(c) If there is significant doubt about the appropriate level of classification, it shall be classified at the lower level.

SECTION 1.3. CLASSIFICATION AUTHORITY.

(a) The authority to classify information originally may be exercised only by:

(1) the President and the Vice President;

(2) agency heads and officials designated by the President; and

(3) United States Government officials delegated this authority pursuant to paragraph (c) of this section.

(b) Officials authorized to classify information at a specified level are also authorized to classify information at a lower level.

(c) Delegation of original classification authority.

(1) Delegations of original classification authority shall be limited to the minimum required to administer this order. Agency heads are responsible for ensuring that designated subordinate officials have a demonstrable and continuing need to exercise this authority.

(2) "Top Secret" original classification authority may be delegated only by the President, the Vice President, or an agency head or official designated pursuant to paragraph (a)(2) of this section.

(3) "Secret" or "Confidential" original classification authority may be delegated only by the President, the Vice President, an agency head or official designated pursuant to paragraph (a)(2) of this section, or the senior agency official designated under section 5.4(d) of this order, provided that official has been delegated "Top Secret" original classification authority by the agency head.

(4) Each delegation of original classification authority shall be in writing and the authority shall not be redelegated except as provided in this order. Each delegation shall identify the official by name or position.

(5) Delegations of original classification authority shall be reported or made available by name or position to the Director of the Information Security Oversight Office.

(d) All original classification authorities must receive training in proper classification (including the avoidance of over-classification) and declassification as provided in this order and its implementing directives at least once a calendar year. Such training must include instruction on the proper safeguarding of classified information and on the sanctions in section 5.5 of this order that may be brought against an individual who fails to classify information properly or protect classified information from unauthorized disclosure. Original classification authorities who do not receive such mandatory training at least once within a calendar year shall have their classification authority suspended by the agency head or the senior agency official designated under section 5.4(d) of this order until such training has taken place. A waiver may be granted by the agency head, the deputy agency head, or the senior agency official if an individual is unable to receive such training due to unavoidable circumstances. Whenever a waiver is granted, the individual shall receive such training as soon as practicable.

(e) Exceptional cases. When an employee, government contractor, licensee, certificate holder, or grantee of an agency who does not have original classification authority originates information believed by that person to require classification, the information shall be protected in a manner consistent with this order and its implementing directives. The information shall be transmitted promptly as provided under this order or its implementing directives to the agency that has appropriate subject matter interest and classification authority with respect to this information. That agency shall decide within 30 days whether to classify this information.

SECTION 1.4. CLASSIFICATION CATEGORIES. Information shall not be considered for classification unless its unauthorized disclosure could reasonably be expected to cause identifiable or describable damage to the national security in accordance with section 1.2 of this order, and it pertains to one or more of the following:

(a) military plans, weapons systems, or operations;

(b) foreign government information;

(c) intelligence activities (including covert action), intelligence sources or methods, or cryptology;

(d) foreign relations or foreign activities of the United States, including confidential sources;

(e) scientific, technological, or economic matters relating to the national security;

(f) United States Government programs for safeguarding nuclear materials or facilities;

(g) vulnerabilities or capabilities of systems, installations, infrastructures, projects, plans, or protection services relating to the national security; or

(h) the development, production, or use of weapons of mass destruction.

SECTION 1.5. DURATION OF CLASSIFICATION.

(a) At the time of original classification, the original classification authority shall establish a specific date or event for declassification based on the duration of the national security sensitivity of the information. Upon reaching the date or event, the information shall be automatically declassified. Except for information that should clearly and demonstrably be expected to reveal the identity of a confidential human source or a human intelligence source or key design concepts of weapons of mass destruction, the date or event shall not exceed the time frame established in paragraph (b) of this section.

(b) If the original classification authority cannot determine an earlier specific date or event for declassification, information shall be marked for declassification 10 years from the date of the original decision, unless the original classification authority otherwise determines that the sensitivity of the information requires that it be marked for declassification for up to 25 years from the date of the original decision.

(c) An original classification authority may extend the duration of classification up to 25 years from the date of origin of the document, change the level of classi-

fication, or reclassify specific information only when the standards and procedures for classifying information under this order are followed.
(d) No information may remain classified indefinitely. Information marked for an indefinite duration of classification under predecessor orders, for example, marked as "Originating Agency's Determination Required," or classified information that contains incomplete declassification instructions or lacks declassification instructions shall be declassified in accordance with part 3 of this order.

SECTION 1.6. IDENTIFICATION AND MARKINGS.
(a) At the time of original classification, the following shall be indicated in a manner that is immediately apparent:

(1) one of the three classification levels defined in section 1.2 of this order;
(2) the identity, by name and position, or by personal identifier, of the original classification authority;
(3) the agency and office of origin, if not otherwise evident;
(4) declassification instructions, which shall indicate one of the following:

(A) the date or event for declassification, as prescribed in section 1.5(a);
(B) the date that is 10 years from the date of original classification, as prescribed in section 1.5(b);
(C) the date that is up to 25 years from the date of original classification, as prescribed in section 1.5(b); or
(D) in the case of information that should clearly and demonstrably be expected to reveal the identity of a confidential human source or a human intelligence source or key design concepts of weapons of mass destruction, the marking prescribed in implementing directives issued pursuant to this order; and

(5) a concise reason for classification that, at a minimum, cites the applicable classification categories in section 1.4 of this order.

(b) Specific information required in paragraph (a) of this section may be excluded if it would reveal additional classified information.
(c) With respect to each classified document, the agency originating the document shall, by marking or other means, indicate which portions are classified, with the applicable classification level, and which portions are unclassified. In accordance with standards prescribed in directives issued under this order, the Director of the Information Security Oversight Office may grant and revoke temporary waivers of this requirement. The Director shall revoke any waiver upon a finding of abuse.
(d) Markings or other indicia implementing the provisions of this order, including abbreviations and requirements to safeguard classified working papers, shall conform to the standards prescribed in implementing directives issued pursuant to this order.
(e) Foreign government information shall retain its original classification markings or shall be assigned a U.S. classification that provides a degree of protection at least equivalent to that required by the entity that furnished the information. Foreign government information retaining its original classification markings need

not be assigned a U.S. classification marking provided that the responsible agency determines that the foreign government markings are adequate to meet the purposes served by U.S. classification markings.
(f) Information assigned a level of classification under this or predecessor orders shall be considered as classified at that level of classification despite the omission of other required markings. Whenever such information is used in the derivative classification process or is reviewed for possible declassification, holders of such information shall coordinate with an appropriate classification authority for the application of omitted markings.
(g) The classification authority shall, whenever practicable, use a classified addendum whenever classified information constitutes a small portion of an otherwise unclassified document or prepare a product to allow for dissemination at the lowest level of classification possible or in unclassified form.
(h) Prior to public release, all declassified records shall be appropriately marked to reflect their declassification.

SEC. 1.7. CLASSIFICATION PROHIBITIONS AND LIMITATIONS.
(a) In no case shall information be classified, continue to be maintained as classified, or fail to be declassified in order to:

(1) conceal violations of law, inefficiency, or administrative error;
(2) prevent embarrassment to a person, organization, or agency;
(3) restrain competition; or
(4) prevent or delay the release of information that does not require protection in the interest of the national security.

(b) Basic scientific research information not clearly related to the national security shall not be classified.
(c) Information may not be reclassified after declassification and release to the public under proper authority unless:

(1) the reclassification is personally approved in writing by the agency head based on a document-by-document determination by the agency that reclassification is required to prevent significant and demonstrable damage to the national security;
(2) the information may be reasonably recovered without bringing undue attention to the information;
(3) the reclassification action is reported promptly to the Assistant to the President for National Security Affairs (National Security Advisor) and the Director of the Information Security Oversight Office; and
(4) for documents in the physical and legal custody of the National Archives and Records Administration (National Archives) that have been available for public use, the agency head has, after making the determinations required by this paragraph, notified the Archivist of the United States (Archivist), who shall suspend public access pending approval of the reclassification action by the Director of the Information Security Oversight Office. Any such decision by the Director may be appealed by the agency head to the President through the National Security Advisor. Public access shall remain suspended pending a prompt decision on the appeal.

(d) Information that has not previously been disclosed to the public under proper authority may be classified or reclassified after an agency has received a request for it under the Freedom of Information Act (5 U.S.C. 552), the Presidential Records Act, 44 U.S.C. 2204(c)(1), the Privacy Act of 1974 (5 U.S.C. 552a), or the mandatory review provisions of section 3.5 of this order only if such classification meets the requirements of this order and is accomplished on a document-by-document basis with the personal participation or under the direction of the agency head, the deputy agency head, or the senior agency official designated under section 5.4 of this order. The requirements in this paragraph also apply to those situations in which information has been declassified in accordance with a specific date or event determined by an original classification authority in accordance with section 1.5 of this order.
(e) Compilations of items of information that are individually unclassified may be classified if the compiled information reveals an additional association or relationship that: (1) meets the standards for classification under this order; and (2) is not otherwise revealed in the individual items of information.

SECTION 1.8. CLASSIFICATION CHALLENGES.
(a) Authorized holders of information who, in good faith, believe that its classification status is improper are encouraged and expected to challenge the classification status of the information in accordance with agency procedures established under paragraph (b) of this section.
(b) In accordance with implementing directives issued pursuant to this order, an agency head or senior agency official shall establish procedures under which authorized holders of information, including authorized holders outside the classifying agency, are encouraged and expected to challenge the classification of information that they believe is improperly classified or unclassified. These procedures shall ensure that:

(1) individuals are not subject to retribution for bringing such actions;

(2) an opportunity is provided for review by an impartial official or panel; and

(3) individuals are advised of their right to appeal agency decisions to the Interagency Security Classification Appeals Panel (Panel) established by section 5.3 of this order.

(c) Documents required to be submitted for prepublication review or other administrative process pursuant to an approved nondisclosure agreement are not covered by this section.

SECTION 1.9. FUNDAMENTAL CLASSIFICATION GUIDANCE REVIEW.
(a) Agency heads shall complete on a periodic basis a comprehensive review of the agency's classification guidance, particularly classification guides, to ensure the guidance reflects current circumstances and to identify classified information that no longer requires protection and can be declassified. The initial fundamental classification guidance review shall be completed within 2 years of the effective date of this order.

(b) The classification guidance review shall include an evaluation of classified information to determine if it meets the standards for classification under section 1.4 of this order, taking into account an up-to-date assessment of likely damage as described under section 1.2 of this order.
(c) The classification guidance review shall include original classification authorities and agency subject matter experts to ensure a broad range of perspectives.
(d) Agency heads shall provide a report summarizing the results of the classification guidance review to the Director of the Information Security Oversight Office and shall release an unclassified version of this report to the public.

PART 2 — DERIVATIVE CLASSIFICATION

SECTION 2.1. USE OF DERIVATIVE CLASSIFICATION.

(a) Persons who reproduce, extract, or summarize classified information, or who apply classification markings derived from source material or as directed by a classification guide, need not possess original classification authority.
(b) Persons who apply derivative classification markings shall:

(1) be identified by name and position, or by personal identifier, in a manner that is immediately apparent for each derivative classification action;
(2) observe and respect original classification decisions; and
(3) carry forward to any newly created documents the pertinent classification markings. For information derivatively classified based on multiple sources, the derivative classifier shall carry forward:

(A) the date or event for declassification that corresponds to the longest period of classification among the sources, or the marking established pursuant to section 1.6(a)(4)(D) of this order; and
(B) a listing of the source materials.

(c) Derivative classifiers shall, whenever practicable, use a classified addendum whenever classified information constitutes a small portion of an otherwise unclassified document or prepare a product to allow for dissemination at the lowest level of classification possible or in unclassified form.
(d) Persons who apply derivative classification markings shall receive training in the proper application of the derivative classification principles of the order, with an emphasis on avoiding over-classification, at least once every 2 years. Derivative classifiers who do not receive such training at least once every 2 years shall have their authority to apply derivative classification markings suspended until they have received such training. A waiver may be granted by the agency head, the deputy agency head, or the senior agency official if an individual is unable to receive such training due to unavoidable circumstances. Whenever a waiver is granted, the individual shall receive such training as soon as practicable.

SECTION 2.2. CLASSIFICATION GUIDES

(a) Agencies with original classification authority shall prepare classification guides to facilitate the proper and uniform derivative classification of information. These guides shall conform to standards contained in directives issued under this order.
(b) Each guide shall be approved personally and in writing by an official who:

(1) has program or supervisory responsibility over the information or is the senior agency official; and

(2) is authorized to classify information originally at the highest level of classification prescribed in the guide.

(c) Agencies shall establish procedures to ensure that classification guides are reviewed and updated as provided in directives issued under this order.

(d) Agencies shall incorporate original classification decisions into classification guides on a timely basis and in accordance with directives issued under this order.

(e) Agencies may incorporate exemptions from automatic declassification approved pursuant to section 3.3(j) of this order into classification guides, provided that the Panel is notified of the intent to take such action for specific information in advance of approval and the information remains in active use.

(f) The duration of classification of a document classified by a derivative classifier using a classification guide shall not exceed 25 years from the date of the origin of the document, except for:

(1) information that should clearly and demonstrably be expected to reveal the identity of a confidential human source or a human intelligence source or key design concepts of weapons of mass destruction; and

(2) specific information incorporated into classification guides in accordance with section 2.2(e) of this order.

PART 3 — DECLASSIFICATION AND DOWNGRADING

SECTION 3.1. AUTHORITY FOR DECLASSIFICATION.

(a) Information shall be declassified as soon as it no longer meets the standards for classification under this order.

(b) Information shall be declassified or downgraded by:

(1) the official who authorized the original classification, if that official is still serving in the same position and has original classification authority;

(2) the originator's current successor in function, if that individual has original classification authority;

(3) a supervisory official of either the originator or his or her successor in function, if the supervisory official has original classification authority; or

(4) officials delegated declassification authority in writing by the agency head or the senior agency official of the originating agency.

(c) The Director of National Intelligence (or, if delegated by the Director of National Intelligence, the Principal Deputy Director of National Intelligence) may, with respect to the Intelligence Community, after consultation with the head of the originating Intelligence Community element or department, declassify, downgrade, or direct the declassification or downgrading of information or intelligence relating to intelligence sources, methods, or activities.

(d) It is presumed that information that continues to meet the classification requirements under this order requires continued protection. In some exceptional cases, however, the need to protect such information may be outweighed by the public interest in disclosure of the information, and in these cases the information should be declassified. When such questions arise, they shall be referred to the agency head or the senior agency official. That official will determine, as an exercise of discretion, whether the public interest in disclosure outweighs the damage to the national security that might reasonably be expected from disclosure. This provision does not:

(1) amplify or modify the substantive criteria or procedures for classification; or

(2) create any substantive or procedural rights subject to judicial review.

(e) If the Director of the Information Security Oversight Office determines that information is classified in violation of this order, the Director may require the information to be declassified by the agency that originated the classification. Any such decision by the Director may be appealed to the President through the National Security Advisor. The information shall remain classified pending a prompt decision on the appeal.

(f) The provisions of this section shall also apply to agencies that, under the terms of this order, do not have original classification authority, but had such authority under predecessor orders.

(g) No information may be excluded from declassification under section 3.3 of this order based solely on the type of document or record in which it is found. Rather, the classified information must be considered on the basis of its content.

(h) Classified nonrecord materials, including artifacts, shall be declassified as soon as they no longer meet the standards for classification under this order.

(i) When making decisions under sections 3.3, 3.4, and 3.5 of this order, agencies shall consider the final decisions of the Panel.

SECTION 3.2. TRANSFERRED RECORDS.

(a) In the case of classified records transferred in conjunction with a transfer of functions, and not merely for storage purposes, the receiving agency shall be deemed to be the originating agency for purposes of this order.

(b) In the case of classified records that are not officially transferred as described in paragraph (a) of this section, but that originated in an agency that has ceased to exist and for which there is no successor agency, each agency in possession of such records shall be deemed to be the originating agency for purposes of this order. Such records may be declassified or downgraded by the agency in possession of the records after consultation with any other agency that has an interest in the subject matter of the records.

(c) Classified records accessioned into the National Archives shall be declassified or downgraded by the Archivist in accordance with this order, the directives issued pursuant to this order, agency declassification guides, and any existing procedural agreement between the Archivist and the relevant agency head.

(d) The originating agency shall take all reasonable steps to declassify classified information contained in records determined to have permanent historical value before they are accessioned into the National Archives. However, the Archivist may require that classified records be accessioned into the National Archives when necessary to comply with the provisions of the Federal Records Act. This provision does not apply to records transferred to the Archivist pursuant to section 2203 of title 44, United States Code, or records for which the National Archives serves as the custodian of the records of an agency or organization that has gone out of existence.

(e) To the extent practicable, agencies shall adopt a system of records management that will facilitate the public release of documents at the time such documents are declassified pursuant to the provisions for automatic declassification in section 3.3 of this order.

SECTION 3.3. AUTOMATIC DECLASSIFICATION.

(a) Subject to paragraphs (b)–(d) and (g)–(j) of this section, all classified records that (1) are more than 25 years old and (2) have been determined to have permanent historical value under title 44, United States Code, shall be automatically declassified whether or not the records have been reviewed. All classified records shall be automatically declassified on December 31 of the year that is 25 years from the date of origin, except as provided in paragraphs (b)–(d) and (g)–(i) of this section. If the date of origin of an individual record cannot be readily determined, the date of original classification shall be used instead.

(b) An agency head may exempt from automatic declassification under paragraph (a) of this section specific information, the release of which should clearly and demonstrably be expected to:

(1) reveal the identity of a confidential human source, a human intelligence source, a relationship with an intelligence or security service of a foreign government or international organization, or a nonhuman intelligence source; or impair the effectiveness of an intelligence method currently in use, available for use, or under development;

(2) reveal information that would assist in the development, production, or use of weapons of mass destruction;

(3) reveal information that would impair U.S. cryptologic systems or activities;

(4) reveal information that would impair the application of state-of-the-art technology within a U.S. weapon system;

(5) reveal formally named or numbered U.S. military war plans that remain in effect, or reveal operational or tactical elements of prior plans that are contained in such active plans;

(6) reveal information, including foreign government information, that would cause serious harm to relations between the United States and a foreign government, or to ongoing diplomatic activities of the United States;

(7) reveal information that would impair the current ability of United States Government officials to protect the President, Vice President, and other protectees for whom protection services, in the interest of the national security, are authorized;

(8) reveal information that would seriously impair current national security emergency preparedness plans or reveal current vulnerabilities of systems, installations, or infrastructures relating to the national security; or

(9) violate a statute, treaty, or international agreement that does not permit the automatic or unilateral declassification of information at 25 years.

(c)(1) An agency head shall notify the Panel of any specific file series of records for which a review or assessment has determined that the information within that file series almost invariably falls within one or more of the exemption categories listed in paragraph (b) of this section and that the agency proposes to exempt from automatic declassification at 25 years.

(2) The notification shall include:

(A) a description of the file series;

(B) an explanation of why the information within the file series is almost invariably exempt from automatic declassification and why the information must remain classified for a longer period of time; and

(C) except when the information within the file series almost invariably identifies a confidential human source or a human intelligence source or key design concepts of weapons of mass destruction, a specific date or event for declassification of the information, not to exceed December 31 of the year that is 50 years from the date of origin of the records.

(3) The Panel may direct the agency not to exempt a designated file series or to declassify the information within that series at an earlier date than recommended. The agency head may appeal such a decision to the President through the National Security Advisor.

(4) File series exemptions approved by the President prior to December 31, 2008, shall remain valid without any additional agency action pending Panel review by the later of December 31, 2010, or December 31 of the year that is 10 years from the date of previous approval.

(d) The following provisions shall apply to the onset of automatic declassification:

(1) Classified records within an integral file block, as defined in this order, that are otherwise subject to automatic declassification under this section shall not be automatically declassified until December 31 of the year that is 25 years from the date of the most recent record within the file block.

(2) After consultation with the Director of the National Declassification Center (the Center) established by section 3.7 of this order and before the records are subject to automatic declassification, an agency head or senior agency official may delay automatic declassification for up to five additional years for classified information contained in media that make a review for possible declassification exemptions more difficult or costly.

(3) Other than for records that are properly exempted from automatic declassification, records containing classified information that originated with other agencies or the disclosure of which would affect the interests or activities of other agencies with respect to the classified information and could reasonably be expected to fall under one or more of the exemptions in paragraph (b) of this section shall be identified prior to the onset of automatic declassification for later referral to those agencies.

(A) The information of concern shall be referred by the Center established by section 3.7 of this order, or by the centralized facilities referred to in section 3.7(e) of this order, in a prioritized and scheduled manner determined by the Center.

(B) If an agency fails to provide a final determination on a referral made by the Center within 1 year of referral, or by the centralized facilities referred to in section 3.7(e) of this order within 3 years of referral, its equities in the referred records shall be automatically declassified.

(C) If any disagreement arises between affected agencies and the Center regarding the referral review period, the Director of the Information Security Oversight Office shall determine the appropriate period of review of referred records.

(D) Referrals identified prior to the establishment of the Center by section 3.7 of this order shall be subject to automatic declassification only in accordance with subparagraphs (d)(3)(A)–(C) of this section.

(4) After consultation with the Director of the Information Security Oversight Office, an agency head may delay automatic declassification for up to 3 years from the date of discovery of classified records that were inadvertently not reviewed prior to the effective date of automatic declassification.

(e) Information exempted from automatic declassification under this section shall remain subject to the mandatory and systematic declassification review provisions of this order.

(f) The Secretary of State shall determine when the United States should commence negotiations with the appropriate officials of a foreign government or international organization of governments to modify any treaty or international agreement that requires the classification of information contained in records affected by this section for a period longer than 25 years from the date of its creation, unless the treaty or international agreement pertains to information that may otherwise remain classified beyond 25 years under this section.

(g) The Secretary of Energy shall determine when information concerning foreign nuclear programs that was removed from the Restricted Data category in order to carry out provisions of the National Security Act of 1947, as amended, may be declassified. Unless otherwise determined, such information shall be declassified when comparable information concerning the United States nuclear program is declassified.

(h) Not later than 3 years from the effective date of this order, all records exempted from automatic declassification under paragraphs (b) and (c) of this section shall be automatically declassified on December 31 of a year that is no more than 50 years from the date of origin, subject to the following:

(1) Records that contain information the release of which should clearly and demonstrably be expected to reveal the following are exempt from automatic declassification at 50 years:

(A) the identity of a confidential human source or a human intelligence source; or

(B) key design concepts of weapons of mass destruction.

(2) In extraordinary cases, agency heads may, within 5 years of the onset of automatic declassification, propose to exempt additional specific information from declassification at 50 years.

(3) Records exempted from automatic declassification under this paragraph shall be automatically declassified on December 31 of a year that is no more than 75 years from the date of origin unless an agency head, within 5 years of that date, proposes to exempt specific information from declassification at 75 years and the proposal is formally approved by the Panel.

(i) Specific records exempted from automatic declassification prior to the establishment of the Center described in section 3.7 of this order shall be subject to the provisions of paragraph (h) of this section in a scheduled and prioritized manner determined by the Center.

(j) At least 1 year before information is subject to automatic declassification under this section, an agency head or senior agency official shall notify the Director of the Information Security Oversight Office, serving as Executive Secretary of the Panel, of any specific information that the agency proposes to exempt from automatic declassification under paragraphs (b) and (h) of this section.

(1) The notification shall include:

(A) a detailed description of the information, either by reference to information in specific records or in the form of a declassification guide;

(B) an explanation of why the information should be exempt from automatic declassification and must remain classified for a longer period of time; and

(C) a specific date or a specific and independently verifiable event for automatic declassification of specific records that contain the information proposed for exemption.

(2) The Panel may direct the agency not to exempt the information or to declassify it at an earlier date than recommended. An agency head may appeal such a decision to the President through the National Security Advisor. The information will remain classified while such an appeal is pending.

(k) For information in a file series of records determined not to have permanent historical value, the duration of classification beyond 25 years shall be the same as the disposition (destruction) date of those records in each Agency Records Control Schedule or General Records Schedule, although the duration of classification shall be extended if the record has been retained for business reasons beyond the scheduled disposition date.

SECTION 3.4. SYSTEMATIC DECLASSIFICATION REVIEW.

(a) Each agency that has originated classified information under this order or its predecessors shall establish and conduct a program for systematic declassification review for records of permanent historical value exempted from automatic declassification under section 3.3 of this order. Agencies shall prioritize their review of such records in accordance with priorities established by the Center.

(b) The Archivist shall conduct a systematic declassification review program for classified records: (1) accessioned into the National Archives; (2) transferred to the Archivist pursuant to 44 U.S.C. 2203; and (3) for which the National Archives serves as the custodian for an agency or organization that has gone out of existence.

SECTION 3.5. MANDATORY DECLASSIFICATION REVIEW.

(a) Except as provided in paragraph (b) of this section, all information classified under this order or predecessor orders shall be subject to a review for declassification by the originating agency if:

(1) the request for a review describes the document or material containing the information with sufficient specificity to enable the agency to locate it with a reasonable amount of effort;

(2) the document or material containing the information responsive to the request is not contained within an operational file exempted from search and review, publication, and disclosure under 5 U.S.C. 552 in accordance with law; and

(3) the information is not the subject of pending litigation.

(b) Information originated by the incumbent President or the incumbent Vice President; the incumbent President's White House Staff or the incumbent Vice President's Staff; committees, commissions, or boards appointed by the incumbent President; or other entities within the Executive Office of the President that solely advise and assist the incumbent President is exempted from the provisions of paragraph (a) of this section. However, the Archivist shall have the authority to review, downgrade, and declassify papers or records of former Presidents and Vice Presidents under the control of the Archivist pursuant to 44 U.S.C. 2107, 2111, 2111 note, or 2203. Review procedures developed by the Archivist shall provide for consultation with agencies having primary subject matter interest and shall be consistent with the provisions of applicable laws or lawful agreements that pertain to the respective Presidential papers or records. Agencies with primary subject matter interest shall be notified promptly of the Archivist's decision. Any final decision by the Archivist may be appealed by the requester or an agency to the Panel. The information shall remain classified pending a prompt decision on the appeal.

(c) Agencies conducting a mandatory review for declassification shall declassify information that no longer meets the standards for classification under this order. They shall release this information unless withholding is otherwise authorized and warranted under applicable law.

(d) If an agency has reviewed the requested information for declassification within the past 2 years, the agency need not conduct another review and may instead inform the requester of this fact and the prior review decision and advise the requester of appeal rights provided under subsection (e) of this section.

(e) In accordance with directives issued pursuant to this order, agency heads shall develop procedures to process requests for the mandatory review of classified information. These procedures shall apply to information classified under this or predecessor orders. They also shall provide a means for administratively appealing a denial of a mandatory review request, and for notifying the requester of the right to appeal a final agency decision to the Panel.

(f) After consultation with affected agencies, the Secretary of Defense shall develop special procedures for the review of cryptologic information; the Director of National Intelligence shall develop special procedures for the review of infor-

mation pertaining to intelligence sources, methods, and activities; and the Archivist shall develop special procedures for the review of information accessioned into the National Archives.
(g) Documents required to be submitted for prepublication review or other administrative process pursuant to an approved nondisclosure agreement are not covered by this section.
(h) This section shall not apply to any request for a review made to an element of the Intelligence Community that is made by a person other than an individual as that term is defined by 5 U.S.C. 552a(a)(2), or by a foreign government entity or any representative thereof.

SEC. 3.6. PROCESSING REQUESTS AND REVIEWS. Notwithstanding section 4.1(i) of this order, in response to a request for information under the Freedom of Information Act, the Presidential Records Act, the Privacy Act of 1974, or the mandatory review provisions of this order:
(a) An agency may refuse to confirm or deny the existence or nonexistence of requested records whenever the fact of their existence or nonexistence is itself classified under this order or its predecessors.
(b) When an agency receives any request for documents in its custody that contain classified information that originated with other agencies or the disclosure of which would affect the interests or activities of other agencies with respect to the classified information, or identifies such documents in the process of implementing sections 3.3 or 3.4 of this order, it shall refer copies of any request and the pertinent documents to the originating agency for processing and may, after consultation with the originating agency, inform any requester of the referral unless such association is itself classified under this order or its predecessors. In cases in which the originating agency determines in writing that a response under paragraph (a) of this section is required, the referring agency shall respond to the requester in accordance with that paragraph.
(c) Agencies may extend the classification of information in records determined not to have permanent historical value or nonrecord materials, including artifacts, beyond the time frames established in sections 1.5(b) and 2.2(f) of this order, provided:

(1) the specific information has been approved pursuant to section 3.3(j) of this order for exemption from automatic declassification; and

(2) the extension does not exceed the date established in section 3.3(j) of this order.

SEC. 3.7. NATIONAL DECLASSIFICATION CENTER
(a) There is established within the National Archives a National Declassification Center to streamline declassification processes, facilitate quality-assurance measures, and implement standardized training regarding the declassification of records determined to have permanent historical value. There shall be a Director of the Center who shall be appointed or removed by the Archivist in consultation with the Secretaries of State, Defense, Energy, and Homeland Security, the Attorney General, and the Director of National Intelligence.

(b) Under the administration of the Director, the Center shall coordinate:

(1) timely and appropriate processing of referrals in accordance with section 3.3(d)(3) of this order for accessioned Federal records and transferred presidential records.

(2) general interagency declassification activities necessary to fulfill the requirements of sections 3.3 and 3.4 of this order;

(3) the exchange among agencies of detailed declassification guidance to enable the referral of records in accordance with section 3.3(d)(3) of this order;

(4) the development of effective, transparent, and standard declassification work processes, training, and quality assurance measures;

(5) the development of solutions to declassification challenges posed by electronic records, special media, and emerging technologies;

(6) the linkage and effective utilization of existing agency databases and the use of new technologies to document and make public declassification review decisions and support declassification activities under the purview of the Center; and

(7) storage and related services, on a reimbursable basis, for Federal records containing classified national security information.

(c) Agency heads shall fully cooperate with the Archivist in the activities of the Center and shall:

(1) provide the Director with adequate and current declassification guidance to enable the referral of records in accordance with section 3.3(d)(3) of this order; and

(2) upon request of the Archivist, assign agency personnel to the Center who shall be delegated authority by the agency head to review and exempt or declassify information originated by their agency contained in records accessioned into the National Archives, after consultation with subject-matter experts as necessary.

(d) The Archivist, in consultation with representatives of the participants in the Center and after input from the general public, shall develop priorities for declassification activities under the purview of the Center that take into account the degree of researcher interest and the likelihood of declassification.

(e) Agency heads may establish such centralized facilities and internal operations to conduct internal declassification reviews as appropriate to achieve optimized records management and declassification business processes. Once established, all referral processing of accessioned records shall take place at the Center, and such agency facilities and operations shall be coordinated with the Center to ensure the maximum degree of consistency in policies and procedures that relate to records determined to have permanent historical value.

(f) Agency heads may exempt from automatic declassification or continue the classification of their own originally classified information under section 3.3(a) of this order except that in the case of the Director of National Intelligence, the Director shall also retain such authority with respect to the Intelligence Community.

(g) The Archivist shall, in consultation with the Secretaries of State, Defense, Energy, and Homeland Security, the Attorney General, the Director of National Intelligence, the Director of the Central Intelligence Agency, and the Director of the Information Security Oversight Office, provide the National Security Advisor with a detailed concept of operations for the Center and a proposed implementing directive under section 5.1 of this order that reflects the coordinated views of the aforementioned agencies.

PART 4 — SAFEGUARDING

SECTION 4.1. GENERAL RESTRICTIONS ON ACCESS.

(a) A person may have access to classified information provided that:

(1) a favorable determination of eligibility for access has been made by an agency head or the agency head's designee;

(2) the person has signed an approved nondisclosure agreement; and

(3) the person has a need-to-know the information.

(b) Every person who has met the standards for access to classified information in paragraph (a) of this section shall receive contemporaneous training on the proper safeguarding of classified information and on the criminal, civil, and administrative sanctions that may be imposed on an individual who fails to protect classified information from unauthorized disclosure.

(c) An official or employee leaving agency service may not remove classified information from the agency's control or direct that information be declassified in order to remove it from agency control.

(d) Classified information may not be removed from official premises without proper authorization.

(e) Persons authorized to disseminate classified information outside the executive branch shall ensure the protection of the information in a manner equivalent to that provided within the executive branch.

(f) Consistent with law, executive orders, directives, and regulations, an agency head or senior agency official or, with respect to the Intelligence Community, the Director of National Intelligence, shall establish uniform procedures to ensure that automated information systems, including networks and telecommunications systems, that collect, create, communicate, compute, disseminate, process, or store classified information:

(1) prevent access by unauthorized persons;

(2) ensure the integrity of the information; and

(3) to the maximum extent practicable, use:

(A) common information technology standards, protocols, and interfaces that maximize the availability of, and access to, the information in a form and manner that facilitates its authorized use; and

(B) standardized electronic formats to maximize the accessibility of information to persons who meet the criteria set forth in section 4.1(a) of this order.

(g) Consistent with law, executive orders, directives, and regulations, each agency head or senior agency official, or with respect to the Intelligence Community, the

Director of National Intelligence, shall establish controls to ensure that classified information is used, processed, stored, reproduced, transmitted, and destroyed under conditions that provide adequate protection and prevent access by unauthorized persons.

(h) Consistent with directives issued pursuant to this order, an agency shall safeguard foreign government information under standards that provide a degree of protection at least equivalent to that required by the government or international organization of governments that furnished the information. When adequate to achieve equivalency, these standards may be less restrictive than the safeguarding standards that ordinarily apply to U.S. "Confidential" information, including modified handling and transmission and allowing access to individuals with a need-to-know who have not otherwise been cleared for access to classified information or executed an approved nondisclosure agreement.

(i)(1) Classified information originating in one agency may be disseminated to another agency or U.S. entity by any agency to which it has been made available without the consent of the originating agency, as long as the criteria for access under section 4.1(a) of this order are met, unless the originating agency has determined that prior authorization is required for such dissemination and has marked or indicated such requirement on the medium containing the classified information in accordance with implementing directives issued pursuant to this order.

(2) Classified information originating in one agency may be disseminated by any other agency to which it has been made available to a foreign government in accordance with statute, this order, directives implementing this order, direction of the President, or with the consent of the originating agency. For the purposes of this section, "foreign government" includes any element of a foreign government, or an international organization of governments, or any element thereof.

(3) Documents created prior to the effective date of this order shall not be disseminated outside any other agency to which they have been made available without the consent of the originating agency. An agency head or senior agency official may waive this requirement for specific information that originated within that agency.

(4) For purposes of this section, the Department of Defense shall be considered one agency, except that any dissemination of information regarding intelligence sources, methods, or activities shall be consistent with directives issued pursuant to section 6.2(b) of this order.

(5) Prior consent of the originating agency is not required when referring records for declassification review that contain information originating in more than one agency.

SECTON 4.2. DISTRIBUTION CONTROLS.

(a) The head of each agency shall establish procedures in accordance with applicable law and consistent with directives issued pursuant to this order to ensure that classified information is accessible to the maximum extent possible by individuals who meet the criteria set forth in section 4.1(a) of this order.

(b) In an emergency, when necessary to respond to an imminent threat to life or in defense of the homeland, the agency head or any designee may authorize the disclosure of classified information (including information marked pursuant to section 4.1(i)(1) of this order) to an individual or individuals who are otherwise not eligible for access. Such actions shall be taken only in accordance with directives implementing this order and any procedure issued by agencies governing the classified information, which shall be designed to minimize the classified information that is disclosed under these circumstances and the number of individuals who receive it. Information disclosed under this provision or implementing directives and procedures shall not be deemed declassified as a result of such disclosure or subsequent use by a recipient. Such disclosures shall be reported promptly to the originator of the classified information. For purposes of this section, the Director of National Intelligence may issue an implementing directive governing the emergency disclosure of classified intelligence information.

(c) Each agency shall update, at least annually, the automatic, routine, or recurring distribution mechanism for classified information that it distributes. Recipients shall cooperate fully with distributors who are updating distribution lists and shall notify distributors whenever a relevant change in status occurs.

SECTION 4.3. SPECIAL ACCESS PROGRAMS.

(a) Establishment of special access programs. Unless otherwise authorized by the President, only the Secretaries of State, Defense, Energy, and Homeland Security, the Attorney General, and the Director of National Intelligence, or the principal deputy of each, may create a special access program. For special access programs pertaining to intelligence sources, methods, and activities (but not including military operational, strategic, and tactical programs), this function shall be exercised by the Director of National Intelligence. These officials shall keep the number of these programs at an absolute minimum, and shall establish them only when the program is required by statute or upon a specific finding that:

(1) the vulnerability of, or threat to, specific information is exceptional; and

(2) the normal criteria for determining eligibility for access applicable to information classified at the same level are not deemed sufficient to protect the information from unauthorized disclosure.

(b) Requirements and limitations.

(1) Special access programs shall be limited to programs in which the number of persons who ordinarily will have access will be reasonably small and commensurate with the objective of providing enhanced protection for the information involved.

(2) Each agency head shall establish and maintain a system of accounting for special access programs consistent with directives issued pursuant to this order.

(3) Special access programs shall be subject to the oversight program established under section 5.4(d) of this order. In addition, the Director of the Information Security Oversight Office shall be afforded access to these programs, in accordance with the security requirements of each program, in order to perform the functions assigned to the Information Security Oversight Office

under this order. An agency head may limit access to a special access program to the Director of the Information Security Oversight Office and no more than one other employee of the Information Security Oversight Office or, for special access programs that are extraordinarily sensitive and vulnerable, to the Director only.

(4) The agency head or principal deputy shall review annually each special access program to determine whether it continues to meet the requirements of this order.

(5) Upon request, an agency head shall brief the National Security Advisor, or a designee, on any or all of the agency's special access programs.

(6) For the purposes of this section, the term "agency head" refers only to the Secretaries of State, Defense, Energy, and Homeland Security, the Attorney General, and the Director of National Intelligence, or the principal deputy of each.

(c) Nothing in this order shall supersede any requirement made by or under 10 U.S.C. 119.

SECTION 4.4. ACCESS BY HISTORICAL RESEARCHERS AND CERTAIN FORMER GOVERNMENT PERSONNEL.

(a) The requirement in section 4.1(a)(3) of this order that access to classified information may be granted only to individuals who have a need to-know the information may be waived for persons who:

(1) are engaged in historical research projects;

(2) previously have occupied senior policy-making positions to which they were appointed or designated by the President or the Vice President; or

(3) served as President or Vice President.

(b) Waivers under this section may be granted only if the agency head or senior agency official of the originating agency:

(1) determines in writing that access is consistent with the interest of the national security;

(2) takes appropriate steps to protect classified information from unauthorized disclosure or compromise, and ensures that the information is safeguarded in a manner consistent with this order; and

(3) limits the access granted to former Presidential appointees or designees and Vice Presidential appointees or designees to items that the person originated, reviewed, signed, or received while serving as a Presidential or Vice Presidential appointee or designee.

PART 5 — IMPLEMENTATION AND REVIEW

SECTION 5.1. PROGRAM DIRECTION.

(a) The Director of the Information Security Oversight Office, under the direction of the Archivist and in consultation with the National Security Advisor, shall issue such directives as are necessary to implement this order. These directives shall be binding on the agencies. Directives issued by the Director of the Information Security Oversight Office shall establish standards for:

(1) classification, declassification, and marking principles;

(2) safeguarding classified information, which shall pertain to the handling, storage, distribution, transmittal, and destruction of and accounting for classified information;

(3) agency security education and training programs;

(4) agency self-inspection programs; and

(5) classification and declassification guides.

(b) The Archivist shall delegate the implementation and monitoring functions of this program to the Director of the Information Security Oversight Office.

(c) The Director of National Intelligence, after consultation with the heads of affected agencies and the Director of the Information Security Oversight Office, may issue directives to implement this order with respect to the protection of intelligence sources, methods, and activities. Such directives shall be consistent with this order and directives issued under paragraph (a) of this section.

SECTION 5.2. INFORMATION SECURITY OVERSIGHT OFFICE.

(a) There is established within the National Archives an Information Security Oversight Office. The Archivist shall appoint the Director of the Information Security Oversight Office, subject to the approval of the President.

(b) Under the direction of the Archivist, acting in consultation with the National Security Advisor, the Director of the Information Security Oversight Office shall:

(1) develop directives for the implementation of this order;

(2) oversee agency actions to ensure compliance with this order and its implementing directives;

(3) review and approve agency implementing regulations prior to their issuance to ensure their consistency with this order and directives issued under section 5.1(a) of this order;

(4) have the authority to conduct on-site reviews of each agency's program established under this order, and to require of each agency those reports and information and other cooperation that may be necessary to fulfill its responsibilities. If granting access to specific categories of classified information would pose an exceptional national security risk, the affected agency head or the senior agency official shall submit a written justification recommending the denial of access to the President through the National Security Advisor within 60 days of the request for access. Access shall be denied pending the response;

(5) review requests for original classification authority from agencies or officials not granted original classification authority and, if deemed appropriate, recommend Presidential approval through the National Security Advisor;

(6) consider and take action on complaints and suggestions from persons within or outside the Government with respect to the administration of the program established under this order;

(7) have the authority to prescribe, after consultation with affected agencies, standardization of forms or procedures that will promote the implementation of the program established under this order;

(8) report at least annually to the President on the implementation of this order; and

(9) convene and chair interagency meetings to discuss matters pertaining to the program established by this order.

SECTION 5.3. INTERAGENCY SECURITY CLASSIFICATION APPEALS PANEL.

(a) Establishment and administration.

(1) There is established an Interagency Security Classification Appeals Panel. The Departments of State, Defense, and Justice, the National Archives, the Office of the Director of National Intelligence, and the National Security Advisor shall each be represented by a senior-level representative who is a full-time or permanent part-time Federal officer or employee designated to serve as a member of the Panel by the respective agency head. The President shall designate a Chair from among the members of the Panel.

(2) Additionally, the Director of the Central Intelligence Agency may appoint a temporary representative who meets the criteria in paragraph (a)(1) of this section to participate as a voting member in all Panel deliberations and associated support activities concerning classified information originated by the Central Intelligence Agency.

(3) A vacancy on the Panel shall be filled as quickly as possible as provided in paragraph (a)(1) of this section.

(4) The Director of the Information Security Oversight Office shall serve as the Executive Secretary of the Panel. The staff of the Information Security Oversight Office shall provide program and administrative support for the Panel.

(5) The members and staff of the Panel shall be required to meet eligibility for access standards in order to fulfill the Panel's functions.

(6) The Panel shall meet at the call of the Chair. The Chair shall schedule meetings as may be necessary for the Panel to fulfill its functions in a timely manner.

(7) The Information Security Oversight Office shall include in its reports to the President a summary of the Panel's activities.

(b) Functions. The Panel shall:

(1) decide on appeals by persons who have filed classification challenges under section 1.8 of this order;

(2) approve, deny, or amend agency exemptions from automatic declassification as provided in section 3.3 of this order;

(3) decide on appeals by persons or entities who have filed requests for mandatory declassification review under section 3.5 of this order; and

(4) appropriately inform senior agency officials and the public of final Panel decisions on appeals under sections 1.8 and 3.5 of this order.

(c) Rules and procedures. The Panel shall issue bylaws, which shall be published in the Federal Register. The bylaws shall establish the rules and procedures that the Panel will follow in accepting, considering, and issuing decisions on appeals.

The rules and procedures of the Panel shall provide that the Panel will consider appeals only on actions in which:

(1) the appellant has exhausted his or her administrative remedies within the responsible agency;

(2) there is no current action pending on the issue within the Federal courts; and

(3) the information has not been the subject of review by the Federal courts or the Panel within the past 2 years.

(d) Agency heads shall cooperate fully with the Panel so that it can fulfill its functions in a timely and fully informed manner. The Panel shall report to the President through the National Security Advisor any instance in which it believes that an agency head is not cooperating fully with the Panel.

(e) The Panel is established for the sole purpose of advising and assisting the President in the discharge of his constitutional and discretionary authority to protect the national security of the United States. Panel decisions are committed to the discretion of the Panel, unless changed by the President.

(f) An agency head may appeal a decision of the Panel to the President through the National Security Advisor. The information shall remain classified pending a decision on the appeal.

SECTION 5.4. GENERAL RESPONSIBILITIES. Heads of agencies that originate or handle classified information shall:

(a) demonstrate personal commitment and commit senior management to the successful implementation of the program established under this order;

(b) commit necessary resources to the effective implementation of the program established under this order;

(c) ensure that agency records systems are designed and maintained to optimize the appropriate sharing and safeguarding of classified information, and to facilitate its declassification under the terms of this order when it no longer meets the standards for continued classification; and

(d) designate a senior agency official to direct and administer the program, whose responsibilities shall include:

(1) overseeing the agency's program established under this order, provided an agency head may designate a separate official to oversee special access programs authorized under this order. This official shall provide a full accounting of the agency's special access programs at least annually;

(2) promulgating implementing regulations, which shall be published in the Federal Register to the extent that they affect members of the public;

(3) establishing and maintaining security education and training programs;

(4) establishing and maintaining an ongoing self inspection program, which shall include the regular reviews of representative samples of the agency's original and derivative classification actions, and shall authorize appropriate agency officials to correct misclassification actions not covered by sections 1.7(c) and 1.7(d) of this order; and reporting annually to the Director of the Information Security Oversight Office on the agency's self-inspection program;

(5) establishing procedures consistent with directives issued pursuant to this order to prevent unnecessary access to classified information, including procedures that:

(A) require that a need for access to classified information be established before initiating administrative clearance procedures; and

(B) ensure that the number of persons granted access to classified information meets the mission needs of the agency while also satisfying operational and security requirements and needs;

(6) developing special contingency plans for the safeguarding of classified information used in or near hostile or potentially hostile areas;

(7) ensuring that the performance contract or other system used to rate civilian or military personnel performance includes the designation and management of classified information as a critical element or item to be evaluated in the rating of:

(A) original classification authorities;

(B) security managers or security specialists; and

(C) all other personnel whose duties significantly involve the creation or handling of classified information, including personnel who regularly apply derivative classification markings;

(8) accounting for the costs associated with the implementation of this order, which shall be reported to the Director of the Information Security Oversight Office for publication;

(9) assigning in a prompt manner agency personnel to respond to any request, appeal, challenge, complaint, or suggestion arising out of this order that pertains to classified information that originated in a component of the agency that no longer exists and for which there is no clear successor in function; and

(10) establishing a secure capability to receive information, allegations, or complaints regarding over-classification or incorrect classification within the agency and to provide guidance to personnel on proper classification as needed.

SECTION 5.5. SANCTIONS

(a) If the Director of the Information Security Oversight Office finds that a violation of this order or its implementing directives has occurred, the Director shall make a report to the head of the agency or to the senior agency official so that corrective steps, if appropriate, may be taken.

(b) Officers and employees of the United States Government, and its contractors, licensees, certificate holders, and grantees shall be subject to appropriate sanctions if they knowingly, willfully, or negligently:

(1) disclose to unauthorized persons information properly classified under this order or predecessor orders;

(2) classify or continue the classification of information in violation of this order or any implementing directive;

(3) create or continue a special access program contrary to the requirements of this order; or

(4) contravene any other provision of this order or its implementing directives.

(c) Sanctions may include reprimand, suspension without pay, removal, termination of classification authority, loss or denial of access to classified information, or other sanctions in accordance with applicable law and agency regulation.

(d) The agency head, senior agency official, or other supervisory official shall, at a minimum, promptly remove the classification authority of any individual who demonstrates reckless disregard or a pattern of error in applying the classification standards of this order.

(e) The agency head or senior agency official shall:

(1) take appropriate and prompt corrective action when a violation or infraction under paragraph (b) of this section occurs; and

(2) notify the Director of the Information Security Oversight Office when a violation under paragraph (b)(1), (2), or (3) of this section occurs.

PART 6 — GENERAL PROVISIONS

SEC. 6.1. DEFINITIONS. For purposes of this order:

(a) "Access" means the ability or opportunity to gain knowledge of classified information.

(b) "Agency" means any "Executive agency," as defined in 5 U.S.C. 105; any "Military department" as defined in 5 U.S.C. 102; and any other entity within the executive branch that comes into the possession of classified information.

(c) "Authorized holder" of classified information means anyone who satisfies the conditions for access stated in section 4.1(a) of this order.

(d) "Automated information system" means an assembly of computer hardware, software, or firmware configured to collect, create, communicate, compute, disseminate, process, store, or control data or information.

(e) "Automatic declassification" means the declassification of information based solely upon:

(1) the occurrence of a specific date or event as determined by the original classification authority; or

(2) the expiration of a maximum time frame for duration of classification established under this order.

(f) "Classification" means the act or process by which information is determined to be classified information.

(g) "Classification guidance" means any instruction or source that prescribes the classification of specific information.

(h) "Classification guide" means a documentary form of classification guidance issued by an original classification authority that identifies the elements of information regarding a specific subject that must be classified and establishes the level and duration of classification for each such element.

(i) "Classified national security information" or "classified information" means information that has been determined pursuant to this order or any predecessor order to require protection against unauthorized disclosure and is marked to indicate its classified status when in documentary form.

(j) "Compilation" means an aggregation of preexisting unclassified items of information.
(k) "Confidential source" means any individual or organization that has provided, or that may reasonably be expected to provide, information to the United States on matters pertaining to the national security with the expectation that the information or relationship, or both, are to be held in confidence.
(l) "Damage to the national security" means harm to the national defense or foreign relations of the United States from the unauthorized disclosure of information, taking into consideration such aspects of the information as the sensitivity, value, utility, and provenance of that information.
(m) "Declassification" means the authorized change in the status of information from classified information to unclassified information.
(n) "Declassification guide" means written instructions issued by a declassification authority that describes the elements of information regarding a specific subject that may be declassified and the elements that must remain classified.
(o) "Derivative classification" means the incorporating, paraphrasing, restating, or generating in new form information that is already classified, and marking the newly developed material consistent with the classification markings that apply to the source information. Derivative classification includes the classification of information based on classification guidance. The duplication or reproduction of existing classified information is not derivative classification.
(p) "Document" means any recorded information, regardless of the nature of the medium or the method or circumstances of recording.
(q) "Downgrading" means a determination by a declassification authority that information classified and safeguarded at a specified level shall be classified and safeguarded at a lower level.
(r) "File series" means file units or documents arranged according to a filing system or kept together because they relate to a particular subject or function, result from the same activity, document a specific kind of transaction, take a particular physical form, or have some other relationship arising out of their creation, receipt, or use, such as restrictions on access or use.
(s) "Foreign government information" means:

(1) information provided to the United States Government by a foreign government or governments,

an international organization of governments, or any element thereof, with the expectation that the information, the source of the information, or both, are to be held in confidence;

(2) information produced by the United States Government pursuant to or as a result of a joint arrangement with a foreign government or governments, or an international organization of governments, or any element thereof, requiring that the information, the arrangement, or both, are to be held in confidence; or

(3) information received and treated as "foreign government information" under the terms of a predecessor order.

(t) "Information" means any knowledge that can be communicated or documentary material, regardless of its physical form or characteristics, that is owned by, is produced by or for, or is under the control of the United States Government.
(u) "Infraction" means any knowing, willful, or negligent action contrary to the requirements of this order or its implementing directives that does not constitute a "violation," as defined below.
(v) "Integral file block" means a distinct component of a file series, as defined in this section, that should be maintained as a separate unit in order to ensure the integrity of the records. An integral file block may consist of a set of records covering either a specific topic or a range of time, such as a Presidential administration or a 5-year retirement schedule within a specific file series that is retired from active use as a group. For purposes of automatic declassification, integral file blocks shall contain only records dated within 10 years of the oldest record in the file block.
(w) "Integrity" means the state that exists when information is unchanged from its source and has not been accidentally or intentionally modified, altered, or destroyed.
(x) "Intelligence" includes foreign intelligence and counterintelligence as defined by Executive Order 12333 of December 4, 1981, as amended, or by a successor order.
(y) "Intelligence activities" means all activities that elements of the Intelligence Community are authorized to conduct pursuant to law or Executive Order 12333, as amended, or a successor order.
(z) "Intelligence Community" means an element or agency of the U.S. Government identified in or designated pursuant to section 3(4) of the National Security Act of 1947, as amended, or section 3.5(h) of Executive Order 12333, as amended.
(aa) "Mandatory declassification review" means the review for declassification of classified information in response to a request for declassification that meets the requirements under section 3.5 of this order.
(bb) "Multiple sources" means two or more source documents, classification guides, or a combination of both.
(cc) "National security" means the national defense or foreign relations of the United States.
(dd) "Need-to-know" means a determination within the executive branch in accordance with directives issued pursuant to this order that a prospective recipient requires access to specific classified information in order to perform or assist in a lawful and authorized governmental function.
(ee) "Network" means a system of two or more computers that can exchange data or information.
(ff) "Original classification" means an initial determination that information requires, in the interest of the national security, protection against unauthorized disclosure.
(gg) "Original classification authority" means an individual authorized in writing, either by the President, the Vice President, or by agency heads or other officials designated by the President, to classify information in the first instance.

(hh) "Records" means the records of an agency and Presidential papers or Presidential records, as those terms are defined in title 44, United States Code, including those created or maintained by a government contractor, licensee, certificate holder, or grantee that are subject to the sponsoring agency's control under the terms of the contract, license, certificate, or grant.
(ii) "Records having permanent historical value" means Presidential papers or Presidential records and the records of an agency that the Archivist has determined should be maintained permanently in accordance with title 44, United States Code.
(jj) "Records management" means the planning, controlling, directing, organizing, training, promoting, and other managerial activities involved with respect to records creation, records maintenance and use, and records disposition in order to achieve adequate and proper documentation of the policies and transactions of the Federal Government and effective and economical management of agency operations.
(kk) "Safeguarding" means measures and controls that are prescribed to protect classified information.
(ll) "Self-inspection" means the internal review and evaluation of individual agency activities and the agency as a whole with respect to the implementation of the program established under this order and its implementing directives.
(mm) "Senior agency official" means the official designated by the agency head under section 5.4(d) of this order to direct and administer the agency's program under which information is classified, safeguarded, and declassified.
(nn) "Source document" means an existing document that contains classified information that is incorporated, paraphrased, restated, or generated in new form into a new document.
(oo) "Special access program" means a program established for a specific class of classified information that imposes safeguarding and access requirements that exceed those normally required for information at the same classification level.
(pp) "Systematic declassification review" means the review for declassification of classified information contained in records that have been determined by the Archivist to have permanent historical value in accordance with title 44, United States Code.
(qq) "Telecommunications" means the preparation, transmission, or communication of information by electronic means.
(rr) "Unauthorized disclosure" means a communication or physical transfer of classified information to an unauthorized recipient.
(ss) "U.S. entity" includes:

(1) State, local, or tribal governments;

(2) State, local, and tribal law enforcement and firefighting entities;

(3) public health and medical entities;

(4) regional, state, local, and tribal emergency management entities, including State Adjutants General and other appropriate public safety entities; or

(5) private sector entities serving as part of the nation's Critical Infrastructure/Key Resources.

(tt) "Violation" means:

(1) any knowing, willful, or negligent action that could reasonably be expected to result in an unauthorized disclosure of classified information;
(2) any knowing, willful, or negligent action to classify or continue the classification of information contrary to the requirements of this order or its implementing directives; or
(3) any knowing, willful, or negligent action to create or continue a special access program contrary to the requirements of this order.

(uu) "Weapons of mass destruction" means any weapon of mass destruction as defined in 50 U.S.C. 1801(p).

SECTION 6.2. GENERAL PROVISIONS.

(a) Nothing in this order shall supersede any requirement made by or under the Atomic Energy Act of 1954, as amended, or the National Security Act of 1947, as amended. "Restricted Data" and "Formerly Restricted Data" shall be handled, protected, classified, downgraded, and declassified in conformity with the provisions of the Atomic Energy Act of 1954, as amended, and regulations issued under that Act.

(b) The Director of National Intelligence may, with respect to the Intelligence Community and after consultation with the heads of affected departments and agencies, issue such policy directives and guidelines as the Director of National Intelligence deems necessary to implement this order with respect to the classification and declassification of all intelligence and intelligence-related information, and for access to and dissemination of all intelligence and intelligence-related information, both in its final form and in the form when initially gathered. Procedures or other guidance issued by Intelligence Community element heads shall be in accordance with such policy directives or guidelines issued by the Director of National Intelligence. Any such policy directives or guidelines issued by the Director of National Intelligence shall be in accordance with directives issued by the Director of the Information Security Oversight Office under section 5.1(a) of this order.

(c) The Attorney General, upon request by the head of an agency or the Director of the Information Security Oversight Office, shall render an interpretation of this order with respect to any question arising in the course of its administration.

(d) Nothing in this order limits the protection afforded any information by other provisions of law, including the Constitution, Freedom of Information Act exemptions, the Privacy Act of 1974, and the National Security Act of 1947, as amended. This order is not intended to and does not create any right or benefit, substantive or procedural, enforceable at law by a party against the United States, its departments, agencies, or entities, its officers, employees, or agents, or any other person. The foregoing is in addition to the specific provisos set forth in sections 1.1(b), 3.1(c) and 5.3(e) of this order.

(e) Nothing in this order shall be construed to obligate action or otherwise affect functions by the Director of the Office of Management and Budget relating to budgetary, administrative, or legislative proposals.

(f) This order shall be implemented subject to the availability of appropriations.

(g) Executive Order 12958 of April 17, 1995, and amendments thereto, including Executive Order 13292 of March 25, 2003, are hereby revoked as of the effective date of this order.

SECTION 6.3. EFFECTIVE DATE. This order is effective 180 days from the date of this order, except for sections 1.7, 3.3, and 3.7, which are effective immediately.

SECTION 6.4. PUBLICATION. The Archivist of the United States shall publish this Executive Order in the Federal Register.

BARACK OBAMA

Executive Order 13549—Classified National Security Information Program for State, Local, Tribal, and Private Sector Entities

75 Fed. Reg. 162 (Aug. 23, 2010)

By the authority vested in me as President by the Constitution and the laws of the United States of America, in order to ensure the proper safeguarding of information shared with State, local, tribal, and private sector entities, it is hereby ordered as follows:

Section 1. *Establishment and Policy.*

Sec. 1.1. There is established a Classified National Security Information Program (Program) designed to safeguard and govern access to classified national security information shared by the Federal Government with State, local, tribal, and private sector (SLTPS) entities.

Sec. 1.2. The purpose of this order is to ensure that security standards governing access to and safeguarding of classified material are applied in accordance with Executive Order 13526 of December 29, 2009 ("Classified National Security Information"), Executive Order 12968 of August 2, 1995, as amended ("Access to Classified Information"), Executive Order 13467 of June 30, 2008 ("Reforming Processes Related to Suitability for Government Employment, Fitness for Contractor Employees, and Eligibility for Access to Classified National Security Information"), and Executive Order 12829 of January 6, 1993, as amended ("National Industrial Security Program"). Procedures for uniform implementation of these standards by SLTPS entities shall be set forth in an implementing directive to be issued by the Secretary of Homeland Security within 180 days of the date of this order, in consultation with affected executive departments and agencies (agencies), and with the concurrence of the Secretary of Defense, the Attorney General, the Director of National Intelligence, and the Director of the Information Security Oversight Office.

Sec. 1.3. Additional policy provisions for access to and safeguarding of classified information shared with SLTPS personnel include the following:
(a) Eligibility for access to classified information by SLTPS personnel shall be determined by a sponsoring agency. The level of access granted shall not exceed the Secret level, unless the sponsoring agency determines on a case-by-case basis that the applicant has a demonstrated and foreseeable need for access to Top Secret, Special Access Program, or Sensitive Compartmented Information.
(b) Upon the execution of a non-disclosure agreement prescribed by the Information Security Oversight Office or the Director of National Intelligence, and absent disqualifying conduct as determined by the clearance granting official, a duly elected or appointed Governor of a State or territory, or an official who has suc-

ceeded to that office under applicable law, may be granted access to classified information without a background investigation in accordance with the implementing directive for this order. This authorization of access may not be further delegated by the Governor to any other person.
(c) All clearances granted to SLTPS personnel, as well as accreditations granted to SLTPS facilities without a waiver, shall be accepted reciprocally by all agencies and SLTPS entities.
(d) Physical custody of classified information by State, local, and tribal (SLT) entities shall be limited to Secret information unless the location housing the information is under the full-time management, control, and operation of the Department of Homeland Security or another agency. A standard security agreement, established by the Department of Homeland Security in consultation with the SLTPS Advisory Committee, shall be executed between the head of the SLT entity and the U.S. Government for those locations where the SLT entity will maintain physical custody of classified information.
(e) State, local, and tribal facilities where classified information is or will be used or stored shall be inspected, accredited, and monitored for compliance with established standards, in accordance with Executive Order 13526 and the implementing directive for this order, by the Department of Homeland Security or another agency that has entered into an agreement with the Department of Homeland Security to perform such inspection, accreditation, and monitoring.
(f) Private sector facilities where classified information is or will be used or stored shall be inspected, accredited, and monitored for compliance with standards established pursuant to Executive Order 12829, as amended, by the Department of Defense or the cognizant security agency under Executive Order 12829, as amended.
(g) Access to information systems that store, process, or transmit classified information shall be enforced by the rules established by the agency that controls the system and consistent with approved dissemination and handling markings applied by originators, separate from and in addition to criteria for determining eligibility for access to classified information. Access to information within restricted portals shall be based on criteria applied by the agency that controls the portal and consistent with approved dissemination and handling markings applied by originators.
(h) The National Industrial Security Program established in Executive Order 12829, as amended, shall govern the access to and safeguarding of classified information that is released to contractors, licensees, and grantees of SLT entities.
(i) All access eligibility determinations and facility security accreditations granted prior to the date of this order that do not meet the standards set forth in this order or its implementing directive shall be reconciled with those standards within a reasonable period.
(j) Pursuant to section 4.1(i)(3) of Executive Order 13526, documents created prior to the effective date of Executive Order 13526 shall not be redisseminated to other entities without the consent of the originating agency. An agency head or

senior agency official may waive this requirement for specific information that originated within that agency.

Sec. 2. Policy Direction.
With policy guidance from the National Security Advisor and in consultation with the Director of the Information Security Oversight Office, the Director of the Office of Management and Budget, and the heads of affected agencies, the Secretary of Homeland Security shall serve as the Executive Agent for the Program. This order does not displace any authorities provided by law or Executive Order and the Executive Agent shall, to the extent practicable, make use of existing structures and authorities to preclude duplication and to ensure efficiency.

Sec. 3. SLTPS Policy Advisory Committee.
(a) There is established an SLTPS Policy Advisory Committee (Committee) to discuss Program-related policy issues in dispute in order to facilitate their resolution and to otherwise recommend changes to policies and procedures that are designed to remove undue impediments to the sharing of information under the Program. The Director of the Information Security Oversight Office shall serve as Chair of the Committee. An official designated by the Secretary of Homeland Security and a representative of SLTPS entities shall serve as Vice Chairs of the Committee. Members of the Committee shall include designees of the heads of the Departments of State, Defense, Justice, Transportation, and Energy, the Nuclear Regulatory Commission, the Office of the Director of National Intelligence, the Central Intelligence Agency, and the Federal Bureau of Investigation. Members shall also include employees of other agencies and representatives of SLTPS entities, as nominated by any Committee member and approved by the Chair.
(b) Members of the Committee shall serve without compensation for their work on the Committee, except that any representatives of SLTPS entities may be allowed travel expenses, including per diem in lieu of subsistence, as authorized by law for persons serving intermittently in the Government service (5 U.S.C. 5701–5707).
(c) The Information Security Oversight Office shall provide staff support to the Committee.
(d) Insofar as the Federal Advisory Committee Act, as amended (5 App. U.S.C.)(the "Act") may apply to this order, any functions of the President under that Act, except that of reporting to the Congress, which are applicable to the Committee, shall be performed by the Administrator of General Services in accordance with guidelines and procedures established by the General Services Administration.

Sec. 4. Operations and Oversight.
(a) The Executive Agent for the Program shall perform the following responsibilities:

(1) overall program management and oversight;

(2) accreditation, periodic inspection, and monitoring of all facilities owned or operated by SLT entities that have access to classified information, except when another agency has entered into an agreement with the Department of Homeland Security to perform some or all of these functions;

(3) processing of security clearance applications by SLTPS personnel, when requested by a sponsoring agency, on a reimbursable basis unless otherwise determined by the Department of Homeland Security and the sponsoring agency;

(4) documenting and tracking the final status of security clearances for all SLTPS personnel in consultation with the Office of Personnel Management, the Department of Defense, and the Office of the Director of National Intelligence;

(5) developing and maintaining a security profile of SLT facilities that have access to classified information; and

(6) developing training, in consultation with the Committee, for all SLTPS personnel who have been determined eligible for access to classified information, which shall cover the proper safeguarding of classified information and sanctions for unauthorized disclosure of classified information.

(b) The Secretary of Defense, or the cognizant security agency under Executive Order 12829, as amended, shall provide program management, oversight, inspection, accreditation, and monitoring of all private sector facilities that have access to classified information.

(c) The Director of National Intelligence may inspect and monitor SLTPS programs and facilities that involve access to information regarding intelligence sources, methods, and activities.

(d) Heads of agencies that sponsor SLTPS personnel and facilities for access to and storage of classified information under section 1.3(a) of this order shall:

(1) ensure on a periodic basis that there is a demonstrated, foreseeable need for such access; and

(2) provide the Secretary of Homeland Security with information, as requested by the Secretary, about SLTPS personnel sponsored for security clearances and SLT facilities approved for use of classified information prior to and after the date of this order, except when the disclosure of the association of a specific individual with an intelligence or law enforcement agency must be protected in the interest of national security, as determined by the intelligence or law enforcement agency.

Sec. 5. Definitions.

For purposes of this order:

(a) "Access" means the ability or opportunity to gain knowledge of classified information.

(b) "Agency" means any "Executive agency" as defined in 5 U.S.C. 105; any military department as defined in 5 U.S.C. 102; and any other entity within the executive branch that comes into possession of classified information.

(c) "Classified National Security Information" or "classified information" means information that has been determined pursuant to Executive Order 13526, or any predecessor or successor order, to require protection against unauthorized disclosure, and is marked to indicate its classified status when in documentary form.

(d) "Information" means any knowledge that can be communicated or documentary material, regardless of its physical form or characteristics, that is owned

by, produced by or for, or is under the control of the United States Government.
(e) "Intelligence activities" means all activities that elements of the Intelligence Community are authorized to conduct pursuant to law or Executive Order 12333, as amended, or a successor order.
(f) "Local" entities refers to "(A) a county, municipality, city, town, township, local public authority, school district, special district, intrastate district, council of governments (regardless of whether the council of governments is incorporated as a nonprofit corporation under State law), regional or interstate government entity, or agency or instrumentality of a local government; and (B) a rural community, unincorporated town or village, or other public entity" as defined in section 2 of the Homeland Security Act of 2002 (6 U.S.C. 101(11)).
(g) "Private sector" means persons outside government who are critically involved in ensuring that public and private preparedness and response efforts are integrated as part of the Nation's Critical Infrastructure or Key Resources (CIKR), including:

(1) corporate owners and operators determined by the Secretary of Homeland Security to be part of the CIKR;
(2) subject matter experts selected to assist the Federal or State CIKR;
(3) personnel serving in specific leadership positions of CIKR coordination, operations, and oversight;
(4) employees of corporate entities relating to the protection of CIKR; or
(5) other persons not otherwise eligible for the granting of a personnel security clearance pursuant to Executive Order 12829, as amended, who are determined by the Secretary of Homeland Security to require a personnel security clearance.

(h) "Restricted portal" means a protected community of interest or similar area housed within an information system and to which access is controlled by a host agency different from the agency that controls the information system.
(i) "Sponsoring Agency" means an agency that recommends access to or possession of classified information by SLTPS personnel.
(j) "State" means any State of the United States, the District of Columbia, the Commonwealth of Puerto Rico, the Virgin Islands, Guam, American Samoa, the Commonwealth of the Northern Mariana Islands, and any possession of the United States, as defined in section 2 of the Homeland Security Act of 2002 (6 U.S.C. 101(15)).
(k) "State, local, and tribal personnel" means any of the following persons:

(1) Governors, mayors, tribal leaders, and other elected or appointed officials of a State, local government, or tribe;
(2) State, local, and tribal law enforcement personnel and firefighters;
(3) public health, radiological health, and medical professionals of a State, local government, or tribe; and
(4) regional, State, local, and tribal emergency management agency personnel, including State Adjutants General and other appropriate public safety personnel and those personnel providing support to a Federal CIKR mission.

(l) "Tribe" means any Indian or Alaska Native tribe, band, nation, pueblo, village, or community that the Secretary of the Interior acknowledges to exist as an Indian tribe as defined in the Federally Recognized Tribe List Act of 1994 (25 U.S.C. 479a(2)).
(m) "United States" when used in a geographic sense, means any State of the United States, the District of Columbia, the Commonwealth of Puerto Rico, the Virgin Islands, Guam, American Samoa, the Commonwealth of the Northern Mariana Islands, any possession of the United States and any waters within the territorial jurisdiction of the United States.

Sec. 6. *General Provisions.*
(a) This order does not change the requirements of Executive Orders 13526, 12968, 13467, or 12829, as amended, and their successor orders and directives.
(b) Nothing in this order shall be construed to supersede or change the authorities of the Secretary of Energy or the Nuclear Regulatory Commission under the Atomic Energy Act of 1954, as amended (42 U.S.C. 2011 *et seq.*); the Secretary of Defense under Executive Order 12829, as amended; the Director of the Information Security Oversight Office under Executive Order 13526 and Executive Order 12829, as amended; the Attorney General under title 18, United States Code, and the Foreign Intelligence Surveillance Act (50 U.S.C. 1801 *et seq.*); the Secretary of State under title 22, United States Code, and the Omnibus Diplomatic Security and Antiterrorism Act of 1986; or the Director of National Intelligence under the National Security Act of 1947, as amended, Executive Order 12333, as amended, Executive Order 12968, as amended, Executive Order 13467, and Executive Order 13526.
(c) Nothing in this order shall limit the authority of an agency head, or the agency head's designee, to authorize in an emergency and when necessary to respond to an imminent threat to life or in defense of the homeland, in accordance with section 4.2(b) of Executive Order 13526, the disclosure of classified information to an individual or individuals who are otherwise not eligible for access in accordance with the provisions of Executive Order 12968.
(d) Consistent with section 892(a)(4) of the Homeland Security Act of 2002 (6 U.S.C. 482(a)(4)), nothing in this order shall be interpreted as changing the requirements and authorities to protect sources and methods.
(e) Nothing in this order shall supersede measures established under the authority of law or Executive Order to protect the security and integrity of specific activities and associations that are in direct support of intelligence operations.
(f) Pursuant to section 892(e) of the Homeland Security Act of 2002 (6 U.S.C. 482(e)), all information provided to an SLTPS entity from an agency shall remain under the control of the Federal Government. Any State or local law authorizing or requiring disclosure shall not apply to such information.
(g) Nothing in this order limits the protection afforded any classified information by other provisions of law. This order is not intended to, and does not, create any right or benefit, substantive or procedural, enforceable at law or in equity by any party against the United States, its departments, agencies, or entities, its officers, employees, or agents, or any other person.

(h) Nothing in this order shall be construed to obligate action or otherwise affect functions by the Director of the Office of Management and Budget relating to budgetary, administrative, or legislative proposals.

(i) This order shall be implemented subject to the availability of appropriations and consistent with procedures approved by the Attorney General pursuant to Executive Order 12333, as amended.

Sec. 7. *Effective Date.* This order is effective 180 days from the date of this order with the exception of section 3, which is effective immediately.

BARACK OBAMA

Executive Order 13581— Blocking Property of Transnational Criminal Organizations

76 Fed. Reg. 44,757 (July 27, 2011)

By the authority vested in me as President by the Constitution and the laws of the United States of America, including section 2656 of title 22, United States Code, and section 3161 of title 5, United States Code, it is hereby ordered as follows:

Section 1. *Policy.* The United States is committed to actively countering the actions and ideologies of al-Qa'ida, its affiliates and adherents, other terrorist organizations, and violent extremists overseas that threaten the interests and national security of the United States. These efforts take many forms, but all contain a communications element and some use of communications strategies directed to audiences outside the United States to counter the ideology and activities of such organizations. These communications strategies focus not only on the violent actions and human costs of terrorism, but also on narratives that can positively influence those who may be susceptible to radicalization and recruitment by terrorist organizations. The purpose of this Executive Order is to reinforce, integrate, and complement public communications efforts across the executive branch that are (1) focused on countering the actions and ideology of al-Qa'ida, its affiliates and adherents, and other international terrorist organizations and violent extremists overseas, and (2) directed to audiences outside the United States. This collaborative work among executive departments and agencies (agencies) brings together expertise, capabilities, and resources to realize efficiencies and better coordination of U.S. Government communications investments to combat terrorism and extremism.

Sec. 2. *Assigned Responsibilities to the Center for Strategic Counterterrorism Communications.*

(a) Under the direction of the Secretary of State (Secretary), the Center for Strategic Counterterrorism Communications (Center) that has been established in the Department of State by the Secretary shall coordinate, orient, and inform Government-wide public communications activities directed at audiences abroad and targeted against violent extremists and terrorist organizations, especially al-Qa'ida and its affiliates and adherents, with the goal of using communication tools to reduce radicalization by terrorists and extremist violence and terrorism that threaten the interests and national security of the United States. Consistent with section 404o of title 50, United States Code, the Center shall coordinate its analysis, evaluation, and planning functions with the National Counterterrorism Center. The Center shall also coordinate these functions with other agencies, as appropriate. Executive branch efforts undertaken through the Center shall draw on all agencies with relevant information or capabilities, to prepare, plan for, and conduct these communications efforts.

(b) To achieve these objectives, the Center's functions shall include:

(i) monitoring and evaluating narratives (overarching communication themes that reflect a community's identity, experiences, aspirations, and concerns) and events abroad that are relevant to the development of a U.S. strategic counterterrorism narrative designed to counter violent extremism and terrorism that threaten the interests and national security of the United States;

(ii) developing and promulgating for use throughout the executive branch the U.S. strategic counterterrorism narratives and public communications strategies to counter the messaging of violent extremists and terrorist organizations, especially al-Qa'ida and its affiliates and adherents;

(iii) identifying current and emerging trends in extremist communications and communications by al-Qa'ida and its affiliates and adherents in order to coordinate and provide thematic guidance to U.S. Government communicators on how best to proactively promote the U.S. strategic counterterrorism narrative and policies and to respond to and rebut extremist messaging and narratives when communicating to audiences outside the United States, as informed by a wide variety of Government and non-government sources, including nongovernmental organizations, academic sources, and finished intelligence created by the intelligence community;

(iv) facilitating the use of a wide range of communications technologies, including digital tools, by sharing expertise among agencies, seeking expertise from external sources, and extending best practices;

(v) identifying and requesting relevant information from agencies, including intelligence reporting, data, and analysis; and

(vi) identifying shortfalls in U.S. capabilities in any areas relevant to the Center's mission and recommending necessary enhancements or changes.

(c) The Secretary shall establish a Steering Committee composed of senior representatives of agencies relevant to the Center's mission to provide advice to the Secretary on the operations and strategic orientation of the Center and to ensure adequate support for the Center. The Steering Committee shall meet not less than every 6 months. The Steering Committee shall be chaired by the Under Secretary of State for Public Diplomacy. The Coordinator for Counterterrorism of the Department of State shall serve as Vice Chair. The Coordinator of the Center shall serve as Executive Secretary. The Steering Committee shall include one senior representative designated by the head of each of the following agencies: the Department of Defense, the Department of Justice, the Department of Homeland Security, the Department of the Treasury, the National Counterterrorism Center, the Joint Chiefs of Staff, the Counterterrorism Center of the Central Intelligence Agency, the Broadcast Board of Governors, and the Agency for International Development. Other agencies may be invited to participate in the Steering Committee at the discretion of the Chair.

Sec. 3. *Establishment of a Temporary Organization.*

(a) There is established within the Department of State, in accordance with section 3161 of title 5, United States Code, a temporary organization to be known as

the Counterterrorism Communications Support Office (CCSO).
(b) The purpose of the CCSO shall be to perform the specific project of supporting agencies in Government-wide public communications activities targeted against violent extremism and terrorist organizations, especially al-Qa'ida and its affiliates and adherents, to audiences abroad by using communication tools designed to counter violent extremism and terrorism that threaten the interests and national security of the United States.
(c) In carrying out its purpose set forth in subsection (b) of this section, the CCSO shall:

(i) support agencies in their implementation of whole-of-government public communications activities directed at audiences abroad, including by providing baseline research on characteristics of these audiences, by developing expertise and studies on aspirations, narratives, information strategies and tactics of violent extremists and terrorist organizations overseas, by designing and developing sustained campaigns on specific areas of interest to audiences abroad, and by developing expertise on implementing highly focused social media campaigns; and

(ii) perform such other functions related to the specific project set forth in subsection (b) of this section as the Secretary may assign.

(d) The CCSO shall be headed by a Director selected by the Secretary, with the advice of the Steering Committee. Its staff may include, as determined by the Secretary: (1) personnel with relevant expertise detailed on a non-reimbursable basis from other agencies; (2) senior and other technical advisers; and (3) such other personnel as the Secretary may direct to support the CCSO. To accomplish this mission, the heads of agencies participating on the Steering Committee shall provide to the CCSO, on a non-reimbursable basis, assistance, services, and other support including but not limited to logistical and administrative support and details of personnel. Non-reimbursable details shall be based on reasonable requests from the Secretary in light of the need for specific expertise, and after consultation with the relevant agency, to the extent permitted by law.
(e) The CCSO shall terminate at the end of the maximum period permitted by section 3161(a)(1) of title 5, United States Code, unless sooner terminated by the Secretary consistent with section 3161(a)(2) of such title.

Sec. 4. *General Provisions.*

(a) Nothing in this order shall be construed to impair or otherwise affect:

(i) authority granted by law to an agency, or the head thereof; or

(ii) functions of the Director of the Office of Management and Budget relating to budgetary, administrative, or legislative proposals.

(b) This order shall be implemented consistent with applicable law and subject to the availability of appropriations.
(c) This order is not intended to, and does not, create any right or benefit, substantive or procedural, enforceable at law or in equity by any party against the United States, its departments, agencies, or entities, its officers, employees, or agents, or any other person.

BARACK OBAMA

Executive Order 13584—Developing an Integrated Strategic Counterterrorism Communications Initiative and Establishing a Temporary Organization to Support Certain Government-wide Communications Activities Directed Abroad

76 Fed. Reg. 56,945 (Sept. 15, 2011)

By the authority vested in me as President by the Constitution and the laws of the United States of America, including section 2656 of title 22, United States Code, and section 3161 of title 5, United States Code, it is hereby ordered as follows:

Section 1. Policy.
The United States is committed to actively countering the actions and ideologies of al- Qa'ida, its affiliates and adherents, other terrorist organizations, and violent extremists overseas that threaten the interests and national security of the United States. These efforts take many forms, but all contain a communications element and some use of communications strategies directed to audiences outside the United States to counter the ideology and activities of such organizations. These communications strategies focus not only on the violent actions and human costs of terrorism, but also on narratives that can positively influence those who may be susceptible to radicalization and recruitment by terrorist organizations.

The purpose of this Executive Order is to reinforce, integrate, and complement public communications efforts across the executive branch that are (1) focused on countering the actions and ideology of al-Qa'ida, its affiliates and adherents, and other international terrorist organizations and violent extremists overseas, and (2) directed to audiences outside the United States. This collaborative work among executive departments and agencies (agencies) brings together expertise, capabilities, and resources to realize efficiencies and better coordination of U.S. Government communications investments to combat terrorism and extremism.

Sec. 2. Assigned Responsibilities to the Center for Strategic Counterterrorism Communications.
(a) Under the direction of the Secretary of State (Secretary), the Center for Strategic Counterterrorism Communications (Center) that has been established in the Department of State by the Secretary shall coordinate, orient, and inform Government-wide public communications activities directed at audiences abroad and targeted against violent extremists and terrorist organizations, especially al-Qa'ida and its affiliates and adherents, with the goal of using communication tools to reduce radicalization by terrorists and extremist violence and terrorism that threaten the interests and national security of the United States. Consistent with section

404o of title 50, United States Code, the Center shall coordinate its analysis, evaluation, and planning functions with the National Counterterrorism Center. The Center shall also coordinate these functions with other agencies, as appropriate.

Executive branch efforts undertaken through the Center shall draw on all agencies with relevant information or capabilities, to prepare, plan for, and conduct these communications efforts.

(b) To achieve these objectives, the Center's functions shall include:

(i) monitoring and evaluating narratives (overarching communication themes that reflect a community's identity, experiences, aspirations, and concerns) and events abroad that are relevant to the development of a U.S. strategic counterterrorism narrative designed to counter violent extremism and terrorism that threaten the interests and national security of the United States;

(ii) developing and promulgating for use throughout the executive branch the U.S. strategic counterterrorism narratives and public communications strategies to counter the messaging of violent extremists and terrorist organizations, especially al-Qa'ida and its affiliates and adherents;

(iii) identifying current and emerging trends in extremist communications and communications by al-Qa'ida and its affiliates and adherents in order to coordinate and provide thematic guidance to U.S. Government communicators on how best to proactively promote the U.S. strategic counterterrorism narrative and policies and to respond to and rebut extremist messaging and narratives when communicating to audiences outside the United States, as informed by a wide variety of Government and non- government sources, including non-governmental organizations, academic sources, and finished intelligence created by the intelligence community;

(iv) facilitating the use of a wide range of communications technologies, including digital tools, by sharing expertise among agencies, seeking expertise from external sources, and extending best practices;

(v) identifying and requesting relevant information from agencies, including intelligence reporting, data, and analysis; and

(vi) identifying shortfalls in U.S. capabilities in any areas relevant to the Center's mission and recommending necessary enhancements or changes.

(c) The Secretary shall establish a Steering Committee composed of senior representatives of agencies relevant to the Center's mission to provide advice to the Secretary on the operations and strategic orientation of the Center and to ensure adequate support for the Center. The Steering Committee shall meet not less than every 6 months. The Steering Committee shall be chaired by the Under Secretary of State for Public Diplomacy. The Coordinator for Counterterrorism of the Department of State shall serve as Vice Chair. The Coordinator of the Center shall serve as Executive Secretary. The Steering Committee shall include one senior representative designated by the head of each of the following agencies: the Department of Defense, the Department of Justice, the Department of Homeland Security, the Department of the Treasury, the National Counterterrorism Center, the Joint Chiefs of Staff, the Counterterrorism Center of the Central Intelligence Agency, the Broadcast Board of Governors, and the Agency for International

Development. Other agencies may be invited to participate in the Steering Committee at the discretion of the Chair.

Sec. 3. Establishment of a Temporary Organization.

(a) There is established within the Department of State, in accordance with section 3161 of title 5, United States Code, a temporary organization to be known as the Counterterrorism Communications Support Office (CCSO).

(b) The purpose of the CCSO shall be to perform the specific project of supporting agencies in Government- wide public communications activities targeted against violent extremism and terrorist organizations, especially al-Qa'ida and its affiliates and adherents, to audiences abroad by using communication tools designed to counter violent extremism and terrorism that threaten the interests and national security of the United States.

(c) In carrying out its purpose set forth in subsection (b) of this section, the CCSO shall:

(i) support agencies in their implementation of whole-of-government public communications activities directed at audiences abroad, including by providing baseline research on characteristics of these audiences, by developing expertise and studies on aspirations, narratives, information strategies and tactics of violent extremists and terrorist organizations overseas, by designing and developing sustained campaigns on specific areas of interest to audiences abroad, and by developing expertise on implementing highly focused social media campaigns; and

(ii) perform such other functions related to the specific project set forth in subsection (b) of this section as the Secretary may assign.

(d) The CCSO shall be headed by a Director selected by the Secretary, with the advice of the Steering Committee. Its staff may include, as determined by the Secretary: (1) personnel with relevant expertise detailed on a non-reimbursable basis from other agencies; (2) senior and other technical advisers; and (3) such other personnel as the Secretary may direct to support the CCSO. To accomplish this mission, the heads of agencies participating on the Steering Committee shall provide to the CCSO, on a non-reimbursable basis, assistance, services, and other support including but not limited to logistical and administrative support and details of personnel. Non-reimbursable details shall be based on reasonable requests from the Secretary in light of the need for specific expertise, and after consultation with the relevant agency, to the extent permitted by law.

(e) The CCSO shall terminate at the end of the maximum period permitted by section 3161(a)(1) of title 5, United States Code, unless sooner terminated by the Secretary consistent with section 3161(a)(2) of such title.

Sec. 4. General Provisions.

(a) Nothing in this order shall be construed to impair or otherwise affect:

(i) authority granted by law to an agency, or the head thereof; or

(ii) functions of the Director of the Office of Management and Budget relating to budgetary, administrative, or legislative proposals.

(b) This order shall be implemented consistent with applicable law and subject to the availability of appropriations.
(c) This order is not intended to, and does not, create any right or benefit, substantive or procedural, enforceable at law or in equity by any party against the United States, its departments, agencies, or entities, its officers, employees, or agents, or any other person.

BARACK OBAMA

Executive Order 13587—Structural Reforms to Improve the Security of Classified Networks and the Responsible Sharing and Safeguarding of Classified Information

76 Fed. Reg. 63,811 (Oct. 13, 2011)

By the authority vested in me as President by the Constitution and the laws of the United States of America and in order to ensure the responsible sharing and safeguarding of classified national security information (classified information) on computer networks, it is hereby ordered as follows:

Section 1. Policy.

Our Nation's security requires classified information to be shared immediately with authorized users around the world but also requires sophisticated and vigilant means to ensure it is shared securely. Computer networks have individual and common vulnerabilities that require coordinated decisions on risk management.

This order directs structural reforms to ensure responsible sharing and safeguarding of classified information on computer networks that shall be consistent with appropriate protections for privacy and civil liberties. Agencies bear the primary responsibility for meeting these twin goals. These structural reforms will ensure coordinated interagency development and reliable implementation of policies and minimum standards regarding information security, personnel security, and systems security; address both internal and external security threats and vulnerabilities; and provide policies and minimum standards for sharing classified information both within and outside the Federal Government. These policies and minimum standards will address all agencies that operate or access classified computer networks, all users of classified computer networks (including contractors and others who operate or access classified computer networks controlled by the Federal Government), and all classified information on those networks.

Sec. 2. General Responsibilities of Agencies.

Sec. 2.1. The heads of agencies that operate or access classified computer networks shall have responsibility for appropriately sharing and safeguarding classified information on computer networks. As part of this responsibility, they shall:

(a) designate a senior official to be charged with overseeing classified information sharing and safeguarding efforts for the agency;

(b) implement an insider threat detection and prevention program consistent with guidance and standards developed by the Insider Threat Task Force established in section 6 of this order;

(c) perform self-assessments of compliance with policies and standards issued pursuant to sections 3.3, 5.2, and 6.3 of this order, as well as other applicable policies and standards, the results of which shall be reported annually to the Senior Information Sharing and Safeguarding Steering Committee established in section 3 of this order;

(d) provide information and access, as warranted and consistent with law and section 7(d) of this order, to enable independent assessments by the Executive Agent for Safeguarding Classified Information on Computer Networks and the Insider Threat Task Force of compliance with relevant established policies and standards; and

(e) detail or assign staff as appropriate and necessary to the Classified Information Sharing and Safeguarding Office and the Insider Threat Task Force on an ongoing basis.

Sec. 3. Senior Information Sharing and Safeguarding Steering Committee.

Sec. 3.1. There is established a Senior Information Sharing and Safeguarding Steering Committee (Steering Committee) to exercise overall responsibility and ensure senior-level accountability for the coordinated interagency development and implementation of policies and standards regarding the sharing and safeguarding of classified information on computer networks.

Sec. 3.2. The Steering Committee shall be co-chaired by senior representatives of the Office of Management and Budget and the National Security Staff. Members of the committee shall be officers of the United States as designated by the heads of the Departments of State, Defense, Justice, Energy, and Homeland Security, the Office of the Director of National Intelligence, the Central Intelligence Agency, and the Information Security Oversight Office within the National Archives and Records Administration (ISOO), as well as such additional agencies as the co-chairs of the Steering Committee may designate.

Sec. 3.3. The responsibilities of the Steering Committee shall include:

(a) establishing Government-wide classified information sharing and safeguarding goals and annually reviewing executive branch successes and shortcomings in achieving those goals;

(b) preparing within 90 days of the date of this order and at least annually thereafter, a report for the President assessing the executive branch's successes and shortcomings in sharing and safeguarding classified information on computer networks and discussing potential future vulnerabilities;

(c) developing program and budget recommendations to achieve Government-wide classified information sharing and safeguarding goals;

(d) coordinating the interagency development and implementation of priorities, policies, and standards for sharing and safeguarding classified information on computer networks;

(e) recommending overarching policies, when appropriate, for promulgation by the Office of Management and Budget or the ISOO;

(f) coordinating efforts by agencies, the Executive Agent, and the Task Force to assess compliance with established policies and standards and recommending corrective actions needed to ensure compliance;

(g) providing overall mission guidance for the Program Manager-Information Sharing Environment (PM-ISE) with respect to the functions to be performed by the Classified Information Sharing and Safeguarding Office established in section 4 of this order; and

(h) referring policy and compliance issues that cannot be resolved by the Steering Committee to the Deputies Committee of the National Security Council in accordance with Presidential Policy Directive/PPD-1 of February 13, 2009 (Organization of the National Security Council System).

Sec. 4. Classified Information Sharing and Safeguarding Office.

Sec. 4.1. There shall be established a Classified Information Sharing and Safeguarding Office (CISSO) within and subordinate to the office of the PM-ISE to provide expert, fulltime, sustained focus on responsible sharing and safeguarding of classified information on computer networks. Staff of the CISSO shall include detailees, as needed and appropriate, from agencies represented on the Steering Committee.

Sec. 4.2. The responsibilities of CISSO shall include:

(a) providing staff support for the Steering Committee;

(b) advising the Executive Agent for Safeguarding Classified Information on Computer Networks and the Insider Threat Task Force on the development of an effective program to monitor compliance with established policies and standards needed to achieve classified information sharing and safeguarding goals; and

(c) consulting with the Departments of State, Defense, and Homeland Security, the ISOO, the Office of the Director of National Intelligence, and others, as appropriate, to ensure consistency with policies and standards under Executive Order 13526 of December 29, 2009, Executive Order 12829 of January 6, 1993, as amended, Executive Order 13549 of August 18, 2010, and Executive Order 13556 of November 4, 2010.

Sec. 5. Executive Agent for Safeguarding Classified Information on Computer Networks.

Sec. 5.1. The Secretary of Defense and the Director, National Security Agency, shall jointly act as the Executive Agent for Safeguarding Classified Information on Computer Networks (the "Executive Agent"), exercising the existing authorities of the Executive Agent and National Manager for national security systems, respectively, under National Security Directive/NSD-42 of July 5, 1990, as supplemented by and subject to this order.

Sec. 5.2. The Executive Agent's responsibilities, in addition to those specified by NSD-42, shall include the following:

(a) developing effective technical safeguarding policies and standards in coordination with the Committee on National Security Systems (CNSS), as redesignated by Executive Orders 13286 of February 28, 2003, and 13231 of October 16, 2001, that address the safeguarding of classified information within national security systems, as well as the safeguarding of national security systems themselves;

(b) referring to the Steering Committee for resolution any unresolved issues delaying the Executive Agent's timely development and issuance of technical policies and standards;

(c) reporting at least annually to the Steering Committee on the work of CNSS, including recommendations for any changes needed to improve the timeliness and effectiveness of that work; and

(d) conducting independent assessments of agency compliance with established safeguarding policies and standards, and reporting the results of such assessments to the Steering Committee.

Sec. 6. Insider Threat Task Force.

Sec. 6.1. There is established an interagency Insider Threat Task Force that shall develop a Government-wide program (insider threat program) for deterring, detecting, and mitigating insider threats, including the safeguarding of classified information from exploitation, compromise, or other unauthorized disclosure, taking into account risk levels, as well as the distinct needs, missions, and systems of individual agencies. This program shall include development of policies, objectives, and priorities for establishing and integrating security, counterintelligence, user audits and monitoring, and other safeguarding capabilities and practices within agencies.

Sec. 6.2. The Task Force shall be co-chaired by the Attorney General and the Director of National Intelligence, or their designees. Membership on the Task Force shall be composed of officers of the United States from, and designated by the heads of, the Departments of State, Defense, Justice, Energy, and Homeland Security, the Office of the Director of National Intelligence, the Central Intelligence Agency, and the ISOO, as well as such additional agencies as the co-chairs of the Task Force may designate. It shall be staffed by personnel from the Federal Bureau of Investigation and the Office of the National Counterintelligence Executive (ONCIX), and other agencies, as determined by the co-chairs for their respective agencies and to the extent permitted by law. Such personnel must be officers or full-time or permanent part-time employees of the United States. To the extent permitted by law, ONCIX shall provide an appropriate work site and administrative support for the Task Force.

Sec. 6.3. The Task Force's responsibilities shall include the following:

(a) developing, in coordination with the Executive Agent, a Government-wide policy for the deterrence, detection, and mitigation of insider threats, which shall be submitted to the Steering Committee for appropriate review;

(b) in coordination with appropriate agencies, developing minimum standards and guidance for implementation of the insider threat program's Government-wide policy and, within 1 year of the date of this order, issuing those minimum standards and guidance, which shall be binding on the executive branch;

(c) if sufficient appropriations or authorizations are obtained, continuing in coordination with appropriate agencies after 1 year from the date of this order to add to or modify those minimum standards and guidance, as appropriate;

(d) if sufficient appropriations or authorizations are not obtained, recommending for promulgation by the Office of Management and Budget or the ISOO any

additional or modified minimum standards and guidance developed more than 1 year after the date of this order; (e) referring to the Steering Committee for resolution any unresolved issues delaying the timely development and issuance of minimum standards;
(f) conducting, in accordance with procedures to be developed by the Task Force, independent assessments of the adequacy of agency programs to implement established policies and minimum standards, and reporting the results of such assessments to the Steering Committee;
(g) providing assistance to agencies, as requested, including through the dissemination of best practices; and
(h) providing analysis of new and continuing insider threat challenges facing the United States Government.

Sec. 7. General Provisions.
(a) For the purposes of this order, the word "agencies" shall have the meaning set forth in section 6.1(b) of Executive Order 13526 of December 29, 2009.
(b) Nothing in this order shall be construed to change the requirements of Executive Orders 12333 of December 4, 1981, 12829 of January 6, 1993, 12968 of August 2, 1995, 13388 of October 25, 2005, 13467 of June 30, 2008, 13526 of December 29, 2009, 13549 of August 18, 2010, and their successor orders and directives.
(c) Nothing in this order shall be construed to supersede or change the authorities of the Secretary of Energy or the Nuclear Regulatory Commission under the Atomic Energy Act of 1954, as amended; the Secretary of Defense under Executive Order 12829, as amended; the Secretary of Homeland Security under Executive Order 13549; the Secretary of State under title 22, United States Code, and the Omnibus Diplomatic Security and Antiterrorism Act of 1986; the Director of ISOO under Executive Orders 13526 and 12829, as amended; the PM-ISE under Executive Order 13388 or the Intelligence Reform and Terrorism Prevention Act of 2004, as amended; the Director, Central Intelligence Agency under NSD-42 and Executive Order 13286, as amended; the National Counterintelligence Executive, under the Counterintelligence Enhancement Act of 2002; or the Director of National Intelligence under the National Security Act of 1947, as amended, the Intelligence Reform and Terrorism Prevention Act of 2004, as amended, NSD-42, and Executive Orders 12333, as amended, 12968, as amended, 13286, as amended, 13467, and 13526.
(d) Nothing in this order shall authorize the Steering Committee, CISSO, CNSS, or the Task Force to examine the facilities or systems of other agencies, without advance consultation with the head of such agency, nor to collect information for any purpose not provided herein.
(e) The entities created and the activities directed by this order shall not seek to deter, detect, or mitigate disclosures of information by Government employees or contractors that are lawful under and protected by the Intelligence Community Whistleblower Protection Act of 1998, Whistleblower Protection

Act of 1989, Inspector General Act of 1978, or similar statutes, regulations, or policies.

(f) With respect to the Intelligence Community, the Director of National Intelligence, after consultation with the heads of affected agencies, may issue such policy directives and guidance as the Director of National Intelligence deems necessary to implement this order.

(g) Nothing in this order shall be construed to impair or otherwise affect:

(1) the authority granted by law to an agency, or the head thereof; or

(2) the functions of the Director of the Office of Management and Budget relating to budgetary, administrative, or legislative proposals

(h) This order shall be implemented consistent with applicable law and appropriate protections for privacy and civil liberties, and subject to the availability of appropriations.

(i) This order is not intended to, and does not, create any right or benefit, substantive or procedural, enforceable at law or in equity by any party against the United States, its departments, agencies, or entities, its officers, employees, or agents, or any other person.

BARACK OBAMA

Executive Order 13603—National Defense Resources Preparedness

77 Fed. Reg. 16,651 (Mar. 22, 2012)

By the authority vested in me as President by the Constitution and the laws of the United States of America, including the Defense Production Act of 1950, as amended (50 U.S.C. App. 2061 et seq.), and section 301 of title 3, United States Code, and as Commander in Chief of the Armed Forces of the United States, it is hereby ordered as follows:

PART I—PURPOSE, POLICY, AND IMPLEMENTATION

Section 101. Purpose.

This order delegates authorities and addresses national defense resource policies and programs under the Defense Production Act of 1950, as amended (the "Act").

Sec. 102. Policy. The United States must have an industrial and technological base capable of meeting national defense requirements and capable of contributing to the technological superiority of its national defense equipment in peacetime and in times of national emergency. The domestic industrial and technological base is the foundation for national defense preparedness. The authorities provided in the Act shall be used to strengthen this base and to ensure it is capable of responding to the national defense needs of the United States.

Sec. 103. General Functions.

Executive departments and agencies (agencies) responsible for plans and programs relating to national defense (as defined in section 801(j) of this order), or for resources and services needed to support such plans and programs, shall:

(a) identify requirements for the full spectrum of emergencies, including essential military and civilian demand;

(b) assess on an ongoing basis the capability of the domestic industrial and technological base to satisfy requirements in peacetime and times of national emergency, specifically evaluating the availability of the most critical resource and production sources, including subcontractors and suppliers, materials, skilled labor, and professional and technical personnel;

(c) be prepared, in the event of a potential threat to the security of the United States, to take actions necessary to ensure the availability of adequate resources and production capability, including services and critical technology, for national defense requirements;

(d) improve the efficiency and responsiveness of the domestic industrial base to support national defense requirements; and

(e) foster cooperation between the defense and commercial sectors for research and development and for acquisition of materials, services, components, and equipment to enhance industrial base efficiency and responsiveness.

Sec. 104. Implementation.

(a) The National Security Council and Homeland Security Council, in conjunction with the National Economic Council, shall serve as the integrated policymaking forum for consideration and formulation of national defense resource preparedness policy and shall make recommendations to the President on the use of authorities under the Act.

(b) The Secretary of Homeland Security shall:

(1) advise the President on issues of national defense resource preparedness and on the use of the authorities and functions delegated by this order;

(2) provide for the central coordination of the plans and programs incident to authorities and functions delegated under this order, and provide guidance to agencies assigned functions under this order, developed in consultation with such agencies; and

(3) report to the President periodically concerning all program activities conducted pursuant to this order.

(c) The Defense Production Act Committee, described in section 701 of this order, shall:

(1) in a manner consistent with section 2(b) of the Act, 50 U.S.C. App. 2062(b), advise the President through the Assistant to the President and National Security Advisor, the Assistant to the President for Homeland Security and Counterterrorism, and the Assistant to the President for Economic Policy on the effective use of the authorities under the Act; and

(2) prepare and coordinate an annual report to the Congress pursuant to section 722(d) of the Act, 50 U.S.C. App. 2171(d).

(d) The Secretary of Commerce, in cooperation with the Secretary of Defense, the Secretary of Homeland Security, and other agencies, shall:

(1) analyze potential effects of national emergencies on actual production capability, taking into account the entire production system, including shortages of resources, and develop recommended preparedness measures to strengthen capabilities for production increases in national emergencies; and

(2) perform industry analyses to assess capabilities of the industrial base to support the national defense, and develop policy recommendations to improve the international competitiveness of specific domestic industries and their abilities to meet national defense program needs.

PART II—PRIORITIES AND ALLOCATIONS

Sec. 201. Priorities and Allocations Authorities.

(a) The authority of the President conferred by section 101 of the Act, 50 U.S.C. App. 2071, to require acceptance and priority performance of contracts or orders (other than contracts of employment) to promote the national defense over performance of any other contracts or orders, and to allocate materials, services, and facilities as deemed necessary or appropriate to promote the national defense, is delegated to the following agency heads:

(1) the Secretary of Agriculture with respect to food resources, food resource facilities, livestock resources, veterinary resources, plant health resources, and the domestic distribution of farm equipment and commercial fertilizer;

(2) the Secretary of Energy with respect to all forms of energy;

(3) the Secretary of Health and Human Services with respect to health resources;

(4) the Secretary of Transportation with respect to all forms of civil transportation;

(5) the Secretary of Defense with respect to water resources; and

(6) the Secretary of Commerce with respect to all other materials, services, and facilities, including construction materials.

(b) The Secretary of each agency delegated authority under subsection (a) of this section (resource departments) shall plan for and issue regulations to prioritize and allocate resources and establish standards and procedures by which the authority shall be used to promote the national defense, under both emergency and non-emergency conditions. Each Secretary shall authorize the heads of other agencies, as appropriate, to place priority ratings on contracts and orders for materials, services, and facilities needed in support of programs approved under section 202 of this order.

(c) Each resource department shall act, as necessary and appropriate, upon requests for special priorities assistance, as defined by section 801(l) of this order, in a time frame consistent with the urgency of the need at hand. In situations where there are competing program requirements for limited resources, the resource department shall consult with the Secretary who made the required determination under section 202 of this order. Such Secretary shall coordinate with and identify for the resource department which program requirements to prioritize on the basis of operational urgency. In situations involving more than one Secretary making such a required determination under section 202 of this order, the Secretaries shall coordinate with and identify for the resource department which program requirements should receive priority on the basis of operational urgency.

(d) If agreement cannot be reached between two such Secretaries, then the issue shall be referred to the President through the Assistant to the President and National Security Advisor and the Assistant to the President for Homeland Security and Counterterrorism.

(e) The Secretary of each resource department, when necessary, shall make the finding required under section 101(b) of the Act, 50 U.S.C. App. 2071(b). This finding shall be submitted for the President's approval through the Assistant to the President and National Security Advisor and the Assistant to the President for Homeland Security and Counterterrorism. Upon such approval, the Secretary of the resource department that made the finding may use the authority of section 101(a) of the Act, 50 U.S.C. App. 2071(a), to control the general distribution of any material (including applicable services) in the civilian market.

Sec. 202. Determinations.
Except as provided in section 201(e) of this order, the authority delegated by section 201 of this order may be used only to support programs that have been determined in writing as necessary or appropriate to promote the national defense:

(a) by the Secretary of Defense with respect to military production and construction, military assistance to foreign nations, military use of civil transportation, stockpiles managed by the Department of Defense, space, and directly related activities;

(b) by the Secretary of Energy with respect to energy production and construction, distribution and use, and directly related activities; and

(c) by the Secretary of Homeland Security with respect to all other national defense programs, including civil defense and continuity of Government.

Sec. 203. Maximizing Domestic Energy Supplies.
The authorities of the President under section 101(c)(1)- (2) of the Act, 50 U.S.C. App. 2071(c)(1)-(2), are delegated to the Secretary of Commerce, with the exception that the authority to make findings that materials (including equipment), services, and facilities are critical and essential, as described in section 101(c)(2)(A) of the Act, 50 U.S.C. App. 2071(c)(2)(A), is delegated to the Secretary of Energy. Sec. 204. Chemical and Biological Warfare. The authority of the President conferred by section 104(b) of the Act, 50 U.S.C. App. 2074(b), is delegated to the Secretary of Defense. This authority may not be further delegated by the Secretary.

PART III—EXPANSION OF PRODUCTIVE CAPACITY AND SUPPLY

Sec. 301. Loan Guarantees.

(a) To reduce current or projected shortfalls of resources, critical technology items, or materials essential for the national defense, the head of each agency engaged in procurement for the national defense, as defined in section 801(h) of this order, is authorized pursuant to section 301 of the Act, 50 U.S.C. App. 2091, to guarantee loans by private institutions.

(b) Each guaranteeing agency is designated and authorized to: (1) act as fiscal agent in the making of its own guarantee contracts and in otherwise carrying out the purposes of section 301 of the Act; and (2) contract with any Federal Reserve Bank to assist the agency in serving as fiscal agent.

(c) Terms and conditions of guarantees under this authority shall be determined in consultation with the Secretary of the Treasury and the Director of the Office of Management and Budget (OMB). The guaranteeing agency is authorized, following such consultation, to prescribe: (1) either specifically or by maximum limits or otherwise, rates of interest, guarantee and commitment fees, and other charges which may be made in connection with such guarantee contracts; and (2) regulations governing the forms and procedures (which shall be uniform to the extent practicable) to be utilized in connection therewith.

Sec. 302. Loans.
To reduce current or projected shortfalls of resources, critical technology items, or materials essential for the national defense, the head of each agency engaged in procurement for the national defense is delegated the authority of the President under section 302 of the Act, 50 U.S.C. App. 2092, to make loans thereunder. Terms and conditions of loans under this authority shall be determined in consultation with the Secretary of the Treasury and the Director of OMB.

Sec. 303. Additional Authorities.

(a) To create, maintain, protect, expand, or restore domestic industrial base capabilities essential for the national defense, the head of each agency engaged in procurement for the national defense is delegated the authority of the President under section 303 of the Act, 50 U.S.C. App. 2093, to make provision for purchases of, or commitments to purchase, an industrial resource or a critical technology item for Government use or resale, and to make provision for the development of production capabilities, and for the increased use of emerging technologies in security program applications, and to enable rapid transition of emerging technologies.

(b) Materials acquired under section 303 of the Act, 50 U.S.C. App. 2093, that exceed the needs of the programs under the Act may be transferred to the National Defense Stockpile, if, in the judgment of the Secretary of Defense as the National Defense Stockpile Manager, such transfers are in the public interest.

Sec. 304. Subsidy Payments.
To ensure the supply of raw or nonprocessed materials from high-cost sources, or to ensure maximum production or supply in any area at stable prices of any materials in light of a temporary increase in transportation cost, the head of each agency engaged in procurement for the national defense is delegated the authority of the President under section 303(c) of the Act, 50 U.S.C. App. 2093(c), to make subsidy payments, after consultation with the Secretary of the Treasury and the Director of OMB.

Sec. 305. Determinations and Findings.

(a) Pursuant to budget authority provided by an appropriations act in advance for credit assistance under section 301 or 302 of the Act, 50 U.S.C. App. 2091, 2092, and consistent with the Federal Credit Reform Act of 1990, as amended (FCRA), 2 U.S.C. 661 et seq., the head of each agency engaged in procurement for the national defense is delegated the authority to make the determinations set forth in sections 301(a)(2) and 302(b)(2) of the Act, in consultation with the Secretary making the required determination under section 202 of this order; provided, that such determinations shall be made after due consideration of the provisions of OMB Circular A- 129 and the credit subsidy score for the relevant loan or loan guarantee as approved by OMB pursuant to FCRA.

(b) Other than any determination by the President under section 303(a)(7)(b) of the Act, the head of each agency engaged in procurement for the national defense is delegated the authority to make the required determinations, judgments, certifications, findings, and notifications defined under section 303 of the Act, 50 U.S.C. App. 2093, in consultation with the Secretary making the required determination under section 202 of this order.

Sec. 306. Strategic and Critical Materials.

The Secretary of Defense, and the Secretary of the Interior in consultation with the Secretary of Defense as the National Defense Stockpile Manager, are each delegated the authority of the President under section 303(a)(1)(B) of the Act, 50 U.S.C. App. 2093(a)(1)(B), to encourage the exploration, development, and mining of strategic and critical materials and other materials.

Sec. 307. Substitutes.

The head of each agency engaged in procurement for the national defense is delegated the authority of the President under section 303(g) of the Act, 50 U.S.C. App. 2093(g), to make provision for the development of substitutes for strategic and critical materials, critical components, critical technology items, and other resources to aid the national defense.

Sec. 308. Government-Owned Equipment.

The head of each agency engaged in procurement for the national defense is delegated the authority of the President under section 303(e) of the Act, 50 U.S.C. App. 2093(e), to:

(a) procure and install additional equipment, facilities, processes, or improvements to plants, factories, and other industrial facilities owned by the Federal Government and to procure and install Government-owned equipment in plants, factories, or other industrial facilities owned by private persons;

(b) provide for the modification or expansion of privately owned facilities, including the modification or improvement of production processes, when taking actions under sections 301, 302, or 303 of the Act, 50 U.S.C. App. 2091, 2092, 2093; and

(c) sell or otherwise transfer equipment owned by the Federal Government and installed under section 303(e) of the Act, 50 U.S.C. App. 2093(e), to the owners of such plants, factories, or other industrial facilities.

Sec. 309. Defense Production Act Fund.

The Secretary of Defense is designated the Defense Production Act Fund Manager, in accordance with section 304(f) of the Act, 50 U.S.C. App. 2094(f), and shall carry out the duties specified in section 304 of the Act, in consultation with the agency heads having approved, and appropriated funds for, projects under title III of the Act.

Sec. 310. Critical Items.
The head of each agency engaged in procurement for the national defense is delegated the authority of the President under section 107(b)(1) of the Act, 50 U.S.C. App. 2077(b)(1), to take appropriate action to ensure that critical components, critical technology items, essential materials, and industrial resources are available from reliable sources when needed to meet defense requirements during peacetime, graduated mobilization, and national emergency. Appropriate action may include restricting contract solicitations to reliable sources, restricting contract solicitations to domestic sources (pursuant to statutory authority), stockpiling critical components, and developing substitutes for critical components or critical technology items.

Sec. 311. Strengthening Domestic Capability.
The head of each agency engaged in procurement for the national defense is delegated the authority of the President under section 107(a) of the Act, 50 U.S.C. App. 2077(a), to utilize the authority of title III of the Act or any other provision of law to provide appropriate incentives to develop, maintain, modernize, restore, and expand the productive capacities of domestic sources for critical components, critical technology items, materials, and industrial resources essential for the execution of the national security strategy of the United States.

Sec. 312. Modernization of Equipment.
The head of each agency engaged in procurement for the national defense, in accordance with section 108(b) of the Act, 50 U.S.C. App. 2078(b), may utilize the authority of title III of the Act to guarantee the purchase or lease of advance manufacturing equipment, and any related services with respect to any such equipment for purposes of the Act. In considering title III projects, the head of each agency engaged in procurement for the national defense shall provide a strong preference for proposals submitted by a small business supplier or subcontractor in accordance with section 108(b)(2) of the Act, 50 U.S.C. App. 2078(b)(2).

PART IV—VOLUNTARY AGREEMENTS AND ADVISORY COMMITTEES

Sec. 401. Delegations.
The authority of the President under sections 708(c) and (d) of the Act, 50 U.S.C. App. 2158(c), (d), is delegated to the heads of agencies otherwise delegated authority under this order. The status of the use of such delegations shall be furnished to the Secretary of Homeland Security.

Sec. 402. Advisory Committees.
The authority of the President under section 708(d) of the Act, 50 U.S.C. App. 2158(d), and delegated in section 401 of this order (relating to establishment of advisory committees) shall be exercised only after consultation with, and in accordance with, guidelines and procedures established by the Administrator of General Services.

Sec. 403. Regulations.
The Secretary of Homeland Security, after approval of the Attorney General, and after consultation by the Attorney General with the Chairman of the Federal Trade Commission, shall promulgate rules pursuant to section 708(e) of the Act, 50 U.S.C. App. 2158(e), incorporating standards and procedures by which voluntary agreements and plans of action may be developed and carried out. Such rules may be adopted by other agencies to fulfill the rulemaking requirement of section 708(e) of the Act, 50 U.S.C. App. 2158(e).

PART V—EMPLOYMENT OF PERSONNEL

Sec. 501. National Defense Executive Reserve.

(a) In accordance with section 710(e) of the Act, 50 U.S.C. App. 2160(e), there is established in the executive branch a National Defense Executive Reserve (NDER) composed of persons of recognized expertise from various segments of the private sector and from Government (except full-time Federal employees) for training for employment in executive positions in the Federal Government in the event of a national defense emergency.

(b) The Secretary of Homeland Security shall issue necessary guidance for the NDER program, including appropriate guidance for establishment, recruitment, training, monitoring, and activation of NDER units and shall be responsible for the overall coordination of the NDER program. The authority of the President under section 710(e) of the Act, 50 U.S.C. App. 2160(e), to determine periods of national defense emergency is delegated to the Secretary of Homeland Security.

(c) The head of any agency may implement section 501(a) of this order with respect to NDER operations in such agency.

(d) The head of each agency with an NDER unit may exercise the authority under section 703 of the Act, 50 U.S.C. App. 2153, to employ civilian personnel when activating all or a part of its NDER unit. The exercise of this authority shall be subject to the provisions of sections 501(e) and (f) of this order and shall not be redelegated.

(e) The head of an agency may activate an NDER unit, in whole or in part, upon the written determination of the Secretary of Homeland Security that an emergency affecting the national defense exists and that the activation of the unit is necessary to carry out the emergency program functions of the agency.

(f) Prior to activating the NDER unit, the head of the agency shall notify, in writing, the Assistant to the President for Homeland Security and Counterterrorism of the impending activation.

Sec. 502. Consultants.
The head of each agency otherwise delegated functions under this order is delegated the authority of the President under sections 710(b) and (c) of the Act, 50 U.S.C. App. 2160(b), (c), to employ persons of outstanding experience and ability without compensation and to employ experts, consultants, or organizations. The authority delegated by this section may not be redelegated.

PART VI—LABOR REQUIREMENTS

Sec. 601. Secretary of Labor.

(a) The Secretary of Labor, in coordination with the Secretary of Defense and the heads of other agencies, as deemed appropriate by the Secretary of Labor, shall:

(1) collect and maintain data necessary to make a continuing appraisal of the Nation's workforce needs for purposes of national defense;

(2) upon request by the Director of Selective Service, and in coordination with the Secretary of Defense, assist the Director of Selective Service in development of policies regulating the induction and deferment of persons for duty in the armed services;

(3) upon request from the head of an agency with authority under this order, consult with that agency with respect to: (i) the effect of contemplated actions on labor demand and utilization; (ii) the relation of labor demand to materials and facilities requirements; and (iii) such other matters as will assist in making the exercise of priority and allocations functions consistent with effective utilization and distribution of labor;

(4) upon request from the head of an agency with authority under this order: (i) formulate plans, programs, and policies for meeting the labor requirements of actions to be taken for national defense purposes; and (ii) estimate training needs to help address national defense requirements and promote necessary and appropriate training programs; and

(5) develop and implement an effective labor-management relations policy to support the activities and programs under this order, with the cooperation of other agencies as deemed appropriate by the Secretary of Labor, including the National Labor Relations Board, the Federal Labor Relations Authority, the National Mediation Board, and the Federal Mediation and Conciliation Service.

(b) All agencies shall cooperate with the Secretary of Labor, upon request, for the purposes of this section, to the extent permitted by law.

PART VII—DEFENSE PRODUCTION ACT COMMITTEE

Sec. 701. The Defense Production Act Committee.

(a) The Defense Production Act Committee (Committee) shall be composed of the following members, in accordance with section 722(b) of the Act, 50 U.S.C. App. 2171(b):

(1) The Secretary of State;

(2) The Secretary of the Treasury;

(3) The Secretary of Defense;

(4) The Attorney General;

(5) The Secretary of the Interior;

(6) The Secretary of Agriculture;

(7) The Secretary of Commerce;

(8) The Secretary of Labor;

(9) The Secretary of Health and Human Services;

(10) The Secretary of Transportation;
(11) The Secretary of Energy;
(12) The Secretary of Homeland Security;
(13) The Director of National Intelligence;
(14) The Director of the Central Intelligence Agency;
(15) The Chair of the Council of Economic Advisers;
(16) The Administrator of the National Aeronautics and Space Administration; and
(17) The Administrator of General Services.

(b) The Director of OMB and the Director of the Office of Science and Technology Policy shall be invited to participate in all Committee meetings and activities in an advisory role. The Chairperson, as designated by the President pursuant to section 722 of the Act, 50 U.S.C. App. 2171, may invite the heads of other agencies or offices to participate in Committee meetings and activities in an advisory role, as appropriate.

Sec. 702. Offsets.
The Secretary of Commerce shall prepare and submit to the Congress the annual report required by section 723 of the Act, 50 U.S.C. App. 2172, in consultation with the Secretaries of State, the Treasury, Defense, and Labor, the United States Trade Representative, the Director of National Intelligence, and the heads of other agencies as appropriate. The heads of agencies shall provide the Secretary of Commerce with such information as may be necessary for the effective performance of this function.

PART VIII—GENERAL PROVISIONS

Sec. 801. Definitions.
In addition to the definitions in section 702 of the Act, 50 U.S.C. App. 2152, the following definitions apply throughout this order:

(a) "Civil transportation" includes movement of persons and property by all modes of transportation in interstate, intrastate, or foreign commerce within the United States, its territories and possessions, and the District of Columbia, and related public storage and warehousing, ports, services, equipment and facilities, such as transportation carrier shop and repair facilities. "Civil transportation" also shall include direction, control, and coordination of civil transportation capacity regardless of ownership. "Civil transportation" shall not include transportation owned or controlled by the Department of Defense, use of petroleum and gas pipelines, and coal slurry pipelines used only to supply energy production facilities directly.

(b) "Energy" means all forms of energy including petroleum, gas (both natural and manufactured), electricity, solid fuels (including all forms of coal, coke, coal chemicals, coal liquification, and coal gasification), solar, wind, other types of renewable energy, atomic energy, and the production, conservation, use, control, and distribution (including pipelines) of all of these forms of energy.

(c) "Farm equipment" means equipment, machinery, and repair parts manufactured for use on farms in connection with the production or preparation for market use of food resources.
(d) "Fertilizer" means any product or combination of products that contain one or more of the elements nitrogen, phosphorus, and potassium for use as a plant nutrient.
(e) "Food resources" means all commodities and products, (simple, mixed, or compound), or complements to such commodities or products, that are capable of being ingested by either human beings or animals, irrespective of other uses to which such commodities or products may be put, at all stages of processing from the raw commodity to the products thereof in vendible form for human or animal consumption. "Food resources" also means potable water packaged in commercially marketable containers, all starches, sugars, vegetable and animal or marine fats and oils, seed, cotton, hemp, and flax fiber, but does not mean any such material after it loses its identity as an agricultural commodity or agricultural product.
(f) "Food resource facilities" means plants, machinery, vehicles (including on farm), and other facilities required for the production, processing, distribution, and storage (including cold storage) of food resources, and for the domestic distribution of farm equipment and fertilizer (excluding transportation thereof).
(g) "Functions" include powers, duties, authority, responsibilities, and discretion.
(h) "Head of each agency engaged in procurement for the national defense" means the heads of the Departments of State, Justice, the Interior, and Homeland Security, the Office of the Director of National Intelligence, the Central Intelligence Agency, the National Aeronautics and Space Administration, the General Services Administration, and all other agencies with authority delegated under section 201 of this order.
(i) "Health resources" means drugs, biological products, medical devices, materials, facilities, health supplies, services and equipment required to diagnose, mitigate or prevent the impairment of, improve, treat, cure, or restore the physical or mental health conditions of the population.
(j) "National defense" means programs for military and energy production or construction, military or critical infrastructure assistance to any foreign nation, homeland security, stockpiling, space, and any directly related activity. Such term includes emergency preparedness activities conducted pursuant to title VI of the Robert T. Stafford Disaster Relief and Emergency Assistance Act, 42 U.S.C. 5195 et seq., and critical infrastructure protection and restoration.
(k) "Offsets" means compensation practices required as a condition of purchase in either government-to-government or commercial sales of defense articles and/or defense services as defined by the Arms Export Control Act, 22 U.S.C. 2751 et seq., and the International Traffic in Arms Regulations, 22 C.F.R. 120.1-130.17.

(l) "Special priorities assistance" means action by resource departments to assist with expediting deliveries, placing rated orders, locating suppliers, resolving production or delivery conflicts between various rated orders, addressing problems that arise in the fulfillment of a rated order or other action authorized by a delegated agency, and determining the validity of rated orders.
(m) "Strategic and critical materials" means materials (including energy) that (1) would be needed to supply the military, industrial, and essential civilian needs of the United States during a national emergency, and (2) are not found or produced in the United States in sufficient quantities to meet such need and are vulnerable to the termination or reduction of the availability of the material.
(n) "Water resources" means all usable water, from all sources, within the jurisdiction of the United States, that can be managed, controlled, and allocated to meet emergency requirements, except "water resources" does not include usable water that qualifies as "food resources."

Sec. 802. General.

(a) Except as otherwise provided in section 802(c) of this order, the authorities vested in the President by title VII of the Act, 50 U.S.C. App. 2151 et seq., are delegated to the head of each agency in carrying out the delegated authorities under the Act and this order, by the Secretary of Labor in carrying out part VI of this order, and by the Secretary of the Treasury in exercising the functions assigned in Executive Order 11858, as amended.
(b) The authorities that may be exercised and performed pursuant to section 802(a) of this order shall include:

(1) the power to redelegate authorities, and to authorize the successive redelegation of authorities to agencies, officers, and employees of the Government; and
(2) the power of subpoena under section 705 of the Act, 50 U.S.C. App. 2155, with respect to (i) authorities delegated in parts II, III, and section 702 of this order, and (ii) the functions assigned to the Secretary of the Treasury in Executive Order 11858, as amended, provided that the subpoena power referenced in subsections (i) and (ii) shall be utilized only after the scope and purpose of the investigation, inspection, or inquiry to which the subpoena relates have been defined either by the appropriate officer identified in section 802(a) of this order or by such other person or persons as the officer shall designate.

(c) Excluded from the authorities delegated by section 802(a) of this order are authorities delegated by parts IV and V of this order, authorities in section 721 and 722 of the Act, 50 U.S.C. App. 2170-2171, and the authority with respect to fixing compensation under section 703 of the Act, 50 U.S.C. App. 2153.

Sec. 803. Authority.

(a) Executive Order 12919 of June 3, 1994, and sections 401(3)-(4) of Executive Order 12656 of November 18, 1988, are revoked. All other previously issued orders, regulations, rulings, certificates, directives, and other actions relating to any function affected by this order shall remain in effect except as they are inconsistent with this order or are subsequently amended or revoked under proper authority. Nothing in this order shall affect the validity or force of anything done under previous delegations or other assignment of authority under the Act.

(b) Nothing in this order shall affect the authorities assigned under Executive Order 11858 of May 7, 1975, as amended, except as provided in section 802 of this order.

(c) Nothing in this order shall affect the authorities assigned under Executive Order 12472 of April 3, 1984, as amended.

Sec. 804. General Provisions.

(a) Nothing in this order shall be construed to impair or otherwise affect functions of the Director of OMB relating to budgetary, administrative, or legislative proposals.

(b) This order shall be implemented consistent with applicable law and subject to the availability of appropriations.

(c) This order is not intended to, and does not, create any right or benefit, substantive or procedural, enforceable at law or in equity by any party against the United States, its departments, agencies, or entities, its officers, employees, or agents, or any other person.

BARACK OBAMA

Executive Order 13606—Blocking the Property and Suspending Entry into the United States of Certain Persons with Respect to Grave Human Rights Abuses by the Governments of Iran and Syria via Information Technology

77 Fed. Reg. 24,571 (Apr. 24, 2012)

By the authority vested in me as President by the Constitution and the laws of the United States of America, including the International Emergency Economic Powers Act (50 U.S.C. 1701 et seq.) (IEEPA), the National Emergencies Act (50 U.S.C. 1601 et seq.), section 212(f) of the Immigration and Nationality Act of 1952, as amended (8 U.S.C. 1182(f)), and section 301 of title 3, United States Code,

I, BARACK OBAMA, President of the United States of America, hereby determine that the commission of serious human rights abuses against the people of Iran and Syria by their governments, facilitated by computer and network disruption, monitoring, and tracking by those governments, and abetted by entities in Iran and Syria that are complicit in their governments' malign use of technology for those purposes, threaten the national security and foreign policy of the United States. The Governments of Iran and Syria are endeavoring to rapidly upgrade their technological ability to conduct such activities. Cognizant of the vital importance of providing technology that enables the Iranian and Syrian people to freely communicate with each other and the outside world, as well as the preservation, to the extent possible, of global telecommunications supply chains for essential products and services to enable the free flow of information, the measures in this order are designed primarily to address the need to prevent entities located in whole or in part in Iran and Syria from facilitating or committing serious human rights abuses. In order to take additional steps with respect to the national emergencies declared in Executive Order 12957 of March 15, 1995, as relied upon for additional steps in subsequent Executive Orders, and in Executive Order 13338 of May 11, 2004, as modified in scope and relied upon for additional steps in subsequent Executive Orders, and to address the situation described above, I hereby order:

Section 1.

(a) All property and interests in property that are in the United States, that hereafter come within the United States, or that are or hereafter come within the possession or control of any United States person, including any foreign branch, of the following persons are blocked and may not be transferred, paid, exported, withdrawn, or otherwise dealt in:

(i) the persons listed in the Annex to this order; and

(ii) any person determined by the Secretary of the Treasury, in consultation with or at the recommendation of the Secretary of State:

(A) to have operated, or to have directed the operation of, information and communications technology that facilitates computer or network disruption, monitoring, or tracking that could assist in or enable serious human rights abuses by or on behalf of the Government of Iran or the Government of Syria;
(B) to have sold, leased, or otherwise provided, directly or indirectly, goods, services, or technology to Iran or Syria likely to be used to facilitate computer or network disruption, monitoring, or tracking that could assist in or enable serious human rights abuses by or on behalf of the Government of Iran or the Government of Syria;
(C) to have materially assisted, sponsored, or provided financial, material, or technological support for, or goods or services to or in support of, the activities described in subsections (a)(ii)(A) and (B) of this section or any person whose property and interests in property are blocked pursuant to this order; or
(D) to be owned or controlled by, or to have acted or purported to act for or on behalf of, directly or indirectly, any person whose property and interests in property are blocked pursuant to this order.

(b) The prohibitions in subsection (a) of this section apply except to the extent provided by statutes, or in regulations, orders, directives, or licenses that may be issued pursuant to this order, and notwithstanding any contract entered into or any license or permit granted prior to the effective date of this order.

Sec. 2.

I hereby determine that the making of donations of the type of articles specified in section 203(b)(2) of IEEPA (50 U.S.C. 1702(b)(2)) by, to, or for the benefit of any person whose property and interests in property are blocked pursuant to this order would seriously impair my ability to deal with the two national emergencies identified in the preamble to this order, and I hereby prohibit such donations as provided by section 1 of this order.

Sec. 3.

The prohibitions in section 1 of this order include but are not limited to:

(a) the making of any contribution or provision of funds, goods, or services by, to, or for the benefit of any person whose property and interests in property are blocked pursuant to this order; and
(b) the receipt of any contribution or provision of funds, goods, or services from any such person.

Sec. 4.

I hereby find that the unrestricted immigrant and nonimmigrant entry into the United States of aliens who meet one or more of the criteria in section 1 of this order would be detrimental to the interests of the United States, and I hereby suspend the entry into the United States, as immigrants or nonimmigrants, of such persons. Such persons shall be treated as persons covered by section 1 of Proclamation 8693 of July 24, 2011 (Suspension of Entry of Aliens Subject to United Nations Security Council Travel Bans and International Emergency Economic Powers Act Sanctions).

Sec. 5.

(a) Any transaction by a United States person or within the United States that evades or avoids, has the purpose of evading or avoiding, causes a violation of, or attempts to violate any of the prohibitions set forth in this order is prohibited.
(b) Any conspiracy formed to violate any of the prohibitions set forth in this order is prohibited.

Sec. 6.

Nothing in section 1 of this order shall prohibit transactions for the conduct of the official business of the United States Government by employees, grantees, or contractors thereof.

Sec. 7.

For the purposes of this order:

(a) the term "person" means an individual or entity;

(b) the term "information and communications technology" means any hardware, software, or other product or service primarily intended to fulfill or enable the function of information processing and communication by electronic means, including transmission and display, including via the Internet;

(c) the term "entity" means a partnership, association, trust, joint venture, corporation, group, subgroup, or other organization;

(d) the term "United States person" means any United States citizen, permanent resident alien, entity organized under the laws of the United States or any jurisdiction within the United States (including foreign branches), or any person in the United States;

(e) the term "Government of Iran" means the Government of Iran, any political subdivision, agency, or instrumentality thereof, including the Central Bank of Iran, and any person owned or controlled by, or acting for or on behalf of, the Government of Iran; and

(f) the term "Government of Syria" means the Government of the Syrian Arab Republic, its agencies, instrumentalities, and controlled entities.

Sec. 8.

For those persons whose property and interests in property are blocked pursuant to this order who might have a constitutional presence in the United States, I find that because of the ability to transfer funds or other assets instantaneously, prior notice to such persons of measures to be taken pursuant to this order would render those measures ineffectual. I therefore determine that for these measures to be effective in addressing the two national emergencies identified in the preamble to this order, there need be no prior notice of a listing or determination made pursuant to section 1 of this order.

Sec. 9.
The Secretary of the Treasury, in consultation with the Secretary of State, is hereby authorized to take such actions, including the promulgation of rules and regulations, and to employ all powers granted to the President by IEEPA as may be necessary to carry out the purposes of this order. The Secretary of the Treasury may redelegate any of these functions to other officers and agencies of the United States Government consistent with applicable law. All agencies of the United States Government are hereby directed to take all appropriate measures within their authority to carry out the provisions of this order.

Sec. 10.
The Secretary of the Treasury, in consultation with the Secretary of State, is hereby authorized to determine that circumstances no longer warrant the blocking of the property and interests in property of a person listed in the Annex to this order and to take necessary action to give effect to that determination.

Sec. 11.
This order is not intended to, and does not, create any right or benefit, substantive or procedural, enforceable at law or in equity by any party against the United States, its departments, agencies, or entities, its officers, employees, or agents, or any other person.

Sec. 12.
The measures taken pursuant to this order with respect to Iran are in response to actions of the Government of Iran occurring after the conclusion of the 1981 Algiers Accords, and are intended solely as a response to those later actions.

Sec. 13. This order is effective at 12:01 a.m. eastern daylight time on April 23, 2012.

BARACK OBAMA

Executive Order 13608—Prohibiting Certain Transactions With and Suspending Entry Into the United States of Foreign Sanctions Evaders With Respect to Iran and Syria

77 Fed. Reg. 26,409 (May 3, 2012))

By the authority vested in me as President by the Constitution and the laws of the United States of America, including the International Emergency Economic Powers Act (50 U.S.C. 1701 *et seq.*) (IEEPA), the National Emergencies Act (50 U.S.C. 1601 *et seq.*), section 212(f) of the Immigration and Nationality Act of 1952, as amended (8 U.S.C. 1182(f)), and section 301 of title 3, United States Code,

I, BARACK OBAMA, President of the United States of America, hereby find that efforts by foreign persons to engage in activities intended to evade U.S. economic and financial sanctions with respect to Iran and Syria undermine our efforts to address the national emergencies declared in Executive Order 12957 of March 15, 1995, as relied on for additional steps in subsequent Executive Orders, in Executive Order 13338 of May 11, 2004, as modified in scope and relied on for additional steps in subsequent Executive Orders, in Executive Order 12938 of November 14, 1994, as relied on for additional steps in subsequent Executive Orders, and in Executive Order 13224 of September 23, 2001, as relied on for additional steps in subsequent Executive Orders, and in order to take additional steps pursuant to these national emergencies, I hereby order:

Section 1. (a) The Secretary of the Treasury, in consultation with the Secretary of State, is hereby authorized to impose on a foreign person the measures described in subsection (b) of this section upon determining that the foreign person:

(i) has violated, attempted to violate, conspired to violate, or caused a violation of any license, order, regulation, or prohibition contained in, or issued pursuant to:

(A) any Executive Order relating to the national emergencies declared in Executive Order 12957 of March 15, 1995, or in Executive Order 13338 of May 11, 2004, as modified in scope in subsequent Executive Orders; or

(B) to the extent such conduct relates to property and interests in property of any person subject to United States sanctions concerning Iran or Syria, Executive Order 13382 of June 28, 2005, any Executive Order subsequent to Executive Order 13382 of June 28, 2005, that relates to the national emergency declared in Executive Order 12938 of November 14, 1994, or any Executive Order relating to the national emergency declared in Executive Order 13224 of September 23, 2001;

(ii) has facilitated deceptive transactions for or on behalf of any person subject to United States sanctions concerning Iran or Syria; or

(iii) is owned or controlled by, or is acting or purporting to act for or on behalf of, directly or indirectly, any person determined to meet the criteria set forth in subsection (a) of this section.

(b) With respect to any foreign person determined to meet the criteria set forth in subsection (a) of this section, the Secretary of the Treasury may prohibit all transactions or dealings, whether direct or indirect, involving such person, including any exporting, reexporting, importing, selling, purchasing, transporting, swapping, brokering, approving, financing, facilitating, or guaranteeing, in or related to (i) any goods, services, or technology in or intended for the United States, or (ii) any goods, services, or technology provided by or to United States persons, wherever located.

(c) The prohibitions in subsection (b) of this section apply except to the extent provided by statutes, or in regulations, orders, directives, or licenses that may be issued pursuant to this order, and notwithstanding any contract entered into or any license or permit granted prior to the date of this order.

Sec. 2. I hereby determine that the making of donations of the type of articles specified in section 203(b)(2) of IEEPA (50 U.S.C. 1702(b)(2)) by, to, or for the benefit of any person subject to the measures described in section 1 of this order would seriously impair my ability to deal with the national emergencies identified in the preamble to this order, and I hereby prohibit such donations as provided by section 1 of this order.

Sec. 3. The prohibitions in section 1 of this order include but are not limited to:

(a) the making of any contribution or provision of funds, goods, or services by, to, or for the benefit of any person subject to the measures described in this order; and

(b) the receipt of any contribution or provision of funds, goods, or services from any such person.

Sec. 4. I hereby find that the unrestricted immigrant and nonimmigrant entry into the United States of aliens determined to meet one or more of the criteria in subsection 1(a) of this order would be detrimental to the interests of the United States, and I hereby suspend the entry into the United States, as immigrants or nonimmigrants, of such persons. Such persons shall be treated as persons covered by section 1 of Proclamation 8693 of July 24, 2011 (Suspension of Entry of Aliens Subject to United Nations Security Council Travel Bans and International Emergency Economic Powers Act Sanctions).

Sec. 5. (a) Any transaction by a United States person or within the United States that evades or avoids, has the purpose of evading or avoiding, causes a violation of, or attempts to violate any of the prohibitions set forth in this order is prohibited.

(b) Any conspiracy formed to violate any of the prohibitions set forth in this order is prohibited.

Sec. 6. Nothing in section 1 of this order shall prohibit transactions for the conduct of the official business of the United States Government by employees, grantees, or contractors thereof.

Sec. 7. For the purposes of this order:

(a) the term "person" means an individual or entity;

(b) the term "entity" means a partnership, association, trust, joint venture, corporation, group, subgroup, or other organization;

(c) the term "United States person" means any United States citizen, permanent resident alien, entity organized under the laws of the United States or any jurisdiction within the United States (including foreign branches), or any person in the United States;

(d) the term "deceptive transaction" means any transaction where the identity of any person subject to United States sanctions concerning Iran or Syria is withheld or obscured from other participants in the transaction or any relevant regulatory authorities;

(e) the term "person subject to United States sanctions concerning Iran or Syria" means (i) any person, including the Government of Iran or the Government of Syria, with whom transactions are restricted pursuant to any Executive Order relating to the national emergencies declared in Executive Order 12957 of March 15, 1995, or in Executive Order 13338 of May 11, 2004, as modified in scope in subsequent Executive Orders, or (ii) any person whose property and interests in property are blocked pursuant to IEEPA in connection with Iran's or Syria's proliferation of weapons of mass destruction or delivery systems for weapons of mass destruction, or Iran's or Syria's support for international terrorism;

(f) the term "Government of Iran" means the Government of Iran, any political subdivision, agency, or instrumentality thereof, including the Central Bank of Iran, and any person owned or controlled by, or acting for or on behalf of, the Government of Iran; and

(g) the term "Government of Syria" means the Government of the Syrian Arab Republic, its agencies, instrumentalities, and controlled entities.

Sec. 8. For those persons subject to the measures described in section 1 of this order who might have a constitutional presence in the United States, I find that because of the ability to transfer funds or other assets instantaneously, prior notice to such persons of measures to be taken pursuant to this order would render those measures ineffectual. I therefore determine that for these measures to be effective in addressing the national emergencies identified in the preamble to this order, there need be no prior notice of a listing or determination made pursuant to section 1 of this order.

Sec. 9. The Secretary of the Treasury, in consultation with the Secretary of State, is hereby authorized to take such actions, including the promulgation of rules and regulations, and to employ all powers granted to the President by IEEPA, as may be necessary to carry out the purposes of this order. The Secretary of the Treasury may redelegate any of these functions to other officers and agencies of the United States Government consistent with applicable law. All agencies of the United States Government are hereby directed to take all appropriate measures within their authority to carry out the provisions of this order.

Sec. 10. This order is not intended to, and does not, create any right or benefit, substantive or procedural, enforceable at law or in equity by any party against the United States, its departments, agencies, or entities, its officers, employees, or agents, or any other person.

Sec. 11. The measures taken pursuant to this order with respect to Iran are in response to actions of the Government of Iran occurring after the conclusion of the 1981 Algiers Accords, and are intended solely as a response to those later actions.

BARACK OBAMA

Executive Order 13611—Prohibiting Certain Transactions with and Suspending Entry into the United States of Foreign Sanctions Evaders with Respect to Iran and Syria

77 Fed. Reg. 26,409 (May 3, 2012)

By the authority vested in me as President by the Constitution and the laws of the United States of America, including the International Emergency Economic Powers Act (IEEPA), the National Emergencies Act (50U.S.C. 1601 *et seq.)* (NEA), and section 301 of title 3, United States Code,

I, BARACK OBAMA, President of the United States of America, find that the actions and policies of certain members of the Government of Yemen and others threaten Yemen's peace, security, and stability, including by obstructing the implementation of the agreement of November 23, 2011, between the Government of Yemen and those in opposition to it, which provides for a peaceful transition of power that meets the legitimate demands and aspirations of the Yemeni people for change, and by obstructing the political process in Yemen. I further find that these actions constitute an unusual and extraordinary threat to the national security and foreign policy of the United States, and I hereby declare a national emergency to deal with that threat. I hereby order:

Section 1. All property and interests in property that are in the United States, that hereafter come within the United States, or that are or hereafter come within the possession or control of any United States person, including any foreign branch, of the following persons are blocked and may not be transferred, paid, exported, withdrawn, or otherwise dealt in: any person determined by the Secretary of the Treasury, in consultation with the Secretary of State, to:

(a) have engaged in acts that directly or indirectly threaten the peace, security, or stability of Yemen, such as acts that obstruct the implementation of the agreement of November 23, 2011, between the Government of Yemen and those in opposition to it, which provides for a peaceful transition of power in Yemen, or that obstruct the political process in Yemen;

(b) be a political or military leader of an entity that has engaged in the acts described in subsection (a) of this section;

(c) have materially assisted, sponsored, or provided financial, material, or technological support for, or goods or services to or in support of, the acts described in subsection (a) of this section or any person whose property and interests in property are blocked pursuant to this order; or

(d) be owned or controlled by, or to have acted or purported to act for or on behalf of, directly or indirectly, any person whose property and interests in property are blocked pursuant to this order.

Sec. 2. I hereby determine that the making of donations of the type of articles specified in section 203(b)(2) of IEEPA by, to, or for the benefit of any person whose property and interests in property are blocked pursuant to section 1 of this order would seriously impair my ability to deal with the national emergency declared in this order, and I hereby prohibit such donations as provided by section 1 of this order.

Sec. 3. The prohibitions in section 1 of this order include but are not limited to:
(a) the making of any contribution or provision of funds, goods, or services by, to, or for the benefit of any person whose property and interests in property are blocked pursuant to this order; and
(b) the receipt of any contribution or provision of funds, goods, or services from any such person.

Sec. 4. The prohibitions in section 1 of this order apply except to the extent provided by statutes, or in regulations, orders, directives, or licenses that may be issued pursuant to this order, and notwithstanding any contract entered into or any license or permit granted prior to the effective date of this order.

Sec. 5. Nothing in section 1 of this order shall prohibit transactions for the conduct of the official business of the United States Government by employees, grantees, or contractors thereof.

Sec. 6. (a) Any transaction that evades or avoids, has the purpose of evading or avoiding, causes a violation of, or attempts to violate any of the prohibitions set forth in this order is prohibited.
(b) Any conspiracy formed to violate any of the prohibitions set forth in this order is prohibited.

Sec. 7. For the purposes of this order:

(a) the term "person" means an individual or entity;

(b) the term "entity" means a partnership, association, trust, joint venture, corporation, group, subgroup, or other organization; and

(c) the term "United States person" means any United States citizen,permanent resident alien, entity organized under the laws of the United States or anyjurisdiction within the United States (including foreign branches), or any person in theUnited States.

Sec. 8. For those persons whose property and interests in propertyare blocked pursuant to this order who might have a constitutional presence in the UnitedStates, I find that because of the ability to transfer funds or other assets instantaneously,prior notice to such persons of measures to be taken pursuant to this order would renderthose measures ineffectual. I therefore determine that for these measures to be effective inaddressing the national emergency declared in this order, there need be no prior notice ofa listing or determination made pursuant to section 1 of this order.

Sec. 9. The Secretary of the Treasury, in consultation with theSecretary of State, is hereby authorized to take such actions, including the promulgationof rules and regulations, and to employ all powers granted to the President by IEEPA asmay be necessary to carry out the purposes of this order. The Secretary of the Treasurymay redelegate any of these functions to other officers and agencies of the United StatesGovernment consistent with applicable law. All agencies of the United StatesGovernment are hereby directed to take all appropriate measures within their authority tocarry out the provisions of this order.

Sec. 10. The Secretary of the Treasury, in consultation with theSecretary of State, is hereby authorized to submit the recurring and final reports to theCongress on the national emergency declared in this order, consistent with section 401(c)of the NEA and section 204(c) of IEEPA.

Sec. 11. This order is not intended to, and does not, create any rightor benefit, substantive or procedural, enforceable at law or in equity by any party againstthe United States, its departments, agencies, or entities, its officers, employees, or agents,or any other person.

BARACK OBAMA

Executive Order 13617—Blocking Property of the Government of the Russian Federation Relating to the Disposition of Highly Enriched Uranium Extracted from Nuclear Weapons

77 Fed. Reg. 38,459 (June 27, 2012)

By the authority vested in me as President by the Constitution and the laws of the United States of America, including the International Emergency Economic Powers Act (IEEPA), the National Emergencies Act (NEA), and section 301 of title 3, United States Code,

I, BARACK OBAMA, President of the United States of America, in view of the policies underlying of November 14, 1994, and of May 26, 1998, and the restrictions put in place pursuant to of June 21, 2000, find that the risk of nuclear proliferation created by the accumulation of a large volume of weapons-usable fissile material in the territory of the Russian Federation continues to constitute an unusual and extraordinary threat to the national security and foreign policy of the United States, and hereby declare a national emergency to deal with that threat. I hereby order:

Section 1. A major national security goal of the United States is to ensure that fissile material removed from Russian nuclear weapons pursuant to various arms control and disarmament agreements is dedicated to peaceful uses, subject to transparency measures, and protected from diversion to activities of proliferation concern. As reflected in the full implementation of the Agreement Between the Government of the United States of America and the Government of the Russian Federation Concerning the Disposition of Highly Enriched Uranium Extracted from Nuclear Weapons, dated February 18, 1993, and related contracts and agreements (collectively, the "HEU Agreements") is essential to the attainment of this goal. The HEU Agreements provide for the conversion of approximately 500 metric tons of highly enriched uranium contained in Russian nuclear weapons into low-enriched uranium for use as fuel in commercial nuclear reactors. In furtherance of our national security goals, all heads of departments and agencies of the United States Government shall continue to take all appropriate measures within their authority to further the full implementation of the HEU Agreements.

Sec. 2. Government of the Russian Federation assets directly related to the implementation of the HEU Agreements currently may be subject to attachment, judgment, decree, lien, execution, garnishment, or other judicial process, thereby jeopardizing the full implementation of the HEU Agreements to the detriment of U.S. foreign policy. In order to ensure the preservation and proper and complete transfer to the Government of the Russian Federation of all payments due to it under the HEU Agreements, and except to the extent provided in regulations, orders, directives, or licenses that may be issued pursuant to this order, or that were issued pursuant to of June 21, 2000, all property and interests in property of the Government of the Russian Federation directly related to the implementation of the HEU Agreements that are in the United States, that hereafter come within the United States, or that are or hereafter come within the possession or control of any United States persons, including any foreign branch, are blocked and may not be transferred, paid, exported, withdrawn, or otherwise dealt in. Unless licensed or authorized pursuant to this order, or of June 21, 2000, any attachment, judgment, decree, lien, execution, garnishment, or other judicial process is null and void with respect to any property or interest in property blocked pursuant to this order.

Sec. 3. (a) Any transaction that evades or avoids, has the purpose of evading or avoiding, causes a violation of, or attempts to violate any of the prohibitions set forth in this order is prohibited.
(b) Any conspiracy formed to violate any of the prohibitions set forth in this order is prohibited.

Sec. 4. For the purposes of this order:

(a) the term "person" means an individual or entity;

(b) the term "entity" means a partnership, association, trust, joint venture, corporation, group, subgroup, or other organization;

(c) the term "United States person" means any United States citizen, permanent resident alien, entity organized under the laws of the United States or any jurisdiction within the United States (including foreign branches), or any person in the United States; and

(d) the term "Government of the Russian Federation" means the Government of the Russian Federation, any political subdivision, agency, or instrumentality thereof, and any person owned or controlled by, or acting for or on behalf of, the Government of the Russian Federation.

Sec. 5. (a) The Secretary of the Treasury, in consultation with the Secretary of State, the Secretary of Energy, and, as appropriate, other agencies, is hereby authorized to take such actions, including the promulgation of rules and regulations, and to employ all powers granted to the President by IEEPA, as may be necessary to carry out the purposes of this order. The Secretary of the Treasury may redelegate any of these functions to other officers and agencies of the United States Government consistent with applicable law. All agencies of the United States Government are hereby directed to take all appropriate measures within their statutory authority to carry out the provisions of this order.
(b) Nothing contained in this order shall relieve a person from any requirement to obtain a license or other authorization from any department or agency of the United States Government in compliance with applicable laws and regulations subject to the jurisdiction of the department or agency.

Sec. 6. The Secretary of the Treasury, in consultation with the Secretary of State, is hereby authorized to submit the recurring and final reports to the Congress on the national emergency declared in this order, consistent with section 401(c) of the NEA and section 204(c) of IEEPA Sec. 7. This order is not intended to, and does not, create any right or benefit, substantive or procedural, enforceable at law or in equity by any party against the United States, its departments, agencies, or entities, its officers, employees, or agents, or any other person.

BARACK OBAMA

Executive Order 13618—Assignment of National Security and Emergency Preparedness Communications Functions

77 Fed. Reg. 40779 (July 11, 2012)

By the authority vested in me as President by the Constitution and the laws of the United States of America, it is hereby ordered as follows:

Section 1. *Policy.* The Federal Government must have the ability to communicate at all times and under all circumstances to carry out its most critical and time sensitive missions. Survivable, resilient, enduring, and effective communications, both domestic and international, are essential to enable the executive branch to communicate within itself and with: the legislative and judicial branches; State, local, territorial, and tribal governments; private sector entities; and the public, allies, and other nations. Such communications must be possible under all circumstances to ensure national security, effectively manage emergencies, and improve national resilience. The views of all levels of government, the private and nonprofit sectors, and the public must inform the development of national security and emergency preparedness (NS/EP) communications policies, programs, and capabilities.

Sec. 2. *Executive Office Responsibilities.*

Sec. 2.1. Policy coordination, guidance, dispute resolution, and periodic in-progress reviews for the functions described and assigned herein shall be provided through the interagency process established in Presidential Policy Directive-1 of February 13, 2009 (Organization of the National Security Council System) (PPD-1).

Sec. 2.2. The Director of the Office of Science and Technology Policy (OSTP) shall: (a) issue an annual memorandum to the NS/EP Communications Executive Committee (established in section 3 of this order) highlighting national priorities for Executive Committee analyses, studies, research, and development regarding NS/EP communications;

(b) advise the President on the prioritization of radio spectrum and wired communications that support NS/EP functions; and

(c) have access to all appropriate information related to the test, exercise, evaluation, and readiness of the capabilities of all existing and planned NS/EP communications systems, networks, and facilities to meet all executive branch NS/EP requirements.

Sec. 2.3. The Assistant to the President for Homeland Security and Counterterrorism and the Director of OSTP shall make recommendations to the President, informed by the interagency policy process established in PPD-1, with respect to the exercise of authorities assigned to the President under section 706 of the Communications Act of 1934, as amended. The Assistant to the President for Homeland Security and Counterterrorism and the Director of OSTP shall also jointly monitor the exercise of these authorities, in the event of any delegation, through the process established in PPD-1 or as the President otherwise may direct.

Sec. 3. *The NS/EP Communications Executive Committee.*

Sec. 3.1. There is established an NS/EP Communications Executive Committee (Executive Committee) to serve as a forum to address NS/EP communications matters.

Sec. 3.2. The Executive Committee shall be composed of Assistant Secretary-level or equivalent representatives designated by the heads of the Departments of State, Defense, Justice, Commerce, and Homeland Security, the Office of the Director of National Intelligence (DNI), the General Services Administration, and the Federal Communications Commission, as well as such additional agencies as the Executive Committee may designate. The designees of the Secretary of Homeland Security and the Secretary of Defense shall serve as Co-Chairs of the Executive Committee.

Sec. 3.3. The responsibilities of the Executive Committee shall be to:

(a) advise and make policy recommendations to the President, through the PPD-1 process, on enhancing the survivability, resilience, and future architecture of NS/EP communications, including what should constitute NS/EP communications requirements;

(b) develop a long-term strategic vision for NS/EP communications and propose funding requirements and plans to the President and the Director of the Office of Management and Budget (OMB), through the PPD-1 process, for NS/EP communications initiatives that benefit multiple agencies or other Federal entities;

(c) coordinate the planning for, and provision of, NS/EP communications for the Federal Government under all hazards;

(d) promote the incorporation of the optimal combination of hardness, redundancy, mobility, connectivity, interoperability, restorability, and security to obtain, to the maximum extent practicable, the survivability of NS/EP communications under all circumstances;

(e) recommend to the President, through the PPD-1 process, the regimes to test, exercise, and evaluate the capabilities of existing and planned communications systems, networks, or facilities to meet all executive branch NS/EP communications requirements, including any recommended remedial actions;

(f) provide quarterly updates to the Assistant to the President for Homeland Security and Counterterrorism and the Director of OSTP, through the Co-Chairs, on the status of Executive Committee activities and develop an annual NS/EP communications strategic agenda utilizing the PPD-1 process;

(g) enable industry input with respect to the responsibilities established in this section; and

(h) develop, approve, and maintain a charter for the Executive Committee.

Sec. 4. *Executive Committee Joint Program Office.*

Sec. 4.1. The Secretary of Homeland Security shall establish an Executive Committee Joint Program Office (JPO) to provide full-time, expert, and administrative support for the Executive Committee's performance of its responsibilities under section 3.3 of this order. Staff of the JPO shall include detailees, as needed and appropriate, from agencies represented on the Executive Committee. The Department of Homeland Security shall provide resources to support the JPO. The JPO shall be responsive to the guidance of the Executive Committee.

Sec. 4.2. The responsibilities of the JPO shall include: coordination of programs that support NS/EP missions, priorities, goals, and policy; and, when directed by the Executive Committee, the convening of governmental and nongovernmental groups (consistent with the Federal Advisory Committees Act, as amended (5 U.S.C. App.)), coordination of activities, and development of policies for senior official review and approval.

Sec. 5. *Specific Department and Agency Responsibilities.*

Sec. 5.1. The Secretary of Defense shall:

(a) oversee the development, testing, implementation, and sustainment of NS/EP communications that are directly responsive to the national security needs of the President, Vice President, and senior national leadership, including: communications with or among the President, Vice President, White House staff, heads of state and government, and Nuclear Command and Control leadership; Continuity of Government communications; and communications among the executive, judicial, and legislative branches to support Enduring Constitutional Government;

(b) incorporate, integrate, and ensure interoperability and the optimal combination of hardness, redundancy, mobility, connectivity, interoperability, restorability, and security to obtain, to the maximum extent practicable, the survivability of NS/EP communications defined in section 5.1(a) of this order under all circumstances, including conditions of crisis or emergency;

(c) provide to the Executive Committee the technical support necessary to develop and maintain plans adequate to provide for the security and protection of NS/EP communications; and

(d) provide, operate, and maintain communication services and facilities adequate to execute responsibilities consistent with Executive Order 12333 of December 4, 1981, as amended.

Sec. 5.2. The Secretary of Homeland Security shall:

(a) oversee the development, testing, implementation, and sustainment of NS/EP communications, including: communications that support Continuity of Government; Federal, State, local, territorial, and tribal emergency preparedness and response communications; non-military executive branch communications systems; critical infrastructure protection networks; and non-military communications networks, particularly with respect to prioritization and restoration;

(b) incorporate, integrate, and ensure interoperability and the necessary combination of hardness, redundancy, mobility, connectivity, interoperability, restorability, and security to obtain, to the maximum extent practicable, the survivability of NS/EP communications defined in section 5.2(a) of this order under all circumstances, including conditions of crisis or emergency;

(c) provide to the Executive Committee the technical support necessary to develop and maintain plans adequate to provide for the security and protection of NS/EP communications;

(d) receive, integrate, and disseminate NS/EP communications information to the Federal Government and State, local, territorial, and tribal governments, as appropriate, to establish situational awareness, priority setting recommendations, and a common operating picture for NS/EP communications information;

(e) satisfy priority communications requirements through the use of commercial, Government, and privately owned communications resources, when appropriate;

(f) maintain a joint industry-Government center that is capable of assisting in the initiation, coordination, restoration, and reconstitution of NS/EP communications services or facilities under all conditions of emerging threats, crisis, or emergency;

(g) serve as the Federal lead for the prioritized restoration of communications infrastructure and coordinate the prioritization and restoration of communications, including resolution of any conflicts in or among priorities, in coordination with the Secretary of Defense when activities referenced in section 5.1(a) of this order are impacted, consistent with the National Response Framework. If conflicts in or among priorities cannot be resolved between the Departments of Defense and Homeland Security, they shall be referred for resolution in accordance with section 2.1 of this order; and

(h) within 60 days of the date of this order, in consultation with the Executive Committee where appropriate, develop and submit to the President, through the Assistant to the President for Homeland Security and Counterterrorism, a detailed plan that describes the Department of Homeland Security's organization and management structure for its NS/EP communications functions, including the Government Emergency Telecommunications Service, Wireless Priority Service, Telecommunications Service Priority program, Next Generation Network Priority program, the Executive Committee JPO, and relevant supporting entities.

Sec. 5.3. The Secretary of Commerce shall:

(a) provide advice and guidance to the Executive Committee on the use of technical standards and metrics to support execution of NS/EP communications;

(b) identify for the Executive Committee requirements for additional technical standards and metrics to enhance NS/EP communications;
(c) engage with relevant standards development organizations to develop appropriate technical standards and metrics to enhance NS/EP communications;
(d) develop plans and procedures concerning radio spectrum allocations, assignments, and priorities for use by agencies and executive offices;
(e) develop, maintain, and publish policies, plans, and procedures for the management and use of radio frequency assignments, including the authority to amend, modify, or revoke such assignments, in those parts of the electromagnetic spectrum assigned to the Federal Government; and
(f) administer a system of radio spectrum priorities for those spectrum-dependent telecommunications resources belonging to and operated by the Federal Government and certify or approve such radio spectrum priorities, including the resolution of conflicts in or among such radio spectrum priorities during a crisis or emergency.

Sec. 5.4. The Administrator of General Services shall provide and maintain a common Federal acquisition approach that allows for the efficient centralized purchasing of equipment and services that meet NS/EP communications requirements. Nothing in this section shall be construed to impair or otherwise affect the procurement authorities granted by law to an agency or the head thereof.

Sec. 5.5. With respect to the Intelligence Community, the DNI, after consultation with the heads of affected agencies, may issue such policy directives and guidance as the DNI deems necessary to implement this order. Procedures or other guidance issued by the heads of elements of the Intelligence Community shall be in accordance with such policy directives or guidelines issued by the DNI.

Sec. 5.6. The Federal Communications Commission performs such functions as are required by law, including:

(a) with respect to all entities licensed or regulated by the Federal Communications Commission: the extension, discontinuance, or reduction of common carrier facilities or services; the control of common carrier rates, charges, practices, and classifications; the construction, authorization, activation, deactivation, or closing of radio stations, services, and facilities; the assignment of radio frequencies to Federal Communications Commission licensees; the investigation of violations of pertinent law; and the assessment of communications service provider emergency needs and resources; and
(b) supporting the continuous operation and restoration of critical communications systems and services by assisting the Secretary of Homeland Security with infrastructure damage assessment and restoration, and by providing the Secretary of Homeland Security with information collected by the Federal Communications Commission on communications infrastructure, service outages, and restoration, as appropriate.

Sec. 6. *General Agency Responsibilities.* All agencies, to the extent consistent with law, shall:

(a) determine the scope of their NS/EP communications requirements, and provide information regarding such requirements to the Executive Committee;

(b) prepare policies, plans, and procedures concerning communications facilities, services, or equipment under their management or operational control to maximize their capability to respond to the NS/EP needs of the Federal Government;

(c) propose initiatives, where possible, that may benefit multiple agencies or other Federal entities;

(d) administer programs that support broad NS/EP communications goals and policies;

(e) submit reports annually, or as otherwise requested, to the Executive Committee, regarding agency NS/EP communications activities;

(f) devise internal acquisition strategies in support of the centralized acquisition approach provided by the General Services Administration pursuant to section 5.4 of this order; and

(g) provide the Secretary of Homeland Security with timely reporting on NS/EP communications status to inform the common operating picture required under (d).

Sec. 7. *General Provisions.*

(a) For the purposes of this order, the word "agency" shall have the meaning set forth in section 6.1(b) of December 29, 2009.

(b) Executive Order 12472 of April 3, 1984, as amended, is hereby revoked.

(c) Executive Order 12382 of September 13, 1982, as amended, is further amended by striking the following language from section 2(e): "in his capacity as Executive Agent for the National Communications System".

(d) Nothing in this order shall be construed to impair or otherwise affect:

(i) the authority granted by law to an agency, or the head thereof; or

(ii) the functions of the Director of the OMB relating to budgetary, administrative, or legislative proposals.

(e) This order shall be implemented consistent with applicable law and subject to the availability of appropriations.

(f) This order is not intended to, and does not, create any right or benefit, substantive or procedural, enforceable at law or in equity by any party against the United States, its departments, agencies, or entities, its officers, employees, or agents, or any other person.

BARACK OBAMA

Executive Order 13622—Authorizing Additional Sanctions with Respect to Iran

77 Fed. Reg. 45,897 (Aug. 2, 2012)

By the authority vested in me as President by the Constitution and the laws of the United States of America, including the International Emergency Economic Powers Act (IEEPA), the National Emergencies Act, and section 301 of title 3, United States Code,

I, BARACK OBAMA, President of the United States of America, in order to take additional steps with respect to the national emergency declared in of March 15, 1995, as relied upon for additional steps in subsequent Executive Orders, particularly in light of the Government of Iran's use of revenues from petroleum, petroleum products, and petrochemicals for illicit purposes, Iran's continued attempts to evade international sanctions through deceptive practices, and the unacceptable risk posed to the international financial system by Iran's activities, hereby order:

Section 1. (a) The Secretary of the Treasury, in consultation with the Secretary of State, is hereby authorized to impose on a foreign financial institution the sanctions described in subsection (b) of this section upon determining that the foreign financial institution has knowingly conducted or facilitated any significant financial transaction:

(i) with the National Iranian Oil Company (NIOC) or Naftiran Intertrade Company (NICO), except for a sale or provision to NIOC or NICO of the products described in section 5(a)(3)(A)(i) of the Iran Sanctions Act of 1996, as amended, provided that the fair market value of such products is lower than the applicable dollar threshold specified in that provision;

(ii) for the purchase or acquisition of petroleum or petroleum products from Iran; or

(iii) for the purchase or acquisition of petrochemical products from Iran.

(b) With respect to any foreign financial institution determined by the Secretary of the Treasury in accordance with this section to meet the criteria set forth in subsection (a)(i), (a)(ii), or (a)(iii) of this section, the Secretary of the Treasury may prohibit the opening, and prohibit or impose strict conditions on the maintaining, in the United States of a correspondent account or a payable-through account by such foreign financial institution.

(c) Subsections (a)(i) and (ii) of this section shall apply with respect to a significant financial transaction conducted or facilitated by a foreign financial institution only if:

(i) the President determines under subparagraphs (4)(B) and (C) of subsection 1245(d) of the National Defense Authorization Act for Fiscal Year 2012 (NDAA) that there is a sufficient supply of petroleum and petroleum products from countries other than Iran to permit a significant reduction in the volume of petroleum and petroleum products purchased from Iran by or through foreign financial institutions; and

(ii) an exception under subparagraph 4(D) of subsection 1245(d) of the NDAA from the imposition of sanctions under paragraph (1) of that subsection does not apply with respect to the country with primary jurisdiction over the foreign financial institution.

(d) Subsection (a) of this section shall not apply with respect to any person for conducting or facilitating a transaction for the sale of food, medicine, or medical devices to Iran or when the underlying transaction has been authorized by the Secretary of the Treasury.

(e) The prohibitions in subsection (b) of this section apply except to the extent provided by statutes, or in regulations, orders, directives, or licenses that may be issued pursuant to this order, and notwithstanding any contract entered into or any license or permit granted prior to the effective date of this order.

Sec. 2. (a) The Secretary of State, in consultation with the Secretary of the Treasury, the Secretary of Commerce, and the United States Trade Representative, and with the President of the Export-Import Bank, the Chairman of the Board of Governors of the Federal Reserve System, and other agencies and officials as appropriate, is hereby authorized to impose on a person any of the sanctions described in section 3 or 4 of this order upon determining that the person:

(i) knowingly, on or after the effective date of this order, engaged in a significant transaction for the purchase or acquisition of petroleum or petroleum products from Iran;

(ii) knowingly, on or after the effective date of this order, engaged in a significant transaction for the purchase or acquisition of petrochemical products from Iran;

(iii) is a successor entity to a person determined by the Secretary of State in accordance with this subsection to meet the criteria in subsection (a)(i) or (a)(ii) of this section;

(iv) owns or controls a person determined by the Secretary of State in accordance with this subsection to meet the criteria in subsection (a)(i) or (a)(ii) of this section, and had knowledge that the person engaged in the activities referred to in that subsection; or

(v) is owned or controlled by, or under common ownership or control with, a person determined by the Secretary of State in accordance with this subsection to meet the criteria in subsection (a)(i) or (a)(ii) of this section, and knowingly participated in the activities referred to in that subsection.

(b) Subsection (a)(i) of this section shall apply with respect to a person only if:

(i) the President determines under subparagraphs (4)(B) and (C) of subsection 1245(d) of the NDAA that there is a sufficient supply of petroleum and petroleum products from countries other than Iran to permit a significant re-

duction in the volume of petroleum and petroleum products purchased from Iran by or through foreign financial institutions; and
(ii) an exception under subparagraph 4(D) of subsection 1245(d) of the NDAA from the imposition of sanctions under paragraph (1) of that subsection does not apply with respect to the country with primary jurisdiction over the person.

Sec. 3. When the Secretary of State, in accordance with the terms of section 2 of this order, has determined that a person meets any of the criteria described in section 2 and has selected any of the sanctions set forth below to impose on that person, the heads of relevant agencies, in consultation with the Secretary of State, shall take the following actions where necessary to implement the sanctions imposed by the Secretary of State:
(a) the Board of Directors of the Export-Import Bank shall deny approval of the issuance of any guarantee, insurance, extension of credit, or participation in an extension of credit in connection with the export of any goods or services to the sanctioned person;
(b) agencies shall not issue any specific license or grant any other specific permission or authority under any statute that requires the prior review and approval of the United States Government as a condition for the export or reexport of goods or technology to the sanctioned person;
(c) with respect to a sanctioned person that is a financial institution:
(i) the Chairman of the Board of Governors of the Federal Reserve System and the President of the Federal Reserve Bank of New York shall take such actions as they deem appropriate, including denying designation, or terminating the continuation of any prior designation of, the sanctioned person as a primary dealer in United States Government debt instruments; or
(ii) agencies shall prevent the sanctioned person from serving as an agent of the United States Government or serving as a repository for United States Government funds; or
(d) agencies shall not procure, or enter into a contract for the procurement of, any goods or services from the sanctioned person.
(e) The prohibitions in subsections (a)-(d) of this section apply except to the extent provided by statutes, or in regulations, orders, directives, or licenses that may be issued pursuant to this order, and notwithstanding any contract entered into or any license or permit granted prior to the effective date of this order.

Sec. 4. (a) When the Secretary of State, in accordance with the terms of section 2 of this order, has determined that a person meets any of the criteria described in section 2 and has selected any of the sanctions set forth below to impose on that person, the Secretary of the Treasury, in consultation with the Secretary of State, shall take the following actions where necessary to implement the sanctions imposed by the Secretary of State:
(i) prohibit any United States financial institution from making loans or providing credits to the sanctioned person totaling more than $10,000,000 in any 12-month period, unless such person is engaged in activities to relieve human

suffering and the loans or credits are provided for such activities;
(ii) prohibit any transactions in foreign exchange that are subject to the jurisdiction of the United States and in which the sanctioned person has any interest;
(iii) prohibit any transfers of credit or payments between financial institutions or by, through, or to any financial institution, to the extent that such transfers or payments are subject to the jurisdiction of the United States and involve any interest of the sanctioned person;
(iv) block all property and interests in property that are in the United States, that come within the United States, or that are or come within the possession or control of any United States person, including any foreign branch, of the sanctioned person, and provide that such property and interests in property may not be transferred, paid, exported, withdrawn, or otherwise dealt in; or
(v) restrict or prohibit imports of goods, technology, or services, directly or indirectly, into the United States from the sanctioned person.

(b) The prohibitions in subsections (a)(i)-(a)(v) of this section apply except to the extent provided by statutes, or in regulations, orders, directives, or licenses that may be issued pursuant to this order, and notwithstanding any contract entered into or any license or permit granted prior to the effective date of this order.

Sec. 5. (a) The Secretary of the Treasury, in consultation with the Secretary of State, is hereby authorized to impose on a person the measures described in subsection (b) of this section upon determining that the person has materially assisted, sponsored, or provided financial, material, or technological support for, or goods or services in support of, NIOC, NICO, or the Central Bank of Iran, or the purchase or acquisition of U.S. bank notes or precious metals by the Government of Iran.

(b) With respect to any person determined by the Secretary of the Treasury in accordance with subsection (a) to meet the criteria set forth in subsection (a) of this section, all property and interests in property that are in the United States, that hereafter come within the United States, or that are or hereafter come within the possession or control of any United States person, including any foreign branch, of such person are blocked and may not be transferred, paid, exported, withdrawn, or otherwise dealt in.

(c) The prohibitions in subsection (b) of this section apply except to the extent provided by statutes, or in regulations, orders, directives, or licenses that may be issued pursuant to this order, and notwithstanding any contract entered into or any license or permit granted prior to the effective date of this order.

Sec. 6. Subsection 1(a), section 2, and subsection 5(a) of this order shall not apply with respect to any person for conducting or facilitating a transaction involving a natural gas development and pipeline project initiated prior to the effective date of this order to bring gas from Azerbaijan to Europe and Turkey in furtherance of a production sharing agreement or license awarded by a sovereign government other than the Government of Iran before the effective date of this order.

Sec. 7. I hereby determine that, to the extent section 203(b)(2) of IEEPA may apply, the making of donations of the type of articles specified in such section by, to, or for the benefit of any person whose property and interests in property are blocked pursuant to subsection (a)(iv) of section 4 or subsection (b) of section 5 of this order would seriously impair my ability to deal with the national emergency declared in and I hereby prohibit such donations as provided by subsection (a)(iv) of section 4 and subsection (b) of section 5 of this order.

Sec. 8. The prohibitions in subsection (a)(iv) of section 4 and subsection (b) of section 5 of this order include, but are not limited to:

(i) the making of any contribution or provision of funds, goods, or services by, to, or for the benefit of any person whose property and interests in property are blocked pursuant to this order; and

(ii) the receipt of any contribution or provision of funds, goods, or services from any such person.

Sec. 9. (a) Any transaction that evades or avoids, has the purpose of evading or avoiding, causes a violation of, or attempts to violate any of the prohibitions set forth in this order is prohibited.

(b) Any conspiracy formed to violate any of the prohibitions set forth in this order is prohibited.

Sec. 10. For the purposes of this order:

(a) the term "person" means an individual or entity;

(b) the term "entity" means a partnership, association, trust, joint venture, corporation, group, subgroup, or other organization;

(c) the term "United States person" means any United States citizen, permanent resident alien, entity organized under the laws of the United States or any jurisdiction within the United States (including foreign branches), or any person in the United States;

(d) the term "financial institution," as used in sections 3 and 4 of this order, includes (i) a depository institution (as defined in section 3(c)(1) of the Federal Deposit Insurance Act), including a branch or agency of a foreign bank (as defined in section 1(b)(7) of the International Banking Act of 1978); (ii) a credit union; (iii) a securities firm, including a broker or dealer; (iv) an insurance company, including an agency or underwriter; and (v) any other company that provides financial services;

(e) the term "foreign financial institution," as used in section 1 of this order, means any foreign entity that is engaged in the business of accepting deposits, making, granting, transferring, holding, or brokering loans or credits, or purchasing or selling foreign exchange, securities, commodity futures or options, or procuring purchasers and sellers thereof, as principal or agent. It includes, but is not limited to, depository institutions, banks, savings banks, money service businesses, trust companies, securities brokers and dealers, commodity futures and options brokers and dealers, forward contract and foreign exchange merchants, securities and commodities exchanges, clearing corporations, investment companies, employee benefit plans, and holding companies, affiliates, or subsidiaries of any of the foregoing. The term does not include the international financial institutions identified in the International Fund for Agricultural Development, the North American Development Bank, or any other international financial institution so notified by the Secretary of the Treasury;

(f) the term "United States financial institution" means a financial institution as defined in subsection (d) of this section (including its foreign branches) organized under the laws of the United States or any jurisdiction within the United States or located in the United States;

(g) the term "Iran" means the Government of Iran and the territory of Iran and any other territory or marine area, including the exclusive economic zone and continental shelf, over which the Government of Iran claims sovereignty, sovereign rights, or jurisdiction, provided that the Government of Iran exercises partial or total de facto control over the area or derives a benefit from economic activity in the area pursuant to international arrangements;

(h) the term "Government of Iran" includes the Government of Iran, any political subdivision, agency, or instrumentality thereof, including the Central Bank of Iran, and any person owned or controlled by, or acting for or on behalf of, the Government of Iran;

(i) the terms "knowledge" and "knowingly," with respect to conduct, a circumstance, or a result, mean that a person has actual knowledge, or should have known, of the conduct, the circumstance, or the result;

(j) the term "sanctioned person" means a person on whom the Secretary of State, in accordance with the terms of section 2 of this order, has determined to impose sanctions pursuant to section 2;

(k) the term "petroleum" (also known as crude oil) means a mixture of hydrocarbons that exists in liquid phase in natural underground reservoirs and remains liquid at atmospheric pressure after passing through surface separating facilities;

(l) the term "petroleum products" includes unfinished oils, liquefied petroleum gases, pentanes plus, aviation gasoline, motor gasoline, naphtha-type jet fuel, kerosene-type jet fuel, kerosene, distillate fuel oil, residual fuel oil, petrochemical feedstocks, special naphthas, lubricants, waxes, petroleum coke, asphalt, road oil, still gas, and miscellaneous products obtained from the processing of: crude oil (including lease condensate), natural gas, and other hydrocarbon compounds. The term does not include natural gas, liquefied natural gas, biofuels, methanol, and other non-petroleum fuels;

(m) the term "petrochemical products" includes any aromatic, olefin, and synthesis gas, and any of their derivatives, including ethylene, propylene, butadiene, benzene, toluene, xylene, ammonia, methanol, and urea;

(n) the terms "National Iranian Oil Company" and "NIOC" mean the National Iranian Oil Company and any entity owned or controlled by, or operating for or on behalf of, the National Iranian Oil Company; and

(o) the terms "Naftiran Intertrade Company" and "NICO" mean the Naftiran Intertrade Company and any entity owned or controlled by, or operating for or on behalf of, the Naftiran Intertrade Company.

Sec. 11. For those persons whose property and interests in property are blocked pursuant to this order who might have a constitutional presence in the United States, I find that because of the ability to transfer funds or other assets instantaneously, prior notice to such persons of measures to be taken pursuant to subsection (a)(iv) of section 4 or subsection (b) of section 5 of this order would render those measures ineffectual. I therefore determine that for these measures to be effective in addressing the national emergency declared in Executive Order 12957, there need be no prior notice of an action taken pursuant to subsection (a)(iv) of section 4 or subsection (b) of section 5 of this order.

Sec. 12. The Secretary of the Treasury, in consultation with the Secretary of State, is hereby authorized to take such actions, including the promulgation of rules and regulations, and to employ all powers granted to the President by IEEPA as may be necessary to carry out the purposes of sections 1, 4, and 5 of this order. The Secretary of the Treasury may redelegate any of these functions to other officers and agencies of the United States Government consistent with applicable law. All agencies of the United States Government are hereby directed to take all appropriate measures within their authority to carry out the provisions of this order.

Sec. 13. This order is not intended to, and does not, create any right or benefit, substantive or procedural, enforceable at law or in equity by any party against the United States, its departments, agencies, or entities, its officers, employees, or agents, or any other person.

Sec. 14. The measures taken pursuant to this order are in response to actions of the Government of Iran occurring after the conclusion of the 1981 Algiers Accords, and are intended solely as a response to those later actions.
Sec. 15. This order is effective at 12:01 a.m. eastern daylight time on July 31, 2012.

BARACK OBAMA

Executive Order 13628—Authorizing the Implementation of Certain Sanctions Set Forth in the Iran Threat Reduction and Syria Human Rights Act of 2012 and Additional Sanctions with Respect to Iran

77 Red. Reg. 62,139 (Oct. 12, 2012)

By the authority vested in me as President by the Constitution and the laws of the United States of America, including the International Emergency Economic Powers Act (IEEPA), the National Emergencies Act, the Iran Sanctions Act of 1996 , as amended (ISA), the Comprehensive Iran Sanctions, Accountability, and Divestment Act of 2010, as amended (CISADA), the Iran Threat Reduction and Syria Human Rights Act of 2012, section 212(f) of the Immigration and Nationality Act of 1952, as amended, and section 301 of title 3, United States Code, and in order to take additional steps with respect to the national emergency declared in Executive Order 12957 of March 15, 1995,

I, BARACK OBAMA, President of the United States of America, hereby order:

Section 1. (a) When the President, or the Secretary of State or the Secretary of the Treasury pursuant to authority delegated by the President and in accordance with the terms of such delegation, has determined that sanctions shall be imposed on a person pursuant to ISA, CISADA, or ITRSHRA and has, in accordance with those authorities, selected one or more of the sanctions set forth in section 6 of ISA to impose on that person, the Secretary of the Treasury, in consultation with the Secretary of State, shall take the following actions with respect to the sanctions selected and maintained by the President, the Secretary of State, or the Secretary of the Treasury:

(i) with respect to section 6(a)(3) of ISA, prohibit any United States financial institution from making loans or providing credits to the sanctioned person consistent with that section;

(ii) with respect to section 6(a)(6) of ISA, prohibit any transactions in foreign exchange that are subject to the jurisdiction of the United States and in which the sanctioned person has any interest;

(iii) with respect to section 6(a)(7) of ISA, prohibit any transfers of credit or payments between financial institutions or by, through, or to any financial institution, to the extent that such transfers or payments are subject to the jurisdiction of the United States and involve any interest of the sanctioned person;

(iv) with respect to section 6(a)(8) of ISA, block all property and interests in property that are in the United States, that come within the United States, or that are or come within the possession or control of any United States person, including any foreign branch, of the sanctioned person, and provide that such property and interests in property may not be transferred, paid, exported, withdrawn, or otherwise dealt in;

(v) with respect to section 6(a)(9) of ISA, prohibit any United States person from investing in or purchasing significant amounts of equity or debt instruments of a sanctioned person;

(vi) with respect to section 6(a)(11) of ISA, impose on the principal executive officer or officers, or persons performing similar functions and with similar authorities, of a sanctioned person the sanctions described in sections 6(a)(3), 6(a)(6), (6)(a)(7), 6(a)(8), 6(a)(9), or 6(a)(12) of ISA, as selected by the President, Secretary of State, or Secretary of the Treasury, as appropriate; or

(vii) with respect to section 6(a)(12) of ISA, restrict or prohibit imports of goods, technology, or services, directly or indirectly, into the United States from the sanctioned person.

(b) The prohibitions in subsection (a) of this section apply except to the extent provided by statutes, or in regulations, orders, directives, or licenses that may be issued pursuant to this order, and notwithstanding any contract entered into or any license or permit granted prior to the date of this order.

Sec. 2. (a) All property and interests in property that are in the United States, that hereafter come within the United States, or that are or hereafter come within the possession or control of any United States person, including any foreign branch, of the following persons are blocked and may not be transferred, paid, exported, withdrawn, or otherwise dealt in: any person determined by the Secretary of the Treasury, in consultation with or at the recommendation of the Secretary of State:

(i) to have knowingly, on or after August 10, 2012, transferred, or facilitated the transfer of, goods or technologies to Iran, any entity organized under the laws of Iran or otherwise subject to the jurisdiction of the Government of Iran, or any national of Iran, for use in or with respect to Iran, that are likely to be used by the Government of Iran or any of its agencies or instrumentalities, or by any other person on behalf of the Government of Iran or any of such agencies or instrumentalities, to commit serious human rights abuses against the people of Iran;

(ii) to have knowingly, on or after August 10, 2012, provided services, including services relating to hardware, software, or specialized information or professional consulting, engineering, or support services, with respect to goods or technologies that have been transferred to Iran and that are likely to be used by the Government of Iran or any of its agencies or instrumentalities, or by any other person on behalf of the Government of Iran or any of such agencies or instrumentalities, to commit serious human rights abuses against the people of Iran;

(iii) to have materially assisted, sponsored, or provided financial, material, or technological support for, or goods or services to or in support of, the activities described in subsection (a)(i) or (a)(ii) of this section or any person whose property and interests in property are blocked pursuant to this section; or

(iv) to be owned or controlled by, or to have acted or purported to act for or on behalf of, directly or indirectly, any person whose property and interests in property are blocked pursuant to this section.

(b) The prohibitions in subsection (a) of this section apply except to the extent provided by statutes, or in regulations, orders, directives, or licenses that may be issued pursuant to this order, and notwithstanding any contract entered into or any license or permit granted prior to the date of this order.

Sec. 3. (a) All property and interests in property that are in the United States, that hereafter come within the United States, or that are or hereafter come within the possession or control of any United States person, including any foreign branch, of the following persons are blocked and may not be transferred, paid, exported, withdrawn, or otherwise dealt in: any person determined by the Secretary of the Treasury, in consultation with or at the recommendation of the Secretary of State:

(i) to have engaged in censorship or other activities with respect to Iran on or after June 12, 2009, that prohibit, limit, or penalize the exercise of freedom of expression or assembly by citizens of Iran, or that limit access to print or broadcast media, including the facilitation or support of intentional frequency manipulation by the Government of Iran or an entity owned or controlled by the Government of Iran that would jam or restrict an international signal;

(ii) to have materially assisted, sponsored, or provided financial, material, or technological support for, or goods or services to or in support of, the activities described in subsection (a)(i) of this section or any person whose property and interests in property are blocked pursuant to this section; or

(iii) to be owned or controlled by, or to have acted or purported to act for or on behalf of, directly or indirectly, any person whose property and interests in property are blocked pursuant to this section.

(b) The prohibitions in subsection (a) of this section apply except to the extent provided by statutes, or in regulations, orders, directives, or licenses that may be issued pursuant to this order, and notwithstanding any contract entered into or any license or permit granted prior to the date of this order.

Sec. 4. (a) No entity owned or controlled by a United States person and established or maintained outside the United States may knowingly engage in any transaction, directly or indirectly, with the Government of Iran or any person subject to the jurisdiction of the Government of Iran, if that transaction would be prohibited by Executive Order 12957, Executive Order 12959 of May 6, 1995, Executive Order 13059 of August 19, 1997, Executive Order 13599 of February 5, 2012, section 5 of Executive Order 13622 of July 30, 2012, or section 12 of this order, or any regulation issued pursuant to the foregoing, if the transaction were engaged in by a United States person or in the United States.

(b) Penalties assessed for violations of the prohibition in subsection (a) of this section, and any related violations of section 12 of this order, may be assessed

against the United States person that owns or controls the entity that engaged in the prohibited transaction.
(c) Penalties for violations of the prohibition in subsection (a) of this section shall not apply if the United States person that owns or controls the entity divests or terminates its business with the entity not later than February 6, 2013.
(d) The prohibitions in subsection (a) of this section apply except to the extent provided by statutes, or in regulations, orders, directives, or licenses that may be issued pursuant to this order, and notwithstanding any contract entered into or any license or permit granted prior to the date of this order.

Sec. 5. The Secretary of State, in consultation with the Secretary of the Treasury, the Secretary of Commerce, and the United States Trade Representative, and with the President of the Export-Import Bank of the United States, the Chairman of the Board of Governors of the Federal Reserve System, and other agencies and officials as appropriate, is hereby authorized to impose on a person any of the sanctions described in section 6 or 7 of this order upon determining that the person:
(a) knowingly, between July 1, 2010, and August 10, 2012, sold, leased, or provided to Iran goods, services, technology, information, or support with a fair market value of $1,000,000 or more, or with an aggregate fair market value of $5,000,000 or more during a 12-month period, and that could directly and significantly facilitate the maintenance or expansion of Iran's domestic production of refined petroleum products, including any direct and significant assistance with respect to the construction, modernization, or repair of petroleum refineries;
(b) knowingly, between July 1, 2010, and August 10, 2012, sold or provided to Iran refined petroleum products with a fair market value of $1,000,000 or more, or with an aggregate fair market value of $5,000,000 or more during a 12-month period;
(c) knowingly, between July 1, 2010, and August 10, 2012, sold, leased, or provided to Iran goods, services, technology, information, or support with a fair market value of $1,000,000 or more, or with an aggregate fair market value of $5,000,000 or more during a 12-month period, and that could directly and significantly contribute to the enhancement of Iran's ability to import refined petroleum products;
(d) is a successor entity to a person determined by the Secretary of State in accordance with this section to meet the criteria in subsection (a), (b), or (c) of this section;
(e) owns or controls a person determined by the Secretary of State in accordance with this section to meet the criteria in subsection (a), (b), or (c) of this section, and had knowledge that the person engaged in the activities referred to in that subsection; or
(f) is owned or controlled by, or under common ownership or control with, a person determined by the Secretary of State in accordance with this section to meet the criteria in subsection (a), (b), or (c) of this section, and knowingly participated in the activities referred to in that subsection.

Sec. 6. (a) When the Secretary of State, in accordance with the terms of section 5 of this order, has determined that a person meets any of the criteria described in section 5 and has selected any of the sanctions set forth below to impose on that person, the heads of relevant agencies, in consultation with the Secretary of State, shall take the following actions where necessary to implement the sanctions imposed by the Secretary of State:

(i) the Board of Directors of the Export-Import Bank shall deny approval of the issuance of any guarantee, insurance, extension of credit, or participation in an extension of credit in connection with the export of any goods or services to the sanctioned person;

(ii) agencies shall not issue any specific license or grant any other specific permission or authority under any statute that requires the prior review and approval of the United States Government as a condition for the export or reexport of goods or technology to the sanctioned person;

(iii) with respect to a sanctioned person that is a financial institution:

(1) the Chairman of the Board of Governors of the Federal Reserve System and the President of the Federal Reserve Bank of New York shall take such actions as they deem appropriate, including denying designation, or terminating the continuation of any prior designation of, the sanctioned person as a primary dealer in United States Government debt instruments; or

(2) agencies shall prevent the sanctioned person from serving as an agent of the United States Government or serving as a repository for United States Government funds; or

(iv) agencies shall not procure, or enter into a contract for the procurement of, any goods or services from the sanctioned person.

(b) The prohibitions in subsections (a)(i)-(a)(iv) of this section apply except to the extent provided by statutes, or in regulations, orders, directives, or licenses that may be issued pursuant to this order, and notwithstanding any contract entered into or any license or permit granted prior to the date of this order.

Sec. 7. (a) When the Secretary of State, in accordance with the terms of section 5 of this order, has determined that a person meets any of the criteria described in section 5 and has selected any of the sanctions set forth below to impose on that person, the Secretary of the Treasury, in consultation with the Secretary of State, shall take the following actions where necessary to implement the sanctions imposed by the Secretary of State:

(i) prohibit any United States financial institution from making loans or providing credits to the sanctioned person totaling more than $10,000,000 in any 12-month period, unless such person is engaged in activities to relieve human suffering and the loans or credits are provided for such activities;

(ii) prohibit any transactions in foreign exchange that are subject to the jurisdiction of the United States and in which the sanctioned person has any interest;

(iii) prohibit any transfers of credit or payments between financial institutions or by, through, or to any financial institution, to the extent that such transfers or payments are subject to the jurisdiction of the United States and involve any interest of the sanctioned person;

(iv) block all property and interests in property that are in the United States, that come within the United States, or that are or come within the possession or control of any United States person, including any foreign branch, of the sanctioned person, and provide that such property and interests in property may not be transferred, paid, exported, withdrawn, or otherwise dealt in; or

(v) restrict or prohibit imports of goods, technology, or services, directly or indirectly, into the United States from the sanctioned person.

(b) The prohibitions in subsections (a)(i)-(a)(v) of this section apply except to the extent provided by statutes, or in regulations, orders, directives, or licenses that may be issued pursuant to this order, and notwithstanding any contract entered into or any license or permit granted prior to the date of this order.

Sec. 8. I hereby determine that, to the extent that section 203(b)(2) of IEEPA may apply, the making of donations of the types of articles specified in such section by, to, or for the benefit of any person whose property and interests in property are blocked pursuant to this order would seriously impair my ability to deal with the national emergency declared in Executive Order 12957, and I hereby prohibit such donations as provided by subsections 1(a)(iv), 2(a), 3(a), and 7(a)(iv) of this order.

Sec. 9. The prohibitions in subsections 1(a)(iv), 2(a), 3(a), and 7(a)(iv) of this order include but are not limited to:

(a) the making of any contribution or provision of funds, goods, or services by, to, or for the benefit of any person whose property and interests in property are blocked pursuant to this order; and

(b) the receipt of any contribution or provision of funds, goods, or services from any such person.

Sec. 10. I hereby find that the unrestricted immigrant and nonimmigrant entry into the United States of aliens who meet one or more of the criteria in subsections 2(a) and 3(a) of this order would be detrimental to the interests of the United States, and I hereby suspend the entry into the United States, as immigrants or nonimmigrants, of such persons. Such persons shall be treated as persons covered by section 1 of Proclamation 8693 of July 24, 2011 (Suspension of Entry of Aliens Subject to United Nations Security Council Travel Bans and International Emergency Economic Powers Act Sanctions).

Sec. 11. The Secretary of the Treasury, in consultation with the Secretary of State, is hereby authorized to take such actions, including the promulgation of rules and regulations, and to employ all powers granted to the President by IEEPA and sections 6(a)(6), 6(a)(7), 6(a)(8), 6(a)(9), 6(a)(11), and 6(a)(12) of ISA, and to employ all powers granted to the United States Government by section 6(a)(3) of ISA, as may be necessary to carry out the purposes of this order. The Secretary of the Treasury may redelegate any of these functions to other officers and agencies of the United States Government consistent with applicable law.

Sec. 12. (a) Any transaction that evades or avoids, has the purpose of evading or avoiding, causes a violation of, or attempts to violate any of the prohibitions set forth in this order or in Executive Order 12957, Executive Order 12959, Executive Order 13059, or Executive Order 13599 is prohibited.
(b) Any conspiracy formed to violate any of the prohibitions set forth in this order or in Executive Order 12957, Executive Order 12959, Executive Order 13059, or Executive Order 13599 is prohibited.

Sec. 13. For the purposes of this order:

(a) the term "entity" means a partnership, association, trust, joint venture, corporation, group, subgroup, or other organization;

(b) the term "Government of Iran" includes the Government of Iran, any political subdivision, agency, or instrumentality thereof, including the Central Bank of Iran, and any person owned or controlled by, or acting for or on behalf of, the Government of Iran;

(c) the term "Iran" means the Government of Iran and the territory of Iran and any other territory or marine area, including the exclusive economic zone and continental shelf, over which the Government of Iran claims sovereignty, sovereign rights, or jurisdiction, provided that the Government of Iran exercises partial or total de facto control over the area or derives a benefit from economic activity in the area pursuant to international arrangements;

(d) the terms "knowledge" and "knowingly," with respect to conduct, a circumstance, or a result, mean that a person has actual knowledge, or should have known, of the conduct, the circumstance, or the result;

(e) the term "person" means an individual or entity;

(f) the term "sanctioned person" means a person that the President, or the Secretary of State or the Secretary of the Treasury pursuant to authority delegated by the President and in accordance with the terms of such delegation, has determined is a person on whom sanctions shall be imposed pursuant to IEEPA, ISA, CISADA, or ITRSHRA, and on whom the President, the Secretary of State, or the Secretary of the Treasury has imposed any of the sanctions in section 6 of ISA;

(g) for the purposes of section 4 of this order, the term "subject to the jurisdiction of the Government of Iran" means a person organized under the laws of Iran or any jurisdiction within Iran, ordinarily resident in Iran, or in Iran, or owned or controlled by any of the foregoing;

(h) the term "United States financial institution" means a financial institution (including its foreign branches) organized under the laws of the United States or any jurisdiction within the United States or located in the United States; and

(i) the term "United States person" means any United States citizen, permanent resident alien, entity organized under the laws of the United States or any jurisdiction within the United States (including foreign branches), or any person in the United States.

Sec. 14. For those persons whose property and interests in property are blocked pursuant to this order who might have a constitutional presence in the United States, I find that because of the ability to transfer funds or other assets instantaneously, prior notice to such persons of measures to be taken pursuant to this order would render those measures ineffectual. I therefore determine that for these measures to be effective in addressing the national emergency declared in Executive Order 12957, there need be no prior notice of an action taken pursuant to subsections 1(a)(iv), 2(a), 3(a), and 7(a)(iv) of this order.

Sec. 15. Executive Order 13622 is hereby amended as follows:

(a) Subsection (1)(c)(ii) is amended by deleting the words "with respect to the country with primary jurisdiction over the foreign financial institution."

(b) Subsection (2)(b)(ii) is amended by deleting the words "with respect to the country with primary jurisdiction over the person."

(c) Subsection 1(d) is amended by inserting the words "agricultural commodities," after the words "sale of."

Sec. 16. The Secretary of the Treasury, in consultation with the Secretary of State, is hereby authorized to take such actions, including the promulgation of rules and regulations, and to employ all powers granted to the President by IEEPA, as may be necessary to carry out section 104A of CISADA. The Secretary of the Treasury may redelegate any of these functions to other officers and agencies of the United States Government consistent with applicable law.

Sec. 17. All agencies of the United States Government are hereby directed to take all appropriate measures within their authority to carry out the provisions of this order.

Sec. 18. This order is not intended to, and does not, create any right or benefit, substantive or procedural, enforceable at law or in equity by any party against the United States, its departments, agencies, or entities, its officers, employees, or agents, or any other person.

Sec. 19. The measures taken pursuant to this order are in response to actions of the Government of Iran occurring after the conclusion of the 1981 Algiers Accords, and are intended solely as a response to those later actions.

BARACK OBAMA

Executive Order 13629—Establishing the White House Homeland Security Partnership Council

77 Fed. Reg. 66,353 (Nov. 2, 2012)

By the authority vested in me as President by the Constitution and the laws of the United States of America, and in order to advance the Federal Government's use of local partnerships to address homeland security challenges, it is hereby ordered as follows:

Section 1. *Policy.* The purpose of this order is to maximize the Federal Government's ability to develop local partnerships in the United States to support homeland security priorities. Partnerships are collaborative working relationships in which the goals, structure, and roles and responsibilities of the relationships are mutually determined. Collaboration enables the Federal Government and its partners to use resources more efficiently, build on one another's expertise, drive innovation, engage in collective action, broaden investments to achieve shared goals, and improve performance. Partnerships enhance our ability to address homeland security priorities, from responding to natural disasters to preventing terrorism, by utilizing diverse perspectives, skills, tools, and resources.

The National Security Strategy emphasizes the importance of partnerships, underscoring that to keep our Nation safe "we must tap the ingenuity outside government through strategic partnerships with the private sector, nongovernmental organizations, foundations, and community-based organizations. Such partnerships are critical to U.S. success at home and abroad, and we will support them through enhanced opportunities for engagement, coordination, transparency, and information sharing." This approach recognizes that, given the complexities and range of challenges, we must institutionalize an all-of-Nation effort to address the evolving threats to the United States.

Sec. 2. *White House Homeland Security Partnership Council and Steering Committee.*

(a) *White House Homeland Security Partnership Council.* There is established a White House Homeland Security Partnership Council (Council) to foster local partnerships—between the Federal Government and the private sector, nongovernmental organizations, foundations, community-based organizations, and State, local, tribal, and territorial government and law enforcement—to address homeland security challenges. The Council shall be chaired by the Assistant to the President for Homeland Security and Counterterrorism (Chair), or a designee from the National Security Staff.

(b) *Council Membership.*

(i) Pursuant to the nomination process established in subsection (b)(ii) of this section, the Council shall be composed of Federal officials who are from field offices of the executive departments, agencies, and bureaus (agencies) that are members of the Steering Committee established in subsection (c) of this section, and who have demonstrated an ability to develop, sustain, and institutionalize local partnerships to address policy priorities.

(ii) The nomination process and selection criteria for members of the Council shall be established by the Steering Committee. Based on those criteria, agency heads may select and present to the Steering Committee their nominee or nominees to represent them on the Council. The Steering Committee shall consider all of the nominees and decide by consensus which of the nominees shall participate on the Council. Each member agency on the Steering Committee, with the exception of the Office of the Director of National Intelligence, may have at least one representative on the Council.

(c) *Steering Committee.* There is also established a Steering Committee, chaired by the Chair of the Council, to provide guidance to the Council and perform other functions as set forth in this order. The Steering Committee shall include a representative at the Deputy agency head level, or that representative's designee, from the following agencies:

(i) Department of State;
(ii) Department of the Treasury;
(iii) Department of Defense;
(iv) Department of Justice;
(v) Department of the Interior;
(vi) Department of Agriculture;
(vii) Department of Commerce;
(viii) Department of Labor;
(ix) Department of Health and Human Services;
(x) Department of Housing and Urban Development;
(xi) Department of Transportation;
(xii) Department of Energy;
(xiii) Department of Education;
(xiv) Department of Veterans Affairs;
(xv) Department of Homeland Security;
(xvi) Office of the Director of National Intelligence;
(xvii) Environmental Protection Agency;
(xviii) Small Business Administration; and
(xix) Federal Bureau of Investigation.

At the invitation of the Chair, representatives of agencies not listed in subsection (c) of this section or other executive branch entities may attend and participate in Steering Committee meetings as appropriate.

(d) *Administration.* The Chair or a designee shall convene meetings of the Council and Steering Committee, determine their agendas, and coordinate their work. The Council may establish subgroups consisting exclusively of Council members or their designees, as appropriate.

Sec. 3. *Mission and Function of the Council and Steering Committee.* (a) The Council shall, consistent with guidance from the Steering Committee:

(i) advise the Chair and Steering Committee members on priorities, challenges, and opportunities for local partnerships to support homeland security priorities, as well as regularly report to the Steering Committee on the Council's efforts;

(ii) promote homeland security priorities and opportunities for collaboration between Federal Government field offices and State, local, tribal, and territorial stakeholders;

(iii) advise and confer with State, local, tribal, and territorial stakeholders and agencies interested in expanding or building local homeland security partnerships;

(iv) raise awareness of local partnership best practices that can support homeland security priorities;

(v) as appropriate, conduct outreach to representatives of the private sector, nongovernmental organizations, foundations, community-based organizations, and State, local, tribal, and territorial government and law enforcement entities with relevant expertise for local homeland security partnerships, and collaborate with other Federal Government bodies; and

(vi) convene an annual meeting to exchange key findings, progress, and best practices.

(b) The Steering Committee shall:

(i) determine the scope of issue areas the Council will address and its operating protocols, in consultation with the Office of Management and Budget;

(ii) establish the nomination process and selection criteria for members of the Council as set forth in section 2(b)(ii) of this order;

(iii) provide guidance to the Council on the activities set forth in subsection (a) of this section; and

(iv) within 1 year of the selection of the Council members, and annually thereafter, provide a report on the work of the Council to the President through the Chair.

Sec. 4. *General Provisions.* (a) The heads of agencies participating in the Steering Committee shall assist and provide information to the Council, consistent with applicable law, as may be necessary to implement this order. Each agency shall bear its own expense for participating in the Council.

(b) Nothing in this order shall be construed to impair or otherwise affect:

(i) the authority granted by law to an executive department, agency, or the head thereof;

(ii) the functions of the Director of the Office of Management and Budget relating to budgetary, administrative, or legislative proposals; or

(iii) the functions of the Overseas Security Advisory Council.

(c) This order shall be implemented consistent with applicable law and appropriate protections for privacy and civil liberties, and subject to the availability of appropriations.

(d) This order is not intended to, and does not, create any right or benefit, substantive or procedural, enforceable at law or in equity by any party against the United States, its departments, agencies, or entities, its officers, employees, or agents, or any other person.

BARACK OBAMA

Executive Order 13637—Administration of Reformed Export Controls

78 Fed. Reg. 16,129 (Mar. 13, 2013)

By the authority vested in me as President by the Constitution and the laws of the United States of America, including the Arms Export Control Act, as amended(the "Act"), and section 301 of title 3, United States Code, it is hereby ordered as follows:

Section 1. *Delegation of Functions.* The following functions conferred upon the President by the Act, and related laws, are delegated as follows:

(a) Those under section 3 of the Act, with the exception of subsections (a)(1), (b), (c)(3), (c)(4), and (f), to the Secretary of State. The Secretary of State, in the implementation of the delegated functions under sections 3(a) and (d) of the Act, is authorized to find, in the case of a proposed transfer of a defense article or related training or other defense service by a foreign country or international organization not otherwise eligible under section 3(a)(1) of the Act, whether the proposed transfer will strengthen the security of the United States and promote world peace.

(b) Those under section 5 to the Secretary of State.

(c) Those under section 21 of the Act, with the exception of the last sentence of subsection (d) and all of subsection (i), to the Secretary of Defense.

(d) Those under sections 22(a), 29, 30, and 30A of the Act, 2769, 2770, and 2770a) to the Secretary of Defense.

(e) Those under section 23 of the Act, and under section 7069 of the Department of State, Foreign Operations, and Related Programs Appropriations Act, 2012, Division I) and any subsequently enacted provision of law that is the same or substantially the same, to the Secretary of Defense to be exercised in consultation with the Secretary of State and, other than the last sentence of section 23(a), in consultation with the Secretary of the Treasury, except that the President shall determine any rate of interest to be charged that is less than the market rate of interest.

(f) Those under sections 24 and 27 of the Act to the Secretary of Defense. The Secretary of Defense shall consult with the Secretary of State and the Secretary of the Treasury in implementing the delegated functions under section 24 and with the Secretary of State in implementing the delegated functions under section 27.

(g) Those under section 25 of the Act to the Secretary of State. The Secretary of Defense shall assist the Secretary of State in the preparation of materials for presentation to the Congress under that section.

(h) Those under section 34 of the Act to the Secretary of State. To the extent the standards and criteria for credit and guaranty transactions are based upon national security or financial policies, the Secretary of State shall obtain the prior concurrence of the Secretary of Defense and the Secretary of the Treasury, respectively.

(i) Those under section 35(a) of the Act to the Secretary of State.

(j) Those under sections 36(a) and 36(b)(1) of the Act, except with respect to the certification of an emergency as provided by subsection (b)(1), to the Secretary of Defense. The Secretary of Defense, in the implementation of the delegated functions under sections 36(a) and (b)(1), shall consult with the Secretary of State. With respect to those functions under sections 36(a)(5) and (6), the Secretary of Defense shall consult with the Director of the Office of Management and Budget.

(k) Those under section 36(b)(1) with respect to the certification of an emergency as provided by subsection (b)(1) and under sections 36(c) and (d) of the Act to the Secretary of State.

(l) Those under section 36(f)(1) of the Act to the Secretary of Defense.

(m) Those under sections 36(f)(2) and (f)(3) of the Act to the Secretary of State.

(n) Those under section 38 of the Act to:

(i) the Secretary of State, except as otherwise provided in this subsection. Designations, including changes in designations, by the Secretary of State of items or categories of items that shall be considered as defense articles and defense services subject to export control under section 38 shall have the concurrence of the Secretary of Defense. The authority to undertake activities to ensure compliance with established export conditions may be redelegated to the Secretary of Defense, or to the head of another executive department or agency as appropriate, who shall exercise such functions in consultation with the Secretary of State;

(ii) the Attorney General, to the extent they relate to the control of the permanent import of defense articles and defense services. In carrying out such functions, the Attorney General shall be guided by the views of the Secretary of State on matters affecting world peace, and the external security and foreign policy of the United States. Designations, including changes in designations, by the Attorney General of items or categories of items that shall be considered as defense articles and defense services subject to permanent import control under section 38 of the Act shall be made with the concurrence of the Secretary of State and the Secretary of Defense and with notice to the Secretary of Commerce; and

(iii) the Department of State for the registration and licensing of those persons who engage in the business of brokering activities with respect to defense articles or defense services controlled either for purposes of export by the Department of State or for purposes of permanent import by the Department of Justice.

(o) Those under section 39(b) of the Act to the Secretary of State. In carrying out such functions, the Secretary of State shall consult with the Secretary of Defense as may be necessary to avoid interference in the application of Department of Defense regulations to sales made under section 22 of the Act.

(p) Those under the portion of section 40A of the Act added by, to the Secretary of State insofar as they relate to commercial exports licensed under the Act, and to the Secretary of Defense insofar as they relate to defense articles and defense services sold, leased, or transferred under the Foreign Military Sales Program.

(q) Those under the portion of section 40A of the Act added by the Antiterrorism and Effective Death Penalty Act of 1996, to the Secretary of State.

(r) Those under sections 42(c) and (f) of the Act to the Secretary of Defense. The Secretary of Defense shall obtain the concurrence of the Secretary of State and the Secretary of Commerce on any determination considered under the authority of section 42(c) of the Act.

(s) Those under section 52(b) of the Act to the Secretary of Defense.

(t) Those under sections 61 and 62(a) of the Act to the Secretary of Defense.

(u) Those under section 2(b)(6) of the Export-Import Bank Act of 1945, as amended to the Secretary of State.

Sec. 2. *Coordination.*

(a) In addition to the specific provisions of section 1 of this order, the Secretary of State and the Secretary of Defense, in carrying out the functions delegated to them under this order, shall consult with each other and with the heads of other executive departments and agencies on matters pertaining to their responsibilities.

(b) Under the direction of the President and in accordance with section 2(b) of the Act, the Secretary of State, taking into account other United States activities abroad, shall be responsible for the continuous supervision and general direction of sales and exports under the Act, including the negotiation, conclusion, and termination of international agreements, and determining whether there shall be a sale to a country and the amount thereof, and whether there shall be delivery or other performance under such sale or export, to the end that sales and exports are integrated with other United States activities and the foreign policy of the United States is best served thereby.

Sec. 3. *Allocation of Funds.* Funds appropriated to the President for carrying out the Act shall be deemed to be allocated to the Secretary of Defense without any further action of the President.

Sec. 4. *Revocation.* Executive Order 11958 of January 18, 1977, as amended, is revoked; except that, to the extent consistent with this order, all determinations, authorizations, regulations, rulings, certificates, orders, directives, contracts, agreements, and other actions made, issued, taken, or entered into under the provisions of Executive Order 11958, as amended, and not revoked, superseded, or otherwise made inapplicable, shall continue in full force and effect until amended, modified, or terminated by appropriate authority.

Sec. 5. *Delegation of Functions under the International Emergency Economic Powers Act.* Executive Order 13222 of August 17, 2001, is amended as follows:

(a) Redesignate section 4 as section 6.

(b) Insert the following new sections 4 and 5 after section 3: "Sec. 4. The Secretary of Commerce shall, to the extent required as a matter of statute or regulation, establish appropriate procedures for when Congress is to be notified of the export of firearms that are subject to the jurisdiction of the Department of Commerce under the Export Administration Regulations and that are controlled for purposes of permanent import by the Attorney General under section 38(a) of the Arms Export Control Act and appropriate procedures for when Congress is to be notified of the export of Major Defense Equipment controlled for purposes of permanent export under the jurisdiction of the Department of Commerce.

Sec. 5. (a) The Secretary of State is hereby authorized to take such actions and to employ those powers granted to the President by the Act as may be necessary to license or otherwise approve the export, reexport, or transfer of items subject to the jurisdiction of the Department of Commerce as agreed to by the Secretary of State and the Secretary of Commerce.

(b) Notwithstanding subsection (a) of this section, items licensed or otherwise approved by the Secretary of State pursuant to this section remain subject to the jurisdiction of the Department of Commerce."

Sec. 6. *General Provisions.*

(a) Nothing in this order shall be construed to impair or otherwise affect:

(i) the authority granted by law to an agency, or the head thereof; or

(ii) the functions of the Director of the Office of Management and Budget relating to budgetary, administrative, or legislative proposals.

(b) This order shall be implemented consistent with applicable law and subject to the availability of appropriations.

(c) This order is not intended to, and does not, create any right or benefit, substantive or procedural, enforceable at law or in equity by any party against the United States, its departments, agencies, or entities, its officers, employees, or agents, or any other person.

BARACK OBAMA

Intelligence Policy Directives and Guidance

KEY INTELLIGENCE COMMUNITY DIRECTIVES

Intelligence Community Directive Number 1

Policy Directive for Intelligence Community Leadership
(Effective: May 1, 2006)

A. AUTHORITY:

The National Security Act (NSA) of 1947, as amended; the Intelligence Reform and Terrorism Prevention Act (IRTPA) of 2004; the Counterintelligence Enhancement Act of 2002, as amended; Executive Order (EO) 12333, as amended, United States Intelligence Activities; EO 13355, Strengthened Management of the Intelligence Community; and other applicable provisions of law.

B. PURPOSE:

This capstone Intelligence Community (IC) Directive (lCD) sets forth the overarching policy and framework for the Director of National Intelligence's (DNI) approach to national intelligence and delineates the authorities and responsibilities of the DNI and the Office of the DNI (ODM). It also establishes a system of ICDs, IC Policy Memoranda (ICPMs), and IC Policy Guidance (ICPGs) for managing the IC. Terms used in this directive are defined in Annex A.

This ICD rescinds all versions of Director of Central Intelligence Directive (DCID) 1/1 and DCID 3/3P.

C. APPLICABILITY:

This directive applies to the IC, as defined by the National Security Act of 1947, as amended, and other departments or agencies that may be designated by the President, or designated jointly by the DNI and the head of the department or agency concerned, as an element of the IC.

D. POLICY:

1. **Background.** The DNI's policies and directives seek to create an integrated and effective intelligence enterprise. The DNI's overarching goal is to ensure that the elements of the IC are working collaboratively to provide accurate, timely, and objective intelligence—independent of political considerations—to support the President and all who make and implement US national security policy, defend our Nation, and enforce our laws.

The DNI relies on the senior leadership of the IC, including the senior leaders of the ODM, to execute his responsibilities for providing national intelligence and to ensure US intelligence continuously upgrades its capabilities to stay ahead of emerging threats. IC senior leaders will measure their success by intelligence outcomes, aligned with DNI strategic objectives, in support of US national security priorities.

The senior leadership of each of the IC elements must lead by example. The senior leadership is responsible for sharing information and ensuring collaboration while protecting the integrity of the intelligence process. IC senior leaders must establish the necessary linkage between planning and execution. In doing so, they must demand results; evaluate their annual budgets in light of established objectives, priorities, and guidance issued; ensure that analytic requirements drive the development and deployment of collection techniques and strategies; and propose bold measures to resolve new challenges. Accordingly, IC leaders will:

- Create a climate that encourages experimentation and risk-taking, and that will reward collectors, intelligence analysts, and leaders for implementing innovative approaches that lead to more effective anticipation and avoidance of strategic surprise.
- Foster an environment of information sharing to the greatest extent possible while ensuring clear, uniform security practices and rules, and enabling effective counterintelligence activities.
- Create and maintain a "joint" environment in which intelligence personnel at every level are fully engaged in achieving community, organizational, and individual goals.
- Develop the ability to adapt quickly to rapidly changing customer needs and situations, to include a flexible, adaptive workforce.
- Develop enterprise-based evaluation criteria and metrics to assess efficiency and effectiveness.
- Continually improve each organization within the IC, and create an environment that fosters integrity, unity of purpose, and high performance across community organizations.

2. National Intelligence Policy System. The National Intelligence Policy System is organized around the DNI' s major responsibilities and calls for nine component series, organized topically. Each series falls under the cognizance of a designated senior official of the ODM (cognizant official), who is responsible for guiding the development of the overarching policy or "capstone" and related policies within the series.

3. DNI Policy Issuances. The DNI will use ICDs, ICPMs, and ICPGs to convey overarching direction, policy and program objectives, and implementing instructions, respectively.

a. **Intelligence Community Directive.** ICDs are the principal issuances through which the DNI provides policy direction to the IC. The DNI, or in his absence, the Principal DDNI (PDDNI), approves all ICDs. ICDs are numbered sequentially within each series.

b. **Intelligence Community Policy Memorandum.** ICPMs are issuances that provide policy direction to the IC prior to formal inclusion in an ICD series. ICPMs will also be used to issue policy on an expeditious basis. An ICPM may reflect a new policy or an update or revision to an existing policy. All ICPMs will contain the following language: *The content of this policy shall be incorporated into an Intelligence Community Directive.* Each ICPM will be assigned a number that incorporates the year, the appropriate series number, and a sequential number (for example, 2005-100-1,2005-100-2). The DNI or the PDDNE approves all ICPMs.

c. **Intelligence Community Policy Guidance.** ICPGs are subsidiary to ICDs and provide more detailed implementation direction to the IC. ICPGs are associated with the appropriate ICD by referencing the ICD number followed by a decimal and a sequential number (for example, the first implementation guidance issued for ICD 201 would be cited as ICPG 201.1). The cognizant official and the Deputy Director of National Intelligence for Management (DDNI/M) approve all ICPGs.

E. AUTHORITIES AND RESPONSIBILITIES OF THE DNI:

This section summarizes the DNI's authorities and responsibilities, as set forth in the NSA of 1947, as amended; the IRTPA; E0 12333, as amended; and other provisions of law and Presidential directives. This summary is not exhaustive and does not change or abrogate the underlying authorities that are controlling. The authorities and responsibilities are listed by general topic, although a number of the authorities and responsibilities cross topic areas. Annex B contains a full citation to the source references.

1. **General.** The DNI serves as head of the US IC; acts as the principal advisor to the President, the National Security Council (NSC), and the Homeland Security Council (HSC) for intelligence matters related to national security; and oversees and directs the implementation of the National Intelligence Program (NIP). (NSA § 102(b); see also IRTPA § 1018)

2. **Enterprise Management**

a. **Program and Budget.** The DNI provides guidance for developing the NIP budget; develops and determines the annual consolidated NIP budget based on budget proposals provided by the heads of agencies and organizations within the IC and the heads of their respective departments and, as appropriate, after obtaining the advice of the Joint Intelligence Community Council; and presents the consolidated NIP budget to the President for approval together with any comments from the heads of departments containing agencies or organizations with the IC. The DNI ensures the effective execution of the annual budget for intelligence and intelligence-related activities and manages NIP appropriations by directing the allotment or allocation of such appropriations through the heads of the departments containing agencies or organizations within the IC and the Director of the Central Intelligence Agency (CIA). In addition, the DNI participates in the development by the Secretary of Defense (SECDEF) of the annual budget for the Military Intelligence Program (MIP). The DNI also provides guidance for the development of the annual budget for each element of the IC that is not within the NIP. (NSA § 102A(c); see also, EO 12333 § 1.5(n))

b. **Transfer and Reprogramming of Funds.** No funds made available under the NIP may be transferred or reprogrammed without the prior approval of the DNI, except in accordance with procedures prescribed by the DNI. SECDEF shall consult with the DNI before transferring or reprogramming funds made available under the MW. The DNI may transfer or reprogram funds appropriated for a program within the NIP to another such program in accordance with section 102A of the National Security Act. (NSA § 102A(d)(1))

c. **Acquisition Authorities.** In carrying out the authorities and responsibilities of section 102A of the National Security Act of 1947, the DNI may exercise the acquisition and appropriations authorities referred to in the CIA Act of 1949, other than the authorities referred to in section 8(b) of that Act, including the authority, notwithstanding any other provision of law, to expend funds to carry out the authorities and responsibilities of section 102A. (NSA § 102A(n))

d. **NIP Responsibility Regarding the Department of Defense (DoD).** Subject to the direction of the President, the DNI after consultation with SECDEF, ensures that NIP budgets for the elements of the IC that are within DoD are adequate to satisfy the national intelligence needs of DoD, including the needs of the Chairman of the Joint Chiefs of Staff and the commanders of the combatant commands, and wherever such elements are performing govemment-wide functions, the needs of other Federal departments and agencies. (NSA § 102A(p))

e. **Acquisitions of Major Systems.** For each intelligence program funded in whole out of amounts within the NIP for the acquisition of a major system, the DNI requires the development and implementation of a program management plan that includes cost, schedule, and performance goals and program milestone criteria, except that with respect to DoD programs the DNI shall consult with SECDEF; serves as exclusive milestone decision authority, except that with respect to DoD programs where the DNI shall serve as milestone decision authority jointly with SECDEF or the designee of the Secretary; and periodically reviews and assesses the progress made toward the achievement of the goals and milestones established in such plan; and submits to Congress a report on the results of such a review and assessment. (NSA § 102A(q))

f. **Advisory Groups.** The DNI is authorized to appoint advisory committees and to employ part-time advisory personnel, as the DNI deems necessary in the execution of DNI functions, consistent with section 303 of the National Security Act. (NSA § 303; see also, EO 12333 § 1.3(a), (b), and 1.5(j)).

g. **Perfonnance of Common Services.** The DNI, in consultation with heads of departments and agencies of the US Government (USG) containing elements within the IC and with the Director of the CIA, coordinates the performance by the elements of the IC within the NIP of such services as are of common concern to the IC, which services the DNI determines can be more efficiently accomplished in a consolidated manner. (NSA § 102A(r); EO 12333 § 1.5(c))

h. **Waste.** The DNI shall ensure the elimination of waste and unnecessary duplication throughout the IC. (NSA § 102A(f)(5))

3. **Intelligence Analysis**

a. **Provision of Intelligence.** The DNI is responsible for ensuring that national intelligence is provided to the President, to heads of departments and agencies of the executive branch, to the Chairman of the Joint Chiefs of Staff and senior military commanders, to the Senate and House of Representatives and the committees, thereof, and to such other persons as the DNI determines to be appropriate. (NSA § 102A(a))

b. **Tasking of Analysis, Production, and Dissemination of National Intelligence.** The DNI establishes objectives, priorities, and guidance for the IC to ensure timely and effective analysis, production, and dissemination of national intelligence; determines requirements and priorities for, and manages and directs the tasking of analysis, production, and dissemination of national intelligence by elements of the IC; and provides advisory tasking to intelligence elements of those agencies and departments not within the NIP. (NSA § 102A(f)(1))

c. **Analysis.** To ensure the most accurate analysis of intelligence is derived from all sources to support national security needs, the DNJ implements appropriate policies and procedures; ensures that resources are allocated to analysis and collection in an appropriately proportional manner to enable collected data to be properly analyzed; ensures that differences in analytic judgment are fully considered and brought to the attention of policymakers; ensures that the IC's analytic tradecraft includes competitive analysis, alternative analysis, and analytic integrity; and ensures that relationships are established between intelligence collectors and analysts to facilitate greater understanding of the needs of analysts. (NSA § 102A(h))

4. **Intelligence Collection and Related Activities**

a. **Tasking of Collection, Processing, and Dissemination of National Intelligence.** The DNI establishes objectives, priorities, and guidance for the IC to ensure timely and effective collection, processing, and dissemination of national intelligence; determines requirements and priorities for, and manages and directs the tasking of, collection, production, and dissemination of national intelligence by elements of the IC; resolves conflicts in collection requirements and in the tasking of national collection assets of the elements of the IC; and provides advisory tasking to intelligence elements of those agencies and departments not within the NIP. (NSA § 102A(t)(1))

b. **Operational Coordination between DoD and CIA.** The DNI, in consultation with SECDEF and the Director, CIA, shall develop joint procedures to improve the coordination and deconfliction of operations involving elements of the Armed Forces and the CIA consistent with national security and the protection of human intelligence sources and methods. (IRTPA § 1013(a))

c. **Access to Intelligence.** The DNI shall have access to all national intelligence and intelligence related to the national security that is collected by any Federal department, agency, or other entity, except as otherwise provided by law or, as appropriate, under guidelines agreed upon by the Attorney General and the DNI, unless otherwise directed by the President. (NSA § 102A(b); see also, EO 12333 § 1.6(a))

d. **Foreign Intelligence Surveillance Act (FISA) of 1978.** The DNI shall establish requirements and priorities for foreign intelligence information to be collected under FISA and provide assistance to the Attorney General to ensure that information derived from electronic surveillance or physical searches under FISA is disseminated so it may be used efficiently and effectively for national intelligence purposes. (NSA § 102A(f)(6))

e. **Open Source Intelligence.** The DNI is responsible for ensuring that the IC makes efficient and effective use of open source information and analysis. (IRTPA § 1052(b))

f. **Space Activities.** The DNI has been assigned authorities and responsibilities for space under the National Space Policy. The DNI oversees certain space activities and jointly oversees other space activities with the SECDEF consistent with their respective responsibilities as set forth in the National Security Act of 1947, as amended; EO 12333, as amended; and other applicable law.

g. **Covert Action.** The DNI has been assigned authorities and responsibilities concerning covert activities. (See NSA §§ 102A, 104A(b), 104A(d)(4), and 503(b); EO 12333 (special activities); IRPTA § 1081).

5. **Customer Outcomes**

a. **Coordination with Foreign Govermnents.** Under the direction of the President and consistent with applicable law, the DNI oversees Director, CIA's, coordination of the relationships between elements of the IC and the intelligence or security services of foreign governments or international organizations on all matters involving intelligence related to the national security or involving intelligence acquired through clandestine means. (NSA §§ 102A(k) and 104A(f); see also EO 12333 § 1.5(e))

b. **Counternarcotics Activities.** The DNI participates in the development of procedures approved by the Attorney General governing criminal narcotics intelligence activities abroad to ensure that these activities are consistent with foreign intelligence programs. (EO 12333 § 1.5(t))

6. **Information Management**

Intelligence Information Sharing and Enterprise Architecture. The DNI has principal authority to ensure maximum availability of and access to intelligence information within the IC consistent with national security requirements. To ensure maximum availability of and access to intelligence information, the DNI establishes uniform security standards and procedures; establishes common information technology standards, protocols, and interfaces; ensures development of information technology systems that include multi-level security and intelligence integration capabilities; establishes policies and procedures to resolve conflicts between the need to share intelligence information and the need to protect intelligence sources and methods; develops an enterprise architecture for the IC and ensures that elements of the IC comply with such architecture; and has procurement approval authority over all enterprise architecture-related information technology items funded in the NIP. (NSA § 102A(g); see also EO 12333 § 1.5(g)).

7. **Human Capital**

a. **Personnel Management.** The DNI prescribes, in consultation with the heads of other agencies or elements of the IC, and the heads of their respective departments, personnel policies and programs applicable to the IC that, among other things: encourage and facilitate assignments and details of personnel to national intelligence centers, and between elements of the IC; set standards for education, training, and career development of personnel of the IC; establish IC scholarship programs; establish and train a National Intelligence Reserve Corps; encourage and facilitate the recruitment and retention by the IC of highly qualified individuals for the effective conduct of nteffigence activities; ensure personnel within the IC are sufficiently diverse for purposes of the collection and analysis of intelligence through the recruitment and training of women, minorities, and individuals with diverse ethnic, cultural, and linguistic backgrounds; make service in more than one element of the IC a condition of promotion to such positions within the IC as the DNI shall specify; and ensure the effective management of IC personnel who are responsible for IC-wide matters. The DNI is responsible for providing incentives for personnel to serve in support of IC management functions and for prescribing mechanisms to facilitate the rotation of personnel throughout the IC. The DNI identifies specific requirements for the range of linguistic skills necessary for the IC, including proficiency in scientific and technical vocabularies of critical foreign languages, and develops a comprehensive plan for the ODNI to meet these requirements through education, recruitment, and training of linguists. (NSA § 102A(f)(l); IRTPA §§ 1041, 1042, 1043, and 1053)

b. **Cross-Disciplinary Education and Training.** The DNI shall establish an integrated framework that brings together the educational components of the IC to promote a more effective and productive IC through cross-disciplinary education and joint training. (IRTPA § 1042)

c. **Transfer of Personnel.** In addition to any other available authorities in the first 12 months after a new national intelligence center is created the DNI, with the approval of the Director of the Office of Management and Budget (OMB) and in consultation with the appropriate committees of Congress, may transfer up to 100 personnel authorized for elements of the IC to such center. The DNI, with the approval of the Director of OMB and in accordance with procedures developed by the DNI and the heads of the departments and agencies concerned, may transfer personnel authorized for an element of the IC to another such element for a period of not more than two years. These transfers will be made only when personnel are being transferred to an activity that is a higher priority intelligence activity; and the transfer supports an emergent need, improves program effectiveness, or increases efficiency. (NSA § 102A(e))

8. **Security and Counterintelligence**

a. **Protection of Intelligence Sources and Methods.** The DNI is responsible for protecting intelligence sources and methods from unauthorized disclosure. To maximize the dissemination of intelligence, the DNI is responsible for establishing and implementing guidelines for the IC for the following purposes:

(1) Classification of information under applicable law, EOs, or other Presidential directives.

(2) Access to and dissemination of intelligence, both in final form and in the form when initially gathered.

(3) Preparation of intelligence products in such a way that source information is removed to allow for dissemination at the lowest level of classification possible or in unclassified form to the extent practicable. (NSA § 102A(i))

b. **Reciprocity of Security Clearance and Access Determinations**

(1) All security clearance background investigations and determinations completed by an authorized investigative agency or authorized adjudicative agency shall be accepted by all agencies. Further, all such security clearance investigations initiated by an authorized investigative agency shall be transferable to any other authorized investigative agency. (IRTPA § 3001(d)(1) and (2)).

(2) An authorized investigative, or adjudicative agency may not establish additional investigative or adjudicative requirements (other than for the conduct of a polygraph examination) that exceed the requirements specified in applicable executive orders without the approval of the Director, OMB. The DNI has been delegated responsibility for developing and, after approval by the Director, OMB, and the Assistant to the President for National Security Affairs, implementing uniform policies and procedures for access to sensitive compartmented information (SCI) and intelligence special access programs (SAPs), which includes policies regarding additional investigative or adjudicative procedures. (IRTPA § 300 1(d)(3)(A) and (B); EO 13381; OMB M-05-17)

(3) No authorized investigative agency or authorized adjudicative agency may conduct an investigation to determine whether to grant a security clearance to an individual where a current investigation or clearance of equal level already exists or has been granted by another authorized adjudicative agency. (IRTPA § 300 1(d)(4))

(4) Only the Director, OMB, may disallow the reciprocal recognition of an individual security clearance by an agency on a case-by-case basis when the Director, OMB, determines that such action is necessary for national security purposes. The DNI has been delegated the authority to develop policies and procedures in this respect with regard to SCI and intelligence SAPs, subject to the approvals noted in paragraph E.8.b.(2). (IRTPA § 3001(a)(1) and (d)(5); EO 13381; OMB M-05-17, Attachment A, paragraph (4))

c. **Counterintelligence.** The DNI provides direction and control over the National Counterintelligence Executive, who serves as the head of national counterintelligence for the USG. (50 USC § 402b)

d. **Uniform Procedures for SCI.** The DNI, subject to the direction of the President, establishes uniform standards and procedures for the granting of access to SCI; ensures the consistent implementation of those standards and procedures; ensures that security clearances granted by individual elements of the IC are recognized by all elements of the IC and under contracts entered into by those agencies; and ensures that the process for investigation and adjudication of an application for access to SCI is performed in the most expeditious manner possible consistent with applicable standards for national security. (NSA § 102A(j))

e. **Special Access Programs.** The DNI is authorized to create SAPs pertaining to intelligence activities (including special activities, but not including military operational, strategic, and tactical programs) or intelligence sources or methods. The DNI shall prescribe security and counterintelligence requirements for the safeguarding of such intelligence. (EO 12958 § 4.3, as amended)

9. **Science and Technology.**

The DNI, with the assistance of the Associate DNI for Science and Technology (ADNI/S&T), is to formulate a long-term strategy for scientific advances in the field of intelligence. (NSA § 103E(c)(3))

10. **Mission Management**

National Intelligence Centers. The DNI shall oversee the National Counterterrorism Center (NCTC) and the National Counterproliferalion Center (NCPC) and may establish such other national intelligence centers as the DNI determines necessary. (NSA § 102A(f)(2))

11. **Other Responsibilities**

a. **Compliance with Laws.** The DNI shall ensure compliance with the Constitution and laws of the United States by the CIA and shall ensure compliance by other elements of the IC through the host executive departments that manage the programs and activities that are part of the NIP. (NSA § 102A(f)(4))

b. **Civil Liberties Protection.** The DNI will, through the Civil Liberties Protection Officer, ensure that the protection of civil liberties and privacy is appropriately incorporated into the policies and procedures of the elements of the IC within the NIP. (NSA § 103D(b)(1))

c. **IC Appointments.** The DNI is responsible for recommending to the President nominees for the positions of PDDNI and Director of the CIA. The concurrence of the DNI is required prior to the appointment or recommendation by the head of the department or agency concerned of individuals to fill vacancies in the positions of Director of the National Security Agency; Director of the National Reconnaissance Office (NRO); Director of the National Geospatial-Intelligence Agency (NGA), the Assistant Secretary of State for Intelligence and Research; the Directors of the Offices of Intelligence and Counterintelligence of the Department of Energy; the Assistant Secretary for Intelligence and Analysis of the Department of the Treasury; the Executive Assistant Director of the National Security Branch of the Federal Bureau of Investigation; and the Assistant Secretary of Homeland Security for Intelligence and Analysis. The DNI must be consulted prior to the appointment or the recommendation of individuals to fill vacancies in the positions of the Director of the Defense Intelligence Agency (DIA) and the Deputy Assistant Commandant of the Coast Guard for Intelligence. (NSA § 106)

d. **Committees.** The DNI chairs or participates in the following committees:

(1) Joint Intelligence Community Council (JICC). The DNI chairs the JICC. (NSA § 101A)

(2) National Security Council. The DNI, in the performance of his duties under the National Security Act, and subject to the direction of the President, may attend and participate in meetings of the NSC. The DNI serves as the principal advisor to the NSC for intelligence matters related to the national security. (NSA §§ 101(j), 102(b)(2)); see also EO 12333 § 1.5(a))

(3) Committee on Foreign Intelligence. The DNI is a member of the Committee on Foreign Intelligence of the NSC. (NSA § 101(h)(2)(A))

(4) Committee on Transnational Threats. The DNI is a member of the Committee on Transnational Threats of the NSC. (NSA § 101(i)(2)(A))

(5) National Homeland Security Council. The DNI serves as the principal advisor to the Homeland Security Council for intelligence matters related to national security. (NSA § 102(b)(2))

e. **Presidential Direction.** The DNI shall perform such other functions as the President may direct. (NSA § 102A(f)(7))

12. **Congressional Reporting Requirements**

a. **Keeping Committees Fully and Currently Informed.** To the extent consistent with due regard for the protection from unauthorized disclosure of classified information relating to sensitive intelligence sources and methods or other exceptionally sensitive matters, the DNI and the heads of all departments, agencies, and other entities of the USG involved in intelligence activities shall keep the congressional intelligence committees fully and currently informed of all intelligence activities, other than covert actions, which are the responsibility of, are engaged by, or are carried out for or on behalf of, any department, agency, or entity of the USG, including any significant anticipated intelligence activity and any significant intelligence failure. (NSA § 502(a)(1))

b. **Provision of Information.** To the extent consistent with due regard for the protection from unauthorized disclosure of classified information relating to sensitive intelligence sources and methods or other exceptionally sensitive matters, the DNI and the heads of all departments, agencies, and other entities of the USG involved in intelligence activities shall furnish the congressional intelligence committees any information or material concerning intelligence activities, other than covert actions, that is within his custody or control, and that is requested by either of the intelligence committees to carry out its authorized responsibilities. (NSA § 502(a)(2))

c. **Covert Action.** To the extent consistent with due regard for the protection from unauthorized disclosure of classified information relating to sensitive intelligence sources and methods or other exceptionally sensitive matters, the DNI and the heads of all departments, agencies, and other entities of the USG involved in a covert action shall keep the intelligence committees fully and currently informed of all covert actions that are the responsibility of, are engaged in by, or are carried out for or on behalf of, any department, agency, or entity of the USG, including significant failures; and shall furnish to the intelligence committees any information or material concerning covert actions that is in the possession, custody, or control of any department, agency, or entity of the USG and that is requested by either of the intelligence committees to carry out its authorized responsibilities. (NSA § 503(b) and EO 12333 § 1.5(d) (special activities))

F. LEADERSHIP OF THE IC:

1. **Director of National Intelligence.** The DNI serves as the head of the IC, as the principal advisor to the President, the NSC, and the Homeland Security Council for intelligence matters related to the national security and, consistent with the IRTPA, oversees and directs the implementation of the NIP. Ultimately, the DNI ensures that

those who defend America, combat terrorism, and advance US national security interests have the best possible information to make the best decisions. To carry out these duties, the DNI is responsible for leading the IC and for working with the respective USG departments and agencies to set intelligence priorities.

2. **Office of the DNI.** The DNI is assisted by the ODM in carrying out each of the duties and responsibilities established under the IRTPA of 2004, the National Security Act of 1947 (50 USC 401 et seq.), other applicable provisions of law, and such other duties as may be prescribed by the President or by law. The ODNI comprises professional staff personnel having expertise in matters relating to each of the duties and responsibilities of the Director, who has the authority to establish permanent positions and appropriate rates of pay with respect to that staff. In addition to the DNI, the ODNI consists of the following positions and associated staffs:

a. **Principal Deputy Director of National Intelligence.** The PDDNI assists the DNI in carrying out the duties and responsibilities of the Director. The PDDNI acts.for and exercises the powers of the DNI during the absence or disability of the DNI or during a vacancy in the DNI position. The DNI has delegated all authorities vested in the DNI to the PDDNI, except as otherwise prohibited by law, ICD, or as the DNI directs.

b. **Deputy Directors of National Intelligence.** There are up to four DDNIs, appointed by the DNI, each of whom exercises such duties, responsibilities, and authorities as the DNI assigns or as specified by law. DDNIs exercise the DNI's authorities and responsibilities over the IC and exercise planning, policy, and strategic oversight over national intelligence policy, plans, and programs. In the exercise of assigned responsibilities, DDNIs serve the DNI and PDDNI as the senior IC intelligence policy and resource officials for their assigned areas. The DNI has established four deputy director positions:

(1) **Deputy Director of National Intelligence for Collection (DDNI/C).** The DDNI/C is charged with the implementation of the responsibilities of the DNI relative to the collection of national intelligence and covert action. The DDNI/C is responsible for the integrated collection enterprise, ensuring timely and effective collection, processing, and dissemination of national intelligence. The DDNI/C establishes collection objectives, priorities, and guidance for and manages and directs the tasking of the collection of national intelligence by elements of the IC. The DDNI/C further resolves conflicts in collection requirements and in the tasking of national collection assets of the elements of the IC. The DDNI/C also provides advisory tasking regarding collection, production, and dissemination of national intelligence to elements of agencies and departments not with the NIP. The DDNI/C provides the DNI with recommendations to reallocate, reprogram, or realign resources or functions of collection activities. The DDNI/C ensures DNI priorities are appropriately reflected in future planning and systems acquisition decisions, and puts into context how those decisions affect the total collection mission. The DDNI/C establishes requirements and priorities for foreign intelligence information to be collected under FISA.

(2) **Deputy Director of National Intelligence for Analysis (DDNI/A).** The DDNI/A is charged with the implementation of the responsibilities of the DNI relative to processing, analysis, and dissemination of national intelligence analytic products. The DDNI/A has responsibility for enhancing the quality, timeliness, and utility of analytic support to intelligence consumers. This responsibility is largely accomplished by increasing expertise and improving analytic tradecraft at individual, agency, and community levels through specialization, collaboration, and cross-fertilization. The DDNI/A is also responsible for identifying gaps in the analytic community's understanding of critical targets and working with the DDNI/C to develop integrated analytic and collection strategies against them. The DDNI/A has responsibility to ensure that this tradecraft includes competitive analysis, alternative analysis, and analytic integrity. The DDNI/A, through the Analytic Ombudsman, will also safeguard objectivity in intelligence analysis. The DDNI/A serves concurrently as the Chairman of the National Intelligence Council (NIC) and also manages the production of the President's Daily Brief.

(3) **Deputy Director of National Intelligence for Customer Outcomes (DDNI/CO).** The DDNI/CO is charged with the implementation of the responsibilities of the DNI relative to understanding the needs of the customers of national intelligence, determining the extent to which the IC is working to address those needs, gauging customer satisfaction throughout, and providing regular reports to the DNI on these responsibilities. In addition, the DDNI/CO is responsible for collecting, validating, and obtaining approval of national intelligence capability requirements, overseeing foreign intelligence relationships, and overseeing the national intelligence priorities process.

(4) **Deputy Director of National Intelligence for Management.** The DDNI/M is charged with the implementation of the responsibilities of the DNI relative to the administrative management of the IC, strategic planning and coordination, and the development and execution of the NIP budget. The DDNI/M oversees all the managerial aspects of the ODM, including the IC Senior Acquisition Executive; the Chancellor of the National Intelligence University and Chief Community Training Officer; the Office of Strategy, Plans, and Policy; the Chief Human Capital Officer; the Chief Financial Officer; Security; and the ODM Office of Administration.

c. **General Counsel.** The General Counsel is the chief legal officer of the ODM and performs such functions as the DM may prescribe. The General Counsel serves as the head of the Office of the General Counsel (OGC). OGC's mission is to provide accurate and timely legal guidance and counsel to the DNI in carrying out his statutory responsibility to ensure compliance with the Constitution and laws of the United States by elements of the IC. To this end, OGC works closely with responsible legal officers across the IC and with legal officers of the departments containing elements of the IC to coordinate the development of legal mechanisms to facilitate the implementation of DNI policies to ensure compliance with applicable law. OGC's mission also includes ensuring all employees and contractors assigned to the ODM comply with US law and any applicable regulations and directives.

d. **Associate Directors of National Intelligence.** The ODM includes several associate director positions who report directly to the DNI:

(1) **Associate Director of National Intelligence for Science and Technology.** The ADNI/S&T is responsible for translating the DNI's priorities into a technology investment strategy, for strengthening the IC's technology workforce, and for orchestrating key community strategies in the S&T arena. The ADNI/S&T chairs the DNI S&T Committee, assists the DNI in formulating a strategy for scientific advances in the field of intelligence, assists the DNI on the S&T elements of the budget, and performs all such duties as may be prescribed by the DNI or specified by law.

(2) **Associate Director of National Intelligence and Chief of Staff (ADNI/COS).** The COS oversees ODM offices that directly support the DM, including the Executive Secretariat, Legislative Affairs, Public Affairs, the Office of Protocol, and the Watch Office.

(3) **Associate Director of National Intelligence and Chief Information Officer (ADNI/CIO).** The ADNI/CIO is responsible for the overall formation, development, and management of the IC's information technology (IT) enterprise required to implement the present and future business directives of the DNI. The ADNT/CIO will closely coordinate with the Department of Defense, Department of Homeland Security, Department of Justice and other US Government Departments to produce compatible architectures, and common standards and policies ensuring the greatest transparency for intelligence support. The CIO shall: manage activities relating to the information technology infrastructure and enterprise architecture of the IC; have procurement approval authority over all information technology items related to the enterprise architectures of all IC elements; direct and manage all information technology-related procurement for the IC; and ensure that all expenditures for information technology and research and development activities are consistent with the IC enterprise architecture and the strategy of the Director for such architecture. The ADNI/CIO will oversee Deputy ADNI's responsible for IC IT Governance, IC IT Management, IC Enterprise services, IC Enterprise Architecture, and Information Sharing and Customer Outreach.

e. **Civil Liberties Protection Officer.** The Civil Liberties Protection Officer advises the leadership, offices, and personnel of the ODM on the protection of privacy and civil liberties; oversees the implementation of the DNI's civil liberties policies, directives, and instructions; and carries out responsibilities designated by law or otherwise assigned by the DNI relating to the protection of privacy and civil liberties within the ODNI and elements of the IC, as appropriate.

f. **National Intelligence Council.** The NIC is composed of senior analysts within the IC and substantive experts from other government agencies and the private sector, who shall be appointed by, report to, and serve at the pleasure of the DNI. Members of the NIC constitute the senior intelligence advisors of the IC for purposes of representing the views of the IC within the USG. The MC is authorized to task IC elements and to coordinate and compile the necessary briefing materials for ODNI participation at all principals and deputies committee meetings, as well as NSC and HSC meetings. The DDNI/A is delegated all authorities and responsibilities of the DNI with respect to the MC.

g. **National Counterintelligence Executive (NCIX) and the Office of the National Counterintelligence Executive (ONCIX).** The NCIX serves as the head of national counterintelligence for the USG. The NCIX and the ONCIX function as components of the ODM and perform duties provided in the Counterintelligence Enhancement Act of 2002, as amended. The NCIX duties include integration of all counterintelligence activities of the USG, acting as chairperson of the Counterintelligence Policy Board, which also serves as the membership of the Policy Coordinating Council on Counterintelligence; the ONCIX is responsible for production of the National Counterintelligence Strategy, the National Threat Identification and Prioritization Assessment, and such other duties as may be prescribed by the DNI or specified by law. The Director of NCIX also serves as DNI Mission Manager for Counterintelligence and as such is the principal advisor to the DNI on issues relating to the overall strategy and performance of the IC relating to counterintelligence. (Intelligence Authorization Act for FY 2003 §§ 901–904 (50 USC 402b and 402c))

h. **Inspector General.** The Inspector General provides policy direction for and plans, conducts, supervises, and coordinates inspections, audits, investigations, and other inquiries relating to the programs and operations of the ODM and the authorities and responsibilities of the DNI. The mission of the Office of the Inspector General is to ensure accountability and integrity in the performance of duties and expenditure of funds, and to provide analyses and insights that enhance the economy, efficiency, and effectiveness of the programs for which ODNI is responsible. The Office also exercises coordination and leadership, working with the inspectors general of the departments and agencies containing elements of the IC and with the inspectors general of the individual IC elements, in carrying out cross-agency projects and fulfilling community-wide objectives established under the IRTPA of 2004.

i. **National Intelligence Centers.** NCTC and NCPC are national intelligence centers. The DNI may establish additional national intelligence centers to address intelligence priorities, including, but not limited to, regional issues. Each national intelligence center shall perform such duties as the DNI assigns. The DNI shall ensure that the head of each national intelligence center has appropriate authority, direction, and control of such center, and of the personnel assigned, to carry out the assigned mission.

(1) **National Counterterrorism Center.** As set forth in the National Security Act of 1947, as amended, the NCTC is the primary organization in the USG for analyzing and integrating all intelligence possessed or acquired by the USG pertaining to terrorism and counterterrorism, except for intelligence pertaining exclusively to domestic terrorists and domestic counterterrorism. The Director of NCTC reports to the DNI with respect to the budget and programs of the NCTC, the activities of the Directorate of Intelligence of the NCTC, and the conduct of intelligence operations implemented by other elements of the IC. In this role, the center performs the following:

- Serves as the central and shared knowledge bank on known and suspected terrorist and terror group information.
- Provides all-source intelligence support to government-wide counterterrorism activities.
- Ensures that agencies, as appropriate, have access to and receive intelligence needed to accomplish their assigned activities, and have access to and receive all-source intelligence support needed to execute their counterterrorism plans or perform independent, alternative analysis.

The Director of NCTC also serves as DNI Mission Manager for Counterterrorism and as such is the principal advisor to the DNI on issues relating to the overall strategy and performance of the IC relating to terrorism and counterterrorism. Overseeing all aspects of national intelligence related to terrorism, the Director, NCTC, in his mission manager role drives community efforts to address key intelligence problems and bring mission focus to the management of community resources to help optimize US counterterrorism capabilities and performance. NCTC is also responsible for conducting strategic operational planning for counterterrorism activities across the USG. The Director of NCTC reports to the President of the United States with respect to his strategc operational planning responsibilities.

(2) **National Counterproliferation Center**. NCPC is the primary organization within the USG for managing, coordinating, and integrating IC planning, collection, exploitation, analysis, interdiction, and other activities related to the proliferation of weapons of mass destruction, their delivery systems, and related materials and technologies and intelligence support to efforts to prevent or impede such proliferation. As the DNI Mission Manager for Counterproliferation, the Director of NCPC serves as the principal advisor to the DNI on issues relating to the overall strategy of the IC relating to such proliferation.

j. **DNI Mission Managers.** Mission managers oversee all aspects of intelligence related to designated priority targets of the IC. In coordination with the DDNIs and with the guidance and oversight of the PDDNI, DNI mission managers set intelligence priorities for collection, analysis, and target development; establish strategic plans for collection and analysis; review/validate research and development and S&T plans; and make resource recommendations to the DNI, as designated by the PDDNI.

National Intelligence Mission Manager Board. The National Intelligence Mission Manager Board shall oversee the activities of the DNI mission managers. The board will be made up of the PDDNI, who will serve as the chair, DDNI/C, DDNI/A, DDNI/CO, DDNI/M, ADNI/S&T, and other senior ODNI representatives, as appropriate.

k. **ODNI Watch Center.** The ODNI Watch Center is the DNI's principal crisis management center and locus for tracking breaking information, Its main duties include:

- Alerting ODM senior leaders to breaking world events and facilitating the IC response

- Anticipating and briefmg the DNI and PDDNI on topics of concern to US decisionmakers
- Providing executive communications support

3. **Committees and Advisory Groups.** The DNI is authorized to appoint advisory committees and to employ part-time advisory personnel, as the DNI deems necessary in the execution of DNI functions, consistent with Section 303 of the National Security Act (NSA § 303; see also, EO 12333 § 1.3(a), (b), 1.5(j)). The DNI has established appropriate committees and councils consistent with the direction contained in the IRTPA to advise and assist, where appropriate, in the overall administration and management of the IC. Some of these bodies established by the DNI as well as others used by the DNI include, but are not limited to:

a. **Joint Intelligence Community Council.** As set forth in the National Security Act of 1947, as amended, the JICC assists the DNI in developing and implementing a joint, unified national intelligence effort to protect national security by: advising the DNI on establishing requirements, developing budgets, managing finances, monitoring and evaluating the performance of the IC, and on other matters, as appropriate, and ensuring the tmely execution of programs, policies, and directives of the DNI. The JICC comprises the DNI, as chair; the Secretary of State; the Secretary of the Treasury; SECDEF; the Attorney General; the Secretary of Energy; the Secretary of Homeland Security; and such other officers as the President may designate.

b. **IC Leadership Committee (ICLC).** The ICLC is the senior IC forum for advising and assisting the DNI in the development and implementation of IC policies, plans, and processes, consistent with applicable laws and regulations. The ICLC comprises the PDDNI, as chair; the heads of the elements of the IC; the DDNIs; the ADNI/COS; and others as directed by the chair.

c. **Program Manager Group.** The Program Manager Group, chaired by the PDDNI, advises and assists the DNI in identifying requirements, developing budgets, managing finance, and monitoring and evaluating the performance of the IC. The Program Manager Group membership consists of the heads of CIA, DIA, NGA, NRO, the National Security Agency, and the Federal Bureau of Investigation (National Security Branch), the DDNIs, the ADNI/COS, and others, as directed by the chair.

4. **Program Manager, Information Sharing Environment (ISE).** The Program Manager, ISE, reports to the President through the DNI The terms "information sharing environment" and "ISE" mean an approach that facilitates the sharing of terrorism information. The program manager has and exercises government-wide authority, in consultation with the Information Sharing Council, to plan for and oversee the implementation of and manage the ISE; assist in the development of policies, procedures, guidelines, rules, and standards, as appropriate, to foster the development and proper operation of the ISE; and assist, monitor, and assess the implementation of the ISE by Federal departments and agencies to ensure adequate progress, technological consistency, and policy compliance; and regularly report findings to Congress.

5. **Intelligence Discipline Managers.** To support the DNI's responsibilities for oversight and management of the IC, enhance the integration, coordination and evaluation of intelligence operations, and ensure the strategic management of resources, the DNI has designated certain officials to lead and manage intelligence disciplines across agencies and programs. Intelligence discipline managers will work with the ODNI to develop, coordinate, and implement policies, procedures, standards, guidance, and techniques for their respective disciplines that ensure appropriate integration, coordination, and collaboration within and across intelligence disciplines consistent with the overall direction of the DNI.

a. **Director of Central Intelligence Agency.** The Director of the CIA (DCIA) serves as the National Human Intelligence (HUMINT) Manager for the IC with the authority to coordinate, deconflict, and evaluate clandestine HUMINT operations across the IC. The DCIA has delegated National HUMINT Manager authorities to the Director of the National Clandestine Service (NCS). The Director of the NCS works with the DDNI/C and agencies engaged in clandestine HUMINT operations for tasking, coordination, budget resources, personnel policies, and information sharing.

b. **Measurement and Signature Intelligence (MASINT) Community Executive (MCE).** The MCE is responsible for MASINT for the entire IC and serves as the IC-wide advocate for the discipline. The MCE reports to the DDNI/C and works to resolve MASINT issues in concert with the relevant IC members. The Under Secretary of Defense for Intelligence designates an individual to serve as Deputy, MCE.

c. **Director, National Geospatial Intelligence Agency.** The Director, NGA, serves as the IC functional manager within the NIP for investment activities related to geospatial intelligence (GEOINT); carries out tasking of imagery and geospatial information collection; coordinates imagery and geospatial information processing and exploitation; ensures the dissemination of imagery and geospatial information in a timely manner to authorized recipients; authorizes foreign disclosures and releases for national satellite imagery consistent with the DNI's delegation of authority to the Director, NGA; prescribes technical architecture and standards related to GEOINT and ensures compliance with such architecture and standards; and develops and fields systems of common concern related to GEOINT. The Director of NGA is responsible for the collection, processing, and dissemination of GEOINT for foreign intelligence purposes in accordance with guidance provided by the DNI through the DDNI/C. (see NSA § 105(b)(2))

d. **Director, National Security Agency.** The Director of the National Security Agency executes the responsibilities of SECDEF as executive agent of the USG for the conduct of signals intelligence (SIGINT), except as otherwise directed by the President or the NSC. The Director of the National Security Agency is responsible for the collection, processing, and dissemination of SIGINT information for foreign intelligence purposes in accordance with guidance provided by the DNI through the DDNI/C. (NSA § 105(b)(1))

e. **DNI Executive Agent for the DNI Open Source Center.** The DCIA serves as the DNI's executive agent for the DNI Open Source Center, with day-to-day management delegated to the Center Director. The Center Director reports directly to the Deputy DCIA in executing strategy, policy, and program guidance established by the DNI. The DDNI/C establishes open source strategy, policy and program guidance for the Center and other IC elements. The Open Source Center advances the IC's exploitation of open source material, including from the Internet, and is responsible for enabling all IC analysts to access and use relevant open source materials.

6. **Director of National Intelligence Representatives.** The DNI appoints representatives to carry out IC responsibilities and functions in foreign countries, at military commands, and at other government agencies, departments, or institutions. These representatives may be drawn from officers serving in other positions within the IC. Where applicable, such representatives continue at the same time to serve and support their parent organizations. The DDNI/CO is the executive agent for DNI representatives and makes appointment recommendations to the DNI for assignment of representatives. The DDNI/CO also serves as the primary point of contact for the representatives to report key IC information, and ODNI management and administration issues and concerns to the DNI.

G. EFFECTIVE DATE: This directive is effective immediately.

ANNEX A—DEFINITIONS

Congressional Intelligence Committees: The Select Committee on Intelligence of the Senate and the Permanent Select Committee on Intelligence of the House of Representatives.

Counterintelligence: Information gathered and activities conducted to protect against espionage, other intelligence activities, sabotage, or assassinations conducted by or on behalf of foreign governments or elements thereof, foreign organizations, or foreign persons, or international terrorist activities, but not including personnel, physical, document, or communications security programs. (EO 12333)

Covert Action: The term "covert action" means an activity or activities of the US Government (USG) to influence political, economic, or military conditions abroad, where it is intended that the role of the USG will not be apparent or acknowledged publicly, but does not include: activities the primary purpose of which is to acquire intelligence, traditional counterintelligence activities, traditional activities to improve or maintain the operational security of USG programs, or administrative activities; traditional diplomatic or military activities or routine support to such activities; traditional law enforcement activities conducted by USG law enforcement agencies or routine support to such activities; or, activities to provide routine support to the overt activities (other than activities described) of other USG agencies abroad. (NSA § 503(e))

Elements of Intelligence Community: The term "Intelligence Community" includes the following:

- Office of the Director of National Intelligence
- Central Intelligence Agency
- National Security Agency
- Defense Intelligence Agency
- National Geospatial-Intelligence Agency
- National Reconnaissance Office
- Other offices within Department of Defense (DoD) for the collection of specialized national intelligence through reconnaissance programs
- The intelligence elements of the Army, Navy, Air Force, Marine Corps, the Federal Bureau of Investigation, and the Department of Energy
- Bureau of Intelligence and Research of the Department of State
- Office of Intelligence and Analysis of the Department of the Treasury
- The elements of the Department of Homeland Security concerned with the analysis of intelligence information, including the Office of Intelligence of the Coast Guard
- Office of National Security Intelligence, Drug Enforcement Administration
- Such other elements of any other department or agency as may be designated by the President, or designated jointly by the Director of National Intelligence and the head of the department or agency concerned, as an element of the Intelligence Community (IC).

(NSA § 3(4); DNI Letter to the IC, February 7, 2006)

Geospatial Intelligence (GEOINT): The exploitation and analysis of imagery and geospatial information to describe, assess, and visually depict physical features and geographically referenced activities on the Earth. Geospatial intelligence consists of imagery, imagery intelligence, and geospatial information.

Human Intelligence (HUMINT): A category of intelligence derived from information collected and provided by human sources.

Intelligence Discipline: A well-defined area of intelligence collection, processing, exploitation, and reporting using a specific category of technical or human resources. There are five major disciplines: HUMINT, GEOINT, measurement and signature intelligence (MASINT), signals intelligence (SIGINT), and open-source intelligence (OSINT).

Major System: The term "major system" means a combination of elements that will function together to produce the capabilities required to fulfill a mission need, which elements may include hardware, equipment, software or any combination thereof, but excludes construction or other improvements to real property. A system shall be considered a major system if:

- DoD is responsible for the system and the total expenditures for research, development, test, and evaluation for the system are estimated to be more than $75,000,000 (based on fiscal year 1980 constant dollars) or the eventual total expenditure for procurement of more than $300,000,000 (based on fiscal year 1980 constant dollars).
- A civilian agency is responsible for the system and total expenditures for the system are estimated to exceed $750,000 (based on fiscal year 1980 constant dollars) or the dollar threshold for a "major system" established by the agency (pursuant to Office of Management and Budget Circular A-109), whichever is greater.
- The system is designated a "major system" by the head of the agency responsible for the system.

(41 USC 403(9))

Measurement and Signature Intelligence: Measurement and Signature Intelligence (MASINT) is information produced by quantitative and qualitative analysis of physical attributes of targets and events in order to characterize and identify them.

National Intelligence: The terms "national intelligence" and "intelligence related to national security" refer to all intelligence, regardless of the source from which derived and including information gathered within or outside the United States, that pertains, as determined consistent with any guidance issued by the President, to more than one USG agency and that involves threats to the United States, its people, property, or interests; the development, proliferation, or use of weapons of mass destruction; or any other matter bearing on US national or homeland security. (NSA § 3(5))

National Intelligence Program: All programs, projects, and activities of the IC, as well as any other programs of the IC designated jointly by the Director of National Intelligence (DNI) and the head of a US department or agency or by the President. It does not include programs, projects, or activities of the military departments to acquire intelligence solely for the planning and conduct of tactical military operations by US armed forces. (NSA § 3(6))

Open-Source Intelligence: Open-Source Intelligence is intelligence produced from publicly available information that is collected, exploited, and disseminated in a timely manner to an appropriate audience for the purpose of addressing a specific intelligence requirement. (National Defense Authorization Act for FY 2006 § 931)

Sensitive Compartmented Information (SCI): SCI is classified national intelligence information concerning or derived from sensitive intelligence sources, methods, or analytical processes, which is to be handled exclusively within formal access control systems established by the DNI.

Signals Intelligence: SIGINT is a category of intelligence comprising either individually or in combination all communications intelligence, electronic intelligence, and foreign instrumentation signals intelligence, however transmitted. In addition, SIGINT is intelligence derived from communications, electronic, and foreign instrumentation signals.

ANNEX B—PRIMARY REFERENCES

1. National Security Act of 1947, 50 U.S.C. § 401 et seq., as amended
2. Intelligence Reform and Terrorism Prevention Act of 2004, Pub. L. No. 108-458, 118 Stat. 3638 (2004)
3. Counterintelligence Enhancement Act of 2002, Pub. L. No. 107-306, §§ 901-904, 116 Stat. 2436 (2002), as amended
4. Executive Order 12333, 46 Federal Regulation 59,941 (December 4, 1981), as amended
5.. Executive Order 13381, 70 Federal Regulation 37,953 (June 30, 2005)
6. Executive Order 13355, 69 Federal Regulation 53,593 (September 1, 2004)
7. Executive Order 12958, 60 Federal Regulation 19,825 (Apr. 20, 1995), as amended
8. Federal Property and Administrative Services Act of 1949, as amended
9. National Defense Authorization Act for FY 2006
10. Office of Management and Budget, Memorandum M-05-17 (June 30, 2005)

Intelligence Community Directive Number 101

Intelligence Community Policy System (Effective: January 16, 2009)
(Amended: June 12, 2009)

A. AUTHORITY: The National Security Act of 1947, as amended; Executive Order (EO) 12333, as amended; and other applicable provisions of law.

B. PURPOSE:
1. To effectively and efficiently promulgate Intelligence Community (lC) policy, this Intelligence Community Directive (lCD) establishes the IC Policy System which is comprised of a hierarchy of policy documents; processes for the development, coordination and evaluation of policy; and a governance structure to advise the Director of National Intelligence (DNI) or the DNI's designees regarding policy issues. This ICD also delegates decision authority for the promulgation of certain policies, and delineates the roles and responsibilities of the Office of the DNI (ODNI), IC elements, and Functional Managers, as designated by EO 12333 or the DNI, in the implementation of the IC Policy System.
2. This Directive rescinds Intelligence Community Policy Memorandum *2006-100-1, The Intelligence Community Policy Process* and supersedes all previous policies, memoranda, or portions thereof, regarding the IC policy process.

C. APPLICABILITY: This Directive applies to the Ie, as defined by the National Security Act of 1947, as amended; and such other elements of any other department or agency as may be designated by the President, or designated jointly by the DNI and the head of the department or agency concerned, as an element of the Ie.

D. POLICY:
1. The DNI shall establish IC policy to achieve a unified, integrated, effective and accountable IC postured to address and advance IC mission objectives to meet United States national security needs. The DNI shall establish IC policy consistent with applicable law, Exef.,:utive Order, National Security policy, and the DNI's strategic intent.
2. The IC Policy System shall be comprised of a hierarchy of policy instruments as defined in Section E.1. These interrelated IC directives, guidance, standards, or correspondence, herein referred to as policies, issued by the DNI, designated ODNI officials, Functional Managers, and other IC officials designated by the DNI are governed by this Directive and any subordinate policies.
3. Policies shall be:
   a. Developed in a collaborative manner to take into account the views of IC elements and others as appropriate;
   b. Deconflicted with any other applicable policies or regulations;
   c. Drafted in accordance with Section E.l, adhering to a common format and using common terms and definitions to the greatest extent possible;
   d. Formulated to be enforceable and implementable;

e. Disseminated electronically and communicated broadly, except where restrictions are required by the classification of the document; and
f. Evaluated for compliance, effectiveness and improvement.

E. FRAMEWORK

1. The IC Policy System shall establish policies applicable to the IC using the following instruments:

a. *Intelligence Community Directive (ICD).* ICDs may be based on statute, regulation, Executive Order, or other policy directives and establish policy and provide definitive direction to the Ie. ICDs may: defme activities, systems or missions; delegate authorities; establish roles and responsibilities; assign decision rights; establish governance structures; include evaluation criteria; or replace or modify previous policy, or provide other such guidance as the DNI deems appropriate. ICDs are developed and coordinated in accordance with ICPG 101.1, *Intelligence Community Directives and Policy Guidance* and are signed by the DNI or, in the DNI's absence, the Principal Deputy DNI (PDDNI).

b. *Intelligence Community Policy Guidance (ICPG).* ICPGs provide further guidance required for the implementation of ICDs. ICPGs are subsidiary to ICDs and may establish subordinate responsibilities, and define procedures, processes, or methodologies that enable ICDs to be implemented effectively. ICPGs shall be within the scope of and consistent with their associated ICDs. ICPGs are coordinated in accordance with ICPG 101.1 and are signed by the Deputy Director of National Intelligence for Policy, Plans, and Requirements (DDNIIPPR).

c. *Intelligence Community Standard (ICS).* ICSs are subordinate to ICDs and ICPGs, and are fully consistent with applicable ICDs and ICPGs. ICSs are policy instruments of the IC Policy System and provide specific procedures, sets of rules, conditions, guidelines, characteristics, or specifications for intelligence or intelligence-related products, processes, or activities in support of effective and uniform implementation of laws, Executive Orders, and IC policies. ICSs shall be developed, coordinated and approved pursuant to ICPG 101.2, *Intelligence Community Standards,* and are signed by officials designated in Section G.1.c.(2) or G.2 of this Directive.

d. *DNI Executive Correspondence (EC).* DNI EC focuses on issues or concerns of the DNI that impact the IC; communicates strategic policy intent, or preliminary approaches of the DNI; and may later culminate in, and contribute to, development of an ICD or ICPG. EC may also be used by the DNI to address emerging, immediate or urgent policy needs. The DNI or, in the DNI's absence, the PDDNI signs all EC.

2. Intelligence Community Policy Memoranda (ICPMs) will no longer be issued. All existing ICPMs will remain in effect until expressly rescinded by the DNI.

F. POLICY ADVISORY BODIES

1. The IC Policy System includes the following bodies, which serve an integral role in the process of developing and coordinating IC policy:

a. *Intelligence Community Policy Review Board (IC-PRB).* The IC-PRB is an advisory board comprised of deputy-level leaders from IC elements. The IC-

PRB is chaired by the DDNIJPPR. The objective of the IC-PRB is to provide a forum for high-level issue discussion and resolution; to ensure that key stakeholders and constituencies have been appropriately engaged on individual policies; to align policies with DNI and IC strategic objectives and intent; and to further identify policy needs and priorities, as well as inconsistencies or gaps in current policy.

b. *Intelligence Policy Advisory Group (IPAG).* The IPAG is comprised of designated senior policy representatives from each IC element and is chaired by the Assistant Deputy DNI for Policy. The objective of the IPAG forum is to inform the development of policy and ensure an inclusive and collaborative process. The IPAG shall serve as the official channel of communication on policy matters, and each IC element is responsible for communicating its respective policy equities and interests and identifying members for working groups.

2. To facilitate the development and coordination of policy, the DDNIJPPR or his or her designee may establish IC policy working groups or consult other advisors, as appropriate, to inform decision making throughout the policy process.

G. ROLES AND RESPONSmILITIES

1. *Office ofthe Director ofNational Intelligence*

a. The DNI or, in the DNI's absence, the PDDNI shall:

(1) Establish, through signature, ICDs and EC;

(2) Review and approve IC policies as required;

(3) Establish or use advisory boards to inform or make decisions regarding policy issues as appropriate;

(4) Ensure policies established under the IC Policy System are consistent with US law, Executive Orders, Presidential Directives, and other applicable provisions of law; and

(5) In coordination with appropriate department or agency heads, establish joint agreements or procedures for issues which fall outside the scope of the IC Policy System, but which may be required for the conduct of the IC mission or activities related to national security.

b. The DDNIJPPR shall serve as the DNI's designee for all matters pertaining to the IC Policy System and, in accordance with ICPG 101.1, shall:

(1) Develop ICDs and ICPGs with Accountable Officials, as established in Section G.1.c.(2), and subject matter experts as appropriate;

(2) Establish, through signature, ICPGs;

(3) Make technical amendments to ICDs and ICPGs through memoranda;

(4) Support ODNI officials, Functional Managers, and other IC officials designated by the DNI, in the development of ICSs where applicable;

(5) Chair the IC-PRB;

(6) Establish working groups to inform or develop specific policies as necessary;

(7) Ensure IC policies are consistent with Section D.3;

(8) Ensure IC policies are coordinated with department-level officials, when appropriate;

(9) Oversee the implementation of this Directive; and

(10) Serve as the office of record for all IC Policy System documents and maintain all comments, drafts and revisions as appropriate.

c. ODNI elements shall:

(1) Participate, as appropriate in the development, coordination and evaluation of IC policies, and provide subject matter expertise to the DNI designee; and

(2) Establish ICSs in accordance with the requirements provided in ICPG 10 1.2.

(a) The Associate DNI (ADNI) and IC Chief Information Officer shall establish ICSs related to information technology, community-level data standards, information security, and information management issues.

(b) The ADNI and IC Chief Human Capital Officer shall establish ICSs related to human capital and the IC workforce.

(c) The ADNI and Chief Financial Officer shall establish ICSs related to the financial and resource management of National Intelligence Program.

(d) The DDNIIPPR shall establish ICSs related to IC security and classification marking.

(e) The National Counterintelligence Executive shall establish ICSs related to counterintelligence.

(f) Other ODNI officials as designated by the DNI or the DNI designee may establish ICSs.

2. *Functional Managers and other officials designated by the DNI* shall:

a. Establish ICSs applicable to their functional or other area, designated in accordance with ICPG 101.2;

b. Participate in the development, coordination and evaluation of IC policies, and provide subject matter expertise to the DNI designee as requested;

c. Ensure implementing standards are in accordance with IC policies; and

d. Inform the DNI designee when there is any IC element policy in conflict with IC policy.

3. *Ie Elements* shall:

a. Participate in the development, coordination and evaluation of IC policies, and provide subject matter expertise to the DNI designee as requested;

b. Develop internal implementing policies, standards, procedures, or processes applicable to their element, in accordance with IC policies;

c. Inform the DNI designee when there is any policy applicable to an IC element in conflict with IC policy; and

d. Designate representatives to the IC-PRB and IPAG at the level described in Section F.1.

H. EFFECTIVE DATE: This Directive becomes effective on the date of signature.

J. M. McConnell
Director of National Intelligence
16 January 2009

Intelligence Community Directive Number 112

Congressional Notification

(Effective: November 16, 2011)

A. AUTHORITY: The National Security Act of 1947, as amended (hereinafter, National Security Act); Executive Order 12333, as amended; and other applicable provisions of law.

B. PURPOSE: This Directive establishes Intelligence Community (IC) policy to provide written notification to the Senate Select Committee on Intelligence and the House Permanent Select Committee on Intelligence (collectively the "Congressional intelligence committees") in order to keep them fully and currently informed of intelligence activities. This Directive replaces and rescinds Intelligence Community Policy Memorandum 2005-100-3, *Reporting of Intelligence Activities to Congress,* dated January 10,2006; *Timely Notification ofSignificant Intelligence Activities,* dated 24 March 2009; and *Follow-up to Reporting Intelligence Matters to Congress,* dated 15 October 2009.

C. APPLICABILITY

1. This Directive applies to the IC, as defined by the National Security Act of 1947, and to elements of any other department or agency as may be designated by the President, or designated jointly by the Director of National Intelligence (DNI) and the head of the department or agency concerned, as an element of the IC.

2. The Directive does not preclude or alter reporting responsibilities to the President's Intelligence Oversight Board as specified in Executive Order 13462 and any successor thereto.

3. This Directive does not apply to reporting of covert actions to the Congressional intelligence committees, to statutory reporting requirements for IC Inspectors General, or to routine informational briefings.

D. POLICY

1. The IC is committed to full and current notification of all intelligence activities as required by the National Security Act, including significant anticipated intelligence actions, significant intelligence failures, and illegal intelligence activities.

2. The provisions of this Directive shall be interpreted with a presumption of notification in fulfIllment of the statutory requirement to keep the Congressional intelligence committees fully and currently informed of all intelligence activities.

3. It is IC policy that IC elements shall, in a timely manner, keep the Congressional intelligence committees fully infonned, in writing, of all significant antici-

pated intelligence activities, significant intelligence failures, significant intelligence activities, and illegal activities.

4. IC element heads are responsible for determining whether an event is reportable under this Directive and are responsible for ensuring that Congress is notified of all intelligence activities in accordance with the provisions of this Directive.

5. Determining whether written notification should be provided of a particular intelligence activity is a judgment based on all the facts and circumstances known to the IC element, and on the nature and extent of previous notifications or briefings to Congress on the same matter. Not every intelligence activity warrants written notification. Facts and circumstances of intelligence activities change over time; therefore, IC elements must continually assess whether there is an obligation to report a matter pursuant to the National Security Act and this Directive.

6. As required by the National Security Act, Congress must receive written notification of significant anticipated intelligence activities and significant intelligence failures. General guidelines for determining the types of intelligence activities that warrant written notification follow:

a. Significant anticipated intelligence activities include:

(1) intelligence activities that entail, with reasonable foreseeability, significant risk of exposure, compromise, and loss of human life;

(2) intelligence activities that are expected to have a major impact on important foreign policy or national security interests;

(3) an IC element's transfer, to a recipient outside that IC element, of defense articles, personnel services, or "controlled equipment" valued in excess of $1 million as provided in Section 505 of the National Security Act;

(4) extensive organizational changes in an IC element;

(5) deployment of new collection techniques that represent a significant departure from previous operations or activities or that result from evidence of significant foreign developments;

(6) significant activities undertaken pursuant to specific direction of the President or the National Security Council (this is not applicable to covert action, which is covered by Section 503 of the National Security Act); or

(7) significant acquisition, reprogramming, or non-routine budgetary actions that are of Congressional concern and that are not otherwise reportable under the National Intelligence Program Procedures for Reprogramming and Transfers.

b. Significant intelligence failures are failures that are extensive in scope, continuing in nature, or likely to have a serious impact on United States (US) national security interests and include:

(l) the loss or compromise of classified information on such a scale or over such an extended period as to indicate a systemic loss or compromise of classified intelligence infonnation that may pose a substantial risk to US national security interests;

(2) a significant unauthorized disclosure of classified intelligence infonnation that may pose a substantial risk to US national security interests;

(3) a potentially pervasive failure, interruption, or compromise of a collection capability or collection system; or

(4) a conclusion that an intelligence product is the result of foreign deception or denial activity, or othefVJise contains major errors in analysis, with a significant impact on US national security policies, programs, or activities.

7. As a matter of policy, IC elements shall provide Congress written notification of other significant intelligence activities and illegal activities. General guidelines for determining these types of intelligence activities warranting notification follow.

a. Significant intelligence activities include:

(1) substantial changes in the capabilities or known vulnerabilities of US intelligence operations or intelligence systems or resources;

(2) programmatic developments likely to be of Congressional interest, such as major cost overruns, a major modification of, or the termination of a significant contract;

(3) developments that affect intelligence programs, projects, or activities that are likely to be of Congressional concern because of their substantial impact on national security or foreign policy;

(4) the loss of life in the perfonnance of an intelligence activity; or

(5) significant developments in, or the resolution of, a matter previously reported under these procedures.

b. illegal activities include:

(1) An intelligence activity believed to be in violation of US law, including any corrective action taken or planned in connection with such activity;

(2) Significant misconduct by an employee of an IC element or asset that is likely to seriously affect intelligence activities or othefVJise is of congressional concern, including human rights violations; or

(3) Other serious violations of US criminal law by an employee of an IC element or asset, which in the discretion of the head of an IC element warrants congressional notification.

8. Criteria described in Sections D.6 and D.7 above are not exhaustive. The absence of any of these criteria shall not be seen as determinative. Each potential determination shall be addressed on its particular merits. If it is unclear whether a notification is appropriate, IC elements should decide in favor of notification.

E. ROLES AND RESPONSIBILITIES:

To ensure full and current written notification of intelligence activities consistent with this Directive, each IC element head shall:

1. Designate as a point of contact a senior official who will have access to all relevant infonnation to assist the IC element head in identifying matters that should

be reported and who will be responsible for ensuring that notifications are full and current.

2. Establish, in writing, internal processes that will ensure timely identification and full and current reporting of intelligence activities, consistent with this Directive.

3. Provide the Office of the Director of National Intelligence Office of Legislative Affairs (ODNIJOLA) with a point of contact pursuant to Section B.1 above and a copy of the procedures established pursu ant to section E.2 above.

4. Ensure that written notifications required under this Directive are provided promptly upon determination that the intelligence activity should be reported under this Directive and the National Security Act.

a. Within 14 days of final determination by an IC element head (or designee) that a significant activity should be reported, an IC element shall provide written notification. If a complete written notification is not possible at that time, an IC element may provide preliminary oral notification and a projected time for further or final notification.

b. Written notifications shall contain a concise statement of the pertinent facts, an explanation of the significance of the intelligence activity, and the role of all departments and agencies involved in the intelligence activity.

c. Oral notifications shall be followed by a written notification, which shall include, in addition to the information described in Section EA.b above, the date of the oral notification, the office responsible for the subject of the oral notification, and the Congressional members and staff orally notified.

d. Notification of routine administrative matters such as reprogrammings, facility lease arrangement and renewals, or contract awards should be made with reference to the element's established timeline for such issues and consistent with Congressional requirements and budget processes.

5. Coordinate, as appropriate, with any other department, agency, or other entity of the US Government involved in the intelligence activity to ensure that an intelligence activity is fully and currently reported to the Congressional intelligence committees.

6. Conduct annual training for element personnel involved in intelligence activities regarding the IC's obligation to provide information to Congress under the National Security Act and this Directive.

7. Provide the ODNIIOLA copies of all Congressional notifications at the time they are provided to Congress, and a summary of any oral notification.

F. COORDINATION WITH THE DEPARTMENT OF JUSTICE REGARDING CRIMINAL INVESTIGATIONS AND PROSECUTIONS: Where intelligence information subject to this Directive relates to criminal investigations and prosecutions or reasonably anticipated criminal investigations and prosecutions, the IC shall comply with the following procedures:

1. IC elements shall consult with the Attorney General's designee or designees prior to providing the information to Congressional committees, members, or staff. With respect to the Congressional intelligence committees, this coordination shall ensure that the IC meets its reporting obligations under the National Security Act in a manner consistent with the integrity and independence of criminal investigations and prosecutions.

2. Disagreements between an IC element and the Department of Justice regarding the application of this section will be referred for resolution to the Attorney General and the DNI.

G. LIMITATION: Nothing in this directive shall be construed to limit an IC element's obligation to report matters to other Congressional committees with oversight jurisdiction or appropriations responsibility for that IC element, subject to the principles identified above regarding criminal matters or potential criminal matters.

H. EFFECTIVE DATE: This Directive becomes effective on the date of signature.

James R, Clapper
Director of National Intelligence
November 16, 2011

Intelligence Community Directive No. 114

Comptroller General Access to Intelligence Community Information

(Effective: June 30, 2011)

A. AUTHORITY: The National Security Act of 1947, as amended; Executive Order (EO) 12333, as amended, and other applicable provisions of law.

B. PURPOSE

1. This Intelligence Community (IC) Directive addresses the requirement in the Intelligence Authorization Act of 2010 (Public Law 111-259, section 348) to establish policy for access to information in the possession of an IC element by the Comptroller General through the Government Accountability Office (GAO).

2. This Directive provides guidance to the IC elements that is consistent with both the National Security Act of 1947, which provides the oversight structure for intelligence activities, and Chapter 7 of Title 31, which provides GAO the jurisdiction and authority to conduct audits and reviews of government programs and activities.

C. APPLICABILITY

1. This Directive applies to the IC, as defined by the National Security Act of 1947, as amended, and to such other elements of any other department or agency as may be designated by the President, or designated jointly by the Director of National Intelligence (DNI) and the head of the department or agency concerned, as an element of the IC.

2. This Directive shall apply to requests by the Comptroller General for information in the possession of an IC element that is related to intelligence activities and programs. Nothing in this Directive is intended to diminish the scope of support that IC elements have provided to GAO. For IC elements within departments, this Directive complements departmental policies governing GAO access to departmental information to the greatest extent possible. Departmental policies shall have primacy except for requests for national intelligence information related to activities and programs funded wholly or in part by the National Intelligence Program (NIP).

3. Nothing in this Directive shall be construed to authorize the Comptroller General or GAO to audit or examine records and expenditures made under the authority of 22 U.S Code 2396(a)(8), 10 U.S Code 127, 7231, or 50 U.S Code 403j(b).

D. POLICY

1. It is IC policy to cooperate with the Comptroller General, through the GAO, to the fullest extent possible, and to provide timely responses to requests for information.

2. To the extent consistent with national security and the protection of intelligence sources and methods, IC elements shall provide GAO access to information that relates to matters that are the subject of announced GAO reviews.

3. IC element heads are responsible for decisions regarding GAO access to information consistent with the guidelines set forth in this Directive. Those decisions apply only to information or documents originated by that particular IC element.

4. IC elements shaH evaluate GAO requests for information on a case-by-case basis.

a. Generally, IC elements shall cooperate with GAO audits or reviews and make information available to appropriately cleared GAO personnel. Finished, disseminated national intelligence information relevant to a GAO review, information relating to the administration of a US government-wide program or activity, and publicly available information shall generally be provided to GAO.

b. Information that falls within the purview of the congressional intelligence oversight committees generally shall not be made available to GAO to support a GAO audit or review of core national intelligence capabilities and activities, which include intelligence collection operations, intelligence analyses and analytical techniques, counterintelligence operations, and intelligence funding. IC elements may on a case-by-case basis provide information in response to any GAO requests not related to GAO audits or reviews of core national intelligence capabilities and activities. Access determinations for all such requests shall be made in a manner consistent with this Directive and applicable Departmental directives.

c. When making access determinations, IC elements shall also consider whether the infonnation is subject to statutory restrictions or executive branch confidentiality interests. Information on intelligence sources and methods, and information related to covert action shall not be provided.

5. IC elements shall not categorically deny GAO access to information, nor shall they withhold information solely because the information relates to a program that is funded by the NIP.

a. IC elements shall carefully consider requests for information based on dialogue with GAO and in a manner consistent with this Directive.

b. IC elements shall work with GAO to explore alternative means to accommodate a request for access to specific information if it is determined that GAO should not have access to the specific information requested.

6. Information provided to GAO shall be made available in a manner consistent with the obligation to protect intelligence sources and methods. Access to information shall be tailored after discussion with GAO to address specific objectives of the particular review. Accordingly,

a. Access by GAO personnel to information held by IC elements shall be consistent with principles of eligibility for access to classified national security information and need-to-know as outlined in EOs 12968 and 13526;

b. Consistent with Section D above, GAO may be afforded access to classifIed or other sensitive information only after GAO:

(1) Identifies the individuals who will have access to documents; and

(2) Verifies that: information and

(a) the individuals being granted access possess the appropriate security clearance, or have obtained a limited security approval and have signed an applicable nondisclosure agreement;

(b) if infonnation is to be retained by GAO it has secure facilities accredited to receive and store such information and holds such information, in accordance with classification, dissemination controls, and other special handling requirements;

(c) it has acknowledged and agreed to abide by the classification, dissemination controls, and other special handling requirements of any provided document or information; and

(d) its retention and dissemination of intelligence information shall comply with EO 12333, part 2, as it pertains to US persons information.

7. IC element responses to GAO products.

a. If GAO provides an IC element an opportunity to comment on a GAO product, the IC element is strongly encouraged to provide GAO with a timely response.

b. When a GAO report contains a recommendation concerning an IC element or intelligence activities, the concerned element shall submit a written statement addressing the recommendations within 60 calendar days of the date of the report to the appropriate House andSenate committees in the same manner as provided by 31 US Code 720. A copy of suchstatement shall also be provided to the ODNI Office of Legislative Affairs (OLA).

E. ROLES AND RESPONSIBILITIES: To ensure that this Directive is fully implemented, each IC element head shall:

1. Engage in dialogue with GAO, as appropriate;

2. Maintain or develop written procedures that detail the element's process for responding to GAO reviews. These procedures shall include at a minimum the following:

a. A presumption of cooperation including a process for exploring alternative means of accommodating GAO requests, to the extent possible, and within a reasonable time;

b. Designation of an appropriate initial point of contact in the element for coordinating GAO reviews. This point of contact shall be responsible for ensuring that GAO is informed of the classification and sensitivity of any infonnation provided as well a, any special handling instructions, as appropriate;

c. A process to assess GAO requests for information that provides for access determinations to be made at the lowest possible level consistent with organizational needs;

d. A requirement that the element respond to GAO requests for access to nformation within a reasonable timeframe to include notification to GAO of any delays;

e. A review process whereby an access issue that is not resolved at the lowest possible level may be elevated within an Ie element in an attempt to facilitate resolution;

f. A process for documenting formal denials of GAO requests for information; and, g. A method of alerting GAO to the confidentiality obligations and penalties at 31 US Code 716(e) and Section 348(b) of Public Law 111-259.

3. Provide the ODNI Office of Legislative Affairs (OLA) a copy of the procedures issued pursuant to Section E.2.

4. Promptly notify the ODNI OLA of GAO requests for engagement with an Ie element and subsequently of Ie element decisions on access. ODNI notification shall not delay Ie element responses to GAO requests.

5. Determine that information made available to GAO is responsive to the GAO review for which the information or record is requested and is supported by a written GAO request that clearly identifies the purpose of the request.

6. Upon receipt of any request for access to information that may affect the joint equities of other IC elements, coordinate responses with other affected offices and elements of the IC.

7. Ensure that any GAO request for access to another agency's information is referred to that agency or that information responsive to such a request is made available to GAO only after obtaining the documented consent of that agency.

8. If after following procedures developed pursuant to Section E.2, the IC element determines that a GAO request. for information cannot be accommodated, the IC element shall promptly advise GAO of the denial of a request for information with a written justification and provide a copy to the ODNI OLA.

F. EFFECTIVE DATE: This ICD becomes effective on June 30, 2011.

James R, Clapper
Director of National Intelligence
April 29, 2011

Intelligence Community Directive Number 116

Intelligence Planning, Programming, Budgeting, and Evaluation System

(Effective: September 14, 2011)

A. AUTHORITY: The National Security Act of'1947, as amended; Executive Order (EO) 12333, as amended; and other applicable provisions of law.

B. PURPOSE: This Intelligence Corrununity Directive (ICD) establishes overarching policy and a management framework relevant to the Director of National Intelligence (DNl) National Intelligence Program (NIP) development and budget execution authorities. This Directive also constitutes in part the procedures called for in EO 12333 Section 1.3(b)(20). This Directive rescinds lCD 106, *Intelligence Community Strategic Enterprise Management,* 20 November 2008.

C. APPLICABILITY: This Directive applies to the Intelligence Corrununity (IC) as defmed by the National Security Act of 1947, as amended; and such other elements of any other department or agencies as may be designated by the President, or designated jointly by the DNl and the head of the department or agency concerned, as an element of the lC.

D. POLICY

1. The Intelligence Planning, Programming, Budgeting, and Evaluation (IPPBE) system is designed to effectively shape and sustain intelligence capabilities through the development of the NIP and budget consistent with the National Intelligence Strategy (NlS) and other applicable National Strategies or Presidential Policy Directives. IPPBE ensures a predictable, transparent, and repeatable end-to-end process to collect and prioritize intelligence mission requirements in the context of the strategic objectives of the DNl and the Ie. In addition, IPPBE supports the DNl's participation in the development of the Military Intelligence Program (MIP).

2. The IPPBE system comprises the interdependent phases of planning, programming, and budgeting that are informed by ongoing evaluation. Each phase is informed and guided by the products and decisions produced in other phases.

a. **Planning:** The planning phase identifies IC strategic priorities and Major Issues to be addressed in the programming phase. Planning includes the following primary activities:

(1) Analyzing impacts of sustaining current capabilities, long-term trends, and alternative future challenges;

(2) Identifying and analyzing strategic issues and future customer needs; and

(3) Identifying gaps and shortfalls by analyzing current IC capabilities.

b. **Programming:** The programming phase provides options to frame DNI resource decisions through analysis of alternatives and studies that assess cost-performance benefits. Programming includes the following primary activities:

(1) Conducting Major Issue Studies, which assess and analyze high impact crosscommunity issues and provide feasible alternatives;

(2) Developing Independent Cost Estimates (ICE), which provide a total life-cycle cost estimate for Major System Acquisitions and other programs of interest;

(3) Developing the Consolidated Intelligence Guidance (CIG), which documents IC strategic priorities and conveys DNI direction for building the United States intelligence program and budget;

(4) Deconflicting and integrating guidance for MIP-funded and joint NIPIMIPfunded activities into the CIG; and

(5) Managing the Strategic Program Briefings (SPB), which provide a strategic-level dialogue between the DNI and each Program Manager regarding incorporation of DNI priorities and other CIG direction into their program build.

c. **Budgeting:** Budgeting and execution activities addressed in IPPBE have the goal of produCing and implementing an annual consolidated NIP budget. Budgeting includes the following primary activities:

(1) Developing the Intelligence Program Budget Submission (IPBS) Procedural Guidance.

(2) Developing and issuing DNI Decision Documents to adjust NIP program resources.

(3) Developing the NIP portion of the President's Budget;

(4) Ensuring the budget submission is executable, aligned with the CIG, and reflects performance-based budget decisions;

(5) Presenting, justifying, and defending the NIP budget to the Office of Management and Budget (OMB) and Congress;

(6) Managing apportionment and reprogramming activities;

(7) Reviewing the execution of the NIP budget and participating in MIP execution reviews; and

(8) Developing supplemental appropriations requests.

d. **Evaluation:** Evaluation assesses the effectiveness of IC programs, activities, major initiatives, and investments in implementing DNI guidance in the context of their original objectives, measures of effectiveness, metrics, outcomes, benefits, shortfalls, and costs. The purpose is to provide insight to inform investment decisions and future guidance, to identify material and non-material solutions to IC challenges, and to identify best practices to improve IC effectiveness. The IPPBE evaluation process leverages existing reports to economize evaluation efforts across the Ie. Evaluation activities include:

(1) Strategic Evaluation Reports—Independent evaluations of prior major issue decisions and intelligence investments to assess their effectiveness relative to expected outcomes, success measures, prior investments, cost benefits, and potential utility;

(2 Budget and Performance Reports—Assessments of IC-wide budget, performance, and execution measures to enable performance-based budget decisions;

(3) NIS Progress Assessment—An assessment of IC progress towards achieving the goals and objectives of the NIS to inform decisions and products in each phase of the IPPBE System; and

(4) IC Strategic Assessment -An annual assessment of the implications for the IC of policy and strategy changes, long-term trends, and alternative future challenges to inform decisions and products in each phase of the IPPBE System.

E. ROLES AND RESPONSffiILITIES

1. The DNI provides guidance and:

a. Exercises final authority over NIP development and budget execution;

b. Approves the planning and programming priorities; and

c. Participates in the development of the MIP.

2. IC Element Heads:

a. Assess mission needs to identify intelligence gaps and shortfalls during the planning phase and identify requirements to the ODNI;

b. Recommend and participate in Major Issue Studies;

c. Develop and present SPBs to the DNI on implementation of the CIG;

d. Notify the *ADNIlCFO* and ADNIISRA when there is a major change from what was presented in the SPB;

e. Develop and submit an IPBS and Congressional Budget Justification Book;

f. Provide representation to staff-level fora for all phases of IPPBE;

g. Provide requested information to the DNI to support development and determination of a performance-based NIP budget;

h. Provide performance assessment information to the DNI detailing accomplishments and challenges in implementing NIS mission and enterprise objectives to support a comprehensive evaluation regime;

i. Manage and oversee the execution of appropriated programs, as applicable; and

j. Advise the DNI on reprogramming proposals required to address changing programs and emerging requirements.

3. ADNUSRA:

a. Manages the integration and synchronization of the IPPBE system;

b. Leads the planning and programming phases of IPPBE and publishes the CIG;

c. Develops the Major Issues List, which documents the Major Issue Studies to be completed in the programming phase;

d. Manages the SPBs;

e. Develops ICEs;

f. Manages the IC Capability Requirements process in accordance with DNI policy and guidance;

g. Produces Strategic Evaluation Reports; and

h. Consolidates and integrates evaluation findings for input to the IPPBE phases of planning, programming, and budgeting.

4. ADNUP&S:

a. Leads the development of the NIS;

b. Conducts NIS Progress Assessments; and

c. Manages the production of Strategic Assessments in consultation with the Deputy DNI for Intelligence Integration (DDNIJII).

5. ADNIJCFO:

a. Leads the budgeting phase;

b. Leads in-depth analysis of the IPBS and other budgets, as appropriate;

c. Leads IC budget and performance management by establishing, tracking, and reporting on goals, measures, and initiatives;

d. Develops and issues DNI Decision Documents;

e. Publishes the NIP portion of the President's Budget;

f. Develops, presents, justifies, and defends the NIP budget to OMB and Congress;

g. Develops Congressional appeal letters;

h. Develops and justifies supplemental appropriation requests;

i. Oversees budget execution by conducting NIP execution reviews and participating in the Office of the Under Secretary of Defense for Intelligence-led MIP execution reviews;

j. Manages financial reporting and analysis of NIP resources; to include apportionment and reprogramming of appropriated funds;

k. Maintains the DNI's budget and execution systems that support the NIP budget requests and historical program of record; and

1. Provides guidance on, and oversees all NIP-related fmancial management operations and reporting for the IC.

6. DDNIIIl:

a. Leads the development, implementation, and assessment of the Unifying Intelligence Strategies;

b. Articulates, prioritizes, and conveys mission requirements identified by the Program Managers, IC Elements, and National Intelligence Mission Managers;

c. Participates in Major Issue Studies and other related studies; and

d. Coordinates, prioritizes, and optimizes intelligence integration capabilities and activities.

F. EFFECTIVE DATE: This Directive becomes effective on the date of signature.

James R, Clapper
Director of National Intelligence
September 14, 2011

Intelligence Community Directive No. 300

Management, Integration, and Oversight of Intelligence Collection and Covert Action

(Effective: October 3, 2006)

A. Authority: The National Security Act of 1947, as amended; Sections 441-467 of Title 10, US code, as amended; The Intelligence Reform and Terrorism Prevention Act of 2004; Executive Order 12333, as amended; and other applicable provisions of law.

B. Purpose

1. This Intelligence Community (IC) directive (ICD) establishes Director of National Intelligence (DNI) policy to integrate, prioritize, and maximize IC collection capabilities and activities to produce timely and useful national intelligence information for policymakers, Defense, and other intelligence consumers. It establishes the Deputy Director of National Intelligence for Collection (DDNI/C) authorities and responsibilities for the coordination, integration, and oversight of the national intelligence collection enterprise; covert action; information operations; and national intelligence-related activities engaged in, by, carried out for or on behalf of any department, agency or entity of the IC. This directive applies to information collected from overt as well as clandestine sources obtained in foreign or domestic arenas. Further, this policy articulates the DDNI/C responsibilities, on behalf of the DNI, to ensure that all national collection activities support national customer priorities, achieve maximum impact, and protect US persons civil liberties, while safeguarding sensitive collection sources and methods and minimizing operational and developmental risk, unnecessary programmatic overlap, and interagency conflict and confusion.

2. The DDNI/C shall ensure the effective implementation of this policy.

3. This ICD rescinds Director of Central Intelligence Directive 3/1, Authorities and Responsibilities of the Assistant Director of Central Intelligence for Collection and the National Intelligence Collection Board, 7 August 2000; IC Policy Memorandum 2005-300-1, DDNI for Collection, 9 November 2005; and the previously signed ICD 300, same subject, 31 August 2006.

C. Applicability: This directive applies to the IC, as defined by the National Security Act of 1947, as amended, and other departments or agencies that may be designated by the President, or designated jointly by the DNI and the head of the department or agency concerned, as an element of the IC.

D. Policy

1. The DDNI/C is charged with the implementation of the responsibilities of the DNI relative to the collection of national intelligence and covert action. For the purposes of this ICD, "collection" is defined as the acquisition of information to meet an intelligence requirement. The DDNI/C will ensure that the IC activities in these areas are conducted in a prioritized, coherent and coordinated manner to have maximum effectiveness in support of US intelligence priorities and are in accordance with all applicable laws and presidential directives.

2. The DDNI/C will carry out these responsibilities through the appointment of four assistant deputy directors: the Assistant Deputy Director of National Intelligence for Collection Strategies (ADDNI/CS). The ADDNI for Human Intelligence (HUMINT) (ADDNI/H), the ADDNI for Technical Means (ADDNI/TM), and the ADDNI for Open Source (ADDNI/OS), as well as additional staff as deemed necessary. In addition, the DDNI/C will oversee IC collection activities via the National Intelligence Collection Board (NICB), the Community Clandestine HUMINT Committee, the Signals Intelligence (SIGINT) Committee, the Geospatial-Intelligence (GEOINT) Committee, the Measurement and Signature Intelligence (MASINT) Executive and the MASINT Committee (MASCOM), the National Open Source Committee, the DNI Mission Managers, and other entities that may be established.

3. Under the guidance of the DDNI/C, IC elements are responsible for the execution of their specific intelligence collection activities and are accountable for the associated programming, performance planning and budget. Community leadership roles for specific areas of responsibilities have been defined by the National Security Act of 1947, as amended; and Executive Order 12333, as amended, and/or clarified by DNI decision memoranda. This directive does not modify the authorities of the heads of executive departments and agencies to exercise, consistent with the authorities and responsibilities of the DNI, their authorities to manage elements of IC within their department and agencies.

E. Authorities and Responsibilities

1. The DDNI/C is delegated the following authorities and responsibilities.

   a. All authorities and responsibilities of the DNI with respect to establishing collection priorities for the IC to ensure timely and effective tasking, collection, processing, analysis, and dissemination of national intelligence. All authorities of the DNI with respect to using national collection assets are used optimally to support national, Defense, and other US government intelligence priorities, through coordination within the IC, with the Defense Joint Intelligence Operations Center (D-JIOC)/Joint Functional Component Command-Intelligence Surveillance, and Reconnaissance (JFCC-ISR) and combatant command JIOCs, and with other appropriate US government elements. These authorities and responsibilities will be exercised in coordination with the DDNI/A and the DDNI/R.

b. Consistent with intelligence priorities identified in the National Intelligence Priorities Framework, all authorities and responsibilities of the DNI with respect to establishing objectives and guidance for the IC to ensure timely and effective collection of national intelligence, and in coordination with the DDNI/A, such authorities and responsibilities with respect to processing and dissemination of national intelligence, including all authorities and responsibilities of the DNI to:

(1) Direct timely, effective and integrated collection of national intelligence through the NICB and to manage and direct the tasking of the collection of national intelligence by elements of the IC.

(2) Provide advisory tasking regarding collection of national intelligence to elements of agencies and departments not within the National Intelligence Program (NIP).

(3) Establish requirements and priorities for foreign intelligence information to be collected under the Foreign Intelligence Surveillance Act of 1978 (50 US Code 1801, et. Seq.). The DDNI/C also has the authority and responsibility of the DNI for providing assistance to the Attorney General to ensure that information is derived from electronic surveillance or physical searches under that Act is disseminated so that it may be used efficiently and effectively for national intelligence purposes.

(4) Oversee open source collection, including providing overall guidance to the DNI Open Source Center and, in coordination with the DDNI/A, the authorities and responsibilities of the DNI with respect to ensuring that the IC makes efficient and effective use of open sources to facilitate collaboration between analysts and collectors in support of all customers to ensure that a systematic effort is made to prioritize the collection of intelligence based on the intelligence gaps and needs that are identified by the policy and analytic communities.

(5) Oversee covert action and national intelligence collection in support of information operations.

c. The responsibility to assist the DDNI/M in establishing competency, qualification, security, training, career development and performance standards to meet the present and future collection and resource needs of the IC.

d. In coordination with the DDNI/M, the responsibility for recommending to the DNI the reallocation or realignment of resources or functions associated with collection activities, whether funded in the NIP or in the Military Intelligence Program, as appropriate, to ensure the optimal level of operational effectiveness and impact on national intelligence priorities.

e. In coordination with the DDNI/M and the Associate DNI and Chief Information Officer, the responsibility and authority to coordinate the performance of services of common concern to the IC with respect to collection responsibilities and authorities.

f. The responsibility to establish and maintain dynamic, mission driven processes that ensure the collection enterprise responds optimally to prioritized intelligence requirements.

2. The following ODNI officers will assist the DDNI/C and exercise authorities and responsibilities delegated to them by the DDNI/C.

a. Assistant Deputy Director of National Intellligence for Collection Strategies. The ADDNI/CS develops and implements integrated IC collection strategies through NICE. In partnership with the DDNI/A, serves as co-mission manager for priority intelligence topics that do not fall under the DNI Mission Managers and devises new assessment and evaluation tools to inform resource allocation decisions. Collaborates with the DNI Mission Managers to optimize the overall US strategic collection posture and tasking, and with the D-JIOC/JFCC-ISR/combatant command JIOCs for defense collection requirements. On behalf of the DDNI/C, establishes requirements and priorities for foreign intelligence information to be collected under the Foreign Intelligence Surveillance Act of 1978. Oversees and provides direction to the Integrated Concepts Development Office to perform tasks and undertake projects to advance Community collaboration, integration and innovation to strengthen the US intelligence collection posture.

b. Assistant Deputy Director of National Intelligence for Human Intelligence. The ADDNI/H exercises the advocacy, integration, evaluation and oversight responsibilities of the HUMINT community to include the enabling by HUMINT of technical collection and covert action. The ADDNI/H will develop and foster greater operational integration and deconfliction among HUMINT collectors across the IC and will oversee the establishment of standards for the validation of the IC's HUMINT sources, HUMINT tradecraft training, and Human Intelligence Reporting. The ADDNI/H oversees the Community Clandestine HUMINT Committee, chaired by the National Clandestine Services (NCS).

c. Assistant Deputy Director of National Intelligence for Technical Means. The ADDNI/TM exercises the advocacy, integration, evaluation and oversight responsibilities for all national technical collection. The ADDNI/TM works with the other ODNI components, agencies, and collection committees and asses current technical collection capabilities and identifies gaps; catalyzes development of and assesses new concepts and strategies for technical collection; develops and facilitates the adoption of IC-wide architecture-level collection system engineering standards and practices; and develops an end-to-end, Community technical collection architecture and mission-driven and focused, repeatable processes to develop, prioritize and evaluate changes and modifications to existing capabilities and architectures. In addition, the ADDNI/TM manages the MASINT Community Executive (MCE), who is responsible for MASINT for the entire IC. The ADDNI/TM exercises his IC leadership of the technical disciplines by the SIGINT, GEOINT and MASCOMs on behalf of the DDNI/C.

d. Assistant Deputy Director of National Intelligence for Open Source. The ADDNI/OS exercises the advocacy, integration, evaluation and oversight responsibilities for the National Open Source Enterprise. The ADDNI/OS provides strategic oversight of and guides strategic investment in Community open source capabilities; encourages Community collaboration and builds public/private partnerships and engages the US government and private sector to close collection capability gaps. The ADDNI/OS chairs the National Open Source Committee and the Open Source of Board Advisors, and oversees the DNI Open Source Center and the distributed National Open Source Enterprise. The ADDNI/OS also exercises responsibility for media and document exploitation and translation for the Community, chairing the Board of Directors, which oversees the National Media Exploitation Center (NMEC) and the National Virtual Translation Center (NVTC).

3. Intelligence Discipline Managers. To support the DNI's responsibilities for oversight and management of the IC, enhance the integration, coordination and evaluation of intelligence operations, and ensure the strategic management of resources, the DNI has designated certain officials to lead the effective and efficient management of intelligence disciplines across agencies and programs. Intelligence Discipline Managers that may be specifically designated by the law or by the DNI will provide the following support to the DNI and the DDNI/C.

a. Director, Central Intelligence Agency (CIA). The Director of CIA serves as the National HUMINT Manager for the IC with the authority coordinate, deconflict and evaluate HUMINT operations across the IC. The Director of CIA has delegated National HUMINT Manager authorities for Clandestine HUMINT to the Director of NCS. The Director of NCS works with the DDNI/C, the ADDNI/H, and agencies engaged in clandestine HUMINT operations for tasking, coordination, budget resources, training and standards for personal policies and information sharing.

b. Director, National Geospatial-Intelligence Agency (NGA). The Director of NGA serves as the National GEOINT Manager for the IC with the authority and responsibility for collecting, processing and disseminating GEOINT for foreign intelligence purposes in accordance with guidance provided by the DNI through the DDNI/C and the ADDNI/TM.

c. Director, National Security Agency (NSA). The Director of NSA is the National SIGINT Manager for the IC with the authority and responsibility for collecting, processing, and disseminating SIGINT information for foreign intelligence purposes in accordance with guidance provided by the DNI through the DDNI/C and the ADDNI/TM.

d. Measurement and Signature Intelligence Community Executive. The MCE is responsible for MASINT and the entire IC and serves as the IC-wide advocate for the discipline. The MCE reports to the DDNI/C and works to resolve MASINT issues in concert with the relevant IC members.

The Under Secretary of Defense for Intelligence designates an individual to serve as the Deputy, MCE.

e. DNI Executive Agent for DNI Open Source Center. The Director of CIA serves as the DNI's executive agent for the DNI Open Source Center, with day-to-day management delegated to the Center Director. The Center Director reports directly to the Deputy Director, CIA, in executing strategy, policy and program guidance for the Center and other IC elements. The Open Source Center advances the IC's exploitation of open source material, including from the Internet, and is responsible for enabling all IC analysts to access and use relevant open sources.

f. DNI Executive Agent for National Virtual Translation Center. The Director of the Federal Bureau of Investigation serves as the DNI's executive agent for the NVTC, an IC element that employs language specialists across the United States for the purpose of augmenting existing government language resources by translating high-priority requests from IC agencies.

g. DNI Executive Agent for the National Media Exploitation Center. The Director of the Defense Intelligence Agency serves as the DNI's executive agent for the NMEC, an IC enterprise for the rapid exploitation and dissemination of documents and other media required on terrorism, Iraq, Afghanistan, and other targets as assigned by the Board of Directors.

4. IC elements, as appropriate, or unless otherwise outlined in statute, executive order, or memorandum of understanding, shall:

a. Ensure effective programming, planning, execution and management of the various collection activities within their domains and represent the needs of their respective areas to the DDNI/C.

b. Provide full access to all activities, operations, and plans in collection, covert action, and intelligence-related clandestine operations to the DDNI/C, and designated oversight staff, regardless of the degree of compartmentalization or operational sensitivity.

c. Ensure the DDNI/C is apprised of critical areas of concern within their areas of responsibility and is fully and currently informed of all US covert actions and activities and their successes and failures.

d. Provide the IC with a single interface for tasking the collection assets (or resources) within their areas of responsibility.

e. Define and implement standards, policies, architectures, security, training, tools, algorithms, signatures, databases and support infrastructures necessary to conduct and support the various activities within their areas of responsibility.

F. EFFECTIVE DATE: This directive becomes effective on the date of the signature

Intelligence Community Directive Number 301

National Open Source Enterprise
(Effective: July 11, 2006)

A. AUTHORITY: The National Security Act of 1947, as amended; the Intelligence Reform and Terrorism Prevention Act (IRTPA) of 2004; Executive Order 12333; the Foreign Service Act of 1980; and other applicable law.

B. PURPOSE

1. This Intelligence Community (IC) Directive (ICD) establishes Director of National Intelligence (DNI) policy and specifies responsibilities for the oversight, management, and implementation of the Assistant Deputy DNI for Open Source (ADDN/OS), the DNI Open Source Center (the Center), and the IC to ensure efficient and effective open source information and analysis.

2. This ICS rescinds the Director of Central Intelligence Directive 1/7 (26 September 2000), Intelligence Community Open Source Program.

C. APPLICABILITY: This directive applies to the IC, as defined by the National Security Act of 1947, as amended, and other departments or agencies that may be designated by the President, or designated jointly by the DNI and the head of the department or agency concerned, as an element of the IC.

D. POLICY

1. Pursuant to IRTPA, the DNI is committed to ensuring the active and efficient use of open source intelligence information, and analysis by the IC through the establishment and maintenance of an effective, reliable, and collaborative capability that provide maximum availability of open source information to all consumer, optimizes resource utilization, and establishes effective burden sharing.

2. Within the IC:

a. Open source strategy development, progammatic oversight, and evaluation will be centralized under the ADDNI/OS. Open source activities will be executed in a distributive manner.

b. Elements will leverage burden sharing, partnerships, and outside capabilities (IC, public, private, other US Government (USG) and foreign partners) to the maximum extent possible.

c. Organizations acquiring and/or exploiting open source information and developing open source specific capabilities/tools will share their information and capabilities to the fullest via the Associate DNI/Chief Information Officer's (ADNI/CIO) information architecture.

(1) Prior to acquiring and/or exploiting any major new capability or

tool, the implementing organization must coordinate with ADDNI/OS to validate consistency with community strategy and to preclude duplication of effort.

(2) After acquiring and/or exploiting a new capability or tool, the implementing organization must tag the information in accordance with IC standards and make available all information (acquired, processed, analyzed) and tools/capabilities to other community elements unless expressly prohibited by law, DNI directive, or contractual obligation.

d. IC open source efforts support a wide range of intelligence activities, including all-source analysis, and human, signals, geospatial, and measurement and signature intelligence. Open source reporting and analysis are also considered intelligence products.

e. All open source exploiters, to include analysts, will exercise appropriate tradecraft and information security practices in accordance with DNI standards and policies.

f. All open source exploitation efforts will establish appropriate source/information validation security practices in accordance with DNI standards and policies.

g. IC elements will develop metrics for overall open source activities and for individual major initiatives. These metrics will be coordinated with the ADNI/OS and will be sued to determine return on investment and customer satisfaction and to inform strategy development and resource decisionmaking.

E. AUTHORITIES AND RESPONSIBILITIES

1. Assistant Deputy DNI for Open Source

a. The ADDNI/OS shall have the following authorities and responsibilities for the National Open Source Enterprise:

(1) Ensuring integrated IC open source collection management strategy and implementation are reflective of Presidential priorities.

(2) Oversight evaluation, policy direction, and tasking of IC open source exploitation organizations.

(3) Advisory tasking regarding acquisition of open source information by agencies and departments not within the National Intelligence program.

(4) Development and oversight of national open source enterprise.

(5) Working with the ADDNI/Chief Financial Officer (CFO) and the Deputy Director of National Intelligence for Customer Outcomes (DDNI/CO) to establish program guidance in accordance with Presidential priorities.

(6) Oversight of Program Manager's compliance with program guidance in concert with the ADDNI/CFO.

(7) Coordination of open source requirements of common concern.

(8) Oversight of the procurement of tools and services to support open source exploitation.

(9) Oversight of interagency sharing of open source information.

(10) Overall guidance on behalf of the DNI and the DDNI for Collection (DDNI/C), to the Director, Central Intelligence Agency (D/CIA), in the role as Executive Agent for DNI Open Source Center.

b. ADDNI/OS will provide the ADDNI/Chief Technology Officer, the ADNI/CIO, and the ADNI for Science and Technology (ADNI/S&T) critical capability requirements, to include those that cannot or will not be met by commercial-off-the-shelf or government off-the-shelf capabilities, and support related development, test, and implementation programs.

c. The ADDNI/OS will chair the National Open Source Committee.

d. The ADDNI/OS will manage the Open Source Board of Advisors (the Board), should such a board be established.

2. National Open Source Committee (NOSC)

a. The NOSC is established to provide guidance to the National Open Source Enterprise under this directive. The NOSC is chaired by the ADDNI/OS and comprises senior executives from the following:

(1) DNI Open Source Center
(2) Office of the Under Secretary of Defense for Intelligence
(3) Department of Homeland Security
(4) CIA
(5) National Security Agency
(6) National Geospatial-Intelligence Agency
(7) Department of State's Bureau of Intelligence and Research
(8) Defense Intelligence Agency
(9) Federal Bureau of Investigation
(10) Office of the IC CIO
(11) Other members as determined by the ADDNI/OS

b. The NOSC will advise and report to the DDNI/C through the ADDNI/OS and, as represented by the DDNI/C, will:

(1) Provide programmatic, strategic, and resource recommendations.

(2) Develop and promulgate appropriate operational standards for areas such as, but not limited to, source/information verification, tradecraft, and training/certification.

(3) Develop and promulgate, in coordination with the ADNI/CIO and, as appropriate, the ADNI/S&T, technology standards for such areas as, but not limited to, interface standards, metadata tagging, and storage standards.

(4) Provide evaluations of the IC's open source gaps and capabilities.

(5) Provide recommendations to optimize future open source exploitation by elements in the IC and, as appropriate, other departments and agencies.

c. The NOSC will establish such working groups as required to facilitate the coordination or execution of specific programs or to address topics of IC interest.

3. Open Source Board of Advisors

a. The DDNI/C is authorized to establish an Open Source Board of Advisors. The Board will be comprised of senior experts from inside and outside the USG, will provide advice to the DDNI/C and the ADDNI/OS on open source matters, and will be available to consult with other ODNI and USG organizations, as needed.

b. When established, the Board will develop and publish a charter for approval by the DDNI/C. The charts and membership will be reviewed by the DDNI/C and ADDNI/OS annually.

4. DNI Open Source Center and D/CIA as Executive Agent

a. The Center serves to advance the IC's exploitation of open source material and nurtures acquisition, procurement, analysis, dissemination, and sharing of open source information, products, and services throughout the ISG.

b. Under the overall guidance of the DNI, the D/CIA serves as the DNI's Executive Agent for the Center, with day-to-day management delegated to the Center director and operating the Center under all relevant authorities available to the CIA. The Center director reports directly to the Deputy D/CIA in executing strategy, policy, and program guidance established by the DNI. The ADDNI/OS established open source strategy, policy, and program guidance for the Center and other IC elements. The CIA ensures the Center consults with and provides insight into Center activities to the ADDNI/OS and other ODNI elements. The DNI provides formal tasking to the CIA for the Center.

c. The Center is established at CIA and builds on the former Foreign Broadcast Information Service. It will include personnel from across the IC and other USG organizations.

d. The center director is selected and appointed by the CIA with the concurrence of the DNI. The Center director reports to the Deputy D/CIA for day-to-day management. The Center director has two deputy directors (at least one of the deputy directors is an IC element other than CIA). The Center director will select Center staff and manage the Center's overall operations.

e. The Center's budget will remain a separate expenditure center with the CIA Program, and it may not be taxed or reprogrammed without DNI approval. The budget for the Center is executed by the D/CIA constituent with DNI guidance. The Center will provide expanded services in response to DNI guidance.

f. As directed by the DNI, the D/CIA will ensure that the Center acts as a service of common concern and:

(1) Supports development of the implementation of the DNI's open source strategic plan, policy, and program decisions.

(2) Participates in the NOSC.

(3) Makes open source information available to all customers and partners in a timely manner and is responsive to their needs.

(4) Facilitates open source exploitation for USG partners and customers.

(5) Secures appropriate licensing and other agreements that ensure necessary access to all open source consumers.

(6) Exports open source expertise to other government entities when requested.

(7) Develops and advocates programs that expose all IC personnel to the benefits of using open source materials and trains them in open source exploitation.

(8) Trains IC personnel in open source exploitation and tradecraft including information security practices in concert with other IC elements.

(9) Unless otherwise directed, will continue existing services of common concern to the Community, including acquisition, analysis, dissemination, media analysis, procurement, and relationships with other USG and non-USG entities. Such services will be delivered consistent with the ADNI/CIO information architecture.

5. Elements

a. In coordination with the ADDNI/OS and consistent with DNI standards IC elements will:

(1) Conduct acquisition, analysis, dissemination or open source materials via the ADNI/CIO information architecture.

(2) Make all open source information, products, and services available across the IC unless expressly prohibited by law, DNI directive, or contractual obligation.

(3) Source material and information, as necessary, to meet unique component requirements.

(4) Keep ADDNI/OS apprised of open source resources and activities to minimize duplication of effort.

(5) Designate a primary open source coordinator in each department/agency who guides its participation in the National Open Source Enterprise.

(6) Provide members for and participate in the deliberations/activities of the NOSC and related working groups, as set forth.

(7) Support staffing requirements of the DNI's Open Source Center.

(8) Make full use of open source information, expertise, and capabilities to conduct analysis and inform collection strategies.

(9) Create a structure to institutionalize sharing across appropriate Federal agency lines to form the most comprehensive repository of open source information,

(10) Implement an open source information technology infrastructure that is in full compliance with IC Enterprise Architecture common policies, services, and standards.

(11) Advise ADDNI/OS, through a formal requirements mechanism to be determined by the ADDNI/OS, of open source information requirements.

(12) Make the ADDNI/OS aware of the unique acquisition and analysis capabilities.

6. Additional Rules and Responsibilities

a. The Department of State (DOS) procures foreign publications, maps, and geographic data through designated DOS personnel at overseas missions as requested by the Center.

b. The National Geospatial-Intelligence Agency is responsible for providing a single agency focus for imagery and geospatial information resources for the Department of Defense, and other Federal departments or agencies on request.

c. The DDNI for Management (DDNI/M) in coordination with the ADDNI/OS executes the DNI's milestone decisions authorities and coordinates program trades for open source activities determined to be of significant IC interest by the NOSC, ADDNI/OS, the DDNI/C, and/or the DDNI/M.

d. The ADNI/CIO, in concert with the ADDNI/OS, the Center, and other open source providers, coordinates across the IC and its customers to ensure technical means and standards are in place to facilitate access to open source information, products, and services.

e. The DDNI for Analysis, with the support of the ADDNI/OS, ensures the IC makes efficient and effective use of open source information.

f. The DDNI/CO, in coordination with the ADDNI/OS, orchestrates customer satisfaction metrics on open source that are then used in strategy development, return-on-investment discussions, and resource decisionmaking.

g. The National Counterintelligence Executive will support open source activities, tradecraft, and information security training to ensure that open source exploiters are cognizant of intelligence-related threats and vulnerabilities.

F. DEFINITIONS

1. **Open Source Acquisition:** The act of gaining possession of, or access to, open source information synonymous with "open source collection." The preferred term is acquisition because by definition, open sources are collected and disseminated by others, open source exploiters acquire previously collected and publicly available information second-hand.

2. **Open Source Collection**: See "Open Source Acquisition."

3. **Open Source Information**: Publicly available information that anyone can lawfully obtain by request, purchase, or observation.

4. **Open Source Intelligence**: Produced from publicly available information that is collected, exploited, disseminated in a timely manner to an appropriate audience for the purpose of addressing a specific intelligence requirment.[1]

F. EFFECTIVE DATE: This ICD becomes effective on the date of signature.

______________________________________ __________
Director of National Intelligence Date

1. As define in Sec. 931 of Public Law 109-163, entitled *"National Defense Authorization Act for Fiscal Year 2006."*

Intelligence Community Directive Number 801

Acquisition

(Effective: August 15, 2006)
(Amended: August 16, 2009)

A. AUTHORITY: The National Security Act of 1947, as amended; Executive Order (EO) 12333, as amended; *Memorandum of Agreement between the Director of National Intelligence and the Secretary of Defense concerning the management of Acquisition Programs Executed at the Department of Defense Intelligence Community Elements*, March 2008; and other applicable provisions of law.

B. PURPOSE: This Directive establishes the overarching policy of the Director of National Intelligence (DNI) relevant to the DNI's acquisition authorities and related procurement authorities. This Directive also establishes the management framework for executing Milestone Decision Authority (MDA) and constitutes in part the procedures called for in EO 12333, Section 1.3(b)(22) and the *Memorandum of Agreement between the Director of National Intelligence and the Secretary of Defense concerning the Management of Acquisition Programs Executed at the Department of Defense Intelligence Community Elements*, March 2008, Section D.2.

C. APPLICABILITY

1. This Directive applies to the Intelligence Community (IC), as defined by the National Security Act of 1947, as amended; and such other elements of any other department or agency as may be designated by the President, or designated jointly by the DNI and the head of the department of agency concerned, as an element of the IC.

2. Specifically, this policy applies to all IC acquisitions funded in whole within the National Intelligence Program (NIP), and all major system acquisitions (MSA) funded in majority part within the NIP that are executed within the Department of Defense (DoD). To the extent formally agreed to by the relevant parties, this Directive shall also apply to other acquisitions funded jointly in the NIP and another funding program. Appendix A defines key terms used in this Directive.

D. POLICY

1. <u>Acquisition Process</u>: The acquisition process model identified in IC Policy Guidance (ICPG) 801.1, *Acquisition,* shall be used for all NIP-funded MSAs. Such acquisitions shall be undertaken using a balanced and proactive risk management approach to create innovative and responsive systems for use by the IC. Proactive risk management is the acceptance of appropriate risk to allow the necessary innovation and technology insertion in an acquisition, while ensuring, through positive means, that the uncertainties of the acquisition are managed within a tolerable range to enable cost, schedule, and performance constraints to be met. The IC

acquisition process shall ensure that a set of validated and approved requirements is implemented through development, integration, and testing within an established schedule and budget. System acquisitions in the IC shall use a disciplined process of responsible management that retains the necessary agility to respond to the urgencies of time and opportunity, while being mindful of the public trust and the need for fiscal responsibility. Achieving agility will prudent, and capable of responding to quick reaction capability needs.

2. Delegation: The DNI has delegated to the Deputy Director of National Intelligence for Acquisition and Technology (DDNI/A&T) all acquisition authorities and responsibilities of the DNI with respect to MSAs, including the DNI's authority to serve as the MDA. DDNI/A&T may delegate any of these authorities, including the authority to further re-delegate, to agency heads, department heads, the Associate DNI and IC Information Officer (ADNI/CIO), or others as he may determine. The Assistant Deputy Director of National Intelligence and Senior Acquisition Executive (ADDNI/SAE) is the principal person supporting the DDNI/A&T's authority to delegate MDA.

3. Procurement Executive: The Office of Federal Procurement Policy Act requires the head of each executive agency to designate a Senior Procurement Executive (SPE). Executive Order 12931 outlines the Federal Procurement Reform roles and responsibilities of the heads of executive agencies and the supporting role of the SPE. The Office of the DNI (ODNI) Procurement Executive (PE) is the SPE for the ODNI, reports to the ADDNI/SAE, and is the principal person supporting the DNI, DDNI/A&T, and the ADDNI/SAE in executing their procurement authorities. In support of the DNI's MSA authorities and the DNI's responsibility to monitor the implementation and execution of the NIP budget, the ODNI PE is responsible for monitoring the IC procurement system and for developing and implementing policies to facilitate the effective monitoring of the IC procurement system. The ODNI PE will chair an IC Procurement Executive Council to identify common IC contracting and procurement issues. Such issues are meant to include, but are not limited to, exploring innovative and flexible procurement practices that assist the IC to accomplish its mission as quickly and efficiently as possible and exploring best government and industry procurement practices, while ensuring that appropriate counterintelligence and security considerations are addressed. The SPE, or equivalent officer, for each IC element that executes NIP-funded procurements shall be a member of the Council. In support of the DNI's authority and responsibility to monitor the implementation and execution of the NIP, elements of the IC shall provide the ODNI PE with all information requested by the ODNI PE concerning NIP-funded procurements.

4. Milestone Decision Authority: The DNI exercises MDA for the acquisition of "major systems" funded in whole by the NIP, except that with respect to wholly or majority NIP-funded acquisitions executed with the DoD, the DNI serves as MDA jointly with the Secretary of Defense (SecDef) or his designee. The DNI

will determine whether the total cost of the combination of elements the function together to produce the capabilities required to fulfill a mission need reach the "major system" threshold. The ADDNI/SAE, in consultation with the ADNI/CIO, for information technology (IT)-related acquisitions, shall conduct a periodic review to determine those acquisitions for which the ODNI will exercise MDA (hereinafter referred to as the DNI MDA), either alone or jointly with the SecDef or his designee. The DNI MDA may delegate MDA for MSAs to IC elements based on the following considerations:

- Adherence to DNI and IC element acquisition policies and implementing instructions
- Program investment magnitude
- Cross-community issues
- Multi-intelligence considerations
- IC element demonstrated performance in managing acquisitions
- Transparency of the management activity and decision process at that IC element to DNI oversight, to include ODNI accessibility to needed data
- Existence of an individual in the IC element with overall authority and responsibility for NIP-funded acquisition activity within that element who is appropriately empowered to fully execute the responsibilities of the position, including the supervision of personnel executing the acquisitions
- Other special interest considerations applicable to a particular acquisition or IC element

Delegations of MDA for NIP-funded acquisition activity shall be made in writing by the DNI MDA on acquisition-by-acquisition basis or other basis as determined by the DNI MDA, and may be changed or withdrawn at the discretion of the DNI MDA, except with respect to NIP-funded acquisitions executed within DoD, the DNI MDA shall act jointly with the SecDef or his designee for all delegations, and for all changes or withdrawals of delegations.

5. Program Management Plans (PMPs): As required by the National Security Act, and to assist the DNI in his execution of his responsibility and authority to monitor the implementation and execution of the NIP, all NIP-funded MSAs shall have a PMP that includes cost, schedule, and performance goals, as well as program milestone criteria. This process will include consultation with the SecDef for wholly or majority NIP-funded MSAs executed by an IC element in DoD. IC elements are responsible for PMP development and maintenance, and must keep each PMP current. Other required data and reporting requirements are contained in ICPG 801.1. The ADDNI/SAE, in consultation with the ADNI/CIO for IT-related acquisitions, will periodically review the PMP for each MSA, review and assess the progress made toward the achievement of the goals and milestones established in each PMP, and submit a report to Congress on the results of these reviews and assessments as required by the National Security Act.

6. User Requirements: NIP-funded MSAs shall be driven by formally established user requirements. Each IC element, or the heads of their respective departments, shall establish processes to develop and manage these requirements. Requirements for NIP-funded MSAs shall be submitted to the DNI, or his designee, for requirements validation and shall be provided in accordance with the acquisition process model specified in ICPG 801.1. Requirements may also be submitted to additional requirements processes for NIP-funded acquisitions executed within a department.

7. Architectural Compliance, Interoperability, and Data Sharing: All MSAs the include the procurement of enterprise architecture-related IT items that are wholly or partially NIP-funded shall adhere to the applicable ADNI/CIO IC enterprise architecture, standards, protocols, and interfaces, and shall support the DNI's IC data- and information-sharing initiatives and shall be so certified. The ADNI/CIO, or the IC element or department CIO when MDA has been delegated to the element or department, shall certify this compliance, as well as compliance with any other similarly applicable statutory provisions (such as the Clinger-Cohen Act) to the MDA, as specified in ICPG 8801.1

8. Independent Cost Assessments/Estimates: In accordance with Title 50, U.S. Code, Section 415a-1, the DNI will prepare and independent cost estimate (ICE) of the full life-cycle cost of the development, integration, and operation of each major system to be acquired by the IC, in consultation with the head of each concerned element if the IC. The DNI Cost Analysis Improvement Group, or its agent, shall prepare an ICE for all NIP-funded MSAs unless the DSI or his designee and the SecDef or his designee jointly designate an alternate entity to prepare an ICE for an IC major system acquisition by an IC element within DoD.

9. Acquisition Oversight: The ODNI, led by the ADDNI/SAE, will conduct oversight of NIP-funded acquisitions (jointly with the Office of the SecDef [OSD] for acquisitions executed within DoD) to ensure effective execution of such acquisitions. The primary oversight function will be to review and assess acquisition execution against MDA-approved baselines for cost, schedule, and performance through periodic program reviews. If an acquisition is not executing against its established baseline, a more detailed review may be conducted by ODNI, or jointly with OSD for acquisitions executed within DoD. The result of this review may be revocation or re-assignment of MDA, or other action to correct performance for the acquisition in question.

10. Professional Acquisition Workforce: Each IC element that executes NIP-funded acquisitions shall develop and maintain a fully proficient acquisition workforce to conduct such acquisitions. The ADDNI/SAE, in coordination with the Associate Director of National Intelligence and IC Chief Human Capital Officer and after consultation with the heads of other agencies or elements of the IC and the heads of their respective departments, shall establish education, training,

and experience standards for acquisition personnel in the IC. These standards shall not be inconsistent with the standards set forth in the Defense Acquisition Workforce Improvement Act (Title 10 U.S. Code, Chapter 87) or with personnel policies and education and training requirements otherwise applicable to members of the uniformed services.

11. Multiple IC Element Acquisitions: Many MSAs are executed through the efforts of multiple IC elements to achieve an end-to-end capability required by the Community. To achieve this end-to-end capability, certain multiple element acquisitions identified by the DNI MDA (or identified jointly by the DNI MDA and the SecDef, or his designee, for NIP-funded acquisitions executed within DoD) shall have a documented agreement for the management structure of the integrated team executing across the IC elements. This agreement shall be coordinated with the ADDNI/SAE, signed by all the IC elements involved, and provided to the ADDNI/SAE prior to beginning the development (normally Milestone B) of the first in the end-to-end chain.

12. ICPG for Acquisition: ICPG 801.1 supports this Directive and establishes a flexible, streamlined, and responsive acquisition model encompassing best practices and facilitating the requisite agility needed by the acquisition management system to ensure timely delivery of needed capabilities. The guidance establishes a National Intelligence Acquisition Board chaired by the DNI MDA and details the board membership, procedures, and decision mechanics. IC elements executing NIP-funded MSAs shall develop written acquisition procedures for such acquisitions conforming to this Directive and ICPG 801.1 and shall execute NIP-funded MSAs under their control according to those written acquisition procedures; except that for NIP-funded MSAs executed within DoD, the acquisition procedures developed by the IC element shall conform to the jointly signed memorandum of agreement as discussed in paragraph D.13.

13. Joint Programs: To the extent formally agreed to by the DNI and the heads of departments and agencies with organizations in the IC, intelligence-related acquisitions funded jointly by the NIP and non-NIP budgets, or NIP-funded but executed with DoD, shall be managed through a joint process and joint decision forum that is adapted from that established under ICPG 801.1 and documented in a jointly signed memorandum of agreement. The ODNI will strive to observe the principle of equal representation in all acquisition decision forums for joint programs.

E. EFFECTIVE DATE: This Directive becomes effective on the date of signature.

//SIGNED// John Negroponte Date: August 15, 2006
Director of National Intelligence

APPENDIX A—DEFINITIONS
ICD 801, *ACQUISITION*

National Intelligence Program (NIP)-funded Acquisition: A NIP-funded activity involving development of new items by one or more contractors to create a required mission system capability within the Intelligence Community (IC). This definition is consistent with the use of the term within the acquisition development community. The broader definition of "acquisition" occurring in the *Federal Acquisition Regulation* is addressed in ICPG 801.2, *Contracting and Procurement Policy.*

IC Element: An organization that is part of the IC as defined in the National Security Act of 1947, as amended.

Major System: The term "major system" is defined by the National Security Act through reference to 41 U.S. Code 403(9); that definition shall be applied to all uses of the term in this document.

Milestone Decision Authority: The authority to approve the transition of a system development from one phase of the acquisition process to the next phase.

NIP-Funded: For IC acquisitions executed within DoD, NIP-finded refers to acquisitions funded in whole or in majority part from the NIP. For all other IC acquisitions, NIP-funded refers to acquisitions funded in whole from the NIP, unless specifically stated otherwise, or unless agreed to by the DNI and the relevant head of department containing an IC element, or in accordance with procedures established pursuant to EO 12333, Section 1.3(b)(22).

CHANGES IN ETHICS LAWS RELATED TO THE INTELLIGENCE COMMUNITY

March 8, 2011 LA-11-02
LEGAL ADVISORY

TO: Designated Agency Ethics Officials
FROM: Robert I. Cusick, Director
SUBJECT: LEGISLATIVE ACTIVITY OF THE 111TH CONGRESS AFFECTING THE EXECUTIVE BRANCH ETHICS PROGRAM

This Legal Advisory updates relevant legislative activity from the recently ended 111th Congress. Two new laws are of particular importance to the Executive Branch ethics community: the re-codification of the Procurement Integrity Act and changes to the ethics laws for the intelligence community, both of which are briefly discussed below. OGE also detected a trend in legislative activity aimed at imposing new post-employment restrictions on certain Executive Branch employees.

The 111th Congress also considered several other ethics-related provisions that did not become law, including: the extension of partner benefits to domestic partnerships and amendments to 18 U.S.C. § 205 that would have exempted qualifying law students from conflict of interest violations when participating in law clinics.

The Procurement Integrity Act

The Procurement Integrity Act was previously codified as 41 U.S.C. § 423. On January 4, 2011, 41 U.S.C. § 423 was repealed and subsequently replaced by 41 U.S.C.A. §§ 2101 – 2107. *See* Pub. L. No. 111-350, sec. 7(b), 124 Stat. 3855 (2011). In the recodification of the Procurement Integrity Act, the post-employment restriction that prohibits certain former federal employees from accepting employment with a contractor for a one-year period was codified into a separate section. *Id.* (to be codified at 41 U.S.C. § 2104).

The House Committee on the Judiciary's Report on H.R. 1107 (which became Public Law No: 111-350) asserts that, in restating the existing law, H.R. 1107 consolidated and reorganized various provisions of law which had been enacted separately over a period of many years, conformed style and terminology, modernized obsolete language, and corrected drafting errors – and that the changes are not intended to have substantive effect, and are not to impair in 2
any way the precedential value of earlier judicial decisions or other interpretations: that is, H.R. 1107 is intended to restate existing law without substantive change. S*ee* H.R. REP. NO. 111-42, *at* 2-3 (2009).

This change may affect training materials and other materials in which a citation may be made to the Procurement Integrity Act.

Changes to Ethics Laws Related to the Intelligence Community

The Intelligence Authorization Act for Fiscal Year 2010, Pub. L. No. 111-259, allows the head of an element of the intelligence community to delete certain information about the receipt and disposition of foreign gifts and decorations if the publication of this information would adversely affect U.S. intelligence sources or methods. Pub. L. No. 111-259, § 361, 124 Stat. 2654 (2010). Any information withheld from the Secretary of State must be transmitted to the Director of National Intelligence, who is required to keep a record of this sensitive information. This Act also requires the Director of National Intelligence to issue outside-employment restrictions for intelligence officers and employees in consultation with OGE. Pub. L. No. 111-259, § 307, 124 Stat. 2654 (2010). The Director of National Intelligence will submit an annual report to the congressional intelligence committees detailing the authorized instances of outside employment for intelligence officers and employees.

Legislative Trends in Post-Employment Restrictions

Legislators in the 111th Congress focused on imposing additional post-employment restrictions for certain government employees, a trend which appears to be surfacing again in the 112th Congress. Proposed legislation directed at the former Minerals Management Service, National Highway Traffic Safety Administration, and the Federal Aviation Administration (FAA) would have either directly prohibited current government employees from working for certain prospective employers or penalized specified prospective employers for hiring certain government employees. The FAA Air Transportation Modernization and Safety Improvement Act proposed in the 111th Congress called for three-year post-employment restriction period for certain former employees and has been reintroduced in the first session of the 112th Congress. S. 223, 112th Cong. (2011); H.R. 658, 112th Cong. (2011). OGE will continue to monitor legislative activity involving post-employment restrictions and provide relevant updates as events unfold.

Conclusion

OGE brings this information to your attention as part of our initiative to keep you apprised of relevant legislative activity. As the 112th Congress engages in ethics-related legislative activity, OGE will provide similar, periodic legislative activity updates. OGE also may be in communication with you directly about agency-specific legislative proposals and provisions that may affect your ethics program as they come to our attention. If you would like to discuss this or other legislative matters, please contact OGE's Associate Director for Legislative Affairs, Shelley Finlayson at (202) 482-9314.

DEPARTMENT OF DEFENSE

Memorandum of Agreement between the Secretary of Defense and the Director of National Intelligence on the Director of Defense Intelligence

Editors comment: *A joint ODNI/DoD press release "Under Secretary of Defense for Intelligence to be Dual-Hatted as Director of Defense Intelligence"* (ODNI News Release No. 16-07, DoD News Release No. 637-07) *is included here. This Memorandum of Agreement has been annotated as "For Official Use Only", a copy of the actual document can be obtained by authorized government users at*: https://usdi.dtic.mil/usdi_docs/keyref/usdi_keyref.cfm

OFFICE OF THE DIRECTOR OF NATIONAL INTELLIGENCE
PUBLIC AFFAIRS OFFICE
WASHINGTON, D.C.
20511
NEWS RELEASE

FOR IMMEDIATE RELEASE ODNI News Release No. 16-07
MAY 24, 2007

Under Secretary of Defense for Intelligence to be Dual-Hatted as Director of Defense Intelligence Secretary of Defense Robert Gates and Director of National Intelligence Mike McConnell signed a memorandum of agreement this week that establishes a role for the under secretary of defense for intelligenceas the director of defense intelligence within the Office of the DNI.

In his role as Under Secretary of Defense for Intelligence, James R. Clapper Jr. will continue to report to the secretary and deputy secretary of defense. The responsibilities and the authorities assigned to this position by the secretary will not change.

As the Director of Defense Intelligence, Clapper will report directly to the DNI and serve as his principal advisor regarding defense intelligence matters. The director of defense intelligence will have responsibilities as determined by the DNI in consultation with the Secretary of Defense and promulgated separately.

The secretary and the director made this agreement in recognition of the crucial importance of coordinated intelligence efforts to the national security of the United States. The defense intelligence components provide a full range of intelligence products and analysis to a broad spectrum of consumers; from military forces in the field to senior policy makers across the federal government. These efforts are intertwined with the national intelligence efforts overseen by the DNI.

"The creation of the Office of the Director of Defense Intelligence is in recognition of the importance of coordinated intelligence efforts to the national security of the United States," said Clapper. "This office will serve to strengthen the relationship between the DNI and the DoD."

At an operational level, there should be no impact on the day-to-day operations and management of defense intelligence agencies, added Clapper.

"The objective here is to facilitate staff interaction and promote synchronization," he said.

The MOA does not alter the statutory responsibilities or authorities of either the secretary of defense or the DNI but will provide a framework to ensure a seamless integration of critical intelligence efforts.

# # #

Memorandum of Agreement between the Secretary of Defense and the Director of National Intelligence on the Director of Defense Intelligence

March 25, 2008

A. PURPOSE

This agreement provides for joint management by the Department of Defense (DoD) and the Office of the Director of National Intelligence (DNI) (hereafter referred to as the "parties") of National Intelligence Program (NIP) funded acquisition programs executed by DoD Intelligence Community (IC) elements. It is intended that a single acquisition process be employed for programs covered by this MOA.

B. SCOPE

The Intelligence Reform and Terrorism Prevention Act (IRTPA) of2004 (see 50 U.S.C. 403-1 (q)) provides that the DNI, or designee, and the Secretary of Defense (SecDef), or designee, shall serve jointly as the Milestone Decision Authority (MDA) for major system acquisitions (MSA) of DoD intelligence programs wholly funded by the NIP. This agreement covers MDA and associated oversight for DoD intelligence programs that are estimated to be majority and minority funded from the NIP.

C. *DEFINITIONS*

The "MDA" is the official or officials with overall responsibility for an acquisition program. The MDA possesses the authority to approve an acquisition program's entry into, or movement into later phases of, the acquisition process and shall be responsible for monitoring acquisition program cost, schedule, and performance. An "MSA" is an acquisition ofa major system as defined at 41 U.S.C. 403(9).

"Wholly NIP-funded acquisition program" is an MSA of a 000 intelligence program wholly funded from the NIP. This includes those wholly NIP-funded acquisition programs that do not meet the dollar thresholds of 41 U.S.C. 403(9) but are designated an MSA by the DNI and the SecDef, or their designees, because the program is of special interest.

"Majority NIP-funded acquisition program" is an MSA for a DoD intelligence program estimated to be funded in the majority from the NIP.

"Majority MIP-funded acquisition program" is an MSA for a DoD intelligence program estimated to be funded in the majority from the MIP.

"DoD IC elements" are the DoD organizations that execute DoD intelligence program acquisitions. They i.nclude the Defense Intelligence Agency, the National GeospatialIntelligence Agency, the National Reconnaissance Office, and the National Security Agency.

D. AGREEMENTS

1. Dual MDA: For wholly NIP-funded acquisition programs, in accordance with IRTPA, the parties shall serve jointly as the MDA. Also, for majority NIP-funded acquisition programs the parties agree to serve jointly as the MDA.

2. General Acquisition Policy: National intelligence acquisitions will be agile, flexible, and responsive to the needs of the IC and its customers. This approach is intended to promote synergy among acquisitions, requirements, and cost disciplines, and shorten the time between when a need or requirement is identified and when a capability is fielded or placed into service.

Wholly and majority NIP-funded acquisition programs shall be executed according to IC acquisition policy. This will be implemented through direct reference of the DNI policy in DoD 5000.

3. Acquisition Oversight: The Deputy Director of National Intelligence for Acquisition (DDNIJAQ) and the Under Secretary of Defense of Acquisition, Technology and Logistics (USD(AT&L)) will conduct joint oversight of all wholly or majority NIP-funded acquisition programs. At least once a quarter, they will jointly review and assess program execution against MDA-approved baselines for cost, schedule, and perfonnance. Ifan acquisition program is not executing to its established baseline, the SecDef or DNI, or their designees, may conduct a more detailed joint program review for that acquisition and take actions as necessary to improve program perfonnance.

For majority MIP-funded acquisition programs executed at the DoD IC elements, the DNI or hislher representative shall have a seat on the Defense Acquisition Board.

4. MDA Delegation: The SeeDef and DNI, or their designees, may jointly delegate MDA to a DoD IC element agency head for a wholly or majority NIP-funded acquisition program. MDA delegation will be captured in a fonnal memorandum and will only be done after a thorough review is conducted by the advisors of the DDNIJAQ and the USD(AT&L) to ensure that a mature, repeatable, and fundamentally sound acquisition program is in place prior to recommending the delegation of MDA. The *DDNII*AQ and the USD(AT&L) will jointly review any program with delegated MDA at least annually (or more often as directed), and may jointly reassign or reclaim delegated MDA for any wholly or majority NIP-funded acquisition program.

5. Exceptions for Specific Projects or Programs: Exceptions to any or all provisions of this agreement for a specific project or program may be agreed to by both parties and documented in a written agreement signed jointly by the DNI and the SecDef, or their designees.

E. IMPLEMENTATION

This agreement is effective upon signature and will continue in effect until modified or tenninated by mutual written agreement of the parties. In the event the parties cannot agree, they shall raise the issue to the President fofthe President's consideration.

DEPARTMENT OF JUSTICE

The Attorney General's Guidelines for Domestic FBI Operations

PREAMBLE

These Guidelines are issued under the authority of the Attorney General as provided in sections 509,510,533, and 534 of title 28, United States Code, and Executive Order 12333. They apply to domestic investigative activities of the Federal Bureau of Investigation (FBI) and other activities as provided herein.

TABLE OF CONTENTS

INTRODUCTION

As the primary investigative agency of the federal government, the Federal Bureau of Investigation (FBI) has the authority and responsibility to investigate all violations of federal law that are not exclusively assigned to another federal agency. The FBI is further vested by law and by Presidential directives with the primary role in carrying out investigations within the United States of threats to the national security. This includes the lead domestic role in investigating international terrorist threats to the United States, and in conducting counterintelligence activities to meet foreign entities' espionage and intelligence efforts directed against the United States. The FBI is also vested with important hctions in collecting foreign intelligence as a member agency of the U.S. Intelligence Community. The FBI accordingly plays crucial roles in the enforcement of federal law and the proper administration of justice in the United States, in the protection of the national security, and in obtaining information needed by the United States for the conduct of its foreign affairs. These roles reflect the wide range of the FBI's current responsibilities and obligations, whch require the FBI to be both an agency that effectively detects, investigates, and prevents crimes, and an agency that effectively protects the national security and collects intelligence.

The general objective of these Guidelines is the full utilization of all authorities and investigative methods, consistent with the Constitution and laws of the United States, to protect the United States and its people from terrorism and other threats to the national security, to protect the United States and its people from victimization by all crimes in violation of federal law, and to further the foreign intelligence objectives of the United States. At the same time, it is axiomatic that the FBI must conduct its investigations and other activities in a lawful and reasonable manner that respects liberty and privacy and avoids unnecessary intrusions into the lives of law-abiding people. The purpose of these Guidelines, therefore, is to establish consistent policy in such matters. They will enable the FBI to perform its duties with effectiveness, certainty, and confidence, and will provide the American people with a firm assurance that the FBI is acting properly under the law.

The issuance of these Guidelines represents the culmination of the hstorical evolution of the FBI and the policies governing its domestic operations subsequent to the September 11,2001, terrorist attacks on the United States. Reflecting decisions and directives of the President and the Attorney General, inquiries and enactments of Congress, and the conclusions of national commissions, it was recognized that the FBI's hctions needed to be expanded and better integrated to meet contemporary realities:

> [Clontinuing coordination . . . is necessary to optimize the FBI's performance in both national security and criminal investigations . . . . [The] new reality requires first that the FBI and other agencies do a better job of gathering intelligence inside the United States, and second that we eliminate the remnants of the old "wall" between foreign intelligence and domestic law enforcement. Both tasks must be accomplished without sacri-

ficing our domestic liberties and the rule of law, and both depend on building a very different FBI from the one we had on September 10,2001. (Report of the Commission on the Intelligence Capabilities of the United States Regarding Weapons of Mass Destruction 466,452 (2005).)

In line with these objectives, the FBI has reorganized and reoriented its programs and missions, and the guidelines issued by the Attorney General for FBI operations have been extensively revised over the past several years. Nevertheless, the principal directives of the Attorney General governing the FBI's conduct of criminal investigations, national security investigations, and foreign intelligence collection have persisted as separate documents involving different standards and procedures for comparable activities. These Guidelines effect a more complete integration and harmonization of standards, thereby providing the FBI and other affected Justice Department components with clearer, more consistent, and more accessible guidance for their activities, and making available to the public in a single document the basic body of rules for the FBI's domestic operations.

These Guidelines also incorporate effective oversight measures involving many Department of Justice and FBI components, which have been adopted to ensure that all FBI activities are conducted in a manner consistent with law and policy.

The broad operational areas addressed by these Guidelines are the FBI's conduct of investigative and intelligence gathering activities, including cooperation and coordination with other components and agencies in such activities, and the intelligence analysis and planning functions of the FBI.

A. FBI Responsibilities—Federal Crimes, Threats to The National Security, Foreign Intelligence

Part 11 of these Guidelines authorizes the FBI to carry out investigations to detect, obtain information about, or prevent or protect against federal crimes or threats to the national security or to collect foreign intelligence. The major subject areas of information gathering activities under these Guidelines—federal crimes, threats to the national security, and foreign intelligence—are not distinct, but rather overlap extensively. For example, an investigation relating to international terrorism will invariably crosscut these areas because international terrorism is included under these Guidelines' definition of "threat to the national security," because international terrorism subject to investigation within the United States usually involves criminal acts that violate federal law, and because information relating to international terrorism also falls within the definition of "foreign intelligence." Likewise, counterintelligence activities relating to espionage are likely to concern matters that constitute threats to the national security, that implicate violations or potential violations of federal espionage laws, and that involve information falling under the definition of "foreign intelligence."

While some distinctions in the requirements and procedures for investigations are necessary in different subject areas, the general design of these Guidelines is to take a uniform approach wherever possible, thereby promoting certainty and consistency regarding the applicable standards and facilitating compliance with those standards. Hence, these Guidelines do not require that the FBI's information gathering activities be differentially labeled as "criminal investigations," "national security investigations," or "foreign intelligence collections," or that the categories of FBI personnel who cany out investigations be segregated fiom each other based on the subject areas in which they operate. Rather, all of the FBI's legal authorities are available for deployment in all cases to which they apply to protect the public fiom crimes and threats to the national security and to further the United States' foreign intelligence objectives. In many cases, a single investigation will be supportable as an exercise of a number of these authorities - i.e., as an investigation of a federal crime or crimes, as an investigation of a threat to the national security, andlor as a collection of foreign intelligence.

1. Federal Crimes

The FBI has the authority to investigate all federal crimes that are not exclusively assigned to other agencies. In most ordinary criminal investigations, the immediate objectives include such matters as: determining whether a federal crime has occurred or is occurring, or if planning or preparation for such a crime is taking place; identifjmg, locating, and apprehending the perpetrators; and obtaining the evidence needed for prosecution. Hence, close cooperation and coordination with federal prosecutors in the United States Attorneys' Offices and the Justice Department litigating divisions are essential both to ensure that agents have the investigative tools and legal advice at their disposal for which prosecutorial assistance or approval is needed, and to ensure that investigations are conducted in a manner that will lead to successful prosecution. Provisions in many parts of these Guidelines establish procedures and requirements for such coordination.

2. Threats to the National Security

The FBI's authority to investigate threats to the national security derives fiom the executive order concerning U.S. intelligence activities, from delegations of functions by the Attorney General, and from various statutory sources. See, e.g., E.O. 12333; 50 U.S.C. 401 et seq.; 50 U.S.C. 1801 et seq. These Guidelines (Part VII.S) specifically define threats to the national security to mean: international terrorism; espionage and other intelligence activities, sabotage, and assassination, conducted by, for, or on behalf of foreign powers, organizations, or persons; foreign computer intrusion; and other matters determined by the Attorney General, consistent with Executive Order 12333 or any successor order.

Activities within the definition of "threat to the national security" that are subject to investigation under these Guidelines commonly involve violations (or potential violations) of federal criminal laws. Hence, investigations of such threats may constitute an exercise both of the FBI's criminal investigation authority and of the FBI's authority to investigate threats to the national security. As with criminal investigations generally, detecting and solving the crimes, and eventually arresting and prosecuting the perpetrators, are likely to be among the objectives of

investigations relating to threats to the national security. But these investigations also often serve important purposes outside the ambit of normal criminal investigation and prosecution, by providing the basis for, and informing decisions concerning, other measures needed to protect the national security. These measures may include, for example: excluding or removing persons involved in terrorism or espionage from the United States; recruitment of double agents; freezing assets of organizations that engage in or support terrorism; securing targets of terrorism or espionage; providing threat information and warnings to other federal, state, local, and private agencies and entities; diplomatic or military actions; and actions by other intelligence agencies to counter international terrorism or other national security threats.

In line with this broad range of purposes, investigations of threats to the national security present special needs to coordinate with other Justice Department components, including particularly the Justice Department's National Security Division, and to share information and cooperate with other agencies with national security responsibilities, including other agencies of the U.S. Intelligence Community, the Department of Homeland Security, and relevant White House (including National Security Council and Homeland Security Council) agencies and entities. Various provisions in these Guidelines establish procedures and requirements to facilitate such coordination.

3. Foreign Intelligence

As with the investigation of threats to the national security, the FBI's authority to collect foreign intelligence derives from a mixture of administrative and statutory sources. See, e.g., E.O. 12333; 50 U.S.C. 401 et seq.; 50 U.S.C. 1801 et seq.; 28 U.S.C. 532 note (incorporating P.L. 108-458 §§ 2001-2003). These Guidelines (Part VI1.E) define foreign intelligence to mean "information relating to the capabilities, intentions, or activities of foreign governments or elements thereof, foreign organizations or foreign persons, or international terrorists."

The FBI's foreign intelligence collection activities have been expanded by legislative and administrative reforms subsequent to the September 11, 2001, terrorist attacks, reflecting the FBI's role as the primary collector of foreign intelligence within the United States, and the recognized imperative that the United States' foreign intelligence collection activities become more flexible, more proactive, and more efficient in order to protect the homeland and adequately inform the United States' crucial decisions in its dealings with the rest of the world:

> The collection of information is the foundation of everything that the Intelligence Community does. Wle successful collection cannot ensure a good analytical product, the failure to collect information . . . turns analysis into guesswork. And as our review demonstrates, the Intelligence Community's human and technical intelligence collection agencies have collected far too little information on many of the issues we care about most. (Report of the Commission on the Intelligence Capabilities of the United States Regafding Weapons of Mass Destruction 35 1 (2005).)

These Guidelines accordingly provide standards and procedures for the FBI's foreign intelligence collection activities that meet current needs and realities and optimize the FBI's ability to discharge its foreign intelligence collection functions.

The authority to collect foreign intelligence extends the sphere of the FBI's information gathering activities beyond federal crimes and threats to the national security, and permits the FBI to seek information regarding a broader range of matters relating to foreign powers, organizations, or persons that may be of interest to the conduct of the United States' foreign affairs. The FBI's role is central to the effective collection of foreign intelligence within the United States because the authorized domestic activities of other intelligence agencies are more constrained than those of the FBI under applicable statutes and Executive Order 12333. In collecting foreign intelligence, the FBI will generally be guided by nationally-determined intelligence requirements, including the National Intelligence Priorities Framework and the National HUMINT Collection Directives, or any successor directives issued under the authority of the Director of National Intelligence (DNI). As provided in Part VII.F of these Guidelines, foreign intelligence requirements may also be established by the President or Intelligence Community officials designated by the President, and by the Attorney General, the Deputy Attorney General, or an official designated by the Attorney General.

The general guidance of the FBI's foreign intelligence collection activities by DNI—authorized requirements does not, however, limit the FBI's authority to -conduct investigations supportable on the basis of its other authorities—to investigate federal crimes and threats to the national security -in areas in which the information sought also falls under the definition of foreign intelligence. The FBI conducts investigations of federal crimes and threats to the national security based on priorities and strategic objectives set by the Department of Justice and the FBI, independent of DNI-established foreign intelligence collection requirements.

Since the authority to collect foreign intelligence enables the FBI to obtain information pertinent to the United States' conduct of its foreign affairs, even if that information is not related to criminal activity or threats to the national security, the information so gathered may concern lawful activities. The FBI should accordingly operate openly and consensually with U.S. persons to the extent practicable when collecting foreign intelligence that does not concern criminal activities or threats to the national security.

B. The FBI as An Intelligence Agency

The FBI is an intelligence agency as well as a law enforcement agency. Its basic functions accordingly extend beyond limited investigations of discrete matters, and include broader analytic and planning functions. The FBI's responsibilities in this area derive fkom various administrative and statutory sources. See, e.g., E.O. 12333; 28 U.S.C. 532 note (incorporating P.L. 108-458 §§ 2001 -2003) and 534 note (incorporating P.L. 109-162 § 1107). Enhancement of the FBI's intelligence analysis capabilities and functions has consistently been recognized as a key priority in the legislative and administrative reform efforts following the

September 1 1,2001, terrorist attacks:

> [Counterterrorism] strategy should . . . encompass specific efforts to . . . enhance the depth and quality of domestic intelligence collection and analysis . . . . [Tlhe FBI should strengthen and improve its domestic [intelligence]

capability as fully and expeditiously as possible by immediately instituting measures to . . . significantly improve strategic analytical capabilities . . . . (Joint Inquiry into Intelligence Community Activities Before and After the Terrorist Attacks of September 11,2001, S. Rep. No. 351 & H.R. Rep. No. 792, 107th Cong., 2d Sess. 4-7 (2002) (errata print).)

A "smart" government would *integrate* all sources of information to see the enemy as a whole. Integrated all-source analysis should also inform and shape strategies to collect more intelligence. . . . The importance of integrated, all-source analysis cannot be overstated. Without it, it is not possible to "connect the dots." (Final Report of the National Commission on Terrorist Attacks Upon the United States 401,408 (2004).)

Part IV of these Guidelines accordingly authorizes the FBI to engage in intelligence analysis and planning, drawing on all lawful sources of information. The functions authorized under that Part include: (i) development of overviews and analyses concerning threats to and vulnerabilities of the United States and its interests, (ii) research and analysis to produce reports and assessments concerning matters relevant to investigative activities or other authorized FBI activities, and (iii) the operation of intelligence systems that facilitate and support investigations through the compilation and analysis of data and information on an ongoing basis.

C. Oversight

The activities authorized by these Guidelines must be conducted in a manner consistent with all applicable laws, regulations, and policies, including those protecting privacy and civil liberties. The Justice Department's National Security Division and the FBI's Inspection Division, Office of General Counsel, and Office of Integrity and Compliance, along with other components, share the responsibility to ensure that the Department meets these goals with respect to national security and foreign intelligence matters. In particular, the National Security Division's Oversight Section, in conjunction with the FBI's Office of General Counsel, is responsible for conducting regular reviews of all aspects of FBI national security and foreign intelligence activities. These reviews, conducted at FBI field offices and headquarter units, broadly examine such activities for compliance with these Guidelines and other applicable requirements.

Various features of these Guidelines facilitate the National Security Division's oversight functions. Relevant requirements and provisions include:

(i) required notification by the FBI to the National Security Division concerning full investigations that involve foreign intelligence collection or investigation of United States persons in relation to threats of the national security,
(ii) annual reports by the FBI to the National Security Division concerning the FBI's foreign intelligence collection program, including information on the scope and nature of foreign intelligence collection activities in each FBI field office, and
(iii) access by the National Security Division to information obtained by the FBI through national security or foreign intelligence activities and general au-

thority for the Assistant Attorney General for National Security to obtain reports from the FBI concerning these activities.

Pursuant to these Guidelines, other Attorney General guidelines, and institutional assignments of responsibility withn the Justice Department, additional Department components—including the Criminal Division, the United States Attorneys' Offices, and the Office of Privacy and Civil Liberties -are involved in the common endeavor with the FBI of ensuring that the activities of all Department components are lawful, appropriate, and ethxal as well as effective. Examples include the involvement of both FBI and prosecutorial personnel in the review of undercover operations involving sensitive circumstances, notice requirements for investigations involving sensitive investigative matters (as defined in Part V1I.N of these Guidelines), and notice and oversight provisions for enterprise investigations, which may involve a broad examination of groups implicated in the gravest criminal and national security threats. These requirements and procedures help to ensure that the rule of law is respected in the Department's activities and that public confidence is maintained in these activities.

I. GENERAL AUTHORITIES AND PRINCIPLES

A. Scope

These Guidelines apply to investigative activities conducted by the FBI within the United States or outside the territories of all countries. They do not apply to investigative activities of the FBI in foreign countries, which are governed by the Attorney General's Guidelines for Extraterritorial FBI Operations.

B. General Authorities

The FBI is authorized to conduct investigations to detect, obtain information about, and prevent and protect against federal crimes and threats to the national security and to collect foreign intelligence, as provided in Part I1 of these Guidelines.

The FBI is authorized to provide investigative assistance to other federal agencies, state, local, or tribal agencies, and foreign agencies as provided in Part III of these Guidelines.

The FBI is authorized to conduct intelligence analysis and planning as provided in Part IV of these Guidelines.

The FBI is authorized to retain and share information obtained pursuant to these Guidelines as provided in Part VI of these Guidelines.

C. Use of Authorities and Methods

1. Protection of the United States and Its People

The FBI shall hlly utilize the authorities provided and the methods authorized by these Guidelines to protect the United States and its people from crimes in violation of federal law and threats to the national security, and to further the foreign intelligence objectives of the United States.

2. *Choice of Methods*

a. The conduct of investigations and other activities authorized by these Guidelines may present choices between the use of different investigative methods that are each operationally sound and effective, but that are more or less intrusive, considering such factors as the effect on the privacy and civil liberties of individuals and potential damage to reputation. The least intrusive method feasible is to be used in such situations. It is recognized, however, that the choice of methods is a matter of judgment. The FBI shall not hesitate to use any lawful method consistent with these Guidelines, even if intrusive, where the degree of intrusiveness is warranted in light of the seriousness of a criminal or national security threat or the strength of the information indicating its existence, or in light of the importance of foreign intelligence sought to the United States' interests. This point is to be particularly observed in investigations relating to terrorism.

b. United States persons shall be dealt with openly and consensually to the extent practicable when collecting foreign intelligence that does not concern criminal activities or threats to the national security.

3. *Respect for Legal Rights*

All activities under these Guidelines must have a valid purpose consistent with these Guidelines, and must be carried out in conformity with the Constitution and all applicable statutes, executive orders, Department of Justice regulations andpolicies, and Attorney General guidelines. These Guidelines do not authorize investigating or collecting or maintaining information on United States persons solely for the purpose of monitoring activities protected by the First Amendment or the lawful exercise of other rights secured by the Constitution or laws of the United States. These Guidelines also do not authorize any conduct prohibited by the Guidance Regarding the Use of Race by Federal Law Enforcement Agencies.

4. *Undisclosed Participation in Organizations*

Undisclosed participation in organizations in activities under these Guidelines shall be conducted in accordance with FBI policy approved by the Attorney General.

5. *Maintenance of Records under the Privacy Act*

The Privacy Act restricts the maintenance of records relating to certain activities of individuals who are United States persons, with exceptions for circumstances in which the collection of such information is pertinent to and within the scope of an authorized law enforcement activity or is otherwise authorized by statute. 5 U.S.C. 552a(e)(7). Activities authorized by these Guidelines are authorized law enforcement activities or activities for which there is otherwise statutory authority for purposes of the Privacy Act. These Guidelines, however, do not provide an exhaustive enumeration of authorized FBI law enforcement activities or FBI activities for which there is otherwise statutory authority, and no restriction is implied with respect to such activities carried out by the FBI pursuant to other authorities. Further questions about the application of the Privacy Act to authorized activities of the FBI should be addressed to the FBI Office of the General Counsel, the FBI Privacy and Civil Liberties Unit, or the Department of Justice Office of Privacy and Civil Liberties.

D. Nature and Application of the Guidelines

1. Repealers

These Guidelines supersede the following guidelines, which are hereby repealed:

a. The Attorney General's Guidelines on General Crimes, Racketeering Enterprise and Terrorism Enterprise Investigations (May 30,2002) and all predecessor guidelines thereto.

b. The Attorney General's Guidelines for FBI National Security Investigations and Foreign Intelligence Collection (October 3 1,2003) and all predecessor guidelines thereto.

c. The Attorney General's Supplemental Guidelines for Collection, Retention, and Dissemination of Foreign Intelligence (November 29, 2006).

d. The Attorney General Procedure for Reporting and Use of Information Concerning Violations of Law and Authorization for Participation in Otherwise Illegal Activity in FBI Foreign Intelligence, Counterintelligence or International Terrorism Intelligence Investigations (August 8, 1988).

e. The Attorney General's Guidelines for Reporting on Civil Disorders and Demonstrations Involving a Federal Interest (April 5, 1976).

2. Status as Internal Guidance

These Guidelines are set forth solely for the purpose of internal Department of Justice guidance. They are not intended to, do not, and may not be relied upon to create any rights, substantive or procedural, enforceable by law by any party in any matter, civil or criminal, nor do they place any limitation on otherwise lawful investigative and litigative prerogatives of the Department of Justice.

3. Departures from the Guidelines

Departures fiom these Guidelines must be approved by the Director of the FBI, by the Deputy Director of the FBI, or by an Executive Assistant Director designated 14 by the Director. If a departure is necessary without such prior approval because of the immediacy or gravity of a threat to the safety of persons or property or to the national security, the Director, the Deputy Director, or a designated Executive Assistant Director shall be notified as soon thereafter as practicable. The FBI shall provide timely written notice of departures fiom these Guidelines to the Criminal Division and the National Security Division, and those divisions shall notify the Attorney General and the Deputy Attorney General. Notwithstanding this paragraph, all activities in all circumstances must be carried out in a manner consistent with the Constitution and laws of the United States.

4. Other Activities Not Limited

These Guidelines apply to FBI activities as provided herein and do not limit other authorized activities of the FBI, such as the FBI's responsibilities to conduct background checks and inquiries concerning applicants and employees under federal personnel security programs, the FBI's maintenance and operation of national criminal records systems and preparation of national crime statistics, and the forensic assistance and administration functions of the FBI Laboratory.

II. INVESTIGATIONS AND INTELLIGENCE GATHERING

This Part of the Guidelines authorizes the FBI to conduct investigations to detect, obtain information about, and prevent and protect against federal crimes and threats to the national security and to collect foreign intelligence.

When an authorized purpose exists, the focus of activities authorized by this Part may be whatever the circumstances warrant. The subject of such an activity may be, for example, a particular crime or threatened crime; conduct constituting a threat to the national security; an individual, group, or organization that may be involved in criminal or national security- threatening conduct; or a topical matter of foreign intelligence interest.

Investigations may also be undertaken for protective purposes in relation to individuals, groups, or other entities that may be targeted for criminal victimization or acquisition, or for terrorist attack or other depredations by the enemies of the United States. For example, the participation of the FBI in special events management, in relation to public events or other activities whose character may make them attractive targets for terrorist attack, is an authorized exercise of the authorities conveyed by these Guidelines. Likewise, FBI counterintelligence activities directed to identifying and securing facilities, personnel, or information that may be targeted for infiltration, recruitment, or acquisition by foreign intelligence services are authorized exercises of the authorities conveyed by these Guidelines.

The identification and recruitment of human sources -who may be able to provide or obtain information relating to criminal activities, information relating to terrorism, espionage, or other threats to the national security, or information relating to matters of foreign intelligence interest -is also critical to the effectiveness of the FBI's law enforcement, national security, and intelligence programs, and activities undertaken for this purpose are authorized and encouraged.

The scope of authorized activities under this Part is not limited to "investigation" in a narrow sense, such as solving particular cases or obtaining evidence for use in particular criminal prosecutions. Rather, these activities also provide critical information needed for broader analytic and intelligence purposes to facilitate the solution and prevention of crime, protect the national security, and further foreign intelligence objectives. These purposes include use of the information in intelligence analysis and planning under Part IV, and dissemination of the information to other law enforcement, Intelligence Community, and White House agencies under Part VI. Information obtained at all stages of investigative activity is accordingly to be retained and disseminated for these purposes as provided in these Guidelines, or in FBI policy consistent with these Guidelines, regardless of whether it furthers investigative objectives in a narrower or more immediate sense.

In the course of activities under these Guidelines, the FBI may incidentally obtain information relating to matters outside of its areas of primary investigative responsibility. For example, information relating to violations of state or local law or foreign law may be incidentally obtained in the course of investigating federal crimes or threats to the national security or in collecting foreign intelligence. These Guidelines do not bar the acquisition of such information in the course of authorized investigative activities, the retention of such information, or its dissemination as appropriate to the responsible authorities in other agencies or jurisdictions. Part VI of these Guidelines includes specific authorizations and requirements for sharing such information with relevant agencies and officials.

This Part authorizes different levels of information gathering activity, which afford the FBI flexibility, under appropriate standards and procedures, to adapt the methods utilized and the information sought to the nature of the matter under investigation and the character of the information supporting the need for investigation.

Assessments, authorized by Subpart A of this Part, require an authorized purpose but not any particular factual predication. For example, to carry out its central mission of preventing the commission of terrorist acts against the United States and its people, the FBI must proactively draw on available sources of information to identifl terrorist threats and activities. It cannot be content to wait for leads to come in through the actions of others, but rather must be vigilant in detecting terrorist activities to the full extent permitted by law, with an eye towards early intervention and prevention of acts of terrorism before they occur. Likewise, in the exercise of its protective functions, the FBI is not constrained to wait until information is received indicating that a particular event, activity, or facility has drawn the attention of those who would threaten the national security. Rather, the FBI must take the initiative to secure and protect activities and entities whose character may make them attractive targets for terrorism or espionage. The proactive investigative authority conveyed in assessments is designed for, and may be utilized by, the FBI in the discharge of these responsibilities. For example, assessments may be conducted as part of the FBI's special events management activities.

More broadly, detecting and interrupting criminal activities at their early stages, and preventing crimes from occurring in the first place, is preferable to allowing criminal plots and activities to come to fruition. Hence, assessments may be undertaken proactively with such objectives as detecting criminal activities; obtaining information on individuals, groups, or organizations of possible investigative interest, either because they may be involved in criminal or national security-threatening activities or because they may be targeted for attack or victimization by such activities; and identifying and assessing individuals who may have value as human sources. For example, assessment activities may involve proactively surfing the Internet to find publicly accessible websites and services through which recruitment by terrorist organizations and promotion of terrorist crimes is openly taking place; through which child pornography is advertised and traded; through which efforts are made by sexual predators to lure children for purposes of sexual abuse; or through which fraudulent schemes are perpetrated against the public. ,

The methods authorized in assessments are generally those of relatively low intrusiveness, such as obtaining publicly available information, checking government records, and requesting information fiom members of the public. These Guidelines do not impose supervisory approval requirements in assessments, given the types of techniques that are authorized at this stage (e.g., perusing the Internet for publicly available information). However, FBI policy will prescribe supervisory approval requirements for certain assessments, considering such matters as the purpose of the assessment and the methods being utilized.

Beyond the proactive information gathering functions described above, assessments may be used when allegations or other information concerning crimes or threats to the national security is received or obtained, and the matter can be checked out or resolved through the relatively non-intrusive methods authorized in assessments. The checking of investigative leads in this manner can avoid the need to proceed to more formal levels of investigative activity, if the results of an assessment indicate that further investigation is not warranted.

Subpart B of this Part authorizes a second level of investigative activity, predicated investigations. The purposes or objectives of predicated investigations are essentially the same as those of assessments, but predication as provided in these Guidelines is needed—generally, allegations, reports, facts or circumstances indicative of possible criminal or national security- threatening activity, or the potential for acquiring information responsive to foreign intelligence requirements -and supervisory approval must be obtained, to initiate predicated investigations. Corresponding to the stronger predication and approval requirements, all lawful methods may be used in predicated investigations. A classified directive provides further specification concerning circumstances supporting certain predicated investigations.

Predicated investigations that concern federal crimes or threats to the national security are subdivided into preliminary investigations and full investigations. Preliminary investigations may be initiated on the basis of any allegation or information indicative of possible criminal or national security-threatening activity, but more substantial factual predication is required for full investigations. Wle time limits are set for the completion of preliminary investigations, full investigations may be pursued without preset limits on their duration.

The final investigative category under this Part of the Guidelines is enterprise investigations, authorized by Subpart C, which permit a general examination of the structure, scope, and nature of certain groups and organizations. Enterprise investigations are a type of full investigations. Hence, they are subject to the purpose, approval, and predication requirements that apply to full investigations, and all lawful methods may be used in carrying them out. The distinctive characteristic of enterprise investigations is that they concern groups or organizations that may be involved in the most serious criminal or national security threats to the public -generally, patterns of racketeering activity, terrorism or other threats to the national security, or the commission of offenses characteristically involved in terrorism as described in 18 U.S.C. 2332b(g)(5)(B). A broad examination of the characteristics of groups satisfying these criteria is authorized in enterprise investigations, including any relationshp of the group to a foreign power, its size and composition, its geographic dimensions and finances, its past acts and goals, and its capacity for harm.

A. Assessments

1. Purposes

Assessments may be canied out to detect, obtain information about, or prevent or protect against federal crimes or threats to the national security or to collect foreign intelligence.

2. Approval

The conduct of assessments is subject to any supervisory approval requirements prescribed by FBI policy.

3. Authorized Activities

Activities that may be canied out for the purposes described in paragraph 1.in an assessment include:

a. seeking information, proactively or in response to investigative leads, relating to:

i. activities constituting violations of federal criminal law or threats to the national security,

..

ii. the involvement or role of individuals, groups, or organizations in such activities; or

. . .

iii. matters of foreign intelligence interest responsive to foreign intelligence requirements;

b. identifying and obtaining information about potential targets of or vulnerabilities to criminal activities in violation of federal law or threats to the national security;

c. seeking information to identifl potential human sources, assess the suitability, credibility, or value of individuals as human sources, validate human sources, or maintain the cover or credibility of human sources, who may be able to provide or obtain information relating to criminal activities in violation of federal law, threats to the national security, or matters of foreign intelligence interest; and

d. obtaining information to inform or facilitate intelligence analysis and planning as described in Part IV of these Guidelines.

4. Authorized Methods

Only the following methods may be used in assessments:

a. Obtain publicly available information.

b. Access and examine FBI and other Department of Justice records, and obtain information from any FBI or other Department of Justice personnel.

c. Access and examine records maintained by, and request information fkom, other federal, state, local, or tribal, or foreign governmental entities or agencies.

d. Use online services and resources (whether nonprofit or commercial).

e. Use and recruit human sources in conformity with the Attorney General's Guidelines Regarding the Use of FBI Confidential Human Sources.

f. Interview or request information from members of the public and private entities.
g. Accept information voluntarily provided by governmental or private entities.
h. Engage in observation or surveillance not requiring a court order.
i. Grand jury subpoenas for telephone or electronic mail subscriber information.

B. Predicated Investigations

1. Purposes

Predicated investigations may be carried out to detect, obtain information about, or prevent or protect against federal crimes or threats to the national security or to collect foreign intelligence.

2. Approval

The initiation of a predicated investigation requires supervisory approval at a level or levels specified by FBI policy. A predicated investigation based on paragraph 3.c. (relating to foreign intelligence) must be approved by a Special Agent in Charge or by an FBI Headquarters official as provided in such policy.

3. Circumstances Warranting Investigation

A predicated investigation may be initiated on the basis of any of the following circumstances:

a. An activity constituting a federal crime or a threat to the national security has or may have occurred, is or may be occurring, or will or may occur and the investigation may obtain information relating to the activity or the involvement or role of an individual, group, or organization in such activity.
b. An individual, group, organization, entity, information, property, or activity is or may be a target of attack, victimization, acquisition, infiltration, or recruitment in connection with criminal activity in violation of federal law or a threat to the national security and the investigation may obtain information that would help to protect against such activity or threat.
c. The investigation may obtain foreign intelligence that is responsive to a foreign intelligence requirement.

4. Preliminary and Full Investigations

A predicated investigation relating to a federal crime or threat to the national security may be conducted as a preliminary investigation or a full investigation. A predicated investigation that is based solely on the authority to collect foreign intelligence may be conducted only as a full investigation.

a. Preliminary investigations
   i. Predication Required for Preliminary Investigations. A preliminary investigation may be initiated on the basis of information or an allegation indicating the existence of a circumstance described in paragraph 3.a.-.b.
   ii. Duration of Preliminary Investigations. A preliminary investigation must be concluded within six months of its initiation, which may be extended

by up to six months by the Special Agent in Charge. Extensions of preliminary investigations beyond a year must be approved by FBI Headquarters.

iii. Methods Allowed in Preliminary Investigations. All lawful methods may be used in a preliminary investigation except for methods within the scope of Part V.A. 1 1 .-.13. of these Guidelines.

b. Full Investigations

i. Predication Required for Full Investigations. A full investigation may be initiated if there is an articulable factual basis for the investigation that reasonably indicates that a circumstance described in paragraph 3 .a.-.b. exists or if a circumstance described in paragraph 3 .c. exists.

ii. Methods Allowed in Full Investigations. All lawful methods may be used in a full investigation.

5. Notice Requirements

a. An FBI field office shall notify FBI Headquarters and the United States Attorney or other appropriate Department of Justice official of the initiation by the field office of a predicated investigation involving a sensitive investigative matter. If the investigation is initiated by FBI Headquarters, FBI Headquarters shall notify the United States Attorney or other appropriate Department of Justice official of the initiation of such an investigation. If the investigation concerns a threat to the national security, an official of the National Security Division must be notified. The notice shall identify all sensitive investigative matters involved in the investigation.

b. The FBI shall notify the National Security Division of:

i. the initiation of any full investigation of a United States person relating to a threat to the national security; and

ii. the initiation of any full investigation that is based on paragraph 3.c. (relating to foreign intelligence).

c. The notifications under subparagraphs a. and b. shall be made as soon as practicable, but no later than 30 days after the initiation of an investigation.

d. The FBI shall notify the Deputy Attorney General if FBI Headquarters disapproves a field office's initiation of a predicated investigation relating to a threat to the national security on the ground that the predication for the investigation is insufficient.

C. Enterprise Investigations

1. Definition

A full investigation of a group or organization may be initiated as an enterprise investigation if there is an articulable factual basis for the investigation that reasonably indicates that the group or organization may have engaged or may be engaged in, or may have or may be engaged in planning or preparation or provision of support for:

a. a pattern of racketeering activity as defined in 18 U.-S.C. 1961 (5);

b. international terrorism or other threat to the national security;
c. domestic terrorism as defined in 18 U.S.C. 2331(5) involving a violation of federal criminal law;
d. futhering political or social goals wholly or in part through activities that involve force or violence and a violation of federal criminal law; or
e. an offense described in 18 U.S.C. 2332b(g)(5)(B) or 18 U.S.C. 43.

2. Scope

The information sought in an enterprise investigation may include a general examination of the structure, scope, and nature of the group or organization including: its relationship, if any, to a foreign power; the identity and relationship of its members, employees, or other persons who may be acting in furtherance of its objectives; its finances and resources; its geographical dimensions; and its past and future activities and goals.

3. Notice and Reporting Requirements

a. The responsible Department of Justice component for the purpose of notification and reports in enterprise investigations is the National Security Division, except that, for the purpose of notifications and reports in an enterprise investigation relating to a pattern of racketeering activity that does not involve an offense or offenses described in 18 U.S.C. 2332b(g)(5)(B), the responsible Department of Justice component is the Organized Crime and Racketeering Section of the Criminal Division.
b. An FBI field office shall notify FBI Headquarters of the initiation by the field office of an enterprise investigation.
c. The FBI shall notify the National Security Division or the Organized Crime and Racketeering Section of the initiation of an enterprise investigation, whether by a field office or by FBI Headquarters, and the component so notified shall notify the Attorney General and the Deputy Attorney General. The FBI shall also notify any relevant United States Attorney's Office, except that any investigation within the scope of Part V1.D.1.d of these Guidelines (relating to counterintelligence investigations) is to be treated as provided in that provision. Notifications by the FBI under this subparagraph shall be provided as soon as practicable, but no later than 30 days after the initiation of the investigation.
d. The Assistant Attorney General for National Security or the Chief of the Organized Crime and Racketeering Section, as appropriate, may at any time request the FBI to provide a report on the status of an enterprise investigation and the FBI will provide such reports as requested.

III. ASSISTANCE TO OTHER AGENCIES

The FBI is authorized to provide investigative assistance to other federal, state, local, or tribal, or foreign agencies as provided in ths Part.

The investigative assistance authorized by this Part is often concerned with the same objectives as those identified in Part II of these Guidelines—investigating federal crimes and threats to the national security, and collecting foreign intelligence. In some cases, however, investigative assistance to other agencies is legally authorized for purposes other than those identified in Part II, such as assistance in certain contexts to state or local agencies in the investigation of crimes under state or local law, see 28 U.S.C. 540, 540A, 540B, and assistance to foreign agencies in the investigation of foreign law violations pursuant to international agreements. Investigative assistance for such legally authorized purposes is permitted under this Part, even if it is not for purposes identified as grounds for investigation under Part II.

The authorities provided by this Part are cumulative to Part II and do not limit the FBI's investigative activities under Part II. For example, Subpart B.2 in this Part authorizes investigative activities by the FBI in certain circumstances to inform decisions by the President concerning the deployment of troops to deal with civil disorders, and Subpart B.3 authorizes investigative activities to facilitate demonstrations and related public health and safety measures. The requirements and limitations in these provisions for conducting investigations for the specified purposes do not limit the FBI's authority under Part II to investigate federal crimes or threats to the national security that occur in the context of or in connection with civil disorders or demonstrations.

A. The Intelligence Community

The FBI may provide investigative assistance (including operational support) to authorized intelligence activities of other Intelligence Community agencies.

B. Federal Agencies Generally

1. In General

The FBI may provide assistance to any federal agency in the investigation of federal crimes or threats to the national security or in the collection of foreign intelligence, and investigative assistance to any federal agency for any other purpose that may be legally authoized, including investigative assistance to the Secret Service in support of its protective responsibilities.

2. The President in Relation to Civil Disorders

a. At the direction of the Attorney General, the Deputy Attorney General, or the Assistant Attorney General for the Criminal Division, the FBI shall collect information relating to actual or threatened civil disorders to assist the President in determining (pursuant to the authority of the President under 10 U.S.C. 331-33) whether use of the armed forces or militia is required and how a decision to commit troops should be implemented. The information sought shall concern such matters as:

i. The size of the actual or threatened disorder, both in number of people involved or affected and in geographic area.

. .

ii. The potential for violence.

iii. The potential for expansion of the disorder in light of community conditions and underlying causes of the disorder.

iv. The relationship of the actual or threatened disorder to the enforcement of federal law or court orders and the likelihood that state or local authorities will assist in enforcing those laws or orders.

v. The extent of state or local resources available to handle the disorder.

b. Investigations under this paragraph will be authorized only for a period of 30 days, but the authorization may be renewed for subsequent 30 day periods.

c. Notwithstanding Subpart E.2 of this Part, the methods that may be used in an investigation under ths paragraph are those described in subparagraphs a.-.d., subparagraph f. (other than pretext interviews or requests), or subparagraph g. of Part II.A.4 of these Guidelines. The Attorney General, the Deputy Attorney General, or the Assistant Attorney General for the Criminal Division may also authorize the use of other methods described in Part II.A.4.

Public Health and Safety Authorities in Relation to Demonstrations

a. At the direction of the Attorney General, the Deputy Attorney General, or the Assistant Attorney General for the Criminal Division, the FBI shall collect information relating to demonstration activities that are likely to require the federal government to take action to facilitate the activities and provide public health and safety measures with respect to those activities. The information sought in such an investigation shall be that needed to facilitate an adequate federal response to ensure public health and safety and to protect the exercise of First Amendment rights, such as:

i. The time, place, and type of activities planned.

..

ii. The number of persons expected to participate.

...

iii. The expected means and routes of travel for participants and expected time of arrival.

iv. Any plans for lodging or housing of participants in connection with the demonstration.

b. Notwithstanding Subpart E.2 of this Part, the methods that may be used in an investigation under this paragraph are those described in subparagraphs a.-.d., subparagraph f. (other than pretext interviews or requests), or subparagraph g. of Part II.A.4 of these Guidelines. The Attorney General, the Deputy Attorney General, or the Assistant Attorney General for the Criminal Division may also authorize the use of other methods described in Part II.A.4.

C. State, Local, or Tribal Agencies

The FBI may provide investigative assistance to state, local, or tribal agencies in the investigation of matters that may involve federal crimes or threats to the national security, or for such other purposes as may be legally authorized.

D. Foreign Agencies

At the request of foreign law enforcement, intelligence, or security agencies, the FBI may conduct investigations or provide assistance to investigations by such agencies, consistent with the interests of the United States (including national security interests) and with due consideration of the effect on any United States person. Investigations or assistance under this paragraph must be approved as provided by FBI policy. The FBI shall notify the National Security Division concerning investigation or assistance under this paragraph where: (i) FBI Headquarters approval for the activity is required pursuant to the approval policy adopted by the FBI for purposes of this paragraph, and (ii) the activity relates to a threat to the national security. Notification to the National Security Division shall be made as soon as practicable but no later than 30 days after the approval. Provisions regarding notification to or coordination with the Central Intelligence Agency by the FBI in memoranda of understanding or agreements with the Central Intelligence Agency may also apply to activities under this paragraph.

The FBI may not provide assistance to foreign law enforcement, intelligence, or security officers conducting investigations within the United States unless such officers have provided prior notification to the Attorney General as required by 18 U.S.C. 951.

The FBI may conduct background inquiries concerning consenting individuals when requested by foreign government agencies.

The FBI may provide other material and technical assistance to foreign governments to the extent not otherwise prohibited by law.

E. Applicable Standards and Procedures

Authorized investigative assistance by the FBI to other agencies under this Part includes joint operations and activities with such agencies.

All lawful methods may be used in investigative assistance activities under this Part. 3. Where the methods used in investigative assistance activities under this Part go beyond the methods authorized in assessments under Part II.A.4 of these Guidelines, the following apply:

a. Supervisory approval must be obtained for the activity at a level or levels specified in FBI policy.

b. Notice must be provided concerning sensitive investigative matters in the manner described in Part II.B.5.

c. A database or records system must be maintained that permits, with respect to each such activity, the prompt retrieval of the status of the activity (open or closed), the dates of opening and closing, and the basis for the activity. This database or records system may be combined with the database or records system for predicated investigations required by Part VI.A.2.

IV. INTELLIGENCE ANALYSIS AND PLANNING

The FBI is authorized to engage in analysis and planning. The FBI's analytic activities enable the FBI to identify and understand trends, causes, and potential indicia of criminal activity and other threats to the United States that would not be apparent from the investigation of discrete matters alone. By means of intelligence analysis and strategic planning, the FBI can more effectively discover crimes, threats to the national security, and other matters of national intelligence interest and can provide the critical support needed for the effective discharge of its investigative responsibilities and other authorized activities. For example, analysis of threats in the context of special events management, concerning public events or activities that may be targeted for terrorist attack, is an authorized activity under this Part.

In carrying out its intelligence functions under this Part, the FBI is authorized to draw on all lawful sources of information, including but not limited to the results of investigative activities under these Guidelines. Investigative activities under these Guidelines and other legally authorized activities through which the FBI acquires information, data, or intelligence may properly be utilized, structured, and prioritized so as to support and effectuate the FBI's intelligence mission. The remainder of this Part provides further specification concerning activities and functions authorized as part of that mission.

A. Strategic Intelligence Analysis

The FBI is authorized to develop overviews and analyses of threats to and vulnerabilities of the United States and its interests in areas related to the FBI's responsibilities, including domestic and international criminal threats and activities; domestic and international activities, circumstances, and developments affecting the national security; and matters relevant to the conduct of the United States' foreign affairs. The overviews and analyses prepared under this Subpart may encompass present, emergent, and potential threats and vulnerabilities, their contexts and causes, and identification and analysis of means of responding to them.

B. Reports and Assessments Generally

The FBI is authorized to conduct research, analyze information, and prepare reports and assessments concerning matters relevant to authorized FBI activities, such as reports and assessments concerning: types of criminals or criminal activities; organized crime groups; terrorism, espionage, or other threats to the national security; foreign intelligence matters; or the scope and nature of criminal activity in particular geographic areas or sectors of the economy.

C. Intelligence Systems

The FBI is authorized to operate intelligence, identification, tracking, and information systems in support of authorized investigative activities, or for such other or additional purposes as may be legally authorized, such as intelligence and tracking systems relating to terrorists, gangs, or organized crime groups.

V. AUTHORIZED METHODS

A. Particular Methods

All lawful investigative methods may be used in activities under these Guidelines as authorized by these Guidelines. Authorized methods include, but are not limited to, those identified in the following list. The methods identified in the list are in some instances subject to special restrictions or review or approval requirements as noted:

1. The methods described in Part II.A.4 of these Guidelines.
2. Mail covers.
3. Physical searches of personal or real property where a warrant or court order is not legally required because there is no reasonable expectation of privacy (e.g., trash covers).
4. Consensual monitoring of communications, including consensual computer monitoring, subject to legal review by the Chief Division Counsel or the FBI Office of the General Counsel. Where a sensitive monitoring circumstance is involved, the monitoring must be approved by the Criminal Division or, if the investigation concerns a threat to the national security or foreign intelligence, by the National Security Division.
5. Use of closed-circuit television, direction finders, and other monitoring devices, subject to legal review by the Chief Division Counsel or the FBI Office of the General Counsel. (The methods described in this paragraph usually do not require court orders or warrants unless they involve physical trespass or non-consensual monitoring of communications, but legal review is necessary to ensure compliance with all applicable legal requirements.)
6. Polygraph examinations.
7. Undercover operations. In investigations relating to activities in violation of federal criminal law that do not concern threats to the national security or foreign intelligence, undercover operations must be carried out in conformity with the Attorney General's Guidelines on Federal Bureau of Investigation Undercover Operations. In investigations that are not subject to the preceding sentence because they concern threats to the national security or foreign intelligence, undercover operations involving religious or political organizations must be reviewed and approved by FBI Headquarters, with participation by the National Security Division in the review process.
8. Compulsory process as authorized by law, including grand jury subpoenas and other subpoenas, National Security Letters (1 5 U.S.C. 168 lu, 168 lv; 18 U.S.C. 2709; 12 U.S.C. 3414(a)(5)(A); 50 U.S.C. 436), and Foreign Intelligence Surveillance Act orders for the production of tangible things (50 U.S.C. 1861-63).
9. Accessing stored wire and electronic communications and transactional records in conformity with chapter 121 of title 18, United States Code (18 U.S.C. 2701- 2712).
10. Use of pen registers and trap and trace devices in conformity with chapter 206 of title 18, United States Code (18 U.S.C. 3121-3127), or the Foreign Intelligence Surveillance Act (50 U.S.C. 1841-1846).
12. Electronic surveillance in conformity with chapter 1 19 of title 18, United States Code (18 U.S.C. 2510-2522), the Foreign Intelligence Surveillance Act, or Executive Order 12333 5 2.5.

13. Physical searches, including mail openings, in conformity with Rule 41 of the Federal Rules of Criminal Procedure, the Foreign Intelligence Surveillance Act, or Executive Order 12333 *5* 2.5. A classified directive provides additional limitation on certain searches.
14. Acquisition of foreign intelligence information in conformity with title VII of the Foreign Intelligence Surveillance Act.

B. Special Requirements

Beyond the limitations noted in the'list above relating to particular investigative methods, the following requirements are to be observed:

1. Contacts with Represented Persons

Contact with represented persons may implicate legal restrictions and affect the admissibility of resulting evidence. Hence, if an individual is known to be represented by counsel in a particular matter, the FBI will follow applicable law and Department procedure concerning contact with represented individuals in the absence of prior notice to counsel. The Special Agent in Charge and the United States Attorney or their designees shall consult periodically on applicable law and Department procedure. Where issues arise concerning the consistency of contacts with represented persons with applicable attorney conduct rules, the United States Attorney's Office should consult with the Professional Responsibility AdvisoryOffice.

2. Use of Classified Investigative Technologies

Inappropriate use of classified investigative technologies may risk the compromise of such technologies. Hence, in an investigation relating to activities in violation of federal criminal law that does not concern a threat to the national security or foreign intelligence, the use of such technologies must be in conformity with the Procedures for the Use of Classified Investigative Technologies in Criminal Cases.

C. Otherwise Illegal Activity

1. Otherwise illegal activity by an FBI agent or employee in an undercover operation relating to activity in violation of federal criminal law that does not concern a threat to the national security or foreign intelligence must be approved in conformity with the Attorney General's Guidelines on Federal Bureau of Investigation Undercover Operations. Approval of otherwise illegal activity in conformity with those guidelines is sufficient and satisfies any approval requirement that would otherwise apply under these Guidelines.
2. Otherwise illegal activity by a human source must be approved in conformity with the Attorney General's Guidelines Regarding the Use of FBI Confidential Human Sources.
3. Otherwise illegal activity by an FBI agent or employee that is not within the scope of paragraph 1.must be approved by a United States Attorney's Office or a Department of Justice Division, except that a Special Agent in Charge may authorize the following:

a. otherwise illegal activity that would not be a felony under federal, state, local, or tribal law;
b. consensual monitoring of communications, even if a crime under state, local, or tribal law;
c. the controlled purchase, receipt, delivery, or sale of drugs, stolen property, or other contraband;
d. the payment of bribes;
e. the making of false representations in concealment of personal identity or the true ownership of a proprietary; and
f. conducting a money laundering transaction or transactions involving an aggregate amount not exceeding $1 million.

However, in an investigation relating to a threat to the national security or foreign intelligence collection, a Special Agent in Charge may not authorize an activity that may constitute a violation of export control laws or laws that concern the proliferation of weapons of mass destruction. In such an investigation, a Special Agent in Charge may authorize an activity that may otherwise violate prohibitions of material support to terrorism only in accordance with standards established by the Director of the FBI and agreed to by the Assistant Attorney General for National Security.

4. The following activities may not be authorized:
a. Acts of violence.
b. Activities whose authorization is prohibited by law, including unlawful investigative methods, such as illegal electronic surveillance or illegal searches. Subparagraph a., however, does not limit the right of FBI agents or employees to engage in any lawful use of force, including the use of force in self-defense or defense of others or otherwise in the lawful discharge of their duties.

An agent or employee may engage in otherwise illegal activity that could be authorized under this Subpart without the authorization required by paragraph 3. if necessary to meet an immediate threat to the safety of persons or property or to the national security, or to prevent the compromise of an investigation or the loss of a significant investigative opportunity. In such a case, prior to engaging in the otherwise illegal activity, every effort should be made by the agent or employee to consult with the Special Agent in Charge, and by the Special Agent in Charge to consult with the United States Attorney's Office or appropriate Department of Justice Division where the authorization of that office or division would be required under paragraph 3., unless the circumstances preclude such consultation. Cases in which otherwise illegal activity occurs pursuant to this paragraph without the authorization required by paragraph 3. shall be reported as soon as possible to the Special Agent in Charge, and by the Special Agent in Charge to FBI Headquarters and to the United States Attorney's Office or appropriate Department of Justice Division.

In an investigation relating to a threat to the national security or foreign intelligence collection, the National Security Division is the approving component for otherwise illegal activity for which paragraph 3. requires approval beyond internal FBI approval. However, officials in other components may approve otherwise illegal activity in such investigations as authorized by the Assistant Attorney General for National Security.

VI. RETENTION AND SHARING OF INFORMATION

A. Retention of Information

The FBI shall retain records relating to activities under these Guidelines in accordance with a records retention plan approved by the National Archives and Records Administration.

The FBI shall maintain a database or records system that permits, with respect to each predicated investigation, the prompt retrieval of the status of the investigation (open or closed), the dates of opening and closing, and the basis for the investigation.

B. Information Sharing Generally

1. Permissive Sharing

Consistent with law and with any applicable agreements or understandings with other agencies concerning the dissemination 'of information they have provided, the FBI may disseminate information obtained or produced through activities under these Guidelines:

a. within the FBI and to other components of the Department of Justice;

b. to other federal, state, local, or tribal agencies if related to their responsibilities and, in relation to other Intelligence Community agencies, the determination whether the information is related to the recipient's responsibilities may be left to the recipient;

c. to congressional committees as authorized by the Department of Justice Office of Legislative Affairs;

d. to foreign agencies if the information is related to their responsibilities and the dissemination is consistent with the interests of the United States (including national security interests) and the FBI has considered the effect such dissemination may reasonably be expected to have on any identifiable United States person;

e. if the information is publicly available, does not identify United States persons, or is disseminated with the consent of the person whom it concerns;

f. if the dissemination is necessary to protect the safety or security of persons or property, to protect against or prevent a crime or threat to the national security, or to obtain information for the conduct of an authorized FBI investigation; or

g. if dissemination of the information is otherwise permitted by the Privacy Act (5 U.S.C. 552a).

2. Required Sharing

The FBI shall share and disseminate information as required by statutes, treaties, Executive Orders, Presidential directives, National Security Council directives, Homeland Security Council directives, and Attorney General-approved policies, memoranda of understanding, or agreements.

C. Information Relating to Criminal Matters

1. Coordination with Prosecutors

In an investigation relating to possible criminal activity in violation of federal law, the agent conducting the investigation shall maintain periodic written or oral contact with the appropriate federal prosecutor, as circumstances warrant and as requested by the prosecutor. When, during such an investigation, a matter appears arguably to warrant prosecution, the agent shall present the relevant facts to the appropriate federal prosecutor. Information on investigations that have been closed shall be available on request to a United States Attorney or his or her designee or an appropriate Department of Justice official.

2. Criminal Matters Outside FBI Jurisdiction

When credible information is received by an FBI field office concerning serious criminal activity not within the FBI's investigative jurisdiction, the field office shall promptly transmit the information or refer the complainant to a law enforcement agency having jurisdiction, except where disclosure would jeopardize an ongoing investigation, endanger the safety of an individual, disclose the identity of a human source, interfere with a human source's cooperation, or reveal legally privileged information. If full disclosure is not made for the reasons indicated, then, whenever feasible, the FBI field office shall make at least limited disclosure to a law enforcement agency or agencies having jurisdiction, and full disclosure shall be made as soon as the need for restricting disclosure is no longer present. Where full disclosure is not made to the appropriate law enforcement agencies within 180 days, the FBI field office shall promptly notify FBI Headquarters in writing of the facts and circumstances concerning the criminal activity. The FBI shall make periodic reports to the Deputy Attorney General on such nondisclosures and incomplete disclosures, in a form suitable to protect the identity of human sources.

3. Reporting of Criminal Activity

a. When it appears that an FBI agent or employee has engaged in criminal activity in the course of an investigation under these Guidelines, the FBI shall notify the United States Attorney's Office or an appropriate Department of Justice Division. When it appears that a human source has engaged in criminal activity in the course of an investigation under these Guidelines, the FBI shall proceed as provided in the Attorney General's Guidelines Regarding the Use of FBI Confidential Human Sources. When information concerning possible criminal activity by any other person appears in the course of an investigation under these Guidelines, the FBI shall initiate an investigation of the criminal activity if warranted, and shall proceed as provided in paragraph 1. or 2.

b. The reporting requirements under this paragraph relating to criminal activity by FBI agents or employees or human sources do not apply to otherwise illegal activity that is authorized in conformity with these Guidelines or other Attorney General guidelines or to minor traffic offenses.

D. Information Relating to National Security and Foreign Intelligence Matters

The general principle reflected in current laws and policies is that there is a responsibility to provide information as consistently and fully as possible to agencies with relevant responsibilities to protect the United States and its people fiom terrorism and other threats to the national security, except as limited by specific constraints on such sharing. The FBI's responsibilities in this area include carrying out the requirements of the Memorandum of Understanding Between the Intelligence Community, Federal Law Enforcement Agencies, and the Department of Homeland Security Concerning, Information Sharing (March 4,2003), or any successor memorandum of understanding or agreement. Specific requirements also exist for internal coordination and consultation with other Department of Justice components, and for provision of national security and foreign intelligence information to White House agencies, as provided in the ensuing paragraphs.

1. Department of Justice

a. The National Security Division shall have access to all information obtained by the FBI through activities relating to threats to the national security or foreign intelligence. The Director of the FBI and the Assistant Attorney General for National Security shall consult concerning these activities whenever requested by either of them, and the FBI shall provide such reports and information concerning these activities as the Assistant Attorney General for National Security may request. In addition to any reports or information the Assistant Attorney General for National Security may specially request under this subparagraph, the FBI shall provide annual reports to the National Security Division concerning its foreign intelligence collection program, including information concerning the scope and nature of foreign intelligence collection activities in each FBI field office.

b. The FBI shall keep the National Security Division apprised of all information obtained through activities under these Guidelines that is necessary to the ability of the United States to investigate or protect against threats to the national security, which shall include regular consultations between the FBI and the National Security Division to exchange advice and information relevant to addressing such threats through criminal prosecution or other means.

c. Subject to subparagraphs d. and e., relevant United States Attorneys' Offices shall have access to and shall receive information from the FBI relating to threats to the national security, and may engage in consultations with the FBI relating to such threats, to the same extent as the National Security Division. The relevant United States Attorneys' Offices shall receive such access and information from the FBI field offices.

d. In a counterintelligence investigation—i.e., an investigation relating to a matter described in Part VII.S.2 of these Guidelines—the FBI's provision of information to and consultation with a United States Attorney's Office are subject to authorization by the National Security Division. In consultation with the Executive Office for United States Attorneys and the FBI, the National Security Division shall establish policies setting forth circumstances in which the FBI will consult with the National Security Division prior to informing relevant United States Attorneys' Offices about such an investigation. The policies established by the National Security Division under this subparagraph shall (among other things) provide that:

i. the National Security Division will, within 30 days, authorize the FBI to share with the United States Attorneys' Offices information relating to certain espionage investigations, as defined by the policies, unless such information is withheld because of substantial national security considerations; and

. .

ii. the FBI may consult freely with United States Attorneys' Offices concerning investigations within the scope of this subparagraph during an emergency, so long as the National Security Division is notified of such consultation as soon as practical after the consultation.

e. Information shared with a United States Attorney's Office pursuant to subparagraph c. or d. shall be disclosed only to the United States Attorney or any Assistant United States Attorneys designated by the United States Attorney as points of contact to receive such information. The United States Attorneys and designated Assistant United States Attorneys shall have appropriate security clearances and shall receive training in the handling of classified information and information derived from the Foreign Intelligence Surveillance Act, including training concerning the secure handling and storage of such information and training concerning requirements and limitations relating to the use, retention, and dissemination of such information.

The disclosure and sharing of information by the FBI under ths paragraph is subject to any limitations required in orders issued by the Foreign Intelligence Surveillance Court, controls imposed by the originators of sensitive material, and restrictions established by the Attorney General or the Deputy Attorney General in particular cases. The disclosure and sharing of information by the FBI under hs paragraph that may disclose the identity of human sources is governed by the relevant provisions of the Attorney General's Guidelines Regarding the Use of FBI Confidential Human Sources.

2. White House

In order to carry out their responsibilities, the President, the Vice President, the Assistant to the President for National Security Affairs, the Assistant to the President for Homeland Security Affairs, the National Security Council and its

staff, the Homeland Security Council and its staff, and other White House officials and offices require information from all federal agencies, including foreign intelligence, and information relating to international terrorism and other threats to the national security. The FBI accordingly may disseminate to the mte House foreign intelligence and national security information obtained through activities under these Guidelines, subject to the following standards and procedures:

a. Requests to the FBI for such information fiom the White House shall be made through the National Security Council staff or Homeland Security Council staff including, but not limited to, the National Security Council Legal and Intelligence Directorates and Office of Combating Terrorism, or through the President's Intelligence Advisory Board or the Counsel to the President.

b. Compromising information concerning domestic officials or political organizations, or information concerning activities of United States persons intended to affect the political process in the United States, may be disseminated to the White House only with the approval of the Attorney General, based on a determination that such dissemination is needed for foreign intelligence purposes, for the purpose of protecting against international terrorism or other threats to the national security, or for the conduct of foreign affairs. However, such approval is not required for dissemination to the mte House of information concerning efforts of foreign intelligence services to penetrate the White House, or concerning contacts by White House personnel with foreign intelligence service personnel.

c. Examples of types of information that are suitable for dissemination to the mte House on a routine basis include, but are not limited to:

i. information concerning international terrorism;

. . .

ii. information concerning activities of foreign intelligence services in the United States;

. . .

iii. information indicative of imminent hostilities involving any foreign power;

iv. information concerning potential cyber threats to the United States or its allies;

v. information indicative of policy positions adopted by foreign officials, governments, or powers, or their reactions to United States foreign policy initiatives;

vi. information relating to possible changes in leadership positions of foreign governments, parties, factions, or powers;

vii. information concerning foreign economic or foreign political matters that might have national security ramifications; and

. . .

viii. information set forth in regularly published national intelligence requirements.

d. Communications by the FBI to the White House that relate to a national security matter and concern a litigation issue for a specific pending case must be made known to the Office of the Attorney General, the Office of the Deputy Attorney General, or the Office of the Associate Attorney General. White House policy may specially limit or prescribe the White House personnel who may request information concerning such issues fiom the FBI.

e. The limitations on dissemination of information by the FBI to the White House under these Guidelines do not apply to dissemination to the White House of information acquired in the course of an FBI investigation requested by the White House into the background of a potential employee or appointee, or responses to requests from the White House under Executive Order 10450.

3. ***Special Statutory Requirements***
   a. Dissemination of information acquired under the Foreign Intelligence Surveillance Act is, to the extent provided in that Act, subject to minimization procedures and other requirements specified in that Act.
   b. Information obtained through the use of National Security Letters under 15 U.S.C. 1681v may be disseminated in conformity with the general standards of this Part. Information obtained through the use of National Security Letters under other statutes may be disseminated in conformity with the general standards of this Part, subject to any applicable limitations in their governing statutory provisions: 12 U.S.C. 3414(a)(5)(B); 15 U.S.C. 1681u(f); 18 U.S.C. 2709(d); 50 U.S.C. 436(e).

VII. DEFINITIONS

A. CONSENSUAL MONITORING: monitoring of communications for which a court order or warrant is not legally required because of the consent of a party to the communication.

B. EMPLOYEE: an FBI employee or an employee of another agency working under the direction and control of the FBI.

C. FOR OR ON BEHALF OF A FOREIGN POWER: the determination that activities are for or on behalf of a foreign power shall be based on consideration of the extent to which the foreign power is involved in:

control or policy direction;
financial or material support; or
leadership, assignments, or discipline.

D. FOREIGN COMPUTER INTRUSION: the use or attempted use of any cyber-activity or other means, by, for, or on behalf of a foreign power to scan, probe, or gain unauthorized access into one or more U.S.-based computers.

E. FOREIGN INTELLIGENCE: information relating to the capabilities, intentions, or activities of foreign governments or elements thereof, foreign organizations or foreign persons, or international terrorists.

F. FOREIGN INTELLIGENCE REQUIREMENTS: national intelligence requirements issued pursuant to authorization by the Director of National Intelligence, including the National Intelligence Priorities Framework and the National HUMINT Collection Directives, or any successor directives thereto; requests to collect foreign intelligence by the President or by Intelligence Community oficials designated by the President; and directions to collect foreign intelligence by the Attorney General, the Deputy Attorney General, or an official designated by the Attorney General.

G. FOREIGN POWER: a foreign government or any component thereof, whether or not recognized by the United States; a faction of a foreign nation or nations, not substantially composed of United States persons; an entity that is openly acknowledged by a foreign government or governments to be directed and controlled by such foreign government or governments; a group engaged in international terrorism or activities in preparation therefor; a foreign-based political organization, not substantially composed of United States persons; or an entity that is directed or controlled by a foreign government or governments.

H. HUMAN SOURCE: a Confidential Human Source as defined in the Attorney General's Guidelines Regarding the Use of FBI Confidential Human Sources.

I. INTELLIGENCE ACTIVITIES: any activity conducted for intelligence purposes or to affect political or governmental processes by, for, or on behalf of a foreign power.

J. INTERNATIONAL TERRORISM: Activities that: involve violent acts or acts dangerous to human life that violate federal, state, local, or tribal criminal law or would violate such law if committed within the United States or a state, local, or tribal jurisdiction; appear to be intended:

i. to intimidate or coerce a civilian population;

. . .

ii. to influence the policy of a government by intimidation or coercion; or

. . .

iii. to affect the conduct of a government by assassination or kidnapping; and

iv. occur totally outside the United States, or transcend national boundaries in terms of the means by which they are accomplished, the persons they appear to be intended to coerce or intimidate, or the locale in whch their perpetrators operate or seek asylum.

K. PROPRIETARY: a sole proprietorship, partnership, corporation, or other business entity operated on a commercial basis, which is owned, controlled, or operated wholly or in part on behalf of the FBI, and whose relationship with the FBI is concealed from thrd parties.

L. PUBLICLY AVAILABLE: information that has been published or broadcast for public consumption, is available on request to the public, is accessible on-line or otherwise to the public, is available to the public by subscription or purchase, could be seen or heard by any casual observer, is made available at a meeting open to the public, or is obtained by visiting any place or attending any event that is open to the public.

M. RECORDS: any records, databases, files, indices, information systems, or other retained information.

N. SENSITIVE INVESTIGATIVE MATTER: an investigative matter involving the activities of a domestic public official or political candidate (involving corruption or a threat to the national security), religious or political organization or individual prominent in such an organization, or news media, or any other matter which, in the judgment of the official authorizing an investigation, should be brought to the attention of FBI Headquarters and other Department of Justice officials.

O. SENSITIVE MONITORING CIRCUMSTANCE: investigation of a member of Congress, a federal judge, a member of the Executive Branch at Executive Level IV or above, or a person who has served in such capacity within the previous two years; investigation of the Governor, Lieutenant Governor, or Attorney General of any state or territory, or a judge or justice of the hghest court of any state or territory, concerning an offense involving bribery, conflict of interest, or extortion related to the performance of official duties; a party to the communication is in the custody of the Bureau of Prisons or the United States Marshals Service or is being or has been afforded protection in the Witness Security Program; or the Attorney General, the Deputy Attorney General, or an Assistant Attorney General has requested that the FBI obtain prior approval for the use of consensual monitoring in a specific investigation.

P. SPECIAL AGENT IN CHARGE: the Special Agent in Charge of an FBI field office (including an Acting Special Agent in Charge), except that the functions authorized for Special Agents in Charge by these Guidelines may also be exercised by the Assistant Director in Charge or by any Special Agent in Charge designated by the Assistant Director in Charge in an FBI field office headed by an Assistant Director, and by FBI Headquarters officials designated by the Director of the FBI.

Q. SPECIAL EVENTS MANAGEMENT: planning and conduct of public events or activities whose character may make them attractive targets for terrorist attack.

R. STATE, LOCAL, OR TRIBAL: any state or territory of the United States or political subdivision thereof, the District of Columbia, or Indian tribe.

S. THREAT TO THE NATIONAL SECURITY: international terrorism; espionage and other intelligence activities, sabotage, and assassination, conducted by, for, or on behalf of foreign powers, organizations, or persons; foreign computer intrusion; and other matters determined by the Attorney General, consistent with Executive Order 12333 or a successor order.

T. UNITED STATES: when used in a geographic sense, means all areas under the territorial sovereignty of the United States.

U. UNITED STATES PERSON: Any of the following, but not including any association or corporation that is a foreign power as defined in Subpart G.1.-.3.: an individual who is a United States citizen or an alien lawfully admitted for permanent residence; an unincorporated association substantially composed of individuals who are United States persons; or a corporation incorporated in the United States.

In applying paragraph 2., if a group or organization in the United States that is affiliated with a foreign-based international organization operates directly under the control of the international organization and has no independent program or activities in the United States, the membership of the entire international organization shall be considered in determining whether it is substantially composed of United States persons. If, however, the U.S.-based group or organization has programs or activities separate fiom, or in addition to, those directed by the international organization, only its membership in the United States shall be considered in determining whether it is substantially composed of United States persons. A classified directive provides firther guidance concerning the determination of United States person status.

V. USE: when used with respect to human sources, means obtaining information fiom, tasking, or otherwise operating such sources.

Report and Recommendations of the Presidential Task Force on Controlled Unclassified Information

(August 25, 2009)

The Task Force on Controlled Unclassified Information
Under the leadership of:

Janet Napolitano
Secretary of Homeland Security

Eric H. Holder,Jr.
Attorney General

Matthew L. Kronisch
Co-Chair Department of Homeland Security

Candace Kelly
Co-Chair Department of Justice

Dr. Josh Weerasinghe
Program Manager for the Information Sharing Environment

Patricia Mantoan
Department of Health and Human Services

Janice C. Haith
Department of Defense

Michael A. Fitzpatrick
Office of Management and Budget

Marguerite R. Coffey
Department of State

John W. Vardaman
Department of Justice

Greg Gardner
Office of the Director of National Intelligence

William J. Bosanko
National Archives and Records Administration

John J. Young
Department Homeland Security

Roland J. Corvington
Federal Bureau of Investigation

Edwin J. McCeney
Department of the Interior

Keith McElfresh
Department of Agriculture

Patricia K. Hammar
Executive Secretary

Table of Contents

Letter from the CUI Task Force Leadership

August 25, 2009

The President
The White House
Washington, DC 20500

Dear Mr. President:

As directed by your May 27, 2009 Memorandum, we established an Interagency Task Force to review current procedures for categorizing and sharing Sensitive but Unclassified ("SBU") information. The Task Force conducted a 90-day review of the Controlled Unclassified Information ("CUI") Framework for terrorism-related information within the information sharing environment established by Presidential Memorandum in 2008, and considered whether that Framework should be expanded to apply to all SBU information under the control of the Executive Branch. Enclosed are the Report and Recommendations resulting from this review.

In addition to analyzing previous studies of SBU and the efforts of the CUI Council, the Task Force met with representatives from federal agencies both within and outside the information sharing environment; State, local, and tribal partners; privacy and open government organizations; and Congress. Informed by these consultations, a significant majority of the Task Force concluded that expanding the CUI Framework to encompass all SBU information will best strike the appropriate balance among the goals of Standardization, Information Sharing, and Government Transparency.

The recommendation of a vastly expanded scope for CUI necessitates a careful and coordinated effort to attain the benefits of standardization without adversely affecting agencies' missions or the security of sensitive information. Accordingly, the report recommends a phased approach to implementation of the proposed CUI Framework that prioritizes training, marking, and oversight.

Taken as a whole, the Task Force's recommendations seek to further information sharing among Executive Branch agencies as well as State, local, tribal and foreign partners by establishing a standard system for designating, marking, and handling all SBU information. The recommendations also enhance government transparency by establishing clear rules that protect information only when there is a compelling need to do so.

We recommend adoption of the Task Force Report and Recommendations, as well as the issuance of a new Executive Order rescinding the 2008 Memorandum on CUI and clearly setting forth the President's intention for this complex but important subject.

Respectfully,
Eric H. Holder, Jr.
Attorney General
Janet Napolitano
Secretary of Homeland Security

Executive Summary

The President's Memorandum of May 27, 2009 on Classified Information and Controlled Unclassified Information, directed a Task Force, led by the Secretary of Homeland Security and the Attorney General, to review the Controlled Unclassified Information ("CUI") Framework established in 2008 for the management of Sensitive but Unclassified[1] ("SBU") terrorism-related information. The Task Force undertook a 90-day study of the CUI Framework, the current regimes for managing SBU information in the Executive Branch, and, by extension, the sharing of that information with our non-federal information-sharing partners.

1. Sensitive but Unclassified (SBU) information refers collectively to the various designations used within the Executive Branch for documents and information that are sufficiently sensitive to warrant some level of protection but that do not meet the standards for classification. CUI Framework refers to the single set of policies and procedures established by the Presidential Memorandum of May 7, 2008, governing the designation, marking, safeguarding, and dissemination of terrorism-related SBU information, which pursuant to that Memorandum, is renamed as "Controlled Unclassified Information." Expanding the scope of the CUI Framework refers to the extension of the CUI Framework governing the designation, marking, safeguarding, and dissemination of CUI to all SBU information in possession or control of the Executive Branch.

The Task Force concluded that Executive Branch performance suffers immensely from interagency inconsistency in SBU policies, frequent uncertainty in interagency settings as to exactly what policies apply to given SBU information, and the inconsistent application of similar policies across agencies. Additionally, the absence of effective training, oversight, and accountability at many agencies results in a tendency to over-protect information, greatly diminishing government transparency.

Although the CUI Framework is intended to improve the sharing of only terrorism-related information, the Task Force concluded that a single, standardized framework for marking, safeguarding, and disseminating all Executive Branch SBU is required to further the goals of:

- standardizing currently disparate terminology and procedures (represented by over 107 distinct SBU regimes);
- facilitating information-sharing through the promulgation of common and understandable rules for information protection and dissemination; and
- enhancing government transparency through policies and training that clarify the standards for protecting information within the Framework.

A simple, concise, and standardized CUI Framework, with effective centralized governance and oversight has the best chance of both wide acceptance within the federal government and broad adoption throughout our State, local, tribal, and private sector partner communities. The successful expansion of the scope of the CUI Framework requires careful consideration of agency missions, requirements, and the processes by which SBU information is currently managed.

Building upon the CUI Framework established in 2008, the Task Force has proposed 40 Recommendations intended to enhance Standardization, Information Sharing, Government Transparency, and the Protection of Information only where there is a compelling requirement to do so, including simplifying the definition of CUI; expanding the scope of the CUI Framework; clarifying that CUI markings have no bearing on releases either under the Freedom of Information Act or to Congress; and phasing implementation of the expanded scope of CUI.

CUI Task Force Recommendations

Recommendation #1	Simplify the Definition of CUI
Recommendation #2	Expand the Scope of the CUI Framework
Recommendation #3	Make the Expanded CUI Framework the Exclusive Means of Protecting SBU
Recommendation #4	Adjust the CUI Council Membership and Roles to Reflect the Expanded Scope
Recommendation #5	Moratorium on New SBU Regimes
Recommendation #6	Engagement of Non-ISE Agencies
Recommendation #7	Phase Implementation of Scope Expansion

Recommendation #8	Designation of CUI
Recommendation #9	Identification of CUI
Recommendation #10	Agency CUI Programs
Recommendation #11	Simplification of Categories and Markings
Recommendation #12	Executive Agent to Establish Standard Markings and Guidance
Recommendation #13	Flexible Marking of CUI
Recommendation #14	Clarify that CUI Has No Bearing on FOIA
Recommendation #15	Safeguarding
Recommendation #16	Consultation on Threat
Recommendation #17	CIO Council as Advisor on Information Standards and Safeguards
Recommendation #18	Standardize Specified Dissemination
Recommendation #19	Dissemination to Congress and the Courts
Recommendation #20	Clarify Decontrol
Recommendation #21	Establish Life Cycle
Recommendation #22	Establish Exception Process
Recommendation #23	Delay in Incorporation of Exceptions into the CUI Framework
Recommendation #24	Amending Regulations or Statutes
Recommendation #25	Establish Training
Recommendation #26	Incentives
Recommendation #27	Accountability and Sanctions
Recommendation #28	Internal Oversight
Recommendation #29	Challenges to Designation and Identification
Recommendation #30	Federal Acquisition Guidance
Recommendation #31	Phase Implementation of Training, Marking, Oversight and Reporting
Recommendation #32	Phase Implementation of Technical Safeguards
Recommendation #33	Marking Initiation
Recommendation #34	Ensure Adequate Resourcing of Executive Agent
Recommendation #35	Synchronize CUI Implementation with Government Processes and Cycles
Recommendation #36	Impact of CUI on the Federal Enterprise Architecture
Recommendation #37	Incorporate CUI into Federal Grant Guidance
Recommendation #38	Annual Report of the Executive Agent
Recommendation #39	Establish a Baseline Measurement of Current SBU Efforts
Recommendation #40	Measure Implementation

Part 1. Overview

In furtherance of the Administration's commitment to openness and transparency in government, the President's Memorandum of May 27, 2009, entitled Classified Information and Controlled Unclassified Information (the "2009 Memorandum") directed that the Attorney General and the Secretary of Homeland Security lead an Interagency Task Force on Controlled Unclassified Information ("CUI")(the "Task Force"). The mission of the Task Force was to review current procedures for categorizing and sharing Sensitive But Unclassified ("SBU")[2] information in order to determine whether such procedures strike the proper balance among certain imperatives. These imperatives include protecting legitimate security, law enforcement, and privacy interests as well as civil liberties; providing clear rules to those who handle SBU information; and ensuring that the handling and dissemination of information is not restricted unless there is a compelling need.

In addition to reviewing current procedures for SBU, the Task Force was charged with considering:

- measures to track agencies' progress with implementing the "CUI Framework"[3]
- other measures to enhance implementation of an effective information sharing environment across agencies and levels of government,[4] and
- whether the scope of the CUI Framework should remain limited to terrorism-related information within the Information Sharing Environment ("ISE") or be expanded to apply to all SBU information.

---

2. As reflected in the 2009 Memorandum, SBU refers collectively to the various designations used within the Federal Government for documents and information that are sufficiently sensitive to warrant some level of protection, but that do not meet the standards for National Security Classification. A process created in 2005 for establishing a single, standardized, comprehensive categorical designation within the Executive Branch for most SBU information culminated with the adoption of the phrase "Controlled Unclassified Information" (CUI) in the Presidential Memorandum of May 7, 2008, entitled *Designation and Sharing of Controlled Unclassified Information* (CUI) (the "2008 Memorandum"). CUI was defined in the 2008 Memorandum as:

> a categorical designation that refers to unclassified information that does not meet the standards for National Security Classification under Executive Order 12958, as amended, but is (i) pertinent to the national interests of the United States or to the important interests of entities outside the Federal Government, and (ii) under law or policy requires protection from unauthorized disclosure, special handling safeguards, or prescribed limits on exchange or dissemination.

The 2008 Memorandum directs that CUI be used in place of SBU as the single categorical designation for information within the scope of the CUI definition to refer generally to such information.

3. The "CUI Framework" refers to the single set of policies and procedures governing the designation, marking, safeguarding, and dissemination of terrorism-related CUI, as established in the 2008 Memorandum.

4. Pursuant to the Memorandum of July 2, 2009, *Strengthening Information Sharing and Access,* the Assistant to the President for Homeland Security and Counterterrorism initiated a comprehensive review of the Information Sharing Environment. The Task Force was advised that it need not report on these measures.

1.1 The CUI Task Force

1. Membership

Led by the Secretary of Homeland Security and the Attorney General, and co-chaired by their senior representatives, the CUI Task Force was comprised of senior representatives of twelve federal agencies. This included representatives of following nine ISE agencies:

- Department of State ("State")
- Office of the Director of National Intelligence ("ODNI")
- Office of Management and Budget ("OMB")
- Federal Bureau of Investigation ("FBI")
- Department of Defense ("DoD")
- Department of Health and Human Services ("HHS")
- Program Manager, Information Sharing Environment ("PM-ISE")
- Department of Homeland Security ("DHS"), and
- Department of Justice ("DOJ").

The Task Force also included the following three non-ISE agencies:

- Department of Agriculture ("USDA")
- Department of the Interior ("DOI"), and
- National Archives and Records Administration ("NARA").

2. Methodology

The Task Force assessed current procedures for categorizing and sharing SBU, both within and outside of the ISE, in light of the imperatives specified in the 2009 Memorandum. The Task Force also analyzed the most significant issues thus far encountered by the Executive Agent ("EA") and the CUI Council in developing the CUI Framework while recognizing the Task Force goals of standardization, information sharing, and government transparency. The Task Force drew upon SBU efforts dating back to 2006, as well as the CUI Council's analysis, findings, draft policy statements, and implementation guidance as the foundation for much of its effort.

The Task Force met with representatives of multiple government entities to assess the many issues raised by implementation of the CUI Framework as described in the 2008 Memorandum, including its impact on agencies outside of the ISE, on the current exceptions to the CUI Framework,[5] on the ability of certain specific

5. Four regimes for the safeguarding of infrastructure protection information were granted "excepted" status under the May 2008 Memorandum, including Protected Critical Infrastructure Information, Sensitive Security Information, Chemical Vulnerability Information, and Safeguards Information. Excepted status requires that the CUI Framework be used to the maximum extent possible, including the most applicable safeguarding marking, and that any additional safeguarding requirements beyond that specified under the CUI Framework shall be appropriately registered in the CUI Registry. Regulatory markings are to follow CUI markings and a specified dissemination instruction is to articulate any additional regulatory requirements.

and discrete communities of interest to support CUI implementation, and on the interests and concerns of Congress. The Task Force also met with representatives of a number of non-government entities to assess various aspects of CUI implementation on entities outside of the federal government, including private sector owners and operators of critical infrastructure, industrial security contractors, open government and privacy advocacy organizations, and our State, local, and tribal information sharing partners. (For a complete list of entities consulted, see Appendix 1.) These consultations were extraordinarily valuable in understanding the concerns of CUI constituents and were critical in developing the Task Force's recommendations.

Part 2. The SBU Challenge

All federal agencies[6] routinely generate, use, store, and share information that, while not appropriate for "classification" under Executive Order 12958,[7] as amended, or other authority,[8] nevertheless requires some level of protection from unauthorized access and release. Protection may be required due to privacy concerns, law enforcement sensitivities, the business proprietary nature of the information, or for other reasons. Currently, across the Executive Branch, this information is identified by over 100 unique markings and at least 130 different labeling or handling regimes, such as "Law Enforcement Sensitive," "For Official Use Only," "Sensitive Security Information," and "Limited Official Use." (A partial listing of SBU markings is attached at Appendix 2.) Although SBU regimes or markings are typically derived from an identifiable authority, be it a statute, regulation, or agency policy, collectively they reflect a disjointed, inconsistent, and unpredictable system for protecting, sharing, and disclosing sensitive information.

2.1 Assessment of Current SBU Procedures

The Task Force reviewed current policies and procedures for categorizing and sharing SBU information to assess these processes against the imperatives identified by the President. The Task Force found that performance under these categories varied greatly. The factors influencing performance included the scope of subject matter

6. As used here and throughout the remainder of this report and its recommendations, the terms "agency," "Agency," or "agencies," shall be deemed to refer to all Executive Branch departments, agencies, offices, components, and entities.

7. *See* Exec. Order No. 12,958, 60 Fed. Reg. 19,823 (Apr. 20, 1995), reprinted as amended by Exec. Order 13292, 68 Fed. Reg. 15,315 (Mar. 28, 2003) (prescribing a uniform system for classifying, safeguarding, and declassifying national security information, including information relating to defense against transnational terrorism).

8. *See e.g.*, Atomic Energy Act of 1954, §§ 4 & 142, 42 U.S.C. §§ 2014(y) & 2162 (2009) (automatically classifying as "Restricted Data" all data concerning (1) the design, manufacture, or utilization of atomic weapons; (2) the production of special nuclear material; or (3) the use of special nuclear material in the production of energy; and automatically classifying as "Formerly Restricted Data" all data the Nuclear Regulatory Commission and the Department of Defense jointly determine relates primarily to the military utilization of atomic weapons and can be adequately safeguarded as defense information).

and personnel covered; the intended purpose for control; the type of information protected; the process for developing policy and procedure; the clarity of policy and procedure; the availability of policy and procedure to persons handling subject information; the quality and frequency of employee training; and the existence of meaningful oversight. For some of these regimes, such as the widely utilized "Law Enforcement Sensitive" or "LES," few of these factors are currently implemented.

Regardless of any individual regime's performance, it is clear that as a whole, Executive Branch performance under these measures suffers immensely from interagency inconsistency in SBU policies, frequent uncertainty in interagency settings as to exactly what policies apply, and inconsistent application of similar policies across agencies.

Additionally, the absence of effective training, oversight, and accountability at many agencies results in a tendency to over-protect information as SBU, thus greatly diminishing government transparency.

Clarity as to what policies apply, as well as access to those policies, is essential to ensuring that a recipient properly handles SBU. Across the Executive Branch, the same type of information may be governed by entirely different, and often unclear, requirements. As a result, even where two agencies use the same marking, such as For Official Use Only ("FOUO"), and separately provide similar information to a recipient, that recipient must distinguish between the FOUO policies of each providing agency.

The Task Force recognized that sharing terrorism-related and other intelligence and law enforcement information with local law enforcement is critical to our national and homeland security.[9] Current SBU policies are generally ill-suited to this purpose. One example is when a State, local, or tribal official properly receives information from the federal government marked as "sensitive," but does not receive any indication of the applicable safeguarding or dissemination policies. This situation can often result in the official's reluctance to further share the information with other local law enforcement or first responders who may also have a need for it.

Another challenge presented by inconsistent, agency-specific SBU regimes is the incidental, yet often unintended effect some markings have on the processing of requests for public release of information under the Freedom of Information Act ("FOIA"). While a number of SBU regimes are based upon, or at least recognize, a specific statute or other legal authority for properly withholding information from public release under FOIA, many do not. Regardless, the markings are sometimes misunderstood as providing an independent basis for withholding documents from the public, Congress, or the courts, which in turn can undermine transparency, as well as public trust in government.

---

9. Final Report of the National Commission on Terrorist Attacks Upon the United States, www.9-11commission.gov.

The lack of standardized Executive Branch procedures for governing SBU information is well-established,[10] the need for those standards well-documented,[11] and the interest of Congress to address the challenge, proven.[12]

2.2 The 2008 CUI Framework

Although the problems associated with SBU have existed for many decades, addressing them assumed greater urgency following the information sharing failures preceding the 9/11 attacks. The 9/11 Commission reported that in the months leading up to the attacks:

> Information was not shared, sometimes inadvertently or because of legal misunderstandings. Analysis was not pooled . . . . Often the handoffs of information were lost across the divide separating the foreign and domestic agencies of government.[13]

In response to these challenges, in 2004, Congress passed and the President signed the Intelligence Reform and Terrorism Prevention Act, Pub. L. 108-458, which

---

10. *See e.g.*, The Constitution Project, *Reining in Excessive Secrecy: Recommendations for the Reform of the Classification and Controlled Unclassified Information Systems* (2009) available at http://www.constitutionproject.org/manage/file/178.pdf; U.S. Gov't. Accountability Off., *Information Security: Federal Agencies Show Mixed Progress in Implementing Statutory Requirements*, GAO-06-527T (Mar. 16, 2006); U.S. Gov't. Accountability Off., *Information Sharing: The Federal Government Needs to Establish Policies and Processes for Sharing Terrorism-Related and Sensitive but Unclassified Information,* GAO-06-385 (Mar. 17, 2006); U.S. Gov't. Accountability Off., *Managing Sensitive Information: DOE and DOD Could Improve Their Policies and Oversight,* GAO-06-531T (Mar. 14, 2006); U.S. Gov't. Accountability Off., *TSA: Clear Policies and Oversight Needed for Designation of Sensitive Security Information,* GAO-05-677 (Jun. 29, 2005); U.S. Gen. Acct. Off., *Selected Agencies' Handling of Personnel Information,* GAO-02-1058 (Sep. 30, 2002); Cong. Res. Serv., *'Sensitive but Unclassified Information' and Other Controls Policy and Options for Scientific and Technical Information,* CRS Rep. RL31845 (Feb. 15, 2006), as updated by CRS Rep. RL33303 (Dec. 29, 2006); Cong. Res. Serv., *Secrecy vs. Openness: New Proposed Arrangements for Balancing Competing Needs,* CRS Rep. 21895 (Aug. 26, 2004), as updated (Oct. 12, 2004).

11. Final Report of the National Commission on Terrorist Attacks Upon the United States, www.9-11commission.gov, 416-419.

12 *See e.g.*, the "Reducing Over-Classification Act of 2009," H.R. 553, 111th Cong. (1st Sess. 2009) (as introduced by Rep. Harman, Jan. 15, 2009); the "Reducing Information Control Designations Act," H.R. 1323, 111th Cong. (1st Sess. 2009) (as introduced by Rep. Driehaus, Mar. 5, 2009); the "Implementing the Controlled Unclassified Information Framework Act of 2008," S. 3662, 110th Cong. (2nd Sess. 2008) (as introduced by Sen. Lieberman, Oct. 1, 2008); the "Reducing Overclassification Act of 2008," H.R. 4806, 110th Cong. (2nd Sess. 2008) (as introduced by Rep. Harman, Dec. 18, 2007); the "Improving the Public Access to Documents Act of 2008," H.R. 6193, 110th Cong. (2nd Sess. 2008) (as introduced by Rep. Harman, Jun. 5, 2008); and the "Reducing Information Control Designations Act," H.R. 6576, 110th Cong. (2nd Sess. 2008) (as introduced by Rep. Waxman, Jul. 23, 2008).

13. Final Report of the National Commission on Terrorist Attacks Upon the United States, www.9-11commission.gov, 353.

mandated the development of an Information Sharing Environment ("ISE") to facilitate the sharing of terrorism-related information among federal, State, local, tribal, private sector, and foreign partner entities. On December 16, 2005, President Bush directed federal agencies to recommend procedures for standardizing the marking, handling, and safeguarding of SBU information.[14] The resulting recommendations[15] were largely reflected in the 2008 Memorandum, which adopted CUI as the single Executive Branch designation for all SBU within the scope of the ISE, and established a corresponding new framework for designating, marking, safeguarding, and disseminating terrorism-related CUI, which became known as the CUI Framework.[16]

The 2008 Memorandum designated the National Archives and Records Administration (NARA) as the Executive Agent (EA) for the CUI Framework and directed that a CUI Council[17] perform an advisory and coordinating role for the development of policy standards and implementation guidance for the CUI Framework. With a May 2013 deadline for full implementation of the CUI Framework, the Archivist of the United States established the CUI Office, which hosted the first monthly meeting of the CUI Council in August 2008.

In the ensuing 12 months, the EA, in consultation with the CUI Council, has conducted data calls and analyses, initiated the development of an implementation plan along with draft guidance in key policy areas, including: designation,

---

14. Memorandum for Heads of Executive Departments and Agencies on the Guidelines and Requirements in Support of the Information Sharing Environment, December 16, 2005. This Memorandum requires the development of recommendations, first, for homeland security information, law enforcement information, and terrorism information and then for all types of information not previously addressed.

15. Presidential Guideline 3 Report, Standardized Procedures for Sensitive But Unclassified (SBU) Information, (Fall 2007).

16. 2008 Memorandum, at 4-6.

17. The CUI Council was established by the National Archives and Records Administration (NARA) in accordance with the 2008 Memorandum, as a subcommittee of the Information Sharing Council (ISC) created by the Intelligence Reform and Terrorism prevention Act of 2004 (Public Law 108-458) (IRTPA). Guidance issued separately by the PM-ISE on July 9, 2008, directed each ISC agency to designate a representative to the CUI Council. The CUI Council effectively represents the needs and equities of ISE participants, providing the EA with advice and recommendations on CUI policies. The membership of the CUI Council currently includes: Department of Commerce, Department of Defense (Office of the Secretary and Joint Staff), Office of the Director of National Intelligence (on behalf of the Intelligence Community), Department of Energy, Federal Bureau of Investigation, Department of Health and Human Services, Department of Homeland Security, Department of the Interior, Office of Management and Budget, Department of Justice, Program Manager for the Information Sharing Environment, Department of State, Department of Transportation, Department of The Treasury, Environmental Protection Agency, and the Nuclear Regulatory Commission. In addition, non-federal participation on the CUI Council includes two members from State, local, and/or tribal government, two members from the private sector, and consultation with the ISC's State, Local, Tribal, and Private Sector Subcommittee, as appropriate.

marking, dissemination, safeguarding, dispute resolution, life cycle, oversight, and exceptions. As a result of these efforts, the emerging CUI Framework is intended to include: a standing Governance Structure under the current EA; two possible levels of safeguarding;[18] two possible levels of dissemination controls;[19] a procedure for designating specific dissemination requirements or limitations, when appropriate; three unique markings to reflect the three combinations of safeguarding and dissemination controls;[20] a publicly available, web based "Registry" of markings that apply to CUI information and certain associated policies; and standardized training requirements across the federal government.

Although implementation of the CUI Framework will be required only within the Executive Branch, it is intentionally being developed to be as accessible as possible to non-federal information sharing partners, such as State, local, tribal, and foreign governments and the private sector. Thus, the promulgation and publication of standard rules across the Executive Branch should not only ease the handling of CUI by our non-federal partners, but it could also encourage the adoption of these rules and facilitate compliance with similar rules by partners outside the Executive Branch. Although adoption by non-federal partners may require modifications to accommodate applicable State, local and tribal law, in meeting with the Task Force, State, local and tribal representatives nonetheless expressed their desire to see the CUI Framework achieve the same broad acceptance and adaptation experienced by the Rules for Criminal Intelligence System Operating Policies promulgated by the Department of Justice.[21]

---

18. "Safeguarding" means measures and controls to protect CUI from unauthorized access resulting from theft, trespass, or carelessness. The current safeguarding levels are "Controlled" and "Controlled Enhanced."

19. Dissemination controls are instructions governing the extent to which dissemination is permitted or limited. The current dissemination controls are "Standard Dissemination" and "Specified Dissemination."

20. The markings include "CONTROLLED WITH STANDARD DISSEMINATION", "CONTROLLED WITH SPECIFIED DISSEMINATION", and "CONTROLLED ENHANCED WITH SPECIFIED DISSEMINATION." At this time, there is no anticipated marking category that would couple "Controlled Enhanced" safeguards with "Standard Dissemination" controls.

21. *See* "Criminal Intelligence Systems Operating Policies," 28 C.F.R. pt. 23 (2009). 28 C.F.R. part 23 is a guideline for federal, State, and local law enforcement agencies to follow in implementing standards for operating federally grant-funded multi-jurisdictional criminal intelligence systems. It was written to both protect the privacy rights of individuals and to encourage and expedite the exchange of criminal intelligence information between and among law enforcement agencies of different jurisdictions. It provides specific guidance in five primary areas: submission and entry of criminal intelligence information, security, inquiry, dissemination, and the review-and-purge process. Only information technology systems operating under or funded through the Omnibus Crime Control and Safe Streets Act of 1968, 42 U.S.C. § 3711, et seq., as amended, must comply with the 28 C.F.R. part 23; however, the underlying "framework" has been widely applied to other activities involving the collection, maintenance, and dissemination of criminal intelligence information.

Part 3. Recommendations

3.1 Expanding the Scope of the Current CUI Framework

The CUI Task Force was specifically directed to consider whether the scope of the CUI Framework should remain limited to terrorism-related information within the ISE, or, be expanded to apply to all SBU information, and by extension, apply beyond the realm of the ISE.

Eleven of the 12 Task Force members concurred in the recommendation to expand the scope of the CUI Framework beyond the ISE and to all SBU information.[22] Even prior to the establishment of the Task Force, DHS and DOD, as well as the FBI and ODNI (on behalf of the National Intelligence Community) had already committed to extending the current CUI Framework to all SBU within their control. It was the consensus of the 11 concurring agencies that maintaining multiple regimes for managing SBU information would be inconsistent with the goals of the Task Force, and that expanding the scope of the current CUI Framework would provide for specificity and consistency in the marking and identification of various types of sensitive information.

A number of Task Force members also endorsed expanding the scope of the current CUI Framework as a means of providing greater clarity in implementation. For example, although the 2008 Memorandum's definition of "CUI" is not limited to terrorism-related information, the scope of the CUI Framework it established is limited to terrorism-related information. Maintaining this discrepancy would force agencies to perform the often difficult task of segregating terrorism-related from non-terrorism-related information, a distinction that is not always clear or static.

The Task Force believes the first step in improving the CUI Framework is to simplify the definition of CUI. CUI should be defined as "All unclassified information for which, pursuant to statute, regulation, or departmental or agency policy, there is a compelling requirement for safeguarding and/or dissemination controls." Next, the scope of the CUI Framework should be expanded to include all information falling within the definition of CUI in the possession or under the control of the Executive Branch. As directed in the 2008 Memorandum, CUI should be used in place of SBU as the single categorical designation for all information falling within the scope of the definition of CUI.

In sum, a strong majority of the Task Force believes that limiting the scope of the CUI Framework to terrorism-related information within the ISE: (1) risks overlooking information with a terrorism nexus that may not be apparent until some later time; (2) fails to address the inefficiencies and confusion in continuing to maintain over 100 discrete SBU markings across the federal government; (3) could result in unintended inefficiencies, such as where agencies that handle sensitive

22. The Department of State opposes scope expansion out of concern that it would dilute the terrorism-related focus of the Framework envisioned in the 2008 Memorandum and the ability to use the CUI marking as a means of identifying solely terrorism-related information.

terrorism-related and non-terrorism-related information would have to maintain at least two separate systems for handling SBU; and (4) creates confusion as to the true scope of CUI.

Expanding the scope of the CUI Framework is not intended to provide agencies with unfettered access to all the sensitive unclassified information within the Executive Branch; rather, it is meant to facilitate appropriate sharing of sensitive unclassified information. It would also promote increased accountability in how information is shared by allowing agencies and the public to know what kind of information is maintained by federal agencies.

Moreover, because of its uniformity, standardized training requirements, and the public availability of the registry, the expanded scope of the CUI Framework can be expected to significantly increase the openness and transparency of government by improving the efficiency of information sharing, where otherwise authorized, between and among federal, State, local, tribal, private sector, and foreign partners. By eliminating the overuse of SBU designations, an expanded CUI Framework would enhance the protection of personal privacy and civil liberties, while continuing to protect sensitive information as appropriate.

The Task Force believes that the efforts of the EA and the CUI Council are enhanced when taking into consideration the perspectives of a wide range of information-sharing partners and incorporating those perspectives into policy development efforts. The EA could achieve this by periodically inviting public interest or private sector entities to attend meetings for the purpose of providing their insights, experiences, observations or opinions on relevant matters.

The Task Forces believes that expansion of the CUI Framework necessitates an expansion of the CUI Council membership, which, under the 2008 Memorandum, was limited to members of the Information Sharing Council,[23] as well as to its roles and functions. Composition of the CUI Council should be adjusted to reflect the scope of CUI under an expanded CUI Framework. To accommodate that expanded scope while optimizing effective representation, the Task Force believes the core composition of the Council should primarily include "capstone" agencies. For example, ODNI would represent all intelligence community agencies; DOD would represent each of the military services and all other DOD elements; DHS would represent all of the component agencies of DHS; DOJ would represent its subordinate agencies, etc. The expanded CUI Council should be recognized as a consensus body for developing CUI policy and should retain the esponsibilities and authorities identified in the 2008 Memorandum, including resolving disputes among agencies concerning the proper designation or marking of CUI. In addition, the Task Force believes that the CUI Council should be empowered to hear appeals from agency dispute/challenge mechanisms.

---

23. The Information Sharing Council has been merged into the Information Sharing and Access Interagency Policy Committee.

The majority of developments in post 9/11 information sharing have impacted terrorism-related information within the context of the ISE. Agencies outside of the ISE have generally had only limited exposure to the CUI Framework directed by the 2008 Memorandum. Task Force outreach to those agencies identified the steeper learning curve many of them would face in implementing the CUI Framework as compared to their peers within the ISE. To begin to understand non-ISE agency requirements, the Task Force believes that the EA should reach out to these agencies and inform them of efforts to implement the Framework in light of the 2008 Memorandum and the recommendations contained herein. The EA should solicit from them any agency-specific needs or considerations relevant to their implementation of the CUI Framework.

Recommendation #1 Simplify the Definition of CUI
The definition of "Controlled Unclassified Information," or CUI, should be simplified to: All unclassified information for which, pursuant to statute, regulation, or departmental or agency policy, there is a compelling requirement for safeguarding and/or dissemination controls.

Recommendation #2 Expand the Scope of the CUI Framework
The scope of the CUI Framework should be expanded to include all information falling within the definition of CUI in the possession or under the control of the Executive Branch of the Federal Government.

Recommendation #3 Make the Expanded CUI Framework the Exclusive Means of Protecting SBU
The expanded CUI Framework should be the single categorical designation used to identify, safeguard, and disseminate unclassified information for which, pursuant to statute, regulation, or departmental or agency policy, there is a compelling requirement for safeguarding and/or dissemination controls, except where a particular regime has been approved by the EA as a temporary exception to the CUI Framework.

Recommendation #4 Adjust the CUI Council Membership and Roles to Reflect the Expanded Scope CUI
Council membership should be adjusted to reflect the expanded scope of the CUI Framework, and membership reassessed to prioritize representation through "capstone" agencies. Additionally, the CUI Council should be empowered to address appeals of agency dispute/challenge mechanisms.

Recommendation #5 Moratorium on New SBU Regimes
Consistent with the imperatives listed in the 2009 Memorandum, the President should impose a moratorium on efforts within the Executive Branch to define or develop new SBU categories outside of the CUI Framework.

Recommendation #6 Engagement of Non-ISE Agencies
The EA should develop a 120-day outreach plan to engage all non-ISE agencies in CUI Framework efforts and the EA should solicit from them any agency-specific needs or considerations relevant to their implementation of the CUI Framework.

Recommendation #7 Phase Implementation of Scope Expansion
Implementation of the CUI Framework should begin with all ISE agencies, and consistent with the 2008 Memorandum, they should complete implementation by May 2013. All other agencies (other than the excepted regimes) should complete implementation by May 2015. The excepted regimes should complete implementation by May 2016. If the excepted regimes believe that implementation by May 2016 would cause serious and demonstrable harm, they may petition the EA, upon identification of their specific concerns and proposals for their remediation, for an extension of time to ensure that exception implementation does not negatively impact those regimes.

3.2 Measures to Enhance the Current CUI Framework

The discussions and recommendations which follow are intended to improve the current CUI Framework, as established in the 2008 Memorandum.

1. Designation and Identification

Since issuance of the 2008 Memorandum, the EA, in coordination with the CUI Council, has worked to define the concepts of "Designation" and "Identification." Designation is currently defined as the determination that a general category of information (e.g. personally identifiable information, law enforcement information, etc.) may be protected as CUI and, if so, the level of protection required and dissemination authorized. It is each agency's responsibility to evaluate its data holdings to determine what information should be designated as CUI. It is foreseeable, based on the revised definition and scope of CUI recommended herein, that some information currently treated as "sensitive" may be found not to warrant CUI designation. Designation may be initiated by the President, statute, regulation, agency head, or appropriately designated senior agency official. Identification is currently defined as recognition by an authorized individual that specific information fits within a general category of information which has been previously designated as CUI.

A key goal of the expanded CUI Framework is reducing the number of existing SBU regimes into the minimum appropriate number of CUI designations. The EA, in coordination with the CUI Council, has already begun the process for designating various general categories of information common to most agencies, including:

- Acquisition-Related Information
- Law Enforcement

- Export Controlled
- Business Proprietary
- Intellectual Property Controls
- Privacy Protected Information
- Restrictions on Non-U.S. Citizens
- Legal Privileges and Restrictions
- Security Information

Accommodation and Flexibility

In exercising their respective responsibilities, the EA and CUI Council should fully consider the mission and requirements of the agency recommending a designation and make all appropriate efforts to accommodate those requirements in the harmonization effort. Similarly, senior officials of agencies recommending designations should be flexible in working with the EA to ensure that harmonization of their designation recommendations with the CUI Framework is achieved.

Recommendation #8 Designation of CUI

CUI designation by the EA should reflect the following four-step process:

Step 1: The agency head, or other appropriately designated senior-level official, determines that there exists a compelling requirement to protect a category of information that the agency routinely handles, and which has not already been designated by the EA.

Step 2: The official submits a designation recommendation, along with supporting and accompanying materials (e.g., statute, regulation, or policy), to the EA for review and consideration.

Step 3: In consultation with the CUI Council, the EA reviews the designation recommendation for the purpose of ensuring that:

a. the description of, authority and justification for, and requested standards for safeguarding and dissemination are clearly articulated;

b. the requested designation is consistent with standards applicable to any similar types of information and harmonized, as appropriate, with those designations; and

c. the submitting agency is aware of and understands any concern of the EA, or of any other agency, that a prospective designation does not warrant the protection levels selected and/or the ensuing loss of government transparency accompanying designation.

Step 4: Upon approval by the EA, designations and supporting information are published, as appropriate, to a public CUI Registry, from which the public and official users of CUI markings may identify the categories of information designated as CUI. To the extent that any of the information supporting a particular designation is, itself, CUI, it will be maintained separately from the public registry by the EA.

Recommendation #9 Identification of CUI

Each agency should establish standards for personnel possessing the authority and/or necessary qualifications for identifying information as CUI. At a minimum, all individuals authorized to identify CUI should meet standardized CUI training requirements, as implemented within that agency.

Recommendation #10 Agency CUI Programs

Each agency should establish a program to manage its CUI. The program should include, at a minimum, Senior Officials responsible on behalf of the agency head for recommending CUI Designations, providing training, CUI management, and oversight of agency CUI activities.

2. Marking

Standardization of Markings Standardization is one of the goals of CUI implementation. The EA should provide the standardized markings and marking requirements with which agencies will comply. The decision regarding how to apply the standardized CUI markings to the various forms of CUI should be left to agency discretion. CUI intended for dissemination must be marked, but agency mission, intended data usage, access policies, established information exchange processes, and means or purposes for disseminating should all inform the agency decision regarding the most appropriate means of marking.

EA approved standardized markings should identify CUI designation, safeguarding and dissemination controls; originating agency; and life cycle, and should be the only markings used to convey this information. The Task Force reviewed the many variations of markings and marking schemes employed in the legacy SBU regimes and concluded that no marking scheme in current use can accommodate all requirements of the expanded scope. For example, some agencies – particularly those outside of the ISE – routinely process and transfer bulk form SBU (e.g., privacy, health, income, etc.) with other agencies, but for a very limited purpose, to a known and limited audience, and under clear processes. In such circumstances, it is possible that simply using a "system-high"[24] marking may be adequate. Alternatively, in the case of finished intelligence products intended for dissemination to our State, local, and tribal partners, it may be irresponsible not to clearly identify the intelligence report as CUI, and to include any warranted portion marking. The Task Force recognized the value of some level of portion marking for specific formats of CUI in information sharing efforts to enable the ready identification of the CUI elements within appropriately marked documents.

The Task Force believes that agencies should consider the full range of marking options – including, as appropriate, system-high, database, application, docu-

24. System High is a means of marking an entire system at the level of the most restricted CUI within the system.

ment, portion, paragraph, and data element identification[25] - as required by mission and information protection and sharing requirements. When shared, all information should be marked consistent with EA issued standards.
Given the likelihood that mission requirements may necessitate occasional deviations from the standards, the EA should be authorized to waive or modify these standards in such circumstances.

Simplification of Markings
The Task Force believes that the CUI Framework, not only across federal agencies, but in the potential for its adoption by State, local, tribal, private sector, and foreign partners, requires the use of terminology which is clear, simple and intuitive. It is likely that while the 2008 Memorandum's categorizing scheme is appropriate, its supporting marking nomenclature ("CONTROLLED WITH STANDARD DISSEMINATION," "CONTROLLED WITH SPECIFIED DISSEMINATION," and "CONTROLLED ENHANCED WITH SPECIFIED DISSEMINATION") can be improved. The Task Force encourages the EA to utilize input from a variety of CUI user focus groups, to try out variations of markings or labels and facilitate development of standard markings. The Task Force believes CUI markings should use plain language, and while abbreviations are appropriate, codes should be discouraged.

Public Registry
The Task Force views the public registry as an important source of government transparency and public insight into CUI designations. While the CUI registry would contain a full description of the requirements for safeguarding and disseminating CUI, the Task Force nonetheless believes it preferable that a given CUI document (such as an intelligence report) itself, to the extent possible, contain any safeguarding and dissemination information necessary to its proper handling.

Distinguish from FOIA
Finally, the Task Force believes it is critical to recognize that the CUI Framework does not alter the requirements of FOIA, and that CUI implementation guidance and training make clear that the presence or absence of a CUI marking has no bearing on whether a record is releasable or exempt from release under FOIA.
Recommendation #11 Simplification of Categories and Markings
The 2008 Memorandum marking nomenclature should be replaced with succinct, informative overall markings, such as:

25. Database marking would identify the most restricted CUI at the database level. Application marking would identify the most restricted CUI at the application level. Document marking would identify the most restricted CUI within a document. Paragraph or portion marking would identify each paragraph or portion containing CUI at the most restricted level found in that paragraph or portion. Data element identification includes the marking only of those discrete data elements or segments of information that are deemed CUI.

- CONTROLLED-ENHANCED
- CONTROLLED-SPECIFIED
- CONTROLLED-STANDARD or

- CONTROLLED-HIGH
- CONTROLLED-MEDIUM
- CONTROLLED-LOW

Recommendation #12 EA to Establish Standard Markings and Guidance
The EA should establish standardized CUI markings that identify CUI designation, safeguarding and dissemination controls; originating agency; and life cycle. The EA should publish the standardized markings and marking guidance to the agencies. Upon agency request, the EA may grant specific waivers or modifications to these standards, and the EA should work with agencies to ensure compliance with both the Framework and agency requirements.

Recommendation #13 Flexible Marking of CUI
CUI intended for dissemination must be marked in accordance with the standardized markings established by the EA. Agency decisions regarding how and when to apply standardized CUI markings should consider the full range of marking options and be driven by agency mission, the medium in which the CUI resides or is conveyed, and information protection and sharing requirements.

Recommendation #14 Clarify that CUI Has No Bearing on FOIA
CUI implementation guidance and CUI training should make clear that the CUI Framework and FOIA are entirely separate and that CUI markings have no bearing on whether records are exempt from release under FOIA.

3. Safeguarding
"Safeguarding" refers to physical or electronic measures that ensure CUI is not accessed inadvertently or improperly. The two levels of safeguarding established in the 2008 Memorandum, "standard"[26] and "enhanced",[27] are believed adequate for the expanded scope of the CUI Framework proposed herein. The Task Force is concerned, however, that incorporating existing federal IT standards directly into the CUI Framework could pose a significant impediment to CUI implementation, as application and adherence have been inconsistent to date. The reasons for the inconsistency include cost, complexity, and some contradiction between overlapping rules.

Mindful of the fact that agencies are obligated to comply with federal IT standards independent of those standards' inclusion in the CUI Framework, the Task Force has concluded that the EA, in consultation with the Federal Chief Informa-

---

26. "'Standard Safeguarding' is a handling instruction that means the information so designated is subject to baseline safeguarding measures that reduce the risks of unauthorized or inadvertent disclosure." 2008 Memorandum, at 3.

27. "'Enhanced Safeguarding' is a handling requirement that means the information so designated is subject to measures more stringent than those normally required because inadvertent or unauthorized disclosure would create a risk of substantial harm." 2008 Memorandum, at 2.

tion Officer (CIO) Council, should develop IT safeguarding standards for the CUI Framework in a phased manner.

The Task Force endorses the position of OMB that phased development of IT standards for the CUI Framework is neither authority for nor endorsement of non-compliance by agencies with federal IT standards. The Task Force believes that Federal CIOs, through the Federal CIO Council, could provide relevant, practical, and objective advice and perspectives given their current responsibilities across government for balancing security requirements with IT planning and implementation. Assistance in aligning metadata tagging and digital identity management with the CUI Framework to manage access to CUI is one goal for such advice.

An additional safeguarding challenge arises when sensitive federal government information is shared with State, local, tribal, private sector, and foreign partners. As non-federal partners, these entities are neither required by law to comply with the same physical or IT safeguarding standards as the federal Executive Branch, nor are they necessarily funded to do so. Nonetheless, the Task Force believes that non-federal entities that receive CUI from the federal government should be encouraged to provide safeguarding protection consistent with the CUI Framework to the maximum extent possible.

Recognizing the need to achieve the parallel goals of information protection and information sharing with these partners, the Task Force concluded that the CUI Framework would likely benefit from the establishment of standardized arrangements to address formal, recurring, and institutionalized information sharing settings as well as informal, irregular, or field conditions. Such means must be based on risk management as informed by operational requirements.

There are useful precedents for formal information sharing arrangements between the federal government and non-federal partners. Despite certain obvious distinctions between them and the CUI Framework, the Task Force was impressed by the procedures implemented by the Chemical-Terrorism Vulnerability Information ("CVI")[28] and Protected Critical Infrastructure Information ("PCII")[29] programs. Both of those programs have well developed guidelines, tailored to mission needs, providing safeguarding standards which can be achieved with reasonable and appropriate efforts by the non-federal partners. The PCII program also contains an "Accreditation" process. The Task Force encourages the EA and CUI Council to review those procedures for any appropriate measures which may benefit the CUI Framework, taking proper account of situations in which non-federal partners may have severe resource constraints.

---

28. Procedures for the CVI program can be found in the CVI Manual, http://www.dhs.gov/xlibrary/assets/chemsec_cvi_proceduresmanual.pdf.

29. Procedures for the PCII program can be found in the April 2009 Protected Critical Infrastructure Information Program Procedures Manual, found at http://www.dhs.gov/xlibrary/assets/pcii_program_procedures_manual.pdf

Information sharing which is informal, irregular, or which occurs under field conditions presents its own set of safeguarding concerns, and in these circumstances, formal procedures, agreements, and compliance mechanisms may serve only to impede information sharing. The Task Force believes that in such circumstances, where information must be shared, but where there is no opportunity for formalizing procedures, federal employees and their non-federal partners should be enabled to identify "equivalent measures," taking into account the sensitivity of the particular CUI and the risks thereto. In such circumstances, a federal employee's training and understanding of the CUI Framework could be critical, both to ensure protection of the information, and to ensure that sharing is not impeded by "non-issues." The Task Force would encourage agencies to develop pocket reference cards and short-form CUI Agreements for use by personnel in the field.

Recommendation #15 Safeguarding
The EA, in consultation with the CUI Council, should develop a means to address safeguarding in formal, recurring, and institutionalized information sharing settings, as well as in informal or irregular situations including field conditions.

Recommendation #16 Consultation on Threat
The EA, in consultation with the CUI Council, should consult with appropriate entities to determine the level at which certain unclassified information on federal government networks and systems is being targeted in order to best allocate resources to protect CUI.

Recommendation # 17 CIO Council as Advisor on Information Standards and Safeguards
The EA should utilize the Federal CIO Council for advice and consultation on:

a. appropriate measures to support a phased approach to the application of information technology standards to the CUI Framework,
b. a balanced set of technology requirements for safeguarding CUI which are consistent with federal guidance and achievable by our non-federal information sharing partners, and
c. metadata standards to promote transparency, facilitate IT functions, and support digital privilege management.

4. Dissemination
The CUI Framework currently contains two dissemination controls - "Standard" and "Specified." Standard dissemination control allows an authorized holder, based on his/her discretion, to provide the CUI to federal, State, local, tribal, private sector, and foreign partners – provided that the dissemination furthers an official mission purpose. Specified Dissemination rules are used when there are compelling requirements to limit the authorized holder's discretion. Specified dissemination requires additional markings describing those limits. These restrictions, based on law, regulation, interagency or intergovernmental agreement, or agency policy,

should define a specified dissemination instruction clearly articulating the discretion authorized the holder, as approved by the EA at designation. Where CUI is marked only to identify it as CUI, without specifying dissemination instructions, standard dissemination applies. Where specified dissemination rules do not lend themselves to effective summarization, they will be maintained by the EA and made easily accessible to handlers of that category of CUI.

Congress and the Judiciary
While the CUI Framework may well include a designation for materials covered by Executive Privilege, the Task Force recognized that Executive accountability requires that CUI markings do not themselves interfere with the checks and balances provided by the legislative and judicial branches. Official activities by those branches constitute "official use" as it does for other authorized recipients of CUI. While those branches often must honor the safeguard and dissemination controls required for CUI of any other recipient, marking as CUI is not itself a basis for withholding information from Congress or the Judiciary.

Recommendation #18 Standardize Specified Dissemination Requirement s
Agencies should work with the EA and CUI Council to standardize specified dissemination instructions. In reviewing agency requests for specified dissemination instructions, the EA should seek to harmonize instructions and thereby limit the total number of CUI specified dissemination instructions to the greatest extent possible.

Recommendation #19 Dissemination to Congress and the Courts
Implementation guidance for the CUI framework should clarify that a CUI marking is not a basis for withholding information from Congress or the Judiciary.

5. Life Cycle
Life Cycle refers to the time period during which information identified as CUI would receive the safeguarding and dissemination controls of the CUI Framework. Appropriate life cycles support government transparency and ensure that resources are focused on protecting information as warranted by the level and anticipated duration of sensitivity.

The Task Force members agreed that given the volume of CUI material within the federal government, it is impracticable to implement a review process prior to decontrol. Hence, the intent is to have the life cycle established as part of the CUI designation, and be tied to either specific events or a specific timeframe.

The broad range of material covered by the CUI Framework poses difficult life cycle challenges. The Task Force believes CUI should be decontrolled as soon as it no longer warrants the safeguarding or dissemination controls of the CUI Framework. While in some cases this time frame would be foreseeable and reasonably short, in other instances, such as situations in which the Privacy Act or the Health Insurance Portability and Accountability Act apply, the timelines for protection may span the life of the protected individual, or longer.

Agency officials who recommend designation of CUI are in the best position to judge how long CUI protection should be required. The designation decisions should therefore address decontrol. Each CUI designation recommendation should specify either the passage of a certain period of time or an event certain (for example, the death of the individuals named, conclusion of prosecution and expiration of appeal rights, etc.) after which the document would be decontrolled and lose its status as CUI.

The Task Force believes that no document should remain subject to CUI controls indefinitely, and identified the requirement for a default lifecycle for any situation where no other life cycle is identifiable. Recognizing that the selection of such a generally applicable time period is both necessary and somewhat arbitrary, the Task Force considered the recommendations of both The Constitution Project (2-10 years)[30] and OMB Watch (not more than 5 years).[31] The Task Force considered these recommendations in light of the anticipated breadth of CUI designations, the significant administrative burden resulting from an overly aggressive decontrol cycle, and the enhanced transparency afforded by separating CUI status from releasability decisions (described below), and concluded that in circumstances where CUI lifecycle is otherwise undetermined, decontrol should occur 10 years following CUI identification. Any CUI whose decontrol is other than 10 years after identification should be clearly marked with the date or event certain upon which decontrol would take place.

The Task Force recognizes that decontrol of CUI is distinct from release of CUI, and that mandatory, pre-release review procedures, particularly when conducted following decontrol, facilitate coordination with the document's originator and awareness of any enduring requirement for control. At no time, pre- or post-decontrol, is a CUI marking itself determinative of whether it may be released. Similarly, the CUI Framework should not impact destruction timelines established through statute, regulation, or records management policy.

Recommendation #20 Clarify Decontrol

"Decontrol" should be identified as the act of removing information previously designated as CUI from the CUI Framework, and it should be made clear that while public release of CUI should be preceded by the CUI's decontrol, decontrol is not itself authorization for public release.

Recommendation #21 Establish Life Cycle

All CUI information should be decontrolled after ten years unless (a) the CUI designation establishes an alternative decontrol requirement by date or event, (b)

---

30. The Constitution Project, *Reining in Excessive Secrecy: Recommendations for the Reform of the Classification and Controlled Unclassified Information Systems* (2009) at 9, available at http://www.constitutionproject.org/manage/file/178.pdf.

31. OMB Watch, *Controlled Unclassified Information: Recommendations for Information Control Reform* (2009) at 10, available at http://www.ombwatch.org/files/info/2009cuirpt.pdf

the alternative decontrol appears in the controlled registry, or (c) the alternative decontrol is clearly identified on the CUI.

6. Exceptions

The 2008 Memorandum lists four critical infrastructure information regimes which are specific exceptions to the CUI Framework. If the scope of CUI is expanded, as per Recommendation # 2, additional temporary exceptions may be required. To limit exceptions to those truly required, the Task Force believes it important that the EA identify specific criteria for establishing exceptions. Possible factors could include that the potential exception contains a significant amount of information not originated by the federal government and provided to the government based upon negotiated criteria that do not conform to the CUI regime, or that the provision of the information to the government is highly dependent on the existence of a trusted regime for data protection.

With respect to the four exceptions listed in the 2008 Memorandum, the relationship between the federal government and the private sector has been negotiated through public rule making. Each of these systems was negotiated and tailored to a particular community and type of information. There is significant interest in these communities that their incorporation into the Framework not negate the currently established trust. A proposal by the excepted regime program offices is to establish and implement the CUI Framework with the intention of bringing the "exceptions" into the CUI Framework once its reliability and trust are established.

The Task Force believes that the exceptions should be incorporated into the CUI Framework in a manner which, to the maximum extent possible, preserves the fundamental elements of the exceptions, and neither harms the trusted relationships nor forces the excepted regimes out of compliance with statutory requirements. As the excepted regimes approach incorporation into the CUI Framework, the Task Force believes the EA should work with the relevant agencies and program offices to amend regulations and, if necessary, with Congress to amend relevant statutes. Incorporating the exceptions into the Framework is not intended to negate established FOIA exemptions.

Any new exceptions should be considered in light of the ability to render them compliant either with existing CUI standards for safeguarding and dissemination or standards for the classification of information for national security or other authorized purposes.

Recommendation #22 Establish Exception Process

In addition to the four existing exceptions within the Presidential guidance on CUI, a process should be developed by the EA, in coordination with the CUI Council, to develop a means of evaluating whether additional categories of information that are covered by the expanded scope of CUI should be treated as temporary exceptions.

Recommendation #23 Delay in Incorporation of Exceptions into the CUI Framework
The CUI Framework should be established, running, and proven, prior to incorporation of the exceptions into the Framework.

Recommendation #24 Amending Regulations or Statutes
The EA should work with the agencies and program offices administering excepted regimes to amend relevant regulations and, if necessary, with Congress to amend relevant statutes, as the excepted regimes are incorporated into the CUI Framework.

7. Training
Effective implementation of the CUI Framework requires changing the way unclassified information protection and sharing is commonly understood. A dedicated, centralized training program is critical to that effort. CUI training is required at various levels of instruction, based upon agency mission and employee duties and seniority. Baseline training should be established by the EA, and agencies should coordinate development of intermediate and advanced level training with the EA. Each agency should be encouraged to create training that is tailored to its particular needs and mission. This is especially true in the ISE agencies, where the tension between sharing and protecting critical information is greatest. Training in this area requires a strong emphasis on the exercise of individual judgment in ensuring that the CUI Framework does not have a chilling effect on information sharing. Additionally, the EA should provide training to the senior officials responsible for CUI designation and agency CUI program management.

Recommendation #25 Establish Training
The EA should establish a baseline training program sufficient to educate federal employees on the key principles underlying the CUI Framework, including the importance of government transparency and public trust in government. Intermediate and advanced level training should be developed by agencies, in consultation with the EA, to address increased requirements for expertise and sophistication in managing CUI. Basic CUI training should be the minimum requirement for an employee to be authorized to identify or disseminate CUI. Additionally, to promote consistency across the Executive Branch the EA should provide training directly to the senior officials responsible for CUI designation and agency CUI program management.

8. Incentives and Accountability
The Task Force believes that getting CUI designation and identification decisions right the first time is as important as ensuring compliance with CUI safeguards and dissemination controls. Like recent efforts with regard to the ISE, compliance with CUI policies should be viewed as routine elements of job performance and considered in employee evaluation, promotion, or award decisions. Moreover, administrative or other appropriate sanctions should be available for re-

peated non-compliance with CUI policies, or with CUI safeguard or dissemination control requirements.

Recommendation #26 Incentives
Agencies should consider employee performance under the CUI Framework in evaluation, promotion, and award decisions.

Recommendation #27 Accountability and Sanctions
Agencies should be authorized to impose administrative sanctions for repeated non-compliance with CUI policies or with CUI safeguard or dissemination control requirements.

9. Standardization, Oversight, and Dispute Resolution
A simple, concise, and standardized CUI Framework, with effective centralized governance and oversight, has the best chance not only for the widest acceptance within the federal government, but for broad adaptation throughout our State, local, tribal, and private sector partner communities.

The Task Force believes it is critical that the CUI Framework bring standardization to current SBU processes to reduce inconsistency and a tendency toward over-protection of information. To accomplish this goal, the Task Force determined that the EA should be appropriately empowered to harmonize and standardize designations across agencies.

The Task Force considers that oversight should begin within the agency, based on procedures to be set out by the agency head. Agencies should establish an effective internal oversight approach, either as part of or parallel with the CUI program.

The EA should maintain oversight authority and the ability to perform on-site reviews of agency CUI programs to support the implementation of an effective Framework across government, and to require of each agency any reports, information, and other cooperation that may be necessary to fulfill its responsibilities. In addition, each agency and the EA should also establish a mechanism for addressing challenges to CUI designation and identification by authorized holders of the information.

CUI dispute resolution requires a balanced approach. The goal is to empower the EA to implement and manage the CUI Framework while recognizing the authority of the agencies to execute their missions. CUI is likely to be fully embedded throughout mission execution, and agencies require a means of assuring that decisions within the CUI Framework do not improperly impact mission execution.

The Task Force also recognizes the significant costs imposed on private entities doing business with the federal government in order to comply with multiple, inconsistent SBU regimes. The Task Force believes the obligation under federal contracts to handle CUI information should be clear, consistent, and reflected in a single Federal Acquisition Regulation (FAR) provision that addresses the handling of CUI across the federal government. The language of this provision should be mirrored in agency-level acquisition regulations and guidance.

Recommendation #28 Internal Oversight
Each agency should identify an internal oversight program to assure the effective implementation of the CUI Framework within the agency.

Recommendation #29 Challenges to Designation and Identification
Each agency head or senior official should establish a mechanism for addressing challenges to CUI designation and identification, to include appeals to the CUI Council. The EA should establish a mechanism by which the CUI Council would address appeals of agency challenges as well as other interagency disputes based upon CUI designation or identification.

Recommendation #30 Federal Acquisition Guidance
The Federal Acquisition Regulations should be revised to reflect one provision or clause that addresses compliance with the CUI Framework by private entities seeking to do business with the federal government. This provision or clause should be mirrored in agency specific acquisition regulations or guidance. 25

10. Implementation Timeline and Resources
Full implementation of the CUI Framework requires significant resources, especially with respect to IT safeguards. Previously released safeguarding guidance required Federal IT systems to make use of encryption, two-factor authentication for remote access, and other secure system and data access procedures. Many agencies are still developing procedures to meet these requirements. Accelerating the implementation of the safeguarding requirements could impact resource constraints at certain agencies.

Raising the level of IT safeguards, however, was not among the factors mandating the replacement of the existing 107 disparate SBU regimes, the development of the CUI Framework, or the expansion of the CUI Framework beyond its current scope. Those actions were mandated by the need to bring standardization, ease information sharing, and increase government transparency to the world of SBU information. If, in the alternative, implementation focuses on the core requirements of training, marking and oversight, while still requiring an extraordinary effort, the mandates of the CUI Framework can likely be achieved for a fraction of the cost anticipated by current planning.

Therefore, to see more immediate improvements without requiring an inordinate and potentially impossible investment, the Task Force believes that implementation should begin with the foundational aspects of the CUI Framework – training, marking, and oversight, while the EA works to identify or develop appropriate IT safeguarding requirements and capabilities. Automated tools could greatly ease the burden of identifying and marking efforts by providing users with clear choices – such as are available through drop-down menus, as well as aiding oversight and CUI management efforts.

Specifically, Federal agencies should prioritize:

- Establishing agency CUI Programs.
- Implementing an EA-provided training program on the fundamentals of CUI and the importance of maintaining public trust in government.
- Adopting the CUI markings and dissemination controls, while phasing out the use of existing markings.
- Deploying automated tools, such as the Intelligence Community's Classification Management Tool, on unclassified networks to enable common and consistent markings.
- Establishing oversight and reporting mechanisms.

The Task Force recognizes that should the recommendation to expand the scope of CUI be accepted, the EA would need to provide extraordinary support to non-ISE agencies to ensure effective implementation of the CUI Framework, and the EA's staffing and resource requirements would have to be addressed. Likewise, even with a phased implementation as recommended herein, successfully implementing the CUI Framework without impeding existing operations and programs would require that the agencies receive clear budgetary guidelines from OMB, and that the necessary resources be made available.

Transitioning to the new markings under CUI will largely be a matter of change management, in which agency leadership should be held accountable for implementing plans and policies to ensure the workforce transitions to CUI in a timely manner.

Implementing compliance and reporting processes and procedures would facilitate a clearer understanding of how much information is being protected, and for what reasons. Further, if made available to the public, the results of these reporting and oversight requirements will further government transparency.

Recommendation #31 Phase Implementation of Training, Marking, Oversight and Reporting
CUI implementation should prioritize:

- Establishing agency CUI Programs.
- Implementing EA-provided baseline training program as well as agency developed intermediate and advanced level training,
- Adopting the CUI markings and dissemination controls, while phasing out the use of existing markings.
- Implementing automated tools on unclassified networks to enable common and consistent markings.
- Establishing oversight and reporting mechanisms.

Recommendation #32 Phase Implementation of Technical Safeguards
Information Technology safeguards should be phased into the CUI Framework pursuant to timelines established by the EA when, in coordination with the CIO

Council, the EA determines that technical safeguards will enhance, and not degrade, the effectiveness of the CUI Framework.

Recommendation #33 Marking Initiation
Marking in accordance with the CUI Framework should begin as directed by the EA. No CUI marking should be done prior thereto. Material previously developed and disseminated, printed, or otherwise memorialized should not be remarked. Information that continues to be disseminated should be remarked at agency discretion.

Recommendation #34 Ensure Adequate Resourcing of Executive Agent
The extraordinary efforts required of the EA to develop and implement the expanded scope CUI Framework, as well as the criticality of EA effectiveness in those efforts to the success of the CUI Framework, should be recognized and appropriately resourced to include funding, permanent staff, and agency detailees.

Recommendation #35 Synchronize CUI Implementation with Government Processes and Cycles
CUI implementation should be incorporated into the appropriate policy, budgetary, and administrative cycles so that the implementation of the CUI Framework better aligns with current agency and Federal government business practices.

Recommendation #36 Impact of CUI on the Federal Enterprise Architecture
Members of the CUI Council should solicit feedback from their agency CIOs on how the CUI Framework can most effectively be incorporated into the Federal Enterprise Architecture ("FEA"), reflecting priorities which support business processes to enhance efficiency in implementation. This feedback should then be reviewed with OMB, and based on OMB feedback, the CUI Council – through agency CIOs and other appropriate policy officials – should work to develop specific input to the FEA within established guidance for review and possible incorporation into government-wide FEA guidance.

Recommendation #37 Incorporate CUI into Federal Grant Guidance
Federal grant guidelines for State, local and tribal government should be amended to facilitate federal grants utilization for implementation of the CUI Framework among our State, local and tribal information sharing partners, as appropriate.

3.3 Measures to Track Progress in Implementation of CUI
The 2009 Memorandum identifies three presumptive goals for implementation of the Framework:

- standardization;
- information sharing; and
- government transparency

Implementation of CUI will require significant cultural changes, including a more proactive balancing of security and openness. Given that an overemphasis of either security or openness will jeopardize these goals, ongoing assessment should be a prominent part of the implementation process.

The Task Force identified three stages of CUI Framework implementation:

- Planning – the Framework is developed, tested, and put in place, including EA and agency policies, the CUI Registry, and the CUI training program;
- Transition – agencies modify existing practices to conform to the Framework; and
- Sustainment – agencies consistently apply the Framework as standard practice

The measures used to track progress will change based on the stage of implementation, but they will always support the overarching goals established by the 2009 Memorandum. In order to fully assess the Framework, the status quo must be understood and documented. It will be critical to perform baseline analysis and develop ongoing measurement programs that fully meet these complex goals. In addition, annual reporting will allow for independent public analysis as to the maintenance of the required balance, thereby improving accountability. The Task Force affirms the importance of measuring and tracking the implementation and effectiveness of the Framework.

Recommendation #38 Annual Report of the Executive Agent
The EA should publish an annual report to the President, that is also made available to the Congress and the public, that provides the status of CUI implementation to include performance measurement data developed pursuant to Recommendation #40, and other information as deemed appropriate by the EA in consultation with the CUI Council.

Recommendation #39 Establish a Baseline Measurement of Current SBU Efforts
Based on the system established above, the EA should immediately undertake to establish a baseline measurement of SBU activity to support future implementation and assessment efforts.

Recommendation #40 Measure Implementation
The EA, in coordination with OMB (including the Chief Performance Officer and the Resource Management Office) and appropriate expert support, should develop a system to measure the implementation of CUI that addresses the various phases of implementation and is effectively tied to the federal budget cycle.

Part 4. Conclusion

Through its 90-day study, the CUI Task Force concluded that within the Executive Branch, information sharing and transparency suffer from inconsistency in SBU policies, uncertainty in interagency settings as to what policies apply to SBU information, and the inconsistent application of even similar policies across agencies. The general lack of effective, standardized training and oversight at many agencies results in a tendency to over-protect information.

The Controlled Unclassified Information (CUI) Framework provided a good start toward addressing these deficiencies, but was intended to do so only with regard to terrorism-related information. The Task Force has concluded that a single, standardized framework for marking, safeguarding, and disseminating all Executive Branch SBU is required to further the goals of standardization, information sharing, and government transparency.

The Task Force recommendations are intended to overlay, and in some cases modify, the CUI Framework established by the 2008 Memorandum. Building upon that Framework, the Task Force has proposed 40 Recommendations, including simplifying the definition of CUI; expanding the scope of the CUI Framework; clarifying that limits of CUI markings – such as with regard to releases under FOIA or to Congress; and phasing implementation of the expanded scope of CUI to ensure no disruption to agencies' mission performance or the security of information.

APPENDIX 1

Entities Consulted by the CUI Task Force

Government Entities

- Controlled Unclassified Information Council
- Department of Energy, Office of Classification
- Deputy to the Director of the Federal CIO Council
  - o Privacy Committee of the Federal CIO Council
- Legislative Staff Representing:
  - o Senate Homeland Security and Governmental Affairs Committee
  - o House Committee on Homeland Security
  - o House Committee on Oversight and Government Reform
  - o House Committee on the Judiciary
  - o House Permanent Select Committee on Intelligence
- Excepted Regime Program Offices
- Concurrent Executive Order 12958 Review
- Office of National Drug Control Policy
- Non-ISE Agencies:
  - o Department of Labor
  - o Department of Agriculture
  - o Department of Education
  - o National Air and Space Administration
  - o Consumer Product Safety Commission

o Federal Energy Regulatory Commission

- State, Local, and Tribal Government Partners
  o International Association of Chiefs of Police
  o Garden Grove, California Police Department
  o Minnehaha County, South Dakota Sheriff's Office
  o Florida Department of Law Enforcement
  o American Probation and Parole Association

Non-Government Entities

- Critical Infrastructure Partnership Advisory Council
- National Industrial Security Program Policy Advisory Committee
- Privacy and Open Government Advocacy Organizations
  o American Civil Liberties Union
  o The Constitution Project o Openthegovernment.org o Federation of American Scientists
  o National Security Archive o Public Citizen o OMB Watch
  o Electronic Frontier Foundation

APPENDIX 2
SBU Markings Currently in Use

1. SENSITIVE
2. DO NOT DISSEMINATE
3. SBU-NF
4. SBU/ NOFORN
5. UNLIMITED RIGHTS
6. GOVERNMENT PURPOSE RIGHTS
7. LIMITED RIGHTS 8. RESTRICTED RIGHTS
9. SPECIAL LICENSE RIGHTS
10. PRE-EXISTING MARKINGS
11. COMMERCIAL MARKINGS
12. CLOSE HOLD
13. RSEN
14. PREDECISIONAL PRODUCT
15. SOURCE SELECTION SENSITIVE
16. DEA SENSITIVE (DEA S)
17. SENSITIVE (SENS)
18. COPYRIGHT (DATE) (OWNER)
19. DELIBERATE PROCESS PRIVILEGE
20. RELIDO
21. EYES ONLY
22. BANK SECRECY ACT INFORMATION (BSA)
23. ACQUISITION SENSITIVE
24. ATTORNEY WORK PRODUCT
25. LIMITED ACCESS

26. RESTRICTED ACCESS
27. MEDICAL RECORDS
28. LAN INFRASTRUCTURE
29. IT SECURITY RELATED
30. LAN BACKUP SENSITIVE INFORMATION
31. SOURCE SELECTION INFORMATION
32. TRADE SECRET
33. ATTORNEY CLIENT
34. BUDGETARY INFORMATION
35. PRE-DECISIONAL
36. FOR INTERNAL USE ONLY
37. NOT FOR DISTRIBUTION SAFEGUARDS INFORMATION (SGI)
38. AGENCY INTERNAL USE ONLY (U//AIUO)
39. TRADE SENSITIVE INFORMATION
40. SENSITIVE BUT UNCLASSIFIED (SBU)
41. HEALTH RELATED INFORMATION (EM)
42. NO DISTRIBUTION (NODIS OR ND)
43. LAW ENFORCEMENT SENSITIVE (LES)
44. EXCLUSIVE DISTRIBUTION (EXDIS OR XD)
45. FOR OFFICIAL USE ONLY (FOUO)
46. SENSITIVE STUDENT RECORDS (STR)
47. CONFIDENTIAL BUSINESS INFORMATION (CBI)
48. LIMITED OFFICIAL USE (LOU)
49. LIMITED DISTRIBUTION
50. LIMITED DISTRIBUTION (LIMDIS)
51. SENSITIVE INFORMATION (SINFO)
52. COVERED BY CONFIDENTIALITY AGREEMENT
53. ORIGINATOR CONTROLLED (ORCON)
54. CONTRACTUAL SENSITIVE INFORMATION
55. ENFORCEMENT CONFIDENTIAL INFORMATION (ECI)
56. LIMITED OFFICIAL USE INFORMATION (LOUI)
57. SUBSTANCE ABUSE RECORDS (SAB)
58. SENSITIVE SECURITY INFORMATION (SSI)
59. TITLE III COMMUNICATIONS (T3)
60. FEDERAL TAXPAYER INFORMATION
61. TECHNOLOGY TRANSFER INFORMATION
62. BOMB TECH SENSITIVE (BTS)
63. CFIUS INFORMATION (CFIUS)
64. RESTRICTED BY COURT ORDER (CO)
65. LIMITED USE ONLY (LUO)
66. PRIVACY ACT PROTECTED INFORMATION (PAPI)
67. PROPRIETARY INFORMATION (PROPIN)
68. CHILD VICTIM/WITNESS (CH)
69. FINANCIAL RECORDS (NON-NSL) (FR)
70. FINANCIAL RECORDS NSL (NSLF)

71. SOURCE SELECTION INFORMATION
72. LIMITED CREDIT INFORMATION NSL (NSLC)
73. SELECT AGENT SENSITIVE INFORMATION (SASI)
74. CALEA COST RECOVERY INFORMATION (CALEA)
75. INNOCENT IMAGES VISUAL INFORMATION (IIVI)
76. SENSITIVE TREATY/MOU/NDA INFORMATION (STM)
77. PRIVILEGED FBI ATTORNEY CLIENT
78. OFFICIAL USE ONLY-SMALL BUSINESS
79. OFFICIAL USE ONLY-PROTECTED COOPERATIVE CENSUS CONFIDENTIAL
80. SBU-GSA-BI
81. OFFICIAL USE ONLY (OUO)
82. ATTORNEY/ CLIENT PRIVILEGED
83. GRAND JURY MATERIAL (FGJ)
84. OFFICIAL USE ONLY-APPLIED TECHNOLOGY
85. DOD UNCLASSIFIED CONTROLLED NUCLEAR INFORMATION (DOD UCNI)
86. OFFICIAL USE ONLY-PATENT CAUTION INFORMATION
87. CONFIDENTIAL CONTRACT PROPOSAL INFORMATION (CCPI)
88. CONTROLLED NUCLEAR INFORMATION (U//DCNI OR U//ECNI)
89. CHEMICAL-TERRORISM VULNERABILITY INFORMATION (CVI)
90. NAVAL NUCLEAR PROPULSION INFORMATION (U-NNPI)
91. OFFICIAL USE ONLY-EXPORT CONTROLLED INFORMATION
92. NAVAL NUCLEAR PROPULSION INFORMATION (NOFORN)
93. SENSITIVE UNCLASSIFIED NON- SAFEGUARDS INFORMATION (SUNSI)
94. PROTECTED CRITICAL INFRASTRUCTURE INFORMATION (PCII)
95. OFFICIAL USE ONLY - SENSITIVE INTERNAL INFORMATION
96. TELEPHONE OR ELECTRONIC COMMUNICATIONS NSL (NSLT)
97. JUVENILE - PROTECT IDENTITY IN ACCORDANCE WITH 18 USC 5031 (JI)
98. SENSITIVE INFORMATION- SPECIAL HANDLING REQUIRED
99. SENSITIVE WATER VULNERABILITY ASSESSMENT INFORMATION
100. LIMITED OFFICIAL USE-LAW ENFORCEMENT SENSITIVE (LOU-LES)
101. EXPORT CONTROLLED INFORMATION (OR MATERIAL) (ECI)
102. SENSITIVE HOMELAND SECURITY INFORMATION (SHSI)
103. OPERATIONS SECURITY PROTECTED INFORMATION (OSPI)
104. DISSEMINATION IS PROHIBITED EXCEPT AS AUTHORIZED BY AR 20–1
105. COMMUNICATION/ ATTORNEY WORK PRODUCT (PRV)
106. RESEARCH AND DEVELOPMENT AGREEMENT INFORMATION
107. INNOVATION RESEARCH INFORMATION AND SMALL BUSINESS
108. CONFIDENTIAL INFORMATION PROTECTION AND STATISTICAL EFFICIENCY ACT OF 2002 (CIPSEA)
109. WITNESS SECURITY PROGRAM - PROTECT IDENTITY IN ACCORDANCE WITH 18 USC 3521 (WS)

110. SENSITIVE DRINKING WATER RELATED INFORMATION (SDWRI)
111. CONTRACTOR ACCESS RESTRICTED INFORMATION (CARI)
112. COMPUTER SECURITY ACT SENSITIVE INFORMATION (CSASI)
113. SMALL BUSINESS INNOVATION RESEARCH (SBIR) PROGRAM
114. PERSONALLY IDENTIFIABLE INFORMATION - PRIVACY ACT OF 1974
115. PERSONNEL DATA, PRIVACY ACT OF 1974 (5 U.S.C. 552A)
116. FOR OFFICIAL USE ONLY- LAW ENFORCEMENT SENSITIVE (FOUO-LES)
117. FOREIGN INTELLIGENCE SURVEILLANCE ACT (FISA)

APPENDIX 3

Acronyms used in this report

CIO	Chief Information Officer
CUI	Controlled Unclassified Information
CVI	Chemical-Terrorism Vulnerability Information
DHS	Department of Homeland Security
DOD	Department of Defense
DOI	Department of Interior
DOJ	Department of Justice
EA	Executive Agent
FAR	Federal Acquisition Regulation
FBI	Federal Bureau of Investigation
FEA	Federal Enterprise Architecture
FOIA	Freedom of Information Act
FOUO	For Official Use Only (FOUO)
HHS	Department of Health and Human Service
HIPAA	Health Insurance Portability and Accountability Act
ISE	Information Sharing Environment
IT	Information Technology
LES	Law Enforcement Sensitive
NARA	National Archives and Records Administration
ODNI	Office of the Director of National Intelligence
OMB	Office of Management and Budget
PCII	Protected Critical Infrastructure Information
PM-ISE	Program Manager, Information Sharing Environment
SBU	Sensitive But Unclassified
SGI	Safeguards Information
SSI	Sensitive Security Information
USDA	Department of Agriculture

Attorney General Memorandum: Guidance for Conducting Interviews Without Providing Miranda Warnings in Arrests of Terrorism Suspects

(Oct. 19, 2010)

With my approval, the Federal Bureau of Investigation (FBI) has issued guidance for law enforcement agents, FBI field offices, and JTTF's concerning custodial interrogation of an operational terrorist arrested with the United States. In particular, that guidance discusses the interrogation of an operational terrorist that is conducted without provision of an advice of rights under *Miranda v. Arizona,* 384 U.S. 436 (1966). This memorandum provides corresponding guidance in federal prosecution if an agent consults about whether to process with unwarned custodial interrogation in the circumstances the FBI guidance addresses.

the FBI guidance primarily concerns the "public safety" exception recognized in *New York V. Quarles*, 467 U.S. 649 (1984), which held that, if law enforcement officials engage in custodial interrogation that is "reasonably prompted by concern for public safety," any statements the individual provides in the course of such interrogation shall not be inadmissible on the ground that the questioning was conducted with Miranda warnings. The FBI guidance explains that in light of the magnitude and complexity of the threat often posed by terrorist organizations, particularly international terrorist organizations, and the nature of their attacks, the circumstances surrounding an arrest of an operational terrorist may warrant significantly more extensive public safety interrogation than would be permissible in an ordinary criminal case. The FBI guidance instructs that, after any and all applicable public safety questions have been exhausted, agents should advise the arrestee of his Miranda rights and seek a waiver of those rights before any further investigation occurs, absent exceptional circumstances. Specifically, there may be exceptional situations in which continued unwarned interrogation is necessary to intelligence—outweighs the disadvantages of proceeding in this fashion. In such a situation, the FBI guidance directs agents to consult, when possible, with FBI Headquarters (including the Office of General Counsel) and Department of Justice attorneys regarding the interrogation strategy to be followed prior to reading the defendant his Miranda rights.[1]

---

[1] Neither the FBI guidance nor this memorandum addresses un-Mirandized questioning of suspects who are under indictment or represented by counsel. In this circumstances, which may present special legal and/or critical concerns, prosecutors should whenever possible consult with the Department's Professional Advisory Office and/or the National Security Division as appropriate prior to advising an agent to conduct unwarned interrogation.

Finally, note that the FBI guidance makes clear that, in all cases, presentment of an arrestee should not be delayed simply to continue interrogation, unless the arrestee has waived prompt presentment.

INFORMATION SHARING

Intelligence Community Policy Guidance 500.2
Attribute-Based Authorization and Access Management

(November 23, 2010)

A. AUTHORITY: The National Security Act of 1947, as amended; Executive Order 12333, as amended; and other applicable provisions of law.

B. PURPOSE: This Intelligence Community Policy Guidance establishes that attributes shall be used by Intelligence Community (IC) elements to authorize and manage access by personnel or processes to information resources in the information environment. This Guidance also addresses the management and protection of attributes.

C. APPLICABILITY: This Guidance applies to the IC, as defined by the National Security Act of 1947, as amended; and such other elements of any other department or agency as may be designated by the President, or designated jointly by the Director of National Intelligence and the head of the department or agency concerned, as an element of the IC.

D. DEFINITIONS

1. Information resources are defined as "information and related resources, such as personnel, equipment, funds, and information technology."[1]

2. Information environment is defined as the "aggregate of individuals, organizations, and/or systems that collect, process, or disseminate information, also included is the information itself."[2]

3. Attributes are distinct characteristics of an object or subject.

a. An object is a "passive information system-related entity (e.g., devices, files, records, tables, processes, programs, domains) containing or receiving information. Access to an object implies access to the information it contains."[3]

b. A subject is an active entity (generally an individual, process, or device) that causes information to flow among objects or changes the system state.[4]

---

1. Committee on National Security Systems Instruction No. 4009, National Information Assurance Glossary

2. *Ibid*

3. *Ibid.*

4. *Ibid.*

E. POLICY

1. The Assistant Director of National Intelligence and Chief Information Officer (IC CIO) shall issue IC Standards) regarding the identification and maintenance of attributes.

2. IC elements shall implement and maintain attributes in accordance with IC Standards) issued by the ADNUIC CIO.

3. IC elements shall use attributes to authorize and manage access by personnel or processes to information resources in the information environment.

4. IC elements shall ensure attributes are:

a. Used by information resources to control access to information by personnel or processes;

b. Attributable to a person or process;

c. Derived from authoritative sources;

d. Readily accessible;

e. Maintained for accuracy and currency;

f. Compatible with Department of Defense and other United States Government formats, to the maximum extent practicable;

g. Managed via an integrated lifecycle approach; and

h. Supportive of Che requirements of IC Directive 501, Discovery anti Dissemination or Retrieval of Information within the Intelligence Community.

5. IC elements shall manage, audit, and protect information resources where attributes are collected, processed, developed, stored, maintained, or disseminated, in accordance with IC Standards) issued by the IC CIO.

E. EFFECTIVE DATE: This Guidance becomes effective on the date of signature.

Assistant Director of National Intelligence for Policy & Strategy
November 23, 2010

Intelligence Community Directive 501
Discovery and Dissemination or Retrieval of Information Within the Intelligence Community

(January 21, 2009)

A. AUTHORITY: The National Security Act of 1947, as amended; Executive Order (EO) 12333, as amended; and other applicable provisions of law.

B. PURPOSE:

1. This Intelligence Community Directive (ICD) establishes in part the Director of National Intelligence (DNI) guidelines called for in Section 1.3(b)(9)(B) of EO 12333, as amended, addresses mandates in the Intelligence Reform and Terrorism Prevention Act of 2004 to strengthen the sharing, integration, and management of information within the Intelligence Community (IC), and establishes policies for: (1) discovery; and (2) dissemination or retrieval of intelligence and intelligence-related information collected or analysis produced by the IC.

2. The overall objectives of this policy are to:

a. Foster an enduring culture of responsible sharing and collaboration within an integrated IC;

b. Provide an improved capacity to warn of and disrupt threats to the United States (U.S.) homeland, and U.S. persons and interests; and

c. Provide more accurate, timely, and insightful analysis to inform decision making by the President, senior military commanders, national security advisers, and other executive branch officials.

3. This Directive rescinds Intelligence Community Policy Memorandum (ICPM) 2007-500-3, *Intelligence Information Sharing*, 22 December 2007. The following three Director of Central Intelligence Directive (DCID) 8 Series documents remain in effect: (1) Policy Memoranda 1, "Intelligence Community Implementation of Releasable by Information Disclosure Official (RELIDO) Dissemination Marking;" (2) Policy Memoranda 2, "Modification to Policy for NonICD 501Title 50 Organizations' Access to Shared IC Services on TS/SCI Information Systems;" and (3) Implementation Issuance Number 1, "Guidelines for Tearline Reporting."

C. APPLICABILITY:

1. This Directive applies to the IC, as defined by the National Security Act of 1947, as amended; and such other elements of any other department or agency as may be designated by the President, or designated jointly by the Director of National Intelligence (DNI) and the head of the department or agency concerned, as an element of the IC.

2. This Directive does not apply to purely law enforcement information. When law enforcement information also contains intelligence or intelligence-related information, this Directive shall apply to the intelligence or intelligence-related information.

D. POLICY:

1. IC elements shall treat information collected and analysis produced as national assets and, as such, shall act as stewards of information who have a predominant "responsibility to provide." In addition, authorized IC personnel have a "responsibility to discover" information believed to have the potential to contribute to their assigned mission need and a corresponding "responsibility to request" relevant information they have discovered.

2. *Responsibility to Provide.*

a. IC elements shall fulfill their "responsibility to provide" by making all intelligence and intelligence-related information (hereinafter referred to as "information") that IC elements are authorized to acquire, collect, hold, or obtain (hereinafter referred to as "information collected") or analysis an IC element is authorized to produce discoverable by automated means by "authorized IC personnel," in accordance with Section D, unless otherwise exempt in accordance with Intelligence Community Policy Guidance (ICPG) 501.1, *Exemption of Information from Discovery*. Authorized IC personnel are individuals identified by their element head and who have an appropriate security clearance and an assigned mission need for information collected or analysis produced. "Discovery," as defined in Appendix A, is the act of obtaining knowledge of the existence, but not necessarily the content, of information collected or analysis produced by any IC element.

b. "Stewards," as defined in Appendix A, shall fulfill their "responsibility to provide" by making all information collected and analysis produced by an IC element available for discovery by automated means by authorized IC personnel, unless otherwise determined by the DNI; by making as much information as possible available for automated retrieval upon discovery; and by presuming that authorized IC personnel who request information discovered possess a "need to know," in accordance with Section F.

3. *Responsibility to Discover.* "Authorized IC personnel," as defined in Appendix A, have a "responsibility to discover" information believed to have the potential to contribute to their assigned mission need. The act of discovery does not itself constitute a request for receipt of the information collected or analysis produced.

4. *Responsibility to Request.*

a. Authorized IC personnel have a corresponding "responsibility to request" relevant information they have discovered that has the potential to contribute to an analytic judgment, to optimize collection, to inform collection strategies and priorities, or to otherwise advance the intelligence mission. Authorized IC personnel who have discovered information collected or analysis produced that is of possible relevance to their assigned mission shall meet in part their responsibility to request such information by taking affirmative steps to request such information collected or analysis produced from the appropriate steward in accordance with Section F if the content of the information is not already available.

b. Stewards shall determine whether authorized IC personnel who have discovered information collected or analysis produced, that may be relevant to an assigned mission need, and who have requested such information, may receive the information in accordance with procedures in Section F.

5. *Subsequent Use of Information.* Authorized IC personnel shall be responsible for the proper handling and use of information received from a steward. Use of information collected or analysis produced shall be in accordance with Section D.6. and ICPG 501.3, *Subsequent Use of* Information.

6. All IC personnel shall carry out their responsibilities under this Directive, including the discovery, dissemination, retrieval, and use of information collected or analysis produced, consistent with applicable law and in a manner that protects fully the privacy rights and civil liberties of all U.S. persons, as required by the Constitution, Federal statutes, Executive Orders, Presidential Directives, court orders, and Attorney General approved guidelines, including those regarding the dissemination of U.S. person information. In addition, the responsibilities under this Directive shall be carried out consistent with the Guidelines to Implement Information Privacy Rights and Other Legal Protections in the Development and Use of the Information Sharing Environment.

7. To achieve the policy objectives in this Directive, the IC Information Sharing Executive (IC ISE) shall develop, in consultation with IC elements, integrated implementation plans that set forth required benchmarks each IC element head shall meet. Integrated implementation plans shall be subject to the approval of the DNI, after consultation with the Executive Committee (EXCOM).

a. These benchmarks shall serve as a minimum baseline and shall not be construed as fulfilling each IC element head's overall obligation to achieve the policy objectives set forth in this Directive in full and as quickly as possible.

b. At a minimum, stewards shall make disseminated analytic products discoverable by, and to the extent possible, available to authorized IC personnel by automated means as soon as possible, but no later than 1 June 2009.

8. Upon enactment of this Directive, IC elements shall ensure that new information technology (IT) systems or significant changes to existing IT systems provide the capability for discovery, dissemination, and retrieval of information collected or analysis produced through automated means. This requirement is not retroactive and shall be implemented in accordance with standards promulgated by the IC Chief Information Officer (IC CIO).

9. The Deputy Director of National Intelligence for Policy, Plans, and Requirements (DDNI/PPR), as the DNI's designee for policy, shall evaluate compliance with this policy as of 1 October 2009, and periodically thereafter, as determined by the DDNI/PPR or designee.Evaluation results shall be provided to the DNI and, at the DNI's discretion, to the EXCOM and others, as appropriate. An IC element that is unable to comply fully or is found to be in violation of this

policy shall report in writing to the DNI the reasons for failing to meet the objectives of this policy and the steps that will be taken to come into compliance.

E. DISCOVERY OF INFORMATION COLLECTED OR ANALYSIS PRODUCED:

1. *Collection Stewards and Analytic Production Stewards ("Stewards").*

a. IC element heads shall appoint one or more "collection steward(s)" for each type of collection activity the IC element is authorized to conduct, and shall appoint one or more "analytic production steward(s)" for all analytic activity it is authorized to conduct. Stewards shall be senior IC element officials.

b. Stewards shall make all information collected and all analysis produced by an IC element available for discovery by automated means by authorized IC personnel consistent with the requirements in Section D.6., including information collected through contracts, arrangements, agreements, or understandings. In some cases, this may mean that only standardized or limited metadata is made discoverable. In such cases, discovery requires that such information be described with sufficient detail to allow authorized IC personnel to make a reasonable determination regarding whether it is relevant to a mission need. In cases where content is not fully available, the steward shall provide instructions concerning how authorized IC personnel may request dissemination or retrieval of the content of the information collected or analysis produced.

c. Should an IC element head determine that discovery of information collected or analysis produced, or the confirmation of the mere existence of such information or analysis, will jeopardize the protection of sources, methods, or activities; compromise a criminal or national security investigation; or be inconsistent with the requirements in Section D.6., the IC element head may exempt such information or analysis from discovery unless and until such time as the DNI makes an exemption decision in accordance with ICPG 501.1.

d. IC elements that acquire or hold information provided by consent or by arrangement or agreement with federal departments; agencies; foreign nations or organizations; corporations; state, local, or tribal entities; or individuals outside the IC; shall seek to acquire or hold the information so as to authorize and provide discovery and dissemination or retrieval by authorized IC personnel, in a manner consistent with applicable Federal statutes, Executive Orders, Presidential Directives, court orders, and Attorney General approved guidelines.

2. *Authorized IC Personnel.*

a. Authorized IC personnel are U.S. persons employed by, assigned to, or acting on behalf of an IC element who, through the course of their duties and employment, have a mission need for information collected or analysis produced by an IC element, and who have an appropriate security clearance. Authorized IC personnel shall be identified by their IC element head.

b. Until such time as an attribute-based identity management capability that enables automated user authorization, discovery, retrieval, and auditing services for IC personnel is approved by the DNI and implemented throughout the IC, IC element heads shall identify authorized IC personnel within their IC element who have discovery rights to information collected and analysis produced by other IC elements.

c. The total number of authorized IC personnel approved by stewards to retrieve information collected or analysis produced may be subject to the IC's ability to adequately audit such activities. The IC ISE, in coordination with relevant stakeholders, shall include an auditing capability as part of an integrated implementation plan, pursuant to Section G.1.a. (1) and (2), and shall advise the DNI of constraints on retrieval, if any. The IC CIO shall promulgate IT system standards to govern audit practices.

F. DISSEMINATION OR RETRIEVAL OF INFORMATION COLLECTED OR ANALYSIS PRODUCED:

1. Dissemination or retrieval of information collected or analysis produced shall be made available to authorized IC personnel through automated means in accordance with Sections D.2. and D.6. Legacy information should be made available for dissemination or retrieval in accordance with Section D.6., to the greatest extent practicable.

2. Upon discovery of information collected or analysis produced that authorized IC personnel believe may fulfill an assigned mission need, authorized IC personnel shall request the information from the appropriate steward. Stewards may designate certain information as preapproved for automatic retrieval upon discovery. When seeking to obtain discovered information that the steward has not pre-approved for retrieval, authorized IC personnel shall provide the steward with information regarding their role, assigned mission need and when established, DNI approved identity attributes.

3. Stewards shall determine whether authorized IC personnel may retrieve or receive discovered information collected or analysis produced in accordance with this section.

4. Absent specific information to the contrary, stewards shall accept the information provided by authorized IC personnel, in accordance with Section F.2. above, as satisfying the "need-to-know" requirement. The steward may determine, based on specific, articulable facts, that the requestor's need for the information is significantly outweighed by the risks of providing it, using the risk management framework in Section F.5., or that providing the information would violate a statutory provision or a court order.

5. Stewards shall meet their responsibility to provide through a risk-managed approach when determining whether to permit the dissemination to or the retrieval by authorized IC personnel of the content of information collected or analysis produced. Stewards shall evaluate the risks associated with providing the content of information collected or analysis produced against the risks associated with denying the request and shall take special care to ensure determinations are made consistent with Section D.6.

a. Risks associated with providing information include, but are not limited to: risks to sources, methods, and activities; and risks of unauthorized or unintentional disclosure.

b. Risks associated with denying a request for information include, but are not limited to: risks to mission performance; and risks of incomplete or erroneous analytic judgments informing policy or other decisions.

6. In accordance with DNI guidelines, an IC element head may stipulate specific security and training requirements for authorized IC personnel to obtain the content of particularly sensitive discovered information. Such requirements shall be established as part of an integrated implementation plan developed and approved in accordance with Section D.7. and consistent with Section D.6.and IC policy. IC element heads may not stipulate specific security or training requirements that exceed those imposed on their authorized IC personnel.

7. Should a steward deny the request, or partially deny the request (such as providing "minimized" content), authorized IC personnel who are not satisfied with the steward's determination may initiate a formal review through his or her Sensitive Review Board (SRB) in accordance with ICPG 501.2, *Sensitive Review Board and Information Sharing Dispute Resolution Process.*

a. Stewards shall provide written justification for denial or partial denial of information to the requestor and appropriate SRBs, in accordance with ICPG 501.2.

b. The requestor's SRB and the steward's SRB shall attempt to resolve the dispute under the direction of the IC element heads. Disputes that cannot be resolved between SRBs shall be forwarded jointly by the affected SRBs to the DNI.

c. The DNI may resolve any risk management dispute that cannot be resolved at a lower level.

d. Disputes involving Attorney General approved guidelines, or court-ordered or statutory restrictions on the dissemination of information, such as dissemination of U.S. person information collected under the Foreign Intelligence Surveillance Act, shall be referred to the Attorney General if the dispute cannot be resolved by the DNI and affected IC element heads, in consultation with their General Counsels.

G. ROLES AND RESPONSIBILITIES:

1. The Office of the Director of National Intelligence (ODNI).

a. The IC ISE is the DNI's senior accountable official for the oversight and financial and program management of IC information integration efforts and shall:

(1) Develop a series of IC integrated implementation plans, in consultation with IC elements, and subject to DNI approval, that ensure all aspects of information sharing are addressed by the appropriate ODNI component or IC element, including but not limited to: IT architecture and standards; policies; human resource and cultural factors; business processes; information assurance; privacy; counterintelligence; risk management and security;

(2) Develop, in consultation with IC elements, a fully resourced, near-term, integrated implementation plan to achieve the policy objective in Section D.7.b.;

(3) Monitor implementation; identify, anticipate, and mitigate obstacles to implementation; and take appropriate steps to ensure any implementation plan developed pursuant to Section G.2.c. is appropriately resourced;

(4) Provide periodic progress reports to the DNI and the EXCOM;

(5) Provide subject matter expertise, as appropriate, to inform the development of IC policies in accordance with ICD 101, *IC Policy System*; ICPG 101.1, *IC Directives and Policy Guidance*; ICPG 101.2, *IC Standards*; and any other policy that may be promulgated pursuant to ICD 101;

(6) Implement, as appropriate, the dispute resolution process in accordance with ICPG 501.2;

(7) Assist the DDNI/PPR, as requested, in monitoring compliance and evaluating the effectiveness of this policy; and

(8) Create such committees, boards, or councils as the IC ISE deems necessary to carry out the responsibilities described herein.

b. The Chancellor of the National Intelligence University (NIU) shall, in coordination with IC elements, develop community-level information sharing training to promote understanding and individual responsibilities with respect to this Directive.

c. The IC CIO shall:

(1) Develop the IT architecture that supports this Directive;

(2) Develop and promulgate standards required to implement this Directive in accordance with ICPG 101.2, to include: documented procedures for the review and analysis of audit data to support security, counterintelligence, and intelligence oversight requirements; standards to allow information to be discoverable; and standards to define new or significant changes to existing IT systems in Section D.8.; and

(3) Maintain the list of designated stewards and authorized IC personnel.

d. The DDNI/PPR shall support policy requirements for implementation plans and shall evaluate and monitor compliance with this policy.

e. The IC Chief Human Capital Officer shall work with the Chancellor of the NIU to ensure information sharing education and training is mandatory for IC personnel and is linked to implementation of ICD 651, *Performance Management System Requirements for the IC Civilian Workforce*, and ICD 656, *Performance Management System Requirements for IC Senior Civilian* Officers.

f. The Deputy Director of National Intelligence for Collection and the Deputy Director of National Intelligence for Analysis shall work with stewards to develop a concept of operations to implement this Directive to inform the IT architecture and integrated implementation plans; and

g. The National Counterintelligence Executive shall provide a counterintelligence mission perspective to inform the IT architecture and any integrated implementation plans.

h. The Civil Liberties Protection Officer shall support IC elements in carrying out their responsibilities to implement this Directive in compliance with applicable requirements to protect privacy and civil liberties.

2. IC Element Heads shall:

a. Designate individuals in their IC element who are "authorized IC personnel." Until such time as an attribute-based identity management capability exists for the IC, provide the list of positions and names to the IC CIO;

b. Name collection steward(s) and analytic production steward(s), and provide the list of positions and names to the IC CIO;

c. Produce a strategy to implement this policy and provide it to the IC ISE, including a specific, appropriately resourced plan to meet the objectives of this Directive;

d. Seek a DNI exemption from discovery for information collected or analysis produced, in accordance with the procedures in ICPG 501.1, when appropriate;

e. Appoint appropriate personnel from their element to SRBs in accordance with Section G.3.;

f. Ensure that new information systems or significant enhancements to information systems comply with Section D.8. of this Directive;

g. Provide assistance, as requested, to the DDNI/PPR in evaluating implementation of this policy;

h. Incorporate mandatory education to collectors, analysts, and others who collect, process, retain, or use information regarding the importance of information sharing in accordance with curriculum developed by the Chancellor of the NIU. Initial training of all relevant IC personnel shall be accomplished within six months after the curriculum is developed;

i. Negotiate arrangements, agreements, understandings, or commercial contracts that shall, to the greatest extent possible, seek to obtain terms that permit discovery, and dissemination or retrieval by authorized IC personnel; and

j. Provide authorized IC personnel in all IC elements specific training recommended by an IC element that is part of an integrated implementation plan, in accordance with F.6.

3. SRBs shall:

a. In accordance with implementation procedures set forth in ICPG 501.2, serve as their respective IC element head's designated body to resolve dissemination and retrieval disputes; and take proactive measures to help ensure information is made available to authorized IC personnel, as appropriate;

b. Be established within the Office of the Director of National Intelligence (ODNI), the Central Intelligence Agency, the National Security Agency, the Defense Intelligence Agency (DIA), the National Geospatial-Intelligence Agency, and the Federal Bureau of Investigation, with limited membership.

(1) The DIA SRB shall include at least one member from the intelligence and counterintelligence elements of the Army, the Navy, the Air Force, and the Marine Corps, and represent the interests of the services;

(2) The ODNI SRB shall include a member from the National Reconnaissance Office; the Office of National Security Intelligence of the Drug Enforcement Administration; the Office of Intelligence and Counterintelligence of the Department of Energy; the Bureau of Intelligence and Research of the Department of State; the Office of Intelligence and Analysis of the Department of the Treasury; the Office of Intelligence and Analysis of the Department of Homeland Security; the intelligence and counterintelligence elements of the Coast Guard; and represent the interests of these elements, as well as those of the ODNI.

c. Consist of members cleared for access to all information, as determined by the DNI in consultation with IC element heads and in accordance with implementation procedures set forth in ICPG 501.2.

4. Stewards shall:

a. Make information collected and analysis produced available for discovery in accordance with this Directive; and

b. Make decisions with respect to information discovered and requested by authorized IC personnel in accordance with this Directive and pursue risk mitigation strategies to the greatest extent possible.

H. EFFECTIVE DATE: This ICD becomes effective on the date of signature.

J.M. McConnell
Director of National Intelligence Date
January 21, 2009

APPENDIX A - DEFINITIONS ICD 501, DISCOVERY AND DISSEMINATION OR RETRIEVAL OF INFORMATION WITHIN THE INTELLIGENCE COMMUNITY

For the purposes of this Directive and all subordinate Policies and Standards, the terms below shall have the following meanings:

1. *Analysis Produced*: A disseminated or undisseminated product, assessment, study, estimate, compilation, or other report created and reviewed or validated by an IC element. It also includes databases comprised of information that may inform analysis. Databases become discoverable as part of a phased implementation plan in accordance with Section D.7.

2. *Authorized IC Personnel*: A U.S. person employed by, assigned to, or acting on behalf of an IC element who, through the course of their duties and employment, has a mission need and an appropriate security clearance. Authorized IC personnel shall be identified by their IC element head and shall have discovery rights to information collected and analysis produced by all elements of the IC. The term may include contractor personnel.

3. *Collected*: Any information, both in its final form and in the form when initially gathered, acquired, held, or obtained by an IC element that is potentially relevant to a mission need of any IC element. This includes information as it is obtained directly from its source, regardless of whether the information has been reviewed or processed.

4. *Discovery*: The act of obtaining knowledge of the existence, but not necessarily the content, of information collected or analysis produced by any IC element. Discovery, as it is applicable under this Directive, is not defined or intended to be interpreted as discovery under the Federal Rules of Civil Procedure, Federal Rules of Criminal Procedure, or other individual state discovery rules regarding non-privileged matter that is relevant to any party's claim or defense.

5. *Dissemination*: The act of a steward providing information collected or analysis produced by an IC element to authorized IC personnel, either through the ordinary course of business or in response to a request following discovery—(information "pushed" to authorized IC personnel).

6. *Information*: Intelligence and intelligence-related information. It does not include information pertaining to the internal administration or management of IC elements, such as IC personnel, medical, administrative, budget or security records.

7. *Intelligence*: As defined in EO 12333, as amended, includes foreign intelligence and counterintelligence.

8. *Mission Need*: A requirement for access to specific information to perform or assist in a lawful and authorized governmental function. Mission needs are determined by the mission and functions of an IC element or the roles and responsibilities of particular IC personnel in the course of their official duties.

9. *Retrieval:* The act of authorized IC personnel obtaining information collected or analysis produced by any IC element in response to a request following discovery through means other than dissemination.

10. *Steward (includes both Collection Steward and Analytic Production Steward):*

a. *Collection Steward*: An appropriately cleared employee of an IC element, who is a senior official, designated by the head of that IC element to represent a collection activity that the IC element is authorized by law or executive order to conduct, and to make determinations regarding the dissemination to or the retrieval by authorized IC personnel of information collected by that activity.

b. *Analytic Production Steward*: An appropriately cleared employee of an IC element, who is a senior official, designated by the head of that IC element to represent the analytic activity that the IC element is authorized by law or executive order to conduct, and to make determinations regarding the dissemination to or the retrieval by authorized IC personnel of analysis produced by that activity.

APPENDIX B – ACRONYM LIST
ICD 501, DISCOVERY AND DISSEMINATION OR RETRIEVAL OF INFORMATION
WITHIN THE INTELLIGENCE COMMUNITY

CIO	Chief Information Officer
DCID	Director of Central Intelligence Directive
DDNI/PPR	Deputy Director of National Intelligence for Policy, Plans, and Requirements
DIA	Defense Intelligence Agency
DNI	Director of National Intelligence
EO	Executive Order
EXCOM	Executive Committee
IC	Intelligence Community
ICD	Intelligence Community Directive
IC ISE	Intelligence Community Information Sharing Executive
ICPG	Intelligence Community Policy Guidance
ICPM	Intelligence Community Policy Memorandum
IT	Information Technology
NIU	National Intelligence University
ODNI	Office of the Director of National Intelligence
RELIDO	Releasable by Information Disclosure Official
SRB	Sensitive Review Board
TS/SCI	TOP SECRET/Sensitive Compartmented Information

Intelligence Community Policy Guidance 501.1
Exemption of Information From Discovery

(May 26, 2009)

A. AUTHORITY: The National Security Act of 1947, as amended; Executive Order 12333, as amended; and other applicable provisions of law.

B. PURPOSE: This Intelligence Community Policy Guidance (ICPG) sets forth the implementing procedures for exemptions from discovery for information collected or analysis produced, as called for in Sections E. 1.c and G.2.d of Intelligence Community Directive (ICD) 501, Discovery and Dissemination or Retrieval of Information within the Intelligence Community.

C. APPLICABILITY

1. This guidance applies to the Intelligence Community (IC), as defined by the National Security Act of 1947, as amended; and such other elements of any other department or agency as may be designated by the President, or designated jointly by the Director of National Intelligence (DNI) and the head of the department or agency concerned, as an element of the IC.

2. This ICPG does not apply to purely law enforcement information. When law enforcement information also contains intelligence or intelligence-related information, this ICPG shall apply to the intelligence or intelligence-related information.

D. POLICY

1. In accordance with ICD 501, information may be exempt from discovery if it is determined that discovery, or the confirmation of the mere existence of such information, will jeopardize the protection of sources, methods, or activities; compromise a criminal or national security investigation; or be inconsistent with the requirements of Section D.6 of ICD 501. The term "information" in this ICPG constitutes "information collected or analysis produced" as used in ICD 501.

2. The definitions in Appendix A of ICD 501 apply to this ICPG.

E. PROCESS

1. Exemptions

a. IC element heads shall submit recommendations to the DNI for the exemption of information from discovery in accordance with timelines established in IC integrated implementation plans. These timelines shall specify that exemption recommendations be submitted no later than 60 days prior to the information in question being made available for discovery, as called for in an IC integrated implementation plan. In recommending an exemption, IC element heads shall provide information in accordance with Section E.l.c.(1-6) of this ICPG.

b. Should an IC element head deem it necessary to exempt information from discovery in advance of a DNI exemption decision, the IC element head shall provide information in accordance with Section E.l.c.(1-6) of this ICPG as soon as possible but no later than 10 business days after the IC element head's action to exempt the information. Information an IC element head has exempted from discovery shall not be discoverable unless and until the DNI makes an exemption decision.

c. Exemptions shall:

(1) Be addressed to the DNI in the form of Executive Correspondence;

(2) Specifically identify and fully describe the information being exempted, to include scope and volume. Exemptions may be submitted for categories of information with common attributes or components, when appropriate;

(3) Include an assessment of the risks to sources, methods, or activities, as well as an assessment of the risks of unauthorized or unintentional disclosure;

(4) Include an assessment of the risks associated with exempting the information from discovery, to include risks to mission performance and risks of incomplete or erroneous analytic judgments informing national security decisions;

(5) Specify the time period over which the exemption should endure; and

(6) Provide any additional information or potential implications the IC element head believes the DNI should consider.

d. Sensitive Review Boards (SRB) shall consist of members cleared for access to all information, as determined by the DNI in consultation with IC element heads. For efficiency, an IC element head may include, as part of a recommendation to exempt information from discovery by authorized IC personnel, a recommendation to restrict SRB member access in accordance with Section F.4 of ICPG 501.2, Sensitive Review Board and Information Sharing Dispute Resolution Process.

2. DNI Decision

a. The DNI may approve an exemption in whole or in part, or deny the exemption, and will provide a written copy of his decision to the IC element head who recommended the exemption, as well as inform the SRBs, as appropriate.

b. Should the DNI deny an exemption in whole or in part, the relevant IC element head shall make the subject information discoverable immediately but no later than five business days after the relevant IC element head is notified of the DNI's decision, or in accordance with an approved IC integrated implementation plan, whichever is later.

3. Information Handling

a. IC element heads shall ensure that all information that is exempted from discovery is marked immediately with control markings unique for discovery exemptions, in accordance with the Controlled Access Program Coordination Office's (CAPCO) Authorized Classification and Control Markings Register.

b. CAPCO shall establish control markings for exempted information in accordance with the IC integrated implementation plans.

c. Information exempted from discovery shall adhere to IC metadata standards promulgated by the IC Chief Information Officer.

4. The Senior Review Group of the Office of the Director of National Intelligence shall:

a. Be chaired by the IC Information Sharing Executive and report to the DNI for matters pertaining to the exemption of information from discovery pursuant to this Guidance.

b. Maintain records of all official communications between the DNI and an IC element head as specified in Section E, the disposition of exemptions, and the results of annual reviews; and

c. Review by 1 June annually all exemptions.

F. EFFECTIVE DATE: This Guidance is effective on the date of signature.

May 26, 2009
Deputy Director of National Intelligence for Policy, Plans, and Requirements

Intelligence Community Policy Guidance 501.2
Sensitive Review Board and Information Sharing Dispute Resolution Process

(May 26, 2009)

A. AUTHORITY: The National Security Act of 1947, as amended; Executive Order 12333, as amended; and other applicable provisions of law.

B. PURPOSE

1. This Intelligence Community Policy Guidance (ICPG):

a. Further defines the process called for in Intelligence Community Directive (ICD) 501, Discovery and Dissemination or Retrieval of Information Within the Intelligence Community, to resolve disputes between authorized Intelligence Community (IC) personnel and stewards regarding the dissemination or retrieval of information discovered.

b. Sets forth the implementing procedures for access to information by Sensitive Review Board (SRB) members as required by Section G.3.c of ICD 501; and

c. Delineates specific roles and responsibilities of the Office of the Director of National Intelligence (ODNI), IC element heads, and SRBs.

C. APPLICABILITY

1. This guidance applies to the IC, as defined by the National Security Act of 1947, as amended; and such other elements of any other department or agency that may be designated by the President, or designated jointly by the Director of National Intelligence (DNI) and the head of the department or agency concerned, as an element of the IC.

2. This ICPG does not apply to purely law enforcement information. When law enforcement information also contains intelligence or intelligence-related information, this ICPG shall apply to the intelligence or intelligence-related information.

D. POLICY

1. Authorized IC personnel have a responsibility to request discovered information that has the potential to contribute to their assigned mission need. Discovery alone does not constitute a request for the content of the information. Stewards shall determine whether authorized IC personnel may receive the information, and shall make as much information as possible available for automated retrieval upon discovery. If a dispute arises regarding a request for information, authorized IC personnel, stewards, and their respective SRBs shall use the process in Section E of this ICPG to resolve the disputes.

2. This Guidance applies to authorized IC personnel seeking the content of information discovered with respect to information made discoverable as a result of an IC integrated implementation plan in accordance with Sections D.7 and G.l.a.(1) of ICD 501. This Guidance is in addition to and does not replace an IC employee's ability to seek information under other policies and procedures.

3. SRBs are comprised of members cleared for access to all information in accordance with Section F of this ICPG to facilitate their roles and responsibilities to resolve dissemination or retrieval disputes; and to take proactive measures to help ensure information is made available to authorized IC personnel, as appropriate.

4. An exemption of information from discovery made in accordance with ICPG 501.1, Exemption of Information from Discovery, does not apply to SRB members' access to said information, unless otherwise determined by the DNI. SRB members may, on behalf of specific personnel in their element, seek information regardless of whether the information has been made discoverable in accordance with an integrated implementation plan, and shall use the dispute resolution process in Section E of this ICPG, should a steward deny an SRB member's request.

5. The definitions in Appendix A of ICD 501 apply to this ICPG. The term "information" in this ICPG constitutes "information collected or analysis produced" as used in ICD 501.

E. INFORMATION SHARING DISPUTE RESOLUTION PROCESS

1. The process for resolving disputes regarding the dissemination or retrieval of IC information discovered and requested by authorized IC personnel shall include the following steps:

a. Authorized IC personnel ("requestor") shall make a written request to the steward to obtain the content of discovered information that has the potential to contribute to their mission need if the steward has not made the information available. The requestor shall provide the steward with information regarding their role, assigned mission need. and, when established, DN I approved identity attributes. Stewards shall accept the information provided by the requestor as satisfying the "need-to-know" requirement, absent specific information to the contrary. The requestor shall simultaneously provide a copy of the request to the steward, the requestor's SRB, and the steward's SRB.

b. In reviewing requests for the content of information discovered by authorized IC personnel, stewards shall apply the risk management principles of Section F.5 of ICD 501. In denying or partially denying requests, stewards shall provide written justification delineating specific, articulable facts that the requestor's mission need for the information is significantly outweighed by the risk of providing the information to the requestor, or that providing the information would violate Attorney General approved guidelines or court ordered or statutory restrictions in accordance with Section F.7.d of ICD 501.

c. The steward shall provide the original request and a written explanation of the rationale for a decision to deny or partially deny a request to the requestor's SRB and the steward's SRB within 10 business days of receiving the request. The requestor's SRB shall promptly notify the requestor of the steward's decision and, as appropriate, the rationale.

d. The requestor's SRB shall consult with the requester within five business days of receipt of the steward's justification for denial or partial denial of a request, and determine whether to dispute the steward's decision. The requestor's SRS shall provide written notice to the steward's SRB of the intent to dispute the steward's decision.

e. Under the direction of the relevant IC element heads, the requestor's SRB and the steward's SRB shall attempt to resolve the dispute by jointly and promptly reviewing the steward's decision to deny the request. SRBs are encouraged to consider multiple options for dispute resolution if providing the full content is not possible, such as providing partial, sanitized, or minimized content. SRBs may contact the requestor and steward for additional information, if needed. Within seven business days after the requestor's SRB initiates a dispute, the respective SRBs shall notify the affected requestor and steward of the outcome of the dispute, along with justification for the decision and disposition of the case.

f. If a dispute cannot be resolved between SRBs within seven business days, the dispute shall be forwarded jointly by the SRBs to the DNI within three business days. The SRBs involved in the dispute must each provide, as applicable, all necessary information to the DNI, through the ODNI Senior Review Group (SRG), including:

(1) Justifications for the request;

(2) Specific, articulable facts for the denial based on risk management principles in Section F.5 of ICD 501;

(3) Reasons for the dispute;

(4) Content of the information discovered and requested: and

(5) Any additional details or potential implications that the SRBs believe the DN I should consider.

g. The SRG shall ensure the information regarding the dispute is complete, and shall forward the dispute to the DNI within 15 business days of receipt.

h. The DNI will issue a written decision resolving the dispute. The SRG shall promptly convey the DNI's decision to the relevant SRBs, and oversee implementation of the decision.

2. At any time, the requestor's SRB may withdraw a dispute through written notification to the steward's SRB and the SRG, as applicable.

3. A requestor or requestor's SRB may request expedited review of the dispute based upon exigent circumstances, including the prevention of loss of life or serious bodily injury, significant threats to national security. informing time-critical intelligence collection or policy requirements, or significant input to a case under investigation or litigation. When an expedited request is submitted, SRBs or the DNI, as the case may be, shall make every effort to resolve the dispute as soon as possible.

4. For disputes involving Attorney General approved guidelines. or court-ordered or statutory restrictions on the dissemination of information, such as dissemination of U.S. persons information collected under the Foreign Intelligence

Surveillance Act, SRBs shall consult with their respective General Counsel. In such cases, the SRBs shall have an additional 10 business days to obtain and integrate the response provided by their General Counsels. The DNI shall refer a dispute to the Attorney General if it cannot be resolved by the DNI and affected IC element heads, in consultation with their General Counsels.

5. SRB members are responsible for ensuring appropriate personnel within their IC element obtain information that is relevant to their assigned mission need, which may include information exempted by the DNI from discovery by authorized IC personnel. SRB members' access is not limited to infounation made discoverable as a result of an IC integrated implementation plan. SRB members may submit a request for information on behalf of specific personnel in their IC element to the appropriate steward for consideration, using procedures set forth in Section E.1 of this ICPG. If the SRB member is not satisfied with the steward's decision on the request, the SRB member and the steward's SRB shall use the dispute resolution procedures in Section E.1 of this ICPG to resolve the dispute.

F. SRB MEMBER ACCESS

1. SRB members shall be cleared for access to all information in accordance with instructions issued by the SRG. Appropriate security personnel in each IC element shall clear SRB members for access in accordance with SRG instructions within 15 business days of the SRB member's appointment to the position, and to any new controlled access program within 15 business days of establishment of the program, unless otherwise restricted by the DNI in accordance with this Section.

2. SRB member access to information is based on their assigned roles and responsibilities as SRB members. The SRG shall maintain a record of each IC element's SRB members, and their specific accesses. When an SRB member's assignment to an SRB ends, each IC element's SRB Chair is responsible for notifying the SRG to ensure unifoiin debriefing in accordance with applicable security procedures.

3. The DNI, in consultation with affected IC element heads, may restrict accesses of SRB members. The DNI may approve a restriction in whole, approve a restriction with conditions, or deny a restriction.

4. IC element heads may recommend the DNI restrict SRB member access to information collected or analysis produced by their element.

a. Such recommendations shall:

(1) Be submitted to the DNI in the form of Executive Correspondence;

(2) Include a description of the access to be restricted;

(3) Provide a compelling justification, including an analysis of whether restricting access detracts from the objectives of the SRB in Section D.3 of this ICPG;

(4) Identify SRB member(s) subject to the recommended access restriction; and

(5) Include any additional details or potential implications the IC element head believes the DNI should consider.

b. As stated in Section E.l.d of ICPG 501.1, an IC element head may include, as part of a recommendation to exempt information from discovery by authorized IC personnel, a recommendation to restrict SRB member access to said information. in accordance with Section F.4.a.(1-5) of this ICPG.

c. The DNI will review the recommendation within 15 business days of receipt and will provide a written copy of his decision to the IC element head who submitted the recommendation.

G. ROLES AND RESPONSIBILITIES

1. Office of the Director of National Intelligence

a. The DNI will:

(1) Resolve disputes regarding dissemination or retrieval of information within the IC that cannot be resolved at a lower level, except that disputes described in Section E.4 of this ICPG shall be referred for resolution to the Attorney General, if necessary; and

(2) Make decisions regarding SRB member access restrictions.

b. The SRG shall:

(1) Be chaired by the IC Information Sharing Executive and report to the DNI for matters pertaining to information sharing dispute resolution and SRB member access pursuant to this Guidance;

(2) Maintain records of: all official communications between the DNI and IC element heads, and between the DNI and SRBs; disposition of disputes referred to the DNI for resolution; the names of SRB members and their specific accesses: and the disposition of recommendations to the DNI to restrict SRB member access to information;

(3) Review by 1 July annually SRB member access restrictions; and

(4) Evaluate, in collaboration with IC element SRBs, the effectiveness of the dispute resolution process established by this ICPG, including a review to identify best practices.

2. IC Element Heads shall:

a. Appoint a limited number of SRB members who:

(1) Are a General Schedule 15 or Band 5 officer. or higher: and are cleared for access to information in accordance with Section F of this ICPG: and

(2) Possess, either individually or collectively, a comprehensive understanding of their IC element's collection and analysis missions, as well as knowledge of collection and analysis missions of other IC elements.

b. Provide their SRB member names to the SRG, and keep their SRB membership roster current.

c. Ensure their respective SRB members are adequately informed, supported, and trained to perform their duties.

d. Ensure their SRB or their SRB member addresses disputes regarding dissemination or retrieval of information, and takes proactive measures to help ensure information is made available to appropriate authorized IC personnel.

e. Ensure any internal regulations established by their element for resolving disputes regarding dissemination or retrieval of information are consistent with the intent and objectives of ICD 501, this ICPG, and other policies as appropriate.

3. Sensitive Review Boards shall:

a. Attempt to resolve disputes regarding dissemination or retrieval of information with other SRBs in accordance with Section E of this ICPG;

b. Take proactive measures to help ensure information is made available to appropriate authorized IC personnel:

c. Assist the SRG in evaluating the effectiveness of the dispute resolution process in Section E of this ICPG;

d. Respond to SRG requests for information regarding dissemination or retrieval of information;

e. Provide quarterly reports as requested by the SRG, including information about disputes regarding dissemination or retrieval of information; and proactive actions taken by the SRB to ensure information is made available to appropriate authorized IC personnel. Reports should contain all relevant data, including the quantity, disposition. and timelines of all requests and disputes; and

f. Maintain records, including records of all requests raised by authorized IC personnel or the SRBs for dissemination or retrieval of information and the disposition thereof.

H. EFFECTIVE DATE: This Guidance is effective on the date of signature.

May 26, 2009
Deputy Director of National Intelligence for Policy, Plans, and Requirements

Intelligence Community Policy Guidance 501.3
Subsequent Use of Information

(May 20, 2010)

A. AUTHORITY: The National Security Act of 1947, as amended; Executive Order 12333, as amended; Executive Order 13526; and other applicable provisions of law.

B. PURPOSE: This Guidance addresses subsequent use, the proper handling and use of information collected or analysis produced that is received by authorized Intelligence Community personnel (AICP) to further a mission need ("received information"), pursuant to the provisions of Intelligence Community Directive (ICD) 501, Discovery and Dissemination or Retrieval of Information within the Intelligence Community. The definitions in Appendix A of ICD 501 apply to this Guidance.

C. APPLICABILITY

1. This Guidance applies to the Intelligence Community (IC), as defined by the National Security Act of 1947, as amended; and such other elements of any other department or agency as may be designated by the President, or designated jointly by the Director of National Intelligence and the head of the department or agency concerned, as an element of the IC.

2. This Guidance does not apply to purely law enforcement information. When law enforcement information also contains intelligence or intelligence-related information, this Guidance shall apply to the intelligence or intelligence-related information.

3. All IC personnel shall carry out their responsibilities under this Guidance consistent with applicable law and in a manner that protects fully the privacy rights and civil liberties of all U.S. persons, as required by the Constitution, Federal statutes, Executive Orders, Presidential Directives, court orders, and Attorney General approved guidelines, including those regarding the dissemination of U.S. person information.

D. POLICY

1. Received information may only be used in accordance with the mission need of the receiving AICP. All received information shall be handled in accordance with existing policy and procedures in the IC, including but not limited to bilateral agreements between IC elements, classification and control markings, retention, handling, destruction, and disclosure and release.

2. In determining possible uses of received information, AICPs are responsible for ascertaining to the best of their ability aspects of the information, includ-

ing its quality and reliability, that would inform decisions on subsequent use by the receiving IC element. AICPs are encouraged to communicate with the originating IC steward in this regard. Similarly, IC stewards in the IC element that originated the information are responsible for fully and substantially assisting AICPs who communicate with them.

3. An IC element must determine if and how to use received information in its analytic products or for other purposes pursuant to its mission need. The receiving IC element shall bear the risks associated with the use of received information.

4. When using received information, AICPs shall cite sufficient details about the information to enable identification of the original information, and shall, to the extent possible, source the information in accordance with ICD 206, Sourcing Requirements for Disseminated Analytic Products.

E. EFFECTIVE DATE: This Guidance becomes effective on the date of signature.

May 20, 2010
Deputy Director of National Intelligence for Policy, Plans, and Requirements

INTELLIGENCE OVERSIGHT REPORTING CRITERIA

MEMORANDUM FOR THE SECRETARY OF STATE
THE SECRETARY OF THE TREASURY
THE SECRETARY OF DEFENSE
THE ATTORNEY GENERAL
THE SECRETARY OF ENERGY
THE SECRETARY OF HOMELAND SECURITY
DIRECTOR, CENTRAL INTELLIGENCE AGENCY

SUBJECT: Intelligence Oversight Reporting Criteria

Executive Order (EO) 13462 tasks the Intelligence Oversight Board (IOB) with issuing criteria on the thresholds for reporting intelligence oversight matters to the IOB and to the Director of National Intelligence (DNI). It also tasks the DNI with issuing instructions relating to the format and scheduling of such reporting. The attached guidance provides those criteria and instructions.

EO 13462 and these criteria acknowledge the establishment of the DNI and seek to infuse a fresh awareness of the importance of intelligence oversight reporting. The criteria also provide guidance on what information the President and the DNI need to execute their respective duties to see that the laws are faithfully executed and that intelligence activities comply with the Constitution and laws of the United States.

To implement EO 13462, the DNI will execute day-to-day intelligence oversight responsibilities. Among other things, this will include reviewing the guidelines by which Intelligence Community (IC) components report intelligence activities to ensure they are consistent with Part I.7(d) of EO 12333 and with EO 13462, reviewing reports submitted to the IOB, and providing the IOB with a quarterly assessment of the content, quality, and timeliness of reporting by the IC.

The IOB continues to act as an independent entity appointed by the President to ensure that the Constitution and laws of the United States are respected and to report to the President in accordance with the functions assigned to the IOB by EO 13462. The IOB will audit, review, and assess the adequacy of the respective processes by which the DNI performs his oversight and review functions and the IC components perform their reporting functions under EO 13461. As necessary, the IOB may conduct its own investigations of intelligence activities. The IOB also will continue to receive and review reports of all matters that may be unlawful or contrary to executive order or presidential directive and to report to the President and the Attorney General concerning those matters.

In addition, a key element of intelligence oversight is the explicit direction that "significant or highly sensitive matters" must be reported immediately. "Significant or highly sensitive matters" are intelligence activities that may or may not be unlawful or contrary to executive order or presidential directive, that could impugn the reputation or integrity of the IC, or that could otherwise call into question the propriety of U.S. intelligence activities. These types of matters, initially articulated by Assistant to the President for National Security Affairs Stephen Hadley in his memorandum of April 17, 2007, are also captured in the accompanying criteria for reporting.

As a reminder, section 8(b)(ii) of EO 13462 provides that the heads of departments with organizations in the IC shall designate offices within their respective organizations that shall submit to the IOB the reports required by executive order and inform the IOB and the DNI of such designations.

Each component of the IC is responsible for reviewing its internal processes, guidelines, and training for reporting intelligence oversight matters to the IOB and DNI and updating them in accordance with EO 13462 and the criteria and instructions set forth in this memorandum. Please provide the IOB and the DNI with a progress report on your review by July 30, 2008.

J. M. McConnell
Director of National Intelligence

Stephen Friedman
Chairman, Intelligence Oversight Board

Attachment
Tab A Reporting Criteria

CRITERIA ON THRESHOLDS FOR REPORTING INTELLIGENCE OVERSIGHT MATTERS AND INSTRUCTIONS RELATING TO FORMATTING AND SCHEDULING

Intelligence oversight reporting serves as an early warning of intelligence activities of which the President should be informed, through either his Intelligence Oversight Board (IOB) or the Director of National Intelligence (DNI), or both, and provides a means by which the Executive Branch may timely identify and correct any deficiencies in the conduct of its intelligence activities. The following criteria on thresholds for reporting intelligence oversight matters to the Intelligence Oversight Board, and instructions on formatting and scheduling of reports, are issued under the authority of Executive Order 13462.

I. Criteria on Thresholds for Reporting. The heads of departments with organizations in the Intelligence Community (IC), or the beads of such organizations, or their designees, shall:

A. Report to the IOB, with copies to the DNI, any intelligence activity with respect to which there is reason to believe may be unlawful or contrary to executive order (EO) or presidential directive (PD). The following guidance applies to determining whether a particular matter should he reported:

1. "Intelligence activities" are defined in Part 34(e) of BC) 12333 and, for purposes of these criteria, include, but are not limited to, the acquisition, collection, retention, analysis, and dissemination of intelligence information,
2. Intelligence activities are reportable if a reasonable person would believe they may he unlawful or contrary to EO or PD without waiting for substantiation, investigation, formal adjudication, or resolution of the issue of whether a particular matter is unlawful or contrary to EO or PD.
3. Intelligence activities to be reported under EOs 13462 and 12333 are not limited to those that concern "United States persons," as defined in Part 3.4(i) of EO 12333 or in any successor EO.
4. "Executive order or presidential directive" means, for purposes of implementing these criteria, a document signed by the President of the United States that has the force of law for the Executive Branch or constitutes the exercise by the President of his Executive authority. Reports may include violations of procedures and guidelines that heads of departments or IC components have established to implement EO 12333, or a successor order, provided, however, that such matters are of potential presidential interest or deemed appropriate for the IOB's review, e.g., because they involve the apparent violation of substantive rights of individuals,
5. Reportable events include the initiation of, and significant developments in, investigations or other inquiries relating to the legality or propriety of intelligence activities.

6. Initial reports made on the basis of incomplete or inaccurate reporting are to be updated as additional information becomes available. Subsequent or updated reports should be identified in such a manner that they can be accurately related to the relevant initial reports.

7. Intelligence activities are reportable to the IOB if such activities are required to be reported or have been reported to the Attorney General as required by law or other directive, including the Memorandum of Understanding on Reporting of Information Concerning Federal Crimes (1995),

8. Any intelligence activity that is to be reported to any congressional committee or member of Congress because it is or may be unlawful or contrary to executive order or otherwise "significant or highly sensitive" (see paragraph B, below) shall also be reported to the IOB and DNI generally before such a congressional report is made, Any report concerning intelligence activities that is submitted to any committee or member of Congress shall also be submitted to the IOB and DNI if the commencement of the investigation or other inquiry regarding such activities was also reportable under these criteria.

B. Report to the DNI, and the IOB as appropriate, significant or highly sensitive matters, whether or not unlawful or contrary to EO or PD.

1. "Significant of highly sensitive matters" are developments or circumstances involving intelligence activities that could impugn the reputation or integrity of the IC, or otherwise call into question the propriety of intelligence activities.
2. Such matters might be manifested in or by:
   a. congressional inquiries or investigations;
   b. adverse media coverage;
   c. impact on foreign relations or foreign partners; or
   d. unauthorized disclosure of protected information.

II. Content of Reports. Intelligence oversight reports should include (to the extent practicable without compromising the timeliness of reporting) the following:

A. A narrative describing each intelligence activity in question.

B. Why the matter is being reported, i.e, it is:

1. a potential violation of law (cite the relevant law, if a judgment has been made);
2. potentially contrary to EO or PD (cite the relevant section or part of the EO or PD);
3. a potential violation of agency procedures implementing EO 12333 (cite the specific rule or procedure, if a judgment has been made);
4. "'significant' because. . ."; or
5. "'highly sensitive' because. . ."

C. An explanation and analysis of how or why the incident occurred.

D. An assessment of any impact of the incident on national security or international relations, as well as any mitigation efforts, including success and failures of such efforts,

E. Any remedial action the IC element has taken or is taking to prevent recurrence of the incident being reported.

F. An assessment of any impact the reported intelligence activity may have on civil liberties or protected privacy rights.

G. How the IC element concerned is addressing any information improperly acquired, handled, used, destroyed, etc., as a consequence of the matter being reported.

H. A summary of the gravity, frequency, trends, and patterns of matters reported for the quarter.

I. Any additional information that the reporting official considers relevant for purposes of fully and completely informing the IOB and the DNI on intelligence oversight matters.

III. Formatting of Reports. Reports may be formatted in accordance with departmental or agency policies, provided all the substantive information described above is included in each report.

IV. Schedule for Reporting.

A. Significant or highly sensitive matters must be reported immediately.

1. Significant of highly sensitive matters may be reported orally, if necessary, and followed up with a written report as soon as possible thereafter. The preference is for written reports.
2. Significant of highly sensitive matters that may be unlawful or contrary to EO or PD shall be reported to the DNI or IOB.
3. Significant of highly sensitive matters that are NOT unlawful or contrary to EO or PD shall be reported to the DNI.

B. Routine reports shall be submitted on a quarterly basis. The first report for the calendar years shall cover 1 January through 31 March, and so for each quarter of the year.

C. Quarterly reports are due the last day of the month following the end of the quarter. For example, a report for the first quarter of the calendar year is due 30 April.

D. All IC elements must submit reports at least quarterly, even if a component has not been made aware of any reportable matter during the reporting period.

Questions concerning the implementation of EO 13462, or intelligence oversight reporting in general, may be submitted to the IOB's General Counsel by calling 202-456-2352, or to the ODNI IOB Team by calling 703-482-6304 (ODNI/OIG) or 703-275-2523 (ODNI/OGC).

Detention Annex

FEDERAL STATUTES

National Defense Authorization Act of 2012

(Pub. L. 112-81, 125 Stat. 1298 (2011))

SEC. 1023. PROCEDURES FOR PERIODIC DETENTION REVIEW OF INDIVIDUALS DETAINED AT UNITED STATES NAVAL STATION, GUANTANAMO BAY, CUBA.

(a) PROCEDURES REQUIRED.—Not later than 180 days after the date of the enactment of this Act, the Secretary of Defense shall submit to the appropriate committees of Congress a report setting forth procedures for implementing the periodic review process required by Executive Order No. 13567 for individuals detained at United States Naval Station, Guantanamo Bay, Cuba, pursuant to the Authorization for Use of Military Force (Public Law 107–40; 50 U.S.C. 1541 note).

(b) COVERED MATTERS.—The procedures submitted under subsection (a) shall, at a minimum—

(1) clarify that the purpose of the periodic review process is not to determine the legality of any detainee's law of war detention, but to make discretionary determinations whether or not a detainee represents a continuing threat to the security of the United States;

(2) clarify that the Secretary of Defense is responsible for any final decision to release or transfer an individual detained in military custody at United States Naval Station, Guantanamo Bay, Cuba, pursuant to the Executive Order referred to in subsection (a), and that in making such a final decision, the Secretary shall consider the recommendation of a periodic review board or review committee established pursuant to such Executive Order, but shall not be bound by any such recommendation;

(3) clarify that the periodic review process applies to any individual who is detained as an unprivileged enemy belligerent at United States Naval Station, Guantanamo Bay, Cuba, at any time; and

(4) ensure that appropriate consideration is given to factors addressing the need for continued detention of the detainee, including—

(A) the likelihood the detainee will resume terrorist activity if transferred or released;

(B) the likelihood the detainee will reestablish ties with al-Qaeda, the Taliban, or associated forces that are engaged in hostilities against the United States or its coalition partners if transferred or released;

(C) the likelihood of family, tribal, or government rehabilitation or support for the detainee if transferred or released;

(D) the likelihood the detainee may be subject to trial by military commission; and

(E) any law enforcement interest in the detainee.

(c) APPROPRIATE COMMITTEES OF CONGRESS DEFINED.—In this section, the term "appropriate committees of Congress" means—

(1) the Committee on Armed Services and the Select Committee on Intelligence of the Senate; and

(2) the Committee on Armed Services and the Permanent Select Committee on Intelligence of the House of Representatives.

SEC. 1024. PROCEDURES FOR STATUS DETERMINATIONS.

(a) IN GENERAL.—Not later than 90 days after the date of the enactment of this Act, the Secretary of Defense shall submit to the appropriate committees of Congress a report setting forth the procedures for determining the status of persons detained pursuant to the Authorization for Use of Military Force (Public Law 107–40; 50 U.S.C. 1541 note) for purposes of section 1021.

(b) ELEMENTS OF PROCEDURES.—The procedures required by this section shall provide for the following in the case of any unprivileged enemy belligerent who will be held in long-term detention under the law of war pursuant to the Authorization for Use of Military Force:

(1) A military judge shall preside at proceedings for the determination of status of an unprivileged enemy belligerent.

(2) An unprivileged enemy belligerent may, at the election of the belligerent, be represented by military counsel at proceedings for the determination of status of the belligerent.

(c) APPLICABILITY.—The Secretary of Defense is not required to apply the procedures required by this section in the case of a person for whom habeas corpus review is available in a Federal court.

(d) REPORT ON MODIFICATION OF PROCEDURES.—The Secretary of Defense shall submit to the appropriate committees of Congress a report on any modification of the procedures submitted under this section. The report on any such modification shall be so submitted not later than 60 days before the date on which such modification goes into effect.

(e) APPROPRIATE COMMITTEES OF CONGRESS DEFINED.—In this section, the term "appropriate committees of Congress" means—

(1) the Committee on Armed Services and the Select Committee on Intelligence of the Senate; and

(2) the Committee on Armed Services and the Permanent Select Committee on Intelligence of the House of Representatives.

SEC. 1026. PROHIBITION ON USE OF FUNDS TO CONSTRUCT OR MODIFY FACILITIES IN THE UNITED STATES TO HOUSE DETAINEES TRANSFERRED FROM UNITED STATES NAVAL STATION, GUANTANAMO BAY, CUBA.

(a) IN GENERAL.—No amounts authorized to be appropriated or otherwise made available to the Department of Defense for fiscal year 2012 may be used to construct or modify any facility in the United States, its territories, or possessions to house any individual detained at Guantanamo for the purposes of detention or imprisonment in the custody or under the control of the Department of Defense unless authorized by Congress.

(b) EXCEPTION.—The prohibition in subsection (a) shall not apply to any modification of facilities at United States Naval Station, Guantanamo Bay, Cuba.

(c) INDIVIDUAL DETAINED AT GUANTANAMO DEFINED.—In this section, the term "individual detained at Guantanamo" has the meaning given that term in section 1028(e)(2).

(d) REPEAL OF SUPERSEDED AUTHORITY.—Section 1034 of the Ike Skelton National Defense Authorization Act for Fiscal Year 2011 (Public Law 111–383; 124 Stat. 4353) is amended by striking subsections (a), (b), and (c).

SEC. 1027. PROHIBITION ON THE USE OF FUNDS FOR THE TRANSFER OR RELEASE OF INDIVIDUALS DETAINED AT UNITED STATES NAVAL STATION, GUANTANAMO BAY, CUBA.

None of the funds authorized to be appropriated by this Act for fiscal year 2012 may be used to transfer, release, or assist Khalid Sheikh Mohammed in the transfer or release to or within the United States, its territories, or possessions of Khalid Sheikh Mohammed or any other detainee who—

(1) is not a United States citizen or a member of the Armed Forces of the United States; and

(2) is or was held on or after January 20, 2009, at United States Naval Station, Guantanamo Bay, Cuba, by the Department of Defense.

SEC. 1028. REQUIREMENTS FOR CERTIFICATIONS RELATING TO THE TRANSFER OF DETAINEES AT UNITED STATES NAVAL STATION, GUANTANAMO BAY, CUBA, TO FOREIGN COUNTRIES AND OTHER FOREIGN ENTITIES.

(a) CERTIFICATION REQUIRED PRIOR TO TRANSFER.—

(1) IN GENERAL.—Except as provided in paragraph (2) and subsection (d), the Secretary of Defense may not use any amounts authorized to be appropriated or otherwise available to the Department of Defense for fiscal year 2012 to transfer any individual detained at Guantanamo to the custody or control of the individual's country of origin, any other foreign country, or any other foreign entity unless the Secretary submits to Congress the certification described in subsection (b) not later than 30 days before the transfer of the individual.

(2) EXCEPTION.—Paragraph (1) shall not apply to any action taken by the Secretary to transfer any individual detained at Guantanamo to effectuate—

(A) an order affecting the disposition of the individual that is issued by a court or competent tribunal of the United States having lawful jurisdiction (which the Secretary shall notify Congress of promptly after issuance); or

(B) a pre-trial agreement entered in a military commission case prior to the date of the enactment of this Act.

(b) CERTIFICATION.—A certification described in this subsection is a written certification made by the Secretary of Defense, with the concurrence of the Secretary of State and in consultation with the Director of National Intelligence, that—

(1) the government of the foreign country or the recognized leadership of the foreign entity to which the individual detained at Guantanamo is to be transferred—

(A) is not a designated state sponsor of terrorism or a designated foreign terrorist organization;

(B) maintains control over each detention facility in which the individual is to be detained if the individual is to be housed in a detention facility;

(C) is not, as of the date of the certification, facing a threat that is likely to substantially affect its ability to exercise control over the individual;

(D) has taken or agreed to take effective actions to ensure that the individual cannot take action to threaten the United States, its citizens, or its allies in the future;

(E) has taken or agreed to take such actions as the Secretary of Defense determines are necessary to ensure that the individual cannot engage or reengage in any terrorist activity; and

(F) has agreed to share with the United States any information that—

(i) is related to the individual or any associates of the individual; and

(ii) could affect the security of the United States, its citizens, or its allies; and

(2) includes an assessment, in classified or unclassified form, of the capacity, willingness, and past practices (if applicable) of the foreign country or entity in relation to the Secretary's certifications.

(c) PROHIBITION IN CASES OF PRIOR CONFIRMED RECIDIVISM.—

(1) PROHIBITION.—Except as provided in paragraph (2) and subsection (d), the Secretary of Defense may not use any amounts authorized to be appropriated or otherwise made available to the Department of Defense to transfer any individual detained at Guantanamo to the custody or control of the individual's country of origin, any other foreign country, or any other foreign entity if there is a confirmed case of any individual who was detained at United States Naval Station, Guantanamo Bay, Cuba, at any time after September 11, 2001, who was transferred to such foreign country or entity and subsequently engaged in any terrorist activity.

(2) EXCEPTION.—Paragraph (1) shall not apply to any action taken by the Secretary to transfer any individual detained at Guantanamo to effectuate—

(A) an order affecting the disposition of the individual that is issued by a court or competent tribunal of the United States having lawful jurisdiction (which the Secretary shall notify Congress of promptly after issuance); or

(B) a pre-trial agreement entered in a military commission case prior to the date of the enactment of this Act.

(d) NATIONAL SECURITY WAIVER.—

(1) IN GENERAL.—The Secretary of Defense may waive the applicability to a detainee transfer of a certification requirement specified in subparagraph (D) or (E) of subsection (b)(1) or the prohibition in subsection (c), if the Secretary certifies the rest of the criteria required by subsection (b) for transfers prohibited by subsection (c) and, with the concurrence of the Secretary of

State and in consultation with the Director of National Intelligence, determines that—

(A) alternative actions will be taken to address the underlying purpose of the requirement or requirements to be waived;

(B) in the case of a waiver of subparagraph (D) or (E) of subsection (b)(1), it is not possible to certify that the risks addressed in the paragraph to be waived have been completely eliminated, but the actions to be taken under subparagraph (A) will substantially mitigate such risks with regard to the individual to be transferred;

(C) in the case of a waiver of subsection (c), the Secretary has considered any confirmed case in which an individual who was transferred to the country subsequently engaged in terrorist activity, and the actions to be taken under subparagraph (A) will substantially mitigate the risk of recidivism with regard to the individual to be transferred; and

(D) the transfer is in the national security interests of the United States.

(2) REPORTS.—Whenever the Secretary makes a determination under paragraph (1), the Secretary shall submit to the appropriate committees of Congress, not later than 30 days before the transfer of the individual concerned, the following:

(A) A copy of the determination and the waiver concerned.

(B) A statement of the basis for the determination, including—

(i) an explanation why the transfer is in the national security interests of the United States; and

(ii) in the case of a waiver of subparagraph (D) or (E) of subsection (b)(1), an explanation why it is not possible to certify that the risks addressed in the subparagraph to be waived have been completely eliminated.

(C) A summary of the alternative actions to be taken to address the underlying purpose of, and to mitigate the risks addressed in, the subparagraph or subsection to be waived.

(D) The assessment required by subsection (b)(2).

(e) DEFINITIONS.—In this section:

(1) The term "appropriate committees of Congress" means—

(A) the Committee on Armed Services, the Committee on Appropriations, and the Select Committee on Intelligence of the Senate; and

(B) the Committee on Armed Services, the Committee on Appropriations, and the Permanent Select Committee on Intelligence of the House of Representatives.

(2) The term "individual detained at Guantanamo" means any individual located at United States Naval Station, Guantanamo Bay, Cuba, as of October 1, 2009, who—

(A) is not a citizen of the United States or a member of the Armed Forces of the United States; and

(B) is—

(i) in the custody or under the control of the Department of Defense; or

(ii) otherwise under detention at United States Naval Station, Guantanamo Bay, Cuba.

(3) The term "foreign terrorist organization" means any organization so designated by the Secretary of State under section 219 of the Immigration and Nationality Act (8 U.S.C. 1189).

(f) REPEAL OF SUPERSEDED AUTHORITY.—Section 1033 of the Ike Skelton National Defense Authorization Act for Fiscal Year 2011 (Public Law 111–383; 124 Stat. 4351) is repealed.

SEC. 1029. REQUIREMENT FOR CONSULTATION REGARDING PROSECUTION OF TERRORISTS.

(a) IN GENERAL.—Before seeking an indictment of, or otherwise charging, an individual described in subsection (b) in a Federal court, the Attorney General shall consult with the Director of National Intelligence and the Secretary of Defense about—

(1) whether the more appropriate forum for prosecution would be a Federal court or a military commission; and

(2) whether the individual should be held in civilian custody or military custody pending prosecution.

(b) APPLICABILITY.—The consultation requirement in subsection (a) applies to—

(1) a person who is subject to the requirements of section 1022, in accordance with a determination made pursuant to subsection (a)(2) of such section; and

(2) any other person who is held in military detention outside of the United States pursuant to the authority affirmed by section 1021.

Cybersecurity Annex

FEDERAL STATUTES

National Defense Authorization Act of 2011

(Pub. L. 111-383, 124 Stat. 4337 (2010))

Subtitle D—Cyber Warfare, Cyber Security, and Related Matters

SEC. 931. CONTINUOUS MONITORING OF DEPARTMENT OF DEFENSE INFORMATION SYSTEMS FOR CYBERSECURITY.

(a) IN GENERAL.—The Secretary of Defense shall direct the Chief Information Officer of the Department of Defense to work, in coordination with the Chief Information Officers of the military departments and the Defense Agencies and with senior cybersecurity and information assurance officials within the Department of Defense and otherwise within the Federal Government, to achieve, to the extent practicable, the following:

(1) The continuous prioritization of the policies, principles, standards, and guidelines developed under section 20 of the National Institute of Standards and Technology Act (15 U.S.C. 278g–3) with agencies and offices operating or exercising control of national security systems (including the National Security Agency) based upon the evolving threat of information security incidents with respect to national security systems, the vulnerability of such systems to such incidents, and the consequences of information security incidents involving such systems.

(2) The automation of continuous monitoring of the effectiveness of the information security policies, procedures, and practices within the information infrastructure of the Department of Defense, and the compliance of that infrastructure with such policies, procedures, and practices, including automation of—

(A) management, operational, and technical controls of every information system identified in the inventory required under section 3505(c) of title 44, United States Code; and

(B) management, operational, and technical controls relied on for evaluations under section 3545 of title 44, United States Code.

(b) DEFINITIONS.—In this section:

(1) The term "information security incident" means an occurrence that—

(A) actually or potentially jeopardizes the confidentiality, integrity, or availability of an information system or the information such system processes, stores, or transmits; or

(B) constitutes a violation or imminent threat of violation of security policies, security procedures, or acceptable use policies with respect to an information system.

(2) The term "information infrastructure" means the underlying framework, equipment, and software that an information system and related assets rely on to process, transmit, receive, or store information electronically.

(3) The term "national security system" has the meaning given that term in section 3542(b)(2) of title 44, United States Code.

SEC. 932. STRATEGY ON COMPUTER SOFTWARE ASSURANCE.

(a) STRATEGY REQUIRED.—The Secretary of Defense shall develop and implement, by not later than October 1, 2011, a strategy for assuring the security of software and software-based applications for all covered systems.

(b) COVERED SYSTEMS.—For purposes of this section, a covered system is any critical information system or weapon system of the Department of Defense, including the following:

(1) A major system, as that term is defined in section 2302(5) of title 10, United States Code.

(2) A national security system, as that term is defined in section 3542(b)(2) of title 44, United States Code.

(3) Any Department of Defense information system categorized as Mission Assurance Category I.

(4) Any Department of Defense information system categorized as Mission Assurance Category II in accordance with Department of Defense Directive 8500.01E.

(c) ELEMENTS.—The strategy required by subsection (a) shall include the following:

(1) Policy and regulations on the following:

(A) Software assurance generally.

(B) Contract requirements for software assurance for covered systems in development and production.

(C) Inclusion of software assurance in milestone reviews and milestone approvals.

(D) Rigorous test and evaluation of software assurance in development, acceptance, and operational tests.

(E) Certification and accreditation requirements for software assurance for new systems and for updates for legacy systems, including mechanisms to monitor and enforce reciprocity of certification and accreditation processes among the military departments and Defense Agencies.

(F) Remediation in legacy systems of critical software assurance deficiencies that are defined as critical in accordance with the Application Security Technical Implementation Guide of the Defense Information Systems Agency.

(2) Allocation of adequate facilities and other resources for test and evaluation and certification and accreditation of software to meet applicable require-

ments for research and development, systems acquisition, and operations.

(3) Mechanisms for protection against compromise of information systems through the supply chain or cyber attack by acquiring and improving automated tools for—

(A) assuring the security of software and software applications during software development;

(B) detecting vulnerabilities during testing of software; and

(C) detecting intrusions during real-time monitoring of software applications.

(4) Mechanisms providing the Department of Defense with the capabilities—

(A) to monitor systems and applications in order to detect and defeat attempts to penetrate or disable such systems and applications; and

(B) to ensure that such monitoring capabilities are integrated into the Department of Defense system of cyber defense-in-depth capabilities.

(5) An update to Committee for National Security Systems Instruction No. 4009, entitled "National Information Assurance Glossary", to include a standard definition for software security assurance.

(6) Either—

(A) mechanisms to ensure that vulnerable Mission Assurance Category III information systems, if penetrated, cannot be used as a foundation for penetration of protected covered systems, and means for assessing the effectiveness of such mechanisms; or

(B) plans to address critical vulnerabilities in Mission Assurance Category III information systems to prevent their use for intrusions of Mission Assurance Category I systems and Mission Assurance Category II systems.

(7) A funding mechanism for remediation of critical software assurance vulnerabilities in legacy systems.

(d) REPORT.—Not later than October 1, 2011, the Secretary of Defense shall submit to the congressional defense committees a report on the strategy required by subsection (a). The report
shall include the following:

(1) A description of the current status of the strategy required by subsection (a) and of the implementation of the strategy, including a description of the role of the strategy in the risk management by the Department regarding the supply chain and in operational planning for cyber security.

(2) A description of the risks, if any, that the Department will accept in the strategy due to limitations on funds or other applicable constraints.

(a) STRATEGY REQUIRED.—The Secretary of Defense, in consultation with the Secretaries of the military departments, shall develop a strategy to provide for the rapid acquisition of tools, applications, and other capabilities for cyber warfare for the United States Cyber Command and the cyber operations components of the military departments.

(b) BASIC ELEMENTS.—The strategy required by subsection (a) shall include the following:

(1) An orderly process for determining and approving operational requirements.

(2) A well-defined, repeatable, transparent, and disciplined process for developing capabilities to meet such requirements, in accordance with the information technology acquisition process developed pursuant to section 804 of the National Defense Authorization Act for Fiscal Year 2010 (Public Law 111–84; 10 U.S.C. 2225 note).

(3) The allocation of facilities and other resources to thoroughly test such capabilities in development, before deployment, and before use in order to validate performance and take into
account collateral damage and other so-called second-order effects.

(c) ADDITIONAL ELEMENTS.—The strategy required by subsection (a) shall also provide for the following:

(1) Safeguards to prevent—

(A) the circumvention of operational requirements and acquisition processes through informal relationships among the United States Cyber Command, the Armed Forces, the National Security Agency, and the Defense Information Systems Agency; and

(B) the abuse of quick-reaction processes otherwise available for the rapid fielding of capabilities.

(2) The establishment of reporting and oversight processes for requirements generation and approval for cyber warfare capabilities, the assignment of responsibility for providing capabilities to meet such requirements, and the execution of development and deployment of such capabilities, under the authority of the Chairman of the Joint Requirements Oversight Council, the Under Secretary of Defense for Policy, and other officials in the Office of the Secretary of Defense, as designated in the strategy.

(3) The establishment and maintenance of test and evaluation facilities and resources for cyber infrastructure to support research and development, operational test and evaluation, operational planning and effects testing, and training by replicating or emulating networks and infrastructure maintained and operated by the military and political organizations of potential United States adversaries, by domestic and foreign telecommunications service providers, and by the Department of Defense.

(4) An organization or organizations within the Department of Defense to be responsible for the operation and maintenance of cyber infrastructure for research, development, test, and evaluation purposes.

(5) Appropriate disclosure regarding United States cyber warfare capabilities to the independent test and evaluation community, and the involvement of that community in the development and maintenance of such capabilities, regardless of classification.

(6) The role of the private sector and appropriate Department of Defense organizations in developing capabilities to operate in cyberspace, and a clear process for determining whether to allocate responsibility for responding to Department of Defense cyber warfare requirements through Federal Government personnel, contracts with private sector entities, or a combination of both.

(7) The roles of each military department, and of the combat support Defense Agencies, in the development of cyber warfare capabilities in support of offensive, defensive, and intelligence
operational requirements.

(8) Mechanisms to promote information sharing, cooperative agreements, and collaboration with international, interagency, academic, and industrial partners in the development of cyber warfare capabilities.

(9) The manner in which the Department of Defense will promote interoperability, share innovation, and avoid unproductive duplication in cyber warfare capabilities through specialization among the components of the Department responsible for developing cyber capabilities.

(d) REPORT ON STRATEGY.—

(1) REPORT REQUIRED.—Not later than 180 days after the date of the enactment of this Act, the Secretary of Defense shall submit to the appropriate committees of Congress a report on the strategy required by subsection (a). The report shall include a comprehensive description of the strategy and plans (including a schedule) for the implementation of the strategy.

(2) APPROPRIATE COMMITTEES OF CONGRESS DEFINED.—In this subsection, the term "appropriate committees of Congress" means—

(A) the Committee on Armed Services, the Committee on Appropriations, and the Select Committee on Intelligence of the Senate; and

(B) the Committee on Armed Services, the Committee on Appropriations, and the Permanent Select Committee on Intelligence of the House of Representatives.

SEC. 933. STRATEGY FOR ACQUISITION AND OVERSIGHT OF DEPARTMENT OF DEFENSE CYBER WARFARE CAPABILITIES.

(a) STRATEGY REQUIRED.—The Secretary of Defense, in consultation with the Secretaries of the military departments, shall develop a strategy to provide for the rapid acquisition of tools, applications, and other capabilities for cyber warfare for the United States Cyber Command and the cyber operations components of the military departments.

(b) BASIC ELEMENTS.—The strategy required by subsection (a) shall include the following:

(1) An orderly process for determining and approving operational requirements.

(2) A well-defined, repeatable, transparent, and disciplined process for developing capabilities to meet such requirements, in accordance with the information technology acquisition process developed pursuant to section 804 of the National Defense Authorization Act for Fiscal Year 2010 (Public Law 111–84; 10 U.S.C. 2225 note).

(3) The allocation of facilities and other resources to thoroughly test such capabilities in development, before deployment, and before use in order to validate performance and take into account collateral damage and other so-called second-order effects.

(c) ADDITIONAL ELEMENTS.—The strategy required by subsection (a) shall also provide for the following:

(1) Safeguards to prevent—

(A) the circumvention of operational requirements and acquisition processes through informal relationships among the United States Cyber Command, the Armed Forces, the National Security Agency, and the Defense Information Systems Agency; and

(B) the abuse of quick-reaction processes otherwise available for the rapid fielding of capabilities.

(2) The establishment of reporting and oversight processes for requirements generation and approval for cyber warfare capabilities, the assignment of responsibility for providing capabilities to meet such requirements, and the execution of development and deployment of such capabilities, under the authority of the Chairman of the Joint Requirements Oversight Council, the Under Secretary of Defense for Policy, and other officials in the Office of the Secretary of Defense, as designated in the strategy.

(3) The establishment and maintenance of test and evaluation facilities and resources for cyber infrastructure to support research and development, operational test and evaluation, operational planning and effects testing, and training by replicating or emulating networks and infrastructure maintained and operated by the military and political organizations of potential United States adversaries, by domestic and foreign telecommunications service providers, and by the Department of Defense.

(4) An organization or organizations within the Department of Defense to be responsible for the operation and maintenance of cyber infrastructure for research, development, test, and evaluation purposes.

(5) Appropriate disclosure regarding United States cyber warfare capabilities to the independent test and evaluation community, and the involvement of that community in the development and maintenance of such capabilities, regardless of classification.

(6) The role of the private sector and appropriate Department of Defense organizations in developing capabilities to operate in cyberspace, and a clear process for determining whether to allocate responsibility for responding to Department of Defense cyber warfare requirements through Federal Government personnel, contracts with private sector entities, or a combination of both.

(7) The roles of each military department, and of the combat support Defense Agencies, in the development of cyber warfare capabilities in support of offensive, defensive, and intelligence operational requirements.

(8) Mechanisms to promote information sharing, cooperative agreements, and collaboration with international, interagency, academic, and industrial partners in the development of cyber warfare capabilities.

(9) The manner in which the Department of Defense will promote interoperability, share innovation, and avoid unproductive duplication in cyber warfare capabilities through specialization among the components of the Department responsible for developing cyber capabilities.

(d) REPORT ON STRATEGY.—

(1) REPORT REQUIRED.—Not later than 180 days after the date of the enactment of this Act, the Secretary of Defense shall submit to the appropriate committees of Congress a report on the strategy required by subsection (a). The report shall include a comprehensive description of the strategy and plans (including a schedule) for the implementation of the strategy.

(2) APPROPRIATE COMMITTEES OF CONGRESS DEFINED.—In this subsection, the term "appropriate committees of Congress" means—

(A) the Committee on Armed Services, the Committee on Appropriations, and the Select Committee on Intelligence of the Senate; and

(B) the Committee on Armed Services, the Committee on Appropriations, and the Permanent Select Committee on Intelligence of the House of Representatives.

SEC. 934. REPORT ON THE CYBER WARFARE POLICY OF THE DEPARTMENT OF DEFENSE.

(a) REPORT REQUIRED.—Not later than March 1, 2011, the Secretary of Defense shall submit to Congress a report on the cyber warfare policy of the Department of Defense.

(b) ELEMENTS.—The report required under this section shall include the following:

(1) A description of the policy and legal issues investigated and evaluated by the Department in considering the range of missions and activities that the Department may choose to conduct in cyberspace.

(2) The decisions of the Secretary with respect to such issues, and the recommendations of the Secretary to the President for decisions on such of those issues as exceed the authority of the Secretary to resolve, together with the rationale and justification of the Secretary for such decisions and recommendations.

(3) A description of the intentions of the Secretary with regard to modifying the National Military Strategy for Cyberspace Operations.

(4) The current use of, and potential applications of, modeling and simulation tools to identify likely cybersecurity vulnerabilities, as well as new protective and remediation means, within the Department.

(5) The application of modeling and simulation technology to develop strategies and programs to deter hostile or malicious activity intended to compromise Department information systems.

(c) FORM.—The report required under this section shall be submitted in unclassified form, but may include a classified annex.

SEC. 935. REPORTS ON DEPARTMENT OF DEFENSE PROGRESS IN DEFENDING THE DEPARTMENT AND THE DEFENSE INDUSTRIAL BASE FROM CYBER EVENTS.

(a) REPORTS ON PROGRESS REQUIRED.—Not later than 180 days after the date of the enactment of this Act, and March 1 every year thereafter through

2015, the Secretary of Defense shall submit to the congressional defense committees a report on the progress of the Department of Defense in defending the Department and the defense industrial base from cyber events (such as attacks, intrusions, and theft).

(b) ELEMENTS.—Each report under subsection (a) shall include the following:

(1) In the case of the first report, a baseline for measuring the progress of the Department of Defense in defending the Department and the defense industrial base from cyber events, including definitions of significant cyber events, an appropriate categorization of various types of cyber events, the basic methods used in various cyber events, the vulnerabilities exploited in such cyber events, and the metrics to be utilized to determine whether the Department is or is not making progress against an evolving cyber threat.

(2) An ongoing assessment of such baseline against key cyber defense strategies (described in subsection (c)) to determine implementation progress.

(3)(A) A description of the nature and scope of significant cyber events against the Department and the defense industrial base during the preceding year, including, for each such event, a description of the intelligence or other Department data acquired, the extent of the corruption or compromise of Department information or weapon systems, and the impact of such event on the Department generally and on operational capabilities.

(B) For any such event that has been investigated by or on behalf of the Damage Assessment Management Office, a synopsis of each damage assessment report, with emphasis on actions needing remediation.

(4) A comparative assessment of the offensive cyber warfare capabilities of current representative potential United States adversaries and nations with advanced cyber warfare capabilities with the capacity of the United States to defend—

(A) military networks and mission capabilities; and

(B) critical infrastructure.

(5) A comparative assessment of the offensive cyber warfare capabilities of the United States with the capacity of current representative potential United States adversaries and nations with advanced cyber warfare capabilities to defend against cyber attacks.

(6) A comparative assessment of the degree of dependency of current representative potential United States adversaries, nations with advanced cyber warfare capabilities, and the United States on networks that can be attacked through cyberspace.

(7) A description of known or suspected identified supply chain vulnerabilities, including known or suspected supply chain attacks, and actions to remediate such vulnerabilities.

(c) KEY CYBER DEFENSE STRATEGIES.—For purposes of subsection (b)(2), key cyber defense strategies include the following:

(1) Relevant valid Homeland Security Presidential Directives and National Security Presidential Directives.

(2) The Comprehensive National Cybersecurity Initiative.

(3) The National Military Strategy for Cyberspace Operations implementation plan.

(d) PERFORMANCE OF CERTAIN ASSESSMENTS.—The comparative assessment of critical infrastructure required by subsection (b)(4)(B) shall be performed by the Secretary of Homeland Security, in
coordination with the Secretary of Defense and the heads of other agencies of the Government with specific responsibility for critical infrastructure.

(e) FORM.—Each report under this section shall be submitted in unclassified form, but may include a classified annex.

National Defense Authorization Act for Fiscal Year 2012

(Pub. L. 112-81, 125 Stat. 1298 (2011))

Subtitle F—Other Matters

SEC. 951. ACTIVITIES TO IMPROVE MULTILATERAL, BILATERAL, AND REGIONAL COOPERATION REGARDING CYBERSECURITY.

(a) ESTABLISHMENT OF CYBERSECURITY PROGRAM.—

(1) IN GENERAL.—Chapter 53 of title 10, United States Code, is amended by inserting after section 1051b the following new section:

"§ 1051c. Multilateral, bilateral, or regional cooperation programs: assignments to improve education and training in information security

"(a) ASSIGNMENTS AUTHORIZED; PURPOSE.—The Secretary of Defense may authorize the temporary assignment of a member of the military forces of a foreign country to a Department of Defense organization for the purpose of assisting the member to obtain education and training to improve the member's ability to understand and respond to information security threats, vulnerabilities of information security systems, and the consequences of information security incidents.

"(b) PAYMENT OF CERTAIN EXPENSES.—To facilitate the assignment of a member of a foreign military force to a Department of Defense organization under subsection (a), the Secretary of Defense may pay such expenses in connection with the assignment as the Secretary considers in the national security interests of the United States.

"(c) PROTECTION OF DEPARTMENT CYBERSECURITY.—In authorizing the temporary assignment of members of foreign military forces to Department of Defense organizations under subsection (a), the Secretary of Defense shall require the inclusion of adequate safeguards to prevent any compromising of Department information security.

"(d) MULTI-YEAR AVAILABILITY OF FUNDS.—Funds available to carry out this section shall be available, to the extent provided in appropriations Acts, for programs and activities under this section that begin in a fiscal year and end in the following fiscal year.

"(e) INFORMATION SECURITY DEFINED.—In this section, the term 'information security' refers to—

"(1) the confidentiality, integrity, or availability of an information system or the information such system processes, stores, or transmits; and

"(2) the security policies, security procedures, or acceptable use policies with respect to an information system.".

(2) CLERICAL AMENDMENT.—The table of sections at the beginning of such chapter is amended by inserting after the item relating to section 1051b the following new item:

"1051c. Multilateral, bilateral, or regional cooperation programs: assignments to improve education and training in information security.".

(b) REPORT ON EXPANSION OF FELLOWSHIP OPPORTUNITIES.— Not later one year after the date of the enactment of this Act, the Secretary of Defense shall submit to Congress a report evaluating the feasibility and benefits of expanding the fellowship program authorized by section 1051c of title 10, United States Code, as added by subsection (a), to include ministry of defense officials, security officials, or other civilian officials of foreign countries.

SEC. 952. REPORT ON UNITED STATES SPECIAL OPERATIONS COMMAND STRUCTURE.

(a) REPORT.—Not later than March 1, 2012, the Secretary of Defense shall submit to the congressional defense committees a study of the United States Special Operations Command sub-unified structure.

(b) ELEMENTS.—The report required under this section shall include, at a minimum, the following:

(1) Recommendations to revise as necessary the present command structure to better support development and deployment of joint special operations forces and capabilities.

(2) Any other matters the Secretary considers appropriate.

(c) FORM.—The report required under this section shall be submitted in unclassified form, but may include a classified annex.

SEC. 953. STRATEGY TO ACQUIRE CAPABILITIES TO DETECT PREVIOUSLY UNKNOWN CYBER ATTACKS.

(a) IN GENERAL.—The Secretary of Defense shall develop and implement a plan to augment the cybersecurity strategy of the Department of Defense through the acquisition of advanced capabilities to discover and isolate penetrations and attacks that were previously unknown and for which signatures have not been developed for incorporation into computer intrusion detection and prevention systems and anti-virus software systems.

(b) CAPABILITIES.—

(1) NATURE OF CAPABILITIES.—The capabilities to be acquired under the plan required by subsection (a) shall—

(A) be adequate to enable well-trained analysts to discover the sophisticated attacks conducted by nation-state adversaries that are categorized as "advanced persistent threats";

(B) be appropriate for—

(i) endpoints or hosts;

(ii) network-level gateways operated by the Defense Information Systems Agency where the Department of Defense network connects to the public Internet; and

(iii) global networks owned and operated by private sector Tier 1 Internet Service Providers;

(C) at the endpoints or hosts, add new discovery capabilities to the Host-Based Security System of the Department, including capabilities such as—

(i) automatic blocking of unauthorized software programs and accepting approved and vetted programs;

(ii) constant monitoring of all key computer attributes, settings, and operations (such as registry keys, operations running in memory, security settings, memory tables, event logs, and files); and

(iii) automatic baselining and remediation of altered computer settings and files;

(D) at the network-level gateways and internal network peering points, include the sustainment and enhancement of a system that is based on full-packet capture, session reconstruction, extended storage, and advanced analytic tools, by—

(i) increasing the number and skill level of the analysts assigned to query stored data, whether by contracting for security services, hiring and training Government personnel, or both; and

(ii) increasing the capacity of the system to handle the rates for data flow through the gateways and the storage requirements specified by the United States Cyber Command; and

(E) include the behavior-based threat detection capabilities of Tier 1 Internet Service Providers and other companies that operate on the global Internet.

(2) SOURCE OF CAPABILITIES.—The capabilities to be acquired shall, to the maximum extent practicable, be acquired from commercial sources. In making decisions on the procurement of such capabilities from among competing commercial and Government providers, the Secretary shall take into consideration the needs of other departments and agencies of the Federal Government, State and local governments, and critical infrastructure owned and operated by the private sector for unclassified, affordable, and sustainable commercial solutions.

(c) INTEGRATION AND MANAGEMENT OF DISCOVERY CAPABILITIES.—The plan required by subsection (a) shall include mechanisms for improving the standardization, organization, and management of the security information and event management systems that are widely deployed across the department of Defense to improve the ability of United States Cyber Command to understand and control the status and condition of Department networks, including mechanisms to ensure that the security information and event management systems of the Department receive and correlate data collected and analyses conducted at the host or endpoint, at the network gateways, and by Internet Service Providers in order to discover new attacks reliably and rapidly.

(d) PROVISION FOR CAPABILITY DEMONSTRATIONS.—The plan required by subsection (a) shall provide for the conduct of demonstrations, pilot projects, and other tests on cyber test ranges and operational networks in order to determine and verify that the capabilities to be acquired pursuant to the plan are effective, practical, and affordable.

(e) REPORT.—Not later than April 1, 2012, the Secretary shall submit to the congressional defense committees a report on the plan required by subsection (a). The report shall set forth the plan and include a comprehensive description of the actions being undertaken by the Department to implement the plan.

SEC. 954. MILITARY ACTIVITIES IN CYBERSPACE.

Congress affirms that the Department of Defense has the capability, and upon direction by the President may conduct offensive operations in cyberspace to defend our Nation, Allies and interests,
subject to—

(1) the policy principles and legal regimes that the Department follows for kinetic capabilities, including the law of armed conflict; and

(2) the War Powers Resolution (50 U.S.C. 1541 et seq.). of United States and foreign civilian and non-defense agency personnel in conducting activities under the State Partnership Program of the National Guard.

SEC. 1090. CYBERSECURITY COLLABORATION BETWEEN THE DEPARTMENT OF DEFENSE AND THE DEPARTMENT OF HOMELAND SECURITY.

(a) INTERDEPARTMENTAL COLLABORATION.—

(1) IN GENERAL.—The Secretary of Defense and the Secretary of Homeland Security shall provide personnel, equipment, and facilities in order to increase interdepartmental collaboration with respect to—

(A) strategic planning for the cybersecurity of the United States;

(B) mutual support for cybersecurity capabilities development; and

(C) synchronization of current operational cybersecurity mission activities.

(2) EFFICIENCIES.—The collaboration provided for under paragraph (1) shall be designed—

(A) to improve the efficiency and effectiveness of requirements formulation and requests for products, services, and technical assistance for, and coordination and performance assessment of, cybersecurity missions executed across a variety of Department of Defense and Department of Homeland Security elements; and

(B) to leverage the expertise of each individual Department and to avoid duplicating, replicating, or aggregating unnecessarily the diverse line organizations across technology developments, operations, and customer support that collectively execute the cybersecurity mission of each Department.

(b) RESPONSIBILITIES.—

(1) DEPARTMENT OF HOMELAND SECURITY.—The Secretary of Homeland Security shall identify and assign, in coordination with the Department of Defense, a Director of Cybersecurity Coordination within the Department

of Homeland Security to undertake collaborative activities with the Department of Defense.
(2) DEPARTMENT OF DEFENSE.—The Secretary of Defense shall identify and assign, in coordination with the Department of Homeland Security, one or more officials within the Department of Defense to coordinate, oversee, and execute collaborative activities and the provision of cybersecurity support to the Department of Homeland Security.

Executive Order 13636—Improving Critical Infrastructure Cybersecurity

78 Fed. Reg. 11,739 (Feb. 19 2013)

By the authority vested in me as President by the Constitution and the laws of the United States of America, it is hereby ordered as follows:

Section 1. *Policy.* Repeated cyber intrusions into critical infrastructure demonstrate the need for improved cybersecurity. The cyber threat to critical infrastructure continues to grow and represents one of the most serious national security challenges we must confront. The national and economic security of the United States depends on the reliable functioning of the Nation's critical infrastructure in the face of such threats. It is the policy of the United States to enhance the security and resilience of the Nation's critical infrastructure and to maintain a cyber environment that encourages efficiency, innovation, and economic prosperity while promoting safety, security, business confidentiality, privacy, and civil liberties. We can achieve these goals through a partnership with the owners and operators of critical infrastructure to improve cybersecurity information sharing and collaboratively develop and implement risk-based standards.

Sec. 2. *Critical Infrastructure.* As used in this order, the term critical infrastructure means systems and assets, whether physical or virtual, so vital to the United States that the incapacity or destruction of such systems and assets would have a debilitating impact on security, national economic security, national public health or safety, or any combination of those matters.

Sec. 3. *Policy Coordination.* Policy coordination, guidance, dispute resolution, and periodic in-progress reviews for the functions and programs described and assigned herein shall be provided through the interagency process established in Presidential Policy Directive-1 of February 13, 2009 (Organization of the National Security Council System), or any successor.

Sec. 4. *Cybersecurity Information Sharing.*

(a) It is the policy of the United States Government to increase the volume, timeliness, and quality of cyber threat information shared with U.S. private sector entities so that these entities may better protect and defend themselves against cyber threats. Within 120 days of the date of this order, the Attorney General, the Secretary of Homeland Security (the "Secretary"), and the Director of National Intelligence shall each issue instructions consistent with their authorities and with the requirements of section 12(c) of this order to ensure the timely production of unclassified reports of cyber threats to the

U.S. homeland that identify a specific targeted entity. The instructions shall address the need to protect intelligence and law enforcement sources, methods, operations, and investigations.

(b) The Secretary and the Attorney General, in coordination with the Director of National Intelligence, shall establish a process that rapidly disseminates the reports produced pursuant to section 4(a) of this order to the targeted entity. Such process shall also, consistent with the need to protect national security information, include the dissemination of classified reports to critical infrastructure entities authorized to receive them. The Secretary and the Attorney General, in coordination with the Director of National Intelligence, shall establish a system for tracking the production, dissemination, and disposition of these reports.

(c) To assist the owners and operators of critical infrastructure in protecting their systems from unauthorized access, exploitation, or harm, the Secretary, consistent with 6 U.S.C. 143 and in collaboration with the Secretary of Defense, shall, within 120 days of the date of this order, establish procedures to expand the Enhanced Cybersecurity Services program to all critical infrastructure sectors. This voluntary information sharing program will provide classified cyber threat and technical information from the Government to eligible critical infrastructure companies or commercial service providers that offer security services to critical infrastructure.

(d) The Secretary, as the Executive Agent for the Classified National Security Information Program created under Executive Order 13549 of August 18, 2010 (Classified National Security Information Program for State, Local, Tribal, and Private Sector Entities), shall expedite the processing of security clearances to appropriate personnel employed by critical infrastructure owners and operators, prioritizing the critical infrastructure identified in section 9 of this order.

(e) In order to maximize the utility of cyber threat information sharing with the private sector, the Secretary shall expand the use of programs that bring private sector subject-matter experts into Federal service on a temporary basis. These subject matter experts should provide advice regarding the content, structure, and types of information most useful to critical infrastructure owners and operators in reducing and mitigating cyber risks.

Sec. 5. *Privacy and Civil Liberties Protections.*

(a) Agencies shall coordinate their activities under this order with their senior agency officials for privacy and civil liberties and ensure that privacy and civil liberties protections are incorporated into such activities. Such protections shall be based upon the Fair Information Practice Principles and other privacy and civil liberties policies, principles, and frameworks as they apply to each agency's activities.

(b) The Chief Privacy Officer and the Officer for Civil Rights and Civil Liberties of the Department of Homeland Security (DHS) shall assess the privacy and civil liberties risks of the functions and programs undertaken by DHS as called for in this order and shall recommend to the Secretary ways to minimize or mitigate such risks, in a publicly available report, to be released within 1 year of the date of this order. Senior agency privacy and civil liberties officials for other agencies engaged in activities under this order shall conduct assessments of their agency activities and provide those assessments to DHS for consideration and inclusion in the report. The report shall be reviewed on an annual basis and revised as necessary. The report may contain a classified annex if necessary. Assessments shall include evaluation of activities against the Fair Information Practice Principles and other applicable privacy and civil liberties policies, principles, and frameworks. Agencies shall consider the assessments and recommendations of the report in implementing privacy and civil liberties protections for agency activities.

(c) In producing the report required under subsection (b) of this section, the Chief Privacy Officer and the Officer for Civil Rights and Civil Liberties of DHS shall consult with the Privacy and Civil Liberties Oversight Board and coordinate with the Office of Management and Budget (OMB).

(d) Information submitted voluntarily in accordance with 6 U.S.C. 133 by private entities under this order shall be protected from disclosure to the fullest extent permitted by law.

Sec. 6. *Consultative Process.* The Secretary shall establish a consultative process to coordinate improvements to the cybersecurity of critical infrastructure. As part of the consultative process, the Secretary shall engage and consider the advice, on matters set forth in this order, of the Critical Infrastructure Partnership Advisory Council; Sector Coordinating Councils; critical infrastructure owners and operators; Sector-Specific Agencies; other relevant agencies; independent regulatory agencies; State, local, territorial, and tribal governments; universities; and outside experts.

Sec. 7. *Baseline Framework to Reduce Cyber Risk to Critical Infrastructure.*

(a) The Secretary of Commerce shall direct the Director of the National Institute of Standards and Technology (the "Director") to lead the development of a framework to reduce cyber risks to critical infrastructure (the "Cybersecurity Framework"). The Cybersecurity Framework shall include a set of standards, methodologies, procedures, and processes that align policy, business, and technological approaches to address cyber risks. The Cybersecurity Framework shall incorporate voluntary consensus standards and industry best practices to the fullest extent possible. The Cybersecurity Framework shall be consistent with voluntary international standards when such international standards will advance the objectives of this order, and shall meet the requirements of the National Institute of Standards and Technology Act, as amended (15 U.S.C. 271 et seq.), the National Technology Transfer and Advancement Act of 1995 (Public Law 104-113), and OMB Circular A-119, as revised.

(b) The Cybersecurity Framework shall provide a prioritized, flexible, repeatable, performance-based, and cost-effective approach, including information security measures and controls, to help owners and operators of critical infrastructure identify, assess, and manage cyber risk. The Cybersecurity Framework shall focus on identifying cross-sector security standards and guidelines applicable to critical infrastructure. The Cybersecurity Framework will also identify areas for improvement that should be addressed through future collaboration with particular sectors and standards-developing organizations. To enable technical innovation and account for organizational differences, the Cybersecurity Framework will provide guidance that is technology neutral and that enables critical infrastructure sectors to benefit from a competitive market for products and services that meet the standards, methodologies, procedures, and processes developed to address cyber risks. The Cybersecurity Framework shall include guidance for measuring the performance of an entity in implementing the Cybersecurity Framework.

(c) The Cybersecurity Framework shall include methodologies to identify and mitigate impacts of the Cybersecurity Framework and associated information security measures or controls on business confidentiality, and to protect individual privacy and civil liberties.

(d) In developing the Cybersecurity Framework, the Director shall engage in an open public review and comment process. The Director shall also consult with the Secretary, the National Security Agency, Sector-Specific Agencies and other interested agencies including OMB, owners and operators of critical infrastructure, and other stakeholders through the consultative process established in section 6 of this order. The Secretary, the Director of National Intelligence, and the heads of other relevant agencies shall provide threat and vulnerability information and technical expertise to inform the development of the Cybersecurity Framework. The Secretary shall provide performance goals for the Cybersecurity Framework informed by work under section 9 of this order.

(e) Within 240 days of the date of this order, the Director shall publish a preliminary version of the Cybersecurity Framework (the "preliminary Framework"). Within 1 year of the date of this order, and after coordination with the Secretary to ensure suitability under section 8 of this order, the Director shall publish a final version of the Cybersecurity Framework (the "final Framework").

(f) Consistent with statutory responsibilities, the Director will ensure the Cybersecurity Framework and related guidance is reviewed and updated as necessary, taking into consideration technological changes, changes in cyber risks, operational feedback from owners and operators of critical infrastructure, experience from the implementation of section 8 of this order, and any other relevant factors.

Sec. 8. *Voluntary Critical Infrastructure Cybersecurity Program.*

(a) The Secretary, in coordination with Sector-Specific Agencies, shall establish a voluntary program to support the adoption of the Cybersecurity Framework by owners and operators of critical infrastructure and any other interested entities (the "Program").

(b) Sector-Specific Agencies, in consultation with the Secretary and other interested agencies, shall coordinate with the Sector Coordinating Councils to review the Cybersecurity Framework and, if necessary, develop implementation guidance or supplemental materials to address sector-specific risks and operating environments.

(c) Sector-Specific Agencies shall report annually to the President, through the Secretary, on the extent to which owners and operators notified under section 9 of this order are participating in the Program.

(d) The Secretary shall coordinate establishment of a set of incentives designed to promote participation in the Program. Within 120 days of the date of this order, the Secretary and the Secretaries of the Treasury and Commerce each shall make recommendations separately to the President, through the Assistant to the President for Homeland Security and Counterterrorism and the Assistant to the President for Economic Affairs, that shall include analysis of the benefits and relative effectiveness of such incentives, and whether the incentives would require legislation or can be provided under existing law and authorities to participants in the Program.

(e) Within 120 days of the date of this order, the Secretary of Defense and the Administrator of General Services, in consultation with the Secretary and the Federal Acquisition Regulatory Council, shall make recommendations to the President, through the Assistant to the President for Homeland Security and Counterterrorism and the Assistant to the President for Economic Affairs, on the feasibility, security benefits, and relative merits of incorporating security standards into acquisition planning and contract administration. The report shall address what steps can be taken to harmonize and make consistent existing procurement requirements related to cybersecurity.

Sec. 9. *Identification of Critical Infrastructure at Greatest Risk.*

(a) Within 150 days of the date of this order, the Secretary shall use a risk-based approach to identify critical infrastructure where a cybersecurity incident could reasonably result in catastrophic regional or national effects on public health or safety, economic security, or national security. In identifying critical infrastructure for this purpose, the Secretary shall use the consultative process established in section 6 of this order and draw upon the expertise of Sector-Specific Agencies. The Secretary shall apply consistent, objective criteria in identifying such critical infrastructure. The Secretary shall not identify any commercial information technology products or consumer information technology services under this section. The Secretary shall review and update the list of identified critical infrastructure under this section on an annual basis, and provide such list to the President, through the Assistant to the President for Homeland Security and Counterterrorism and the Assistant to the President for Economic Affairs.

(b) Heads of Sector-Specific Agencies and other relevant agencies shall provide the Secretary with information necessary to carry out the responsibilities under this section. The Secretary shall develop a process for other relevant stakeholders to submit information to assist in making the identifications required in subsection (a) of this section.

(c) The Secretary, in coordination with Sector-Specific Agencies, shall confidentially notify owners and operators of critical infrastructure identified under subsection (a) of this section that they have been so identified, and ensure identified owners and operators are provided the basis for the determination. The Secretary shall establish a process through which owners and operators of critical infrastructure may submit relevant information and request reconsideration of identifications under subsection (a) of this section.

Sec. 10. *Adoption of Framework.*

(a) Agencies with responsibility for regulating the security of critical infrastructure shall engage in a consultative process with DHS, OMB, and the National Security Staff to review the preliminary Cybersecurity Framework and determine if current cybersecurity regulatory requirements are sufficient given current and projected risks. In making such determination, these agencies shall consider the identification of critical infrastructure required under section 9 of this order. Within 90 days of the publication of the preliminary Framework, these agencies shall submit a report to the President, through the Assistant to the President for Homeland Security and Counterterrorism, the Director of OMB, and the Assistant to the President for Economic Affairs, that states whether or not the agency has clear authority to establish requirements based upon the Cybersecurity Framework to sufficiently address current and projected cyber risks to critical infrastructure, the existing authorities identified, and any additional authority required.

(b) If current regulatory requirements are deemed to be insufficient, within 90 days of publication of the final Framework, agencies identified in subsection (a) of this section shall propose prioritized, risk-based, efficient, and coordinated actions, consistent with Executive Order 12866 of September 30, 1993 (Regulatory Planning and Review), Executive Order 13563 of January 18, 2011 (Improving Regulation and Regulatory Review), and Executive Order 13609 of May 1, 2012 (Promoting International Regulatory Cooperation), to mitigate cyber risk.

(c) Within 2 years after publication of the final Framework, consistent with Executive Order 13563 and Executive Order 13610 of May 10, 2012 (Identifying and Reducing Regulatory Burdens), agencies identified in subsection (a) of this section shall, in consultation with owners and operators of critical infrastructure, report to OMB on any critical infrastructure subject to ineffective, conflicting, or excessively burdensome cybersecurity requirements. This report shall describe efforts made by agencies, and make recommendations for further actions, to minimize or eliminate such requirements.

(d) The Secretary shall coordinate the provision of technical assistance to agencies identified in subsection (a) of this section on the development of their cybersecurity workforce and programs.

(e) Independent regulatory agencies with responsibility for regulating the security of critical infrastructure are encouraged to engage in a consultative process with the Secretary, relevant Sector-Specific Agencies, and other affected parties to consider prioritized actions to mitigate cyber risks for critical infrastructure consistent with their authorities.

Sec. 11. *Definitions.*

(a) "Agency" means any authority of the United States that is an "agency" under 44 U.S.C. 3502(1), other than those considered to be independent regulatory agencies, as defined in 44 U.S.C. 3502(5).

(b) "Critical Infrastructure Partnership Advisory Council" means the council established by DHS under 6 U.S.C. 451 to facilitate effective interaction and coordination of critical infrastructure protection activities among the Federal Government; the private sector; and State, local, territorial, and tribal governments.

(c) "Fair Information Practice Principles" means the eight principles set forth in Appendix A of the National Strategy for Trusted Identities in Cyberspace.

(d) "Independent regulatory agency" has the meaning given the term in 44 U.S.C. 3502(5).

(e) "Sector Coordinating Council" means a private sector coordinating council composed of representatives of owners and operators within a particular sector of critical infrastructure established by the National Infrastructure Protection Plan or any successor.

(f) "Sector-Specific Agency" has the meaning given the term in Presidential Policy Directive-21 of February 12, 2013 (Critical Infrastructure Security and Resilience), or any successor.

Sec. 12. *General Provisions.*

(a) This order shall be implemented consistent with applicable law and subject to the availability of appropriations. Nothing in this order shall be construed to provide an agency with authority for regulating the security of critical infrastructure in addition to or to a greater extent than the authority the agency has under existing law. Nothing in this order shall be construed to alter or limit any authority or responsibility of an agency under existing law.

(b) Nothing in this order shall be construed to impair or otherwise affect the functions of the Director of OMB relating to budgetary, administrative, or legislative proposals.

(c) All actions taken pursuant to this order shall be consistent with requirements and authorities to protect intelligence and law enforcement sources and methods. Nothing in this order shall be interpreted to supersede measures established under authority of law to protect the security and integrity of specific activities and associations that are in direct support of intelligence and law enforcement operations.

(d) This order shall be implemented consistent with U.S. international obligations.

(e) This order is not intended to, and does not, create any right or benefit, substantive or procedural, enforceable at law or in equity by any party against the United States, its departments, agencies, or entities, its officers, employees, or agents, or any other person.

Barack Obama

Policy Directives and Guidance

Presidential Policy Directive 21—Critical Infrastructure Security and Resilience

SUBJECT: Critical Infrastructure Security and Resilience

The Presidential Policy Directive (PPD) on Critical Infrastructure Security and Resilience advances a national unity of effort to strengthen and maintain secure, functioning, and resilient critical infrastructure.

Introduction

The Nation's critical infrastructure provides the essential services that underpin American society. Proactive and coordinated efforts are necessary to strengthen and maintain secure, functioning, and resilient critical infrastructure—including assets, networks, and systems—that are vital to public confidence and the Nation's safety, prosperity, and well-being.

The Nation's critical infrastructure is diverse and complex. It includes distributed networks, varied organizational structures and operating models (including multinational ownership), interdependent functions and systems in both the physical space and cyberspace, and governance constructs that involve multi-level authorities, responsibilities, and regulations. Critical infrastructure owners and operators are uniquely positioned to manage risks to their individual operations and assets, and to determine effective strategies to make them more secure and resilient.

Critical infrastructure must be secure and able to withstand and rapidly recover from all hazards. Achieving this will require integration with the national preparedness system across prevention, protection, mitigation, response, and recovery.

This directive establishes national policy on critical infrastructure security and resilience. This endeavor is a shared responsibility among the Federal, state, local, tribal, and territorial (SLTT) entities, and public and private owners and operators of critical infrastructure (herein referred to as "critical infrastructure owners and operators"). This directive also refines and clarifies the critical infrastructure-related functions, roles, and responsibilities across the Federal Government, as well as enhances overall coordination and collaboration. The Federal Government also has a responsibility to strengthen the security and resilience of its own critical infrastructure, for the continuity of national essential functions, and to organize itself to partner effectively with and add value to the security and resilience efforts of critical infrastructure owners and operators.

Policy

It is the policy of the United States to strengthen the security and resilience of its critical infrastructure against both physical and cyber threats. The Federal Government shall work with critical infrastructure owners and operators and SLTT entities to take proactive steps to manage risk and strengthen the security and resilience of the Nation's critical infrastructure, considering all hazards that could have a debilitating impact on national security, economic stability, public health and safety, or any combination thereof. These efforts shall seek to reduce vulnerabilities, minimize consequences, identify and disrupt threats, and hasten response and recovery efforts related to critical infrastructure.

The Federal Government shall also engage with international partners to strengthen the security and resilience of domestic critical infrastructure and critical infrastructure located outside of the United States on which the Nation depends.

U.S. efforts shall address the security and resilience of critical infrastructure in an integrated, holistic manner to reflect this infrastructure's interconnectedness and interdependency. This directive also identifies energy and communications systems as uniquely critical due to the enabling functions they provide across all critical infrastructure sectors.

Three strategic imperatives shall drive the Federal approach to strengthen critical infrastructure security and resilience:

1) Refine and clarify functional relationships across the Federal Government to advance the national unity of effort to strengthen critical infrastructure security and resilience;

2) Enable effective information exchange by identifying baseline data and systems requirements for the Federal Government; and

3) Implement an integration and analysis function to inform planning and operations decisions regarding critical infrastructure.

All Federal department and agency heads are responsible for the identification, prioritization, assessment, remediation, and security of their respective internal critical infrastructure that supports primary mission essential functions. Such infrastructure shall be addressed in the plans and execution of the requirements in the National Continuity Policy.

Federal departments and agencies shall implement this directive in a manner consistent with applicable law, Presidential directives, and Federal regulations, including those protecting privacy, civil rights, and civil liberties. In addition, Federal departments and agencies shall protect all information associated with carrying out this directive consistent with applicable legal authorities and policies.

Roles and Responsibilities

Effective implementation of this directive requires a national unity of effort pursuant to strategic guidance from the Secretary of Homeland Security. That national effort must include expertise and day-to-day engagement from the Sector-Specific Agencies (SSAs) as well as the specialized or support capabilities from other Federal departments and agencies, and strong collaboration with critical infrastructure owners and operators and SLTT entities. Although the roles and responsibilities identified in this directive are directed at Federal departments and agencies, effective partnerships with critical infrastructure owners and operators and SLTT entities are imperative to strengthen the security and resilience of the Nation's critical infrastructure.

Secretary of Homeland Security

The Secretary of Homeland Security shall provide strategic guidance, promote a national unity of effort, and coordinate the overall Federal effort to promote the security and resilience of the Nation's critical infrastructure. In carrying out the responsibilities assigned in the Homeland Security Act of 2002, as amended, the Secretary of Homeland Security evaluates national capabilities, opportunities, and challenges in protecting critical infrastructure; analyzes threats to, vulnerabilities of, and potential consequences from all hazards on critical infrastructure; identifies security and resilience functions that are necessary for effective public-private engagement with all critical infrastructure sectors; develops a national plan and metrics, in coordination with SSAs and other critical infrastructure partners; integrates and coordinates Federal cross-sector security and resilience activities; identifies and analyzes key interdependencies among critical infrastructure sectors; and reports on the effectiveness of national efforts to strengthen the Nation's security and resilience posture for critical infrastructure.

Additional roles and responsibilities for the Secretary of Homeland Security include:

1) Identify and prioritize critical infrastructure, considering physical and cyber threats, vulnerabilities, and consequences, in coordination with SSAs and other Federal departments and agencies;

2) Maintain national critical infrastructure centers that shall provide a situational awareness capability that includes integrated, actionable information about emerging trends, imminent threats, and the status of incidents that may impact critical infrastructure;

3) In coordination with SSAs and other Federal departments and agencies, provide analysis, expertise, and other technical assistance to critical infrastructure owners and operators and facilitate access to and exchange of information and intelligence necessary to strengthen the security and resilience of critical infrastructure;

4) Conduct comprehensive assessments of the vulnerabilities of the Nation's critical infrastructure in coordination with the SSAs and in collaboration with SLTT entities and critical infrastructure owners and operators;

5) Coordinate Federal Government responses to significant cyber or physical incidents affecting critical infrastructure consistent with statutory authorities;

6) Support the Attorney General and law enforcement agencies with their responsibilities to investigate and prosecute threats to and attacks against critical infrastructure;

7) Coordinate with and utilize the expertise of SSAs and other appropriate Federal departments and agencies to map geospatially, image, analyze, and sort critical infrastructure by employing commercial satellite and airborne systems, as well as existing capabilities within other departments and agencies; and

8) Report annually on the status of national critical infrastructure efforts as required by statute.

Sector-Specific Agencies

Each critical infrastructure sector has unique characteristics, operating models, and risk profiles that benefit from an identified Sector-Specific Agency that has institutional knowledge and specialized expertise about the sector. Recognizing existing statutory or regulatory authorities of specific Federal departments and agencies, and leveraging existing sector familiarity and relationships, SSAs shall carry out the following roles and responsibilities for their respective sectors:

1) As part of the broader national effort to strengthen the security and resilience of critical infrastructure, coordinate with the Department of Homeland Security (DHS) and other relevant Federal departments and agencies and collaborate with critical infrastructure owners and operators, where appropriate with independent regulatory agencies, and with SLTT entities, as appropriate, to implement this directive;

2) Serve as a day-to-day Federal interface for the dynamic prioritization and coordination of sector-specific activities;

3) Carry out incident management responsibilities consistent with statutory authority and other appropriate policies, directives, or regulations;

4) Provide, support, or facilitate technical assistance and consultations for that sector to identify vulnerabilities and help mitigate incidents, as appropriate; and

5) Support the Secretary of Homeland Security's statutorily required reporting requirements by providing on an annual basis sector-specific critical infrastructure information.

Additional Federal Responsibilities

The following departments and agencies have specialized or support functions related to critical infrastructure security and resilience that shall be carried out by, or along with, other Federal departments and agencies and independent regulatory agencies, as appropriate.

1) The Department of State, in coordination with DHS, SSAs, and other Federal departments and agencies, shall engage foreign governments and international organizations to strengthen the security and resilience of critical infrastructure located outside the United States and to facilitate the overall exchange of best practices and lessons learned for promoting the security and resilience of critical infrastructure on which the Nation depends.

2) The Department of Justice (DOJ), including the Federal Bureau of Investigation (FBI), shall lead counterterrorism and counterintelligence investigations and related law enforcement activities across the critical infrastructure sectors. DOJ shall investigate, disrupt, prosecute, and otherwise reduce foreign intelligence, terrorist, and other threats to, and actual or attempted attacks on, or sabotage of, the Nation's critical infrastructure. The FBI also conducts domestic collection, analysis, and dissemination of cyber threat information, and shall be responsible for the operation of the National Cyber Investigative Joint Task Force (NCIJTF). The NCIJTF serves as a multi-agency national focal point for coordinating, integrating, and sharing pertinent information related to cyber threat investigations, with representation from DHS, the Intelligence Community (IC), the Department of Defense (DOD), and other agencies as appropriate. The Attorney General and the Secretary of Homeland Security shall collaborate to carry out their respective critical infrastructure missions.

3) The Department of the Interior, in collaboration with the SSA for the Government Facilities Sector, shall identify, prioritize, and coordinate the security and resilience efforts for national monuments and icons and incorporate measures to reduce risk to these critical assets, while also promoting their use and enjoyment.

4) The Department of Commerce (DOC), in collaboration with DHS and other relevant Federal departments and agencies, shall engage private sector, research, academic, and government organizations to improve security for technology and tools related to cyber-based systems, and promote the development of other efforts related to critical infrastructure to enable the timely availability of industrial products, materials, and services to meet homeland security requirements.

5) The IC, led by the Director of National Intelligence (DNI), shall use applicable authorities and coordination mechanisms to provide, as appropriate, intelligence assessments regarding threats to critical infrastructure and coordinate on intelligence and other sensitive or proprietary information related to critical infrastructure. In addition, information security policies, directives, standards, and guidelines for safeguarding national security systems shall be overseen as directed by the President, applicable law, and in accordance with that direction, carried out under the authority of the heads of agencies that operate or exercise authority over such national security systems.

6) The General Services Administration, in consultation with DOD, DHS, and other departments and agencies as appropriate, shall provide or support government-wide contracts for critical infrastructure systems and ensure that such contracts include audit rights for the security and resilience of critical infrastructure.

7) The Nuclear Regulatory Commission (NRC) is to oversee its licensees' protection of commercial nuclear power reactors and non-power nuclear reactors used for research, testing, and training; nuclear materials in medical, industrial, and academic settings, and facilities that fabricate nuclear fuel; and the transportation, storage, and disposal of nuclear materials and waste. The NRC is to collaborate, to the extent possible, with DHS, DOJ, the Department of Energy, the Environmental Protection Agency, and other Federal departments and agencies, as appropriate, on strengthening critical infrastructure security and resilience.

8) The Federal Communications Commission, to the extent permitted by law, is to exercise its authority and expertise to partner with DHS and the Department of State, as well as other Federal departments and agencies and SSAs as appropriate, on: (1) identifying and prioritizing communications infrastructure; (2) identifying communications sector vulnerabilities and working with industry and other stakeholders to address those vulnerabilities; and (3) working with stakeholders, including industry, and engaging foreign governments and international organizations to increase the security and resilience of critical infrastructure within the communications sector and facilitating the development and implementation of best practices promoting the security and resilience of critical communications infrastructure on which the Nation depends.

9) Federal departments and agencies shall provide timely information to the Secretary of Homeland Security and the national critical infrastructure centers necessary to support cross-sector analysis and inform the situational awareness capability for critical infrastructure.

Three Strategic Imperatives

1) Refine and Clarify Functional Relationships across the Federal Government to Advance the National Unity of Effort to Strengthen Critical Infrastructure Security and Resilience

An effective national effort to strengthen critical infrastructure security and resilience must be guided by a national plan that identifies roles and responsibilities and is informed by the expertise, experience, capabilities, and responsibilities of the SSAs, other Federal departments and agencies with critical infrastructure roles, SLTT entities, and critical infrastructure owners and operators.

During the past decade, new programs and initiatives have been established to address specific infrastructure issues, and priorities have shifted and expanded. As a result, Federal functions related to critical infrastructure security and resilience shall be clarified and refined to establish baseline capabilities that will reflect this evolution of knowledge, to define relevant Federal program functions, and to facilitate collaboration and information exchange between and among the Federal Government, critical infrastructure owners and operators, and SLTT entities.

As part of this refined structure, there shall be two national critical infrastructure centers operated by DHS—one for physical infrastructure and another for cyber infrastructure. They shall function in an integrated manner and serve as focal points for critical infrastructure partners to obtain situational awareness and integrated, actionable information to protect the physical and cyber aspects of critical infrastructure. Just as the physical and cyber elements of critical infrastructure are inextricably linked, so are the vulnerabilities. Accordingly, an integration and analysis function (further developed in Strategic Imperative 3) shall be implemented between these two national centers.

The success of these national centers, including the integration and analysis function, is dependent on the quality and timeliness of the information and intelligence they receive from the SSAs and other Federal departments and agencies, as well as from critical infrastructure owners and operators and SLTT entities.

These national centers shall not impede the ability of the heads of Federal departments and agencies to carry out or perform their responsibilities for national defense, criminal, counterintelligence, counterterrorism, or investigative activities.

2) Enable Efficient Information Exchange by Identifying Baseline Data and Systems Requirements for the Federal Government

A secure, functioning, and resilient critical infrastructure requires the efficient exchange of information, including intelligence, between all levels of governments and critical infrastructure owners and operators. This must facilitate the timely exchange of threat and vulnerability information as well as information that allows for the development of a situational awareness capability during incidents. The goal is to enable efficient information exchange through the identification of requirements for data and information formats and accessibility, system interoperability, and redundant systems and alternate capabilities should there be a disruption in the primary systems.

Greater information sharing within the government and with the private sector can and must be done while respecting privacy and civil liberties. Federal departments and agencies shall ensure that all existing privacy principles, policies, and procedures are implemented consistent with applicable law and policy and shall include senior agency officials for privacy in their efforts to govern and oversee information sharing properly.

3) Implement an Integration and Analysis Function to Inform Planning and Operational Decisions Regarding Critical Infrastructure

The third strategic imperative builds on the first two and calls for the implementation of an integration and analysis function for critical infrastructure that includes operational and strategic analysis on incidents, threats, and emerging risks. It shall reside at the intersection of the two national centers as identified in Strategic Imperative 1, and it shall include the capability to collate, assess, and integrate vulnerability and consequence information with threat streams and hazard information to:

a. Aid in prioritizing assets and managing risks to critical infrastructure;

b. Anticipate interdependencies and cascading impacts;

c. Recommend security and resilience measures for critical infrastructure prior to, during, and after an event or incident; and

d. Support incident management and restoration efforts related to critical infrastructure.

This function shall not replicate the analysis function of the IC or the National Counterterrorism Center, nor shall it involve intelligence collection activities. The IC, DOD, DOJ, DHS, and other Federal departments and agencies with relevant intelligence or information shall, however, inform this integration and analysis capability regarding the Nation's critical infrastructure by providing relevant, timely, and appropriate information to the national centers. This function shall also use information and intelligence provided by other critical infrastructure partners, including SLTT and nongovernmental analytic entities.

Finally, this integration and analysis function shall support DHS's ability to maintain and share, as a common Federal service, a near real-time situational awareness capability for critical infrastructure that includes actionable information about imminent threats, significant trends, and awareness of incidents that may affect critical infrastructure.

Innovation and Research and Development

The Secretary of Homeland Security, in coordination with the Office of Science and Technology Policy (OSTP), the SSAs, DOC, and other Federal departments and agencies, shall provide input to align those Federal and Federally-funded research and development (R&D) activities that seek to strengthen the security and resilience of the Nation's critical infrastructure, including:

1) Promoting R&D to enable the secure and resilient design and construction of critical infrastructure and more secure accompanying cyber technology;

2) Enhancing modeling capabilities to determine potential impacts on critical infrastructure of an incident or threat scenario, as well as cascading effects on other sectors;

3) Facilitating initiatives to incentivize cybersecurity investments and the adoption of critical infrastructure design features that strengthen all-hazards security and resilience; and

4) Prioritizing efforts to support the strategic guidance issued by the Secretary of Homeland Security.

Implementation of the Directive

The Secretary of Homeland Security shall take the following actions as part of the implementation of this directive.

1) Critical Infrastructure Security and Resilience Functional Relationships. Within 120 days of the date of this directive, the Secretary of Homeland Security shall develop a description of the functional relationships within DHS and across the Federal Government related to critical infrastructure security and resilience. It should include the roles and functions of the two national critical infrastructure centers and a discussion of the analysis and integration function. When complete, it should serve as a roadmap for critical infrastructure owners and operators and SLTT entities to navigate the Federal Government's functions and primary points of contact assigned to those functions for critical infrastructure security and resilience against both physical and cyber threats. The Secretary shall coordinate this effort with the SSAs and other relevant Federal departments and agencies. The Secretary shall provide the description to the President through the Assistant to the President for Homeland Security and Counterterrorism.

2) Evaluation of the Existing Public-Private Partnership Model. Within 150 days of the date of this directive, the Secretary of Homeland Security, in coordination with the SSAs, other relevant Federal departments and agencies, SLTT entities, and critical infrastructure owners and operators, shall conduct an analysis of the existing public-private partnership model and recommend options for improving the effectiveness of the partnership in both the physical and cyber space. The evaluation shall consider options to streamline processes for collaboration and exchange of information and to minimize duplication of effort. Furthermore, the analysis shall consider how the model can be flexible and adaptable to meet the unique needs of individual sectors while providing a focused, disciplined, and effective approach for the Federal Government to coordinate with the critical infrastructure owners and operators and with SLTT governments. The evaluation shall result in recommendations to enhance partnerships to be approved for implementation through the processes established in the Organization of the National Security Council System directive.

3) Identification of Baseline Data and Systems Requirements for the Federal Government to Enable Efficient Information Exchange. Within 180 days of the date of this directive, the Secretary of Homeland Security, in coordination

with the SSAs and other Federal departments and agencies, shall convene a team of experts to identify baseline data and systems requirements to enable the efficient exchange of information and intelligence relevant to strengthening the security and resilience of critical infrastructure. The experts should include representatives from those entities that routinely possess information important to critical infrastructure security and resilience; those that determine and manage information technology systems used to exchange information; and those responsible for the security of information being exchanged. Interoperability with critical infrastructure partners; identification of key data and the information requirements of key Federal, SLTT, and private sector entities; availability, accessibility, and formats of data; the ability to exchange various classifications of information; and the security of those systems to be used; and appropriate protections for individual privacy and civil liberties should be included in the analysis. The analysis should result in baseline requirements for sharing of data and interoperability of systems to enable the timely exchange of data and information to secure critical infrastructure and make it more resilient. The Secretary shall provide that analysis to the President through the Assistant to the President for Homeland Security and Counterterrorism.

4) Development of a Situational Awareness Capability for Critical Infrastructure. Within 240 days of the date of this directive, the Secretary of Homeland Security shall demonstrate a near real-time situational awareness capability for critical infrastructure that includes threat streams and all-hazards information as well as vulnerabilities; provides the status of critical infrastructure and potential cascading effects; supports decision making; and disseminates critical information that may be needed to save or sustain lives, mitigate damage, or reduce further degradation of a critical infrastructure capability throughout an incident. This capability should be available for and cover physical and cyber elements of critical infrastructure, and enable an integration of information as necessitated by the incident.

5) Update to National Infrastructure Protection Plan. Within 240 days of the date of this directive, the Secretary of Homeland Security shall provide to the President, through the Assistant to the President for Homeland Security and Counterterrorism, a successor to the National Infrastructure Protection Plan to address the implementation of this directive, the requirements of Title II of the Homeland Security Act of 2002 as amended, and alignment with the National Preparedness Goal and System required by PPD-8. The plan shall include the identification of a risk management framework to be used to strengthen the security and resilience of critical infrastructure; the methods to be used to prioritize critical infrastructure; the protocols to be used to synchronize communication and actions within the Federal Government; and a metrics and analysis process to be used to measure the Nation's ability to manage and reduce risks to critical infrastructure. The updated plan shall also reflect the

identified functional relationships within DHS and across the Federal Government and the updates to the public-private partnership model. Finally, the plan should consider sector dependencies on energy and communications systems, and identify pre-event and mitigation measures or alternate capabilities during disruptions to those systems. The Secretary shall coordinate this effort with the SSAs, other relevant Federal departments and agencies, SLTT entities, and critical infrastructure owners and operators.

6) National Critical Infrastructure Security and Resilience R&D Plan. Within 2 years of the date of this directive, the Secretary of Homeland Security, in coordination with the OSTP, the SSAs, DOC, and other Federal departments and agencies, shall provide to the President, through the Assistant to the President for Homeland Security and Counterterrorism, a National Critical Infrastructure Security and Resilience R&D Plan that takes into account the evolving threat landscape, annual metrics, and other relevant information to identify priorities and guide R&D requirements and investments. The plan should be issued every 4 years after its initial delivery, with interim updates as needed.

Policy coordination, dispute resolution, and periodic in-progress reviews for the implementation of this directive shall be carried out consistent with PPD-1, including the use of Interagency Policy Committees coordinated by the National Security Staff.

Nothing in this directive alters, supersedes, or impedes the authorities of Federal departments and agencies, including independent regulatory agencies, to carry out their functions and duties consistent with applicable legal authorities and other Presidential guidance and directives, including, but not limited to, the designation of critical infrastructure under such authorities.

This directive revokes Homeland Security Presidential Directive/HSPD-7, Critical Infrastructure Identification, Prioritization, and Protection, issued December 17, 2003. Plans developed pursuant to HSPD-7 shall remain in effect until specifically revoked or superseded.

Designated Critical Infrastructure Sectors and Sector-Specific Agencies

This directive identifies 16 critical infrastructure sectors and designates associated Federal SSAs. In some cases co-SSAs are designated where those departments share the roles and responsibilities of the SSA. The Secretary of Homeland Security shall periodically evaluate the need for and approve changes to critical infrastructure sectors and shall consult with the Assistant to the President for Homeland Security and Counterterrorism before changing a critical infrastructure sector or a designated SSA for that sector. The sectors and SSAs are as follows:

Chemical:
Sector-Specific Agency: Department of Homeland Security

Commercial Facilities:
Sector-Specific Agency: Department of Homeland Security

Communications:
Sector-Specific Agency: Department of Homeland Security

Critical Manufacturing: Sector-Specific Agency: Department of Homeland Security

Dams:
Sector-Specific Agency: Department of Homeland Security

Defense Industrial Base:
Sector-Specific Agency: Department of Defense

Emergency Services:
Sector-Specific Agency: Department of Homeland Security

Energy:
Sector-Specific Agency: Department of Energy

Financial Services:
Sector-Specific Agency: Department of the Treasury

Food and Agriculture:
Co-Sector-Specific Agencies: U.S. Department of Agriculture and Department of Health and Human Services

Government Facilities:
Co-Sector-Specific Agencies: Department of Homeland Security and General Services Administration

Healthcare and Public Health:
Sector-Specific Agency: Department of Health and Human Services

Information Technology:
Sector-Specific Agency: Department of Homeland Security

Nuclear Reactors, Materials, and Waste:
Sector-Specific Agency: Department of Homeland Security

Transportation Systems:
Co-Sector-Specific Agencies: Department of Homeland Security and Department of Transportation

Water and Wastewater Systems:
Sector-Specific Agency: Environmental Protection Agency

Definitions

For purposes of this directive:

The term "all hazards" means a threat or an incident, natural or manmade, that warrants action to protect life, property, the environment, and public health or safety, and to minimize disruptions of government, social, or economic activities. It includes natural disasters, cyber incidents, industrial accidents, pandemics, acts of terrorism, sabotage, and destructive criminal activity targeting critical infrastructure.

The term "collaboration" means the process of working together to achieve shared goals.

The terms "coordinate" and "in coordination with" mean a consensus decision-making process in which the named coordinating department or agency is responsible for working with the affected departments and agencies to achieve consensus and a consistent course of action.

The term "critical infrastructure" has the meaning provided in section 1016(e) of the USA Patriot Act of 2001 (42 U.S.C. 5195c(e)), namely systems and assets, whether physical or virtual, so vital to the United States that the incapacity or destruction of such systems and assets would have a debilitating impact on security, national economic security, national public health or safety, or any combination of those matters.

The term "Federal departments and agencies" means any authority of the United States that is an "agency" under 44 U.S.C. 3502(1), other than those considered to be independent regulatory agencies, as defined in 44 U.S.C. 3502(5).

The term "national essential functions" means that subset of Government functions that are necessary to lead and sustain the Nation during a catastrophic emergency.

The term "primary mission essential functions" means those Government functions that must be performed in order to support or implement the performance of the national essential functions before, during, and in the aftermath of an emergency.

The term "national security systems" has the meaning given to it in the Federal Information Security Management Act of 2002 (44 U.S.C. 3542(b)).

The term "resilience" means the ability to prepare for and adapt to changing conditions and withstand and recover rapidly from disruptions. Resilience includes the ability to withstand and recover from deliberate attacks, accidents, or naturally occurring threats or incidents.

The term "Sector-Specific Agency" (SSA) means the Federal department or agency designated under this directive to be responsible for providing institutional knowledge and specialized expertise as well as leading, facilitating, or supporting the security and resilience programs and associated activities of its designated critical infrastructure sector in the all-hazards environment.

The terms "secure" and "security" refer to reducing the risk to critical infrastructure by physical means or defense cyber measures to intrusions, attacks, or the effects of natural or manmade disasters.

PRIVACY ANNEX

FEDERAL STATUTES

The Privacy Act of 1974

5 USC § 552
As Amended

5 USC § 552a—Records maintained on individuals

(a) Definitions.—For purposes of this section—

(1) the term "agency" means agency as defined in section 552 (e) of this title;

(2) the term "individual" means a citizen of the United States or an alien lawfully admitted for permanent residence;

(3) the term "maintain" includes maintain, collect, use, or disseminate;

(4) the term "record" means any item, collection, or grouping of information about an individual that is maintained by an agency, including, but not limited to, his education, financial transactions, medical history, and criminal or employment history and that contains his name, or the identifying number, symbol, or other identifying particular assigned to the individual, such as a finger or voice print or a photograph;

(5) the term "system of records" means a group of any records under the control of any agency from which information is retrieved by the name of the individual or by some identifying number, symbol, or other identifying particular assigned to the individual;

(6) the term "statistical record" means a record in a system of records maintained for statistical research or reporting purposes only and not used in whole or in part in making any determination about an identifiable individual, except as provided by section 8 of title 13;

(7) the term "routine use" means, with respect to the disclosure of a record, the use of such record for a purpose which is compatible with the purpose for which it was collected;

(8) the term "matching program"—

(A) means any computerized comparison of—

(i) two or more automated systems of records or a system of records with non- Federal records for the purpose of—

(I) establishing or verifying the eligibility of, or continuing compliance with statutory and regulatory requirements by, applicants for, recipients or beneficiaries of, participants in, or providers of services with respect to, cash or in-kind assistance or payments under Federal benefit programs, or

(II) recouping payments or delinquent debts under such Federal benefit programs, or

(ii) two or more automated Federal personnel or payroll systems of records or a system of Federal personnel or payroll records with non-Federal records,

(B) but does not include—

(i) matches performed to produce aggregate statistical data without any personal identifiers;

(ii) matches performed to support any research or statistical project, the specific data of which may not be used to make decisions concerning the rights, benefits, or privileges of specific individuals;

(iii) matches performed, by an agency (or component thereof) which performs as its principal function any activity pertaining to the enforcement of criminal laws, subsequent to the initiation of a specific criminal or civil law enforcement investigation of a named person or persons for the purpose of gathering evidence against such person or persons;

(iv) matches of tax information

(I) pursuant to section 6103(d) of the Internal Revenue Code of 1986,

(II) for purposes of tax administration as defined in section 6103(b)(4) of such Code,

(III) for the purpose of intercepting a tax refund due an individual under authority granted by section 404(e), 464, or 1137 of the Social Security Act; or

(IV) for the purpose of intercepting a tax refund due an individual under any other tax refund intercept program authorized by statute which has been determined by the Director of the Office of Management and Budget to contain verification, notice, and hearing requirements that are substantially similar to the procedures in section 1137 of the Social Security Act;

(v) matches—

(I) using records predominantly relating to Federal personnel, that are performed for routine administrative purposes (subject to guidance provided by the Director of the Office of Management and Budget pursuant to subsection (v)); or

(II) conducted by an agency using only records from systems of records maintained by that agency;

if the purpose of the match is not to take any adverse financial, personnel, disciplinary, or other adverse action against Federal personnel;

(vi) matches performed for foreign counterintelligence purposes or to produce background checks for security clearances of Federal personnel or Federal contractor personnel;

(vii) matches performed incident to a levy described in section 6103(k)(8) of the Internal Revenue Code of 1986;

(viii) matches performed pursuant to section 202(x)(3) or 1611(e)(1) of the Social Security Act (42 U.S.C. 402 (x)(3), 1382 (e)(1)); or

(ix) matches performed by the Secretary of Health and Human Services or the Inspector General of the Department of Health and Human Services with respect to potential fraud, waste, and abuse, including matches of a system of records with non- Federal records;

(9) the term "recipient agency" means any agency, or contractor thereof, receiving records contained in a system of records from a source agency for use in a matching program;

(10) the term "non-Federal agency" means any State or local government, or agency thereof, which receives records contained in a system of records from a source agency for use in a matching program;

(11) the term "source agency" means any agency which discloses records contained in a system of records to be used in a matching program, or any State or local government, or agency thereof, which discloses records to be used in a matching program;

(12) the term "Federal benefit program" means any program administered or funded by the Federal Government, or by any agent or State on behalf of the Federal Government, providing cash or in-kind assistance in the form of payments, grants, loans, or loan guarantees to individuals; and

(13) the term "Federal personnel" means officers and employees of the Government of the United States, members of the uniformed services (including members of the Reserve Components), individuals entitled to receive immediate or deferred retirement benefits under any retirement program of the Government of the United States (including survivor benefits).

(b) Conditions of Disclosure.—No agency shall disclose any record which is contained in a system of records by any means of communication to any person, or to another agency, except pursuant to a written request by, or with the prior written consent of, the individual to whom the record pertains, unless disclosure of the record would be—

(1) to those officers and employees of the agency which maintains the record who have a need for the record in the performance of their duties;

(2) required under section 552 of this title;

(3) for a routine use as defined in subsection (a)(7) of this section and described under subsection (e)(4)(D) of this section;

(4) to the Bureau of the Census for purposes of planning or carrying out a census or survey or related activity pursuant to the provisions of title 13;

(5) to a recipient who has provided the agency with advance adequate written assurance that the record will be used solely as a statistical research or reporting record, and the record is to be transferred in a form that is not individually identifiable;

(6) to the National Archives and Records Administration as a record which has sufficient historical or other value to warrant its continued preservation by the United States Government, or for evaluation by the Archivist of the United States or the designee of the Archivist to determine whether the record has such value;

(7) to another agency or to an instrumentality of any governmental jurisdic-

tion within or under the control of the United States for a civil or criminal law enforcement activity if the activity is authorized by law, and if the head of the agency or instrumentality has made a written request to the agency which maintains the record specifying the particular portion desired and the law enforcement activity for which the record is sought;

(8) to a person pursuant to a showing of compelling circumstances affecting the health or safety of an individual if upon such disclosure notification is transmitted to the last known address of such individual;

(9) to either House of Congress, or, to the extent of matter within its jurisdiction, any committee or subcommittee thereof, any joint committee of Congress or subcommittee of any such joint committee;

(10) to the Comptroller General, or any of his authorized representatives, in the course of the performance of the duties of the Government Accountability Office;

(11) pursuant to the order of a court of competent jurisdiction; or

(12) to a consumer reporting agency in accordance with section 3711 (e) of title 31.

(c) Accounting of Certain Disclosures.—Each agency, with respect to each system of records under its control, shall—

(1) except for disclosures made under subsections (b)(1) or (b)(2) of this section, keep an accurate accounting of—

(A) the date, nature, and purpose of each disclosure of a record to any person or to another agency made under subsection (b) of this section; and

(B) the name and address of the person or agency to whom the disclosure is made;

(2) retain the accounting made under paragraph (1) of this subsection for at least five years or the life of the record, whichever is longer, after the disclosure for which the accounting is made;

(3) except for disclosures made under subsection (b)(7) of this section, make the accounting made under paragraph (1) of this subsection available to the individual named in the record at his request; and

(4) inform any person or other agency about any correction or notation of dispute made by the agency in accordance with subsection (d) of this section of any record that has been disclosed to the person or agency if an accounting of the disclosure was made.

(d) Access to Records.—Each agency that maintains a system of records shall—

(1) upon request by any individual to gain access to his record or to any information pertaining to him which is contained in the system, permit him and upon his request, a person of his own choosing to accompany him, to review the record and have a copy made of all or any portion thereof in a form comprehensible to him, except that the agency may require the individual to furnish a written statement authorizing discussion of that individual's record in the accompanying person's presence;

(2) permit the individual to request amendment of a record pertaining to him and—

(A) not later than 10 days (excluding Saturdays, Sundays, and legal public holidays) after the date of receipt of such request, acknowledge in writing such receipt; and

(B) promptly, either—

(i) make any correction of any portion thereof which the individual believes is not accurate, relevant, timely, or complete; or

(ii) inform the individual of its refusal to amend the record in accordance with his request, the reason for the refusal, the procedures established by the agency for the individual to request a review of that refusal by the head of the agency or an officer designated by the head of the agency, and the name and business address of that official;

(3) permit the individual who disagrees with the refusal of the agency to amend his record to request a review of such refusal, and not later than 30 days (excluding Saturdays, Sundays, and legal public holidays) from the date on which the individual requests such review, complete such review and make a final determination unless, for good cause shown, the head of the agency extends such 30-day period; and if, after his review, the reviewing official also refuses to amend the record in accordance with the request, permit the individual to file with the agency a concise statement setting forth the reasons for his disagreement with the refusal of the agency, and notify the individual of the provisions for judicial review of the reviewing official's determination under subsection (g)(1)(A) of this section;

(4) in any disclosure, containing information about which the individual has filed a statement of disagreement, occurring after the filing of the statement under paragraph (3) of this subsection, clearly note any portion of the record which is disputed and provide copies of the statement and, if the agency deems it appropriate, copies of a concise statement of the reasons of the agency for not making the amendments requested, to persons or other agencies to whom the disputed record has been disclosed; and

(5) nothing in this section shall allow an individual access to any information compiled in reasonable anticipation of a civil action or proceeding.

(e) Agency Requirements.—Each agency that maintains a system of records shall—

(1) maintain in its records only such information about an individual as is relevant and necessary to accomplish a purpose of the agency required to be accomplished by statute or by executive order of the President;

(2) collect information to the greatest extent practicable directly from the subject individual when the information may result in adverse determinations about an individual's rights, benefits, and privileges under Federal programs;

(3) inform each individual whom it asks to supply information, on the form which it uses to collect the information or on a separate form that can be retained by the individual—

(A) the authority (whether granted by statute, or by executive order of the President) which authorizes the solicitation of the information and whether disclosure of such information is mandatory or voluntary;

(B) the principal purpose or purposes for which the information is intended to be used;

(C) the routine uses which may be made of the information, as published pursuant to paragraph (4)(D) of this subsection; and

(D) the effects on him, if any, of not providing all or any part of the requested information;

(4) subject to the provisions of paragraph (11) of this subsection, publish in the Federal Register upon establishment or revision a notice of the existence and character of the system of records, which notice shall include—

(A) the name and location of the system;

(B) the categories of individuals on whom records are maintained in the system;

(C) the categories of records maintained in the system;

(D) each routine use of the records contained in the system, including the categories of users and the purpose of such use;

(E) the policies and practices of the agency regarding storage, retrievability, access controls, retention, and disposal of the records;

(F) the title and business address of the agency official who is responsible for the system of records;

(G) the agency procedures whereby an individual can be notified at his request if the system of records contains a record pertaining to him;

(H) the agency procedures whereby an individual can be notified at his request how he can gain access to any record pertaining to him contained in the system of records, and how he can contest its content; and

(I) the categories of sources of records in the system;

(5) maintain all records which are used by the agency in making any determination about any individual with such accuracy, relevance, timeliness, and completeness as is reasonably necessary to assure fairness to the individual in the determination;

(6) prior to disseminating any record about an individual to any person other than an agency, unless the dissemination is made pursuant to subsection (b)(2) of this section, make reasonable efforts to assure that such records are accurate, complete, timely, and relevant for agency purposes;

(7) maintain no record describing how any individual exercises rights guaranteed by the First Amendment unless expressly authorized by statute or by the individual about whom the record is maintained or unless pertinent to and within the scope of an authorized law enforcement activity;

(8) make reasonable efforts to serve notice on an individual when any record on such individual is made available to any person under compulsory legal process when such process becomes a matter of public record;

(9) establish rules of conduct for persons involved in the design, development, operation, or maintenance of any system of records, or in maintaining any record, and instruct each such person with respect to such rules and the requirements of this section, including any other rules and procedures adopted pursuant to this section and the penalties for noncompliance;

(10) establish appropriate administrative, technical, and physical safeguards to insure the security and confidentiality of records and to protect against any

anticipated threats or hazards to their security or integrity which could result in substantial harm, embarrassment, inconvenience, or unfairness to any individual on whom information is maintained;

(11) at least 30 days prior to publication of information under paragraph (4)(D) of this subsection, publish in the Federal Register notice of any new use or intended use of the information in the system, and provide an opportunity for interested persons to submit written data, views, or arguments to the agency; and

(12) if such agency is a recipient agency or a source agency in a matching program with a non- Federal agency, with respect to any establishment or revision of a matching program, at least 30 days prior to conducting such program, publish in the Federal Register notice of such establishment or revision.

(f) Agency Rules.—In order to carry out the provisions of this section, each agency that maintains a system of records shall promulgate rules, in accordance with the requirements (including general notice) of section 553 of this title, which shall—

(1) establish procedures whereby an individual can be notified in response to his request if any system of records named by the individual contains a record pertaining to him;

(2) define reasonable times, places, and requirements for identifying an individual who requests his record or information pertaining to him before the agency shall make the record or information available to the individual;

(3) establish procedures for the disclosure to an individual upon his request of his record or information pertaining to him, including special procedure, if deemed necessary, for the disclosure to an individual of medical records, including psychological records, pertaining to him;

(4) establish procedures for reviewing a request from an individual concerning the amendment of any record or information pertaining to the individual, for making a determination on the request, for an appeal within the agency of an initial adverse agency determination, and for whatever additional means may be necessary for each individual to be able to exercise fully his rights under this section; and

(5) establish fees to be charged, if any, to any individual for making copies of his record, excluding the cost of any search for and review of the record.

The Office of the Federal Register shall biennially compile and publish the rules promulgated under this subsection and agency notices published under subsection (e)(4) of this section in a form available to the public at low cost.

(g)(1) Civil Remedies.—Whenever any agency

(A) makes a determination under subsection (d)(3) of this section not to amend an individual's record in accordance with his request, or fails to make such review in conformity with that subsection;

(B) refuses to comply with an individual request under subsection (d)(1) of this section;

(C) fails to maintain any record concerning any individual with such accuracy, relevance, timeliness, and completeness as is necessary to assure fairness in any determination relating to the qualifications, character, rights, or opportunities of, or benefits to the individual that may be made on the basis of such record, and consequently a determination is made which is adverse to the individual; or

(D) fails to comply with any other provision of this section, or any rule promulgated thereunder, in such a way as to have an adverse effect on an individual,

the individual may bring a civil action against the agency, and the district courts of the United States shall have jurisdiction in the matters under the provisions of this subsection.

(2)(A) In any suit brought under the provisions of subsection (g)(1)(A) of this section, the court may order the agency to amend the individual's record in accordance with his request or in such other way as the court may direct. In such a case the court shall determine the matter de novo.

(B) The court may assess against the United States reasonable attorney fees and other litigation costs reasonably incurred in any case under this paragraph in which the complainant has substantially prevailed.

(3)(A) In any suit brought under the provisions of subsection (g)(1)(B) of this section, the court may enjoin the agency from withholding the records and order the production to the complainant of any agency records improperly withheld from him. In such a case the court shall determine the matter de novo, and may examine the contents of any agency records in camera to determine whether the records or any portion thereof may be withheld under any of the exemptions set forth in subsection (k) of this section, and the burden is on the agency to sustain its action.

(B) The court may assess against the United States reasonable attorney fees and other litigation costs reasonably incurred in any case under this paragraph in which the complainant has substantially prevailed.

(4) In any suit brought under the provisions of subsection (g)(1)(C) or (D) of this section in which the court determines that the agency acted in a manner which was intentional or willful, the United States shall be liable to the individual in an amount equal to the sum of—

(A) actual damages sustained by the individual as a result of the refusal or failure, but in no case shall a person entitled to recovery receive less than the sum of $1,000; and

(B) the costs of the action together with reasonable attorney fees as determined by the court.

(5) An action to enforce any liability created under this section may be brought in the district court of the United States in the district in which the complainant resides, or has his principal place of business, or in which the agency records are situated, or in the District of Columbia, without regard to the amount in controversy, within two years from the date on which the cause of action arises, except that where an agency has materially and willfully misrepresented any information required under this section to be disclosed to an individual and the information so misrepresented is material to establishment of the liability of the

agency to the individual under this section, the action may be brought at any time within two years after discovery by the individual of the misrepresentation. Nothing in this section shall be construed to authorize any civil action by reason of any injury sustained as the result of a disclosure of a record prior to September 27, 1975.

(h) Rights of Legal Guardians.—For the purposes of this section, the parent of any minor, or the legal guardian of any individual who has been declared to be incompetent due to physical or mental incapacity or age by a court of competent jurisdiction, may act on behalf of the individual.

(i)(1) Criminal Penalties.—Any officer or employee of an agency, who by virtue of his employment or official position, has possession of, or access to, agency records which contain individually identifiable information the disclosure of which is prohibited by this section or by rules or regulations established thereunder, and who knowing that disclosure of the specific material is so prohibited, willfully discloses the material in any manner to any person or agency not entitled to receive it, shall be guilty of a misdemeanor and fined not more than $5,000.

(2) Any officer or employee of any agency who willfully maintains a system of records without meeting the notice requirements of subsection (e)(4) of this section shall be guilty of a misdemeanor and fined not more than $5,000.

(3) Any person who knowingly and willfully requests or obtains any record concerning an individual from an agency under false pretenses shall be guilty of a misdemeanor and fined not more than $5,000.

(j) General Exemptions.—The head of any agency may promulgate rules, in accordance with the requirements (including general notice) of sections 553 (b)(1), (2), and (3), (c), and (e) of this title, to exempt any system of records within the agency from any part of this section except subsections (b), (c)(1) and (2), (e)(4)(A) through (F), (e)(6), (7), (9), (10), and (11), and (i) if the system of records is—

(1) maintained by the Central Intelligence Agency; or

(2) maintained by an agency or component thereof which performs as its principal function any activity pertaining to the enforcement of criminal laws, including police efforts to prevent, control, or reduce crime or to apprehend criminals, and the activities of prosecutors, courts, correctional, probation, pardon, or parole authorities, and which consists of

(A) information compiled for the purpose of identifying individual criminal offenders and alleged offenders and consisting only of identifying data and notations of arrests, the nature and disposition of criminal charges, sentencing, confinement, release, and parole and probation status;

(B) information compiled for the purpose of a criminal investigation, including reports of informants and investigators, and associated with an identifiable individual; or

(C) reports identifiable to an individual compiled at any stage of the process of enforcement of the criminal laws from arrest or indictment through release from supervision.

At the time rules are adopted under this subsection, the agency shall include in the statement required under section 553 (c) of this title, the reasons why the system of records is to be exempted from a provision of this section.

(k) Specific Exemptions.—The head of any agency may promulgate rules, in accordance with the requirements (including general notice) of sections 553 (b)(1), (2), and (3), (c), and (e) of this title, to exempt any system of records within the agency from subsections (c)(3), (d), (e)(1), (e)(4)(G), (H), and (I) and (f) of this section if the system of records is—

(1) subject to the provisions of section 552 (b)(1) of this title;

(2) investigatory material compiled for law enforcement purposes, other than material within the scope of subsection (j)(2) of this section: Provided, however, That if any individual is denied any right, privilege, or benefit that he would otherwise be entitled by Federal law, or for which he would otherwise be eligible, as a result of the maintenance of such material, such material shall be provided to such individual, except to the extent that the disclosure of such material would reveal the identity of a source who furnished information to the Government under an express promise that the identity of the source would be held in confidence, or, prior to the effective date of this section, under an implied promise that the identity of the source would be held in confidence;

(3) maintained in connection with providing protective services to the President of the United States or other individuals pursuant to section 3056 of title 18;

(4) required by statute to be maintained and used solely as statistical records;

(5) investigatory material compiled solely for the purpose of determining suitability, eligibility, or qualifications for Federal civilian employment, military service, Federal contracts, or access to classified information, but only to the extent that the disclosure of such material would reveal the identity of a source who furnished information to the Government under an express promise that the identity of the source would be held in confidence, or, prior to the effective date of this section, under an implied promise that the identity of the source would be held in confidence;

(6) testing or examination material used solely to determine individual qualifications for appointment or promotion in the Federal service the disclosure of which would compromise the objectivity or fairness of the testing or examination process; or

(7) evaluation material used to determine potential for promotion in the armed services, but only to the extent that the disclosure of such material would reveal the identity of a source who furnished information to the Government under an express promise that the identity of the source would be held in confidence, or, prior to the effective date of this section, under an implied promise that the identity of the source would be held in confidence.

At the time rules are adopted under this subsection, the agency shall include in the statement required under section 553 (c) of this title, the reasons why the system of records is to be exempted from a provision of this section.

(l)(1) Archival Records.—Each agency record which is accepted by the Archivist of the United States for storage, processing, and servicing in accordance with section 3103 of title 44 shall, for the purposes of this section, be considered to be maintained by the agency which deposited the record and shall be subject to the provisions of this section. The Archivist of the United States shall not disclose the record except to the agency which maintains the record, or under rules established by that agency which are not inconsistent with the provisions of this section.

(2) Each agency record pertaining to an identifiable individual which was transferred to the National Archives of the United States as a record which has sufficient historical or other value to warrant its continued preservation by the United States Government, prior to the effective date of this section, shall, for the purposes of this section, be considered to be maintained by the National Archives and shall not be subject to the provisions of this section, except that a statement generally describing such records (modeled after the requirements relating to records subject to subsections (e)(4)(A) through (G) of this section) shall be published in the Federal Register.

(3) Each agency record pertaining to an identifiable individual which is transferred to the National Archives of the United States as a record which has sufficient historical or other value to warrant its continued preservation by the United States Government, on or after the effective date of this section, shall, for the purposes of this section, be considered to be maintained by the National Archives and shall be exempt from the requirements of this section except subsections (e)(4)(A) through (G) and (e)(9) of this section.

(m)(1) Government Contractors.—When an agency provides by a contract for the operation by or on behalf of the agency of a system of records to accomplish an agency function, the agency shall, consistent with its authority, cause the requirements of this section to be applied to such system. For purposes of subsection (i) of this section any such contractor and any employee of such contractor, if such contract is agreed to on or after the effective date of this section, shall be considered to be an employee of an agency.

(2) A consumer reporting agency to which a record is disclosed under section 3711 (e) of title 31 shall not be considered a contractor for the purposes of this section.

(n) Mailing Lists.—An individual's name and address may not be sold or rented by an agency unless such action is specifically authorized by law. This provision shall not be construed to require the withholding of names and addresses otherwise permitted to be made public.

(o) Matching Agreements.—

(1) No record which is contained in a system of records may be disclosed to a recipient agency or non-Federal agency for use in a computer matching program except pursuant to a written agreement between the source agency and the recipient agency or non-Federal agency specifying—

(A) the purpose and legal authority for conducting the program;

(B) the justification for the program and the anticipated results, including a specific estimate of any savings;

(C) a description of the records that will be matched, including each data element that will be used, the approximate number of records that will be matched, and the projected starting and completion dates of the matching program;

(D) procedures for providing individualized notice at the time of application, and notice periodically thereafter as directed by the Data Integrity Board of such agency (subject to guidance provided by the Director of the Office of Management and Budget pursuant to subsection (v)), to—

(i) applicants for and recipients of financial assistance or payments under Federal benefit programs, and

(ii) applicants for and holders of positions as Federal personnel,

that any information provided by such applicants, recipients, holders, and individuals may be subject to verification through matching programs;

(E) procedures for verifying information produced in such matching program as required by subsection (p);

(F) procedures for the retention and timely destruction of identifiable records created by a recipient agency or non-Federal agency in such matching program;

(G) procedures for ensuring the administrative, technical, and physical security of the records matched and the results of such programs;

(H) prohibitions on duplication and redisclosure of records provided by the source agency within or outside the recipient agency or the non-Federal agency, except where required by law or essential to the conduct of the matching program;

(I) procedures governing the use by a recipient agency or non-Federal agency of records provided in a matching program by a source agency, including procedures governing return of the records to the source agency or destruction of records used in such program;

(J) information on assessments that have been made on the accuracy of the records that will be used in such matching program; and

(K) that the Comptroller General may have access to all records of a recipient agency or a non-Federal agency that the Comptroller General deems necessary in order to monitor or verify compliance with the agreement.

(2)(A) A copy of each agreement entered into pursuant to paragraph (1) shall—

(i) be transmitted to the Committee on Governmental Affairs of the Senate and the Committee on Government Operations of the House of Representatives; and

(ii) be available upon request to the public.

(B) No such agreement shall be effective until 30 days after the date on which such a copy is transmitted pursuant to subparagraph (A)(i).

(C) Such an agreement shall remain in effect only for such period, not to exceed 18 months, as the Data Integrity Board of the agency determines is appropriate in light of the purposes, and length of time necessary for the conduct, of the matching program.

(D) Within 3 months prior to the expiration of such an agreement pursuant to subparagraph (C), the Data Integrity Board of the agency may, without additional review, renew the matching agreement for a current, ongoing matching program for not more than one additional year if—

(i) such program will be conducted without any change; and

(ii) each party to the agreement certifies to the Board in writing that the program has been conducted in compliance with the agreement.

(p) Verification and Opportunity to Contest Findings.—

(1) In order to protect any individual whose records are used in a matching program, no recipient agency, non-Federal agency, or source agency may suspend, terminate, reduce, or make a final denial of any financial assistance or payment under a Federal benefit program to such individual, or take other adverse action against such individual, as a result of information produced by such matching program, until—

(A)(i) the agency has independently verified the information; or

(ii) the Data Integrity Board of the agency, or in the case of a non-Federal agency the Data Integrity Board of the source agency, determines in accordance with guidance issued by the Director of the Office of Management and Budget that—

(I) the information is limited to identification and amount of benefits paid by the source agency under a Federal benefit program; and

(II) there is a high degree of confidence that the information provided to the recipient agency is accurate;

(B) the individual receives a notice from the agency containing a statement of its findings and informing the individual of the opportunity to contest such findings; and

(C)(i) the expiration of any time period established for the program by statute or regulation for the individual to respond to that notice; or

(ii) in the case of a program for which no such period is established, the end of the 30-day period beginning on the date on which notice under subparagraph (B) is mailed or otherwise provided to the individual.

(2) Independent verification referred to in paragraph (1) requires investigation and confirmation of specific information relating to an individual that is used as a basis for an adverse action against the individual, including where applicable investigation and confirmation of—

(A) the amount of any asset or income involved;

(B) whether such individual actually has or had access to such asset or income for such individual's own use; and

(C) the period or periods when the individual actually had such asset or income.

(3) Notwithstanding paragraph (1), an agency may take any appropriate action otherwise prohibited by such paragraph if the agency determines that the public health or public safety may be adversely affected or significantly threatened during any notice period required by such paragraph.

(q) Sanctions.—

(1) Notwithstanding any other provision of law, no source agency may disclose any record which is contained in a system of records to a recipient

agency or non-Federal agency for a matching program if such source agency has reason to believe that the requirements of subsection (p), or any matching agreement entered into pursuant to subsection (o), or both, are not being met by such recipient agency.

(2) No source agency may renew a matching agreement unless—

(A) the recipient agency or non-Federal agency has certified that it has complied with the provisions of that agreement; and

(B) the source agency has no reason to believe that the certification is inaccurate.

(r) Report on New Systems and Matching Programs.—Each agency that proposes to establish or make a significant change in a system of records or a matching program shall provide adequate advance notice of any such proposal (in duplicate) to the Committee on Government Operations of the House of Representatives, the Committee on Governmental Affairs of the Senate, and the Office of Management and Budget in order to permit an evaluation of the probable or potential effect of such proposal on the privacy or other rights of individuals.

(s) Biennial Report.—The President shall biennially submit to the Speaker of the House of Representatives and the President pro tempore of the Senate a report—

(1) describing the actions of the Director of the Office of Management and Budget pursuant to section 6 of the Privacy Act of 1974 during the preceding 2 years;

(2) describing the exercise of individual rights of access and amendment under this section during such years;

(3) identifying changes in or additions to systems of records;

(4) containing such other information concerning administration of this section as may be necessary or useful to the Congress in reviewing the effectiveness of this section in carrying out the purposes of the Privacy Act of 1974.

(t)(1) Effect of Other Laws.—No agency shall rely on any exemption contained in section 552 of this title to withhold from an individual any record which is otherwise accessible to such individual under the provisions of this section.

(2) No agency shall rely on any exemption in this section to withhold from an individual any record which is otherwise accessible to such individual under the provisions of section 552 of this title.

(u) Data Integrity Boards.—

(1) Every agency conducting or participating in a matching program shall establish a Data Integrity Board to oversee and coordinate among the various components of such agency the agency's implementation of this section.

(2) Each Data Integrity Board shall consist of senior officials designated by the head of the agency, and shall include any senior official designated by the head of the agency as responsible for implementation of this section, and the inspector general of the agency, if any. The inspector general shall not serve as chairman of the Data Integrity Board.

(3) Each Data Integrity Board—

(A) shall review, approve, and maintain all written agreements for receipt or disclosure of agency records for matching programs to ensure compliance with subsection (o), and all relevant statutes, regulations, and guidelines;

(B) shall review all matching programs in which the agency has participated during the year, either as a source agency or recipient agency, determine compliance with applicable laws, regulations, guidelines, and agency agreements, and assess the costs and benefits of such programs;

(C) shall review all recurring matching programs in which the agency has participated during the year, either as a source agency or recipient agency, for continued justification for such disclosures;

(D) shall compile an annual report, which shall be submitted to the head of the agency and the Office of Management and Budget and made available to the public on request, describing the matching activities of the agency, including—

(i) matching programs in which the agency has participated as a source agency or recipient agency;

(ii) matching agreements proposed under subsection (o) that were disapproved by the Board;

(iii) any changes in membership or structure of the Board in the preceding year;

(iv) the reasons for any waiver of the requirement in paragraph (4) of this section for completion and submission of a cost-benefit analysis prior to the approval of a matching program;

(v) any violations of matching agreements that have been alleged or identified and any corrective action taken; and

(vi) any other information required by the Director of the Office of Management and Budget to be included in such report;

(E) shall serve as a clearinghouse for receiving and providing information on the accuracy, completeness, and reliability of records used in matching programs;

(F) shall provide interpretation and guidance to agency components and personnel on the requirements of this section for matching programs;

(G) shall review agency recordkeeping and disposal policies and practices for matching programs to assure compliance with this section; and

(H) may review and report on any agency matching activities that are not matching programs.

(4)(A) Except as provided in subparagraphs (B) and (C), a Data Integrity Board shall not approve any written agreement for a matching program unless the agency has completed and submitted to such Board a cost-benefit analysis of the proposed program and such analysis demonstrates that the program is likely to be cost effective.

(B) The Board may waive the requirements of subparagraph (A) of this paragraph if it determines in writing, in accordance with guidelines prescribed by the Director of the Office of Management and Budget, that a cost-benefit analysis is not required.

(C) A cost-benefit analysis shall not be required under subparagraph (A) prior to the initial approval of a written agreement for a matching program that is specifically required by statute. Any subsequent written agreement for such a program shall not be approved by the Data Integrity Board unless the agency has submitted a cost-benefit analysis of the program as conducted under the preceding approval of such agreement.

(5)(A) If a matching agreement is disapproved by a Data Integrity Board, any party to such agreement may appeal the disapproval to the Director of the Office of Management and Budget. Timely notice of the filing of such an appeal shall be provided by the Director of the Office of Management and Budget to the Committee on Governmental Affairs of the Senate and the Committee on Government Operations of the House of Representatives.

(B) The Director of the Office of Management and Budget may approve a matching agreement notwithstanding the disapproval of a Data Integrity Board if the Director determines that—

(i) the matching program will be consistent with all applicable legal, regulatory, and policy requirements;

(ii) there is adequate evidence that the matching agreement will be cost-effective; and

(iii) the matching program is in the public interest.

(C) The decision of the Director to approve a matching agreement shall not take effect until 30 days after it is reported to committees described in subparagraph (A).

(D) If the Data Integrity Board and the Director of the Office of Management and Budget disapprove a matching program proposed by the inspector general of an agency, the inspector general may report the disapproval to the head of the agency and to the Congress.

(6) In the reports required by paragraph (3)(D), agency matching activities that are not matching programs may be reported on an aggregate basis, if and to the extent necessary to protect ongoing law enforcement or counterintelligence investigations.

(v) Office of Management and Budget Responsibilities.—The Director of the Office of Management and Budget shall—

(1) develop and, after notice and opportunity for public comment, prescribe guidelines and regulations for the use of agencies in implementing the provisions of this section; and

(2) provide continuing assistance to and oversight of the implementation of this section by agencies.

(w) Applicability to Bureau of Consumer Financial Protection.—Except as provided in the Consumer Financial Protection Act of 2010, this section shall apply with respect to the Bureau of Consumer Financial Protection.

Electronic Communications Privacy Act

As amended

18 USC § 2510—Definitions

As used in this chapter—

(1) "wire communication" means any aural transfer made in whole or in part through the use of facilities for the transmission of communications by the aid of wire, cable, or other like connection between the point of origin and the point of reception (including the use of such connection in a switching station) furnished or operated by any person engaged in providing or operating such facilities for the transmission of interstate or foreign communications or communications affecting interstate or foreign commerce;

(2) "oral communication" means any oral communication uttered by a person exhibiting an expectation that such communication is not subject to interception under circumstances justifying such expectation, but such term does not include any electronic communication;

(3) "State" means any State of the United States, the District of Columbia, the Commonwealth of Puerto Rico, and any territory or possession of the United States;

(4) "intercept" means the aural or other acquisition of the contents of any wire, electronic, or oral communication through the use of any electronic, mechanical, or other device.

(5) "electronic, mechanical, or other device" means any device or apparatus which can be used to intercept a wire, oral, or electronic communication other than—

(a) any telephone or telegraph instrument, equipment or facility, or any component thereof,

(i) furnished to the subscriber or user by a provider of wire or electronic communication service in the ordinary course of its business and being used by the subscriber or user in the ordinary course of its business or furnished by such subscriber or user for connection to the facilities of such service and used in the ordinary course of its business; or

(ii) being used by a provider of wire or electronic communication service in the ordinary course of its business, or by an investigative or law enforcement officer in the ordinary course of his duties;

(b) a hearing aid or similar device being used to correct subnormal hearing to not better than normal;

(6) "person" means any employee, or agent of the United States or any State or political subdivision thereof, and any individual, partnership, association, joint stock company, trust, or corporation;

(7) "Investigative or law enforcement officer" means any officer of the United States or of a State or political subdivision thereof, who is empowered by law

to conduct investigations of or to make arrests for offenses enumerated in this chapter, and any attorney authorized by law to prosecute or participate in the prosecution of such offenses;

(8) "contents", when used with respect to any wire, oral, or electronic communication, includes any information concerning the substance, purport, or meaning of that communication;

(9) "Judge of competent jurisdiction" means—

(a) a judge of a United States district court or a United States court of appeals; and

(b) a judge of any court of general criminal jurisdiction of a State who is authorized by a statute of that State to enter orders authorizing interceptions of wire, oral, or electronic communications;

(10) "communication common carrier" has the meaning given that term in section 3 of the Communications Act of 1934;

(11) "aggrieved person" means a person who was a party to any intercepted wire, oral, or electronic communication or a person against whom the interception was directed;

(12) "electronic communication" means any transfer of signs, signals, writing, images, sounds, data, or intelligence of any nature transmitted in whole or in part by a wire, radio, electromagnetic, photoelectronic or photooptical system that affects interstate or foreign commerce, but does not include—

(A) any wire or oral communication;

(B) any communication made through a tone-only paging device;

(C) any communication from a tracking device (as defined in section 3117 of this title); or

(D) electronic funds transfer information stored by a financial institution in a communications system used for the electronic storage and transfer of funds;

(13) "user" means any person or entity who—

(A) uses an electronic communication service; and

(B) is duly authorized by the provider of such service to engage in such use;

(14) "electronic communications system" means any wire, radio, electromagnetic, photooptical or photoelectronic facilities for the transmission of wire or electronic communications, and any computer facilities or related electronic equipment for the electronic storage of such communications;

(15) "electronic communication service" means any service which provides to users thereof the ability to send or receive wire or electronic communications;

(16) "readily accessible to the general public" means, with respect to a radio communication, that such communication is not—

(A) scrambled or encrypted;

(B) transmitted using modulation techniques whose essential parameters have been withheld from the public with the intention of preserving the privacy of such communication;

(C) carried on a subcarrier or other signal subsidiary to a radio transmission;

(D) transmitted over a communication system provided by a common carrier, unless the communication is a tone only paging system communication; or

(E) transmitted on frequencies allocated under part 25, subpart D, E, or F of part 74, or part 94 of the Rules of the Federal Communications Commission, unless, in the case of a communication transmitted on a frequency allocated under part 74 that is not exclusively allocated to broadcast auxiliary services, the communication is a two-way voice communication by radio;

(17) "electronic storage" means—

(A) any temporary, intermediate storage of a wire or electronic communication incidental to the electronic transmission thereof; and

(B) any storage of such communication by an electronic communication service for purposes of backup protection of such communication;

(18) "aural transfer" means a transfer containing the human voice at any point between and including the point of origin and the point of reception;

(19) "foreign intelligence information", for purposes of section 2517 (6) of this title, means—

(A) information, whether or not concerning a United States person, that relates to the ability of the United States to protect against—

(i) actual or potential attack or other grave hostile acts of a foreign power or an agent of a foreign power;

(ii) sabotage or international terrorism by a foreign power or an agent of a foreign power; or

(iii) clandestine intelligence activities by an intelligence service or network of a foreign power or by an agent of a foreign power; or

(B) information, whether or not concerning a United States person, with respect to a foreign power or foreign territory that relates to—

(i) the national defense or the security of the United States; or

(ii) the conduct of the foreign affairs of the United States;

(20) "protected computer" has the meaning set forth in section 1030; and

(21) "computer trespasser"—

(A) means a person who accesses a protected computer without authorization and thus has no reasonable expectation of privacy in any communication transmitted to, through, or from the protected computer; and

(B) does not include a person known by the owner or operator of the protected computer to have an existing contractual relationship with the owner or operator of the protected computer for access to all or part of the protected computer.

18 USC § 2511—Interception and disclosure of wire, oral, or electronic communications prohibited

(1) Except as otherwise specifically provided in this chapter any person who—

(a) intentionally intercepts, endeavors to intercept, or procures any other person to intercept or endeavor to intercept, any wire, oral, or electronic communication;

(b) intentionally uses, endeavors to use, or procures any other person to use or endeavor to use any electronic, mechanical, or other device to intercept any oral communication when—

(i) such device is affixed to, or otherwise transmits a signal through, a wire, cable, or other like connection used in wire communication; or

(ii) such device transmits communications by radio, or interferes with the transmission of such communication; or

(iii) such person knows, or has reason to know, that such device or any component thereof has been sent through the mail or transported in interstate or foreign commerce; or

(iv) such use or endeavor to use (A) takes place on the premises of any business or other commercial establishment the operations of which affect interstate or foreign commerce; or (B) obtains or is for the purpose of obtaining information relating to the operations of any business or other commercial establishment the operations of which affect interstate or foreign commerce; or

(v) such person acts in the District of Columbia, the Commonwealth of Puerto Rico, or any territory or possession of the United States;

(c) intentionally discloses, or endeavors to disclose, to any other person the contents of any wire, oral, or electronic communication, knowing or having reason to know that the information was obtained through the interception of a wire, oral, or electronic communication in violation of this subsection;

(d) intentionally uses, or endeavors to use, the contents of any wire, oral, or electronic communication, knowing or having reason to know that the information was obtained through the interception of a wire, oral, or electronic communication in violation of this subsection; or

(e)(i) intentionally discloses, or endeavors to disclose, to any other person the contents of any wire, oral, or electronic communication, intercepted by means authorized by sections 2511 (2)(a)(ii), 2511 (2)(b)–(c), 2511(2)(e), 2516, and 2518 of this chapter,

(ii) knowing or having reason to know that the information was obtained through the interception of such a communication in connection with a criminal investigation,

(iii) having obtained or received the information in connection with a criminal investigation, and

(iv) with intent to improperly obstruct, impede, or interfere with a duly authorized criminal investigation,

shall be punished as provided in subsection (4) or shall be subject to suit as provided in subsection (5).

(2)(a)(i) It shall not be unlawful under this chapter for an operator of a switchboard, or an officer, employee, or agent of a provider of wire or electronic communication service, whose facilities are used in the transmission of a wire or electronic communication, to intercept, disclose, or use that communication in the normal course of his employment while engaged in any activity which is a necessary incident to the rendition of his service or to the protection of the rights or property of the provider of that service, except that a provider of wire communication service to the public shall not utilize service observing or random monitoring except for mechanical or service quality control checks.

(ii) Notwithstanding any other law, providers of wire or electronic communication service, their officers, employees, and agents, landlords, custodians, or other persons, are authorized to provide information, facilities, or technical assistance to persons authorized by law to intercept wire, oral, or electronic communications or to conduct electronic surveillance, as defined in section 101 of the Foreign Intelligence Surveillance Act of 1978, if such provider, its officers, employees, or agents, landlord, custodian, or other specified person, has been provided with—

(A) a court order directing such assistance or a court order pursuant to section 704 of the Foreign Intelligence Surveillance Act of 1978 signed by the authorizing judge, or

(B) a certification in writing by a person specified in section 2518 (7) of this title or the Attorney General of the United States that no warrant or court order is required by law, that all statutory requirements have been met, and that the specified assistance is required, setting forth the period of time during which the provision of the information, facilities, or technical assistance is authorized and specifying the information, facilities, or technical assistance required. No provider of wire or electronic communication service, officer, employee, or agent thereof, or landlord, custodian, or other specified person shall disclose the existence of any interception or surveillance or the device used to accomplish the interception or surveillance with respect to which the person has been furnished a court order or certification under this chapter, except as may otherwise be required by legal process and then only after prior notification to the Attorney General or to the principal prosecuting attorney of a State or any political subdivision of a State, as may be appropriate. Any such disclosure, shall render such person liable for the civil damages provided for in section 2520. No cause of action shall lie in any court against any provider of wire or electronic communication service, its officers, employees, or agents, landlord, custodian, or other specified person for providing information, facilities, or assistance in accordance with the terms of a court order, statutory authorization, or certification under this chapter.

(iii) If a certification under subparagraph (ii)(B) for assistance to obtain foreign intelligence information is based on statutory authority, the certification shall identify the specific statutory provision and shall certify that the statutory requirements have been met.

(b) It shall not be unlawful under this chapter for an officer, employee, or agent of the Federal Communications Commission, in the normal course of his employment and in discharge of the monitoring responsibilities exercised by the Commission in the enforcement of chapter 5 of title 47 of the United States Code, to intercept a wire or electronic communication, or oral communication transmitted by radio, or to disclose or use the information thereby obtained.

(c) It shall not be unlawful under this chapter for a person acting under color of law to intercept a wire, oral, or electronic communication, where such person is a party to the communication or one of the parties to the communication has given prior consent to such interception.

(d) It shall not be unlawful under this chapter for a person not acting under color of law to intercept a wire, oral, or electronic communication where such person is a party to the communication or where one of the parties to the communication has given prior consent to such interception unless such communication is intercepted for the purpose of committing any criminal or tortious act in violation of the Constitution or laws of the United States or of any State.

(e) Notwithstanding any other provision of this title or section 705 or 706 of the Communications Act of 1934, it shall not be unlawful for an officer, employee, or agent of the United States in the normal course of his official duty to conduct electronic surveillance, as defined in section 101 of the Foreign Intelligence Surveillance Act of 1978, as authorized by that Act.

(f) Nothing contained in this chapter or chapter 121 or 206 of this title, or section 705 of the Communications Act of 1934, shall be deemed to affect the acquisition by the United States Government of foreign intelligence information from international or foreign communications, or foreign intelligence activities conducted in accordance with otherwise applicable Federal law involving a foreign electronic communications system, utilizing a means other than electronic surveillance as defined in section 101 of the Foreign Intelligence Surveillance Act of 1978, and procedures in this chapter or chapter 121 and the Foreign Intelligence Surveillance Act of 1978 shall be the exclusive means by which electronic surveillance, as defined in section 101 of such Act, and the interception of domestic wire, oral, and electronic communications may be conducted.

(g) It shall not be unlawful under this chapter or chapter 121 of this title for any person—

(i) to intercept or access an electronic communication made through an electronic communication system that is configured so that such electronic communication is readily accessible to the general public;

(ii) to intercept any radio communication which is transmitted—

(I) by any station for the use of the general public, or that relates to ships, aircraft, vehicles, or persons in distress;

(II) by any governmental, law enforcement, civil defense, private land mobile, or public safety communications system, including police and fire, readily accessible to the general public;

(III) by a station operating on an authorized frequency within the bands allocated to the amateur, citizens band, or general mobile radio services; or

(IV) by any marine or aeronautical communications system;

(iii) to engage in any conduct which—

(I) is prohibited by section 633 of the Communications Act of 1934; or

(II) is excepted from the application of section 705(a) of the Communications Act of 1934 by section 705(b) of that Act;

(iv) to intercept any wire or electronic communication the transmission of which is causing harmful interference to any lawfully operating station or consumer electronic equipment, to the extent necessary to identify the source of such interference; or

(v) for other users of the same frequency to intercept any radio communication made through a system that utilizes frequencies monitored by individuals engaged in the provision or the use of such system, if such communication is not scrambled or encrypted.

(h) It shall not be unlawful under this chapter—

(i) to use a pen register or a trap and trace device (as those terms are defined for the purposes of chapter 206 (relating to pen registers and trap and trace devices) of this title); or

(ii) for a provider of electronic communication service to record the fact that a wire or electronic communication was initiated or completed in order to protect such provider, another provider furnishing service toward the completion of the wire or electronic communication, or a user of that service, from fraudulent, unlawful or abusive use of such service.

(i) It shall not be unlawful under this chapter for a person acting under color of law to intercept the wire or electronic communications of a computer trespasser transmitted to, through, or from the protected computer, if—

(I) the owner or operator of the protected computer authorizes the interception of the computer trespasser's communications on the protected computer;

(II) the person acting under color of law is lawfully engaged in an investigation;

(III) the person acting under color of law has reasonable grounds to believe that the contents of the computer trespasser's communications will be relevant to the investigation; and

(IV) such interception does not acquire communications other than those transmitted to or from the computer trespasser.

(3)(a) Except as provided in paragraph (b) of this subsection, a person or entity providing an electronic communication service to the public shall not intentionally divulge the contents of any communication (other than one to such person or entity, or an agent thereof) while in transmission on that service to any person or entity other than an addressee or intended recipient of such communication or an agent of such addressee or intended recipient.

(b) A person or entity providing electronic communication service to the public may divulge the contents of any such communication—

(i) as otherwise authorized in section 2511 (2)(a) or 2517 of this title;

(ii) with the lawful consent of the originator or any addressee or intended recipient of such communication;

(iii) to a person employed or authorized, or whose facilities are used, to forward such communication to its destination; or

(iv) which were inadvertently obtained by the service provider and which appear to pertain to the commission of a crime, if such divulgence is made to a law enforcement agency.

(4)(a) Except as provided in paragraph (b) of this subsection or in subsection (5), whoever violates subsection (1) of this section shall be fined under this title or imprisoned not more than five years, or both.

(b) Conduct otherwise an offense under this subsection that consists of or relates to the interception of a satellite transmission that is not encrypted or scrambled and that is transmitted—

(i) to a broadcasting station for purposes of retransmission to the general public; or

(ii) as an audio subcarrier intended for redistribution to facilities open to the public, but not including data transmissions or telephone calls,

is not an offense under this subsection unless the conduct is for the purposes of direct or indirect commercial advantage or private financial gain.

(5)(a)(i) If the communication is—

(A) a private satellite video communication that is not scrambled or encrypted and the conduct in violation of this chapter is the private viewing of that communication and is not for a tortious or illegal purpose or for purposes of direct or indirect commercial advantage or private commercial gain; or

(B) a radio communication that is transmitted on frequencies allocated under subpart D of part 74 of the rules of the Federal Communications Commission that is not scrambled or encrypted and the conduct in violation of this chapter is not for a tortious or illegal purpose or for purposes of direct or indirect commercial advantage or private commercial gain, then the person who engages in such conduct shall be subject to suit by the Federal Government in a court of competent jurisdiction.

(ii) In an action under this subsection—

(A) if the violation of this chapter is a first offense for the person under paragraph (a) of subsection (4) and such person has not been found liable in a civil action under section 2520 of this title, the Federal Government shall be entitled to appropriate injunctive relief; and

(B) if the violation of this chapter is a second or subsequent offense under paragraph (a) of subsection (4) or such person has been found liable in any prior civil action under section 2520, the person shall be subject to a mandatory $500 civil fine.

(b) The court may use any means within its authority to enforce an injunction issued under paragraph (ii)(A), and shall impose a civil fine of not less than $500 for each violation of such an injunction.

18 USC § 2512—Manufacture, distribution, possession, and advertising of wire, oral, or electronic communication intercepting devices prohibited

(1) Except as otherwise specifically provided in this chapter, any person who intentionally—

(a) sends through the mail, or sends or carries in interstate or foreign commerce, any electronic, mechanical, or other device, knowing or having reason to know that the design of such device renders it primarily useful for the purpose of the surreptitious interception of wire, oral, or electronic communications;

(b) manufactures, assembles, possesses, or sells any electronic, mechanical, or other device, knowing or having reason to know that the design of such device renders it primarily useful for the purpose of the surreptitious interception of wire, oral, or electronic communications, and that such device or any component thereof has been or will be sent through the mail or transported in interstate or foreign commerce; or

(c) places in any newspaper, magazine, handbill, or other publication or disseminates by electronic means any advertisement of—

(i) any electronic, mechanical, or other device knowing or having reason to know that the design of such device renders it primarily useful for the purpose of the surreptitious interception of wire, oral, or electronic communications; or

(ii) any other electronic, mechanical, or other device, where such advertisement promotes the use of such device for the purpose of the surreptitious interception of wire, oral, or electronic communications,

knowing the content of the advertisement and knowing or having reason to know that such advertisement will be sent through the mail or transported in interstate or foreign commerce,

shall be fined under this title or imprisoned not more than five years, or both.

(2) It shall not be unlawful under this section for—

(a) a provider of wire or electronic communication service or an officer, agent, or employee of, or a person under contract with, such a provider, in the normal course of the business of providing that wire or electronic communication service, or

(b) an officer, agent, or employee of, or a person under contract with, the United States, a State, or a political subdivision thereof, in the normal course of the activities of the United States, a State, or a political subdivision thereof, to send through the mail, send or carry in interstate or foreign commerce, or manufacture, assemble, possess, or sell any electronic, mechanical, or other device knowing or having reason to know that the design of such device renders it primarily useful for the purpose of the surreptitious interception of wire, oral, or electronic communications.

(3) It shall not be unlawful under this section to advertise for sale a device described in subsection (1) of this section if the advertisement is mailed, sent, or carried in interstate or foreign commerce solely to a domestic provider of wire or electronic communication service or to an agency of the United States, a State, or a political subdivision thereof which is duly authorized to use such device.

18 USC § 2513 —Confiscation of wire, oral, or electronic communication intercepting devices

Any electronic, mechanical, or other device used, sent, carried, manufactured, assembled, possessed, sold, or advertised in violation of section 2511 or section 2512 of this chapter may be seized and forfeited to the United States. All provisions of law relating to

(1) the seizure, summary and judicial forfeiture, and condemnation of vessels, vehicles, merchandise, and baggage for violations of the customs laws contained in title 19 of the United States Code,

(2) the disposition of such vessels, vehicles, merchandise, and baggage or the proceeds from the sale thereof,

(3) the remission or mitigation of such forfeiture,

(4) the compromise of claims, and

(5) the award of compensation to informers in respect of such forfeitures, shall apply to seizures and forfeitures incurred, or alleged to have been incurred, under the provisions of this section, insofar as applicable and not inconsistent with the provisions of this section; except that such duties as are imposed upon the collector of customs or any other person with respect to the seizure and forfeiture of vessels, vehicles, merchandise, and baggage under the provisions of the customs laws contained in title 19 of the United States Code shall be performed with respect to seizure and forfeiture of electronic, mechanical, or other intercepting devices under this section by such officers, agents, or other persons as may be authorized or designated for that purpose by the Attorney General.

18 USC § 2514 —Repealed.

18 USC § 2515 —Prohibition of use as evidence of intercepted wire or oral communications

Whenever any wire or oral communication has been intercepted, no part of the contents of such communication and no evidence derived therefrom may be received in evidence in any trial, hearing, or other proceeding in or before any court, grand jury, department, officer, agency, regulatory body, legislative committee, or other authority of the United States, a State, or a political subdivision thereof if the disclosure of that information would be in violation of this chapter.

18 USC § 2516 —Authorization for interception of wire, oral, or electronic communications

(1) The Attorney General, Deputy Attorney General, Associate Attorney General, or any Assistant Attorney General, any acting Assistant Attorney General, or any Deputy Assistant Attorney General or acting Deputy Assistant Attorney General in the Criminal Division or National Security Division specially designated by the Attorney General, may authorize an application to a Federal judge of competent jurisdiction for, and such judge may grant in conformity with section 2518 of this chapter an order authorizing or approving the interception of wire or oral communications by the Federal Bureau of Investigation, or a Federal agency having responsibility for the investigation of the offense as to which the application is made, when such interception may provide or has provided evidence of—

(a) any offense punishable by death or by imprisonment for more than one year under sections 2122 and 2274 through 2277 of title 42 of the United States Code (relating to the enforcement of the Atomic Energy Act of 1954), section 2284 of title 42 of the United States Code (relating to sabotage of nuclear facilities or fuel), or under the following chapters of this title: chapter 10 (relating to biological weapons) chapter 37 (relating to espionage), chapter 55 (relating to kidnapping), chapter 90 (relating to protection of trade secrets), chapter 105 (relating to sabotage), chapter 115 (relating to treason), chapter 102 (relating to riots), chapter 65 (relating to malicious mischief), chapter 111 (relating to destruction of vessels), or chapter 81 (relating to piracy);

(b) a violation of section 186 or section 501 (c) of title 29, United States Code (dealing with restrictions on payments and loans to labor organizations), or any offense which involves murder, kidnapping, robbery, or extortion, and which is punishable under this title;

(c) any offense which is punishable under the following sections of this title: section 37 (relating to violence at international airports), section 43 (relating to animal enterprise terrorism), section 81 (arson within special maritime and territorial jurisdiction), section 201 (bribery of public officials and witnesses), section 215 (relating to bribery of bank officials), section 224 (bribery in sporting contests), subsection (d), (e), (f), (g), (h), or (i) of section 844 (unlawful use of explosives), section 1032 (relating to concealment of assets), section 1084 (transmission of wagering information), section 751 (relating to escape), section 832 (relating to nuclear and weapons of mass destruction threats), section 842 (relating to explosive materials), section 930 (relating to possession of weapons in Federal facilities), section 1014 (relating to loans and credit applications generally; renewals and discounts), section 1114 (relating to officers and employees of the United States), section 1116 (relating to protection of foreign officials), sections 1503, 1512, and 1513 (influencing or injuring an officer, juror, or witness generally), section 1510 (obstruction of criminal investigations), section 1511 (obstruction of State or local law enforcement), section 1591 (sex trafficking of children by force, fraud, or coercion), section 1751 (Presidential and Presidential staff assassination, kidnapping, and assault), section 1951 (interference with commerce by threats or violence), section 1952 (interstate and foreign travel or transportation in aid of racketeering enterprises), section 1958 (relating to use of interstate commerce facilities in the commission of murder for hire), section 1959 (relating to violent crimes in aid of racketeering activity), section 1954 (offer, acceptance, or solicitation to influence operations of employee benefit plan), section 1955 (prohibition of business enterprises of gambling), section 1956 (laundering of monetary instruments), section 1957 (relating to engaging in monetary transactions in property derived from specified unlawful activity), section 659 (theft from interstate shipment), section 664 (embezzlement from pension and welfare funds), section 1343 (fraud by wire, radio, or television), section 1344 (relating to bank fraud), section 1992 (relating to terrorist attacks against mass transportation), sections 2251 and 2252 (sexual exploitation of children), section 2251A (selling or buying of children), section 2252A (relating to material constituting or containing child pornography), section 1466A (relating to child obscenity), section 2260 (production of sexually explicit depictions of a minor for importation into the United States), sections 2421, 2422, 2423, and 2425 (relating to transportation for illegal sexual activity and related crimes), sections 2312, 2313, 2314, and 2315 (interstate transportation of stolen property), section 2321 (relating to trafficking in certain motor vehicles or motor vehicle parts), section 2340A (relating to torture), section 1203 (relating to hostage taking), section 1029 (relating to fraud and related activity in connection with access devices), section 3146 (relating to penalty for failure to appear), section 3521 (b)(3) (relating to witness relocation and assistance), section 32 (relating to destruction of aircraft or aircraft facilities), section 38 (relating to aircraft parts fraud), section 1963 (violations with respect to racketeer influenced and corrupt organizations), section 115 (relating to threatening or retaliating against a Federal official), section 1341 (relating to mail fraud), a felony violation of section 1030 (relating to computer fraud and abuse), section 351 (violations with respect to congressional, Cabinet, or Supreme Court assassinations, kidnapping, and assault), section 831 (relating to prohibited transactions involving nuclear materials), section 33 (relating to destruction of motor vehicles or motor vehicle facilities), section 175 (relating to biological weapons), section 175c (relating to variola virus), section 956 (conspiracy to harm persons or property overseas), section a felony violation of section 1028 (relating to production of false identification documentation),

section 1425 (relating to the procurement of citizenship or nationalization unlawfully), section 1426 (relating to the reproduction of naturalization or citizenship papers), section 1427 (relating to the sale of naturalization or citizenship papers), section 1541 (relating to passport issuance without authority), section 1542 (relating to false statements in passport applications), section 1543 (relating to forgery or false use of passports), section 1544 (relating to misuse of passports), or section 1546 (relating to fraud and misuse of visas, permits, and other documents);
(d) any offense involving counterfeiting punishable under section 471, 472, or 473 of this title;
(e) any offense involving fraud connected with a case under title 11 or the manufacture, importation, receiving, concealment, buying, selling, or otherwise dealing in narcotic drugs, marihuana, or other dangerous drugs, punishable under any law of the United States;
(f) any offense including extortionate credit transactions under sections 892, 893, or 894 of this title;
(g) a violation of section 5322 of title 31, United States Code (dealing with the reporting of currency transactions), or section 5324 of title 31, United States Code (relating to structuring transactions to evade reporting requirement prohibited);
(h) any felony violation of sections 2511 and 2512 (relating to interception and disclosure of certain communications and to certain intercepting devices) of this title;
(i) any felony violation of chapter 71 (relating to obscenity) of this title;
(j) any violation of section 60123(b) (relating to destruction of a natural gas pipeline,) section 46502 (relating to aircraft piracy), the second sentence of section 46504 (relating to assault on a flight crew with dangerous weapon), or section 46505(b)(3) or (c) (relating to explosive or incendiary devices, or endangerment of human life, by means of weapons on aircraft) of title 49;
(k) any criminal violation of section 2778 of title 22 (relating to the Arms Export Control Act);
(l) the location of any fugitive from justice from an offense described in this section;
(m) a violation of section 274, 277, or 278 of the Immigration and Nationality Act (8 U.S.C. 1324, 1327, or 1328) (relating to the smuggling of aliens);
(n) any felony violation of sections 922 and 924 of title 18, United States Code (relating to firearms);
(o) any violation of section 5861 of the Internal Revenue Code of 1986 (relating to firearms);
(p) a felony violation of section 1028 (relating to production of false identification documents), section 1542 (relating to false statements in passport applications), section 1546 (relating to fraud and misuse of visas, permits, and other documents, section 1028A (relating to aggravated iden-

tity theft)) of this title or a violation of section 274, 277, or 278 of the Immigration and Nationality Act (relating to the smuggling of aliens); or

(q) any criminal violation of section 229 (relating to chemical weapons) or section 2332, 2332a, 2332b, 2332d, 2332f, 2332g, 2332h, 2339, 2339A, 2339B, 2339C, or 2339D of this title (relating to terrorism);

(r) any criminal violation of section 1 (relating to illegal restraints of trade or commerce), 2 (relating to illegal monopolizing of trade or commerce), or 3 (relating to illegal restraints of trade or commerce in territories or the District of Columbia) of the Sherman Act (15 U.S.C. 1, 2, 3); or

(s) any conspiracy to commit any offense described in any subparagraph of this paragraph.

(2) The principal prosecuting attorney of any State, or the principal prosecuting attorney of any political subdivision thereof, if such attorney is authorized by a statute of that State to make application to a State court judge of competent jurisdiction for an order authorizing or approving the interception of wire, oral, or electronic communications, may apply to such judge for, and such judge may grant in conformity with section 2518 of this chapter and with the applicable State statute an order authorizing, or approving the interception of wire, oral, or electronic communications by investigative or law enforcement officers having responsibility for the investigation of the offense as to which the application is made, when such interception may provide or has provided evidence of the commission of the offense of murder, kidnapping, gambling, robbery, bribery, extortion, or dealing in narcotic drugs, marihuana or other dangerous drugs, or other crime dangerous to life, limb, or property, and punishable by imprisonment for more than one year, designated in any applicable State statute authorizing such interception, or any conspiracy to commit any of the foregoing offenses.

(3) Any attorney for the Government (as such term is defined for the purposes of the Federal Rules of Criminal Procedure) may authorize an application to a Federal judge of competent jurisdiction for, and such judge may grant, in conformity with section 2518 of this title, an order authorizing or approving the interception of electronic communications by an investigative or law enforcement officer having responsibility for the investigation of the offense as to which the application is made, when such interception may provide or has provided evidence of any Federal felony.

18 USC § 2517 —Authorization for disclosure and use of intercepted wire, oral, or electronic communications

(1) Any investigative or law enforcement officer who, by any means authorized by this chapter, has obtained knowledge of the contents of any wire, oral, or electronic communication, or evidence derived therefrom, may disclose such contents to another investigative or law enforcement officer to the extent that such disclosure is appropriate to the proper performance of the official duties of the officer making or receiving the disclosure.

(2) Any investigative or law enforcement officer who, by any means autho-

rized by this chapter, has obtained knowledge of the contents of any wire, oral, or electronic communication or evidence derived therefrom may use such contents to the extent such use is appropriate to the proper performance of his official duties.

(3) Any person who has received, by any means authorized by this chapter, any information concerning a wire, oral, or electronic communication, or evidence derived therefrom intercepted in accordance with the provisions of this chapter may disclose the contents of that communication or such derivative evidence while giving testimony under oath or affirmation in any proceeding held under the authority of the United States or of any State or political subdivision thereof.

(4) No otherwise privileged wire, oral, or electronic communication intercepted in accordance with, or in violation of, the provisions of this chapter shall lose its privileged character.

(5) When an investigative or law enforcement officer, while engaged in intercepting wire, oral, or electronic communications in the manner authorized herein, intercepts wire, oral, or electronic communications relating to offenses other than those specified in the order of authorization or approval, the contents thereof, and evidence derived therefrom, may be disclosed or used as provided in subsections (1) and (2) of this section. Such contents and any evidence derived therefrom may be used under subsection (3) of this section when authorized or approved by a judge of competent jurisdiction where such judge finds on subsequent application that the contents were otherwise intercepted in accordance with the provisions of this chapter. Such application shall be made as soon as practicable.

(6) Any investigative or law enforcement officer, or attorney for the Government, who by any means authorized by this chapter, has obtained knowledge of the contents of any wire, oral, or electronic communication, or evidence derived therefrom, may disclose such contents to any other Federal law enforcement, intelligence, protective, immigration, national defense, or national security official to the extent that such contents include foreign intelligence or counterintelligence (as defined in section 3 of the National Security Act of 1947 (50 U.S.C. 401a)), or foreign intelligence information (as defined in subsection (19) of section 2510 of this title), to assist the official who is to receive that information in the performance of his official duties. Any Federal official who receives information pursuant to this provision may use that information only as necessary in the conduct of that person's official duties subject to any limitations on the unauthorized disclosure of such information.

(7) Any investigative or law enforcement officer, or other Federal official in carrying out official duties as such Federal official, who by any means authorized by this chapter, has obtained knowledge of the contents of any wire, oral, or electronic communication, or evidence derived therefrom, may disclose such contents or derivative evidence to a foreign investigative or law enforcement officer to the extent that such disclosure is appropriate to the proper performance of the official duties of the officer making or receiving

the disclosure, and foreign investigative or law enforcement officers may use or disclose such contents or derivative evidence to the extent such use or disclosure is appropriate to the proper performance of their official duties.

(8) Any investigative or law enforcement officer, or other Federal official in carrying out official duties as such Federal official, who by any means authorized by this chapter, has obtained knowledge of the contents of any wire, oral, or electronic communication, or evidence derived therefrom, may disclose such contents or derivative evidence to any appropriate Federal, State, local, or foreign government official to the extent that such contents or derivative evidence reveals a threat of actual or potential attack or other grave hostile acts of a foreign power or an agent of a foreign power, domestic or international sabotage, domestic or international terrorism, or clandestine intelligence gathering activities by an intelligence service or network of a foreign power or by an agent of a foreign power, within the United States or elsewhere, for the purpose of preventing or responding to such a threat. Any official who receives information pursuant to this provision may use that information only as necessary in the conduct of that person's official duties subject to any limitations on the unauthorized disclosure of such information, and any State, local, or foreign official who receives information pursuant to this provision may use that information only consistent with such guidelines as the Attorney General and Director of Central Intelligence shall jointly issue.

18 USC § 2518 —Procedure for interception of wire, oral, or electronic communications

(1) Each application for an order authorizing or approving the interception of a wire, oral, or electronic communication under this chapter shall be made in writing upon oath or affirmation to a judge of competent jurisdiction and shall state the applicant's authority to make such application. Each application shall include the following information:

(a) the identity of the investigative or law enforcement officer making the application, and the officer authorizing the application;

(b) a full and complete statement of the facts and circumstances relied upon by the applicant, to justify his belief that an order should be issued, including

(i) details as to the particular offense that has been, is being, or is about to be committed,

(ii) except as provided in subsection (11), a particular description of the nature and location of the facilities from which or the place where the communication is to be intercepted,

(iii) a particular description of the type of communications sought to be intercepted,

(iv) the identity of the person, if known, committing the offense and whose communications are to be intercepted;

(c) a full and complete statement as to whether or not other investigative procedures have been tried and failed or why they reasonably appear to be unlikely to succeed if tried or to be too dangerous;

(d) a statement of the period of time for which the interception is required to be maintained. If the nature of the investigation is such that the authorization for interception should not automatically terminate when the described type of communication has been first obtained, a particular description of facts establishing probable cause to believe that additional communications of the same type will occur thereafter;

(e) a full and complete statement of the facts concerning all previous applications known to the individual authorizing and making the application, made to any judge for authorization to intercept, or for approval of interceptions of, wire, oral, or electronic communications involving any of the same persons, facilities or places specified in the application, and the action taken by the judge on each such application; and

(f) where the application is for the extension of an order, a statement setting forth the results thus far obtained from the interception, or a reasonable explanation of the failure to obtain such results.

(2) The judge may require the applicant to furnish additional testimony or documentary evidence in support of the application.

(3) Upon such application the judge may enter an ex parte order, as requested or as modified, authorizing or approving interception of wire, oral, or electronic communications within the territorial jurisdiction of the court in which the judge is sitting (and outside that jurisdiction but within the United States in the case of a mobile interception device authorized by a Federal court within such jurisdiction), if the judge determines on the basis of the facts submitted by the applicant that—

(a) there is probable cause for belief that an individual is committing, has committed, or is about to commit a particular offense enumerated in section 2516 of this chapter;

(b) there is probable cause for belief that particular communications concerning that offense will be obtained through such interception;

(c) normal investigative procedures have been tried and have failed or reasonably appear to be unlikely to succeed if tried or to be too dangerous;

(d) except as provided in subsection (11), there is probable cause for belief that the facilities from which, or the place where, the wire, oral, or electronic communications are to be intercepted are being used, or are about to be used, in connection with the commission of such offense, or are leased to, listed in the name of, or commonly used by such person.

(4) Each order authorizing or approving the interception of any wire, oral, or electronic communication under this chapter shall specify—

(a) the identity of the person, if known, whose communications are to be intercepted;

(b) the nature and location of the communications facilities as to which, or the place where, authority to intercept is granted;

(c) a particular description of the type of communication sought to be intercepted, and a statement of the particular offense to which it relates;

(d) the identity of the agency authorized to intercept the communications, and of the person authorizing the application; and

(e) the period of time during which such interception is authorized, including a statement as to whether or not the interception shall automatically terminate when the described communication has been first obtained.

An order authorizing the interception of a wire, oral, or electronic communication under this chapter shall, upon request of the applicant, direct that a provider of wire or electronic communication service, landlord, custodian or other person shall furnish the applicant forthwith all information, facilities, and technical assistance necessary to accomplish the interception unobtrusively and with a minimum of interference with the services that such service provider, landlord, custodian, or person is according the person whose communications are to be intercepted. Any provider of wire or electronic communication service, landlord, custodian or other person furnishing such facilities or technical assistance shall be compensated therefor by the applicant for reasonable expenses incurred in providing such facilities or assistance. Pursuant to section 2522 of this chapter, an order may also be issued to enforce the assistance capability and capacity requirements under the Communications Assistance for Law Enforcement Act.

(5) No order entered under this section may authorize or approve the interception of any wire, oral, or electronic communication for any period longer than is necessary to achieve the objective of the authorization, nor in any event longer than thirty days. Such thirty-day period begins on the earlier of the day on which the investigative or law enforcement officer first begins to conduct an interception under the order or ten days after the order is entered. Extensions of an order may be granted, but only upon application for an extension made in accordance with subsection (1) of this section and the court making the findings required by subsection (3) of this section. The period of extension shall be no longer than the authorizing judge deems necessary to achieve the purposes for which it was granted and in no event for longer than thirty days. Every order and extension thereof shall contain a provision that the authorization to intercept shall be executed as soon as practicable, shall be conducted in such a way as to minimize the interception of communications not otherwise subject to interception under this chapter, and must terminate upon attainment of the authorized objective, or in any event in thirty days. In the event the intercepted communication is in a code or foreign language, and an expert in that foreign language or code is not reasonably available during the interception period, minimization may be accomplished as soon as practicable after such interception. An interception under this chapter may be conducted in whole or in part by Government personnel, or by an individual operating under a contract with the Government, acting under the supervision of an investigative or law enforcement officer authorized to conduct the inter-

ception.

(6) Whenever an order authorizing interception is entered pursuant to this chapter, the order may require reports to be made to the judge who issued the order showing what progress has been made toward achievement of the authorized objective and the need for continued interception. Such reports shall be made at such intervals as the judge may require.

(7) Notwithstanding any other provision of this chapter, any investigative or law enforcement officer, specially designated by the Attorney General, the Deputy Attorney General, the Associate Attorney General, or by the principal prosecuting attorney of any State or subdivision thereof acting pursuant to a statute of that State, who reasonably determines that—

(a) an emergency situation exists that involves—

(i) immediate danger of death or serious physical injury to any person,

(ii) conspiratorial activities threatening the national security interest, or

(iii) conspiratorial activities characteristic of organized crime,

that requires a wire, oral, or electronic communication to be intercepted before an order authorizing such interception can, with due diligence, be obtained, and

(b) there are grounds upon which an order could be entered under this chapter to authorize such interception, may intercept such wire, oral, or electronic communication if an application for an order approving the interception is made in accordance with this section within forty-eight hours after the interception has occurred, or begins to occur. In the absence of an order, such interception shall immediately terminate when the communication sought is obtained or when the application for the order is denied, whichever is earlier. In the event such application for approval is denied, or in any other case where the interception is terminated without an order having been issued, the contents of any wire, oral, or electronic communication intercepted shall be treated as having been obtained in violation of this chapter, and an inventory shall be served as provided for in subsection (d) of this section on the person named in the application.

(8)(a) The contents of any wire, oral, or electronic communication intercepted by any means authorized by this chapter shall, if possible, be recorded on tape or wire or other comparable device. The recording of the contents of any wire, oral, or electronic communication under this subsection shall be done in such a way as will protect the recording from editing or other alterations. Immediately upon the expiration of the period of the order, or extensions thereof, such recordings shall be made available to the judge issuing such order and sealed under his directions. Custody of the recordings shall be wherever the judge orders. They shall not be destroyed except upon an order of the issuing or denying judge and in any event shall be kept for ten years. Duplicate recordings may be made for use or disclosure pursuant to the provisions of subsections (1) and (2) of section 2517 of this chapter for investigations. The presence of the seal provided for by this subsection, or a satisfactory explanation for the absence thereof, shall be a prerequisite for the use or disclosure of the contents of any wire, oral, or electronic communication or evidence derived therefrom under subsection (3) of section 2517.

(b) Applications made and orders granted under this chapter shall be sealed by the judge. Custody of the applications and orders shall be wherever the judge directs. Such applications and orders shall be disclosed only upon a showing of good cause before a judge of competent jurisdiction and shall not be destroyed except on order of the issuing or denying judge, and in any event shall be kept for ten years.

(c) Any violation of the provisions of this subsection may be punished as contempt of the issuing or denying judge.

(d) Within a reasonable time but not later than ninety days after the filing of an application for an order of approval under section 2518 (7)(b) which is denied or the termination of the period of an order or extensions thereof, the issuing or denying judge shall cause to be served, on the persons named in the order or the application, and such other parties to intercepted communications as the judge may determine in his discretion that is in the interest of justice, an inventory which shall include notice of—

(1) the fact of the entry of the order or the application;

(2) the date of the entry and the period of authorized, approved or disapproved interception, or the denial of the application; and

(3) the fact that during the period wire, oral, or electronic communications were or were not intercepted.

The judge, upon the filing of a motion, may in his discretion make available to such person or his counsel for inspection such portions of the intercepted communications, applications and orders as the judge determines to be in the interest of justice. On an ex parte showing of good cause to a judge of competent jurisdiction the serving of the inventory required by this subsection may be postponed.

(9) The contents of any wire, oral, or electronic communication intercepted pursuant to this chapter or evidence derived therefrom shall not be received in evidence or otherwise disclosed in any trial, hearing, or other proceeding in a Federal or State court unless each party, not less than ten days before the trial, hearing, or proceeding, has been furnished with a copy of the court order, and accompanying application, under which the interception was authorized or approved. This ten-day period may be waived by the judge if he finds that it was not possible to furnish the party with the above information ten days before the trial, hearing, or proceeding and that the party will not be prejudiced by the delay in receiving such information.

(10)(a) Any aggrieved person in any trial, hearing, or proceeding in or before any court, department, officer, agency, regulatory body, or other authority of the United States, a State, or a political subdivision thereof, may move to suppress the contents of any wire or oral communication intercepted pursuant to this chapter, or evidence derived therefrom, on the grounds that—

(i) the communication was unlawfully intercepted;

(ii) the order of authorization or approval under which it was intercepted is insufficient on its face; or

(iii) the interception was not made in conformity with the order of authorization or approval.

Such motion shall be made before the trial, hearing, or proceeding unless there was no opportunity to make such motion or the person was not aware of the grounds of the motion. If the motion is granted, the contents of the intercepted wire or oral communication, or evidence derived therefrom, shall be treated as having been obtained in violation of this chapter. The judge, upon the filing of such motion by the aggrieved person, may in his discretion make available to the aggrieved person or his counsel for inspection such portions of the intercepted communication or evidence derived therefrom as the judge determines to be in the interests of justice.

(b) In addition to any other right to appeal, the United States shall have the right to appeal from an order granting a motion to suppress made under paragraph (a) of this subsection, or the denial of an application for an order of approval, if the United States attorney shall certify to the judge or other official granting such motion or denying such application that the appeal is not taken for purposes of delay. Such appeal shall be taken within thirty days after the date the order was entered and shall be diligently prosecuted.

(c) The remedies and sanctions described in this chapter with respect to the interception of electronic communications are the only judicial remedies and sanctions for nonconstitutional violations of this chapter involving such communications.

(11) The requirements of subsections (1)(b)(ii) and (3)(d) of this section relating to the specification of the facilities from which, or the place where, the communication is to be intercepted do not apply if—

(a) in the case of an application with respect to the interception of an oral communication—

(i) the application is by a Federal investigative or law enforcement officer and is approved by the Attorney General, the Deputy Attorney General, the Associate Attorney General, an Assistant Attorney General, or an acting Assistant Attorney General;

(ii) the application contains a full and complete statement as to why such specification is not practical and identifies the person committing the offense and whose communications are to be intercepted; and

(iii) the judge finds that such specification is not practical; and

(b) in the case of an application with respect to a wire or electronic communication—

(i) the application is by a Federal investigative or law enforcement officer and is approved by the Attorney General, the Deputy Attorney

General, the Associate Attorney General, an Assistant Attorney General, or an acting Assistant Attorney General;

(ii) the application identifies the person believed to be committing the offense and whose communications are to be intercepted and the applicant makes a showing that there is probable cause to believe that the person's actions could have the effect of thwarting interception from a specified facility;

(iii) the judge finds that such showing has been adequately made; and

(iv) the order authorizing or approving the interception is limited to interception only for such time as it is reasonable to presume that the person identified in the application is or was reasonably proximate to the instrument through which such communication will be or was transmitted.

(12) An interception of a communication under an order with respect to which the requirements of subsections (1)(b)(ii) and (3)(d) of this section do not apply by reason of subsection (11)(a) shall not begin until the place where the communication is to be intercepted is ascertained by the person implementing the interception order. A provider of wire or electronic communications service that has received an order as provided for in subsection (11)(b) may move the court to modify or quash the order on the ground that its assistance with respect to the interception cannot be performed in a timely or reasonable fashion. The court, upon notice to the government, shall decide such a motion expeditiously.

18 USC § 2519 —Reports concerning intercepted wire, oral, or electronic communications

(1) In January of each year, any judge who has issued an order (or an extension thereof) under section 2518 that expired during the preceding year, or who has denied approval of an interception during that year, shall report to the Administrative Office of the United States Courts—

(a) the fact that an order or extension was applied for;

(b) the kind of order or extension applied for (including whether or not the order was an order with respect to which the requirements of sections 2518 (1)(b)(ii) and 2518 (3)(d) of this title did not apply by reason of section 2518 (11) of this title);

(c) the fact that the order or extension was granted as applied for, was modified, or was denied;

(d) the period of interceptions authorized by the order, and the number and duration of any extensions of the order;

(e) the offense specified in the order or application, or extension of an order;

(f) the identity of the applying investigative or law enforcement officer and agency making the application and the person authorizing the application; and

(g) the nature of the facilities from which or the place where communications were to be intercepted.

(2) In March of each year the Attorney General, an Assistant Attorney General specially designated by the Attorney General, or the principal prosecuting attorney of a State, or the principal prosecuting attorney for any political subdivision of a State, shall report to the Administrative Office of the United States Courts—

(a) the information required by paragraphs (a) through (g) of subsection (1) of this section with respect to each application for an order or extension made during the preceding calendar year;

(b) a general description of the interceptions made under such order or extension, including

(i) the approximate nature and frequency of incriminating communications intercepted,

(ii) the approximate nature and frequency of other communications intercepted,

(iii) the approximate number of persons whose communications were intercepted,

(iv) the number of orders in which encryption was encountered and whether such encryption prevented law enforcement from obtaining the plain text of communications intercepted pursuant to such order, and

(v) the approximate nature, amount, and cost of the manpower and other resources used in the interceptions;

(c) the number of arrests resulting from interceptions made under such order or extension, and the offenses for which arrests were made;

(d) the number of trials resulting from such interceptions;

(e) the number of motions to suppress made with respect to such interceptions, and the number granted or denied;

(f) the number of convictions resulting from such interceptions and the offenses for which the convictions were obtained and a general assessment of the importance of the interceptions; and

(g) the information required by paragraphs (b) through (f) of this subsection with respect to orders or extensions obtained in a preceding calendar year.

(3) In June of each year the Director of the Administrative Office of the United States Courts shall transmit to the Congress a full and complete report concerning the number of applications for orders authorizing or approving the interception of wire, oral, or electronic communications pursuant to this chapter and the number of orders and extensions granted or denied pursuant to this chapter during the preceding calendar year. Such report shall include a summary and analysis of the data required to be filed with the Administrative Office by subsections (1) and (2) of this section. The Director of the Administrative Office of the United States Courts is authorized to issue binding regu-

lations dealing with the content and form of the reports required to be filed by subsections (1) and (2) of this section.

18 USC § 2520 —Recovery of civil damages authorized

(a) In General.— Except as provided in section 2511 (2)(a)(ii), any person whose wire, oral, or electronic communication is intercepted, disclosed, or intentionally used in violation of this chapter may in a civil action recover from the person or entity, other than the United States, which engaged in that violation such relief as may be appropriate.

(b) Relief.— In an action under this section, appropriate relief includes—

(1) such preliminary and other equitable or declaratory relief as may be appropriate;

(2) damages under subsection (c) and punitive damages in appropriate cases; and

(3) a reasonable attorney's fee and other litigation costs reasonably incurred.

(c) Computation of Damages.—

(1) In an action under this section, if the conduct in violation of this chapter is the private viewing of a private satellite video communication that is not scrambled or encrypted or if the communication is a radio communication that is transmitted on frequencies allocated under subpart D of part 74 of the rules of the Federal Communications Commission that is not scrambled or encrypted and the conduct is not for a tortious or illegal purpose or for purposes of direct or indirect commercial advantage or private commercial gain, then the court shall assess damages as follows:

(A) If the person who engaged in that conduct has not previously been enjoined under section 2511 (5) and has not been found liable in a prior civil action under this section, the court shall assess the greater of the sum of actual damages suffered by the plaintiff, or statutory damages of not less than $50 and not more than $500.

(B) If, on one prior occasion, the person who engaged in that conduct has been enjoined under section 2511 (5) or has been found liable in a civil action under this section, the court shall assess the greater of the sum of actual damages suffered by the plaintiff, or statutory damages of not less than $100 and not more than $1000.

(2) In any other action under this section, the court may assess as damages whichever is the greater of—

(A) the sum of the actual damages suffered by the plaintiff and any profits made by the violator as a result of the violation; or

(B) statutory damages of whichever is the greater of $100 a day for each day of violation or $10,000.

(d) Defense.— A good faith reliance on—

(1) a court warrant or order, a grand jury subpoena, a legislative authorization, or a statutory authorization;

(2) a request of an investigative or law enforcement officer under section 2518 (7) of this title; or

(3) a good faith determination that section 2511 (3) or 2511 (2)(i) of this title permitted the conduct complained of;

is a complete defense against any civil or criminal action brought under this chapter or any other law.

(e) Limitation.— A civil action under this section may not be commenced later than two years after the date upon which the claimant first has a reasonable opportunity to discover the violation.

(f) Administrative Discipline.— If a court or appropriate department or agency determines that the United States or any of its departments or agencies has violated any provision of this chapter, and the court or appropriate department or agency finds that the circumstances surrounding the violation raise serious questions about whether or not an officer or employee of the United States acted willfully or intentionally with respect to the violation, the department or agency shall, upon receipt of a true and correct copy of the decision and findings of the court or appropriate department or agency promptly initiate a proceeding to determine whether disciplinary action against the officer or employee is warranted. If the head of the department or agency involved determines that disciplinary action is not warranted, he or she shall notify the Inspector General with jurisdiction over the department or agency concerned and shall provide the Inspector General with the reasons for such determination.

(g) Improper Disclosure Is Violation.— Any willful disclosure or use by an investigative or law enforcement officer or governmental entity of information beyond the extent permitted by section 2517 is a violation of this chapter for purposes of section 2520 (a).

18 USC § 2521 —Injunction against illegal interception

Whenever it shall appear that any person is engaged or is about to engage in any act which constitutes or will constitute a felony violation of this chapter, the Attorney General may initiate a civil action in a district court of the United States to enjoin such violation. The court shall proceed as soon as practicable to the hearing and determination of such an action, and may, at any time before final determination, enter such a restraining order or prohibition, or take such other action, as is warranted to prevent a continuing and substantial injury to the United States or to any person or class of persons for whose protection the action is brought. A proceeding under this section is governed by the Federal Rules of Civil Procedure, except that, if an indictment has been returned against the respondent, discovery is governed by the Federal Rules of Criminal Procedure.

18 USC § 2522 —Enforcement of the Communications Assistance for Law Enforcement Act

(a) Enforcement by Court Issuing Surveillance Order.— If a court authorizing an interception under this chapter, a State statute, or the Foreign Intelligence

Surveillance Act of 1978 (50 U.S.C. 1801 et seq.) or authorizing use of a pen register or a trap and trace device under chapter 206 or a State statute finds that a telecommunications carrier has failed to comply with the requirements of the Communications Assistance for Law Enforcement Act, the court may, in accordance with section 108 of such Act, direct that the carrier comply forthwith and may direct that a provider of support services to the carrier or the manufacturer of the carrier's transmission or switching equipment furnish forthwith modifications necessary for the carrier to comply.

(b) Enforcement Upon Application by Attorney General.— The Attorney General may, in a civil action in the appropriate United States district court, obtain an order, in accordance with section 108 of the Communications Assistance for Law Enforcement Act, directing that a telecommunications carrier, a manufacturer of telecommunications transmission or switching equipment, or a provider of telecommunications support services comply with such Act.

(c) Civil Penalty.—

(1) In general.— A court issuing an order under this section against a telecommunications carrier, a manufacturer of telecommunications transmission or switching equipment, or a provider of telecommunications support services may impose a civil penalty of up to $10,000 per day for each day in violation after the issuance of the order or after such future date as the court may specify.

(2) Considerations.— In determining whether to impose a civil penalty and in determining its amount, the court shall take into account—

(A) the nature, circumstances, and extent of the violation;

(B) the violator's ability to pay, the violator's good faith efforts to comply in a timely manner, any effect on the violator's ability to continue to do business, the degree of culpability, and the length of any delay in undertaking efforts to comply; and

(C) such other matters as justice may require.

(d) Definitions.— As used in this section, the terms defined in section 102 of the Communications Assistance for Law Enforcement Act have the meanings provided, respectively, in such section.

USG GUIDELINES

National Counterterrorism Center Guidelines for Access, Retention, Use, and Dissemination by the National Counterterrorism Center and Other Agencies of Information in Datasets Containing Non-Terrorism Information

I. Background

A. Pursuant to section 119(d) of the National Security Act of 1947, as amended, the National Counterterrorism Center (NCTC) shall "serve as the primary organization in the United States Government for analyzing and integrating all intelligence possessed or acquired by the United States Government pertaining to terrorism and counterterrorism, excepting intelligence pertaining exclusively to domestic terrorists and domestic counterterrorism." NCTC shall also "serve as the central and shared knowledge bank on known and suspected terrorists and international terror groups, as well as their goals, strategies, capabilities. and networks of contacts and support"; ensure that agencies "have access to and receive all-source intelligence support needed to execute their counterterrorism plans or perform independent, alternative analysis"; and "ensure that such agencies have access to and receive intelligence needed to accomplish their assigned activities." Furthermore, any agency "authorized to conduct counterterrorism activities may request information" from NCTC ''to assist it in its responsibilities." *ld.* § 119(e)(2). Finally, the Director of National Intelligence (DNI) also has significant responsibilities for information sharing. He has "principal authority to ensure maximum availability of and access to intelligence information" within the Intelligence Community (IC). *ld.* §.102A(g)(1). When he establishes standards for facilitating access to and dissemination of information and intelligence, the DNI should give ''the highest priority to detecting. preventing, preempting and disrupting terrorist threats and activities." Executive Order 12333 § 1.3(b)(6)(A).

B. NCTC's analytic and integration efforts concerning terrorism and counterterrorism, as well as its role as the central and shared knowledge bank for known and suspected terrorists. at times require it to access and review datasets that are identified as including non-terrorism information in order to identity and obtain ''terrorism information," as defined in section 1016 of the Intelligence Reform and Terrorism Prevention Act (IRTPA) of 2004 as amended.)[1]

"Nonterrorism information" for purposes of these Guidelines includes information pertaining exclusively to domestic terrorism, as well as information maintained by other executive departments and agencies that has not been identified as ''terrorism information" as defined by IR TP A. Included within those datasets identified as including non-terrorism information may be information concerning "United States persons," as defined in Executive Order 12333 of December 4, 1981, as amended. The President authorized the sharing of terrorism information in Executive Order 13388 of October 25, 2005, and required that agencies place the "highest priority" on the "interchange of terrorism information" in order to "strengthen the effective conduct of United States counterterrorism activities and protect the territory, people, and interests of the United States of America" That order further requires that the "head of each agency that possesses or acquires terrorism information ... shall promptly give access to the terrorism information to the head of each other agency that has counterterrorism functions, and provide the terrorism information to each such agency," consistent with law and statutory responsibilities. In the National Security Act of 1947, as amended, Congress recognized that NCTC must have access to a broader range of information than it has primary authority to analyze and integrate if it is to achieve its missions. The Act thus provides that NCTC "may, consistent with applicable law, the direction of the President, and the guidelines referred to in section 102A(b), receive intelligence pertaining exclusively to domestic counterterrorism from any Federal, State, or local government or other source necessary to fulfill its responsibilities and retain and disseminate such intelligence." National Security Act of 1947, as amended, § 119(e). Further, the Act envisions that NCTC, as part of the office of the Director of National Intelligence (ODNI), *id.* § 119(a), would have the broadest possible access to national intelligence relevant to terrorism and counterterrorism. Section 102A(b) of the National Security Act of 1947, as amended, provides that "[u]nless otherwise directed by the President, the Director of National Intelligence shall have access to all national intelligence and intelligence related to the national security which is collected by any federal department, agency, or other entity, except as otherwise provided by law or, as appropriate, under guidelines agreed upon by the Attorney General and the Director of National Intelligence."

---

1. "The term 'terrorism information'—

(A) means all information, whether collected. produced, or distributed by intelligence, law enforcement, military. homeland security, or other activities relating to

(i) the existence, organization, capabilities, plans, intentions, vulnerabilities. means of finance or material support, or activities of foreign or international terrorist groups or individuals, or of domestic groups or individuals involved in transnational terrorism;

(ii) threats posed by such groups or individuals to the United States, United States persons, or United States interests, or to those of other nations;

(iii) communications of or by such groups or individuals; or

(iv) groups or individuals reasonably believed to be assisting or associated with such groups or individuals; and

(B) includes weapons of mass destruction information." 6 U.S.C. § 485(a)(5).

C. These Guidelines are established between the Attorney General and the Director of National Intelligence pursuant to section 102A(b) of the National Security Act of 1947, as amended, to govern the access, retention, use, and dissemination by NCTC of terrorism information that is contained within datasets maintained within other executive departments or agencies that are identified as including non-terrorism information. These Guidelines do not supersede the arrangements in place under the Memorandum of Agreement for the Interagency Threat Assessment and Coordination Group (ITACG). *See* Homeland Security Act of 2002, as amended, section 2100, and the September 27, 2007 Memorandum of Agreement on the Establishment and Operation of the Interagency Threat Assessment and Coordination Group (hereinafter the "ITACG MOA"). The procedures for the IT ACG MOA will be implemented consistent with these Guidelines. These Guidelines also constitute procedures pursuant to section 2.3 of Executive Order 12333 for NCTC's access to and acquisition of data concerning United States persons within the datasets explicitly covered by these Guidelines, and the retention and dissemination of such information from these datasets. The Attorney General approved procedures pursuant to section 2.3 generally governing NCTC's and ODNI's access and acquisition activities (reference (0), below) are hereby superseded insofar as they apply to NCTC's retention, use, and dissemination of data and datasets governed by these Guidelines. NCTC's retention, use, and dissemination of information contained in the datasets governed by these Guidelines and all other NCTC activities remain subject to all other applicable laws and regulations. The terms and conditions of each specific information access or acquisition (hereinafter ''Terms and Conditions") from another department or agency (hereinafter a "data provider") shall be developed in accordance with the provisions in section III.B.2 below, and shall be consistent with the Information Sharing Environment (IS E) guidelines issued pursuant to section 1016 of the IRTPA, to include the guidelines to protect privacy and civil liberties in the development and use of the information sharing environment.

II. References

a) National Security Act of 1947, as amended
b) Intelligence Reform and Terrorism Prevention Act (IRTPA) of 2004, as amended
c) Homeland Security Act of 2002, as amended
d) Federal Agency Data Mining Reporting Act of 2oo7 (42 U.S.C. § 2000ee-3)
e) 18 U.S.C. § 2332b(f) (Acts of terrorism transcending national boundaries-investigative authority)
f) Executive Order 12333 of December 4, 1981, as amended, "United States Intelligence Activities"
g) Executive Order 13388 of October 25, 2005, "Further Strengthening the Sharing of Terrorism Information to Protect Americans"

h) Intelligence Community Directive (ICD) 501 of January 21, 2009, "Discovery and Dissemination or Retrieval of Information within the Intelligence Community"
i) ICD 503 of September 15, 2008, "Intelligence Community Information Technology Systems Security Risk Management, Certification and Accreditation"
j) Director of Central Intelligence Directive (OCID) *6/3 of* June 5, 1999, "Protecting Sensitive Compartmented Information within Information Systems," appendix E (or successor ICD and Policies)
k) DCID *6/6 of* July 11, 2001, "Security Controls on the Dissemination of Intelligence Information," (or successor ICD and Policies)
l) December 4, 2006 Guidelines to Ensure that the Information Privacy and Other Legal Rights of Americans are Protected in the Development and Use of the Information Sharing Environment
m) March 4, 2003 Memorandum of Understanding Between the Intelligence Community, Federal Law Enforcement Agencies, and the Department of Homeland Security Concerning Information Sharing
n) September 27, 2007 Memorandum of Agreement on the Establishment and Operation of the Interagency Threat Assessment and Coordination Group
o) The Attorney General-approved procedures promulgated through Central Intelligence Agency Headquarters Regulation 7-1 of December 23, 1987, "Law and Policy Governing the Conduct of Intelligence Activities," as adopted by ODNIINCTC, including any successor procedures (hereinafter "NCTC's EO 12333, § 2.3 Procedures")
p) National Counterterrorism Center Information Sharing Policy of February 27, 2006, "Rules of the Road" (NCTC Policy Document 11.2) (or successor Policy)
q) National Counterterrorism Center Role-Based Access Policy of July 13, 2009 (NCTC Policy Document 11. 7) (or successor Policy)
r) ODNI Instruction 80.05, Implementation of Privacy Guidelines for Sharing Protected Information, September 2, 2009 (hereinafter ''ODNI ISE Privacy Instruction")
s) ODNI Instruction 80.02, Managing Breaches of Personally Identifiable Information, February 20, 2008.

III. Guidelines

A. Authority for and Scope of NCTC Data Access and Acquisitions

1. Purpose and Authority. NCTC's access to, and acquisition, retention, use, and dissemination of , information covered by these Guidelines will be for authorized NCTC purposes. Pursuant to Executive Order 13388 and consistent with the National Security Act of 1947, as amended, and the March 4, 2003 Memorandum of Understanding between the Intelligence Community, Federal Law Enforcement Agencies, and the Department of Homeland Security Concerning Information Sharing, NCTC shall be afforded prompt access to all federal information and datasets that may constitute or contain terrorism information. NCTC may access or acquire datasets that may constitute or contain terrorism information, including those identified as containing non-terrorism information, such as information pertaining exclusively to domestic terrorism and other information maintained by executive departments and agencies that has not been identified as terrorism information, in order to acquire, retain, and disseminate terrorism information pursuant to NCTC's statutory authorities consistent with these Guidelines.

2. *United States Person Information.* These Guidelines permit NCTC to access and acquire United States person information for the purpose of determining whether the information is reasonably believed to constitute terrorism information and thus may be permanently retained, [2] used, and disseminated. Any United States person information acquired must be reviewed for such purpose in accordance with the procedures below. Information is '1"easonably believed to constitute terrorism information" if, based on the knowledge and experience of counterterrorism analysts as well as the fa~and practical considerations of everyday life on which reasonable and prudent persons act, there are facts giving rise to a reasonable, articulable suspicion that the information is terrorism information.

3. *Erroneously Provided Information and Errors in Information.* Any United States person information that has been erroneously provided to NCTC will not be retained, used, or disseminated by NCTC. Such information will be promptly removed from NCTC's systems, unless such removal is otherwise prohibited by applicable law or court order or by regulation or policy approved by the Attorney General. Information in NCTC systems found to contain errors will be promptly corrected to ensure information integrity and accuracy, and the data provider shall be notified of the error when feasible.

4. *Applicable Laws and Policies.*

a) NCTC will access, acquire, retain, use, and disseminate information, including United States person information,

(i) pursuant to the relevant standards of Executive Order 12333, as amended;

(ii) as consistent with the National Security Act of 1947, as amended; and (iii) as authorized by law or regulations, including applicable privacy laws. These Guidelines do not apply to information the retention, use, and dissemination of which is governed by court order or court-approved procedures.

b) NCTC shall not access, acquire, retain, use, or disseminate United States person information solely for the purpose of monitoring activities protected by the First Amendment or monitoring the lawful exercise of other rights secured by the Constitution or other laws of the United States. NCTC

---

2. For purposes of these Guidelines, "permanently retained" does not mean that the information is retained indefinitely, but rather that it is retained in accordance with NCTC's records retention policies.

users of acquired information will be subject at all times to NCTC's Role-Based Access and Information Sharing Policies, to applicable ODNI Instructions, and to additional audit and oversight authorities and requirements, as applicable. In implementing these Guidelines, NCTC shall consult with the ODNI General Counsel and the ODNI Civil Liberties Protection officer, as appropriate.

5. Responsibility for Compliance. The Director of NCTC, in consultation with the ODNI office of General Counsel, shall be the responsible official for ensuring that NCTC complies with these Guidelines. The ODNI Civil Liberties Protection officer shall oversee compliance with these Guidelines and compliance with other applicable laws, regulations, guidelines, and instructions as they relate to civil liberties and privacy.

B. General Procedures for NCTC Data Access and Acquisitions

1. Identification of Datasets. NCTC will coordinate with the data provider to identify datasets that are reasonably believed to contain terrorism information, including those identified as containing non-terrorism information.

2. Establishing Terms and Conditions for Information Access.

a) For access to or acquisition of specific datasets, the DNI, or the DNI's designee, shall collaborate with the data provider to identify any legal· constraints, operational considerations, privacy or civil rights or civil liberties concerns and protections, or other issues, and to develop appropriate Terms and Conditions that will govern NCTC's access to or acquisition of datasets under these Guidelines. If either party believes that the Terms and Conditions do not adequately address the matters identified during that collaboration, that party may raise those concerns in accordance with the procedures in section III.B.2(d), below. These Guidelines do not alter any other obligations of a data provider to provide information to the DNI or NCTC. All Terms and Conditions shall incorporate these Attorney General-approved Guidelines, and shall ensure that information is transmitted, stored, retained, accessed, used, and disseminated in a manner that (i) protects privacy and civil liberties and information integrity and security, and (ii) is in accordance with applicable laws, regulations, guidelines and instructions (including the ODNI ISE Privacy Instruction). NCTC and the data provider will establish procedures to ensure the data provider notifies NCTC of any information the data provider believes, or subsequently determines to be, materially inaccurate or unreliable. NCTC will ensure mechanisms are in place at NCTC to correct or document the inaccuracy or unreliability of such information, and supplement incomplete information to the extent additional information becomes available. NCTC will work with the data provider to ensure that data acquired by NCTC under these Guidelines is updated and verified throughout its retention and use by NCTC, in accordance with the data quality, data notice, redress, and other applicable provisions of the ODNI ISE Privacy Instruction.

b) NCTC shall consult with the data provider to identify and put in place additional measures as necessary to honor obligations under applicable international agreements governing the information.
c) Any safeguards, procedures, or oversight mechanisms that go beyond those specified in these Guidelines shall be documented in the Terms and Conditions, and may include protections for sensitive sources and methods, pending investigations, law enforcement equities, foreign government interests, privacy and civil liberties, and similar considerations that apply to the use of the information. Any additional protective measures -such as the degree of advance coordination, if any, for dissemination of information obtained from a data provider-shall also be specified in the Terms and Conditions.
d) If the head of the department or agency providing the information or the DNI objects to providing data to NCTC, objects to the "track" under which NCTC intends to acquire the data, or objects to the Terms and Conditions developed after consultation *(e.g.,* he or she believes that the Terms and Conditions do not adequately ensure that information is transmitted, stored, retained, accessed, used, and disseminated in a manner that protects privacy and civil liberties and information integrity and security; do not adequately addresses operational equities; unnecessarily restrict sharing and use of the information; or are not in accordance with applicable laws, international agreements, and regulations), the head of the department or agency or the DNI may raise any concerns, in writing, with the other party. The head of the department or agency and the DNI shall attempt to resolve any such concern. Failing resolution, either party may refer a dispute concerning constitutional or other legal matters to the Attorney General and may seek the resolution of any other disputes through the National Security Council process. In connection with such disputes, the Attorney General or National Security Council may seek the advice of the Privacy and Civil Liberties Oversight Board.

3. Training. NCTC shall ensure that all NCTC employees, NCTC contractors, and detailees and assignees to NCTC from other agencies (hereinafter "NCTC personnel") provided access to datasets under these Guidelines receive training in the use of each dataset to which they will have access to ensure that these personnel use the datasets only for authorized NCTC purposes and understand the baseline and enhanced safeguards, dissemination restrictions, and other privacy and civil liberties protections they must apply to each such dataset. These personnel will also receive ongoing training to ensure understanding of these Guidelines and civil liberties and privacy expectations and requirements involved in the access to and use of datasets governed by these Guidelines. The training required by this paragraph shall be in person whenever practicable and refreshed at least annually.

4. Authorized Uses of Information. Subject to any additional protections, requirements, or provisions in applicable Terms and Conditions, terrorism information, including terrorism information concerning United States persons, properly acquired and retained by NCTC may be used for all authorized NCTC purposes. These include, but are not limited to: analysis and integration purposes, inclusion in finished analytic products and pieces, enhancement of records contained within the Terrorist Identities Datamart Environment (TIDE), operational support, strategic operational planning, and appropriate dissemination to Intelligence Community elements, as well as federal and other counterterrorism partners. Specific provisions on use and dissemination are set forth in sections III.C and IV below, and any additional protections or provisions shall be specified in the Terms and Conditions.

5. Information Access Requests. For information acquired pursuant to the tracks outlined in section III.C below, it shall be the responsibility of the data provider to make determinations regarding the Freedom of Information Act and first-party access under the Privacy Act, and discovery or other requests for such information in any legal proceeding, unless a different arrangement is agreed upon between NCTC and the data provider and specified in the Terms and Conditions or is required by law. Information derived from an operational file exempted from search and review, publication, and disclosure under 5 U.S.C. § 552 in accordance with law shall remain under the control of the data provider and be handled as coordinated in advance with the data provider and specified in the Terms and Conditions for that information.

C. Specific Procedures for NCTC Data Access and Acquisitions

General. NCTC may acquire information contained within datasets governed by these Guidelines in one or more of the three ways outlined below. NCTC, in coordination with the data providers, will determine which information acquisition track, or tracks, provides the most effective means of ensuring NCTC access to terrorism information contained in the relevant datasets, consistent with the protection of privacy and civil liberties of United States persons, and any applicable legal requirements affecting provision of the specific data.

1. Track I Information Acquisition: Account-Based Access

a) *Type of Access.* NCTC personnel may be provided account-based access to the datasets of data providers that contain or may contain terrorism information (hereinafter ''Track I" access).

b) *Standard.* NCTC will access information in such datasets identified as containing nonterrorism information only to determine if the dataset contains terrorism information. NCTC may acquire, retain, use, and disseminate terrorism information for all authorized NCTC purposes, as described in these Guidelines. If the information acquired by NCTC is subsequently determined not to constitute terrorism information, NCTC will promptly purge any information the retention, use, or dissemination of which is not authorized by sections IV and V below.

c) *Terrorism Datapoints.* Consistent with section 119 of the National Security Act of 1947, as amended, and section 1016(a)(5) of the IRTPA, as amended, the initial query term for NCTC Track 1 access shall be a known or suspected terrorist identifier or other piece of terrorism information (hereinafter ''terrorism datapoints"). In order to follow up on positive query results, subsequent terrorism datapoints may be used to explore a known or suspected terrorist's network of contacts and support. NCTC's activities in Track 1 shall be designed to identify information that is reasonably believed to constitute terrorism information. NCTC is not otherwise permitted under these Guidelines to query, use, or exploit such datasets. For example, analysts may not browse through records in the dataset that do not match a query with terrorism datapoints, or conduct pattern-based queries or analyses without terrorism datapoints.

d) *Protection of Sources and Methods.* NCTC shall work with the data provider to ensure that terrorism datapoints and matching records from the dataset are provided, received, stored, and used in a secure manner that appropriately protects intelligence sources and methods and related sensitivities, consistent with the requirements of Appendix E of DCID *6/3* and ICD 503, or successor ICD.

2. Track 2 Information Acquisition: Search and Retention

a) *Type of Access.* NCTC may provide the owner of a dataset that contains or that may contain terrorism information with query terms - either singly or in batches -consisting of terrorism datapoints so that a search of the dataset may be run (hereinafter ''Track 2" access).

b) *Standard.* Information from the dataset that is responsive to queries using NCTC-provided terrorism datapoints will be given by the data provider to NCTC. NCTC may acquire, retain, use, and disseminate information acquired under Track 2 for all authorized NCTC purposes, as described in these Guidelines. NCTC's activities in Track 2 shall be designed solely to identify information that is reasonably believed to be terrorism information. If the information given by a data provider to NCTC does not constitute terrorism information, NCTC will promptly purge any information whose retention, use, or dissemination is not authorized by sections IV and V below .

c) *Protection of Sources and Methods.* NCTC shall work with the data provider to ensure that terrorism datapoints and responsive records from the dataset are provided, received, stored, and used in a secure manner that appropriately protects intelligence sources and methods and related sensitivities, consistent with the requirements of DCID *6/3* and ICD 503, or successor ICD.

3. Track 3 Information Acquisition: NCTC Dataset Acquisition

a) *Type of Access.* NCTC may acquire and replicate portions or the entirety of a dataset when necessary to identify the information that constitutes terrorism information within the dataset (hereinafter ''Track 3" access).

b) *Standard and Process.* Replication of data is appropriate when the Director of NCTC, or a designee who serves as Principal Deputy Director or as a Deputy Director (hereinafter "Designee"), determines in writing, after coordination with the data provider, that a dataset is likely to contain significant terrorism information and that NCTC's authorized purposes cannot effectively be served through Tracks 1 or 2. When making a determination, the Director or Designee also shall consider whether NCTC's authorized purposes can effectively be served by the replication of a portion of a dataset. Datasets received in accordance with Track 3 may not be accessed or used by NCTC prior to replication, except as directly necessary to make the determination above or to accomplish such replication, subject to procedures agreed upon with the data provider. Measures will be put in place to ensure that the dataset is received and stored in a manner to prevent unauthorized access and use prior to the completion of replication.

c) *Identification of United States Person Information and Temporary Retention Period.* For all datasets received pursuant to Track 3, NCTC will use reasonable measures to identify and mark or tag United States person information contained within those datasets. Any United States person information acquired pursuant to Track 3 may be retained and continually assessed for a period of up to five years by NCTC to determine whether the United States person information is reasonably believed to constitute terrorism information (hereinafter ''temporary retention period"). The Terms and Conditions shall establish the temporary retention period for continual assessment of such information. The temporary retention period specified in the Terms and Conditions may be up to five years unless a shorter period is required by law, including any statute, executive order, or regulation. In no event may NCTC retain the information for longer than is permitted by law. The temporary retention period shall commence when the data is made generally available for access and use following both the determination period discussed in section III.C.3(b) immediately above, and any necessary testing and formatting. United States person information that is reasonably believed to constitute terrorism information may be permanently retained and used for all authorized NCTC purposes, as described in these Guidelines.

d) *Baseline Safeguards. Procedures. and Oversight Mechanisms.* During the temporary retention period, the following baseline safeguards, procedures, and oversight mechanisms shall apply to all datasets acquired pursuant to Track 3 that have been determined to contain United States person information:

(1) These datasets will be maintained in a secure, restricted-access repository.

(2) Access to these datasets will be limited to those NCTC personnel who are acting under, and agree to abide by, NCTC's informa-

tion sharing and use rules, including these Guidelines; who have the requisite security clearance and a need-to-know in the course of their official duties; and who have received the training required by section 11I.B.3.

(3) Access to these datasets will be monitored, recorded, and audited. This includes tracking of logons and logoffs, file and object manipulation and changes, and queries executed, in accordance with audit and monitoring standards applicable to the Intelligence Community. Audit records will be protected against unauthorized access, modifications, and deletion, and will be retained for a sufficient period to enable verification of compliance with rules applicable to the data for which audit records apply.

(4) NCTC's queries or other activities to assess information contained in datasets acquired pursuant to Track 3 shall be designed solely to identify information that is reasonably believed to constitute terrorism information. NCTC shall query the data in a way designed to minimize the review of information concerning United States persons that does not constitute terrorism information. To identify information reasonably believed to constitute terrorism information contained in Track 3 data, NCTC may conduct (i) queries that do not consist of , or do not consist exclusively of , terrorism data points, and (ii) pattern-based queries and analyses. To the extent that these activities constitute "data mining" as that term is defined in the Federal Agency Data Mining Reporting Act of 2007, the DNI shall report these activities as required by that Act.

(5) NCTC will conduct compliance reviews as described below in section VI.

e) *Enhanced Safeguards, Procedures, and Oversight Mechanisms.* In addition to the requirements of paragraph (d), at the time when NCTC acquires a new dataset or a new portion of a dataset, the Director of NCTC or Designee shall determine, in writing, whether enhanced safeguards, procedures, and oversight mechanisms are needed. In making such a determination, the Director of NCTC or Designee shall (i) consult with the ODNI General Counsel and the ODNI Civil Liberties Protection officer, and (ii) consider the sensitivity of the data; the purpose for which the data was originally collected by the data provider; the types of queries to be conducted; the means by which the information was acquired; any request or recommendation from the data provider for enhanced safeguards, procedures, or oversight mechanisms; the terms of any applicable international agreement regarding the data; the potential harm or embarrassment to a United States person that could result from improper use or disclosure of the information; practical and technical issues associated with implementing any enhanced safeguards, procedures, or oversight mechanisms; and all other relevant considerations. If the Director of NCTC or Designee determines that enhanced safeguards, procedures, and oversight mechanisms are appropriate, the determination shall include a description of the specific enhanced safeguards, procedures, or oversight mechanisms that will govern the continued retention and assessment of the dataset. These enhanced safeguards, procedures, or oversight mechanisms may include the following:

(1) Additional procedures for review, approval, and/or auditing of any access or searches;

(2) Additional procedures to restrict searches, access, or dissemination, such as procedures limiting the number of personnel with access or authority to search, establishing a requirement for higher-level authorization or review before or after access or search, or requiring a legal review before or after United States person identities are unmasked or disseminated;

(3) Additional use of privacy enhancing technologies or techniques, such as techniques that allow United States person information or other sensitive information to be "discovered" without providing the content of the information, until the appropriate standard is met;

(4) Additional access controls, including data segregation, attribute-based access, or other physical or logical access controls;

(5) Additional, particularized training requirements for NCTC personnel given access or authority to search the dataset; and

(6) More frequent or thorough reviews of retention policies and practices to address the privacy and civil liberties concerns raised by continued retention of the dataset.

Any enhanced safeguards, procedures, and oversight mechanisms must be included in the Terms and Conditions, or specified in writing and appended to the Terms and Conditions, and shall be kept on file as required by NCTC's record retention schedule.

f) *Removal of Information.* NCTC shall remove from NCTC's systems all identified information concerning United States persons that NCTC does not reasonably believe constitutes terrorism information within five years from the date the data is generally available for assessment by NCTC (or within the time period identified in the Terms and Conditions If the Terms and Conditions specify a shorter temporary retention period), unless such removal is otherwise prohibited by applicable law or court order or by regulation or policy approved by the Attorney General, or unless the information is retained for administrative purposes as authorized in section V below.

g) *Protection of Sources and Methods.* NCTC shall work with the data provider to ensure that information for dataset replications is provided, received, stored, and used in a secure manner that appropriately protects intelligence sources and methods and related sensitivities, consistent with the requirements of DCID 6/3 and ICD 503, or successor ICD.

IV. **Dissemination**

A. **General Dissemination Requirements**

1. Definition. For purposes of these Guidelines, dissemination means transmitting, communicating, sharing, passing, or providing access to information outside NCTC by any means, to include oral, electronic, or physical means.

2. Terms and Conditions and Privacy Act. All disseminations under these Guidelines must be:

(i) compatible with any applicable Terms and Conditions or, if not compatible, the data provider must have otherwise consented to the dissemination; and (ii) permissible under the Privacy Act, 5 U.S.C. § 552a, if applicable.

3. Dissemination to State. Local, or Tribal Authorities or Private-Sector Entities. These Guidelines are not intended to alter or otherwise impact pre-existing information sharing relationships by federal agencies with state, local, or tribal authorities or private-sector entities, whether such relationships arise by law, Presidential Directive, MOU, or other formal agreement (including, but not limited to, those listed in section II above). To the extent that these Guidelines allow for dissemination to state, local, tribal, or private sector entities, such dissemination will continue to be made, consistent with section l19(f)(1)(E) of the National Security Act (50 U.S.C. § 4040(f)(1)(E», in support of the Department of Justice (including the FBI) or the Department of Homeland Security responsibilities to disseminate terrorism information to these entities, and conducted under agreements with those Departments.

B. Dissemination of United States Person Information Acquired Under Tracks 1, 2, or 3

NCTC may disseminate United States person information properly acquired under Tracks 1, 2, or 3 If the General Dissemination Requirements are met, and if:

(1) Dissemination of Terrorism Information. The United States person information reasonably appears to constitute terrorism information, or reasonably appears to be necessary to understand or assess terrorism information, and NCTC is disseminating the information to a federal, state, local, tribal, or foreign or international entity, or to any other appropriate entity that is reasonably believed to have a need to receive such information for the performance of a lawful function;

(2) Dissemination for Limited Purposes. The United States person information is disseminated to other elements of the Intelligence Community or to a federal, state, local, tribal, or foreign or international entity, or to any other appropriate entity, for the limited purpose of assisting NCTC in determining whether the United States person information constitutes

terrorism information. Any such recipients may only use the information for this limited purpose, and may not use the information for any other purpose or disseminate the information further without the prior approval of NCTC. Recipients of information under this paragraph must promptly provide the requested assistance to NCTC and promptly thereafter return the information to NCTC or destroy it unless NCTC authorizes continued retention after the specific information is determined by NCTC to meet the dissemination criteria in section IV.C.1 of these Guidelines. Recipients of information under this paragraph may not retain the information for purposes of continual assessment of whether it constitutes terrorism information unless such retention would be permitted by the dissemination criteria in section IV.C.1. Any access to or dissemination under this paragraph of any bulk dataset or significant portion of a dataset believed to contain United States person information must be: (i) approved by the Director of NCTC; and (ii) expressly allowed by the Terms and Conditions or otherwise expressly approved by the data provider. In addition, the recipient of any bulk dataset or significant portion of a dataset under this provision must agree in writing that it: (i) will not disseminate the information further without prior approval by NCTC; (ii) will use the data solely for the limited purpose specified in this provision; (iii) will promptly return the data to NCTC or destroy it after providing the required assistance to NCTC, unless NCTC authorizes continued retention of specific information after it is determined by NCTC to meet the dissemination criteria in section IV.C.1 of these Guidelines; (iv) will comply with any safeguards and procedures deemed appropriate by the ODNI General Counsel and ODNI Civil Liberties Protection officer; and (v) will report to NCTC any significant data breach or failure to comply with the terms of its agreement. In deciding whether to approve dissemination under this paragraph of any bulk dataset or significant portion of a dataset, the Director of NCTC shall consider whether the limited purpose of this paragraph can be satisfied by allowing access to the data while it remains under NCTC's control and whether the recipient of the data has the capabilities necessary to comply with the requirements specified above;

(3) Dissemination Based on Consent. The United States person whom the information concerns consents to the dissemination; or

(4) Dissemination of Publicly Available Information. The United States person information is publicly available.

C. Dissemination of United States Person Information Acquired Under Track 3

1. Standard (Non-bulk) Dissemination of Specific Information Acquired Under Track 3. In addition to the provisions above for dissemination under all three tracks, NCTC may disseminate specific United States person information acquired under Track 3 that has been handled and subsequently identified in accordance with applicable Track 3 safeguards and procedures,[3] If the General Dissemination Requirements are met, and If the United States person information:

a) Reasonably appears to be foreign intelligence or counterintelligence, or information concerning foreign aspects of international narcotics activities, or reasonably appears to be necessary to understand or assess foreign intelligence, counterintelligence, or foreign aspects of international narcotics activities, and NCTC is disseminating the information to another federal, state, local, tribal, or foreign or international entity that is reasonably believed to have a need to receive such information for the performance of a lawful function, provided they agree to such further restrictions on dissemination as may be necessary;

b) Reasonably appears to be evidence of a crime, and NCTC is disseminating the information to another federal, state, local, tribal, or foreign agency that is reasonably believed to have jurisdiction or responsibility for the investigation or prosecution to which the information relates and a need to receive such information for the performance of a lawful governmental function;

c) Is disseminated to a Congressional Committee to perform its lawful oversight functions, after approval by the ODNI office of General Counsel;

d) Is disseminated to a federal, state, local, tribal, or foreign or international entity, or to an individual or entity not part of a government, and is reasonably believed to be necessary to: (i) protect the safety or security of persons, property, or organizations; or (ii) protect against or prevent a crime or a threat to the national security, provided they agree to such further restrictions on dissemination as may be necessary;

e) Is disseminated to another federal, state, local, tribal, or foreign or international entity for the purpose of determining the suitability or credibility of persons who are reasonably believed to be potential sources or contacts, provided they agree to such further restrictions on dissemination as may be necessary;

t) Is disseminated to another federal, state, local, tribal, or foreign or international entity for he purpose of protecting foreign intelligence or counterintelligence sources and methods from unauthorized disclosure;

g) Is disseminated to other recipients, If the subject of the information provides prior consent in writing;

---

3. This paragraph does not authorize NCTC to search for the additional categories of information. but rather allows NCTC to disseminate specific United States person information discovered while performing counterterrorism analysis and searches in accordance with these Guidelines and the applicable Terms and Conditions.

h) Is otherwise required to be disseminated by statutes; treaties; executive orders; Presidential directives; National Security Council directives; Homeland Security Council directives; or Attorney General-approved policies, memoranda of understanding, or agreements; or

i) Is disseminated to appropriate elements of the Intelligence Community for the purposes of allowing the recipient element to determine whether the information is relevant to its responsibilities and can be retained by it.

The identity of a United States person may be disseminated outside the Intelligence Community only if it is necessary or if it is reasonably believed that it may become necessary to understand and assess such information.

2. *Bulk Dissemination of Information Acquired Under Track* 3 *to IC Elements.* If the General Dissemination Requirements in section IV.A above are met, NCTC also may disseminate United States person information acquired under Track 3 to other IC elements under the following conditions:

a) *General Requirements.* Any dissemination under these Guidelines of any bulk dataset or significant portion of a dataset believed to contain United States person information, which has not been assessed as constituting terrorism information, must be approved by the Director of NCTC and must be expressly allowed by the applicable Terms and Conditions for that dataset or otherwise expressly approved by the data provider. IC elements that receive or access bulk datasets or significant portions of a dataset under these Guidelines are not authorized to make further bulk disseminations of that information.

b) *Bulk Dissemination in Support of Counterterrorism Missions:* The Director of NCTC shall only approve such dissemination to IC elements in support of a legally authorized counterterrorism mission If the receiving element head agrees in writing to abide by the provisions of the Appendix to these Guidelines and any enhanced safeguards, procedures, and oversight mechanisms identified in the Terms and Conditions for the particular dataset or otherwise required by the Director of NCTC.[4] The agreement must specify, by name or position, the persons responsible for oversight and reporting, consistent with these Guidelines. The ODNI General Counsel and the ODNI Civil Liberties Protection Officer, in consultation with the Assistant Attorney General for National Security, shall verify that the receiving IC ele-

---

4. If an element with a counterterrorism mission requests changes to provisions in the Appendix to address agency-specific circumstances (e.g., technological capabilities), such changes may be adopted if expressly approved by the data provider and by the DNI and the Attorney General or their delegees, provided that any agency-specific Appendix shall retain safeguards, procedures, and oversight mechanisms substantially similar to those contained in the original Appendix.

ment has the capabilities and technology in place to accomplish the necessary oversight and compliance.

c) *Bulk Dissemination in Support of Other Intelligence Missions:* The Director of National Intelligence shall only approve such dissemination to IC elements in support of lawful intelligence missions other than counterterrorism missions if: such dissemination is expressly allowed by the applicable Terms and Conditions; the receiving element has Attorney General-approved procedures in place for the collection, retention, and dissemination of United States person information, as required by the opening paragraph of section 2.3 of Executive Order 12333; and the receiving element head agrees in writing to abide by safeguards, procedures, and oversight mechanisms substantially similar to the safeguards, procedures, and oversight mechanisms identified in the Appendix to these Guidelines, as well as any enhanced safeguards, procedures, and oversight mechanisms identified in the Terms and Conditions for .the particular datasets or otherwise required by the Director of NCTC. In addition, the Director of National Intelligence may only approve bulk dissemination to IC elements in support of intelligence missions other than counterterrorism missions If the Director of National Intelligence, in consultation with the ODNI General Counsel, determines that the proposed dissemination is necessary to a lawful mission of the IC element and that the IC element's need for the information cannot be fulfilled through dissemination of specific information under the standard dissemination provisions of section IV.C.l; through dissemination of a smaller portion of the data proposed for dissemination; or by allowing access to the data while it remains within NCTC's control. The Director of National Intelligence will provide a copy of this determination to the Assistant Attorney General for National Security. The agreement must specify, by name or position, the persons responsible for oversight and reporting, consistent with these Guidelines. The ODNI General Counsel and the ODNI Civil Liberties Protection officer shall verify that the receiving IC element has the capabilities and technology in place to accomplish the necessary oversight and compliance. Any such agreement must be approved by the Attorney General or his delegee prior to allowing such dissemination, and the National Security Division of the Department of Justice may conduct an independent assessment of the element's oversight and compliance capabilities.

D. Foreign Disseminations

For any dissemination of United States person information to a foreign or international entity, in addition to complying with the dissemination provisions of section IV., NCTC must find that: (i) the dissemination is consistent with the interests of the United States, including U.S. national security interests; (ii) the dissemination complies with DCID 6/6 or any successor ICO[5];

5. ICD 403 is currently in draft. Once signed, any foreign dissemination would be required to comply with ICD 403 and any implementing ICPGs and IC Standards.

(iii) the foreign or international entity agrees not to disseminate the information further without approval by NCTC; and (iv) NCTC, in consultation with OONI General Counsel, has considered the effect such dissemination may reasonably be expected to have on any identifiable United States person to determine whether any additional safeguards are needed.

E. Other Disseminations

If NCTC properly acquires any United States person information under Tracks 1 and 2 that would be authorized for dissemination pursuant to section IV.c.1 if it were acquired under Track 3, it shall consult with the data provider and advise the data provider of the existence of such information. The data provider may disseminate the information or authorize NCTC to do so.

V. Retention of Information for Administrative Purposes

To the extent consistent with law, United States person information acquired pursuant to these Guidelines may be retained if necessary to conduct the oversight, auditing, redress, or compliance activities required by these Guidelines, if required by law or court order to be retained, or if necessary to determine whether the requirements of these Guidelines or applicable laws are satisfied. Any information retained under this paragraph beyond the temporary retention period may not be used for purposes other than those specified in the preceding sentence and must be promptly removed from NCTC's systems once retention is no longer necessary or required for those purposes, except that NCTC may retain any oversight, audit, redress, or compliance records or reports in accordance with its records retention policies.

VI. Compliance

A. Periodic Compliance Reviews

Subject to oversight by the OONI Civil Liberties Protection officer, NCTC shall conduct periodic reviews to verify continued compliance with these Guidelines, including compliance with the Terms and Conditions, and with all baseline and enhanced safeguards, procedures, and oversight mechanisms. These reviews shall include spot checks, reviews of audit logs, and other appropriate measures.

B. Periodic Reviews of the Need for Continued Assessment

NCTC, in coordination with the ODNI Civil Liberties Protection officer, shall conduct periodic reviews of all datasets replicated under Track 3 to determine whether retention and continued assessment of the United States person information in those datasets remains appropriate. In conducting this review, consideration shall be given to the purpose for which the dataset was acquired, the success of that dataset in fulfilling legitimate counterterrorism purposes, whether those purposes can now be fulfilled through Track 1 or 2 access to the dataset, through the use of other datasets in NCTC's possession, or through other appropriate means. and privacy and civil liberties considerations applicable to the particular dataset. NCTC shall also conduct periodic reviews of the continued necessity and efficacy of bulk disseminations permitted under the Guidelines. NCTC shall report the results of these periodic reviews to the IC Inspector General.

C. NCTC's Computer Systems

In designing its computer systems, NCTC shall take reasonable steps to enhance its ability to monitor activity involving United States person information and other sensitive information, and to facilitate compliance with. and the auditing and reporting required by, these Guidelines.

D. Reporting

1. NCTC shall promptly report, in writing, to the Director of NCTC, the ODNI General Counsel, the ODNI Civil Liberties Protection officer, the Department of Justice, and the IC Inspector General upon discovery of any significant failure to comply with: (i) these Guidelines; (ii) baseline or enhanced safeguards, procedures, or other oversight mechanisms; or (iii) any Terms and Conditions. For the purposes of these Guidelines, a "significant failure" is a failure that constitutes a violation of the Constitution or other law, including any executive order, and/or a failure that leads to unauthorized access, use, or dissemination of personally identifiable information about a United States person. NCTC shall report to any data provider whose information was affected by the noncompliance, in accordance with the Terms and Conditions for that data.

2. The Director of NCTC shall report annually in writing to the ODNI Civil Liberties Protection officer on the measures that NCTC is taking to ensure that its access to, and retention, use, and dissemination of, United States person information is appropriate under these Guidelines and in compliance with the baseline and enhanced safeguards, procedures, and oversight mechanisms, and all applicable Terms and Conditions. The report shall include:

(1) For datasets replicated under Track 3, the results of the review required in section VI.B above, regarding whether replication continues to be appropriate;

(2) A general description of NCTC's compliance and audit processes;

(3) A description of the audits, spot checks, and other reviews NCTC conducted during the previous year, and the results of those audits, spot checks, or other reviews, to include any shortcomings identified;

(4) A description of how NCTC ensures that it promptly purges United States person information that does not meet the standards for retention under these Guidelines;

(5) An assessment of United States person information disseminated by NCTC directly to foreign, international, state, local, tribal, or private sector entities or individuals; the restrictions, ifany, that NCTC imposed on the entities' use or further dissemination of such information; and any known misuse of such information by a recipient, data breach, or significant failure by the recipient to comply with the terms of the certification required under section *N.B.2;*

(6) A description of any approvals by the DNI or Director of NCTC, in accordance with sections N.B.2 and *N.C.2* above, to provide access to or to disseminate bulk datasets or significant portions of a dataset;
(7) An assessment of whether there is a need for enhanced safeguards, procedures, or oversight regarding the handling of United States person information or other sensitive information, or whether any other reasonable measures that should be taken to improve the handling of information;
(8) A description of measures that NCTC has taken to comply with the requirements of section VI.C with respect to its data processing systems; and
(9) A description of any material changes or improvements NCTC implemented, or is considering implementing, to improve compliance with these Guidelines.

3. NCTC shall provide a copy of this report to the ODNI General Counsel and the IC Inspector General, and shall make the report available upon request to the Assistant Attorney General for National Security. NCTC shall also make available to the IC Inspector General any other reports or documentation necessary to ensure compliance with these Guidelines.

4. The reporting required by these Guidelines does not replace any other reporting required by statute, executive order, or regulation.

E. Privacy and Civil Liberties Oversight Board

Pursuant to section 1061 of the Intelligence Reform and Terrorism Prevention Act of 2004, the Privacy and Civil Liberties Oversight Board shall have access to all relevant NCTC records, reports, audits, reviews, documents, papers, recommendations, and other material that it deems relevant to its oversight of NCTC activities.

VII. Interpretation and Departures

A. NCTC shall refer all questions relating to the interpretation of these Guidelines to the ODNI office of General Counsel. The ODNI General Counsel shall consult with the Assistant Attorney General for National Security regarding any novel or significant interpretations.

B. The ODNI General Counsel and the Assistant Attorney General for National Security must approve any departures from these Guidelines. If there is not time for such approval and a departure from these Guidelines is necessary because of the immediacy or gravity of a threat to the safety of persons or property or to the national security, the Director of NCTC or the Director's senior representative present may approve a departure from these Guidelines. The ODNI General Counsel shall be notified as soon thereafter as possible. The ODNI General Counsel shall provide prompt written notice of any such departures to the Assistant Attorney General for National Security. Notwithstanding this paragraph, all activities in all circumstances must be carried out in a manner consistent with the Constitution and laws of the United States.

VIII. Status as Internal Guidance

These Guidelines are set forth solely for the purpose of internal NCTC and ODNI guidance. They are not intended to, and do not, create any rights, substantive or procedural, enforceable at law or in equity, by any party against the United States, its departments, agencies, or entities, its officers, employees, agents, or any other person, nor do they place any limitation on otherwise lawful investigative or litigation prerogatives of the United States.

IX. Revocations, Transitions, and Effective Date.

These Guidelines supersede and revoke the Memorandum of Agreement signed by the Director of National Intelligence and Attorney General on October 1, 2008 and November 4, 2008, respectively, along with any amendments to that Agreement. Terms and Conditions entered pursuant to that Memorandum of Agreement, or similar information sharing agreements to which NCTC is currently a party, remain in effect until revoked or until amended or replaced consistent with these Guidelines. As applied to NCTC, these Guidelines also supersede NCTC's EO 12333, § 2.3 Procedures with respect to the data and datasets covered by these Guidelines. These Guidelines shall be effective upon the approval of the Attorney General, the Director of National Intelligence, and the Director of NCTC.

Matthew G. Olsen
Director, National Counterterrorism Center

James R. Clapper, Jr.
Director of National Intelligence

Eric H. Holder, Jr.
Attorney General of the United States of America

Appendix
Safeguards, Procedures, and Oversight Mechanisms for Bulk Dissemination of Information Acquired Under Track 3 to Ie Elements

I. Purpose

This Appendix contains the safeguards, procedures, and oversight mechanisms that an Intelligence Community (lC) element head, or designee, must agree to, in writing, before NCTC may disseminate any bulk dataset or significant portion of a dataset (hereinafter referred to in this Appendix as "a dataset" or "data") that includes United States Person information in accordance with section *N.C.2(b) of* the NCTC Guidelines. NCTC may only disseminate datasets under this Appendix in support of the receiving IC element's legally authorized counterterrorism mission.

II. Implementation

Prior to NCTC's dissemination of any bulk dataset to an IC element, the element head must agree in writing to abide by the provisions of this Appendix, and any enhanced safeguards, procedures, and oversight mechanisms identified in the

Terms and Conditions for the particular dataset or otherwise required by the Director of NCTC (hereinafter ''written agreement"). All requirements shall be described, referenced, or appended to the written agreement, which the Director of NCTC shall develop in consultation with the ODNI General Counsel and Civil Liberties Protection officer. Ifan IC element is provided access to NCTC's systems in support of its legally authorized counterterrorism mission and NCTC will undertake any of the requirements in this Appendix on behalf of the IC element, the IC element head and the Director of NCTC shall specify in the written agreement the persons, by name or position, responsible for all training, oversight, and related compliance measures and reporting.

III. Definitions

For the purposes of this Appendix, the following definitions apply:

A. Dissemination: Dissemination means transmitting, communicating, sharing, passing, or providing access to information outside NCTC and/or the IC element by any means, to include oral, electronic, or physical means.

B. IC Element: The term "IC element" refers to the specific IC element that is provided data in accordance with section *N.C.2(b) of* the NCTC Guidelines in support of the IC element's legally authorized counterterrorism mission.

C. Terrorism Information: The term "terrorism information"

(1) means all information, whether collected, produced, or distributed by intelligence, law enforcement, military, homeland security, or other activities relating to-

(i) the existence, organization, capabilities, plans, intentions, vulnerabilities, means of finance or material support, or activities of foreign or international terrorist groups or individuals, or of domestic groups or individuals involved in transnational terrorism;

(ii) threats posed by such groups or individuals to the United States, United States persons, or United States interests, or to those of other nations;

(iii) communications of or by such groups or individuals; or

(iv) groups or, individuals reasonably believed to be assisting or associated with such groups or individuals; and

(2) includes weapons of mass destruction information. 6 U.S.C. § 48S(a)(S).

D. United States Person. For an IC element receiving information under this Appendix, this term has the meaning given the term in that element's guidelines approved by the Attorney General under section 2.3 of Executive Order 12333. For an element without such Attorney General-approved guidelines, or whose guidelines do not contain such a definition, this term means a United States citizen, an alien known by the intelligence element concerned to be a permanent resident alien, an unincorporated association substantially composed of United States citizens or permanent resident aliens, or a corporation incorporated in the United States, except for a corporation directed and controlled by a foreign government or governments. *See* Executive Order 12333 § 3.S(k).

IV. General Provisions

A. Authorized Purpose. The IC element may access and acquire United States person information in the dataset for the purpose of determining whether the information is reasonably believed to constitute terrorism information and thus may be permanently retained,[1] used, and disseminated. Any United States person information acquired must be reviewed for such purpose in accordance with the procedures in this Appendix, the applicable Terms and Conditions for that dataset, and any other measures specified in the written agreement. Information is "reasonably believed to constitute terrorism information" if, based on the knowledge and experience of counterterrorism analysts as well as the factual and practical considerations of everyday life on which reasonable and prudent persons act, there are facts giving rise to a reasonable, articulable suspicion that the information is terrorism information.

B. Erroneously Provided Information and Errors in Information. Any United States person information that has been erroneously disseminated to the IC element will not be retained, used, or further disseminated by the IC element. Such information will be promptly removed from the IC element's systems, unless such removal is otherwise prohibited by applicable law or court order or by regulation or policy approved by the Attorney General. Information in the IC element's systems found to contain errors will be promptly corrected to ensure information integrity and accuracy, and NCTC shall be notified of the error promptly.

C. Removal of Information. The IC element shall remove from the IC element's systems all identified information concerning United States persons that the IC element does not reasonably believe constitutes terrorism information within five years from the date the data is generally available for assessment by NCTC (or within the time period identified in the written agreement ifit specifies a shorter temporary retention period), unless such removal is otherwise prohibited by applicable law or court order or by regulation or policy approved by the Attorney General, or unless the information is retained for administrative purposes as authorized in section VII below.

D. Training. The IC element shall ensure that all employees and contractors of the IC element and detailees and assignees to the IC element from other agencies (hereinafter "IC element personnel") provided access to the data under this Appendix will receive training in the use of each dataset to which they will have access to ensure that they use the data only for the IC element's authorized counterterrorism purposes and in accordance with this Appendix and other applicable requirements. The training shall also ensure that they understand the baseline and enhanced safeguards, dissemination restrictions, and other privacy and civil liberties protections they must apply to each dataset. This training shall be in person, whenever practical, and refreshed at least

---

1. For purposes of this Appendix, "permanently retained" does not mean that the information is retained indefinitely, but rather that it is retained in accordance with the IC element's records retention policies.

annually. IC element personnel provided access to data under this Appendix will also receive ongoing training to ensure understanding of this Appendix and other applicable agreements and the civil liberties and privacy expectations and requirements involved in the access to and use of the data.

E. Authorized Uses of Information and Time Periods. For all datasets or data received pursuant to this Appendix, the IC element will use reasonable measures to identify and mark or tag United States person information contained within those datasets (to the extent not already done so by the data provider and NCTC). Any United States person information accessed or acquired in accordance with this Appendix may be continually assessed for up to five years by IC element personnel to determine whether the United States person information is reasonably believed to constitute terrorism information unless a shorter temporary retention period is specified in the written agreement with NCTC. The written agreement signed by the IC element head or designee shall specify the applicable temporary retention period for the dataset or data as required by the Terms and Conditions or otherwise required by the Director of NCTC. The temporary retention period shall commence when the data is made generally available for access and use by NCTC; the period is not restarted at the time of dissemination to or access by the IC element. United States person information that is reasonably believed to constitute terrorism information may be permanently retained and used for all authorized IC element purposes. These include, but are not limited to: analysis and integration purposes, inclusion in finished analytic products and pieces, enhancement of records contained within the Terrorist Identities Datamart Environment (TIDE), operational support and planning. and appropriate dissemination to Intelligence Community elements, as well as federal and other counterterrorism partners. Specific provisions on use and dissemination are set forth below. Any additional protections or provisions required by the Terms and Conditions for that dataset or otherwise required by the Director of NCTC must be included in the written agreement signed by the IC element head or designee.

F. Applicable Laws and Policies. The IC element shall access, acquire, retain, use, and disseminate information, including United States person information, (i) pursuant to the relevant standards of Executive Order 12333, as amended; (ii) as consistent with the National Security Act of 1947, as amended; and (iii) as authorized by law or regulations, including applicable privacy laws. This Appendix does not apply to information whose retention, use, and dissemination is governed by court order or court-approved procedures. If the IC element has Attorney General-approved procedures pursuant to section 2.3 of Executive Order 12333, those are hereby superseded as applied to the collection, retention, and dissemination of United States person information in data and datasets governed by this Appendix, except as otherwise specifically provided herein.

G. Limitation. The IC element shall not access, acquire, retain, use, or disseminate United States person information solely for the purpose of monitoring activities protected by the First Amendment or monitoring the lawful exercise of other rights secured by the Constitution or other laws of the United States. IC element personnel who access NCTC's databases will be subject at all times to NCTC's Role-Based Access and Information Sharing Policies, and to additional audit and oversight requirements, as applicable and as specified in the written agreement signed by the IC element head or designee. IC elements may be required to adopt or apply similar role-based access and information sharing policies prior to receiving and storing data from NCTC; any such requirements will be specified in the written agreement signed by the IC element head or designee.

H. Information Access Requests. For information governed by this Appendix, it shall be the responsibility of the data provider who provided the data to NCTC to make determinations regarding the Freedom of Information Act and first-party access under the Privacy Act, and discovery or other requests for such information in any legal proceeding, unless a different arrangement was agreed upon between NCTC and the data provider and specified in the Terms and Conditions or is required by law. Information derived from an operational file exempted from search and review, publication, and disclosure under 5 U.S.C. § 552 in accordance with law shall remain under the control of the data provider and be handled as coordinated in advance with the data provider and as specified in the Terms and Conditions for that information.

I. Baseline Safeguards, Procedures, and Ovenight Mechanisms. During the temporary retention period, the IC element shall adhere to the following baseline safeguards, procedures, and oversight mechanisms for any dataset disseminated by NCTC under this Appendix:

1. The data will be maintained in a secure, restricted-access repository.
2. Access to the data will be limited to those IC element personnel, who:(i) access the data for the purpose authorized in section *N.A;* (ii) are acting under, and agree to abide by, the IC element's information sharing and use rules, including this Appendix and the written agreement; (iii) have the requisite security clearance and a need-to-know in the course of their official duties; and (iv) have received the training required by section *N.D.*
3. Access to the data will be monitored, recorded, and audited. This includes tracking of logons and logoffs, file and object manipulation and changes, and queries executed, in accordance with audit and monitoring standards applicable to the Intelligence Community. Audit records will be protected against unauthorized access, modifications, and deletion, and will be retained for a sufficient period to enable verification of compliance with the rules applicable to the data for which audit records apply.
4. The IC element's queries or other activities to assess information contained in the data disseminated pursuant to this Appendix shall be designed solely to identify information that is reasonably believed to constitute terrorism information.
5. The IC element shall query the data in a way designed to minimize the review of information concerning United States persons that does not

constitute terrorism information. To identify information reasonably believed to constitute terrorism information contained in data disseminated pursuant to this Appendix, the IC element may conduct (i) queries that do not consist of , or do not consist exclusively of , terrorism data points, which are known or suspected terrorist identifiers or other pieces of terrorism information, and (ii) pattern-based queries and analyses. To the extent that these activities constitute "data mining" as that term is defined in the Federal Agency Data Mining Reporting Act of 2007, the IC element shall coordinate with NCTC to ensure proper reporting and to identify which element should report these activities as required by that Act.

6. The IC element will conduct compliance reviews as described below in section IX.

J. Enhanced Safeguards, Procedures, and Oversight Mechanisms. The IC element must also comply with any enhanced safeguards, procedures, and oversight mechanisms identified in the Terms and Conditions for the particular dataset or otherwise required by the Director of NCTC and specified in the written agreement signed by the IC element head or designee. See NCTC Guidelines, section III.C.3(e).

V. Dissemination of United States Person Information

A. General Dissemination Requirements.

1. Terms and Conditions and Privacy Act. All disseminations under this Appendix must be: (i) compatible with this Appendix; (ii) any applicable Terms' and Conditions, and any other measures identified or specified in the written agreement or, if not compatible, the data provider must have otherwise consented to the dissemination; and (iii) permissible under the Privacy Act, 5 U.S.C. § 552a, if applicable.

2. Dissemination to State, Local, or Tribal Authorities or Private-Sector Entities. The NCTC Guidelines and this Appendix are not intended to alter or otherwise impact pre-existing information sharing relationships by federal agencies with state, local, or tribal authorities or private-sector entities, whether such relationships arise by law, Presidential Directive, MOU, or other formal agreement (including, but not limited to, those listed in section II of the NCTC Guidelines). To the extent that the NCTC Guidelines, this Appendix, and the written agreement allow for dissemination to state, local, tribal, or private sector entities, such dissemination will continue to be made, consistent with section I 19(f)(l)(E) of the National Security Act (50 U.S.C. 4040(f)(l)(E), in support of the Department of Justice (including the FBI) or the Department of Homeland Security responsibilities to disseminate terrorism information to these entities, and conducted under agreements with those Departments. This Appendix is not intended to, does not, and shall not be relied upon to create a grant of new or additional authority for information sharing with or dissemination of information to state, local, or tribal authorities or private-sector entitles.

3. Bulk Disseminations Prohibited. In no case may the IC element make a further bulk dissemination of any dataset or any significant portion of a dataset. However, specific United States person information may be disseminated pursuant to the dissemination provisions in sections V.B or V.C below.

B. Basic Dissemination Requirements. The IC element may disseminate United States person information from datasets provided by NCTC If the General Dissemination Requirements are met, and if:

1. Dissemination of Terrorism Information. The United States person information reasonably appears to constitute terrorism information, or reasonably appears to be necessary to understand or assess terrorism information, and the IC element is disseminating the information to a federal, state, local, tribal, or foreign or international entity, or to any other appropriate entity or individual, that is reasonably believed to have a need to receive such information for the performance of a lawful function;

2. Dissemination for Limited Purposes. The United States person information is disseminated to other elements of the Intelligence Community or to a federal, state, local, tribal, or foreign or international entity, or to any other appropriate entity, for the limited purpose of assisting the IC element in determining whether the United States person information constitutes terrorism information. Before disseminating information under this paragraph, the IC element should consider approaching NCTC for this type of assistance. Any such recipients may only use the information for the limited purpose identified in this paragraph, and may not use the information for any other purpose or disseminate the information further without the prior approval of NCTC. Recipients of information under this paragraph must promptly provide the requested assistance to the IC element and promptly thereafter return the information to the IC element or destroy it unless the IC element authorizes continued retention after the specific information continued retention after the specific information is determined by the IC element to meet the dissemination criteria in section V.C of this Appendix. Recipients of information under this paragraph may not retain the information for continual assessment of whether it constitutes terrorism information unless such retention is permitted by the dissemination criteria in section V.C of this Appendix. This paragraph does not authorize the IC element to disseminate any bulk dataset or significant portion of a dataset believed to contain United States person information;

3. Dissemination Based on Consent. The United States person whom the information concerns consents to the dissemination; or

4. Dissemination of Publicly Available Information. The United States person information is publicly available.

C. Dissemination of Non-Terrorism Information. In addition, the IC element may disseminate United States person information contained in datasets provided by NCTC if that United States person information has been handled and subsequently identified in accordance with applicable safeguards and procedures,[2] If the General Dissemination Requirements are met, and If the United States person information:

1. Reasonably appears to be foreign intelligence or counterintelligence, or information concerning foreign aspects of international narcotics activities, or reasonably appears to be necessary to understand or assess foreign intelligence or counterintelligence or foreign aspects of international narcotics activities, and the IC element is disseminating the information to another federal, state, local, tribal, or foreign or international entity that is reasonably believed to have a need to receive such information for the performance of a lawful function, provided they agree to such further restrictions on dissemination as may be necessary;
2. Reasonably appears to be evidence of a crime, and the IC element is disseminating the information to another federal, state, local, tribal, or foreign agency that is reasonably believed to have jurisdiction or responsibility for the investigation or prosecution to which the information relates and a need to receive such information for the performance of a lawful governmental function;
3. Is disseminated to a Congressional Committee to perform its lawful oversight functions, after approval by the IC element's office of General Counsel or senior legal advisor;
4. Is disseminated to a federal, state, local, tribal, or foreign or international entity, or to an individual or entity not part of a government, and is reasonably believed to be necessary to: (i) protect the safety or security of persons, property, or organizations; or (ii) protect against or prevent a crime or a threat to the national security, provided they agree to such further restrictions on dissemination as may be necessary;
5. Is disseminated to another federal, state, local, tribal, or foreign or international entity for the purpose of determining the suitability or credibility of persons who are reasonably believed to be potential sources or contacts, provided they agree to such further restrictions on dissemination as may be necessary;
6. Is disseminated to another federal, state, local, tribal, or foreign or international entity for the purpose of protecting foreign intelligence or counterintelligence sources and methods from unauthorized disclosure;
7. Is disseminated to other recipients, If the subject of the information provides prior consent in writing;
8. Is otherwise required to be disseminated by statutes; treaties; executive orders; Presidential directives; National Security Council directives; Home-

2. Note that this dissemination category does not authorize the IC element to search for additional categories of information, but rather allows the IC element to disseminate certain United States person information uncovered while performing counterterrorism analysis and searches in accordance with this Appendix, the applicable Terms and Conditions, and the written agreement.

land Security Council directives; or Attorney General-approved policies, memoranda of understanding, or agreements; or

9. Is disseminated to appropriate elements of the IC for the purposes of allowing the recipient element to determine whether the information is relevant to its responsibilities and can be retained by it.

The identity of a United States person may be disseminated outside the Intelligence Community only if it is necessary or if it is reasonably believed it may become necessary to understand and assess such United States person information described above.

VI. Foreign Disseminations

For any dissemination of United States person information to a foreign or international entity, in addition to complying with the dissemination provisions of section V, the IC element must find that:

A. the dissemination is consistent with the interests of the United States, including U.S. national security interests;

B. the dissemination complies with DCID 6/6 or any successor ICD[3];

C. the foreign or international entity has agreed not to disseminate the information further without approval by the IC element; and

D. the IC element, in consultation with its General Counselor senior legal advisor, has considered the effect such dissemination may reasonably be expected to have on any identifiable United States person to determine whether any additional safeguards are needed.

VII. Retention of Information for Administrative Purposes

To the extent consistent with law, United States person information acquired pursuant to this Appendix may be retained if necessary to conduct the oversight, auditing, redress, or compliance activities required by these Guidelines, if required by law or court order to be retained, or if necessary to determine whether the requirements of these Guidelines or applicable laws are satisfied. Any information retained under this paragraph beyond the temporary retention period may not be used for purposes other than those specified in the preceding sentence and must be promptly removed from the IC element's systems once retention is no longer necessary or required for those purposes, except that the IC element may retain any oversight, audit, redress, or compliance records or reports in accordance with its records retention policies.

VIII. The IC Element's Computer Systems

In designing its computer systems, the IC element shall take reasonable steps to enhance its ability to monitor activity involving United States person information and other sensitive information, and to facilitate compliance with, and the auditing and reporting required by, this Appendix.

---

3. ICD 403 is currently in draft. Once signed, any foreign dissemination would be required to comply with ICD 403 and any implementing IC Policy Guidance and IC Standards.

IX. **Oversight and Compliance**

A. Subject to oversight by the IC element's Civil Liberties and/or Privacy officer, if applicable, and the ODNI Civil Liberties Protection officer, the IC element shall conduct periodic reviews to verify continued compliance with this Appendix, including compliance with any Terms and Conditions and any measures specified in the written agreement. These reviews shall include spot checks, reviews of audit logs, and other appropriate measures.

B. The IC element, in coordination with the IC element's Civil Liberties and/or Privacy officer (or other appropriate official as identified in the written agreement), shall conduct periodic reviews of its continued need for access to each dataset disseminated pursuant to the NCTC Guidelines and this Appendix to determine whether such access remains necessary and appropriate. In conducting this review, consideration shall be given to the purpose for which the dataset was disseminated; the success of that dataset in fulfilling legitimate counterterrorism purposes; whether those purposes can now be fulfilled through the use of other data in the IC element's possession, or through other appropriate means; and privacy and civil liberties considerations applicable to the particular dataset.

C. The IC element shall promptly report, in writing, to the IC element head, the Director of NCTC, the ODNI General Counsel, the ODNI Civil Liberties Protection officer, the Department of Justice, and the IC Inspector General upon discovery of any significant failure to comply with (i) this Appendix; (ii) baseline or enhanced safeguards, procedures, or other oversight mechanisms; or (iii) any Terms and Conditions or the written agreement. For the purposes of this Appendix, a "significant failure" is a failure that constitutes a violation of the Constitution, or other law, including any executive order, and/or a failure that leads to unauthorized access, use, or dissemination of personally identifiable information about a United States person. NCTC shall then report to any data provider whose information was affected by the noncompliance, in accordance with the Terms and Conditions for that data.

D. The IC element shall report annually in writing to the IC element head and to the ODNI Civil Liberties Protection officer on the measures that the IC element is taking to ensure that its access to, and retention, use, and dissemination of , United States person information is appropriate under this Appendix, and in compliance with all Terms and Conditions and written agreement. The report shall include:

1. The results of the review required in section IX.B. above, regarding whether access to the bulk dataset continues to be appropriate;
2. A general description of the IC element's compliance and audit processes;
3. A description of the audits, spot checks, and other reviews the IC element conducted during the previous year, and the results of those audits, spot checks or other reviews, to include any shortcomings identified;
4. A description of how the IC element ensures that it promptly purges United States person information that does not meet the standards for re-

tention under this Appendix, related Terms and Conditions, and any other measures specified in the written agreement;

5. An assessment of the United States person information disseminated by the IC element directly to foreign, international, state, local, tribal, or private sector entities or individuals; the restrictions, if any, that the IC element imposed on the entities' use or further dissemination of such information; and any known misuse of such information by a recipient, data breach, or significant failure by the recipient to comply with the terms of the certification required under section VI.C of this Appendix;

6. An assessment of whether there is a need for enhanced safeguards, procedures, or oversight regarding the handling of United States person information or other sensitive information, or any other reasonable measures that should be taken to improve the handling of information;

7. Measures the IC element has taken to comply with the requirements of section VIII with respect to its computer systems; and

8. A description of any material changes or improvements the IC element implemented, or is considering implementing, to improve compliance with this Appendix.

E. The IC element shall provide a copy of this report to the IC element General Counsel, the IC element Civil Liberties and/or Privacy officer, the Director of NCTC, the ODNI General Counsel, the IC element's Inspector General, and the IC Inspector General, and shall make the report available upon request to the Assistant Attorney General for National Security. The IC element shall also make available to the IC element's Inspector General and the IC Inspector General any other reports or documentation necessary to ensure compliance with this Appendix.

F. The reporting required by this Appendix does not replace any other reporting required by statute, executive order, or regulation.

X. Interpretation and Departures

A. The IC element shall refer all questions relating to the interpretation of these Guidelines to the IC element's office of General Counselor other senior legal advisor. The IC element's General Counsel shall consult with the ODNI General Counsel regarding any novel or significant interpretations, and the ODNI General Counsel shall then consult with the Assistant Attorney General for National Security to the extent required by the NCTC Guidelines.

B. The ODNI General Counsel and the Assistant Attorney General for National Security must approve in advance any departures from this Appendix. If there is not time for such approval and a departure from this Appendix is necessary because of the immediacy or gravity of a threat to the safety of persons or property or to the national security, the IC element head, other senior IC element personnel identified in the written agreement with NCTC, the Director of NCTC, or the NCTC Director's senior representative present may approve a departure from these Guidelines. The ODNI General Counsel shall be notified as soon thereafter as possible. The ODNI General Counsel shall provide prompt written notice of any such departures to the Assistant Attorney General for National Security. Notwithstanding this paragraph, all activities in all circumstances must be carried out in a manner consistent with the Constitution and laws of the United States.

XI. Status as Internal Guidance

The provisions in this Appendix are set forth solely for the purpose of internal IC element and ODNI guidance. They are not intended to, do not, and may not be relied upon to create any rights, substantive or procedural, enforceable at law or in equity, by any party in any matter, civil or criminal, nor do they place any limitation on otherwise lawful investigative and litigation prerogatives of the U.S. Government.

RELATED USG REPORTS

Office of the Director of National Intelligence 2010 Data Mining Report

For the Period January 1, 2010 through December 31, 2010 2
Office of the Director of National Intelligence
2010 Data Mining Report
January 1, 2010 through December 31, 2010

I. Introduction

The Office of the Director of National Intelligence (ODNI) provides this report pursuant to Section 804 of the *Implementing the Recommendations of the 9/11 Commission Act of 2007*, entitled *The Federal Agency Data Mining Reporting Act of 2007* (Data Mining Reporting Act).

A. Scope.

This report covers the activities of all ODNI components from January 1, 2010 through December 31, 2010. Constituent elements of the Intelligence Community (IC) will report their activities to Congress through their own departments or agencies.[1]

B. Reporting Requirement.

The Data Mining Reporting Act requires "the head of each department or agency of the Federal Government that is engaged in an activity to use or develop data mining shall submit a report to Congress on all such activities of the department or agency."[2] This is an annual requirement. Under the Act, "data mining" is defined as:

> "... a program involving pattern-based queries, searches or other analyses of one or more electronic databases, where —
>
> (A) a department or agency of the Federal Government, or a non-Federal entity acting on behalf of the Federal Government, is conducting the queries, searches, or other analyses to discover or locate a predictive pattern or anomaly indicative of terrorist or criminal activity on the part of any individual or individuals;
>
> (B) the queries, searches, or other analyses are not subject-based and do not use personal identifiers of a specific individual, or inputs associated

1. Section 804(c)(1) of the Data Mining Reporting Act.
2. Section 804(c)(1) of the Data Mining Reporting Act.

with a specific individual or group of individuals, to retrieve information from the database or databases; and
(C) the purpose of the queries, searches, or other analyses is not solely—(i) the detection of fraud, waste, or abuse in a Government agency or program; or (ii) the security of a Government computer system.[3]"

When focusing on individuals or groups, the ODNI typically uses analytic tools and techniques that rely on "personal identifiers of a specific individual, or inputs associated with a specific individual or group of individuals," such as link-analysis tools. Unlike the predictive, pattern-based technologies envisioned by the Act, these tools and techniques start with a known or suspected terrorist, or other subject of foreign intelligence interest, and use various methods to uncover links or relationships between the known subject and potential associates or other persons with whom that subject has a "link" (a contact or relationship). Thus, such analytic tools and techniques do not fall within the statutory definition of data mining.

C. Format and Content.
The format of this year's report has been reworked for clarity and readability. Part II reports on those ODNI programs, if any, that meet reporting requirements of the Data Mining Act. Part III reports on non-data mining programs that are included in the interest of transparency, for the reasons explained below. For programs included under Part III, descriptions are provided in a continuous narrative form, with information that is generally responsive to the reporting elements of the Data Mining Reporting Act.

In this year's report, there are no programs included in Part II, and five programs included in Part III. Three of those programs were described in last year's report: two Intelligence Advanced Research Projects Activity (IARPA) programs – Knowledge Discovery and Dissemination (KDD) and Automated Low-level Analysis and Description of Diverse Intelligence Video (ALADDIN Video) – and one ODNI Chief Information Officer (CIO) program – Catalyst. The fourth program is IARPA's Automatic Privacy Protection (APP) program, which includes discussion of the follow-on Security and Privacy Assurance Research (SPAR) program, and the fifth is the National Counterterrorism Center's (NCTC's) program known as DataSphere.

Although these five programs are not "data mining" programs, information is nonetheless provided in the interest of transparency. As with last year's report, KDD and ALADDIN Video are included because technologies investigated by, or later developed from, those programs could be used to support data mining (such technologies would then be subject to reporting under the Data Mining Reporting Act). Catalyst and DataSphere are in development stages and, while such development does

3. Section 804(b)(1)(A) of the Data Mining Reporting Act.

not currently include pattern-based functionality, both programs contemplate potential pattern-based functionality in future stages. The APP and SPAR programs are included to provide information on programs that may have applicability in enhancing security and privacy protections in data mining activities.

D. Protection of Privacy and Civil Liberties.
The ODNI Civil Liberties and Privacy Office (CLPO) works closely with the ODNI Office of General Counsel, ODNI components and the IC elements to ensure appropriate legal, privacy, and civil liberties safeguards are incorporated into policies, processes and procedures that support the intelligence mission. The CLPO is led by the Civil Liberties Protection Officer, a position established by the IRTPA. The duties of this Officer are set forth in that Act, and include: ensuring that the protection of civil liberties and privacy is appropriately incorporated in the policies of the ODNI and the IC; overseeing compliance by the ODNI with legal requirements relating to civil liberties and privacy; reviewing complaints about potential abuses of privacy and civil liberties in ODNI programs and activities; and ensuring that technologies sustain, and do not erode, privacy protections relating to the use, collection, and other disclosure of personal information."[4]

The IC has in place a protective infrastructure built in principle part on a core set of U.S. Person rules derived from Executive Order (EO) 12333. This EO requires each IC element to maintain procedures, approved by the Attorney General, governing the collection, retention and dissemination of U.S. Person information. These procedures limit the type of information that may be collected, retained or disseminated to the categories listed in part 2.3 of the EO. Each IC element's Attorney-General approved U.S. Persons guidance is interpreted, applied, and overseen by that element's Office of General Counsel and Office of Inspector General. Violations are reported to the Intelligence Oversight Board of the President's Intelligence Advisory Board. In addition to EO 12333, IC elements are subject to the requirements of the Privacy Act, which protects information about U.S. citizens and permanent resident aliens that a government agency maintains and retrieves by name or unique identifier.

The IC's privacy and civil liberties protective infrastructure is bolstered also by guidance and directives issued by the Office of Management and Budget, including memoranda regarding the reporting of and response to incidents involving personally identifiable information and the minimization of Social Security Numbers.

Before any tool or technology could be used in an operational setting, the use of the tool or technology would need to be examined pursuant to EO 12333, the Privacy Act, and other applicable requirements to determine how the tool could be used consistent with the framework for protecting information about Americans and other U.S. Persons.

---

4. National Security Act of 1947, as amended by the Intelligence Reform and Terrorism Prevention Act of 2004 (IRTPA), 50 § 403-3d.

CLPO has been considering how advanced technologies, employed in accordance with proper laws and policies, enable sharing and use of information while protecting privacy and civil liberties. Such privacy-enhancing technologies (PETs) also prove useful in providing protections for data mining activities. CLPO is making available the results of its PET-related research to IC elements and other government offices with which CLPO collaborates. During 2010, CLPO began follow-on work to identify specific activities within the ODNI as to which PETs could be applied, as a means to better understand the practical utility, functionality, and potential of PETs for intelligence activities.

II. ODNI Data Mining Activities

The ODNI did not engage in any activities to use or develop data mining functionality in the reporting period.

III. Other Programs

The following programs are reported in the interest of transparency.

A. <u>CATALYST</u>

The CIO manages the Catalyst program. During Fiscal Year 2010, Catalyst focused on pre-Phase A research activities, which did not include development of pattern-matching functionality. Catalyst Phase A alternative analysis and technology development activities are planned through Fiscal Year 2011. Pattern-matching functionality is contemplated for a later phase of development, currently scheduled to begin in 2013.

Catalyst will support IC information sharing and integration objectives as laid out in Intelligence Community Directive (ICD) 501 and the 2009 National Intelligence Strategy (NIS). In January 2009, the ODNI released ICD 501, establishing policies for discovery and dissemination/retrieval of intelligence and intelligence-related information. The NIS recommended making more information accessible or discoverable, while recognizing the need to protect aspects of sensitive reporting. The NIS highlighted the continuing difficulties analysts face in finding and accessing the universe of relevant data and information across large and diverse data sources, setting "Improving Information Integration and Sharing" as its fourth Enterprise Objective.

As the need for the sharing of intelligence data increases, the volume of data that analysts must interpret is expected to increase dramatically, further impeding efficient and effective access, discovery, and use of that data for analysis. Analysts will encounter data that was collected for different purposes, protected in different ways, and described using different terminologies. The Catalyst program was established to address information overload and improve inter-agency, multi-intelligence (multi-INT) information sharing by providing IC analysts with capabilities for entity disambiguation, correlation, and co-referencing.

Catalyst will provide IC intelligence professionals the ability to discover intelligence information correlated from the IC's vast data holdings. The Catalyst program will address analytic information overload and enable IC enterprise correlation of entity information. The three primary goals for Phase A of Catalyst's development are to: (1) systematically derive entity information from across vast information holdings and share it using consistent standards and processes that ease the time and effort required to exploit the data upon receipt; (2) provide a means of correlating entity data acquired from disparate sources to enable more rapid discovery and understanding of the data; and (3) provide an enterprise-wide system that allows a user to query for a given person or organization of interest using fragmentary intelligence to discover all that the IC knows about that entity and access that portion of intelligence information for which the user is authorized to access.

In its end-state, Catalyst will enable data fusion/analytic programs to share disparate repositories with each other, to disambiguate and cross-correlate the different agencies' holdings, and to discover and visualize relationship/network links, geospatial patterns, temporal patterns and related correlations. Data access controls will be in place to safely exchange essential data elements amongst authorized IC personnel with appropriate credentials. If an analyst does not have access to view a record, the system will provide the analyst with the necessary information to enable that analyst to efficiently request access to the critical information needed.

A key component of Catalyst will be the National Information Correlation Service (NICS). The NICS will maintain ingested source data, data resulting from Catalyst Data Preparation Services (CDPS) processing, assertions made by humans, and information derived through further processing and correlation analytics. CDPS services support systematic data preparation, extraction, and transformation for the NICS. The NICS correlation analytics will include entity disambiguation and automated knowledge inferencing, and will allow users to find attributes and relationships for entities of interest.

The data to be used in the Catalyst program is from IC sources. The NICS enables its data correlation services, through the application and exclusive use of the metadata associated with IC shared, multi-intelligence data sources. As such, the NICS entity correlation processing does not contain the substance or content of the external data sources, only the metadata associated with the data sourced. In implementing Catalyst, each agency's system will be stand-alone, and will reside on its own network. Catalyst will apply the metadata associated with the data provider's data source and use that metadata in its services to make it discoverable and accessible to the entire community. It is anticipated that Catalyst data sources will be modified and changed as the program moves forward.

As stated, pattern matching functionality for Catalyst is contemplated, but has not yet been designed and is, therefore, not currently in development. Such functionality is anticipated in a later phase of development. Currently, functional requirements for pattern matching are expected to be developed in the latter half of 2012. It is anticipated that the Catalyst program's pattern matching functionality will be primarily resident in the NICS data correlation services component. For example, such functionality might enable the use of pattern matching to identify a set of entities for further review by analysts, in response to a threat stream.

ODNI will provide additional detail in a future report when and if such functionality is developed.

CIO works closely with CLPO, as well as the ODNI Office of General Counsel (OGC), to build in privacy and civil liberties protections in its activities, and will do so with respect to the design of any pattern matching functionality. Safeguards include policies and training on the rules regarding the collection, retention, and dissemination of U.S. Person information, guidance on Constitutional limitations, and technical integration of oversight and compliance measures on access and use of data (e.g., PKI-enabled attributed based access controls, audit processes, data export management controls).

B. DATASPHERE

NCTC uses tools that do not fit the definition of data mining as defined by the Data Mining Reporting Act. NCTC uses network analysis tools to discover relationships between known and suspected terrorists (KST) and their associates. These activities are conducted using the personal identifiers of a KST as the starting point. Additionally, NCTC uses entity resolution tools to efficiently discover all data in its holdings pertaining to a given individual. The subjects of NCTC's entity resolution tool include persons already known to have a terrorism nexus, persons seeking entrance into the United States, and persons being assessed for a nexus to terrorism.

NCTC is currently developing a tool – DataSphere – which, once completed, will enhance data fusion and entity resolution, as well as discovery of unknown relationships. DataSphere, enables analysis of the activities of terrorists such as their communication networks and travel. The goal of DataSphere is to provide analysts with a tool to aid in the discovery of unknown terrorism relationships and the identification of previously undetected terrorist and terrorism information. DataSphere development work in 2010 does not fit the definition of data mining as defined by the Data Mining Reporting Act because the data set loaded into the tool is comprised entirely of terrorism information. Queries and searches in DataSphere, thus, begin with known identifiers (such as identifiers of known or suspected terrorists or terrorist groups) based upon threat-based reports. However, it is contemplated that Pattern-matching functionality using data not yet known to be terrorism information will be included in future development phases.

DataSphere draws upon data in NCTC's data holdings. Upon acquisition, each dataset utilized by NCTC is tagged, as appropriate, under existing interagency agreements addressing the provision of the information, as well as pursuant to Attorney General-approved guidelines for the handling of U.S. Person information. Additionally, all datasets are appropriately marked for retention, U.S. Person content, operational sensitivity, and whether there is a "filter" caveat associated with data use. A filter caveat is any data that must be preprocessed, i.e., technically compared against datasets with a pre-existing terrorism nexus prior to only the "terrorism-linked" results being made available to an appropriate limited set of NCTC analysts.

DataSphere will be able to detect patterns in data that links individuals with events and actions including identifying a set of individuals that fit the parameters described in a threat intelligence report. These results will be complemented with other tools and manual analysis for validation purposes. Details regarding such functionality will be provided in a future report, once such functionality is designed and in development.

As DataSphere's pattern matching capabilities are developed and tested, NCTC will continue to work closely with CLPO, as well as OGC, to ensure appropriate privacy and civil liberties protections are taken into account.

The legal and policy foundation for DataSphere is based on IRTPA and the National Security of 1947, as amended. These statutory authorities establish NCTC as the "primary organization in the United States government for analyzing and integrating all intelligence possessed or acquired by the United States government pertaining to terrorism and counterterrorism, excepting intelligence pertaining exclusively to domestic terrorists and domestic counterterrorism." Further, NCTC shall also "serve as the central and shared knowledge bank on known and suspected terrorists and international terror groups, as well as their goals, strategies, capabilities, and networks of contacts and support." Moreover, EO 12333 requires each IC element to maintain procedures, approved by the Attorney General, governing the collection, retention and dissemination of U.S. Person information, thereby protecting the rights and privacy of U.S. Persons. These procedures limit the type of information that may be collected, retained or disseminated to the categories listed in part 2.3 of EO 12333. NCTC currently operates under Attorney General Approved Guidelines that govern NCTC's access, retention, use and dissemination of Terrorism Information contained within datasets. 8

NCTC has instituted the following measures to guard against improper use of data, which would also provide protection in the context of any future data mining activities:

- Mandatory training on the proper handling of U.S. Persons information for everyone who has access to such information. The training includes descriptions of specific uses of U.S. Persons data that are prohibited.
- Strict access control over all information about U.S. Persons limiting access to only those charged with seeking to identify a terrorism nexus.

• Oversight by the OGC and CLPO of all NCTC use, retention and dissemination of data about U.S. Persons. This oversight includes reviews of procedures for determining whether an individual has a terrorism nexus, whether information about an individual can be shared with partner organizations to determine if there is a terrorism nexus, and how decisions are made to use data about individuals determined to have a terrorism nexus.

C. IARPA Research Programs

The mission of IARPA is to invest in high-risk/high payoff research programs that have the potential to provide the United States with an overwhelming intelligence advantage over its future adversaries. It does not have an operational mission and it does not deploy technologies directly to the field. As a scientific research funding organization, IARPA does not use, nor does it expect to make use of, data mining technology. IARPA programs are by nature experimental and are designed to produce new capabilities. The end goal of an IARPA program is typically a proof-of-concept experiment or prototype of an entirely new capability. Due to their experimental nature, IARPA programs do not always achieve their end goals, and when they do, further steps are required to transform the results into real world applications. Any results from IARPA research programs that do get incorporated into future operational programs within the IC, or other parts of the United States government, will be subject to appropriate legal, privacy, civil liberties and policy safeguards.

As with last year's report, the KDD and ALADDIN Video programs below are reported in the interest of transparency, due to the potential that technologies investigated by, or later developed from, those programs could be used to support data mining (such technologies would then be subject to reporting under the Data Mining Reporting Act).

1. *Knowledge Discovery and Dissemination (KDD) Program.* The KDD scientific research program is an IARPA program, begun in 2009. A Broad Agency Announcement (BAA) for KDD was released on December 22, 2009 and KDD research contracts were awarded in September 2010.

The objective of the KDD program is to enable an analyst to utilize large, complex and varied data sets that he has not seen before to produce actionable intelligence in a timely manner. KDD tackles two significant technical areas: (1) how to quickly understand the novel data sets so that the contents can be correctly integrated with data sets that are already in use (this is termed"alignment"); (2) how to construct automatic analysis tools that are able to work effectively across aligned data sets. KDD research results will be evaluated using realistic challenge problems throughout the program.

In evaluations of research teams' prototypes, the KDD scientific research program will utilize real-world, classified data sets that are large and complex. KDD researchers' work will be evaluated in the context of challenge problems using these data sets. The challenge problems will not be problems that require data mining technology as defined by the Act. The data sets used by researchers will be highly varied, and may include, for example, regional biographic data, incident reports, translated newspaper articles, etc. The use of all data sets will be consistent with all U.S. laws and regulations.

For more information on the KDD Program, see http://www.iarpa.gov/solicitations_kdd.html

2. *Automated Low-level Analysis and Description of Diverse Intelligence Video (ALADDIN Video) Program.* The Automated Low-level Analysis and Description of Diverse Intelligence Video (ALADDIN Video) scientific research program is an IARPA program that is expected to award research contracts in early 2011. A BAA for ALADDIN was released on June 10, 2010.

The objective of the ALADDIN program is to enable an analyst to query large video data sets to quickly and reliably locate those video clips that show a specific type of event. The ALADDIN program will research technologies designed to automatically search large numbers of video data files for analyst-defined events of interest and direct the analyst to those video data files that are likely to contain occurrences of those events. ALADDIN's technologies, if successful, will help to automate a triage process that is currently performed largely manually by analysts. Although this is not "data mining," technologies that result from ALADDIN research could, potentially, be applied by operational organizations to support capabilities that involve pattern recognition.

ALADDIN addresses three significant technical areas: (1) High-speed processing of large amounts of video clips to extract information that can later be used to support queries about each clip's contents; (2) Generation of effective queries from small sets of example video clips and a textual description; (3) Robust query processing that identifies the clips of interest and summarizes the rationale for their selection. ALADDIN research results will be evaluated by IARPA and the National Institute for Standards and Technology (NIST).

The ALADDIN program will use video data files in its research and evaluations that are acquired by NIST for its annual, international, Video Retrieval video search technology research program (TRECVID). TRECVID sponsors public evaluations of video and multimedia search technologies that are open to worldwide participation. ALADDIN performers will participate in these evaluations to demonstrate objective progress in their research. The data collections used in the TRECVID evaluations are made available to all participants through an evaluation participation agreement that stipulates that the TRECVID data collections are to be used for research purposes only. The TRECVID data is collected using a rigorous process that protects privacy.

For more information on the TRECVID Program, see http://www-nlpir.nist.gov/projects/trecvid

For more information on ALADDIN, see http://www.iarpa.gov/open_solicitations.html

3. *Automatic Privacy Protection (APP) Program.* The 2009 ODNI Data Mining Report included a discussion of the APP program that, while not specifically focused on data mining, may enhance security and protect privacy in data mining activities.

In the 2010 reporting period, APP research achieved two complementary goals. First, it developed secure distributed private information retrieval (PIR) protocols that permit an organization (Client) to query a cooperating data provider (Server) so that the Server cannot learn about the query posed or the results returned. At the same time, the Server is assured that only information relevant to the query is returned to the Client. These protocols add minimal overheads for computation and communication for simple queries and databases using a trusted third party. Second, APP demonstrated algorithms to compare database queries with privacy policies so that a Client's auditor can verify that only authorized queries have been submitted to the Server.

A follow-on program began with solicitation of proposals for Security and Privacy Assurance Research (SPAR, http://www.iarpa.gov/solicitations_spar.html) in December 2010. This research will build on the APP program's results to handle complex queries, large datasets, and three new information sharing architectures: publish-subscribe systems, message queue (mailbox) systems, and outsourced data storage systems. Furthermore, SPAR will develop policy compliance checking algorithms that work on encrypted queries, enabling the Server to verify that Client queries are authorized. In addition, the SPAR program will explore efficient homomorphic encryption techniques to implement queries on encrypted data. If successful, the SPAR program will benefit the IC by securing and protecting the privacy interests of both those who search and those who own databases. The technology may enhance cooperative information sharing within the IC, and among governments and the private sector. Efficient private information retrieval may expand policy options for reconciliation of privacy and security concerns when information is shared. Furthermore, the program could enable both Clients and Servers to enforce restrictions on data mining activities.

Unclassified Report on the President's Surveillance Program

(July 10, 2009)

Preface

Title III of the Foreign Intelligence Surveillance Act Amendments Act of 2008 required the Inspectors General (IGs) of the elements of the Intelligence Community that participated in the President's Surveillance Program (PSP) to conduct a comprehensive review of the program. The IGs of the Department of Justice, the Department of Defense, the Central Intelligence Agency, the National Security Agency, and the Office of the Director of National Intelligence participated in the review required under the Act. The Act required the IGs to submit a comprehensive report on the review to the Senate Select Committee on Intelligence, the Senate Committee on the Judiciary, the House Permanent Select Committee on Intelligence, and the House Committee on the Judiciary.

In response to Title III requirements, we have prepared this unclassified report on the PSP, which summarizes the collective results of our reviews. Because many aspects of the PSP remain classified, and in order to provide the Congressional committees the complete results of our reviews, we also prepared, and have bound separately, a classified report on the PSP. The individual reports detailing the results of each IG's review are annexes to the classified report.

Glenn A. Fine
Inspector General
Department of Justice

Gordon S. Heddell
Acting Inspector General
Department of Defense

Patricia A. Lewis
Acting Inspector General
Central Intelligence Agency

George Ellard
Inspector General
National Security Agency

Roslyn A. Mazer
Inspector General
Office of the Director of National Intelligence

Unclassified Report on the President's Surveillance Program

I. INTRODUCTION

In the weeks following the terrorist attacks of September 11, 2001, the President authorized the National Security Agency (NSA) to conduct a classified program to detect and prevent further attacks in the United States. As part of the NSA's classified program, several different intelligence activities were authorized in Presidential Authorizations, and the details of these activities changed over time. The program was reauthorized by the President approximately every 45 days, with certain modifications. Collectively, the activities carried out under these Authorizations are referred to as the "President's Surveillance Program" or "PSP."[1]

One of the activities authorized as part of the PSP was the interception of the content of communications into and out of the United States where there was a reasonable basis to conclude that one party to the communication was a member of al-Qa'ida or related terrorist organizations. This aspect of the PSP was publicly acknowledged and described by the President, the Attorney General, and other Administration officials beginning in December 2005 following a series of articles published in The New York Times. The Attorney General subsequently publicly acknowledged the fact that other intelligence activities were also authorized under the same Presidential Authorization, but the details of those activities remain classified.

The President and other Administration officials labeled the publicly disclosed interception of the content of certain international communications by the NSA as the "Terrorist Surveillance Program."

Several different agencies had roles in the PSP. At the request of the White House, the NSA was involved in providing the technical expertise necessary to create the program. The NSA also was responsible for conducting the actual collection of information under the PSP and disseminating intelligence reports to other agencies such as the Federal Bureau of Investigation (FBI), the Central Intelligence Agency (CIA), and the Office of the Director of National Intelligence (ODNI) National Counterterrorism Center (NCTC) for analysis and possible investigation.[2] In addition, the NSA Office of General Counsel and Office of the

---

1. In Title III of the Foreign Intelligence Surveillance Act Amendments Act of 2008 (FISA Amendments Act), the President's Surveillance Program is defined as

> the intelligence activity involving communications that was authorized by the President during the period beginning on September 11, 2001, and ending on January 17, 2007, including the program referred to by the President in a radio address on December 17, 2005 (commonly known as the Terrorist Surveillance Program).

FISA Amendments Act, Title III, Sec. 301(a)(3).

2. The National Counterterrorism Center was made a subcomponent of the Office of the Director of National Intelligence by the Intelligence Reform and Terrorism Prevention Act of 2004 and is charged with being the primary U.S. Government organization for analyzing and integrating counterterrorism intelligence, except for intelligence pertaining exclusively to domestic terrorists and domestic counterterrorism.

Inspector General were responsible for reviewing and monitoring the NSA's PSP operation. With the exception of the NSA, the Department of Defense (DoD) had limited involvement in the PSP.

Components of the Department of Justice (DOJ) other than the FBI also were involved in the program. Most significantly, DOJ's Office of Legal Counsel (OLC) provided advice to the White House and the Attorney General on the overall legality of the PSP. In addition, DOJ's Office of Intelligence Policy and Review (now called the Office of Intelligence in DOJ's National Security Division) worked with the FBI and the NSA to address the impact PSP-derived information had on proceedings under the Foreign Intelligence Surveillance Act (FISA). DOJ's National Security Division also handled potential discovery issues that may have involved PSP-related information in international terrorism prosecutions.

The CIA, in addition to receiving intelligence reports as PSP consumers, requested information from the program and utilized this information in its analyses. The CIA also initially prepared threat assessment memoranda that were used to support the periodic Presidential Authorizations.

Beginning in 2005, the newly-created ODNI assumed responsibility for preparing these threat assessment memoranda. In addition, NCTC analysts received program information for possible use in analytical products prepared for the President, senior policymakers, and other Intelligence Community (IC) analysts and officers.

A. Scope of Report

Title III of the Foreign Intelligence Surveillance Act of 1978 Amendments Act of 2008 (FISA Amendments Act)—signed into law on July 10, 2008-required the Inspectors General of Intelligence Community agencies that participated in the PSP to conduct a comprehensive review of the program. The review required to be conducted under the Act was to examine:

(A) all of the facts necessary to describe the establishment, implementation, product, and use of the product of the Program;

(B) access to legal reviews of the Program and access to information about the Program;

(C) communications with, and participation of, individuals and entities in the private sector related to the Program;

(D) interaction with the Foreign Intelligence Surveillance Court and transition to court orders related to the Program; and

(E) any other matters identified by any such Inspector General that would enable that Inspector General to complete a review of the Program, with respect to such Department or element.

The Inspectors General (IGs) of the DoD, DOJ, CIA, NSA, and ODNIcollectively the "PSP IG Group"—conducted the review required under the Act. This unclassified report summarizes the portions of the collective results of the IG reviews that can be released in unclassified form. A separate classified report summarizes the classified results of the individual IG reviews. In addition, the individual IG reports that document the results of each of the participating IGs' reviews and investigations, which provide additional classified details concerning the PSP and each agency's role in the PSP, are included as attachments to the classified report.

Title III of the FISA Amendments Act required that the report of any investigation of matters relating to the PSP conducted by the DOJ Office of Professional Responsibility (OPR) be provided to the DOJ Inspector General, and that the findings and conclusions of such investigation be included in the DOJ OIG review. OPR has initiated a review of whether any standards of professional conduct were violated in the preparation of the first series of legal memoranda supporting the PSP. OPR has not completed its review.

B. Methodology of this Review

The PSP IG Group collectively interviewed approximately 200 government and private sector personnel as part of this review. Most of the interviews were conducted separately by the individual OIGs as part of their agency-specific reviews, although some interviews were conducted jointly. Among the interviewees were former and current senior government officials, including Director of National Intelligence (DNI) John D. Negroponte, NSA Director Keith Alexander, and DNI Michael McConnell, NSA and CIA Director and Principal Deputy DNI (PDDNI) Michael V. Hayden, White House Counsel and Attorney General Alberto Gonzales, FBI Director Robert Mueller, and Secretary of Defense Donald Rumsfeld. Certain senior officials either declined or did not respond to our requests to be interviewed for this review, including Counsel to the Vice President David Addington, White House Chief of Staff Andrew Card, Attorney General John Ashcroft, DOJ Office of Legal Counsel Deputy Assistant Attorney General John Yoo, and former Director of Central Intelligence George Tenet.

The OIGs also interviewed many agency managers and personnel, including attorneys, NSA operational personnel, FBI special agents and analysts, and CIA officials and analysts who were responsible for the day-to-day operation of the PSP, including the legal issues associated with the program.

In addition to these interviews, the PSP IG Group reviewed thousands of documents and electronic records, including the Presidential Authorizations and Threat Assessments supporting reauthorization of the program, OLC legal memoranda, contemporaneous notes and e-mails of various senior officials describing significant events during the program, Foreign Intelligence Surveillance Court (FISC) pleadings and orders, and documents that were used to disseminate PSP-derived leads to FBI field offices and CIA stations for investigation and for other purposes related to the PSP. Finally, there were previous NSA OIG reports and supporting documentation to use as additional sources.

II. INCEPTION OF THE PRESIDENT'S SURVEILLANCE PROGRAM (PSP)

A. Expansion of NSA's Collection Activities

Prior to September 11, 2001, the Foreign Intelligence Surveillance Act of 1978 and Executive Order 12333 were generally viewed as the principal governing authorities for conducting electronic surveillance for national security purposes.[3] The Foreign Intelligence Surveillance Act, 50 U.S.C. § 1801, et *seq.,* was enacted in 1978 to "provide legislative authorization and regulation for all electronic surveillance conducted within the United States for foreign intelligence purposes." S. Rep. No. 95-701, at 9 (1978), reprinted in 1978 U.S.C.C.A.N. 3973,3977. Executive Order 12333 placed restrictions on intelligence collection activities engaged in by Executive Branch agencies, including the NSA, while also seeking to foster "full and free exchange of information" among these agencies. In 2000 the NSA reported to Congress that

The applicable legal standards for the collection, retention, or dissemination of information concerning u.s. persons reflect a careful balancing between the needs of the government for such intelligence and the protection of the rights of U.S. persons, consistent with the reasonableness standard of the Fourth Amendment, as determined by factual circumstances.

In the Foreign Intelligence Surveillance Act (FISA) and Executive Order (E.O.) 12333, Congress and the Executive have codified this balancing. (Citations omitted.)[4]

As explained below, the PSP expanded the NSA's authority by allowing it to conduct electronic surveillance within the United States without an order from the FISC when certain factual conditions and legal standards were met.

B. Presidential Authorization of the PSP

In the days immediately after September 11, 2001, the NSA used its existing authorities to gather intelligence information in response to the terrorist attacks. When Director of Central Intelligence Tenet, on behalf of the White House, asked NSA Director Hayden whether the NSA could do more against terrorism, Hayden replied that nothing more could be done within existing authorities. When asked what he might do with more authority, Hayden said he put together information on what was operationally useful and technologically feasible. This information formed the basis of the PSP.

Shortly thereafter, the President authorized the NSA to undertake a number of new, highly classified intelligence activities.[5] All of these activities were authorized in a single Presidential Authorization that was periodically reauthorized.

---

3. Executive Order 12333 was amended on July 30, 2008 by Executive Order 13470. This report refers to Executive Order 12333 as it existed prior to that amendment. The Foreign Intelligence Surveillance Act (FISA), 50 U.S.C. § 1801, et *seq.* also was amended by the FISA Amendments Act of 2008. Unless otherwise indicated, this report refers to FISA as it existed prior to 2008.

4. Legal Standards for the Intelligence Community in Conducting Electronic Surveillance, Report to Congress pursuant to Fiscal Year 2000 Intelligence Authorization Act.

5. See Letter from Attorney General Alberto Gonzales to Senator Patrick Leahy, Chairman, Committee on the Judiciary (Gonzales Letter), August 1, 2007.

The specific intelligence activities that were permitted by the Presidential Authorizations remain highly classified, except that beginning in December 2005 the President and other Administration officials acknowledged that these activities included the interception without a court order of certain international communications where there is "a reasonable basis to conclude that one party to the communication is a member of al-Qa'ida, affiliated with al-Qa'ida, or a member of an organization affiliated with al-Qa'ida."6 The President and other Administration officials referred to this publicly disclosed activity as the "Terrorist Surveillance Program," a convention we follow in this unclassified report. We refer to other intelligence activities authorized under the Presidential Authorizations as the "Other Intelligence Activities." The specific details of the Other Intelligence Activities remain highly classified, although the Attorney General publicly acknowledged the existence of such activities in August 2007.[7] Together, the Terrorist Surveillance Program and the Other Intelligence Activities comprise the PSP.

The Presidential Authorizations were issued at intervals of approximately every 45 days. As described in the next section, with each reauthorization the CIA and later the NCTC prepared an assessment of current potential terrorist threats and a summary of intelligence gathered through the PSP and other means during the previous authorization period. The Department of Justice's Office of Legal Counsel reviewed this information to assess whether there was "a sufficient factual basis demonstrating a threat of terrorist attacks in the United States for it to continue to be reasonable under the standards of the Fourth Amendment for the President to [continue] to authorize the warrantless searches involved" in the program. The Office of Legal Counsel then advised the Attorney General whether the constitutional standard of reasonableness had been met and whether the Presidential Authorization could be certified "as to form and legality." Each of the Presidential Authorizations included a finding to the effect that an extraordinary emergency continued to exist, and that the circumstances "constitute an urgent and compelling governmental interest" justifying the activities being authorized without a court order.

Each Presidential Authorization also included a requirement to maintain the secrecy of the activities carried out under the program. The President also noted his intention to inform appropriate members of the Senate and the House of Representatives of the program "as soon as I judge that it can be done consistently with national defense needs." As discussed in Section III.B.2. below, beginning on October 25, 2001, White House officials and Hayden provided briefings on the PSP to members of Congress and their staffs.

Although there was no legal requirement that the Authorizations be certified by the Attorney General or other Department of Justice official, current and former

6. Press Briefing by Attorney General Alberto Gonzales and General Michael Hayden, Principal Deputy Director for National Intelligence (December 19, 2005) (statement of Attorney General Gonzales).

7. Gonzales Letter, August 1, 2007.

DOJ officials told us that this certification added value by giving the program a sense of legitimacy. Former Attorney General Gonzales stated that the NSA was being asked to do something it had not done before, and it was important to assure the NSA that the Attorney General had approved the legality of the program. He also stated that it was important that the cooperating private sector personnel know that the Attorney General had approved the program. In addition, Gonzales said that for "purely political considerations" the Attorney General's approval of the program would have value "prospectively" in the event of congressional or inspector general reviews of the program.

C. Threat Assessment Memoranda Supporting Authorization of the PSP

The CIA initially prepared the threat assessment memoranda that were used to support the Presidential Authorization and periodic reauthorizations of the PSP. The memoranda documented intelligence assessments of the terrorist threats to the United States and to U.S. interests abroad from al-Qa'ida and affiliated terrorist organizations. These assessments were prepared approximately every 45 days to correspond with the President's Authorizations of the PSP.

The Director of Central Intelligence's (DCI) Chief of Staff was the initial focal point for preparing the threat assessment memoranda. According to the former DCI Chief of Staff, he directed CIA terrorism analysts to prepare objective appraisals of the current terrorist threat, focusing primarily on threats to the U.S. homeland, and to document those appraisals in a memorandum. Initially, the analysts who prepared the threat assessments were not read into the PSP and did not know how the threat assessments would be used. CIA's terrorism analysts drew upon all sources of intelligence in preparing these threat assessments.

After the terrorism analysts completed their portion of the memoranda, the DCI Chief of Staff added a paragraph at the end of the memoranda stating that the individuals and organizations involved in global terrorism (and discussed in the memoranda) possessed the capability and intention to' undertake further terrorist attacks within the United States. The DCI Chief of Staff recalled that the paragraph was provided to him initially by a senior White House official. The paragraph included the DCI's recommendation to the President that he authorize the NSA to conduct surveillance activities under the PSP. CIA Office of General Counsel (OGC) attorneys reviewed the draft threat assessment memoranda to determine whether they contained sufficient threat information and a compelling case for reauthorization of the PSP. If either was lacking, an OGC attorney would request that the analysts provide additional threat information or make revisions to the draft memoranda.

The threat assessment memoranda were then signed by the DCI. George Tenet signed most of the threat memoranda prepared during his tenure as DCI. On the few occasions when he was unavailable, the Deputy Director of Central Intelligence, John E. McLaughlin, signed the memoranda on behalf of Tenet. McLaughlin also signed the memoranda in the capacity of Acting DCI in August and September 2004.

In November 2004, Porter J. Goss became DCI and assumed responsibility for signing the memoranda. There were no occasions when the DCI or Acting DCI withheld their signatures from the threat assessment memoranda. The memoranda were co-signed by the Secretary of Defense, reviewed by the Attorney General, and delivered to the White House to be attached to the PSP Presidential Authorizations signed by the President.

Responsibility for drafting the threat assessment memoranda was transferred from the CIA to the newly established Terrorist Threat Integration Center (TIIC) in May 2003. This responsibility subsequently was retained by TIIC's successor organization, the NCTC. The DCI continued to sign the threat assessment memoranda through April 2005.

The ODNI was established in April 2005, and the NCTC became a subcomponent of the ODNI. Once Ambassador Negroponte was confirmed as the DNI, senior IC officials believed that DNI Negroponte, as the President's new senior intelligence advisor, should make the IC's recommendation to the President regarding the need to renew the PSP.

The preparation and approval of the threat assessments became the ODNI's primary role in the PSP. Beginning in April 2005, and continuing at specific intervals until the program's termination in early 2007, ODNI personnel prepared and approved threat assessments in support of the periodic renewal of the PSP.

The ODNI OIG found that the ODNI threat assessments were drafted by experienced NCTC personnel who prepared the documents in a memorandum style following an established DOJ format used in earlier PSP renewals. Throughout the ODNI preparation and approval process, the threat assessments were also subject to varying degrees of review and comment by DOJ and ODNI attorneys. Each threat assessment was designed to set forth the DNI's view regarding the current threat of an al-Qa'ida attack against the United States and to provide the DNI's recommendation whether to renew the PSP. NCTC personnel involved in preparing the threat assessments told the ODNI OIG that the danger of a terrorist attack described in the threat assessments was sobering and "scary," resulting in the threat assessments becoming known by ODNI and IC personnel involved in the PSP as the "scary memos." During interviews, ODNI personnel said they were aware the threat assessments were relied upon by DOJ and White House personnel as the basis for continuing the PSP, and understood that if a threat assessment identified a threat against the United States the PSP was likely to be renewed. NCTC analysts also reported that on a less frequent basis they prepared a related document that set forth a list of al-Qa'ida affiliated groups that they understood were targets of the PSP. The ODNI OIG found that the threat assessments and the less frequent list of al-Qa'ida-affiliated groups underwent the same ODNI approval process.

The ODNI OIG also determined that the ODNI threat assessments were prepared using evaluated intelligence information chosen from a wide variety of IC sources. ODNI personnel told the ODNI OIG that during the period when the ODNI prepared the threat assessments, the IC had access to fully evaluated intelligence that readily supported the ODNI assessments that al-Qa'ida terrorists remained a significant threat to the United States. The ODNI OIG found that once the ODNI threat assessments were approved within NCTC and by the NCTC Director, the documents were forwarded through an established approval chain to senior ODNI personnel who independently satisfied themselves that the documents were accurate, properly prepared, and in the appropriate format.

Once the draft threat assessments were subjected to this systematic and multilayered management and legal review, the documents were provided to the DNI or his Principal Deputy (PDDNI) for consideration and, if appropriate, approval. Overall, the ODNI OIG found that the ODNI process used to prepare and obtain approval of the threat assessments was straightforward, reasonable, and consistent with the preparation of other documents requiring DNI or PDDNI approval.

NCTC analysts involved in preparing the threat assessments told the ODNI OIG that only a portion of the PSP information was ever used in the ODNI threat assessments because other intelligence sources were available that provided more timely or detailed information about the al-Qa'ida threat to the United States. During interviews, the NCTC analysts noted that PSP information was only one of several valuable sources of intelligence information available to them. The NCTC analysts also told ODNI OIG staff that during the period when the NCTC prepared the threat memoranda, the intelligence demonstrating the al-Qa'ida threat to the United States was overwhelming and readily available to the IC.

D. Department of Justice Office of Legal Counsel's Early Memoranda Supporting the Legality of the PSP

From the outset of the program, access to the PSP for non-operational personnel was tightly restricted. Former White House Counsel and Attorney General Alberto Gonzales told the DOJ OIG that it was the President's decision to keep the program a "close hold." Gonzales stated that the President made the decision on all requests to "read in" any non-operational persons, including DOJ officials.[8]

DOJ Office of Legal Counsel (OLC) Deputy Assistant Attorney General John Yoo was responsible for drafting the first series of legal memoranda supporting the program.[9] Yoo was the only OLC official "read into" the PSP from the program's inception in October 2001 until Yoo left DOJ in May 2003.[10] The only other non-

8. Gonzales testified before the Senate Judiciary Committee on July 18, 2006, that "[a]s with all decisions that are non-operational in terms of who has access to the program, the President of the United States makes the decisions, because this is such an important program[.]"

9. The Office of Legal Counsel (OLC) typically drafts memoranda for the Attorney General and the Counsel to the President, usually on matters involving significant legal issues or constitutional questions, and in response to legal questions raised by Executive Branch agencies. In addition, all Executive Orders proposed to be issued by the President are reviewed by the Office of Legal Counsel as to form and legality, as are other matters that require the President's formal approval.

10. The process of being "read into" a compartmented program generally entails being approved for access to particularly sensitive and restricted information about a classified program, receiving a briefing about the program, and formally acknowledging the briefing, usually by signing a nondisclosure agreement describing restrictions on the handling and use of information concerning the program.

FBI DOJ officials read into the program during this period were Attorney General Ashcroft and Counsel for Intelligence Policy James Baker.

Jay Bybee was OLC Assistant Attorney General from November 2001 through March 2003, and Yoo's supervisor. Bybee told the DOJ OIG that in early July 2001, before he was confirmed, he learned that Yoo was already under consideration for one of OLC Deputy Assistant Attorney General slots. Bybee said he was "enthusiastic" about Yoo and later agreed to Yoo's request to be assigned to the "national security portfolio" because Y00 had more national security experience than any of the other OLC deputies.

However, Bybee stated he was never read into the PSP and could shed no further light on how Yoo came to draft the OLC opinions on the program. He said that Yoo had responsibility for supervising the drafting of opinions related to other national security issues when the September 11 attacks occurred.[11] Bybee described Yoo as "articulate and brilliant," and said he had a "golden resume" and was "very well connected" with officials in the White House. Bybee said that from these connections, in addition to Yoo's scholarship in the area of executive authority during wartime, it was not surprising that Yoo "became the White House's guy" on national security matters.

In September and early October 2001, Yoo prepared several preliminary opinions relating to hypothetical random domestic electronic surveillance activities, but the first OLC opinion explicitly addressing the legality of the PSP was not drafted until after the program had been formally authorized by President Bush in October 2001. Attorney General Ashcroft approved the first Presidential Authorization for the PSP as to "form and legality" on the same day that he was read into the program.

The first OLC opinion directly supporting the legality of the PSP was dated November 2, 2001, and was drafted by Yoo. As discussed in Section IV of this report, deficiencies in Yoo's memorandum identified by his successors in the Office of Legal Counsel and the Office of the Deputy Attorney General later became critical to DOJ's decision to reassess the legality of the program in 2003.

Yoo's November 2, 2001 memorandum focused almost exclusively on the activity that the President later publicly confirmed as the Terrorist Surveillance Program. Y00 acknowledged that FISA "purports to be the exclusive statutory means for conducting electronic surveillance for foreign intelligence," but opined that "[s]uch a reading of FISA would be an unconstitutional infringement on the President's Article II authorities." Yoo characterized FISA as merely providing a "safe harbor for electronic surveillance," adding that it "cannot restrict the

11. As noted above, Yoo, Ashcroft, Card, and Addington declined or did not respond to the DOJ OIG's request for interviews, and the DOJ OIG does not know how Yoo came to deal directly with the White House on legal issues related to the PSP. In his book "War by Other Means," Yoo wrote that "[a]s a deputy to the assistant attorney general in charge of the office, I was a Bush Administration appointee who shared its general constitutional philosophy.... I had been hired specifically to supervise OLC's work on [foreign affairs and national security]." "War by Other Means," by John Yoo, at 19-20.

President's ability to engage in warrantless searches that protect the national security." According to Yoo, the ultimate test of whether the government may engage in warrantless electronic surveillance activities is whether such conduct is consistent with the Fourth Amendment, not whether it meets the standards of FISA. Yoo wrote that "unless Congress made a clear statement in FISA that it sought to restrict presidential authority to conduct warrantless searches in the national security area—which it has not—then the statute must be construed to avoid such a reading."[12]

Yoo's analysis of this point would later raise serious concerns for other officials in OLC and the Office of the Deputy Attorney General (ODAG) in late 2003 and early 2004. Among other concerns, Y00 did not address the section of FISA that creates an explicit exemption from the requirement to obtain a judicial warrant for 15 days following a congressional declaration of war. See 50 U.S.C. § 1811. Yoo's successors in OLC criticized this omission in Yoo's memorandum because they believed that by including this provision in FISA Congress arguably had demonstrated an explicit intention to restrict the government's authority to conduct electronic surveillance during wartime.

Yoo's memorandum also analyzed Fourth Amendment issues raised by the Presidential Authorizations. Yoo dismissed Fourth Amendment concerns regarding the PSP to the extent that the Authorizations applied to non-U.S. persons outside the United States. Regarding those aspects of the program that involved interception of the international communications of

U.S. persons in the United States, Yoo asserted that Fourth Amendment jurisprudence allowed for searches of persons crossing the border and that interceptions of communications into or out of the United States fell within the "border crossing exception." Yoo further opined that electronic surveillance in "direct support of military operations" did not trigger constitutional rights against illegal searches and seizures, in part because the Fourth Amendment is primarily aimed at curbing law enforcement abuses.

Yoo also wrote that the activity described in the Presidential Authorizations was "reasonable" under the Fourth Amendment and therefore did not require a

12. On March 2, 2009, DOJ released nine opinions written by OLC from 2001 through 2003 regarding "the allocation of authorities between the President and Congress in matters of war and national security" containing certain propositions that no longer reflect the views of OLC and "should not be treated as authoritative for any purpose." Memorandum for the Files from Steven G. Bradbury, Principal Deputy Assistant Attorney General, Office of Legal Counsel, "Re: Status of Certain OLC Opinions Issued in the Mtermath of the Terrorist Attacks of September 11, 2001" (January 15, 2009), at 1, 11. Among these opinions was a classified February 2002 memorandum written by Yoo which asserted that Congress had not included a clear statement in FISA that it sought to restrict presidential authority to conduct warrantless surveillance activities in the national security area and that the FISA statute therefore does not apply to the President's exercise of his Commander-in-Chief authority. In Bradbury's unclassified January 15, 2009, memorandum (included among those released in March 2009), Bradbury stated that this proposition "is problematic and questionable, given FISA's express references to the President's authority" and is "not supported by convincing reasoning."

warrant. In support of this position, Yoo cited Supreme Court opinions upholding warrantless searches in a variety of contexts, such as drug testing of employees and sobriety checkpoints to detect drunk drivers, and in other circumstances "when special needs, beyond the normal need for law enforcement, make the warrant and probable-cause requirement impracticable." *Veronia School Dist. 47J v. Acton,* 515 u.S. 464, 652 (1995)(as quoted in November 2, 2001 Memorandum at 19). Yoo wrote that in these situations the government's interest was found to have outweighed the individual's privacy interest, and that in this regard "no governmental interest is more compelling than the security of the Nation." *Haig v. Agee,* 435 U.S. 280, 307 (1981). According to Yoo, the activity authorized by the Presidential Authorizations advanced this governmental security interest.

Yoo's legal memoranda omitted any discussion of *Youngstown Sheet & Tube Co. v. Sawyer,* 343 U.S. 579 (1952), a leading case on the distribution of government powers between the Executive and Legislative Branches. Justice Jackson's analysis of President Truman's Article II Commander-in-Chief authority during wartime in the *Youngstown* case was an important factor in OLC's subsequent reevaluation of Yoo's opinions on the legality of the PSP.

Yoo also discussed in his memoranda the legal rationale for Other Intelligence Activities authorized as part of the PSP. To the extent that particular statutes might appear to preclude these activities, Yoo concluded that "we do not believe that Congress may restrict the President's inherent constitutional powers, which allow him to gather intelligence necessary to defend the nation from direct attack."

However, as detailed in Chapter Three of the DOJ OIG report, Yoo's discussion of some of the Other Intelligence Activities did not accurately describe the scope of these activities. Yoo's factual discussion of these activities was later identified by his successors in the Office of Legal Counsel and ODAG in late 2003 as insufficient and presenting a serious impediment to recertification of the program as to form and legality.

The President continued to reauthorize the PSP periodically during late 2001 and 2002, with some modifications of the scope of the intelligence activities being authorized. In October 2002, at Attorney General Ashcroft's request, Yoo drafted another opinion concerning the PSP. This memorandum, dated October 11, 2002, reiterated the same basic analysis contained in Yoo's November 2, 2001, memorandum in support of the legality of the PSP.

As the only OLC official read into the PSP through early 2003, Yoo consulted directly with White House officials about the PSP during this period. Because the DOJ OIG was unable to interview Yoo, it could not determine the exact nature and extent of these consultations. The DOJ OIG was also unable to determine whether Attorney General Ashcroft was fully aware of the advice Y00 was providing directly to the White House about the PSP.

Former Attorney General Gonzales and former OLC Assistant Attorney· General Bybee both told the DOJ OIG that they did not know how Yoo became responsible for analyzing the legality of the PSP. Bybee told us that he was "surprised" and "a little disappointed" to learn through media accounts that Yoo had worked on the PSP without Bybee's knowledge. Bybee said that it would not be unusual for a Deputy Assistant Attorney General such as Yoo to have direct contact with the White House for the purpose of rendering legal advice, but that the OLC Assistant Attorney General must be aware of all opinions that issue from OLC. Other senior DOJ officials also criticized the assignment of a single OLC attorney to draft the legal rationale for the program. These officials noted that OLC traditionally adheres to a rigorous peer review process for all legal memoranda it issues. They also cited the importance of having the OLC Assistant Attorney General, a Senate-confirmed official accountable for the work of that office, be aware of all OLC legal memoranda.

Gonzales told the DOJ OIG that the Yoo opinions represented the legal opinion of DOJ, and that it was Ashcroft's decision as to how to satisfy his obligations as Attorney General. Gonzales told the DOJ OIG that Ashcroft complained to the White House that it was "inconvenient" not to have the Deputy Attorney General or Ashcroft's Chief of Staff read into the PSP, but Gonzales also stated that he never got the sense from Ashcroft that this affected the quality of the legal advice about the program that DOJ provided to the White House. As noted, Ashcroft declined the DOJ OIG's request for an interview. The DOJ OIG therefore was unable to determine from Ashcroft whether he sought additional DOJ read-ins to assist in the legal analysis of the program, how hard he may have pressed for these additional read-ins, or whether he believed he was receiving adequate legal advice about the program from Yoo alone during this early phase of the PSP.

III. IMPLEMENTATION OF THE PRESIDENT'S SURVEILLANCE PROGRAM

A. NSA Intelligence Activities under the PSP

According to the NSA OIG report, the first Presidential Authorization was the product of discussions between former NSA Director Hayden and White House officials. Hayden also consulted with NSA senior technical experts and experienced attorneys from the NSA's Office of General Counsel. While he consulted with NSA personnel in identifying critical intelligence gaps, only Hayden knew about and participated in the development of the Presidential Authorization by serving as a technical advisor. After the Authorization was signed, NSA attorneys supported the lawfulness of the resulting program. Hayden stated that DOJ did not participate in his early meetings about the NSA's collection activities. As noted, the Attorney General was read into the program on the same day he signed the first Authorization as to form and legality.

When the NSA received the first Presidential Authorization, Hayden noted that he was assured by the signature of the Attorney General that the program was iawful and had been reviewed by the White House and DOJ.

After Hayden received the first Authorization, he assembled 80 to 90 people in a conference room and explained what the President had authorized. Hayden said: "We're going to do exactly what he said and not one photon or electron more." The NSA's purpose in implementing the PSP was to collect foreign intelligence. According to Hayden, the activities were targeted and focused with the purpose of "hot pursuit" of communications entering or leaving the United States involving individuals believed to be associated with al-Qa'ida, not to intercept conversations between people in the United States. The intercepted communications had to be reasonably believed to be al-Qa'ida communications, one end of which was in the United States.

According to the NSA OIG, the PSP had standards for targeting al-Qa'ida. There were several layers of review, starting with an NSA management review, and the NSA OIG conducted a review of target folders to ensure compliance with program standards and additional management controls.[13] A sample of target folders was tested to determine whether targeting decisions were adequately supported. Any ambiguities were discussed with analysts and adequately resolved.

The NSA OIG reported that the NSA's conduct of the PSP was reviewed and monitored by the NSA Office of General Counsel and the NSA OIG. According to the NSA OIG, NSA employees involved in the program received tailored training and their work was overseen to ensure that all activities were consistent with the letter and intent of the Authorization and with the protection of civil liberties. The NSA OIG report concluded that it found no evidence of intentional misuse of the PSP.

Hayden stated that although he understood that the PSP activities were more aggressive than those available traditionally under FISA, he believed that the PSP was less intrusive because the period of time in which collection was conducted was, in most cases, far less than was authorized in a typical FISC order. Additionally, the sole purpose of the overall PSP was to detect and prevent terrorism against the United States. According to Hayden, the program was designed to provide the NSA with the operational agility to cover terrorism-related targets.

B. Access to the PSP

1. Executive Branch Personnel

Knowledge of the PSP was strictly controlled and limited at the express direction of the White House. Further information about the number of Executive Branch employees who were read into the program is provided in the classified report.

As discussed below and in more detail in the DOJ OIG report, the DOJ OIG found that overly restrictive limitations on the number of DOJ personnel read into the program created several problems. Among other things, these limitations prevented DOJ from adequately reviewing the PSP's legality during the earliest phase of the program's operation. The subsequent identification of what DOJ officials perceived to be serious factual and legal flaws in Yoo's early legal analysis of the PSP also precipitated a major dispute between DOJ and the White House over reauthorization of the program that nearly led to the resignations of several senior DOJ

13. Internal control, or management control, comprises the plans, methods, and procedures used to meet missions, goals, and objectives. It provides reasonable assurance that an entity is effective and efficient in its operations, reliable in its reporting, and compliant with applicable laws and regulations.

and FBI officials in March 2004. In addition, the ODNI OIG found that the opportunity for ODNI oversight components to participate in oversight of the PSP was limited by ODNI oversight personnel not being granted timely access to the PSP.

2. Congressional Briefings

On October 25, 2001, White House officials and Hayden conducted a briefing on the PSP for the Chairman and Ranking Member of the House Permanent Select Committee on Intelligence, Nancy P. Pelosi and Porter J. Goss; and the Chairman and Vice Chairman of the Senate Select Committee on Intelligence, D. Robert Graham and Richard J. Shelby. According to the NSA, between October 25, 2001, and January 17, 2007, Hayden and current NSA Director Keith Alexander, sometimes supported by other NSA personnel, conducted approximately 49 briefings to members of Congress and their staff, 17 of which took place before the December 2005 media reports regarding what was called the "Terrorist Surveillance Program." Hayden told us that during the many PSP briefings to members of Congress no one ever suggested that NSA should stop the program.

3. Foreign Intelligence Surveillance Court Briefings

From January 2002 to January 2006, only FISC Presiding Judge Royce Lamberth, followed by Presiding Judge Colleen Kollar-Kotelly, were read into the PSP. The classified report and the full DOJ OIG report describe the circumstances under which the Presiding Judge was notified of the existence of the PSP and read into the program, and the measures subsequently taken to address the effect of the PSP on the government's relationship with the FISC.

4. FBI Participation in the PSP

The DOJ OIG report also describes the FBI's participation in the PSP, particularly as a recipient of intelligence collected under the program. The DOJ OIG addresses the challenges the FBI faced in disseminating this information to FBI field offices for investigation without revealing the source of the information, as well as the efforts the FBI made to improve cooperation with the NSA to enhance the usefulness of PSP-derived information to FBI agents. Further details about these topics are classified and therefore cannot be discussed here. The DOJ OIG generally found that the FBI implemented reasonable procedures for expeditiously disseminating PSP-derived information to FBI field offices for investigation while protecting the sources and methods by which the information was obtained. However, the DOJ OIG also found that the highly compartmented nature of the PSP created obstacles for the FBI's process for handling program-derived information and understandably frustrated FBI agents responsible for investigating the information.

5. CIA Participation in the PSP

The CIA OIG report describes the CIA's participation in the PSP. CIA officials, as PSP consumers, requested information from the program and utilized this information in their analyses. The CIA OIG found that CIA officials appeared to have had an adequate understanding of the justification needed to request PSP-derived information, and that CIA requests were adequately justified.

Senior CIA officials, including former Directors of Central Intelligence (DCI) Hayden and Goss, and former Acting Director McLaughlin, stated that the PSP addressed a gap in intelligence collection. Following the terrorist attacks on September 11, 2001, there was concern that additional acts of terrorism would be perpetrated by terrorist cells already inside the United States. Senior IC officials believed that providing IC analysts access to increased signals intelligence could lead to the discovery of terrorists in the

U.S. and planned terrorist attacks. However, collection of such communications required authorization under FISA, and there was widespread belief among senior IC and CIA officials that the process for obtaining FISA authorization was too cumbersome and time consuming to address the current threat. CIA officials stated that FISA required extensive paperwork and high-level reviews and approvals by the DCI and the Attorney General and the FISC did not always approve FISA applications in a timely manner. Hayden and other senior IC officials also told the CIA OIG that, at the time that the PSP operated, Congress had not updated FISA since its 1978 enactment to reflect changes in communication technologies.

6. ODNI Participation in the PSP

PSP-derived information was closely held within the ODNI and was made available to a limited number of NCTC analysts for review or, if appropriate, use in preparing NCTC analytical products. Generally, the NCTC analysts approved for PSP access received PSP-derived information in the form of NSA intelligence products. NCTC analysts told the ODNI OIG that they generally obtained access to the PSP-derived information from a secure IC database or directly from an NSA representative. NCTC analysts told the ODNI OIG that the PSP-derived information was subject to stringent security protections. The NCTC analysts said that they received training regarding the proper handling of IC signals intelligence, and they reported that they handled all such information, including PSP-derived information, consistent with standard rules and procedures.

C. Impact of PSP-Derived Information on the FISA Process

Chapters Three and Six of the DOJ OIG report describe how DOJ and the FISC addressed the impact PSP-derived information had on the FISA process. The DOJ OIG concluded that it was foreseeable that such information might impact the process and that the initial delay in reading anyone from DOJ's Office of Intelligence Policy and Review (OIPR) or the FISC into the PSP unnecessarily jeopardized DOJ's relationship with the Court. In addition, overly restrictive limitations on the number of OIPR attorneys and FISC judges who were read into the program created significant and avoidable problems of workload imbalance in the functioning both of OIPR and the FISC. The DOJ OIG concluded that once the PSP began to affect the functioning of the FISA process, the number of OIPR staff and FISC judges read into the PSP to manage the program's impact should have increased.

D. Discovery Issues

The DOJ OIG reviewed DOJ's handling of PSP information with respect to its discovery obligations in international terrorism prosecutions. DOJ was aware as early as 2002 that information collected under the PSP could have implications for DOJ's litigation responsibilities under Federal Rule of Criminal Procedure Rule 16 and *Brady v. Maryland,* 37:3 U.S. 83 (1963).

Analysis of this discovery issue was first assigned to OLC Deputy Assistant Attorney General Yoo in 2003: However, no DOJ attorneys with terrorism prosecution responsibilities were read into the PSP until mid-2004, and as a result DOJ continued to lack the advice of attorneys who were best equipped to identify and examine the discovery issues in connection with the PSP.

Since then, DOJ has taken steps to address discovery issues with respect to the PSP, which is discussed in the DOJ OIG classified report. Based upon its review of DOJ's handling of these issues, the DOJ OIG recommends that DOJ assess its discovery obligations regarding PSP-derived information, if any, in international terrorism prosecutions. The DOJ OIG also recommends that DOJ carefully consider whether it must re-examine past cases to see whether potentially discoverable but undisclosed Rule 16 or *Brady* material was collected under the PSP, and take appropriate steps to ensure that it has complied with its discovery obligations in such cases. In addition, the DOJ OIG recommends that DOJ implement a procedure to identify PSP-derived information, if any, that may be associated with international terrorism cases currently pending or likely to be brought in the future and evaluate whether such information should be disclosed in light of the government's discovery obligations under Rule 16 and *Brady.*

IV. LEGAL REASSESSMENT OF THE PRESIDENT'S SURVEILLANCE PROGRAM

Chapter Four of the DOJ OIG's report describes the period in late 2003 and early 2004 when DOJ determined that aspects of the PSP were not supported by law and advised the President that the program should be modified.

A. Justice Department Attorneys Become Concerned About the Legality of Some Activities under the PSP

As noted above, John Yoo was the sole OLC attorney who advised Attorney General Ashcroft and White House officials on the PSP from the program's inception in October 2001 through Yoo's resignation from DOJ in May 2003. Upon Yoo's departure, another DOJ official, Patrick Philbin, was selected by the White House to be read into the PSP to assume Yoo's role as advisor to the Attorney General concerning the program. In addition, Jack Goldsmith replaced Jay Bybee as the Assistant Attorney General for OLC on October 6, 2003. Even though Bybee had never been read into the PSP, Philbin persuaded Counsel to the Vice President David Addington to read in Goldsmith, Bybee's replacement.

After being read into the PSP, Goldsmith and Philbin became concerned about the factual and legal basis for Yoo's legal memoranda supporting the program. For example, FISA prohibits persons from intentionally engaging in electronic surveillance "under color of law except as authorized by statute[.]" 50 U.S.C. § 1809(a). Yoo's analysis concluded that this provision did not implicate the legality of the PSP because FISA did not expressly apply to wartime operations. However, Yoo's memoranda omitted any reference to the FISA provision allowing the interception of electronic communications without a warrant for a period of 15 days following a congressional declaration of war. See 50 U.S.C. § 1811. Goldsmith and Philbin were concerned that this provision contradicted Yoo's assertion that Congress did not intend FISA to apply to wartime operations. They also were troubled by other aspects ofYoo's legal analysis and by the lack of an adequate factual description in his memoranda of how the PSP operated.

B. OLC Begins Developing a New Legal Analysis for the PSP

Goldsmith and Philbin began developing an analysis to more fully address the FISA statute with respect to the PSP. This new analysis relied on the legal argument that the Congressional Authorization for Use of Military Force Joint Resolution (AUMF), enacted shortly after the attacks of September 11, 2001, effectively exempted some of the activities under the PSP from FISA. However, Goldsmith and Philbin became concerned that this revised analysis would not be sufficient to support the legality of certain aspects of the Other Intelligence Activities that the President had authorized under the PSP.

Beginning in August 2003, Philbin and later Goldsmith brought their concerns about the OLC legal opinions to Attorney General Ashcroft. With Ashcroft's approval, Philbin began preparing a new OLC memorandum assessing the legality of the PSP. During this period in late 2003, Goldsmith and Philbin advised Ashcroft to continue to certify as to form and legality the Presidential Authorizations for the PSP pending completion of the new legal analysis.

C. DOJ Officials Convey Concerns to the White House

In December 2003, Goldsmith and Philbin met with Counsel to the Vice President Addington and White House Counsel Gonzales at the White House to express their growing concerns about the legal underpinnings of the program. Goldsmith said he told them that OLC was not sure the program could survive in its current form. According to Goldsmith's contemporaneous notes of these events, these discussions did not contemplate an interruption of the program, although the White House officials represented that they would "agree to pull the plug" if the problems with the program were found to be sufficiently serious.

In late January 2004, at Goldsmith's request, the White House agreed to allow Deputy Attorney General James Comey to be read into the PSP following Comey's confirmation as the Deputy Attorney General in December 2003. After being briefed, Comey agreed that the concerns about Yoo's legal analysis were well-founded.[14] Comey told the DOJ OIG that of particular concern to him and

14. Corney also discussed DOJ's concerns about the legality of the program with FBI Director Mueller on March 1, 2004. Mueller told the DOJ OIG that this was the first time he had been made aware of DOJ's concerns.

Goldsmith was the notion that Yoo's legal analysis entailed ignoring an act of Congress, and doing so without full congressional notification.

D. Conflict Between DOJ and the White House

Comey told the DOJ OIG that he met with Attorney General Ashcroft on March 4, 2004, to discuss the PSP and that Ashcroft agreed with Comey and the other DOJ officials' assessment of the potential legal problems with the PSP. Later that day, Ashcroft was struck with severe gallstone pancreatitis and was admitted to the George Washington University Hospital in Washington, D.C.[15]

On March 5, 2004, Goldsmith advised Comey by memorandum that under the circumstances of Ashcroft's medical condition and hospitalization, a "clear basis" existed for Comey to determine that "this is a case of 'absence or disability' of the Attorney General" within the meaning of 28 U.S.C. § 508(a). The "cc" line of Goldsmith's memorandum to Comey indicated that a copy of the memorandum was also sent to White House Counsel Gonzales.

Later on March 5, Gonzales called Goldsmith to request a letter from OLC stating that Yoo's prior OLC opinions "covered the program," meaning the PSP. Philbin told the DOJ OIG that Gonzales was not requesting a new opinion that the program itself was legal, but only that the prior opinions had concluded that it was. As a result of Gonzales's request, Goldsmith, Philbin, and Comey re-examined Yoo's memoranda with a view toward determining whether they adequately described the actual intelligence activities of the NSA under the Authorizations. Goldsmith, Philbin, and Corney concluded that Yoo's memoranda did not accurately describe some of the Other Intelligence Activities that were being conducted under the Presidential Authorizations implementing the PSP, and that the memoranda therefore did not provide a basis for finding that these activities were legal.

On Saturday, March 6, Goldsmith and Philbin, with Corney's concurrence, met with Addington and Gonzales at the White House to convey their conclusions that certain activities in the PSP should cease. According to Goldsmith's notes, Addington and Gonzales "reacted calmly and said they would get back with us."

On Sunday, March 7, 2004, Goldsmith and Philbin met again with Addington and Gonzales at the White House. According to Goldsmith, the White House officials informed Goldsmith and Philbin that they disagreed with their interpretation of Yoo's memoranda and on the need to change any of the NSA's intelligence activities under the PSP.

On March 9 Gonzales called Goldsmith to the White House in an effort to persuade him that his criticisms of Yoo's memoranda were incorrect and that Yoo's analysis provided sufficient legal support for the program. After Goldsmith disagreed, Gonzales next argued for a "30-day bridge" to get past the expiration of the current Presidential Authorization on March 11, 2004. Gonzales reasoned that Ashcroft, who was still hospitalized, was not in any condition to sign a renewal of the Authorization, and that a "30-day bridge" would move the situation to a point

15. Ashcroft's doctors did not clear Ashcroft to resume his duties as Attorney General until March 31, 2004.

where Ashcroft would be well enough to approve the program. Goldsmith told Gonzales he could not agree to recommend an extension because aspects of the program lacked legal support.

At noon that day, another meeting was held in the White House office of Andrew Card, the President's Chief of Staff. According to Director Mueller's notes, Mueller, Card, Vice President Cheney, CIA Deputy Director McLaughlin, Hayden, Gonzales, and other unspecified officials were present. Corney, Goldsmith, and Philbin were not invited to this meeting. After a presentation on the value of the PSP by NSA and CIA officials, it was then explained to the group that Corney "has problems" with some activities authorized under the program. Mueller's notes state that Vice President Cheney suggested that "the President may have to reauthorize without [the] blessing of DOJ," to which Mueller responded, "I could have a problem with that," and that the FBI would "have to review legality of continued participation in the program."

Another meeting at the White House was held on March 9, this time with Corney, Goldsmith, and Philbin present. Gonzales told the DOJ OIG that the meeting was held to make sure that Corney understood what was at stake with the PSP and to demonstrate the program's value. Corney said Vice President Cheney stressed that the PSP was "critically important" and warned that Corney would risk "thousands" of lives if Corney did not agree to recertify the program. Corney said he stated at the meeting that he, as Acting Attorney General, could not support reauthorizing certain intelligence activities unless they were modified. According to Corney, the White House officials said they could not agree to that modification.

Goldsmith, Philbin, and Corney met in the early afternoon of March 10, 2004, to discuss the meeting at the White House the day before and how DOJ should proceed. Goldsmith and Philbin confirmed their position to Corney that some of the Other Intelligence Activities under the PSP could not be legally supported and would have to be changed or shut down.

Gonzales told the DOJ OIG that after President Bush was advised of the results of the March 9, 2004, meeting, the President instructed Vice President Cheney on the morning of Wednesday, March 10, to call a meeting with congressional leaders to advise them of the impasse with DOJ. On the afternoon of March 10, at approximately 4:00 or 5:00 p.m., Gonzales and other White House and intelligence agency officials, including Vice President Cheney, Card, Hayden, McLaughlin, and Tenet, convened an "emergency meeting" with congressional leaders in the White House Situation Room. The congressional leaders in attendance were Senate Majority and Minority Leaders William H. "Bill" Frist and Thomas A. Daschle; Senate Select Committee on Intelligence Chairman Pat Roberts and Vice Chairman Jay Rockefeller; Speaker of the House Dennis Hastert and House Minority Leader Nancy Pelosi; and House Permanent Select Committee on Intelligence Chair Porter Goss and Ranking Member Jane Harman. This congressional group was known informally as the "Gang of Eight." No officials from DOJ were asked to attend the meeting.

According to Gonzales's notes of the meeting, individual congressional leaders expressed thoughts and concerns related to the program. However, Gonzales told the DOJ OIG that the consensus of the congressional leaders was that the program should continue.[16]

Gonzales told the DOJ OIG that following the meeting with the congressional leaders on March 10, President Bush instructed him and Card to go to the George Washington University Hospital to speak to Ashcroft, who was in the intensive care unit recovering from surgery.

According to notes from Ashcroft's FBI security detail, at 6:20 p.m. that evening Card called the hospital and spoke with an agent in Ashcroft's security detail, advising him that President Bush would be calling shortly to speak with Ashcroft. Ashcroft's wife told the agent that Ashcroft would not accept the call. Ten minutes later, the agent called Ashcroft's Chief of Staff David Ayres at DOJ to request that Ayres speak with Card about the President's intention to call Ashcroft. The agent conveyed to Ayres Mrs. Ashcroft's desire that no calls be made to Ashcroft for another day or two. However, at 6:45 p.m., Card and the President called the hospital and, according to the agent's notes, "insisted on speaking [with Attorney General Ashcroft]." According to the agent's notes, Mrs. Ashcroft took the call from Card and the President and was informed that Gonzales and Card were coming to the hospital to see Ashcroft regarding a matter involving national security.

At approximately 7:00 p.m., after learning that Gonzales and Card were on their way to the hospital, Ayres relayed this information to Corney. According to Corney's May 2007 testimony before the Senate Judiciary Committee, Corney called his Chief of Staff and directed him to "get as many of my people as possible to the hospital immediately." Corney next called FBI Director Mueller and told him that Gonzales and Card were on their way to the hospital to see Ashcroft, and that Ashcroft was in no condition to receive guests, much less make a decision about whether to recertify the PSP. According to Mueller's notes, Corney asked Mueller to come to the hospital to "witness [the] condition of AG." Mueller told Corney he would go to the hospital right away.

Philbin said he was leaving work that evening when he received a call from Corney, who told Philbin that he needed to get to the hospital right away because Gonzales and Card were on their way there "to get Ashcroft to sign something." Corney also directed Philbin to call Goldsmith and tell him what was happening.

---

16. When Gonzales testified before the Senate Judiciary Committee on July 24, 2007, he essentially described the congressional leaders' reactions to the March 10, 2004, "Gang of Eight" briefing as he did in his handwritten notes of the briefing, stating, "The consensus in the room from the congressional leadership is that we should continue the activities, at least for now." However, after Gonzales testified Representative Pelosi, Senator Rockefeller, and Senator Daschle issued statements sharply disputing Gonzales's characterization of their statements at the March 10, 2004, meeting, stating that there was no consensus at the meeting that the program should proceed. Pelosi's office also issued a statement that she "made clear my disagreement with what the White House was asking" concerning the program. The DOJ OIG did not attempt to interview the congressional leaders and obtain their recollections as to what was said at this meeting because this was beyond the scope of its review.

Corney arrived at the hospital between 7: 10 and 7:30 p.m. In his congressional testimony, Corney said he ran up the stairs with his security detail to Ashcroft's floor, and he entered Ashcroft's room, which he described as darkened, and found Ashcroft lying in bed and his wife standing by his side. Corney said he began speaking to Ashcroft, and that it was not clear that Ashcroft could focus and that he "seemed pretty bad off[.]"

Goldsmith and Philbin arrived at the hospital within a few minutes of each other. Corney, Goldsmith, and Philbin met briefly in an FBI "command post" that had been set up in a room adjacent to Ashcroft's room. Moments later, the command post was notified that Card and Gonzales had arrived at the hospital and were on their way upstairs to see Ashcroft. Corney, Goldsmith, and Philbin entered Ashcroft's room and, according to Goldsmith's notes, Corney and the others advised Ashcroft "not to sign anything."

Gonzales and Card entered Ashcroft's hospital room at 7:35 p.m., according to the FBI agent's notes. The two stood across from Mrs. Ashcroft at the head of the bed, with Corney, Goldsmith, and Philbin behind them. Gonzales told the DOJ OIG that he carried with him in a manila envelope the March 11, 2004, Presidential Authorization for Ashcroft to sign. According to Philbin, Gonzales first asked Ashcroft how he was feeling and Ashcroft replied, "Not well." Gonzales then said words to the effect, "You know, there's a reauthorization that has to be renewed ...." Gonzales told us that he may also have told Ashcroft that White House officials had met with congressional leaders "to pursue a legislative fix."

Corney testified to the Senate Judiciary Committee that at this point Ashcroft told Gonzales and Card "in very strong terms" about his legal concerns with the PSP, which Corney testified Ashcroft drew from his meeting with Corney about the program a week earlier. Corney testified that Ashcroft next stated:

> "But that doesn't matter, because I'm not the Attorney General. There is the Attorney General," and he pointed to me—I was just to his left. The two men [Gonzales and Card] did not acknowledge me; they turned and walked from the room.

Records kept by the Attorney General's security detail indicate that Gonzales and Card left Ashcroft's room at 7:40 p.m. Moments after Gonzales and Card departed, Mueller arrived at the hospital. At approximately 8:00 p.m., Mueller went into Ashcroft's room for 5 to 10 minutes. Mueller wrote in his notes: "AG in chair; is feeble, barely articulate, clearly stressed."

Before leaving the hospital, Corney received a call from White House Chief of Staff Card. Corney testified that Card was very upset and demanded that Corney come to the White House immediately. Corney told Card that he would meet with him, but not without a witness, and that he intended that witness to be DOJ Solicitor General Ted Olson. Corney and

Olson subsequently went to the White House at about 11:00 p.m. that evening and met with Gonzales and Card. Gonzales told the DOJ OIG that little more was achieved at this meeting other than a general acknowledgement that a "situation" continued to exist because of the disagreement between DOJ and the White House regarding legal authorization for the program.

E. White House Counsel Certifies Presidential Authorization Without Department of Justice Concurrence

On the morning of March 11, 2004, with the Presidential Authorization set to expire, President Bush signed a new Authorization for the PSP. In a departure from the past practice of having the Attorney General certify the Authorization as to form and legality, the March 11 Authorization was certified by White House Counsel Gonzales. The March 11 Authorization also differed markedly from prior Authorizations in three other respects. It explicitly asserted that the President's exercise of his Article II Commander-in-Chief authority displaced any contrary provisions of law, including FISA. It clarified the description of certain Other Intelligence Activities being conducted under the PSP to address questions regarding whether such activities had actually been authorized explicitly in prior Authorizations. It also stated that in approving the prior Presidential Authorizations as to form and legality, the Attorney General previously had authorized the same activities now being approved under the March 11 Authorization.[17]

White House Chief of Staff Card informed Corney by telephone on the morning of March 11, 2004, that the President had signed the new Authorization that morning. At approximately noon, Gonzales called Goldsmith to inform him that the President, in issuing the Authorization, had made an interpretation of law concerning his authorities and that DOJ should not act in contradiction of the President's determinations.

Also at noon on March 11, Director Mueller met with Card at the White House. According to Mueller's notes, Card told Mueller that if no "legislative fix" could be found by May 6, 2004, when the March 11 Authorization was set to expire, the program would be discontinued.

Mueller wrote that he told Card that the failure to have DOJ representation at the congressional briefing and the attempt to have Ashcroft certify the Authorization without going through Corney "gave the strong perception that the [White House] was trying to do an end run around the Acting [Attorney General] whom they knew to have serious concerns as to the legality of portions of the program." Card responded that he and Gonzales were unaware at the time of the hospital visit that Corney was the Acting Attorney General, and that they had only been following the directions of the President.

F. Department of Justice and FBI Officials Consider Resigning

Several senior DOJ and FBI officials considered resigning after the Presiden-

17. The DOJ OIG determined that this statement subsequently was removed from future Authorizations after Ashcroft complained to Gonzales that the statement was "inappropriate." In a May 20, 2004 memorandum, Ashcroft wrote that it was not until Philbin and later Goldsmith explained to him that aspects of the NSA's Other Intelligence Activities were not accurately described in the prior Authorizations that he realized that he had been certifying the Authorizations prior to March 2004 based on a misimpression of those activities.

tial Authorization was signed without DOJ's concurrence. Corney told the DOJ OIG that he drafted a letter of resignation because he believed it was impossible for him to remain with DOJ if the President would do something DOJ said was not legally supportable. Corney also testified that Ashcroft's Chief of Staff David Ayres believed Ashcroft also was likely to resign and thus Ayres urged Corney to wait until Ashcroft was well enough to resign with him.[18]

Goldsmith told the DOJ OIG he drafted a resignation letter at around the same time as Corney. According to his contemporaneous notes, Goldsmith cited the "shoddiness" of the prior OLC legal review, the "over-secrecy" of the PSP, and the "shameful" incident at the hospital as among his grievances.

At approximately 1:30 a.m. on March 12, 2004, FBI Director Mueller drafted by hand a letter stating, in part: "[A]fter reviewing the plain language of the FISA statute, and the order issued yesterday by the President ... and in the absence of further clarification of the legality of the program from the Attorney General, I am forced to withdraw the FBI from participation in the program. Further, should the President order the continuation of the FBI's participation in the program, and in the absence of further legal advice from the AG, I would be constrained to resign as Director of the FBI." Mueller told the DOJ OIG that he planned on having the letter typed and then tendering it, but that based on subsequent events his resignation was not necessary.

On the morning of March 12, 2004, Corney and Mueller attended the regular daily threat briefing with the President in the Oval Office. Corney said that following the briefing President Bush called him into the President's private study for an "unscheduled meeting." Corney told the President of DOJ's legal concerns regarding the PSP. According to Corney, the President's response indicated that he had not been fully informed of these concerns. Corney told the President that the President's staff had been advised of these issues "for weeks." According to Corney, the President said that he just needed until May 6 (the date of the next Authorization), and that if he could not get Congress to fix FISA by then he would shut down the program. The President emphasized the importance of the program and that it "saves lives."

The President next met with Mueller. According to Mueller's notes, Mueller told the President of his concerns regarding the FBI's continued participation in the program without an opinion from the Attorney General as to its legality, and that he was considering resigning if the FBI were directed to continue to participate without the concurrence of the Attorney General. Mueller wrote that he explained to the President that he had an "independent obligation to the FBI and to DOJ to assure the legality of actions we undertook, and that a presidential order alone could not do that." According to Mueller's notes, the President then directed Mueller to. meet with Corney and other PSP principals to address the legal

---

18. In written responses to Senator Charles Schumer following his testimony, Corney wrote that he believed that several senior DOJ officials, including Chuck Rosenberg, Daniel Levin, James Baker, David Ayres, and Deputy Chief of Staff to the Attorney General David Israelite, were also prepared to resign. Corney wrote that he believed that "a large portion" of his staff also would have resigned if he had.

concerns so that the FBI could continue participating in the program "as appropriate under the law."

On the morning of March 12, 2004, Corney decided not to direct the FBI to cease cooperating with the NSA in conjunction with the program. Corney's decision is documented in a one-page memorandum from Goldsmith to Corney in which Goldsmith explained that the President, as Commander in Chief and Chief Executive with the constitutional duty to "take care that the laws are faithfully executed," made a determination that the PSP, as practiced, was lawful. Goldsmith concluded that this determination was binding on the entire Executive Branch, including Corney in his exercise of the powers of the Attorney General.

On March 12, 2004 an interagency working group led by OLC was convened to continue reanalyzing the legality of the PSP. In the days that followed, Goldsmith continued to express doubt that a viable legal rationale could be found for some of the Other Intelligence Activities being conducted under the PSP.

On March 16, 2004 Corney drafted a memorandum to White House Counsel Gonzales setting out his advice to the President. According to the memorandum, Corney advised that DOJ remained unable to find a legal basis to support certain Other Intelligence Activities that had been authorized as part of the program and that such activities should be discontinued immediately. Comey cautioned that he believed some ongoing activities under the program raised "serious issues" about congressional notification, "particularly where the legal basis for the program is the President's decision to assert his authority to override an otherwise applicable Act of Congress."

Gonzales replied by letter on the evening of March 16. The letter stated, in part:

> Your memorandum appears to have been based on a misunderstanding of the President's expectations regarding the conduct of the Department of Justice. While the President was, and remains, interested in any thoughts the Department of Justice may have on alternative ways to achieve effectively the goals of the activities authorized by the Presidential Authorization of March 11, 2004, the President has addressed definitively for the Executive Branch in the Presidential Authorization the interpretation of the law.

G. White House Agrees to Modify the PSP

Notwithstanding Gonzales's letter, on March 17, 2004 the President decided to modify certain PSP intelligence-gathering activities and to discontinue certain Other Intelligence Activities that DOJ believed were legally unsupported. The President's directive was expressed in two modifications to the March 11, 2004 Presidential Authorization.

On May 6, 2004 Goldsmith and Philbin completed an OLC legal memorandum assessing the legality of the PSP as it was operating at that time. The lOB-page memorandum traced the history of the program and analyzed the legality of all of the intelligence activities conducted under the program in light of applicable statutes, Executive Orders, cases, and constitutional provisions. Much of the legal reasoning in the May 6, 2004 OLC memorandum was publicly released by DOJ in a "White Paper" issued after one aspect of the program was revealed in The New York Times and publicly confirmed by the President in December 2005 as the Terrorist Surveillance Program. The OLC memorandum stated that the Authorization for Use of Military Force (AUMF) passed by Congress shortly after the attacks of September 11, 2001 gave the President authority to use both domestically and abroad "all necessary and appropriate force," including signals intelligence capabilities, to prevent future acts of international terrorism against the United States. According to the memorandum, the AUMF was properly read as an express authorization to conduct targeted electronic surveillance against al-Qa'ida and its affiliates, the entities responsible for attacking the United States, thereby supporting the President's directives to conduct these activities under the PSP.

H. Department of Justice OIG Conclusions

The DOJ OIG concluded that it was extraordinary and inappropriate that a single DOJ attorney, John Yoo, was relied upon to conduct the initial legal assessment of the PSP, and that the lack of oversight and review of Yoo's work, as customarily is the practice of OLC, contributed to a legal analysis of the PSP that at a minimum was factually flawed. Deficiencies in the legal memoranda became apparent once additional DOJ attorneys were read into the program in 2003 and when those attorneys sought a greater understanding of the PSP's operation. The DOJ OIG concluded that the White House's strict controls over DOJ access to the PSP undermined DOJ's ability to perform its critical legal function during the PSP's early phase of operation.

The DOJ OIG also concluded that the circumstances plainly called for additional DOJ resources to be applied to the legal review of the program and that it was the Attorney General's responsibility to be aware of this need and to take steps to address it. Ashcroft's request during this period that his chief of staff David Ayres and Deputy Attorney General Larry Thompson be read into the program was not approved. However, the DOJ OIG could not determine whether Attorney General Ashcroft aggressively sought additional read-ins to assist with DOJ's legal review of the program during this period because Ashcroft did not agree to be interviewed.

V. TRANSITION OF CERTAIN PROGRAM ACTIVITIES TO FOREIGN INTELLIGENCE SURVEILLANCE COURT ORDERS

Certain activities that were originally authorized as part of the PSP have subsequently been authorized under orders issued by the Foreign Intelligence Surveillance Court (FISC). The activities transitioned in this manner included the interception of certain international communications that the President publicly described as the "Terrorist Surveillance Program."

As a result of this transition, the President decided not to reauthorize these activities and the final Presidential Authorization expired on February 1, 2007. The White House stated that work on the transition of authority over a two-year period addressed Administration concerns about preserving the speed and agility that the Terrorist Surveillance Program provided.

The transition of certain PSP-authorized activities to FISC orders is described in detail in Section 5 of the classified report and Chapter Five of the DOJ OIG Report. Further details regarding this transition are classified and therefore cannot be addressed in this unclassified report.

In August 2007, the Protect America Act was enacted, amending FISA to address the government's ability to conduct electronic surveillance in the United States of persons reasonably believed to be located outside the United States. This legislation expired in early 2008, and in July 2008 the FISA Amendments Act of 2008 was enacted. This latter law authorized the government to intercept inside the United States any communications of non-U.S. persons reasonably believed to be located outside the United States, provided a significant purpose of the acquisition pertains to foreign intelligence. This legislation gave the government even broader authority to intercept international communications than did the provisions of the Presidential Authorizations governing the activities that the President acknowledged in December 2005 as the Terrorist Surveillance Program.

The DOJ OIG review concluded that several considerations favored initiating the process of transitioning the PSP to FISA authority earlier than had been done, especially as the program became less a temporary response to the September 11 terrorist attacks and more a permanent surveillance tool. These considerations included the PSP's effect on privacy interests of

U.S. persons, the instability of the legal reasoning on which the program rested for several years, and the substantial restrictions placed on FBI agents' access to and use of program-derived information due to the highly classified status of the PSP.

VI. IMPACT OF THE PRESIDENT'S SURVEILLANCE PROGRAM ON INTELLIGENCE COMMUNITY COUNTERTERRORISM EFFORTS

A. NSA's Assessment of the PSP

The NSA OIG reported that Hayden, referring to portions of the PSP in 2005, said there had probably been no communications more important to NSA efforts to defend the nation than those involving al-Qa'ida. NSA collected communications when one end was inside the United States and one end was associated with al-Qa'ida or terrorist groups associated with al Qa'ida in order to detect and prevent attacks inside the United States. Hayden stated that "the program in this regard has been successful." During the May 2006 Senate hearing on his nomination to be CIA Director, Hayden said that, had the PSP been in place before the September 2001 attacks, hijackers Khalid Almihdhar and Nawaf Alhazmi almost certainly would have been identified and located.

In May 2009, Hayden told NSA OIG that the value of the Program was in knowing that NSA signals intelligence activities under the PSP covered an important "quadrant" of terrorist communications. NSA's Deputy Director echoed Hayden's comment when he said that the value of the PSP was in the confidence it provided that someone was looking at the seam between the foreign and domestic intelligence domains.

B. DOJ OIG's Assessment of the PSP

In 2004 and 2006, the FBI's Office of General Counsel (OGC) attempted to assess the value of PSP information on FBI counterterrorism efforts. Neither of these efforts represented a comprehensive assessment of the PSP's value. The FBI conducted a more comprehensive survey of the impact of PSP-derived information, also in 2006. The results of these surveys are summarized in the DOJ OIG Report. Based in part on the results of one study, FBI management, including Director Mueller and Deputy Director John Pistole, concluded that the PSP was "of value."

The DOJ OIG sought as part of its review to assess the role of PSP-derived information and its value to the FBI's overall counterterrorism efforts. Director Mueller told the DOJ OIG that he believes the PSP was useful. Mueller said that the FBI must follow every lead it receives in order to prevent future terrorist attacks and that to the extent such information can be gathered and used legally it must be exploited. Mueller also stated that he "would not dismiss the potency of a program based on the percentage of hits."

The DOJ OIG interviewed FBI officials, agents, and analysts responsible for handling PSP information about their experiences with the program. These assessments, more fully described in Chapter Six of the DOJ OIG's report, generally were supportive of the program as "one tool of many" in the FBI's anti-terrorism efforts that "could help move cases forward." Even though most PSP leads were determined not to have any connection to terrorism, many of the FBI witnesses believed the mere possibility of the leads producing useful information made investigating the leads worthwhile.

However, the DOJ OIG also found that the exceptionally compartmented nature of the program created some frustration for FBI personnel. Some agents and analysts criticized the PSP-derived information they received for providing insufficient details, and the agents who managed counterterrorism programs at the FBI field offices the DOJ OIG visited said the FBI's process for disseminating PSP-derived information failed to adequately prioritize the information for investigation.

The DOJ OIG also examined several cases that have frequently been cited as examples of the PSP's contribution to the IC's counterterrorism efforts. These assessments, more fully described in Chapter Six of the DOJ OIG's report, generally were supportive of the program as "one tool of many" in the FBI's anti-terrorism efforts.

In sum, the DOJ OIG found it difficult to assess or quantify the overall effectiveness of the PSP program as it relates to the FBI's counterterrorism activities. However, based on the interviews conducted and documents reviewed, the DOJ OIG concluded that although PSP-derived information had value in some counterterrorism investigations, it generally played a limited role in the FBI's overall counterterrorism efforts. The reasons for this conclusion are classified and are described in the classified report and Chapter Six of the DOJ OIG report.

As noted above, certain activities that were originally authorized as part of the PSP have subsequently been authorized under orders issued by the FISC. The

DOJ OIG believes that DOJ and other IC agencies should continue to assess the value of information derived from such activities to the government's counterterrorism efforts.

C. CIA OIG's Assessment of the PSP

The CIA OIG reviewed the impact of the PSP on the CIA's counterterrorism efforts.

The CIA OIG reported that senior administration officials considered the PSP to be a valuable counterterrorism tool. In his December 2005 press conference, President Bush also said that there was an on-going debate in Washington, D.C. that criticized his, and previous, administrations for not "connecting the dots" prior to the attacks of September 11, 2001. He went on to say that the USA PATRIOT Act and the NSA program (the PSP) are helping to connect the dots as best as his administration possibly can. During a December 2005 press briefing, Hayden said that information had been obtained through this program that would not otherwise have been available. Senior CIA officials also told the CIA OIG that they had received PSP reporting with information that was previously unavailable. One senior official told the CIA OIG that the program eliminated some of the impediments that the CIA had encountered in accessing and analyzing communications between foreign and domestic locations. Another said that the PSP was a key resource, and without it there would have been a missing piece of the picture.

The CIA OIG determined that the CIA did not implement procedures to assess the usefulness of the product of the PSP and did not routinely document whether particular PSP reporting had contributed to successful counterterrorism operations. CIA officials, including Hayden, told the CIA OIG that PSP reporting was used in conjunction with reporting from other intelligence sources; consequently, it is difficult to attribute the success of particular counterterrorism case exclusively to the PSP. In a May 2006 briefing to the Senate Select Committee on Intelligence, a senior CIA official said that PSP reporting was rarely the sole basis for an intelligence success, but that it frequently played a supporting role. He went on to state that the program was an additional resource to enhance the CIA's understanding of terrorist networks and to help identify potential threats to the U.S. homeland. Other officials told the CIA OIG that the PSP was one of many tools available to them, and that the tools were often used in combination.

NSA disseminated PSP-derived information in its normal reporting channels when it could be done without revealing the source of the information. As such, CIA officers, even those read into the program, would have been unaware of the full extent of PSP reporting. In the course of this review, the CIA OIG learned of numerous PSP reports that provided leads. However, because there is no means to comprehensively track how PSP information was incorporated into CIA analysis, officials were able to provide only limited information on how program reporting contributed to successful operations, and the CIA OIG was unable to independently draw any conclusion on the overall effectiveness of the program to the CIA.

The CIA OIG determined that several factors hindered the CIA in making full use of the product of the PSP. Many CIA officials stated that too few CIA personnel at the working level were read into the PSP. At the program's inception, a disproportionate number' of the CIA personnel who were read into the PSP were senior CIA managers. According to one CIA manager, the tight control over access to the PSP prevented some officers who could have made effective use of the program reporting from being read in. Another official stated that the disparity between the number of senior CIA managers read into PSP and the number of working-level CIA personnel resulted in too few CIA personnel to fully utilize PSP information for targeting and analysis.

Officials also told the CIA OIG that working-level CIA analysts and targeting officers who were read into the PSP had too many competing priorities, and too many other information sources and analytic tools available to them, to fully utilize PSP reporting. Officials also stated that much of the PSP reporting was vague or without context, which led analysts and targeting officers to rely more heavily on other information sources and analytic tools, which were more easily accessed and timely than the PSP.

CIA officers also told the CIA OIG that the PSP would have been more fully utilized if analysts and targeting officers had obtained a better understanding of the program's capabilities. There was no formal training on the use of the PSP beyond the initial read-in to the program. Many CIA officers stated that the instruction provided in the read-in briefing was not sufficient and that they were surprised and frustrated by the lack of additional guidance. Some officers told the CIA OIG that there was insufficient legal guidance on the use of PSP-derived information.

The CIA OIG concluded that the factors that hindered the CIA in making full use of the PSP might have been mitigated if the CIA had designated an individual at an appropriate level of managerial authority who possessed knowledge of both the PSP and CIA counterterrorism activities to be responsible and accountable for overseeing CIA involvement in the program.

D. ODNI's Assessment of the PSP

Hayden told the PSP IG Group that during his tenure as Director of the NSA, he sought to disseminate PSP information within the IC while also protecting the PSP as the source of the information. Hayden said this policy likely resulted in IC analysts not having a full appreciation of the PSP's value because they likely did not realize that some NSA reporting was derived from the PSP. NCTC analysts confirmed that they often did not know if the NSA intelligence available to them was derived from the PSP. The NCTC analysts said they understood that NSA marked PSP information in a manner that protected the source of the information.

On those occasions when the NCTC analysts knew that a particular NSA intelligence product was derived from the PSP, the analysts said they reviewed the PSP information in the same manner as other NSA intelligence products and, if appropriate, incorporated the PSP information into analytical products being prepared for the DNI and other senior intelligence officials. NCTC analysts with access to PSP information told the ODNI OIG that they had broad access to a wide variety of high-quality and fully evaluated terrorism related intelligence, including some of the most sensitive and valuable terrorism intelligence available to the IC. In this context, NCTC analysts characterized the PSP information as being a useful tool, but noted that the information was only one of several valuable sources of information available to them. During ODNI OIG interviews, some NCTC analysts and ODNI personnel described the PSP information as "one tool in the tool box" or used equivalent descriptions to explain their view that the PSP information was not of greater value than other sources of intelligence. The NCTC analysts noted that the NSA policy protecting the source of the PSP information would have resulted in them not fully understanding the value of the PSP information.

Hayden said the PSP information allowed IC leaders to make valuable judgments regarding the allocation of national security resources. Hayden described the PSP as an "early warning system" for terrorist threats. Hayden told the ODNI OIG that the PSP was extremely valuable in protecting the United States from an al-Qa'ida terrorist attack. He cited several examples of where he said the PSP information was used to disrupt al-Qa'ida operatives or assist in terrorism investigations.

E. Intelligence Community Activities Supported by the PSP

Most IC officials interviewed by the PSP IG Group had difficulty citing specific instances where PSP reporting had directly contributed to counterterrorism successes. Although it was difficult for a variety of reasons already discussed to independently identify instances where PSP reporting contributed to successful counterterrorism efforts, there are several cases identified by IC officials and in IC documentation where PSP reporting may have contributed to a counterterrorism success. These cases cannot be discussed in this unclassified report, but are described in the classified report and accompanying individual OIG reports.

VII. PUBLIC STATEMENTS ABOUT THE PRESIDENT'S SURVEILLANCE PROGRAM

As noted above, aspects of the PSP were first disclosed publicly in a series of articles in The New York Times in December 2005. Subsequently, Attorney General Gonzales was questioned about NSA surveillance activities in two public hearings before the Senate Judiciary Committee in February 2006 and July 2007. As part of its review, the DOJ OIG examined whether Attorney General Gonzales made false, inaccurate, or misleading statements to Congress related to the PSP in those hearings.

Through media accounts and former Deputy Attorney General Corney's Senate Judiciary Committee testimony in May 2007, it was publicly revealed that DOJ and the White House had a major disagreement related to the PSP in March 2004. As discussed in Section IV of this unclassified report, this dispute—which resulted in the visit to Attorney General Ashcroft's hospital room by Gonzales and Card and brought several senior DOJ and FBI officials to the brink of resignation—concerned certain of the Other Intelligence Activities that were different from the communication interception activities that the President later publicly acknowledged as the Terrorist Surveillance Program, but that had been implemented through the same Presidential Authorizations.

In testimony before the Senate Judiciary Committee, Gonzales stated that the dispute at issue between DOJ and the White House did not relate to the Terrorist Surveillance Program that the President had confirmed, but rather pertained to other intelligence activities. The DOJ OIG concluded that this testimony created the misimpression that the dispute concerned activities entirely unrelated to the Terrorist Surveillance Program, which was not accurate. As previously noted, both activities had been authorized by the President in a single Presidential Authorization.

In addition, the DOJ OIG concluded that Gonzales's testimony that DOJ attorneys did not have "reservations" or "concerns" about the program the "President has confirmed" (the Terrorist Surveillance Program) was incomplete and confusing. As detailed in Chapter Four of the DOJ OIG report, there also was a dispute about this portion of the program. Although this dispute was not the subject of the hospital room confrontation or the threatened resignations, DOJ's concerns over this issue were communicated to the White House in several meetings over a period of months prior to and including March 2004 before the issue was resolved.

The DOJ OIG recognized that Attorney General Gonzales was in the difficult position of testifying before the Senate Judiciary Committee about a highly classified program in an open forum. However, the DOJ OIG concluded that Gonzales, as a participant in the March 2004 dispute between the White House and DOJ and, more importantly, as the nation's chief law enforcement officer, had a duty to balance his obligation not to disclose classified information with the need not to be misleading in his testimony about the events that nearly led to resignations of several senior officials at DOJ and the FBI. The DOJ OIG concluded that Gonzales did not intend to mislead Congress, but it found that his testimony was confusing, inaccurate, and had the effect of misleading those who were not knowledgeable about the program.

VIII. CONCLUSION

Pursuant to the FISA Amendments Act of 2008, the Inspectors General of the DOJ, DoD, ODNI, NSA, and CIA conducted reviews of the PSP. In this report, the classified report, and the accompanying individual reports of the participating IGs, we describe how, following the terrorist attacks of September 11, 2001, the President directed that the NSA's signals intelligence collection capabilities be used to detect and prevent acts of terrorism within the United States.

Pursuant to this authority the NSA conducted new intelligence activities, including the collection of the content of communications into and out of the United States, where one party to the communication was reasonably believed to be a member of al-Qa'ida or its affiliates. The NSA analyzed this information for dissemination as leads to the IC, principally to the CIA and the FBI. As described in the IG reports, the scope of this collection authority changed over the course of the PSP.

The IG reports describe the role of each of the participating agencies in the PSP, including the NSA's management and oversight of the collection and analysis process, the CIA's and FBI's use of the PSP-derived intelligence in their counterterrorism efforts, the ODNI's involvement in the program by providing periodic threat assessments and using the program intelligence to produce analytical products, and DOJ's role in analyzing and certifying the legality of the PSP. With the exception of the NSA, the DoD had limited involvement in the PSP.

The IG reports also describe the conflicting views surrounding the legality of aspects of the PSP during 2004, the confrontation between officials from DOJ and the White House about the legal basis for parts of the program, as well as the resolution of that conflict. The ensuing transition of the PSP from presidential authority to statutory authority under FISA is also described in the IG reports.

The IGs also examined the impact of PSP information on counterterrorism efforts. Many senior IC officials believe that the PSP filled a gap in intelligence collection thought to exist under the FISA statute shortly after the al-Qa'ida terrorist attacks against the United States. Others within the IC, including FBI agents, CIA analysts and officers, and other officials had difficulty evaluating the precise contribution of the PSP to counterterrorism efforts because it was most often viewed as one source among many available analytic and intelligence-gathering tools in these efforts. The IG reports describe several examples of how PSP-derived information factored into specific investigations and operations.

Finally, the collection activities pursued under the PSP, and under FISA following the PSP's transition to that authority, involved unprecedented collection activities. We believe the retention and use by IC organizations of information collected under the PSP and FISA should be carefully monitored.

III. Congress and Signifcant Proposed Legislation in 2013

Rules of the Congressional Intelligence Committee
Senate Select Committee on Intelligence

Rules of Procedure of the Select Committee on Intelligence

(Amended February 15, 2011) (S. Prt. 112-14)

RULE 1. CONVENING OF MEETINGS

1.1. The regular meeting day of the Select Committee on Intelligence for the transaction of Committee business shall be every other Tuesday of each month, unless otherwise directed by the Chairman.

1.2. The Chairman shall have authority, upon notice, to call such additional meetings of the Committee as the Chairman may deem necessary and may delegate such authority to any other member of the Committee.

1.3. A special meeting of the Committee may be called at any time upon the written request of five or more members of the Committee filed with the Clerk of the Committee.

1.4. In the case of any meeting of the Committee, other than a regularly scheduled meeting, the Clerk of the Committee shall notify every member of the Committee of the time and place of the meeting and shall give reasonable notice which, except in extraordinary circumstances, shall be at least 24 hours in advance of any meeting held in Washington, D.C. and at least 48 hours in the case of any meeting held outside Washington, D.C.

1.5. If five members of the Committee have made a request in writing to the Chairman to call a meeting of the Committee, and the Chairman fails to call such a meeting within seven calendar days thereafter, including the day on which the written notice is submitted, these members may call a meeting by filing a written notice with the Clerk of the Committee who shall promptly notify each member of the Committee in writing of the date and time of the meeting.

RULE 2. MEETING PROCEDURES

2.1. Meetings of the Committee shall be open to the public except as provided in paragraph 5(b) of Rule XXVI of the Standing Rules of the Senate.

2.2. It shall be the duty of the Staff Director to keep or cause to be kept a record of all Committee proceedings.

2.3. The Chairman of the Committee, or if the Chairman is not present the Vice Chairman, shall preside over all meetings of the Committee. In the absence of the Chairman and the Vice Chairman at any meeting, the ranking majority member, or if no majority member is present the ranking minority member present, shall preside.

2.4. Except as otherwise provided in these Rules, decisions of the Committee shall be by a majority vote of the members present and voting. A quorum for the transaction of Committee business, including the conduct of executive sessions, shall consist of no less than one third of the Committee members, except that for the purpose of hearing witnesses, taking sworn testimony, and receiving evidence under oath, a quorum may consist of one Senator.

2.5. A vote by any member of the Committee with respect to any measure or matter being considered by the Committee may be cast by proxy if the proxy authorization (1) is in writing; (2) designates the member of the Committee who is to exercise the proxy; and (3) is limited to a specific measure or matter and any amendments pertaining thereto. Proxies shall not be considered for the establishment of a quorum.

2.6. Whenever the Committee by roll call vote reports any measure or matter, the report of the Committee upon such measure or matter shall include a tabulation of the votes cast in favor of and the votes cast in opposition to such measure or matter by each member of the Committee.

RULE 3. SUBCOMMITTEES

Creation of subcommittees shall be by majority vote of the Committee. Subcommittees shall deal with such legislation and oversight of programs and policies as the Committee may direct. The subcommittees shall be governed by the Rules of the Committee and by such other rules they may adopt which are consistent with the Rules of the Committee. Each subcommittee created shall have a chairman and a vice chairman who are selected by the Chairman and Vice Chairman, respectively.

RULE 4. REPORTING OF MEASURES OR RECOMMENDATIONS

4.1. No measures or recommendations shall be reported, favorably or unfavorably, from the Committee unless a majority of the Committee is actually present and a majority concur.

4.2. In any case in which the Committee is unable to reach a unanimous decision, separate views or reports may be presented by any member or members of the Committee.

4.3. A member of the Committee who gives notice of intention to file supplemental, minority, or additional views at the time of final Committee approval of a measure or matter, shall be entitled to not less than three working days in which to file such views, in writing with the Clerk of the Committee. Such views shall then be included in the Committee report and printed in the same volume, as a part thereof, and their inclusion shall be noted on the cover of the report.

4.4. Routine, non-legislative actions required of the Committee may be taken in accordance with procedures that have been approved by the Committee pursuant to these Committee Rules.

RULE 5. NOMINATIONS

5.1. Unless otherwise ordered by the Committee, nominations referred to the Committee shall be held for at least 14 days before being voted on by the Committee.

5.2. Each member of the Committee shall be promptly furnished a copy of all nominations referred to the Committee.
5.3. Nominees who are invited to appear before the Committee shall be heard in public session, except as provided in Rule 2.1. 5.4. No confirmation hearing shall be held sooner than seven days after receipt of the background and financial disclosure statement unless the time limit is waived by a majority vote of the Committee. 5.5. The Committee vote on the confirmation shall not be sooner than 48 hours after the Committee has received transcripts of the confirmation hearing unless the time limit is waived by unanimous consent of the Committee.
5.6. No nomination shall be reported to the Senate unless the nominee has filed a background and financial disclosure statement with the Committee.

RULE 6. INVESTIGATIONS
No investigation shall be initiated by the Committee unless at least five members of the Committee have specifically requested the Chairman or the Vice Chairman to authorize such an investigation. Authorized investigations may be conducted by members of the Committee and/or designated Committee staff members.

RULE 7. SUBPOENAS
Subpoenas authorized by the Committee for the attendance of witnesses or the production of memoranda, documents, records, or any other material may be issued by the Chairman, the Vice Chairman, or any member of the Committee designated by the Chairman, and may be served by any person designated by the Chairman, Vice Chairman or member issuing the subpoenas. Each subpoena shall have attached thereto a copy of S. Res. 400 of the 94th Congress, and a copy of these rules.

RULE 8. PROCEDURES RELATED TO THE TAKING OF TESTIMONY
8.1. NOTICE.—Witnesses required to appear before the Committee shall be given reasonable notice and all witnesses shall be furnished a copy of these Rules.
8.2. OATH OR AFFIRMATION.—At the direction of the Chairman or Vice Chairman, testimony of witnesses shall be given under oath or affirmation which may be administered by any member of the Committee.
8.3. INTERROGATION.—Committee interrogation shall be conducted by members of the Committee and such Committee staff as are authorized by the Chairman, Vice Chairman, or the presiding member.
8.4. COUNSEL FOR THE WITNESS.—(a) Any witness may be accompanied by counsel. A witness who is unable to obtain counsel may inform the Committee of such fact. If the witness informs the Committee of this fact at least 24 hours prior to his or her appearance before the Committee, the Committee shall then endeavor to obtain voluntary counsel for the witness. Failure to obtain such counsel will not excuse the witness from appearing and testifying. (b) Counsel shall conduct themselves in an ethical and professional manner. Failure to do so shall, upon a finding to that effect by a majority of the members present, subject such counsel to disciplinary action which may include warning, censure, removal, or a

recommendation of contempt proceedings. (c) There shall be no direct or cross-examination by counsel. However, counsel may submit any question in writing to the Committee and request the Committee to propound such question to the counsel's client or to any other witness. The counsel also may suggest the presentation of other evidence or the calling of other witnesses. The Committee may use or dispose of such questions or suggestions as it deems appropriate.

8.5. STATEMENTS BY WITNESSES.—Witnesses may make brief and relevant statements at the beginning and conclusion of their testimony. Such statements shall not exceed a reasonable period of time as determined by the Chairman, or other presiding members. Any witness required or desiring to make a prepared or written statement for the record of the proceedings shall file a paper and electronic copy with the Clerk of the Committee, and insofar as practicable and consistent with the notice given, shall do so at least 48 hours in advance of his or her appearance before the Committee.

8.6. OBJECTIONS AND RULINGS.—Any objection raised by a witness or counsel shall be ruled upon by the Chairman or other presiding member, and such ruling shall be the ruling of the Committee unless a majority of the Committee present overrules the ruling of the chair.

8.7. INSPECTION AND CORRECTION.—All witnesses testifying before the Committee shall be given a reasonable opportunity to inspect, in the office of the Committee, the transcript of their testimony to determine whether such testimony was correctly transcribed. The witness may be accompanied by counsel. Any corrections the witness desires to make in the transcript shall be submitted in writing to the Committee within five days from the date when the transcript was made available to the witness. Corrections shall be limited to grammar and minor editing, and may not be made to change the substance of the testimony. Any questions arising with respect to such corrections shall be decided by the Chairman. Upon request, the Committee may provide to a witness those parts of testimony given by that witness in executive session which are subsequently quoted or made part of a public record, at the expense of the witness.

8.8. REQUESTS TO TESTIFY.—The Committee will consider requests to testify on any matter or measure pending before the Committee. A person who believes that testimony or other evidence presented at a public hearing, or any comment made by a Committee member or a member of the Committee staff, may tend to affect adversely that person's reputation, may request to appear personally before the Committee to testify or may file a sworn statement of facts relevant to the testimony, evidence, or comment, or may submit to the Chairman proposed questions in writing for the cross-examination of other witnesses. The Committee shall take such action as it deems appropriate.

8.9. CONTEMPT PROCEDURES.—No recommendation that a person be cited for contempt of Congress or that a subpoena be otherwise enforced shall be forwarded to the Senate unless and until the Committee has, upon notice to all its members, met and considered the recommendation, afforded the person an opportunity to oppose such contempt or subpoena enforcement proceeding either in writing or in person, and agreed by majority vote of the Committee to forward such recommendation to the Senate.

8.10. RELEASE OF NAME OF WITNESS.—Unless authorized by the Chairman, the name of any witness scheduled to be heard by the Committee shall not be released prior to, or after, appearing before the Committee. Upon authorization by the Chairman to release the name of a witness under this paragraph, the Vice Chairman shall be notified of such authorization as soon as practicable thereafter. No name of any witness shall be released if such release would disclose classified information, unless authorized under Section 8 of S. Res. 400 of the 94th Congress or Rule 9.7.

RULE 9. PROCEDURES FOR HANDLING CLASSIFIED OR COMMITTEE SENSITIVE MATERIAL

9.1. Committee staff offices shall operate under strict precautions. At least one United States Capitol Police Officer shall be on duty at all times at the entrance of the Committee to control entry. Before entering the Committee office space all persons shall identify themselves and provide identification as requested.

9.2. Classified documents and material shall be stored in authorized security containers located within the Committee's Sensitive Compartmented Information Facility (SCIF). Copying, duplicating, or removing from the Committee offices of such documents and other materials is prohibited except as is necessary for the conduct of Committee business, and in conformity with Rule 10.3 hereof. All classified documents or materials removed from the Committee offices for such authorized purposes must be returned to the Committee's SCIF for overnight storage.

9.3. "Committee sensitive" means information or material that pertains to the confidential business or proceedings of the Select Committee on Intelligence, within the meaning of paragraph 5 of Rule XXIX of the Standing Rules of the Senate, and is: (1) in the possession or under the control of the Committee; (2) discussed or presented in an executive session of the Committee; (3) the work product of a Committee member or staff member; (4) properly identified or marked by a Committee member or staff member who authored the document; or (5) designated as such by the Chairman and Vice Chairman (or by the Staff Director and Minority Staff Director acting on their behalf). Committee sensitive documents and materials that are classified shall be handled in the same manner as classified documents and material in Rule 9.2. Unclassified committee sensitive documents and materials shall be stored in a manner to protect against unauthorized disclosure.

9.4. Each member of the Committee shall at all times have access to all papers and other material received from any source. The Staff Director shall be responsible for the maintenance, under appropriate security procedures, of a document control and accountability registry which will number and identify all classified papers and other classified materials in the possession of the Committee, and such registry shall be available to any member of the Committee.

9.5. Whenever the Select Committee on Intelligence makes classified material available to any other committee of the Senate or to any member of the Senate not a member of the Committee, such material shall be accompanied by a verbal or written notice to the recipients advising of their responsibility to protect such materials pursuant to section 8 of S. Res. 400 of the 94th Congress. The Security Director of the Committee shall ensure that such notice is provided and shall maintain a written record identifying the particular information transmitted and the committee or members of the Senate receiving such information.

9.6. Access to classified information supplied to the Committee shall be limited to those Committee staff members with appropriate security clearance and a need-to-know, as determined by the Committee, and, under the Committee's direction, the Staff Director and Minority Staff Director.

9.7. No member of the Committee or of the Committee staff shall disclose, in whole or in part or by way of summary, the contents of any classified or committee sensitive papers, materials, briefings, testimony, or other information in the possession of the Committee to any other person, except as specified in this rule. Committee members and staff do not need prior approval to disclose classified or committee sensitive information to persons in the Executive branch, the members and staff of the House Permanent Select Committee on Intelligence, and the members and staff of the Senate, provided that the following conditions are met: (1) for classified information, the recipients of the information must possess appropriate security clearances (or have access to the information by virtue of their office); (2) for all information, the recipients of the information must have a need-to-know such information for an official governmental purpose; and (3) for all information, the Committee members and staff who provide the information must be engaged in the routine performance of Committee legislative or oversight duties. Otherwise, classified and committee sensitive information may only be disclosed to persons outside the Committee (to include any congressional committee, Member of Congress, congressional staff, or specified non-governmental persons who support intelligence activities) with the prior approval of the Chairman and Vice Chairman of the Committee, or the Staff Director and Minority Staff Director acting on their behalf, consistent with the requirements that classified information may only be disclosed to persons with appropriate security clearances and a need-to-know such information for an official governmental purpose. Public disclosure of classified information in the possession of the Committee may only be authorized in accordance with Section 8 of S. Res. 400 of the 94th Congress.

9.8. Failure to abide by Rule 9.7 shall constitute grounds for referral to the Select Committee on Ethics pursuant to Section 8 of S. Res. 400 of the 94th Congress. Prior to a referral to the Select Committee on Ethics pursuant to Section 8 of S. Res. 400, the Chairman and Vice Chairman shall notify the Majority Leader and Minority Leader.

9.9. Before the Committee makes any decision regarding the disposition of any testimony, papers, or other materials presented to it, the Committee members shall have a reasonable opportunity to examine all pertinent testimony, papers, and other materials that have been obtained by the members of the Committee or the Committee staff.

9.10. Attendance of persons outside the Committee at closed meetings of the Committee shall be kept at a minimum and shall be limited to persons with appropriate security clearance and a need-to-know the information under consideration for the execution of their official duties. The Security Director of the Committee may require that notes taken at such meetings by any person in attendance shall be returned to the secure storage area in the Committee's offices at the conclusion of such meetings, and may be made available to the department, agency, office, committee, or entity concerned only in accordance with the security procedures of the Committee.

RULE 10. STAFF

10.1. For purposes of these rules, Committee staff includes employees of the Committee, consultants to the Committee, or any other person engaged by contract or otherwise to perform services for or at the request of the Committee. To the maximum extent practicable, the Committee shall rely on its full-time employees to perform all staff functions. No individual may be retained as staff of the Committee or to perform services for the Committee unless that individual holds appropriate security clearances.

10.2. The appointment of Committee staff shall be approved by the Chairman and Vice Chairman, acting jointly, or, at the initiative of both or either be confirmed by a majority vote of the Committee. After approval or confirmation, the Chairman shall certify Committee staff appointments to the Financial Clerk of the Senate in writing. No Committee staff shall be given access to any classified information or regular access to the Committee offices until such Committee staff has received an appropriate security clearance as described in Section 6 of S. Res. 400 of the 94th Congress.

10.3. The Committee staff works for the Committee as a whole, under the supervision of the Chairman and Vice Chairman of the Committee. The duties of the Committee staff shall be performed, and Committee staff personnel affairs and day-to-day operations, including security and control of classified documents and material, shall be administered under the direct supervision and control of the Staff Director. All Committee staff shall work exclusively on intelligence oversight issues for the Committee. The Minority Staff Director and the Minority Counsel shall be kept fully informed regarding all matters and shall have access to all material in the files of the Committee.

10.4. The Committee staff shall assist the minority as fully as the majority in the expression of minority views, including assistance in the preparation and filing of additional, separate, and minority views, to the end that all points of view may be fully considered by the Committee and the Senate. 10.5. The members of the Committee staff shall not discuss either the substance or procedure of the work of the Committee with any person not a member of the Committee or the Committee staff for any purpose or in connection with any proceeding, judicial or otherwise, either during their tenure as a member of the Committee staff or at any time thereafter, except as directed by the Committee in accordance with Section 8 of S. Res. 400 of the 94th Congress and the provisions of these rules, or in the event of the termination of the Committee, in such a manner as may be determined by the Senate. The Chairman may authorize the Staff Director and the Staff Director's designee, and the Vice Chairman may authorize the Minority Staff Director and the Minority Staff Director's designee, to communicate with the media in a manner that does not divulge classified or committee sensitive information.

10.6. No member of the Committee staff shall be employed by the Committee unless and until such a member of the Committee staff agrees in writing, as a condition of employment, to abide by the conditions of the nondisclosure agreement promulgated by the Select Committee on Intelligence, pursuant to Section 6 of S. Res. 400 of the 94th Congress, and to abide by the Committee's code of conduct.

10.7. As a precondition for employment on the Committee staff, each member of the Committee staff must agree in writing to notify the Committee of any request for testimony, either during service as a member of the Committee staff or at any time thereafter with respect to information obtained by virtue of employment as a member of the Committee staff. Such information shall not be disclosed in response to such requests except as directed by the Committee in accordance with Section 8 of S. Res. 400 of the 94th Congress and the provisions of these rules or, in the event of the termination of the Committee, in such manner as may be determined by the Senate.

10.8. The Committee shall immediately consider action to be taken in the case of any member of the Committee staff who fails to conform to any of these Rules. Such disciplinary action may include, but shall not be limited to, immediate dismissal from the Committee staff.

10.9. Within the Committee staff shall be an element with the capability to perform audits of programs and activities undertaken by departments and agencies with intelligence functions. The audit element shall conduct audits and oversight projects that have been specifically authorized by the Chairman and Vice Chairman of the Committee, acting jointly through the Staff Director and Minority Staff Director. Staff shall be assigned to such element jointly by the Chairman and Vice Chairman, and staff with the principal responsibility for the conduct of an audit shall be qualified by training or experience in accordance with accepted auditing standards.

10.10. The workplace of the Committee shall be free from illegal use, possession, sale, or distribution of controlled substances by its employees. Any violation of such policy by any member of the Committee staff shall be grounds for termination of employment. Further, any illegal use of controlled substances by a member of the Committee staff, within the workplace or otherwise, shall result in reconsideration of the security clearance of any such staff member and may constitute grounds for termination of employment with the Committee.

10.11. All personnel actions affecting the staff of the Committee shall be made free from any discrimination based on race, color, religion, sex, national origin, age, handicap, or disability.

RULE 11. PREPARATION FOR COMMITTEE MEETINGS

11.1. Under direction of the Chairman and the Vice Chairman designated Committee staff members shall brief members of the Committee at a time sufficiently prior to any Committee meeting to assist the Committee members in preparation for such meeting and to determine any matter which the Committee member might wish considered during the meeting. Such briefing shall, at the request of a member, include a list of all pertinent papers and other materials that have been obtained by the Committee that bear on matters to be considered at the meeting.

11.2. The Staff Director and/or Minority Staff Director shall recommend to the Chairman and the Vice Chairman the testimony, papers, and other materials to be presented to the Committee at any meeting. The determination whether such testimony, papers, and other materials shall be presented in open or executive session shall be made pursuant to the Rules of the Senate and Rules of the Committee.

11.3. The Staff Director shall ensure that covert action programs of the U.S. Government receive appropriate consideration by the Committee no less frequently than once a quarter.

RULE 12. LEGISLATIVE CALENDAR

12.1. The Clerk of the Committee shall maintain a printed calendar for the information of each Committee member showing the measures introduced and referred to the Committee and the status of such measures; nominations referred to the Committee and their status; and such other matters as the Committee determines shall be included. The Calendar shall be revised from time to time to show pertinent changes. A copy of each such revision shall be furnished to each member of the Committee.

12.2. Measures referred to the Committee may be referred by the Chairman and/or Vice Chairman to the appropriate department or agency of the Government for reports thereon.

RULE 13. COMMITTEE TRAVEL

13.1. No member of the Committee or Committee Staff shall travel abroad on Committee business unless specifically authorized by the Chairman and Vice Chairman. Requests for authorization of such travel shall state the purpose and extent of the trip. A full report shall be filed with the Committee when travel is completed.

13.2. No member of the Committee staff shall travel within this country on Committee business unless specifically authorized by the Chairman and Vice Chairman.

RULE 14. CHANGES IN RULES

These Rules may be modified, amended, or repealed by the Committee, provided that a notice in writing of the proposed change has been given to each member at least 48 hours prior to the meeting at which action thereon is to be taken.

APPENDIX A

S. RES. 400, 94TH CONG., 2D SESS. (1976)[1]

Resolved, That it is the purpose of this resolution to establish a new select committee of the Senate, to be known as the Select Committee on Intelligence, to oversee and make continuing studies of the intelligence activities and programs of the United States Government, and to submit to the Senate appropriate proposals for legislation and report to the Senate concerning such intelligence activities and programs. In carrying out this purpose, the Select Committee on Intelligence shall make every effort to assure that the appropriate departments and agencies of the United States provide informed and timely intelligence necessary for the executive and legislative branches to make sound decisions affecting the security and vital interests of the Nation. It is further the purpose of this resolution to provide vigilant legislative oversight over the intelligence activities of the United States to assure that such activities are in conformity with the Constitution and laws of the United States.

SEC. 2. (a)(1) There is hereby established a select committee to be known as the Select Committee on Intelligence (hereinafter in this resolution referred to as the "Select Committee"). The Select Committee shall be composed of not to exceed fifteen Members appointed as follows:

(A) two members from the Committee on Appropriations;

(B) two members from the Committee on Armed Services;

(C) two members from the Committee on Foreign Relations;

(D) two members from the Committee on the Judiciary; and

(E) not to exceed seven members to be appointed from the Senate at large.

(2) Members appointed from each committee named in clauses (A) through (D) of paragraph (1) shall be evenly divided between the two major political parties and shall be appointed by the President pro tempore of the Senate upon the recommendations of the majority and minority leaders of the Senate. Of any members appointed under paragraph (1)(E), the majority leader shall appoint the majority members and the minority leader shall appoint the minority members, with the majority having a one vote margin. (3)(A) The majority leader of the Senate and the minority leader of the Senate shall be ex officio members of the Select Committee but shall have no vote in the Committee and shall not be counted for purposes of determining a quorum. (B) The Chairman and Ranking Member of the Committee on Armed Services (if not already a member of the Select Committee) shall be ex officio members of the Select Committee but shall have no vote in the Committee and shall not be counted for purposes of determining a quorum. (b) At the beginning of each Congress, the Majority Leader of the Senate shall select a chairman of the Select Committee and the Minority Leader shall select a vice chairman for the Select Committee. The vice chairman shall act in

1, As amended by S. Res. 4, 95th Cong., 1st Sess. (1977), S. Res, 445, 108th Cong., 2d Sess. (2004), Pub. L. No. 109–177, § 506, 120 Stat. 247 (2005), and S. Res. 50, 110th Cong., 1st Sess. (2007).

the place and stead of the chairman in the absence of the chairman. Neither the chairman nor the vice chairman of the Select Committee shall at the same time serve as chairman or ranking minority member of any other committee referred to in paragraph 4(e)(1) of rule XXV of the Standing Rules of the Senate. (c) The Select Committee may be organized into subcommittees. Each subcommittee shall have a chairman and a vice chairman who are selected by the Chairman and Vice Chairman of the Select Committee, respectively.

SEC. 3. (a) There shall be referred to the Select Committee all proposed legislation, messages, petitions, memorials, and other matters relating to the following:

(1) The Office of the Director of National Intelligence and the Director of National Intelligence.

(2) The Central Intelligence Agency and the Director of the Central Intelligence Agency.

(3) Intelligence activities of all other departments and agencies of the Government, including, but not limited to, the intelligence activities of the Defense Intelligence Agency, the National Security Agency, and other agencies of the Department of Defense; the Department of State; the Department of Justice; and the Department of the Treasury.

(4) The organization or reorganization of any department or agency of the Government to the extent that the organization or reorganization relates to a function or activity involving intelligence activities.

(5) Authorizations for appropriations, both direct and indirect, for the following:

(A) The Office of the Director of National Intelligence and the Director of National Intelligence.

(B) The Central Intelligence Agency and the Director of the Central Intelligence Agency.

(C) The Defense Intelligence Agency.

(D) The National Security Agency.

(E) The intelligence activities of other agencies and subdivisions of the Department of Defense.

(F) The intelligence activities of the Department of State.

(G) The intelligence activities of the Federal Bureau of Investigation.

(H) Any department, agency, or subdivision which is the successor to any agency named in clause (A). (B). (C) or (D); and the activities of any department, agency, or subdivision which is the successor to any department, agency, bureau, or subdivision named in clause (E). (F), or (G) to the extent that the activities of such successor department, agency, or subdivision are activities described in clause (E). (F), or (G).

(b)(1) Any proposed legislation reported by the Select Committee except any legislation involving matters specified in clause (1). (2). (5)(A), or (5)(B) of subsection (a), containing any matter otherwise within the jurisdiction of any standing committee shall, at the request of the chairman of such standing committee, be referred to such standing committee for its consideration of such matter and be reported to the Senate by such standing committee within 10 days after the day on which such proposed legislation, in its entirety and including annexes, is referred to such standing committee; and any proposed legislation reported by any committee, other than the Select Committee, which contains any matter within the jurisdiction of the Select Committee shall, at the request of the chairman of the Select Committee, be referred to the Select Committee for its consideration of such matter and be reported to the Senate by the Select Committee within 10 days after the day on which such proposed legislation, in its entirety and including annexes, is referred to such committee.

(2) In any case in which a committee fails to report any proposed legislation referred to it within the time limit prescribed in this subsection, such Committee shall be automatically discharged from further consideration of such proposed legislation on the 10th day following the day on which such proposed legislation is referred to such committee unless the Senate provides otherwise, or the Majority Leader or Minority Leader request, prior to that date, an additional 5 days on behalf of the Committee to which the proposed legislation was sequentially referred. At the end of that additional 5 day period, if the Committee fails to report the proposed legislation within that 5 day period, the Committee shall be automatically discharged from further consideration of such proposed legislation unless the Senate provides otherwise.

(3) In computing any 10 or 5 day period under this subsection there shall be excluded from such computation any days on which the Senate is not in session.

(4) The reporting and referral processes outlined in this subsection shall be conducted in strict accordance with the Standing Rules of the Senate. In accordance with such rules, committees to which legislation is referred are not permitted to make changes or alterations to the text of the referred bill and its annexes, but may propose changes or alterations to the same in the form of amendments.

(c) Nothing in this resolution shall be construed as prohibiting or otherwise restricting the authority of any other committee to study and review any intelligence activity to the extent that such activity directly affects a matter otherwise within the jurisdiction of such committee. (d) Nothing in this resolution shall be construed as amending, limiting, or otherwise changing the authority of any standing committee of the Senate to obtain full and prompt access to the product of the intelligence activities of any department or agency of the Government relevant to a matter otherwise within the jurisdiction of such committee.

SEC 4. (a) The Select Committee, for the purposes of accountability to the Senate, shall make regular and periodic, but not less than quarterly, reports to the Senate on the nature and extent of the intelligence activities of the various departments and agencies of the United States. Such committee shall promptly call to the attention of the Senate or to any other appropriate committee or committees of the Senate any matters requiring the attention of the Senate or such other committee

or committees. In making such report, the Select Committee shall proceed in a manner consistent with section 8(c)(2) to protect national security.
(b) The Select Committee shall obtain an annual report from the Director of National Intelligence, the Director of the Central Intelligence Agency, the Secretary of Defense, the Secretary of State, and the Director of the Federal Bureau of Investigation. Such reports shall review the intelligence activities of the agency or department concerned and the intelligence activities of foreign countries directed at the United States or its interest. An unclassified version of each report may be made available to the public at the discretion of the Select Committee. Nothing herein shall be construed as requiring the public disclosure in such reports of the names of individuals engaged in intelligence activities for the United States or the divulging of intelligence methods employed or the sources of information on which such reports are based or the amount of funds authorized to be appropriated for intelligence activities.
(c) On or before March 15 of each year, the Select Committee shall submit to the Committee on the Budget of the Senate the views and estimates described in section 301(c) of the Congressional Budget Act of 1974 regarding matters within the jurisdiction of the Select Committee.

SEC. 5. (a) For the purposes of this resolution, the Select Committee is authorized in its discretion

(1) to make investigations into any matter within its jurisdiction.
(2) to make expenditures from the contingent fund of the Senate.
(3) to employ personnel.
(4) to hold hearings.
(5) to sit and act at any time or place during the sessions, recesses, and adjourned periods of the Senate.
(6) to require, by subpoena or otherwise, the attendance of witnesses and the production of correspondence, books, papers, and documents.
(7) to take depositions and other testimony.
(8) to procure the service of individual consultants or organizations thereof, in accordance with the provisions of section 202(i) of the Legislative Reorganization Act of 1946, and
(9) with the prior consent of the government department or agency concerned and the Committee on Rules and Administration, to use on a reimbursable basis the services of personnel of any such department or agency. (b) The chairman of the Select Committee or any member thereof may administer oaths to witnesses.

(c) Subpoenas authorized by the Select Committee may be issued over the signature of the chairman, the vice chairman or any member of the Select Committee designated by the chairman, and may be served by any person designated by the chairman or any member signing the subpoenas.

SEC. 6. No employee of the Select Committee or any person engaged by contract or otherwise to perform services for or at the request of such committee shall be given access to any classified information by such committee unless such employee or person has (1) agreed in writing and under oath to be bound by the rules of the Senate (including the jurisdiction of the Select Committee on Ethics) and of such committee as to the security of such information during and after the period of his employment or contractual agreement with such committee; and (2) received an appropriate security clearance as determined by such committee in consultation with the Director of National Intelligence. The type of security clearance to be required in the case of any such employee or person shall, within the determination of such committee in consultation with the Director of National Intelligence, be commensurate with the sensitivity of the classified information to which such employee or person will be given access by such committee.

SEC. 7. The Select Committee shall formulate and carry out such rules and procedures as it deems necessary to prevent the disclosure, without the consent of the person or persons concerned, of information in the possession of such committee which unduly infringes upon the privacy or which violates the constitutional rights of such person or persons. Nothing herein shall be construed to prevent such committee from publicly disclosing any such information in any case in which such committee determines the national interest in the disclosure of such information clearly outweighs any infringement on the privacy of any person or persons.

SEC. 8. (a) The Select Committee may, subject to the provisions of this section, disclose publicly any information in the possession of such committee after a determination by such committee that the public interest would be served by such disclosure. Whenever committee action is required to disclose any information under this section, the committee shall meet to vote on the matter within five days after any member of the committee requests such a vote. No member of the Select Committee shall disclose any information, the disclosure of which requires a committee vote, prior to a vote by the committee on the question of the disclosure of such information or after such vote except in accordance with this section.

(b)(1) In any case in which the Select Committee votes to disclose publicly any information which has been classified under established security procedures, which has been submitted to it by the Executive branch, and which the Executive branch requests be kept secret, such committee shall—

(A) first, notify the Majority Leader and Minority Leader of the Senate of such vote; and

(B) second, consult with the Majority Leader and Minority Leader before notifying the President of such vote.

(2) The Select Committee may disclose publicly such information after the expiration of a 5-day period following the day on which notice of such vote is transmitted to the Majority Leader and the Minority Leader and the President, unless, prior to the expiration of such 5-day period, the President, personally in writing, notifies the committee that he objects to the disclosure of such information, provides his reasons therefore, and certifies that the threat to the

national interest of the United States posed by such disclosure is of such gravity that it outweighs any public interest in the disclosure.
(3) If the President, personally, in writing, notifies the Majority Leader and Minority Leader of the Senate and the Select Committee of his objections to the disclosure of such information as provided in paragraph (2), the Majority Leader and Minority Leader jointly or the Select Committee, by majority vote, may refer the question of the disclosure of such information to the Senate for consideration. (4) Whenever the Select Committee votes to refer the question of disclosure of any information to the Senate under paragraph (3), the Chairman shall not later than the first day on which the Senate is in session following the day on which the vote occurs, report the matter to the Senate for its consideration. (5) One hour after the Senate convenes on the fourth day on which the Senate is in session following the day on which any such matter is reported to the Senate, or at such earlier time as the majority leader and the minority leader of the Senate jointly agree upon in accordance with paragraph 5 of rule XVII of the Standing Rules of the Senate, the Senate shall go into closed session and the matter shall be the pending business. In considering the matter in closed session the Senate may—

(A) approve the public disclosure of all or any portion of the information in question, in which case the committee shall publicly disclose the information ordered to be disclosed.

(B) disapprove the public disclosure of all or any portion of the information in question, in which case the committee shall not publicly disclose the information ordered not to be disclosed, or

(C) refer all or any portion of the matter back to the committee, in which case the committee shall make the final determination with respect to the public disclosure of the information in question. Upon conclusion of the consideration of such matter in closed session, which may not extend beyond the close of the ninth day on which the Senate is in session following the day on which such matter was reported to the Senate, or the close of the fifth day following the day agreed upon jointly by the majority and minority leaders in accordance with paragraph 5 of rule XVII of the Standing Rules of the Senate (whichever the case may be), the Senate shall immediately vote on the disposition of such matter in open session, without debate, and without divulging the information with respect to which the vote is being taken. The Senate shall vote to dispose of such matter by one or more of the means specified in clauses (A). (B), and (C) of the second sentence of this paragraph. Any vote of the Senate to disclose any information pursuant to this paragraph shall be subject to the right of a Member of the Senate to move for reconsideration of the vote within the time and pursuant to the procedures specified in rule XIII of the Standing Rules of the Senate, and the disclosure of such information shall be made consistent with that right.

(c)(1) No information in the possession of the Select Committee relating to the lawful intelligence activities of any department or agency of the United States which has been classified under established security procedures and which the Select Committee, pursuant to subsection (a) or (b) of this section, has determined should not be disclosed shall be made available to any person by a Member, officer, or employee of the Senate except in a closed session of the Senate or as provided in paragraph (2).

(2) The Select Committee may, under such regulations as the committee shall prescribe to protect the confidentiality of such information, make any information described in paragraph (1) available to any other committee or any other Member of the Senate. Whenever the Select Committee makes such information available, the committee shall keep a written record showing, in the case of any particular information, which committee or which Members of the Senate received such information. No Member of the Senate who, and no committee which, receives any information under this subsection, shall disclose such information except in a closed session of the Senate.

(d) It shall be the duty of the Select Committee on Ethics to investigate any unauthorized disclosure of intelligence information by a Member, officer or employee of the Senate in violation of subsection (c) and to report to the Senate concerning any allegation which it finds to be substantiated.

(e) Upon the request of any person who is subject to any such investigation, the Select Committee on Ethics shall release to such individual at the conclusion of its investigation a summary of its investigation together with its findings. If, at the conclusion of its investigation, the Select Committee on Ethics determines that there has been a significant breach of confidentiality or unauthorized disclosure by a Member, officer, or employee of the Senate, it shall report its findings to the Senate and recommend appropriate action such as censure, removal from committee membership, or expulsion from the Senate, in the case of a Member, or removal from office or employment or punishment for contempt, in the case of an officer or employee.

SEC.9. The Select Committee is authorized to permit any personal representative of the President, designated by the President to serve as a liaison to such committee, to attend any closed meeting of such committee.

SEC. 10. Upon expiration of the Select Committee on Governmental Operations With Respect to Intelligence Activities, established by Senate Resolution 21, Ninety-fourth Congress, all records, files, documents, and other materials in the possession, custody, or control of such committee, under appropriate conditions established by it, shall be transferred to the Select Committee.

SEC. 11. (a) It is the sense of the Senate that the head of each department and agency of the United States should keep the Select Committee fully and currently informed with respect to intelligence activities, including any significant anticipated activities, which are the responsibility of or engaged in by such department or agency: Provided, That this does not constitute a condition precedent to the implementation of any such anticipated intelligence activity.

(b) It is the sense of the Senate that the head of any department or agency of the United States involved in any intelligence activities should furnish any information or document in the possession, custody, or control of the department or agency, or person paid by such department or agency, whenever requested by the Select Committee with respect to any matter within such committee's jurisdiction.
(c) It is the sense of the Senate that each department and agency of the United States should report immediately upon discovery to the Select Committee any and all intelligence activities which constitute violations of the constitutional rights of any person, violations of law, or violations of Executive orders, Presidential directives, or departmental or agency rules or regulations; each department and agency should further report to such committee what actions have been taken or are expected to be taken by the departments or agencies with respect to such violations.
SEC. 12. Subject to the Standing Rules of the Senate, no funds shall be appropriated for any fiscal year beginning after September 30, 1976, with the exception of a continuing bill or resolution, or amendment thereto, or conference report thereon, to, or for use of, any department or agency of the United States to carry out any of the following activities, unless such funds shall have been previously authorized by a bill or joint resolution passed by the Senate during the same or preceding fiscal year to carry out such activity for such fiscal year:

(1) The activities of the Office of the Director of National Intelligence and the Director of National Intelligence.
(2) The activities of the Central Intelligence Agency and the Director of the Central Intelligence Agency.
(3) The activities of the Defense Intelligence Agency.
(4) The activities of the National Security Agency.
(5) The intelligence activities of other agencies and subdivisions of the Department of Defense.
(6) The intelligence activities of the Department of State.
(7) The intelligence activities of the Federal Bureau of Investigation.

SEC. 13. (a) The Select Committee shall make a study with respect
to the following matters, taking into consideration with respect to each such matter, all relevant aspects of the effectiveness of planning, gathering, use, security, and dissemination of intelligence:

(1) the quality of the analytical capabilities of United States foreign intelligence agencies and means for integrating more closely analytical intelligence and policy formulation;
(2) the extent and nature of the authority of the departments and agencies of the Executive branch to engage in intelligence activities and the desirability of developing charters for each intelligence agency or department;
(3) the organization of intelligence activities in the Executive branch to maximize the effectiveness of the conduct, oversight, and accountability of intelligence activities; to reduce duplication or overlap; and to improve the morale of the personnel of the foreign intelligence agencies;

(4) the conduct of covert and clandestine activities and the procedures by which Congress is informed of such activities;
(5) the desirability of changing any law, Senate rule or procedure, or any Executive order, rule, or regulation to improve the protection of intelligence secrets and provide for disclosure of information for which there is no compelling reason for secrecy;
(6) the desirability of establishing a standing committee of the Senate on intelligence activities;
(7) the desirability of establishing a joint committee of the Senate and the House of Representatives on intelligence activities in lieu of having separate committees in each House of Congress, or of establishing procedures under which separate committees on intelligence activities of the two Houses of Congress would receive joint briefings from the intelligence agencies and coordinate their policies with respect to the safeguarding of sensitive intelligence information;
(8) the authorization of funds for the intelligence activities of the Government and whether disclosure of any of the amounts of such funds is in the public interest; and
(9) the development of a uniform set of definitions for terms to be used in policies or guidelines which may be adopted by the executive or legislative branches to govern, clarify, and strengthen the operation of intelligence activities. (b) The Select Committee may, in its discretion, omit from the special study required by this section any matter it determines has been adequately studied by the Select Committee To Study Governmental Operations With Respect to Intelligence Activities, established by Senate Resolution 21, Ninety-fourth Congress.

(c) The Select Committee shall report the results of the study provided for by this section to the Senate, together with any recommendations for legislative or other actions it deems appropriate, no later than July 1, 1977, and from time to time thereafter as it deems appropriate.

SEC. 14. (a) As used in this resolution, the term "intelligence activities" includes'
(1) the collection, analysis, production, dissemination, or use of information which relates to any foreign country, or any government, political group, party, military force, movement, or other association in such foreign country, and which relates to the defense, foreign policy, national security, or related policies of the United States, and other activity which is in support of such activities;
(2) activities taken to counter similar activities directed against the United States;
(3) covert or clandestine activities affecting the relations of the United States with any foreign government, political group, party, military force, movement or other association;
(4) the collection, analysis, production, dissemination, or use of information about activities of persons within the United States, its territories and posses-

sions, or nationals of the United States abroad whose political and related activities pose, or may be considered by any department, agency, bureau, office, division, instrumentality, or employee of the United States to pose, a threat to the internal security of the United States, and covert or clandestine activities directed against such persons. Such term does not include tactical foreign military intelligence serving no national policymaking function. (b) As used in this resolution, the term "department or agency" includes any organization, committee, council, establishment, or office within the Federal Government.

(c) For purposes of this resolution, reference to any department, agency, bureau, or subdivision shall include a reference to any successor department, agency, bureau, or subdivision to the extent that such successor engages in intelligence activities now conducted by the department, agency, bureau, or subdivision referred to in this resolution.

SEC. 15. (a) In addition to other committee staff selected by the Select Committee, the Select Committee shall hire or appoint one employee for each member of the Select Committee to serve as such Member's designated representative on the Select Committee. The Select Committee shall only hire or appoint an employee chosen by the respective Member of the Select Committee for whom the employee will serve as the designated representative on the Select Committee. (b) The Select Committee shall be afforded a supplement to its budget, to be determined by the Committee on Rules and Administration, to allow for the hire of each employee who fills the position of designated representative to the Select Committee. The designated representative shall have office space and appropriate office equipment in the Select Committee spaces. Designated personal representatives shall have the same access to Committee staff, information, records, and databases as Select Committee staff, as determined by the Chairman and Vice Chairman. (c) The designated employee shall meet all the requirements of relevant statutes, Senate rules, and committee security clearance requirements for employment by the Select Committee.

(d) Of the funds made available to the Select Committee for personnel—

(1) not more than 60 percent shall be under the control of the Chairman; and

(2) not less than 40 percent shall be under the control of the Vice Chairman.

SEC. 16. Nothing in this resolution shall be construed as constituting acquiescence by the Senate in any practice, or in the conduct of any activity, not otherwise authorized by law.

SEC. 17. (a)(1) Except as otherwise provided in subsection (b), the Select Committee shall have jurisdiction for reviewing, holding hearings, and reporting the nominations of civilian persons nominated by the President to fill all positions within the intelligence community requiring the advice and consent of the Senate.

(2) Other committees with jurisdiction over the nominees' executive branch department may hold hearings and interviews with such persons, but only the Select Committee shall report such nominations. (b)(1) With respect to the confirmation of the Assistant Attorney General for National Security, or any successor position, the nomination of any individual by the President to serve in such position shall be referred to the Committee on the Judiciary and, if and when reported, to the Select Committee for not to exceed 20 calendar days, except that in cases when the 20-day period expires while the Senate is in recess, the Select Committee shall have 5 additional calendar days after the Senate reconvenes to report the nomination. (2) If, upon the expiration of the period described in paragraph (1), the Select Committee has not reported the nomination, such nomination shall be automatically discharged from the Select Committee and placed on the Executive Calendar.

APPENDIX B

INTELLIGENCE PROVISIONS IN S. RES. 445, 108TH CONG., 2D SESS. (2004) WHICH WERE NOT INCORPORATED IN S. RES. 400, 94TH CONG., 2D SESS. (1976)

TITLE III—COMMITTEE STATUS

* * * * * * *

SEC. 301(b) INTELLIGENCE.—The Select Committee on Intelligence shall be treated as a committee listed under paragraph 2 of rule XXV of the Standing Rules of the Senate for purposes of the Standing Rules of the Senate.

TITLE IV—INTELLIGENCE-RELATED SUBCOMMITTEES SEC. 401. SUBCOMMITTEE RELATED TO INTELLIGENCE OVERSIGHT.

(a) ESTABLISHMENT.—There is established in the Select Committee on Intelligence a Subcommittee on Oversight which shall be in addition to any other subcommittee established by the Select Committee.

(b) RESPONSIBILITY.—The Subcommittee on Oversight shall be responsible for ongoing oversight of intelligence activities.

SEC. 402. SUBCOMMITTEE RELATED TO INTELLIGENCE APPROPRIATIONS.

(a) ESTABLISHMENT.—There is established in the Committee on Appropriations a Subcommittee on Intelligence. The Committee on Appropriations shall reorganize into 13 subcommittees as soon as possible after the convening of the 109th Congress.

(b) JURISDICTION.—The Subcommittee on Intelligence of the Committee on Appropriations shall have jurisdiction over funding for intelligence matters, as determined by the Senate Committee on Appropriations.

APPENDIX C

RULE 26.5(B) OF THE STANDING RULES OF THE SENATE (REFERRED TO IN COMMITTEE RULE 2.1)

Each meeting of a committee, or any subcommittee thereof, including meetings to conduct hearings, shall be open to the public, except that a meeting or series of meetings by a committee or a subcommittee thereof on the same subject for a period of no more than fourteen calendar days may be closed to the public on a motion made and seconded to go into closed session to discuss only whether the matters enumerated in clauses (1) through (6) would require the meeting to be closed, followed immediately by a record vote in open session by a majority of the members of the committee or subcommittee when it is determined that the matters to be discussed or the testimony to be taken at such meeting or meetings—

(1) will disclose matters necessary to be kept secret in the interests of national defense or the confidential conduct of the foreign relations of the United States;

(2) will relate solely to matters of committee staff personnel or internal staff management or procedure;

(3) will tend to charge an individual with crime or misconduct, to disgrace or injure the professional standing of an individual, or otherwise to expose an individual to public contempt or obloquy, or will represent a clearly unwarranted invasion of the privacy of an individual;

(4) will disclose the identity of any informer or law enforcement agent or will disclose any information relating to the investigation or prosecution of a criminal offense that is required to be kept secret in the interests of effective law enforcement;

(5) will disclose information relating to the trade secrets of financial or commercial information pertaining specifically to a given person if—

(A) an Act of Congress requires the information to be kept confidential by Government officers and employees; or

(B) the information has been obtained by the Government on a confidential basis, other than through an application by such person for a specific Government financial or other benefit, and is required to be kept secret in order to prevent undue injury to the competitive position of such person; or

(6) may divulge matters required to be kept confidential under other provisions of law or Government regulations.

House Permanent Select Committee on Intelligence

Rules of Procedure for the Permanent Select Committee on Intelligence

112th Congress

1. MEETING DAY
Regular Meeting Day for the Full Committee.
The regular meeting day of the Committee for the transaction of Committee business shall be the first Thursday of each month, unless otherwise directed by the Chair.
2. NOTICE FOR MEETINGS
(a) Generally. In the case of any meeting of the Committee, the Chief Clerk of the Committee shall provide reasonable notice to every member of the Committee. Such notice shall provide the time, place, and subject matter of the meeting, and shall be made consistent with the provisions of clause 2(g)(3) of House Rule XI.
(b) Hearings. Except as provided in subsection (d), a Committee hearing may not commence earlier than one week after such notice.
(c) Business Meetings. Except as provided in subsection (d), a Committee business meeting may not commence earlier than the third day on which Members have notice thereof.
(d) Exception. A hearing or business meeting may begin sooner than otherwise specified in either of the following circumstances (in which case the Chair shall provide the notice at the earliest possible time):

(1) the Chair, with the concurrence of the Ranking Minority Member, determines there is good cause; or

(2) the Committee so determines by majority vote in the presence of the number of members required under the rules of the committee for the transaction of business.

(e) Definition. For purposes of this rule, "notice" means:

(1) Written notification; or

(2) Notification delivered by facsimile transmission, regular mail, or electronic mail.

3. PREPARATIONS FOR COMMITTEE MEETINGS
(a) Generally. Designated Committee Staff, as directed by the Chair, shall brief members of the Committee at a time sufficiently prior to any Committee meeting in order to:

(1) Assist Committee members in preparation for such meeting; and

(2) Determine which matters members wish considered during any meeting.

(b) Briefing Materials.

(1) Such a briefing shall, at the request of a member, include a list of all pertinent papers, and such other materials, that have been obtained by the Committee that bear on matters to be considered at the meeting; and

(2) The Staff Director shall also recommend to the Chair any testimony, papers, or other materials to be presented to the Committee at the meeting of the Committee.

4. OPEN MEETINGS

(a) Generally. Pursuant to House Rule XI, but subject to the limitations of subsections (b) and (c), Committee meetings held for the transaction of business and Committee hearings shall be open to the public.

(b) Meetings. Any meeting or portion thereof, for the transaction of business, including the markup of legislation, or any hearing or portion thereof, shall be closed to the public, if the Committee determines by record vote in open session, with a majority of the Committee present, that disclosure of the matters to be discussed may:

(1) Endanger national security;

(2) Compromise sensitive law enforcement information;

(3) Tend to defame, degrade, or incriminate any person; or

(4) Otherwise violate any law or Rule of the House.

(c) Hearings. The Committee may vote to close a Committee hearing pursuant to clause 11(d)(2) of House Rule X, regardless of whether a majority is present, so long as at least two members of the Committee are present, one of whom is a member of the Minority and votes upon the motion.

(d) Briefings. Committee briefings shall be closed to the public.

5. QUORUM

(a) Hearings. For purposes of taking testimony, or receiving evidence, a quorum shall consist of two Committee members, at least one of whom is a member of the Majority.

(b) Other Committee Proceedings. For purposes of the transaction of all other Committee business, other than the consideration of a motion to close a hearing as described in rule 4(c), a quorum shall consist of a majority of members.

6. PROCEDURES FOR AMENDMENTS AND VOTES

(a) Amendments. When a bill or resolution is being considered by the Committee, members shall provide the Chief Clerk in a timely manner with a sufficient number of written copies of any amendment offered, so as to enable each member present to receive a copy thereof prior to taking action. A point of order may be made against any amendment not reduced to writing. A copy of each such amendment shall be maintained in the public records of the Committee.

(b) Reporting Record Votes. Whenever the Committee reports any measure or matter by record vote, the report of the Committee upon such measure or matter shall include a tabulation of the votes cast in favor of, and the votes cast in opposition to, such measure or matter.

(c) Postponement of Further Proceedings. In accordance with clause 2(h) of House Rule XI, the Chair is authorized to postpone further proceedings when a record vote is ordered on the question of approving a measure or matter or adopting an amendment. The Chair may resume proceedings on a postponed request at any time after reasonable notice. When proceedings resume on a postponed question, notwithstanding any intervening order for the previous question, an underlying proposition shall remain subject to further debate or amendment to the same extent as when the question was postponed.

(d) Availability of Record Votes on Committee Website. In addition to any other requirement of the Rules of the House, the Chair shall make the record votes on any measure or matter on which a record vote is taken, other than a motion to close a Committee hearing, briefing, or meeting, available on the Committee's website not later than 2 business days after such vote is taken. Such record shall include an unclassified description of the amendment, motion, order, or other proposition, the name of each member voting in favor of, and each member voting in opposition to such amendment, motion, order, or proposition, and the names of those members of the Committee present but not voting.

7. SUBCOMMITTEES

(a) Generally.

(1) Creation of subcommittees shall be by majority vote of the Committee.

(2) Subcommittees shall deal with such legislation and oversight of programs and policies as the Committee may direct.

(3) Subcommittees shall be governed by these rules.

(4) For purposes of these rules, any reference herein to the "Committee" shall be interpreted to include subcommittees, unless otherwise specifically provided.

(b) Establishment of Subcommittees. The Committee establishes the following subcommittees:

(1) Subcommittee on Terrorism, Human Intelligence, Analysis, and Counterintelligence;

(2) Subcommittee on Technical and Tactical Intelligence; and,

(3) Subcommittee on Oversight and Investigations.

(c) Subcommittee Membership.

(1) Generally. Each member of the Committee may be assigned to at least one of the subcommittees.

(2) Ex Officio Membership. In the event that the Chair and Ranking Minority Member of the full Committee do not choose to sit as regular voting members of one or more of the subcommittees, each is authorized to sit as an ex officio member of the subcommittees and participate in the work of the subcommittees. When sitting ex officio, however, they:

(A) Shall not have a vote in the subcommittee; and

(B) Shall not be counted for purposes of determining a quorum.

(d) Regular Meeting Day for Subcommittees. There is no regular meeting day for subcommittees.

8. PROCEDURES FOR TAKING TESTIMONY OR RECEIVING EVIDENCE

(a) Notice. Adequate notice shall be given to all witnesses appearing before the Committee.

(b) Oath or Affirmation. The Chair may require testimony of witnesses to be given under oath or affirmation.

(c) Administration of Oath or Affirmation. Upon the determination that a witness shall testify under oath or affirmation, any member of the Committee designated by the Chair may administer the oath or affirmation.

(d) Questioning of Witnesses.

(1) Generally. Questioning of witnesses before the Committee shall be conducted by members of the Committee.

(2) Exceptions.

(A) The Chair, in consultation with the Ranking Minority Member, may determine that Committee Staff will be authorized to question witnesses at a hearing in accordance with clause (2)(j) of House Rule XI.

(B) The Chair and Ranking Minority Member are each authorized to designate Committee Staff to conduct such questioning.

(e) Counsel for the Witness.

(1) Generally. Witnesses before the Committee may be accompanied by counsel, subject to the requirements of paragraph (2).

(2) Counsel Clearances Required. In the event that a meeting of the Committee has been closed because the subject to be discussed deals with classified information, counsel accompanying a witness before the Committee must possess the requisite security clearance and provide proof of such clearance to the Committee at least 24 hours prior to the meeting at which the counsel intends to be present.

(3) Failure to Obtain Counsel. Any witness who is unable to obtain counsel should notify the Committee. If such notification occurs at least 24 hours prior to the witness' appearance before the Committee, the Committee shall then endeavor to obtain voluntary counsel for the witness. Failure to obtain counsel, however, will not excuse the witness from appearing and testifying.

(4) Conduct of Counsel for Witnesses. Counsel for witnesses appearing before the Committee shall conduct themselves ethically and professionally at all times in their dealings with the Committee.

(A) A majority of members of the Committee may, should circumstances warrant, find that counsel for a witness before the Committee failed to conduct himself or herself in an ethical or professional manner.

(B) Upon such finding, counsel may be subject to appropriate disciplinary action.

(5) Temporary Removal of Counsel. The Chair may remove counsel during any proceeding before the Committee for failure to act in an ethical and professional manner.

(6) Committee Reversal. A majority of the members of the Committee may vote to overturn the decision of the Chair to remove counsel for a witness.

(7) Role of Counsel for Witness.

(A) Counsel for a witness:

(i) Shall not be allowed to examine witnesses before the Committee, either directly or through cross-examination; but

(ii) May submit questions in writing to the Committee that counsel wishes propounded to a witness; or

(iii) May suggest, in writing to the Committee, the presentation of other evidence or the calling of other *witnesses.

(B) The Committee may make such use of any such questions, or suggestions, as the Committee deems appropriate.

(f) Statements by Witnesses.

(1) Generally. A witness may make a statement, which shall be brief and relevant, at the beginning and at the conclusion of the witness' testimony.

(2) Length. Each such statement shall not exceed five minutes in length, unless otherwise determined by the Chair.

(3) Submission to the Committee. Any witness desiring to submit a written statement for the record of the proceeding shall submit a copy of the statement to the Chief Clerk of the Committee.

(A) Such statements shall ordinarily be submitted no less than 48 hours in advance of the witness' appearance before the Committee and shall be submitted in written and electronic format.

(B) In the event that the hearing was called with less than 24 hours notice, written statements should be submitted as soon as practicable prior to the hearing.

(g) Objections and Ruling.

(1) Generally. Any objection raised by a witness, or counsel for the witness, shall be ruled upon by the Chair, and such ruling shall be the ruling of the Committee.

(2) Committee Action. A ruling by the Chair may be overturned upon a majority vote of the Committee.

(h) Transcripts.

(1) Transcript Required. A transcript shall be made of the testimony of each witness appearing before the Committee during any hearing of the Committee.

(2) Opportunity to Inspect. Any witness testifying before the Committee shall be given a reasonable opportunity to inspect the transcript of the hearing, and may be accompanied by counsel to determine whether such testimony was correctly transcribed. Such counsel:

(A) May review the transcript only if he or she has the appropriate security clearances necessary to review any classified aspect of the transcript; and

(B) Should, to the extent possible, be the same counsel that was present for such classified testimony.

(3) Corrections.

(A) Pursuant to Rule XI of the House Rules, any corrections the witness desires to make in a transcript shall be limited to technical, grammatical, and typographical corrections. (B) Corrections may not be made to change the substance of the Testimony.

(C) Such corrections shall be submitted in writing to the Committee within 7 days after the transcript is made available to the witnesses. (D) Any questions arising with respect to such corrections shall be decided by the Chair.

(4) Copy for the Witness. At the request of the witness, any portion of the witness' testimony given in executive session shall be made available to that witness if that testimony is: subsequently quoted or intended to be made part of a public record. Such testimony shall be made available to the witness at the witness' expense.

(i) Requests to Testify.

(1) Generally. The Committee will consider requests to testify on any matter or measure pending before the Committee.

(2) Recommendations for Additional Evidence. Any person who believes that testimony, other evidence, or commentary, presented at a public hearing may tend to affect adversely that person's reputation may submit to the Committee, in writing:

(A) A request to appear personally before the Committee;

(B) A sworn statement of facts relevant to the testimony, evidence, or commentary; or

(C) Proposed questions for the cross-examination of other witnesses.

(3) Committee Discretion. The Committee may take those actions it deems appropriate with respect to such requests.

(j) Contempt Procedures. Citations for contempt of Congress shall be forwarded to the House only if:

(1) Reasonable notice is provided to all members of the Committee of a meeting to be held to consider any such contempt recommendations;

(2) The Committee has met and considered the contempt allegations;

(3) The subject of the allegations was afforded an opportunity to state either in writing or in person, why he or she should not be held in contempt; and

(4) The Committee agreed by majority vote to forward the citation recommendations to the House.

(k) Release of Name of Witness.

(1) Generally. At the request of a witness scheduled to be heard by the Committee, the name of that witness shall not be released publicly prior to, or after, the witness' appearance before the Committee.

(2) Exceptions. Notwithstanding paragraph (1), the Chair may authorize the release to the public of the name of any witness scheduled to appear before the Committee.

9. INVESTIGATIONS

(a) Commencing Investigations. The Committee shall conduct investigations only if approved by the Chair, in consultation with the Ranking Minority Member.

(b) Conducting Investigations. An authorized investigation may be conducted by members of the Committee or Committee Staff designated by the Chair, in consultation with the Ranking Minority Member, to undertake any such investigation.

10. SUBPOENAS

(a) Generally. All subpoenas shall be authorized by the Chair of the full Committee, upon consultation with the Ranking Minority Member, or by vote of the Committee.

(b) Subpoena Contents. Any subpoena authorized by the Chair of the full Committee, or the Committee, may compel:

(1) The attendance of witnesses and testimony before the Committee; or

(2) The production of memoranda, documents, records, or any other tangible item.

(c) Signing of Subpoena. A subpoena authorized by the Chair of the full Committee, or the Committee, may be signed by the Chair, or by any member of the Committee designated to do so by the Committee.

(d) Subpoena Service. A subpoena authorized by the Chair of the full Committee, or the Committee, may be served by any person designated to do so by the Chair.

(e) Other Requirements. Each subpoena shall have attached thereto a copy of these rules.

11. COMMITTEE STAFF

(a) Definition. For the purpose of these rules, "Committee Staff" or "Staff of the Committee" means:

(1) Employees of the Committee;

(2) Consultants to the Committee;

(3) Employees of other Government agencies detailed to the Committee; or

(4) Any other person engaged by contract, or otherwise, to perform services for, or at the request of, the Committee.

(b) Appointment of Committee Staff and Security Requirements.

(1) Chair's Authority. Except as provided in paragraph (2), the Committee Staff shall be appointed, and may be removed, by the Chair and shall work under the general supervision and direction of the Chair.

(2) Staff Assistance to Minority Membership. Except as provided in paragraphs (3) and (4), and except as otherwise provided by Committee Rules, the Committee Staff provided to the Minority Party members of the Committee shall be appointed, and may be removed, by the Ranking Minority Member of the Committee, and shall work under the general supervision and direction of such member.

(3) Security Clearance Required. All offers of employment for prospective Committee Staff positions shall be contingent upon:

(A) The results of a background investigation; and

(B) A determination by the Chair that requirements for the appropriate security clearances have been met.

(4) Security Requirements. Notwithstanding paragraph (2), the Chair shall supervise and direct the Committee Staff with respect to the security and nondisclosure of classified information. Committee Staff shall comply with requirements necessary to ensure the security and nondisclosure of classified information as determined by the Chair in consultation with the Ranking Minority Member.

12. LIMIT ON DISCUSSION OF CLASSIFIED WORK OF THE COMMITTEE

(a) Prohibition.

(1) Generally. Except as otherwise provided by these rules and the Rules of the House of Representatives, members of the Committee and Committee Staff

shall not at any time, either during that person's tenure as a member of the Committee or as Committee Staff, or anytime thereafter, discuss or disclose, or cause to be discussed or disclosed:

(A) The classified substance of the work of the Committee;

(B) Any information received by the Committee in executive session;

(C) Any classified information received by the Committee from any source; or

(D) The substance of any hearing that was closed to the public pursuant to these rules or the Rules of the House.

(2) Non-Disclosure in Proceedings.

(A) Members of the Committee and the Committee Staff shall not discuss either the substance or procedure of the work of the Committee with any person not a member of the Committee or the Committee Staff in connection with any proceeding, judicial or otherwise, either during the person's tenure as a member of the Committee, or of the Committee Staff, or at any time thereafter, except as directed by the Committee in accordance with the Rules of the House and these rules.

(B) In the event of the termination of the Committee, members and Committee Staff shall be governed in these matters in a manner determined by the House concerning discussions of the classified work of the Committee.

(3) Exceptions.

(A) Notwithstanding the provisions of subsection (a)(1), members of the Committee and the Committee Staff may discuss and disclose those matters described in subsection (a)(1) with:

(i) Members and staff of the Senate Select Committee on Intelligence designated by the chair of that committee;

(ii) The chairmen and ranking minority members of the House and Senate Committees on Appropriations and staff of those committees designated by the chairmen of those committees; and,

(iii) The chair and ranking minority member of the Subcommittee on Defense of the House Committee on Appropriations and staff of that subcommittee as designated by the chair of that subcommittee, or Members of that subcommittee designated by the Chair pursuant to clause (g)(1) of Committee Rule 12.

(B) Notwithstanding the provisions of subsection (a)(1), members of the Committee and the Committee Staff may discuss and disclose only that budget-related information necessary to facilitate the enactment of the annual defense authorization bill with the chairmen and ranking minority members of the House and Senate Committees on Armed Services and the staff of those committees as designated by the chairmen of those committees.

(C) Notwithstanding the provisions of subsection (a)(1), members of the Committee and the Committee Staff may discuss with and disclose to the chair and ranking minority member of a subcommittee of the House Appropriations Committee with jurisdiction over an agency or program within the National Intelligence Program (NIP), and staff of that subcommittee as designated by the chair of that subcommittee, only that budget-related information necessary to facilitate the enactment of an appropriations bill within which is included an appropriation for an agency or program within the NIP.

(D) The Chair may, in consultation with the Ranking Minority Member, upon the written request to the Chair from the Inspector General of an element of the Intelligence Community, grant access to Committee transcripts or documents that are relevant to an investigation of an allegation of possible false testimony or other inappropriate conduct before the Committee, or that are otherwise relevant to the Inspector General's investigation.

(E) Upon the written request of the head of an Intelligence Community element, the Chair may, in consultation with the Ranking Minority Member, make available Committee briefing or hearing transcripts to that element for review by that element if a representative of that element testified, presented information to the Committee, or was present at the briefing or hearing the transcript of which is requested for review.

(F) Members and Committee Staff may discuss and disclose such matters as otherwise directed by the Committee.

(4) Records of Closed Proceedings: Any records or notes taken by any person memorializing material otherwise prohibited from disclosure by members of the Committee and Committee staff under these rules, including information received in executive session and the substance of any hearing or briefing that was closed to the public, shall remain Committee material subject to these rules and may not be publicly discussed, disclosed, or caused to be publicly discussed or disclosed, unless authorized by the Committee consistent with these rules.

(b) Non-Disclosure Agreement.

(1) Generally. All Committee Staff must, before joining the Committee Staff, agree in writing, as a condition of employment, not to divulge or cause to be divulged any classified information which comes into such person's possession while a member of the Committee Staff, to any person not a member of the Committee or the Committee Staff, except as authorized by the Committee in accordance with the Rules of the House and these rules.

(2) Other Requirements. In the event of the termination of the Committee, members and Committee Staff must follow any determination by the House of Representatives with respect to the protection of classified information received while a member of the Committee or as Committee Staff.

(3) Requests for Testimony of Staff.

(A) All Committee Staff must, as a condition of employment, agree in writing to notify the Committee immediately of any request for testimony received while a member of the Committee Staff, or at any time thereafter, concerning any classified information received by such person while a member of the Committee Staff.

(B) Committee Staff shall not disclose, in response to any such request for testimony, any such classified information, except as authorized by the Committee in accordance with the Rules of the House and these rules.

(C) In the event of the termination of the Committee, Committee Staff will be subject to any determination made by the House of Representatives with respect to any requests for testimony involving classified information received while a member of the Committee Staff.

13. CLASSIFIED MATERIAL

(a) Receipt of Classified Information.

(1) Generally. In the case of any information that has been classified under established security procedures and submitted to the Committee by any source, the Committee shall receive such classified information as executive session material.

(2) Staff Receipt of Classified Materials. For purposes of receiving classified information, the Committee Staff is authorized to accept information on behalf of the Committee.

(b) Non-Disclosure of Classified Information. Any classified information received by the Committee, from any source, shall not be disclosed to any person not a member of the Committee or the Committee Staff, or otherwise released, except as authorized by the Committee in accordance with the Rules of the House and these rules.

(c) Exception for Non-Exclusive Materials.

(1) Non-Exclusive Materials. Any materials provided to the Committee by the executive branch, if provided in whole or in part for the purpose of review by members who are not members of the Committee, shall be received or held by the Committee on a non-exclusive basis. Classified information provided to the Committee shall be considered to have been provided on an exclusive basis unless the executive branch provides a specific, written statement to the contrary.

(2) Access for Non-Committee Members. In the case of materials received on a non-exclusive basis, the Chair, in consultation with the Ranking Minority Member, may grant non-Committee members access to such materials in accordance with the requirements of Rule 14(f)(4), notwithstanding paragraphs (1), (2), and (3) of Rule 14.

14. PROCEDURES RELATED TO HANDLING OF CLASSIFIED INFORMATION

(a) Security Measures.

(1) Strict Security. The Committee's offices shall operate under strict security procedures administered by the Director of Security and Registry of the Committee under the direct supervision of the Staff Director.

(2) U.S. Capitol Police Presence Required. At least one U.S. Capitol Police officer shall be on duty at all times outside the entrance to Committee offices to control entry of all persons to such offices.

(3) Identification Required. Before entering the Committee's offices all persons shall identify themselves to the U.S. Capitol Police officer described in paragraph (2) and to a member of the Committee or Committee Staff.

(4) Maintenance of Classified Materials. Classified documents shall be segregated and maintained in approved security storage locations.

(5) Examination of Classified Materials. Classified documents in the committee's possession shall be examined in an appropriately secure manner.

(6) Prohibition on Removal of Classified Materials. Removal of any classified document from the Committee's offices is strictly prohibited, except as provided by these rules.

(7) Exception. Notwithstanding the prohibition set forth in paragraph (6), a classified document, or copy thereof, may be removed from the Committee's offices in furtherance of official Committee business. Appropriate security procedures shall govern the handling of any classified documents removed from the Committee's offices.

(b) Access to Classified Information by Members. All members of the Committee shall at all times have access to all classified papers and other material received by the Committee from any source.

(c) Need-to-know.

(1) Generally. Committee Staff shall have access to any classified information provided to the Committee on a strict "need-to-know" basis, as determined by the Committee, and under the Committee's direction by the Staff Director.

(2) Appropriate Clearances Required. Committee Staff must have the appropriate clearances prior to any access to compartmented information.

(d) Oath.

(1) Requirement. Before any member of the Committee, or the Committee Staff, shall have access to classified information, the following oath shall be executed:

"I do solemnly swear (or affirm) that I will not disclose or cause to be disclosed any classified information received in the course of my service on the House Permanent Select Committee on Intelligence, except when authorized to do so by the Committee or the House of Representatives."

(2) Copy. A copy of such executed oath shall be retained in the files of the Committee.

(e) Registry.

(1) Generally. The Committee shall maintain a registry that:

(A) Provides a brief description of the content of all classified documents provided to the Committee by the executive branch that remain in the possession of the Committee; and

(B) Lists by number all such documents.

(2) Designation by the Staff Director. The Staff Director shall designate a member of the Committee Staff to be responsible for the organization and daily maintenance of such registry.

(3) Availability. Such registry shall be available to all members of the Committee and Committee Staff.

(f) Requests by Members of Other Committees. Pursuant to the Rules of the House, members who are not members of the Committee may be granted access to such classified transcripts, records, data, charts, or files of the Committee, and be admitted on a non-participatory basis to classified hearings of the Committee involving discussions of classified material in the following manner:

(1) Written Notification Required. Members who desire to examine classified materials in the possession of the Committee, or to attend Committee hearings or briefings on a non-participatory basis, must notify the Chief Clerk of the Committee in writing. Such notification shall state with specificity the justification for the request and the need for access.

(2) Committee Consideration. The Committee shall consider each such request by non-Committee members at the earliest practicable opportunity. The Committee shall determine, by record vote, what action it deems appropriate in light of all of the circumstances of each request. In its determination, the Committee shall consider:

(A) The sensitivity to the national defense or the confidential conduct of the foreign relations of the United States of the information sought;

(B) The likelihood of its being directly or indirectly disclosed;

(C) The jurisdictional interest of the member making the request; and

(D) Such other concerns, constitutional or otherwise, as may affect the public interest of the United States.

(3) Committee Action. After consideration of the member's request, the Committee may take any action it deems appropriate under the circumstances, including but not limited to:

(A) Approving the request, in whole or part;

(B) Denying the request;

(C) Providing the requested information or material in a different form than that sought by the member; or

(D) Making the requested information or material available to all members of the House.

(4) Requirements for Access by Non-Committee Members. Prior to a non-Committee member being given access to classified information pursuant to this subsection, the requesting member shall:

(A) Provide the Committee a copy of the oath executed by such member pursuant to House Rule XXIII, clause 13; and

(B) Agree in writing not to divulge any classified information provided to the member, pursuant to this subsection, to any person not a member of the Committee or the Committee Staff, except as otherwise authorized by the Committee in accordance with the Rules of the House and these rules.

(5) Consultation Authorized. When considering member's request, the Committee may consult the Director of National Intelligence and such other officials it considers necessary.

(6) Finality of Committee Decision.

(A) Should the member making such a request disagree with the Committee's determination with respect to that request, or any part thereof, that member must notify the Committee in writing of such disagreement.

(B) The Committee shall subsequently consider the matter and decide, by record vote, what further action or recommendation, if any, the Committee will take.

(g) Admission of Designated Members of the Subcommittee on Defense of the Committee on Appropriations. Notwithstanding the provisions of subsection (f), the Chair may admit no more than three designated Members of the Subcommittee on Defense of the Committee on Appropriations to classified hearings and briefings of the Committee involving discussions of classified material. Such Members may also be granted access to classified transcripts, records, data, charts or files of the Committee incident to such attendance.

(1) Designation. The Chair may designate three Members of the Subcommittee to be eligible for admission in consultation with the Ranking Minority Member, of whom not more than two may be from the same political party. Such designation shall be effective for the entire Congress.

(2) Admission. The Chair may determine whether to admit designated Members at each hearing or briefing of the Committee involving discussions of classified material. If the Chair admits any of the designated Members to a particular hearing or briefing, all three of the designated Members shall be admitted to that hearing or briefing. Designated Members shall not be counted for quorum purposes and shall not have a vote in any meeting.

(3) Requirements for Access. Prior to being given access to classified information pursuant to this subsection, a designated Member shall:

(A) Provide the Committee a copy of the oath executed by such Member pursuant to House Rule XXIII, clause 13; and

(B) Agree in writing not to divulge any classified information provided to the Member pursuant to this subsection to any person not a Member of the Committee or a designated Member or authorized Staff of the Subcommittee on Defense of the Committee on Appropriations, except as otherwise authorized by the Committee in accordance with the Rules of the House and these rules.

(h) Advising the House or Other Committees. Pursuant to Section 501 of the National Security Act of 1947 (50 U.S.C. 413), and to the Rules of the House, the Committee shall call to the attention of the House, or to any other appropriate committee of the House, those matters requiring the attention of the House, or such other committee, on the basis of the following provisions:

(1) By Request of Committee Member. At the request of any member of the Committee to call to the attention of the House, or any other committee, executive session material in the Committee's possession, the Committee shall meet at the earliest practicable opportunity to consider that request.

(2) Committee Consideration of Request. The Committee shall consider the following factors, among any others it deems appropriate:

(A) The effect of the matter in question on the national defense or the foreign relations of the United States;

(B) Whether the matter in question involves sensitive intelligence sources and methods;

(C) Whether the matter in question otherwise raises questions affecting the national interest; and

(D) Whether the matter in question affects matters within the jurisdiction of another Committee of the House.

(3) Views of Other Committees. In examining such factors, the Committee may seek the opinion of members of the Committee appointed from standing committees of the House with jurisdiction over the matter in question, or submissions from such other committees.

(4) Other Advice. The Committee may, during its deliberations on such requests, seek the advice of any executive branch official.

(i) Reasonable Opportunity to Examine Materials. Before the Committee makes any decision regarding any request for access to any classified information in its possession, or a proposal to bring any matter to the attention of the House or another committee, members of the Committee shall have a reasonable opportunity to examine all pertinent testimony, documents, or other materials in the Committee's possession that may inform their decision on the question.

(j) Notification to the House. The Committee may bring a matter to the attention of the House when, after consideration of the factors set forth in this rule, it considers the matter in question so grave that it requires the attention of all members of the House, and time is of the essence, or for any reason the Committee finds compelling.

(k) Method of Disclosure to the House.

(1) Should the Committee decide by record vote that a matter requires the attention of the House as described in subsection (i), it shall make arrangements to notify the House promptly.

(2) In such cases, the Committee shall consider whether:

(A) To request an immediate secret session of the House (with time equally divided between the Majority and the Minority); or

(B) To publicly disclose the matter in question pursuant to clause 11(g) of House Rule X.

(l) Requirement to Protect Sources and Methods. In bringing a matter to the attention of the House, or another committee, the Committee, with due regard for the protection of intelligence sources and methods, shall take all necessary steps to safeguard materials or information relating to the matter in question.

(m) Availability of Information to Other Committees. The Committee, having determined that a matter shall be brought to the attention of another committee, shall ensure that such matter, including all classified information related to that matter, is promptly made available to the chair and ranking minority member of such other committee.

(n) Provision of Materials. The Director of Security and Registry for the Committee shall provide a copy of these rules, and the applicable portions of the Rules of the House of Representatives governing the handling of classified information, along with those materials determined by the Committee to be made available to such other committee of the House or non-Committee member.

(o) Ensuring Clearances and Secure Storage. The Director of Security and Registry shall ensure that such other committee or non-Committee member receiving such classified materials may properly store classified materials in a manner consistent with all governing rules, regulations, policies, procedures, and statutes.

(p) Log. The Director of Security and Registry for the Committee shall maintain a written record identifying the particular classified document or material provided to such other committee or non-Committee member, the reasons agreed upon by the Committee for approving such transmission, and the name of the committee or non-Committee member receiving such document or material.

(q) Miscellaneous Requirements.

(1) Staff Director's Additional Authority. The Staff Director is further empowered to provide for such additional measures, which he or she deems necessary, to protect such classified information authorized by the Committee to be provided to such other committee or non-Committee member.

(2) Notice to Originating Agency. In the event that the Committee authorizes the disclosure of classified information provided to the Committee by an agency of the executive branch to a non-Committee member or to another committee, the Chair may notify the providing agency of the Committee's action prior to the transmission of such classified information.

15. LEGISLATIVE CALENDAR

(a) Generally. The Chief Clerk, under the direction of the Staff Director, shall maintain a printed calendar that lists:

(1) The legislative measures introduced and referred to the Committee;

(2) The status of such measures; and

(3) Such other matters that the Committee may require.

(b) Revisions to the Calendar. The calendar shall be revised from time to time to show pertinent changes.

(c) Availability. A copy of each such revision shall be furnished to each member, upon request.

(d) Consultation with Appropriate Government Entities. Unless otherwise directed by the Committee, legislative measures referred to the Committee may be referred by the Chief Clerk to the appropriate department or agency of the Government for reports thereon.

16. COMMITTEE WEBSITE

The Chair shall maintain an official Committee web site for the purpose of furthering the Committee's legislative and oversight responsibilities, including communicating information about the Committee's activities to Committee members and other members of the House.

17. MOTIONS TO GO TO CONFERENCE

In accordance with clause 2(a) of House Rule XI, the Chair is authorized and directed to offer a privileged motion to go to conference under clause 1 of House Rule XXII whenever the Chair considers it appropriate.

18. COMMITTEE TRAVEL

(a) Authority. The Chair may authorize members and Committee Staff to travel on Committee business.

(b) Requests.

(1) Member Requests. Members requesting authorization for such travel shall state the purpose and length of the trip, and shall submit such request directly to the Chair.

(2) Committee Staff Requests. Committee Staff requesting authorization for such travel shall state the purpose and length of the trip, and shall submit such request through their supervisors to the Staff Director and the Chair.

(c) Notification to Members.

(1) Generally. Members shall be notified of all foreign travel of Committee Staff not accompanying a member.

(2) Content. All members are to be advised, prior to the commencement of such travel, of its length, nature, and purpose.

(d) Trip Reports.

(1) Generally. A full report of all issues discussed during any travel shall be submitted to the Chief Clerk of the Committee within a reasonable period of time following the completion of such trip.

(2) Availability of Reports. Such report shall be:

(A) Available for review by any member or appropriately cleared Committee Staff; and

(B) Considered executive session material for purposes of these rules.

(e) Limitations on Travel.

(1) Generally. The Chair is not authorized to permit travel on Committee business of Committee Staff who have not satisfied the requirements of subsection (d) of this rule.

(2) Exception. The Chair may authorize Committee Staff to travel on Committee business, notwithstanding the requirements of subsections (d) and (e) of this rule,

(A) At the specific request of a member of the Committee; or

(B) In the event there are circumstances beyond the control of the Committee Staff hindering compliance with such requirements.

(f) Definitions. For purposes of this rule the term "reasonable period of time" means:

(1) No later than 60 days after returning from a foreign trip; and

(2) No later than 30 days after returning from a domestic trip.

19. DISCIPLINARY ACTIONS

(a) Generally. The Committee shall immediately consider whether disciplinary action shall be taken in the case of any member of the Committee Staff alleged to have failed to conform to any rule of the House of Representatives or to these rules.

(b) Exception. In the event the House of Representatives is:

(1) In a recess period in excess of 3 days; or

(2) Has adjourned sine die; the Chair of the full Committee, in consultation with the Ranking Minority Member, may take such immediate disciplinary actions deemed necessary.

(c) Available Actions. Such disciplinary action may include immediate dismissal from the Committee Staff.

(d) Notice to Members. All members shall be notified as soon as practicable, either by facsimile transmission or regular mail, of any disciplinary action taken by the Chair pursuant to subsection (b).

(e) Reconsideration of Chair's Actions. A majority of the members of the full Committee may vote to overturn the decision of the Chair to take disciplinary action pursuant to subsection (b).

PROPOSED FEDERAL STATUTES

Cybersecurity Enhancement Act of 2013m H.R. 756

AN ACT

To advance cybersecurity research, development, and technical standards, and for other purposes.

Be it enacted by the Senate and House of Representatives of the United States of America in Congress assembled,

SECTION 1. SHORT TITLE.

This Act may be cited as the 'Cybersecurity Enhancement Act of 2013'.

TITLE I—RESEARCH AND DEVELOPMENT

SEC. 101. DEFINITIONS.

In this title:

(1) NATIONAL COORDINATION OFFICE—The term National Coordination Office means the National Coordination Office for the Networking and Information Technology Research and Development program.

(2) PROGRAM—The term Program means the Networking and Information Technology Research and Development program which has been established under section 101 of the High-Performance Computing Act of 1991 (15 U.S.C. 5511).

SEC. 102. FINDINGS.

Section 2 of the Cyber Security Research and Development Act (15 U.S.C. 7401) is amended—

(1) by amending paragraph (1) to read as follows:

'(1) Advancements in information and communications technology have resulted in a globally interconnected network of government, commercial, scientific, and education infrastructures, including critical infrastructures for electric power, natural gas and petroleum production and distribution, telecommunications, transportation, water supply, banking and finance, and emergency and government services.';

(2) in paragraph (2), by striking 'Exponential increases in interconnectivity have facilitated enhanced communications, economic growth,' and inserting 'These advancements have significantly contributed to the growth of the United States economy,';

(3) by amending paragraph (3) to read as follows:

'(3) The Cyberspace Policy Review published by the President in May, 2009, concluded that our information technology and communications infrastructure is vulnerable and has 'suffered intrusions that have allowed criminals to steal hundreds of millions of dollars and nation-states and other entities to steal intellectual property and sensitive military information'.'; and

(4) by amending paragraph (6) to read as follows:

'(6) While African-Americans, Hispanics, and Native Americans constitute 33 percent of the college-age population, members of these minorities comprise less than 20 percent of bachelor degree recipients in the field of computer sciences.'.

SEC. 103. CYBERSECURITY STRATEGIC RESEARCH AND DEVELOPMENT PLAN.

(a) In General—Not later than 12 months after the date of enactment of this Act, the agencies identified in subsection 101(a)(3)(B)(i) through (x) of the High-Performance Computing Act of 1991 (15 U.S.C. 5511(a)(3)(B)(i) through (x)) or designated under section 101(a)(3)(B)(xi) of such Act, working through the National Science and Technology Council and with the assistance of the National Coordination Office, shall transmit to Congress a strategic plan based on an assessment of cybersecurity risk to guide the overall direction of Federal cybersecurity and information assurance research and development for information technology and networking systems. Once every 3 years after the initial strategic plan is transmitted to Congress under this section, such agencies shall prepare and transmit to Congress an update of such plan.

(b) Contents of Plan—The strategic plan required under subsection (a) shall—

(1) specify and prioritize near-term, mid-term and long-term research objectives, including objectives associated with the research areas identified in section 4(a)(1) of the Cyber Security Research and Development Act (15 U.S.C. 7403(a)(1)) and how the near-term objectives complement research and development areas in which the private sector is actively engaged;

(2) describe how the Program will focus on innovative, transformational technologies with the potential to enhance the security, reliability, resilience, and trustworthiness of the digital infrastructure, and to protect consumer privacy;

(3) describe how the Program will foster the rapid transfer of research and development results into new cybersecurity technologies and applications for the timely benefit of society and the national interest, including through the dissemination of best practices and other outreach activities;

(4) describe how the Program will establish and maintain a national research infrastructure for creating, testing, and evaluating the next generation of secure networking and information technology systems;

(5) describe how the Program will facilitate access by academic researchers to the infrastructure described in paragraph (4), as well as to relevant data, including event data;

(6) describe how the Program will engage females and individuals identified in section 33 or 34 of the Science and Engineering Equal Opportunities Act (42 U.S.C. 1885a or 1885b) to foster a more diverse workforce in this area; and

(7) describe how the Program will help to recruit and prepare veterans for the Federal cybersecurity workforce.

(c) Development of Roadmap—The agencies described in subsection (a) shall develop and annually update an implementation roadmap for the strategic plan required in this section. Such roadmap shall—

(1) specify the role of each Federal agency in carrying out or sponsoring research and development to meet the research objectives of the strategic plan, including a description of how progress toward the research objectives will be evaluated;

(2) specify the funding allocated to each major research objective of the strategic plan and the source of funding by agency for the current fiscal year; and

(3) estimate the funding required for each major research objective of the strategic plan for the following 3 fiscal years.

(d) Recommendations—In developing and updating the strategic plan under subsection (a), the agencies involved shall solicit recommendations and advice from—

(1) the advisory committee established under section 101(b)(1) of the High-Performance Computing Act of 1991 (15 U.S.C. 5511(b)(1)); and

(2) a wide range of stakeholders, including industry, academia, including representatives of minority serving institutions and community colleges, National Laboratories, and other relevant organizations and institutions.

(e) Appending to Report—The implementation roadmap required under subsection (c), and its annual updates, shall be appended to the report required under section 101(a)(2)(D) of the High-Performance Computing Act of 1991 (15 U.S.C. 5511(a)(2)(D)).

(f) Cybersecurity Research Database—The agencies involved in developing and updating the strategic plan under subsection (a) shall establish, in coordination with the Office of Management and Budget, a mechanism to track ongoing and completed Federal cybersecurity research and development projects and associated funding, and shall make such information publically available.

SEC. 104. SOCIAL AND BEHAVIORAL RESEARCH IN CYBERSECURITY.

Section 4(a)(1) of the Cyber Security Research and Development Act (15 U.S.C. 7403(a)(1)) is amended—

(1) by inserting ‘and usability’ after ‘to the structure’;

(2) in subparagraph (H), by striking ‘and’ after the semicolon;

(3) in subparagraph (I), by striking the period at the end and inserting ‘; and’; and

(4) by adding at the end the following new subparagraph:

‘(J) social and behavioral factors, including human-computer interactions, usability, and user motivations.’.

SEC. 105. NATIONAL SCIENCE FOUNDATION CYBERSECURITY RESEARCH AND DEVELOPMENT PROGRAMS.

(a) Computer and Network Security Research Areas—Section 4(a)(1) of the Cyber Security Research and Development Act (15 U.S.C. 7403(a)(1)) is amended—

(1) in subparagraph (A) by inserting 'identity management,' after 'cryptography,'; and
(2) in subparagraph (I), by inserting ', crimes against children, and organized crime' after 'intellectual property'.

(b) Computer and Network Security Research Grants—Section 4(a)(3) of such Act (15 U.S.C. 7403(a)(3)) is amended by striking subparagraphs (A) through (E) and inserting the following new subparagraphs:
'(A) $119,000,000 for fiscal year 2014;
'(B) $119,000,000 for fiscal year 2015; and
'(C) $119,000,000 for fiscal year 2016.'.

(c) Computer and Network Security Research Centers—Section 4(b) of such Act (15 U.S.C. 7403(b)) is amended—
(1) in paragraph (4)—
(A) in subparagraph (C), by striking 'and' after the semicolon;
(B) in subparagraph (D), by striking the period and inserting '; and'; and
(C) by adding at the end the following new subparagraph:
'(E) how the center will partner with government laboratories, for-profit entities, other institutions of higher education, or nonprofit research institutions.'; and
(2) in paragraph (7) by striking subparagraphs (A) through (E) and inserting the following new subparagraphs:
'(A) $5,000,000 for fiscal year 2014;
'(B) $5,000,000 for fiscal year 2015; and
'(C) $5,000,000 for fiscal year 2016.'.

(d) Computer and Network Security Capacity Building Grants—Section 5(a)(6) of such Act (15 U.S.C. 7404(a)(6)) is amended by striking subparagraphs (A) through (E) and inserting the following new subparagraphs:
'(A) $25,000,000 for fiscal year 2014;
'(B) $25,000,000 for fiscal year 2015; and
'(C) $25,000,000 for fiscal year 2016.'.

(e) Scientific and Advanced Technology Act Grants—Section 5(b)(2) of such Act (15 U.S.C. 7404(b)(2)) is amended by striking subparagraphs (A) through (E) and inserting the following new subparagraphs:
'(A) $4,000,000 for fiscal year 2014;
'(B) $4,000,000 for fiscal year 2015; and
'(C) $4,000,000 for fiscal year 2016.'.

(f) Graduate Traineeships in Computer and Network Security—Section 5(c)(7) of such Act (15 U.S.C. 7404(c)(7)) is amended by striking subparagraphs (A) through (E) and inserting the following new subparagraphs:
'(A) $32,000,000 for fiscal year 2014;
'(B) $32,000,000 for fiscal year 2015; and
'(C) $32,000,000 for fiscal year 2016.'.

(g) Cyber Security Faculty Development Traineeship Program—Section 5(e) of such Act (15 U.S.C. 7404(e)) is repealed.

SEC. 106. FEDERAL CYBER SCHOLARSHIP FOR SERVICE PROGRAM.

(a) In General—The Director of the National Science Foundation shall continue a Scholarship for Service program under section 5(a) of the Cyber Security Research and Development Act (15 U.S.C. 7404(a)) to recruit and train the next generation of Federal cybersecurity professionals and to increase the capacity of the higher education system to produce an information technology workforce with the skills necessary to enhance the security of the Nation's communications and information infrastructure.

(b) Characteristics of Program—The program under this section shall—

(1) provide, through qualified institutions of higher education, including community colleges, scholarships that provide tuition, fees, and a competitive stipend for up to 2 years to students pursing a bachelor's or master's degree and up to 3 years to students pursuing a doctoral degree in a cybersecurity field;

(2) provide the scholarship recipients with summer internship opportunities or other meaningful temporary appointments in the Federal information technology workforce; and

(3) increase the capacity of institutions of higher education throughout all regions of the United States to produce highly qualified cybersecurity professionals, through the award of competitive, merit-reviewed grants that support such activities as—

(A) faculty professional development, including technical, hands-on experiences in the private sector or government, workshops, seminars, conferences, and other professional development opportunities that will result in improved instructional capabilities;

(B) institutional partnerships, including minority serving institutions and community colleges;

(C) development and evaluation of cybersecurity-related courses and curricula; and

(D) public-private partnerships that will integrate research experiences and hands-on learning into cybersecurity degree programs.

(c) Scholarship Requirements—

(1) ELIGIBILITY—Scholarships under this section shall be available only to students who—

(A) are citizens or permanent residents of the United States;

(B) are full-time students in an eligible degree program, as determined by the Director, that is focused on computer security or information assurance at an awardee institution; and

(C) accept the terms of a scholarship pursuant to this section.

(2) SELECTION—Individuals shall be selected to receive scholarships primarily on the basis of academic merit, with consideration given to financial need, to the goal of promoting the participation of females and individuals identified in section 33 or 34 of the Science and Engineering Equal Opportu-

nities Act (42 U.S.C. 1885a or 1885b), and to veterans. For purposes of this paragraph, the term 'veteran' means a person who—

(A) served on active duty (other than active duty for training) in the Armed Forces of the United States for a period of more than 180 consecutive days, and who was discharged or released therefrom under conditions other than dishonorable; or

(B) served on active duty (other than active duty for training) in the Armed Forces of the United States and was discharged or released from such service for a service-connected disability before serving 180 consecutive days. For purposes of subparagraph (B), the term 'service-connected' has the meaning given such term under section 101 of title 38, United States Code.

(3) SERVICE OBLIGATION—If an individual receives a scholarship under this section, as a condition of receiving such scholarship, the individual upon completion of their degree must serve as a cybersecurity professional within the Federal workforce for a period of time as provided in paragraph (5). If a scholarship recipient is not offered employment by a Federal agency or a federally funded research and development center, the service requirement can be satisfied at the Director's discretion by—

(A) serving as a cybersecurity professional in a State, local, or tribal government agency; or

(B) teaching cybersecurity courses at an institution of higher education.

(4) CONDITIONS OF SUPPORT—As a condition of acceptance of a scholarship under this section, a recipient shall agree to provide the awardee institution with annual verifiable documentation of employment and up-to-date contact information.

(5) LENGTH OF SERVICE—The length of service required in exchange for a scholarship under this subsection shall be 1 year more than the number of years for which the scholarship was received.

(d) Failure To Complete Service Obligation-

(1) GENERAL RULE—If an individual who has received a scholarship under this section—

(A) fails to maintain an acceptable level of academic standing in the educational institution in which the individual is enrolled, as determined by the Director;

(B) is dismissed from such educational institution for disciplinary reasons;

(C) withdraws from the program for which the award was made before the completion of such program;

(D) declares that the individual does not intend to fulfill the service obligation under this section; or

(E) fails to fulfill the service obligation of the individual under this section,

such individual shall be liable to the United States as provided in paragraph (3).

(2) MONITORING COMPLIANCE—As a condition of participating in the program, a qualified institution of higher education receiving a grant under this section shall—

(A) enter into an agreement with the Director of the National Science Foundation to monitor the compliance of scholarship recipients with respect to their service obligation; and

(B) provide to the Director, on an annual basis, post-award employment information required under subsection (c)(4) for scholarship recipients through the completion of their service obligation.

(3) AMOUNT OF REPAYMENT—

(A) LESS THAN ONE YEAR OF SERVICE—If a circumstance described in paragraph (1) occurs before the completion of 1 year of a service obligation under this section, the total amount of awards received by the individual under this section shall be repaid or such amount shall be treated as a loan to be repaid in accordance with subparagraph (C).

(B) MORE THAN ONE YEAR OF SERVICE—If a circumstance described in subparagraph (D) or (E) of paragraph (1) occurs after the completion of 1 year of a service obligation under this section, the total amount of scholarship awards received by the individual under this section, reduced by the ratio of the number of years of service completed divided by the number of years of service required, shall be repaid or such amount shall be treated as a loan to be repaid in accordance with subparagraph (C).

(C) REPAYMENTS—A loan described in subparagraph (A) or (B) shall be treated as a Federal Direct Unsubsidized Stafford Loan under part D of title IV of the Higher Education Act of 1965 (20 U.S.C. 1087a and following), and shall be subject to repayment, together with interest thereon accruing from the date of the scholarship award, in accordance with terms and conditions specified by the Director (in consultation with the Secretary of Education) in regulations promulgated to carry out this paragraph.

(4) COLLECTION OF REPAYMENT—

(A) IN GENERAL—In the event that a scholarship recipient is required to repay the scholarship under this subsection, the institution providing the scholarship shall—

(i) be responsible for determining the repayment amounts and for notifying the recipient and the Director of the amount owed; and

(ii) collect such repayment amount within a period of time as determined under the agreement described in paragraph (2), or the repayment amount shall be treated as a loan in accordance with paragraph (3)(C).

(B) RETURNED TO TREASURY—Except as provided in subparagraph (C) of this paragraph, any such repayment shall be returned to the Treasury of the United States.

(C) RETAIN PERCENTAGE—An institution of higher education may retain a percentage of any repayment the institution collects under this paragraph to defray administrative costs associated with the collection. The

Director shall establish a single, fixed percentage that will apply to all eligible entities.

(5) EXCEPTIONS—The Director may provide for the partial or total waiver or suspension of any service or payment obligation by an individual under this section whenever compliance by the individual with the obligation is impossible or would involve extreme hardship to the individual, or if enforcement of such obligation with respect to the individual would be unconscionable.

(e) Hiring Authority-

(1) APPOINTMENT IN EXCEPTED SERVICE—Notwithstanding any provision of chapter 33 of title 5, United States Code, governing appointments in the competitive service, an agency shall appoint in the excepted service an individual who has completed the academic program for which a scholarship was awarded.

(2) NONCOMPETITIVE CONVERSION—Except as provided in paragraph (4), upon fulfillment of the service term, an employee appointed under paragraph (1) may be converted noncompetitively to term, career-conditional or career appointment.

(3) TIMING OF CONVERSION—An agency may noncompetitively convert a term employee appointed under paragraph (2) to a career-conditional or career appointment before the term appointment expires.

(4) AUTHORITY TO DECLINE CONVERSION—An agency may decline to make the noncompetitive conversion or appointment under paragraph (2) for cause.

SEC. 107. CYBERSECURITY WORKFORCE ASSESSMENT.

Not later than 180 days after the date of enactment of this Act the President shall transmit to the Congress a report addressing the cybersecurity workforce needs of the Federal Government. The report shall include—

(1) an examination of the current state of and the projected needs of the Federal cybersecurity workforce, including a comparison of the different agencies and departments, and an analysis of the capacity of such agencies and departments to meet those needs;

(2) an analysis of the sources and availability of cybersecurity talent, a comparison of the skills and expertise sought by the Federal Government and the private sector, an examination of the current and future capacity of United States institutions of higher education, including community colleges, to provide current and future cybersecurity professionals, through education and training activities, with those skills sought by the Federal Government, State and local entities, and the private sector, and a description of how successful programs are engaging the talents of females and individuals identified in section 33 or 34 of the Science and Engineering Equal Opportunities Act (42 U.S.C. 1885a or 1885b);

(3) an examination of the effectiveness of the National Centers of Academic Excellence in Information Assurance Education, the Centers of Academic Ex-

cellence in Research, and the Federal Cyber Scholarship for Service programs in promoting higher education and research in cybersecurity and information assurance and in producing a growing number of professionals with the necessary cybersecurity and information assurance expertise, including individuals from States or regions in which the unemployment rate exceeds the national average;

(4) an analysis of any barriers to the Federal Government recruiting and hiring cybersecurity talent, including barriers relating to compensation, the hiring process, job classification, and hiring flexibilities; and

(5) recommendations for Federal policies to ensure an adequate, well-trained Federal cybersecurity workforce.

SEC. 108. CYBERSECURITY UNIVERSITY-INDUSTRY TASK FORCE.

(a) Establishment of University-Industry Task Force—Not later than 180 days after the date of enactment of this Act, the Director of the Office of Science and Technology Policy shall convene a task force to explore mechanisms for carrying out collaborative research, development, education, and training activities for cybersecurity through a consortium or other appropriate entity with participants from institutions of higher education and industry.

(b) Functions—The task force shall—

(1) develop options for a collaborative model and an organizational structure for such entity under which the joint research and development activities could be planned, managed, and conducted effectively, including mechanisms for the allocation of resources among the participants in such entity for support of such activities;

(2) identify and prioritize at least three cybersecurity grand challenges, focused on nationally significant problems requiring collaborative and interdisciplinary solutions;

(3) propose a process for developing a research and development agenda for such entity to address the grand challenges identified under paragraph (2);

(4) define the roles and responsibilities for the participants from institutions of higher education and industry in such entity;

(5) propose guidelines for assigning intellectual property rights and for the transfer of research and development results to the private sector; and

(6) make recommendations for how such entity could be funded from Federal, State, and nongovernmental sources.

(c) Composition—In establishing the task force under subsection (a), the Director of the Office of Science and Technology Policy shall appoint an equal number of individuals from institutions of higher education, including minority-serving institutions and community colleges, and from industry with knowledge and expertise in cybersecurity.

(d) Report—Not later than 12 months after the date of enactment of this Act, the Director of the Office of Science and Technology Policy shall transmit to the Congress a report describing the findings and recommendations of the task force.

(e) Termination—The task force shall terminate upon transmittal of the report required under subsection (d).
(f) Compensation and Expenses—Members of the task force shall serve without compensation.

SEC. 109. CYBERSECURITY AUTOMATION AND CHECKLISTS FOR GOVERNMENT SYSTEMS.

Section 8(c) of the Cyber Security Research and Development Act (15 U.S.C. 7406(c)) is amended to read as follows:

'(c) Security Automation and Checklists for Government Systems—

'(1) IN GENERAL—The Director of the National Institute of Standards and Technology shall develop, and revise as necessary, security automation standards, associated reference materials (including protocols), and checklists providing settings and option selections that minimize the security risks associated with each information technology hardware or software system and security tool that is, or is likely to become, widely used within the Federal Government in order to enable standardized and interoperable technologies, architectures, and frameworks for continuous monitoring of information security within the Federal Government.

'(2) PRIORITIES FOR DEVELOPMENT—The Director of the National Institute of Standards and Technology shall establish priorities for the development of standards, reference materials, and checklists under this subsection on the basis of—

'(A) the security risks associated with the use of the system;

'(B) the number of agencies that use a particular system or security tool;

'(C) the usefulness of the standards, reference materials, or checklists to Federal agencies that are users or potential users of the system;

'(D) the effectiveness of the associated standard, reference material, or checklist in creating or enabling continuous monitoring of information security; or

'(E) such other factors as the Director of the National Institute of Standards and Technology determines to be appropriate.

'(3) EXCLUDED SYSTEMS—The Director of the National Institute of Standards and Technology may exclude from the application of paragraph (1) any information technology hardware or software system or security tool for which such Director determines that the development of a standard, reference material, or checklist is inappropriate because of the infrequency of use of the system, the obsolescence of the system, or the inutility or impracticability of developing a standard, reference material, or checklist for the system.

'(4) DISSEMINATION OF STANDARDS AND RELATED MATERIALS—The Director of the National Institute of Standards and Technology shall ensure that Federal agencies are informed of the availability of any standard, reference material, checklist, or other item developed under this subsection.

'(5) AGENCY USE REQUIREMENTS—The development of standards, reference materials, and checklists under paragraph (1) for an information technology hardware or software system or tool does not—

'(A) require any Federal agency to select the specific settings or options recommended by the standard, reference material, or checklist for the system;

'(B) establish conditions or prerequisites for Federal agency procurement or deployment of any such system;

'(C) imply an endorsement of any such system by the Director of the National Institute of Standards and Technology; or

'(D) preclude any Federal agency from procuring or deploying other information technology hardware or software systems for which no such standard, reference material, or checklist has been developed or identified under paragraph (1).'.

SEC. 110. NATIONAL INSTITUTE OF STANDARDS AND TECHNOLOGY CYBERSECURITY RESEARCH AND DEVELOPMENT.

Section 20 of the National Institute of Standards and Technology Act (15 U.S.C. 278g-3) is amended by redesignating subsection (e) as subsection (f), and by inserting after subsection (d) the following:

'(e) Intramural Security Research—As part of the research activities conducted in accordance with subsection (d)(3), the Institute shall—

'(1) conduct a research program to develop a unifying and standardized identity, privilege, and access control management framework for the execution of a wide variety of resource protection policies and that is amenable to implementation within a wide variety of existing and emerging computing environments;

'(2) carry out research associated with improving the security of information systems and networks;

'(3) carry out research associated with improving the testing, measurement, usability, and assurance of information systems and networks;

'(4) carry out research associated with improving security of industrial control systems; and

'(5) carry out research associated with improving the security and integrity of the information technology supply chain.'.

SEC. 111. RESEARCH ON THE SCIENCE OF CYBERSECURITY.

The Director of the National Science Foundation and the Director of the National Institute of Standards and Technology shall, through existing programs and activities, support research that will lead to the development of a scientific foundation for the field of cybersecurity, including research that increases understanding of the underlying principles of securing complex networked systems, enables repeatable experimentation, and creates quantifiable security metrics.

TITLE II—ADVANCEMENT OF CYBERSECURITY TECHNICAL STANDARDS

SEC. 201. DEFINITIONS.

In this title:

(1) DIRECTOR—The term 'Director' means the Director of the National Institute of Standards and Technology.

(2) INSTITUTE—The term 'Institute' means the National Institute of Standards and Technology.

SEC. 202. INTERNATIONAL CYBERSECURITY TECHNICAL STANDARDS.

(a) In General—The Director, in coordination with appropriate Federal authorities, shall—

(1) as appropriate, ensure coordination of Federal agencies engaged in the development of international technical standards related to information system security; and

(2) not later than 1 year after the date of enactment of this Act, develop and transmit to the Congress a plan for ensuring such Federal agency coordination.

(b) Consultation With the Private Sector—In carrying out the activities specified in subsection (a)(1), the Director shall ensure consultation with appropriate private sector stakeholders.

SEC. 203. CLOUD COMPUTING STRATEGY.

(a) In General—The Director, in collaboration with the Federal CIO Council, and in consultation with other relevant Federal agencies and stakeholders from the private sector, shall continue to develop and encourage the implementation of a comprehensive strategy for the use and adoption of cloud computing services by the Federal Government.

(b) Activities—In carrying out the strategy developed under subsection (a), the Director shall give consideration to activities that—

(1) accelerate the development, in collaboration with the private sector, of standards that address interoperability and portability of cloud computing services;

(2) advance the development of conformance testing performed by the private sector in support of cloud computing standardization; and

(3) support, in consultation with the private sector, the development of appropriate security frameworks and reference materials, and the identification of best practices, for use by Federal agencies to address security and privacy requirements to enable the use and adoption of cloud computing services, including activities—

(A) to ensure the physical security of cloud computing data centers and the data stored in such centers;

(B) to ensure secure access to the data stored in cloud computing data centers;

(C) to develop security standards as required under section 20 of the National Institute of Standards and Technology Act (15 U.S.C. 278g-3); and

(D) to support the development of the automation of continuous monitoring systems.

SEC. 204. PROMOTING CYBERSECURITY AWARENESS AND EDUCATION.

(a) Program—The Director, in collaboration with relevant Federal agencies, industry, educational institutions, National Laboratories, the National Coordination Office of the Networking and Information Technology Research and Development program, and other organizations, shall continue to coordinate a cybersecurity awareness and education program to increase knowledge, skills, and awareness of cybersecurity risks, consequences, and best practices through—

(1) the widespread dissemination of cybersecurity technical standards and best practices identified by the Institute;

(2) efforts to make cybersecurity best practices usable by individuals, small to medium-sized businesses, State, local, and tribal governments, and educational institutions;

(3) improving the state of cybersecurity education at all educational levels;

(4) efforts to attract, recruit, and retain qualified professionals to the Federal cybersecurity workforce; and

(5) improving the skills, training, and professional development of the Federal cybersecurity workforce.

(b) Strategic Plan—The Director shall, in cooperation with relevant Federal agencies and other stakeholders, develop and implement a strategic plan to guide Federal programs and activities in support of a comprehensive cybersecurity awareness and education program as described under subsection (a).

(c) Report to Congress—Not later than 1 year after the date of enactment of this Act and every 5 years thereafter, the Director shall transmit the strategic plan required under subsection (b) to the Committee on Science, Space, and Technology of the House of Representatives and the Committee on Commerce, Science, and Transportation of the Senate.

SEC. 205. IDENTITY MANAGEMENT RESEARCH AND DEVELOPMENT.

The Director shall continue a program to support the development of technical standards, metrology, testbeds, and conformance criteria, taking into account appropriate user concerns, to—

(1) improve interoperability among identity management technologies;

(2) strengthen authentication methods of identity management systems;

(3) improve privacy protection in identity management systems, including health information technology systems, through authentication and security protocols; and

(4) improve the usability of identity management systems.

SEC. 206. AUTHORIZATIONS.

No additional funds are authorized to carry out this Act, and the amendments made by this Act. This Act, and the amendments made by this Act, shall be carried out using amounts otherwise authorized or appropriated.

Passed the House of Representatives April 16, 2013.

Cyber Intelligence Sharing and Protection Act

H.R. 624

AN ACT

To provide for the sharing of certain cyber threat intelligence and cyber threat information between the intelligence community and cybersecurity entities, and for other purposes.

Be it enacted by the Senate and House of Representatives of the United States of America in Congress assembled,

SECTION 1. SHORT TITLE.

This Act may be cited as the 'Cyber Intelligence Sharing and Protection Act'.

SEC. 2. FEDERAL GOVERNMENT COORDINATION WITH RESPECT TO CYBERSECURITY.

(a) Coordinated Activities—The Federal Government shall conduct cybersecurity activities to provide shared situational awareness that enables integrated operational actions to protect, prevent, mitigate, respond to, and recover from cyber incidents.

(b) Coordinated Information Sharing—

(1) DESIGNATION OF COORDINATING ENTITY FOR CYBER THREAT INFORMATION—The President shall designate an entity within the Department of Homeland Security as the civilian Federal entity to receive cyber threat information that is shared by a cybersecurity provider or self-protected entity in accordance with section 1104(b) of the National Security Act of 1947, as added by section 3(a) of this Act, except as provided in paragraph (2) and subject to the procedures established under paragraph (4).

(2) DESIGNATION OF A COORDINATING ENTITY FOR CYBERSECURITY CRIMES—The President shall designate an entity within the Department of Justice as the civilian Federal entity to receive cyber threat information related to cybersecurity crimes that is shared by a cybersecurity provider or self-protected entity in accordance with section 1104(b) of the National Security Act of 1947, as added by section 3(a) of this Act, subject to the procedures under paragraph (4).

(3) SHARING BY COORDINATING ENTITIES—The entities designated under paragraphs (1) and (2) shall share cyber threat information shared with such entities in accordance with section 1104(b) of the National Security Act of 1947, as added by section 3(a) of this Act, consistent with the procedures established under paragraphs (4) and (5).

(4) PROCEDURES—Each department or agency of the Federal Government receiving cyber threat information shared in accordance with section 1104(b)

of the National Security Act of 1947, as added by section 3(a) of this Act, shall establish procedures to—

(A) ensure that cyber threat information shared with departments or agencies of the Federal Government in accordance with such section 1104(b) is also shared with appropriate departments and agencies of the Federal Government with a national security mission in real time;

(B) ensure the distribution to other departments and agencies of the Federal Government of cyber threat information in real time; and

(C) facilitate information sharing, interaction, and collaboration among and between the Federal Government; State, local, tribal, and territorial governments; and cybersecurity providers and self-protected entities.

(5) PRIVACY AND CIVIL LIBERTIES—

(A) POLICIES AND PROCEDURES—The Secretary of Homeland Security, the Attorney General, the Director of National Intelligence, and the Secretary of Defense shall jointly establish and periodically review policies and procedures governing the receipt, retention, use, and disclosure of non-publicly available cyber threat information shared with the Federal Government in accordance with section 1104(b) of the National Security Act of 1947, as added by section 3(a) of this Act. Such policies and procedures shall, consistent with the need to protect systems and networks from cyber threats and mitigate cyber threats in a timely manner—

(i) minimize the impact on privacy and civil liberties;

(ii) reasonably limit the receipt, retention, use, and disclosure of cyber threat information associated with specific persons that is not necessary to protect systems or networks from cyber threats or mitigate cyber threats in a timely manner;

(iii) include requirements to safeguard non-publicly available cyber threat information that may be used to identify specific persons from unauthorized access or acquisition;

(iv) protect the confidentiality of cyber threat information associated with specific persons to the greatest extent practicable; and

(v) not delay or impede the flow of cyber threat information necessary to defend against or mitigate a cyber threat.

(B) SUBMISSION TO CONGRESS—The Secretary of Homeland Security, the Attorney General, the Director of National Intelligence, and the Secretary of Defense shall, consistent with the need to protect sources and methods, jointly submit to Congress the policies and procedures required under subparagraph (A) and any updates to such policies and procedures.

(C) IMPLEMENTATION—The head of each department or agency of the Federal Government receiving cyber threat information shared with the Federal Government under such section 1104(b) shall—

(i) implement the policies and procedures established under subparagraph (A); and

(ii) promptly notify the Secretary of Homeland Security, the Attorney General, the Director of National Intelligence, the Secretary of Defense, and the appropriate congressional committees of any significant violations of such policies and procedures.

(D) OVERSIGHT—The Secretary of Homeland Security, the Attorney General, the Director of National Intelligence, and the Secretary of Defense shall jointly establish a program to monitor and oversee compliance with the policies and procedures established under subparagraph (A).

(6) INFORMATION SHARING RELATIONSHIPS—Nothing in this section shall be construed to—

(A) alter existing agreements or prohibit new agreements with respect to the sharing of cyber threat information between the Department of Defense and an entity that is part of the defense industrial base;

(B) alter existing information-sharing relationships between a cybersecurity provider, protected entity, or self-protected entity and the Federal Government;

(C) prohibit the sharing of cyber threat information directly with a department or agency of the Federal Government for criminal investigative purposes related to crimes described in section 1104(c)(1) of the National Security Act of 1947, as added by section 3(a) of this Act; or

(D) alter existing agreements or prohibit new agreements with respect to the sharing of cyber threat information between the Department of Treasury and an entity that is part of the financial services sector.

(7) TECHNICAL ASSISTANCE—

(A) DISCUSSIONS AND ASSISTANCE—Nothing in this section shall be construed to prohibit any department or agency of the Federal Government from engaging in formal or informal technical discussion regarding cyber threat information with a cybersecurity provider or self-protected entity or from providing technical assistance to address vulnerabilities or mitigate threats at the request of such a provider or such an entity.

(B) COORDINATION—Any department or agency of the Federal Government engaging in an activity referred to in subparagraph (A) shall coordinate such activity with the entity of the Department of Homeland Security designated under paragraph (1) and share all significant information resulting from such activity with such entity and all other appropriate departments and agencies of the Federal Government.

(C) SHARING BY DESIGNATED ENTITY—Consistent with the policies and procedures established under paragraph (5), the entity of the Department of Homeland Security designated under paragraph (1) shall share with all appropriate departments and agencies of the Federal Government all significant information resulting from—

(i) formal or informal technical discussions between such entity of the Department of Homeland Security and a cybersecurity provider or self-protected entity about cyber threat information; or

(ii) any technical assistance such entity of the Department of Homeland Security provides to such cybersecurity provider or such self-protected entity to address vulnerabilities or mitigate threats.

(c) Reports on Information Sharing—

(1) INSPECTOR GENERAL OF THE DEPARTMENT OF HOMELAND SECURITY REPORT—The Inspector General of the Department of Homeland Security, in consultation with the Inspector General of the Department of Justice, the Inspector General of the Intelligence Community, the Inspector General of the Department of Defense, and the Privacy and Civil Liberties Oversight Board, shall annually submit to the appropriate congressional committees a report containing a review of the use of information shared with the Federal Government under subsection (b) of section 1104 of the National Security Act of 1947, as added by section 3(a) of this Act, including—

(A) a review of the use by the Federal Government of such information for a purpose other than a cybersecurity purpose;

(B) a review of the type of information shared with the Federal Government under such subsection;

(C) a review of the actions taken by the Federal Government based on such information;

(D) appropriate metrics to determine the impact of the sharing of such information with the Federal Government on privacy and civil liberties, if any;

(E) a list of the departments or agencies receiving such information;

(F) a review of the sharing of such information within the Federal Government to identify inappropriate stovepiping of shared information; and

(G) any recommendations of the Inspector General of the Department of Homeland Security for improvements or modifications to the authorities under such section.

(2) PRIVACY AND CIVIL LIBERTIES OFFICERS REPORT—The Officer for Civil Rights and Civil Liberties of the Department of Homeland Security, in consultation with the Privacy and Civil Liberties Oversight Board, the Inspector General of the Intelligence Community, and the senior privacy and civil liberties officer of each department or agency of the Federal Government that receives cyber threat information shared with the Federal Government under such subsection (b), shall annually and jointly submit to Congress a report assessing the privacy and civil liberties impact of the activities conducted by the Federal Government under such section 1104. Such report shall include any recommendations the Civil Liberties Protection Officer and Chief Privacy and Civil Liberties Officer consider appropriate to minimize or mitigate the privacy and civil liberties impact of the sharing of cyber threat information under such section 1104.

(3) FORM—Each report required under paragraph (1) or (2) shall be submitted in unclassified form, but may include a classified annex.

(d) Definitions—In this section:

(1) APPROPRIATE CONGRESSIONAL COMMITTEES—The term 'appropriate congressional committees' means—

(A) the Committee on Homeland Security, the Committee on the Judiciary, the Permanent Select Committee on Intelligence, and the Committee on Armed Services of the House of Representatives; and

(B) the Committee on Homeland Security and Governmental Affairs, the Committee on the Judiciary, the Select Committee on Intelligence, and the Committee on Armed Services of the Senate.

(2) CYBER THREAT INFORMATION, CYBER THREAT INTELLIGENCE, CYBERSECURITY CRIMES, CYBERSECURITY PROVIDER, CYBERSECURITY PURPOSE, AND SELF-PROTECTED ENTITY—The terms 'cyber threat information', 'cyber threat intelligence', 'cybersecurity crimes', 'cybersecurity provider', 'cybersecurity purpose', and 'self-protected entity' have the meaning given those terms in section 1104 of the National Security Act of 1947, as added by section 3(a) of this Act.

(3) INTELLIGENCE COMMUNITY—The term 'intelligence community' has the meaning given the term in section 3(4) of the National Security Act of 1947 (50 U.S.C. 401a(4)).

(4) SHARED SITUATIONAL AWARENESS—The term 'shared situational awareness' means an environment where cyber threat information is shared in real time between all designated Federal cyber operations centers to provide actionable information about all known cyber threats.

SEC. 3. CYBER THREAT INTELLIGENCE AND INFORMATION SHARING.

(a) In General—Title XI of the National Security Act of 1947 (50 U.S.C. 442 et seq.) is amended by adding at the end the following new section:

'CYBER THREAT INTELLIGENCE AND INFORMATION SHARING

'Sec. 1104. (a) Intelligence Community Sharing of Cyber Threat Intelligence With Private Sector and Utilities-

'(1) IN GENERAL—The Director of National Intelligence shall establish procedures to allow elements of the intelligence community to share cyber threat intelligence with private-sector entities and utilities and to encourage the sharing of such intelligence.

'(2) SHARING AND USE OF CLASSIFIED INTELLIGENCE—The procedures established under paragraph (1) shall provide that classified cyber threat intelligence may only be—

'(A) shared by an element of the intelligence community with—

'(i) a certified entity; or

'(ii) a person with an appropriate security clearance to receive such cyber threat intelligence;

'(B) shared consistent with the need to protect the national security of the United States;

'(C) used by a certified entity in a manner which protects such cyber threat intelligence from unauthorized disclosure; and

'(D) used, retained, or further disclosed by a certified entity for cybersecurity purposes.

'(3) SECURITY CLEARANCE APPROVALS—The Director of National Intelligence shall issue guidelines providing that the head of an element of the intelligence community may, as the head of such element considers necessary to carry out this subsection—

'(A) grant a security clearance on a temporary or permanent basis to an employee, independent contractor, or officer of a certified entity;

'(B) grant a security clearance on a temporary or permanent basis to a certified entity and approval to use appropriate facilities; and

'(C) expedite the security clearance process for a person or entity as the head of such element considers necessary, consistent with the need to protect the national security of the United States.

'(4) NO RIGHT OR BENEFIT—The provision of information to a private-sector entity or a utility under this subsection shall not create a right or benefit to similar information by such entity or such utility or any other private-sector entity or utility.

'(5) RESTRICTION ON DISCLOSURE OF CYBER THREAT INTELLIGENCE—Notwithstanding any other provision of law, a certified entity receiving cyber threat intelligence pursuant to this subsection shall not further disclose such cyber threat intelligence to another entity, other than to a certified entity or other appropriate agency or department of the Federal Government authorized to receive such cyber threat intelligence.

'(b) Use of Cybersecurity Systems and Sharing of Cyber Threat Information-

'(1) IN GENERAL-

'(A) CYBERSECURITY PROVIDERS—Notwithstanding any other provision of law, a cybersecurity provider, with the express consent of a protected entity for which such cybersecurity provider is providing goods or services for cybersecurity purposes, may, for cybersecurity purposes—

'(i) use cybersecurity systems to identify and obtain cyber threat information to protect the rights and property of such protected entity; and

'(ii) share such cyber threat information with any other entity designated by such protected entity, including, if specifically designated, the entities of the Department of Homeland Security and the Department of Justice designated under paragraphs (1) and (2) of section 2(b) of the Cyber Intelligence Sharing and Protection Act.

'(B) SELF-PROTECTED ENTITIES—Notwithstanding any other provision of law, a self-protected entity may, for cybersecurity purposes—

'(i) use cybersecurity systems to identify and obtain cyber threat information to protect the rights and property of such self-protected entity; and

'(ii) share such cyber threat information with any other entity, including the entities of the Department of Homeland Security and the Department of Justice designated under paragraphs (1) and (2) of section 2(b) of the Cyber Intelligence Sharing and Protection Act.

'(2) USE AND PROTECTION OF INFORMATION—Cyber threat information shared in accordance with paragraph (1)—

'(A) shall only be shared in accordance with any restrictions placed on the sharing of such information by the protected entity or self-protected entity authorizing such sharing, including appropriate anonymization or minimization of such information and excluding limiting a department or agency of the Federal Government from sharing such information with another department or agency of the Federal Government in accordance with this section;

'(B) may not be used by an entity to gain an unfair competitive advantage to the detriment of the protected entity or the self-protected entity authorizing the sharing of information;

'(C) may only be used by a non-Federal recipient of such information for a cybersecurity purpose;

'(D) if shared with the Federal Government—

'(i) shall be exempt from disclosure under section 552 of title 5, United States Code (commonly known as the 'Freedom of Information Act');

'(ii) shall be considered proprietary information and shall not be disclosed to an entity outside of the Federal Government except as authorized by the entity sharing such information;

'(iii) shall not be used by the Federal Government for regulatory purposes;

'(iv) shall not be provided to another department or agency of the Federal Government under paragraph (2)(A) if—

'(I) the entity providing such information determines that the provision of such information will undermine the purpose for which such information is shared; or

'(II) unless otherwise directed by the President, the head of the department or agency of the Federal Government receiving such cyber threat information determines that the provision of such information will undermine the purpose for which such information is shared; and

'(v) shall be handled by the Federal Government consistent with the need to protect sources and methods and the national security of the United States; and

'(E) shall be exempt from disclosure under a law or regulation of a State, political subdivision of a State, or a tribe that requires public disclosure of information by a public or quasi-public entity.

'(3) EXEMPTION FROM LIABILITY—

'(A) EXEMPTION—No civil or criminal cause of action shall lie or be maintained in Federal or State court against a protected entity, self-protected entity, cybersecurity provider, or an officer, employee, or agent of a protected entity, self-protected entity, or cybersecurity provider, acting in good faith—

'(i) for using cybersecurity systems to identify or obtain cyber threat information or for sharing such information in accordance with this section; or

'(ii) for decisions made for cybersecurity purposes and based on cyber threat information identified, obtained, or shared under this section.

'(B) LACK OF GOOD FAITH—For purposes of the exemption from liability under subparagraph (A), a lack of good faith includes any act or omission taken with intent to injure, defraud, or otherwise endanger any individual, government entity, private entity, or utility.

'(4) RELATIONSHIP TO OTHER LAWS REQUIRING THE DISCLOSURE OF INFORMATION—The submission of information under this subsection to the Federal Government shall not satisfy or affect—

'(A) any requirement under any other provision of law for a person or entity to provide information to the Federal Government; or

'(B) the applicability of other provisions of law, including section 552 of title 5, United States Code (commonly known as the 'Freedom of Information Act'), with respect to information required to be provided to the Federal Government under such other provision of law.

'(5) RULE OF CONSTRUCTION—Nothing in this subsection shall be construed to provide new authority to—

'(A) a cybersecurity provider to use a cybersecurity system to identify or obtain cyber threat information from a system or network other than a system or network owned or operated by a protected entity for which such cybersecurity provider is providing goods or services for cybersecurity purposes; or

'(B) a self-protected entity to use a cybersecurity system to identify or obtain cyber threat information from a system or network other than a system or network owned or operated by such self-protected entity.

'(c) Federal Government Use of Information—

'(1) LIMITATION—The Federal Government may use cyber threat information shared with the Federal Government in accordance with subsection (b)—

'(A) for cybersecurity purposes;

'(B) for the investigation and prosecution of cybersecurity crimes;

'(C) for the protection of individuals from the danger of death or serious bodily harm and the investigation and prosecution of crimes involving such danger of death or serious bodily harm; or

'(D) for the protection of minors from child pornography, any risk of sexual exploitation, and serious threats to the physical safety of minors, including kidnapping and trafficking and the investigation and prosecution of crimes involving child pornography, any risk of sexual exploitation, and serious threats to the physical safety of minors, including kidnapping and trafficking, and any crime referred to in section 2258A(a)(2) of title 18, United States Code.

'(2) AFFIRMATIVE SEARCH RESTRICTION—The Federal Government may not affirmatively search cyber threat information shared with the Federal Government under subsection (b) for a purpose other than a purpose referred to in paragraph (1).

'(3) ANTI-TASKING RESTRICTION—Nothing in this section shall be construed to permit the Federal Government to—

'(A) require a private-sector entity or utility to share information with the Federal Government; or

'(B) condition the sharing of cyber threat intelligence with a private-sector entity or utility on the provision of cyber threat information to the Federal Government.

'(4) PROTECTION OF SENSITIVE PERSONAL DOCUMENTS—The Federal Government may not use the following information, containing information that identifies a person, shared with the Federal Government in accordance with subsection (b):

'(A) Library circulation records.

'(B) Library patron lists.

'(C) Book sales records.

'(D) Book customer lists.

'(E) Firearms sales records.

'(F) Tax return records.

'(G) Educational records.

'(H) Medical records.

'(5) NOTIFICATION OF NON-CYBER THREAT INFORMATION—If a department or agency of the Federal Government receiving information pursuant to subsection (b)(1) determines that such information is not cyber threat information, such department or agency shall notify the entity or provider sharing such information pursuant to subsection (b)(1).

'(6) RETENTION AND USE OF CYBER THREAT INFORMATION—No department or agency of the Federal Government shall retain or use information shared pursuant to subsection (b)(1) for any use other than a use permitted under subsection (c)(1).

'(d) Federal Government Liability for Violations of Restrictions on the Disclosure, Use, and Protection of Voluntarily Shared Information-

'(1) IN GENERAL—If a department or agency of the Federal Government intentionally or willfully violates subsection (b)(3)(D) or subsection (c) with respect to the disclosure, use, or protection of voluntarily shared cyber threat information shared under this section, the United States shall be liable to a person adversely affected by such violation in an amount equal to the sum of—

'(A) the actual damages sustained by the person as a result of the violation or $1,000, whichever is greater; and

'(B) the costs of the action together with reasonable attorney fees as determined by the court.

'(2) VENUE—An action to enforce liability created under this subsection may be brought in the district court of the United States in—

'(A) the district in which the complainant resides;

'(B) the district in which the principal place of business of the complainant is located;

'(C) the district in which the department or agency of the Federal Government that disclosed the information is located; or

'(D) the District of Columbia.

'(3) STATUTE OF LIMITATIONS—No action shall lie under this subsection unless such action is commenced not later than two years after the date of the violation of subsection (b)(3)(D) or subsection (c) that is the basis for the action.

'(4) EXCLUSIVE CAUSE OF ACTION—A cause of action under this subsection shall be the exclusive means available to a complainant seeking a remedy for a violation of subsection (b)(3)(D) or subsection (c).

'(e) Federal Preemption—This section supersedes any statute of a State or political subdivision of a State that restricts or otherwise expressly regulates an activity authorized under subsection (b).

'(f) Savings Clauses—

'(1) EXISTING AUTHORITIES—Nothing in this section shall be construed to limit any other authority to use a cybersecurity system or to identify, obtain, or share cyber threat intelligence or cyber threat information.

'(2) LIMITATION ON MILITARY AND INTELLIGENCE COMMUNITY INVOLVEMENT IN PRIVATE AND PUBLIC SECTOR CYBERSECURITY EFFORTS—Nothing in this section shall be construed to provide additional authority to, or modify an existing authority of, the Department of Defense or the National Security Agency or any other element of the intelligence community to control, modify, require, or otherwise direct the cybersecurity efforts of a private-sector entity or a component of the Federal Government or a State, local, or tribal government.

'(3) INFORMATION SHARING RELATIONSHIPS—Nothing in this section shall be construed to—

'(A) limit or modify an existing information sharing relationship;

'(B) prohibit a new information sharing relationship;

'(C) require a new information sharing relationship between the Federal Government and a private-sector entity or utility;

'(D) modify the authority of a department or agency of the Federal Government to protect sources and methods and the national security of the United States; or

'(E) preclude the Federal Government from requiring an entity to report significant cyber incidents if authorized or required to do so under another provision of law.

'(4) LIMITATION ON FEDERAL GOVERNMENT USE OF CYBERSECURITY SYSTEMS—Nothing in this section shall be construed to provide additional authority to, or modify an existing authority of, any entity to use a cybersecurity system owned or controlled by the Federal Government on a private-sector system or network to protect such private-sector system or network.

'(5) NO LIABILITY FOR NON-PARTICIPATION—Nothing in this section shall be construed to subject a protected entity, self-protected entity, cyber security provider, or an officer, employee, or agent of a protected entity, self-protected entity, or cybersecurity provider, to liability for choosing not to engage in the voluntary activities authorized under this section.

'(6) USE AND RETENTION OF INFORMATION—Nothing in this section shall be construed to authorize, or to modify any existing authority of, a department or agency of the Federal Government to retain or use information shared pursuant to subsection (b)(1) for any use other than a use permitted under subsection (c)(1).

'(7) LIMITATION ON SURVEILLANCE—Nothing in this section shall be construed to authorize the Department of Defense or the National Security Agency or any other element of the intelligence community to target a United States person for surveillance.

'(g) Definitions—In this section:

'(1) AVAILABILITY—The term 'availability' means ensuring timely and reliable access to and use of information.

'(2) CERTIFIED ENTITY—The term 'certified entity' means a protected entity, self-protected entity, or cybersecurity provider that—

'(A) possesses or is eligible to obtain a security clearance, as determined by the Director of National Intelligence; and

'(B) is able to demonstrate to the Director of National Intelligence that such provider or such entity can appropriately protect classified cyber threat intelligence.

'(3) CONFIDENTIALITY—The term 'confidentiality' means preserving authorized restrictions on access and disclosure, including means for protecting personal privacy and proprietary information.

'(4) CYBER THREAT INFORMATION—

'(A) IN GENERAL—The term 'cyber threat information' means information directly pertaining to—

'(i) a vulnerability of a system or network of a government or private entity or utility;

'(ii) a threat to the integrity, confidentiality, or availability of a system or network of a government or private entity or utility or any information stored on, processed on, or transiting such a system or network;

'(iii) efforts to deny access to or degrade, disrupt, or destroy a system or network of a government or private entity or utility; or

'(iv) efforts to gain unauthorized access to a system or network of a government or private entity or utility, including to gain such unauthorized access for the purpose of exfiltrating information stored on, processed on, or transiting a system or network of a government or private entity or utility.

'(B) EXCLUSION—Such term does not include information pertaining to efforts to gain unauthorized access to a system or network of a government or private entity or utility that solely involve violations of consumer terms of service or consumer licensing agreements and do not otherwise constitute unauthorized access.

'(5) CYBER THREAT INTELLIGENCE-

'(A) IN GENERAL—The term 'cyber threat intelligence' means intelligence in the possession of an element of the intelligence community directly pertaining to—

'(i) a vulnerability of a system or network of a government or private entity or utility;

'(ii) a threat to the integrity, confidentiality, or availability of a system or network of a government or private entity or utility or any information stored on, processed on, or transiting such a system or network;

'(iii) efforts to deny access to or degrade, disrupt, or destroy a system or network of a government or private entity or utility; or

'(iv) efforts to gain unauthorized access to a system or network of a government or private entity or utility, including to gain such unauthorized access for the purpose of exfiltrating information stored on, processed on, or transiting a system or network of a government or private entity or utility.

'(B) EXCLUSION—Such term does not include intelligence pertaining to efforts to gain unauthorized access to a system or network of a government or private entity or utility that solely involve violations of consumer terms of service or consumer licensing agreements and do not otherwise constitute unauthorized access.

'(6) CYBERSECURITY CRIME—The term 'cybersecurity crime' means—

'(A) a crime under a Federal or State law that involves—

'(i) efforts to deny access to or degrade, disrupt, or destroy a system or network;

'(ii) efforts to gain unauthorized access to a system or network; or '(iii) efforts to exfiltrate information from a system or network without authorization; or

'(B) the violation of a provision of Federal law relating to computer crimes, including a violation of any provision of title 18, United States Code, created or amended by the Computer Fraud and Abuse Act of 1986 (Public Law 99-474).

'(7) CYBERSECURITY PROVIDER—The term 'cybersecurity provider' means a non-Federal entity that provides goods or services intended to be used for cybersecurity purposes.

'(8) CYBERSECURITY PURPOSE—

'(A) IN GENERAL—The term 'cybersecurity purpose' means the purpose of ensuring the integrity, confidentiality, or availability of, or safeguarding, a system or network, including protecting a system or network from—

'(i) a vulnerability of a system or network;

'(ii) a threat to the integrity, confidentiality, or availability of a system or network or any information stored on, processed on, or transiting such a system or network;

'(iii) efforts to deny access to or degrade, disrupt, or destroy a system or network; or

'(iv) efforts to gain unauthorized access to a system or network, including to gain such unauthorized access for the purpose of exfiltrating information stored on, processed on, or transiting a system or network.

'(B) EXCLUSION—Such term does not include the purpose of protecting a system or network from efforts to gain unauthorized access to such system or network that solely involve violations of consumer terms of service or consumer licensing agreements and do not otherwise constitute unauthorized access.

'(9) CYBERSECURITY SYSTEM-

'(A) IN GENERAL—The term 'cybersecurity system' means a system designed or employed to ensure the integrity, confidentiality, or availability of, or safeguard, a system or network, including protecting a system or network from—

'(i) a vulnerability of a system or network;

'(ii) a threat to the integrity, confidentiality, or availability of a system or network or any information stored on, processed on, or transiting such a system or network;

'(iii) efforts to deny access to or degrade, disrupt, or destroy a system or network; or

'(iv) efforts to gain unauthorized access to a system or network, including to gain such unauthorized access for the purpose of exfiltrating information stored on, processed on, or transiting a system or network.

'(B) EXCLUSION—Such term does not include a system designed or employed to protect a system or network from efforts to gain unauthorized access to such system or network that solely involve violations of consumer terms of service or consumer licensing agreements and do not otherwise constitute unauthorized access.

'(10) INTEGRITY—The term 'integrity' means guarding against improper information modification or destruction, including ensuring information nonrepudiation and authenticity.

'(11) PROTECTED ENTITY—The term 'protected entity' means an entity, other than an individual, that contracts with a cybersecurity provider for goods or services to be used for cybersecurity purposes.

'(12) SELF-PROTECTED ENTITY—The term 'self-protected entity' means an entity, other than an individual, that provides goods or services for cybersecurity purposes to itself.

'(13) UTILITY—The term 'utility' means an entity providing essential services (other than law enforcement or regulatory services), including electricity, natural gas, propane, telecommunications, transportation, water, or wastewater services.'.

(b) Procedures and Guidelines—The Director of National Intelligence shall—

(1) not later than 60 days after the date of the enactment of this Act, establish procedures under paragraph (1) of section 1104(a) of the National Security Act of 1947, as added by subsection (a) of this section, and issue guidelines under paragraph (3) of such section 1104(a);

(2) in establishing such procedures and issuing such guidelines, consult with the Secretary of Homeland Security to ensure that such procedures and such guidelines permit the owners and operators of critical infrastructure to receive all appropriate cyber threat intelligence (as defined in section 1104(h)(5) of such Act, as added by subsection (a)) in the possession of the Federal Government; and

(3) following the establishment of such procedures and the issuance of such guidelines, expeditiously distribute such procedures and such guidelines to appropriate departments and agencies of the Federal Government, private-sector entities, and utilities (as defined in section 1104(h)(13) of such Act, as added by subsection (a)).

(c) Privacy and Civil Liberties Policies and Procedures—Not later than 60 days after the date of the enactment of this Act, the Director of National Intelligence, in consultation with the Secretary of Homeland Security and the Attorney General, shall establish the policies and procedures required under section 1104(c)(7)(A) of the National Security Act of 1947, as added by subsection (a) of this section.

(d) Initial Reports—The first reports required to be submitted under paragraphs (1) and (2) of subsection (e) of section 1104 of the National Security Act of 1947, as added by subsection (a) of this section, shall be submitted not later than 1 year after the date of the enactment of this Act.

(e) Table of Contents Amendment—The table of contents in the first section of the National Security Act of 1947 is amended by adding at the end the following new item:

'Sec. 1104. Cyber threat intelligence and information sharing.'.

SEC. 4. SUNSET.

Effective on the date that is 5 years after the date of the enactment of this Act—

(1) section 1104 of the National Security Act of 1947, as added by section 2(a) of this Act, is repealed; and

(2) the table of contents in the first section of the National Security Act of 1947, as amended by section 2(d) of this Act, is amended by striking the item relating to section 1104, as added by such section 2(d).

SEC. 5. SENSE OF CONGRESS ON INTERNATIONAL COOPERATION.

It is the sense of Congress that international cooperation with regard to cybersecurity should be encouraged wherever possible under this Act and the amendments made by this Act.

SEC. 6. RULE OF CONSTRUCTION RELATING TO CONSUMER DATA.

Nothing in this Act or the amendments made by this Act shall be construed to provide new or alter any existing authority for an entity to sell personal information of a consumer to another entity for marketing purposes.

SEC. 7. SAVINGS CLAUSE WITH REGARD TO CYBERSECURITY PROVIDER OBLIGATION TO REPORT CYBER THREAT INCIDENT INFORMATION TO FEDERAL GOVERNMENT.

Nothing in this Act or the amendments made by this Act shall be construed to provide authority to a department or agency of the Federal Government to require a cybersecurity provider that has contracted with the Federal Government to provide information services to provide information about cybersecurity incidents that do not pose a threat to the Federal Government's information.

Passed the House of Representatives April 18, 2013.

Oversight of Sensitive Military Operations Act

H.R. 1904

A BILL

To amend title 10, United States Code, to require the Secretary of Defense to notify the congressional defense committees of certain sensitive military operations, and for other purposes.

Be it enacted by the Senate and House of Representatives of the United States of America in Congress assembled,

SECTION 1. SHORT TITLE.

This Act may be cited as the 'Oversight of Sensitive Military Operations Act'.

SEC. 2. CONGRESSIONAL NOTIFICATION OF SENSITIVE MILITARY OPERATIONS.

(a) Notification Required—

(1) IN GENERAL—Chapter 3 of title 10, United States Code, is amended by adding at the end the following new section:

'Sec. 130f. Congressional notification of sensitive military operations

'(a) In General—The Secretary of Defense shall promptly submit to the congressional defense committees notice in writing of any sensitive military operation following such operation.

'(b) Procedures—(1) The Secretary of Defense shall establish and submit to the congressional defense committees procedures for complying with the requirements of subsection (a) consistent with the national security of the United States and the protection of operational integrity.

'(2) The congressional defense committees shall ensure that committee procedures designed to protect from unauthorized disclosure classified information relating to national security of the United States are sufficient to protect the information that is submitted to the committees pursuant to this section.

'(c) Sensitive Military Operation Defined—The term 'sensitive military operation' means a lethal operation or capture operation conducted by the armed forces outside the United States pursuant to—

'(1) the Authorization for Use of Military Force (Public Law 107-40; 50 U.S.C. 1541 note); or

'(2) any other authority except—

'(A) a declaration of war; or

'(B) a specific authorization for the use of force other than the authorization referred to in paragraph (1).

'(d) Exception—The notification requirement under subsection (a) shall not apply with respect to a sensitive military operation executed within the territory of Afghanistan pursuant to the Authorization for Use of Military Force (Public Law 107-40; 50 U.S.C. 1541 note).

'(e) Rule of Construction—Nothing in this section shall be construed to provide any new authority or to alter or otherwise affect the War Powers Resolution (50 U.S.C. 1541 et seq.) or the Authorization for Use of Military Force (Public Law 107-40; 50 U.S.C. 1541 note).'.

(2) CLERICAL AMENDMENT—The table of sections at the beginning of such chapter is amended by inserting after the item relating to section 130e the following new item:

'130f. Congressional notification regarding sensitive military operations.'.

(b) Effective Date—Section 130f of title 10, United States Code, as added by subsection (a), shall apply with respect to any sensitive military operation (as defined in subsection (c) of such section) executed on or after the date of the enactment of this Act.

(c) Deadline for Submittal of Procedures—The Secretary of Defense shall submit to the congressional defense committees the procedures required under section 130f(b) of title 10, United States Code, as added by subsection (a), by not later than 60 days after the date of the enactment of this Act.

SEC. 3. REPORT ON PROCESS FOR DETERMINING TARGETS OF LETHAL OPERATIONS.

(a) Report Required—Not later than 60 days after the date of the enactment of this Act, the Secretary of Defense shall submit to the congressional defense committees a report containing an explanation of the legal and policy considerations and approval processes used in determining whether an individual or group of individuals could be the target of a lethal operation or capture operation conducted by the Armed Forces of the United States outside the United States.

(b) Congressional Defense Committees Defined—In this section, the term 'congressional defense committees' means—

(1) the Committee on Armed Services and the Committee on Appropriations of the Senate; and

(2) the Committee on Armed Services and the Committee on Appropriations of the House of Representatives.

SEC. 4. COUNTERTERRORISM OPERATIONAL BRIEFINGS.

(a) Briefings Required—Chapter 23 of title 10, United States Code, is amended by adding at the end the following new section:

'Sec. 492. Quarterly briefings: counterterrorism operations

'(a) Briefings Required—The Secretary of Defense shall provide to the congressional defense committees quarterly briefings outlining Department of Defense counterterrorism operations and related activities involving special operations forces.

'(b) Elements—Each briefing under subsection (a) shall include each of the following:

'(1) A global update on activity within each geographic combatant command.

'(2) An overview of authorities and legal issues including limitations.

'(3) An outline of interagency activities and initiatives.

'(4) Any other matters the Secretary considers appropriate.'.

(b) Clerical Amendment—The table of sections at the beginning of such chapter is amended by adding at the end the following new item:

'492. Quarterly briefings: counterterrorism operations.'.